AB
LONDON
street atlas

Key and Legend for Central London Maps   ii
Légende des plans du Centre de Londres
Legende für Innenstadtkarten

Legend for London Maps   iv
Légende des cartes autres que le Centre de Londres
Legende für karten ausser London-Innenstadt

Places of Entertainment   vi

Major Hotels   viii

Maps of Central London at 6 inches to 1 mile   1-10

Maps of London at 3½ inches to 1 mile   11-112

Index and Reference system explanations and abbreviations   113

Selected Bus Routes in Central London   Following index

Key to Maps   Inside back cover

London Underground Map   Back cover

Newnes Books
Ordnance Survey

CENTRAL LONDON

Key and Legend for Maps 1-10

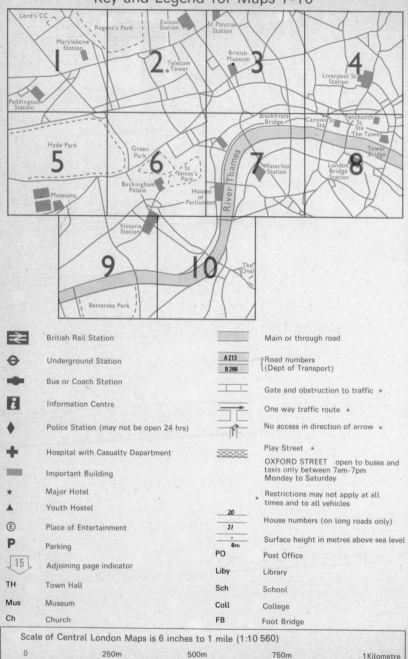

Lord's CC / Marylebone Station / Regent's Park / Paddington Station **1**	Euston Station / Telecom Tower **2**	St Pancras Station / British Museum **3**	Liverpool St Station **4**
Hyde Park / Museums **5**	Green Park / St James's Park / Buckingham Palace / Victoria Station **6**	Blackfriars Bridge / River Thames / Waterloo Station / Houses of Parliament **7**	Cannon St Sta / Fenchurch St Sta / The Tower / Tower Bridge / London Bridge Station **8**
	9 Battersea Park	**10** The Oval	

Symbol	Meaning	Symbol	Meaning
⇄	British Rail Station	(road)	Main or through road
⊖	Underground Station	A 213 / B 266	Road numbers (Dept of Transport)
🚌	Bus or Coach Station		Gate and obstruction to traffic *
𝐢	Information Centre	→	One way traffic route *
♦	Police Station (may not be open 24 hrs)	↱	No access in direction of arrow *
✚	Hospital with Casualty Department	▨▨▨	Play Street *
▬	Important Building		OXFORD STREET open to buses and taxis only between 7am-7pm Monday to Saturday
★	Major Hotel		
▲	Youth Hostel	*	Restrictions may not apply at all times and to all vehicles
Ⓔ	Place of Entertainment	20 / 21	House numbers (on long roads only)
P	Parking	• 8m	Surface height in metres above sea level
15	Adjoining page indicator	PO	Post Office
TH	Town Hall	Liby	Library
Mus	Museum	Sch	School
Ch	Church	Coll	College
		FB	Foot Bridge

Scale of Central London Maps is 6 inches to 1 mile (1:10 560)

0	250m	500m	750m	1 Kilometre
0	¼		½ Mile	

CENTRE DE LONDRES

LONDON INNENSTADT

Légende

Legende

⇌	Gare ferroviaire (British Rail)	British Rail-Bahnhof
⊖	Station de métro	Untergrundbahnstation
●	Gare d'autobus ou d'autocar	Busbahnhof
𝒊	Bureau de renseignements	Informationsbüro
♦	Poste de police (une permanence de 24 heures ne sera pas toujours assurée)	Polizeiwache (u.U. nicht 24-stündig in Betrieb)
✚	Centre hospitalier pour accidentés	Krankenhaus mit Unfallstation
▬	Edifice important	Bedeutendes Bauwerk
★	Grand Hôtel	Grosses Hotel
▲	Auberge de jeunesse	Jugendherberge
Ⓔ	Lieu de distraction	Vergnügungsstätte
P	Parking	Parkplatz
15	Index de la page suivante	Nummer der angrenzenden Kartenseite
▬▬	Route principale ou route prioritaire	Haupstrasse, Durchfahrtsstrasse
A 213 / B 266	Numérotation des routes (Ministère du Transport)	Strassennummern (Verkehrsministerium)
⊤⊤	Grille et obstacle à la circulation *	Schranke, Verkehrssperre *
→	Voie de circulation en sens unique *	Einbahnstrasse *
⇞	Pas d'accès dans la direction de la flèche *	In Pfeilrichtung keine Zufahrt *
▨▨	Rue réservée aux jeux des enfants *	Als Kinderspielplatz benutzte Strasse *
	OXFORD STREET- Circulation interdite (sauf autobus et taxis) du lundi au samedi, de 7 heures à 19 heures	OXFORD STREET- Nur für Autobusse und Taxis frei 07.00-19.00 Uhr Montag bis Samstag
	* Les restrictions ne s'appliqueront pas tout le temps et à tous les véhicules	* Streckenverbote:z.T.nicht ganzzeitig bzw. für alle Fahrzeuge in Kraft
20 / 21	Numéros de maisons (seulement sur les routes longues)	Hausnummern (nur bei langen Strassen)
· / 8m	Altitude en mètres au-dessus du niveau de la mer	Oberflächenhöhe in Metern über NN
TH	Hôtel de ville	Rathaus
Mus	Musée	Museum
Ch	Eglise	Kirche
PO	Bureau de poste	Postamt
Liby	Bibliothèque	Bibliothek
Coll	Collège	Lehranstalt, Hochschule
Sch	Ecole	Schule
FB	Passerelle	Fussgängerüberführung

LEGEND
For Maps 11-112

For key to Maps see inside back cover

≷ British Rail Station

⊖ Underground Station

▬ Bus or Coach Station

🅸 Information Centre

♦ Police Station
(may not be open 24 hrs)

✚ Hospital
with Casualty Department

+ Church

▬ Important Building

★ Major Hotel

▲ Youth Hostel

Ⓛ Library

Ⓔ Place of Entertainment

□ Post Office

P Parking

15 Adjoining page indicator

TH Town Hall

Mus Museum

Dual Carriageway

Main or through road

A 213
B 266 Road numbers
(Dept of Transport)

Gate and obstruction to traffic *

One way traffic route *

No access in direction of arrow *

Play Street *

* Restrictions may not apply at all
times and to all vehicles

20
21 House numbers
(on long roads only)

Poly   Polytechnic

Coll   College

Sch   School

Mkt   Market

CH   Club House

LC   Level Crossing

FB   Foot Bridge

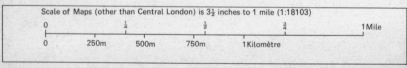

Scale of Maps (other than Central London) is 3½ inches to 1 mile (1:18103)

0   ¼   ½   ¾   1 Mile

0   250m   500m   750m   1 Kilomètre

(iv)

LEGENDE   LEGENDE

Pour les légendes des schémas, voir à l'intérieur de la couverture arrière   Zeichenerklärung siehe Innenseite des Umschlages hinten

⇌	Gare ferroviaire (British Rail)	British Rail-Bahnhof
⊖	Station de métro	Untergrundbahnstation
➤	Gare d'autobus ou d'autocar	Busbahnhof
🛈	Bureau de renseignements	Informationsbüro
◆	Poste de police (une permanence de 24 heures ne sera pas toujours assurée)	Polizeiwache (u.U. nicht 24-stündig in Betrieb)
✚	Centre hospitalier pour accidentés	Krankenhaus mit Unfallstation
+	Eglise	Kirche
▬	Edifice important	Bedeutendes Bauwerk
★	Grand Hôtel	Grosses Hotel
▲	Auberge de jeunesse	Jugendherberge
Ⓛ	Bibliothèque	Bibliothek
Ⓔ	Lieu de distraction	Vergnügungsstätte
☐	Bureau de poste	Postamt
P	Parking	Parkplatz
15	Index de la page suivante	Nummer der angrenzenden Kartenseite
═══	Double chaussée	Zweibahnig
───	Route principale ou route prioritaire	Hauptstrasse, Durchfahrtsstrasse
A 213 / B 266	Numérotation des routes (Ministère du Transport)	Strassennummern (Verkehrsministerium)
⊥⊥	Grille et obstacle à la circulation *	Schranke, Verkehrssperre *
←	Voie de circulation en sens unique *	Einbahnstrasse *
⇂	Pas d'accès dans la direction de la flèche *	In Pfeilrichtung keine Zufahrt *
▨▨▨	Rue réservée aux jeux des enfants *	Als Kinderspielplatz benutzte Strasse *
	* Les restrictions ne s'appliqueront pas tout le temps et à tous les véhicules	*Streckenverbote:z.T. nicht ganzzeitig bzw. für alle Fahrzeuge in Kraft
20 / 21	Numéros de maisons (seulement sur les routes longues)	Hausnummern (nur bei langen Strassen)
TH	Hôtel de ville	Rathaus
Mus	Musée	Museum
Poly	Institut universitaire de technologie	Technische Hochschule
Coll	Collège	Lehranstalt, Hochschule
Sch	Ecole	Schule
Mkt	Marché	Markt
CH	Club	Clubhaus
LC	Passage à niveau	Niveau-Ubergang
FB	Passerelle	Fussgängerüberführung

(v)

PLACES OF ENTERTAINMENT

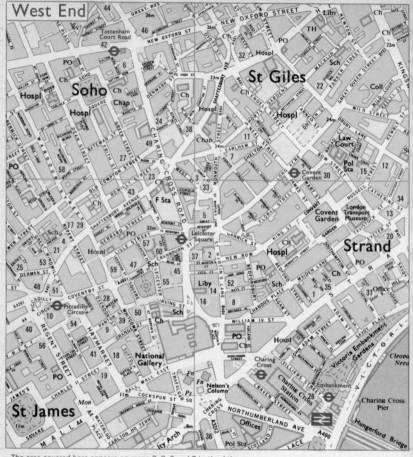

The area covered here appears on maps 2, 3, 6 and 7 in the Atlas

INDEX TO WEST END MAP

THEATRES

1 Adelphi
2 Albery
3 Ambassadors
4 Apollo
5 Arts Theatre
6 Astoria
7 Cambridge
8 Coliseum
9 Comedy
10 Criterion
11 Donmar W'House
12 Drury Lane Theatre Royal
13 Duchess
14 Duke of Yorks
15 Fortune
16 Garrick
17 Globe
18 Haymarket Theatre Royal
19 Her Majesties

20 Lyceum
21 Lyric
22 New London
23 Palace
24 Phoenix
25 Piccadilly
26 Players
27 Prince Edward
28 Prince of Wales
29 Queens
30 Royal Opera House
31 Savoy
32 Shaftesbury
33 St Martins
34 Strand
35 Vaudeville
36 Whitehall
37 Wyndhams

CINEMAS

38 ABC
39 Cinecenta
40 Cinecenta
41 Classic
42 Classic
43 Classic
44 Classic
45 Classic Royal
46 Dominion
47 Empire
48 Eros Cinema
49 Film Centa Cinema
50 Leicester Square Theatre
51 London Pavilion
52 Lumiere Cinema
53 Moulin
54 Odeon
55 Odeon
56 Plaza

57 Prince Charles
58 Roxy
59 Scenes
60 Warner

OTHER CINEMAS, THEATRES AND CONCERT HALLS

An explanation of the referencing system, and abbreviations used are on page 113

CINEMAS

ABC, Edgware Rd. W2	*1*	26	81	B
ABC, Fulham SW10	*62*	26	78	C
ABC (Bayswater), Bishop's Bridge Rd. W2	*1*	25	81	D
ABC (Beckenham), High St.	*98*	37	69	C
ABC (Bexleyheath), The Broadway	*79*	48	75	D
ABC (Catford), Bromley Rd. SE6	*88*	37	73	B
ABC (Croydon), London Rd.	*105*	31	66	B
ABC (Ealing), Uxbridge Rd. W5	*54*	17	80	B
ABC (Elephant & Castle), New Kent Rd. SE1	*63*	32	79	C
ABC (Enfield), Southbury Rd.	*13*	33	96	A
ABC (Ewell), Kingston Rd.	*109*	21	63	B
ABC (Golders Green), Golders Green Rd. NW11	*35*	24	87	A
ABC (Hammersmith), King St. W6	*61*	22	78	B
ABC (Harrow), Station Rd.	*33*	15	88	B
ABC (Ilford), High Rd.	*40*	44	86	A
ABC (Mile End), Mile End Rd. E1	*57*	35	82	C
ABC (Putney), High St. SW15	*73*	24	75	A
ABC (Romford), South St.	*42*	51	88	C
ABC (Sidcup). High St.	*90*	46	71	A
ABC (Streatham), Streatham High Rd. SW16	*86*	30	72	A
ABC (Turnpike Lane), Turnpike Parade. N15	*25*	31	89	B
ABC (Woodford), High Rd. E18	*27*	40	90	C
Academy Cinema, Oxford St. W1	*2*	29	81	C
Ace, Rayner's Lane. Har.	*32*	13	87	C
Ace (Peckham), Peckham High St.	*75*	33	76	B
Ace (Stoke Newington), Stoke Newington Rd. N16	*48*	33	85	D
Ace State (Barkingside), Fairlop Rd.	*28*	44	90	C
Barbican, Barbican Centre Silk St. EC2	*4*	32	81	A
Battersea Arts Centre, Lavender Hill. SW11	*74*	27	75	B
Bloomsbury Theatre, Gordon St. WC1	*3*	29	82	C
Camden Plaza, Camden High St. NW1	*47*	28	88	B
Chelsea Cinema, Kings Road. SW3	*9*	27	78	C
Classic, Praed St. W2	*1*	27	81	A
Classic (Chelsea), Kings Rd. SW3	*9*	26	77	B
Classic (Hampstead), Pond St. NW3	*47*	27	85	C
Classic (Hendon), Central Circus. NW4	*34*	22	88	B
Classic (Kilburn), Kilburn High Rd.	*46*	24	84	B
Coronet (Elephant & Castle), New Kent Rd. SE1	*63*	32	79	C
Coronet (Northfields), Northfield Ave. W5	*60*	17	79	C
Coronet (Notting Hill), Westbourne Gr. W11	*56*	25	81	C
Coronet (Well Hall), Well Hall Rd. SE9	*77*	42	75	C
Coronet (Woolwich), John Wilson St.	*66*	43	79	C
Curzon, Curzon St. W1	*6*	28	80	D
Curzon (Haringey), Frobisher High St.	*25*	31	89	D
Everyman Cinema, Holly Bush Vale. NW3	*46*	26	85	A
Film Location (Acton), The Railway High St. W3	*55*	20	80	D
Gate (Bloomsbury), Brunswick Sq. WC1	*3*	30	82	C
Gate (Mayfair), Mayfair Hotel Stratton St. W1	*6*	26	82	D
Gate (Notting Hill), Notting Hill Gate. W11	*56*	25	80	C
Granada (Kingston), Clarence St.	*93*	18	69	C
Granada (Harrow), Sheepcote Rd.	*33*	15	88	D
Granada (Walthamstow), Hoe St.	*26*	37	89	C
Institute of Cont Arts, Nash.House The Mall. SW1	*6*	29	80	D
Ionic (Golders Green), Finchley Rd. NW11	*35*	25	87	C
Minema, Knightsbridge. SW1	*6*	28	79	A
National Film Theatre, South Bank. SE1	*7*	30	80	D
Odeon, High St. Kensington W8	*62*	25	79	C
Odeon, Marble Arch. W1	*1*	26	82	D
Odeon (Barking), Longbridge Rd.	*51*	44	84	D
Odeon (Barnet), Western Parade.	*11*	25	95	A
Odeon (Bromley), Bromley High St.	*99*	40	69	C
Odeon (Croydon), North End.	*105*	32	65	A
Odeon (Hammersmith), Queen Caroline St. W6.	*62*	23	78	C
Odeon (Holloway), Holloway Rd. N7	*47*	30	85	B
Odeon (Ilford), Gants Hill.	*40*	43	88	C
Odeon (Muswell Hill), Fortis Green Rd. N10	*24*	28	89	D
Odeon (Richmond), Hill St.	*71*	17	74	B
Odeon (Romford), South St.	*42*	51	88	A
Odeon (Streatham), Streatham High Rd.	*86*	30	72	C
Odeon (Swiss Cottage), Finchley Rd.	*46*	26	84	D
Odeon (Wimbledon). The Broadway.	*95*	25	70	C
Phoenix, High Rd East Finchley. N2	*24*	27	89	C
Rio Cinema, Kingsland High St. Hackney N16	*48*	33	85	D
Ritzy (Brixton), Brixton Oval Coldharbour La. SW2	*75*	31	75	C
Scala, Pentonville Rd. WC1	*3*	30	82	A
Screen on the Green, Upper St. N1	*48*	31	83	B
Screen on the Hill, Haverstock Hill. NW3	*47*	27	85	C
Studios, Oxford St. W1	*2*	29	81	C
Studios (Ealing), Northfield Ave. W13	*54*	16	80	D
Studios (Lewisham), Lewisham High St. SE13	*76*	38	75	A
Studios (Sutton). Cheam Rd.	*110*	25	64	D
Times Centa Cinema, Marylebone Rd. NW1	*2*	28	82	C

THEATRES

Albany Empire, Douglas Way. SE8	*64*	37	77	C
Aldwych, Aldwych. WC2	*3*	30	81	D
Apollo Vic. Wilton Rd. SW1	*6*	29	79	C
Ashcroft, Fairfield Halls High St. Croy.	*105*	32	65	D
Barbican RSC, Barbican Centre Silk St. EC2	*4*	32	81	A
Bloomsbury, Gordon St. WC1	*2*	29	82	D
Bush, Shepherds Bush Green. W12	*62*	23	79	A
Churchill, High St. Brom.	*99*	40	69	C
Cockpit, Gateforth St. NW8	*1*	27	82	C
Cottesloe, South Bank. SE1	*7*	30	80	D
Drill Hall, Chenies St. WC1	*2*	29	81	B
Greenwich, Crooms Hill. SE10	*64*	38	77	C
Half Moon, Mile End Rd. E1	*57*	35	82	D
Hampstead Theatre Club, Swiss Cottage Centre. NW3	*46*	26	84	D
Jeannetta Cochrane, Theobalds Rd. WC1	*3*	30	81	B
Jacksons Lane, Archway Rd. N6.	*36*	28	88	D
Kings Head, Upper St. N1	*48*	31	83	B
Lyric (Hammersmith), King St. W6	*62*	23	78	A
Lyttleton, South Bank. SE1	*7*	30	80	D
Mayfair, Stratton St. W1	*6*	28	80	D
Mermaid, Puddle Dock. EC4	*7*	31	80	B
National Theatre, South Bank. SE1	*7*	30	80	D
New End, New End. NE3	*35*	26	86	C
Old Vic, The Cut. SE1	*63*	31	79	A
Olivier, South Bank. SE1	*7*	30	80	D
Oval House, Kennington Oval. SE11	*63*	31	77	A
Palladium, Argyle St. W1	*2*	29	81	C
Questors, Mattock Lane. W5	*54*	17	80	A
Regents Park (Open Air), Inner Circle. NW1	*2*	28	82	A
Riverside Studios, Crisp Rd. W6	*62*	23	78	C
Round House, Chalk Farm Rd. NW1	*47*	28	84	C
Royal Court, Sloane Sq. SW1	*9*	28	78	A
Royalty, Portugal St. WC2	*3*	30	81	D
Shaw, Euston Rd. NW1	*2*	29	82	B
St Georges, Tufnell Park Rd. N7	*47*	30	85	A
Theatre Royal, Gerry Raffles Sq. E15	*49*	38	84	B
The Green, Richmond Green. Rich	*71*	17	75	D
Tower, Cannonbury Tower Cannonbury Pl. N1	*48*	31	84	B
Vanbrugh Theatre Club, Malet St. WC1	*2*	29	81	B
Victoria Palace, Victoria St. SW1	*6*	29	79	C
Westminster, Palace St. SW1	*6*	29	79	C
Wimbledon, The Broadway. SW19	*95*	25	70	C
Young Vic, The Cut. SE1	*7*	31	79	A

CONCERT HALLS

Barbican, Barbican Centre Silk St. EC2	*4*	32	81	A
Central Hall, Storeys Gate. SW1	*6*	29	79	B
Conway Hall, Red Lion Sq. WC1	*3*	30	81	B
Fairfield Halls, Park La. Croy	*105*	32	65	D
Hammersmith Palais, Shepherds Bush Rd. W6	*62*	23	78	A
Institute of Cont Arts, Nash House The Mall. SW1	*6*	29	80	D
The Place, Dukes Rd. WC1	*2*	29	82	B
Purcell Room, Q E Hall South Bank. SE1	*7*	30	80	D
Queen Elizabeth Hall, South Bank. SE1	*7*	30	80	D
Royal Albert Hall, Kensington Gore. SW7	*5*	26	79	B
Royal College of Music, Prince Consort Rd. SW7	*5*	26	79	D
Royal Festival Hall, South Bank. SE1	*7*	30	80	D
Royal Military Sch of Music, Kneller Rd. Twick	*70*	14	74	D
Sadlers Wells, Rosebery Ave. EC1	*3*	31	82	A
St Johns, Smith Sq. SW1	*7*	30	79	C
Wigmore Hall, Wigmore St. W1	*2*	28	81	C

MAJOR HOTELS

An explanation of the referencing system, and abbreviations used are on page 113.

Aerial Hotel, Bath Rd. Hay	69	08 76	B
Antoinette of Kingston Hotel, 26 Beaufort Rd. King	93	18 68	C
Athenaeum Hotel, 116 Piccadilly. W1	6	28 80	D
Baileys Hotel, 140 Gloucester Rd. SW7	62	26 78	A
Barbican City Hotel, Central St. EC1	4	32 82	A
Bayswater Fairway Inn, 8-16 Princes Sq. W2	5	25 80	B
Belgravia Sheraton Hotel, 20 Chesham Pl. SW1	6	28 79	C
Berkeley, Wilton Pl. SW1	6	28 79	A
Bloomsbury Crest Hotel, Coram St. WC1	3	30 82	C
Britannia Hotel, 42 Grosvenor Sq. W1	6	28 80	A
Bromley Court Hotel, Bromley Hill. Brom	99	39 70	A
Brown's Hotel, Albemarle St. W1	6	29 80	A
Cavendish Hotel, Jermyn St. SW1	6	29 80	C
Central Park Hotel, 49 Queensborough Terr. W2	5	26 80	A
Charing Cross, Strand. WC2	7	30 80	C
Charles Dickens, 66 Lancaster Gate. W2	5	26 80	A
The Churchill, Portman Sq. W1	2	27 81	D
Clarendon Hotel, 8-16 Montpelier Row. SE3	77	39 76	D
Clarendon Court Hotel, Maida Vale. W9	1	26 82	C
Claridge's, Brook St. W1	6	28 80	B
Crest Hotel, Empire Way. Wem	44	18 85	D
Cumberland Hotel, Marble Arch. W1	1	27 81	D
Dorchester, Park La. W1	6	28 80	C
Eden Park Hotel, 35 Inverness Terr. W2	5	25 80	B
Europa, Grosvenor Sq. W1	6	28 80	A
Flemings Hotel, 7-12 Half Moon St. W1	6	28 80	D
The Gloucester, Harrington Gdns. SW7	62	26 78	A
Goring Hotel, 15 Beeston Pl. SW1	6	28 79	D
Great Eastern Hotel, Liverpool St. EC2	4	33 81	A
Great Western Royal Hotel, Praed St. W2	1	26 81	D
Grosvenor Hotel, Buckingham Palace Rd. SW1	6	28 79	D
Grosvenor House, Park La. W1	6	28 80	A
Heathrow Penta, Bath Rd. Houn	69	08 76	A
Henry VIII Hotel, 19 Leinster Gdns. W2	5	26 80	A
London Hilton, 22 Park La. W1	6	28 80	C
Hilton International (Kensington), 179-199 Holland Park Ave. W11	62	24 79	A
Holiday Inn (Chelsea), 17-25 Sloane St. SW1	5	27 79	D
Holiday Inn (Marble Arch), 134 George St. W1	1	27 81	D
Holiday Inn (Swiss Cottage), King Henry's Rd. NW2	47	27 84	C
Hotel Bristol, Berkeley St. W1	6	29 80	C
Hotel George, Templeton Pl. SW5	62	25 78	A
Hotel Russell, Russell Sq. WC1	3	30 82	C
Howard Hotel, Temple Pl. WC2	7	30 80	B
The Hyatt Carlton Tower Hotel, Cadogan Pl. SW1	5	27 79	D
Hyde Park Hotel, Knightsbridge. SW1	6	27 79	B
Imperial Hotel, Russell Sq. WC1	3	30 81	A
Inn on the Park, Hamilton Pl Park La. W1	6	28 80	A
Inter-Continental, 1 Hamilton Pl Hyde Park Cnr	6	28 79	A
Kenilworth Hotel, Great Russell St. WC1	2	29 81	B
Kensington Close Hotel, Wrights La. W8	62	25 79	D
Kensington Palace Hotel, De Vere Gdns. W8	6	26 79	A
Kingsley Hotel, Bloomsbury Way. WC1	3	30 81	A
Ladbroke Westmoreland Hotel, 18 Lodge Rd. NW8	1	27 82	A
Leinster Towers Hotel, 25 Leinster Gdns. W2	5	26 80	A
London Embassy Hotel, Bayswater Rd. W2	56	25 80	B
London Forum Hotel, 97 Cromwell Rd. SW5	62	26 78	A
London International, Cromwell Rd. SW5	62	25 78	B
London Metropole Hotel, Edgware Rd. W2	1	27 81	A
London Penta Hotel, Cromwell Rd. SW5	62	26 78	A
London Ryan Hotel, Gwynne Pl Kings Cross. WC1	3	30 82	B
London Tara Hotel, Scarsdale Pl Wrights La. W8	62	25 79	D
Londoner Hotel, Welbeck St. W1	2	28 81	D
Mayfair, Stratton St. W1	6	28 80	D
Mostyn Hotel, Bryanston St. W1	1	27 81	D
Mount Royal Hotel, Bryanston St. W1	1	27 81	D
Novotel London, Shortlands, W6	62	23 78	B
Onslow Court Hotel, 109-113 Queens Gate. SW7	62	26 78	B
Park Lane, 111 Piccadilly. W1	6	28 80	D
Park Court Hotel, 75 Lancaster Gate. W2	5	26 80	A
Park Plaza Hotel, 5 Lancaster Gate. W2	5	26 80	B
Phoenix Hotel, 1-8 Kensington Gdns Sq. W2	56	25 80	B
Piccadilly Hotel, 24 Piccadilly. W1	6	29 80	A
The Portman Intercontinental, Portman Sq. W1	2	27 81	D
Post House Hotel, 104 Bayswater Rd. W2	5	26 80	A
Post House Hotel, Haverstock Hill. NW3	47	27 85	C
Regency Hotel, 100-105 Queens Gate. SW7	62	26 78	A
Regent Crest Hotel, Carburton St. W1	2	28 82	D
Rembrandt Hotel, 11 Thurloe Pl. SW7	5	27 79	C
Richmond Hill Hotel, 146-150 Richmond Hill, Rich	83	18 73	A
The Ritz, Piccadilly. W1	6	29 80	C
Royal Court Hotel, Sloane Sq. SW1	9	28 78	A
Royal Garden Hotel, Kensington High St. W8	62	25 79	B
Royal Horseguards Hotel, Whitehall Ct. SW1	7	30 80	C
Royal Kensington Hotel, 380 Kensington High St. W14	62	24 79	D
Royal Lancaster Hotel, Lancaster Terr. W2	5	26 80	B
Royal Scot Hotel, Kings Cross Rd. WC1	3	30 82	B
Royal Trafalgar Hotel, Whitcomb St. WC2	6	29 80	B
Royal National, Bedford Way. WC1	3	30 82	C
Royal Westminster Hotel, Buckingham Palace Rd. SW1	6	28 79	D
Rubens Hotel, 39-41 Buckingham Palace Rd. SW1	6	28 79	D
The Savoy, Savoy Pl. WC2	7	30 80	B
Savoy Court Hotel, Granville Pl. W1	6	28 81	C
The Selfridge Hotel, Orchard St. W1	2	28 81	C
Sheraton Park Hotel, 101 Knightsbridge. SW1	5	27 79	B
Sherlock Holmes Hotel, Baker St. W1	1	27 81	B
Skyway Hotel, Bath Rd. Hay	69	08 76	A
St Ermins, Caxton St. SW1	6	29 79	D
St James, Buckingham Gate. SW1	6	29 79	C
Strand Palace Hotel, Strand. WC2	7	30 80	A
Tower Hotel, St Katherine's Way. E1	8	33 80	D
Vanderbilt Hotel, 76-86 Cromwell Rd. SW7	62	26 78	A
Waldorf Hotel, Aldwych. WC2	6	30 80	B
Washington Hotel, Curzon St. W1	6	28 80	D
Westbury Hotel, New Bond St. W1	6	28 80	B
West Centre Hotel, Lillie Rd. SW6	62	25 77	A
The White House, Osnaburgh Terr. NW1	2	28 82	D

Central London
Maps 1-10
scale 6 inches to 1 mile

London
Maps 11-112
scale 3½ inches to 1 mile

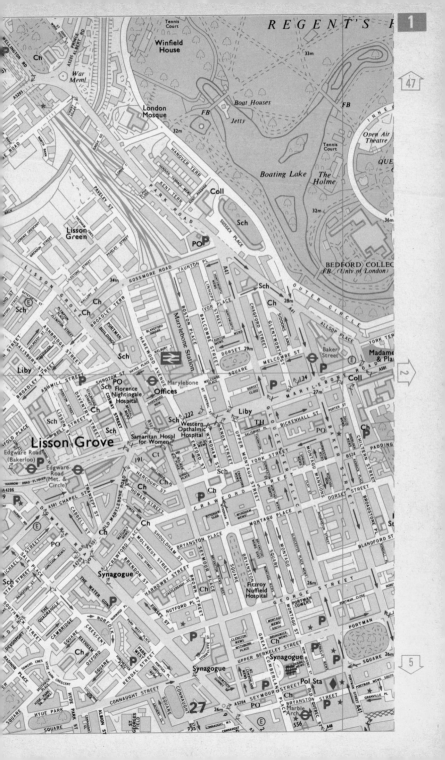

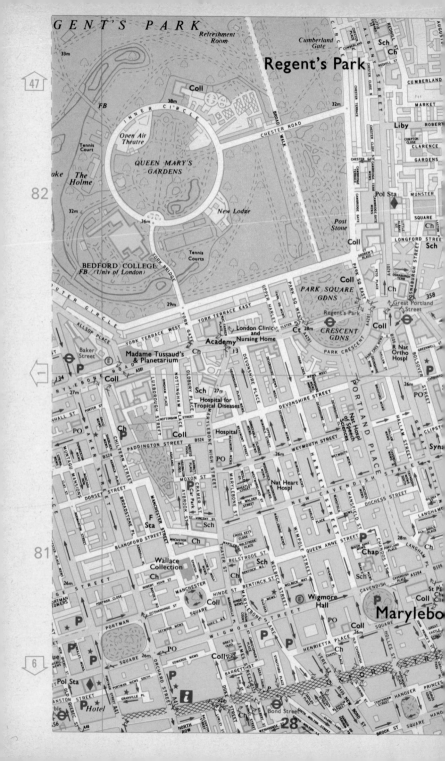

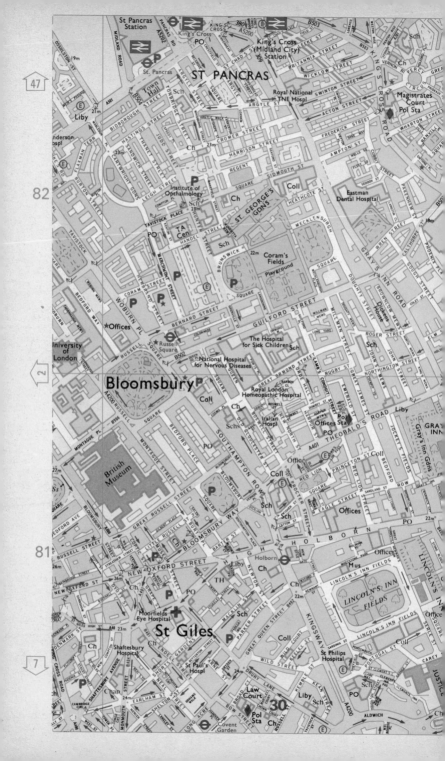

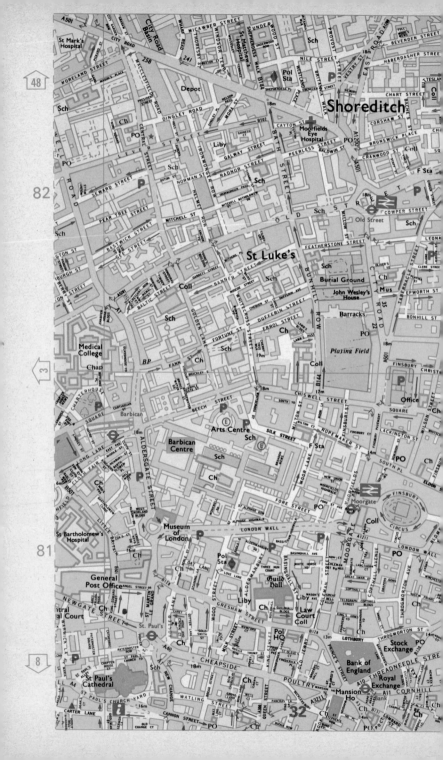

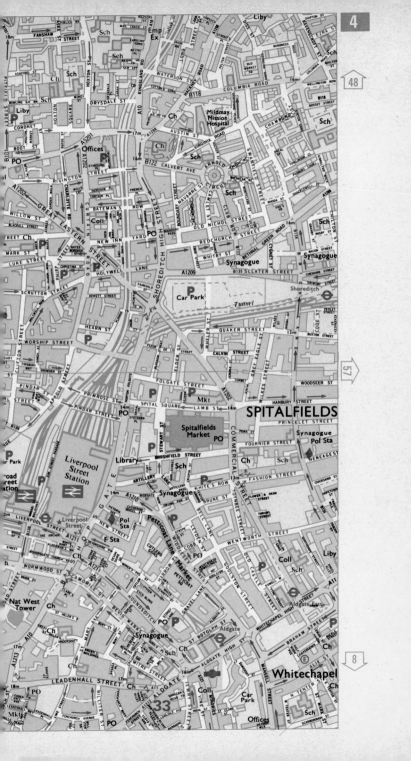

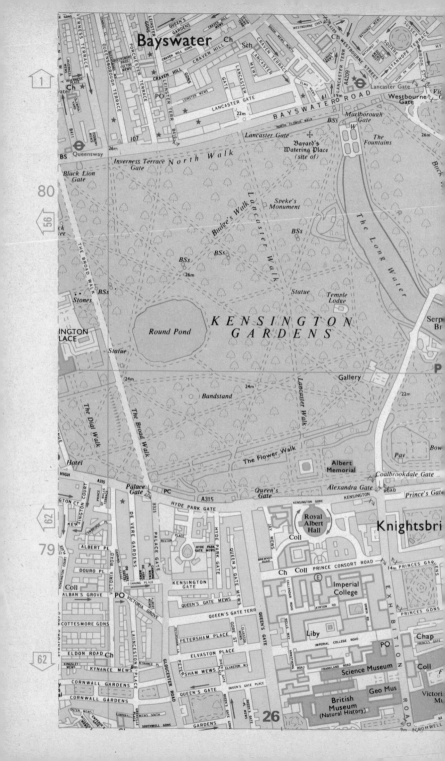

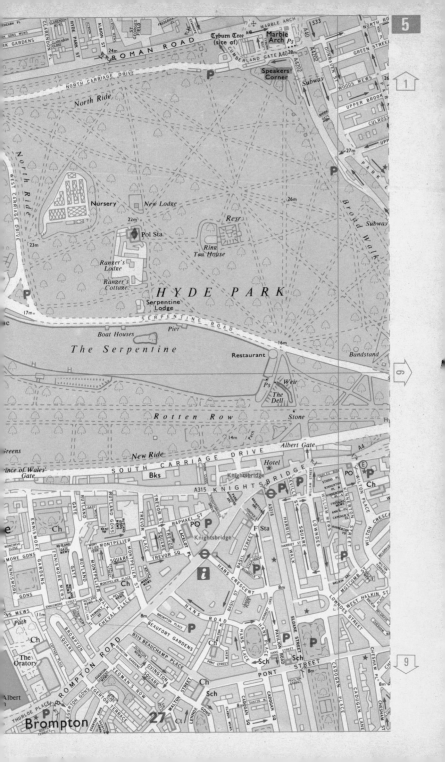

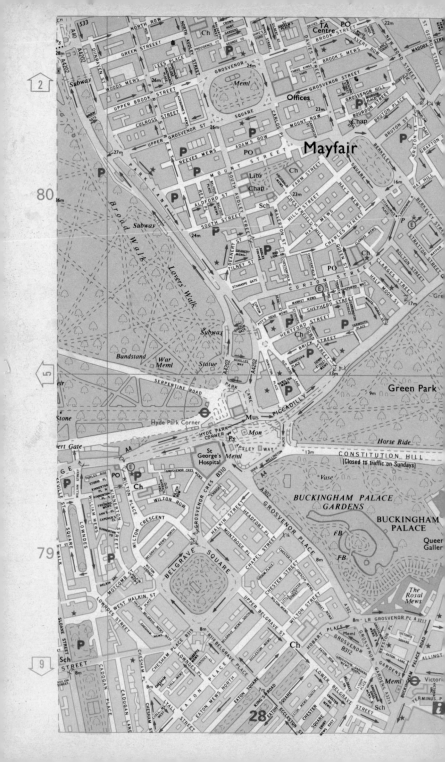

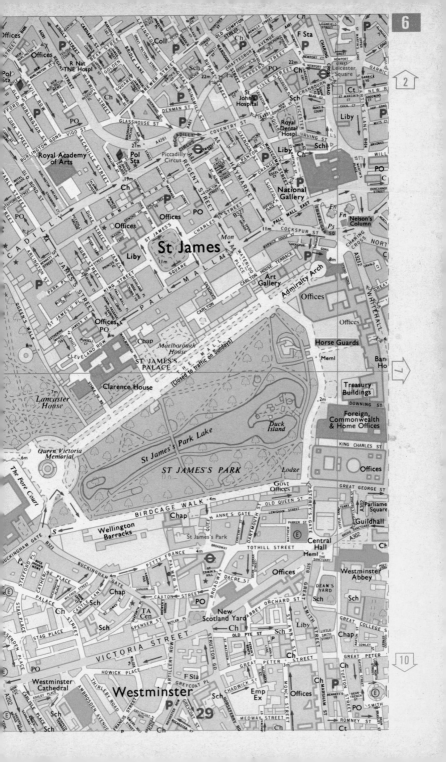

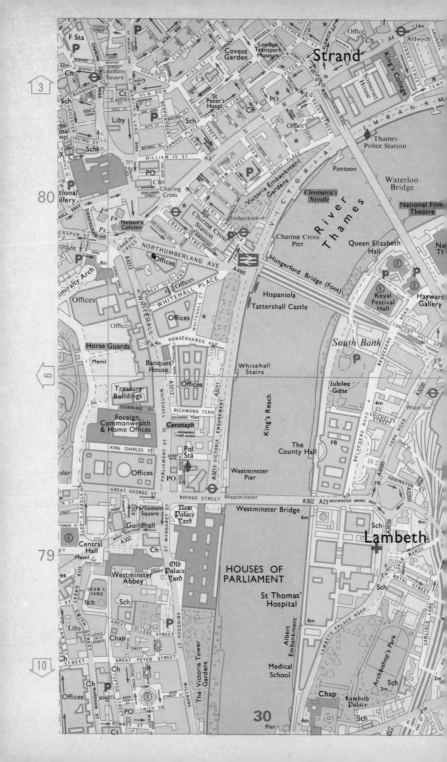

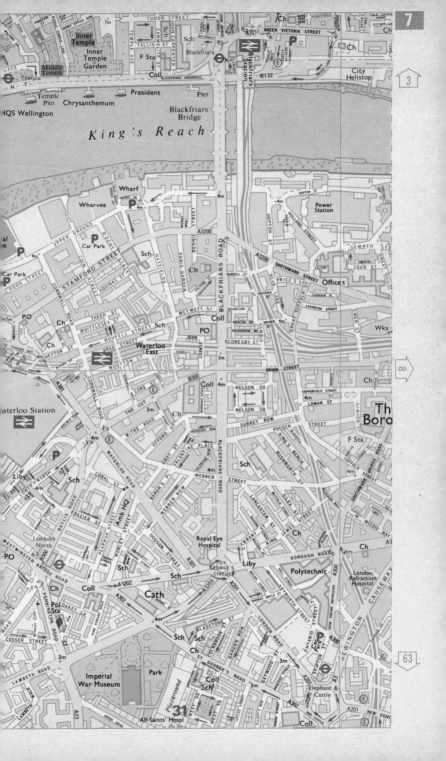

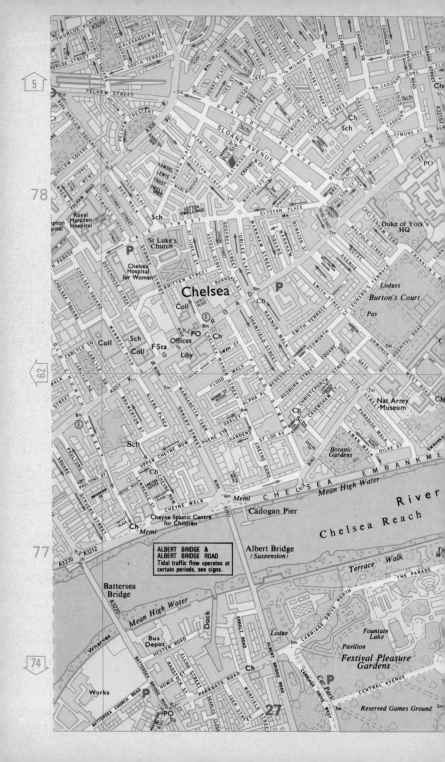

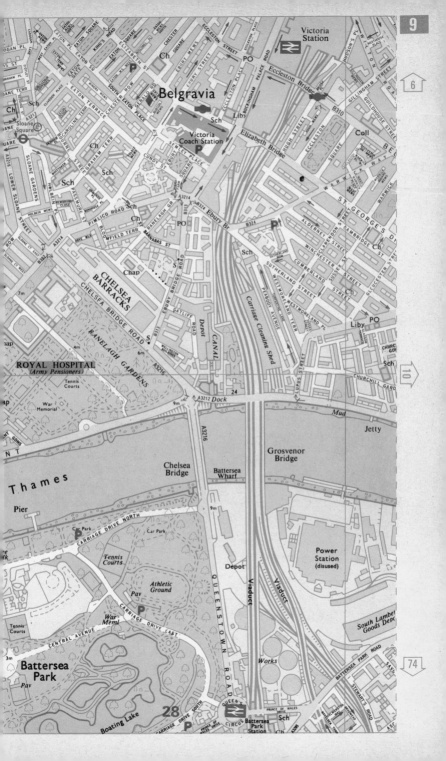

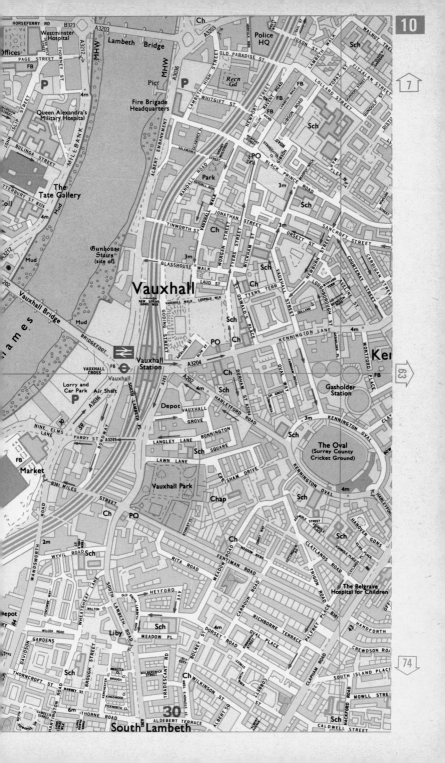

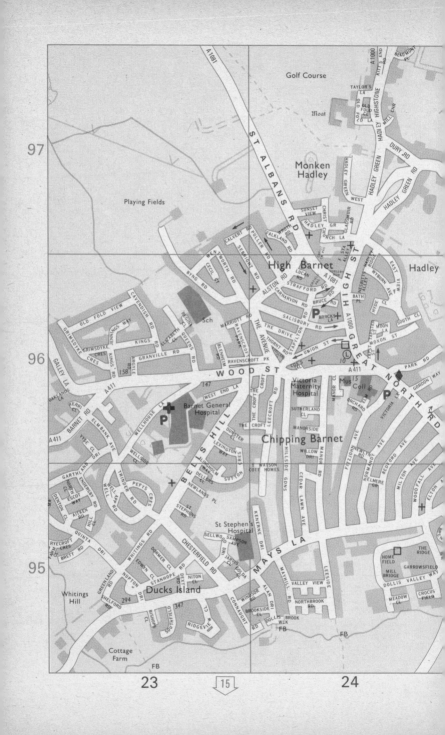

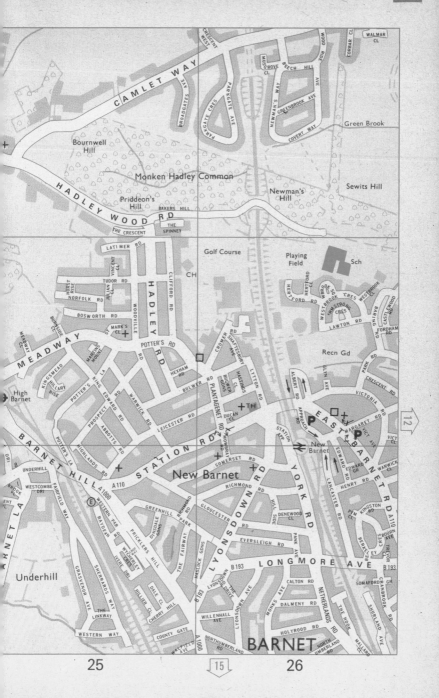

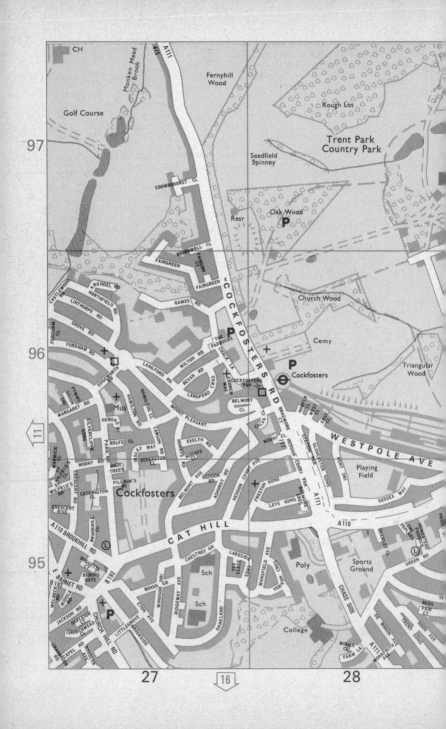

Camlet Hill

Enfield Chase

Icehouse
Wood

Poly

Williams
Wood

Shaws
Wood

HADLEY RD

Vicarage Farm

Leeging Beech Gutter

Salmon's Brook

Hog Hill

RIDGE CREST

Golf Course

Merryhills Brook

TRENTWOOD SIDE

GRAFTON RD

ELMER AVE

A110

BINCOTE RD

ENFIELD RD

Sch

Sch

Boxer's
Lake

COTSWOLD WAY

GLENBROOK

CHITTEN

SOUTH CL
LODGE

LAKESIDE

5TH
LODGE
CL

GREYSTOKE GDNS

LOWTHER DRI

NETHERBY GDNS

CULGAITH GDNS

BEWCASTLE GDNS

CORBY CRES N

CH

227

MERRYHILLS DRI

BRAXTON GDNS

CURTHWAITE GDNS

BRANTWOOD GDNS

CLIFTON GDNS

WOODEND GDNS

LONSDALE DRIVE

SILVERDALE

LINDAL CRES

ROUNDHILL DRI

RUSHEY HILL

Sch

WORLD'S END LA

SNAKES LA

BRAMLEY RD

CHASE RD

BELGRAVE GDNS

GROSVENOR GDNS

Oakwood

GERRARDS CL

BELGRAVE
CL

CARLTON AVE

SOUTH LODGE DRI

KENWOOD

OAKWOOD

LONSDALE DRI

TARNBANK

South Lodge
Hospl

Highlands Hospl

STAFFORD CL

TREGENNA CL

CATHERINE CT

ASHCONISBEE CT

WOLVERTON

CHESTNUT CL

PRINCE GEORGE AVE

OVERTON RD

CHASEVILLE PARK RD

GREEN
DRAGON
LA

RESERVOIR RD

THE VINERIES

AVENUE CL

ASHMEAD

LAKENHEATH

MERRIVALE

SHE

PINGHAM AVE

Oakwood Park

Sch

OAKWOOD CRES

THE BIRCHES

HOLLY HILL

WILLOW WLK

EVERSLEY PARK RD

MAPLIN

EVE CALLIS

EVERSLEY CRES

AIRWAY

LINDEN CT

WPER GDNS

BEARDOW CL

WAYSIDE CL

SAXON WAY

WRIGHTFIELD

OAKWOOD CL

FAIRLAWN CL

Oakwood

AVENUE RD

ORCHARD AVE

LINDEN WAY

CHARTER WAY

OAKWOOD PARK RD

THE VALE

SPRINGBANK

SEYMOUR CT

MEADOWBANK

BROOKSIDE

HOUNDSDEN RD

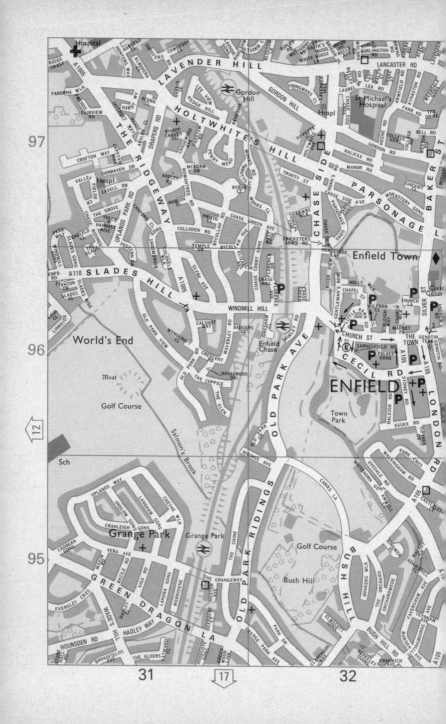

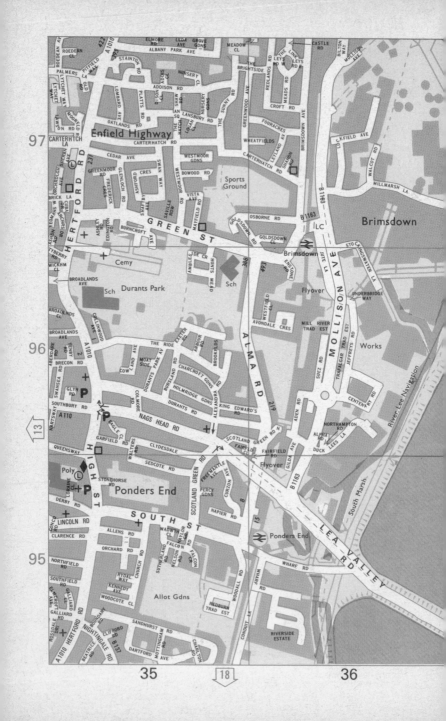

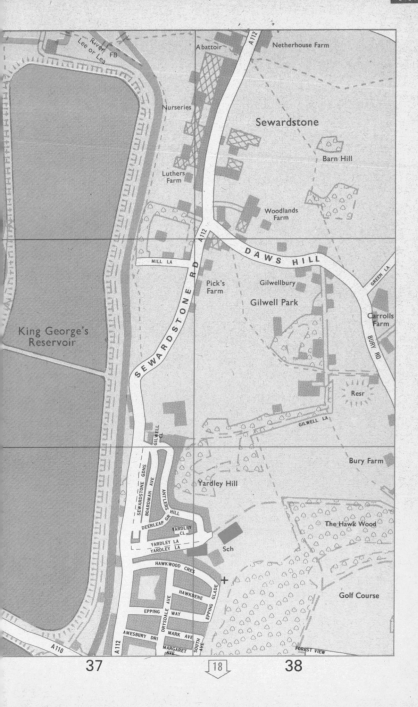

River Lee or Lea

FB

Abattoir

Netherhouse Farm

A 112

Nurseries

Sewardstone

Barn Hill

Luthers Farm

Woodlands Farm

A 112

DAWS HILL

MILL LA

GREEN LA

SEWARDSTONE RD

Pick's Farm

Gilwellbury

Gilwell Park

Carrolls Farm

BURY RD

King George's Reservoir

Resr

GILWELL LA

GILWELL CL

Bury Farm

SEWARDSTONE GDNS

BOARDMAN AVE

ANTLERS HILL

Yardley Hill

The Hawk Wood

DEERLEAP GR

YARDLEY CL

YARDLEY LA

YARDLEY LA

Sch

HAWKWOOD CRES

+

HAWKDENE

Golf Course

DRYSDALE AVE

EPPING GLADE

EPPING WAY

AMESBURY DRI

MARK AVE

SOUTH AVE

MARGARET AVE

A 110

A 112

FOREST VIEW

MAY'S LA

Dollis Brook

Sch

OAKLANDS RD

Totteridge

94

Fairlight
Cottage

GRANGE AVE

PRIORY CL

WHITE
ORCHARDS

BARNET LA

LIME GR

BADGERS
CROFT

THE PASTURES

HORSESHOE LA

WYKEHAM RISE

TOTTERIDGE

Abattoir

TOTTERIDGE COMMON

NORTHCLIFFE DRI

HARMSWORT

A 5109

CHESTNUT LA

VILLAGE

THE CLOSE

Ellern Mede
Farm

Windyridge

93

Coll

Laurel Farr

Folly Brook

Burtonhole
Farm

BURTONHOLE LA

MCKEL

BURTONHOLE CL

HILLVIEW RD

92

B 552

ELEANOR CRES

THE RIDGEWAY

Frith Manor
Farm

LULLINGTON GART

PYCOM

ROSEHILL

OPTHAM SLOPE

Drivers Hill

Oakfields

PARTINGDALE LA

FOLKINGTON CNR

CYPR

READING WAY

HOLMES

FRITH LA

CHARLES
SEVRIGHT
DRI

Inglis Barracks

LIDBURY RD

BITTACY
PARK

HENRY DARLOT DRI

B 552

WOODCOTE AVE

HENRY LANE W

GAWTHORNE AVE

11

NORTHUMBERLAND RD
HOLLAND CL
MALLARD CL
Oakleigh Park

WALFIELD AVE
FARNHAM CL
MACARET CL
Allot Gdns
FRIERN MOUNT DRI
BUCKINGHAM AVE
LANGTON AVE
TEMPLE AVE
CHANDOS AVE
Hosp

Golf Course

Brook Farm Open Space
Allot Gdns
DOWNLAND CL
THE GRANGE
OAKLEIGH GDNS
Playing Fields
ATHENAEUM RD
OXFORD GDNS
THE FIRS
OAKLEIGH PARK N

CH
BELMONT CL
ROWBEN CL
WEST HILL WAY
LINKS DRI
OAK TREE DRI
GREAT BUSHEY DRI
Totteridge & Whetstone
ST MARGARETS
BLAMEREY
MANUS WAY
ILLIUM WAY
OAKLEIGH RD
Oakleigh Park
SHRUB LANDS
PINE GR

TOTTERIDGE LA
L
A5109
HILL CRES
A109
HIGH RD
OAKLEIGH RD N
A109
Totteridge
Whetstone
CAMERON CL
1250
SWEETS WAY

Greenway
NAYLOR RD
BIRLEY RD
BAXENDALE
THE MOUNT
B550
ORCHARD AVE
QUEENS AVE
MYDDELTON PARK
WILLOW END
ELMSTEADW END
GREENWAY RD
SOUTHWAY
LYNTON MEAD
VENTNOR DRI
LONGLAND DRI
HAYWARD RD
RASPER RD
FRIERN BARNET LA
B550

COPPICE WLK
RIDGEVIEW RD
SWAN LA
GREEN RD
CAPEL CL
Denis Brook

LAUREL WAY
CHARNWOOD PL
HARLEY CT
CONISTON CL
Golf Course

CHIDDINGFOLD
LAUREL VIEW
ROGERS WLK
WOODSIDE LA
WOODSIDE GR
DERWENT CRES
BRITTANNIA RD
PARK CL

NORTHIAM
FARMFIELD CL
BROOK MEADOW
CLAIRE CL
LIMES AVE
Finchley Park
MAYFIELD AVE

NORTHIAM
LORIAN CL
GUILDOWN RD
HOLDEN RD
LITTLE CEDARS
SQUIRRELS
HIGHWOOD
ANDREW'S CL
LYNTON RD
GREAT NORTH RD
A1000

DOWN
GREEN BANK ST
GRANGE GDNS
WATNANSEN VILLAGE
THEO FRED BALD'S ERICK'S AVE PL
FRIERN WATCH AVE

SOUTHOVER
TILLINGHAM GREEN WAY
SONIA GDNS
CLIVEDEN RD
CHURCH PATH
AVENUE RD
RAVENSDALE AVE
FRIARY RD
VALLEY AVE

Woodside Park
STATION CL
HOLDEN
THE OAKS
WOODSIDE
ASHBOURNE CL
FAIRFIELD CL
TORRINGTON PARK
CARDREW CL

CHANCTONBURY WAY
GARDEN CT
HOLDEN RD
WOODSIDE PARK RD
LODGE LA
VICTORIA GR
FRIERN PARK
BEECH LAWNS
GLENHURST
CARDEN AVE
Woodside Park

NES
EAGLETON SCARP
WESTBURY RD
SPRINGFIELD RD
GANSBOROUGH RD
NETHER GRANGE AVE
PERCY RD
ALBERT RD
STANHOPE RD
NORTHWOOD GDNS
GROVE RD
THE LINDENS
TORRINGTON AVE
HILTON AVE

SADDLESCOMBE WAY
SUSSEX RING
AVONDALE
GAINS BOROUGH AVE
COLERIDGE RD
DERBY AVE
HALL ST
REGENT
STANHOPE RD
CASTLE LAMBERT WAY
FENSTANTON AVE

POYNINGS WAY
STEYNINGS WAY
BALLINGTON FOLD
ARGYLE RD
HUTTON GR
DALE GR
ALEXANDRA GR
NETHER ST
North Finchley
A598
BALFOUR RD
A1000

25
23
26

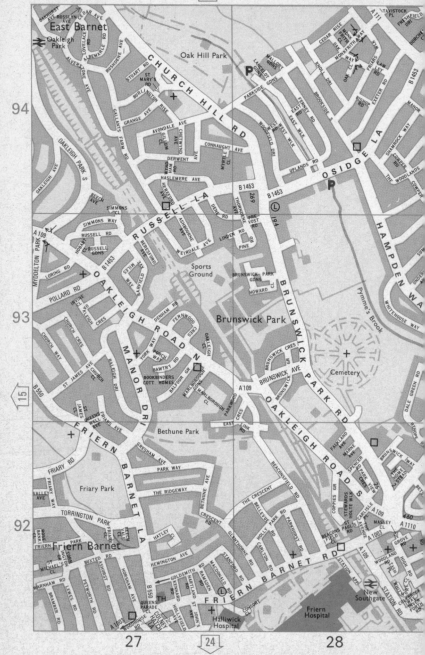

Grovelands Park

Grovelands
Hospital

Boating
Lake

Southgate

WOODCROFT

Osidge

Cricket
Ground

Cemy

A 1003 THE GREEN

WHITE
HOUSE
CT

Palmers Green

Southgate

THE BOURNE

HIGH ST

FOX LA

A 111

P

Poly

STATION
PAR

Southgate

Coll

Sch

CHASE SIDE

CHASE RD

CROWN LA

A 1004

MORTON
CRES

Broomfield
Park

Mus

ALDERMAN'S HILL

Palmers
Green

A 1004

A 1004

New Southgate

Arnos Park

Arnos
Grove

MORTON WAY

WATERFALL RD

POWYS LA

WILLMER WAY

BROOMFIELD LA

TH

North Circular Rd

A 1110 (T)

BOWES RD

A 406(T)

NORTH CIRCULAR RD

A 406(T)

15

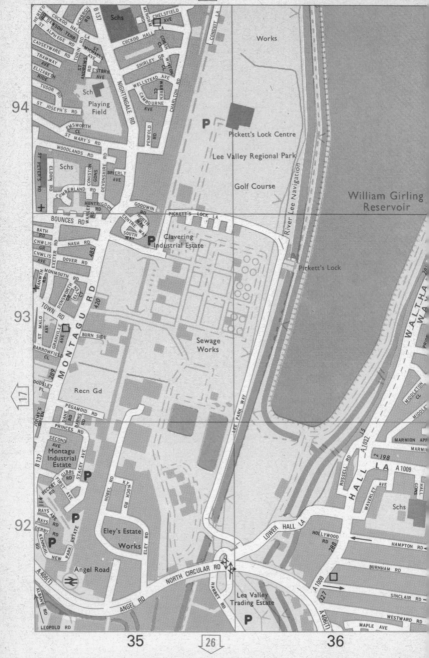

14

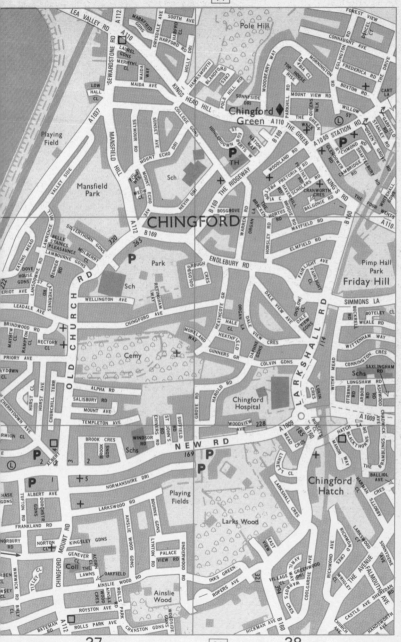

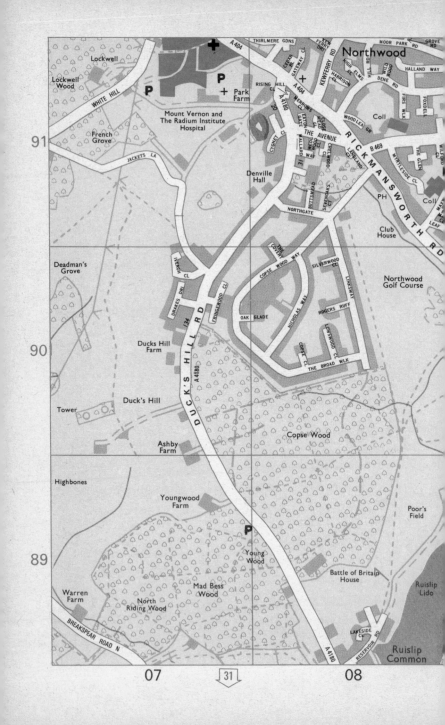

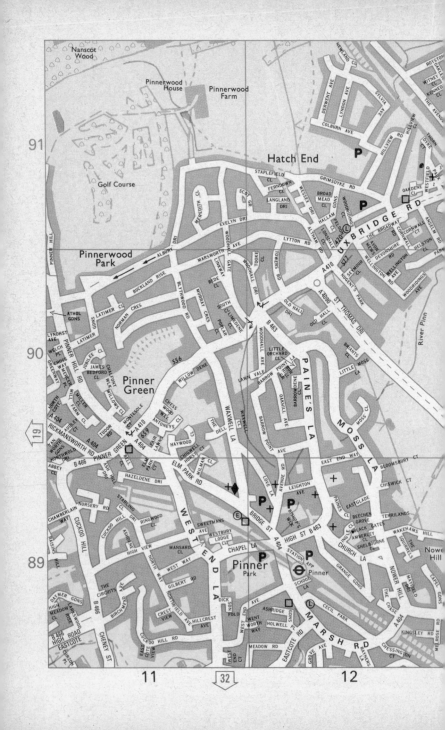

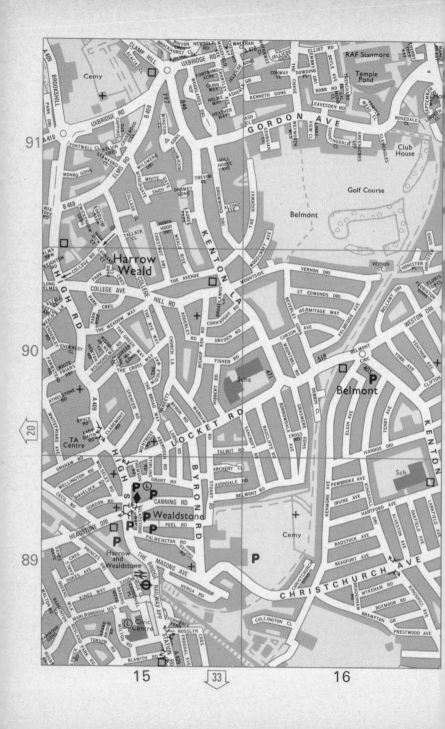

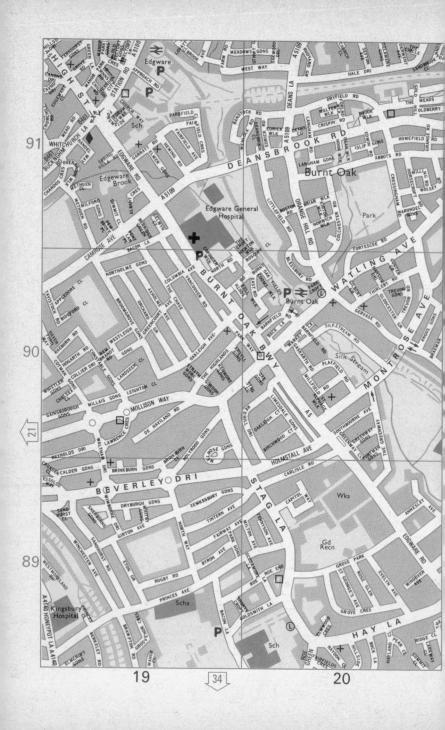

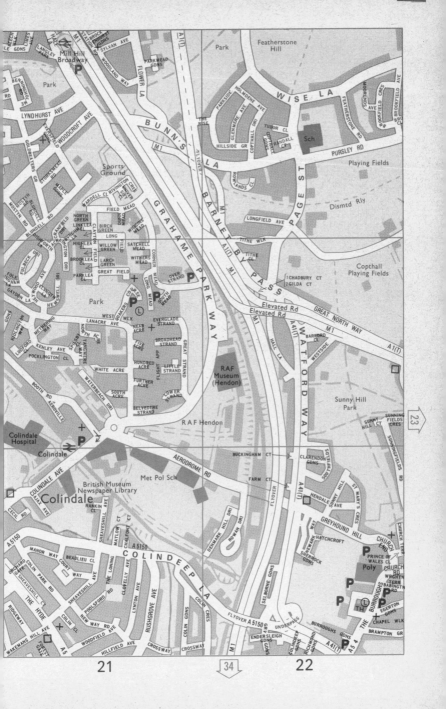

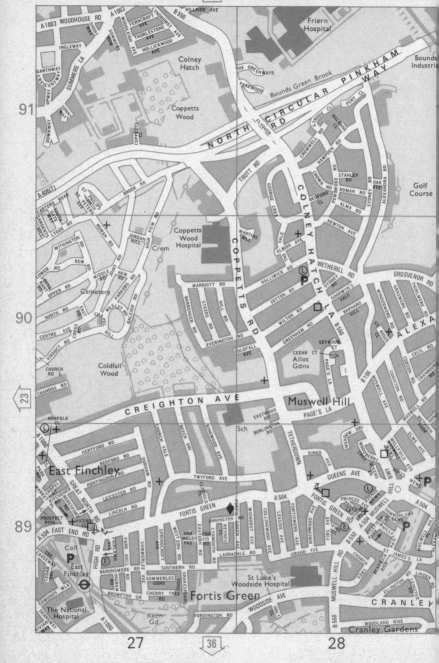

A1003 WOODHOUSE RD
A1003
HILLSIDE AVE
B 550

Friern
Hospital

FERNSCROFT AVE
THURLESTONE AVE
HOLLICKWOOD AVE
WOOLLEIGH AVE
LYNDHURST AVE
INGLEWAY
SUMMERS ROW
SUMMERS LA
GARTHWAY
CRESCENTWAY
UPWAY
DOWNWAY
RUNWAY
SHORT WAY

Colney
Hatch

THE GREENWAYS
PARKWOOD

Bounds Green Brook

Bounds
Industria

91

Coppetts
Wood

COPPETTS CL

NORTH CIRCULAR RD PINKHAM WAY

FLOWER

TROTT RD

SPODE CL
CROWLAND RD
HALDANE CL
PERT CL
HAMPDEN RD

A 406 (T)
CARTERS RD
SARGENTS SOUTH
SQUIRES HILLS
WITHINGTON RD
KEW RD
LOWER RD
UPPER RD
ST PHILLIPS
ST IVES
LTGOE RD
BROOK RD
JORDAN RILL
HIGH VIEW RD
ROMAN RD

GEORGE CRES

CROMWELL RD
PEMBROKE RD
STANLEY RD
ROMAN RD
ALMA RD
BEDFORD CL
CRONY
OAK AVE
ALEXANDRA RD
SYDNEY RD

Golf
Course

Coppetts
Wood
Hospital

MARTINS WALK

NEWTON AVE

ALBION AVE
THE VALE
VALE

WETHERILL RD

GROSVENOR RD

Crem

MIDDLE RD
SAINT RD
NEW RD
PARXERS RD
RALEIGH RD
WESLEY RD
CH PEEL HILL

MARRIOTT RD
BARRENGER RD
STEEDS RD
HILL RD

HALLIWICK RD
SUTTON RD
WILTON RD

SYDNEY RD
GOODWYN'S VALE
BARNARD HILL
ST REGIS

WINDERMERE RD
GRASMERE RD
THIRLMERE RD

90

Cemetery

NORTH RD
EAST RD
CENTRE AVE
CROSS RD
VIADUCT RD
CHURCH RD S
CHANDOS RD

EVERINGTON RD
COLDFALL AVE

GREENHAM RD

SEYMOUR CT
CEDAR CT
Allot
Gdns
PAGE'S LA

B 106
MUSWELL AVE
CONISTON RD
CURZON RD
CECIL RD
CRANMOUR RD

ALEXA

Coldfall
Wood

23

NORFOLK CL

CREIGHTON AVE

Muswell Hill

CHURCH VALE
BEECH DRI
RINGWOOD AVE

EASTWOOD RD
BURLINGTON RD
PAGE'S LA

TETHERDOWN

MEADOW DRI
WOODBERRY CRES
QUEENS
DUKES AVE
WELLFIELD AVE
ELMS AVE
MEXFIELD

East Finchley
A 1000

HERTFORD RD
BEDFORD RD
HUNTINGDON RD
DURHAM RD

TWYFORD AVE
CLISSOLD RD

Sch

KINGS AVE

QUEENS AVE

AMB
DIKES RD
MEWS

P

89

PARK
MARKET PL
CHAPEL
KITCHENER RD
BRIMSDOWN
GREAT NORTH RD
HIGH RD
PROSPECT RING
VICEROY
A 504 EAST END RD
FAIRLYNN
PARK HALL RD
SUMMERLEE AVE
BARONSMERE RD
INGRAM RD
BROMPTON GR

Coll
East Finchley

LEICESTER RD
LINCOLN RD
FORTIS GREEN

CHAPEL
SPRINGFIELD
WEST FERN RD
WELLS RD
NAB
FRANCIS RD
LYNMOUTH RD
ANNINGTON
KEYNES

EASTERN RD
SOUTHERN RD
SHAKESPEARE

LAURADALE RD

MIDHURST AVE
LEASIDE AVE
COLLINGWOOD AVE

FORTIS GREEN RD
FORTISMERE AVE
GRAND AVE

PRINCES AVE
FIR AVE

DOGMODIB

A 504
FORTIS GREEN RD

A 504 MUSWELL
B 550
CHURCH
PRIORY

SUMMERLAND GDNS
A 504

P

The
National
Hospital

P
East
Finchley

EDMUNDS WLK
CEDARS
THE CAUSEWAY
GREATWAY
VIVIAN WAY

A 1000

SUMMERLEE GDNS
CHERRY TREE RD
Recn Gd
FORDINGTON RD

St Luke's
Woodside Hospital

Fortis Green

WOODSIDE AVE

HOLT CL

MUSWELL HILL RD

ST JAMES'S LA
ST JAMES'S
BECKTOR RISE
PRIORY
RISE
LINDEN RD
ELLINGTON RD
HINTERY
ROSTERY

CRANLEY

WOODLAND RISE

Cranley Gardens

25

Traffic Restriction
PARK VIEW RD
HAVELOCK RD
ROSEBERY AVE
SHELBOURNE RD
WILLOUGHBY LA
DYSON'S RD

Vehicle access to these roads
is restricted at certain times
Observe road signs.
Beware of traffic barriers.

Tottenham

Tottenham Hale

Works

Works

LEA VALLEY
TRADING ESTATE

HARBET RD

P

A 406(T)

MAPLE AVE

SILVER BIRCH AV

LILAC

HAZEL

LABURNUM

MARIGOLD
WAY

Wks

W A L T H A

LEESIDE RD

91

LEESIDE
INDUSTRIAL
ESTATE

GARMAN RD

MOWLEM
TRADING ESTATE

Pymme's Brook

River Lee Navigation

Banbury Reservoir

FOLLY LA

STO
CRES

P

Tottenham Marshes

COGAN AVE

COOPER AVE

VALLOUES

AUBE

ASCHAM
END

CHENEY ROW

DURRANT

KIMBERLEY

SINNOTT RD

LAWRENCE AVE

MC ENTEE AVE

210

B I L L E T   R D

GUILDSWAY

LYNE

WIGTON

FAIR VIEW
CL

SHAW
SQ

161

90

LEE 414

249

SUTTON RD

THE
MILE

WORCESTER RD

1 ROMANY GDNS
2 SWANSLAND GDNS
3 GARNETT WAY

MILLFIELD AVE

NORTH COUNTESS

WILLIAMS
AVE

KEITH

THORPE

ANGEL RD

NUSHORD

RIVERHEAD

WOODSTON
CL

LOCKWOOD
WAY

GLOUCESTER RD

CLARENCE RD

MAYFIELD RD

MECHAM
CL

NORFOLK RD

CARLTON RD

MANOR RD

MANOR
CL

WARWICK RD

RODNEY PL

WINDSOR

PLEASANT RD

MOUNT
PL

CUMBER
LAND

OAKFIELD
RD

HERON

PENNANT

FLEMING
CL

TERR

Lockwood
Reservoir

LANCASTER RD

GOLDSMITH RD

SHAKESPEARE RD

ST ANDREWS RD

Higham Hill

CHURCH
HILL

CLAREMONT
RD

BRAMLEY
CL

HILLYFIELD

GATLAND

HAMILTON

COLVILLE

PRIORS CROFT

PRIORY

ELPHINSTONE RD

FLEMING RD

Allot
Gdns

THE
QUAD
RANGLE

UPLANDS
AVE

UPLANDS TRADING
ESTATE

STIRLING
PATH

SUTHERLAND RD

STIRLING RD

BROAD INDS

HIGHAM
RD

GREEN
POND
RD

WINNS   AVE

HOLMES
RD

BELMSTED RD

WERSLEY RD

89

RICKFORD
WAY

A 503

Low Maynard Reservoir

High Maynard Reservoir

PRIESTLEY
WAY

HOOKER'S
RD

Wks

HIGH AM. ST

BLENHEIM RD

TAVISTOCK AVE

KENMARE AVE

FARNBOROUGH

KING EDWARD RD

CENTURY RD

QUEEN ELIZABETH RD

CHATHAM RD

ROMA RD

PASQUIER RD

BENNESS RD

LUTON RD

SOUTH
COUNTESS RD

WILLIAM
MORRIS
CL

RUSSELL RD

BOXWICK

ROSEBANK

WOLSEY RD

GREEN LE

B 179

CLIFTON AVE

65

CANNING RD

WELLINGTON RD

MELBOURNE RD

COLERIDGE RD

MELVILLE

P

26

ESSEX
CL

ORCHARD
ST

LIME
STONE
RD

DUKE
RD

LINKS
RD

BRISTOL
PARK RD

MAYNARD
PARK RD

SUFFOLK
PARK RD

WALPOLE RD

GAINSFORD RD

ELMSDALE RD

COTTENHA

CAMPBELL RD

Blackhorse
Road

STONEYDOWN
HOUSE

BLACKHORSE RD

A 1006

HAWARDEN
RD

LLOYD RD

CORNWALLIS RD

EDWARD RD

COURTENAY RD

LONGFELLOW AVE

PRETORIA AVE

A 1006

CHEWTON RD

NORTHCOTE AVE

WARNER RD

BRAXTON RD

MELFORD RD

WOODVILLE RD

OSBORNE
GR

PALMERSTON RD

MANSFIELD RD

SOMERS

ELDON RD

STOREY RD

HIGH

25

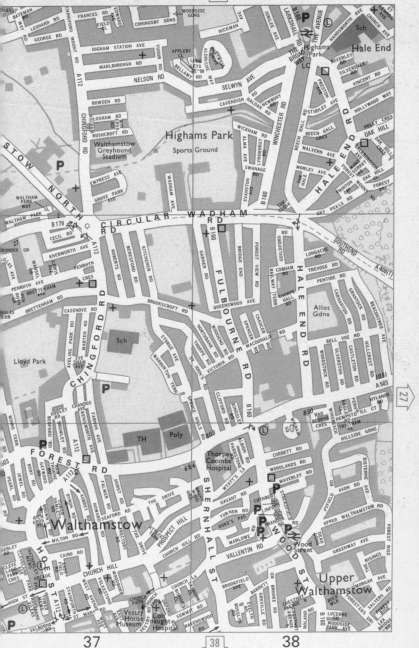

Hale End

Highams Park
Sports Ground

Walthamstow
Greyhound
Stadium

WALTHAM
PARK WAY

CIRCULAR — WADHAM — RD

SOUTHEND RD

A 408(T)

Highams Park

HALE END RD

FULBOURNE RD

Allot
Gdns

Lloyd Park

CHINGFORD RD

Sch

27

A 503

TH Poly

Thorpe
Coombe
Hospital

FOREST RD

SHERNHALL ST

PROSPECT HILL

Walthamstow

WOOD ST

Wood
Street

Upper
Walthamstow

CHURCH HILL

Vestry
House
Museum

Con
Connaught
Hospital

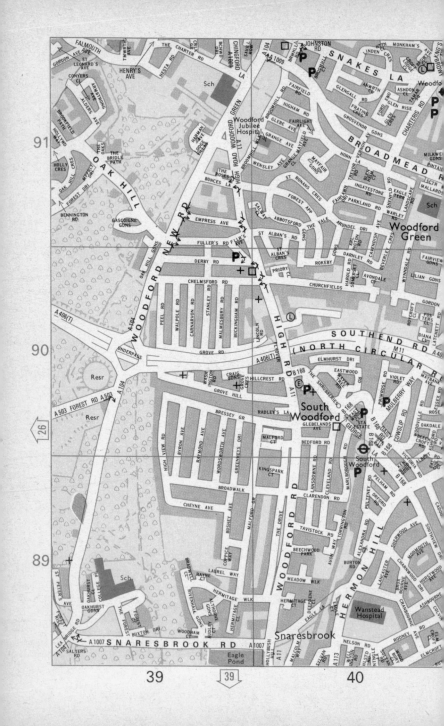

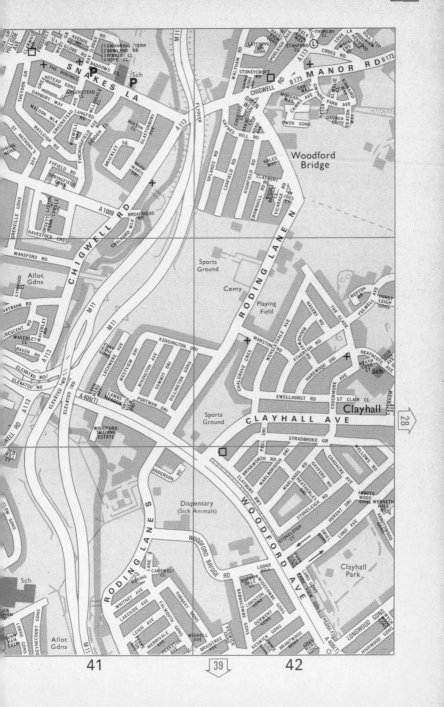

Woodford
Bridge

Clayhall

Clayhall
Park

Sports
Ground

Cemy

Playing
Field

Sports
Ground

Woodford
Trading
Estate

Dispensary
(Sick Animals)

Sch

Allot
Gdns

Allot
Gdns

Sch

41   39   42

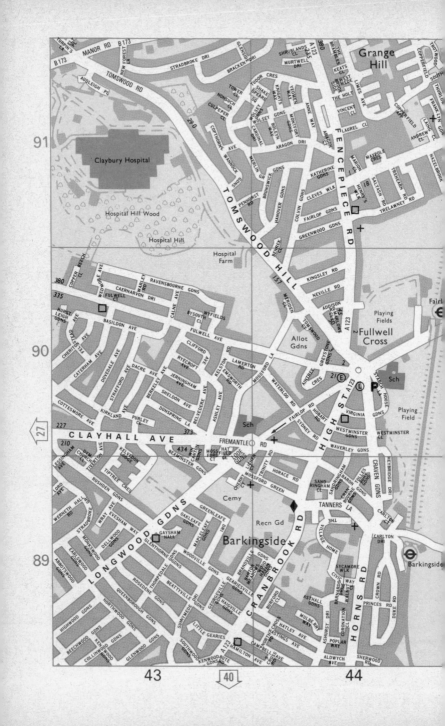

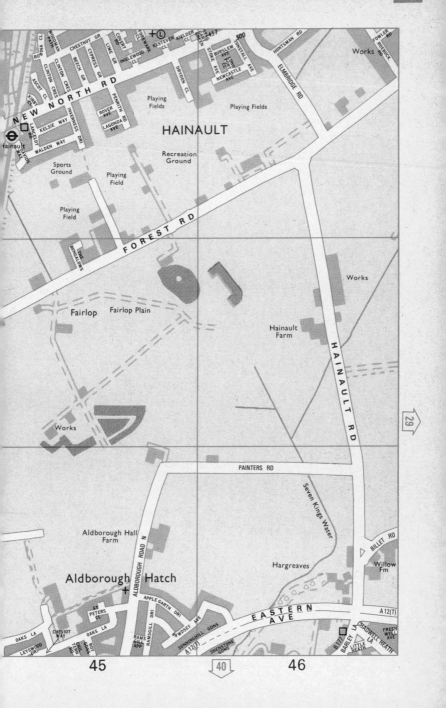

HAINAULT

Works

NEW NORTH RD

ELMBRIDGE RD

HUNTSMAN RD

FOWLER RD

RODUCK

Playing Fields

Playing Fields

Recreation Ground

Sports Ground

Playing Field

Playing Field

THE BUNGALOWS

FOREST RD

Works

Fairlop

Fairlop Plain

Hainault Farm

HAINAULT RD

Works

29

PAINTERS RD

Aldborough Hall Farm

Seven Kings Water

BILLET RD

Willow Fm

ALDBOROUGH ROAD N

Aldborough Hatch

Hargreaves

A12(T)

ST PETERS CL

APPLE GARTH DRI

EASTERN AVE

CHADWELL HEATH

FRESH WELL AVE

CHEVIOT WAY

OAKS LA

OAKS LA

RAMSGILL DRI

TWDSET AVE

SUNNINGHILL GDNS

SHENSTONE GDNS

A12(T)

BARLEY LA

LITTLE HEATH

LEYSWOOD DRI

RAMS GILL APP

ROY GDNS

CHILL TERN RD

B177

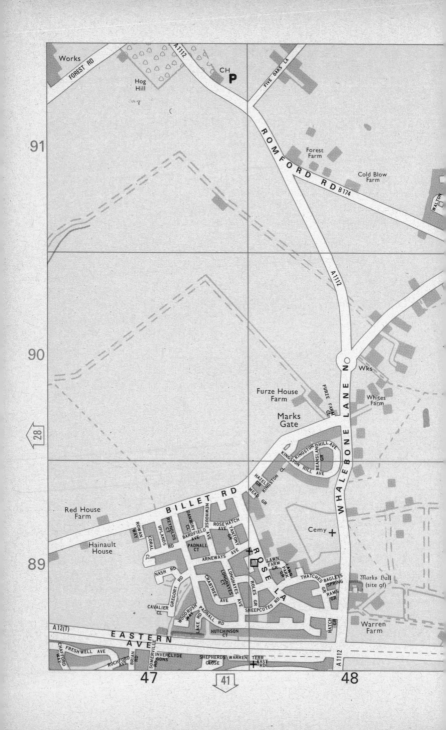

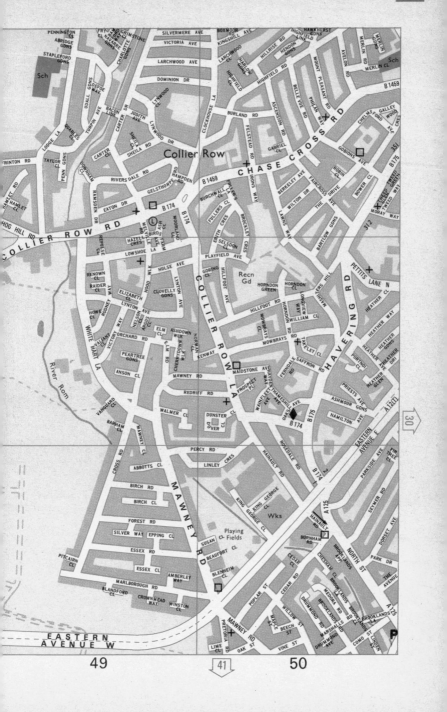

Collier Row

CHASE CROSS RD

B 1459

B 174

COLLIER ROW RD

HOG HILL RD

COLLIER ROW

WHITE HART LA

River Rom

COLLIER ROW LA

HAVERING RD

PETTITS LANE N

MAWNEY RD

EASTERN AVENUE W

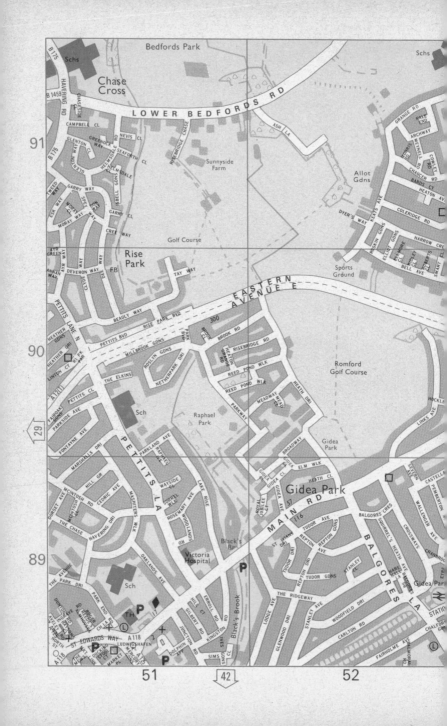

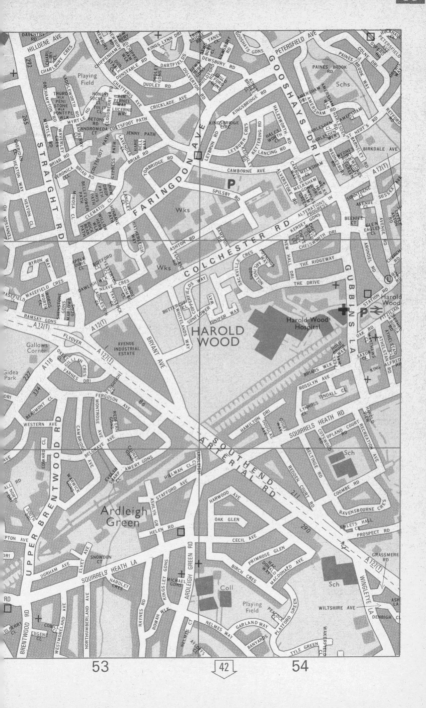

HAROLD WOOD

Harold Wood Hospital

Ardleigh Green

Willow Tree Farm

Bayhurst Wood Country Park

BREAKSPEAR RD N

FINE BUSH LA

Crem

DELL FARM RD

DUCKS HILL RD

WITHY LA

RESERVOIR RD

88

BREAKSPEAR RD

STANDALE GR

ST CATHERINES RD

BURY AVE

BOSTON GR

HOWLETTS LA

OLD HOWLETT'S LA

LABURNUM GR

KESWICK GDNS

ST EDMUNDS RD

BURY ST

STOWE CRES

LESBONE

WAYEL

WYTELEA CL

DIBDIN CL

WALLINGTON CL

HOWLETTS LA

ARLINGTON DRI

MEADWAY WAY

NEWYEARS GREEN LA

Elm Tree Farm

Newyears Green

Crows Nest Farm

BREAKSPEAR RDS

MAYFLOWER CL

WESTWOOD CL

St CATHERINES FARM CT

NAYBORNE

HANKE

HWYTE CL

STAFFORD CL

MARLBOROUGH AVE

COPPICE

ST MARGARETS

MEAD

LADYGATE LA

WHITCLEATH AVE

GRASMERE

RAVENSCOURT CL

ANSLEY

WOODVILLE GDNS

FAIRFIELD AVE

GLENHOLME

HEATHFIELD RISE

ELLESMERE RD

ROUNDHILL

GLENFIELD CRES

VICARAGE CL

GLENHURST

WESTCOTE RISE

ORCHARD CL

SOUTHCOTE RISE

NEATS ACRE

87

TILE KILNS LA

FIELD WAY

HILL LA

FIELD HILL RISE

CHARFS LA

COTTAGE CL

MANOR RD

KING EDW

CHURCH AVE

CLACK LA

Golf Course

West Ruislip

ICKENHAM R

MARWELL CL

FAIRFIELD RD

SEAFORD CL

WHITSTABL

CHICA

THE GREENWAY

BEAUFORT RD

GRINDLEY RD

SWINDER RD

ICKENHAM CL

GOODYER RD

LYMINGTON DRI

BLENHEIM CRES

WE

West Ruislip

86

Moat

PINCHESTER CL

HOTLAKE CRES

THE MEAD

BUSHEY RD

BUSHEY CL

CHITTERN CL

FIELD CL

WOODLAND CL

MALVERN CL

CHARLTON GR

FARM CL

THE GREENWAY

OAK AVE

PARKFIELD RD

RECTORY RD

ASH WAY

RCHAM AVE

HIGH ROAD ICKENHAM

PENTLAND

TWEEDALE GR

ANNANDALE GR

AUSTIN'S LA

ST GEORGE'S DRI

COPHALL RD W

ELG'R CL

KENBURY CL

DERWENT AVE

GREENACRES AVE

WALLASEY CRES

COPHALL RD E

BROADACRE

ELEANOR GR

BONIFACE RD

THE TILES

RAF Station

B 467

SWAKELEYS RDS

B 467

VINLAKE AVE

THORNHILL CL

STEDMAN CL

BELLAMY CL

THE AVENUE

IVYHOUSE RD

MILTON RD

ALMOND AVE

EDINBURGH DRI

CLAY

LONG LA

COMMUNITY

WILLOW TREE LA

P

Ickenham

07   08

Eastcote Village

Ruislip

Eastcote

EASTCOTE RD

Ruislip Manor

Ruislip

WEST END RD

VICTORIA RD

20

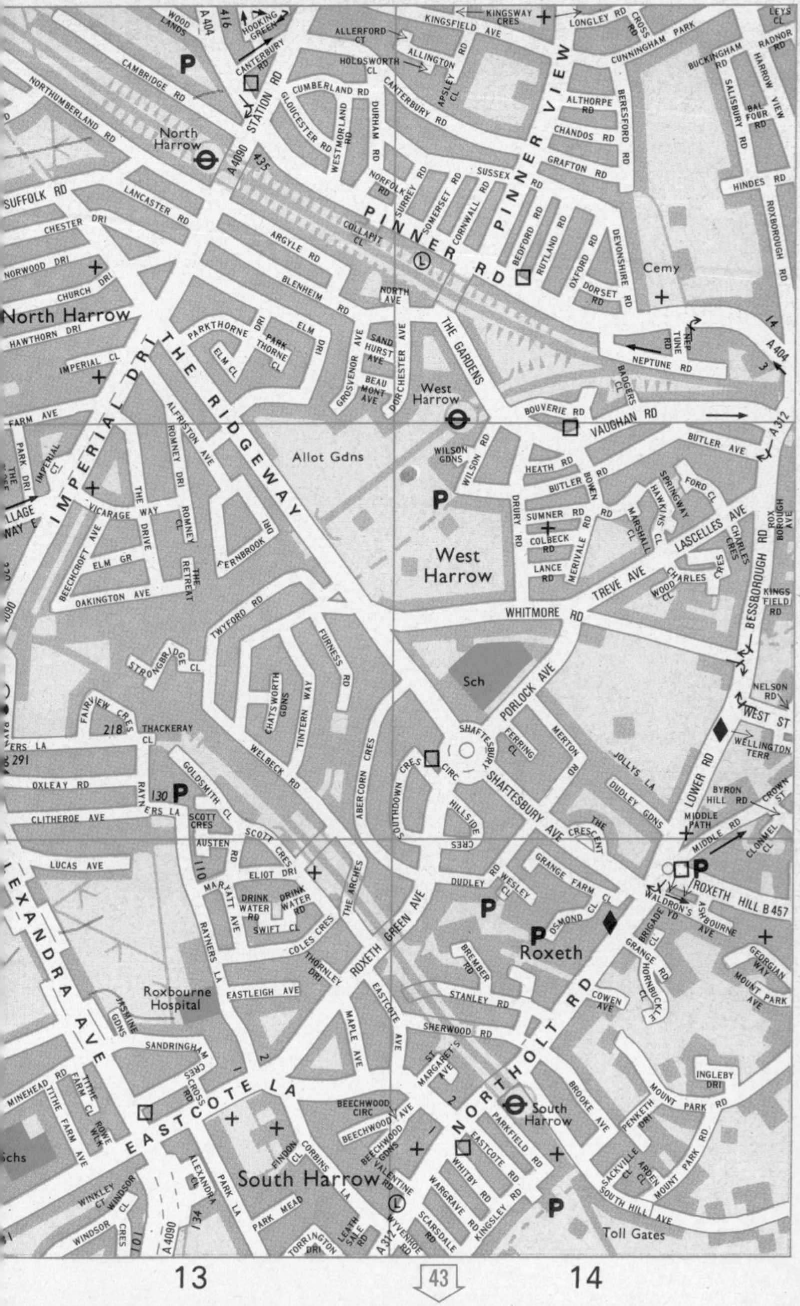

WOOD LANDS
A 404
416
HOOKING GREEN
CANTERBURY RD
CAMBRIDGE RD
NORTHUMBERLAND RD
STATION RD
North Harrow
A 4090
435
SUFFOLK RD
LANCASTER RD
CHESTER DRI
NORWOOD DRI
CHURCH DRI
North Harrow
HAWTHORN DRI
IMPERIAL CL
IMPERIAL DRI
FARM AVE
PARK DRI
IMPERIAL CT
VILLAGE WAY E
KINGSWAY CRES
KINGSFIELD AVE
ALLERFORD CT
ALLINGTON CL
HOLDSWORTH CL
APSLEY CL
CUMBERLAND RD
GLOUCESTER RD
WESTMORLAND RD
DURHAM RD
CANTERBURY RD
NORFOLK RD
SURREY RD
SOMERSET RD
CORNWALL RD
SUSSEX RD
COLLAPIT CL
PINNER RD
ARGYLE RD
BLENHEIM RD
NORTH AVE
LONGLEY RD
CROSS RD
CUNNINGHAM PARK
LEYS CL
RADNOR RD
BUCKINGHAM RD
HARROW VIEW
SALISBURY RD
BAL FOUR RD
ALTHORPE RD
BERESFORD RD
CHANDOS RD
GRAFTON RD
PINNER VIEW
HINDES RD
ROXBOROUGH RD
BEDFORD RD
RUTLAND RD
OXFORD RD
DEVONSHIRE RD
DORSET RD
Cemy
NEP TUNE RD
NEPTUNE RD
A 404
BADGERS CL
PARKTHORNE DRI
PARK THORNE CL
ELM CL
ELM DRI
GROSVENOR AVE
SANDHURST AVE
BEAUMONT AVE
DORCHESTER AVE
THE GARDENS
West Harrow
THE RIDGEWAY
ALFRISTON AVE
ROMNEY DRI
BOUVERIE RD
VAUGHAN RD
A 312
BUTLER AVE
WILSON GDNS
WILSON RD
Allot Gdns
HEATH RD
BUTLER RD
BOWEN RD
SPRINGWAY
HAWKINS CL
FORD CL
DRURY RD
SUMNER RD
COLBECK RD
MARSHALL CL
MERIVALE RD
LASCELLES AVE
CHARLES CRES
ROX BOROUGH AVE
West Harrow
LANCE RD
TREVE AVE
WOOD CL
BESSBOROUGH RD
KINGSFIELD RD
VICARAGE WAY
THE DRIVE
ROMNEY CL
BEECHCROFT AVE
ELM GR
FERNBROOK DRI
OAKINGTON AVE
THE RETREAT
WHITMORE RD
TWYFORD RD
STRONGBRIDGE CL
FURNESS RD
CHATSWORTH GDNS
TINTERN WAY
Sch
PORLOCK AVE
NELSON RD
WEST ST
FAIRVIEW CRES
218
THACKERAY CL
RAYNERS LA
291
OXLEAY RD
WELBECK RD
ABERCORN CRES
SOUTHDOWN CRES
SHAFTESBURY CIRC
FERRING CL
MERTON RD
JOLLYS LA
WELLINGTON TERR
LOWER RD
130
GOLDSMITH CL
CLITHEROE AVE
SCOTT CRES
HILLSIDE CRES
SHAFTESBURY AVE
DUDLEY GDNS
BYRON HILL RD
CROWN ST
MIDDLE PATH
MIDDLE RD
THE CRESCENT
LUCAS AVE
AUSTEN RD
110
SCOTT CRES
ELIOT DRI
THE ARCHES
DUDLEY RD
WESLEY CL
GRANGE FARM CL
CLONMEL CL
ROXETH HILL B 457
MARYATT AVE
DRINK WATER RD
SWIFT CL
ROXETH GREEN AVE
OSMOND CL
WALDRON'S YD
ASHBOURNE AVE
BRIGADE CL
ALEXANDRA AVE
COLES CRES
THORNLEY DRI
BREMBER RD
Roxeth
GRANGE RD
GEORGIAN WAY
HORNBUCKLE CL
MOUNT PARK AVE
Roxbourne Hospital
EASTLEIGH AVE
EASTCOTE AVE
MAPLE AVE
STANLEY RD
COWEN AVE
JASMINE GDNS
SHERWOOD RD
NORTHOLT RD
SANDRINGHAM CRES
CROSS RD
ST. MARGARET'S AVE
BROOKE AVE
INGLEBY DRI
MINEHEAD RD
TITHE FARM CL
EASTCOTE LA
BEECHWOOD CIRC
BEECHWOOD AVE
South Harrow
MOUNT PARK RD
PENKETH DRI
ROWE WLK
TITHE FARM AVE
BEECHWOOD GDNS
EASTCOTE RD
PARKFIELD RD
Schs
SACKVILLE CL
ARDEN CL
WINKLEY CT
WINDSOR CL
ALEXANDRA CL
PARK LA
FINDON CL
CORBINS LA
South Harrow
VALENTINE RD
WHITBY RD
KINGSLEY RD
SOUTH HILL AVE
WINDSOR CRES
101
A 4090
134
PARK MEAD
TORRINGTON DRI
LEATHSALE RD
A 312
WYVENHOE RD
SCARSDALE RD
WARGRAVE RD
Toll Gates

33

13 14

43

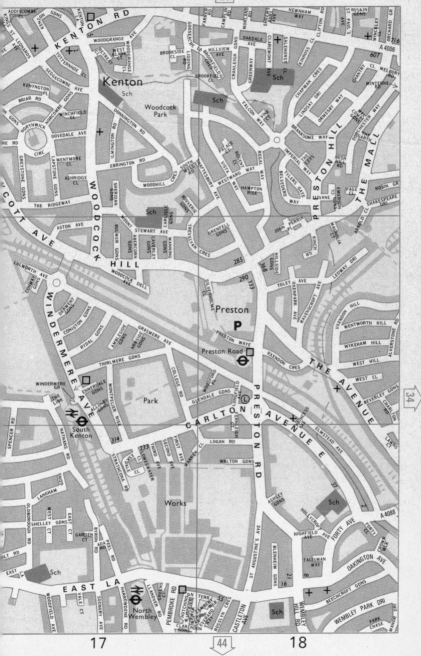

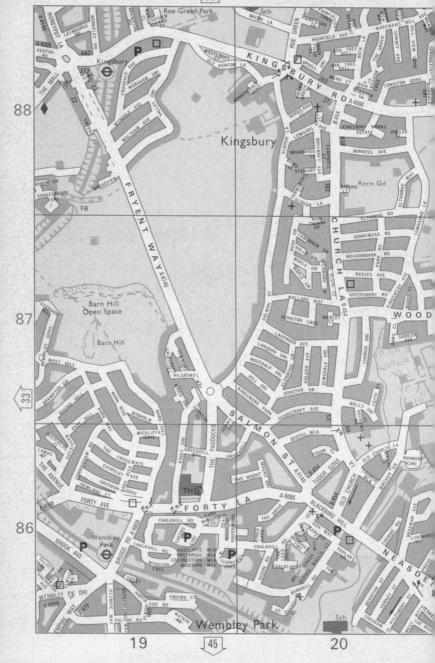

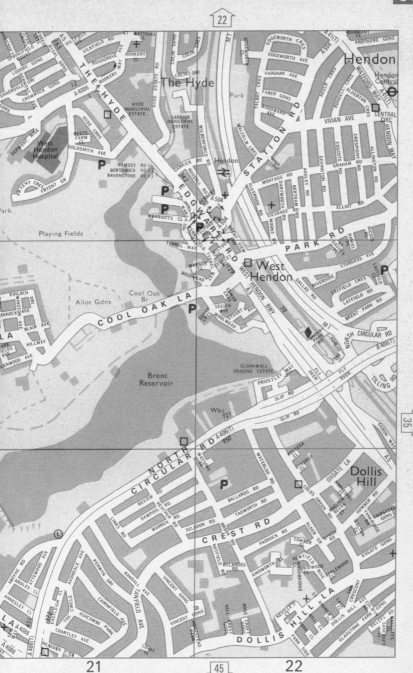

Hendon

The Hyde

West Hendon Hospital

West Hendon

Brent Reservoir

Cool Oak La

COOL OAK LA

Playing Fields

Allot Gdns

Dollis Hill

NORTH CIRCULAR RD A406(T)

CREST RD

DOLLIS HILL LA

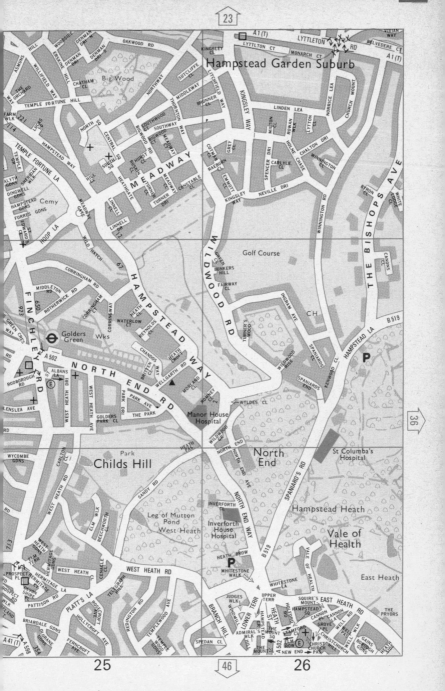

DEANS WAY
THE BISHOPS AVE
CONNAUGHT
TERESA
HOUSE
WOODLAND GDNS
ONSLOW GDNS
CONNAUGHT WK
A 1000
DRIVE
THE DRIVE
ACTON
WOODSIDE AVE
LANCHESTER RD
B 550
BANCROFT AVE
GREAT NORTH RD
CHERRY TREE HILL
MANSFIELD
A 1000
DESK'S GDNS
Highgate Wood
Queen's Wood
AYLMER RD
WHITTINGTON CT
A 1(T)
B 517
TOTNE
KENWOOD
BAKER'S
NORTH HILL AVE
MUSWELL HILL RD
SUMMERSBY RD
SOUTH CL
QUEEN'S WOOD RD

88

BISHOPS GR
Golf Course
CH
SHELDON AVE
YEATMAN RD
CHURCH RD
B 517
STOREY
BASKELL
TALBOT RD
CROMWELL RD
NORTH HILL
BISHOPSWOOD RD
BISHOPS RD
HILLSIDE GDNS
THE PARK
Highgate
P L
E
SHEPHERD'S
WOOD LA
PRIORY GDNS
HOLMESDALE RD
ORCHARD

WHITE LODGE CL
DENEWOOD RD
VIEW CL
VIEW RD
GRANGE RD
BROADLANDS RD
WOODLANDS
HILLCREST
PARK WLK
PARK WLK
SOUTHWOOD LA
SOUTHWOOD
SOUTHWOOD AVE
JACKSON'S
LAWN RD
ARCHWAY RD
CROMWELL
A 1

COURTENAY AVE
COMPTON AVE
STORMONT RD
BROADLANDS RD
WOODLANDS
PARK HOUSE PAS
HIGHPOINT
Highgate
CASTLE YD
KINGSLEY
DORSET GDNS
Southwood Hospital
CHOLMELEY PARK
PEA WLK
CAUSTON RD
B 519
HAMPSTEAD LA
BISHOPSWOOD RD
HIGHGATE CL
B 519 NORTH RD
KINGSLEY PL
HIGH RD
B 550
DUKE'S HEAD
WINCHESTER PL
WELLEY CRES

87

The Iveagh Bequest Kenwood
Middlesex Hospital Recovery Unit Athlone House
FITZROY PARK
THE GROVE
SOUTH GR
BACON'S LA
BISHAM
HIGHGATE HIGH ST
THE BANK
NETHERLEIGH CL
DARTMOUTH

35

Ken Wood
FITZROY CL
FITZROY PARK
WEST HILL
HIGHGATE
HOLLY TERR
HOLLY LODGE
MERTON LANE
WEST HILL PARK
ROBIN LA
ST JAMES'S
Highgate Cemetery
Whittington Hosp (St Mary's Wing)
Whittington Hospital (Highgate Wing)
Dartmouth
Highgate Cemetery
CULOT
RETCAR CL
SANDSTONE RD
STONELEIGH TERR
RAYDON ST

86

Highgate Ponds
Tumulus
Parliament Hill
MILLFIELD LA
MILLFIELD PL
OAKESHOTT AVE
MAKEPEACE AVE
LANGBOURNE AVE
BROMWICH AVE
ST ANNE'S
WEST HILL
BROOKFIELD
HIGHGATE RD
ST ALBAN
BROOKFIELD PARK RD
KINGWEAR RD
CROUCH
DOYNTON ST
BALMOR
CHESTER RD
BRAMSHILL
BELLTREE
WINSCOMBE
PARK
YORK RISE
BRAMSHILL GDNS
PARK AVE
LAURIER RD

Parliament Hill
SOUTH HILL PARK
PARLIAMENT HILL
WOODSOME RD
GROVE TERRACE
BOSCASTLE RD
YORK RISE
LAURIER RD
DARTMOUTH PARK ROW
BELLGATE MEWS
CHETWYND RD
SPENCER
Schs
Sch

27
28

24

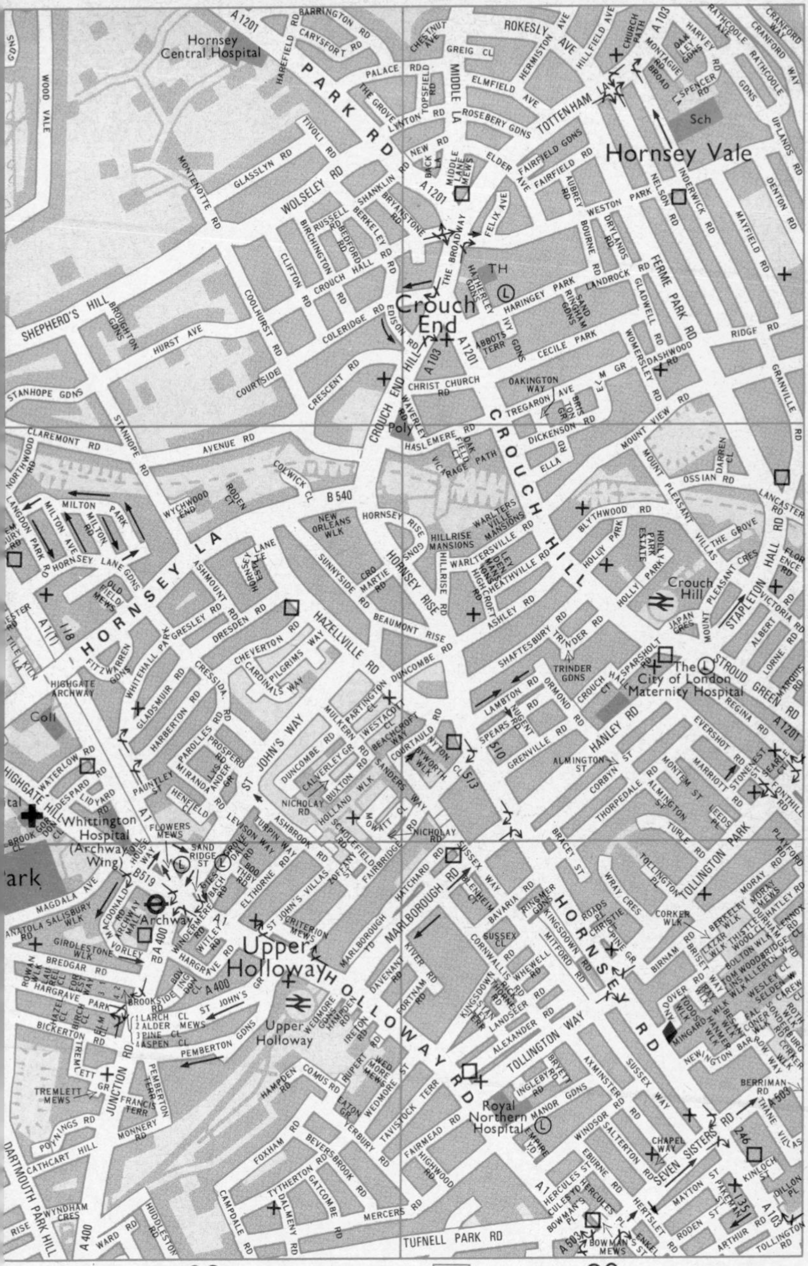
Hornsey Central Hospital
Hornsey Vale
Crouch End
Crouch Hill
The City of London Maternity Hospital
Whittington Hospital (Archway Wing)
Archway
Upper Holloway
Royal Northern Hospital
PARK RD
TOTTENHAM LA
HORNSEY LA
CROUCH HILL
HORNSEY RD
HOLLOWAY RD
TUFNELL PARK RD
SHEPHERD'S HILL
CROUCH END HILL
HORNSEY RISE
STROUD GREEN RD
SEVEN SISTERS RD
DARTMOUTH PARK HILL
JUNCTION RD
TOLLINGTON WAY
TOLLINGTON PARK
FERME PARK RD
MOUNT PLEASANT VILLAS
ST JOHN'S WAY
HAZELLVILLE RD
MARLBOROUGH RD
CAMPDALE RD
WOOD VALE

37

29 30

47

EFFINGHAM RD
BERESFORD RD
B 138
A 105
COLINAS RD
HARRINGAY RD
GLENWOOD RD
AVONDALE RD
CRANLEIGH RD
FALMER RD
CLARENCE RD
GORDON RD
GONVILLE RD
NEWSAM AVE
ST ANNS RD

ALLISON RD
HARINGEY
B 152
WOODLANDS PARK
CONWAY
RD
THERLEY RD
RITCHES RD
ROWLEY RD
BLACK BOY LA
CORNWALL
ALEXANDRA
PENRITH RD
NORTH
AVENUE
OULTON

HEWITT RD
SALISBURY RD
BRAMPTON RD
ASCOT RD
SOUTH
CISSBURY

SEYMOUR RD PAS
WARHAM RD
KIMBERLEY GDNS
WARWICK RD
SUFFOLK RD

88
Harringay
PEMBERTON RD
MATTISON RD
CHESTERFIELD RD
St Ann's
General Hospital

DUCKETT
HARINGEY
ROSEBERRY
ELEVINGTON GDNS
ESTON
RUTLAND GDNS
OAKDALE RD
TEMPLETON RD
REMINGTON
MORETON RD
MOSELAN
MANOR

CAVENDISH RD
STANHOPE GDNS
ASHFIELD
BEECHFIELD RD
TIVERTON RD
MORETON RD
PULEORD
HEYSHAM RD

CHETTLE CL
BURGOYNE RD
GRAFTON GDNS
TAVISTOCK
FINSBURY RD
BERKELEY RD
NETHERTON RD

CRANFORD WAY
UPLANDS RD
BEXTON
OAKFIELD RD
Harringay
UMFREVILLE RD
HARRINGAY
STADIUM
ARENA
VALE TERR
HERMITAGE RD
A 503
SAMUEL LEWIS

MOUNT
QUENNMORE RD
WOODCLOSE RD
Harringay
Stadium
VALE RD
EADE RD

ALBANY
LODDIGES RD
STAPLETON HALL RD
CONNINGSBY RD
LOTHAIR ROAD N
B 150
FINSBURY PARK
LINK WAY
A 107
A

Stroud Green
LOTHAIR RD
TANCRED RD
VENETIA RD
NEWTON

LANCASTER
CORNWALL RD
ENDYMION RD
New River
ROWLEY GDNS
WOODBERRY GR
SEVEN SISTERS RD
LINCOLN CT

DAGMAR RD
BEATRICE RD
CARL
CARLISLE RD
Park
WOODBERRY DOWN

87
LOWE
FLORENCE RD
VICTORIA
SCARTHO
GREEN LANES
SPRING PARK
Sch
East Reservoir

MARQUIS
UPPER TOLLINGTON PARK B150
OXFORD RD
Manor House
WOODBERRY GR
WOODCOURT PATH

DULAS ST
PERTH RD
QUINN'S RD
WOODSTOCK RD
PORTLAND RISE
BIRTLE CT
FAIRHOLT RD
ST ANDREWS
PAGET

36
STROUD GREEN
CHATERIS RD
PORTLAND RD
ALEXANDRA
GR
HENRY RD
West Reservoir
LORDSHIP RD

MARCUS RD
CLIFTON RD
WAVERLEY
ADOLPHUS RD
GLOUCESTER DRI
Bearsted Memorial Hospital

LENNOX RD
NORRIS
WELLS TERR
PRINCESS CS
3RD S
QUEEN'S DRI
ALLERTON RD
LORDSHIP PARK MEWS
B 105

FONTHILL RD
GOODWIN RD
ROCK ST
FINSBURY RD
WILBERFORCE RD
DIGBY CRES
LORDSHIP PARK
QUEEN ELIZABETH'S WLK
GRAZEBROOK
CHESTNUT CL

PLAYFORD RD
BIGGERSTAFF RD
TWHICON
Finsbury Park
SOMERFIELD RD
PARK RD
BROWNSWOOD RD
GREENWAY CL
Park
LORDSHIP

86
A 503
DURHAM RD
ISLEDON RD
PRAH RD
ROMILLY RD
BLACKSTOCK RD
B 105
KING'S CRES
LORDSHIP

ROTH WLK
MEDINA GR
WAVERS
THANE VILLAS
ST THOMAS'S RD
MONSELL RD
CHATTERTON RD
MOUNTGROVE RD
HERRICK RD
PRIESTLEY
CHURCH WLK

TOLLINGTON RD
A 503
Arsenal
GILLESPIE RD
HURLOCK ST
CANNING RD
A 1201
BLACKDALE RD
HIGHBURY QUADRANT
NEW PARK
ADEN TERR
CARTSFORD RD

THANE VILLAS
Arsenal FC
ELWOOD ST
VENELL RD
CONEWOOD ST
HIGHBURY
BIRCHMORE WLK
BIRCHMORE WLK
HIGHBURY QUADRANT
COLLINS
CLISSOLD

DRAYTON PARK
SOTHEBY RD
HIGHBURY
CATHERALL RD
A 105

SEAFORD RD
BRUNSWICK RD
ROSLYN RD
WESTERFIELD RD
SUFFIELD RD
ASHMOUNT RD
EARLSMEAD
HAROLD
NEWTON RD
HERBERT RD
PEMBROKE RD
NORMAN RD
BERNARD RD
CONSTABLE CRES
MANFIELD RD
FM
KESSOCK CRES

SOUTHEY RD
GREENFIELD RD
Seven Sisters
A603
COLLESS RD
PAGE GREEN RD

Seven Sisters
HIGH RD
PAGE GREEN TERR
TOWNSEND RD
South Tottenham
PAGE GREEN RD

Copsmill Stream

B152
KERSWELL
CULVERT RD
A10(T)
CROWLAND RD
FERNDALE RD
LEALAND RD
South Tottenham

Sch

Warwick Reservoir East

South Tottenham

PLEVNA CRES
SHERBORD RD
ERMINE RD
GLADESMORE RD
ELM RD
LEMSFORD CL
GROVELANDS
LEABANK VIEW

CANDLER ST
FRANKLIN RD
THORPE RD
B152
FAIRVIEW RD
WARGRAVE AVE
WELLINGTON AVE
KINGSLAND RD
RIVERSIDE RD
LOCKWOOD RD
THISTLEWAITE RD

Stamford Hill
NORFOLK AVE
CLIFTON GDNS
CASTLEWOOD RD
LEONARD RD
FAIRWEATHER
MAPLE CL

ROSTREVOR AVE
ARRY AVE
CRAVEN PARK RD
MOUNDFIELD RD
LEABOURNE RD

TRUST ESTATE
JOSEPH CT
HILLSIDE
OLINDA RD
PRIESTLEY
RAVENSDALE RD
ROOKWOOD RD

River Lea or Lee

Warwick Reservoir West

MHURST PARK
NORTHDENE GDNS
HURSTDENE GDNS
AMHURST PARK
EGERTON RD

BERGHOLT CRES
STANARD CL
TOWER
CRAVEN CL
CASTLEWOOD RD
CRAVEN
ASHTEAD RD
LINGWOOD RD
SPRING HILL

DENVER RD
A107
BROAD LANE
NORTHFIELD RD
CLAPTON COMMON
OVER LEA RD
BUCKLEBURY
CLAPTON COMMON

BETHUNE RD
WEST BANK
EAST BANK
LINTHORPE RD
Stamford Hill
THE GARDENS
WEBB ESTATE

Park

CLAPTON PATH

COLBERG PL
SUMMIT ESTATE

HEATHLAND RD
DUNSMURE RD
PORTLAND
BRAYDON
SWA
FIRSBY
STAMFORD HILL
CLARKE PATH
FAWCETT ESTATE

HAWKWOOD MOUNT
HOLMBURY VIEW
SPRINGFIELD GDNS

HOLMLEIGH RD
DARENTH RD
STAMFORD GROVE E
OLDHILL ST

GRANGECOURT RD
SANDFORD
MONTEFIORE CT
KYVERDALE RD
STAMFORD GROVE W
OSBALDESTON RD
FORBURN RD

SPRINGFIELD
LEA VIEW HOUSE
JESSAM AVE

GUINNESS
TRUST
MORESBY RD

KILDA's
MANOR RD
LYNMOUTH RD
LAMPARD GR
MARGARET RD
CHARDMORE RD
GILDA CRES

WARWICK GR

Upper Clapton

GRAYLING RD
BOUVERIE RD
B105
WINDUS RD
WINDUS WLK
FILEY AVE

HALBERD MEWS
WREN'S CT
KNIGHTLAND RD
PARK HOUSE
SACH RD

YOAKLEY RD
LISTRIA PK
BELFAST RD
CAZENOVE RD
MORLEY HOUSE
WEALD SQ

MOUNT PLEASANT LA

Stoke Newington
Cemy
MART ABAN RD
Stoke Newington
GEORGE DOWNING ESTATE
FOUNTAYNE RD
BURTLESTON RD
ROSSINGTON ST
UPPER CLAPTON RD

CLAPTON

BOUVERIE MEWS
FLEETWOOD ST
GIBSON RD
ALEHAM
ALKHAM RD
OSBALDESTON RD
HOGAN RD
GELDESTON RD
B111

MOUNT
CHESTER
BRAMPTON RD

SUMMERHOUSE RD
ADAM PL
WILL PL
GARNHAM
Northwold
RYMHOLE RD
Northwold RD

DEFOE RD
Newington Church St
SANFORD WLK
KEATS ESTATE
Stoke Newington Common
ALCONBURY RD
HARTFORD RD
REIGHTON RD

ICKBURGH ESTATE

STOKE NEWINGTON HIGH ST

KERSLEY RD
DUMONT RD
SLINDON
SANFORD
CLEVEDON
NORCOTT RD
GUNTON RD

ALBION RD
BROOK RD
CRESSINGTON RD
KYNASTON AVE
NEVILL RD
LAVERS RD
BROOKE RD
BENTHAL RD
MAURY RD
EVERING RD
CLEVELEYS RD
CASIMIR RD

SANDBROOK RD
OLDFIELD RD
JENNER RD
WALSINGHAM RD

BARBAULD RD
YORKSHIRE CL
TYSSEN RD
DARVILLE RD
BAYSTON RD
HOLLAR RD
LESWIN RD
RECTORY RD
Rectory Road
BROOKE RD
NIGHTINGALE RD
KENNINGHALL RD

LEA BRIDGE RD

ORPEN WLK
VICTORIAN RD
GLADDING TERR
STOKE NEWINGTON
EVERING
MANSE RD
STELLMAN CL
OTTAWAY ROW
RENDLESHAM
MONTAGUE
DELLA PATH
FERRON RD
POWELL RD
CLAPTON WAY
CHARNOCK RD

THISTLE

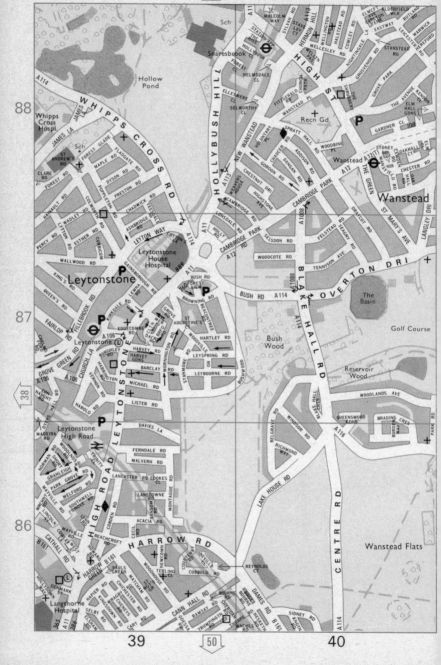

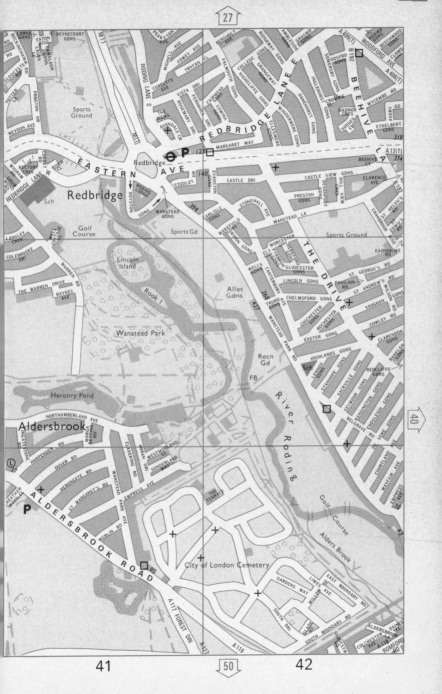

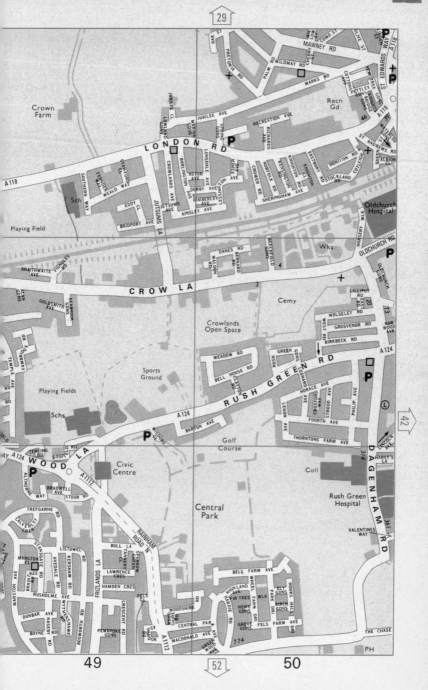

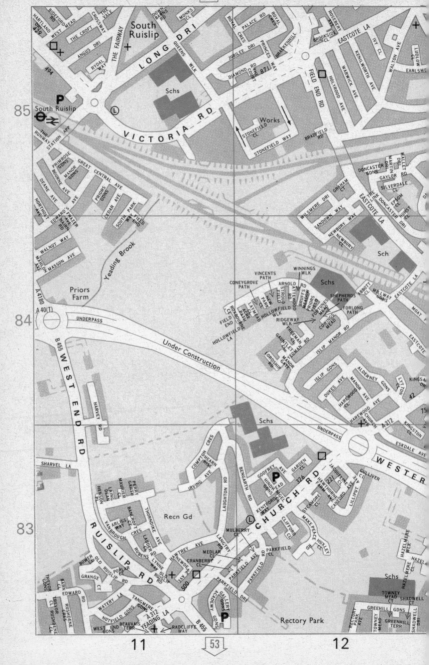

A 4739
EMPIRE WAY
Palace of Industry
Palace of Arts
RUTHERFORD WAY
OLYMPIC WAY
FOURTH WAY
FOURTH WAY
ATLAS RD
ENGINEERS WAY
Wembley Arena
LAKESIDE WAY
Conference Centre
STADIUM WAY
FULTON RD
FIRST WAY
SECOND WAY
THIRD WAY
FOURTH WAY

85
★ P
Empire Stadium
SOUTH WAY
Wembley Complex

PARK VIEW
GROVE WAY
R. Brent
LOVETT WAY
BENTHAM WAY
HARDIE CL
WLK
ASCOT PARK
HERNE

VIVIAN GD
GRAND CRES
HEELD AVE
OAKINGTON MANOR DRI
BESANT
ST RAPHAEL'S WAY
LEWIS CR
A 404
CLIFTON AVE
TUDOR COURT N
TUDOR COURT S
GRAND AVE
VIVIAN AVE
CHIPPENHAM AVE
LANSBURY CL
DORMAN WLK
WAY
A 406(T)
JESMOND AVE
BERKHAMSTED A
ST MICHAEL'S
GEORGIAN CT
VICTORIA AVE
VICTORIA AVE
WYLD
BRENT WAY
WEMBLEY WAY
MONKS PARK
OWEN WAY
GARDEN WAY
FINCH CL
Neasden Hospital

NORTHCHURCH RD
NETTLEDEN AVE
TRING AVE
VICTORIA CT
BABINGTON RISE
HARROW RD
Tokyngton
CHALFONT AVE
STONE BRIDGE AVE
RAINBOROUGH CL
HENDERSON
LILBURNE WLK
MEAD PLAT
WRIGHTS PL
NORMANS MEAD
NORTH CIRCULAR RD
BRENTFIELD RD
Sch

84
FLAMSTED AVE
BOVINGDON AVE
WIGGINTON AVE
Wembley Brook
ALDBURY AVE
SYLVIA GDNS
DEREK AVE
MONKS PARK GDNS
GRITTLETON AVE
L
TILLETT CL
OVERTON CL
MITCHELL WAY
DRYFIELD CL
NORMANS CL
MEADOW GARTH
CROUCH
P
Sch

A 404
A 406(T)
A 404
BRENTFIELD
Stonebridge Park
DURAND CL
CONDUIT WAY
RUSSELL CL
WYBORNE WAY
JAMES DUDSON CT
WYBRENE HOUSE
TWYBRIDGE WAY
MANDELA CL
EXTON CRES
TATAM RD
BEECH WAY
BARRY RD
FANWOOD
STILTON CRES
KING'S RD
GLOUCESTER RD
MELVILLE AVE
STONEBRIDGE PARK
LEICESTER CL
ALRIC AV
HAZELDEN
CASSLE
BRUCE RD

44
MARQUIS CL
THE GRANGE
HEATHER PARK DRI
SUNNY CRES
FOOTHILL
AYRES CRES
BRENT CRES
Stonebridge
HILLSIDE
A 404
KNATCHBULL RD
WINCHELSEA

HIGHCROFT AVE
KENMERE GDNS
BERESFORD AVE
WYCOMBE RD
Brent Junction
WESLEY SHAKESPEARE AVE
SHAKESPEARE CRES
SHREWSBURY CRES
MILTON AVE
CARLTYLE CR
MORDAUNT RD
BRACKEN

83
QUEENSBURY RD
A 406(T)
INEAGH AVE
ABBEYDALE RD
NORTHFIELD INDUSTRIAL ESTATE
ELYEDEN PL
ELYEDEN RD
IVERE RD
TUDOR ESTATE
Wks
Wks
WAXLOW RD
Harlesden

TWYFORD ABBEY RD
MOYNE PL
RAINSFORD RD
GRAND UNION INDUSTRIAL ESTATE
ABBEY RD
ELDON WAY
COMMERCIAL WAY
Lower Place
DISRAELI RD
STEELE RD
COBBOLD RD
BABBRETT'S GREEN RD
NORTH ACTON
B 4492

Neasden

GLADSTONE PARK

Dudden Hill

Dollis Hill

Willesden

Church End

Cemetery

Willesden Green

Willesden General Hospital

Park

Harlesden

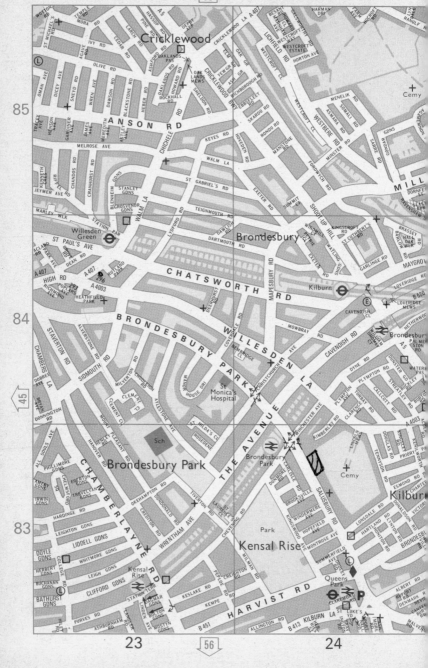

Arsenal F.C.

DRAYTON PARK

Highbury

Poly

A 103

HORNSEY

85

HOLLOWAY RD

Highbury & Islington

84

LIVERPOOL RD

Canonbury

ST PAUL'S RD

A 1199

A 1199

Islington

UPPER ST

ESSEX RD

DOW

Royal Free Hospital (Annexe)

83

SOUTHGATE RD

NEW NORTH RD

PENTONVILLE RD

Pentonville

PENTONVILLE

A 501

City Road Basin

CITY RD

GREEN LANES

47

Wks RUCKHOLT RD

Sports
Ground

Temple
Mills

Stratford New Town

Arena
Field

Stadium

Hackney Wick

Hackney Wick

Bow Industrial Park

Carpenter's Rd

Stratford

Stratford Centre

Stratford Marsh

Heron Industrial Estate

Underpass

Blackwall Tunnel Northern Approach

Works

Bow

Mill Meads

Pumping Stn

BARKING

Mayesbrook Park

Boating Lakes

Barking Hospital

Poly

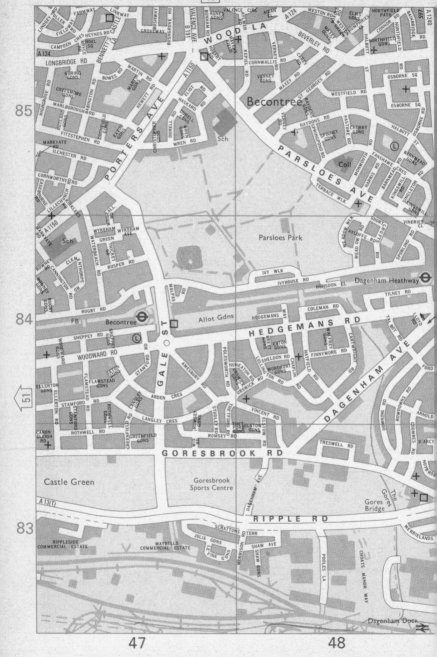

ROBINSON RD

OXLOW LA

GLENCOE DRI
SEDGEMOOR DRI
MARSTON AVE
EDGEFIELD AVE
FRIZLANDS LA
JORDANS
CRESCENT
MUGGERIDGE RD
KINGSLEY CL

GREENWOOD AVE
RAINWOOD AVE
RAINHAM ROAD N A1112
DAGENHAM RD

EASTBROOK AVE
DELVERS M'BAD
Sch

Playing Field

POWELL GDNS
EASTFIELD GDNS
HILL GDNS
WAYSIDE GDNS
STREET CRES

HUNTER SQ
CROPPATH RD
HUNTER SQ
HUNTER RD
WANTZ RD

MANCHESTER WAY
Wks

239
FELHURST

CRANMER GDNS

Sports Ground

ALBION RD
HUNTERS HALL RD
SNEYD RD
WITHAM RD
DUNBAR GDNS
STANDFIELD GDNS
ROCKWELL RD

Recn Gd

BURY RD

VICTORIA RD

FOXLANDS CRES
GAY GDNS
WINSTEAD GDNS

Works

LAKE GDNS
STERRY RD
PETTIT'S RD
PETTIT'S PL
ROGERS RD
ROGERS GDNS
WATERS GDNS
HOLGATE
STERRY GDNS
STANDFIELD GDNS

SURREY RD
KENT RD
NORFOLK RD
SUFFOLK RD
ESSEX RD
DURHAM RD

HEATHWAY

REEDE RD

FB
FB

VINE WAY
ROGERS RD
PARK WAY

FOXLANDS CL
CAMBEYS RD

Dagenham East

RAINHAM ROAD S

SHAFTER RD
DEWEY RD
KILDENER
SANDOWN AVE

WESTERN AVE

MAYSWOOD GDNS

AURIEL AVE
ROOSEVELT WAY

MILLARD TERR
THE MALL
SPENLOW
HUNTINGS
CRANE CL RD
HARRISON
HAMPSTEAD
BLACKBORNE RD
INGLEBY
CHARLOTTE RD
BUTTFIELD RD
GLEN RD
EXETER RD

CROWN AVE
ISCOTT CL
CRISPIN
ALDBOROUGH RD
CADIZ RD
234

CHARLES RD
GORING RD
NORTON RD
MANOR RD
MANOR CL

CHURCH ELM LA
LANGHORNE RD
BROAD ST
MANNING RD
FORD RD
ARMSTEAD WLK
MORGAN CU

ROGERS RD
VIC RD
SALISBURY RD
VICARAGE RD
RECTORY RD
MOSS RD

CRANE CL RD
CHARLOTTE RD

SALISBURY RD

CHURCH ST
ST GILES CL
JOHN PARKER CL
SIVITER WAY
ST STEPHENS RD
ROOK CR ACRE
ROOKERY
CROWN ST
CHURCH LA
REEDE RD
STRATFORD RD

DAGENHAM

RAINHAM ROAD
BEAMWAY
910

WHILL WLK

B 178
BIRDBROOK RD
WELLINGTON CL
TRINIDAD GDNS
CANBERRA CRES
DUNBAR GDNS
KOTTS CL
OTTAWA GDNS

DAGENHAM RD A1112

MORGAN CU WLK
MORLAND RD
DIGBY GDNS
LOWER BROAD ST
BADDOW WLK
MARSH GREEN RD
NORTH CL

Broad Street Market
Playing Field

Dagenham Old Park

BALLARDS RD

WELL RD
300 RD
BALLARDS RD

WELLINGTON RD
LEYS AVE

SCHOOL RD
ORCHARD RD
WHITEARN RD

CROSBY RD
OVAL ROAD N

Dagenham Hospital

Beam River

A 13 (T)
A 1240

SOUTH CL
KENT AVE
REVIEW LA
LINK RD
B 178
OVAL ROAD E
OVAL ROAD S

BEAM AVE
SECOND AVE
FIRST AVE
CENTRE RD
FIFTH AVE
CLAVE
THIRD AVE

CHANTRY AVE
LOWER MARLOWE AVE
LOWEN RD
PERRY RD
ROMAN CL
FREDERICK RD

CHEQUERS LA
CRES

Works

NEW RD

Works

A 13 (T)
THAMES WAY

SOUTH ST
WALDEN AVE
QUEENS GDNS
MARLOWE AVE
LYNBROOK CL
ASKWITH RD
SPENCER RD

RUSHDENE CRES
GURNEY RD
KINGSHILL AVE
OWEN RD
BRYANT RD
WEST END GDNS
EDWARD GDNS
HIGHENDEN GDNS
MERLIN GDNS
BROOMCROFT AVE
BEAUVAIS TER
RADCLIFFE WAY
KITTY CL
A.312
CANBERRA DRI
B.455

1 DILSTON CL
2 WELLS CL
3 FRIARS CL
4 WILLETT CL
5 BRETT CL

1 VALIANT CL
2 MAYFLY GDNS
3 SEASPRITE CL
4 CONVAIR WLK
5 DELTA GR

RECTORY PARK AVE
SHADWELL DRI
COURT MEAD
HOME CL
THORN CL
CRAWFORD

370
ABBEY CL
BRUNEL GR
INVICTA GR
DOWNSIDE
HAYWOOD
TAYWOOD RD
345

ADRIENNE AVE
KENT GDNS
NEAL AVE
BALMORAL DRI

82

YEADING LA
Yeading
MAPLE RD
PERTH AVE
DUNEDIN WAY
BARNHILL RD
271
HARRIES RD
NORCOTT RD
NORWOOD GDNS
MIDDLE WAY
DOUGLAS CRES
HOBART RD
MARIAN CL
FRIAR RD
WILLOW TREE LA

JETSTAR WAY
ARGUS WAY
SEALAND RD
JAVELIN RD
BYRON WAY
HAZELTREE
ASPEN LA
MAYTREE RD
BROADMEAD RD

SEALAND RD
FRIENDSHIP WAY
WAYFARER RD
DALE
LANATA WLK

1 ARROWSCOUT WLK
2 CHIPMUNK GR
3 DAKOTA GDNS
4 MONTGOLFIER WLK
5 BEAVER GR
6 FLAMINGO GDNS
7 TRIDENT GDNS
8 GEMINI GR
9 MARTLET GR

10 TOMAHAWK GDNS
11 CARAVELLE GDNS
12 FARMAN GR
13 VISCOUNT GR

Wks
P

BALMORAL DRI

SHAKESPEARE AVE
AVON RD
ERROLL GDNS
MASSFIELD GDNS
YEADING FORK
MIMOSA RD
LARCH CRES
HORNBEAM RD
LARCH CRES
WILLOW TREE CL

GLENCOE RD
STIPULARIS DRI
RHAMNUS DRI
LAPPONUM WLK
PENDULA DRI
TRESTIS LA
JOLLYS LA
TRIANDRA WAY
SAXTON TER

81

A.312
720
SHAFTESBURY AVE
WINE BONNE
KILWORTH WAY
EDMUNDS CL
X
131
CARLYON RD
Schs
BLANFORD WAYE

Warren
Park

KINGSBRIDGE CRES
CRAVEN GDNS
LYN WOOD AVE
FAIRFIELD GR
CHANNELSEA
SUTHERLAND GDNS
EVELYN GR
TRING AVE
DENBIGH RD
CHEPSTOW GDNS
JOURDAN RD
SHELLEY

LADY MARGARET RD
MAPLE GR
WIND

80

ALLWIN
SMITH
YNAGE WAYE
DORCHESTER WAYE
CRANBORNE WAYE
FERNE WAYE
ASHFORD AVE
BROOKSIDE RD
CAMDEN AVE
BERWICK AVE
DELAMERE RD

QUEBECOURT WAYE
A.4020
CERNE
LONGFORD GDNS

Works

UXBRIDGE RD

SPRINGFIELD RD
BULLSBROOK RD

BEACONSFIELD RD

SPIKES BRIDGE RD
NORMAN AVE
SAXON GDNS
WEST AVE
CARLYLE AVE
EAST AVE
SOUTH AVENUE GDNS
GREENFORD RD
NORTH AVE
CARLYLE AVE
SOUTHALL CT
SHACKLETON RD

LOWDEN RD
LIVINGSTONE RD
ALMA RD
RUSKIN RD
STANLEY RD
TUDOR RD
LANCASTER RD
DANE RD
SAXON RD
NORTHCOTE AVE
SOUTH RD

SOUTHALL

THE BROADWAY
ALFRED GDNS
BEECH AVE
HERBERT RD
HAMILTON RD
CAMBRIDGE RD

BANKSIDE
BERESFORD RD
RANELAGH RD
WOODLANDS RD
TRINITY RD
TOWNSEND RD
WEST END RD
HAMBROUGH RD
ABBOTTS RD
OSWALD RD
ST JOSEPH'S DRI
ORCHARD AVE
RAYNOR CL
BEATRICE RD
SOUTH RD
OXFORD RD
AVENUE RD
VILLIERS RD
4 FAIRLAWN RD
A.3005

CHERRY AVE
BEACONSFIELD RD
Coll

KENSINGTON RD
MARLEY CL
FISHER CL
FERRYMEAD AVE
GOSLING CL
FRESHWATER RD
Sch
ROSEDENE AVE
CROSSMEAD AVE
GREENWAY GDNS
BEECHWOOD AVE
EASTMEAD AVE
MARNHAM CRES
MILLET RD
BARNHAM RD
GREENFORD GDNS
GORING WAY
FARNDALE CRES
OLDFIELD LA
COSTONS LA
A 4127
716
SILVER TREE CL
DEERHURST GDNS
COMBE RD
WOOD CL
WEST AVE
CARDHAW RD
SHELLEY AVE
HOWCROFT LA
RUISLIP RD
475
448
ALLENBY CL
STICKLETON CL
RAVENOR PARK RD
Ravenor Park
LYNDHURST GDNS
PEMBROK
STANHOPE
P
CROYDE AVE
BROMFIELD CT
PARK RD
OAKFIELD GDNS
LOCARNO LA
SHELLEY GDNS
COSTONS AVE
WEDMORE RD
BETHAM RD
HILLSIDE RD
ENMORE RD
TOWERS RD
VERULAN
RUISLIP CL
AVON RD
AVON RD
WARREN DRI
GARRICK RD
THE BROADWAY
CLIFTON RD
RUISLIP ROAD E
B 455
Greenford
CRESSAGE CL
LAWSON RD
BURNHAM GR
ROSE GDNS
SELBY GDNS
WESTBURY AVE
ROSECROFT RD
BYCROFT RD
UPPER TOWN RD
BRAUND AVE
MORNINGTON RD
FERMOY RD
MASSELL RD
PORTLAND CRES
ELLESMERE RD
WINDMILL LA
OTTER RD
RMERE RD
DEVONSHIRE RD
RUTLAND RD
SUNNYCROFT RD
ASH GR
CEDAR GR
PURCELL
STANHOPE
ASCOT GDNS
CORNWALL AVE
HARE AVE
SOMERSET RD
ALLENBY RD
Jubilee Park
DALE RD
KEATS WAY
HURLEY RD
CANTERBURY CL
Cemy
Recn Gd
GREENFORD RD
CORNWALL AVE
ST PETER'S RD
JUBILEE GDNS
ST URSULA RD
SASSET WAY
BARRICAN RD
PRINCE'S AVE
Queen's AVE
THE GROVE
BRIDGE AVE
BROOKBANK AVE
ELM BANK WAY
CUCKOO DENE
GIFFORD GDNS
BEECHMOUNT AVE
BERESFORD AVE
MAYFIELD GDNS
HANWAY RD
HOBBAYNE RD
STUDLAND RD
STERLIN'S
DERWENT RD
KELVIN GDNS
WAXLOW CRES
LOVELL RD
WHITTLE RD
WALLIS
SWAN RD
KING'S AVE
DARWIN DRI
HOWARD AVE
FISBORN
SUNNINGDALE
HIGH LA
ALLENDALE RD
DORMER'S AVE
Sch
Mount Pleasant Hospital
MOUNT AVE
2
EDISON DRI
LONGBRIDGE
MARCONI
DORMERS
WHITECOTE RD
FLEMING RD
SMYTH RD
REDCROFT RD
Golf Course
GREENFIELDS
MASEFIELD AVE
DORMER'S WELLS LA
TELFORD RD
BRINDLEY WAY
FARADAY RD
PANHARD PL
BRUNEL
RISE
BAIRD AVE
NORTH RD
BURNS AVE
SHELLEY RD
KENTON AVE
LONGFORD AVE
Dormer's Wells
CHURCH RD
P
PALGRAVE AVE
KINGSLEY AVE
OAKWOOD AVE
MILFORD RD
ATHERTON AVE
Golf Course
Weir
SHRUBBERY CL
PARK VIEW RD
MELROSE AVE
STAMFORD CL
GREEN DRI
UXBRIDGE RD
A 4127
WHARNCLIFFE DRI
BRENTVALE AVE
BLACKMORE AVE
HIGH ST
BOYD AVE
ARGYLL AVE
KNOWSLEY AVE
MORLAND GDNS
WINDMILL LA
A 4127
St Bernard's Wing
The Ealing Hospital
A 4020
Sch
PARK AVE
RICKARDS

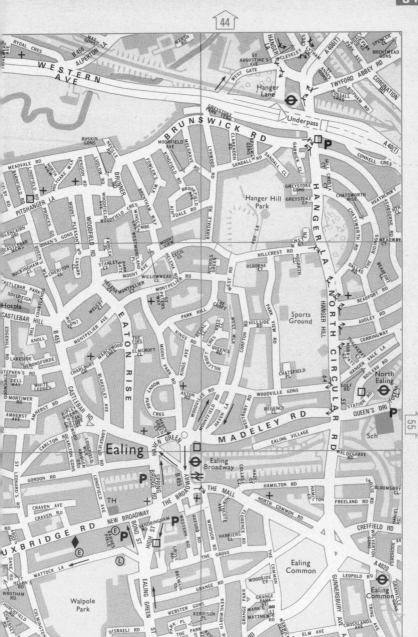

45

Park Royal

Central Middlesex
County Hospital

TWYFORD ABBEY RD.
ELDON WAY
RAINSFORD RD.
WHITBY AVE
PENNY RD.
CUMBERLAND AVE
COMMERCIAL WAY
ABBEY RD.
ACTON LA.
GARRATT GREEN RD.
B 4492
WESLEY AVE
HAROLD RD.
NORTH ACTON RD.
EVERITT RD.
NEWARK CRES.
CONRAD
BASHLEY RD.
THE MILL
TRADING ESTATE

82

CORONATION RD.
BRITANNIA WAY
WESTERN RD.
STANDARD RD.
GREEN RD.
MINERVA RD.
GORST RD.
SUNBEAM RD.
CHASE RD.
LEONARD'S
SCHOOL
BETHUNE RD.

A 4011

RANGER'S GREEN
HEATH
HANGER Park Royal
EAST LO.
ROTHERWICK
MASON'S GREEN LA.
DUKES RD.
MASON'S RD.

Trading Estate

TRADING ESTATE PARK ROYAL RD.
CULLEN WAY
400
North Acton

North Acton
Cemy

ASHBURNHAM
CORRINGWAY
BEAUFORT RD.
BOURNE AVE
AUGLE RD.
PRINCES GDNS
KENDAL AVE
CONCORD RD.
ALLIANCE RD.
MANSFIELD RD.
CANADA RD.
HIGHFIELD RD.
CANADA RD.
VICTOR RD.
KATHLEEN RD.
ALLAN WAY
WESTERN AVE
VICTORIA RD. A 4000
Cemy
A 4000

81

HANGER VALE
HANGER VIEW
MONK'S DRI
TUDOR
PRINCES GDNS
SAXON DRI
WALTON DRI
WALTON WAY
WESTFIELDS RD.
NORMAN WAY
MOATAN LA.
THE HOWARD CL.
NORTHFIELDS RD.
EASTFIELDS RD.
COURT WAY
PARK VIEW
CLOISTER RD.
BALFOUR RD.
CECIL RD.
A 4000
LEAMINGTON PARK
Leamington
Park
Hospital

West
Acton

West Acton

NOEL RD.
LOWFIELD RD.
YORK RD.
ROSEBANK WAY

KENT RD.
LINKS RD.
BRITANNIA RD.
QUEEN'S DRI
CHURCHILL GDNS

Acton
Main Line

FRIARY RD.
THE DRIVE
FRIARY

54

GARAGE

LYNTON RD.
HORNLA.
EMANUEL AVE
BROUGHAM RD.
FARADAY RD.
MESSALINE AVE
WESTON
EASTMEARE
FRIARS PLACE
FRIARS AVE

OAKLEY AVE
BLOOMSBURY
WESTERN GDNS
MONTPELIER GDNS
MAYFIELD RD.
SHALIMAR RD.
ESSEX RD.
HEREFORD RD.
SHALIMAR GDNS
ACACIA RD.
GRAFTON RD.
CRANE AVE
GROSVENOR AVE
GDNS
DUNSTAN'S RD.
ST DUNSTAN'S AVE
PRIDEAUX
FYNE RD.

CREFFIELD RD.
TWYFORD AVE
CRESWICK RD.
ROSEMONT RD.
NEMOURE RD.
CUMBERLAND RD.
HIGHLANDS AVE
MALDON RD.
CUMBERLAND RD.
GOLDSMITH AVE
PERRYN RD.
SHAA RD.
GOLDSMITHS

80

LAYER GDNS
BYRON
A 4020
WOODSTREAM RD.
BIRCH GR.
STANWAY GDNS
HALE GDNS
FOX
LODGE GDNS
CHATSWORTH RD.
BUXTON GDNS
LEIDEN RD.
WOODHURST RD.
SPENCER RD.
SHAKESPEARE RD.
SUTHERLANDS RD.
CHAUCER RD.
MYRTLE RD.
MILTON RD.
EAST CHURCHFIELD RD.
LC

UXBRIDGE RD.
HART LA.
WHITEHALL GDNS
KING ST
WILLCOTT RD.
HILLCREST RD.
STEYNE RD.
BARLOW RD.
RECTORY RD.
STUART RD.
WATER RD.
TOWN RD.
GROVE PL.
CHURCHFIELD RD.
BURLINGTON RD.
SPOONER'S MEWS
Acton
Central

P

Acton

Brunel
Univ.
Acton Hospital

HIGH ST.
MILL HILL RD.
CROWN ST.
CHURCHFIELD RD.
BURLINGTON RD.
BIRKBECK RD.
GOLDSMITH RD.
MELVILLE VILLAS
VAL E
(E)

19

61

20

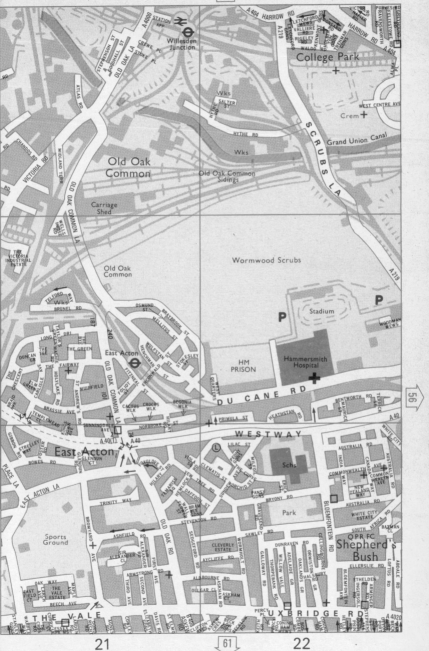

A 404 HARROW RD

VICTOR
ROAD
RAVENSWORTH RD
PURVES
FELIXSTOWE RD

LETFORD
VALLIERE
RIGELEY
TUBBS
WALDO
TREMAR
HARROW RD
A 404

College Park

STATION APP
A 4000
CREWE PL
STEPHENSON ST
STONE PL
GOODHALL ST
CREWE PL
OLD OAK LA

Willesden
Junction

WEST CENTRE AVE

ATLAS RD

Crem

Wks
SALTER ST

SCRUBS LA

HYTHE RD

Grand Union Canal

VICTORIA RD
MIDLAND TERR
CHANDOS RD

Old Oak
Common

Wks

Old Oak Common
Sidings

RD

OLD OAK COMMON LA

Carriage
Shed

WELLS HOUSE RD

THE
VICTORIA
INDUSTRIAL
ESTATE

Old Oak
Common

Wormwood Scrubs

A 219

TELFORD WAY
Wks
BRUNEL RD

OSMUND ST
BRAYBROOK ST

P
Stadium
P
WOODMAN MEWS

187
240
LONG DRIVE
LARDEN RD
MACFARLANE RD
THE GREEN
DUNCAN
THE TEE

MELLITSS ST

HENCHMAN ST
WULFSTAN ST
STOKESLEY ST

East Acton

HM
PRISON

Hammersmith
Hospital

THE FAIRWAY
ELM
CARLISLE
HOLYLAKE
ST ANDREW'S
MUIRFIELD
101

OLD OAK COMMON LA
FITZNEAL ST
ERCONWALD ST

QUARTERS
BEGONIA WLK

BRASSIE AVE
CACTUS WLK
CROCUS WLK

DU CANE RD

BENTWORTH RD

TEPRICK
ST MAURICE

TEMPLEMEAD
SUNNINGDALE AVE
NORBROKE ST
HILARY ST

PRIMULA ST
HEATHSTAN RD

A 40

STREELEY WAY
GIBBON RD
POSTER
BOWES RD
GLENBURN CT
FOXGLOVE RD
HILARY RD
NEW TARE RD
HESLOP

A 40 (T)

L
LILAC ST
CLEMATIS ST
ORCHID ST
THE CURVE
MILROSE ST
PERRY
WESTWAY
BECK
PERRY

WHITE CITY
AUSTRALIA RD
INDIA WAY
COMMONWEALTH
CANADA WAY
AUSTRALIA
COMMON WAY

PLACE LA
EAST ACTON LA
TRINITY WAY

TAMARISK
BRAMLEY
GRAVESEND
PANSY GDNS
BRYONY RD

Schs

Park

NEW ZEALAND WAY
SOUTH AFRICA RD
AUSTRALIA

WHITE CITY
ESTATE
BLOEMFONTEIN RD
BAZMAN CL

Sports
Ground

ASHFIELD RD
SIR ALEXANDER CL
SIR ALEXANDER
FIRST AVE
BROMYARD AVE

STEVENTON RD
AYCLIFFE RD
CLEVERLY ESTATE
WORMHOLT RD
SAWLEY RD
DUNRAVEN RD
GALLOWAY RD
WILLOW VALE
THORPEBANK RD
OAKLANDS GR
ADELAIDE GR
ORMISTON GR
HALSBURY
COLLINGBOURNE

QPR FC
Shepherd's
Bush
ELLERSLIE RD

SOUTH AFRICA RD

EAST
FIELD CT
THE VALE ESTATE
BEECH AVE
OAK WAY
THIRD AVE
SECOND AVE
ARMSTRONG RD
ALABOURNE RD
OILGAR CL
ASKHAM RD
ASKHAM

PERCY
ETHELDEN RD
INGERSOLL RD
BLOEMFONTEIN
STEPHENDALE
ARMINGER
BELINDER
ABDALE RD
LOFTUS RD

THE VALE

UXBRIDGE RD
A 4020

Maida Vale

Westbourne Green

Paddington
General Hospital

WESTWAY

Little
Venice

Royal Oak

Paddington

Bayswater

Lancaster Gate

Notting
Hill Gate

Queensway

BAYSWATER RD

Kensington Gardens

Kensington
Palace

THE BROAD WALK

Lord's
Cricket
Ground

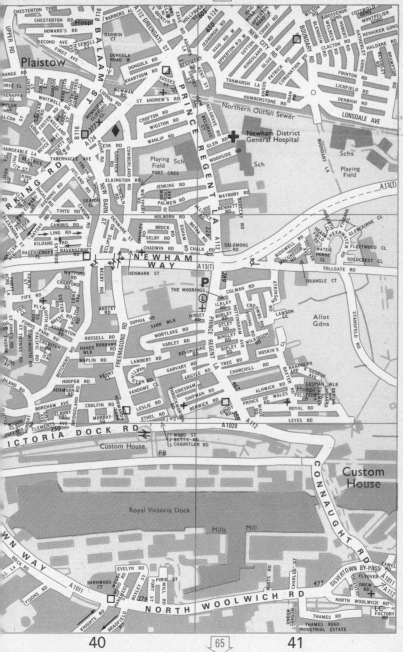

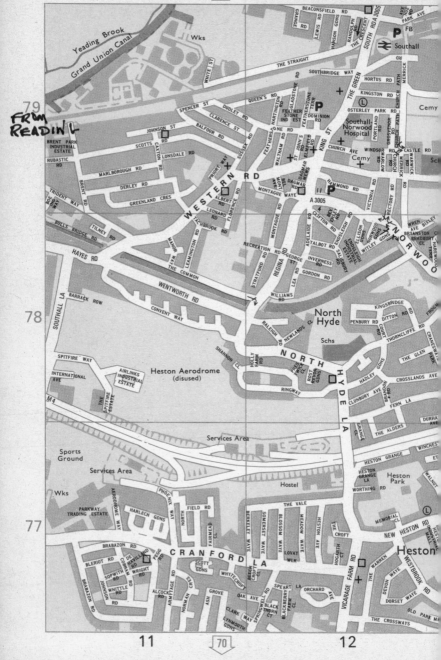

Yeading Brook
Grand Union Canal
Wks

Wks
WHITE ST
THE STRAIGHT
SOUTHBRIDGE WAY
BEACONSFIELD RD
LEWIS GDNS
HANSON RD
GINNIS RD
RANDOLPH
THE CRESCENT
SOUTH RD A 3005
PARK AVE
MERRICK
FB
P
Southall

QUEEN'S RD
GLADSTONE RD
FEATHERSTONE TERR
DOMINION IND EST
HORTUS RD
THE GREEN
KINGSTON RD
OSTERLEY PARK RD
PORTLAND RD
GROSVENOR
CHURCH PATH
MERRICK RD

FROM
READING

SPENCER ST
DUDLEY RD
CLARENCE ST
BALFOUR RD
JOHNSON ST
SCOTTS RD
CAXTON RD
LONSDALE RD
MARLBOROUGH RD
DERLEY RD
GREENLAND CRES
PRIORY RD
SUSSEX RD
WESTERN RD
ALBERT RD
FLORENCE RD
LEONARD RD
TACHBROOK RD

BRENT PARK INDUSTRIAL ESTATE
RUBASTIC RD
BRENT RD
TRIDENT WAY
BULL'S BRIDGE RD
TILNEY RD

HARTINGTON RD
FEATHERSTONE IND EST
WALTHAM RD
ST JOHN'S RD
REDFERN RD
DAGMAR MEWS
MONTAGUE WAYE
MONTAGUE RD
KING ST
CHURCH AVE
WINDSOR RD
Cemy
Cemy
P
A 3005
HAMMOND RD
VICTORIA RD
RECTORY RD
CASTLE RD
WARWICK RD
CHURCH RD
MERRICK RD

Southall-Norwood Hospital

RECREATION RD
REGINA RD
STRATFORD RD
MONTAGUE RD
ADELAIDE RD
TALBOT RD
GEORGE ST
INVERNESS RD
LEA RD
GORDON RD
SALISBURY RD
CLIFTON RD
SIDLESLEIGH RD
BERLEY RD
ALLISON RD
WITLEY GDNS
BRYANSTON AVE
WREN AVE
BRADBURY
BIXLEY RD
NORWOOD RD
TANGLEWOOD
SHERWOOD

WILLIAMS RD

HAYES RD
SOUTHALL LA
BARRACK ROW
MANOR WAY
LEXINGTON RD
THE COMMON
WENTWORTH RD
CONVENT WAY

North Hyde
Schs
PENBURY RD
KINGSBRIDGE
DITTON RD
FROGMORE RD

RALEIGH RD
NEWLANDS CL
SHANNON CL
HOLLY FARM RD
PINES
MOAT
ROOST
REDDONS GDNS
RINGWAY
NORTH
HYDE LA
THORNCLIFFE RD
COURT
HADLEY GDNS
CROSSLANDS AVE
FERN LA
THE GLEN
CRANES PARK

SPITFIRE WAY
INTERNATIONAL AVE
M 4
THE SPITFIRE ESTATE
AIRLINKS INDUSTRIAL ESTATE

Heston Aerodrome
(disused)

CLUNBURY RD
BRANDON RD
GRANGE CL
THE ALDERS
DURHAM RD

Services Area

Sports Ground

Services Area

Wks

PARKWAY TRADING ESTATE
AERODROME WAY
HARLECH GDNS
PHOENIX WAY
NORTH FIELD RD
FIELD RD
FAIRMEAD CL
BERKELEY WAYE
SOMERSET WAYE
BLOSSOM WAYE
MEADOW WAYE
HESTON AVE
Hostel
HESTON GRANGE LA
WORTHING RD
THE VALE
Heston Grange
Heston Park
MEMORIAL CL
NEW HESTON RD
Heston

BRABAZON RD
BLERIOT RD
DE HAVILLAND RD
SOPWITH RD
WHITTLE RD
JOHNSON RD
PAGE RD
WRIGHT RD
CORNWALL RD
BRABAZON RD
ARMITAGE RD
NORMAN CRES
ALCOCK RD
ASH GROVE
SCOTT GDNS
WHYTECROFT
BEECH
CROFT
C R A N F O R D   L A
LOVAT WLK
SPRINGWELL RD
CLARK WAY
LYNMOUTH GDNS
OAK AVE
BLACKTHORN CT
SPEART LA
BLACKBERRY FARM RD
ORCHARD
VICARAGE FARM RD
THE CROFT
HOGARTH RD
THE WARREN
DEVON WAYE
DORSET WAYE
WESTBROOK RD
OLD PARK RD
THE CROSSWAYS

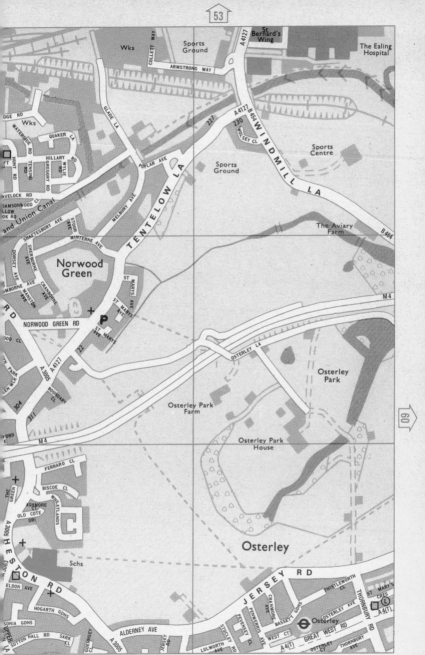

VICTORIA CT

Acton Hospital

A 4000 MILL HILL LANGLEY DRI
CLANDON CL

Sch

AVENUE RD

CHELTENHAM

BUCKLAND WLK
OTTERSHAW
CHURCH RD
OLDHAM

SAIS GLOUCESTER
MANCHESTER
NEVILLE

BIRKBECK
MANSELL

EASTMAN

ACTON IND.

BEARDSLEY WAY

CARBERRY AVE
TUDOR AVE
A 406(T)
LILIAN RD
A 4000

GUNNERSBURY LA
GUNNERSBURY GDNS
THE RIDGEWAY

GUNNERSBURY

ENFIELD RD
373
HANBURY RD

HEATHFIELD RD

AVENUE CRES
AVENUE GDNS

PARK RD E

BELGRAVE CL

MEON RD
LEYTHE RD
NEW RD

BROMYARD AVE

ACTON LA

B 491 SOUTHFIELD RD

ST GEORGES
ALEXANDRA RD
BONHEUR RD

HATFI

CLOVELLY RD
GRAHAM RD
SOMERSET RD

STRAUSS
BROOKFIE
SPELDHU

79
A 406(T)

P
Acton Town

OSBORNE RD

BOLLO BRIDGE RD
STRATFORD RD
PALMERSTON
STANLEY RD

RAMSAY RD
BOLLO CT
CHURCH PATH
FLETCHER RD
REYNOLDS RD

CARLTON RD
BAYHAM RD

POPE'S LA
B 4491
P

GUNNERSBURY AVE
(NORTH CIRCULAR RD)

PRINCES AVE
PARK DRI

South Acton

ROSLIN RD
STIRLING RD
COLVILE RD

P **P**
South Acton

VINCENT RD
BRIDGMAN RD

KENT RD

BEAUMONT RD
STEELE RD

CHURCH PATH

BERRYMEDE RD
SAVILLE RD

ST ALBANS RD

EVERIDGE AVE

P **L**
Mus

South Acton

BOLLO LA

STANLEY RD

MELROSE RD
WESTON RD
TEMPLE RD
ROTHSCHILD RD

KINGSWOOD RD

EVELYN RD
GLADSTONE RD

KINGSCOTE RD

RAMILLIES

BUSTHALL AVE
ESMOND

LC

ANTROBUS RD
SEYMOUR RD

CLEVE RD

BEACONSFIELD RD

SOUTH

A 406(T)

Wks

LC

IVY CRES

MONTGOMERY RD
FAIRLAWN
FAIRLAWN AVE

LENNINGTON GR ST

ACTON'S LA

HARDWICKE RD

DISRAELI RD
WINSTON
CLEMENT

WALK

X B 409

78
M4
A 4(T)
A 4(T)

Cerny

A 406(T)

POWER RD
POWER RD
THORNEY HEDGE RD
SILVER CRES

BRENTHAM WAY
A 315

Acton Green

Chiswick Park

GUNNERSBURY MEWS

CHISWICK

KINGS RD
GRANGE RD
MARLBOROUGH

CHISWICK HIGH RD B 490

B 490

ARLINGTON GDNS

B 490

MILL'S ROW
BRIDGE ST
BEL MONT TERR

ESSEX
PLACE

TOWN HALL AVE

CHISWICK

DOLMAN RD
CLENNS

HEATHFIELD TERR

BARLEY
MOW PAS

L

BOURNE

Elevated Road M4

SURREY CRES
Gunnersbury

OXFORD RD
BURLINGTON

Q ≠ A 3000

WELLESLEY RD
Gunnersbury

WALPOLE GDNS

SUTTON

A 3000

HORTICULTURAL PL

WATCHFIELD CT

P

ALWYN AVE

HADLEY GDNS

FOSTER RD

DUKE'S AVE

NORTH CIRCULAR RD CHISWICK

STONEHILL RD
MELVILLE RD
CAMBRIDGE RD

P
A 3000

GROSVENOR RD

BEL
SONS
LA

HARVARD RD

WAVENDON AVE

60
LIONEL RD
A 205

KEW BRIDGE

STILE HALL GDNS
REGENT ST

OXFORD GDNS
OXFORD ROAD S

HARVARD HILL

A 4(T) GREAT

BURLINGTON LA
HEATHFIELD RD

SUTTON COURT RD

WEST RD

BARROWGATE RD

PARK ROAD E

SPRING GR
MARNE

WALDECK RD
PIERMONT

BROOKS
GRESHAM

CHISWICK VILLAGE

HARVARD RD

CEDARS RD

SUTTON COURT ROUNDABOUT

GARTH RD

ELLESMERE RD

STRAND ON-THE-GREEN

STRAND on the Green

WOLSELEY GDNS
WHITEHALL
WHITEHALL GDNS
DEANS CL
ST MARY'S
GORDON
ST MARY'S GR

HAZLEDENE RD
ELMWOOD RD

SUTTON LANE

FAIRCLOUGH RD
COMPTON RD

EAST BOURNE RD

CHARA PL

MILNTHORPE RD

CHESTERFIELD RD

PARK RD

A 205 KEW RD

KEW BRIDGE CT

WATERLOO
KEW GREEN

BUSHWOOD RD
PRIORY RD

HAVERFIELD RD
FOREST RD

KEW

MORTLAKE RD

CAMBRIDGE COTTAGES
OLD DOCK

GRASMERE

POST OFFICE ALLEY
THAMES RD

SHIP ALLEY STRAND-ON-THE-GREEN

HERBERT GDNS
RHODA

LORRAINE
ERNEST GDNS

RIVERVIEW GR

BURNABY GDNS
FLORENCE GDNS
KNIGHTSBRIDGE

NIGHTINGALE RD

ST THOMAS

CHATSWORTH RD

STAVELEY RD

Chisw Hous

SPRING
WATERLOO

A 205 KEW RD

KEW GREEN

GLOUCESTER
CAMBRIDGE
LETHBRIDGE

OVER
CUMBERLAND RD

MORTLAKE RD

B 353
KEW GARDENS RD

RUSKIN
A 205
DYER'S AVE

RIVERVIEW GDNS

GROVE PARK RD

RANELAGH GDNS
GROVE PARK GDNS

LAWFORD RD

GROVE PARK MEWS

Sch

STATION
BOLTON RD

SPENCER RD

Chiswick
≠
STATION APPROACH

WILMINGTON AVE

BURLINGTON LA

Sch

HARTINGTON RD

GROVE PARK RD

KINNAIRD AVE
DEVONSHIRE GDNS

CONISTON CL

WINDRUSH CL

A 318 GR

55

62

72

Kensington Palace

KENSINGTON RD HYDE PARK GATE KENSINGTON GORE A315 KENSINGTON RD

High Street
Kensington

Hospital
Kensington

CROMWELL

Gloucester
Rd

South
Kensington

Coll
QUEENS
BERRY WAY

Hospitals

Earl's
Court

South Kensington

Earl's Court

KENSINGTON
MANSIONS

Earls Court
Exhibition Building

WHARFEDALE
ST
West
Brompton

**West
Brompton**

St Stephen's
Hospital

Cerny

Western Hospital
&
Royal Hospital
(Western Annexe)

SAMUEL LEWIS
TRUST DWELLINGS

Chelsea
F.C.

Fulham
Broadway

KINGS RD

CREMORNE RD

1 WORLD'S END PL
2 DARTREY WLK
3 EDITH YD
4 WHISTLER WLK
5 WORLD'S END PASS
6 BLANTYRE WLK
7 UPPER BERENGER WLK
8 BERENGER WLK
9 UPPER BLANTYRE WLK
10 MIDDLE DARTREY WLK
11 UPPER DARTREY WLK
12 UPPER WHISTLER WLK

**Walham
Green**

Coll

River Thames

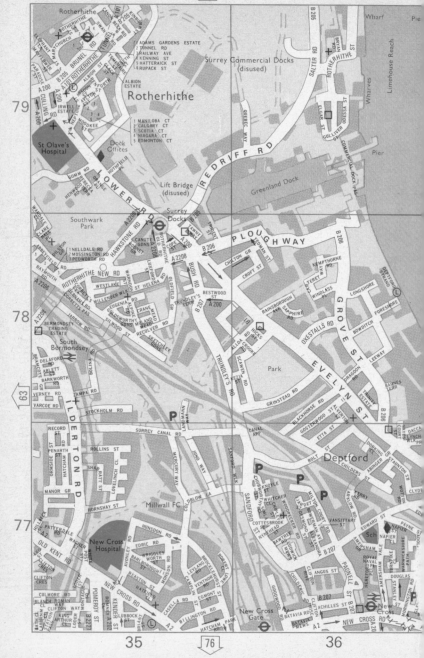

Rotherhithe

ELEPHANT LA
ROTHERHITHE ST
CHURCH
BRUNEL RD
ROTHERHITHE TUNNEL
A101
KINBURN ST
CANON BECK RD
SWAN RD
B205

1 ADAMS GARDENS ESTATE
2 TUNNEL RD
3 RAILWAY AVE
4 KENNING ST
5 HATTERAICK ST
6 RUPACK ST

Surrey Commercial Docks
(disused)

B205
SALTER RD
ROTHERHITHE ST
BRYAN RD
Wharf
Pie
ELGAR ST
GULLIVER ST
KEPPEL ST
Limehouse Reach
Wharves
ALBION
ESTATE
PARADISE ST
CULLING RD
A200
A200
B205
A101 ROTHERHITHE TUNNEL
ALBION ST
NEPTUNE ST
FORTH
MOODKEE ST
IRWELL
ESTATE

Rotherhithe

1 MANILOBA CT
2 CALGARY CT
3 SCOTIA CT
4 NIAGARA CT
5 EDMONTON CT

QUEBEC WAY
REDRIFF RD
Pier
COMMERCIAL DOCK RD

St Olave's Hospital

Dock Offices

HOTHFIELD

COMM RD
HENWOOD
REBECCA
GRANGE

Lift Bridge
(disused)

Greenland Dock

LOWER RD

Southwark Park

A2206
WESTFIELD
CLIFTON
CLARE
Surrey Docks
PLOUGHWAY
B206

Southwark Park

AMBLESIDE
RAYMOUTH RD
HAWKSTONE RD
CANUTE GDNS
NEILDALE RD
ROTHERHITHE OLD RD

1 NEILDALE RD
2 MOSSINGTON RD
3 PEDWORTH

CANUTE
OLD RD
COVE
ROPE
A2206
BUSH RD
A2206
LAWN
TROUT
FOWAN ST
KEMPTHORNE
DESTERET
WINDLASS
Longshore
Foreshore

ROTHERHITHE NEW RD
A2206
JARROW RD
RENFORTH ST
GATAKER ST
WESTLANE
ST HELENA
CRANE
MEAD
MOLAND
RECULVER RD
CHILTON GR
CROFT ST
BESTWOOD ST
CROFT ST
RAINSBOROUGH AVE
SAPPHIRE

BERMONDSEY
TRADING ESTATE

South Bermondsey

A2208
DELAFORD
ABLETT
BARKWORTH
VERNEY RD
VARCOE RD

EUGENIA
MILLENDER WLK
GOLDSWORTHY
SILWOOD ST
TRUNDLEY'S
OLD FIELD
A200
DRUMMOND RD

SKETCHLEY
GDNS
TRUNDLEY'S RD

Park

ALGA RD
SCAWEN
KETZA
HICKS
CROWN

OXESTALLS RD
BOWDITCH
LEEWAY
DRAGGON RD
TANNER
BARNES
ELIR
B206
EVELYN ST
GROVE ST

STOCKHOLM RD

SURREY CANAL RD

P

GRINSTEAD RD

BLACKHORSE RD
GOSTENWOOD RD
SILVERTON
RD
ETTA ST
DORKING
DACCA
LYNCH
COURT
NAPIER

Deptford

CANAL APP

RECORD
PENARTH
HAWTHORN
DR
ALDERTON RD
ROLLINS ST
SHARRATT ST
LOVELINCH CL
MANOR GR
HORNSHAY ST

SURREY CANAL RD

MERCURY WAY
JUNO WAY

P
BOLT
CHILDERS ST
ABINGER
STAUNTON
CLYDE
P
P
P

OLD KENT RD
A2
PATTERDALE RD
HILLIER
CLIFTON
NEW CROSS RD

New Cross Hospital

Millwall FC

HUNSDON RD
EDRIC RD
WRIGGLESWORTH
BARLBOROUGH
AVONLEY RD
REASTON ST
CULMORE RD
BLANCH ROMAN
CL
CLIFTON WAY
KING ARTHUR
CT
POMEROY ST
B2172
KENDER ST
SLUBOCK ST
BRYANT
A2

COLDBLOW LA
SANDFORD ST
SANDFORD
GOSTERWOOD
WHITCHER
WOODPECKER
COTTESBROOK
RAWTHMELL
HUNTER
DET
B207
MILTON COURT
BRUNSWICK
ESMOND
ALEXANDRA
VANSITTART ST
CLIFTON
ANGUS ST
CHILDERIC RD
GOODWOOD
B207
BATAVIA RD
BATAVIA
MEWS
NEW CROSS RD

LEYLAND
BROCKLEHURST
ROMBERG
CAMPLIN
VENTNOR
EGMONT ST
CASELLA RD
BILLINGTON RD
HATCHAM PARK
New Cross Gate
A2

ROYAL NAVAL
VICTUALLING
MERSHAM
TURNPIKE
Sch
PAYNE ST
EDWARD
NAPIER
HEREFORD
DOUGLAS
WARWICKSHIRE
PAGNELL ST
ACHILLES ST
New Cross
PELL
DACCA
PELL

57
58
65

South Dock

COLDHARBOUR

Drawbridge Jetties

SOUTH WEST INDIA DOCK ENTRANCE

BLACKWALL TUNNEL AVE A102

A1206

CHIPKA ST

FOLLY WALL

CASTALIA SQ

ROSERTON

CAPSTAN SQ

RIVER BARGE CL

Wharf

Blackwall Reach

West India & Millwall Docks

MANILLA ST

BYNG ST

STRAFFORD ST

HAVANNAH ST

MALABAR GR

ALPHA GR

CHEVAL ST

JANET ST

MELLISH ST

TILLER RD

STARBOARD WAY

CUBA ST
A1206

SOCIETY RD

HUTCHING'S

QUARTERDECK

MILLWALL DOCK RD

GLENGALL CSWY

Millwall

WEST FERRY RD

EAST FERRY RD

ASTER RD

ROCKET ST

CARDALE ST

PLEVNA ST

MICKLE ST

KING GALBRAITH

STRATTONDALE ST

MARSHFIELD

GLENGALL GR

MANCHESTER RD

A379

CASTLE

Wharf

NEW UNION CL

OVEX CL

DAGMAR CT

Pier

BIRCHFIELD CRES
OLLEFFE

PIER ST

SEYSSEL ST

KINGFIELD ST

BILLSON ST

GLENWORTH AVE

PARSONAGE ST

STEBONDALE ST

GLENGARNOCK AVE

GLENAFFRIC AVE

NESS ST

SAUNDERS NESS RD

EMPIRE WHARF

GROSVENOR WHARF

Isle of Dogs

Cubitt Town

GAVERICK ST

CHEWS

CLAUDE ST

MASTMAKER RD

HARINGTON RD

HESPERUS

CAHIR ST

MARSH WALL

THORNE HOUSE ST

MAQUAIRE

THERMOPYLAE GATE

CHAPEL HOUSE ST

JULIAN PL

MANCHESTER RD

JOHNSON'S DRAWDOCK

Park

455

308

A1206

FACTORY

FERRY ST

LIVINGSTONE PL

MIDLAND PL

Jetty

BALLAST

DEPTFORD FERRY RD

Wharves

Landing Stages

RIVER THAMES

HWM

Tunnel

Pier

HOSKINS ST

HIGH BRIDGE

COBLINGTON ST

CRANE ST

EASTNEY ST

Pier

Greenwich Reach

HWM

Cutty Sark

OLD WOOLWICH RD

TRENCHARD ST

TRAFALGAR RD

Royal Naval College

Seaman's Hospital Society

GRAND SQ

PARK

ROMNEY RD A206

PARK ROW

PARK VISTA

National Maritime Museum

BORTHWICK

TRENCHARD

MEWS

CREWS

NEW KING ST

BENBOW

FRIGATE MEWS

CARRICK MEWS

BRIG MEWS

ARMADA

MCMILLAN

WATERGATE

A341

BARQUE MEWS

A200

Coll

STOWAGE

GONSON

DEPTFORD GREEN

WOOD WHARF

NORWAY

THAMES ST

CLAVELL ST

HORSEFERRY

COLLEGE APP

KING WILLIAM WALK

GREENWICH CHURCH ST

A206

ROYAL HILL

CREEK RD

BARDSLEY LA

A200

NELSON RD

TURNPIN LA

LAMERTON

ALBURY ST

MARY ANN BUILDINGS

HAMILTON

COPPERAS ST

BERTHON ST

BRONZE ST

THORNHAM

CLAREMONT

NORMAN RD

B208

JORDAN ST

TARVES WAY

RANDALL PL

GLAISHER ST

STRAIGHTSMOUTH

PRINCE OF ORANGE

HARBOUR

NEVADA

STOCKWELL ST

A2211

A206

Deptford

P

FFINCH

CROSSFIELD ST

DEPTFORD HIGH ST

MECHANIC'S PATH

GIFFIN ST

FRANKHAM ST

HALES

REGINALD RD

A2209

HUGHAN

WILLIAMS

COMET

SPEEDWELL ST

CREEKSIDE

Greenwich

GREENWICH TRADING ESTATE

GREENWICH HIGH RD

A2211

MAITLAND PL

ASHBURNHAM PL

A206

DEVONSHIRE DRI

EGERTON DRI

ASHBURNHAM GR

GLOUCESTER CIRC

PELTON RD

B208

BRAND ST

PRIOR ST

ROYAL HILL

ROYAL PL

GLOUCESTER CIRC

KING GEORGE ST

CROOM'S HILL

CROOM'S HILL GR

GLOUCESTER

BURNEY ST

CROOM'S HILL

HAWKS MEWS

WELLINGTON

HYDE VALE B209

THE AVENUE

Greenwich Observatory

Greenwich Park

PARK VISTA

GREAT ROSS AVE

CONDUIT AVE

37
76
38

201 A
ORDNANCE CRES
ORDNANCE CRES
BLACKWALL TUNNEL APP
TUNNEL AVE

Gas Works

79

River Way

INDUSTRIAL ESTATE

R I V E R   T H

Bugsby's Reach

Jetty

Wharf

Jetties

BOORD ST
DREADNOUGHT ST
A 2203

MORDEN WHARF RD

BLACKWALL LA
TUNNEL AVE
A 102

BRADFIELD RD
YT'S RD

BUGSBY'S WAY

ALTERATIONS IN PROGRESS

HORN LA

BUGSBY'S WAY

LOMBARD WALL

MERIDAN TRADING ESTATE

LOMBARD TRADIN ESTATE

River Thames

Wharves

RIVERSIDE WLK

WHARF WLK

Wks

MAURITIUS RD

AZOF ST

78

CADET PL
DERWENT ST
CHRISTCHURCH WAY
BELLOT ST

BANNING ST
PELTON RD

COMMERELL ST
A 2203
WHITWORTH RD

BENDISH RD
HORN FAIR
LENTHORP RD
BROOKE WAY
ARMITAGE RD
DAVERN CL
HATCLIFF
MERCERS CL
GLENISTER ST
CALVERT
GLENFORTH ST
DENHAM ST
WILLIAMSON CL
HAMRIOTT

TUNNEL AVE
FINGAL ST
MARLTON ST
CHILVER ST
COMMERELL
COLLERSTON RD
SELCROFT ST
SCHORP ST

DENTON ST

A 206
CHEVENING RD
22

GREENWICH INDUSTRIAL ESTATE

LOMBARD WALL

MARITIME INDUSTRIAL ESTATE

A 206
WOO
330
TROUGHTON
RATHMORE
DUPREE RD
RAINTON RD
HARDMAN
FAIRTHORN
GURDON RD
FELLTRAM WAY
ELLITOR
ALDE
FEARON ST
BURGH ST

64

WOODHILL
GUILDFORD RD
BANNING ST
CARDWELL RD
MORDEN
THORNLEY
KING WILLIAM LA
TRAFALGAR RD
PELTON RD
RODMERE ST
WALNUT TREE RD
EARLSWOOD ST
WOODLAND CRES
TYLER ST
ANNANDALE RD
LASSELL ST
WOODLANDS PARK RD
TUSKAR ST

P
Greenwich District Hospital

Cemy

KEMSING RD
ORMISTON
HALSTOW
STATION CRES
WESTERDALE
Westcombe Park
COMMERELL
FAREDALE
WESTCOMBE HILL

DELAFIE
DENVER
FOSSDENE RD
CALYDON RD
VICTOR

A 206
PARK VISTA
FROBISHER ST
Maze Hill
GREENWICH

WOODLANDS PARK RD
RESTELL CL
DINSDALE

VANBRUGH HILL
HUMBER RD
PEACHUM RD
WEBB
FOYLE RD
COLERAINE RD
HARDY RD
INGLESIDE
BEACONSFIELD
MYCENE RD

KIRKSIDE
GLENLUCE RD
RUTHIN RD
SIEBERT

EASTCOMBE AVE
SANDTOFT RD
EVERSLEY RD
TALLIS GR
BRAMSHOT AVE
MAYHILL RD
HOPEDALE RD
SHERINGTON
FURRE RD
HIGHCOMBE
WYNDCLIFF

CHARLTO

77

LOVERS' WLK

Greenwich Park

MAZE HILL
HIGHMORE RD
LYNDALE CL
VANBRUGH FIELDS
WESTCOMBE PARK RD
PAYNE
VANBRUGH PARK RD
VANBRUGH HILL

VICTORIA WAY
INVERMORE

SCHOFIELD WLK
DORNBERG RD
DORNBERG
BROAD BRIDGE
B 210

CONTHURST
HASSENDEAN RD
BANCROFT RD
LYVEDEN RD

LIZBAN ST
BOWATER
SUNFIELDS
B 211

GREAT CROSS AVE
BOWER AVE
SAMS CT
VANBRUGH PARK RD EAST
VANBRUGH PARK
PARKSIDE
VANBRUGH PARK

B 210
B 211
P
OLD DOVER RD
A 102(M)

Sch

BLACKHEATH AVE
CHARLTON WAY
B 210
VANBRUGH PARK RD
VANBRUGH
MANOR WAY
ANGER STEIN
ST JOHN'S PARK
HEATHWAY
VICARAGE RD
B 212 STRATHEDE RD
LANGTON WAY
A 207
L
B 211
REYNOLDS
EAST BROOK

58

THAMESIDE
INDUSTRIAL ESTATE

A 1011 ALBERT RD
FACTORY RD
HENLEY RD

Mean High Water

STANDARD
INDUSTRIAL ESTATE

PIER RD

Silvertown

Jetty

North
Woolwich

T H A M E S

The Thames Barrier

Woolwich Reach

Jetties

Slipway

CHURCH HILL

UNITY WAY HARRINGTON WAY

WARSPITE RD

DEFIANCE WLK

RESOLUTION WLK

A 206

RIVERSIDE HERRINGHAM RD

BOWATER RD

ANTELOPE RD

VENUS

CHURCH HILL

FARADAY WAY

WOOLWICH CHURCH ST

KINGSMAN PAR

WARWICK ST

KINGSMAN ST

NEW LYDENBURG ST

WESTMOOR ST

HARDENS MANORWAY

SIEMENS RD

PETT ST

LORD

MARY BANK

LAMPORT ST

ST MARY

EAST MOOR ST

RUSTON RD

B15

TMARTON

Woolwich
Dockyard

BELSON ST

BORGARD

GORMAN RD

MIRFIELD ST

EASTMOOR ST

FERRANT ST

HARDEN CT

MARSHALLS

FRANCES ST

PARK

CLANCEY CL

FLY CL

TIVOLI GDNS

PROSPECTS VALE

Hosp

SAMUEL ST

ARTILLERY PL

GLUON WAY

LYFORD ST

ELLANBY WLK

GODFREY HILL

ARGOUT RD

FRONT GROVE

MARTON RD

WOODHILL

MARTON

GODFREY RD

OGILBY ST

B 210

WICH RD

HICKIN CL

PRENTISS CT

POUND PARK RD

WOODLAND TERR

WOODVILLE ST

WOODROW

PELHAM RD

GREENHILL TERR

REPOSITORY RD

99

Park

GALLON

HANSON

HARVEY GDNS

MASTED PARK RD

COXMOUNT RD

HEATHWOOD GDNS

KIDD PL

LENNOX

HILLREACH

GREEN HILL

Charlton

BARNEY CL

FLOYD RD

CEDAR

Charlton
FC

THORNTREE RD

WOLFE CRES

KINVEACHY GDNS

CANNON

GREEN HILL

VALLEY GR

SAM BARTRAM

LANSDOWNE MEWS

CHARLTON LA

Mus

DORNE RD

WELLINGTON GDNS

MADINE ST

THE HEIGHTS

LANSDOWNE LA

FAIRFIELD

ST PAULS

BEACHEY

PLUMSTEAD RD

LITTLE HEATH

Royal Military
Repository

FLETCHING RD

CHARLTON LA

OLD

ST ALFEGE RD

PARK DRI

CEMETERY LA

WARREN WLK

COOMBE LODGE

ELLISCOMBE RD

THE VILLAGE

P

CHARLTON PARK RD

HA-HA RD

MARGOT GIBBINS

SPRINGFIELD GR

B 210

Charlton
House

L

Sch

Cemy

MASCALLS CT

CANBERRA RD

Park

CHARLTON PARK LA

CHERRY ORCHARD

HORNFAIR RD

MONTCALM

MERIDIAN

INIGO JONES RD

The
Queen Elizabeth
Military Hospital

FAIRLAWN

SHIRLEY HOUSE DRI

KASHMIRR RD

STADIUM RD

Woolwich
Common

BLAKER CT

MARLBOROUGH LA

NIGERIA RD

GREENBAY WAY

STONEFIELD WAY

PRINCE HENRY RD

SHRAPNEL CL

ACADEMY RD

THE GLADE

CHARLTON DENE

GRENADA RD

KENYA RD

INDUS

STANET WAY

MANSERGH CL

BAKER RD

A 205

RECTORY FIELD CRES

OOTERS HILL RD

HERVEY

PORTWAY GDNS

VALLET WAY

MASTER GUNNER'S PL

A 207

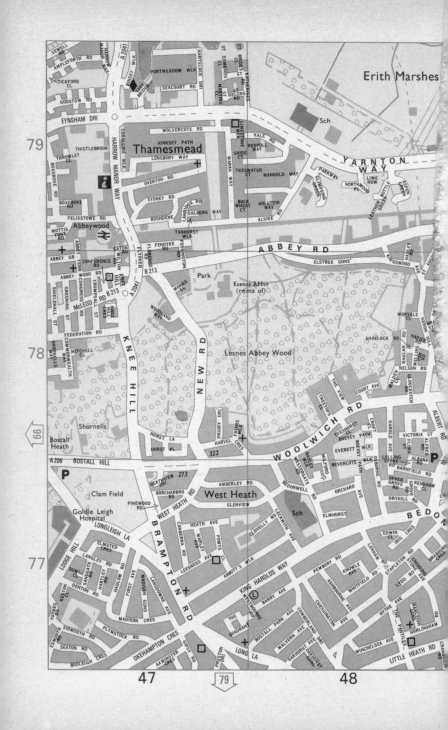

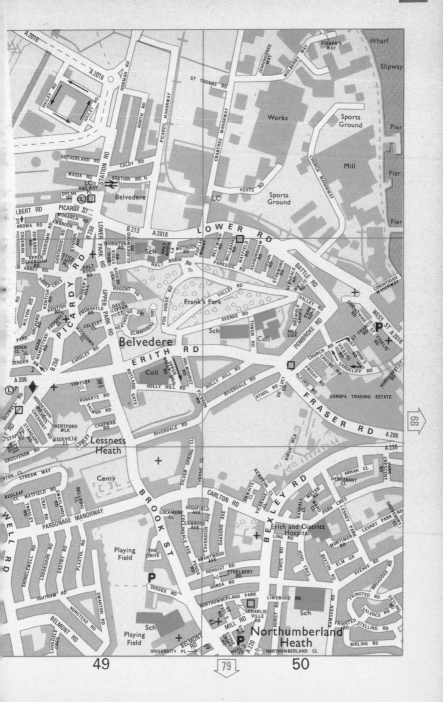

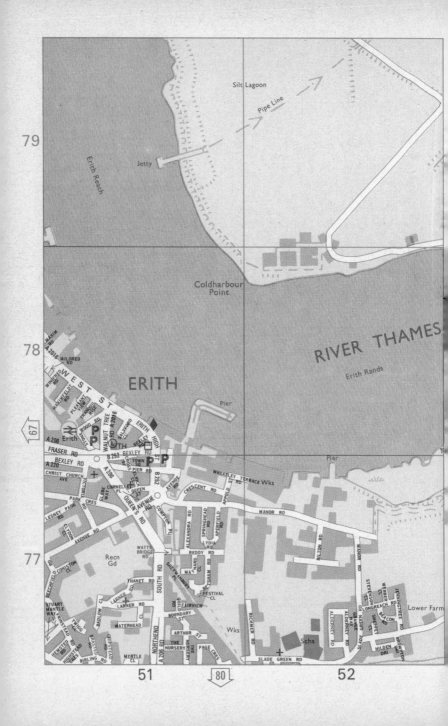

79

Silt Lagoon

Pipe Line

Erith Reach

Jetty

Coldharbour
Point

78

MAXIM RD
A 2016
MILDRED RD
WINIFRED RD
WEST ST
MAXIMFELD RD
PLEASANT
PLATANOS RISE
WOOD STREET
WALNUT TREE RD
BALFOUR RD A 2016
BEXLEY RD
ERITH HIGH ST

ERITH

RIVER THAMES

Erith Rands

Pier

67 ◁

A 206 Erith ⊕
TH
FRASER RD
A 220 BEXLEY RD
B 252 BEXLEY ST
CHRIST CHURCH AVE
PARK CRES
LESHEY PARK RD
CLYFON AVENUE RD
GLEBE WAY
CORNELLY
A 206
QUEEN'S ROAD
QUEEN ST
COMPTON PL
QUEEN'S AVENUE
P P
TOWN
PIER RD
B 252
AVENUE RD
WHEATLEY TERRACE Wks
CRESCENT RD
ALEXANDRA RD
SPRINGHEAD RD
APPFIELD
APPOLD RD
MANOR RD
BILTON RD
MANOR RD

Pier

Pier

77
BEECHFIELD CONISTON RD
Recn Gd
WATTS BRIDGE RD
THANET RD
SOUTH RD
SMITH ANBURY
HURD CL
MAY CL
REDDY
LYDIA RD
CRESHAM RD
FESTIVAL CL
STEVENSON'S
LONGREACH
WEBBER CL
BEACON
GRANGE
SHEPFEY CL
ALDERNEY RD
SLADE RD
JENNINGS STREET RD
BRAMPTON RD
Lower Farm
STUART MANTLE WAY
FRINSTEAD RD
BADLOW CL
LARNER RD
WATERHEAD CL
HEMSTED RD
HIGHSTEAD
BIRLING RD
TWIGG
BRASTED RD
CHISLET CL
MYRTLE RD
NORTHEND RD
A 206
ARTHUR ST
THE NURSERY
FAIRVIEW
OTHER BOUNDARY
PAGE CRES
Wks
BICHNER RD
Schs
SLADE GREEN RD
ALDERNEY RD
HILDEN DRI

51   ▽ 80 △   **52**

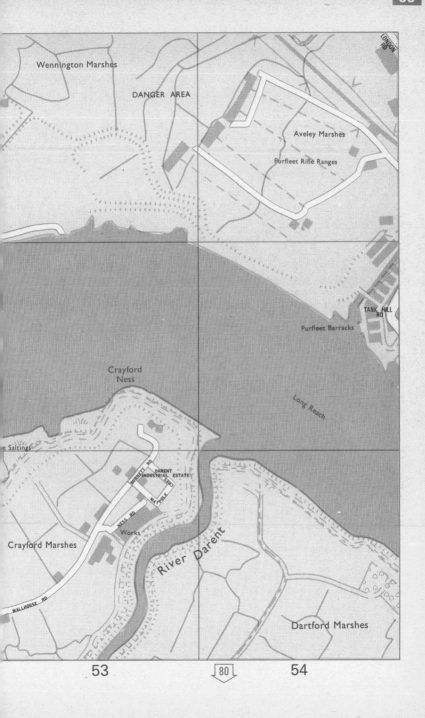

Wennington Marshes

DANGER AREA

Aveley Marshes

Purfleet Rifle Ranges

TANK HILL RD

Purfleet Barracks

Crayford Ness

Long Reach

e Saltings

DARENT INDUSTRIAL ESTATE

NESS RD.

Works

Crayford Marshes

WALLHOUSE RD.

River Darent

Dartford Marshes

53

80

54

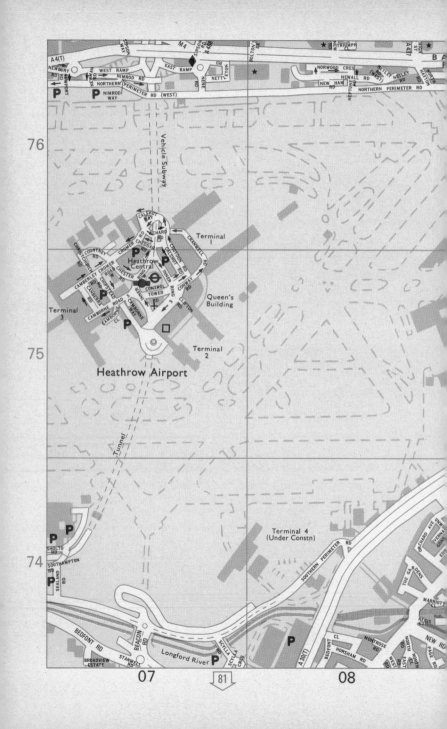

Heathrow Airport

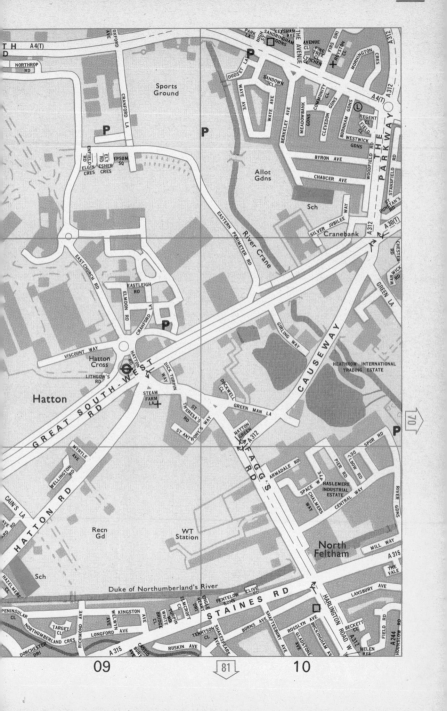

TH A4(T)
D

NORTHROP
RD

OXFORD AVE

CRANFORD LA

Sports
Ground

P

ENFIELD RD
ELGIN CRES

ELY RD
ESHER CRES

EPSOM SQ

PARK LA
HIGH
SANDRINGHAM GDNS
KEYSHAM AVE
THE AVENUE

AVENUE
FIRS DRI
CL
LYNCHEN

MORNINGTON CRES

A 312

A4(T)

A 312

DUDSET LA
SANDOWN CL
WAYE AVE
WAVE AVE

BERKELEY AVE
MEADOWBANK GDNS
COMMUNITY CL
CLEVEDON GDNS
BURNHAM GDNS
WESTWICK GDNS

REGENT
FIELD
L

STANSFIELD RD
DURHAM'S RD
THE PARKWAY

Allot
Gdns

BYRON AVE
WOODFIELD RD

CHAUCER AVE

Sch

SILVER JUBILEE WAY

EASTERN PERIMETER RD

River Crane

Cranebank
A 312

A30(T)

CHESTER RD

WARWICK RD

EAST CHURCH RD

EASTLEIGH RD
ELMDON RD
CRANFORD LA

P

GREEN LA

GIRLING WAY

CAUSEWAY

HEATHROW INTERNATIONAL
TRADING ESTATE

VISCOUNT WAY

Hatton
Cross

LITHGOW'S RD

GREAT SOUTH - WEST RD

HATTON RD

DICK TURPIN WAY
DICKWELL CL
ST THERESA'S WAY
ST ANTHONY'S WAY

STEAM
FARM LA

GREEN MAN LA

HATTON
GREEN A 312

FAGG'S RD

70

P

Hatton

MYRTLE AVE
WELLINGTON RD

ARMADALE RD
SPACE WAY
CHALKERS WAY

SPUR RD
PIER RD

NEW RD
CENTRAL WAY

HASLEMERE
INDUSTRIAL
ESTATE

RIVER GDNS

CAIN'S LA

Recn
Gd

WT
Station

North
Feltham

MILL WAY

A 315

THE
VALE

HATTON RD

HAZELMERE CL

Sch

Duke of Northumberland's River

STAINES RD

HARLINGTON ROAD W

A 315
A 312

LANSBURY AVE

BECKETT RD

PENINSULAR CL
DORCHESTER DRI
NORTHUMBERLAND CRES
TARGET CL
KINGSTON AVE
RICHMOND AVE
LONGFORD AVE
WELWYN AVE
BRIDGE RD
WHITE BRIDGE CL
ELMCROFT AVE
TENNYSON AVE
SHAKESPEARE AVE
RUSKIN AVE
BURNS AVE
SHAFTSBURY AVE
ROSSLYN AVE
BECKINGHAM AVE
GLADSTONE AVE
PENTELOW GDNS
ENGLE HEART
CLIVE RD

FIELD RD
HOUNSLOW RD
NELEN AVE
A 244

09

81

10

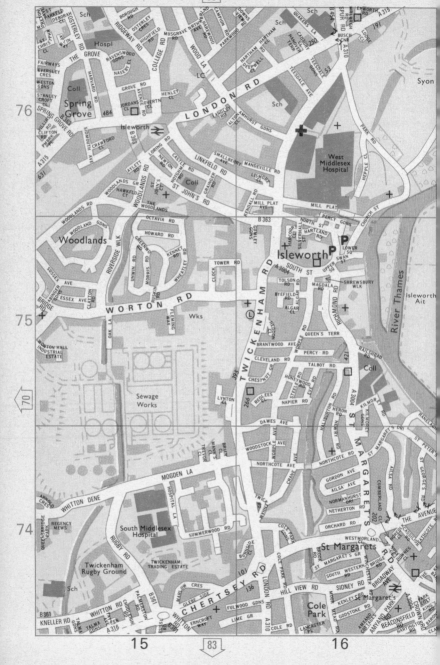

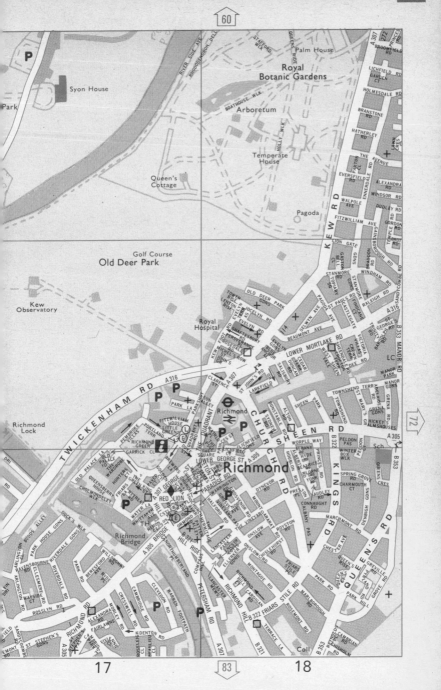

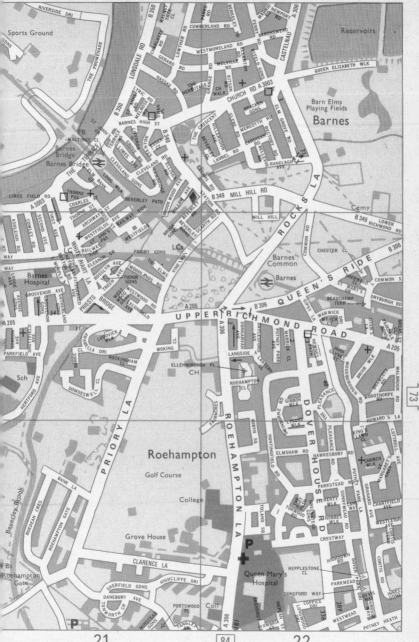

Sports Ground

RIVERSIDE DRI

THE PROMENADE

Reservoirs

QUEEN ELIZABETH WLK

Barn Elms
Playing Fields

Barnes

LONSDALE RD

B 350

WILLOW
CHARLOTTE RD

LOWTHER RD

PLANE
CUMBERLAND RD

BEKELEY RD

WESTMORELAND RD

FERRY RD

MADRID RD

NEWPORT RD

NASSAU RD

GERARD RD

MELVILLE RD

ELLERTON RD

REED GDNS

KITSON RD

BARONSMEAD RD

CASTELNAU

A 306

THE HERMITAGE

CHURCH RD A 3003

CH WALK

GRANGE RD

BRACKEN GDNS

ELM GROVE RD

LYRIC RD

THE CRESCENT

HILLERSDON RD

GLEBE RD

MEREDYTH RD

CARDIGAN RD

RECTORY RD

RANELAGH AVE

BARNES HIGH ST

B 350

B 349

BEVERLEY RD

LAUREL RD

BELLEVUE RD

FB

MALTINGS CL

Barnes
Bridge

Barnes Bridge

THE TERRACE

CLEVELAND GDNS

CLEVELAND RD

LIMES FIELD RD

A 3003

CHARLES
THORNE PAS

THORNE ST

ARCHWAY

BARN ELMS

ELM BANK
LONG WLK

BROOKWOOD AVE

WILLOW
BEVERLEY

STATION RD

B 349 MILL HILL RD

MILL HILL

ROCKS LA

Cemy

B 349 LOWER
RICHMOND RD

LIMES FIELD RD

COWLEY RD

FIRST AVE

SECOND AVE

WHITE HART LA

WESTFIELDS AVE

ANN'S
RAILWAY SIDE

WESTFIELDS

BROOK GDNS

BEVERLEY PATH

BEVERLEY

SCARTH RD

B 306

CHESTER CL

ASHLEIGH RD

WAY

WAY

WESTMORE

ROSSLYN AVE

THE ELMS

VINE RD

LCs

Barnes
Common

SHERWOOD

COMMON S

Barnes Hospital

GROSVENOR AVE

ELEANOR
GDNS

TUDOR GDNS

WOODLANDS RD

WESTWOOD RD

PRIORY GDNS

St MARY'S

Barnes

BEAUCHAMP TERR

DRYBURGH RD

PRIESTS BRIDGE

54

SUTHERLAND

LEONFIELD

A 205

A 205

B 306

UPPER RICHMOND ROAD

A 306

QUEEN'S RIDE

GIPSY LA

WARWICK DRI

MARCH DRI

DYER'S

BREALEY

PARKE'S
AVE

A 205

PARKFIELD AVE

SHEFFIELD AVE

Sch

LUDOVICK WLK

BIRKE
CL

ISABELLA DRI

ROCKINGHAM CL

WOKING

DOWDESWELL

HERTFORD AVE

FAIRACRES

ELLENBOROUGH PL

CH

DUNGARVAN AVE

LANGSIDE

THE LANTERN

LANGSIDE AVE

DANVESTFORD RD

PUTNEY PARK AVE

MATTOCK CL

ROEHAMPTON CL

NEPEAN'S
PATH

WOODBOROUGH RD

BRIAR WLK

WESTCOTE

MALBROOK RD

JOHN GLYNES'S

WOODTHORPE RD

73

GIBBON WLK

MYRTN SQ

NEUMEAD RD

LYSONS RD

THE PLEASANCE

HOWARD'S LA

KING'S LAWN CL

LUTTRELL AVE

Roehampton

Golf Course

College

Grove House

FAIRACRES

ROEHAMPTON LA

HUNTINGFIELD RD

ELMSHAW RD

HAWKESBURY RD

DOVER HOUSE ROAD

PLEASANCE

PARKSTEAD RD

PUTNEY

CHURCH WLK

MARGARET'S RD

WESTLEIGH AVE

CORTIS TERR

CHARTFIELD AVE

Beverley Brook

BANK LA

PRIORY LA

RNEDEAN CRES

ROEHAMPTON GATE

TOLAND SQ

CREST
GDNS

HENTY
WLK

TORWOOD
WLK

HOBBES
WLK

SUNNYMEAD RD

LANE WAY

PARK LA

GRANARD AVE

CRESTWAY

HIGHDOWN RD

CORTIS RD

WESTLEIGH AVE

INNES GDNS

FBs

Roehampton
Gate

CLARENCE LA

HIGHCLIFFE DRI

HEPPLESTONE CL

DOVER PARK DRI

P

DANEBURY AVE

SHERFIELD GDNS

MINSTEAD GDNS

TILEHURST

TWORTH CR

TANGLEY RD

PORTSWOOD PL

Coll

A 306

Queen Mary's
Hospital

DUNSFORD WAY

ARTHUR'S

NEPEAN'S

CUMBRIA

COPPICE DRI

LONGWOOD

WESTMEAD

PARKMEAD

DAVIS'S
DRI

289

336

PUTNEY HEATH

P

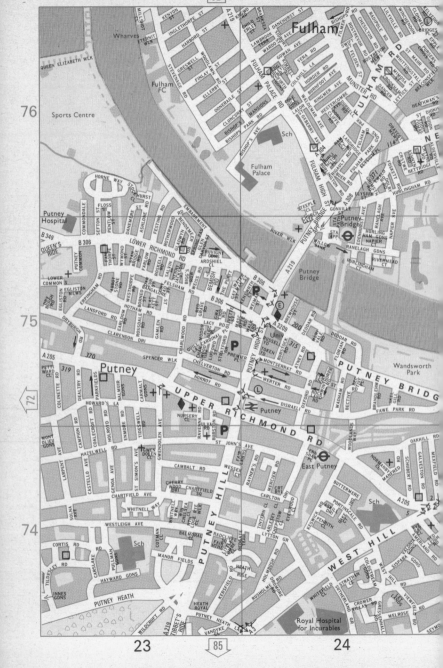

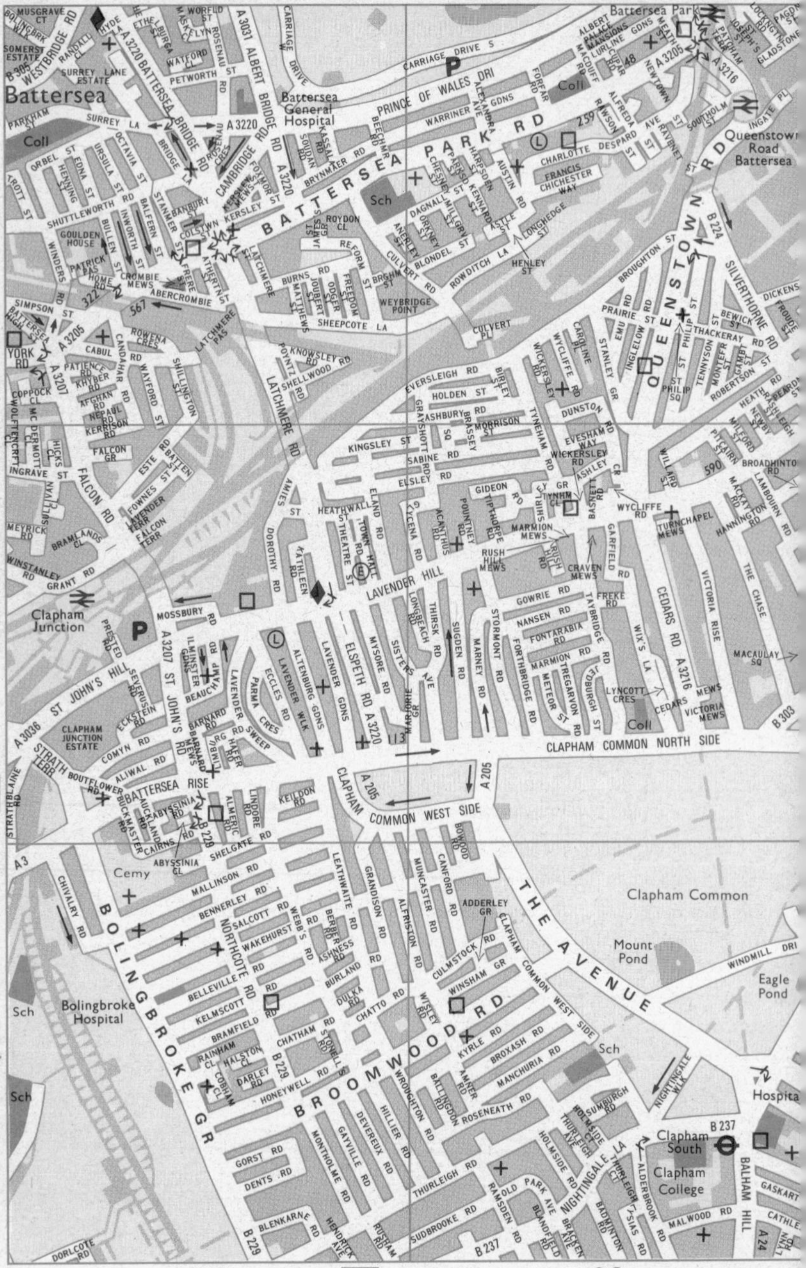

Battersea

BATTERSEA PARK RD

BATTERSEA PARK

Battersea General Hospital

PRINCE OF WALES DRI

Carriage Drive S

Battersea Park

Queenstown Road Battersea

QUEENSTOWN RD

SURREY LANE ESTATE

ALBERT BRIDGE RD

CAMBRIDGE RD

LATCHMERE RD

YORK RD

FALCON RD

Clapham Junction

ST JOHN'S HILL

Clapham Junction Estate

Battersea Rise

Lavender Hill

LAVENDER HILL

ELSPETH RD

CLAPHAM COMMON NORTH SIDE

CLAPHAM COMMON WEST SIDE

Clapham Common

Mount Pond

Eagle Pond

THE AVENUE

WINDMILL DRI

BOLINGBROKE GR

Bolingbroke Hospital

BROOMWOOD RD

NIGHTINGALE LA

Clapham South

Clapham College

BALHAM HILL

Cemy

76

75

73

74

77

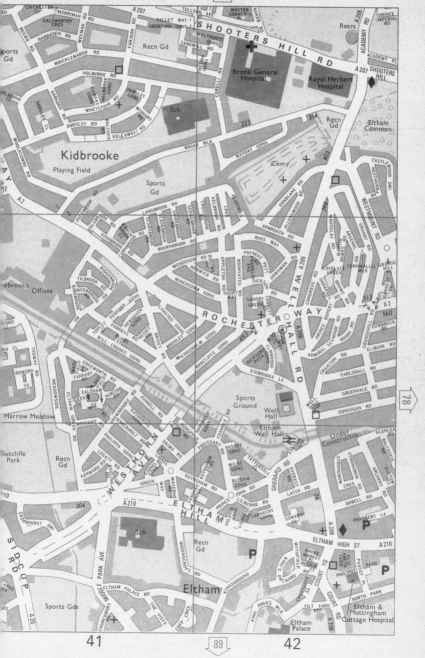

66

PRINCE IMPERIAL RD

RED LION LA
ACADEMY RD
CAMPBELL
CONSTITUTION RISE
DONALDSON RD
ANKERDINE CRES
MOORDOWN
CUPATION LA
MAYPLES
SHREWSBURY LA
FOXCROFT RD
CLEANTHUS RD
CLEANTHUS CL
BUSHMOOR CRES
KINLET RD
EAGLESFIELD RD
MEREWORTH DRI
L
CH

Hospital

Springwater
BARRINGTON VILLAS
27
HILL END
A 207
CRAIGHOLM
STONEY ALLEY

76

Shooters Hill

Golf Course

SHOOTERS HILL DOVER RD
ROMAN ROAD
Woodlands Farm
353
316
415

Woolwich War Memorial Hospital
Severndroog Castle
KENILWORTH GDNS

Jackwood

OXLEAS CL
EASTCOTE RD
SUNDRA

CASTLEWOOD DRI
LITTLECROFT

CROOKSTON RD
DAIRSIE RD
GLENMORE
GLENLEE
GLENESK
BERRYHILL

Oxleas Wood
P

ROCHESTER WAY
A 209

WELLIN

547
A2
664
DUMBRECK RD
ELIBANK RD

Eltham Park

Falconwood Field
Falconwood

LINGFIELD
MILLBROOK AVE
BRAYWOOD CRES
WINCROFTS DRI
A2

75

WESTMOUNT RD
EARLSHALL RD
GREENVALE RD
ELTHAM PARK GDNS
DUNVEGAN RD
GLENLEA
GLENLYON RD

Eltham Park

RIEFIELD RD
Cemy
RIEFIELD

77

GLENHOUSE RD
BEECHHILL RD
GLENSHIEL RD
GLENURE RD
ELDERSLIE RD
GREENHOLM RD

Golf Course
GRAVEL PIT LA
Sch

COLEPITS WOOD RD
CROWN WOODS WAY
FAIROAK DRI
RENNETS WOOD RD
PACKMA

BALCASKIE RD
GOUROCK RD

CH

BEXLEY RD

74

L
TH
ELTHAM HIGH ST A 210
MARLOWE GDNS
WOODINGTON
NORTH PARK
P
ROPER ST
PHILIPOT PATH
MESSETER
A 211
W.ATHENS WLK
OAKWAYS
BUTTERFLY LA
CONTEND
COURTFIELD CRES
FOOTSCRAY RD
GREEN
NEWLANDS CT
LADYSMITH RD
A 211

96
LE MONWELL DRI
Coll
Avery Hill

Avery Hill

B 2214
AVERY HILL RD
ANSTRIDGE RD
ALDERWOOD RD
OSPRIN
B 2214

43
90
44

East Wickham
Open Space

Schs

WARLAND RD
DRYDEN RD
MILTON RD
KEATS RD
TENNYSON CL
EDISON RD
GLENMORE RD
WORDSWORTH RD
BROWNING
SHELLEY RD
BLAKE
CHAUCER RD
WYCLIFFE
BLENHEIM DRI
BURNS ST
ROSEMARY
OKEHAMPTON CRES
A 209
AXMINSTER CRES
ELIOT
ART
KAY ST
MILLS
LYME RD
BRUCE
DOUGLAS
CHARMOUTH RD
BERWICK RD
Sch

WICKHAM ST
BEAL
DARENTH RD
RIDLEY RD
ANTHONY RD
CLINTON RD
EAST RD

WICKHAM ST
EXETER RD
HONITON RD
MONKTON RD
RAWLSCOMBE RD
TIDFORD RD
CAMBORNE RD
CLEVELAND RD
DOVEDALE CL
RIPPLESLEY
STREET
NORFOLK
LOVEL AVE
LEIGH PL
OLIFFE AVE
BENNETT
BURNELL AVE
QUEEN'S RD
CHURCH RD
DUNSTALL WELLING ESTATE
GRAVES ESTATE
ELSA RD
BALLIOL RD
SOMERHILL RD
LYNMERE RD

MARINA DRI
SANDRINGHAM DRI
NEWLYN RD
LULWORTH RD
BALTIMORE PL
BELLEGROVE RD
A 209
MONTROSE RD
STATION APP
Welling
RUSKIN GR
STATION APP
RUSKIN AVE
DEEPDENE
EDMUND RD
COTON RD
12
NEW RD
WESTBROOKE RD
ORCHARD RD
SPRINGFIELD RD
NAGS HEAD
A 209
CARE
Welling

FALCONWOOD AVE
BELMONT RD
SHERWOOD RD
DELMORE RD
SOUTHCROFT
WAY
MONTROSE AVE
FB
ST QUENTIN RD
DARWIN RD
TYNDALL RD
CAVENDISH RD
HUXLEY RD
FARADAY RD
MARNE RD
NEWTON RD
KELTIE
27
L
A 207
WELLING HIGH ST
EMBASSY
MARWOOD
ST MICHAEL'S RD
BULL ALLEY
JOHN NEWTON
WELLING HIGH ST
SCHOOL LA
PENPOOL

NORTHUMBERLAND AVE
WESTMORELAND AVE
CORNWALL AVE
CUMBERLAND AVE
Schs
BUCKINGHAM AVE
CAMBRIDGE AVE
DORSET AVE
YORKLAND AVE
WESTHOOK LA
CHURCHFIELD RD
ST LEONARDS RD
ST JOHN'S RD
DANSON RD
MAKWELL RD
CLINTON AVE
BRADENHAM AVE
MONKBERRY
PORTHKERRY AVE
LANCELOT RD
DANSINGTON RD
MERLIN CL
PARK APP
SELWYN CRES
LAKERN
DANSON LA
ROSEACRE

falconwood
Falconwood
THE GREEN
FALCONWOOD PAR
SUTHERLAND AVE
GLOUCESTER AVE
KENT AVE
SOMERSET AVE
FAIRWATER AVE
BIRCH GR
WENDOVER WAY
223
COWPER CL
INGLETON AVE
Sch
Playing Field
79

ORCHARD RISE W
RIDGEWAY W
B 2213
CHESTER RD
RIDGEWAY
LEECHCROFT AVE
ORCHARD RISE W
BOUNDARY RD
GORDON RD
BLAIR
B 2213
WAVELL DRI
FERNBANK
MONTGOMERY
ALEXANDER
LYNDON AVE
CURRAN AVE
BURLEIGH AVE
EAST ROCHESTER WAY
296
656
GROOMBRIDGE
TYRRELL AVE
RADNOR AVE
FLYOVER
WELLAN CL
A 2(T)
GWILLIM CL

THANINGTON CRES
ONS CRES
ODEN
RONALDSTONE RD
REABURN RD
QUEENSWOOD RD
FEN GR
CRISTOPHER
MONTGOMERY
FERNWOOD RD
HOLBEACH GDNS
CLOVERDALE GDNS
CAITHNESS GDNS
BERWICK CRES
HARMAN DRI
ENE GR
DAYS LA
BLACKFEN RD
Blackfen
ELMCROFT AVE
BURNT OAK LA
CEDAR AVE
WILLOW ASHGROVE CRES
LEAFIELD
SYCAMORE AVE
WELLINGTON AVE
MAPLE
ASHCROFT CRES
PENHURST AVE
BURNS AVE
PORTLAND AVE
374
A 210
RAMILLIES RD
PARK MEAD
ROCHESTER
SHORE
OVERCOURT
WESTERHAM
A 1311
Schs
SHERWOOD PARK AVE

76

75

78

74

BEXLEY

Bexleyheath

Bexleyheath

BROADWAY

Bexleyheath

OKEHAMPTON CRES
AXMINSTER CRES
CHARMOUTH RD
BERWICK RD
TENBY RD
SELSEY CRES
BRIXHAM RD
Park
WROTHAM RD
SWANLEY RD
FARNHAM RD
TEIGNMOUTH RD
ELSA RD
HAZELDENE RD
IVEDON RD
AVONDALE RD
SUTCLIFFE RD
STEVEDALE RD
NORTHDOWN RD
KENMERE RD
LYNMERE RD

NORMANHURST AVE
WINCHESTER RD
ALEXANDER RD
HOLMESDALE RD
FAIRLAWN AVE
BARRINGTON RD
PRESTON DRI
BERKELEY AVE
MAYFAIR AVE

BRAMPTON RD
PICKFORD LA
JENTON AVE
ALBURY AVE
DORCIS AVE
PICKFORD CL
BASILDON RD

KINGSGATE CL
SHAKESPEARE RD
ORCHARD CL
BOWFORD AVE
BRISTOW RD
HEATHSIDE AVE
HAMILTON RD
HARDING RD
HERBERT
SOMERSHAM RD
OLDFIELD
PERCY RD

FRANKLIN RD
HARRIS RD
CANNON RD
STANHOPE RD
CYRIL RD

CUMBERLAND DRI
NORFOLK CONS
ROMNEY RD
CRANBR
PENCHURST RD
DUNWICH RD

SHELDON RD
FAIRFIELD
GRACE AVE
HASLEM

BELVEDERE RD

STATION APP
Bexleyheath STATION RD

FB

MARLBOROUGH RD
PALMEIRA RD
BLACKTHORN
BEECHWOOD CRES
CHESTNUT DRI
WOODLANDS RD
SHERIDAN RD
GLENGALL RD
HARLINGTON RD
CHURCH RD
UPLAND RD
BOSTALL ROW

MAY FIELD
Sch

WEST BROOKE CRES
WESTBROOKE
CLIFTON RD
WARWICK RD
DENHAM
SHARP BROOKE
LEWIS RD
GRANVILLE RD
BETHEL RD
STUART EVANS
PARK VIEW RD
A 207

GLYNDE RD
SPORTMAN CL
REGENCY WAY
ADAMS SQ
CROOK LOG
THOMSONS
GREEN WAY
BOROUGH

PICKFORD RD
SANDFORD RD
BETHRONVI RD
ROWAN RD
HARCOURT
STRATTON RD
BYRON AVE
PRINCES ST
QUEEN ST
ABBEY RD
WEST ST
BANKS LA
TRINITY PL

P

DANSON RD
A 221

THE GROVE
HOWTH CL
SOUTH
DALLIN
BRUNSWICK RD
SYDNEY RD
ASKERN CL
BEAN RD
RED HOUSE LA
WINDSOR RD
TURNPIKE
BRUNS WICK
CLARE COTT
VILLA
STANDARD
PADDOCK
DEVONSHIRE RD
HEATHFIELD RD
IZANE RD
OAKLANDS RD
METHUEN

BROADWAY
P

Danson Park
The Lake
Swimming Pool
Allot Gdns
IVYHURST
GREEN VALE
DITTON RD
CUXTON CL
HANSOL RD
BAFTON
MOUNT RD
YOUNG DRI
FAIRWAY
ROBIN HOOD LA
LEWIN RD
BELLEVUE RD
FRETA RD
MARTIN DENE
MARTIN RISE
HIGHFIE
OAKLANDS RD
ROYAL OAK

UPTON RD
TOWNLEY RD

A 2(T)
LAKESIDE CL
UNDERPASS
Flyover
PARK MEAD
WESTERHAM DRI
BLACKFEN RD A 210
A 210
LODGE LA
SANDHURST
BRASTED RD
GROSVENOR RD
BROOK
KESMARK
PENN RD
OLKON CRES
CORONATION RD
PENN RD
FERGRAVH
Golf Course
IRIS AVE
UPTON RD
UPTON CL
ARNHEL

EAST ROCHESTER WAY
FLYOVER
ARBUTHNOT LA
CHESTNUT
WELDON WIEN
BASING DRI
WILLOW
UPTON RD

DANSON
A 221
PENHILL RD
A 221
SHERWOOD RD
HARCOURT
SHERWOOD PARK AVE
BLEDLO
KESMARK
BANWELL RD
B 2210
BLENDON RD
WOODSIDE LA
THE CEDAR GR
THE DRIVE
THE SANCTUARY
BLENDON DRI
ELMWOOD DRI
ARCADIAN
ARCADIAN CL
B 2210 BRIDGEN
ARCA
WOODALE CL
SOUTH
RIVERDALE RD
SHUTTLE
Sch

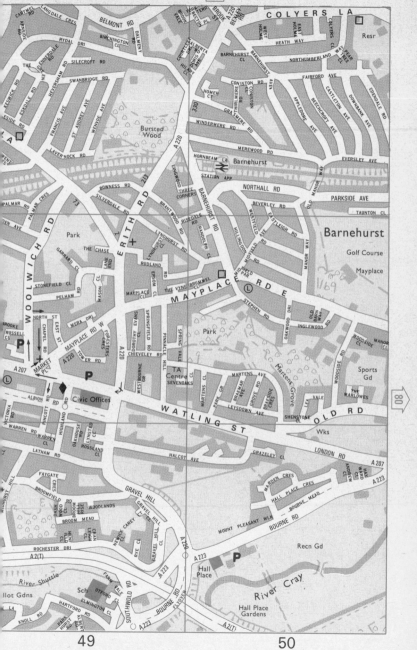

COLYERS LA

CARTMEL RD
LANGDALE CRES
BELMONT RD
Resr

ARNSIDE
RD
RYDAL DRI
BIRCHINGTON CL
DALMENY
WEST HOLME
EAST HOLME
HEATH WAY

THE
PINEDALE
SILECROFT RD
BARNEHURST CL
BARNEHURST AVE
NORTHUMBERLAND
WAY FRELL PEIR

KESWICK RD
HEVERSHAM RD
SWANBRIDGE RD
FAIRFORD AVE

ESDALE RD
FRANCES AVE
ST AUDREY AVE
WENVOE AVE
CONISTON RD
CASTLETON AVE
BEECHCROFT AVE
DOWNBANK RD
ESPENDALE RD

HOMER CT
CONISTON RD
APPLEDORE AVE

Bursted Wood

LAYER NOCK RD
GRASMERE RD
WINDERMERE RD

330
HORNBEAM LA
Barnehurst
EVERSLEY AVE

HOMBEAM LA
MEREWOOD RD

BOWNESS RD
STATION APP
NORTHALL RD
MANOR WAY
PARKSIDE AVE

THREE CORNERS
TAUNTON CL

PALMAR RD
PALMAR CRES
SILVERDALE RD
BRANTWOOD RD
RISEDALE RD
BEVERLEY RD
ESTLEIGH RD

73
Park
THE CHASE
LYNDHURST RD
RANDOLPH RD
WESTFIELD
HILLINGDON

OPEN AVE
ERITH RD
GARRARD CL
LANE END
RUDLAND RD
LYNDHURST RD
MOFIELD
Barnehurst
Golf Course
Mayplace

STONEFIELD CL
MASSON
EPSOM CL
THE VYNE
BRUMMEL CL
MAYPLACE RD E

PELHAM
MAYPLACE CL
MAYPLACE
RDE

NORTH ST
MERA DRI
MAYPLACE RD W
STEPHEN RD
OLD MANOR WAY

BROOKE
RUSSELL CL
CHAPEL RD
EAST ST
FORESTERS CRES
SPRINGFIELD
DOROTHY EVANS
Park
OAKWOOD DRI
INGLEWOOD
WOODSIDE CL

P
A 220
TOWER RD
CHIEVELEY AV
PINNACLE HILL
SPRING VALE
WOODSIDE RD
MANOR CL

A 207
MARKET PL
P
WESTBOURNE GR
TA Centre
SEVENOAKS
MARTENS AVE
MARTENS Grove
Sports Gd

L
ALBION
HIGHLAND
Civic Offices
MARTENS CL
PARK GR
BRAEMAR AVE
GROVE RD
BIRSIDE CRES
LEA VALE
SHENSTONE
THE MARLOWES

VICTORIA
WARREN RD
WARREN CL
HINCROFT
LEYSDOWN AVE
OLD RD

LATHAM RD
ROSSLAND CL
LYNSTED
WATLING ST
Wks

FAYGATE RD
OAKHOUSE RISE
HALCOT AVE
GRAZELEY RD
LONDON RD
A 207

BROOMFIELD RD
GRAVEL HILL
MARDEN CRES
HALL PLACE CRES
ANDREW CL
HAWARD CL
A 223

DASH WOOD CL
WOODLANDS
GRAVEL HILL
BOURNE MEAD
MOUNT PLEASANT WLK
BOURNE RD

BROOM MEAD
HENFIELD
NEW CAREY RD
CRANLEIGH

ROCHESTER DRI
A 2(T)
RYE CL
GRAVEL HILL
A 220
A 223
P
Hall Place
Recn Gd

River Shuttle
Sch
OTFORD RD
FARM VALE
SOUTHWOLD RD
River Cray

llot Gdns
ELMINGTON CL
HARTFORD RD
BOURNE RD
Hall Place Gardens

KNOLL RD
PARK HURST RD
ALBERT
A 223
SOUTHWOLD RD
A 2(T)

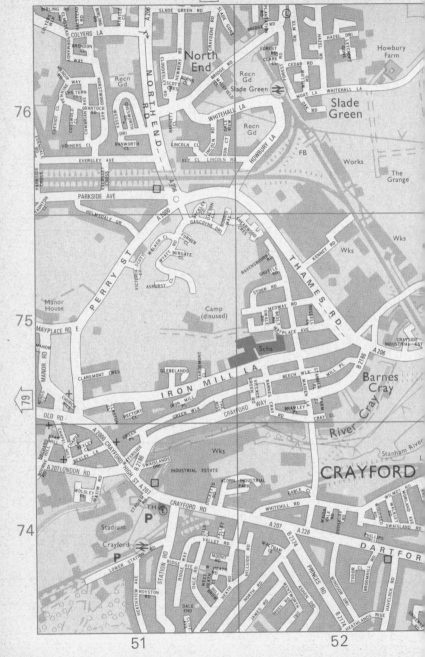

Works

Crayford Marshes

Dartford Creek

Joyce Green Hospital

JOYCE GREEN LA

Crayford Creek

River Darent

Southfield House

East House

STRICKLAND AVE

STRICK LAND AVE

SHARP WAY

BONDFIELD WLK

CHAUCER WAY

WESTINGTON

HENDERSON DRI

JOYCE GREEN RD

AUSTEN GDNS

BROWNING

BLACKS

Wks

Wks

Sandpit Rd

WILLOW WLK

BURNHAM RD

SHIRLEY CL

WINMIR PL

VIVMAR CRES

CHATSWORTH RD

LAWSON RD

Mill

Dartford Fresh Marshes

Temple Hill

WILMCOTE AVE

TRENITHICK DRI

HALL DRI

SPIELMAN RD

FARTHING

STEBBENS RD

BRONTE'S RD

JOYCE GREEN WLK

TREVELYAN

JOYCE GREEN GR

KEYES

HILLTOP GDNS

MARSH

Sports Gd

MAYFAIR RD

SANDY RD

P

CAIRNS CRES

PRIORY RD

RIVERSIDE WAY

RIVERSIDE INDUSTRIAL ESTATE

Wks

P

FRANCIS RD

GROSVENOR CRES

CENTRAL RD

Sch

GAINSBOROUGH

LAWFORD GDNS

MARGARET RD

CRATFORD RD

PRIORY CL

HALLFORD WAY

KINGS DRI

RUFFORD GDNS

CLIVES CT

PRIORY HILL

PRIORY RD

VICTORIA RD

HYTHE ST

MILL POND RD

TEMPLE HILL

TEMPLE HILL SQ

New Town

FULWICH RD

JERMIN RD

LAWRENCE HILL GDNS

LAWRENCE RD

WEST HILL DRI

KINGS DRI

LODGE AVE

KING EDWARD AVE

PRIORY HILL

WEST GATE RD

STATION APP

A 226

GLADSTONE RD

MOUNT PLEASANT

ST MARTIN'S RD

CARRING

THE HOMESTEAD

SANCTUARY CL

West Hill Hospital

A 226

HOME ORCHARD

BULLACE

HOME GDNS

OVERY ST

LAVINIA RD

GREAT QUEEN RD

ST ALBAN'S RD

ROSS HILL

CHURCH HILL

BLENHEIM CL

A 2018

SHEPHERDS LA

TOWER RD

SUMMERHILL

HOMEFIELD RD

ESSEX RD

ORCHARD ST

SPITA ST

KENT RD

HYTHE ST

PRIORY RD

FIELDING CT

LOWFIELD ST

HIGH ST

HOME GDNS

A 226

TUFNAIL RD

WHITE

COLNEY RDN'S CL

WALDECK

53   54

West
Bedfont

Heathrow
Airport **P**

STANWELL RD

Stanwell RD

East
Bedfont

Garages

Homers
Farm

778

A30(T) LONDON RD

Wks

73

WKS

Wks

Cemy

Gravel
Pit

Wks

Wks

BEDFON

CLOCKHOUSE LA

ASCOT RD

ASCOT RD

Wks

Bridge
Farm

72

HM Youth Custody
Centre

ANGLESEY

GLEN AVE

PARKLAND
GR

REEDSFIELD RD

GRAYS LA

Recn
Gd

Chattern
Hill

ASHFORD
INDUSTRIAL ESTATE

CHALLENGE RD

SHIELD
RD

VILLAGE

PARKLAND GR

CLIFFORD GR

CHESTNUT

B 3003

CHATTERN HILL

FERNHURST RD

ANDERSON DRI

71

B 378 CHURCH

MUNCASTER

B 377

FELTHAM RD

WYE RD

WREN'S
AVE

SANDELL'S AVE

NEIL RD

B 3782

TOWN
TREE RD

CONVENT RD

MUNCASTER RD

OAKFIELD

ST MARGARETS

CHALMERS

LYNEGROVE AVE

COOLGARDIE RD

KENNEDY

FAIRVIEW
CT

MANOR RD

REX AVE

GILMORE
CRES

FELTHAM HILL
RD

ELM TREE
CL

DINGLE

HAWLEY
WAY

METCALF RD

BURLEIGH

ROMNEY

MONTROSE RD

JUNCTION RD

MORNINGTON RD

PEAR TREE RD

STAINFORD

ASHGROVE RD

CHESTER
CL

NEWHAVEN
CRES

CHICHESTER WAY
SPARROW FARM DRI
TYNE HAM CLO
CARLTON AVE
FARM DRI
EDGAR RD
A 314

THE DRIVE
BRANTON
SPARROW FARM DRI
FINCH DRI
CYGNET
Feltham Junction
HARVEY RD
Cemy
THEOBALD RD
HEATHSIDE

73
A.312 HARLINGTON ROAD E.
QUEEN'S WALK
CROMWELL RD
KING'S RD
B3377
DURHAM RD
GLOUCESTER
HERFORD RD
NORFOLK RD
Sch
Crematorium
Wks
GODFREY WAY
MILLFIELD RD
FARM RD
TILIN
FARM CRES
GRAFTON CL
HANWORTH RD
PEMBROKE AVE
CHESTER AVE
GLASBROOK AVE
VILLIERS AVE
CHEYNE AVE
ELLERMAN AVE

HANWORTH RD
CAMDEN AVE
SALISBURY RD
BOUNDARIES RD
Sch
ELTHORNE CT
WIGLEY RD
PEVENSEY RD

DANESBURY RD
ALFRED RD
CLYFFONE
Sch
BROWELLS LA
WIGLEY RD
MARLBOROUGH RD
AMESBURY RD
EASTBOURNE RD
WEST BURY RD
BEXHILL CL
LITTLE PARK
MEADOW RD
BRAID CL
NORMAN AVE
COWFIELD RD
SAXON AVE
Sch
FOUNTAINS

UXBRIDGE RD
WOODLAWN DRI
OAKS AVE
SUNNINGDALE AVE
CANTERBURY RD
LORDS CL
FOUNTAINS

72
FOREST RD
Wks
Hanworth Park House
HOUNSLOW RD
L P
MOUNT RD
BARNLEA CL
NEWGATE
HAMPTON INDUSTRIAL ESTATE
HAMPTON ROAD W.
Wks
WINCHESTER RD
YORK WAY
SUN RISE
EXETER RD

ROOKERIES
FERN SIDE AVE
ELMWOOD AVE
CLIFTON AVE
ELM CL
Hanworth Park
RIDGE WAY
HANWORTH TRADING ESTATE
Wks
POPHAM CL
A 312
ELEVATED RD

81
CAMROSE AVE
FERNSIDE AVE
Hanworth
Schs
WINSLOW WAY
Sch
DEVONSHIRE
TWICKENHAM RD
STOURTON AVE
FAIRLAWN AVE
HAMPTON RD E
RECTORY

SEYMOUR SONS
ELIZABETH AVE
PARR CT
TUDOR CT
CASTLE WAY
SWIN
COTTINGTON RD
CRESSWELL RD
DUNMOW CL
GARNET RD
ORIEL
SWIFT RD
CHAMBERLAIN WLK
MILBOURNE RD
RIVERDALE RD
MASEFIELD RD
WORDSWORTH RD
LOXLEY

MOAT SIDE WAY
QUEENS WAY
BLACKWOOD
Rectory Meadow
THE HOLLANDS
PARK RD
CRISPEN RD
CROSS RD
CYGNETS CRES
SWAN RD
HAMPTON LA
THE ALDERS
DUKES
REGENCY CL
BUCKINGHAM CL
GLENMILL

71
QUEENS AVE
RALEIGH WAY
SHAKESPEARE AVE
SUNBURY WAY
ST. GEORGE'S RD
BEAR RD
NEW RD
GREEN LA
OAK AVE
PLUMER RD
BRIAR
MORLAND
EMBLETON WLK
MASLE
DENNING CL

FELTHAM HILL RD
ELEVATED ROAD
A 316
CHURCH RD
NALLHEAD RD
DICKINSON RD
MC CARTHY
OXFORD WAY
MALT ST
ALBANY
CONNAUGHT RD
MAIN ST
FIR RD
FINCH RD
SOUTH RD
FORGE LA
FEARNLEY CRES
STEVENS
STEWART
SHORE CL

11
12

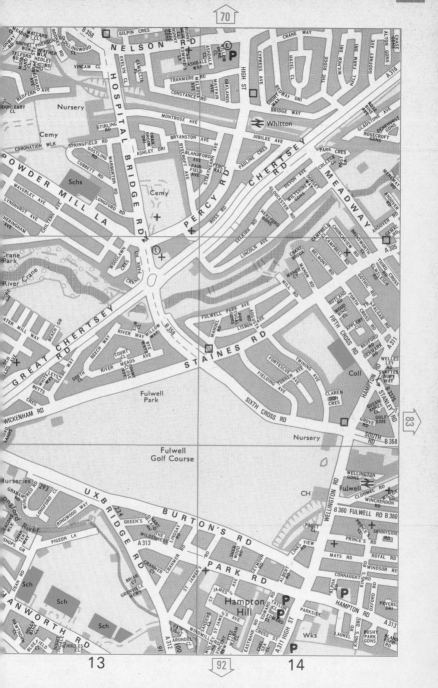

71

84

Marble Hill Park

Marble Hill

Ham House

NORMAN AVE
SANDYCOOMBE RD
A 305 CMBRDG PARK
TELVERTON RD
BEAUFORT RD
MEADOWSIDE
CAMBRIDGE PK
CAMBRIDGE PARK CT
CAMBRIDGE PARK POWDERS
HAVERSHAM CL

CHAPEL RD
MONTPELIER ROW
ORLEANS RD

WARREN FOOTPATH
RIVER LA
RUTLAND DRI

Coll B 353
NIGHTINGALE LA
RICHMOND HILL
QUEEN'S RD
STAFFORD
CHISHOLM RD

A 307

Star & Garter Home

A 307 PETERSHAM RD

B 353 STAR & GARTER HILL

PETERSHAM

Petersham

TREE CL
MEADOW CL
ASHFIELD
CEDAR HTS
SUDBROOK
WHITE AVE

Petersham Park

Richmond Park

Pembroke Lodge

MEADLANDS DRI
BUCKINGHAM RD
PETER SHAM CL
CLIFFORD RD
SANDFITS RD
DICKENS LA
HAZEL LA

SANDY LA
ARLINGTON RD
ASHLEY GDNS
LAUDERDALE DRI

Sch

MURRAY RD
RUSSELL RIDINGS
STRETTON RD
BACK LA
HAM ST

NEVILLE RD

CH

Sudbrook Park

HORNBEAM WLK

Golf Course

MARTIN
GALES CL
EVELYN RD

HAM CL
ASHBURNHAM RD
SHERIDAN RD
MURRAY
LONELL
BACK LA
CLEVES RD
THE BENCH
MEAD RD

A 307

BISHOPS CL

SUDBROOK LA

SKIFF

Ham

WATER WILL
FISHER DRI

LOCK RD
NEW RD

B 352

HAM GATE AVE

Ham Bottom

SIMPSON RD
BROUGHTON AVE
HANDSWORTH RD
CRAIG RD
LAWRENCE
RANDLE RD
LANGHAM GDNS
MORNINGTON WLK
LANGHAM HOUSE

UPPER HAM RD

HAM FARM RD

Ham Common

B 352

DUKES AVE
ANGLERS CL
FAN
SHAWE RD
MAGUIRE RD
BEAUFORT RD
FISHER RD
VAN COWPER RD
LAMMAS RD
DESART AVE

Cassel Hospital for Functional Nervous Disorders

DRYDEN CT

PARKLEYS
PARKLEYS
MILTON CT

BEECH ROW
THE SHIRES
CHURCH RD
GARTHSIDE

Parkgate House

HAM RIDINGS

BURNELL AVE
BARNFIELD AVE
BARNFIELD GDNS

COWPER RD
HM Remand Centre
BEARD RD

Wks

TUDOR DRI

RICHMOND RD
LANCASTER GDNS
FERNHILL RD
LOWER HAM RD
A 307
ARAGON RD
FERNHILL GDNS
WOLSELY DRI
CRANMER RD
ROLEY'S LATCHMERE
LATCHMERE LA
GARTH RD
CARDINAL AVE
HOLLYBUSH
GARTH RD
WOODCOTE
PARKFIELDS RD
WILMER CL
WILMER CRES
PARK GDNS

Sch

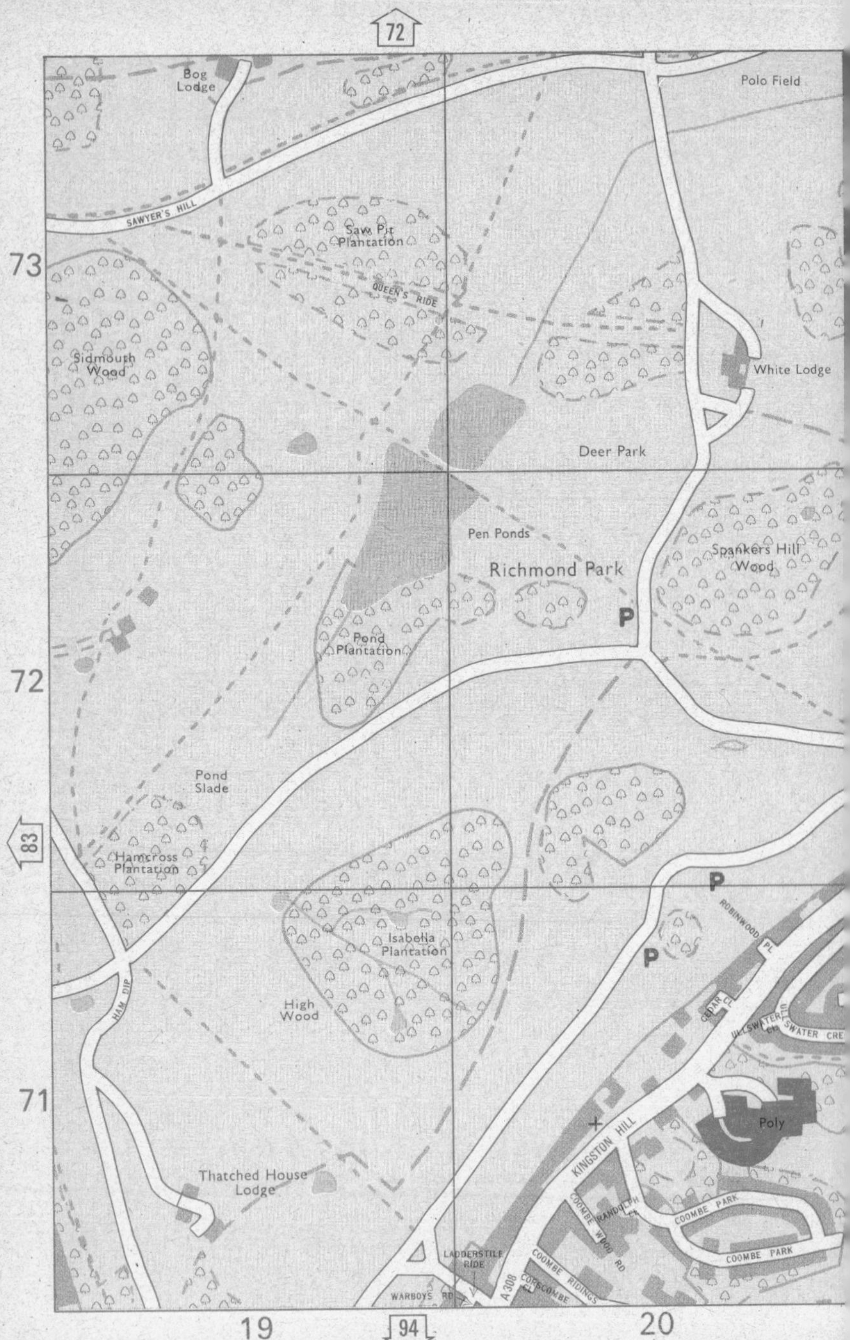

72
Bog Lodge
Polo Field
SAWYER'S HILL
Saw Pit Plantation
QUEEN'S RIDE
73
Sidmouth Wood
White Lodge
Deer Park
Pen Ponds
Spankers Hill Wood
Richmond Park
P
Pond Plantation
72
Pond Slade
83
Hamcross Plantation
P
ROBINWOOD PL
P
Isabella Plantation
HAM DIP
High Wood
CEDAR CL
ULLSWATER CL
ULLSWATER CRE
71
KINGSTON HILL
Poly
Thatched House Lodge
COOMBE WOOD RD
RANDOLPH CL
COOMBE PARK
COOMBE PARK
LADDERSTILE RIDE
COOMBE RIDINGS
A 308
CORSCOMBE CL
WARBOYS RD
19
94
20

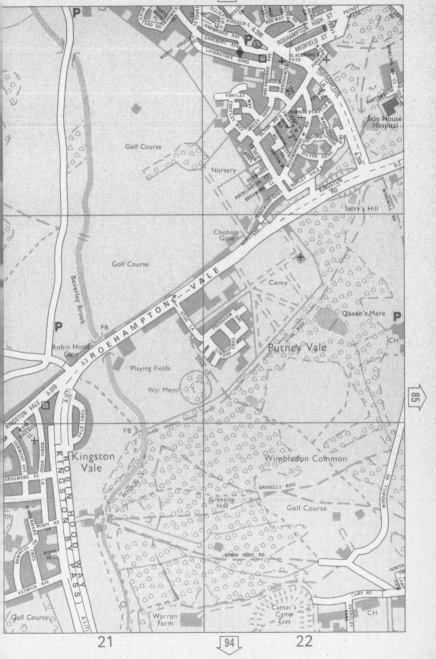

P

MOUNT ANGELUS RD

ELLISFIELD
KINGSCR C A 306
HARBRIDGE AVE
DANEBURY AVE
LAVERSTOKE GDNS

KEECH

ROD WAY

ROEHAMPTON HIGH ST

PUTNEY
HEATH

P
L

BLACKFORD
PATH

MEDFIELD ST

BOWLING GN CL

PORTSMUTH

Scio House
Hospital

FONTLEY
WAY

FONTLEY WAY

IBSLEY GDNS

HOLYBOURNE AVE

HERSHAM

ROEHAMPTON LA

FRIERN

ALTON RD

HORNOR PTR'S FLD DR

WANBOROUGH RD

OXFORD CORCH RD

BRITTWA

OXFORD RD

A 306

A 3

Golf Course

Nursery

REDWOODS

POCKLINGTON CL
BREAMORE CL

RINGWOOD GDNS

DILTON GDNS

NORLEY VALE

KINGSTON RD

WINDMILL RD

Jerry's Hill

Chohole
Gate

NORSTEAD PL

+

Golf Course

Beverley Brook

A3 ROEHAMPTON VALE

STAG LA

FRENSHAM DRI

STROUD CRES

STAG RIDE

Cemy

Queen's Mere

P
CH

Putney Vale

P
FB

Robin Hood
Gate

A 308

A 3011

VALE CRES

Playing Fields

STAG LA

War Meml

WINDROM RD

Kingston Vale

DERWENT AVE

ADELAIDE CL

ROBIN HD

+

GRASMERE AV

FB

Kingston
Vale

K I N G S T O N   V A L E

ROBIN HD
LA

BEVERL

Wimbledon Common

GRAVELLY RIDE

BOWNESS
CRES

WINDERMERE CR

RYDAL GLNS

Gravelly
Hill

Golf Course

WINDHAM RD

KESWICK AVE

A 3(T)

R O B I N   H O O D   W A Y   (K I N G S T O N   B Y   P A S S)

ROBIN HOOD RD

NORTH
VW

Golf Course

Warren
Farm

Caesar's
Camp Fort

CAMP RD

EYVISLEY

CH

85

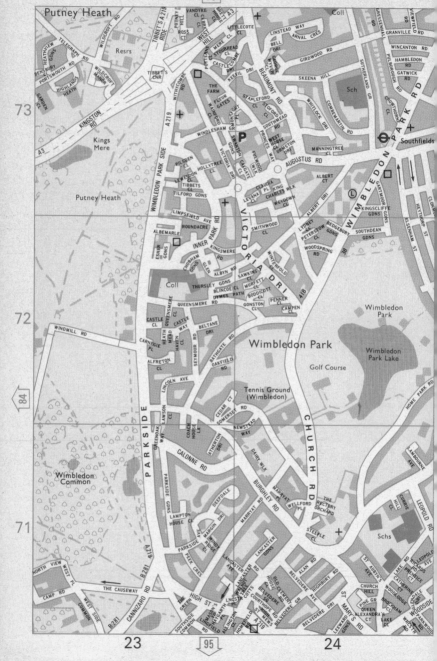

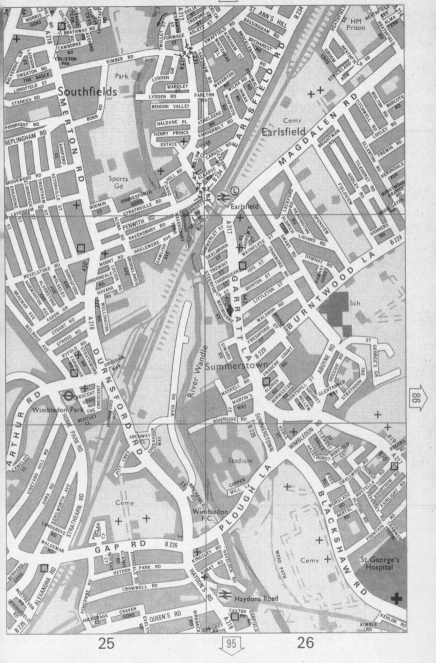

73

Southfields

Earlsfield

Cemy

Earlsfield

HM Prison

Sch

Summerstown

River Wandle

Wimbledon Park

Wimbledon F.C.

Stadium

Cemy

GAP RD

Haydons Road

Cemy

St George's Hospital

86

87

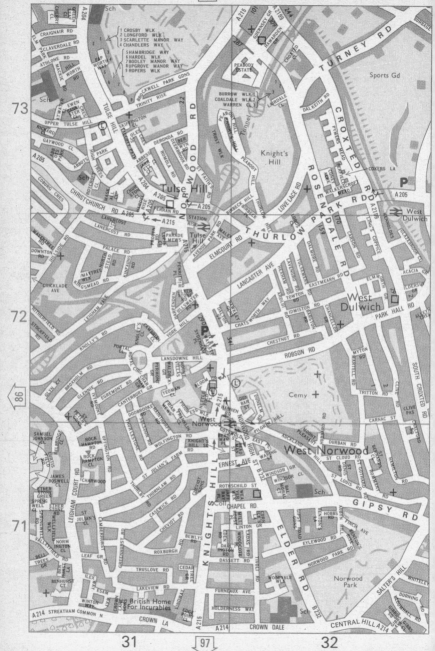

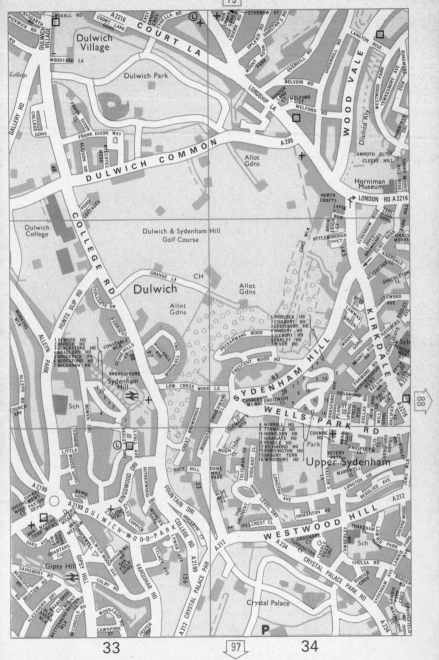

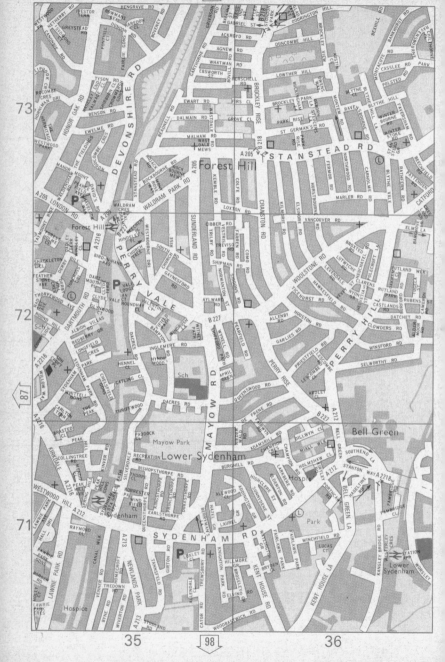

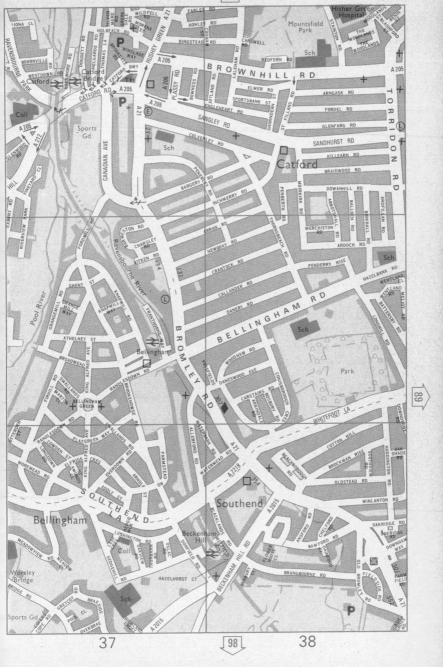

IONA CL
RAVENSBOURNE PARK
BOURNVILLE
WESTDOWN RD
ARDMORE RD
DOGGETT RD
DELGARDE RD
HOLBEACH RD
THOMAS LA
HILVER ST
BROOK
MORENA
WILDFELL RD
WINSLADE WAY
RUSHEY GREEN A21
FABLEY RD
HONLEY RD
CUDHAM
RINGSTEAD RD
LALEHAM RD
CARSWELL
REDFERN RD

Hither Green Hospital
WOODLANDS
BLACKFORD
BENN
THE WOODLANDS
Mountsfield Park
STANTON RD
Sch
A205

BROWNHILL RD

Catford Bridge
Catford
CATFORD RD
A205
A205
A21
P
E
25
A205
PLASSY RD
BOWNESS RD
ENGLEHEART RD
SANGLEY RD
RUTLAND RD
SPORTSBANK ST
ST FILLANS RD
SHORNDEAN ST
ELMER RD
ARNGASK RD
FORDEL RD
GLENFARG RD
SANDHURST RD
KILLEARN RD
BRAIDWOOD RD

TORRIDON RD
A205
L

Coll
A205
A212
EXBURY HILL
GLENFARG RD
VINEYARD CL
RIVERVIEW PARK
Sports Gd
CANADIAN AVE
Sch
CULVERLEY RD
FENWICK RD
BARGERY RD
INCHMERRY RD
PENERTH RD
MUIRKIRK RD
MERCHISTON RD
DOWANHILL RD
BALLOCH RD
ABBOTSHALL RD
ARDGOWAN RD
BIRKHALL RD
ARDFILLAN RD
ARDOCH RD
Sch

Catford

FORDMILL RD
WESTON RD
CHARLEY
AITKEN RD
RAVENSBOURNE RIVER
Ravensbourne River
ARRAN RD
NEWQUAY RD
CRANTOCK RD
CALLANDER RD
DANEBY RD
THORNSBEACH RD
PENDERRY RISE
HAZELBANK RD
WENTLAND RD
WESTLAND RD
MELIOT RD
BATTERSBY RD
LONGHILL RD

Pool River
GHENT ST
GRANGEHILL RD
GRINGE MILL WAY
KNAPMILL WAY
FRANTHORNE WAY
BROMLEY RD
BELLINGHAM RD
WOODHAM RD
DANESWOOD AVE
Sch
Park
WHITEFOOT LA
DOWNDERRY

ATHELNEY ST
BROADMEAD
FIRHILL RD
MARTON RD
SWALLANDS
KING ALFRED AVE
RANDLESDOWN RD
BROOKEHOWSE RD
BELLINGHAM GREEN

Bellingham

PASSFIELDS
307
CARSTAIRS RD
WISBURY RD
ARKINDALE
CONISBOROUGH CRES

OTTERFIELD
RANDLESDOWN RD
COWDEN RD
LONGDOWN
ELFRIDA CRES
KING ALFRED AVE
MOREMEAD RD
PLAYGREEN WAY
OVERDOWN RD
ARNULF ST
ADOLF ST
FARMSTEAD RD
WATERBANK RD
ALLERFORD RD
WATERMEAD RD
A21
A2218
BEECKBOROUGH RD
COTTON HILL
BROCKMAN RISE
OLDSTEAD RD
WINLANTON RD
SOUTHEY RD
HADDINGTON RD
OAK SHADE RD

SOUTHEND LA

Bellingham
MEADOWVIEW RD
MEADOW
Worsley Bridge
BRIDGE RD
Sports Gd
COPE RD
COPT RD
OVERBRAE
HIGHLAND
A2015
Sch
GREYCOT RD
BRAESIDE
SEDGEHILL RD
LUSHINGTON RD
DAVILLE
THORNBANK
HAZELHURST CT
Coll
DUNFIELD RD
BLACKLANDS RD
Beckenham Hill
BECKENHAM HILL RD
FLOWER HOUSE CL
BENBURY
BRANGBOURNE RD
ANGFORD RD
CHELFORD
BAMFORD RD
FIELDSIDE RD
OLD BROMLEY
A21
A2015
DOWNHAM WAY
OAKRIDGE RD
OAKRIDGE CL
NORMANFIELD
P

Southend

A205 BROWNHILL RD

TORRIDON RD
WELLMEADOW RD
SPRINGBANK RD
HITHER GREEN LA
MILNBROUGH CRES
MANOR LA
PARKCROFT RD
NEWSTEAD RD
STONE CL
BIRCH GR
WILDWOOD
ST MILDREDS RD
LONGHURST RD

PICCOLO
WESTHORNE AVE
A205
HORNCASTLE CL
HORNCASTLE RD
KINGSHURST RD
WOODYATES RD
SIMNEL RD
GAVESTONE RD
ALNWICK RD
HENDURST RD
PASTON CRES

A205 BROWNHILL RD

ARDGOWAN RD
SANDHURST RD
KINARD RD
BROADFIELD RD
WELLMEADOW RD
FURTHER GREEN RD
DOWANHILL RD
VERDANT LA

HELDER ST
RAYFORD AVE
LINCHMERE RD
WAITE DAVIES RD
SUMMERFIELD ST
RONVER RD

BARING RD
A2212

CORONA RD
ELWILL
WAY
DANESCOMBE

GAVESTONE CRES
Sch

WINN RD

Park

HARLAND RD
BURNT ASH HILL
GRIMAL RD
SENLAC RD
JEVINGTON WAY
ASHDALE RD

FARMCOTE RD
BRAMDEAN
GDNS
BRAMDEAN CRES
ASHWATER RD
HEATHER RD
EXFORD GDNS
EXFORD RD
WEST

73

PASTURE
OAK COTTAGE
SOUTH PARK CRES
SERGE
WAY
HAFTON RD

HAZELBANK RD

MORDRED RD
BALDWIN RD
PELINORE RD
PERSANT RD
CASTILLON RD
WINDROSE
CASTILLON RD
BOUNDFIELD RD
CRITCHLEY
EVANS RD
GILTON RD

Cemy

Crem

FB

HOSER AVE
PALACE VIEW
BARING
KINGSAND
PRAGNELL RD
PEGLEY GDNS
215
292
251

BARING RD

COOPERS LA
Grove Park Hospital

SANDSTONE RD
SUMMERTREES RD

72

SCARLET RD
HEKAL RD
BATTERY RD
Sch
WATERS RD

WHITEFOOT LA

WHITEFOOT TERR
BIDEFORD RD
CRANMORE RD
BILLERACOMBE RD
LINCOMBE RD
LENTMEAD RD
WOODNAN RD
UNDERSHAW RD
SHAW RD

NORTHOVER

REIGATE RD
JENNIFER RD
BALLAMORE RD
BEDIVERE RD
PENDRAGON RD
MAGNET RD
DISCOUNT
KANGLEY BRIDGE RD
MERLIN RD
THE GREEN

TA Centre
A2212
DILHORNE CL
Grove Park

LE MAY AVE
HOPE RD
GARDEN CL
LUFFMAN RD

B226 CHINBROOK

BROOK
GLEN
ALMBECOTE RD

88

Playing Field

WOODLAND WLK
SHAW PATH

589
648
Grove Park

Sch
Sch
Sch

SHROFFOLD RD
MOORSIDE RD
DURHAM HILL
LAMEROCK RD
CAPSTONE RD
CAMLAN RD

IVORY DOWN
GARETH GR
GERAINT RD

GALAHAD RD

Sch

WAVERY
MARY RD

DOWNHAM WAY

DUNOBERRY RD
Sch
WOODLAND WLK
WRENTHORPE RD
RAVENSCAR RD
WHINTON RD
BANKHOOT RD
CINDERFORD RD
OAKRIDGE RD

Downham Fields

LAUNCELOT RD
WELBECK AVE
CHATSWORTH AVE
THORNTON RD
WYDEVILLE CL
MARBROOK CL
BROADLANDS RD
RIDGEWAY
TREEWALL GDNS

71

65
52
Downham

GOUDHURST RD
ELMSCOTT RD
CHURCHDOWN
KEEDONWOOD RD
PORTLEBACK RD
RANGEFIELD RD
BOLDERWOOD RD

DOWNHAM WAY
SOUTHOVER
379
377
HILLCREST RD

Playing Field
POWSTER RD
POWSTER
COPSE
Resr
BRIARY GDNS

SANDPIT RD
BEECHMONT RD
KENDALE RD
FARMFIELD RD
CLAVELL RD
CLINTLE RD
ARCH RD
KELLERTON RD
KESSLEY
BOYLAND RD
SUNDRY
CRES
Sch
KYNASTON RD
SANDRINGHAM RD
RANGEFIELD RD
ROSLIN RD
OAK TREE GDNS

Park
Sch

P

BURNT ASH LA

RYDER CL
A2212

77

Eltham
Palace

CH

Playing
Fields

TIBTHORPE RD
HORSA RD

CHURCHBURY RD
CAMPFIELD RD
KINGSGROUND
ELM BROOK RD
EGG DOWN HILL
GREGORY CRES

NEWMARKET
GREEN

THE VISTA

WOODMERE
TARNWOOD
PARK

TARNWOOD

COURT RD

MOTTINGHAM LA
MOTTINGHAM LA

JOAN CRES

KING JOHN'S WALK
MIDDLE PARK AVE

KING JOHN'S WK

SIDCUP RD

FB

Mottingham

471

STATION

The Tarn

CARTERS
HILL CL

Mottingham
Farm

CEDAR MOUNT

MOTTINGHAM LA

COLEVIEW

Coll

KEPPINGTON RD
MOTTINGHAM RD
LAZELL

WEST HALLOWES

480

LUXFIELD

WEST PARK

PICKWICK
HINTON

CROSSMEAD

603
A 20
598

JEAN AVE
DEAN

Quaggy River

Playing Fields

B 226

DEVONSHIRE RD

B 226
A 208

L
L

PORCUPINE

HARTSMEAD

LETSDOWN RD
DOWNLEY'S

BOWMEAD

BURBETTS RD

CHAPEL FARM RD

ALTASH WAY

THE CROSSWAY

HALL VIEW

DORSET RD
PORTLAND RD
PORTLAND CRES

CLARENCE RD

LULWORTH RD
ELMHURST RD
COURT FARM RD

AVONDALE

MODEL
FARM CL

ALBERT RD

SHOTTERY CL

BEACONSFIELD RD

BELTON

BLENCHARD

SENNEN
WLK

MOTTINGHAM RD

NUNNINGTON

WIDECOMBE RD

THURSLEY RD

LAXDALE

UNDERWOOD
THE GLADE

WAY

WYNFORD
WAY

WOODCROFT

LITTLEMEDE

KINGSLEY
ORT

BROADRIDGE
WOOD

LONGCROFT

WOODHAM RD

SEEKHILL

A 208

Mottingham
Sports Grounds

P

Sports
Ground

GROVE PARK RD

MARVELS LA

MARBROOK
CT

B 226
CHURCHFIELD RD

ALDERSGROVE AVE
STOFIELD GDNS

AMBERLEY
LAMBSCROFT AVE

LIONS CL

GRACE

LONSDALE RD

HENRY
COOPER
WAY

WICKS

Playing
Field

DUNKERRY RD

HARTING RD

SMARDEN
GR

Sch

PRESTBURY
STONEHAM

90

ROBINS

LEAF
O'NEILL RD
ROSSLARE RD

RIDDONS RD

MAYESWOOD RD

CLAYHILL CRES

DRAGONFLY

CASTLETON RD
BILSBY RD

CHARMINSTER RD

CALDOTT
WLK

HASSOP
WLK
NERSEY
GDNS

KIMMERIDGE

DITTISHAM

RUDGET RD
BECONSFIELD RD
KINWOODGE
HORNING CL

SICKLETON RD

KETTERING

FRAMLINGHAM RD
RAVENSWORTH

STEYNING

CRESTON
FENTON

WINSIDE GR

STEYNING
SQ
STONEHAM

RD

WALDEN AVE

A 208

ELMSTEAD LA

MARVELS LA
COPLAND

LEAMINGTON
AVE

PORTLAND RD

LEAMINGTON AVE

NEW STREET HILL

CHILHAM RD

Marvells
Wood

CASTLECOMBE RD

Sch

CATTISTOCK RD

CRANMORE AVE

ELMSTEAD RD

BROADHEATH
FENTON CL

FOSTERS

DOWNS AVE
HALLAM CL

MELANDRA
CL

Coll

Elmstead Wood

Tunnels

Elmstead

41
99
42

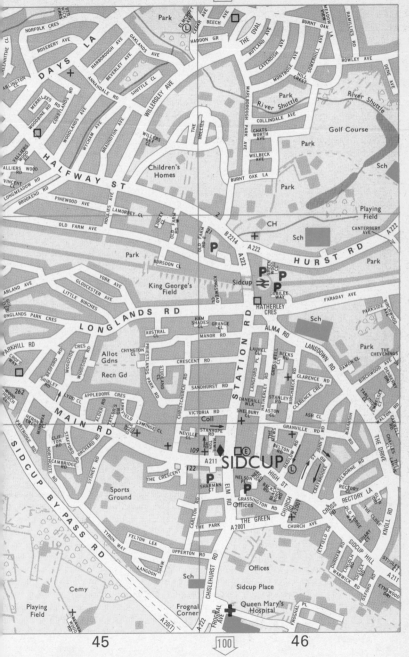

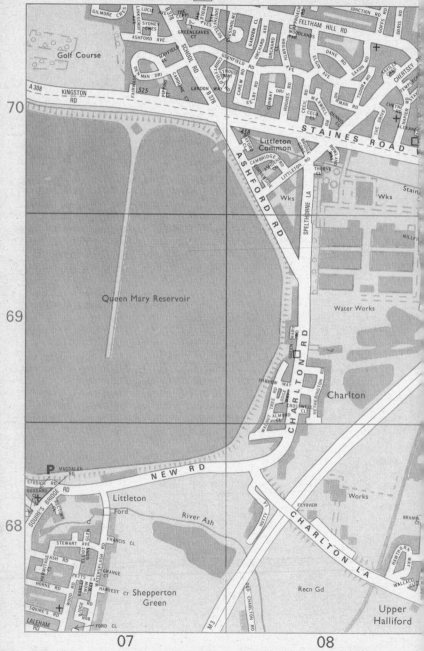

Golf Course

GILMORE CRES

LUCIE
SYDNEY
CRES
LINKSCROFT AVE
THE COPSE
REDLEES AVE
REDLEES
HIGHFIELDS
PRESSHOLME
FELTHAM HILL RD

ASHFORD AVE

GREENLEAVES CT

GARDEN CL
ORCHARD AVE
ORCHARD RD
WOODLANDS PAR

JUNCTION RD
GOFFS RD
DORIS RD

MAYFIELDS
SCHOOL RD

GLENFIELD RD
CAREW RD

STROUD
CRES

ELGIN AVE
DANE RD
SAXON RD

TUDOR RD

CHERTSEY

DENMAN DRI

FAIRWAYS

PIPPIN CT

CARBINE CT

A 308
KINGSTON RD

FAIRWAYS

525

CONWAY RD

SELBY
DRI

HUGHES RD

CECIL RD
CONWAY RD

MAXWELL RD
CECIL RD

DENNES CL

NORMAN RD

SAVILL
TEMPLECROFT

CHEYNE RD

NAPIER RD
ALEXANDRA

70

STAINES ROAD

THE DRIVE

458

Littleton Common

ACORN
CL

CAMBRIDGE RD
ASHFORDSIDE

ASHLEA RD
LITTLETON RD
LITTLETON RD

THORNE CL

Wks

Wks

Stains

A
S
H
F
O
R
D

R
D

S
P
E
L
T
H
O
R
N
E

L
A

MILLFI

Queen Mary Reservoir

Water Works

69

C
H
A
R
L
T
O
N

R
D

QUEEN MARY

Charlton

HARROW RD

WALNUT TREE RD

CROSSWELL CL

HETHERINGTON RD

ALMOND CL

P
Magdalen
RD

STUDIOS RD

GODDARD CL

SQUIRE'S BRIDGE RD

RECTORY

NEW RD

Littleton

Ford

River Ash

Works

FLYOVER

C
H
A
R
L
T
O
N

L
A

BRAMBL

HAWTHORN
AVN

WALLACE

STEWART AVE

ASH RD

ELLIOT GDNS

GREEN CL

GRANGE CT

FRANCIS CL

68

HERMITAGE CT

HORNE RD

WOOD RD

PETTS

BARLEY
MOW
WAY

BROKE RD

WATERSPLASH CT

BOB

HARVEST CT

Shepperton Green

NUTTY LA

M3

Recn Gd

OLD CHARLTON RD

Upper
Halliford

SQUIRE'S RD

LALEHAM RD

FORD CL

09   10

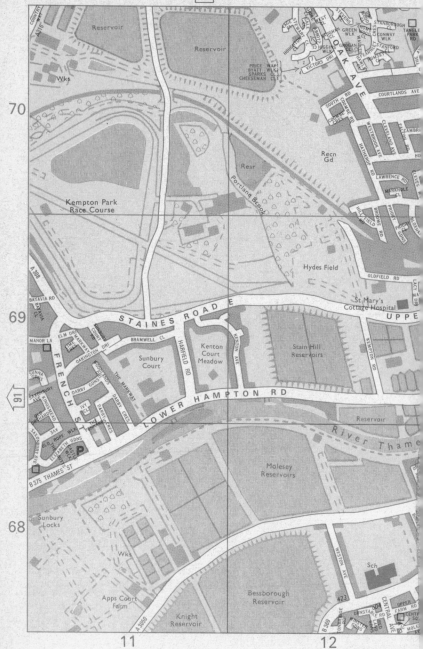

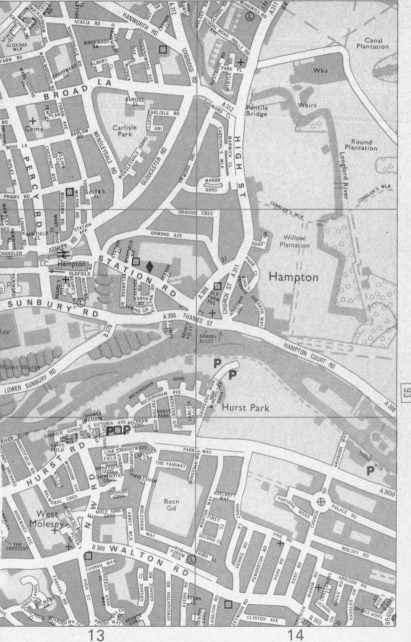

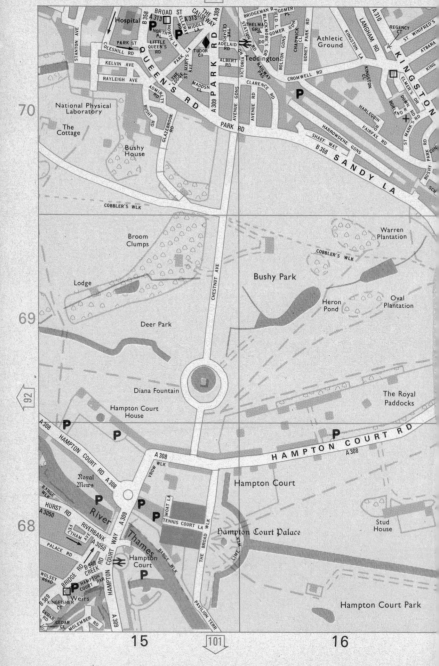

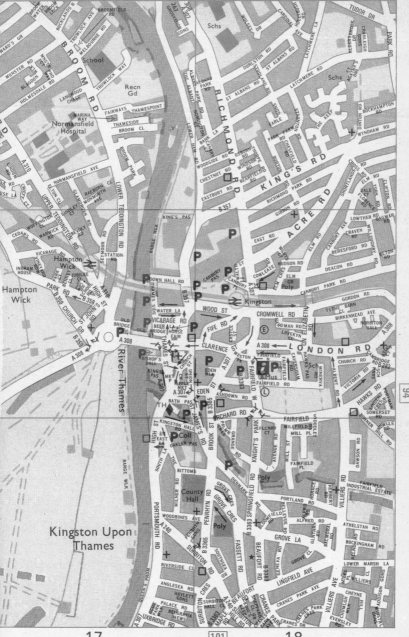

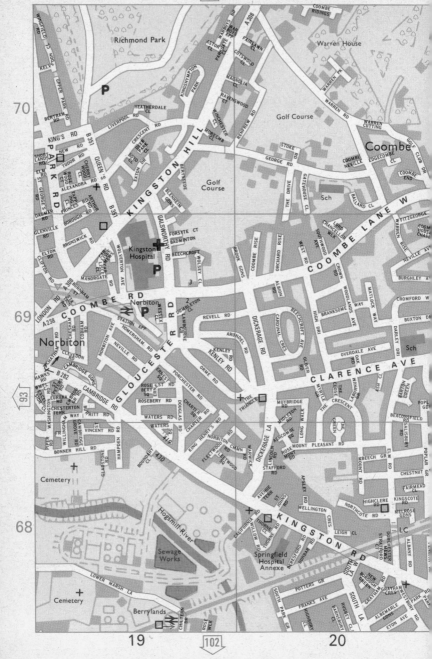

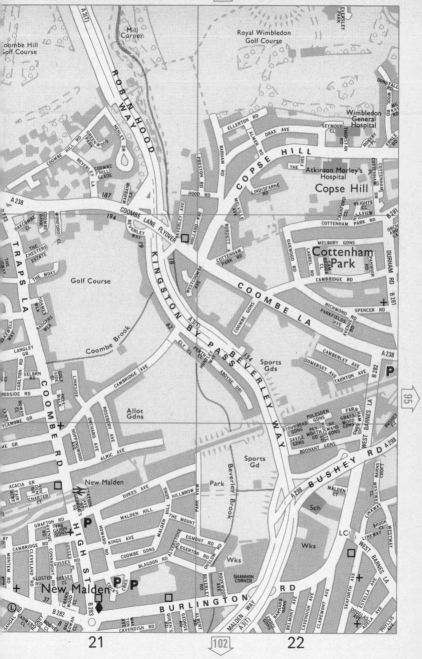

Coombe Hill
Golf Course

Mill Corner

Royal Wimbledon
Golf Course

EVERSLEY PARK

ROBIN HOOD WAY

A 3(T)

DUNSTALL RD

WOOL RD

MC RAY

Wimbledon
General
Hospital

SEYMOUR CL

THURSTAN

MORLEY PL

ERNLE RD

Coombe Hill
Golf Course

GREENWOOD
PARK

COOMBE HILL RD

HENLEY DR

BEVERLEY LA

COOMBE HILL GLADE

WARBAN

187

ELLERTON RD

DRAX AVE

BARHAM RD

ALMER RD

COPSE HILL

The FIRS
Atkinson Morley's
Hospital

Copse Hill

CRANFORD

HEIGHTS CL

LVIEW

DUNSTALL

B 281

COTTENHAM DR

COTTENHAM

A 238

OAKCOMBE CL

COOMBE BANK

WOOFORD CL

COOMBE LANE FLYOVER

194

BEVERLEY WAY

9

PRESTON RD

HOOD RD

BEVERLEY AVE

HOLLAND AVE

MELVILLE AVE

LINDISFARNE RD

COTTENHAM PARK RD

MELBURY GDNS

Cottenham
Park

PANHUR

DURHAM RD

ORCH LA

B 281

TRAPS LA

THE CHESTERS ESTATE

THE HWAY

THE MOAT

Golf Course

SOMME'S WALK

BAUGER'S WALK

194

18

WESTCOMBE AVE

COOMBE GDNS

COTTENHAM PARK RD

BURDETT RD

OAKWOOD RD

LAUREL RD

CAMBRIDGE RD

RICHMOND RD

PARKFIELD AVE

SPENCER RD

COOMBE LA

B 281

MAKEWELL

LANGLEY GR

SELBRN RD

CARLTON RD

WOODSIDE RD

SYCAMORE

COOMBE RD

GOLF SIDE

LINKSIDE

ORCHARD AVE

HOPPINGWOOD

ALRIC AVE

CAMBRIDGE AVE

ROSEBERY AVE

Allot
Gdns

Coombe Brook

KINGSTON BY PASS

62

A 3(T)

154

ELY CL

PERTH

HUNTLEY

ABOYNE DRI

BEVERLEY WAY

Sports
Gds

CAMBERLEY AVE

SOMERSET AVE

TAUNTON AVE

A 238

B 282

BUSHEY CL

POLESDEN GDNS

STOUFHEAD GDNS

SAVILL

WORTH

PENT

MANS

GD

BODNANT GDNS

FARA

GRAYS

HAM

WOOD

WEST BARNES LA

BUSHEY RD

A 238

P

LANGLEY GR

NEW MALDEN

STATION

ST GEORGE'S SQ

DUKES AVE

SANDY

HILLBROW

ANNFIELD

MALDEN WAY

Sports
Gd

Park

Beverley Brook

MALDEN CT

Sch

LINKWAY

BROOK

WEST BARNES LA

LINKWAY

WESTWAY

WESTWAY

ACACIA GR

FAIR ACRE

DEN GDN

CHARTER CL

GRAFTON RD

MONTEM RD

CLEVELAND RD

GLOSTER RD

CAMBRIDGE

CAION GDNS

THE

HIGH ST

HOWARD RD

MALDEN HILL

KINGS AVE

COOMBE GDNS

BLAGDON RD

ALVERSTONE

EGERTON RD

THE MOUNT

ROSTON

WARD

ROOKWOOD AVE

BEVERLEY RD

Wks

Wks

SHANNON CORNER

LC

Wks

SEAFORTH AVE

ESTELLA AVE

CLAREMONT AVE

CAVENDISH AVE

BELMONT AVE

DOUGLAS AVE

ADELA AVE

PHYLLIS AVE

WEST BARNES LA

WESTWAY

37

New Malden

SANDAL RD

CADMER

CRESCENT RD

RODNEY RD

B 282

B 283

CAVENDISH RD

QUEEN'S RD

GEORGE RD

ALBERT RD

BURLINGTON

RD

MALDEN WAY

A 3(T)

BARNARD GDNS

L

P

P

P

95

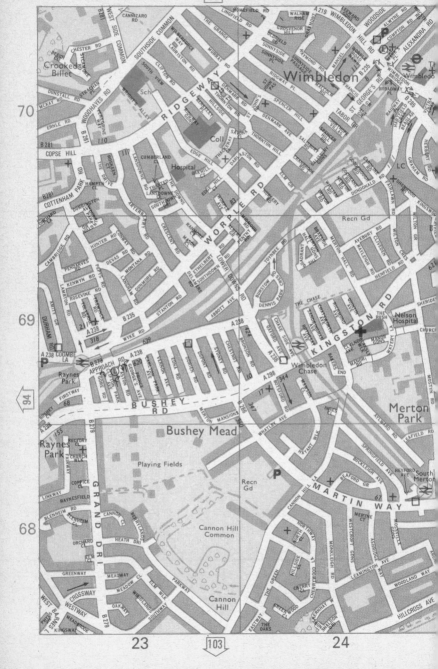

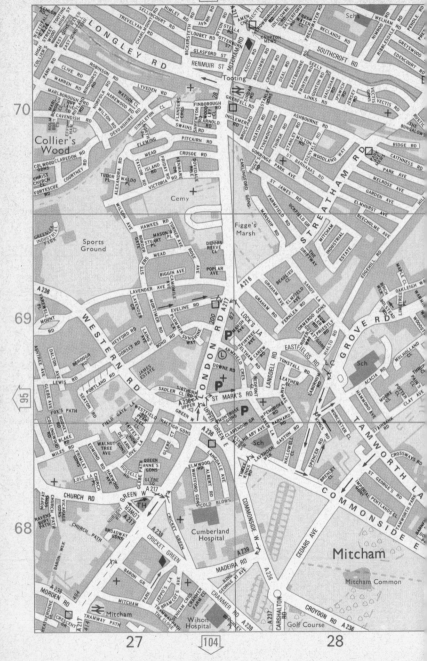

Streatham Common

Streatham Common S

WESTWELL ROAD APP

P

B 272

A 23

MITCHAM LA A216

EARDLEY RD

GREYHOUND LA

Streatham Common

STREATHAM HIGH RD

GREEN LA B 273

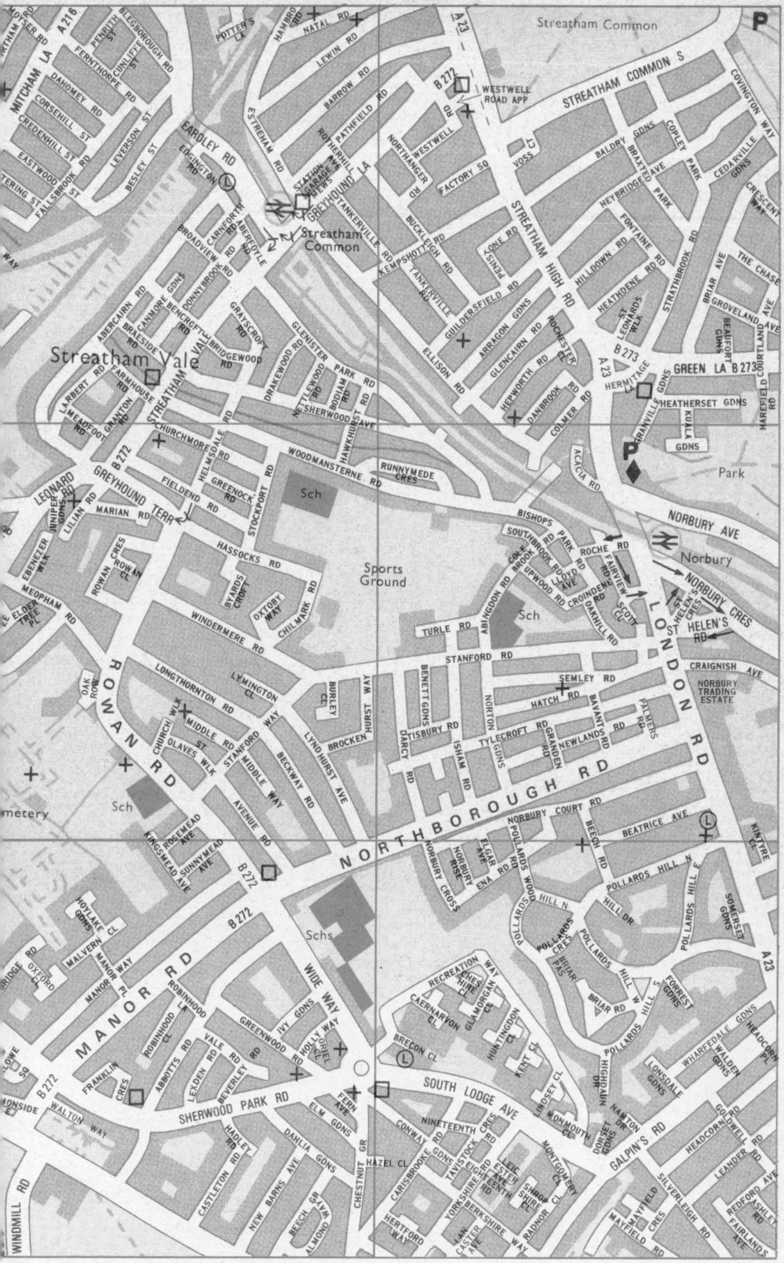

A 23

HERMITAGE

HEATHERSET GDNS

KILRAVOCK GDNS

Park

P

Streatham Vale

B 272

GREYHOUND TERR

LEONARD

WOODMANSTERNE RD

RUNNYMEDE CRES

Sch

NORBURY AVE

BISHOPS PARK RD

ROCHE RD

Norbury

NORBURY CRES

Sports Ground

Sch

ST HELEN'S RD

LONDON RD

CRAIGNISH AVE

NORBURY TRADING ESTATE

TURLE RD

STANFORD RD

SEMLEY RD

ROWAN RD

LONGTHORNTON RD

WINDERMERE RD

LYMINGTON RD

NORTHBOROUGH RD

TYLECROFT RD

NORBURY COURT RD

BEATRICE AVE

BEECH RD

Cemetery

Sch

B 272

MANOR RD

HOTLANE CL

MALVERN CL

B 272

WIDE WAY

Schs

POLLARDS HILL N

POLLARDS HILL E

POLLARDS HILL W

POLLARDS HILL S

RECREATION WAY

CAERNARVON RD

BREDON CL

SOUTH LODGE AVE

SHERWOOD PARK RD

GALPIN'S RD

A 23

WINDMILL RD

Upper Norwood

Norwood Cottage Hospital

JERVISTON GDNS
CROWN LA
CROWN DALE
A214
WOODEND
A205
A215
316
GRECIAN CRES
PRESTON RD
QUEEN MARY RD
MOORE RD
BRADLEY RD
CONVENT HILL
RYEFIELD RD
HERMITAGE RD
OXFORD RD
DOYER
NORBURY
CRYSTAL TERR
HANCOCK RD
TREDOWN RD
Coll
RYECROFT RD
ARNULL'S RD
BEAUMONT RD
PYTCHLEY CRES
HERMITAGE GDNS
CHEVENING
Recn Gd
AVENUE
LEAFIELD
HOLLMAN GDNS
WHITE LODGE
LITTLE HAVEN
WOODFIELD CL
FOUNDERS GDNS
EVERSLEY RD
BEULAH HILL

Norwood Grove

CRESCENT WAY
COVINGTON WAY
GIBSON'S WAY
CHRISTIAN FIELDS
NORBURY HILL
MARSTON RD
DOWNSVIEW RD
WOODLANDS
PRIORY CRES
MENLO GDNS
ELLERY RD
RYELANDS
A215
SPA HILL

70

THE CHASE AVE
GROVELAND AVE
LINKS GDNS
B273
GREEN LA
NORBURY CL
CROFT RD
BIGGINWOOD RD
ST OSWALD'S RD
ARKELL
COVINGTON WAY
WOODMAN
BIGGIN WAY
DOWNS VIEW GDNS
GLENHURST RISE
WADDINGTON WAY
WESTMORLAND
SHIRLEY
DALE PARK AVE
THE LAWNS

Park
Norbury
Sch
262
269

KEN SINGTON AVE
Sch
HAWTHORN AVE
VIRGINIA RD
FLORIDA RD
MARYLAND RD
BRICKFIELD RD
SPRINGFIELD RD
DOWNS RD
INGRAM RD
Allot Gdns
BEAUCHAMP RD

69

BUCKINGHAM
BUCKINGHAM GDNS
WESTMINSTER AVE
GEORGIA RD
CAROLINA RD
OSTERLEY GDNS
GREEN LANE
NORTHWOOD RD
CRANBROOK RD
HOWBERRY RD
UPTON RD
WEST BROOK
PENRITH RD
ROSEBERY RD
BURLINGTON RD
LAYARD RD

MANOR FARM
CRAIGNISH AVE
HIGHBURY AVE
COUNTY RD
PARCHMORE WAY
PARK LAWN
QUEENSBURY RD
BENSHAM MANOR RD
OSBORNE RD
OSGOOD RD
STEERE RD
MOFFAT RD
LIVINGSTONE RD
MERSHAM RD
LENHAM RD

96

NORBURY CRES
NORBURY AVE
DUNBAR AVE
DALMENY AVE
WINDSOR RD
CAMDEN WAY
SN09
FOUNTAIN RD
SAND-SAND FIELD
BEULAH CRES
BEULAH AVE
NORBURY RD
MYTHE RD
GRANGER

EDERLINE AVE
MELROSE AVE
ARDFERN AVE
KILMARTIN AVE
STRATHYRE AVE
MELFORT RD
SANDFIELD RD
WYCH ELM
SANDFIELD GDNS
PARCHMORE RD
BEULAH RD
HEATH RD
MAIN CHESTER
HAMILTON RD
KITCHENER RD
HUNTER RD
BULLER RD
MYTHE RD

STEPHEN'S CRES
WARWICK RD
BRAEMAR AVE
BRIDPORT RD
FB
ATLANTA CT
ST PAUL'S RD
NORFOLK RD
LUNA RD
FOUNTAIN
HOBART RD
NATAL RD

68

A23
HEADFORT RD
GOSTON GDNS
OAKLANDS AVE
WINTERBOURNE RD
TOTTON RD
WILSTONE
STRATFORD RD
RICHMOND RD
BEECHWOOD AVE
LINDEN AVE
FERNHAM RD
BELLEVUE PARK
NORWICH RD
BULGANAK RD
WOODVILLE RD
GRANGE PARK RD
OBAN RD
DUN
HIGH ST
B266
A212

LONDON RD
LENDER RD
REDFORD AVE
GROTTO RD
COLDWELL
HEATHVIEW RD
LANGDALE RD
FOXLEY RD
QUADRANT RD
BROOK RD
ATLANTA
COVENT
STUART
EARNE
CROWLAND
ELM RD
PRIDHAM RD

ASHLEY RD
A23
MALVERN RD
WOODLAND RD
MAPLETHORPE RD
WARLINGHAM RD
NUTFIELD RD
ELLIOTT RD
BRIGSTOCK RD
SENECA RD
BENSHAM
LUCERNE RD
JARVATT
MANOR RD
GILLETT RD
NURSERY RD
ZION
WHITEHORSE RD
Schs

Thornton Heath
P
B273
Coll
P
B266

L

DOVER COURT
WEBBRIDGE RD
COLLIERS WATER LA
B266
GENEVA RD
BOSWELL
BOURNE RD
ZION RD

31
32

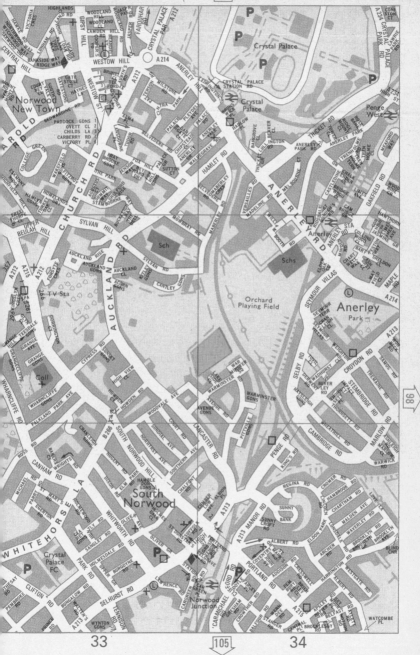

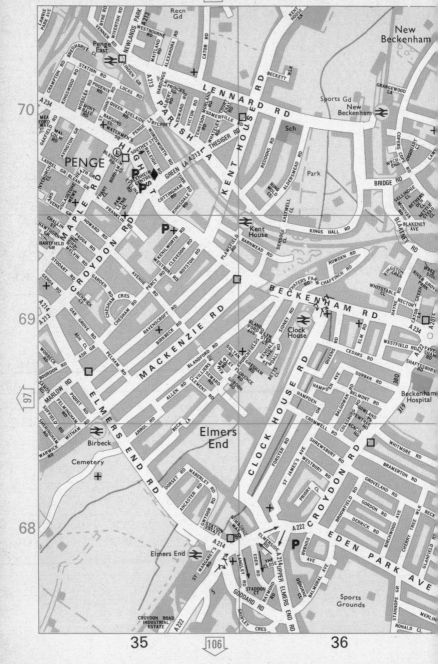

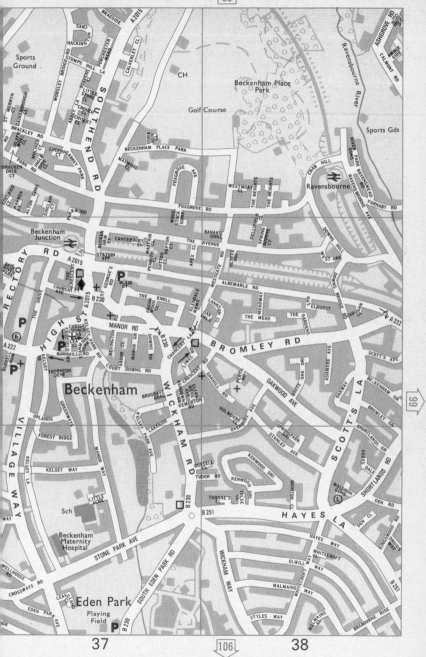

Sports Ground

BRAESIDE

A 2015

HACKING

ASHGROVE RD CONN

AMBLE SIDE

CALMONT RD

CH

Beckenham Place Park

Ravensbourne River

Golf Course

Sports Gds

WORSLEY RD
BRIDGE AV
STUMPS HILL LA
PORCHESTER MEAD
CALVERLEY CL
SOUTHEND RD

ST MERRYN
MAINSBROUGH RD
BRACKLEY RD
MOLINER CL
SINGLE CT
LITTLE STONE
CROUCH CL
CHISLEHURST RD
ABBEY LA
STEVENS RD

BECKENHAM PLACE PARK

FOXGROVE AVE

WESTMOAT CL

THE HEIGHTS
THE HEIGHTS

CRAB HILL

Ravensbourne

RIVER PARK GDNS
RAVENSMEAD
RAVENSBOURNE AVE
FARNABY RD

ADELAIDE RD
SABREN
ALTON GDNS
SINCLAIR CT
LICENSE ABBEY CT
LUCELINE CT
BRACKEN DALE CT
PARK LA
WOOD

MAXWOOD

FOXGROVE RD

FOXGROVE GDNS

WOOD STOCK GDNS

BANAVIE GDNS

DELLIFIELD
SPRING BOURNE

DOWNS HILL

WEST OAK

Beckenham Junction

RECTORY RD

BECKENHAM LA
CANTERBURY CL
STATION APP

PENRITH
SUTCLIFFE
REPTON
APEX CL
THE AVENUE
WESTGATE RD
OLD TYE
OLYTTE GDN

ALBEMARLE RD

ELHURST
BRIDGE RD
LOGAN

A 222

A 2015
THE CRESCENT
CHURCH AVE
ST GEORGE'S RD
BLAIR CL
A 2015
B 230
THE DRIVE
HIGH ST

MAYFAIR

GLENDALE MEWS
LANSDN DALE CL

THE MEADWAY

THE MEAD

THE GARDENS

CHRIST CHURCH RD
MANOR RD
BEVINGTON RD
ABBOT CL
MANOR GR
DOWNS RD
KNOLL
WOOD
CHANCERY LA
LIMES
OAK
B 230

BROMLEY RD

ASHMERE AVE
SCOTT'S AVE
OAKWAY
SCOTT'S LA

P
A 222
BURRELL ROW
BURNHILL RD
KELSEY
THORNTON DENE

COURT DOWNS RD

BROGRAVE GDNS

CRESCENT
ALBERS
AVENUE
KEMERTON
OAKHILL
PERTH RD

OAKWOOD AVE

WHITE OAK DRI

BE-KENHAM
BROMLEY GR
FOXES DALE

Beckenham

WICKHAM RD

HOLMDENE AVE
OVERBURY AVE

SPRINGPARK DRI
STANLEY AVE

SHORTLANDS GR

UPLANDS
GREENWAYS
FOREST RIDGE

KELSEY PARK AVE
LAKESIDE

QUINTON CL

WALDRON GDNS

SHORTLANDS RD

VILLAGE WAY
KELSEY LA
MANOR WAY
KELSEY WAY

RUSSELL
TUDOR RD
KENWOOD DRI
KENWOOD DRI

DEN RD

L

LITTLE ACRE
Sch

B 230

THORNE'S CL
TULSE GR

HAYES LA

DEN CL

KINGSWOOD RD
B 251

WAY
WELLHOUSE RD
CROSSWAYS RD

Beckenham Maternity Hospital

STONE PARK AVE

SOUTH EDEN PARK RD

B 251

WICKHAM WAY

HAYES WAY

WHITECROFT
ELWILL WAY

WHITECROFT WAY

BRABOURNE RISE

EDEN PARK AVE
LEAVE LAND
GR

Eden Park

Playing Field

P
B 230

MALMAINS RD
MALMAINS WAY

STYLES WAY

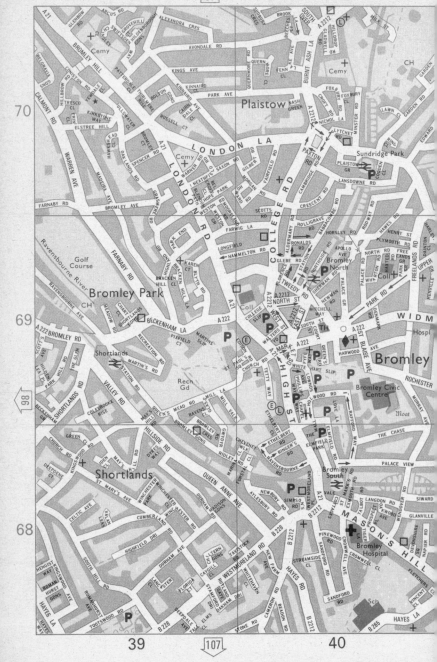

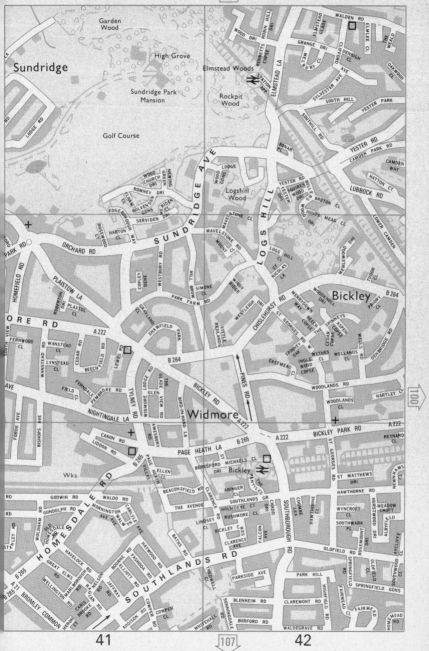

89

Garden Wood

High Grove

Elmstead Woods

WOOD DRI

ROBIN HILL

BENNETTS COPSE

ELMSTEAD LA

ELMSTEAD GLADE

WALDEN RD

ELMLEE CL

THE WELLS

Sundridge

Sundridge Park Mansion

Rockpit Wood

STATION APP

GRANGE DRI

MERBURY

CLIFFORD

DENBIGH CL

OAKWOOD

SILVESTER AVE

SOUTH HILL

YESTER PARK

Golf Course

LODGE RD

SOUTHILL RD

SOUTHILL

YESTER RD

YESTER RD

CAMDEN PARK RD

CAMDEN WAY

BONAR PL

HATTON CT

LUBBOCK RD

WOOD CHURCH DRI

NEWING

ROMNEY DRI

GREEN

EDGE

BURROUGH WAY

GDNS

MEIDEN DRI

SERVIDEN DRI

LINAN

ROLVENDEN

LODGE

WOOD RISE

Logshill Wood

YESTER RD

SQUIRES YESTER

WOOD DRI

MILLER

BIRTON CL

HUNTS MEAD CL

MERLEWOOD DRI

LOWER CAMDEN

ROSEWOOD

HARTON CL

ORCHARD RD

MAVELSTONE RD

LOGS HILL

MAVELSTONE RD

ST NICOLAS LA

LOGS HILL

TUDOR CL

PARK HILL

HOMEFIELD RD

FORD

PLAISTOW LA

ROBERTON

PLAXTOL CL

COPLEY DENE

WESTBURY RD

GRAYLAND CL

PARK FARM

BROW HILL

SIMONE

MOUNT

WINDY RIDGE

LITTLE REDLANDS

WESTLEIGH DRI

CHISLEHURST RD

ST GEORGES

MERRIDOWN WAY

BEECH COPSE

WOODKNOLL DRI

Bickley

B 264

PRIORY CL

ORE RD

SOUTH VIEW

FERNWOOD CL

A 222

WANSTEAD CL

CEDAR AVE

BEECH

LEWES RD

SHAWFIELD PARK

THE SPINNEYS

ASHEN

CEDAR

SPINNEY OAK

WELLS RD

DENBRIDGE RD

LYNSTEAD CL

WANSTEAD

FERNDALE

PEMBROKE RD

GDNS

B 264

WIDMORE LODGE RD

GLADE VIEW RD

THE

GLEN

BICKLEY RD

PINES RD

MERRIDOWN

SPINNEY OAK

INGLE WOOD COPSE

EASTMEAD

WYTHES CL

WELLANDS CL

WOODLANDS RD

FIELD

FORDE AVE

AVE

BISHOPS AVE

NIGHTINGALE LA

TYLNEY RD

BIRD-IN-HAND LA

AMESBURY RD

Widmore A.222

WOODLANDS CL

HARTLEY CL

100

CANON RD

LIDDON RD

B 285

PAGE VILLAS

PAGE HEATH LA

BERESFORD DRI

MICHAELS CL

B 285

A 222

BICKLEY PARK RD

ST GEORGES RD

A 222

REYNARD CL

NEWNHAMS CL

Wks

ELLEN CL

PAGE HEATH

BEACONSFIELD RD

THE AVENUE

ABINGER CT

CLARENCE RD

Bickley

ST PAULS

CRAY

SOUTHLANDS GR

HOLMDENE CT

RUSHMORE CL

CHADO

SOUTHBOROUGH RD

COOMBE

HAWTHORNE RD

ST MATTHEWS DRI

HAWTHORNE RD

WYNCROFT CL

SOUTHWARK PL

MEADOW CROFT

ALBYE

GOODWOOD

HIRSTWOOD DRI

GODWIN RD

WOLDHAM

GUNDULPH RD

MORNINGTON AVE

WALDO RD

CARLISLE AVE

HAYWOOD RD

LINDSEY CL

BICKLEY CRES

CLARENCE AVE

FALCON

ROSEMOUNT DRI

AYCLIFFE

OLDFIELD

SPRINGFIELD RD

OLDFIELD DRI

SOUTHWOOD RD

FAIRMEAD

SPRINGFIELD GDNS

OLD HOMESDALE RD

HOMESDALE RD

HAVELOCK RD

GREAT ELMS RD

MARLBOROUGH RD

ELLIOTT RD

BOURNE RD

FASHODA RD

BATHS RD

SOUTHLANDS RD

TREWELL CL

PARKSIDE AVE

PARK HILL

CLAREMONT RD

HIGHFIELD

FAIRMEAD

HOME MEAD RD

WELLINGTON RD

MENON CT

CARLILE

RAGLAN RD

BROOKE

JASTRAY RD

COWPER CL

WHITEHALL RD

BLENHEIM RD

SUNNINGDALE

BURFORD RD

WALDEGRAVE RD

B 285

B 285 2)

BROMLEY COMMON

A 222

ADDISON RD

COWPER RD

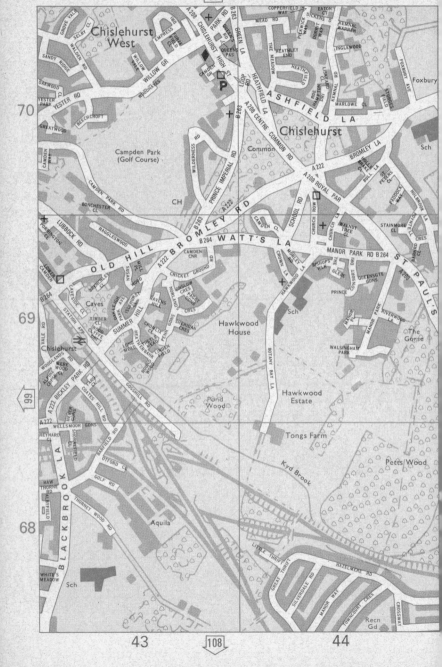

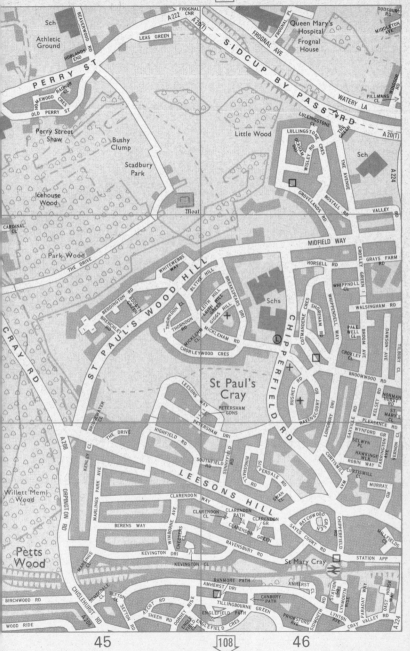

Sch
Athletic
Ground
BEAVERWOOD RD
HOBLANDS END
A 222 FROGNAL CNR
LEAS GREEN
A 20(T)
FROGNAL PL
Queen Mary's
Hospital
Frognal
House
DUDSBURY RD
MIDDLETON AVE

PERRY ST
HOMEWOOD
RADNOR RD CRES
OLD PERRY ST
SIDCUP BY PASS A 20 (T)
FROGNAL AVE
WATERY LA
A 20(T)
PILLMANS CL
BROMPTON RD

Perry Street
Shaw
Bushy
Clump
Scadbury
Park
Little Wood
LULLINGSTONE CL
LULLINGSTONE DRI
WESLEY RD CRES
OCKHAM
THE GLADE
Sch
A 224

Icehouse
Wood
Moat
GROVELANDS RD
BOSTALL RD
THE AVENUE
VALLEY RD

CARDINAL CL
Park Wood
THE DRIVE
MIDFIELD WAY
HORSELL RD
CROXLEY GREEN
GRAYS FARM RD
WALSINGHAM RD

CRAY RD
BEDDINGTON RD
BIRCHLEY RD
ST PAUL'S WOOD HILL
WHITEWEBBS WAY
BLYTH HILL
LEITH HILL
LEITH HILL GREEN
GIGGS HILL
THORNDON RD
THORNDON
WICKLEPH
MICKLEHAM RD
CHORLEYWOOD CRES
BREAKSPEARS DRI
Schs
L
SHOREHAM RD
COTMANDENE CRES
WHIPPENDELL CL
WHIPPENDELL WAY
PALE WELL CL
BROOM AVE
DAWSON AVE
CROXLEY CL
TILBURY CL
BROOMWOOD RD

St Paul's
Cray
LEESONS WAY
PETERSHAM GDNS
PETERSHAM DRI
CHIPPERFIELD RD
RUSHETT RD
BATENS COURT RD
LONGBURY DRI
SAXVILLE RD
NORMAN RD
ST MARY'S CL
PLEASANCE RD

BRIDGEWATER CL
THE DRIVE
KENLEY CL
HIGHFIELD RD
SOUTHFIELD RD
SUNNYFIELD RD
TYNEHAM RD
RINGSHALL RD
RIVERDALE RD
SWAN CL
SELWYN PL
WYNFORD GR
CURTISMILL WAY
FARRINGTON CL
HAWKINGE WLK
ROBIN WAY
CURTISMILL WAY
VERNON CL
MURRAY RD

A 208
ORPINGTON RD
MARLINGS PARK AVE
LEESONS HILL
CLARENDON WAY
CLARENDON CL
CLARENDON PATH
CLARENDON GR
CLARENDON GREEN
SAYES COURT RD
BATCHWOOD GR
CHIPPERFIELD
MILLFIELDS

Willett Mem
Wood
Petts
Wood
BERENS WAY
WIMBORNE AVE
THEYDONS
KEVINGTON DRI
KEVINGTON CL
RAVENSBURY RD
St Mary Cray
STATION APP

MARLINGS
ROSEDALE CL
CHISLEHURST RD
BIRCHWOOD RD
WOOD RIDE
A 208
ASCOT RD
DORNALY RISE
SEFTON RD
SHEEN RD
RANMORE PATH
AMHERST DRI
TILLINGBOURNE GREEN
ENGLEFIELD PATH
ENGLEFIELD CRES
CANBURY PATH
AMHERST
PROSSFORD AVE
LYNTON AVE
STATION RD
SIDMOUTH RD
MORNINGTON
OAST HOUSE
CRAY VALLEY RD
FARADAY AVE
A 224

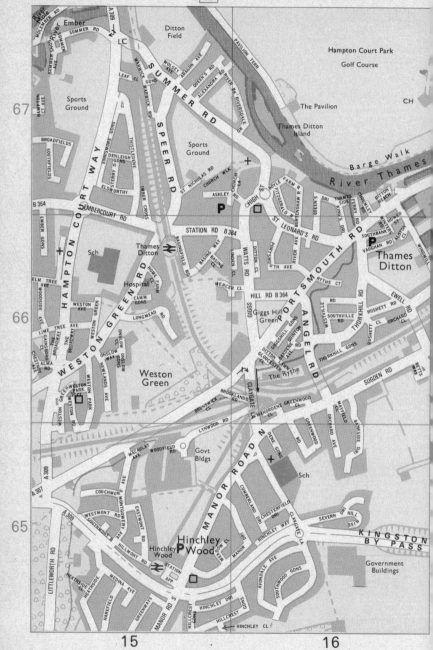

67

River Mole
River Ember
MOLEMBER RD
SUMMER RD
Ember
LC
A 309
SUMMER SHORE
Ditton Field
WOLSEY AVE
ARAGON AVE
QUEEN'S RD
ALEXANDRA RD
PAVILION TERR
RIVER BK
RIVERSDALE
Hampton Court Park
Golf Course

HAMPTON CT AVE
Sports Ground
LEAF CL
WARWICK GDNS
WARWICK RD

SUMMER RD
SPEER RD

The Pavilion
Thames Ditton Island
CH

River Thames
Barge Walk

BROADFIELDS
SOUTHFIELDS
B 364
EMBERCOURT RD
ENDSMORE GDNS
DENLEIGH GDNS
STERRY D
THISTLEDENE
ELSWORTHY
IMBER CROSS

HAMPTON COURT WAY
WESTON GREEN RD

St NICHOLAS RD
CHURCH WLK
CHURCH
ASHLEY RD
P
CHIGH ST
STATION RD B 364
BASINGFIELD RD
HOME FARM
BASING WAY
BASING CL
LINDEN CL
WATTS RD
DITTON CL
9TH AVE

BOTTLE FARM R
FITZGERALD RD
ST LEONARD'S RD
BURTENSHAW R
QUEEN'S DRI
KING'S DRI
CHUMLEY
THAMES SIDE
FERRY RD
DITTON REACH
SOUTHBANK

Thames Ditton

P
VAUGHAN RD
HOWRD
ALFTON CL

66

ELM TREE AVE
WOODSIDE
LIME TREE AVE
THE BROADWAY
GAINSBOROUGH CL
CHESTNUT AVE
ALMA RD

WESTON AVE
WESTON GREEN
CAMM GDNS
LONGMEAD RD
ONSLOW WAY
ONSLOW GDNS
NEWLANDS AVE
WESTON GREEN RD
WESTON PARK
WESTON HOLM
P

Sch
Thames Ditton
Hospital

MERCER RD

Weston Green

HILL RD B 364
Giggs Hill Green
GIGGSHILL GDNS
BAYDEN QUINTON
DITTON LAWN
GLOUCESTER CL
The Rythe

RYTHE CT
SOUTHVILLE RD
THORKHILL RD
THORKHILL GDNS

PORTSMOUTH RD
ANGEL RD
RUSHETT
RD
RUSHETT CL
ORCHARD
EWELL
BETTS WAY
SUGDEN RD

BROOKLANDS RD
BRUNSWICK CL
CLAYGATE LA
MANORDENE
GREENWOOD CL
GREENWOOD CL
MAYFIELD
ORCHARD AVE
BANKSIDE DRI

LYNWOOD CL
MACAULAY AVE
WOODFIELD RD
Govt Bldgs

DENE GDNS

MANOR ROAD

65

A 309
A 307

LITTLEWORTH RD
HEATHSIDE CL
MEDINA AVE
HAREFIELD
GREENWAYS
WESTMONT RD
SOUTHMONT RD
MONTGOMERY AVE
EASTMONT RD
HILLMONT RD

Hinchley Wood
P
Hinchley Wood
STATION APP
WILLOW CL

CUMBERLAND DRI
CHESTERFIELD
DRI
CLAYGATE LA
Sch
X
Hinchley Way
MANOR RD

AVONDALE AVE
SOUTHWOOD GDNS
SNIPE
HINCHLEY DRI
HINCHLEY DRI
HILLCREST
HILLCREST GDNS
HINCHLEY CL

SEVERN DRI
HILL RISE
KINGSTON BY PASS
Government Buildings

MANOR RD S

15   16

Seething Wells

Water Works

Long Ditton

Surbiton

Claremont Hospital

Surbiton General Hospital

Royal Eye Hospl

Southborough

Manor House

Coll

DITTON RD

HOOK RD

FULLERS WAY S

A 3(T)

FLYOVER

HOOK UNDERPASS

HOOK RISE N

HOOK RISE S

ELMCROFT DRI

WOODSTOCK LA S

A 309

KING CHARLES RD

EWELL RD

SURBITON HILL PARK

94

103

95

West
Barnes

Sch

B 279

GRAND DRI

EDINBURGH CT

QUEEN MARY AV

CANNON HILL LA

GLENTHORPE RD

CAMBORNE RD

ELM
EASTWAY

THE
OAKS

THIRLESTONE WAY

TEMPLECOMBE WAY

SHALDON DRI

HILLCROSS AVE

A 239

Playing Fields

P

Col

67

Sports
Gd

CHURTON DRI

Morden
Park

PARK

Cemetery

BUTT
CT
WENT
CL

COLSTON RD

GROVE RD

CRANMERE

A 239

LOWER MORDEN LA

L

P

WYDELL
CL.

EARLINGFORD RD

ROSEBERY

B 279

CRANMER

CARDINAL AVE

CARDINAL RD

TUDOR DRI

WOLSEY
CRES

EPSOM RD

ELM

LITCHFIELD

ROAD W.

RUSTINGTON

HARP

Cemy

Essex
CL.

GARTH CL.

Schs

P

ARAGON RD

SEYMOUR
RISE

CLEVELAND
AVE

DUDLEY DRI

NOVA MEWS

HILL TOP

WOODSTOCK

THE CLOSE

MIDWAY

THE CHATRIN

GILLIAN PARK RD

SELWOOD RD

WOODSTOCK RD

66

GARTH RD

LYNMOUTH AVE

KINGSBRIDGE RD

SALCOMBE DRI

DUNSTER AVE

HILL TOP

TA
Centre

HASLAM
AVE

ASH

POPLAR

TONFIELD

B 279

A 24 STONECOT HILL

WELLESLEY

BURLEIGH RD

STONECOT

BEECHES RD

FIR RD

RIDGE RD

102

BUCKLAND WAY

DELORAINE

MERRILANDS RD

DORCHESTER RD

CAMBERLEY

ROSCOMBE RD

BISLEY CL

CONRAD DRI

CHARMINSTER RD

 RISE

INVERNESS

SOUTHWOOD

WIMBORNE

STANTON

TRAFALGAR AVE

CATERS CROYDON

WAY

L

St Anthony's
Hospital

WARNER

WEST
BOURNE

Cheam
Hospital

BROWNING

RUSKIN DRI

EBBISHAM RD

BEVERLEY RD

MORNINGSIDE RD

COLBORNE
WAY

GRANDISON RD

ANDREWS
CL.

GARETH
CL.

LANGLEY AVE

PERKING AVE

CLARKES AVE

HILL CRES

BEDFORD RD

EDWARDS
CL.

GLYN RD

BURNTWM
CL.

LONDON RD

MARLOW DRI

BEECHCROFT RD

SHAM AVE

STANLEY

PRETORIA

STANES

CHEAM AVE

EGHAM
CRES

HAMILTON AVE

WATSON

SANDFORD RD

GANDER GREEN

WEATHERTYNE

KIMPTON RD

Sewage
Works

65

B 283

WOODBINE

CHEAM COMMON RD

KINGSMEAD AVE

TRENT WAY

ELM WAY

FARM

LAVENDER AVE

PACKMAN

WELLINGTON

A 24

B 283

SCHOOLS

CHURCH HILL RD

COURTENAY RD

LLOYD RD

North
Cheam

P

HILSERT RD

WRAYFIELD

FROGMORE
CL.

ESHER AVE

THE
MEADS

SURBURY RD

HENLEY AVE

MOLESEY DRI

BROCKS

CHERTSEY DRI

ST MARGARET'S AVE

KINGSTON RD

KEW CRES

WALTON RD

WINDSOR AVE

A 217

KIMPTON RD

WILLOW

WHITTAKER RD

DUNSTAN'S

ABBOTTS

Cemy

23

110

24

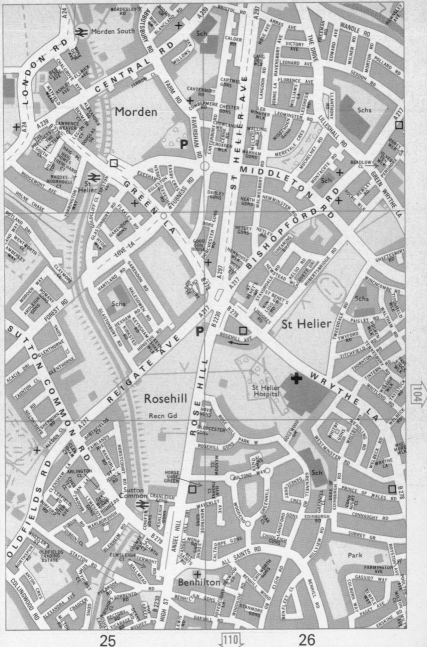

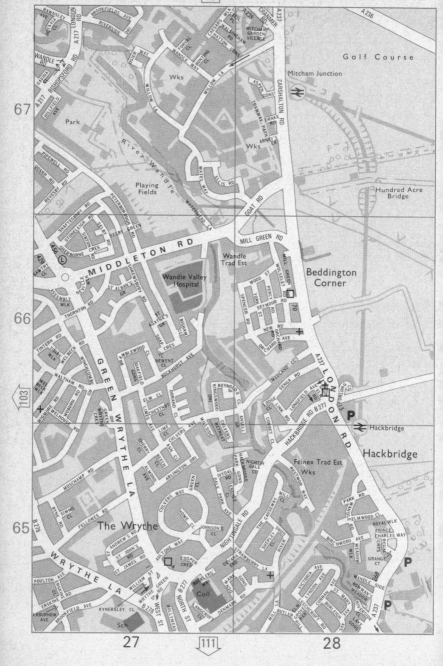

67

66

103

65

A 236

Golf Course

RAMNSLEY AVE
OCTAVIA CL
BROOKFIELDS AVE
RIVERSIDE DRI
A 217 LONDON RD
A 258
CRANMER RD
A 237
MITCHAM GARDEN VILLAGE
CALSANG WLK
CROCIL PL
WALSINGHAM
HATTON GDNS
LOVEL WAY
FOSTER WAY
WANDLE WAY
BUNTING CL
WILLOW LA
WILLOW LA
ASPEN GDNS
TRAMWAY PATH
DRAKE RD
ARNEY LA
Wks

WANDLE RD
A 217
BISHOPSFORD RD
GRAVEL
HILLSFIELD AVE
Park

River Wandle

Mitcham Junction

CARSHALTON RD
GOAT RD
Wks

PIPEWELL RD
QUARR RD
REVESBY RD
PETERBOROUGH RD
Playing Fields
WATES WAY
WATERMEAD LA
ELLIS RD

Hundred Acre Bridge

SHAFTESBURY RD
STONELEIGH RD
SELBY RD
SIRTON CRES
SELBY RD
GREEN
A 296
A 297
SHERBORNE RD
SAWTRY CL
L
NEVILLE
MIDDLETON RD
MILL GREEN RD
Wandle Trad Est
Wandle Valley Hospital
WOOD ST
WOLSELEY RD
MILL GREEN
PERCY RD
Beddington Corner

ASSEMBLY WLK
THORNTON RD
ST ALBAN'S GR
ST AGATHA'S GR
SHERBURN RD
BUSHAM RD
SHRP CRES
SPENCER RD
YORK ST
SEYMOUR RD
NEW RD
ORCHARD RD
OR CHARD
70

TINTERN RD
TORR WLK
WELBECK RD
WINCHCOMBE RD
WEST WLK
WIGMORE WLK
WELHOUSE RD
WOBURN RD
WALTHAM
GREEN WRYTHE LA
AMBLEWOOD
OAKFIELD GDNS
NEWENT CL
BUCKHURST AVE
ELM CL
DURAND CL
LIMES AVE
CHESTNUT CL
GRETHE CRES
REYNOLD'S CL
KINGSWOOD
CULVERS AVE
KINGSWOOD
RETREAT
ANSELL
LODGE LA
LINK RD
LONGSFIELD AVE
MEDLAND CL
SENGA RD
A 237 LONDON RD
BUILDINGS
HACKBRIDGE RD
B 277
P

Hackbridge

WEST WLK
WIGMORE
ARLINGTON DRI
GREEN CL
DALE PARK AVE
LIME
ASH CL
BEECH CL
ALMOND RD
MUSCHAMP RD
CHERRY RD
LENDLE
HACKBRIDGE
PARK GDNS
NIGHTINGALE
HYDALE
Felnex Trad Est
Wks
BESTMOR WAY
MILL CL
PARK RD
WANDLE RD
ELMWOOD CL
ROYAL WLK
BIRCHWOOD AVE
CHARLES WAY
PRINCE
REGAL
GRANGE CT

BINK
SIMMS CL
FELLOWES RD
B 278
The Wrythe
HOME CL
JOHNSON'S CL
CULVERS WAY
NIGHTINGALE RD
THE CAUSEWAY
SHEPLEY CL
SNOS
STRAWBERRY LA
RIVER
VICTORIA AVE
LYNDON AVE
ST MARY'S RD
BIRCHWOOD AVE
MEADOW WLK
BORHAM MEADOW
WANDLE SIDE
P

Hackbridge

POULTON AVE
ERSKINE RD
LABURNUM AVE
BROOKFIELD AVE
WRYTHE LA
ST ANDREW'S WAY
ST JOHN'S RD
ST JAMES RD
WILLIAM RD
WRYTHE GREEN
B 278
WEST ST
KYNERSLEY CL
Sch
AIRLTONE WAY
COOPER CRES
NORTH ST
HOLLYWD
LANGCROFT
Coll
BUCKLERS WAY
DENMARK RD
ORCHARD
STRAWBERRY LA
GDNS
ORYAM WAY
BUTLER AVE
MILL LA
CORRAM RD
ESCHERCOFT RD
ELM
BURLEIGH
GROVE
LAKE GDNS
A 237

96

Mitcham
Common

Mill House

WINDMILL RD
B 272

CROYDON RD
B 272

WATNEYS RD

COMMONSIDE E

WESTMORLAND WAY
SOUTHWAY
NORTHUMBERLAND GDNS
LINCOLN RD
MIDDLESEX RD
GALPIN'S RD

1 LANCASTER AVE
2 BUCKINGHAM RD
3 BERKSHIRE WAY

MAYFIELD RD
SILVERLEIGH RD

GONVILLE RD
DENEHURST
TRAFFORD RD

Crem

Cemy

AURELIA GDNS
LIMPSFIELD AVE

A 23

WINGATE CRES

Sch

RED HOUSE LA

BROOKMEAD RD
HOMEMEAD RD
OAKMEAD RD

LC

Beddington Lane

JESSOPS WAY

BROOM RD T2

ELBERON AVE

ROCHFORD WAY

LAVENDER RD

THORNTON RD

SHAMROCK RD

AURELIA RD
PEALL RD
WKS

MARDEN CRES
MARDEN RD
BOSTON RD
LANCING RD
DONALD RD

MITCHAM RD

RODDING
ROSECOURT
CECIL RD

COOMBER WAY

THERAPIA

THERAPIA LA

THERAPIA LA
ALFRISTON AVE
STONECROFT WAY
LION WAY
DACRE RD
RINGWOOD AVE
WESTCOMBE AVE

ROSEDENE AVE

OCKLEY RD

A 236

A 23

A 23

A 238
L
DRAKE RD
EFFINGHAM RD

BEDDINGTON LA

Beddington

Waddon
Hospital

NEWMAN RD

PURLEY WAY

MILE RD

Sewage
Works

BEDDINGTON FARM RD

BATH
HOUSE RD

WADDON MARSH WAY

GURNEY CRES

Waddon
Marsh

105

A 23

P

P

Beddington Park

CHURCH RD

BLOXWORTH CL

CHURCH LA

BAMPFYLDE CL

CROYDON RD
A 232

A 232

HARRINGTON CL

CRISPIN CRES
CRISPIN CL
MALLINSON RD

MELLER RD
DERRY RD

WHELAN WAY

GUY RD

THE BRANDRIES

HILLIER'S LA
B 272

WANDLE BANK

WANDLE COURT GDNS

BLANDFORD RD

RICHMOND RD

MORTLAKE RD
CHISHOLM RD

RICHMOND GREEN

CEDARS RD

BRIDLE PATH

BRIDGES LA

BRIDLE PATH

WADDON RD
ELSCOTT RD
ALDWICK RD

THACKERAN RD

PROGRESS WAY

COMMERCE WAY

Waddon

MILL LA

RIDGEWAY
HILL

29

111

30

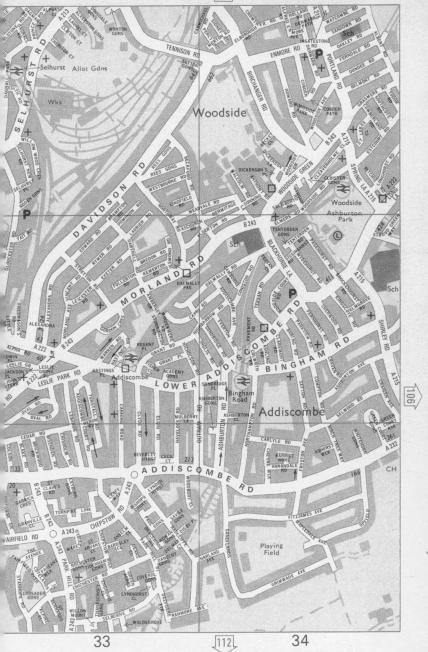

97

Woodside

Woodside Green

Woodside
Ashburton
Park

Addiscombe

LOWER

ADDISCOMBE RD

Bingham
Road

Playing
Field

Schs
KINGSWORTH
ADAMS RD A 214
157
RONALD CL
ERNEST
LONGHEATH GDNS
A 222 LONDON
ABBOTS WAY
LLOYDS WAY
STANHOPE GR

LONGHEATH GDNS
AMBLESIDE AVE
UPPER ELMERS END RD
LODGE GDNS
HOLLY CRES

MACCLE 2
ALBER
SHOREHAM
RUSTMALL
CHAFFINCH RD
MEDWAY
MARGILL RD
CHAFFINCH AVE
FAIRFORD AVE
FAIR FORD CL
FAIRWAY CL
AYLESFORD AVE
AVIEMORE WAY
AVIEMORE CL
AVIEMORE
ALTYRE
ELMDENE CL
ALTYRE'S WAY
ALTYRE RD
HILLCREST VIEW

67

Long Lane Wood
OAK WAY
STONELEIGH WAY
ASH TREE WAY
PARK WAY
GREEN VIEW
BURRELL CL
HILLCREST VIEW

LONG LA
BYWOOD
THE ROPERY
BROOKSIDE AVE
ALDERSMEAD WAY
AVE
GREENVIEW AVE
BARON'S WLK
SLOANE WLK

STOCKBURY
WINCHFIELD WAY
CANDLE
GLADESIDE
HOMER RD
STOKES RD
KEMPTON WLK
HAM VIEW
REGENCY WLK

LONGHURST RD
WOODSIDE WAY
A 222
KEATS WAY
GREEN WAY
THE GLADE
FAIRHAVEN AVE
LAVENDER WAY
GLADESIDE
INGLEWOOD WAY
LORNE AVE
DARLEY CL
RADNOR WLK

STROUD DELAMARE CRES
SWINBURNE CRES
COL
GWYNNE AVE
LORNE AVE GDNS
ROUND
KELVINGTON CL
OVERSTONE GDNS
Monks Orchard

STROUD GREEN
GDNS
GLADESIDE
LORNE AVE
ELSTAN WAY
ORCHARD GR
ORCHARD
ORCHARD WAY

CHAUCER GREEN
Playing Fields
WOODMERE AVE
WOODMERE AVE
MERE END RD
Sch

WOODMERE GDNS
WOODMERE AVE
MERE
TOWER VIEW
LYCONBY GDNS
COVERACK CL

66
SHIRLEY PARK RD
BLACKTHORNE AVE
SHIRLEY GDNS
EDGEWOOD GREEN
TOWER VIEW
HIGH TREES
ORCHARD AVE
ORCHARD RISE
PIPPIN
OAKVIEW GR
PRESHFIELDS
PARKFIELDS
Park Farm

GLENTHORNHOLME AVE
Allot Gdns
WOODLAND WAY

FIRSBY AVE
CHESTON AVE
485

105
A 215
SHIRLEY AVE
VALLEY WLK
BARNFIELD AVE
VERDAYNE AVE
RIDGEMOUNT AVE
WICKHAM AVE
ORCHARD AVE
WICKHAM RD
489

ADDISCOMBE RD
A 232
SHIRLEY RD
ELDON AVE
A 232
2
NURSERY CL
WEST WAY GDNS
SPRING PARK RD
HARTLAND WAY
L
MONNI CL
MEAD WAY
PHILIP GDNS
ADDISON'S CL
LAKE RD
DEVONSHIRE WAY
LANGLAND GDNS
THE GRANGE
FARM LA
THE LEES
FARM DRI

Sch
17
BARMOUTH RD
THE VALE
SPRING PARK RD
THE GLEN
WEST WAY
BENNETTS WAY
EAST WAY
MIDHOLM RD
TEMPLE AVE
SHIRLEY WAY

65
Golf Course
NURSERY CL
CANONS WLK
GMS LA
UPPER SHIRLEY RD
MILL VIEW
TANGLEWOOD
SHIRLEY CHURCH RD
COLIN CL
SANDY WAY
POPES GR
PLEASANT GR
SPRING PARK WAY
BERNEL DRI
HIGHWAY
Spring Park

Shirley
Sch
Sch
Sch
PINEWOOD CL
Sch
SOUTH WAY
GREENWAY GDNS
FERRIS AVE
PALACE VIEW
STUART CRES
ANNESLEY DRI
LIME TREE GR

35
36

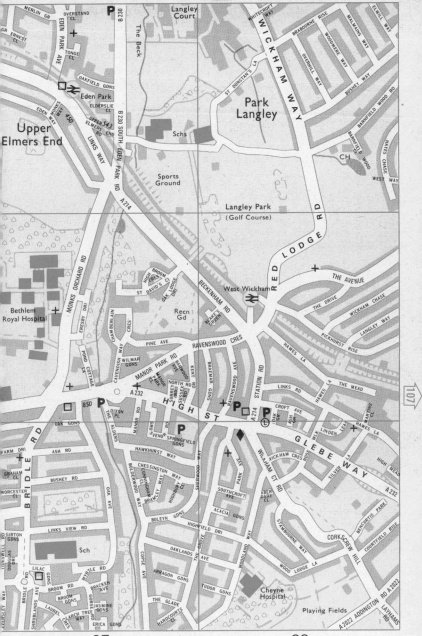

106

107

TOP PARK · B 251 HAYES LA · WESTMORELAND RD B 228 · B 228 · TALL ELMS CL · BROAD OAKS WAY · STONE RD · APPLEDENE · TENHAM GREEN · BEADON RD · HAYES RD · B 2212 · 22 · B 265 · 39

ELMFIELD · BARNFIELD WOOD RD · WOODLEA DRI · PICKHURST PARK · MEREWORTH DRI · PARK DRI · ELVINGTON GREEN · KNOWLTON GREEN · CAMERON RD · HURSTFIELD · LETCHWORTH CL · LETCHWORTH DRI

313 · 316 · PICKHURST DRI · PENSHURST GREEN · HAYESFORD PARK DRI · CHERITON AVE · BENEDEN GREEN · LEYSDOWN

HAYES CHASE · PENSHURST WLK · PICKHURST PARK · BRAMBLEDOWN CL · CULVERSTONE CL · BARNHILL AVE · OTTERDEN · STANSTED · BRACKLEY · MALTON RD · CORNFORD CL · AIR ACRES · P · FISHER'S WOOD

67

MEADWAY

THE AVENUE · THE CRESCENT · GOODHART WAY · LINKFIELD · HEATH RISE · CUPOLA WOOD · Sch · EASTRY AVE · SHERWAY · MARDEN AVE · HAZELMERE WAY · WOLFE CL · CRANBROOK CL · MONTCALM CL · NORMAN PARK · P

WICKHAM CH · PICKHURST LA · KINGSDOWN WAY · OAKMEAD AVE · HAYES LA · SOCKET LA

LANGLEY WAY · 193 · 198 · PICKHURST GREEN · PICKHURST MEAD · SEDGEWOOD · MALLING WAY · BOUGHTON AVE · FARLEIGH AVE · PEMBURY AVE · CHILHAM WAY · NORTHBOURNE RD · DARTMOUTH RD · EASTWAY · KECHILL GDNS · CLUB GARDENS RD · Hayes · 167

PICKHURST RISE · CREST RD · MOUNTHURST RD · TREVOR CL · BOURNE VALE · SOUTH HILL · THE WHITSMEAD · SOUTHBOURNE · GREEN AVE · 246 · B 265 · Hayes Street Farm

66

Sports Gds · HILLDOWN RD · COURTLANDS RD · CONSTANCE CRES · CHATHAM AVE · SACKVILLE AVE · STUART AVE · CHERRY WLK · HAMBRO AVE · BEVERARD AVE · HAYES ST · GEORGIAN CL · GEORGE LA

West Wickham · PONDFIELD RD · HAYES HILL RD · B 251 · BRIAR DENE AVE · CECIL WAY · STANHOPE AVE · EVE · 62 · ESSEYWELL CL · ALEXANDER CL · 8 · HAYES WOOD AVE

HAYES MEAD · HURSTDENE AVE · HURST CL · 31 · STATION APP · B 251 · FORGE · THE KNOLL · GLEBE HOUSE

HAYES HILL · HEPBURN GDNS · P · Hayes · KEMSING CL · HAYES GDN · BURWOOD AVE

106 · TIEPIGS LA · PRIGGLY WOOD · BOURNE WAY · LARKFIELD CL · HILLSIDE LA · STATION HILL · RIDGEWAY · HAWTHORNDENE CL · HAWTHORNDENE RD · WARREN RD

MOUNT CT · KESWICK RD · WINDERMERE RD · WESTLAND DRI · HOLLAND WAY · HOLLAND HAWTHORNDENE · SANDILAND CRES · WARREN CL · WARREN RD · PRESTONS RD · GROVE CL · HAYES · WEST COMMON RD · Sch · REDGATES DRI · BASTON RD

HIGH MEAD · BEARBROOK DRI · HAMBES LA · LITTLE RD · CONEY HILL RD · ABBOTSBURY · POLE CAT ALLEY · Hayes Court

A 232 · LENNARD RD · GLEBE WAY · LENNARD AVE · DUKES WAY · P · Hayes Common

65 · COURTFIELD RISE · ADDINGTON · A 2022 · SOUTH WLK · P · FARM CL · ROSSLYN CL · GATES GREEN RD · COLIN DRI · Hayes Common

P · CHURCH DRI · QUEENSWAY · CHESTNUT AVE · KINGSWAY · PRICES · HARVEST BANK RD · ROBINS GR · HARTFIELD CRES · BASTON MANOR RD · A 232 · CROY · P

Coney Hall

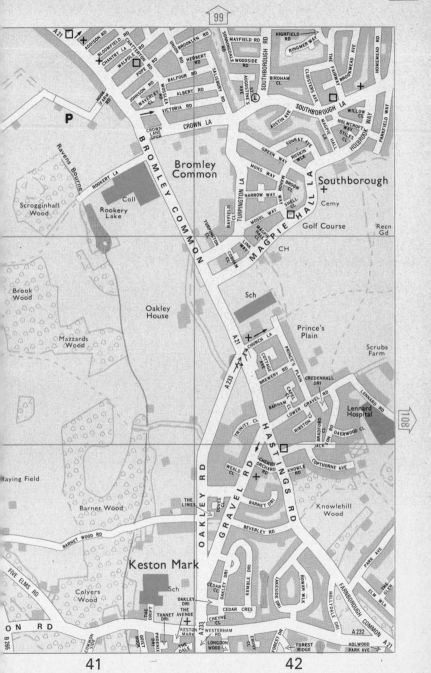

A21

Addison Rd

Bloomfield Rd
Chatterton Rd
Chantry La
Walpole Rd
Pope Rd
Johnson Rd
Waverley Cl
Mosslea Rd
Balfour Rd
Herbert Rd
Albert Rd
Union Rd
Brooklyn Rd
Salisbury Rd
Woodside Rd
Mayfield Rd
Sunningdale Rd
Augustine's Ave

P

Crown La Spur

CROWN LA

Ravens Bourne

Rookery La

ROOKERY LA

Coll

Rookery
Lake

Scrogginhall
Wood

BROMLEY COMMON

Bromley
Common

Highfield
Rd

Ringmer Way

THE FAIRWAY

Brookmead Ave

Homemead Rd

Birdham
Cl

Cloisters Rd

SOUTHBOROUGH LA

Willow
Cl

Parkfield Way

HOLBROOK LA

Holmcroft
Way
Styles
Cl

Austin Ave

Green Way

Sunray Ave

Ruskin Wlk

Mons Way

Broom Cl

Magpie La

Southborough

+

MAGPIE HALL LA

Turpington La

Narrow Way

Mosul Way

Rayfield Cl

Magpie Cl

Turpington Cl

Link La

Cobham

Shell La

Cemy

Golf Course

Recn
Gd

CH

Brook
Wood

Mazzards
Wood

Oakley
House

Sch

Prince's
Plain

Scrubs
Farm

A21

CHURCH LA

Cottage Ave

Brewery Rd

Prince's Plain

Barham

Capel Cl

Lower Gravel Rd

Credenhall
Dri

Lennard Rd

A233

Trinity Cl

Ribston Cl

Bradford Cl

Jackson Rd

Daerwood Cl

Lennard
Hospital

108

laying Field

Barnet Wood

The
Limes

Doves

Oakley
Rd

Gravel Rd

Cherry
Orchard
Rd

Weald
Cl

+

Knowle
Rd

Barnet Dri

Copthorne Ave

Beverley Rd

Knowlehill
Wood

BARNET WOOD RD

Five Elms Rd

Colyers
Wood

Keston Mark

Sch

Oakley
Dri

The
Drift

Thanet
Dri

Oakley
Dri

Cedar
Cl

Kemble Dri

Cedar Cres

Lakeside Dri

Roman Wlk

Park Ave

Elm Wla

The
Glen

FARNBOROUGH COMMON

Hollydale Dri

ON RD

B265

Common
Side

Quiet
Nook

Phoenix
Dri

The
Avenue

+

Keston
Mark

A233

The
Dale

Cheyne
Rd

Westerham
Rd

Longdon
Wood

Ebury
Cl

Forest Dri

Forest
Ridge

Holwood
Park Ave

A232

A21

41

42

Thornet Wood

P

P

L P

PETTS

BLACKBROOK LA

GDNS
NORDEN

GOOSE
GREEN
DRI

CREST VIEW DRI

SOUTHBOROUGH LA

WOODLAND WAY

TOWNCOURT CRES

CROSSWAY

KINGS

STATION
SQ

WEST WAY

MAPLE CL

ACACIA

POSTMILL DRI

Sch

Recn
Gd

FRANKS WOOD AVE

WEST
WAY

ASH CL

P

HAWTHORN

TUDOR WAY

PRIORY AVE

ST GEORG

67

OXHAWTH CRES

THORN

LOVELACE AVE

MAYBURY
CL

LANGLEY

GDNS

LAKESWOOD RD

WOODHURST AVE

NIGHTINGALE RD

CRESCENT DRI

QUEENSWAY

Petts
Wood

P

KENILWORTH
RD

ADDISON CL

JERSEY DRI

EASTBURY
RD

BEAUMONT RD

FIELIWAY

FA

ASH ROW

HAZEL WLK

HORNBEAM

WHITEBEAM WAY

BIRCH

FARTINGDON WAY

THORN
WAY

CHESHAM AVE

CRESCENT DRI

DIAMETER RD

TRANS
MERE
CL

SHEPPERTON RD

RYECROFT

RD

PRESCOTT AVE

FELTON CL

ROLLESTON AVE

HOLLINGWORTH RD

ROLLESTON

FAIRWAY

EMBER CL

ENSFIELD RD

KIRKBROOK

TOWN
COURT LA

BUSHEY
AVE

Sch

Sch

LARCH WAY

ALMOND WAY

LABURNUM WAY

Recn
Gd

DERWENT DRI

GREENFIELD
GDNS

CROFTON

L

ALMOND

BROADCROFT RD

BIRCHME

S

66

Sparrow Wood

Roundabout
Wood

Crofton
Heath

HEATH SIDE

HONOR
OAK

BOURNE

CRANSTON CRES

KENNEDY CL

SPARROW DRI

ABBOTS

MONKS WAY

ST THOMAS DRI

RIDGE DRI

TANDY
RIDGE

GLEN
EAGLES
GREEN

OWN

DARK

107

LENNARD RD

Lennard
Hospital

Hospl

BRAMLEY
CL

LANSDOWNE AVE

DRAYTON AVE

WYNDHAM
CL

ST THOMAS DRI

ROMANY RISE

OREGON SQ

ECCLES
CL

PINEWOOD

65

BIRCH
MEAD

JASMINE CL

ROSE
DALE

WISTARIA

POPLAR AVE

MURLEY
ANTHONY'S

ORMONDE AVE

LYOTH
RD

GUMPING RD

CLAREVILLE RD

134

Crofton

WOOD WAY

LARCH
DENE

SUNNYDALE

MERESIDE

NITFIELD WAY

ERE
CL

BURLINGTON
CL

GLEN
BROWNE

PERCIVAL
RD

BLUEBELL

HIGHWOOD

HIGHWOOD
RD

OAKWOOD RD

CROFTON RD

OAK

WOOD
RD

WOOD RD

FOXFIELD RD

POUND CL

THE GLEN

PARK AVE

GR DALE
AVE

RED OAK CL

PILKINGTON RD

PONDFIELD RD

WESSELS
RD

CROFTON AVE

GRANGE RD

BROUGHTON RD

TORVER
WAY

RUSLAND AVE

HAVERYTHWAITE
AVE

MEADOW WAY

WINDERMERE
AVE

GRASMERE
AVE

GRASMERE GDNS

MADA RD

LOWLANDS RD

PARTRIDGE DRI

MASEFIELD
VIEW

AVEBURY RD

Sch

TILE VILLAGE

WINTERBORNE
RD

ELM WLK

358

360

409

A 21

A 232

368

PRINCESS
PAR

ST GILES
CL

STARTS HILL RD

WILLOW WLK

Locksbottom

SLOANE
GDNS

LYSANDER
WAY

STABLES
END

NURS

OAK

BALLANT

P

Farnborough
Hospital

Darrick
Wood

Playing
Field

CRE

100

Poverest

45   46

64

63

62

109

23   24

London Rd
Malden Rd
Church Hill Rd
St Dunstan's Hill
Cheam
Priory Rd
Priory Ave
Kenley Wlk
The Spinney
Fairlight Ct
Kingswood Lr Ctr
Willowhayne Gdns
Hayes Cl
Frogmore Gdns
Buxton Cres
Carlton Cres
Chartwell Pl
Abbotts Rd
Hanover Rd
Sunningdale Rd
Westfield Rd
Elmbrook Rd
St Albans Rd
Hilldale Rd
Frederick Rd
Denbig Hill
Bourne Way
Love La
Carlisle Rd
Quarry Park Rd
Rosebery Rd
Cecil Rd
Salisbury Ave
Recn Gd
Tilehurst Rd
Tingsdown Rd
Fromondes Rd
Lumley Rd
Springclose La
Mickleham Gdns
Cheam Park Way
Park
Parkside
The Broadway
High St
Tabor
Cheam Mansions
Scotsdale Cl
Ewell Rd
Nonsuch Park
The Avenue
Sch
Harefield Bridge
Holmwood Cl
Kingsway Rd
Station Way
Cheam
Upper Mulgrave Rd
Old Barn Cl
The Lawns
Arundel Rd
Hillside Cl
Beresford Rd
Belmont
Burdon La
Sandy La
Glebe Rd
West Dri
Devon Rd
The Glade
Meadowside Rd
South Dri
Chesham Cl
The Avenue
Wray Rd
Warren Ave
Wilbury Rd
Onslow Rd
Cuddington Way
Chetham Way
Northey Ave
Howell Hill
East Ewell
Sports Ground
Seymour Ave
Arundel Ave
Weepsmead Ave
Hillside Rd
Springfield Rd
Howell Hill
Birchfield Gr
A 232
Cheam Rd
Nonsuch Wlk
Cheyham Gdns
Rugby Lane
Harefield Ave
Holmwood Rd
Bramley Rd
Wonersh Way
Ranmore Rd Way
Merrow Rd
Buckland Rd
Gomshall Rd
Shere Ave
Westcott Way
Alburn Rd
P

111

25   26

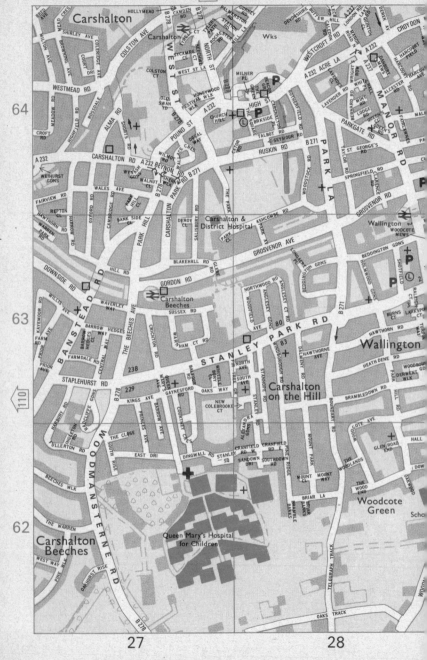

THE HOLT
BOND GDNS
EVELYN WAY
CROYDON RD
SANDHILLS
HALLOWELL RD
BRIDGES LA
TRITTON AVE
GARRATT
CEDARS AVE
SALCOTT
LAVINGTON
ALDWICK
THE COURT DRI

A 232
CROYDON RD
A 232

CLIFFORD AVE
FERRERS AVE
QUEEN ELIZABETH'S WK
ROYSTON AVE
IBERIAN AVE
A 232
B 272
COLLYER AVE
OAKLEY AVE
BEDLOW WAY
WILLOUGHBY AVE
CHERRY HILL
LYNWOOD GDNS

NORTHWAY
DARCY
SOUTHWAY
RECTORY LA
RALEIGH AVE
ROOKWOOD AVE
QUEENSWOOD AVE
BRISTOW RD
KINGSWOOD AVE
BANSTEAD RD
REGATE WAY
GUILDFORD
GODALMING AVE
SHEEN AVE
HEADLEY AVE
MERRIBANK AVE
STARLING

Sports Ground

DEMESNE RD
CRICHTON AVE
Cemy
HINDHEAD WAY
GOMSHALL AVE
CAPEL

MONTAGU GDNS
MORTON GDNS
THE BRIDLE WAY
Allot Gdns

THE CHASE

OSMOND GDNS
BUTE GDNS
THARP RD
PEDDINGTON LA
UPPER RD
HIGH VIEW
EAST AVE
318

MONT RD
BUTE GDNS W
MELLOWS RD
B 272
GARDEN CL
WEST AVE
279

ROSS RD
RUSSELL CT
ROBIN TEAL
CL
Bandonhill
Park
HASLEMERE CL
ABINGER CL
176
B 271

CLYDE RD
CAREW
WALETON ALDES
BANDO
STAFFORD RD
277

ELGIN
CHARLOTTE RD
FRANCIS RD
CHARLIE
B 271
B 272
LINK LA
LYSANDER RD

HINTON RD
MILTON RD
LAVENDER VALE
South Beddington
IMPERIAL WAY

COPER GDNS
WORDSWORTH RD
THE MEAD

STANLEY GDNS
WATERER RISE

BLENHEIM GDNS
COEDACH AV
REDFORD
COBHAM CL

GROSVENOR
ONSLOW GDNS
HILLSIDE
FORESTERS CL
HERMES WAY
BARLOW
MCINTOSH
DOUGLAS
ROE WAY
HINCHLIFFE CL

MARCHMONT RD
AVENUE RD
TUDOR CL
THE NEWLANDS
MAYLAND RD
ROWELL CL
FIREFLY CL
AVRO
DE HAVILLAND
HAWKER CL

SANDY LA S
FORESTERS DRI
INGLEBY WAY
Park
LINDBERGH CL
MOORE
KINGSFORD
HELENA AV
DUNCAN

CARLETON AVE
LAWFORD CL
SUNKIST WAY
MARIETTE WAY

WOODCOTE GN
BUCKINGHAM WAY
HAMILTON WAY
HARMONY
APELDOORN DRI
PLEASANT WAY

SHIRLEY HILL
STRATTON AVE
CLARICE WAY

B 272

THE DRIVE
SPRUCEDALE GDNS
Sch

LORDSBURY FIELD
RIDGE PARK
GREAT WOODCOTE PARK
HILLCREST RD
PLOUGH LA
HIGHFIELD RD

FARM
LINDEN
THE RIDGE
GOLD CREST
CHURCH HILL
CHURCH RD
RUSSELL HILL
THE CLOSE

GREEN LA
A 2022
PEAKS HILL
THE BRIDLE RD
Russell Hill

A 237
FOXLEY LA
A 2022
B 272

29
30

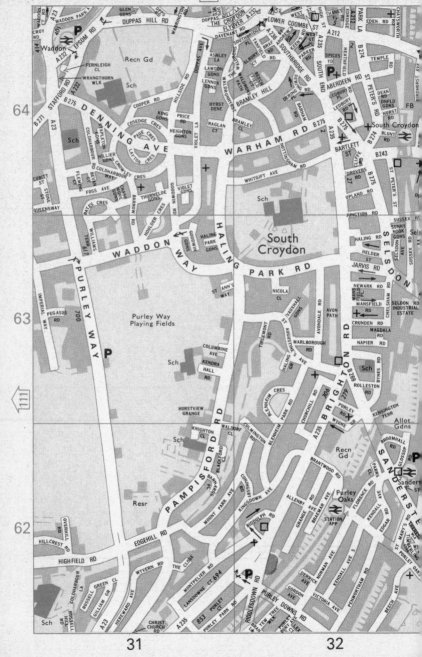

South Croydon

Purley Way
Playing Fields

64

63

62

31   32

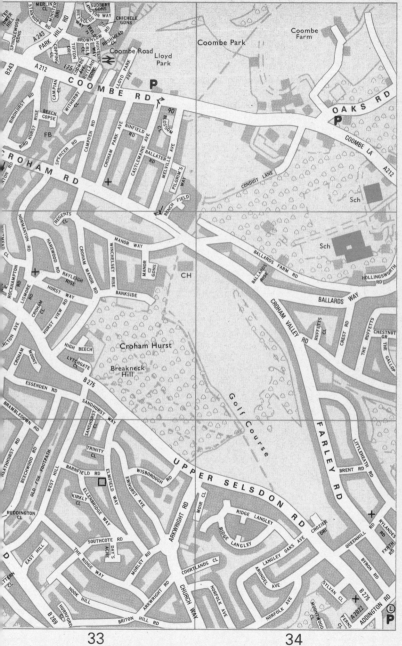

Coombe Park

Coombe Farm

MERLIN CL
STANHOPE GDNS
MINSTER
LANGTON WAY
REYNOLDS RD
SUDBURY GDNS
CHICHELE GDNS
RUSHMEAD
PARK HILL RD
A 243
TIPPTON
BROWNLOW RD
CRLN
ROLLINS
B243
A 212
CAMPIAN RD
175
LLOYD PARK
Coombe Road
Lloyd Park
P

Coombe Park

OAKS RD
P
COOMBE LA
A212

BIRDHURST RD
BEECH COPSE
BIRD HURST RISE
FB

C O O M B E   R D
90
550M
WITHERBY
SPENCER RD
CAMPDEN RD
CROHAM PARK AVE
BINFIELD RD
CASTLEMAINE AVE
BALLATER AVE
MELVILLE AVE
PILGRIM'S WAY
BANCH FIELD

CONDUIT LANE
Sch

C R O H A M   R D

REGENTS CL
NORMANTON RD
HAREWOOD RD
CROHAM MANOR RD
WINCHELSEA RISE
MANOR WAY
MANOR GDNS
CH

Sch

BALLARDS FARM RD
BALLARDS RD
HOLLINGSWORTH RD
BALLARDS WAY

ROCKHAMPTON RD
LISMORE RD
RAYLEIGH RISE
HURST WAY
BANKSIDE
HURST VIEW RD
CROHAM CL

CROHAM VALLEY RD
RUFFETTS CL
CREST RD
THE RUFFETTS
CHESTNUT GR
THE GALLOP

CARLTON AVE
CROHAM MOUNT
HIGH BEECH
LYTHGATE CL
ESSENDEN RD
B 275
SANDHURST WAY
BRAMBLEDOWN RD

Croham Hurst
Breakneck Hill

Golf Course

FARLEY RD

HEATHHURST RD
BEECHWOOD RD
OLD FOX FOOTPATH
WEST HILL
SAUNDERS WAY
TRINITY CL
BARNFIELD RD
ELMFIELD WAY
WISBOROUGH RD
EWHURST AVE

U P P E R   S E L S D O N   R D

REDDINGTON CL
KIRKLY CL
ELLENBRIDGE WAY
EAST HILL
THE RIDGE WAY
SOUTHCOTE RD
DAY'S ACRE
MORLEY RD
ARKWRIGHT RD
MOIR CL
RIDGE LANGLEY
RIDGE LANGLEY
CROZIER DRI
QUEENHILL RD
RYLANDES RD
FARLEY RD
BYRON RD

HOOK HILL
HURNFORD CL
B 269
BRITON HILL RD
ARKWRIGHT RD
CHURCH WAY
COURTLANDS CL
NORFOLK AVE
ARUNDEL AVE
LANGLEY OAKS AVE
SYLVAN CL
SMONTH WOOD
B 275
A 2022
FERNS
ADDINGTON RD
L
P

33

34

EXPLANATION OF STREET INDEX
AND REFERENCE SYSTEM

Example:—   * Haybridge Gdns Mews. Croy........*19*   18 **26** A
               ①   ②   ③   ④   ⑤

① The asterisk indicates that only the first two letters of the name have been shown on the map e.g. HA.

② This is the full street name, which may have been abbreviated on the map.

③ This is the postal code or town in which the street falls, Standard postal codes have been used for street names in the London Postal Districts.
For all other street names Post Town abbreviations have been used as a guide to the location of the street name.

④ This is the map number on which the street name appears

⑤ The four figures and the letter are the reference system for locating the position of the name on the map.
The four figures show in which square the centre of the street falls.
The first two figures can be found along the bottom edge of each map in blue and these apply to the vertical columns. The second two figures can be found along the left or right hand side of each map in brown and these apply to the horizontal rows.
The letter provides a more precise location within the square. The parts of the square to which each letter refers are indicated below.

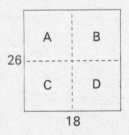

The numerical part of the referencing is based on the National Grid

ABBREVIATIONS USED IN THE INDEX

Road Names

App	Approach
Arc	Arcade
Ave	Avenue
Bvd	Boulevard
Bwy	Broadway
Bldg/s	Building/s
By Ps	By Pass
Cswy	Causeway
Circ	Circle
Circ	Circus
Cl	Close
Cnr	Corner
Ct	Court
Cres	Crescent
Dri	Drive
Dro	Drove
E	East
Emb	Embankment
Espl	Esplanade
Fly	Flyover
Gdns	Gardens
Gr	Grove
Hts	Heights
Junc	Junction
La	Lane
N	North
Par	Parade
Pas	Passage
Pl	Place
Prec	Precinct
Prom	Promenade
Rd	Road
S	South
Sq	Square
Strs	Stairs
Stps	Steps
St	Street
Terr	Terrace
Wlk	Walk
W	West
Yd	Yard

Postal Districts and Towns

Ashf	Ashford
Bark	Barking
Barn	Barnet
Beck	Beckenham
Belv	Belvedere
Bex	Bexley
Bexh	Bexleyheath
Brent	Brentford
Brom	Bromley
Buck H	Buckhurst Hill
Cars	Carshalton
Chess	Chessington
Chig	Chigwell
Chis	Chislehurst
Croy	Croydon
Dag	Dagenham
Dart	Dartford
E Mol	East Molesey
Edg	Edgware
Enf	Enfield
Eps	Epsom
Eri	Erith
Esh	Esher
Felt	Feltham
Grnf	Greenford
Hamp	Hampton
Har	Harrow
Hay	Hayes
Horn	Hornchurch
Houn	Hounslow
Ilf	Ilford
Islw	Isleworth
King	Kingston on Thames
Loug	Loughton
Mit	Mitcham
Mord	Morden
N Mal	New Malden
Nthlt	Northolt
Orp	Orpington
Pnr	Pinner
Pur	Purley
Rain	Rainham
Rich	Richmond
Rom	Romford
Ruis	Ruislip
Shep	Shepperton
Sid	Sidcup
Sthl	Southall
S Croy	South Croydon
Stan	Stanmore
Sun	Sunbury-on-Thames
Surb	Surbiton
Sutt	Sutton
Stai	Staines
Tedd	Teddington
Th Hth	Thornton Heath
Twick	Twickenham
Uxb	Uxbridge
Wall	Wallington
Walt	Walton on Thames
Well	Welling
Wem	Wembley
W Dray	West Drayton
Wdf Gr	Woodford Green
W Wick	West Wickham
Wor Pk	Worcester Park

Name	Page	Grid
Abbess Cl. SW2	87	31 73 D
Abbeville Rd. N8	24	29 89 D
Abbeville Rd. SW4	74	29 74 A
Abbey Ave. Wem	44	18 83 C
Abbey Cl. Nthlt	53	12 82 B
Abbey Cl. Pnr	20	11 89 A
Abbey Cres. Belv	45	49 78 A
Abbeydale Rd. Wem	45	19 83 A
Abbeyfield Rd. SE16	64	35 78 A
Abbey Gdns. NW8		26 83 C
Abbey Gr. SE2	67	47 78 A
Abbey La. Beck	98	37 70 C
Abbey La. E15	49	18 83 D
Abbey Orchard St. SW1	6	29 79 D
Abbey Park. Beck	98	37 70 C
Abbey Rd. Bark	51	44 83 A
Abbey Rd. Belv	67	48 78 A
Abbey Rd. Bexh	79	48 75 C
Abbey Rd. Croy	105	31 65 D
Abbey Rd. E15	50	39 83 A
Abbey Rd. Enf	13	33 95 A
Abbey Rd. Ilf	40	44 88 B
Abbey Rd. NW6		25 83 B
Abbey Rd. NW6	46	25 84 D
Abbey Rd. NW8	46	26 83 C
Abbey Rd. SE2	67	47 78 A
Abbey Rd. SW19	95	26 69 A
Abbey St. E13	58	40 82 C
Abbey St. SE1	8	33 79 D
Abbey Terr. SE2	67	47 78 A
Abbey Wlk. E Mol	92	13 68 B
Abbey Wood Rd. SE2	67	47 78 A
Abbot Cl. Beck	98	37 69 D
Abbot Cl. Ruis	32	11 86 D
Abbotsbury Cl. E15	49	38 83 C
Abbotsbury Cl. W14	62	24 79 B
Abbotsbury Gdns. Pnr	32	11 88 C
Abbotsbury Rd. Brom	107	39 65 B
Abbotsbury Rd. Mord	95	25 68 D
Abbotsbury Rd. W14	62	24 79 B
Abbots Cl. N1	48	32 84 A
Abbots Cl. Orp	108	44 66 C
Abbotsford Ave. N15	25	32 89 C
Abbotsford Gdns. Wdf Gn	27	40 91 C
Abbotsford Rd. Ilf	40	44 88 B
Abbots Gdns. N2	23	26 89 D
Abbotshall Ave. N14	16	29 93 C
Abbotshall Rd. SE6	88	38 72 B
Abbots La. SE1	8	33 80 C
Abbotsleigh Cl. Sutt	110	25 63 D
Abbotsleigh Rd. SW16	86	29 71 C
Abbots Park. SW2		31 73 C
Abbot's Pl. NW6	46	25 83 B
Abbots Rd. E6	50	41 83 D
Abbots Rd. Edg	22	20 91 D
Abbot St. E8		33 84 B
Abbots Terr. N8	36	30 88 C
Abbotstone Rd. SW15	73	23 75 A
Abbots Way. Beck	106	36 67 A
Abbotswell Rd. SE4		36 74 B
Abbotswood Gdns. Ilf	27	42 89 B
Abbotswood Gdns. Ilf		43 89 C
Abbotswood Rd. SW16	86	29 72 D
Abbott Ave. SW20	95	23 69 B
Abbott Cl. Hamp	92	12 70 A
Abbott Cl. Nthlt	43	12 84 B
Abbott Rd. E14	58	38 81 D
Abbotts Cres. E4	18	40 93 C
Abbotts Cres. Enf	13	31 97 D
Abbotts Dri. Wem		16 86 B
Abbotsmede Cl. Twick	83	15 72 B
Abbotts Park Rd. E10	38	38 87 A
Abbotts Rd. Barn	11	25 96 D
Abbotts Rd. Mit	96	29 68 B
Abbotts Rd. Sthl		12 80 C
Abbotts Rd. Sutt	110	24 64 A
Abbotts Rd. Sutt	103	24 65 D
Abbott's Wlk. Bexh	67	47 77 D
Abbs Cross Gdns. Horn	42	53 87 B
Abbs Cross. Horn	42	53 87 B
Abbs Cross. Horn	42	53 86 C
Abbs Cross La. Horn	42	53 86 C
Abchurch La. EC4		32 80 B
Abchurch Yd. EC4	8	32 80 B
Abdale Rd. W12	55	22 80 D
Aberavon Rd. E3	57	36 82 A
Abercairn Rd. SW16	96	29 70 C
Aberconway Rd. Mord	95	25 68 D
Abercorn Cl. NW7	23	24 91 C
Abercorn Cl. NW8	1	26 82 A
Abercorn Cres. Har	32	13 87 D
Abercorn Gdns. Har	33	17 87 B
Abercorn Gdns. Rom	40	46 88 D
Abercorn Pl. NW8	46	26 83 C
Abercorn Rd. NW7		23
Abercorn Rd. Stan	21	17 91 C
Abercrombie St. SW11	74	27 76 C
Aberdare Cl. W Wick	106	38 65 A
Aberdare Gdns. NW6	46	26 84 A
Aberdare Gdns. NW7	23	23 91 D
Aberdare Rd. Enf	14	35 96 C
Aberdeen La. N5	48	32 85 C
Aberdeen Park. N5	48	32 85 C
Aberdeen Pl. NW8	1	26 82 D
Aberdeen Rd. Croy	112	32 64 B
Aberdeen Rd. Har	21	15 90 D
Aberdeen Rd. N18	17	34 92 D
Aberdeen Rd. N5	48	32 85 A
Aberdeen Rd. NW10	45	21 85 D
Aberdeen Terr. SE3	76	38 76 D
Aberdour Rd. Ilf		46 86 B
Aberdour St. SE1	8	33 79 C
Aberfeldy St. E14	58	38 81 C
Aberford Gdns. SE18	77	42 76 A
Aberfoyle Rd. SW16	96	29 70 D
Abergeldie Rd. SE12	77	40 74 D
Abernethy Rd. SE13	77	39 75 C
Abersham Rd. E8	48	33 85 D
Abery St. SE18	66	45 78 A
Abingdon Cl. NW1	47	29 84 B
Abingdon Cl. SW19	95	26 70 A
Abingdon Rd. N3	23	26 90 C
Abingdon Rd. SW16	96	30 69 A
Abingdon Rd. W8	62	25 79 C
Abingdon St. SE1	7	30 79 C
Abingdon Villas. W8	62	25 79 C
Abinger Ave. Sutt	110	23 62 D
Abinger Cl. Bark	51	46 85 A
Abinger Cl. Brom	99	42 68 A
Abinger Cl. Wall	111	30 64 C
Abinger Cl. W5	54	17 80 A
Abinger Gdns. Islw	71	15 75 A
Abinger Gr. SE8	64	36 77 B
Abinger Mews. W9	56	25 82 C
Abinger Rd. W4	61	21 79 C
Ablett St. SE16		35 78 C
Abney Rd. N16	37	33 86 B
Aboyne Dri. SW20	94	22 69 C
Aboyne Rd. NW10	34	21 86 C
Aboyne Rd. SW17	85	26 72 D
Abridge Gdns. Rom	29	49 91 A
Abridge Way. Bark	51	46 83 D
Abyssinia Cl. SW11	74	27 75 C
Abyssinia Rd. SW11	74	27 75 C
Acacia Ave. Brent	60	16 77 D
Acacia Ave. Horn	42	51 86 B
Acacia Ave. N17	31	32 91 D
Acacia Ave. Ruis	31	10 87 B
Acacia Ave. Wem	44	18 85 C
Acacia Cl. Orp	108	44 67 B
Acacia Cl. Stan		15 91 A
Acacia Dri. Sutt	103	25 66 C
Acacia Gdns. NW8	46	26 83 D
Acacia Gdns. W Wick	106	38 65 A
Acacia Gr. N Mal	94	21 68 A
Acacia Gr. SE21	87	32 72 B
Acacia Pl. NW8	46	26 83 D
Acacia Rd. Beck	98	36 68 B
Acacia Rd. E11	39	39 86 B
Acacia Rd. E17	38	36 88 C
Acacia Rd. Enf	13	32 97 B
Acacia Rd. Hamp	92	13 70 A
Acacia Rd. Mit	96	28 69 D
Acacia Rd. N22	25	31 90 A
Acacia Rd. NW8	46	26 83 D
Acacia Rd. W3	55	20 80 A
Acacia Wlk. SW10	62	26 77 C
Academy Gdns. Croy	105	33 66 D
Academy Gdns. Nthlt	43	11 83 D
Academy Pl. SE18	77	42 76 B
Academy Rd. SE18	65	42 77 D
Acanthus Rd. SW11	74	28 75 A
Accommodation Rd. NW11	35	24 87 D
Acfold Rd. SW6	73	25 76 B
Achilles Rd. NW6	46	25 85 C
Achilles St. SE14	64	36 77 D
Achilles Way. W1	6	28 80 C
Acklam Rd. W10	56	24 81 B
Acklington Dri. NW9	22	21 90 A
Ackmar Rd. SW6	73	25 76 A
Ackroyd Dri. E3	57	36 81 B
Ackroyd Rd. SE23	88	36 73 A
Acland Cres. SE5	75	32 75 B
Acland Rd. NW2	45	22 84 B
Acol Rd. NW6	46	26 84 A
Aconbury Rd. Dag	51	46 83 B
Acorn Cl. Chis	90	44 71 C
Acorn Cl. E4	18	37 92 D
Acorn Cl. Enf	13	31 97 B
Acorn Ct. Ilf	40	45 88 A
Acorn Gdns. SE19	97	33 69 B
Acorn Gdns. W3	55	20 81 B
Acorn Wlk. SE16	57	36 80 C
Acre La. Cars	111	28 64 A
Acre La. SW2	74	30 75 C
Acre La. Wall	111	28 64 B
Acre Rd. Dag	52	49 84 D
Acre Rd. King	93	18 69 B
Acre Rd. SW19	95	26 70 B
Acre Way. Nthwd	19	09 90 B
Acris St. SW18	73	26 74 A
Acton La. NW10	45	20 83 D
Acton La. W3	61	20 79 A
Acton La. W4	61	20 79 D
Acton Mews. E8	48	33 83 B
Acton St. WC1	3	30 82 B
Acuba Rd. SW18	85	25 72 B
Ada Gdns. E14	58	38 81 D
Ada Gdns. E15	50	39 83 B
Adair Rd. W10	56	24 82 C
Adam and Eve Ct. W1	2	29 81 C
Adam and Eve Mews. W8	62	25 79 C
Adam Pl. N16	37	33 86 B
Adams Cl. NW9	34	19 86 B
Adams Ct. EC2	4	32 81 D
Adams Gardens Estate. SE16	64	35 79 A
Adamson Rd. E16	58	40 81 C
Adamson Rd. NW3	46	26 84 D
Adams Rd. Beck	106	36 67 A
Adams Rd. N17	25	33 90 C
Adamsrill Rd. Enf	13	32 95 D
Adamsrill Rd. SE26	88	36 71 A
Adam's Row. W1	6	28 80 A
Adams Sq. Bexh	79	48 75 A
Adam St. WC2	7	30 80 A
Ada Pl. E2		34 83 A
Ada Rd. SE5	63	33 77 C
Ada Rd. Wem	33	17 86 D
Adare Wlk. SW16	86	30 72 B
Ada St. E8	48	34 83 B
Adderley Gdns. SE9	90	43 71 A
Adderley Gr. SW11	74	28 74 A
Adderley Rd. Har	21	15 90 B
Adderley St. E14	58	38 81 C
Addington Dri. N12	23	26 91 B
Addington Gr. SE26	88	36 71 A
Addington Rd. Croy	105	31 66 C
Addington Rd. E16	58	39 82 C
Addington Rd. E3	57	37 82 A
Addington Rd. N4	37	31 88 C
Addington Rd. S Croy	112	34 62 D
Addington Rd. W.Wick	107	39 65 C
Addington Sq. SE5	63	32 77 C
Addington St. SE1	7	30 79 B
Addis Cl. Enf	14	35 97 B
Addiscombe Ave. Croy	105	34 66 A
Addiscombe Cl. Har	33	17 88 A
Addiscombe Court Rd. Croy	105	33 65 A
Addiscombe Gr. Croy	105	33 65 A
Addiscombe Rd. Croy	105	34 65 A
Addison Ave. Houn	70	14 76 A
Addison Ave. N14	12	28 95 D
Addison Ave. W11	56	24 80 C
Addison Bridge Pl. W14	62	24 78 B
Addison Cl. Nthwd	19	10 90 A
Addison Cl. Orp	108	44 67 C
Addison Cres. W14	62	24 79 C
Addison Gdns. Surb	93	18 68 D
Addison Gdns. W14	62	23 79 B
Addison Gr. W4	61	21 79 C
Addison Pl. W11	56	24 80 C
Addison Rd. Brom	107	41 67 B
Addison Rd. E11	39	40 88 C
Addison Rd. E17	38	38 88 A
Addison Rd. Enf	14	35 97 B
Addison Rd. Ilf	28	44 90 A
Addison Rd. SE25	97	34 68 C
Addison Rd. W14	62	24 79 A
Addison's Cl. Croy	106	36 65 B
Addison Way. Nthwd	19	09 90 B
Addison Way. NW11	23	25 89 C
Addle Hill. EC4	3	31 81 D
Addle St. EC2	4	32 81 A
Adecroft Way. E Mol	92	14 68 A
Adela Ave. N Mal	94	22 68 D
Adelaide Ave. SE4	76	37 75 C
Adelaide Ct. Beck	98	37 70 C
Adelaide Gdns. Rom	41	48 88 A
Adelaide Gr. W12	55	22 80 C
Adelaide Rd. Chis	90	43 71 D
Adelaide Rd. E10	38	38 86 C
Adelaide Rd. Houn	70	12 76 A
Adelaide Rd. Ilf	40	43 86 B
Adelaide Rd. NW3	47	27 84 C

Adelaide Rd. Rich 71   18 75 D
Adelaide Rd. Sthl 59   12 78 A
Adelaide Rd. Surb 101   18 67 A
Adelaide Rd. Tedd 93   15 70 B
Adelaide Rd. W13 60   16 79 A
Adelaide St. WC2 7   30 80 A
Adela St. W10 56   31 75 C
Adelina Gr. E1 57   24 82 C
Adeline Pl. WC1 2   35 81 A
Adelphi Cres. Horn 42   29 81 B
Adelphi Terr. WC2 7   52 86 A
Adeney Cl. W6 62   30 80 A
Aden Gr. N16 48   23 77 B
Adenmore Rd. SE6 88   32 85 B
Aden Rd. Enf 14   33 73 A
Aden Rd. Ilf 40   36 96 C
Aden Terr. N16 48   44 87 A
Adie Rd. W6 62   32 85 B
Adine Rd. E13 58   23 79 C
Adler St. E1 57   40 82 D
Adley St. E5 49   34 81 C
Admaston Rd. SE18 66   36 85 C
Admiral Mews. W10 56   44 77 A
Admiral Seymour Rd. SE9 7   23 82 D
Admiral St. SE8 76   42 75 D
Admiral's Wlk. NW3 35   37 76 A
Admiralty Rd. Tedd 93   26 86 C
Adolf St. SE6 88   15 70 B
Adolphus Rd. N4 37   37 71 B
Adolphus St. SE8 64   31 87 D
Adomar Rd. Dag 41   36 77 D
Adpar St. W2 1   48 86 C
Adrian Ave. NW2 34   26 81 B
Adrian Mews. SW10 62   22 87 D
Adrienne Ave. Sthl 53   25 77 B
Adys Rd. SE15 75   12 82 B
Aerodrome Rd. NW4 22   34 75 A
Aerodrome Rd. NW9 22   22 89 A
Aerodrome Way. Houn 59   21 89 B
Aeroville. NW9 22   11 77 A
Affleck St. N1 47   21 90 C
Afghan Rd. SW11 74   30 83 D
Agamemnon Rd. NW6 46   27 76 C
Agar Cl. Surb 101   24 85 D
Agar Gr. NW1 47   18 65 B
Agar Pl. NW1 47   29 84 D
Agar St. WC2 7   29 84 C
Agate Rd. W6 62   30 80 A
Agatha Cl. E1 57   23 79 C
Agaton Path. SE9 90   34 80 D
Agaton Rd. SE9 90   44 72 A
Agave Rd. NW2 46   44 72 A
Agdon St. EC1 3   23 85 A
Agincourt Rd. NW3 47   31 82 D
Agnes Ave. Ilf 51   27 85 B
Agnes Gdns. Dag 52   43 85 B
Agnes Rd. W3 61   47 85 B
Agnes St. E14 58   21 79 B
Agnew Rd. SE23 88   36 81 D
Agricola Pl. Enf 13   35 73 B
Aidan Cl. Dag 52   33 95 B
Aileen Wlk. E15 50   48 85 A
Ailsa Ave. Twick 71   39 84 D
Ailsa Rd. Twick 71   16 74 B
Ailsa St. E14 58   16 74 B
Ainger Mews. NW3 47   38 81 A
Ainger Rd. NW3 47   27 84 D
Ainsdale Cl. Orp 108   27 84 D
Ainsdale Cres. Pnr 20   44 66 D
Ainsdale Rd. W5 54   13 89 A
Ainsley Ave. Rom 41   17 82 D
Ainsley St. E2 57   50 88 C
Ainslie Wlk. SW12 86   34 82 B
Ainslie Wood Cres. E4 18   28 73 B
Ainslie Wood Gdns. E4 18   37 92 D
Ainslie Wood Rd. E4 18   37 92 D
Ainsworth Cl. NW2 34   37 92 D
Ainsworth Estate. NW8 46   22 86 C
Ainsworth Rd. Croy 105   26 83 A
Ainsworth Rd. E9 49   31 65 B
Ainsworth Way. NW8 46   35 84 C
Aintree Ave. E6 50   26 83 A
Aintree Cres. Ilf 28   42 83 A
Aintree Gr. Horn 42   44 90 C
Aintree Rd. Grnf 44   54 86 D
Aintree St. SW6 62   16 83 B
Airdrie Cl. N1 47   30 84 D
Airedale Avenue S. W4 61   21 78 D
Airedale Ave. W4 61   21 78 D
Airedale Rd. SW12 86   27 73 B
Airedale Rd. W5 60   17 79 D
Airlie Gdns. Ilf 40   43 87 D
Airlie Gdns. W8 56   25 80 C
Air St. W1 6   29 80 A

Airthrie Rd. Ilf 40   46 86 B
Aisgill Ave. SW5 62   24 78 D
Aislibie Rd. SE12 77   39 75 C
Aitken Cl. E8 48   34 83 A
Aitken Rd. Barn 11   23 95 A
Aitken Rd. SE6 88   37 72 B
Ajax Ave. NW9 22   21 89 A
Ajax Rd. NW6 46   25 85 C
Akehurst St. SW15 84   22 73 A
Akenside Rd. NW3 46   26 85 D
Akerman Rd. Surb 101   17 67 C
Akerman Rd. SW9 75   31 76 B
Alabama St. SE18 66   45 77 C
Alacross Rd. W5 60   17 79 B
Alan Cl. Dart 80   53 75 C
Alandale Dri. Pnr 19   10 90 B
Alan Dri. Barn 11   24 95 C
Alan Gdns. Rom 41   49 87 A
Alan Rd. SW19 85   24 71 C
Alanthus Cl. SE12 77   39 74 D
Alaska St. SE1 7   31 80 C
Albacore Cres. SE13 76   37 74 D
Alba Gdns. NW11 35   24 88 C
Albany Cl. N15 25   32 89 C
Albany Cl. SW14 72   19 75 D
Albany Courtyard. W1 6   29 80 A
Albany Cres. Edg 22   19 91 C
Albany Mews. SE5 63   32 77 A
Albany Park Ave. Enf 14   35 97 B
Albany Park Rd. King 93   18 70 A
Albany Pas. Rich 71   18 74 B
Albany Pl. Brent 60   18 77 A
Albany Pl. N7 47   31 85 A
Albany Rd. Belv 67   48 77 B
Albany Rd. Brent 60   17 77 B
Albany Rd. Chis 90   43 71 D
Albany Rd. E10 38   37 87 A
Albany Rd. E12 50   41 85 B
Albany Rd. E17 38   36 88 C
Albany Rd. Horn 42   52 87 C
Albany Rd. N18 41   35 92 C
Albany Rd. N4 37   31 88 C
Albany Rd. N Mal 94   20 68 D
Albany Rd. Rich 71   18 74 A
Albany Rd. Rom 41   48 88 D
Albany Rd. SE5 63   33 77 A
Albany Rd. SW19 85   25 71 D
Albany Rd. W13 46   16 80 B
Albany St. NW1 2   28 82 B
Albany The. Tedd 93   17 70 B
Alba Pl. W11 56   24 81 D
Albatross St. SE18 66   45 77 C
Albemarle App. Ilf 40   43 88 D
Albemarle Gdns. Twick 71   12 73 D
Albemarle Gdns. Ilf 40   43 88 D
Albemarle Rd. Barn 16   27 94 A
Albemarle Rd. Beck 88   38 69 A
Albemarle St. W1 6   29 80 A
Albemarle Way. EC1 3   23 72 B
Alberon Gdns. NW11 23   24 89 D
Alberta Ave. Sutt 110   24 64 D
Alberta Rd. Enf 14   34 95 C
Alberta Rd. Eri 79   50 76 A
Alberta St. SE17 63   31 78 D
Albert Ave. E4 18   37 92 A
Albert Ave. SW8 10   30 77 D
Albert Bridge Rd. SW11 74   27 76 B
Albert Bridge Rd. SW11 9   27 77 D
Albert Bridge. SW3 9   27 77 A
Albert Carr Gdns. SW16 86   30 71 C
Albert Cl. N22 24   29 90 B
Albert Cres. E4 18   37 92 A
Albert Ct. SW19 85   24 73 C
Albert Dri. SW19 85   24 73 C
Albert Emb. SE1 10   30 78 A
Albert Gdns. E1 57   35 81 D
Albert Gr. SW20 95   23 69 B
Albert Mews. W8 5   26 79 C
Albert Palace Mansions. SW11 74   28 76 A
Albert Pl. N3 23   25 90 A
Albert Pl. W8 5   25 79 B
Albert Rd. Barn 11   26 96 C
Albert Rd. Belv 67   48 78 D
Albert Rd. Bex 79   49 74 C
Albert Rd. Brom 107   42 67 A
Albert Rd. Dag 41   49 87 C
Albert Rd. E10 38   38 87 C
Albert Rd. E16 66   43 79 A
Albert Rd. E17 38   37 88 A
Albert Rd. E18 27   40 89 B
Albert Rd. Hamp 82   14 71 C
Albert Rd. Har 20   14 89 A
Albert Rd. Houn 70   13 75 C

Albert Rd. Ilf 40   44 86 C
Albert Rd. King 93   18 69 D
Albert Rd. Mit 96   27 68 B
Albert Rd. N15 37   33 88 C
Albert Rd. N22 24   29 90 A
Albert Rd. N4 36   30 87 B
Albert Rd. N.Mal 102   21 67 B
Albert Rd. NW6 46   24 83 D
Albert Rd. Orp 108   46 67 D
Albert Rd. Rich 71   18 74 B
Albert Rd. Rom 42   51 88 D
Albert Rd. SE20 98   35 70 B
Albert Rd. SE25 105   34 67 B
Albert Rd. SE25 98   34 68 C
Albert Rd. SE9 89   42 72 C
Albert Rd. Sthl 59   11 79 D
Albert Rd. Sutt 110   26 64 D
Albert Rd. Tedd 93   15 70 B
Albert Rd. Twick 83   15 73 D
Albert Rd. W5 54   16 82 D
Albert Sq. E15 50   39 85 C
Albert Sq. SW8 74   30 76 B
Albert St. N12 15   26 92 C
Albert St. NW1 47   28 83 B
Albert Terrace Mews. NW1 7   28 83 A
Albert Terr. NW1 47   28 83 A
Albert Wlk. E16 66   43 79 A
Albion Ave. N10 4   28 90 A
Albion Ave. SW8 74   29 76 D
Albion Bldgs. EC1 4   32 81 A
Albion Cl. Rom 41   50 88 D
Albion Cl. W2 5   27 80 A
Albion Dri. E8 48   34 84 C
Albion Estate. SE16 64   35 79 A
Albion Gdns. Dag 52   49 85 C
Albion Gdns. W6 61   22 78 B
Albion Gr. N16 48   33 85 A
Albion Mews. N1 48   31 84 C
Albion Mews. W2 5   27 80 A
Albion Pl. EC1 3   31 81 B
Albion Pl. EC2 4   32 81 B
Albion Pl. SE25 97   34 68 A
Albion Rd. Bexh 79   49 75 C
Albion Rd. Dag 52   49 85 C
Albion Rd. E17 26   38 89 A
Albion Rd. Houn 70   13 75 C
Albion Rd. N16 48   32 85 B
Albion Rd. N17 25   34 90 C
Albion Rd. N Mal 94   20 69 A
Albion Rd. Sutt 110   26 63 D
Albion Rd. Twick 83   15 73 C
Albion Sq. E8 48   33 84 D
Albion St. Croy 105   31 66 D
Albion St. SE16 64   35 79 A
Albion St. W2 5   27 80 A
Albion Terr. E8 48   33 84 D
Albion Villas Rd. SE26 98   35 72 C
Albion Way. SE13 76   38 75 C
Albion Way. Wem 34   19 86 D
Albrighton Rd. SE22 75   33 75 A
Albuhera Cl. Enf 13   31 97 A
Albury Ave. Bexh 79   48 76 C
Albury Ave. Islw 60   15 77 D
Albury Ave. Sutt 110   23 62 C
Albury Cl. Hamp 92   13 70 B
Albury Ct. S Croy 112   32 64 A
Albury Ct. Sutt 110   26 64 A
Albury Dri. Pnr 20   11 91 D
Albury Rd. SE8 64   37 77 A
Albyfield. Brom 99   42 68 B
Albyn Rd. SE8 76   37 76 A
Albyn Rd. SE8 76   37 76 D
Alcester Cres. E5 37   34 86 B
Alcester Rd. Wall 111   28 64 B
Alcock Cl. Wall 111   29 63 D
Alcock Rd. Houn 50   11 77 D
Alconbury Rd. E5 37   34 86 A
Alcorn Cl. Sutt 103   25 65 A
Aldborough Rd. Dag 52   50 84 A
Aldborough Rd. Horn 42   54 86 B
Aldborough Road N. Ilf 28   45 89 D
Aldborough Road S. Ilf 40   45 87 A
Aldbourne Rd. W12 55   22 80 C
Aldbridge St. SE17 63   33 78 C
Aldbury Ave. Wem 45   19 84 D
Aldbury Mews. N9 17   32 94 B
Aldebert Terr. SW8 10   30 77 D
Aldeburgh St. SE10 65   40 78 C
Alden Ave. E15 58   39 82 B
Aldenham St. NW1 47   29 83 D
Aldensley Rd. W6 61   22 79 D
Alderbrook Rd. SW12 86   28 73 B
Alderbury Rd. SW13 61   22 77 A
Alder Gr. NW2 34   22 86 B

Alderholt Way (off Lydney Cl). SE15	...63	33 77 C
Aldermanbury. EC2	...4	33 81 C
Aldermanbury Sq. EC2	...4	32 81 A
Alderman's Hill. N13	...16	30 92 B
Alderman's Wlk. EC2	...4	33 81 A
Aldermary Rd. Brom	...99	40 69 A
Aldermaston St. W10	...56	23 81 D
Alder Mews. N19	...36	29 86 A
Alderminster Rd. SE1	...63	34 78 C
Aldermoor Rd. SE6	...88	36 72 D
Alderney Ave. Houn	...59	13 77 D
Alderney Gdns. Nthlt	...43	12 84 D
Alderney Rd. E1	...57	35 82 D
Alderney Rd. Eri	...68	52 77 C
Alderney St. SW1	...9	28 78 D
Alder Rd. Sid	...90	45 72 D
Alder Rd. SW14	...72	20 75 B
Alders Ave. Wdf Gn	...27	39 91 A
Aldersbrook Ave. Enf	...13	33 97 C
Aldersbrook Dr. King	...93	18 70 B
Aldersbrook La. E12	...39	42 86 D
Aldersbrook Rd. E11	...39	40 86 B
Aldersbrook Rd. E12	...39	41 86 A
Aldersey Gdns. Bark	...51	44 84 B
Aldersgate St. EC1	...4	32 81 A
Aldersgrove Ave. SE9	...89	41 72 D
Aldershot Rd. NW6	...46	24 83 B
Aldersmead Ave. Croy	...106	33 67 D
Aldersmead Rd. Beck	...98	36 70 C
Alderson St. W10	...56	24 82 C
Alders The. Felt	...82	12 71 A
Alders The. Houn	...59	12 77 B
Alders The. N21	...13	31 95 C
Alders The. SW16	...86	29 71 A
Alders The. W Wick	...106	37 65 B
Alderton Cres. NW4	...34	22 88 B
Alderton Rd. Croy	...105	34 66 A
Alderton Rd. SE24	...75	32 75 A
Alderville Rd. SW6	...73	24 76 D
Alderwick Dri. Houn	...70	14 75 B
Alderwood Rd. SE9	...78	44 74 D
Aldford St. W1	...6	28 80 C
Aldgate Ave. EC3	...4	33 81 D
Aldgate. EC3	...4	33 81 C
Aldgate High St. EC3	...4	33 81 D
Aldine St. W12	...62	23 79 A
Aldington Rd. SE18	...65	41 79 D
Aldis Mews. SW17	...86	27 71 C
Aldis St. SW17	...86	27 71 C
Aldred Rd. NW6	...46	25 85 C
Aldren Rd. SW17	...85	26 72 C
Aldriche Way. E4	...26	38 91 A
Aldrich Terr. SW18	...85	26 72 A
Aldridge Ave. Ruis	...32	11 86 B
Aldridge Ave. Stan	...21	18 90 A
Aldridge Rd Villas. W11	...56	24 81 B
Aldridge Rise. N.Mal	...102	21 67 C
Aldridge Wlk. N14	...16	29 94 A
Aldrington Rd. SW16	...86	29 71 A
Aldsworth Cl. W9	...56	25 82 D
Aldwick Cl. SE9	...90	44 72 D
Aldwick Rd. Croy	...111	30 64 B
Aldworth Gr. SE13	...76	38 74 C
Aldworth Rd. E15	...50	39 84 C
Aldwych Ave. Ilf	...28	44 89 C
Aldwych Cl. Horn	...42	52 86 A
Aldwych. WC2	...3	30 81 D
Alers Rd. Bexh	...79	47 76 D
Alexander Ave. NW10	...45	22 84 D
Alexander Cl. Brom	...107	40 66 C
Alexander Cl. Sid	...78	45 74 C
Alexander Cl. Twick	...83	15 72 B
Alexander Ct. SE3	...77	40 76 D
Alexander Mews. W2	...56	25 81 D
Alexander Pl. SW7	...7	27 78 A
Alexander Rd. Bexh	...79	47 76 D
Alexander Rd. Chis	...90	43 71 D
Alexander Rd. N19	...36	30 86 A
Alexander Sq. SW3	...9	27 78 A
Alexander St. W2	...56	25 81 D
Alexandra Ave. Har	...32	13 88 A
Alexandra Ave. N22	...24	29 90 B
Alexandra Ave. Sthl	...53	12 80 B
Alexandra Ave. Sutt	...103	25 65 C
Alexandra Ave. SW11	...74	28 76 A
Alexandra Cl. Ashf	...91	08 70 D
Alexandra Cl. Har	...32	13 86 D
Alexandra Cottages. SE14	...76	36 76 B
Alexandra Cres. Brom	...99	39 70 B
Alexandra Ct. Wem	...44	18 85 B
Alexandra Dri. SE19	...97	33 70 A
Alexandra Dri. SE19	...87	33 71 C
Alexandra Dri. Surb	...102	19 66 A
Alexandra Gdns. Cars	...111	28 62 A
Alexandra Gdns. Houn	...70	13 76 D
Alexandra Gdns. N10	...24	28 89 D
Alexandra Gdns. W4	...61	21 77 C
Alexandra Gr. N12	...23	25 91 B
Alexandra Gr. N4	...37	31 87 D
Alexandra Park Rd. N10	...24	28 90 D
Alexandra Park Rd. N22	...24	29 90 B
Alexandra Pl. Croy	...105	33 66 C
Alexandra Pl. NW8	...46	26 83 A
Alexandra Pl. SE25	...105	32 67 B
Alexandra Rd. Ashf	...91	09 70 A
Alexandra Rd. Brent	...60	17 77 B
Alexandra Rd. Croy	...105	33 66 A
Alexandra Rd. E10	...38	38 86 C
Alexandra Rd. E17	...38	36 87 B
Alexandra Rd. E18	...27	40 89 B
Alexandra Rd. Enf	...14	35 96 D
Alexandra Rd. Eri	...68	51 77 B
Alexandra Rd. Houn	...70	13 76 D
Alexandra Rd. King	...94	19 70 C
Alexandra Rd. Mit	...96	27 70 C
Alexandra Rd. N10	...24	28 91 D
Alexandra Rd. N15	...37	32 88 B
Alexandra Rd. N8	...25	31 89 A
Alexandra Rd. N9	...17	34 94 B
Alexandra Rd. NW4	...23	23 89 D
Alexandra Rd. NW8	...46	26 84 C
Alexandra Rd. Rich	...71	18 76 D
Alexandra Rd. Rom	...41	48 88 C
Alexandra Rd. Rom	...42	51 88 D
Alexandra Rd. SE26	...98	35 70 B
Alexandra Rd. Surb	...101	15 67 B
Alexandra Rd. SW14	...72	20 75 B
Alexandra Rd. SW19	...95	24 70 B
Alexandra Rd. Twick	...71	17 74 C
Alexandra Rd. W4	...61	20 79 B
Alexandra Sq. Mord	...103	25 67 A
Alexandra St. E16	...58	40 81 A
Alexandra St. SE14	...64	36 77 C
Alexandra Wlk. SE19	...87	33 71 C
Alexandra Yd. E9	...49	35 83 B
Alexandria Rd. W13	...54	16 80 B
Alexis St. SE16	...63	34 78 A
Alfearn Rd. E5	...49	35 85 A
Alford Pl. N1	...48	32 83 C
Alford Rd. Eri	...67	50 78 C
Alfoxton Ave. N15	...25	31 89 D
Alfreda St. SW11	...74	28 76 B
Alfred Gdns. Sthl	...53	12 80 A
Alfred Mews. W1	...2	29 81 B
Alfred Pl. WC1	...2	29 81 B
Alfred Rd. Belv	...67	48 78 D
Alfred Rd. E15	...50	39 85 D
Alfred Rd. Felt	...82	11 72 A
Alfred Rd. King	...93	18 68 B
Alfred Rd. SE25	...105	34 67 A
Alfred Rd. Sutt	...110	26 64 C
Alfred Rd. W2	...56	25 81 A
Alfred Rd. W3	...55	20 80 C
Alfred Salter Rise. SE1	...63	33 78 B
Alfred's Gdns. Bark	...51	45 83 C
Alfred St. E16	...58	39 80 B
Alfred St. E3	...57	37 82 A
Alfred's Way. Bark	...51	45 83 C
Alfreton Cl. SW19	...85	23 72 D
Alfriston Ave. Croy	...104	30 66 A
Alfriston Ave. Har	...32	13 87 A
Alfriston Rd. SW11	...74	27 74 B
Alfriston. Surb	...101	18 67 D
Algar Cl. Islw	...71	16 75 A
Algar Rd. Islw	...71	16 75 A
Algarve Rd. SW18	...85	25 73 D
Algernon Rd. NW4	...34	22 88 C
Algernon Rd. NW6	...46	25 83 A
Algernon Rd. SE13	...76	37 75 D
Algiers Rd. SE13	...75	37 75 C
Alguin Ct. Stan	...21	17 91 C
Alice Gilliatt Ct. W14	...62	24 77 B
Alice St. SE1	...8	33 79 C
Alicia Ave. Har	...21	17 89 C
Alicia Cl. Har	...21	17 89 C
Alicia Gdns. Har	...21	17 89 C
Alie St. E1	...4	33 81 D
Alington Cres. NW9	...34	20 87 C
Alington Gr. Wall	...111	29 62 B
Aliwal Rd. SW11	...74	27 75 C
Alkerden Rd. W4	...61	21 78 C
Alkham Rd. N16	...37	33 86 B
Allan Cl. N.Mal	...102	20 67 B
Allandale Ave. N3	...23	24 89 B
Allandale Rd. Horn	...42	51 87 B
Allan Way. W3	...55	20 81 A
Allardyce St. SW4	...74	30 75 D
Allbrook Cl. Tedd	...83	15 71 C
Allcroft Rd. NW5	...47	28 84 A
Allenby Ave. S Croy	...112	32 62 A
Allenby Cl. Grnf	...53	13 82 A
Allenby Dri. Horn	...42	54 87 D
Allenby Rd. SE23	...88	36 72 C
Allenby Rd. Sthl	...53	13 81 B
Allen Cl. Sun	...91	10 69 B
Allendale Ave. Sthl	...53	13 81 C
Allendale Cl. SE26	...88	35 71 D
Allendale Cl. SE5	...75	32 76 B
Allendale Rd. Grnf	...44	16 84 B
Allen Edwards Dri. SW8	...74	30 76 A
Allen Rd. Beck	...98	35 68 D
Allen Rd. Croy	...105	31 66 C
Allen Rd. E3	...49	36 83 D
Allen Rd. N16	...48	33 85 A
Allen Rd. Sun	...91	10 69 D
Allensbury Pl. N7	...47	29 84 D
Allens Rd. Enf	...14	35 95 A
Allen St. W8	...62	25 79 C
Allenswood Rd. SE9	...77	42 76 D
Allerford Ct. Har	...32	14 88 A
Allerford Rd. SE6	...88	37 71 B
Allerton Rd. N16	...37	32 86 A
Allerton Wlk. N7	...36	30 86 B
Allestree Rd. SW6	...62	24 77 C
Alleyn Cres. SE21	...87	32 72 B
Alleyndale Rd. Dag	...41	47 86 A
Alleyn Park. SE21	...87	32 72 B
Alleyn Park. Sthl	...59	13 78 C
Alleyn Rd. SE21	...87	32 72 D
Allfarthing La. SW18	...73	26 74 C
Allgood Cl. Mord	...103	23 67 D
Allgood St. E2	...48	33 83 D
Allhallows La. EC4	...8	32 80 B
All Hallows Rd. N17	...25	33 90 A
Alliance Ct. Ashf	...81	08 71 A
Alliance Rd. E13	...58	41 81 A
Alliance Rd. SE18	...66	46 77 C
Alliance Rd. W3	...55	19 82 D
Allingham Cl. W7	...54	15 80 B
Allingham Ct. NW3	...47	27 85 C
Allingham Ct. NW3	...47	27 85 C
Allingham St. N1	...48	32 83 C
Allington Ave. N17	...25	33 91 A
Allington Cl. SW19	...85	23 71 D
Allington Rd. Har	...32	14 88 A
Allington Rd. NW4	...34	22 88 D
Allington Rd. Orp	...108	45 66 C
Allington Rd. W10	...46	24 83 C
Allington St. SW1	...6	28 79 D
Allison Cl. SE10	...76	38 76 A
Allison Gr. SE21	...87	33 73 C
Allison Rd. N8	...37	31 88 B
Allison Rd. W3	...55	20 80 A
Allitsen Rd. NW8	...47	27 83 C
Allnutt Way. SW4	...74	29 74 B
Alloa Rd. Ilf	...40	46 86 A
Alloa Rd. SE8	...64	36 78 C
Allonby Gdns. Wem	...33	17 87 C
Alloway Rd. E3	...57	36 82 A
All Saints Cl. N9	...17	34 93 A
All Saints Dri. SE3	...77	39 76 C
All Saints Pas. SW18	...73	25 74 A
All Saints Rd. Sutt	...103	26 65 C
All Saints Rd. SW19	...95	26 70 C
All Saints Rd. W11	...56	24 81 D
All Saints' Rd. W3	...61	20 79 C
All Saints St. N1	...47	30 83 D
Allsop Pl. NW1	...1	27 82 D
All Souls' Ave. NW10	...45	22 83 B
All Souls Pl. W1	...2	28 81 B
Alium Way. N20	...15	26 94 C
Allwood Cl. SE26	...88	35 71 B
Alma Ave. E4	...26	38 91 C
Alma Ave. Horn	...42	54 86 C
Almack Rd. E5	...49	35 85 A
Alma Cottages. SW9	...74	30 75 A
Alma Cres. Sutt	...110	24 64 C
Alma Gr. SE1	...63	33 78 B
Alma Pl. NW10	...55	22 82 B
Alma Pl. SE19	...97	33 70 D
Alma Pl. Th Hth	...105	31 67 A
Alma Rd. Cars	...111	27 64 C
Alma Rd. Enf	...14	36 96 C
Alma Rd. Esh	...101	15 66 C
Alma Rd. N10	...24	28 91 D
Alma Rd. Sid	...90	46 72 C
Alma Rd. Sthl	...53	12 80 A
Alma Rd. SW18	...73	26 74 A
Alma Rd. SW18	...73	26 75 C
Alma Row. Har	...20	14 90 B
Alma Sq. NW8	...1	26 82 A
Alma Sq. NW8	...46	26 83 C
Alma St. E15	...49	38 84 B

Street	Pg	Ref
Alma St. NW5	47	28 84 B
Alma Terr. SW18	86	26 72 B
Almeida St. N1	48	31 84 D
Almeric Rd. SW11	74	27 75 D
Almer Rd. SW20	94	22 70 C
Almington St. N4	36	30 87 D
Almond Ave. Cars	104	27 65 B
Almond Ave. Uxb	37	07 86 D
Almond Ave. W5	60	18 79 C
Almond Cl. Brom	108	43 66 A
Almond Cl. Ruis	37	09 86 D
Almond Cl. SE15	75	34 76 C
Almond Cl. Shep	91	08 69 C
Almond Gr. Brent	60	16 77 D
Almond Rd. N17	25	34 91 C
Almond Rd. SE16	63	34 78 B
Almond Way. Brom	108	43 66 A
Almond Way. Har	20	14 90 C
Almond Way. Mit	96	29 68 D
Almorah Rd. Houn	70	11 76 B
Almorah Rd. N1	48	32 84 D
Alnwick Gr. Mord	95	25 68 D
Alnwick Rd. E16	58	41 81 C
Alnwick Rd. SE12	89	40 73 B
Alperton La. Wem	44	17 83 D
Alperton St. W10	56	24 82 D
Alpha Cl. NW1	1	27 82 C
Alpha Ct. SE25	105	33 67 A
Alpha Gr. E14	64	37 79 A
Alpha Pl. NW6	46	25 83 C
Alpha Pl. SW3	9	27 77 A
Alpha Rd. E4	18	37 93 D
Alpha Rd. Enf	14	36 96 C
Alpha Rd. N18	17	34 92 C
Alpha Rd. SE14	73	36 76 B
Alpha Rd. Surb	101	18 67 D
Alpha Rd. Tedd	82	14 71 D
Alpha St. SE15	75	34 76 C
Alpine Ave. Surb	102	20 65 A
Alpine Cl. Croy	105	33 66 C
Alpine Copse. Brom	107	43 69 C
Alpine Rd. SE16	64	35 78 D
Alpna Rd. Croy	107	33 66 C
Alric Ave. N Mal	94	21 68 A
Alric Ave. NW10	46	20 84 D
Alroy Rd. N4	37	31 87 A
Alsace Rd. SE17	63	33 78 C
Alscot Rd. SE1	63	33 79 D
Alscot Way. SE1	63	33 78 B
Alsike Rd. Belv	67	48 79 C
Alsom Ave. Wor Pk	109	22 64 A
Alston Cl. Surb	101	16 66 B
Alston Rd. Barn	11	24 96 A
Alston Rd. N18	17	34 92 D
Alston Rd. SW17	85	26 71 B
Altair Cl. N17	25	33 91 B
Altash Way. SE9	89	42 72 B
Altash Way. SE9	90	43 72 A
Altenburg Ave. W13	60	16 79 D
Altenburg Gdns. SW11	74	27 75 D
Alt Gr. SW19	95	24 70 D
Altham Rd. Pnr	20	12 91 C
Althea St. SW6	73	25 76 D
Althorne Gdns. E18	27	39 89 D
Althorne Way. Dag	41	49 86 A
Althorpe Mews. SW11	73	26 76 B
Althorpe Rd. Har	32	14 88 A
Althorp Rd. SW17	86	27 73 D
Altmore Ave. E6	50	42 84 D
Alton Ave. Stan	21	15 91 D
Alton Cl. Islw	71	15 76 D
Alton Gdns. Beck	98	37 70 C
Alton Gdns. Twick	82	14 73 B
Alton Rd. Croy	105	31 65 C
Alton Rd. N17	25	32 89 B
Alton Rd. Rich	71	18 75 C
Alton Rd. SW15	84	22 73 C
Alton St. E14	57	37 81 B
Altyre Cl. Beck	106	36 67 B
Altyre Rd. Croy	105	32 65 B
Altyre Way. Beck	106	36 67 B
Alvanley Gdns. NW6	46	25 85 D
Alverstoke Rd. Rom	30	54 91 C
Alverstone Ave. Barn	16	27 94 A
Alverstone Ave. SW19	85	25 72 A
Alverstone Gdns. SE9	90	44 73 C
Alverstone Rd. E12	51	43 85 A
Alverstone Rd. N Mal	94	21 68 D
Alverstone Rd. NW2	46	23 84 C
Alverstone Rd. Wem	33	18 87 D
Alverston Gdns. SE25	105	33 67 A
Alverton St. SE8	64	36 78 D
Alveston Ave. Har	21	16 89 B
Alvey St. SE17	63	33 78 C
Alvington Cres. E8	48	33 85 D
Alway Ave. Eps	109	20 64 D
Alwold Cres. SE12	77	40 74 D
Alwyn Ave. W4	61	20 76 D
Alwyne La. N1	48	31 84 D
Alwyne Pl. N1	48	32 84 C
Alwyne Rd. N1	48	32 84 C
Alwyne Rd. SW19	95	24 70 B
Alwyne Rd. W7	54	15 80 A
Alwyne Sq. N1	48	32 84 A
Alwyne Villas. N1	48	31 84 D
Alwyn Gdns. W3	55	19 81 D
Alyth Gdns. NW11	35	25 88 C
Amalgamated Dri. Brent	60	16 77 B
Amazon St. E1	57	34 81 D
Ambassador Cl. Houn	70	12 76 C
Amber Ave. E17	26	36 90 A
Amberden Ave. N3	23	25 89 A
Ambergate St. SE17	63	31 78 D
Amberley Cl. Pnr	20	12 89 B
Amberley Gdns. Enf	17	33 94 A
Amberley Gdns. Eps	109	21 64 B
Amberley Gr. Croy	105	33 66 B
Amberley Gr. SE26	87	34 71 D
Amberley Rd. E10	37	37 87 B
Amberley Rd. Enf	17	33 94 B
Amberley Rd. N13	16	30 93 D
Amberley Rd. SE2	67	47 77 B
Amberley Rd. W9	56	25 82 D
Amberley Way. Houn	70	11 74 A
Amberley Way. Mord	103	25 66 A
Amberley Way. Rom	29	49 89 D
Amber St. E15	49	38 84 B
Amberwood Rise. N Mal	102	21 67 C
Amblecote Cl. SE12	89	40 72 D
Amblecote Rd. SE12	89	40 72 D
Ambler Rd. N4	37	31 86 D
Ambleside Ave. Beck	106	36 67 A
Ambleside Ave. SW16	86	29 71 B
Ambleside. Brom	88	38 70 B
Ambleside Cl. E9	49	35 85 C
Ambleside Cres. Enf	14	35 96 B
Ambleside Gdns. Ilf	39	42 88 A
Ambleside Gdns. Sutt	110	26 63 A
Ambleside Gdns. Wem	33	17 87 D
Ambleside Rd. Bexh	79	49 76 C
Ambleside Rd. NW10	46	21 84 D
Ambrey Way. Wall	111	29 62 B
Ambrook Rd. Belv	67	49 79 C
Ambrosden Ave. SW1	6	29 79 C
Ambrose Cl. Orp	108	45 65 D
Ambrose Cl. SE16	64	34 78 B
Ambrose Wlk. E3	49	37 83 C
Amelia St. SE17	63	32 78 C
Amen Cnr. EC4	5	31 81 D
Amen Cnr. SW17	96	28 70 A
Amen Ct. EC4	5	31 81 D
America Sq. EC3	8	33 80 B
America St. SE1	8	32 80 C
Amerland Rd. SW18	73	24 74 D
Amersham Ave. N18	25	33 91 A
Amersham Ave. N18	17	33 92 C
Amersham Cl. Rom	30	54 91 B
Amersham Dri. Rom	30	54 91 B
Amersham Gr. SE14	64	36 77 D
Amersham Rd. Croy	105	32 67 D
Amersham Rd. Har	15	88 C
Amersham Rd. Rom	30	54 91 B
Amersham Rd. SE14	76	36 76 B
Amersham Vale. SE14	64	36 77 D
Amersham Wlk. Rom	30	54 91 B
Amery Gdns. NW10	46	23 83 A
Amery Gdns. Rom	30	53 89 B
Amery Rd. Har	33	16 86 A
Amesbury Ave. SW2	86	30 72 B
Amesbury Cl. Wor Pk	103	23 66 C
Amesbury Dri. E4	14	37 95 D
Amesbury Rd. Brom	99	41 68 B
Amesbury Rd. Dag	52	47 84 D
Amesbury Rd. Felt	82	11 72 B
Amethyst Rd. E15	49	38 85 B
Amherst Ave. W13	54	17 81 C
Amherst Cl. Orp	100	46 68 D
Amherst Dri. Orp	100	46 68 C
Amherst Rd. W13	54	17 81 C
Amhurst Gdns. Islw	71	16 76 C
Amhurst Park. N16	37	33 87 A
Amhurst Pas. N15	37	33 87 B
Amhurst Pas. E8	48	34 85 C
Amhurst Rd. E8	48	34 85 C
Amhurst Rd. N16	48	33 85 B
Amhurst Terr. E8	48	34 85 A
Amidas Gdns. Dag	51	46 85 B
Amiel St. E1	57	35 82 C
Amies St. SW11	74	27 75 B
Amina Way. SE16	63	34 79 C
Amis Ave. Eps	109	19 64 D
Amity Gr. SW20	95	23 69 C
Amity Rd. E15	50	39 84 D
Amner Rd. SW11	74	28 74 C
Amor Rd. W6	62	23 79 C
Amos Estate. SE16	57	35 80 D
Amott Rd. SE15	75	34 75 A
Amour Cl. N7	47	30 84 B
Amoy Pl. E14	57	37 80 A
Ampleforth Rd. SE2	67	47 79 A
Ampthill Rd. N8	24	30 89 B
Ampton Pl. WC1	3	30 82 B
Ampton St. WC1	3	30 82 B
Amroth Cl. SE23	87	34 73 D
Amwell Cl. Enf	13	32 95 B
Amwell St. EC1	3	31 82 A
Amyand Cottages. Twick	71	16 74 D
Amyand La. Twick	83	16 73 B
Amyand Park Gdns. Twick	83	16 73 B
Amyand Park Rd. Twick	83	16 73 A
Amyruth Rd. SE4	76	37 74 A
Anatola Rd. N19	36	28 86 B
Ancaster Cres. N Mal	102	22 67 C
Ancaster Rd. Beck	98	35 68 C
Ancaster St. SE18	66	45 77 C
Anchorage Cl. SW19	85	25 71 C
Anchor and Hope La. SE7	65	41 78 A
Anchor St. SE16	63	34 78 B
Anchor Yd. EC1	4	32 82 C
Ancill Cl. W6	62	24 77 A
Ancona Rd. NW10	55	22 83 C
Ancona Rd. SE18	66	44 78 D
Andalus Rd. SW9	74	30 75 A
Ander Cl. Wem	44	17 85 B
Anderson Dri. Ashf	81	08 71 A
Anderson Rd. E9	49	35 84 B
Anderson Rd. Ilf	27	41 89 D
Anderson's Pl. Houn	70	13 75 D
Anderson St. SW3	9	27 78 D
Anderton Cl. SE5	75	32 75 B
Anderton Ct. N22	23	29 90 D
Andover Cl. Eps	109	20 62 D
Andover Pl. NW6	46	25 83 D
Andover Rd. N7	36	30 86 B
Andover Rd. Orp	100	45 66 C
Andover Rd. Twick	82	14 73 D
Andre St. E8	48	34 85 C
Andrew Borde St. WC2	2	29 81 D
Andrew Cl. Dart	79	50 74 A
Andrew Cl. Ilf	28	44 91 B
Andrew Pl. SW8	74	29 76 B
Andrews Cl. Wor Pk	103	23 65 B
Andrews Crosse. WC2	3	31 81 C
Andrew's Rd. E8	48	34 83 B
Andrew St. E14	58	38 81 C
Andrews Wlk. SE17	63	31 77 B
Andromeda Ct. Rom	30	53 91 A
Andwell Cl. SE2	68	46 79 B
Anerley Gr. SE19	97	33 70 D
Anerley Hill. SE19	97	33 70 B
Anerley Park Rd. SE20	97	34 70 D
Anerley Park. SE20	97	34 70 D
Anerley Rd. SE19	97	34 70 C
Anerley Rd. SE20	97	34 69 B
Anerley Station Rd. SE20	97	34 69 B
Anerley St. SW11	74	27 76 D
Anerley Vale SE19	97	34 70 C
Aneurin Bevan Ct. NW2	34	22 86 B
Anfield Cl. SW12	86	29 73 A
Angel Alley. E1	4	33 81 D
Angel Cl. N18	17	34 92 A
Angel Cl. EC2	4	32 81 D
Angel Ct. SW1	6	29 80 C
Angelfield. Houn	70	13 74 B
Angel Hill Dri. Sutt	103	25 65 D
Angel Hill. Sutt	103	25 65 B
Angel La. E15	49	38 84 B
Angell Park Gdns. SW9	75	31 75 A
Angell Rd. SW9	75	31 75 B
Angel Mews. N1	48	31 83 C
Angel Pas. EC4	2	32 80 B
Angel Pl. N18	17	34 92 C
Angel Pl. SE1	8	32 79 B
Angel Rd. Har	32	15 88 C
Angel Rd. Surb	101	16 66 C
Angel St. EC1	4	32 81 C
Angel Way. Rom	42	51 88 A
Angel Wlk. W6	62	23 78 C
Angerstein La. SE3	79	39 76 B
Angle Green. Dag	41	47 87 C
Anglers Cl. Rich		17 71 A
Anglers La. NW5	47	28 84 B
Anglesea Ave. SE18	66	43 78 B
Anglesea Rd. King	93	17 68 D

Name	Page	Ref
Anglesea Rd. Orp	108	46 67 D
Anglesea Rd. SE18	66	43 78 B
Anglesea St. E1	57	34 82 C
Anglesey Cl. Ashf	81	07 72 C
Anglesey Ct Rd. Cars	111	28 63 A
Anglesey Gdns. Cars	111	28 63 A
Anglesey Rd. Enf	13	34 96 D
Anglesmede Cres. Pnr	20	13 89 A
Anglesmede Way. Pnr	20	13 89 A
Angles Rd. SW16	86	30 71 A
Anglia Wlk. E6	51	43 83 A
Anglo Rd. E3	49	36 83 D
Angns St. SE14	64	36 77 C
Angrave Pas. E8	48	33 83 B
Angus Cl. Chess	109	19 64 C
Angus Dri. Ruis	11	35 A
Angus Gdns. NW9	22	20 90 B
Angus Rd. E13	58	41 82 A
Anhalt Rd. SW11		27 77 C
Ankerdine Cres. SE18	78	43 76 B
Anlaby Rd. Tedd	83	15 71 C
Anley Rd. W14	62	23 79 B
Anmersh Gr. Stan	21	17 90 B
Annabel Cl. E14	57	37 81 D
Annandale Gr. Ruis	31	08 86 C
Annandale Rd. Croy	105	34 65 A
Annandale Rd. E10	65	39 78 D
Annandale Rd. Sid	90	45 73 B
Annandale Rd. W4	61	21 78 C
Annan Way. Rom	30	53 90 A
Anne Boleyn's Wlk. King	83	18 71 C
Anne Boleyn's Wlk. Sutt	110	24 63 C
Anne of Cleves Rd. Dart	80	53 74 D
Annesley Ave. NW9	22	20 89 B
Annesley Cl. NW10	34	21 86 C
Annesley Dri. Croy	106	36 65 D
Annesley Rd. SE3	77	40 76 B
Anne St. E13	58	40 82 C
Annett Cl. Shep	91	09 68 C
Annette Cl. Har	21	15 90 C
Annette Rd. N7	47	30 85 B
Anne Way. E Mol	92	13 68 D
Anne Way. Ilf	28	44 91 A
Annie Besant Cl. E3	49	36 83 B
Anning St. EC2	4	33 82 C
Annington Rd. N2	24	27 89 B
Annis Rd. E9	49	36 84 A
Ann La. SW10	62	26 77 B
Ann's Cl. SW1	6	28 79 A
Ann St. SE18	58	44 78 B
Annsworthy Ave. Th Hth	97	32 68 B
Ansdell Rd. SE15	76	35 76 C
Ansdell St. W8	62	25 79 D
Ansdell Terr. W8	62	25 79 D
Ansell Gr. Cars	104	28 65 A
Ansell Rd. SW17	86	27 72 D
Anselm Cl. Croy	105	33 65 D
Anselm Rd. Pnr	20	12 91 D
Anselm Rd. SW6	62	25 77 A
Ansford Rd. Brom	88	38 71 B
Ansleigh Pl. W11	23	23 80 B
Anson Cl. Rom	29	49 90 D
Anson Rd. N7	47	29 85 B
Anson Rd. NW2	46	23 85 C
Anstey Rd. E16	58	40 81 B
Anstey Rd. SE15	75	34 75 A
Anstey Wlk. N15	29	32 89 C
Anstice Cl. W4	61	21 77 C
Anstridge Path. SE9	78	44 74 D
Anstridge Rd. SE9	78	44 74 D
Antelope Rd. SE18	66	42 79 D
Anthony Rd. Grnf	44	15 83 C
Anthony Rd. SE25	105	34 67 C
Anthony Rd. Well	78	46 76 A
Anthony St. E1	57	34 81 D
Antill Rd. E3	57	36 82 A
Antill Rd. E3	49	36 83 D
Antill Rd. N15	25	34 89 C
Antill Terr. E1	57	35 81 D
Antlers Hill. E4	14	37 95 B
Anton Cres. Sutt	103	25 65 C
Antoneys Cl. Pnr	20	11 90 D
Anton St. E8	48	34 85 C
Antrim Gr. NW3	47	27 84 B
Antrim Rd. NW3	47	27 84 B
Antrobus Cl. Sutt	110	24 64 D
Antrobus Rd. W4	61	20 79 C
Anvil Rd. Sun	91	10 68 A
Anworth Cl. Wdf Gn	27	40 91 B
Apeldoorn Dri. Wall	111	30 62 A
Aperfield Rd. Eri	68	51 77 B
Apex Cl. Beck	98	37 69 B
Aplin Way. Islw	71	15 76 A
Apollo Ave. Brom	99	40 69 B
Apollo Cl. Horn	42	52 86 A
Apollo Pl. SW10	62	26 77 D
Apothecary St. EC4	3	31 81 D
Appach Rd. SW2	75	31 74 C
Appleby Cl. E4	26	38 91 A
Appleby Cl. N15	37	32 88 B
Appleby Cl. Twick	82	14 72 B
Appleby Rd. E16	58	40 81 C
Appleby Rd. E8	48	34 84 C
Appleby St. E2	48	33 83 D
Appledore Ave. Bexh	79	50 76 D
Appledore Ave. Ruis	32	11 86 C
Appledore Cl. Brom	107	40 67 A
Appledore Cl. Edg	22	19 90 A
Appledore Cl. Rom	30	53 90 A
Appledore Cl. SW17	86	27 72 B
Appledore Cres. Sid	90	45 72 D
Appleford Rd. W10	56	24 82 C
Apple Garth. Brent	60	17 78 B
Applegarth Dri. Ilf	28	45 89 D
Applegarth Rd. W14	62	23 79 D
Apple Gr. Enf	13	33 96 A
Apple Market. King	93	17 69 D
Appleton Gdns. N Mal	102	22 67 C
Appleton Rd. SE9	77	42 75 A
Appleton Way. Horn	42	53 87 D
Apple Tree Yd. SW1	6	29 80 C
Applewood Cl. NW2	34	22 86 D
Appold St. EC2	4	32 79 D
Appold St. Eri	68	51 77 B
Approach Cl. N16	48	33 85 A
Approach Rd. Ashf	91	08 70 A
Approach Rd. Barn	11	26 96 D
Approach Rd. E2	49	35 83 C
Approach Rd. Edg	22	19 91 A
Approach Rd. SW20	95	23 69 C
Approach The. Enf	12	34 97 D
Approach The. NW4	35	23 88 B
Approach The. Orp	108	45 65 B
Approach The. W3	55	20 81 D
Aprey Gdns. NW4	23	23 89 C
April Cl. Felt	81	10 72 C
April Cl. W7	54	15 80 A
April Glen. SE23	88	35 72 D
April St. E8	48	33 85 B
Apsley Cl. Har	32	14 88 A
Apsley Rd. N Mal	94	20 68 A
Apsley Rd. SE25	97	34 68 D
Apsley Rd. SW18	73	25 74 B
Apsley Way. W1	7	28 79 A
Aquinas St. SE1	7	31 80 C
Arabella Dri. SW15	72	21 75 C
Arabia Cl. E4	18	38 94 B
Arabin Rd. SE4	76	36 75 D
Aragon Ave. Eps	109	22 62 B
Aragon Ave. Surb	101	15 67 B
Aragon Ct. Ilf	28	44 91 C
Aragon Dri. Ilf	28	44 91 C
Aragon Dri. Ruis	32	11 87 D
Aragon Rd. King	83	18 71 C
Aragon Rd. Mord	103	24 66 A
Arandora Cres. Rom	30	46 88 D
Arbery Rd. E3	49	36 83 C
Arbor Ct. N16	31	32 86 B
Arbor Rd. E4	18	38 93 D
Arbour Rd. Enf	14	35 96 B
Arbour Sq. E1	57	35 81 D
Arbroath Rd. SE9	77	42 75 A
Arbury Terr. SE26	87	34 72 D
Arbuthnot La. Bex		48 74 C
Arbuthnot Rd. SE14	76	35 76 D
Arbutus St. E8	48	33 83 B
Arcade Pl. Rom	42	51 88 A
Arcade The. Bark	51	44 84 C
Arcade The. E17	26	38 88 B
Arcade. The EC2	4	33 81 A
Arcadia Ave. N3	23	25 90 C
Arcadian Ave. Bex	79	48 74 C
Arcadian Cl. Bex	79	48 74 C
Arcadian Gdns. N22	25	31 91 C
Arcadian Rd. Bex	79	48 74 C
Arcadia St. E14	57	37 81 C
Archbishop's Pl. SW2	86	30 73 B
Archdale Rd. SE22	75	30 75 D
Archel Rd. W14	62	24 77 B
Archer Rd. Orp	108	46 67 A
Archer Rd. SE25	97	34 68 D
Archers Dri. Enf	14	35 97 C
Archer St. W1	6	29 80 B
Archers Wlk. SE15	75	33 76 B
Archery Cl. Har	21	15 89 B
Archery Cl. W2	1	27 81 C
Archery Rd. SE9	77	42 74 B
Arches The. Har	32	13 86 B
Arches. The WC2	6	30 80 C
Archibald Mews. W1	6	28 80 B
Archibald Rd. N7	47	29 85 B
Archibald St. E3	57	37 82 A
Arch St. SE1	8	32 79 C
Archway Cl. SW19	85	25 71 B
Archway Mall. N19	36	29 86 A
Archway Rd. N19	36	29 87 C
Archway Rd. N6	36	28 87 B
Archway. Rom	30	52 91 B
Archway St. SW13	72	21 75 A
Arcola St. E8	48	33 85 D
Arctic St. NW5	47	28 85 D
Arcus Rd. Brom	99	39 70 A
Ardbeg Rd. SE24	75	32 74 B
Arden Cl. Har	32	14 86 D
Arden Cres. Dag	52	47 84 D
Arden Mhor. Pnr	19	10 89 D
Arden Rd. N3	23	24 89 B
Arden Rd. W13	54	17 80 A
Ardfern Ave. SW16	97	31 68 A
Ardfillan Rd. SE6	88	38 72 B
Ardgowan Rd. SE6	88	39 73 C
Ardhay Gdns. Surb	101	18 67 A
Ardilaun Rd. N5	48	32 85 A
Ardleigh Cl. Horn	30	53 89 B
Ardleigh Gdns. Sutt	103	25 66 A
Ardleigh Green Rd. Horn	30	53 89 D
Ardleigh Mews. Ilf	40	43 86 D
Ardleigh Rd. E17	26	36 90 B
Ardleigh Rd. N1	48	33 84 A
Ardleigh Terr. E17	26	36 90 B
Ardley Cl. NW10	34	21 86 C
Ardley Cl. Ruis	31	08 87 A
Ardley Cl. SE6	88	36 72 C
Ardlui Rd. SE27	87	32 72 A
Ardmere Rd. SE13	76	38 74 D
Ardoch Rd. SE6	88	38 72 B
Ardrossan Gdns. Wor Pk	102	22 65 C
Ardshiel Cl. SW15	73	23 75 B
Ardwell Ave. Ilf	40	44 88 A
Ardwell Rd. SW2	86	30 72 A
Ardwick Rd. NW2	46	25 85 A
Argall Ave. E10	38	35 67 D
Argon Mews. SW6	62	25 77 C
Argus Cl. Rom	29	49 90 B
Argus Way. Nthlt	53	12 82 A
Argyle Ave. Houn	70	13 74 C
Argyle Cl. W3	54	16 82 C
Argyle Pass. N17	25	33 90 B
Argyle Pl. W6	61	22 78 B
Argyle Rd. Barn	11	23 96 C
Argyle Rd. E15	50	39 85 A
Argyle Rd. E16	58	41 81 C
Argyle Rd. E1	57	35 82 D
Argyle Rd. Har	32	13 88 D
Argyle Rd. Houn	70	13 74 B
Argyle Rd. Ilf	40	43 86 A
Argyle Rd. N12	15	25 92 D
Argyle Rd. N17	25	34 90 A
Argyle Rd. N18	17	34 92 A
Argyle Rd. W13	54	16 81 A
Argyle Sq. WC1	3	30 82 A
Argyle St. WC1	3	30 82 A
Argyle Wlk. WC1	3	30 82 A
Argyll Ave. Sthl	53	13 80 D
Argyll Cl. SW9	74	30 75 B
Argyll Gdns. Edg	22	19 90 B
Argyll Rd. W8	62	25 79 A
Argyll St. W1	2	29 81 C
Arica Rd. SE4	76	36 75 A
Ariel Rd. NW6	46	25 84 A
Ariel Way. W12	56	23 80 C
Aristotle Rd. SW4	74	29 75 D
Arkell Gr. SE19	97	31 70 D
Arkindale Rd. SE6	88	38 72 C
Arkley Cres. E17	38	36 88 B
Arkley Rd. E17	38	36 88 B
Arklow Rd. SE14	64	36 77 B
Arkwright Rd. NW3	46	26 85 C
Arkwright Rd. S Croy	112	33 62 B
Arlesey Cl. SW15	73	24 74 A
Arlesford Rd. SW9	74	30 75 A
Arlingford Rd. SW2	75	31 74 C
Arlington Ave. N1	48	32 83 C
Arlington Cl. Sid	90	45 73 A
Arlington Cl. Sutt	103	25 65 A
Arlington Cl. Twick	71	17 74 A
Arlington Dri. Cars	104	27 65 B
Arlington Dri. Ruis	31	08 88 D
Arlington Gdns. Ilf	40	43 87 C
Arlington Gdns. Rom		54 90 A
Arlington Gdns. W4	61	20 78 B
Arlington. N12	15	25 93 C
Arlington Rd. N14	16	29 94 C
Arlington Rd. NW1	47	28 83 B
Arlington Rd. Rich	83	17 72 B

Street	Page	Grid
Arlington Rd. Surb	101	17 67 D
Arlington Rd. Tedd	83	15 71 B
Arlington Rd. Twick	71	17 74 C
Arlington Rd. W13	54	16 81 D
Arlington Rd. Wdf Gn	27	40 91 D
Arlington Sq. N1	48	32 83 A
Arlington St. SW1	6	29 80 C
Arlington Way. EC1	3	31 82 A
Arliss Way. Nthlt	43	11 83 A
Arlow Rd. N21	17	31 94 C
Armada Ct. SE8	64	37 77 A
Armadale Cl. N15	25	34 89 D
Armadale Rd. Felt	69	10 74 A
Armadale Rd. SW6	62	25 77 A
Armada St. SE8	64	37 77 A
Armagh Rd. E3	49	36 83 D
Armfield Cres. Mit	96	27 69 D
Armfield Rd. Enf	13	32 97 B
Arminger Rd. W12	55	22 80 D
Armitage Rd. E10	65	39 78 D
Armitage Rd. NW11	35	24 87 D
Armoury Way. SW18	73	25 74 A
Armstage Rd. Houn	59	11 77 D
Armstead Wlk. Dag	52	49 84 C
Armstrong Ave. Wdf Gn	27	39 91 A
Armstrong Cl. Pnr	21	10 88 C
Armstrong Cres. Barn	11	26 96 B
Armstrong Rd. Felt	82	12 71 C
Armstrong Rd. SW7	5	26 79 D
Armstrong Rd. W3	55	21 80 D
Armstrong Way. Sthl	59	13 79 B
Arnal Cres. SW18	85	24 73 A
Arndale Centre The. Dart	80	54 74 C
Arndale Centre The. SW18	73	25 74 D
Arndale Wlk. SW18	73	25 74 B
Arne Gr. Orp	108	45 65 D
Arne St. WC2	3	30 81 C
Arneways Ave. Rom	29	47 89 B
Arneway St. SW1	6	29 79 D
Arne Wlk. SE3	77	39 75 D
Arnewood Ct. SW15	84	22 73 C
Arney's La. Mit	104	28 67 C
Arngask Rd. SE6	88	38 73 B
Arnhem Way. SE22	75	33 74 A
Arnison Rd. E Mol	92	14 68 D
Arnold Circ. E2	4	33 82 B
Arnold Cl. Har	23	18 87 B
Arnold Cres. Islw	70	14 74 B
Arnold Gdns. N13	17	31 92 D
Arnold Rd. Dag	52	48 84 D
Arnold Rd. E3	57	37 82 A
Arnold Rd. N15	25	33 89 B
Arnold Rd. Nthlt	43	12 84 A
Arnold Rd. SW17	96	27 70 D
Arnos Gr. N14	16	29 93 D
Arnos Rd. N11	16	29 92 A
Arnott Cl. W4	61	20 78 B
Arnould Ave. SE5	75	32 75 D
Arnside Gdns. Wem	33	17 87 D
Arnside Rd. Bexh	79	49 76 A
Arnside St. SE17	63	32 77 B
Arnulf St. SE6	88	37 71 B
Arnull's Rd. SW16	97	31 70 B
Arodene Rd. SW2	74	30 74 D
Arragon Gdns. SW16	96	30 70 C
Arragon Gdns. W Wick	106	37 65 D
Arragon Rd. E6	50	41 83 B
Arragon Rd. Twick	83	16 73 A
Arran Cl. Eri	67	50 77 B
Arran Cl. Wall	111	29 64 A
Arran Dri. E12	39	41 86 B
Arran Rd. SE6	88	38 72 A
Arran Wlk. N1	48	32 84 C
Arras Ave. Mord	103	26 67 A
Arrol Rd. Beck	93	35 68 B
Arrow Rd. E3	57	37 82 B
Arrowscout Wlk (off Wayfarer Rd). Nthlt	53	12 82 A
Arsenal Rd. SE9	77	42 75 B
Arterberry Rd. SW20	95	23 69 B
Artesian Cl. Horn	42	51 87 B
Artesian Rd. W2	56	25 81 C
Arthingworth St. E15	58	39 83 A
Arthurdon Rd. SE4	76	37 74 A
Arthur Gr. SE18	66	44 78 A
Arthur Rd. E6	50	42 83 D
Arthur Rd. King		19 70 C
Arthur Rd. N7	36	30 86 D
Arthur Rd. N9	17	33 93 B
Arthur Rd. N.Mal	102	22 67 B
Arthur Rd. Rom		47 88 D
Arthur Rd. SW19	85	25 71 A
Arthur St. EC4	4	32 80 B
Arthur St. Eri	68	51 77 D
Artichoke Hill. E1	57	34 80 B
Artichoke Pl. SE5	75	32 76 B
Artillery Cl. Ilf	40	44 88 C
Artillery La. E1		33 81 A
Artillery Pas. E1		33 81 B
Artillery Pl. SE18	66	43 78 A
Artillery Row. SW1		29 79 D
Artizan St. E1		33 81 C
Arundel Ave.	109	22 62 D
Arundel Ave. Mord	95	24 68 D
Arundel Ave. S Croy	112	34 62 C
Arundel Cl. Bex	79	48 74 D
Arundel Cl. Croy	105	31 65 D
Arundel Cl. E15	50	39 85 A
Arundel Cl. Hamp	82	13 71 D
Arundel Ct. N17	25	34 90 A
Arundel Dri. Har	43	13 85 A
Arundel Dri. Wdf Gn	27	40 91 C
Arundel Gdns. Edg	22	20 91 D
Arundel Gdns. Ilf	40	46 86 A
Arundel Gdns. N21	31	31 94 C
Arundel Gdns. W11	56	24 80 B
Arundel Gr. N16	48	33 85 C
Arundel Pl. N1	48	31 84 A
Arundel Rd. Barn	12	27 96 A
Arundel Rd. Croy	105	32 67 D
Arundel Rd. Houn	70	11 75 A
Arundel Rd. King	94	20 69 C
Arundel Rd. Rom	30	54 90 B
Arundel Rd. Sutt	110	24 63 D
Arundel Sq. N1	48	31 84 A
Arundel Sq. N7	48	31 84 A
Arundel St. WC2	7	30 80 B
Arundel Ter. SW13	61	22 77 B
Arvon Rd. N5	48	31 85 C
Ascalon St. SW8	10	29 77 C
Ascension Rd. Rom	29	50 91 A
Ascham Dri. E4	26	37 91 C
Ascham End. E17	26	36 90 A
Ascham St. NW5	47	29 85 C
Aschurch Rd. Croy	105	33 66 B
Ascot Cl. Nthlt	43	13 85 C
Ascot Gdns. Sthl	53	13 81 A
Ascot Park. NW10	45	20 85 D
Ascot Rd. Felt	81	07 72 B
Ascot Rd. N15	37	32 88 B
Ascot Rd. N18	17	34 92 A
Ascot Rd. Orp	100	45 68 D
Ascot Rd. SW17	96	28 70 A
Ascott Ave. W5	60	18 79 A
Ashbourne Ave. Bexh	67	48 77 C
Ashbourne Ave. E18	27	40 89 D
Ashbourne Ave. Har	32	14 86 B
Ashbourne Ave. N20	16	27 93 B
Ashbourne Ave. NW11	35	24 88 B
Ashbourne Cl. N12	15	25 92 B
Ashbourne Cl. W5	55	19 81 A
Ashbourne Gr. SE22	75	33 75 D
Ashbourne Gr. W4	61	21 78 C
Ashbourne Rd. Mit	96	28 70 C
Ashbourne Rd. W5	54	18 82 D
Ashbourne Sq. Nthwd	19	09 91 A
Ashbourne Terr. SW19	95	25 70 C
Ashbourne Way. NW11	35	24 88 B
Ashbridge Rd. E11	39	39 87 B
Ashbridge St. NW8	1	27 82 C
Ashbrook Rd. Dag	52	49 86 D
Ashbrook Rd. N19	36	29 86 B
Ashburn Gdns. SW7	62	26 78 A
Ashburnham Ave. Har	32	15 88 D
Ashburnham Cl. N2	23	26 89 D
Ashburnham Gdns. Har	32	15 88 D
Ashburnham Gr. SE10	64	37 77 D
Ashburnham Pl. SE10	64	37 77 D
Ashburnham Rd. Belv	67	50 78 A
Ashburnham Rd. NW10	46	23 83 C
Ashburnham Rd. SW10	62	26 77 C
Ashburnham Retreat. SE10	64	37 77 D
Ashburn Mews. SW7	62	26 78 A
Ashburn Pl. SW7	62	26 78 A
Ashburton Ave. Croy	105	34 66 D
Ashburton Ave. Ilf	45	45 85 B
Ashburton Cl. Croy	105	34 66 C
Ashburton Gdns. Croy	105	34 65 A
Ashburton Gr. N7	48	31 85 A
Ashburton Rd. Croy	105	34 66 C
Ashburton Rd. E16	58	40 81 C
Ashburton Rd. Ruis	31	10 86 A
Ashburton Terr. E13	50	40 83 C
Ashbury Dri. Uxb	31	07 86 D
Ashbury Gdns. Rom	41	47 88 B
Ashbury Rd. SW11	74	28 76 C
Ashby Ave. Chess	109	19 63 A
Ashby Gr. N1	48	32 84 C
Ashby Mews. SE4	76	36 76 D
Ashby Rd. N15	37	34 88 A
Ashby Rd. SE4	76	36 76 D
Ashby St. EC1	3	31 82 B
Ashby Wlk. Croy	105	32 67 C
Aschurch Gr. W12	22	22 79 C
Aschurch Park Villas. W12	61	22 79 C
Aschurch Terr. W12	61	22 79 A
Ash Cl. Cars	104	27 65 B
Ash Cl. N Mal	94	20 69 D
Ash Cl. Orp	108	44 67 B
Ash Cl. Rom	29	49 91 D
Ash Cl. SE20	98	35 69 C
Ash Cl. Sid	90	46 72 D
Ash Cl. Stan	21	16 91 A
Ashcombe Ave. Surb	101	17 66 B
Ashcombe Park. NW2	34	21 86 C
Ashcombe Rd. Cars	111	28 63 A
Ashcombe Rd. SW19	85	25 71 C
Ashcombe Sq. N Mal	94	20 68 A
Ashcombe St. SW6	62	25 76 D
Ashcroft Ave. Sid	78	46 74 C
Ashcroft Cres. Sid	78	46 74 C
Ashcroft. Pnr	20	13 91 A
Ashcroft Rd. Chess	101	18 65 D
Ashcroft Rd. E3	57	36 82 A
Ashcroft Sq. W6	62	23 78 A
Ash Ct. Eps	109	20 64 A
Ashdale Cl. Twick	82	14 73 A
Ashdale Gr. Stan	21	15 91 B
Ashdale Rd. SE12	89	40 73 D
Ashdale Way. Twick	82	13 73 B
Ashdene Cl. Ashf	91	08 70 C
Ashdene. Pnr	20	11 89 A
Ashdon Cl. Wdf Gn	27	40 91 B
Ashdon Rd. NW10	45	21 83 B
Ashdown Cl. Beck	98	37 69 D
Ashdown Cres. NW5	28	28 85 C
Ashdown Rd. Enf	14	35 97 C
Ashdown Rd. King	93	18 69 C
Ashdown Wlk. Rom	29	49 90 B
Ashenden Rd. E5	49	36 85 C
Ashen Dri. Dart	80	52 74 C
Ashen Gr. SW19	85	25 72 A
Ashentree Ct. EC4	3	31 81 C
Ashfield Ave. Felt	81	10 73 D
Ashfield Cl. Rich	83	18 73 C
Ashfield La. Chis	100	44 70 C
Ashfield Par. N14	16	29 94 D
Ashfield Rd. N14	16	29 93 C
Ashfield Rd. N4	37	32 88 C
Ashfield Rd. W3	55	21 80 D
Ashfield St. E1	57	34 81 B
Ashford Ave. Ashf	91	07 70 B
Ashford Ave. Hay	53	11 81 D
Ashford Ave. N8	24	30 89 C
Ashford Cl. E17	38	36 88 D
Ashford Cres. Enf	14	35 97 C
Ashford Rd. Ashf	91	08 70 C
Ashford Rd. E18	27	40 90 D
Ashford Rd. E6	51	43 84 C
Ashford Rd. Felt	81	09 71 A
Ashford Rd. NW2	46	23 85 B
Ashford St. N1	4	33 82 A
Ash Gr(off Andrew's Rd). E8	49	34 83 B
Ash Gr(off Mare St). E8	48	34 83 B
Ash Gr. Enf	17	33 94 A
Ash Gr. Felt	81	09 73 C
Ash Gr. Houn	70	11 76 B
Ash Gr. N13	17	32 93 C
Ash Gr. NW2	46	24 85 A
Ashgrove Rd. Ashf	81	08 71 D
Ashgrove Rd. Brom	99	38 70 B
Ashgrove Rd. Ilf	40	46 87 C
Ash Gr. SE 20	98	35 69 C
Ash Gr. Sthl	53	13 81 A
Ash Gr. Wem	44	16 85 A
Ash Gr. W Wick	106	38 66 C
Ash Hill Dri. Pnr	20	11 89 A
Ash Hse. SE1	63	33 78 B
Ashington Rd. SW6	73	24 76 D
Ash La. Horn	30	54 89 D
Ashlake Rd. SW16	86	30 71 A
Ashland Pl. W1	2	28 81 A
Ash La. Rom	30	52 91 A
Ashlar Pl. SE18	66	43 78 B
Ashleigh Gdns. Sutt	103	25 65 B
Ashleigh Rd. SE20	97	34 68 B
Ashleigh Rd. SW14	72	21 75 A
Ashley Ave. Ilf	28	43 90 D
Ashley Ave. Mord	103	25 67 A
Ashley Cl. NW4	23	23 90 B
Ashley Cl. Pnr	19	10 90 D
Ashley Cres. N22	25	31 90 C

Ashley Cres. SW11 ... 74 — 28 75 A
Ashley Ct. NW4 ... 23 — 23 90 C
Ashley Dri. Twick ... 82 — 13 73 D
Ashley Gdns. N13 ... 17 — 32 92 A
Ashley Gdns. Rich ... 83 — 17 72 B
Ashley Gdns. Wem ... 33 — 18 86 A
Ashley La. Croy ... 112 — 31 64 B
Ashley La. NW4 ... 23 — 23 89 A
Ashley La. NW7 ... 23 — 23 91 D
Ashley Pl. SW1 ... 6 — 29 79 C
Ashley Rd. E4 ... 26 — 37 91 A
Ashley Rd. E7 ... 50 — 41 84 C
Ashley Rd. Enf ... 14 — 35 97 C
Ashley Rd. Hamp ... 92 — 13 69 A
Ashley Rd. N17 ... 25 — 34 89 A
Ashley Rd. N19 ... 36 — 30 87 A
*Ashley Rd. Rich ... 71 — 18 75 A
Ashley Rd. Surb ... 101 — 15 67 D
Ashley Rd. SW19 ... 95 — 25 70 B
Ashley Rd. Th Hth ... 96 — 30 68 D
Ashling Rd. Croy ... 105 — 34 66 C
Ashlin Rd. E15 ... 49 — 38 85 B
Ashlone Rd. SW15 ... 73 — 23 75 B
Ashlyn Gr. Horn ... 30 — 53 89 B
Ashmead. N14 ... 12 — 29 95 A
Ashmead Rd. Felt ... 81 — 10 73 C
Ashmead Rd. SE8 ... 76 — 37 76 C
Ashmere Ave. Beck ... 98 — 38 69 D
Ashmere Cl. Sutt ... 110 — 23 64 D
Ashmere Gr. SW2 ... 74 — 30 75 C
Ashmill St. NW1 ... 1 — 27 81 A
Ashmole Pl. SW8 ... 10 — 30 77 B
Ashmole St. SW8 ... 10 — 30 77 B
Ashmore Ct. Houn ... 59 — 13 71 A
Ashmore Gr. Well ... 78 — 45 75 A
Ashmore Rd. W9 ... 56 — 24 82 B
Ashmount Rd. N15 ... 37 — 33 88 B
Ashmount Rd. N19 ... 30 — 29 87 D
Ashmour Gdns. Rom ... 23 — 50 90 D
Ashness Gdns. Grnf ... 44 — 16 84 B
Ashness Rd. SW11 ... 74 — 27 74 B
Ash Rd. Croy ... 106 — 37 65 A
Ash Rd. E15 ... 50 — 31 85 D
Ash Rd. Shep ... 91 — 07 68 C
Ash Rd. Sutt ... 103 — 24 66 D
Ashridge Cl. Har ... 33 — 17 88 C
Ashridge Cres. SE18 ... 60 — 41 77 C
Ashridge Ct. N14 ... 12 — 29 95 A
Ashridge Gdns. N13 ... 16 — 30 92 C
Ashridge Gdns. Pnr ... 20 — 12 89 C
Ashridge Way. Mord ... 95 — 24 68 D
Ashridge Way. Sun ... 91 — 10 70 A
Ash Row. Brom ... 100 — 43 67 C
Ashtead Rd. E5 ... 37 — 34 87 A
Ashton Cl. Sutt ... 110 — 25 64 A
Ashton Gdns. Houn ... 70 — 12 75 D
Ashton Gdns. Rom ... 41 — 48 88 C
Ashton Rd. E15 ... 49 — 38 85 D
Ashton Rd. Rom ... 30 — 53 90 B
Ashton St. E14 ... 58 — 38 80 A
Ashtree Ave. Mit ... 96 — 27 69 C
Ash Tree Cl. Croy ... 106 — 34 67 C
Ash Tree Cl. Surb ... 101 — 18 66 C
Ash Tree Dell. NW9 ... 34 — 20 88 B
Ash Tree Way. Croy ... 106 — 36 67 A
Ashurst Cl. Dart ... 80 — 51 75 B
Ashurst Cl. Nthwd ... 19 — 09 91 C
Ashurst Cl. SE20 ... 97 — 34 69 B
Ashurst Dri. Ilf ... 40 — 43 88 B
Ashurst Rd. Barn ... 12 — 27 95 B
Ashurst Rd. N12 ... 16 — 27 92 C
Ashurst Wlk. Croy ... 105 — 34 65 B
Ashvale Rd. SW17 ... 86 — 27 71 D
Ashville Rd. E11 ... 38 — 38 86 B
Ashwater Rd. SE12 ... 89 — 40 73 C
Ashwin St. E8 ... 48 — 33 84 B
Ashwood Rd. E4 ... 18 — 38 93 D
Ashworth Rd. W9 ... 56 — 25 82 B
Aske St. N1 ... 4 — 33 82 A
Askew Bldgs. W12 ... 61 — 22 79 A
Askew Cres. W12 ... 61 — 21 79 B
Askew Rd. W12 ... 61 — 22 79 A
Askham Ct. W12 ... 55 — 22 80 C
Askham Rd. W12 ... 55 — 22 80 C
Askill Dri. SW15 ... 73 — 24 74 A
Askwith Rd. Rain ... 52 — 50 83 D
Asland Rd. E15 ... 50 — 39 83 A
Aslett St. SW18 ... 85 — 26 73 A
Aslett St. SW18 ... 73 — 26 74 C
Asmara Rd. NW2 ... 46 — 24 85 C
Asmuns Hill. NW11 ... 35 — 24 88 B
Asmuns Pl. NW11 ... 35 — 24 88 B
Aspen Cl. N19 ... 36 — 29 86 A
Aspen Cl. W5 ... 60 — 18 79 B
Aspen Copse. Brom ... 99 — 42 69 D

Aspen Dri. Wem ... 33 — 16 86 C
Aspen Gdns. Mit ... 104 — 28 67 A
Aspen Gdns. W6 ... 61 — 22 78 D
Aspen Green. Belv ... 67 — 48 79 D
Aspen La. Nthlt ... 53 — 12 82 A
Aspenlea Rd. W6 ... 62 — 23 77 B
Aspinall Rd. SE4 ... 76 — 35 75 B
Aspinden Rd. SE16 ... 63 — 34 78 B
Aspley Rd. SW18 ... 73 — 26 74 C
Asplins Rd. N17 ... 25 — 34 90 B
Assam St. E1 ... 57 — 34 81 C
Assembly Pas. E1 ... 57 — 35 81 A
Assembly Wlk. Cars ... 104 — 27 66 A
Astall Cl. Har ... 21 — 15 90 A
Astbury Rd. SE15 ... 76 — 35 76 A
Astell St. SW3 ... 9 — 27 78 C
Astern Cl. Bexh ... 79 — 47 75 D
Aste St. E14 ... 64 — 38 79 A
Astey's Row. N1 ... 48 — 32 84 C
Asthall Gdns. Ilf ... 28 — 44 89 C
Astle St. SW11 ... 74 — 28 76 C
Astley Ave. NW2 ... 46 — 23 85 C
Aston Ave. Har ... 33 — 17 87 A
Aston Cl. Sid ... 90 — 46 72 C
Aston Green. Houn ... 70 — 11 76 C
Aston Rd. SW20 ... 95 — 23 69 C
Aston Rd. W5 ... 54 — 17 81 D
Aston St. E14 ... 57 — 36 81 A
Astonville St. SW18 ... 85 — 25 73 C
Astor Ave. Rom ... 41 — 50 88 C
Astor Cl. King ... 94 — 19 70 B
Astoria Wlk. SW9 ... 75 — 31 75 A
Astrop Mews. W6 ... 62 — 23 79 C
Astrop Terr. W12 ... 62 — 23 79 A
Astwood Mews. SW7 ... 62 — 26 78 A
Asylum Rd. SE15 ... 63 — 34 77 D
Atalanta St. SW6 ... 62 — 23 77 D
Atbara Rd. Tedd ... 93 — 16 70 B
Atcham Rd. Houn ... 70 — 14 75 C
Atheldene Rd. SW18 ... 85 — 26 73 C
Athelney St. SE6 ... 88 — 37 72 C
Athelstan Cl. Rom ... 30 — 54 90 D
Athelstane Gr. E3 ... 49 — 36 83 D
*Athelstane Mews. N4 ... 37 — 31 87 C
Athelstan Rd. King ... 93 — 18 68 D
Athelstan Rd. Rom ... 30 — 54 90 D
Athelstone Rd. Har ... 20 — 14 90 D
Athenaeum Ct. N5 ... 48 — 32 85 A
Athenaeum Pl. N10 ... 24 — 28 89 B
Athenaeum Rd. N20 ... 15 — 26 94 D
Athena Pl. Nthwd ... 19 — 09 90 B
Athenlay Rd. SE15 ... 76 — 35 74 B
Atherden Rd. E5 ... 49 — 35 85 A
Atherfold Rd. SW9 ... 74 — 30 75 A
Atherley Way. Houn ... 82 — 12 73 B
Atherstone Mews. SW7 ... 62 — 26 78 A
Atherton Dri. SW19 ... 85 — 23 71 B
Atherton Hts. Wem ... 44 — 17 84 A
Atherton Mews. E7 ... 50 — 39 84 B
Atherton Pl. Har ... 20 — 14 89 B
Atherton Pl. Sthl ... 53 — 13 80 A
Atherton Rd. E7 ... 50 — 39 84 B
Atherton Rd. Ilf ... 27 — 27 77 C
Atherton Rd. SW13 ... 61 — 27 76 C
Atherton St. SW11 ... 74 — 34 85 D
Athlone Cl. E5 ... 48 — 31 73 A
Athlone Rd. SW2 ... 87 — 28 84 A
Athlone St. NW5 ... 47 — 17 83 D
Athlon Rd. Wem ... 44 — 10 90 B
Athol Cl. Pnr ... 19 — 33 95 A
Athol Gdns. Enf ... 13 — 10 90 B
Athol Gdns. Pnr ... 19 — 50 78 C
Athol Rd. Eri ... 67 — 46 87 A
Athol Rd. Ilf ... 40 — 38 81 C
Athol St. E14 ... 58 — 41 81 A
Atkinson Rd. E16 ... 58 — 37 88 D
Atkins Rd. E10 ... 38 — 29 73 B
Atkins Rd. SW12 ... 86 — 32 68 A
Atlanta Ct. Th Hth ... 97 — 41 78 A
Atlas Gdns. SE7 ... 65 — 30 84 B
Atlas Mews. N7 ... 47 — 40 83 C
Atlas Rd. E13 ... 50 — 21 82 A
Atlas Rd. NW10 ... 55 — 20 85 A
Atlas Rd. Wem ... 45 — 37 83 A
Atley Rd. E3 ... 49 — 24 75 C
Atney Rd. SW15 ... 73 — 31 88 D
Atterbury Rd. N4 ... 37 — 30 78 A
Atterbury St. SW1 ... 10 — 28 86 C
Attewood Ave. NW10 ... 34 — 12 84 A
Attewood Rd. Nthlt ... 43 — 34 72 B
Attleborough Ct. SE23 ... 87 — 37 89 D
Attlee Terr. E17 ... 26 — 31 82 A
Attneave St. WC1 ... 3 — 31 73 C
Atwater Cl. SW2 ... 87 — 34 76 C
Atwell Rd. SE15 ... 75 — (—)

Atwood Ave. Rich ... 72 — 19 76 C
Atwood Ho. SE21 ... 87 — 34 72 C
Atwood Rd. W6 ... 61 — 22 78 B
Aubert Ct. N5 ... 48 — 31 85 B
Aubert Park N5 ... 48 — 31 85 B
Aubert Rd. N5 ... 48 — 31 85 B
Aubrey Pl. NW8 ... 46 — 26 83 C
Aubrey Rd. E17 ... 26 — 37 89 A
Aubrey Rd. N8 ... 36 — 30 88 A
Aubrey Rd. W14 ... 56 — 24 80 D
Aubrey Wlk. W14 ... 56 — 24 80 D
Aubyn Hill. SE27 ... 87 — 32 71 A
Aubyn Sq. SW15 ... 72 — 22 74 A
Auckland Cl. SE19 ... 97 — 33 69 B
Auckland Gdns. SE19 ... 97 — 33 69 B
Auckland Hill. SE27 ... 87 — 32 71 A
Auckland Rd. E10 ... 38 — 37 86 D
Auckland Rd. Ilf ... 40 — 44 87 A
Auckland Rd. King ... 93 — 16 68 D
Auckland Rd. SE19 ... 97 — 33 69 B
Auckland Rd. SW11 ... 74 — 27 75 C
Auckland Rise. SE19 ... 97 — 33 69 A
Auckland St. SE11 ... 10 — 30 78 D
Auden Pl. NW1 ... 47 — 28 83 A
Audleigh Pl. Chig ... 28 — 43 91 A
Audley Ct. E18 ... 27 — 39 88 D
Audley Ct. Pnr ... 20 — 11 90 C
Audley Gdns. Ilf ... 40 — 45 86 B
Audley Pl. Sutt ... 110 — 25 63 D
Audley Rd. Enf ... 13 — 31 97 D
Audley Rd. NW4 ... 34 — 22 88 D
Audley Rd. Rich ... 72 — 18 74 B
Audley Rd. W5 ... 54 — 18 81 B
Audley Sq. W1 ... 6 — 28 80 C
Audrey Gdns. Wem ... 33 — 16 86 B
Audrey Rd. Ilf ... 40 — 43 86 D
Audrey St. E2 ... 48 — 34 83 C
Augurs La. E13 ... 58 — 40 82 B
Augusta Rd. Twick ... 82 — 14 72 A
Augusta St. E14 ... 57 — 37 81 D
Augustine Rd. Har ... 20 — 14 90 A
Augustine Rd. W14 ... 62 — 23 79 D
Augustus Cl. Brent ... 60 — 17 77 D
Augustus Cl. SE19 ... 97 — 33 70 C
Augustus Rd. SW19 ... 85 — 24 72 S
Augustus St. NW1 ... 2 — 28 83 B
Auila St. NW6 ... 46 — 26 83 D
Aultone Way. Cars ... 104 — 27 63 D
Aultone Way. Sutt ... 103 — 26 65 A
Aulton Pl. SE11 ... 63 — 31 78 C
Aurelia Gdns. Croy ... 104 — 30 67 D
Aurelia Rd. Croy ... 104 — 30 67 D
Auriel Ave. Dag ... 52 — 50 84 B
Auriga Mews. N16 ... 48 — 33 85 C
Auriol Cl. Wor Pk ... 102 — 21 65 C
Auriol Dri. Grnf ... 43 — 14 84 D
Auriol Park Rd. Wor Pk ... 102 — 21 65 C
Auriol Rd. W14 ... 62 — 24 78 A
Austen Gdns. Dart ... 80 — 54 75 D
Austen Rd. Har ... 32 — 13 86 B
Austin Ave. Brom ... 107 — 42 67 A
Austin Cl. SE6 ... 88 — 36 73 B
Austin Cl. E6 ... 50 — 41 83 A
Austin Friars. EC2 ... 4 — 32 81 D
Austin Friars Sq. EC2 ... 4 — 32 81 D
Austin Rd. Orp ... 108 — 46 67 A
Austin Rd. SW11 ... 74 — 28 76 A
Austin's La. Uxb ... 31 — 08 86 C
Austin St. E2 ... 4 — 33 82 B
Austral Cl. Sid ... 90 — 45 72 D
Austral Dr. Horn ... 42 — 53 87 B
Austral St. SE11 ... 63 — 31 78 B
Australia Rd. W12 ... 55 — 22 80 B
Austyn Gdns. Surb ... 102 — 19 66 D
Autumn Cl. Enf ... 13 — 34 97 A
Autumn St. E3 ... 49 — 37 83 A
Avalon Cl. Enf ... 13 — 31 97 C
Avalon Cl. W13 ... 54 — 16 81 A
Avalon Rd. Orp ... 108 — 46 65 B
Avalon Rd. SW6 ... 73 — 25 76 B
Avalon Rd. W3 ... 54 — 16 82 C
Avarn Rd. SW17 ... 96 — 27 70 B
Avebury Park. Surb ... 101 — 17 66 B
Avebury Rd. E11 ... 38 — 38 87 D
Avebury Rd. Orp ... 108 — 44 65 D
Avebury Rd. SW19 ... 95 — 24 69 B
Avebury St. N1 ... 48 — 32 83 B
Aveley Rd. Rom ... 30 — 51 89 C
Aveline St. SE11 ... 63 — 31 78 C
Aveling Park Rd. E17 ... 26 — 37 90 C
Avelon Rd. Rom ... 29 — 50 91 B
Ave Maria La. EC4 ... 3 — 31 81 D
Avenell Rd. N5 ... 48 — 31 85 B
Avenell Rd. N5 ... 37 — 31 86 D
Avening Terr. SW18 ... 85 — 25 73 A

Avening Terr. SW18	.85	25	73	A	Avery Hill Rd. SE9	.90	44	73	D	Ayres St. SE1	.8	32	79	A
Avenons Rd. E13	.58	40	82	C	Avery Hill Rd. SE9	.78	44	74	D	Ayr Green. Rom	.30	51	90	A
Avenue Cl. Houn	.69	10	76	B	Avery Row. W1	.6	28	80	B	Ayrsome Rd. N16	.37	33	86	C
Avenue Cl. N14	.12	29	95	C	Aviary Cl. E16	.58	39	81	B	Ayrton Rd. SW7	.5	26	79	D
Avenue Cl. NW8	.47	27	83	A	Aviemore Cl. Beck	.106	36	67	B	Ayr Way. Rom	.30	51	90	A
Avenue Cl. Rom	.30	54	91	D	Aviemore Way. Beck	.106	36	67	A	Aysgarth Ct. Surb	.103	25	65	D
Avenue Cres. W3	.61	19	79	B	Avignon Rd. SE4	.96	35	75	B	Aysgarth Rd. SE21	.87	33	73	A
Avenue Elmers. Surb	.101	18	67	A	Avington Gr. SE20	.98	35	70	C	Aytoun Pl. SW9	.74	30	76	D
Avenue Gdns. SE25		34	69	C	Avington Way (off Daniel Gdns).					Aytoun Rd. SW9	.74	30	76	D
Avenue Gdns. SW14	.72	21	75	A	SE15	.63	33	77	D	Azalea Cl. W7	.54	15	80	D
Avenue Gdns. Tedd	.93	15	70	B	Avis Sq. E1	.57	35	81	D	Azalea Wlk. Pnr	.31	10	88	D
Avenue Gdns. W3	.61	19	79	B	Avoca Rd. SW17	.86	28	71	A	Azof St. E10	.65	39	78	A
Avenue Mews. N10	.24	28	89	B	Avon Cl. Hay		11	82	C					
Avenue Park Rd. SE27	.87	31	72	B	Avon Cl. Sutt	.110	26	64	A	Baalbec Rd. N5	.48	31	85	D
Avenue Par. N21	.17	29	94	B	Avon Cl. Wor Pk	.105	22	65	A	Babbacombe Gdns. Ilf	.27	42	89	C
Avenue Rd. Beck	.98	35	69	B	Avon Ct. Grnf	.53	13	82	D	Babbacombe Rd. Brom	.99	40	69	A
Avenue Rd. Belv		50	78	A	Avondale Ave. Barn		27	94	D	Baber Dri. Felt	.70	11	74	C
Avenue Rd. Bexh	.79	48	75	A	Avondale Ave. Esh	.101	16	65	C	Babington Rd. Dag	.52	47	85	A
Avenue Rd. Brent	.60	17	78	C	Avondale Ave. N12	.15	25	92	D	Babington Rd. Horn	.42	52	87	D
Avenue Rd. E7	.50	40	85	B	Avondale Ave. NW2	.34	21	86	C	Babington Rd. NW4	.22	22	89	D
Avenue Rd. Eri	.68	51	77	A	Avondale Ave. Wor Pk	.102	21	66	C	Babington Rd. SW16	.86	29	71	D
Avenue Rd. Eri	.68	51	77	B	Avondale Cres. Enf	.14	36	96	A	Babington Rise. Wem	.45	19	84	A
Avenue Rd. Felt	.81	09	72	D	Avondale Cres. Ilf	.39	41	88	B	Babmaes St. SW1	.6	29	80	B
Avenue Rd. Hamp	.92	13	69	B	Avondale Ct. E16	.58	39	81	A	Bacchus Wlk. N1	.48	33	83	C
Avenue Rd. Islw	.71	15	76	B	Avondale Ct. E18	.27	40	90	B	Bache's St. N1	.4	32	82	B
Avenue Rd. King	.93	18	68	A	Avondale Gdns. Houn		12	74	B	Back Alley. EC3	.4	33	81	C
Avenue Rd. N12	.15	26	92	A	Avondale Park Gdns. W11	.56	24	80	A	Back Church La. E1	.57	34	81	C
Avenue Rd. N14	.14	29	94	A	Avondale Park Rd. W11	.56	24	80	A	Back Hill. EC1	.3	31	82	C
Avenue Rd. N15	.37	32	88	B	Avondale Rd. Brom	.99	39	70	B	Backhouse Pl. SE17	.63	33	78	A
Avenue Rd. N6	.36	29	87	B	Avondale Rd. E16		39	81	A	Back La. Bark	.51	44	83	A
Avenue Rd. N Mal	.94	21	68	C	Avondale Rd. E17	.38	37	87	A	Back La. Brent	.60	17	77	B
Avenue Rd. NW10	.46	21	83	D	Avondale Rd. Har	.21	15	89	B	Back La. Edg	.22	20	90	A
Avenue Rd. NW3	.46	26	84	D	Avondale Rd. N13	.17	31	93	A	Back La. N8	.36	30	88	A
Avenue Rd. NW8	.47	27	83	A	Avondale Rd. N15	.37	31	88	B	Back La. NW3	.46	26	85	A
Avenue Rd. Pnr	.20	12	89	A	Avondale Rd. N3	.23	26	90	A	Back La. Rich		17	72	C
Avenue Rd. Rom	.47	47	87	A	Avondale Rd. S Croy	.112	32	63	A	Back La. Rom	.41	47	87	B
Avenue Rd. Rom	.30	54	90	B	Avondale Sq. SE1	.89	42	72	A	Back Rd. Sid	.90	46	71	A
Avenue Rd. SE20	.98	35	69	A	Avondale Rd. SW14		20	75	B	Bacon Gr. SE1	.8	33	79	D
Avenue Rd. SE25	.97	34	69	C	Avondale Rd. SW19	.85	25	71	D	Bacon La. Edg	.22	19	90	A
Avenue Rd. Sthl	.53	12	80	D	Avondale Rd. Well	.79	47	76	C	Bacon La. NW9	.22	19	89	D
Avenue Rd. Sutt	.110	25	62	C	Avondale Rise. SE15	.75	33	75	B	Bacon La. NW9	.34	20	88	A
Avenue Rd. SW16	.96	29	69	D	Avondale Sq. SE1	.63	34	78	C	Bacon Link. Rom	.29	49	91	B
Avenue Rd. SW20		22	69	D	Avonley Rd. SE14	.64	35	77	C	Bacon La. N6	.36	28	87	C
Avenue Rd. Tedd	.93	16	70	A	Avon Mews. Pnr	.20	12	90	B	Bacon St. E2	.4	33	82	D
Avenue Rd. W3	.61	19	79	B	Avonmore Pl. W14		24	78	B	Bacon St. E2	.57	34	82	C
Avenue Rd. Wall	.111	29	63	C	Avonmore Rd. W14	.62	24	78	A	Bacton. NW5	.47	28	85	C
Avenue Rd. Wdf Gn	.27	41	91	A	Avonmouth St. SE1		32	79	C	Bacton St. E2	.57	35	82	A
Avenue S. Surb	.102	19	66	A	Avon Path. S Croy	.112	32	63	A	Baddow Cl. Dag	.52	49	83	A
Avenue Terr. N Mal	.94	20	68	A	Avon Pl. SE1	.8	32	79	A	Baddows Cl. Wdf Gn	.27	41	91	B
Avenue The. Barn	.11	24	96	A	Avon Rd. E17	.26	38	89	B	Baddow Wlk (off Popham Rd). N1				
Avenue The. Beck	.98	36	69	A	Avon Rd. Grnf		13	82	D			32	83	A
Avenue The. Bex	.79	47	74	D	Avon Rd. SE4	.76	37	75	A	Baden Pl. SE1	.8	32	79	B
Avenue The. Brom	.99	41	65	D	Avon Rd. Sun		09	70	D	Baden Powell Cl. Surb	.101	18	65	B
Avenue The. Brom	.99	41	68	B	Avon Way. E18	.27	40	89	A	Baden Rd. Ilf	.51	43	85	D
Avenue The. Croy	.105	33	65	C	Avonwick Rd. Houn		13	76	D	Baden Rd. N8	.24	29	89	D
Avenue The. E11	.39	40	88	B	Avril Way. E4	.18	38	92	C	Badger Cl. Houn		11	75	A
Avenue The. E4	.18	38	92	D	Avro Way. Wall	.111	30	63	C	Badger Cl. Enf	.13	31	96	B
Avenue The. Eps	.109	22	63	D	Awlfield Ave. N17	.25	32	90	B	Badgers Cl. Har	.32	14	88	D
Avenue The. Hamp	.92	12	70	B	Awliscombe Rd. Well	.78	45	76	D	Badgers Cl. Enf	.13	31	96	B
Avenue The. Har	.21	15	90	B	Axe St. Bark	.51	44	83	A	Badgers Copse. Orp	.108	45	65	B
Avenue The. Horn	.42	52	86	B	Axholme Ave. Edg	.22	19	90	B	Badgers Copse. Wor Pk	.102	21	65	B
Avenue The. Houn	.69	10	76	A	Axminster Cres. Well	.79	47	76	A	Badgers Croft. N20	.15	24	94	C
Avenue The. Houn	.70	13	74	B	Axminster Rd. N7	.47	30	86	D	Badgers Croft. SE9	.90	43	72	C
Avenue The. N10	.24	29	90	C	Aybrook St. W1	.2	28	81	A	Badgers Wlk. N Mal	.94	21	69	C
Avenue The. N11	.16	28	92	D	Aycliffe Cl. Brom	.99	42	68	D	Badlis Rd. E17	.26	37	89	A
Avenue The. N17	.37	33	90	C	Aycliffe Rd. W12	.55	22	80	C	Badlow Cl. Eri	.68	51	77	C
Avenue. The. N3	.23	25	90	C	Aylesbury Cl. E7	.50	39	84	B	Badminton Cl. Har	.21	15	89	C
Avenue The. N8	.25	31	89	A	Aylesbury Rd. Brom	.99	40	68	A	Badminton Cl. Nthlt	.43	13	84	A
Avenue. The. Nthwd	.19	08	91	A	Aylesbury Rd. SE17	.63	32	78	D	Badminton King	.94	19	69	B
Avenue The. NW6		24	83	A	Aylesbury St. EC1	.3	31	82	D	Badminton Rd. SW12	.74	28	74	C
Avenue The. Orp	.108	45	65	B	Aylesbury St. NW10	.34	20	86	D	Badric Ct. SW11	.73	26	76	D
Avenue The. Orp	.100	46	70	D	Aylesbury Ave. Beck	.106	36	67	A	Badsworth Rd. SE5	.63	32	77	C
Avenue The. Pnr	.32	12	88	D	Aylesford St. SW1	.10	29	78	D	Bagleys La. SW6	.73	25	76	B
Avenue The. Pnr	.20	12	91	B	Aylesham Rd. Orp	.100	45	66	B	Bagleys Spring. Rom	.29	48	89	C
Avenue The. Rich	.71	18	76	D	Aylestone Ave. NW6	.46	23	84	D	Bagshot Rd. Enf	.13	33	95	D
Avenue The. Rom	.29	50	89	D	Aylett Rd. Islw	.71	15	76	C	Bagshot St. SE17	.63	33	78	C
Avenue The. SE10	.64	39	77	C	Aylett Rd. SE25	.97	34	68	D	Bahram Rd. Eps	.109	20	62	D
Avenue The. Sun	.91	10	69	D	Ayley Croft. Enf		34	95	A	Baildon St. SE8	.64	37	77	C
Avenue The. Surb	.101	18	67	D	Aylmer Rd. Dag	.41	48	86	C	Baillie's Wlk. W5	.60	17	79	B
Avenue The. Sutt	.110	23	63	D	Aylmer Rd. N2	.36	27	88	A	Bainbridge Rd. Dag	.52	48	85	B
Avenue. The. Sutt	.110	24	62	B	Aylmer Rd. W12	.61	21	79	B	Bainbridge St. WC1	.2	29	81	D
Avenue The. SW4		28	74	A	Ayloffe Rd. Dag	.52	48	84	B	Baird Ave. Sthl	.53	14	80	A
Avenue The. Twick	.71	16	74	B	Ayloffs Cl. Horn	.30	54	88	D	Baird Cl. NW9	.34	20	88	C
Avenue The. Uxb	.31	07	86	D	Ayloff's Wlk. Horn	.42	54	88	B	Baird Gdns. SE19	.87	33	71	A
Avenue The. W13	.54	16	81	D	Aylton Estate. SE16	.64	35	79	B	Baird Rd. Enf	.13	34	96	D
Avenue The. W4	.61	21	79	C	Aylward Rd. SE23	.98	35	72	B	Baird St. EC1	.4	32	82	C
Avenue The. Wem	.33	18	87	D	Aylward Rd. SW20	.95	24	68	B	Baizdon Rd. SE3	.77	39	76	C
Avenue The. Wor Pk	.102	21	65	B	Aylward St. E1	.57	35	81	C	Baker La. Mit	.96	28	68	A
Avenue The. W.Wick	.106	39	66	A	Aylward St. E1		35	81	D	Baker Pas. NW10	.45	21	83	C
Averill Gr. SW16	.97	31	70	B	Aynescombe Path. SW14	.72	20	76	C	Baker Rd. NW10	.45	21	83	A
Averill St. W6		23	77	B	Aynhoe Rd. W14		23	79	D	Baker Rd. SE18	.77	42	76	A
Avern Cl. E Mol	.92	13	68	D	Aynscombe Angle. Orp	.108	46	66	A	Bakers Ave. E17	.38	37	88	D
Avern Rd. E Mol	.92	13	68	D	Ayr Ct. W3	.55	19	81	A	Bakers End. SW20	.95	24	69	C
Avery Farm Row. SW1	.9	28	78	B	Ayres Cl. E13	.58	40	82	A	Bakers Field. N7	.47	30	85	A
Avery Gdns. Ilf	.39	42	88	B	Ayres Cres. NW10	.45	20	84	D					

Name	Page	Grid
Bakers Hall Ct. EC3	8	33 80 A
Bakers Hill. Barn	11	25 97 D
Bakers Hill. E5	38	35 87 C
Baker's La. N6	36	27 88 D
Baker's Mews. W1	2	28 81 C
Bakers Row. E15	50	39 83 C
Baker's Row. EC1	3	31 82 C
Baker St. Enf	13	32 97 B
Baker St. W1	1	27 81 B
Bakewell Way. N Mal	94	21 69 C
Balaams La. N14	16	29 93 B
Balaam St. E13	58	40 82 A
Balaclava Rd. SE1	3	33 78 B
Balaclava Rd. Surb	101	17 67 C
Balben Path. E9	49	35 84 C
Balcaskie Rd. SE9	77	42 74 B
Balchen Rd. SE3	77	41 76 D
Balchier Rd. SE22	75	34 74 D
Balcombe St. NW1	1	27 80 D
Balcorne St. E9	49	35 84 C
Balder Rise. SE12	89	40 72 B
Balderton St. W1	2	28 81 C
Baldewyne Ct. N17	25	34 90 A
Baldock St. E3	49	37 83 D
Baldry Gdns. SW16	96	30 70 B
Baldwin Cres. SE5	73	32 76 A
Baldwin's Gdns. EC1	3	31 81 A
Baldwin St. EC1	4	32 82 B
Baldwin Terr. N1	48	32 84 A
Baldwyn Gdns. W3	55	20 80 B
Balfern Gr. W4	61	21 78 C
Balfern St. SW11	74	27 76 C
Balfe St. N1	47	30 83 C
Balfour App. Ilf	87	43 86 B
Balfour Ave. W7	60	15 80 D
Balfour Gr. N20	16	27 93 D
Balfour Mews. N9	17	34 93 C
Balfour Mews. W1	2	28 80 C
Balfour Pl. W1	6	28 80 A
Balfour Rd. Brom	107	41 67 B
Balfour Rd. Cars	111	27 63 D
Balfour Rd. Har	32	14 88 B
Balfour Rd. Houn	70	13 75 B
Balfour Rd. Ilf		44 87 C
Balfour Rd. N5	48	32 85 A
Balfour Rd. SE25	97	34 68 C
Balfour Rd. Sthl	52	11 79 D
Balfour Rd. SW19	95	25 70 D
Balfour Rd. W13	60	16 79 B
Balfour Rd. W3	55	20 81 A
Balfour St. SE17	63	32 78 B
Balgonie Rd. E4	18	38 94 D
Balgores Cres. Rom	30	52 89 B
Balgores La. Rom	30	52 89 D
Balgores Sq. rom	30	52 89 D
Balgowan Cl. N Mal	94	21 68 C
Balgowan Rd. Beck	98	36 69 D
Balgowan St. SE18	66	45 78 B
Balham Gr. SW12	86	28 73 A
Balham High Rd. SW12	86	28 73 D
Balham High Rd. SW17	86	28 72 A
Balham Hill. SW12	86	28 73 B
Balham New Rd. SW12	86	28 73 B
Balham Park Rd. SW12	86	28 73 C
Balham Rd. N9	17	34 93 A
Balham Station Rd. SW12	86	28 73 D
Ballamore Rd. Brom	89	40 72 C
Ballance Rd. E9	49	36 84 A
Ballantine St. SW18	73	26 75 C
Ballard Cl. King	94	20 70 D
Ballards Cl. Dag	52	49 83 B
Ballards Farm Rd. S Croy	112	34 63 A
Ballard's La. N12	23	26 91 A
Ballards La. N3	23	25 91 D
Ballards Rd. Dag	52	49 83 B
Ballards Rd. NW2	34	22 86 A
Ballards Rise. S Croy	112	34 63 A
Ballards Way. Croy	112	34 63 B
Ballards Way. S Croy	112	34 63 B
Ballast Quay. SE10		38 78 D
Ballater Rd. S Croy	112	33 64 D
Ballater Rd. SW2		30 75 C
Ball Ct. EC3	4	32 81 D
Ballina St. SE23		35 73 B
Ballingdon Rd. SW11	74	28 74 C
Balliol Ave. E4	18	38 92 B
Balliol Rd. N17	25	33 90 A
Balliol Rd. W10		23 81 D
Balliol Rd. Well	78	46 76 D
Balloch Rd. SE6		38 72 B
Ballogie Ave. NW10	45	21 85 A
Ballow Cl. SE5		33 77 C
Ball's Pond Pl. N1	48	32 84 B
Ball's Pond Rd. N1	48	33 84 A
Balmain Cl. W5	54	17 80 D
Balmer Rd. E3	49	36 83 D
Balmes Rd. N1	48	32 83 B
Balmoral Ave. Beck	98	36 68 C
Balmoral Cl. SW15	73	23 74 D
Balmoral Cres. E Mol	92	13 68 A
Balmoral Ct. SE27	87	32 71 A
Balmoral Dri. Sthl	53	12 82 D
Balmoral Gdns. Ilf	40	45 87 D
Balmoral Gdns. W13	60	16 79 A
Balmoral Gr. N7	47	30 84 B
Balmoral Mews. W12		21 79 D
Balmoral Rd. E10	38	37 86 B
Balmoral Rd. E7	50	41 85 C
Balmoral Rd. Har	43	13 85 A
Balmoral Rd. Horn	42	53 86 D
Balmoral Rd. King	93	18 68 D
Balmoral Rd. NW2	45	22 84 B
Balmoral Rd. Rom	42	52 88 B
Balmoral Rd. Wor Pk	102	22 65 B
Balmoral Way. Sutt	110	25 62 C
Balmore St. N19	36	28 86 B
Balmuir Gdns. SW15	73	23 75 C
Balnacraig Ave. NW10	45	21 85 A
Baltic Cl. SW19	95	26 70 D
Baltic St. EC1	4	32 82 C
Baltimore Pl. Well	78	45 76 D
Balvernie Gr. SW18		25 73 A
Bamborough Gdns. W12	62	23 79 A
Bamford Ave. Wem		18 83 D
Bamford Rd. Bark	51	44 84 A
Bamford Rd. Brom		38 71 D
Bampfylde Cl. Wall	104	29 65 C
Bampton Rd. Rom	30	54 90 A
Bampton Rd. SE23		35 72 D
Banavie Gdns. Beck	98	38 69 A
Banbury Cl. Sutt	110	25 63 C
Banbury Ct. WC2	7	30 80 A
Banbury Rd. E9	49	35 84 D
Banbury St. SW11	74	27 76 C
Banchory Rd. SE3	65	40 77 D
Bancroft Ave. N2	36	27 88 A
Bancroft Cl. Ashf	81	07 71 C
Bancroft Cl. Nthlt	43	11 83 A
Bancroft Gdns. Har	20	14 90 A
Bancroft Gdns. Orp	108	45 66 D
Bancroft Rd. E1	57	35 82 B
Bancroft Rd. Har	20	14 90 C
Bandon Rise. Wall	111	29 64 D
Bangalore St. SW15	63	23 75 B
Bangor Cl. Nthlt	43	13 85 D
Bangor Rd. Brent		18 77 B
Banim St. W6	61	22 78 B
Banister House. E9		35 85 D
Banister Rd. W10	56	23 82 B
Bank Ave. Mit	95	26 69 D
Bank Ct. Dart		54 74 C
Bank End. SE1		32 80 C
Bankfoot Rd. Brom		39 71 A
Bankhurst Rd. SE6	88	36 73 B
Bank La. King	93	18 70 C
Bank La. SW15	72	21 74 A
Bank Mews. Sutt	110	26 63 A
Bank Side Cl. Cars	111	27 63 A
Bankside Dri. Surb	101	16 65 B
Bankside. Enf	13	31 97 B
Bankside. S Croy	112	32 63 B
Bankside. SE1	8	32 80 A
Bankside. Sthl	53	11 80 D
Bankside Way. SE19	97	33 70 A
Banks La. Bexh		48 75 D
Bank The. N6	36	28 87 D
Bankton Rd. SW2		31 75 C
Bankwell Rd. SE13	77	39 75 C
Banner St. EC1	4	32 82 C
Banning St. E10	65	39 78 C
Bannister Cl. Grnf		14 85 D
Bannister Cl. SW2	87	31 73 C
Bannockburn Rd. SE18		45 78 B
Banstead Ct. N4	37	32 87 C
Banstead Gdns. N9		33 93 C
Banstead Rd. Cars	111	27 63 C
Banstead Rd. Eps	109	22 62 D
Banstead Rd. S Sutt	110	26 62 D
Banstead St. SE15		35 75 A
Banstead Way. Wall	111	30 64 C
Banstock Rd. Edg		19 91 B
Banton Cl. Enf	13	34 97 D
Bantry St. SE5	63	32 77 D
Banwell Rd. Bex	79	47 74 D
Banyard Rd. SE16		34 79 D
Banyards. Horn	30	54 89 C
Baptist Gdns. NW5	47	28 84 A
Barandon Wlk. W11	56	23 80 B
Barbauld Rd. N16	37	33 86 C
Barbel St. SE1	7	31 79 C
Barber Cl. N21	17	31 94 A
Barberry Cl. Rom	30	53 91 C
Barbers Alley. E13	58	40 82 B
Barbers Rd. E15	49	37 83 D
Barbican Rd. Grnf	53	13 81 D
Barb Mews. W6	62	23 79 C
Barbot St. N9	17	34 93 C
Barchard St. SW18	73	25 74 B
Barchester Rd. Har	20	14 90 D
Barchester St. E14	57	37 81 B
Barclay Cl. SW6	62	25 77 C
Barclay Rd.Croy	105	32 65 D
Barclay Rd. E11	39	39 87 D
Barclay Rd. E13	58	41 82 C
Barclay Rd. E17	38	38 88 A
Barclay Rd. N18		33 91 A
Barclay Rd. SW6	62	25 77 C
Barcombe Ave. SW2	86	30 72 B
Barden St. SE18	66	45 77 C
Bardfield Ave. Rom	29	47 89 B
Bardney Rd. Mord	95	25 68 D
Bardolph Rd. N7	47	30 85 A
Bardolph Rd. Rich	71	18 75 B
Bard Rd. W10	56	23 80 B
Bards Ct. Rom	30	52 91 D
Bardsey Pl. E1	57	35 82 C
Bardsey Wlk. N1	48	32 84 A
Bardsley Cl. Croy	105	33 65 D
Bardsley La. SE10	64	38 77 A
Barfett St. W10	56	24 82 D
Barfield Ave. N20	16	27 93 B
Barfield Rd. Brom	100	43 68 A
Barfield Rd. E11	39	39 87 D
Barford Cl. NW4	22	22 90 A
Barford St. N1	48	31 83 A
Barforth Rd. SE15	75	34 75 B
Barfreston Way. SE20	97	34 69 B
Bargate Cl. N.Mal	102	22 66 A
Bargate Cl. SE18	66	45 78 D
Barge House Rd. E16	66	43 79 B
Barge House St. SE1	7	31 80 C
Bargery Rd. SE6	88	38 73 C
Barge Wlk. E M01	93	15 68 A
Barge Wlk. E Mol		14 68 B
Barge Wlk. E Mol		15 68 D
Barge Wlk. King	93	17 68 B
Barge Wlk. King		17 69 B
Bargrove Cl. SE20	97	34 70 C
Bargrove Cres. SE6		36 72 B
Barham Cl. Brom	107	42 66 C
Barham Cl. Chis	90	43 71 D
Barham Cl. Grnf	44	17 84 A
Barham Cl. Rom	29	49 90 D
Barham Cl. Wem		18 84 B
Barham Rd. Chis	90	43 71 D
Barham Rd. S Croy	112	32 64 C
Barham Rd. SW20	94	22 70 C
Baring Cl. SE12	89	40 72 A
Baring Rd. Barn	11	26 96 B
Baring Rd. Croy	105	34 66 C
Baring Rd. SE12	89	40 72 A
Baring St. N1	48	32 83 B
Barker Ho. SE21	87	34 72 C
Barker Wlk. SW16	86	29 72 D
Barkham Rd. N17	25	33 91 C
Bark Hart Rd. Orp	108	44 66 D
Barking Rd. E16	58	39 81 B
Barking Rd. E6	50	42 83 C
Barkis Way. SE16		34 78 D
Bark Pl. W2	56	25 80 B
Barkston Gdns. SW5	62	25 78 B
Barkworth Rd. SE16	64	35 78 C
Barlborough St. SE14	64	35 77 D
Barlby Gdns. W10	56	23 82 D
Barlby Rd. W10	56	23 81 B
Barleycorn Way. E14	57	36 80 B
Barleycorn Way. Horn		54 88 D
Barley La. Ilf	40	46 88 C
Barley La. Rom	28	46 89 D
Barley Mow Pas. EC1	3	31 81 B
Barley Mow Pas. W4	61	20 78 D
Barley Mow Way. Shep	91	07 68 C
Barlow Cl. Wall	111	30 63 C
Barlow Pl. W1	6	28 80 B
Barlow Rd. Hamp	92	13 70 C
Barlow Rd. NW6	46	24 84 B
Barlow Rd. W3	55	19 80 D
Barlow St. SE17	63	32 78 B
Barmeston Rd. SE6	88	37 72 B
Barmor Cl. Har	20	13 90 D
Barmouth Ave. Grnf	44	15 83 D
Barmouth Rd. Croy	106	33 65 B
Barmouth Rd. SW18	73	26 74 C
Barnabas Rd. E9	49	35 84 B

Name	Page	Grid
Barnard Cl. Chis	*100*	44 69 B
Barnard Cl. Sun	*91*	10 70 D
Barnard Cl. Wall	*111*	29 63 D
Barnard Gdns. N Mal	*94*	22 68 C
Barnard Gr. E15	*50*	39 84 D
Barnard Hill. N10	*24*	28 90 B
Barnard Mews. SW11	*74*	27 75 C
Barnardo Dri. Ilf	*28*	44 89 C
Barnardo St. E1	*57*	35 81 D
Barnard Rd. Enf	*13*	34 97 D
Barnard Rd. Mit	*96*	28 69 C
Barnard Rd. SW11	*74*	27 75 C
Barnard's Inn. EC4	*3*	31 81 A
Barnards Pl. S Croy	*112*	31 62 B
Barnby Sq. E15	*50*	39 83 A
Barnby St. E15	*50*	39 83 A
Barnby St. NW1	*2*	29 82 A
Barn Cl. Ashf	*81*	07 71 D
Barn Cl. Nthlt	*43*	11 83 C
Barn Cres. Stan	*21*	17 91 A
Barnehurst Ave. Bexh	*79*	50 76 C
Barnehurst Ave. Eri	*79*	50 76 A
Barnehurst Cl. Eri	*79*	50 76 A
Barnehurst Rd. Bexh	*79*	50 76 C
Barnes Alley. Hamp	*92*	14 69 C
Barnes Ave. SW13	*61*	22 77 C
Barnes Cl. E12	*41*	85 B
Barnes Cray Rd. Dart	*80*	52 75 C
Barnesdale Cres. Orp	*108*	46 67 A
Barnes End. N.Mal	*102*	22 67 A
Barnes High St. SW13	*72*	21 76 D
Barnes Pikle. W5	*54*	17 80 B
Barnes Rd. Ilf	*51*	44 85 C
Barnes Rd. N18	*18*	35 92 A
Barnes St. E14	*57*	36 81 C
Barnes Terr. SE8	*64*	36 78 D
Barnes Wallis Ct. Wem	*34*	20 86 C
Barnet By Pass. NW7	*22*	21 91 D
Barnet Dri. Brom	*107*	42 65 A
Barnet Gr. E2	*57*	34 82 A
Barnet Hill. Barn	*11*	25 96 C
Barnet La. Barn	*11*	25 95 C
Barnet La. N20	*15*	24 94 B
Barnet Rd. Barn	*11*	23 96 C
Barnett Cl. Eri		51 76 D
Barnett St. E1	*57*	34 81 D
Barnet Wood Rd. Brom	*107*	41 65 A
Barney Ct. E7	*65*	34 85 A
Barnfield Ave. Croy	*106*	35 65 A
Barnfield Ave. King	*83*	18 71 C
Barnfield Ave. Mit	*96*	28 68 B
Barnfield Gdns. King	*83*	18 71 C
Barnfield Gdns. SE18	*66*	43 77 B
Barnfield. N.Mal	*102*	21 67 C
Barnfield Rd. Belv	*67*	48 77 B
Barnfield Rd. Edg	*22*	20 90 A
Barnfield Rd. S Croy	*112*	33 62 A
Barnfield Rd. SE18	*66*	43 77 B
Barnfield Rd. W5	*54*	17 82 C
Barnfield Wood Cl. Beck	*106*	38 67 D
Barnfield Wood Rd. Beck	*106*	38 67 B
Barnham Rd. Grnf	*53*	14 82 A
Barnham St. SE1	*8*	33 79 A
Barnhill Ave. Brom	*107*	39 67 B
Barnhill. Pnr	*32*	11 88 A
Barnhill Rd. Hay		11 82 C
Barnhill Rd. Wem	*34*	20 86 C
Barn Hill. Wem	*34*	19 87 D
Barnlea Cl. Felt	*82*	12 72 A
Barnmead Gdns. Dag	*52*	48 85 D
Barnmead Rd. Beck	*98*	36 69 A
Barnmead Rd. Dag	*52*	48 85 D
Barn Rise. Wem	*34*	19 86 A
Barnsbury Cl. N Mal	*94*	20 68 C
Barnsbury Cres. Surb	*102*	20 66 C
Barnsbury Gro. N7	*48*	31 84 C
Barnsbury La. Surb	*102*	19 66 D
Barnsbury Park. N1	*48*	31 84 C
Barnsbury Rd. N1	*48*	31 83 A
Barnsbury Sq. N1	*48*	31 84 C
Barnsbury St. N1	*48*	31 84 C
Barnsbury Terr. N1	*48*	31 84 C
Barnscroft. SW20	*94*	22 68 B
Barnsdale Rd. W9	*56*	24 82 D
Barnsley Rd. Rom	*30*	54 91 D
Barnsley St. E1	*57*	34 82 D
Barnstaple La. SE13		38 75 C
Barnstaple Rd. Ruis	*32*	11 86 C
Barn St. N16		33 86 A
Barnston Wlk. N1	*48*	32 83 A
Barn Way. Wem	*34*	19 87 C
Barnwell Rd. SW2	*75*	31 74 A
Barnwood Cl. Ruis	*31*	08 86 B
Barnwood Cl. W9		25 82 D
Barnwood Ct. E16	*58*	40 80 D
Baroness Rd. E2	*4*	33 82 B
Baronet Gr. N17	*25*	34 90 A
Baronet Rd. N17	*25*	34 90 A
Baron Gdns. Ilf		44 89 B
Baron Gr. Mit	*96*	27 68 C
Baron Rd. Dag	*41*	47 87 D
Baron's Court Rd. W14	*62*	24 78 C
Barons Ct. NW9	*34*	20 88 D
Baronsfield Rd. Twick	*71*	16 74 D
Barons Gate. Barn	*12*	27 95 C
Barons Keep. W14	*62*	24 78 C
Barons Mead. Har	*21*	15 89 C
Baronsmead Rd. SW13	*72*	22 76 A
Baronsmede. W5		18 79 B
Baronsmere Rd. N2	*24*	27 89 C
Baron's Pl. SE1	*3*	31 79 A
Barons The. Twick	*71*	16 74 D
Baron St. N1	*48*	31 83 C
Baron Wlk. E16	*58*	39 81 B
Baron Wlk. Mit	*96*	27 68 C
Barque Mews. SE8	*64*	37 77 A
Barrack Rd. Houn	*70*	12 75 C
Barracks La. Barn	*11*	11 78 A
Barratt Ave. N22	*24*	30 90 D
Barratt Way. Har		14 89 B
Barrenger Rd. N10	*24*	27 90 D
Barrett Rd. E17	*26*	38 89 C
Barrett's Green Rd. NW10	*45*	20 83 D
Barrett's Gr. N16		33 85 C
Barrett St. W1	*2*	28 81 C
Barrhill Rd. SW2		30 72 A
Barriedale. SE14	*76*	36 76 C
Barringer Sq. SW17		28 71 A
Barrington Cl. NW5	*47*	28 85 C
Barrington Ct. NW5	*47*	28 85 C
Barrington Rd. Bexh	*79*	47 76 D
Barrington Rd. E12	*41*	43 84 A
Barrington Rd. N8	*36*	29 88 B
Barrington Rd. Sutt	*103*	25 66 C
Barrington Rd. SW9	*75*	31 75 B
Barrington Villas. SE18	*78*	43 76 A
Barrow Ave. Cars	*111*	27 62 B
Barrow Cl. N21		31 93 B
Barrowdene Cl. Pnr	*20*	12 90 C
Barrowell Green. N21	*17*	32 93 A
Barrowfield Cl. N9	*18*	35 93 C
Barrowgate Rd. W4	*61*	20 78 D
Barrow Hedges Cl. Cars	*111*	27 63 C
Barrow Hedges Way. Cars	*111*	27 63 C
Barrow Hill Cl. Wor Pk	*102*	21 65 A
Barrow Hill Estate. NW8		27 83 C
Barrow Hill Rd. NW8		27 83 C
Barrow Hill. Wor Pk	*102*	21 65 A
Barrow Point Ave. Pnr	*20*	12 90 C
Barrow Point La. Pnr	*20*	12 90 C
Barrow Rd. Croy	*112*	31 64 C
Barrow Rd. SW16	*96*	29 70 B
Barrs Rd. NW10	*45*	20 84 D
Barry Ave. Bex h		48 77 C
Barry Ave. N15	*37*	33 88 D
Barry Cl. Orp	*108*	45 65 C
Barry Rd. NW10	*45*	20 84 C
Barry Rd. SE22	*75*	34 74 A
Barset Rd. SE15	*76*	35 75 A
Barson Rd. SE27		35 70 C
Barstow Cres. SW2	*86*	30 73 D
Barter St. WC1	*3*	30 81 A
Bartholomew Cl. EC1	*4*	32 81 A
Bartholomew Cl. SW18	*73*	26 75 C
Bartholomew La. EC2	*4*	32 81 B
Bartholomew Pl. EC1	*4*	32 81 A
Bartholomew Rd. NW5	*47*	29 84 A
Bartholomew St. SE1	*8*	32 79 D
Bartholomew Villas. NW5	*47*	29 84 A
Barth Rd. SE18	*66*	45 78 A
Bartle Ave. E6	*50*	42 83 C
Bartle Rd. W11	*56*	24 81 C
Bartlett Ct. EC4	*3*	31 81 C
Bartlett St. E14	*57*	37 81 B
Bartlett St. S Croy	*112*	32 64 D
Bartlow Gdns. Rom	*29*	50 90 B
Bartolomew Sq. EC1		32 82 C
Barton Ave. Rom	*41*	49 87 D
Barton Cl. Bexh	*79*	48 74 A
Barton Cl. E9	*49*	35 85 C
Barton Cl. SE15		34 75 B
Barton Green. N Mal	*94*	20 69 D
Barton Meadows. Ilf	*28*	44 89 C
Barton Rd. Horn	*42*	52 87 C
Barton Rd. W14	*62*	24 78 C
Barton St. SE1		30 79 C
Bartram Rd. SE4	*76*	36 74 C
Bartrip St. E9	*49*	36 84 B
Barwick Rd. E7	*50*	40 85 B
Barwood Ave. W Wick	*106*	37 66 D
Basedale Rd. Dag		46 84 D
Bashley Rd. NW10	*55*	20 82 D
Basildene Rd. Houn	*70*	11 75 B
Basildon Ave. Ilf	*28*	43 90 A
Basildon Cl. Sutt	*110*	25 62 B
Basildon Rd. Bexh		48 76 C
Basildon Rd. SE2	*66*	46 78 A
Basil St. SW3		27 79 B
Basil St. SW3		27 79 D
Basing Cl. Surb	*101*	15 66 B
Basing Ct. SE15	*75*	33 76 B
Basingdon Way. SE5		32 75 D
Basing Dri. Bex		49 74 D
Basingfield Rd. Surb	*101*	15 66 B
Basinghall Ave. EC2	*4*	32 81 D
Basinghall Gdns. Sutt	*110*	25 62 B
Basinghall St. EC2	*4*	32 81 D
Basing Hill. NW11	*35*	24 87 D
Basing Hill. Wem	*34*	19 87 C
Basing House Yd. E2	*4*	33 82 A
Basing Pl. E2	*4*	33 82 A
Basing St. W11	*56*	24 81 D
Basing Way. N3	*23*	25 89 B
Basing Way. Surb	*101*	15 66 B
Basire St. N1	*48*	32 83 A
Baskerville Rd. SW18	*86*	27 73 A
Basket Gdns. SE9	*77*	42 74 A
Baslow Cl. Har	*20*	14 90 B
Baslow Wlk. E5	*49*	35 85 B
Basnett Rd. SW11	*74*	28 75 A
Bassano St. SE22	*75*	33 74 B
Bassant Rd. SE18	*66*	45 77 B
Bassein Park Rd. W12	*61*	21 79 B
Bassett Cl. Sutt	*110*	25 62 B
Bassett Gdns. Islw		14 77 C
Bassett Rd. W10	*56*	23 81 D
Bassett St. NW5	*47*	28 84 A
Bassett Way. Grnf	*53*	13 81 D
Bassingham Rd. SW18	*85*	26 73 A
Bassingham Rd. Wem	*44*	17 84 B
Bassishaw Highwalk. EC2	*4*	32 81 B
Basswood Cl. SE15	*75*	34 75 B
Bastable Ave. Bark		45 83 D
Bastion Rd. SE2	*66*	46 78 C
Baston Manor Rd. Brom	*107*	40 65 D
Baston Rd. Brom	*107*	40 65 B
Bastwick St. EC1		32 82 C
Basuto Rd. SW6	*73*	25 76 A
Batavia Cl. Sun	*92*	11 69 A
Batavia Mews. SE14	*64*	36 77 C
Batavia Rd. SE14	*64*	36 77 C
Batavia Rd. Sun	*91*	10 69 B
Batchelor St. N1	*48*	31 83 A
Batchwood Green. Orp	*100*	46 68 B
Bateman Cl. Bark	*51*	44 84 A
Bateman Rd. E4	*26*	37 91 A
Bateman's Bldgs. W1	*2*	29 81 D
Bateman's Row. EC2		33 82 C
Bateman St. W1	*2*	29 81 D
Bates Cres. Croy	*112*	31 64 C
Bateson St. SE18	*66*	45 78 A
Bate St. E14	*57*	36 80 B
Bath Cl. SE15	*64*	35 77 C
Bath Ct. EC1	*3*	31 82 C
Bathgate Rd. SW19	*85*	23 72 D
Bath Gr. E2		34 83 C
Bath House Rd. Croy	*104*	30 66 D
Bath Pas. King	*93*	17 69 D
Bath Pas. SE5	*63*	31 77 D
Bath Pl. Barn	*11*	24 96 B
Bath Pl. EC2		33 82 A
Bath Rd. E7	*50*	41 84 B
Bath Rd. Hay	*69*	08 76 A
Bath Rd. Houn	*70*	12 76 C
Bath Rd. Mit		26 68 B
Bath Rd. N9	*18*	35 93 A
Bath Rd. Rom	*41*	48 88 C
Bath Rd. W4	*61*	21 78 A
Baths App. SW6	*62*	24 77 D
Baths Rd. Brom	*99*	41 68 D
Bath St. EC1		32 82 B
Bath Terr. SE1	*8*	32 79 C
Bathurst Ave. SW19		25 69 B
Bathurst Gdns. NW10	*45*	22 83 D
Bathurst Mews. W2		26 80 B
Bathurst Rd. Ilf		43 87 D
Bathurst St. W2		26 80 B
Bathway. SE18	*66*	43 78 A
Batley Pl. N16		33 86 D
Batley Rd. Enf	*13*	32 97 B
Batley Rd. N16		33 86 D
Batman Cl. W12	*55*	22 80 D

Batoum Gdns. W6 ...62 23 79 C
Batson St. W12 ...61 22 79 A
Battenberg Wlk. SE19 ...87 33 71 C
Batten St. SW11 ...74 27 75 A
Battersby Rd. SE6 ...88 38 72 D
Battersea Bridge Rd. SW11 ...74 27 76 A
Battersea Bridge Rd. SW11 ...9 27 77 C
Battersea Church Rd. SW11 ...73 26 76 B
Battersea High St. SW11 ...74 26 76 D
Battersea High St. SW11 ...74 27 76 C
Battersea Park Rd. SW11 ...74 27 76 A
Battersea Park Rd. SW8 ...10 29 77 C
Battersea Rise. SW11 ...74 27 75 C
Battishill St. N1 ...48 31 84 D
Battle Bridge La. SE1 ...33 80 C
Battle Bridge Rd. NW1 ...47 30 83 C
Battle Cl. SW19 ...26 70 A
Battledean Rd. N5 ...48 31 85 D
Battle Rd. Belv. ...50 78 A
Battle Rd. Eri ...50 78 B
Batty St. E1 ...57 34 81 C
Baudwin Rd. SE6 ...89 39 72 A
Baulk The. SW18 ...25 73 A
Bavant Rd. SW16 ...96 30 69 D
Bavaria Rd. N19 ...30 86 A
Bavent Rd. SE5 ...75 32 76 C
Bawdale Rd. SE22 ...33 74 B
Bawdsey Ave. Ilf ...28 45 89 D
Bawtree Cl. Sutt ...110 26 62 C
Bawtree Rd. SE14 ...64 36 77 C
Bawtry Rd. N20 ...16 27 93 D
Baxendale. N20 ...15 26 93 A
Baxendale St. E2 ...57 34 82 A
Baxter Rd. E16 ...41 81 C
Baxter Rd. Ilf ...57 43 85 D
Baxter Rd. N17 ...34 89 A
Baxter Rd. N18 ...17 34 92 B
Baxter Rd. N1 ...48 32 84 B
Bayfield Rd. SE9 ...77 41 75 D
Bayford Rd. NW10 ...56 23 82 B
Bayford St. E8 ...48 34 84 D
Bayham Pl. NW1 ...47 29 83 C
Bayham Rd. Mord ...95 26 68 C
Bayham Rd. W13 ...54 16 80 D
Bayham Rd. W4 ...61 20 79 D
Bayham St. NW1 ...47 29 83 A
Bayhurst Dri. Nthwd ...19 09 91 B
Bayley St. WC1 ...2 29 81 B
Bayley Wlk. SE2 ...67 48 78 C
Baylis Rd. SE1 ...31 79 A
Baynes Cl. Enf ...13 34 97 A
Baynes Mews. NW3 ...26 84 B
Baynes St. NW1 ...47 29 84 C
Bayonne Rd. W6 ...62 24 77 A
Bayston Rd. N16 ...37 33 86 D
Bayswater Rd. W2 ...5 26 80 B
Baythorne St. E3 ...36 81 B
Baytree Rd. SW2 ...74 30 75 D
Bazalgette Cl. N.Mal ...102 20 67 B
Bazalgette Gdns. N.Mal ...102 20 67 B
Bazely St. E14 ...38 80 A
Bazile Rd. N21 ...13 31 95 C
Beacham Cl. SE7 ...41 77 B
Beachborough Rd. Brom ...88 38 71 A
Beachcroft Rd. E11 ...39 39 86 C
Beachcroft Way. N19 ...36 29 87 D
Beach Gr. Felt. ...13 72 A
Beachy Rd. E3 ...37 84 C
Beaconfield Terrace Rd. W14 ...24 79 C
Beacon Gr. Cars ...111 28 64 A
Beacon Hill. N7 ...30 85 C
Beacon Rd. Eri ...68 52 77 D
Beacon Rd. Houn ...07 74 C
Beacon Rd. SE13 ...76 38 74 D
Beaconsfield Cl. N11 ...16 28 92 C
Beaconsfield Cl. SE3 ...65 40 77 A
Beaconsfield Cl. W4 ...20 78 C
Beaconsfield Rd. Brom ...99 41 68 B
Beaconsfield Rd. Croy ...105 32 67 D
Beaconsfield Rd. E10 ...38 38 86 C
Beaconsfield Rd. E16 ...39 82 D
Beaconsfield Rd. E17 ...38 36 88 D
Beaconsfield Rd. Hay ...11 80 C
Beaconsfield Rd. N11 ...16 28 92 A
Beaconsfield Rd. N15 ...33 89 C
Beaconsfield Rd. N9 ...17 34 93 C
Beaconsfield Rd. N.Mal ...94 20 69 D
Beaconsfield Rd. NW10 ...45 21 84 B
Beaconsfield Rd. SE17 ...63 33 78 C
Beaconsfield Rd. SE3 ...65 40 77 A
Beaconsfield Rd. SE9 ...89 42 71 A
Beaconsfield Rd. Sthl ...12 80 C
Beaconsfield Rd. Surb ...101 18 66 B
Beaconsfield Rd. Twick ...16 74 D
Beaconsfield Gdns. W4 ...61 20 79 D

Beaconsfield Rd. W5 ...60 17 79 B
Beaconsfield Terr. Rom ...41 47 88 D
Beaconsfield Wlk. SW6 ...73 24 76 B
Beacontree Ave. E17 ...26 38 90 D
Beacontree Rd. E11 ...39 39 87 D
Beadlow Cl. Cars ...103 26 67 D
Beadman Pl. SE27 ...87 31 71 B
Beadman St. SE27 ...87 31 71 B
Beadnell Rd. SE23 ...88 35 73 D
Beadon Rd. Brom ...107 40 67 A
Beadon Rd. Brom ...99 40 68 C
Beadon Rd. W6 ...62 23 78 B
Beaford Gr. SW20 ...95 24 68 B
Beagle Cl. Felt ...81 10 71 B
Beak St. W1 ...29 80 A
Beal Cl. Well ...78 46 76 A
Beale Cl. N13 ...31 92 D
Beale Pl. E3 ...36 83 D
Beale Rd. E3 ...36 83 C
Beal Rd. Ilf ...40 43 86 A
Beam Ave. Dag ...52 49 83 B
Beaminster Gdns. Ilf ...28 43 89 B
Beamish Rd. N9 ...17 34 94 C
Beamway. Dag ...52 50 84 D
Beanacre Cl. E9 ...49 36 84 B
Bean Rd. Bexh ...79 47 75 D
Beanshaw. SE9 ...90 43 71 A
Beansland Gr. Rom ...29 48 89 A
Bear Alley. EC4 ...3 31 81 D
Beardell St. SE19 ...97 33 70 B
Beardow Gr. N14 ...29 95 C
Beard Rd. King ...83 18 71 D
Beardsfield. E13 ...50 40 83 C
Beard's Hill Cl. Hamp ...92 13 69 A
Beard's Hill. Hamp ...92 13 69 A
Beardsley Way. W3 ...61 20 79 B
Beard's Rd. Ashf ...93 18 70 C
Bearfield Rd. King ...83 18 72 C
Bear Gdns. SE1 ...32 80 C
Bear La. SE1 ...7 31 80 D
Bear Rd. Felt. ...11 71 B
Bearstead Rise. SE4 ...76 36 74 B
Bear St. WC2 ...6 29 80 B
Beatrice Ave. SW16 ...96 30 69 C
Beatrice Ave. Wem ...44 18 85 D
Beatrice Cl. E13 ...58 40 82 C
Beatrice Cl. Pnr ...19 10 89 C
Beatrice Rd. E17 ...38 37 88 A
Beatrice Rd. Enf ...14 35 95 C
Beatrice Rd. N4 ...37 31 87 A
Beatrice Rd. Rich ...71 18 74 B
Beatrice Rd. SE1 ...63 34 78 A
Beatrice Rd. Sthl ...53 12 80 D
Beatson Wlk. SE16 ...36 E3 C
Beattock Rise. N10 ...24 28 89 D
Beatty Rd. N16 ...33 85 A
Beatty Rd. Stan ...17 91 A
Beatty St. NW1 ...29 83 C
Beattyville Gdns. Ilf ...28 43 89 D
Beauchamp Pl. SW3 ...27 79 C
Beauchamp Rd. E7 ...50 40 84 D
Beauchamp Rd. SE19 ...32 69 B
Beauchamp Rd. Sutt ...110 25 64 A
Beauchamp Rd. SW11 ...74 27 75 D
Beauchamp Rd. Twick ...83 16 73 A
Beauchamp St. EC1 ...3 31 81 A
Beauchamp Terr. SW15 ...72 22 75 B
Beauclerc Rd. W6 ...23 79 C
Beaufort Ave. Har ...21 16 89 B
Beaufort Cl. Rom ...29 50 89 C
Beaufort Cl. W5 ...54 18 81 B
Beaufort Ct. Rich ...83 17 71 A
Beaufort Dri. NW11 ...23 25 89 C
Beaufort Gdns. Houn ...12 76 A
Beaufort Gdns. Ilf ...40 43 87 C
Beaufort Gdns. NW4 ...35 23 88 C
Beaufort Gdns. SW16 ...96 30 70 D
Beaufort Gdns. SW3 ...5 27 79 D
Beaufort Mansions. SW3 ...26 77 B
Beaufort Mews. SW6 ...62 24 77 B
Beaufort Park. NW11 ...23 25 89 C
Beaufort Rd. King ...93 18 68 C
Beaufort Rd. Rich ...83 17 71 A
Beaufort Rd. Ruis ...31 08 86 B
Beaufort Rd. Twick ...83 17 73 A
Beaufort Rd. W5 ...54 18 81 B
Beaufort St. SW3 ...26 77 B
Beaufort Way. Eps ...109 22 63 C
Beaufoy Rd. N17 ...33 91 C
Beaufoy Wlk. SE11 ...10 30 78 B
Beaulieu Ave. SE26 ...34 71 B
Beaulieu Cl. Mit ...96 28 69 C
Beaulieu Cl. NW9 ...22 21 89 C
Beaulieu Cl. SE5 ...32 75 B

Beaulieu Cl. Twick ...71 17 74 D
Beaulieu Dri. Pnr ...32 11 87 B
Beaulieu Gdns. N21 ...17 32 94 A
Beauly Way. Rom ...30 51 90 A
Beaumaner Gdns. SE9 ...43 71 A
Beaumaris Dri. Wdf Gn ...27 41 91 D
Beaumont Ave. Har. ...13 88 D
Beaumont Ave. Rich ...71 18 75 B
Beaumont Ave. W14 ...62 24 78 D
Beaumont Ave. Wem. ...44 17 85 A
Beaumont Cl. Rom ...30 53 90 C
Beaumont Cres. W14 ...62 24 78 D
Beaumont Dri. Ashf ...81 08 71 D
Beaumont Gr. E1 ...57 35 82 D
Beaumont Mews. W1 ...2 28 81 A
Beaumont Pl. Barn ...11 24 97 B
Beaumont Pl. W1 ...2 29 82 C
Beaumont Rd. E10 ...38 37 87 B
Beaumont Rd. E10 ...38 38 87 A
Beaumont Rd. E13 ...58 40 82 D
Beaumont Rd. Orp ...108 44 67 D
Beaumont Rd. SE19 ...97 32 70 A
Beaumont Rd. SW19 ...85 24 73 A
Beaumont Rise. N19 ...36 30 87 C
Beaumont Sq. E1 ...57 35 81 B
Beaumont St. W1 ...2 28 81 A
Beaumont Wlk. NW3 ...47 27 84 D
Beauvais Terr. Nthlt ...53 11 82 B
Beauval Rd. SE22 ...75 33 74 D
Beaverbank Rd. SE9 ...90 44 73 D
Beaver Cl. Hamp ...92 13 69 B
Beaver Cl. SE20 ...97 34 70 C
Beaver Gr (off Jetstar Way). Nthlt
...53 12 82 A
Beavers Cres. Houn ...70 11 75 D
Beavers La. Houn ...70 11 75 A
Beaverwood Rd. Chis ...100 45 70 A
Beavor La. W6 ...61 22 78 A
Bebbington Rd. SE18 ...66 45 78 A
Beccles Dri. Bark ...51 45 84 B
Beccles St. E14 ...57 36 80 B
Bec Cl. Ruis ...32 11 86 D
Beckenham Ct. Beck ...37 69 A
Beckenham Gdns. N9 ...17 33 93 C
Beckenham Gr. Brom ...98 38 69 D
Beckenham Hill Rd. Beck ...88 37 71 D
Beckenham Hill Rd. SE6 ...88 38 71 C
Beckenham La. Brom ...99 39 69 D
Beckenham Place Park. Beck. ...98 37 70 D
Beckenham Rd. Beck ...98 36 69 A
Beckenham Rd. W Wick ...106 38 66 A
Beckers The. N16 ...48 34 85 A
Becket Cl. SE25 ...105 34 67 C
Becket Rd. N18 ...18 35 92 A
Becket St. SE1 ...32 79 D
Beckett Cl. Felt ...69 10 74 D
Beckett Cl. SW16 ...86 29 72 B
Becketts Cl. Orp ...108 45 65 D
Beckett Wlk. Beck ...36 70 A
*Beckford Pl. SE17 ...63 32 78 C
Beckford Rd. Croy ...105 33 67 D
Beck La. Beck ...98 35 68 B
Becklow Gdns. W12 ...61 22 79 A
Becklow Gdns. W12 ...55 22 80 C
Becklow Rd. W12 ...61 21 79 B
Becklow Rd. W12 ...61 22 79 A
Beck Rd. E8 ...48 34 83 B
Beck River Park. Beck ...98 35 69 C
Beckton Rd. E16 ...58 39 81 B
Beck Way. Beck ...98 37 68 A
Beckway Rd. SW16 ...96 29 69 D
Beckway St. SE17 ...63 33 78 A
Beckwith Rd. SE24 ...75 32 74 B
Beclands Rd. SW17 ...96 28 70 A
Becmead Ave. Har ...33 16 88 B
Becmead Ave. SW16 ...96 29 71 B
Becondale Rd. SE19 ...87 33 71 C
Becontree Ave. Dag ...41 47 86 B
Bective Pl. SW15 ...73 24 75 D
Bective Rd. E7 ...50 40 85 A
Bective Rd. SW15 ...73 24 75 D
Becton Pl. Eri ...79 50 76 A
Bedale St. SE1 ...8 32 80 D
Beddington Farm Rd. Croy ...104 30 66 C
Beddington Gdns. Cars ...111 28 63 A
Beddington Gdns. Wall ...111 28 63 A
Beddington Green. Orp ...100 45 69 B
Beddington Gr. Wall ...111 29 64 D
Beddington La. Croy ...104 29 66 D
Beddington Rd. Ilf ...40 45 89 B
Beddington Rd. Orp ...100 45 69 B
Bede Cl. Pnr ...20 11 90 B

Entry	Page	Grid
Bedenham Way (off Daniel Gdns). SE15	63	33 77 D
Bede Rd. Rom	41	47 88 C
Bedfont Cl. Felt	69	08 74 C
Bedfont Cl. Mit	96	28 69 C
Bedfont La. Felt	81	09 73 B
Bedfont Rd. Felt	81	08 72 B
Bedfont Rd. Stai	69	07 74 C
Bedford Ave. Barn	11	24 95 B
Bedford Ave. WC1	2	29 81 B
Bedfordbury. WC2	7	30 80 A
Bedford Cl. N10	24	28 91 C
Bedford Ct. WC2	7	30 80 A
Bedford Gdns. Horn	42	53 86 A
Bedford Gdns. W8	56	25 80 C
Bedford Hill. SW12	86	28 72 B
Bedford Hill. SW16	86	29 72 C
Bedford Park. Croy	105	32 66 C
Bedford Pas. SW6	62	24 77 C
Bedford Pl. Croy	105	32 66 D
Bedford Pl. WC1	3	30 81 A
Bedford Pl. E17	26	37 89 A
Bedford Pl. E18	27	40 90 C
Bedford Rd. E6	51	43 83 A
Bedford Rd. Har	32	14 88 C
Bedford Rd. Ilf	40	43 86 D
Bedford Rd. N15	25	33 89 C
Bedford Rd. N22	24	30 90 C
Bedford Rd. N2	24	27 89 A
Bedford Rd. N8	36	29 88 D
Bedford Rd. N9	17	34 94 B
Bedford Rd. Orp	108	46 66 D
Bedford Rd. Sid	90	45 72 C
Bedford Rd. SW4	30	30 75 C
Bedford Rd. Twick	82	14 72 D
Bedford Rd. W13	54	16 80 B
Bedford Rd. W4	61	21 79 C
Bedford Rd. Wor Pk	103	23 65 A
Bedford Row. WC1	3	30 81 B
Bedford Sq. WC1	2	29 81 B
Bedford St. WC2	7	30 80 A
Bedford Way. WC1	2	29 82 D
Bedgebury Gdns. SW19	85	24 72 A
Bedgebury Rd. SE9	77	41 75 D
Bedivere Rd. Brom	89	40 72 C
Bedlow Way. Croy	111	30 64 B
Bedonwell Rd. Bexh	67	48 77 B
Bedonwell Rd. SE2	67	48 77 A
Bedser Dri. Grnf	43	14 85 D
Bedster Gdns. E Mol	92	13 69 D
Bedwardine Rd. SE19	97	33 70 C
Bedwell Rd. Belv	67	49 78 C
Bedwell Rd. N17	25	33 90 A
Bedwin Way. SE16	63	34 78 D
Beeby Rd. E13	58	40 81 B
Beech Ave. Brent	60	16 77 D
Beech Ave. N20	24	27 94 C
Beech Ave. Ruis	31	10 86 D
Beech Ave. S Croy	112	32 62 D
Beech Ave. Sid	90	46 73 A
Beech Ave. W3	55	21 80 C
Beech Cl. Ashf	81	08 71 D
Beech Cl. Cars	104	27 65 B
Beech Cl. Horn	42	52 86 D
Beech Cl. N9	34	34 95 D
Beech Cl. SW15	84	22 73 A
Beech Cl. SW19	95	23 70 A
Beech Copse. Brom	99	42 69 D
Beech Copse. S Croy	112	33 64 C
Beechcroft Ave. Bexh	79	50 76 D
Beechcroft Ave. Har	32	13 87 A
Beechcroft Ave. N Mal	94	20 69 C
Beechcroft Ave. NW11	35	24 87 B
Beechcroft Ave. Sthl	53	12 80 D
Beechcroft. Chis	100	43 70 C
Beechcroft. Cl. Houn	59	12 77 C
Beechcroft Gdns. Wem	33	18 86 D
Beechcroft. King	93	19 69 B
Beechcroft Rd. Chess	101	18 65 D
Beechcroft Rd. E18	27	40 90 D
Beechcroft Rd. SW14	72	20 75 A
Beechcroft Rd. SW17	86	27 72 A
Beechdale. N21	16	30 93 B
Beechdale Rd. SW2	74	30 74 D
Beech Dri. N2	24	27 89 B
Beechengrove. Pnr	20	12 89 B
Beeches The. Cars	111	27 63 C
Beeches Ct. Brom	99	40 70 A
Beeches Rd. Sutt	103	24 66 C
Beeches Rd. SW17	86	27 72 D
Beeches Wlk. Cars	111	27 62 A
Beechfield Ct. S Croy	112	32 64 A
Beechfield Gdns. Rom	41	50 87 A
Beechfield Rd. Brom	99	41 69 C
Beechfield Rd. Eri	68	51 77 C
Beechfield Rd. N4	37	32 88 C
Beechfield Rd. SE6	88	36 73 D
Beech Gdns. Dag	52	50 84 C
Beech Gdns. W5	60	18 79 C
Beech Gr. Ilf	28	45 91 A
Beech Gr. Mit	96	29 68 D
Beech Gr. N Mal	94	20 68 B
Beech Hall Cres. E4	26	38 91 D
Beech Hall Rd. E4	26	38 91 D
Beech Hill Ave. Barn	11	26 97 B
Beechhill Rd. SE9	78	43 74 A
Beech House Rd. Croy	105	32 65 D
Beech Lawns. N12	15	26 92 D
Beechmont Cl. Brom	89	39 71 C
Beechmore Gdns. Sutt	103	23 65 B
Beechmore Rd. SW11	74	27 76 B
Beechmount Ave. W7	54	15 81 A
Beecholme Ave. Mit	96	28 69 B
Beech Rd. Felt	81	09 73 A
Beech Rd. N11	24	30 91 A
Beech Rd. SW16	96	30 68 B
Beechrow. King	83	18 71 A
Beech St. EC2	4	32 81 A
Beech St. Rom	29	50 89 C
Beech Tree Pl. Sutt	110	25 64 D
Beechvale Cl. N12	16	27 92 C
Beechway. Bex	79	47 74 D
Beech Way. NW10	45	20 84 D
Beech Way. Twick	82	13 72 C
Beech Wlk. Dart	79	52 75 C
Beech Wlk. NW7	22	21 91 A
Beechwood Ave. Grnf	53	13 82 B
Beechwood Ave. Har	32	14 86 C
Beechwood Ave. N3	23	25 89 A
Beechwood Ave. Rich	72	19 76 A
Beechwood Ave. Ruis	31	09 86 B
Beechwood Ave. Sun	91	10 70 A
Beechwood Ave. T Hth	97	31 68 D
Beechwood Circ. Har	32	13 86 D
Beechwood Cl. Surb	101	17 66 B
Beechwood Cres. Bexh	79	48 75 A
Beechwood Dri. Cars	111	27 64 B
Beechwood Dri. Wdf Gn	27	39 91 B
Beechwood Gdns. Har	32	14 86 C
Beechwood Gdns. Ilf	28	42 88 B
Beechwood Gdns. Ilf	28	43 89 C
Beechwood Park. E18	27	40 89 A
Beechwood Rd. E8	48	33 84 B
Beechwood Rd. N8	24	30 89 C
Beechwood Rd. S Croy	112	33 62 A
Beecroft Rd. SE4	76	36 74 A
Beehive Ct. Ilf	39	42 88 D
Beehive Ct. Rom	30	54 91 D
Beehive La. Ilf	39	42 88 D
Beehive Pl. SW9	74	31 74 C
Beeleigh Rd. Mord	95	25 68 D
Beer La. King	93	17 69 C
Beer La. King	93	17 69 D
Beeston Cl. E8	48	34 85 C
Beeston Pl. SW1	6	28 79 D
Beeston Rd. Barn	11	26 95 D
Beeston Way. Felt	71	11 74 C
Beethoven St. W10	56	24 82 A
Beeton Cl. Pnr	20	13 91 C
Begbie Rd. SE3	77	41 76 A
Begonia Pl. Hamp	92	13 70 A
Begonia Wlk. W12	55	21 81 D
Beira St. SW12	86	28 73 B
Bekesbourne St. E14	57	36 81 C
Beldham Gdns. E Mol	92	13 68 B
Belfairs Dri. Rom	41	47 87 A
Belfast Rd. N16	37	33 86 B
Belfast Rd. SE25	97	34 68 D
Belfield Rd. Eps	109	21 63 C
Belford Gr. SE18	64	43 78 A
Belfort Rd. SE15	76	35 76 C
Belgrade Rd. Hamp	92	13 69 B
Belgrade Rd. N16	37	33 85 A
Belgrave Ave. Rom	30	53 89 A
Belgrave Cl. N14	16	29 95 A
Belgrave Cl. W3	61	20 79 A
Belgrave Cres. Sun	91	10 69 B
Belgrave Gdns. E13	58	41 82 C
Belgrave Gdns. N14	16	29 96 D
Belgrave Gdns. NW8	46	25 83 B
Belgrave Mews N. SW1	6	28 79 A
Belgrave Mews S. SW1	6	28 79 C
Belgrave Mews W. SW1	6	28 79 C
Belgrave Rd. E10	38	38 87 C
Belgrave Rd. E11	39	40 86 A
Belgrave Rd. E13	58	41 82 C
Belgrave Rd. E17	38	37 88 C
Belgrave Rd. Houn	70	12 75 B
Belgrave Rd. Ilf	39	42 87 D
Belgrave Rd. Ilf	40	43 86 A
Belgrave Rd. Mit	95	26 68 B
Belgrave Rd. SE25	97	33 68 D
Belgrave Rd. Sun	91	10 69 B
Belgrave Rd. SW13	61	21 77 D
Belgrave Rd. SW1	10	29 78 A
Belgrave Sq. SW1	6	28 79 C
Belgrave St. E1	57	35 81 D
Belgrave Wlk. Mit	95	26 68 B
Belgrave Yd. SW1	6	28 79 D
Belgravia Gdns. Brom	99	39 70 A
Belgravia Mews. King	93	17 68 D
Belgrove St. WC1	3	30 82 A
Belham Wlk. SE5	75	32 76 B
Belhaven St. E3	57	36 82 A
Belinda Rd. SW9	75	31 75 B
Belitha Villas. N1	48	31 84 C
Bellamy Cl. SW5	62	24 78 D
Bellamy Cl. Uxb	11	07 86 C
Bellamy Rd. E4	26	37 91 B
Bellamy St. SW12	86	28 73 B
Bellany Dri. Stan	21	16 90 B
Bellasis Ave. SW2	86	30 72 A
Bell Ave. Rom	30	52 90 B
Bell Cl. Pnr	20	11 89 A
Bell Cl. Ruis	31	09 86 D
Bell Ct. Surb	102	19 65 B
Bell Dri. SW18	85	24 73 A
Bellefield Rd. Orp	108	46 67 B
Bellefields Rd. SW9	74	30 75 B
Bellegrove Cl. Well	78	45 76 D
Bellegrove Rd. Well	78	45 76 C
Bellenden Rd. SE15	75	33 76 D
Belle Staines Pleasaunce. E4	18	37 93 A
Belleville Rd. SW11	74	27 74 B
Belle Vue. Grnf	43	14 83 B
Bellevue Park. T Hth	97	32 68 C
Bellevue Pl. E1	57	35 82 C
Bellevue Rd. Bexh	79	48 74 B
Bellevue Rd. Horn	42	54 87 D
Bellevue Rd. King	93	18 68 C
Bellevue Rd. N11	16	28 92 B
Belle Vue Rd. Rom	29	50 91 B
Bellevue Rd. SW13	61	22 76 C
Bellevue Rd. SW17	86	27 73 D
Bellevue Rd. W13	54	16 82 D
Bellew St. SW17	85	26 72 C
Bell Farm Ave. Dag	41	50 86 C
Bellfield Ave. Har	20	14 91 B
Bellflower Path. Rom	30	53 91 C
Bellgate Mews. NW5	36	28 86 D
Bell Green. La SE26	88	36 71 B
Bell Green. SE26	88	36 71 B
Bell Hill. Croy	105	32 65 A
Bell House Rd. Rom	41	50 87 C
Bellingham Green. SE6	88	37 72 C
Bellingham Rd. SE6	88	38 72 A
Bell Inn Yd. EC3	4	32 81 D
Bell La. E16	58	40 80 C
Bell La. E1	4	33 81 B
Bell La. NW4	23	23 89 D
Bell La. Twick	83	16 73 C
Bell Meadow. SE19	87	33 71 A
Bellot St. E10	15	39 78 C
Bell Rd. Enf	13	32 97 B
Bell Rd. Houn	70	13 75 D
Bellring Cl. Belv	67	49 77 A
Bell's Alley. SW6	73	25 76 C
Bells Hill. Barn	11	23 96 D
Bell St. NW1	1	27 81 A
Belltrees Gr. SW16	87	31 71 C
Bell Vue Rd. E17	26	38 90 D
Bell Water Gate. SE18	66	43 79 C
Bell Wharf La. EC4	4	32 80 A
Bellwood Rd. SE15	76	35 75 D
Bell Yd. WC2	7	31 81 C
Belmont Ave. Barn	12	27 95 B
Belmont Ave. Horn	42	54 86 B
Belmont Ave. N13	16	30 92 D
Belmont Ave. N17	25	32 89 A
Belmont Ave. N9	17	34 94 C
Belmont Ave. N Mal	94	22 68 C
Belmont Ave. Sthl	59	12 79 C
Belmont Ave. Well	78	45 75 A
Belmont Ave. Wem	44	18 83 B
Belmont Circ. Har	21	16 90 D
Belmont Circ. Stan	21	16 90 B
Belmont Cl. Barn	12	27 96 D
Belmont Cl. N20	15	25 94 D
Belmont Cl. SW4	74	29 75 A
Belmont Gr. SE13	76	38 75 B
Belmont Hill. SE13	76	38 75 B
Belmont La. Chis	90	44 71 C

Name	Page	Ref
Belmont La. Chis	90	44 71 C
Belmont La. Stan	21	17 91 C
Belmont Park Cl. SE13	77	39 75 C
Belmont Park Rd. E10	38	38 88 C
Belmont Park. SE13	77	39 75 C
Belmont Rd. Beck	98	36 69 D
Belmont Rd. Eri	79	49 76 B
Belmont Rd. Har	21	16 89 A
Belmont Rd. Horn	40	53 86 D
Belmont Rd. Ilf	40	44 86 C
Belmont Rd. N15	25	32 89 C
Belmont Rd. N17	25	32 89 A
Belmont Rd. SE25	105	34 67 B
Belmont Rd. Sutt	110	25 62 C
Belmont Rd. SW4	74	29 75 A
Belmont Rd. Twick	82	14 72 B
Belmont Rd. W4	61	20 78 B
Belmont Rd. Wall	111	29 64 C
Belmont Rise. Sutt	110	24 62 B
Belmont St. NW1	47	28 84 C
Belmont Terr. W4	61	20 78 B
Belmore St. SW8	74	29 76 B
Belsham St. E9	49	35 84 A
Belsize Ave. N13	24	30 91 B
Belsize Ave. NW3	47	27 85 C
Belsize Ave. W13	60	16 79 D
Belsize Cres. NW3	46	26 85 B
Belsize Ct Garages. NW3	46	26 85 D
Belsize Ct. NW3	46	26 85 D
Belsize Gdns. Sutt	110	25 64 B
Belsize Gr. NW3	47	27 84 A
Belsize La. NW3	47	27 85 C
Belsize Mews. NW3	46	26 84 B
Belsize Park Gdns. NW3	47	27 84 A
*Belsize Park Mews. NW3	46	26 84 B
Belsize Park. NW3	46	26 84 B
Belsize Pl. NW3	46	26 85 D
Belsize Rd. Har	20	14 91 D
Belsize Rd. NW6	46	26 84 C
Belsize Sq. NW3	46	26 84 B
Belsize Terr. NW3	46	26 84 B
Belson Rd. SE18	65	42 78 B
Beltane Dri. SW19	85	23 72 D
Belthorn Cres. SW12	86	29 73 A
Beltinge Rd. Rom	30	54 89 B
Belton Rd. E11	50	39 85 A
Belton Rd. E7	50	40 84 D
Belton Rd. N17	25	33 89 A
Belton Rd. NW2	45	22 84 A
Belton Rd. Sid	90	46 71 A
Belton Way. E3	57	37 81 A
Beltran Rd. SW6	73	25 76 D
Beltwood Rd. Belv	67	50 78 A
Belvedere Ave. Ilf	28	43 90 D
Belvedere Ave. SW19	85	24 71 C
Belvedere Bldgs. SE1	7	31 79 B
Belvedere Ct. Tedd	83	15 71 C
Belvedere Ct. N2	35	26 88 B
Belvedere Dri. SW19	85	24 71 C
Belvedere Gr. SW19	85	24 71 C
Belvedere Pl. SE1	7	31 79 B
Belvedere Rd. Bexh	79	48 76 D
Belvedere Rd. E10	38	36 87 C
Belvedere Rd. SE19	87	33 70 D
Belvedere Rd. SE1	7	30 79 B
Belvedere Sq. SW19	85	24 71 C
Belvedere Strand. NW9	22	21 90 D
Belvedere Way. Har	22	18 88 C
Belvill Allen Cl. SW17	86	27 71 D
Belvoir Cl. SE9	89	42 72 C
Belvoir Rd. SE22	87	34 73 A
Belvue Cl. Nthlt	43	13 84 C
Belvue Rd. Nthlt	43	13 84 C
Bembridge Cl. NW6	46	24 84 C
Bembridge Gdns. Ruis	31	08 86 B
Bemerton St. N1	47	30 83 B
Bemish Rd. SW15	73	23 75 B
Bempton Dri. Ruis	31	10 86 D
Bemsted Rd. E17	26	36 89 B
Benares Rd. SE18	66	45 78 B
Benbow Rd. W6	61	22 79 D
Benbow St. SE8	64	37 77 A
Benbury Cl. Brom	88	38 71 C
Bench Field. S Croy	122	33 64 D
Bench The. Rich	83	17 72 C
Bencroft Rd. SW16	96	29 70 C
Bencurtis Park. W Wick	106	38 65 D
Bendall Mews. NW1	1	27 81 A
Bendemeer Rd. SW15	73	23 75 B
Bendish Rd. E6	50	42 84 C
Bendmore Ave. SE2	66	46 78 A
Bendon Valley. SW18	85	25 73 A
Benedict Cl. Orp	108	45 65 C
Benedict Dri. Felt	81	08 73 B
Benedict Rd. Mit	95	26 68 B
Benedict Rd. SW9	74	30 75 B
Benedict Way. N2	23	26 89 A
Benenden Green. Brom	107	40 67 A
Benett Gdns. SW16	96	30 69 C
Benfleet Cl. Sutt	103	26 65 C
Bengal Ct. EC3	4	32 81 D
Bengal Rd. Ilf	40	43 86 D
Bengarth Dri. Har	20	14 90 D
Bengarth Rd. Nthlt	43	12 83 A
Bengeworth Rd. Har	33	16 86 C
Bengeworth Rd. SE5	75	32 75 A
Benham Cl. SW11	74	26 75 B
Benham Rd. W7	54	15 81 A
Benhill Ave. Sutt	110	25 64 B
Benhill Ave. Sutt	110	26 64 A
Benhill Rd. SE5	76	32 76 B
Benhill Rd. Sutt	110	26 64 B
Benhill Wood Rd. Sutt	110	26 64 A
Benhilton Gdns. Sutt	103	25 65 D
Benhurst Ave. Horn	42	52 86 D
Benhurst Ct. SW16	87	31 71 C
Benhurst La. SW16	87	31 71 C
Benin St. SE13	88	38 73 B
Benjamin Cl. E8	34	34 83 A
Benjamin Cl. Rom	42	52 87 D
Benjamin St. EC1	3	31 81 B
Ben Jonson Rd. E1	57	36 81 C
Benledi St. E14	58	38 81 D
Bennerley Rd. SW11	74	27 74 B
Bennet Cl. King	93	17 69 A
Bennett Cl. Nthwd	19	09 91 D
Bennett Cl. Well	78	46 76 C
Bennett Gr. SE13	76	37 76 B
Bennett Park. SE3	77	39 75 B
Bennett Rd. E13	58	41 82 C
Bennett Rd. Rom	41	48 87 A
Bennetts Ave. Croy	106	36 65 A
Bennetts Ave. Grnf	44	15 83 A
Bennett's Castle La. Dag	52	47 85 A
Bennett's Castle La. Dag	41	47 85 A
Bennetts Cl. N17	25	33 91 B
Bennetts Copse. Chis	99	39 68 A
Bennett's Hill. EC4	8	32 80 A
Bennett St. SW1	6	29 80 C
Bennett St. W4	61	21 77 A
Bennetts Way. Croy	106	36 65 B
Bennett's Yd. SW1	6	29 79 D
Benningholme Rd. Edg	22	21 91 A
Bennington Rd. N17	25	33 90 A
Bennington Rd. Wdf Gn	27	39 91 C
Benn's Alley. Hamp	92	13 69 D
Benn St. E9	49	36 84 B
Benrek Cl. Ilf	28	44 90 A
Bensbury Cl. SW15	85	23 73 A
Bensham Cl. Th Hth	97	32 68 C
Bensham Gr. Th Hth	97	32 69 C
Bensham La. Croy	105	31 67 D
Bensham La. Th Hth	97	31 67 D
Bensham Manor Rd. Th Hth	97	32 68 C
Ben Smith Way. SE16		34 79 C
Benson Ave. E6	50	41 83 D
Benson Cl. Houn		13 75 C
Benson Rd. Croy	105	31 65 C
Benson Rd. SE23		35 73 C
Bentfield Gdns. SE9	89	41 72 D
Benthal Rd. N16		34 86 C
Bentham Ct. N1	48	32 84 C
Bentham Rd. E9	49	35 84 B
Bentham Wlk. N10	45	20 85 D
Ben Tillet Cl. Bark	51	46 84 C
Bentinck Mews. W1	2	28 81 C
Bentinck St. W1	2	28 81 C
Bentley Cl. SW19	85	25 72 C
Bentley Dri. Ilf	40	44 88 C
Bentley Rd. N1	48	33 84 A
Benton Gdns. Ilf	40	44 87 D
Benton Rd. Ilf	40	44 87 D
Benton's La. SE27	87	32 71 A
Benton's Rise. SE27	87	32 71 D
Bentry Cl. Dag	41	48 86 A
Bentry Rd. Dag	41	48 86 A
Bentworth Rd. W12	55	22 81 D
Benwell Rd. N5		31 85 C
Benwick Ct. SE20	103	35 69 A
Benwood Ct. Sutt	103	26 65 C
Benworth St. E3	57	36 82 B
Benyon Rd. N1	48	32 83 B
Berber Rd. SW11		27 74 B
Bercta Rd. SE9	90	44 72 A
Berenger Wlk. SW10	62	26 77 D
Berenger Wlk. SW10	62	26 77 D
Berens Rd. NW10		23 82 B
Berens Way. Chis	100	45 68 B
Beresford Ave. N20	16	27 93 B
Beresford Ave. NW10	45	19 83 A
Beresford Ave. Surb	102	20 66 A
Beresford Ave. Twick	71	17 74 C
Beresford Ave. W7	54	15 81 A
Beresford Dri. Brom	99	42 68 A
Beresford Gdns. Enf	13	33 96 C
Beresford Gdns. Houn	70	12 74 B
Beresford Gdns. Rom	41	48 88 A
Beresford Ho. SE21	87	34 72 C
Beresford Rd. E17	26	37 90 B
Beresford Rd. Har	32	16 88 C
Beresford Rd. King	93	18 69 B
Beresford Rd. N2	24	27 89 A
Beresford Rd. N5	48	32 85 D
Beresford Rd. N8	37	31 88 B
Beresford Rd. N Mal	94	20 68 C
Beresford Rd. Sthl	53	11 80 D
Beresford Rd. Sutt	110	24 63 D
Beresford Sq. SE18	66	43 78 B
Beresford St. SE18	66	43 79 D
Beresford Terr. N5	48	32 85 C
Bere St. E1	57	35 80 B
Berestede Rd. W6	61	21 78 D
Berger Cl. Orp	108	45 67 C
Berger Rd. E9	49	35 84 B
Berghem Mews. W14	62	23 79 D
Bergholt Ave. Ilf	39	42 88 A
Bergholt Cres. N16	37	33 87 A
Bering Wlk. E16	58	41 81 C
Berkeley Ave. Bexh	79	47 76 B
Berkeley Ave. Grnf	44	15 84 A
Berkeley Ave. Houn	69	10 76 A
Berkeley Ave. Ilf	28	43 90 D
Berkeley Ave. Rom	29	50 91 C
Berkeley Cl. Brent	60	16 77 A
Berkeley Cl. Ruis	31	10 86 C
Berkeley Cres. Barn	11	26 95 D
Berkeley Ct. N14	16	29 94 A
Berkeley Dri. E Mol	92	13 68 A
Berkeley Gdns. N21	17	32 94 B
Berkeley Gdns. W8	56	25 80 C
Berkeley Mews. W1	1	27 81 D
Berkeley Pl. SW19	95	23 70 B
Berkeley Rd. E12	50	42 85 C
Berkeley Rd. N15	37	32 88 D
Berkeley Rd. N8	36	29 88 D
Berkeley Rd. NW9	34	19 88 A
Berkeley Rd. SW13	72	22 76 A
Berkeley Sq. W1	6	28 80 B
Berkeley St. W1	6	28 80 D
Berkeley Waye. Houn	59	12 77 C
Berkeley Wlk. N7	36	30 86 B
Berkely Cl. Orp	108	45 66 A
Berkhampstead Rd. Belv	67	49 78 C
Berkhamsted Ave. Wem	45	19 84 A
Berkley Gr. NW1	47	28 84 C
*Berkley Rd. NW1	47	27 84 D
Berkshire Gdns. N13	25	31 91 A
Berkshire Gdns. N18	17	34 92 D
Berkshire Rd. E9	49	36 84 B
Berkshire Way. Mit	104	30 67 A
Berkshire Way. Mit	96	30 68 C
Bermans Way. NW10	45	21 85 B
Bermondsey St. SE1	8	33 79 A
Bermondsey Trading Estate. SE16	64	35 78 C
Bermondsey Wall E. SE16	63	34 79 B
Bermondsey Wall W. SE16	63	34 79 A
Bermonsey Sq. SE1	8	33 79 C
Bernard Ave. W13	60	16 79 D
Bernard Cassidy St. E16	58	39 81 B
Bernard Gdns. SW19	85	25 71 C
Bernard Rd. N15	37	33 88 B
Bernard Rd. Rom	41	50 87 A
Bernard Rd. Wall	111	28 64 B
Bernard St. WC1	3	30 82 C
Bernard's Cl. Stan	21	17 91 A
Bernays Cl. Stan	21	17 91 A
Bernay's Gr. SW9	74	30 75 D
Bernel Dri. Croy	106	36 65 D
Berne Rd. Th Hth	97	32 67 A
Berners Mews. W1	2	29 81 A
Berners Pl. W1	2	29 81 C
Berners Rd. N1	48	31 83 B
Berners Rd. N22	25	31 90 C
Berners St. W1	2	29 81 C
Berney Rd. Croy	105	32 66 B
Berridge Green. Edg	22	19 91 C
Berridge Rd. SE19	87	33 71 C
Berriman Rd. N7	36	30 86 D
Berriton Rd. Har	32	12 87 D
Berry Cl. N21	17	31 94 D
Berry Cl. NW10	45	21 84 C
Berryfield Rd. SE17	63	31 78 D
Berryhill Gdns. SE9	78	43 75 D
Berryhill. SE9	78	43 75 D
Berrylands Rd. Surb	101	18 67 D

Berrylands. Surb *102* 19 67 A
Berrylands. SW20 *95* 23 68 C
Berryman Cl. Dag *41* 47 86 C
Berryman's La. SE26 *88* 35 71 B
Berrymead Gdns. W3 *61* 20 79 A
Berrymede Rd. W4 *61* 20 79 D
Berry Pl. EC1 *3* 31 82 B
Berry St. EC1 *3* 31 82 D
Berry Way. W5 *60* 18 79 C
Bertal Rd. SW17 *85* 26 71 B
Berther Rd. Horn *42* 54 87 A
Berthon St. SE8 *64* 37 77 B
Bertie Rd. NW10 *45* 22 84 A
Bertram Cottages. SW19 *95* 25 70 C
Bertram Rd. Enf *13* 34 96 C
Bertram Rd. King *94* 19 70 C
Bertram Rd. NW4 *34* 22 88 C
Bertram St. N19 *36* 28 86 B
Bertrand St. SE13 *76* 37 75 B
Bert Rd. Th Hth *105* 32 67 A
Bert Way. Enf *13* 33 96 D
Berwick Ave. Hay *53* 11 80 B
Berwick Cres. Sid *78* 45 74 C
Berwick Rd. E16 *58* 41 81 C
Berwick Rd. E17 *26* 36 89 D
Berwick Rd. N22 *25* 31 90 B
Berwick Rd. Well *78* 46 76 B
Berwick St. W1 *2* 29 81 C
Berwyn Ave. Houn *70* 13 76 B
Berwyn Rd. Rich *72* 19 75 D
Berwyn Rd. SE24 *87* 31 73 D
Beryl Rd. W6 *62* 23 78 D
Berystede. King *94* 19 70 D
Besant Ct. N1 *48* 32 85 D
Besant Rd. NW2 *46* 24 85 A
Besant Way. NW10 *45* 20 85 C
Besant Wlk. N7 *36* 30 86 B
Besley St. SW16 *96* 29 70 A
Bessborough Gdns. SW1 *10* 29 78 D
Bessborough Mews. SW1 *10* 29 78 D
Bessborough Pl. SW1 *10* 29 78 D
Bessborough Rd. Har *32* 14 87 B
Bessborough Rd. SW15 *84* 22 73 C
Bessborough St. SW1 *10* 29 78 D
Bessborough Way. SW1 *10* 29 78 D
Bessemer Rd. SE5 *75* 32 76 D
Bessingby Rd. Ruis *31* 10 86 B
Bessingham Wlk. SE4 *76* 35 75 D
Besson St. SE14 *76* 35 76 B
Bessy St. E2 *57* 35 82 A
Bestwood St. SE8 *64* 35 78 B
Beswick Mews. NW3 *46* 25 84 B
Betchworth Cl. Sutt *110* 26 64 D
Betchworth Rd. Ilf *40* 45 86 C
Betham Rd. Grnf *53* 14 82 B
Bethany Waye. Felt *81* 09 73 A
Bethecar Rd. Har *33* 15 88 A
Bethell Ave. E16 *58* 39 82 D
Bethell Ave. Ilf *40* 43 87 A
Bethel Rd. Well *79* 47 75 A
Bethersden Cl. Beck *98* 36 70 D
Bethnal Green Rd. E1 *4* 33 82 D
Bethnal Green Rd. E2 *57* 34 82 A
Bethune Ave. N11 *16* 27 92 B
Bethune Rd. N16 *37* 33 87 A
Bethune Rd. NW10 *55* 20 82 D
Bethwin Rd. SE5 *63* 32 77 C
Betony Rd. Rom *30* 53 91 B
Betsham Rd. Eri *68* 51 77 D
Betstyle Rd. N11 *16* 28 92 B
Betterton St. WC2 *3* 30 81 C
Bettons Park. E15 *50* 39 83 A
Bettridge Rd. SW6 *73* 24 76 D
Betts Cl. Beck *98* 36 69 C
Betts Rd. E16 *58* 40 80 B
Betts St. E1 *57* 34 80 B
Betts Way. Surb *101* 16 66 C
Beulah Ave. Th Hth *97* 32 69 C
Beulah Cres. Th Hth *97* 32 69 C
Beulah Gr. Croy *105* 32 67 C
Beulah Hill. SE19 *97* 32 70 D
Beulah Path. E17 *38* 37 88 B
Beulah Rd. E17 *38* 37 88 B
Beulah Rd. Horn *42* 53 86 C
Beulah Rd. Sutt *110* 25 64 A
Beulah Rd. SW19 *95* 24 70 D
Beulah Rd. Th Hth *97* 32 68 A
Beult Rd. Dart *80* 52 75 C
Bevan Ave. Bark *51* 46 84 C
Bevan Ct. Croy *112* 31 64 C
Bevan Rd. Barn *12* 27 96 D
Bevan Rd. SE2 *66* 46 78 D
Bevan St. N1 *48* 32 83 A
Bevan Way. Horn *42* 54 86 D
Bevenden St. N1 *4* 32 82 B

Bevercote Wlk. Belv *67* 48 77 B
Beverley Ave. Houn *70* 12 75 D
Beverley Ave. Sid *90* 45 73 B
Beverley Ave. SW20 *94* 21 69 B
Beverley Cl. Enf *13* 33 96 C
Beverley Cl. Horn *42* 54 87 B
Beverley Cl. N21 *17* 32 94 C
Beverley Cl. SW11 *73* 26 75 D
Beverley Cl. SW13 *72* 22 76 C
Beverley Cres. Wdf Gn *27* 40 91 D
Beverley Ct. SE4 *76* 36 75 B
Beverley Dri. Edg *22* 19 89 A
Beverley Gdns. Horn *42* 54 87 B
Beverley Gdns. NW11 *35* 24 87 A
Beverley Gdns. Stan *21* 16 90 A
Beverley Gdns. SW13 *72* 21 75 B
Beverley Gdns. Wem *34* 19 87 C
Beverley Gdns. Wor Pk *102* 22 66 C
Beverley Hyrst. Croy *105* 33 65 B
Beverley La. King *94* 21 70 C
Beverley La. SW19 *84* 21 71 B
Beverley Path. SW13 *72* 21 76 D
Beverley Rd. Bexh *79* 50 76 C
Beverley Rd. Brom *107* 42 65 A
Beverley Rd. Dag *52* 48 85 A
Beverley Rd. E4 *26* 38 91 B
Beverley Rd. E6 *58* 41 82 B
Beverley Rd. King *93* 17 69 A
Beverley Rd. Mit *96* 29 68 D
Beverley Rd. N Mal *94* 22 68 C
Beverley Rd. Ruis *31* 10 86 B
Beverley Rd. SE20 *97* 34 69 D
Beverley Rd. Sthl *59* 12 79 C
Beverley Rd. Sun *91* 09 68 B
Beverley Rd. SW13 *72* 21 75 B
Beverley Rd. Wor Pk *103* 23 65 A
Beverley Way. N Mal *94* 22 68 C
Beverley Way. SW20 *94* 22 69 C
Beverly Ct. N14 *16* 29 94 A
Beversbrook Rd. N19 *36* 29 86 D
Beverstone Rd. SW2 *74* 30 74 B
Beverstone Rd. Th Hth *97* 31 68 D
Bevington Rd. Beck *98* 37 69 D
Bevington Rd. W10 *56* 24 81 A
Bevington St. SE16 *63* 34 79 A
Bevin Way. WC1 *3* 31 82 A
Bevis Marks. EC3 *4* 33 81 C
Bewcastle Gdns. Enf *12* 30 96 C
Bewdley St. N1 *48* 31 84 C
Bewick St. SW8 *74* 28 76 D
Bewley St. E1 *57* 35 80 A
Bewlys Rd. SE27 *87* 31 71 D
Bexhill Cl. Felt *82* 12 72 A
Bexhill Rd. N11 *16* 29 92 D
Bexhill Rd. SE4 *76* 36 74 D
Bexhill Rd. SW14 *72* 20 75 A
Bexley Cl. Dart *80* 51 74 A
Bexley Gdns. N9 *17* 32 92 D
Bexley La. Dart *80* 51 74 A
Bexley Rd. Eri *67* 50 77 A
Bexley Rd. SE9 *78* 44 74 A
Beynon Rd. Cars *111* 27 64 D
Bianca Rd. SE15 *63* 34 77 A
Bibsworth Rd. N3 *23* 24 90 D
Bibury Cl. SE15 *63* 33 77 A
Bicester Rd. Rich *72* 19 75 B
Bickenhall St. W1 *1* 27 81 B
Bickersteth Rd. SW17 *96* 27 70 B
Bickersteth Rd. SW17 *86* 27 71 D
Bickerton Rd. N19 *36* 29 86 A
Bickley Cres. Brom *99* 42 68 B
Bickley Park Rd. Brom *99* 42 68 B
Bickley Rd. Brom *99* 42 69 C
Bickley Rd. E10 *38* 37 87 B
Bickley St. SW17 *86* 27 71 D
Bicknell Rd. SE5 *75* 32 75 A
Bicknoller Cl. Sutt *110* 25 62 D
Bicknoller Rd. Enf *13* 33 97 B
Bicknor Rd. Orp *108* 45 66 B
Bidborough Cl. Brom *107* 39 67 B
Bidborough St. WC1 *3* 30 82 A
Biddenden Way. SE9 *90* 43 71 A
Bidder St. E16 *58* 39 81 A
Bidder St. E16 *58* 39 82 C
Biddestone Rd. N7 *47* 30 85 B
Biddulph Rd. S Croy *112* 32 62 A
Biddulph Rd. W9 *56* 25 82 B
Bideford Ave. Grnf *44* 16 83 D
Bideford Cl. Edg *22* 19 90 A
Bideford Cl. Felt *82* 12 72 D
Bideford Cl. Rom *30* 53 90 A
Bideford Gdns. Enf *17* 33 94 A
Bideford Rd. Brom *89* 39 72 D
Bideford Rd. Ruis *32* 11 86 C

Bideford Rd. SE2 *66* 46 77 D
Bidwell Gdns. N11 *24* 29 91 C
Bidwell St. SE15 *75* 34 76 B
Bigbury Cl. N17 *25* 33 91 C
Biggerstaff Rd. E15 *49* 38 83 A
Biggerstaff St. N4 *37* 31 86 A
Biggin Ave. Mit *96* 27 69 B
Biggin Hill. SE19 *97* 31 70 D
Biggin Way. SE19 *97* 32 70 C
Bigginwood Rd. SW16 *97* 31 70 D
Bigg's Row. SW15 *73* 23 75 B
Big Hill. E5 *37* 34 87 D
Bigland St. E1 *57* 34 81 D
Bignold Rd. E7 *50* 40 85 A
Bigwood Rd. NW11 *35* 25 88 D
Billet La. Horn *42* 53 87 D
Billet Rd. E17 *26* 36 90 B
Billet Rd. Rom *29* 47 89 B
Billingford Cl. SE4 *76* 35 75 D
Billing Pl. SW10 *62* 25 77 D
Billing Rd. SW10 *62* 25 77 D
Billing St. SW10 *62* 25 77 D
Billington Rd. SE14 *64* 35 77 D
Billiter Sq. EC3 *4* 33 81 C
Billiter St. EC3 *4* 33 81 C
Billson St. E14 *64* 38 78 A
Bilsby Gr. SE9 *89* 41 71 B
Bilton Rd. Eri *68* 52 77 A
Bilton Rd. Grnf *44* 16 83 B
Bilton Way. Enf *14* 36 97 A
Bina Gdns. SW5 *62* 26 78 A
Bincote Rd. Enf *12* 30 96 B
Binden Rd. W12 *71* 21 79 D
Bindon Green. Mord *95* 25 68 D
Binfield Rd. S Croy *112* 33 64 D
Binfield Rd. SW4 *74* 30 76 A
Bingfield St. N1 *47* 30 83 B
Bingham Pl. W1 *2* 28 81 A
Bingham Rd. Croy *105* 34 66 D
Bingham St. N1 *48* 32 84 B
Bingley Rd. E16 *58* 41 81 C
Bingley Rd. Grnf *53* 14 81 A
Bingley Rd. Sun *91* 10 70 C
Binney St. W1 *2* 28 81 C
Binns Rd. W4 *61* 21 78 C
Binsey Wlk. SE2 *67* 47 79 A
Binton Rd. SW19 *95* 26 70 B
Binyon Cres. Stan *21* 15 91 B
Birbeck Gr. W3 *61* 20 79 B
Birbeck Hill. SE21 *87* 31 73 D
Birbeck Pl. SE21 *87* 32 72 A
Birbeck Rd. N12 *15* 26 92 C
Birbetts Rd. SE9 *89* 42 72 B
Bircham Path. SE4 *76* 35 75 D
Birchanger Rd. SE25 *105* 34 67 A
Birch Ave. N13 *17* 32 93 C
Birchbeck Rd. Sid *90* 46 72 C
Birch Cl. Brent *60* 16 77 D
Birch Cl. E16 *58* 39 81 A
Birch Cl. N19 *36* 29 86 A
Birch Cl. Rom *29* 49 89 B
Birch Cl. SE15 *75* 34 76 C
Birch Cres. Horn *30* 54 89 C
Birchdale Gdns. Rom *41* 47 87 B
Birchdale Rd. E7 *50* 41 85 C
Birchen Cl. NW9 *34* 20 86 B
Birchen Gr. NW9 *34* 20 86 B
Birches Cl. Pnr *32* 12 88 A
Birches The. N21 *12* 30 95 D
Birches The. SE7 *65* 40 77 B
Birchfield Gr. Eps *110* 23 62 C
Birchfield St. E14 *57* 37 80 A
Birch Gdns. Dag *41* 50 86 C
Birch Green. NW9 *22* 21 91 C
Birch Gr. SE12 *89* 39 73 B
Birch Gr. Shep *91* 09 69 C
Birch Gr. W3 *61* 19 80 A
Birch Gr. Well *78* 46 75 C
Birchington Cl. Bexh *79* 49 76 B
Birchington Rd. N8 *36* 29 88 D
Birchington Rd. NW6 *46* 25 83 A
Birchington Rd. Surb *101* 18 66 B
Birchin La. EC3 *4* 32 81 D
Birchlands Ave. SW12 *86* 27 73 B
Birchmead Ave. Pnr *20* 11 89 C
Birch Mead. Orp *108* 43 65 A
Birchmere Row. SE3 *77* 39 76 D
Birchmore Wlk. N5 *37* 32 86 C
Birch Park. Har *20* 14 91 C
Birch Rd. Felt *82* 11 71 C
Birch Rd. Rom *29* 49 89 B
Birch Row. Brom *108* 43 66 A
Birch Tree Way. Croy *105* 34 65 B
Birch Wlk. Eri *67* 50 77 A
Birch Wlk. Mit *96* 28 69 B

Name	Page	Grid
Birchwood Ave. Beck	98	36 68 D
Birchwood Ave. N10	24	28 89 C
Birchwood Ave. Sid	90	46 72 B
Birchwood Ave. Sid	90	46 72 D
Birchwood Ave. Wall	104	28 65 C
Birchwood Ct. Edg	22	20 90 C
Birchwood Gr. Hamp	92	13 70 B
Birchwood Rd. Orp	100	45 68 C
Birchwood Rd. SW17	86	28 71 D
Birdbrook Cl. Dag	52	50 84 C
Birdbrook Rd. SE3	77	41 75 A
Birdcage Wlk. SW1	6	29 79 B
Birdham Dri. Brom	107	42 67 A
Birdhurst Ave. S Croy	112	32 64 B
Birdhurst Ct. Wall	111	29 63 C
Birdhurst Gdns. S Croy	112	32 64 B
Birdhurst Rd. S Croy	112	33 64 C
Birdhurst Rd. SW18	73	26 74 A
Birdhurst Rd. SW19	96	27 70 A
Birdhurst Rise. S Croy	112	33 64 C
Bird-in-Bush Rd. SE15	63	34 77 C
Bird-in-hand La. Brom	99	41 69 D
Bird-in-hand Pas. SE23	88	35 72 A
Bird in Hand Path. Croy	105	32 66 B
*Bird In Hand Yd. NW3	46	26 85 A
Birdlip Cl. SE15	63	33 77 A
Birds Farm Ave. Rom	29	49 90 B
Bird St. W1	2	28 81 C
Bird Wlk. Twick	82	12 73 D
Birdwood Cl. Tedd	83	15 71 A
Birkbeck Ave. Grnf	43	14 83 B
Birkbeck Ave. W3	55	20 80 A
Birkbeck Mews. E8	48	33 85 D
Birkbeck Rd. Beck	98	35 69 D
Birkbeck Rd. E8	48	33 85 D
Birkbeck Rd. Enf	13	32 97 B
Birkbeck Rd. Ilf	40	44 88 B
Birkbeck Rd. N17	25	33 90 B
Birkbeck Rd. N8	24	30 89 C
Birkbeck Rd. Rom	41	50 87 D
Birkbeck Rd. SW19	95	25 70 B
Birkbeck Rd. W3	55	20 80 D
Birkbeck Rd. W5	60	17 78 A
Birkbeck St. E2	57	34 82 B
Birkbeck Way. Grnf	43	14 83 B
Birkdale Ave. Pnr	20	13 89 A
Birkdale Ave. Rom	30	54 91 D
Birkdale Cl. Orp	108	44 66 B
Birkdale Rd. SE2	66	46 78 A
Birkdale Rd. W5	54	18 82 C
Birkenhead Ave. King	93	18 69 B
Birkenhead St. WC1	3	30 82 A
Birkhall Rd. SE6	88	38 72 B
Birkwood Cl. SW12	86	29 73 B
Birley Rd. N20	15	26 93 A
Birley St. SW11	74	28 76 C
Birling Rd. Eri	80	51 76 A
Birnam Rd. N4	36	30 86 B
Biscay Rd. W6	62	23 78 D
Biscoe Cl. Houn	59	13 77 A
Biscoe Way. SE13	76	38 75 B
Bisenden Rd. Croy	105	33 65 A
Bisham Cl. Cars	104	27 66 D
Bisham Gdns. N6	36	28 87 D
Bishop Butt Cl. Orp	108	45 65 D
Bishop Craven Cl. Enf	13	31 97 B
Bishopsford Rd. Mord	103	26 67 D
Bishop Gr. N2	36	27 88 C
Bishop Ken Rd. Har	21	15 90 B
Bishop King's Rd. W14	62	24 78 A
Bishop Rd. N14	16	28 94 B
Bishops Ave. Brom	99	41 68 A
Bishops Ave. E13	50	40 83 B
Bishops Ave. Rom	41	47 88 C
Bishop's Ave. SW6	73	24 76 C
Bishops Ave The. N2	35	26 88 D
Bishop's Bridge Rd. W2	2	26 81 C
Bishops Cl. Barn	11	23 95 D
Bishop's Cl. E17	26	37 89 D
Bishop's Cl. Enf	13	34 97 D
Bishops Close. Sutt	103	25 65 C
Bishops Cl. Rich	83	17 72 D
Bishops Cl. SE9	90	44 72 A
Bishopscourt. Croy	105	33 65 B
Bishop's Ct. EC4	3	31 81 D
Bishop's Ct. WC2	3	31 81 C
Bishopsgate Church Yd. EC2	4	33 81 C
Bishopsgate. EC2	4	33 81 A
Bishops Gr. Hamp	82	12 71 B
Bishops Gr. N2	36	27 88 C
Bishop's Hall. King	93	17 69 D
Bishop's Mansions. SW6	73	23 76 D
Bishops Park Rd. SW16	96	30 69 A
Bishops Park Rd. SW6	73	24 76 C
Bishops Pl. Sutt	110	26 64 C
Bishop's Rd. Croy	105	31 66 B
Bishops Rd. N6	36	28 88 C
Bishop's Rd. SW6	62	24 77 D
Bishop's Rd. SW6	62	24 77 D
Bishop's Rd. W7	60	15 79 A
Bishop's Terr. SE11	63	31 78 A
Bishopsthorpe Rd. SE26	88	35 71 B
Bishop St. N1	4	32 83 A
Bishop's Way. E2	49	35 83 C
Bishops Wlk. Chis	100	44 69 A
Bishop's Wlk. Pnr	20	12 89 A
Bishopswood Rd. N6	36	27 87 B
Bishop Way. NW10	45	21 84 C
Bisley Cl. Wor Pk	103	23 66 C
Bispham Rd. NW10	54	18 82 B
Bisson Rd. E15	49	38 83 C
Bisterne Ave. E17	26	38 89 B
Bittacy Cl. NW7	23	23 91 B
Bittacy Ct. NW7	23	24 91 C
Bittacy Hill. NW7	23	23 91 B
Bittacy Park Ave. NW7	23	23 92 D
Bittacy Rd. NW7	23	23 91 B
Bittacy Rise. NW7	23	23 91 B
Bittern Pl. N22	24	30 90 D
Bittern St. SE1	7	32 79 A
Bittoms The. King	93	17 68 B
Bixley Cl. Sthl	53	12 78 B
Blackall St. EC2	4	33 82 C
Blackberry Cl. Shep	91	09 68 C
Blackberry Farm Cl. Houn	59	12 77 C
Blackbird Hill. NW9	34	20 86 A
Blackborne Rd. Dag	52	49 84 B
Black Boy La. N15	37	32 88 A
Blackbrook La. Brom	100	43 68 C
Blackburn Rd. NW6	46	25 84 B
Blackbush Ave. Rom	41	47 88 B
Blackbush Cl. Sutt	110	25 63 D
Blackett St. SW15	73	23 75 B
Blackfen Rd. Sid	78	46 74 C
Blackford Cl. S Croy	112	31 62 B
Blackford's Path. SW15	84	22 73 A
Blackfriars Bridge. EC4	7	31 80 B
Blackfriars Ct. EC4	7	31 80 B
Black Friars La. EC4	3	31 81 D
Blackfriars Pas. EC4	7	31 80 A
Blackfriars Rd. SE1	7	31 80 D
Blackfriars Underpass. EC4	7	31 80 B
Black Gates. Pnr	20	12 89 B
Blackheath Ave. SE10	65	39 77 C
Blackheath Gro. SE3	77	39 76 D
Blackheath Hill. SE10	76	38 76 A
Blackheath Park. SE3	77	40 75 A
Blackheath Rise. SE13	76	37 76 B
Blackheath Vale. SE3	77	39 76 C
Blackheath Village. SE3	77	39 76 D
Black Horse Ct. SE1	7	32 79 D
Blackhorse La. Croy	105	34 66 A
Blackhorse La. E17	26	35 89 B
Blackhorse Rd. E17	26	36 89 C
Blackhorse Rd. SE8	64	36 78 C
Black Horse Rd. Sid	90	46 71 A
Blacklands Rd. SE6	88	38 71 A
Black Lion La. W6	61	22 78 A
Blackmore Ave. Sthl	53	14 80 D
Blackmore's Gr. Tedd	93	16 70 A
Blackpool Rd. SE15	75	34 76 D
Black Prince Rd. SE11	10	30 78 B
Black Prince Rd. SE1	10	30 78 B
Blackshaw Pl. N1	48	33 84 C
Blackshaw Rd. SW17	85	26 71 D
Blackshaw Rd. SW17	96	27 70 A
Black's Rd. W6	62	23 78 A
Blackstock Rd. N4	37	31 86 B
Blackstock Rd. N5	37	31 86 D
Blackstone Ho. SE21	87	34 72 C
Blackstone Rd. NW2	45	23 85 A
Black Swan Yd. SE1	8	33 79 A
Blackthorn Ct. Houn	59	12 77 C
Blackthorne Ave. Croy	106	35 66 C
Blackthorne Dri. E4	18	38 92 B
Blackthorn Gr. Bexh	79	48 75 A
Blackthorn St. E3	57	37 82 C
Blacktree Mews. SW9	75	31 75 A
Blackwall La. E10	65	39 78 B
Blackwall Tunnel App. E14	58	38 81 C
Blackwall Tunnel App. SE10	65	37 79 A
Blackwall Tunnel Northern App. E14		38 81 A
Blackwall Tunnel Northern App. E3		38 82 C
Blackwall Tunnels. SE10	58	39 80 A
Blackwall Way. E14	58	38 80 A
Blackwater Rd. Sutt	110	25 64 D
Blackwater St. SE22	75	33 74 B
Blackwell Cl. E5	49	36 85 A
Blackwell Cl. Har	20	14 91 D
Blackwood St. SE17	63	32 78 D
Blagden's Cl. N14	16	29 93 B
Blagden's La. N14	16	29 93 B
Blagdon Rd. N Mal	94	21 68 D
Blagdon Rd. SE13	76	37 74 D
Blagdon Wlk. Tedd	93	17 70 A
Blagrove Rd. W10	56	24 81 B
Blair Ave. NW9	34	21 87 A
Blair Cl. Sid	78	45 74 A
Blair Ct. Beck	98	37 69 B
Blairderry Rd. SW2	86	30 72 A
Blair St. E14	58	38 81 D
Blake Ave. Bark	51	45 83 B
Blake Cl. Well	78	48 76 A
Blake Gdns. Dart	80	54 75 D
Blake Gdns. SW6	73	25 76 B
Blake Hall Cres. E11	39	40 87 C
Blakehall Rd. Cars	111	27 63 B
Blake Hall Rd. E11	39	40 87 A
Blakemore Rd. SW16	86	30 72 C
Blakemore Rd. Th Hth	104	30 67 B
Blakeney Ave. Beck	98	36 69 B
Blakeney Cl. E8	48	34 85 C
Blakeney Cl. N20	15	26 94 C
Blakeney Rd. Beck	98	36 69 B
Blakenham Rd. SW17	86	27 71 B
Blaker Ct. SE7	65	41 77 C
Blake Rd. Croy	105	33 65 A
Bledlow Rd. E16	58	39 82 D
Blake Rd. Mit	96	27 68 A
Blake Rd. N11	24	29 91 C
Blaker Rd. E15	49	38 83 C
Blakes Ave. N Mal	102	21 67 D
Blake's Green. W Wick	106	38 66 C
Blakes La. N Mal	102	21 67 B
Blakesley Ave. W5	54	17 81 C
Blakesley Wlk. SW20	95	24 69 D
Blake's Rd. SE15	63	33 77 C
Blakes Terr. N Mal	102	22 67 A
Blakesware Gdns. N9	17	32 94 B
Blakewood Cl. Felt	82	11 71 A
Blanchard Cl. SE9	89	42 72 C
Blanchard Way. E8	48	34 84 A
Blanch Cl. SE15	64	35 77 C
Blanchedowne. SE5	75	32 75 B
Blanche St. E16	58	39 82 D
Blanchland Rd. Mord	103	25 67 B
Blandfield Rd. SW12	86	28 73 A
Blandford Ave. Beck	98	36 69 C
Blandford Ave. Twick	82	13 73 D
Blandford Cl. Croy	104	30 65 C
Blandford Cl. N2	23	26 89 C
Blandford Cl. Rom	29	49 89 D
Blandford Cres. E4	18	38 94 A
Blandford Rd. N1	48	33 84 C
Blandford Rd. Beck	98	35 69 D
Blandford Rd. Sthl	59	13 78 A
Blandford Rd. Tedd	83	15 71 C
Blandford Rd. W4	61	21 79 C
Blandford Rd. W5	60	17 79 B
Blandford Sq. NW1	1	27 82 C
Blandford St. W1	2	28 81 A
Blandford Waye. Hay	53	11 81 C
Bland St. SE9	77	41 75 D
Blanmerle Rd. SE9	90	43 73 D
Blantyre St. SW10	73	26 77 D
Blantyre Wlk. SW10	62	26 77 D
Blashford St. SE13	88	38 73 B
Blawith Rd. Har	21	15 89 D
Blaydon Cl. Ruis	31	09 87 A
Blaydon Wlk. N17	25	34 91 D
Bleak Hill La. SE18	66	45 77 B
Blean Gr. SE20	98	35 70 C
Bleasdale Ave. Grnf	44	16 83 C
Blechynden St. W10	56	23 81 D
Bleddyn Cl. Sid	79	47 74 C
Bledow Rise. Grnf	43	14 83 C
Bleeding Heart Yd. EC1	3	31 81 A
Blegborough Rd. SW16	96	29 70 A
Blendon Dri. Bex	79	47 74 D
Blendon Path. Brom	89	39 70 D
Blendon Rd. Bex	79	47 74 D
*Blendon Row. SE17	63	32 78 D
Blendon Terr. SE18	66	44 77 A
Blendworth Way (off Lydney Cl). SE15	63	33 77 C
Blenheim Ave. Ilf	40	43 88 C
Blenheim Centre. SE20	98	35 70 D
Blenheim Cl. Dart	80	53 74 C
Blenheim Cl. Grnf	43	14 83 D
Blenheim Cl. N21	17	32 94 C
Blenheim Cl. Rom	29	50 89 C

Blenheim Cl. SW20	95	23 68 A
Blenheim Cl. Wall	111	29 63 C
Blenheim Cres. Ruis	31	08 86 B
Blenheim Cres. S Croy	112	32 63 C
Blenheim Cres. W11	56	24 81 C
Blenheim Ct. N19	48	30 86 A
Blenheim Ct. Sid	90	44 72 D
Blenheim Ct. Wdf Gn	27	40 91 D
Blenheim Dri. Well	78	45 76 B
Blenheim Gdns. King	94	19 70 D
Blenheim Gdns. NW2	46	23 85 C
Blenheim Gdns. SW2	74	30 74 D
Blenheim Gdns. Wall	111	29 63 C
Blenheim Gdns. Wem	33	18 86 C
Blenheim Gr. SE15	75	34 76 C
Blenheim Park Rd. S Croy	112	32 63 C
Blenheim Pas. NW8	46	26 83 C
Blenheim Rd. Barn	11	23 96 D
Blenheim Rd. Brom	99	42 68 C
Blenheim Rd. Dart	80	53 74 C
Blenheim Rd. E15	50	39 85 A
Blenheim Rd. E17	26	36 89 A
Blenheim Rd. E6	58	41 82 B
Blenheim Rd. Eps	109	21 62 C
Blenheim Rd. Har	32	13 88 D
Blenheim Rd. Nthlt	43	13 84 B
Blenheim Rd. NW8	46	26 83 C
Blenheim Rd. SE20	98	35 70 C
Blenheim Rd. Sutt	103	25 65 D
Blenheim Rd. SW20	95	23 68 A
Blenheim Rd. W4	61	21 79 C
Blenheim St. W1	2	28 81 D
Blenheim Terr. NW8	46	26 83 C
Blenkarne Rd. SW11	74	27 74 D
Bleriot Rd. Houn	59	11 77 C
Blessbury Rd. Edg	22	20 90 A
Blessington Cl. SE13	76	38 75 B
Blessington Rd. SE13	76	38 75 D
Bletchley Ct. N1	48	32 83 D
Bletchley St. N1	48	32 83 C
Bletsoe Wlk. N1	48	32 83 C
Blincoe Cl. SW19	85	23 72 B
Blind Cnr. SE25	97	34 68 D
Blisset St. SE10	76	38 76 A
Blithbury Rd. Dag	51	46 84 B
Blithdale Rd. SE2	66	46 78 A
Blithfield St. W8	62	25 79 D
Blockley Rd. Wem	33	16 86 B
Bloemfontein Ave. W12	55	22 80 D
Bloemfontein Rd. W12	55	22 80 B
Blomfield Rd. W9	1	26 81 A
Blomfield St. EC2	4	32 81 B
Blomfield Villas. W2	1	26 81 A
Blomvill Rd. Dag	41	48 86 C
Blondel St. SW11	74	28 76 C
Blondin Ave. W5	60	17 78 A
Blondin St. E3	49	37 83 C
Bloomburg St. SW1	10	29 78 A
Bloomfield Cres. Ilf	40	43 88 D
Bloomfield Pl. W1	6	28 80 B
Bloomfield Rd. Brom	107	41 67 B
Bloomfield Rd. King	93	18 68 A
Bloomfield Rd. N6	36	28 88 C
Bloomfield Rd. SE18	65	43 78 D
Bloomfield Terr. SW1	9	28 78 C
Bloom St. SW8	87	31 72 D
Bloomhall Rd. SE19	96	32 71 D
Bloom Park Rd. SW6	62	24 77 D
Bloomsbury Cl. Eps	109	20 62 D
Bloomsbury Cl. W5	54	18 80 B
Bloomsbury Ct. Pnr	20	12 89 B
Bloomsbury Ct. WC1	3	30 81 A
Bloomsbury Pl. WC1	3	30 81 A
Bloomsbury Sq. WC1	3	30 81 A
Bloomsbury St. WC1	3	29 81 B
Bloomsbury Way. WC1	3	30 81 A
Blore Cl. SW8	74	29 76 B
Blore Ct. W1	6	29 80 B
Blossom Cl. S Croy	112	33 64 D
Blossom Cl. W5	60	18 79 A
Blossom La. Enf	13	32 97 A
Blossom St. E1	4	33 82 C
Blossom Waye. Houn	59	12 77 C
Blount St. E14	57	36 81 C
Bloxam Gdns. SE9	77	42 74 A
Bloxhall Rd. E10	38	36 87 D
Bloxham Cres. Hamp	92	12 69 B
Bloxworth Cl. Wall	104	29 65 C
Blucher Rd. SE5	63	32 77 C
Blue Anchor Alley. Rich	71	18 75 C
Blue Anchor La. SE16	63	34 78 B
Blue Anchor Yd. E1	57	34 80 A
Blue Ball Yd. SW1	6	29 80 C
Bluebell Cl. Orp	108	44 65 A
Bluebell Cl. SE26	87	33 71 A
Bluebell Cl. SE26	87	33 71 B
Bluebell Cl. SE26	87	33 71 B
Bluebird Wlk. Wem	34	19 86 D
Bluefield Cl. Hamp	82	13 71 C
Blundell Rd. Edg	22	21 91 C
Blundell St. N7	47	30 84 A
Blunt Rd. S Croy	112	32 64 D
Blunts Rd. SE9	78	43 74 A
Blurton Rd. E5	49	35 85 B
Blythe Cl. SE6	88	36 73 B
Blythe Hill La. SE6	88	36 73 D
Blythe Hill. Orp	100	46 69 A
Blythe Hill. SE6	88	36 73 B
Blythe Rd. Brom	99	39 69 B
Blythe Rd. W14	62	23 79 D
Blythe Rd. W14	62	24 78 A
Blythe St. E2	57	34 82 B
Blythe Vale. SE6	88	36 73 D
Blyth Rd. E17	38	36 87 B
Blythswood Rd. Ilf	40	46 87 A
Blythwood Rd. N4	36	30 87 B
Blythwood Rd. Pnr	11	90 B
Boadicea St. N1	47	30 83 B
Boardman Ave. E4	14	37 95 B
Boar's Head Yd. Brent	60	17 77 D
Boathouse Wlk. Rich	71	18 76 A
Boathouse Wlk. SE15	63	33 77 D
Bobbin Cl. SW4	74	29 75 A
Bockhampton Rd. King	93	18 70 D
Bocking St. E8	48	34 83 B
Boddicott Cl. SW19	85	24 72 A
Bodiam Cl. Enf	13	33 97 C
Bodiam Rd. SW16	96	29 70 D
Bodley Cl. N.Mal	102	21 67 A
Bodley Manor Way. SE24	87	31 73 A
Bodley Rd. N.Mal	102	21 67 A
Bodmin Gr. Mord	103	26 67 B
Bodmin St. SW18	85	25 73 C
Bodnant Gdns. SW20	94	22 68 B
Bodney Rd. E8	48	34 85 D
Boeing Way. Sthl	59	11 79 C
Boevey Path. Belv	67	48 78 D
Bognor Rd. Well	79	47 76 B
Bohemia Pl. E8	49	35 84 A
Bohun Gr. Barn	12	27 95 D
Boileau Rd. SW13	61	22 77 B
Boileau Rd. W5	54	18 81 D
Bolden St. SE8	76	37 76 D
Bolderwood Way. W Wick	106	37 65 B
Boldmere Rd. Pnr	32	11 87 A
Boleyn Ave. Eps	109	22 62 D
Boleyn Ave. Enf	13	34 97 B
Boleyn Dri. E Mol	92	12 68 B
Boleyn Dri. Ruis	32	11 86 B
Boleyn Gdns. Dag	52	50 84 C
Boleyn Gdns. W Wick	106	37 65 B
Boleyn Rd. E6	50	41 83 D
Boleyn Rd. E7	50	40 84 D
Boleyn Rd. N16	48	33 85 C
Boleyn Way. Ilf	28	44 91 A
Bolina Rd. SE16	64	35 78 C
Bolingbroke Gr. SW11	86	27 73 B
Bolingbroke Gr. SW11	74	27 74 A
Bolingbroke Rd. W14	62	23 79 D
Bolingbroke Wlk. SW11	74	27 76 A
Bollo Bridge Rd. W3	61	20 79 C
Bollo Ct. W3	61	20 79 C
Bollo La. W3	61	19 79 D
Bollo La. W4	61	20 78 A
Bolney St. SW8	10	30 77 D
Bolsover St. W1	2	28 82 D
Bolstead Rd. Mit	96	28 69 B
Bolt Ct. EC4	4	31 81 C
Boltmore Cl. NW4	23	23 89 B
Bolton Cres. SE5	63	31 77 D
Bolton Gdns. Brom	99	39 70 B
Bolton Gdns. NW10	46	23 83 D
Bolton Gdns. SW5	62	25 78 D
Bolton Gdns. SW5	62	26 78 C
Bolton Gdns. Tedd	93	16 70 A
Bolton Rd. E15	50	39 84 B
Bolton Rd. Har	20	14 89 D
Bolton Rd. N18	17	33 92 D
Bolton Rd. NW10	45	20 83 A
Bolton Rd. NW8	46	25 83 B
Bolton Rd. W4	61	20 77 C
Bolton's La. Hay	69	08 76 A
Boltons The. Wem	44	15 85 B
Bolton St. W1	6	28 80 D
Bolton The. SW10	62	26 78 C
Bolton Wlk. N7	36	30 86 B
Bombay St. SE16	63	34 78 B
Bomore Rd. W11	56	24 80 A
Bonar Pl. Chis	99	42 70 C
Bonar Rd. SE15	63	34 77 C
Bonchester Cl. Chis	100	43 70 C
Bonchurch Rd. W10	56	24 81 A
Bonchurch Rd. W13	54	16 80 D
Bond Ct. EC4	4	32 81 D
Bondfield Wlk. Dart	80	54 75 B
Bond Gdns. Wall	111	29 64 A
Bond Rd. Mit	96	27 69 D
Bond Rd. Surb	101	18 65 B
Bond St. E15	50	39 85 C
Bond St. W5	54	17 80 B
Bondway. SW8	10	30 77 A
Boneta Rd. SE18	65	42 79 D
Bonfield Rd. SE13	88	38 75 C
Bonham Gdns. Dag	41	47 86 B
Bonham Rd. Dag	41	47 86 D
Bonham Rd. SW2	74	30 74 B
Bonheur Rd. W4	61	20 79 B
Bonhill St. EC2	4	32 82 D
Boniface Gdns. Har	21	13 91 C
Boniface Rd. Uxb	31	07 86 D
Boniface Wlk. Har	21	13 91 C
Bon Marché Terrace Mews. SE27	87	33 71 A
Bonner Hill Rd. King	94	19 68 A
Bonner Rd. E2	49	35 83 C
Bonnersfield Cl. Har	33	16 88 C
Bonnersfield La. Har	33	16 88 C
Bonner St. E2	49	35 83 C
Bonneville Gdns. SW4	74	29 74 C
Bonnington Sq. SW8	10	30 77 B
Bonny St. NW1	47	29 84 C
Bonser Rd. Twick	83	15 72 B
Bonsor St. SE5	63	33 77 C
Bonville Rd. Brom	89	39 71 D
Bookbinders Cott Homes. N20	16	27 93 D
Booker Cl. E14	57	36 81 B
Booker Rd. N18	17	34 92 C
Boones Rd. SE13	77	39 75 C
Boone St. SE13	77	39 75 C
Boord St. SE10	58	39 79 C
Boothby Rd. N19	36	29 86 B
Booth Rd. Croy	105	31 65 B
Booth Rd. NW9	22	21 90 C
Booth's Pl. W1	2	29 81 A
Boot St. N1	4	33 82 A
Bordars Rd. W7	54	15 81 B
Bordars Wlk. W7	54	15 81 A
Borden Ave. Enf	13	32 95 D
Border Cres. SE26	87	34 71 D
Border Gate. Mit	96	27 69 B
Border Rd. SE26	87	34 71 D
Bordesley Rd. Mord	103	25 67 B
Bordesley Rd. Mord	95	25 68 D
Bordon Wlk. SW15	84	22 73 A
Boreas Wlk. N1	48	31 83 D
Boreham Ave. E16	58	40 81 C
Boreham Cl. E10	38	38 87 C
Boreham Rd. N22	25	32 90 C
Borer's Pas. E1	4	33 81 C
Borgard Rd. SE18	65	42 78 B
Borland Rd. SE15	76	35 75 C
Borland Rd. Tedd	93	16 70 D
Borneo St. SW15	73	23 75 A
Borough High St. SE1	8	32 79 A
Borough Hill Croy	105	31 65 D
Borough Rd. Islw	71	15 76 B
Borough Rd. King	94	19 69 A
Borough Rd. Mit	96	27 69 C
Borough Rd. SE1	7	31 79 D
Borough Sq. SE1	8	32 79 D
Borrett Cl. SE17	63	32 78 C
Borrodaile Rd. SW18	73	25 74 D
Borrodale Rd. SW18	73	25 74 D
Borrowdale Ave. Har	21	16 90 D
Borrowdale Cl. Ilf	27	42 89 C
Borthwick Mews. E15	50	39 85 A
Borthwick Rd. E15	50	39 85 A
Borthwick Rd. NW9	34	21 88 D
Borthwick St. SE8	64	37 78 C
Borwick Ave. E17	26	36 89 B
Bosbury Rd. SE6	88	38 72 C
Boscastle Rd. NW5	36	28 86 D
Boscobel Pl. SW1	9	28 78 B
Boscobel St. NW8	1	26 82 D
Boscombe Ave. E10	38	38 87 B
Boscombe Ave. Horn	42	53 87 B
Boscombe Cl. E5	49	36 85 C
Boscombe Rd. SW17	95	28 70 A
Boscombe Rd. SW19	95	25 69 B
Boscombe Rd. W12	61	22 79 A
Boscombe Rd. Wor Pk	103	23 66 D
Bosgrove. E4	18	38 94 C
Boss St. SE1	8	33 79 B
Bostall Hill. SE2	66	46 78 D
Bostall La. SE2	66	46 78 D

Street	Pg	Grid
Bostall Manorway. SE2	66	46 75 B
Bostall Park Ave. Bexh	67	48 77 C
Bostall Rd. Orp	100	48 70 D
Bostal Row. Bexh	79	48 75 B
Boston Gdns. Brent	60	16 78 B
Boston Gdns. W4	61	21 77 A
Boston Gr. Ruis	31	08 88 C
Boston Manor Rd. Brent	60	16 78 D
Boston Park Rd. Brent	60	17 78 C
Boston Pl. NW1	1	27 82 D
Boston Rd. Croy	105	31 67 C
Boston Rd. Edg	22	20 91 C
Boston Rd. W7	60	15 79 D
Boston St. E2	4	34 83 C
Bostonthorpe Rd. W7	60	15 79 A
Boston Vale. W7	60	16 78 A
Boswell Ct. WC1	3	30 81 A
Boswell Rd. Th Hth	97	32 68 C
Boswell St. WC1	3	30 81 A
Bosworth Cl. E17	26	36 90 B
Bosworth Rd. Barn	11	25 96 B
Bosworth Rd. Dag	41	49 86 C
Bosworth Rd. N11	16	29 92 D
Bosworth Rd. W10	56	24 82 C
Botany Bay La. Chis	100	44 69 C
Boteley Cl. E4	18	38 93 B
Botha Rd. E13	58	41 81 A
Bothwell Cl. E16	58	39 81 B
Bothwell St. W6	62	23 77 B
Botolph Alley. EC3	8	33 80 A
Botolph La. EC3	8	33 80 A
Botsford Rd. SW20	95	24 69 C
Botton Gdns Mews	62	26 78 C
Bott's Mews. W2	56	25 81 C
Boucher Cl. Tedd	83	15 71 D
Boughton Ave. Brom	107	39 66 B
Boughton Rd. SE28	66	45 79 C
Boulcott St. E1	57	35 81 D
Boulogne Rd. Croy	105	32 67 C
Boulton Rd. Dag	41	48 86 D
Bounces La. N9	17	34 93 B
Bounces Rd. N9	18	35 93 A
Boundaries Rd. Felt	82	11 73 C
Boundaries Rd. SW12	86	28 73 C
Boundary Ave. E17	38	36 87 B
Boundary Cl. Ilf	51	45 85 A
Boundary Cl. King	19	19 68 B
Boundary Cl. Sthl	59	13 78 C
Boundary La. E13	58	41 82 D
Boundary La. SE17	63	32 77 A
Boundary Mews. NW8	46	26 83 A
Boundary Pas. E2	4	33 82 D
Boundary Rd. Bark	51	44 83 B
Boundary Rd. Bark	51	44 83 C
Boundary Rd. Cars	111	28 63 C
Boundary Rd. E17	38	37 88 C
Boundary Rd. E6	58	41 82 B
Boundary Rd. Enf	14	35 95 C
Boundary Rd Estate. NW8	46	26 83 A
Boundary Rd. N22	25	32 90 C
Boundary Rd. N2	23	26 90 B
Boundary Rd. NW8	46	26 83 A
Boundary Rd. Pnr	32	11 87 B
Boundary Rd. Rom	42	52 88 C
Boundary Rd. Sid	78	45 74 A
Boundary Rd. SW19	95	26 70 B
Boundary Rd. Wall	111	28 63 C
Boundary Row. SE1	7	31 79 B
Boundary St. E2	4	33 82 D
Boundary St. Eri	8	51 77 D
Boundfield Rd. SE6	89	39 72 A
Bounds Green Rd. N11	24	29 91 B
Bounds Green Rd. N22	24	30 90 A
Bourchier St. W1	6	29 80 B
Bourdon Pl. W1	6	28 80 B
Bourdon Rd. SE20	98	35 69 C
Bourdon St. W1	6	28 80 B
Bourke Cl. NW10	45	21 84 A
Bourke Cl. SW4	74	30 74 C
Bourlet Cl. W1	2	29 81 A
Bourn Ave. Barn	11	26 95 B
Bourn Ave. N15	25	32 89 D
Bournbrook Rd. SE3	77	41 75 B
Bourne Ave. N14	16	30 93 A
Bourne Ave. Ruis	43	11 85 C
Bourne Gdns. E4	18	37 92 B
Bourne Hill. N13	16	30 93 B
Bourne Mead. Bex	79	50 74 B
Bournemouth Rd. SE15	75	34 76 C
Bournemouth Rd. SW19	95	25 69 A
Bourne Pl. W4	61	20 78 D
Bourne Rd. Bex	79	49 74 D
Bourne Rd. Bex	79	50 74 C
Bourne Rd. Brom	99	41 68 D
Bourne Rd. Dart	79	50 74 B
Bourne Rd. E7	39	39 86 D
Bourne Rd. N8	36	30 88 C
Bourne St. Croy	105	31 65 B
Bourne St. SW1	9	28 78 A
Bourne Terr. W2	56	25 81 B
Bourne Terr. W2	56	25 81 B
Bourne The. N14	16	30 94 C
Bourne Vale. Brom	107	40 66 A
Bournevale Rd. SW16	88	30 71 A
Bourne View. Grnf	44	15 85 D
Bourne Way. Brom	107	39 65 B
Bourne Way. Eps	109	20 64 A
Bourne Way. Sutt	110	24 64 D
Bournewood Rd. Orp	108	46 68 B
Bournewood Rd. SE18	66	46 77 C
Bournville Rd. SE6	88	38 73 A
Bournwell Cl. Barn	12	27 97 D
Bousfield Rd. SE14	76	35 76 D
Boutflower Rd. SW11	74	27 75 C
Bouverie Gdns. Har	33	17 88 D
Bouverie Mews. N16	37	33 86 A
Bouverie Pl. W2	1	26 81 D
Bouverie Rd. Har	32	14 88 C
Bouverie Rd. N16	37	33 86 A
Bouverie St. EC4	3	31 81 C
Bovay Pl. N7	47	30 85 B
Bovay St. N7	47	30 85 B
Boveney Rd. SE23	88	35 73 B
Bovill Rd. SE23	88	35 73 B
Bovingdon Ave. Wem	45	19 84 A
Bovingdon La. NW9	22	21 90 A
Bovingdon Rd. SW6	73	25 76 B
Bowater Cl. NW9	34	20 88 B
Bowater Cl. SW4	74	30 74 C
Bowater Pl. SE3	65	40 77 D
Bowater Rd. SE18	65	41 79 D
Bow Churchyard. EC4	4	32 81 C
Bow Common La. E3	57	36 82 D
Bowden Dri. Horn	42	54 87 C
Bowden St. SE11	63	31 78 C
Bowditch. SE8	64	36 78 D
Bowdon Rd. E17	38	37 87 A
Bowen Dri. SE21	87	33 72 C
Bowen Rd. Har	32	14 87 A
Bowen St. E14	57	37 81 D
Bower Ave. SE10	65	39 77 C
Bower Cl. Nthlt	43	11 03 C
Bower Cl. Rom	29	50 91 D
Bowerdean St. SW6	73	25 76 D
Bowerman Ave. SE14	76	36 77 A
Bower St. E1	57	35 81 D
Bowes Cl. Sid	78	46 74 D
Bowes Rd. Dag	52	47 85 A
Bowes Rd. N11	16	29 92 D
Bowes Rd. W3	55	21 80 A
Bowfell Rd. W6	62	23 77 A
Bowford Ave. Bexh	78	48 76 A
Bowie Cl. SW4	86	29 73 B
Bow La. EC4	4	32 81 C
Bow La. Mord	103	24 67 C
Bow La. N12	15	26 91 C
Bowland Rd. SW4	74	29 75 D
Bowland Rd. Wdf Gn	27	41 91 A
Bowl Ct. EC2	4	33 82 C
Bowles Rd. SE1	63	34 77 A
Bowley St. E14	57	36 80 B
Bowling Green Cl. SW15	84	22 73 B
Bowling Green La. EC1	3	31 82 C
Bowling Green Pl. SE1	7	32 79 B
Bowling Green Row. SE18	65	42 78 B
Bowling Green St. SE11	63	31 77 A
Bowling Green Wlk. N1	4	33 82 A
Bowman Ave. E16	58	39 80 B
Bowmans Cl. W13	54	16 80 D
Bowmans Lea. SE23	88	35 73 A
Bowman's Meadow. Wall	104	28 65 D
Bowman's Mews. N7	47	30 86 C
Bowman's Pl. N7	47	30 86 C
Bowmead. SE9	89	42 72 B
Bowmore Wlk. N7	47	29 84 D
Bowness Cl. E8	48	33 84 B
Bowness Cres. SW15	84	21 71 C
Bowness Dri. Houn	70	12 75 C
Bowness Rd. Bexh	79	49 76 D
Bowness Rd. SE6	89	37 73 B
Bowood Rd. Enf	14	35 97 D
Bowood Rd. SW11	74	28 74 A
Bow Rd. E3	57	37 82 A
Bowrons Ave. Wem	44	18 84 C
Bow St. E15	50	39 85 C
Bow St. WC2	3	30 81 C
Bowyer Pl. SE5	63	32 77 C
Bowyer St. SE5	63	32 77 C
Boxall Rd. SE21	87	33 73 A
Boxall Rd. SE21	75	33 74 C
Boxgrove Rd. SE2	67	47 79 C
Boxley Rd. Mord	103	26 68 C
Boxley St. E16	58	40 80 D
Boxmoor Rd. Har	21	16 89 D
Boxmoor Rd. Rom	29	50 91 A
Boxoll Rd. Dag	52	48 86 D
Boxtree La. Har	20	14 91 D
Boxtree Rd. Har	20	14 91 D
Boxworth Gr. N1	47	30 83 B
Boyard Rd. SE18	65	43 78 D
Boyce St. SE1	7	31 80 C
Boyce Way. E13	58	40 82 C
Boycroft Ave. NW9	34	20 88 C
Boyd Ave. Sthl	53	12 80 D
Boyd Cl. King	94	19 70 C
Boydell Ct. NW8	46	26 84 D
Boyd Rd. SW19	95	26 70 B
Boyd St. E1	57	34 81 C
Boyfield St. SE1	7	31 79 B
Boyland Rd. Brom	89	39 71 D
Boyle Ave. Stan	21	16 91 A
Boyle Farm Rd. Surb	101	16 67 C
Boyle St. W1	6	29 80 A
Boyne Ave. NW4	23	23 89 D
Boyne Rd. Dag	41	49 86 C
Boyne Rd. SE13	76	38 75 B
Boyne Terr Mews. W11	56	24 80 D
Boyson Rd. SE17	63	32 77 A
Boythorn Way. SE16	63	34 78 D
Boyton Cl. E1	57	35 82 D
Boyton Cl. N8	24	30 89 A
Boyton Rd. N8	24	30 89 A
Brabant Rd. N22	24	30 90 D
Brabazon Ave. Wall	111	30 63 C
Brabazon Rd. Houn	59	11 77 C
Brabazon Rd. Nthlt	43	13 83 C
Brabazon St. E14	57	37 81 B
Braborne Cl. SE19	87	33 71 C
Braborne Cres. Bex h	67	48 87 B
Braborne Rise. Beck	106	38 67 B
Braburn St. SE15	76	35 78 A
Bracewell Ave. Grnf	44	16 84 A
Bracewell Rd. W10	56	23 81 A
Bracewood Gdns. Croy	105	33 65 D
Bracey St. N4	36	30 86 A
Bracken Ave. Croy	106	37 65 C
Bracken Ave. SW12	86	28 73 A
Brackenbridge Dri. Ruis	32	11 86 D
Brackenbury Gdns. W6	61	22 79 D
Brackenbury Rd. N2	23	26 89 A
Brackenbury Rd. W6	61	22 79 A
Bracken Cl. Houn	82	13 73 A
Brackendale Cl. Houn	70	13 76 B
Brackendale Ct. Beck	98	37 70 C
Brackendale. N21	16	30 93 B
Bracken Dri. Chig	28	43 91 B
Bracken End. Islw	70	14 74 B
Brackenfield Cl. E5	48	34 85 B
Brackenfield Cl. E5	57	34 86 D
Bracken Gdns. SW13	72	22 76 C
Bracken Hill Cl. Brom	99	39 69 B
Bracken Hill La. Brom	99	39 69 B
Brackenhill. Ruis	43	12 85 A
Brackens The. Enf	17	33 94 A
Bracken The. E4	18	38 93 A
Brackenwood. Sun	91	10 69 A
Brackley Cl. Wall	111	30 63 C
Brackley Rd. Beck	98	37 70 C
Brackley Rd. W4	61	21 78 C
Brackley Sq. Wdf Gn	27	41 91 D
Brackley St. EC1	4	32 81 A
Brackley Terr. W4	61	21 78 C
Bracklyn Ct. N1	48	32 83 D
Bracklyn St. N1	48	32 83 D
Bracknell Cl. N22	25	31 90 A
Bracknell Gdns. NW3	46	25 85 B
Bracknell Way. NW3	46	25 85 B
Bracondale Rd. SE2	66	46 78 A
Bradbourne St. SW6	73	25 76 C
Bradbury Cl. Sthl	59	12 78 B
Bradbury St. N16	48	33 85 C
Braddon Rd. Rich	72	18 75 B
Braddyll St. E10	65	39 78 C
Braden Rd. Har	21	16 89 D
Bradenham Ave. Well	46	46 75 C
Bradenham Rd. Har	21	16 89 D
Braden St. W9	56	25 82 D
Bradfield Dri. Bark	51	46 85 C
Bradfield Rd. E16	58	40 79 A
Bradfield Rd. Ruis	43	12 85 C
Bradford Cl. Brom	107	42 66 D
Bradford Cl. SE26	87	34 71 B
Bradford Dri. Eps	109	21 63 B
Bradford Rd. Ilf	40	44 87 D

Bradford Rd. W3....61 21 79 A
Bradgate Rd. SE6....76 37 74 D
Brading Cres. E11....39 40 86 B
Brading Rd. Croy....104 30 67 D
Brading Rd. SW2....86 30 73 B
Bradiston Rd. W9....56 24 82 B
Bradley Cl. N7....47 30 84 B
Bradley Gdns. W13....54 16 81 D
Bradley Rd. N22....24 30 90 D
Bradley Rd. SE19....97 32 70 A
Bradley's Bldgs. N1....48 31 83 C
Bradlord Ho. SE21....87 34 72 C
Bradmead. SW8....10 29 77 C
Bradmore Park Rd. W6....61 22 78 B
Bradstock Rd. E9....49 35 84 B
Bradstock Rd. Eps....109 22 64 D
Brad St. SE1....7 31 80 C
Bradwell Ave. Dag....41 49 86 A
Bradwell Cl. E18....27 39 89 D
Bradwell Mews. N18....17 34 92 A
Brady St. E1....57 34 82 D
Braemar Ave. Bexh....79 50 75 C
Braemar Ave. N22....24 30 90 A
Braemar Ave. NW10....34 20 86 B
Braemar Ave. S Croy....112 32 62 A
Braemar Ave. SW19....85 25 72 A
Braemar Ave. Th Hth....97 31 68 B
Braemar Ave. Wem....44 18 84 C
Braemar Gdns. NW9....22 20 90 B
Braemar Gdns. Sid....90 44 72 D
Braemar Gdns. W Wick....106 38 66 C
Braemar Rd. Brent....60 17 77 B
Braemar Rd. E13....58 39 82 D
Braemar Rd. N15....37 33 88 A
Braemar Rd. Wor Pk....102 22 65 D
Braemore Ct. Barn....12 28 96 C
Braeside Ave. SW19....95 24 69 A
Braeside. Beck....88 37 71 D
Braeside Cl. Pnr....20 13 91 C
Braeside Cres. Bexh....79 50 75 C
Braeside Rd. SW16....96 29 70 C
Braes St. N1....48 31 84 D
Braesyde Cl. Belv....67 48 78 B
Brafferton Rd. Croy....112 32 64 A
Braganza St. SE17....63 31 78 D
Braham St. E1....4 33 81 D
Braid Ave. W3....55 21 81 C
Braid Cl. Felt....82 12 72 B
Braidwood Rd. SE6....88 38 73 D
Braidwood St. SE1....8 33 80 C
Brailsford Rd. SW2....75 31 74 C
Brainton Ave. Felt....82 11 73 A
Braintree Ave. Ilf....27 42 89 C
Braintree Rd. Dag....41 49 86 C
Braintree St. E2....57 35 82 A
Braithwaite Ave. Rom....41 49 87 A
Braithwaite Gdns. Stan....21 17 90 A
Bramalea Cl. N6....36 28 88 C
Bramall Cl. E15....50 39 85 D
Bramber Rd. N12....16 27 92 C
Bramber Rd. W14....62 24 77 B
Bramble Banks. Cars....111 28 62 A
Bramblebury Rd. SE18....66 44 78 C
Bramble Cl. Shep....91 08 68 B
Bramble Cl. Stan....21 17 91 D
Bramble Croft. Eri....67 50 78 A
Brambledown Cl. W.Wick....107 39 67 A
Brambledown Rd. Cars....111 28 63 C
Brambledown Rd. S Croy....112 33 63 C
Brambledown Rd. Wall....111 28 63 D
Bramble Gdns. W12....55 21 80 B
Brambles Cl. Brent....60 16 77 D
Brambles The. Chig....28 44 91 A
Bramblewood Cl. Cars....104 27 66 C
Bramblings The. E4....18 38 92 B
Bramcote Ave. Mit....96 27 68 D
Bramcote Gr. SE16....64 35 78 C
Bramcote Rd. SW15....72 22 75 D
Bramdean Cres. SE12....89 40 73 C
Bramdean Gdns SE12....89 40 73 C
Bramerton Rd. Beck....98 36 68 B
Bramerton St. SW3....9 27 77 A
Bramfield Rd. SW11....74 27 74 B
Bramford Rd. SW18....73 26 75 C
Bramham Gdns. SW5....62 25 78 D
Bramhope La. SE7....65 40 77 B
Bramlands Cl. SW11....74 27 75 A
Bramley Cl. E17....26 36 90 C
Bramley Cl. N14....12 28 95 B
Bramley Cl. Orp....108 43 66 D
Bramley Cl. S Croy....112 32 64 C
Bramley Cl. Twick....70 14 74 C
Bramley Cres. Ilf....40 43 88 C
Bramley Hill. S Croy....112 32 64 A
Bramley Pl. Dart....80 52 75 C

Bramley Rd. Barn....12 29 95 A
Bramley Rd. Sutt....110 23 62 B
Bramley Rd. Sutt....110 26 64 D
Bramley Rd. W11....56 23 80 B
Bramley Rd. W5....60 17 79 C
Bramley St. W10....56 23 81 D
Bramley Way. W Wick....106 37 65 B
Brampton Cl. E5....37 34 86 B
Brampton Gr. Har....21 16 89 D
Brampton Gr. NW4....23 23 89 C
Brampton Gr. Wem....34 19 87 C
Brampton Park Rd. N8....25 31 89 A
Brampton Rd. Bexh....79 48 76 A
Brampton Rd. Croy....79 33 67 D
Brampton Rd. E6....58 41 82 B
Brampton Rd. N15....22 32 88 A
Brampton Rd. NW9....22 19 89 C
Brampton Rd. SE2....47 77 A
Bramshaw Rd. E9....49 35 84 B
Bramshaw Rise. N.Mal....102 21 67 C
Bramshill Gdns. NW5....36 28 86 D
Bramshill Rd. NW10....45 21 83 D
Bramshot Ave SE7....65 40 77 B
Bramshot Rd. NW10....45 22 83 C
Bramwell Cl. Sun....92 11 69 D
Brancaster La. Pur....112 32 62 C
Brancaster Rd. E12....40 42 85 B
Brancaster Rd. Ilf....40 45 88 C
Brancaster Rd. SW16....86 30 72 C
Branch Hill. NW3....35 26 86 C
Branch Pl. N1....48 32 83 B
Branch Rd. E14....57 36 81 C
Brancker Cl. Wall....111 30 63 C
Brancker Rd. Har....21 17 89 B
Brandlehow Rd. SW15....74 24 75 D
Brandon Mews. EC2....4 32 81 B
Brandon Rd. E17....26 38 89 A
Brandon Rd. N7....47 30 84 C
Brandon Rd. Sthl....59 12 78 D
Brandon Rd. Sutt....110 25 64 B
Brandon St. SE17....63 32 78 A
Brandram Rd. SE13....77 39 75 C
Brandreth Rd. SW17....86 28 72 B
Brandries The. Wall....104 29 65 D
Brand St. SE10....64 38 77 C
Brandville Gdns. Ilf....28 43 89 B
Brandy Way. Sutt....110 25 63 C
Brangbourne Rd. Brom....88 38 71 D
Brangton Rd. SE11....10 30 78 D
Brangwyn Cres. SW19....95 26 69 D
Branksea St. SW6....73 24 76 A
Branksome Ave. N18....17 33 92 D
Branksome Rd. SW19....95 25 69 A
Branksome Rd. SW2....74 30 74 A
Branksome Way. Har....33 18 88 D
Branksome Way. N Mal....20 69 B
Branscombe Gdns. N21....17 31 94 A
Branscombe St. SE13....77 37 75 B
Bransdale Cl. NW6....46 25 83 A
Bransgrove Rd. Edg....21 18 91 D
Branston Cres. Orp....108 44 66 D
Branstone Rd. Rich....71 18 76 B
Brants Wlk. W7....54 15 82 C
Brantwood Ave. Eri....67 50 77 C
Brantwood Ave. Islw....71 16 75 C
Brantwood Cl. E17....26 37 89 B
Brantwood Gdns. Enf....12 30 96 C
Brantwood Gdns. Ilf....27 42 89 C
Brantwood Rd. Bexh....79 49 75 B
Brantwood Rd. N17....25 34 91 A
Brantwood Rd. S Croy....112 32 62 A
Brantwood Rd. SE24....75 32 74 A
Brassey Rd. NW6....46 24 84 B
Brassey Sq. SW11....74 28 75 A
Brassie Ave. W3....55 21 81 C
Brasted Cl. Bexh....79 47 74 B
Brasted Cl. Orp....108 46 65 A
Brasted Cl. SE26....88 35 71 A
Brasted Rd. Eri....68 51 77 C
Brathway Rd. SW18....85 25 73 A
Bratley St. E1....34 82 C
Braund Ave. Grnf....53 13 82 D
Braundton Ave. Sid....90 45 73 D
Bravington Pl. W10....56 24 82 D
Bravington Rd. W9....56 24 82 B
Braxfield Rd. SE4....76 36 75 D
Braxted Park. SW16....96 30 70 B
Brayard's. SE15....75 34 76 D
Brayard's. SE15....75 34 76 D
Braybrooke Gdns. SE19....97 33 70 D
Braybrook St. W12....55 21 81 B
Brayburne Ave. SW4....74 29 76 C
Braydon Rd. N16....37 34 87 C
Bray Dr. E16....58 39 80 B
Brayfield Terr. N1....48 31 84 C

Brayford Sq. E1....57 35 81 C
Bray Pl. SW3....9 27 78 B
Bray Rd. NW7....23 23 91 B
Brayton Gdns. Enf....12 29 96 D
Braywood Rd. SE9....78 44 75 D
Bread St. EC4....4 32 81 C
Breakspeare. SE21....87 33 72 D
Breakspear Rd N. Uxb....31 07 88 B
Breakspear Rd. Ruis....31 07 88 D
Breakspear Rd S. Uxb....31 07 87 B
Bream's Bldgs. EC4....3 31 81 C
Bream St. E3....49 37 84 C
Breamwater Gdns. Rich....83 16 72 D
Breasley Cl. SW15....72 22 75 D
Brechin Pl. SW7....62 26 78 A
Brecknock Rd. N19....47 29 85 A
Brecknock Rd. N7....47 29 85 D
Brecknock Road Estate. N7....29 85 D
Brecon Cl. Mit....96 30 68 A
Brecon Cl. Enf....11 35 96 C
Brecon Rd. W6....62 24 77 A
Bredgar Rd. N19....36 29 86 A
Bredhurst Cl. SE20....88 35 70 A
Bredon Rd. Croy....105 33 66 B
Bredon Rd. SE5....75 32 75 A
Breer St. SW6....73 25 75 B
Breezer's Hill. E1....57 34 80 A
Brember Rd. Har....32 14 86 A
Bremner Rd. SW7....5 26 79 C
Brenchley Cl. Brom....107 39 67 D
Brenchley Cl. Chis....100 43 69 A
Brenchley Gdns. SE23....76 35 74 D
Brenchley Rd. Orp....100 45 69 D
Brendans Cl. Horn....62 54 87 C
Brenda Rd. SW17....86 27 72 B
Brende Gdns. E Mol....92 13 68 D
Brendon Ave. NW10....45 21 85 A
Brendon Cl. Eri....80 51 76 A
Brendon Gdns. Har....31 13 85 B
Brendon Gdns. Ilf....40 45 88 A
Brendon Rd. Dag....31 49 87 C
Brendon Rd. SE9....90 44 72 B
Brendon St. W1....1 27 81 C
Brendon Way. Enf....17 33 94 A
Brenley Cl. Mit....96 28 68 A
Brenley Gdns. SE9....77 41 75 D
Brentcot Cl. W13....54 16 82 D
Brent Cres. NW10....44 18 83 D
Brent Cross Fly. NW2....35 23 87 B
Brent Cross Fly. NW4....35 23 88 C
Brent Ct. NW11....35 23 87 B
Brentfield Cl. NW10....45 20 84 B
Brentfield Gdns. NW11....35 23 87 B
Brentfield. NW10....45 20 84 C
Brentfield Rd. NW10....45 20 84 D
Brentford High St. Brent....60 17 77 D
Brent Green. NW4....35 23 88 B
Brent Green Wlk. Wem....34 20 86 C
Brentham Way. W5....54 17 82 D
Brenthouse Rd. E9....49 35 84 A
Brenthurst Rd. NW10....45 21 84 B
Brent Lea. Brent....60 17 77 C
Brentmead Cl. W7....54 15 80 A
Brentmead Gdns. NW10....44 18 83 D
Brentmead Pl. NW11....35 23 88 D
Brenton St. E14....57 36 81 C
Brent Park Rd. NW4....34 22 87 B
Brent Pl. Barn....11 25 95 A
Brent Rd. Brent....60 17 77 A
Brent Rd. E16....58 40 81 A
Brent Rd. S Croy....112 34 62 B
Brent Rd. SE18....66 43 77 D
Brent Rd. Sthl....59 11 79 C
Brentside. Brent....60 17 77 A
Brentside Cl. W3....54 16 82 C
Brent St. NW4....35 23 88 B
Brent Terr. NW2....35 23 86 A
Brentvale Ave. Sthl....53 14 80 D
Brentvale Ave. Wem....44 18 83 B
Brent View Rd. NW9....23 22 87 A
Brent Way. Brent....60 17 77 D
Brent Way. N3....23 25 91 A
Brent Way. Wem....45 19 84 B
Brentwick Gdns. Brent....60 18 76 A
Brentwood Cl. SE9....90 44 73 C
Brentwood Rd. Rom....42 52 88 D
Brereton Rd. N17....25 33 91 D
Bressenden Pl. SW1....6 29 79 C
Bressey Gr. E18....27 39 90 D

Brett Cl. N16	37	33 86 A
Brett Cl. Nthlt	53	11 82 B
Brett Cres. NW10	45	20 84 D
Brettell St. SE17	63	32 78 D
Brettenham Ave. E17	26	37 90 A
Brettenham Rd. E17	26	37 90 A
Brettenham Rd. N18	17	34 92 B
Brett Gdns. Dag	52	48 84 C
Brettgrave. Eps	109	20 62 C
Brett House Cl. SW15	85	23 73 B
Brett House Cl. SW15	73	23 74 D
Brett Pas. E8	48	34 85 D
Brett Rd. Barn	11	23 95 A
Brett Rd. E8	48	34 85 D
Brewer's Green. SW1	6	29 79 C
Brewers La. Rich	71	17 74 B
Brewer St. W1	6	29 80 A
Brewery Rd. Brom	107	42 66 C
Brewery Rd. N7	47	30 84 A
Brewery Rd. SE18	66	44 78 D
Brewhouse La. E1	57	34 80 D
Brewhouse St. SW15	73	24 75 A
Brewhouse Wlk. SE16	57	36 80 C
Brewhouse Yd. EC1	3	31 82 D
Brewood Rd. Dag	51	46 84 B
Brewster Gdns. W10	56	23 81 A
Brewster Rd. E10	38	37 87 D
Briane Rd. Eps	109	20 62 D
Brian Rd. Rom	41	47 88 A
Briants Cl. Pnr	20	12 90 D
Briant St. SE14	76	35 76 B
Briar Ave. SW16	96	30 70 D
Briarbank Rd. W13	54	16 81 C
Briar Banks. Cars	111	28 62 A
Briar Cl. Hamp	82	12 71 D
Briar Cl. Islw	71	15 74 B
Briar Cl. N13	17	32 93 C
Briar Cl. N2	23	25 89 B
Briar Cres. Nthlt	43	13 84 B
Briar Ct. Hamp	82	13 71 D
Briar Ct. Sutt	110	23 64 A
Briardale Gdns. NW3	35	25 86 C
Briarfield Ave. N2	23	25 89 B
Briarfield Ave. N3	23	25 90 D
Briar Gdns. Brom	107	39 66 D
Briaris Cl. N17	25	34 91 D
Briar La. Cars	111	28 62 A
Briar Pas. SW16	96	30 68 A
Briar Rd. Har	33	17 88 A
Briar Rd. Rom	30	53 91 C
Briar Rd. SW16	96	30 68 B
Briar Rd. Twick	83	15 73 C
Briars Wlk. Rom	30	54 90 D
Briar Wlk. Edg	22	20 91 C
Briar Wlk. SW15	72	22 75 D
Briar Wlk. W10	56	24 82 C
Briarwood Cl. NW9	34	20 88 C
Briarwood Dri. Nthwd	19	10 90 C
Briarwood Rd. Eps	109	22 63 A
Briarwood Rd. SW4	74	29 74 B
Briary Cl. NW3	47	27 84 C
Briary Ct. Sid	90	46 71 D
Briary Gdns. Brom	89	40 71 D
Briary La. N9	17	33 93 D
Brick Cl. EC4	3	31 81 C
Brickett Cl. Ruis	31	08 88 A
Brick Farm Cl. Rich	72	19 76 B
Brickfield Cl. Brent	60	17 77 C
Brickfield Cottages. SE18	66	45 77 B
Brickfield Rd. E3	57	37 82 D
Brickfield Rd. SW19	85	25 71 B
Brickfield. Th Hth	97	31 69 B
Brickfields. Har	33	15 86 A
Brick La. E1	4	33 82 D
Brick La. E2	4	34 97 D
Brick St. W1	6	28 80 D
Brickwall La. Ruis	31	09 87 D
Brickwood Cl. SE26	87	34 72 D
Brickwood Rd. Croy	105	33 65 A
Bride Ct. EC4	3	31 81 D
Bride La. EC4	3	31 81 D
Bride St. N7	48	31 84 A
Bridewell Pl. EC4	3	31 81 D
Bridford Mews. W1	2	28 81 B
Bridge App. NW1	47	28 84 C
Bridge Ave. W6	62	23 78 C
Bridge Ave. W7	53	14 81 B
Bridge Cl. Enf	13	34 97 D
Bridge Cl. Rom	42	51 88 C
Bridge Cl. Tedd	83	15 71 B
Bridge End. E17	26	38 90 A
Bridgefield. Sutt	110	25 63 A
Bridgefoot. SE1	10	30 78 C
Bridge Foot. Sun	91	10 69 A
Bridge Gate. N21	17	32 94 A
Bridge Gdns. Ashf	91	08 70 C
Bridge Gdns. E Mol	92	14 68 D
Bridgeland Rd. E16	58	40 81 C
Bridge La. NW11	35	24 88 B
Bridge La. SW11	74	27 76 A
Bridgeman Rd. N1	47	30 84 D
Bridgeman Rd. Tedd	93	16 70 A
Bridgeman St. NW8	47	27 83 C
Bridgend Rd. SW18	73	26 75 C
Bridgenhall Rd. Enf	13	33 97 B
Bridgen Rd. Bex	79	48 74 C
Bridge Pl. Croy	105	32 66 D
Bridge Pl. SW1	9	28 78 B
Bridge Rd. Beck	98	36 70 D
Bridge Rd. Bexh	79	48 76 C
Bridge Rd. E15	49	38 83 B
Bridge Rd. E17	38	36 87 B
Bridge Rd. E6	50	42 84 D
Bridge Rd. E Mol	92	14 68 D
Bridge Rd. E Mol	93	15 68 C
Bridge Rd. Eri	80	51 76 B
Bridge Rd. Houn	70	14 75 B
Bridge Rd. Islw	70	14 75 B
Bridge Rd. N22	24	30 90 A
Bridge Rd. N9	17	34 93 C
Bridge Rd. NW10	45	21 84 A
Bridge Rd. Orp	108	46 67 D
Bridge Rd. Sthl	59	13 79 A
Bridge Rd. Sutt	110	25 63 B
Bridge Rd. Twick	71	16 74 D
Bridge Rd. Wall	111	29 64 C
Bridge Rd. Wem	34	19 86 C
Bridge Row. Croy	105	32 66 D
Bridges Cl. SW11	73	26 75 B
Bridges Ct. SW11	73	26 76 D
Bridges La. Croy	111	30 64 A
Bridges Pl. SW6	73	24 76 B
Bridges Rd. SW19	95	25 70 B
Bridges Road Mews. SW19	95	25 70 B
Bridge St. Pnr	20	12 89 A
Bridge St. Rich	71	17 74 B
Bridge St. SW1	7	30 79 A
Bridge St. W4	61	20 78 B
Bridge Ter. E15	49	38 84 D
Bridge The. Har	21	15 89 D
Bridge View. W6	62	23 78 C
Bridgewater Cl. Chis	100	45 68 A
Bridgewater St. Wem	44	17 84 A
Bridgewater Gdns. Edg	21	18 90 D
Bridgewater Rd. E15	49	38 83 A
Bridgewater Rd. Wem	44	17 84 C
Bridgewater Sq. EC2	4	32 81 A
Bridgewater St. EC2	4	32 81 A
Bridgeway. Bark	51	45 84 D
Bridge Way. N11	16	29 93 C
Bridge Way. NW11	35	24 88 B
Bridgeway St. NW1	47	29 83 C
Bridge Way. Twick	82	14 73 A
Bridgeway. Wem	44	18 84 D
Bridgewood Cl. SE20	97	34 70 D
Bridgewood Rd. SW16	96	29 70 D
Bridgewood Rd. Wor Pk	102	22 65 C
Bridgford St. SW18	85	26 72 C
Bridgman Rd. W4	61	20 79 C
Bridgwater Rd. Ruis	31	10 86 D
Bridle Cl. Eps	109	20 64 D
Bridle Cl. Sun	91	10 68 A
Bridle La. W1	6	29 80 A
Bridle Path. Croy	104	30 65 C
Bridle Path The. Wdf Gn	27	39 91 C
Bridlepath Way. Felt	81	09 73 A
Bridle Rd. Croy	106	37 65 A
Bridle Rd. Pnr	32	11 88 A
Bridle Rd The. Pur	111	30 62 C
Bridle Way The. Wall	111	29 64 C
Bridlington Rd. N9	17	34 94 B
Bridport Ave. Rom	41	49 88 D
Bridport Pl. N1	48	32 83 B
Bridport Rd. Grnf	43	13 83 B
Bridport Rd. N18	17	33 92 D
Bridport Rd. Th Hth	97	31 68 A
Bridstow Pl. W2	56	25 81 C
Brief St. SE5	75	31 76 B
Brierley Ave. N9	18	35 94 C
Brierley Cl. SE25	97	34 68 C
Brierley Cl. W7	54	15 80 A
Brierley Rd. E11	49	38 85 B
Brierley Rd. SW12	86	29 72 A
Brierly Gdns. E2	49	35 83 C
Brigade Cl. Har	32	14 86 B
Brigade St. SE3	77	39 76 D
Brigadier Ave. Enf	13	32 97 A
Brigadier Hill. Enf	13	32 97 A
Briggeford Cl. E5	37	34 86 A
Brightfield Rd. SE12	77	39 74 B
Brightling Rd. SE4	76	36 74 D
Brightlingsea Pl. E14	57	36 80 B
Brightman Rd. SW18	85	26 73 D
Brighton Ave. E17	38	36 88 B
Brighton Dri. Nthlt	43	13 84 A
Brighton Gr. SE14	76	36 76 A
Brighton Rd. N16	48	33 85 A
Brighton Rd. N2	23	26 90 C
Brighton Rd. Pur	112	31 62 D
Brighton Rd. S Croy	112	32 63 D
Brighton Rd. Surb	101	17 67 D
Brighton Rd. Sutt	110	25 62 B
Brighton Terr. SW9	74	30 75 C
Brightside Rd. SE13	76	38 74 D
Brightside The. Enf	14	36 97 A
Bright St. E14	57	37 81 D
Brightwell Cres. SW17	86	27 71 D
Brig Mews. SE8	64	37 77 A
Brig St. E14	64	38 78 D
Brim Hill. N2	23	26 89 D
Brimpsfield Cl. SE2	66	46 79 D
Brimsdown Ave. Enf	14	36 97 A
Brindley Cl. SE14	76	36 76 B
Brindley Way. Sthl	53	13 80 B
Brindwood Rd. E4	18	37 93 C
Brinkburn Cl. Edg	22	19 89 B
Brinkburn Cl. SE2	66	46 78 A
Brinkburn Gdns. Edg	22	19 89 A
Brinkley Rd. Wor Pk	102	22 66 D
Brinklow Cres. SE18	66	43 77 D
Brinkworth Rd. Ilf	27	42 89 A
Brinkworth Way. E9	49	36 84 B
Brinsdale Rd. NW4	23	23 89 D
Brinsley Rd. Har	20	14 90 D
Brinsley St. E1	57	35 81 C
Brinsworth Cl. Twick	82	14 72 B
Brinton Wlk. SE1	7	31 80 D
Brion Pl. E14	58	38 81 A
Brisane St. SE5	63	32 77 D
Brisbane Ave. SW19	95	25 69 B
Brisbane Rd. E10	38	37 86 B
Brisbane Rd. Ilf	40	44 87 C
Briscoe Rd. SW19	95	26 70 B
Briset Rd. SE9	77	41 75 D
Briset St. EC1	3	31 82 D
Briset Way. N7	36	30 86 B
Bristol Gdns. W9	56	25 82 D
Bristol Mews. W9	56	25 82 D
Bristol Park Rd. E17	26	36 89 C
Bristol Rd. E7	50	41 84 B
Bristol Rd. Grnf	43	13 83 B
Bristol Rd. Mord	103	26 67 A
Briston Gr. N8	36	30 88 C
Bristow Rd. Bexh	79	48 76 A
Bristow Rd. Croy	111	30 64 A
Bristow Rd. Houn	70	14 75 A
Bristow Rd. SE19	87	33 71 C
Britannia Cl. SW4	74	29 75 D
Britannia Rd. Ilf	40	43 86 D
Britannia Rd. N12	15	26 93 C
Britannia Rd. Surb	101	18 66 B
Britannia Rd. SW6	73	25 77 D
Britannia Row. N1	48	32 83 A
Britannia St. WC1	3	30 82 B
Britannia Way. NW10	55	19 82 D
Britannia Way. SW6	62	25 77 D
Britannia Wlk. N1	4	32 82 B
Britannia Wlk. N1	4	32 82 B
Britannia Wlk. N1	48	32 83 D
British Grove Pas. W4	61	21 78 D
British Grove Pas. W6	61	21 78 D
British Grove S. W6	61	21 78 D
British Gr. W4	61	21 78 D
British St. E3	57	36 82 B
Briton Hill Rd. S Croy	112	33 62 D
Brittain Rd. Dag	41	48 86 D
Britten Cl. NW11	35	25 87 D
Britten's Ct. E1	57	34 80 B
Britten St. SW3	9	27 78 C
Britton's Ct. EC4	3	31 81 C
Britton St. EC1	3	31 82 D
Brixham Cres. Ruis	31	10 87 C
Brixham Gdns. Ilf	51	45 85 C
Brixham Rd. Well	79	47 76 B
Brixton Hill Cl. SW2	74	30 74 B
Brixton Hill Pl. SW2	86	30 73 A
Brixton Hill. SW2	74	30 74 D
Brixton Oval. SW2	75	31 75 C
Brixton Rd. SW9	75	31 76 C
Brixton Station Rd. SW9	75	31 75 C
Brixton Water La. SW2	75	31 74 A

Name	Page	Grid
Broadacre Cl. Uxb	31	07 86 D
Broadbent St. W1	6	28 80 B
Broadberry Ct. N18	17	34 92 D
Broadbridge Cl. SE3	65	40 77 C
Broadcroft Ave. Stan	21	17 90 D
Broadcroft Rd. Orp	108	44 66 B
Broad Ct. WC2	3	30 81 C
Broadfield Cl. NW2	35	23 86 C
Broadfield Cl. Rom	42	51 88 B
Broadfield La. N7	47	30 84 C
Broadfield Rd. SE6	89	39 73 C
Broadfields Ave. N21	17	31 94 A
Broadfields. E Mol	101	15 67 C
Broadfields. Har	20	13 90 D
Broadfield Sq. Enf	13	34 96 B
Broadgates Ave. Barn	11	25 97 B
Broadgates Rd. SW18	85	26 73 D
Broad Green Ave. Croy	105	31 66 B
Broadhead Strand. NW9	22	21 90 B
Broadheath Dri. Chis	85	42 71 D
Broadhinton Rd. SW4	74	28 75 B
Broadhurst Ave. Ilf	51	45 85 B
Broadhurst Cl. NW6	46	26 84 A
Broadhurst Gdns. NW6	46	25 84 B
Broadhurst Gdns. Ruis	32	11 86 A
Broad La. Hamp	92	13 70 A
Broad La. N15	25	34 89 C
Broad La. N8	36	30 88 B
Broadlands Ave. Enf	13	34 96 B
Broadlands Ave. SW16	86	30 72 A
Broadlands Cl. Enf	14	35 96 A
Broadlands Cl. N6	36	28 87 A
Broadlands Cl. SW16	86	30 72 A
Broadlands. E17	26	36 89 A
Broadlands. Felt	82	13 72 C
Broadlands Rd. Brom	89	40 71 B
Broadlands Rd. N6	36	28 87 A
Broadlands Way. N.Mal	102	21 67 D
Broadlawns Ct. Har	21	15 90 B
Broad Lawn. SE9	90	43 73 C
Broadley St. NW8	1	27 81 A
Broadley Terr. NW1	1	27 82 C
Broadmead Ave. Wor Pk	102	22 66 A
Broadmead Cl. Hamp	92	13 70 A
Broadmead Cl. Pnr		12 91 C
Broadmead Rd. Hay	53	12 82 C
Broadmead Rd. Wdf Gn	27	40 91 D
Broadmead. SE6	88	37 72 C
Broadoak Rd. Eri	67	50 77 D
Broad Oaks. Surb	102	19 65 B
Broad Oaks Way. Brom	107	39 67 B
Broad Sanctuary. SW1	7	30 79 A
Broad St. Ave. EC2	4	33 81 A
Broad St Bldgs. EC2	4	33 81 A
Broad St. Dag	52	49 84 C
Broadstone Pl. W1	2	28 81 A
Broadstone Rd. Horn	42	52 86 A
Broad Street Market. Dag	52	49 84 C
Broad St. Tedd	93	15 70 B
Broadview. NW9	34	19 88 C
Broadview Rd. SW16	96	29 70 D
Broadwalk. E18	27	39 89 B
Broadwalk La. NW11	35	24 87 B
Broad Walk. N21	16	30 94 D
Broad Walk The. W8	56	25 80 D
Broadwater Rd. N17	25	33 90 C
Broadwater Rd. SW17	86	27 71 A
*Broadway Arc. W6	62	23 78 A
Broadway Ave. Croy	105	32 67 B
Broadway Ave. Twick	71	16 74 D
Broadway. Bexh	79	48 75 D
Broadway Ci. Wdf Gn	27	40 91 B
Broadway Ct. SW19	95	25 70 A
Broadway. E15	49	38 84 D
Broadway. Eps	109	22 64 C
Broadway Gdns. Mit	96	27 68 C
Broadway Market. E8	48	34 83 B
Broadway Mews. N16	37	33 87 B
Broadway Mews. N21	17	31 94 D
Broadway Pl. SW19	95	24 70 B
Broadway. Rom	30	52 90 C
Broadway. Surb	102	19 66 D
Broadway. SW1	6	29 79 B
Broadway The. Dag	41	49 86 A
Broadway The. E13	50	40 83 D
Broadway The. E4	26	38 91 B
Broadway The. Grnf	53	14 82 C
Broad Way The. Har	21	15 90 D
Broadway The. N8	36	30 88 C
Broadway The. N9	17	34 93 C
Broadway The. Pnr	20	12 91 D
Broadway The. Sthl	53	12 80 C
Broadway The. Surb	101	15 66 C
Broadway The. Sutt	110	24 63 A
Broadway The. Sutt	110	26 64 A
Broadway The. SW19	95	25 70 C
Broadway The. W5	54	17 80 B
Broadway The. Wdf Gn	27	40 91 B
Broadway. W13	54	16 80 C
Broadway. W7	54	15 80 C
Broadwick St. W1	2	29 81 C
Broad Wlk. Houn	70	12 76 A
Broad Wlk. Rich	60	18 77 D
Broad Wlk. SE3	77	42 76 C
Broad Wlk The. E M01	93	15 68 D
Broad Wlk The. Nthwd	19	08 90 C
Broadwood Ave. Ruis	31	09 88 C
Broad Yd. EC1	3	31 82 D
Brocas Cl. NW3	47	27 84 C
Brockdish Ave. Bark	51	45 85 D
Brockenhurst Ave. Wor Pk	102	21 66 C
Brockenhurst Gdns. Ilf	51	44 85 C
Brockenhurst Gdns. NW7	22	21 91 A
Brockenhurst Rd. Croy	105	34 66 B
Brockenhurst Way. SW16	96	29 69 D
Brockham Dri. Ilf	40	44 88 A
Brockham Dri. SW2	86	30 73 B
Brockham St. SE1	8	32 79 C
Brockhurst Cl. Stan	21	15 91 B
Brockill Cres. SE4	76	36 75 C
Brocklebank Rd. SW18	85	26 73 A
Brocklehurst St. SE14	64	35 77 D
Brocklesby Rd. SE25	97	34 68 D
Brockley Cres. Rom	29	50 91 C
Brockley Cross. SE4	76	36 75 A
Brockley Footpath. SE15	76	35 75 C
Brockley Footpath. SE4	76	36 74 A
Brockley Gr. SE4	76	36 74 B
Brockley Hall Rd. SE4	76	36 74 A
Brockley Park. SE23	88	36 73 A
Brockley Rd. SE4	76	35 75 D
Brockley Rise. SE23	88	36 73 A
Brockley View. SE23	88	36 73 A
Brockley Way. SE4	76	36 74 A
Brockman Rise. Brom	88	38 71 B
Brock Pl. E3	57	37 82 D
Brock Rd. E13	58	40 81 B
Brocks Dri. Sutt	103	24 65 C
Brockshot Cl. Brent	60	17 77 B
Brock St. SE15	76	35 75 A
Brockwell Cl. Orp	108	45 67 B
Brockwell Park Gdns. SE24	87	31 73 B
Brockworth Cl. SE15	63	33 77 A
Broderick Ho. SE21	87	34 72 C
Brodia Rd. N16	37	33 86 C
Brodie Rd. E4	18	38 93 A
Brodie St. SE1	63	33 78 D
Brodlove La. E1	57	35 80 B
Brodrick Gr. SE2	66	46 78 B
Brodrick Rd. SW17	86	27 72 A
Brograve Gdns. Beck	98	37 69 D
Brograve Rd. N17	25	34 89 A
Broken Wharf. EC4	8	32 80 A
Brokesley St. E3	57	36 82 B
Broke Wlk. E8	48	34 83 A
Bromar Rd. SE5	75	33 75 A
Bromefield. Stan	21	17 90 A
Bromehead Rd. E1	57	35 81 C
Bromehead St. E1	57	35 81 C
Brome Rd. SE9	78	42 75 B
Bromfelde Rd. SW4	74	29 76 D
Bromfelde Wlk. SW4	74	30 76 C
Bromfield St. N1	48	31 83 C
Bromhall Rd. Dag	51	46 84 B
Bromhedge. SE9	89	42 72 D
Bromleigh Ct. SE23	87	34 72 B
Bromley Ave. Brom	99	39 70 C
Bromley Common. Brom	107	41 67 D
Bromley Cres. Brom	99	39 68 B
Bromley Ct. Brom	99	39 70 D
Bromley Gdns. Brom	99	39 68 B
Bromley Gr. Brom	98	38 69 D
Bromley Hall Rd. E14	58	38 81 A
Bromley High St. E3	57	37 82 B
Bromley Hill. Brom	99	39 70 A
Bromley La. Chis	100	44 70 D
Bromley Rd. Beck	98	38 69 C
Bromley Rd. Brom	99	39 69 C
Bromley Rd. Chis	100	44 70 C
Bromley Rd. E10	38	37 88 D
Bromley Rd. E17	26	37 89 A
Bromley Rd. N17	25	34 90 A
Bromley Rd. N18	17	32 92 D
Bromley Rd. SE6	88	37 72 D
Bromley St. E1	57	35 81 D
Brompton Arcade. SW3	5	27 79 B
Brompton Cl. Houn	70	12 74 B
Brompton Dri. Eri	68	52 77 D
Brompton Gr. N2	24	27 89 C
Brompton Pl. SW3	5	27 79 C
Brompton Rd. SW3	5	27 79 C
Brompton Sq. SW3	5	27 79 C
Bromwell's Rd. SW4	74	29 75 C
Bromwich Ave. N6	36	28 86 A
Bromyard Ave. W3	55	21 80 C
Brondesbury Mews. NW6	46	25 84 C
Brondesbury Park. NW2	46	23 84 C
Brondesbury Park. NW6	46	24 84 C
Brondesbury Rd. NW6	46	24 83 D
Brondesbury Villas. NW6	46	25 83 C
Bronholm Rd. SE2	66	46 79 D
Bronsart Rd. SW6	62	24 77 C
Bronson Rd. SW20	95	24 69 C
Bronte Gr. Dart	80	54 75 D
Bronti Cl. SE17	63	32 78 C
Bronze St. SE8	64	37 77 C
Brook Ave. Dag	52	49 84 D
Brook Ave. Edg	22	19 91 B
Brook Ave. Wem	34	19 86 C
Brookbank Ave. W7	53	14 81 B
Brookbank Rd. SE13	76	37 75 B
Brook Cl. Rom	30	51 90 B
Brook Cl. Ruis	31	09 87 A
Brook Cl. SW20	94	22 68 B
Brook Cres. E4	18	37 92 B
Brook Cres. N9	17	34 92 B
Brookdale. N11	16	29 92 A
Brookdale Rd. Bex	79	43 74 C
Brookdale Rd. E17	26	37 89 A
Brookdale Rd. SE6	88	37 73 B
Brookdale Rd. SE6	88	37 74 D
Brookdene Dri. Nthwd	19	09 91 B
Brookdene Rd. SE18	66	45 78 B
Brook Dri. Har	20	14 89 C
Brook Dri. Ruis	31	09 87 A
Brook Dri. SE11	8	31 78 B
Brook Dri. SE11	8	31 79 C
Brook Dri. Sun	91	09 70 A
Brooke Ave. Har	32	14 86 C
Brookehowse Rd. SE6	88	37 72 D
Brookend Rd. Sid	90	45 73 C
Brooke Rd. E17	26	38 89 C
Brooke Rd. E5	37	34 86 D
Brooke Rd. N16	37	34 86 C
Brookes Ct. EC1	3	31 81 A
Brooke's Market. EC1	3	31 81 A
Brooke St. EC1	3	31 81 A
Brookfield Ave. E17	26	38 89 C
Brookfield Ave. NW7	22	22 91 B
Brookfield Ave. NW7	22	22 91 B
Brookfield Ave. Sutt	104	27 65 C
Brookfield Ave. W5	54	17 82 D
Brookfield Cl. Har	33	18 88 A
Brookfield Cl. NW7	22	22 91 B
Brookfield Cres. Har	33	18 88 A
Brookfield Cres. NW7	22	22 91 B
Brookfield Ct. Grnf	53	14 82 A
Brookfield. N6	36	28 86 C
Brookfield Path. NW5	26	28 86 D
Brookfield Path. Wdf Gn	27	39 91 A
Brookfield Rd. E9	49	36 84 A
Brookfield Rd. N9	17	34 93 D
Brookfield Rd. W4	61	20 79 B
Brookfields Ave. Mit	104	27 67 A
Brookfields. Enf	14	35 96 D
Brook Gate. Belv	67	49 78 D
Brook Gate. W1	5	27 80 B
Brook Gdns. E4	18	37 92 B
Brook Gdns. King	92	20 69 A
Brook Gdns. SW13	72	21 75 B
Brook Green. W6	62	23 78 B
Brookhill Cl. Barn	12	27 95 A
Brook Hill Cl. SE18	66	43 78 D
Brookhill Rd. Barn	12	27 95 A
Brooking Rd. E7	50	40 85 A
Brook La. Bex	79	47 74 D
Brook La. Bexh	79	47 74 B
Brook La. Brom	99	40 70 A
Brookland Cl. NW11	23	25 89 C
Brookland Garth. NW11	23	25 89 C
Brookland Hill. NW11	23	25 89 D
Brookland Rise. NW11	23	25 89 C
Brooklands App. Rom	29	50 89 D
Brooklands Ave. SE9	90	44 72 B
Brooklands Ave. SW19	85	25 72 B
Brooklands Cl. Rom	29	50 89 D
Brooklands Cl. Sun	91	09 69 A
Brooklands Dri. Grnf	41	17 83 B
Brooklands Gdns. Horn	42	53 88 C
Brooklands La. Rom	29	50 89 D
Brooklands Park. SE3	77	40 75 A
Brooklands Pas. SW8	74	29 76 B
Brooklands Rd. Rom	29	50 89 D
Brooklands Rd. Surb	101	16 66 C

Street	Page	Grid
Brook Lane N. Brent	60	
Brook La. SE3	77	
Brooklea Cl. NW9	22	
Brooklyn Ave. SE25	97	
Brooklyn Gr. SE25	97	
Brooklyn Rd. SE25	97	
Brooklyn Rd. Brom	107	
Brooklyn Rd. Brom	107	
Brooklyn Rd. SE25	97	
Brookmead Ave. Brom	107	
Brookmead Cl. Orp	108	
Brookmead. Croy	109	
Brook Mead. Eps	109	
Brook Meadow. N12	15	
Brookmead Rd. Croy	104	
Brookmead Way. Orp	108	
Brook Mews N. W2	5	
Brookmill Rd. SE8	76	
Brook Pl. Barn	11	
Brook Rd. Ilf	40	
Brook Rd. N22	24	
Brook Rd. N2	24	
Brook Rd. N8	24	
Brook Rd. NW2	34	
Brook Rd. Rom	30	
Brook Rd. Surb	101	
Brook Rd. Th Hth	97	
Brook Rd. Twick	71	
Brook Road S. Brent	60	
Brooksbank St. E9	49	
Brooksby Mews. N1	48	
Brooksby St. N1	48	
Brooksby's Wlk. E9	49	
Brookscroft Rd. E17	26	
Brookshill. Har	21	
Brookside. Barn	12	
Brookside. Cars	111	
Brookside Cl. Barn	11	
Brookside Cl. Har	43	
Brookside Cl. Har	33	
Brookside Cres. Wor Pk	102	
Brookside. Horn	42	
Brookside. Ilf	28	
Brookside. N21	12	
Brookside. Orp	108	
Brookside Rd. Hay	53	
Brookside Rd. N19	36	
Brookside Rd. N9	17	
Brookside Rd. NW11	35	
Brookside S. Barn	16	
Brookside Way. Croy	106	
Brookside Wlk. N3	23	
Brooks La. W4	61	
Brook's Rd. E13	50	
Brooks Rd. W4	61	
Brook St. Eri	67	
Brook St. King	93	
Brook St. N17	25	
Brook St. W1	6	
Brook St. W2	5	
Brooksville Ave. NW6	46	
Brook Vale. Eri	79	
Brookview Rd. SW16	86	
Brookville Rd. SW6	62	
Brookway. SE3	77	
Brook Wlk. Edg	22	
Brook Wlk. N2	23	
Brookwood Ave. SW13	61	
Brookwood Rd. Houn	70	
Brookwood Rd. SW18	85	
Broom Ave. Orp	100	
Broom Cl. Brom	93	
Broom Cl. Tedd	93	
Broomcroft Ave. Nthlt	53	
Broome Rd. Hamp	92	
Broome Way. SE5	63	
Broomfield Ave. N13	16	
Broomfield. E17	38	
Broomfield La. N13	16	
Broomfield Pl. W13	54	
Broomfield Rd. Beck	98	
Broomfield Rd. Bexh	79	
Broomfield Rd. N13	16	
Broomfield Rd. Rich	71	
Broomfield Rd. Rom	41	
Broomfield Rd. Surb	101	
Broomfield Rd. Tedd	93	
Broomfield Rd. W13	54	
Broomfield St. E14	50	
Broomfield. Sun	91	
Broom Gdns. Croy	106	
Broomgrove Gdns. Edg	22	
Broomgrove Rd. SW9	74	
Broomhall Rd. S Croy	112	
Broomhill Ct. Wdf Gn	27	
Broomhill Rd. Dart	80	
Broomhill Rd. Ilf	40	17 78 D
Broomhill Rd. Orp	108	40 76 D
Broomhill Rd. SW18	73	25 74 A
Broomhill Rd. Wdf Gn	27	40 91 A
Broomhill Rise. Bexh	79	49 74 A
Broomhill Wlk. Wdf Gn	27	39 91 D
Broomhouse La. SW6	73	25 75 A
Broomhouse Rd. SW6	73	25 76 C
Broomloan La. Sutt	103	25 65 A
Broom Lock. Tedd	93	17 70 A
Broom Mead. Bexh	79	49 74 A
Broom Park. Tedd	93	17 70 D
Broom Rd. Croy	106	37 65 C
Broom Rd. Tedd	93	17 70 A
Broomsleigh St. NW6	46	24 85 D
Broom Water. Tedd	83	17 71 C
Broom Water W. Tedd	83	17 71 C
Broomwood Rd. Orp	100	46 69 D
Broomwood Rd. SW11	74	27 74 D
Broseley Gr. SE26	88	36 71 C
Brougham Rd. E8	48	34 83 A
Brougham Rd. W3	55	20 81 C
Brougham St. SW11	74	27 76 D
Brough Cl. SW8	10	30 77 C
Brough Cl. SW8	10	30 77 C
Broughton Ave. N3	23	24 89 A
Broughton Ave. Rich	83	17 71 A
Broughton Ct. W13	54	16 80 B
Broughton Dri. SW9	75	31 75 C
Broughton Gdns. N6	36	29 88 C
Broughton Rd. Orp	108	44 65 B
Broughton Rd. SW6	73	25 76 D
Broughton Rd. Th Hth	105	31 67 C
Broughton Rd. W13	54	16 80 B
Broughton Road App. SW6	73	25 76 D
Broughton St. SW8	74	28 76 D
Brouncker Rd. W3	61	20 79 A
Browell's La. Felt	81	10 72 B
Brown Cl. Wall	111	30 63 C
Brownfield St. E14	58	38 81 C
Brown Hart Gdns. W1	6	28 80 A
Brownhill Rd. SE6	88	38 73 B
Browning Ave. Sutt	111	27 64 A
Browning Ave. W7	54	15 81 D
Browning Ave. Wor Pk	102	22 66 D
Browning Cl. Hamp	82	12 71 B
Browning Cl. W9	1	26 82 C
Browning Cl. Well	78	45 76 A
Browning Mews. W1	2	28 81 A
Browning Rd. Dart	80	54 75 D
Browning Rd. E11	39	39 87 B
Browning Rd. E12	50	42 84 B
Browning Rd. Enf	13	32 97 B
Browning St. SE17	63	32 78 A
Browning Way. Houn	70	11 76 B
Brownlea Gdns. Ilf	40	46 86 A
Brownlow Mews. WC1	3	30 82 D
Brownlow Rd. Croy	112	33 64 A
Brownlow Rd. E7	50	40 85 A
Brownlow Rd. E8	48	34 83 A
Brownlow Rd. N11	24	30 91 A
Brownlow Rd. N3	23	25 91 D
Brownlow Rd. NW10	45	21 84 C
Brownlow Rd. W13	54	16 80 C
Brownlow St. WC1	3	30 81 B
Brownrigg Rd. Ashf	81	07 71 A
Brown's Bldgs. EC3	4	33 81 C
Brownspring Dri. SE9	90	44 72 C
Brown's Rd. E17	26	37 89 A
Brown's Rd. Surb	101	18 66 B
Brown St. W1	1	27 81 D
Brownswell Rd. N2	23	26 90 D
Brownswood Rd. N4	37	32 86 A
Broxash Rd. SW11	74	28 74 C
Broxbourne Ave. E18	27	40 89 D
Broxbourne Rd. E7	39	40 86 C
Broxbourne Rd. Orp	108	45 66 B
Broxholm Rd. SE27	87	31 72 C
Broxted Rd. SE6	88	36 72 B
Bruce Ave. Horn	42	53 86 B
Bruce Castle Rd. N17	25	33 90 B
Bruce Cl. Well	78	46 76 B
Bruce Gr. N17	25	33 90 D
Bruce Gr. Orp	108	46 66 C
Bruce Rd. Barn	11	24 96 A
Bruce Rd. E3	57	37 82 B
Bruce Rd. Har	21	15 90 C
Bruce Rd. Mit	96	28 70 C
Bruce Rd. NW10	45	20 84 D
Bruce Rd. SE25	97	32 68 D
Brudenell Rd. SW17	86	28 71 A
Bruffs Meadow. Nthlt	43	12 84 A
Brumfield Rd. Eps	109	20 64 C
Brummel Cl. Bexh	79	50 75 A
Brumwill Rd. W5	44	18 83 C
Brunel Cl. Nthlt	53	12 82 B
Brunel Cl. SE19	97	33 70 B
Brunel Estate. W2	56	25 81 A
Brunel Pl. Sthl	53	13 81 D
Brunel Rd. SE16	64	35 79 A
Brunel Rd. W3	55	21 81 A
Brunel St. E16	58	39 81 D
Brunel Wlk. Houn	82	13 73 A
Brunel Wlk. N15	25	33 89 C
Brune St. E1	4	33 81 B
Brunner Cl. NW11	35	26 88 A
Brunner Rd. E17	38	38 88 B
Brunner Rd. W5	54	17 82 D
Brunswick Ave. N11	16	28 93 C
Brunswick Cl. Bexh	79	47 75 D
Brunswick Cl. Pnr	32	12 88 D
Brunswick Cl. Snb	101	15 66 D
Brunswick Cres. N11	16	28 93 C
Brunswick Gdns. Ilf	28	44 91 C
Brunswick Gdns. W5	54	18 82 C
Brunswick Gdns. W8	56	25 80 C
Brunswick Gr. N11	16	28 93 C
Brunswick Mews. W1	1	27 81 D
Brunswick Park Gdns. N11	16	28 93 C
Brunswick Park Rd. N11	16	28 93 C
Brunswick Park. SE5	75	33 76 A
Brunswick Pl. N1	4	32 82 B
Brunswick Pl. SE19	97	34 70 C
Brunswick Rd. Bexh	79	48 75 C
Brunswick Rd. E10	38	38 87 C
Brunswick Rd. E14	58	38 81 C
Brunswick Rd. King	94	19 69 A
Brunswick Rd. N15	25	33 89 C
Brunswick Rd. Sutt	110	25 64 B
Brunswick Rd. W5	54	18 82 A
Brunswick Sq. WC1	3	30 82 C
Brunswick St. E17	38	38 88 A
Brunswick Villas. SE5	75	33 76 A
Brunswick Way. N11	16	28 92 B
Brunton Pl. E14	57	36 81 C
Brushfield St. E1	4	33 81 B
Brussels Rd. SW11	73	26 75 D
Bruton Cl. Chis	99	42 70 D
Bruton La. W1	6	28 80 B
Bruton Pl. W1	6	28 80 B
Bruton Rd. Mord	95	26 68 C
Bruton St. W1	6	28 80 B
Bruton Way. W13	54	16 81 A
Bryan Ave. NW10	45	22 84 D
Bryan Cl. Sun	91	10 70 C
Bryan Rd. SE16	64	36 79 B
Bryan's Alley. SW6	73	25 76 D
Bryanston Ave. Twick	82	13 73 D
Bryanston Cl. Sthl	59	12 78 B
Bryanstone Rd. N8	36	29 88 D
Bryanston Mews E. W1	1	27 81 B
Bryanston Mews W. W1	1	27 81 D
Bryanston Pl. W1	1	27 81 B
Bryanston Sq. W1	1	27 81 D
Bryanston St. W1	1	27 81 D
Bryant Ave. Rom	30	53 90 D
Bryant Cl. Barn	11	24 95 B
Bryant Ct. E2	48	33 83 D
Bryant Rd. Nthlt	53	11 82 A
Bryant St. E15	50	39 84 C
Bryantwood Rd. N7	48	31 85 C
Brycedale Cres. N14	16	29 93 D
Bryce Rd. Dag	52	47 85 A
Bryden Cl. SE26	88	36 71 C
Brydges Pl. WC2	7	30 80 A
Brydges Rd. E15	49	38 85 D
Brydon Wlk. N1	47	30 83 A
Bryett Rd. N7	36	30 86 C
Brynmaer Rd. SW11	74	27 76 B
Bryn-y-mawr Rd. Enf	13	33 96 D
Bryony Rd. W12	55	22 80 A
Buccleuch House. E5	37	34 87 A
Buchanan Gdns. NW10	45	22 83 D
Buchanan Ho. SE21	87	34 72 C
Buchan Rd. SE15	76	35 75 A
Bucharest Rd. SW18	85	26 73 A
Buckbean Path. Rom	30	53 91 C
Buckden Cl. SE12	77	39 74 D
Buckfast Rd. Mord	95	25 68 D
Buckfast St. E2	57	34 82 A
Buckhold Rd. SW18	73	25 74 C
Buckhurst Ave. Cars	104	27 66 D
Buckhurst St. E1	57	34 82 D
Buckingham Arc. WC2	7	30 80 A
Buckingham Ave. E Mol	92	13 69 D
Buckingham Ave. Felt	69	10 74 D
Buckingham Ave. Grnf	44	16 83 A
Buckingham Ave. N20	15	26 94 B
Buckingham Ave. Th Hth	97	31 69 A

Buckingham Ave. Well ......78 45 75 C
Buckingham Cl. Enf ......13 33 97 C
Buckingham Cl. Hamp ......82 12 71 D
Buckingham Cl. Horn ......42 53 88 B
Buckingham Cl. Orp ......108 45 66 A
Buckingham Cl. W5 ......54 17 81 A
Buckingham Ct. NW4 ......22 22 89 A
Buckingham Ct. Sutt ......110 25 62 A
Buckingham Gate. SW1 ......6 29 79 C
Buckingham Gdns. Edg ......21 18 91 C
Buckingham Gdns. E Mol ......92 13 69 D
Buckingham Gdns. Th Hth ......97 31 69 C
Buckingham La. SE23 ......88 36 73 A
Buckingham Mews. NW10 ......45 21 83 D
Buckingham Mews. SW1 ......6 29 79 C
Buckingham Palace Rd. SW1 ......9 28 78 B
Buckingham Pl. SW1 ......6 29 79 C
Buckingham Rd. E10 ......38 37 86 D
Buckingham Rd. E11 ......39 41 88 A
Buckingham Rd. E15 ......50 39 85 D
Buckingham Rd. E18 ......27 39 90 B
Buckingham Rd. Edg ......21 18 91 D
Buckingham Rd. Hamp ......82 12 71 D
Buckingham Rd. Har ......32 14 88 B
Buckingham Rd. Ilf ......40 44 86 B
Buckingham Rd. King ......93 18 68 D
Buckingham Rd. Mit ......104 30 67 A
Buckingham Rd. N1 ......48 33 84 A
Buckingham Rd. N22 ......24 30 90 A
Buckingham Rd. NW10 ......45 21 83 D
Buckingham Rd. Rich ......83 17 72 B
Buckingham St. WC2 ......7 30 80 C
Buckingham Way. Wall ......111 29 62 A
Buckland Cres. NW3 ......46 26 84 A
Buckland Rd. E10 ......38 38 86 A
Buckland Rd. Sutt ......110 23 62 B
Buckland Rise. Pnr ......20 11 90 B
Bucklands Rd. Tedd ......93 17 70 A
Buckland St. N1 ......48 33 83 C
Buckland Way. Wor Pk ......103 23 66 C
Buckland Wlk. Mord ......95 26 68 C
Buckland Wlk. W3 ......61 20 79 A
Buck La. NW9 ......34 20 88 B
Buck La. NW9 ......22 20 89 D
Buckleigh Ave. SW20 ......95 24 68 B
Buckleigh Rd. SW16 ......96 30 70 C
Buckleigh Way. SW19 ......97 33 70 D
Bucklers Alley. SW6 ......62 24 77 D
Bucklersbury. EC4 ......4 32 81 D
Bucklers' Way. Cars ......104 27 65 D
Buckle St. E1 ......33 81 D
Buckley Cl. Dart ......80 51 76 D
Buckley Rd. NW6 ......46 24 84 D
Buckley St. SE1 ......7 31 80 C
Buckmaster Rd. SW11 ......74 27 75 C
Bucknall St. WC2 ......3 30 81 C
Buckner Rd. SW2 ......74 30 75 D
Buckrell Rd. E4 ......18 38 93 B
Buck St. NW1 ......47 28 84 D
Buckstone Cl. SE23 ......76 35 74 C
Buckstone Rd. N18 ......17 34 92 C
Buckters Rents. SE16 ......57 36 80 C
Buckthorne Rd. SE4 ......76 36 74 A
Buckwheat Ct. Belv ......67 47 79 D
Buck Wlk. E17 ......26 38 89 D
Buddings Circ. Wem ......34 20 86 C
Budds Alley. Twick ......71 17 74 A
Budge Row. EC4 ......4 32 81 D
Budleigh Cres. Well ......79 47 76 A
Budleigh Cres. Well ......67 47 77 C
Budoch Ct. Ilf ......40 46 86 A
Budoch Dri. Ilf ......40 46 86 A
Buer Rd. SW6 ......73 24 76 C
Bugsby's Way. E10 ......65 39 78 B
Bugsby's Way. SE7 ......65 40 78 B
Bulganak Rd. Th Hth ......97 32 68 C
Bulinga St. SW1 ......10 30 78 A
Bullace La. Dart ......80 54 74 C
Bullace La. Dart ......80 54 74 C
Bullace Row. SE5 ......75 32 76 B
Bull Alley. Well ......78 46 75 B
Bullards Pl. E2 ......57 35 82 B
Bullbanks Rd. Belv ......67 50 78 A
Bullen St. SW11 ......74 27 76 C
Buller Cl. SE15 ......63 34 77 C
Buller Rd. Bark ......51 45 84 C
Buller Rd. N17 ......25 34 90 C
Buller Rd. N22 ......25 31 90 C
Buller Rd. NW10 ......56 23 82 B
Buller Rd. Th Hth ......97 32 68 B
Bullers Wood Dri. Chis ......99 42 70 D
Bull Inn Ct. WC2 ......7 30 80 A
Bullivant St. E14 ......58 38 80 A
Bull La. Chis ......100 44 70 D
Bull La. Dag ......41 49 86 D

Bull La. N18 ......17 33 92 C
Bull Rd. E15 ......50 39 83 D
Bulls Alley. SW14 ......72 20 75 B
Bulls Bridge Rd. Sthl ......59 11 78 A
Bullsbrook Rd. Hay ......53 11 80 C
Bull's Gdn. SW3 ......9 27 78 A
Bulls Head Pas. EC3 ......4 33 81 C
Bulls Head Yd. Dart ......80 54 74 C
Bull Wharf La. EC4 ......8 32 80 A
Bull Yd. SE15 ......75 34 76 A
Bulmer Gdns. Har ......33 17 87 B
Bulmer Mews. W11 ......56 25 80 C
Bulstrode Ave. Houn ......70 13 75 A
Bulstrode Gdns. Houn ......70 13 75 A
Bulstrode Pl. W1 ......2 28 81 A
Bulstrode Rd. Houn ......70 13 75 A
Bulstrode St. W1 ......2 28 81 C
Bulwer Court Rd. E11 ......38 38 87 D
Bulwer Gdns. Barn ......11 26 96 C
Bulwer Rd. Barn ......11 25 96 D
Bulwer Rd. E11 ......38 38 87 D
Bulwer Rd. N18 ......17 33 92 A
Bulwer St. W12 ......56 23 80 C
Bunces La. Wdf Gn ......27 39 91 D
Bungalow Rd. SE25 ......97 33 68 C
Bungalows The. SW16 ......96 28 70 D
Bungalow The. Ilf ......28 45 90 A
Bunhill Row. EC1 ......4 32 82 D
Bunhouse Pl. SW1 ......9 28 78 C
Bunker's Hill. Belv ......67 49 78 A
Bunkers Hill. NW11 ......35 26 87 A
Bunn's La. NW7 ......22 21 91 D
Bunsen St. E3 ......49 36 83 C
Buntingbridge Rd. Ilf ......40 44 88 B
Bunting Cl. Mit ......104 27 67 B
Bunton St. SE18 ......66 43 79 C
Bunyan Rd. E17 ......26 36 89 A
Buonaparte Mews. SW1 ......10 29 78 D
Burbage Cl. SE1 ......8 32 79 D
Burbage Rd. SE21 ......87 32 73 B
Burberry Cl. N Mal ......94 21 69 C
Burbidge Rd. Shep ......91 07 58 C
Burbridge Way. N17 ......25 33 90 D
Burcham St. E14 ......58 38 81 C
Burcharbro Rd. SE2 ......67 47 77 B
Burchell Rd. E10 ......38 37 87 D
Burchell Rd. SE15 ......75 34 76 B
Burchett Way. Rom ......41 44 88 D
Burchwall Cl. Rom ......29 50 91 C
Burcote Rd. SW18 ......85 26 73 B
Burden Cl. Brent ......60 17 78 C
Burdenshott Ave. Rich ......72 19 75 D
Burden Way. E11 ......39 40 86 B
Burder Cl. N1 ......48 33 84 A
Burder Rd. N1 ......48 33 84 A
Burdett Ave. SW20 ......94 21 69 C
Burdett Mews. NW3 ......46 26 84 B
Burdett Mews. W2 ......56 25 81 D
Burdett Rd. Croy ......105 32 67 D
Burdett Rd. E14 ......57 36 81 D
Burdett Rd. E3 ......57 36 82 D
Burdett Rd. Rich ......71 18 75 B
Burdon La. Sutt ......110 24 62 B
Burdon Park. Sutt ......110 24 62 B
Burfield Cl. SW17 ......85 26 71 B
Burford Cl. Dag ......41 47 86 C
Burford Cl. Ilf ......28 44 89 C
Burford Gdns. N13 ......16 30 93 D
Burford Rd. Brent ......60 18 78 C
Burford Rd. Brom ......99 42 68 C
Burford Rd. E15 ......49 38 83 B
Burford Rd. SE6 ......88 36 72 B
Burford Rd. Sutt ......103 25 65 A
Burford Rd. Wor Pk ......102 22 66 A
Burgate Cl. Dart ......80 51 75 B
Burges Cl. Horn ......42 50 89 B
Burges Rd. E6 ......50 42 84 D
Burges Rd. E6 ......51 43 84 C
Burgess Ave. NW9 ......34 20 88 D
Burgess Cl. Felt ......82 12 71 A
Burgess Hill. NW2 ......46 25 85 A
Burgess Rd. E15 ......50 39 85 A
Burgess Rd. Sutt ......110 25 64 B
Burgess St. E14 ......57 37 81 A
Burge St. SE1 ......8 32 79 D
Burghill Rd. SE26 ......88 36 71 A
Burghley Ave. N Mal ......94 20 69 B
Burghley Pl. Mit ......96 27 68 D
Burghley Rd. E11 ......39 39 87 C
Burghley Rd. N8 ......25 31 89 A
Burghley Rd. NW5 ......47 28 85 B
Burghley Rd. SW19 ......85 24 71 A
Burgh St. N1 ......48 31 83 D
Burgon St. EC4 ......3 31 81 D

Burgos Gr. SE10 ......76 37 76 B
Burgoyne Rd. Ashf ......91 09 70 B
Burgoyne Rd. N4 ......37 31 88 D
Burgoyne Rd. SE25 ......97 33 68 D
Burgoyne Rd. SW9 ......74 30 75 B
Burgundy St. SE1 ......63 33 78 D
Burham Cl. SE20 ......98 35 70 C
Burhill Gr. Pnr ......20 12 90 C
Burke Cl. SW15 ......72 21 75 C
Burke St. E16 ......58 39 81 B
Burland Rd. Rom ......29 50 91 A
Burland Rd. SW11 ......74 27 74 B
Burleigh Ave. Sid ......78 45 74 B
Burleigh Ave. Wall ......104 28 65 D
Burleigh Gdns. Ashf ......81 08 71 C
Burleigh Gdns. N14 ......16 29 94 C
Burleigh Rd. Enf ......13 33 96 C
Burleigh Rd. Sutt ......103 24 66 D
Burleigh St. WC2 ......7 30 80 B
Burleigh Way. Enf ......13 32 96 B
Burley Cl. E4 ......18 37 92 C
Burley Cl. SW16 ......96 29 69 D
Burley Rd. E16 ......58 41 81 A
Burlington Arc. W1 ......6 29 80 A
Burlington Ave. Rich ......72 19 76 A
Burlington Ave. Rom ......41 49 88 D
Burlington Cl. Felt ......81 08 73 B
Burlington Cl. Orp ......108 43 65 B
Burlington Cl. W9 ......56 25 82 C
Burlington Gdns. Rom ......41 48 87 A
Burlington Gdns. W1 ......6 29 80 A
Burlington Gdns. W3 ......55 20 80 C
Burlington Gdns. W4 ......61 20 78 C
Burlington La. W4 ......61 20 77 D
Burlington La. W4 ......61 21 77 A
Burlington Mews. W3 ......55 20 80 C
Burlington Pl. SW6 ......73 24 76 C
Burlington Rd. Enf ......13 32 97 B
Burlington Rd. Islw ......70 14 76 B
Burlington Rd. N10 ......24 28 89 A
Burlington Rd. N17 ......25 34 90 A
Burlington Rd. N Mal ......94 22 68 C
Burlington Rd. SW6 ......73 24 76 C
Burlington Rd. Th Hth ......97 32 69 D
Burlington Rd. W4 ......61 20 78 B
Burlington Rise. Barn ......16 27 94 B
Burma Ct. N16 ......48 32 85 B
Burma Rd. N16 ......48 32 85 B
Burmester Rd. SW17 ......85 26 72 C
Burnaby Cres. W4 ......61 20 77 A
Burnaby Gdns. W4 ......61 19 77 B
Burnaby St. SW10 ......62 26 77 C
Burnbrae Cl. N3 ......23 25 91 B
Burnbury Rd. SW12 ......86 29 73 C
Burncroft Ave. Enf ......14 35 97 D
Burnell Ave. Rich ......83 17 71 C
Burnell Ave. Well ......78 46 76 C
Burnell Gdns. Stan ......21 17 90 D
Burnell Rd. Sutt ......110 25 64 B
Burness Cl. N7 ......47 30 84 B
Burne St. NW1 ......1 27 81 A
Burnett Cl. E9 ......49 35 85 C
Burnett Rd. Eri ......68 53 77 B
Burney Ave. Surb ......101 18 67 B
Burney St. SE10 ......64 38 77 C
Burnfoot Ave. SW6 ......73 24 76 A
Burnham Cres. Dart ......80 53 75 C
Burnham Cres. E11 ......27 41 89 C
Burnham Ct. NW4 ......23 23 89 C
Burnham Dri. Wor Pk ......103 23 65 B
Burnham Estate. E2 ......57 35 82 A
Burnham Gdns. Houn ......69 10 76 B
Burnham Rd. Dag ......51 46 83 B
Burnham Rd. Dart ......80 53 75 D
Burnham Rd. E4 ......18 36 92 D
Burnham Rd. Mord ......95 25 68 D
Burnham Rd. Rom ......29 50 89 B
Burnham St. E2 ......57 35 82 A
Burnham St. King ......94 19 69 A
Burnham Way. W13 ......60 16 79 D
Burnhill Rd. Beck ......98 37 69 C
Burnley Rd. NW10 ......45 22 85 C
Burnley Rd. SW9 ......74 30 76 D
Burnsall St. SW3 ......9 27 78 C
Burns Ave. Felt ......69 10 74 C
Burns Ave. Sid ......78 46 74 D
Burns Ave. Sthl ......53 13 80 A
Burns Cl. Eri ......80 51 76 B
Burns Cl. Well ......78 45 76 B
Burns Ct. Wall ......111 28 63 D
Burnside Cl. Barn ......11 25 96 A
Burnside Cl. Twick ......71 16 74 C
Burnside Cres. Wem ......44 17 83 B
Burn Side. N9 ......18 35 93 C
Burnside Rd. Dag ......41 47 87 C

Name	Pg	Ref
Burnside St. E3	57	36 82 A
Burn's Rd. NW10	45	21 83 B
Burns Rd. SW11	74	27 76 D
Burns Rd. W13	60	16 79 B
Burns Rd. Wem	44	18 83 C
Burns Way. Houn	70	11 76 B
Burnt Ash Hill SE12	89	40 73 C
Burnt Ash La. Brom	89	40 71 D
Burnt Ash Rd. SE12	77	39 74 B
Burnthwaite Rd. SW6	62	25 77 C
Burnt Oak Bwy. Edg	22	19 90 B
Burnt Oak Fields. Edg	22	20 90 A
Burnt Oak La. Sid	90	46 73 B
Burntwood Ave. Horn	42	54 88 C
Burntwood Cl. SW18	86	27 73 C
Burntwood Grange Rd. SW18	5	27 79 C
Burntwood La. SW18	85	26 72 B
Burnway. Horn	42	54 87 A
Buross St. E1	57	34 81 D
Burrage Gr. SE18	66	44 78 A
Burrage Pl. SE18	66	43 78 D
Burrage Rd. SE18	66	44 78 B
Burrard Rd. E16	58	40 81 D
Burrard Rd. NW6	46	25 85 A
Burr Cl. Bexh	79	48 75 B
Burr Cl. E1	57	34 80 C
Burrell Cl. Croy	106	36 67 C
Burrell Row. Beck	98	37 69 C
Burrell St. SE1	31	31 80 D
Burritt Rd. King	94	19 69 C
Burroughs Gdns. NW4	22	22 89 D
Burroughs The. NW4	22	22 89 D
Burrows Mews. SE1	7	31 79 B
Burrows Rd. NW10	55	23 82 A
Burrow Wlk. SE21	87	32 73 A
Burr Rd. SW18	85	25 73 A
Bursar St. SE1	8	33 80 C
Bursdon Cl. Sid	90	45 72 B
Bursland Rd. Enf	14	35 96 D
Burslem Ave. Ilf	28	46 91 A
Burslem St. E1	57	34 81 D
Burstall Rd. N15	37	33 88 A
Burstock Rd. SW15	73	24 75 C
Burston Rd. SW15	73	23 75 D
Burstow Rd. SW20	95	24 69 A
Burtenshaw Rd. Surb	101	16 67 C
Burtley Cl. N4	37	32 87 C
Burton Gdns. Houn	70	12 76 B
Burton Gr. SE17	63	32 78 D
Burtonhole Cl. NW7	15	23 92 B
Burtonhole La. NW7	15	23 92 B
Burton La. SW9	75	31 76 C
Burton Mews. SW1	9	28 78 A
Burton Pl. WC1	2	29 82 B
Burton Rd. E18	27	40 89 B
Burton Rd. King	93	18 70 C
Burton Rd. NW6	46	24 84 D
Burton Rd. SW9	75	31 76 C
Burton Rd. SW9	75	31 76 D
Burtons Crt. E15	49	38 84 D
Burton's Rd. Hamp	82	13 71 B
Burton St. WC1	2	29 82 D
Burts Rd. E16	58	41 80 C
Burwash Rd. SE18	66	44 78 D
Burwell Ave. Grnf	44	15 84 A
Burwell Cl. E1	57	34 81 D
Burwell Rd. E10	38	36 87 C
Burwell Wlk. E3	57	37 82 C
Burwood Ave. Brom	107	40 65 B
Burwood Ave. Pnr	32	11 88 A
Burwood Pl. W2	1	27 81 C
Bury Ave. Ruis	31	08 88 C
Bury Ct. EC3	4	33 81 C
Bury Gr. Mord	103	25 67 B
Bury Pl. WC1	3	30 81 A
Bury Rd. Dag	52	50 85 C
Bury Rd. Enf	14	38 96 B
Bury Rd. N22	25	31 89 A
Bury St. EC3	4	33 81 C
Bury St. N9	17	34 94 C
Bury Street W. N9	17	33 94 A
Bury St. Ruis	31	08 88 D
Bury St. SW1	6	29 80 C
Bury Wlk. SW3	9	27 78 C
Busby Pl. NW5	47	29 84 B
Busby St. E2	4	33 82 D
Busch Cnr. Islw	71	16 76 B
Bushberry Rd. E9	49	36 84 A
Bush Cl. Ilf	40	44 88 B
Bush Cottages. SW18	73	25 74 A
Bushell Cl. SW2	86	30 72 B
Bushell St. E1	57	34 80 C
Bushell Way. Chis	90	43 71 C
Bush Elms Rd. Horn	42	52 87 A
Bushey Ave. E18	27	39 89 B
Bushey Ave. Orp	108	44 66 B
Bushey Cl. Uxb	31	07 86 A
Bushey Ct. SW20	94	22 68 B
Bushey Ct. SW20	95	23 69 C
Bushey Down. SW12	86	28 72 B
Bushey Hill Rd. SE5	75	33 76 B
Bushey La. Sutt	110	25 64 A
Bushey Rd. Croy	106	37 65 A
Bushey Rd. E13	50	41 83 C
Bushey Rd. N15	37	33 88 C
Bushey Rd. Sutt	110	25 64 B
Bushey Rd. SW20	94	22 68 B
Bushey Rd. Uxb	31	07 86 A
Bushey Way. Beck	106	38 67 B
Bush Fair Ct. N14	12	28 95 D
Bush Gr. NW9	34	20 87 A
Bushgrove Rd. Dag	52	47 85 B
Bush Gr. Stan	21	17 90 B
Bush Hill. N21	17	32 94 A
Bush Hill. N21	13	32 95 C
Bush Hill Par. Enf	17	32 94 B
Bush Hill Rd. Har	18	18 88 D
Bush Hill Rd. N21	13	32 95 D
Bush La. EC4	8	32 80 B
Bushmoor Cres. SE18	66	43 77 D
Bushnell Rd. SW17	86	28 72 D
Bush Rd. E11	39	40 87 A
Bush Rd. E8	48	34 83 B
Bush Rd. Rich	60	18 77 B
Bush Rd. SE8	64	35 78 B
Bushway. Dag	52	47 85 B
Bushwood. E11	39	40 87 C
Bushwood Rd. Rich	61	19 77 A
Bushy Park Gdns. Tedd	82	14 71 D
Bushy Park Rd. Tedd	93	16 70 D
Bushy Rd. Tedd	93	15 70 D
Butcher Row. E14	57	35 80 B
Butcher Row. E1	57	35 81 D
Butchers Rd. E16	58	40 81 C
Bute Ave. Rich	83	18 73 C
Bute Ct. Wall	111	29 64 C
Bute Gdns. W6	62	23 78 B
Bute Gdns. Wall	111	29 64 C
Bute Gdns. W. Wall	111	29 64 C
Bute Rd. Croy	105	31 66 C
Bute Rd. Ilf	40	44 88 A
Bute St. SW7	9	27 78 B
Bute Wlk. N1	48	32 84 B
Butler Ave. Har	32	14 87 B
Butler Pl. SW1	6	29 79 D
Butler Rd. Dag	51	46 85 B
Butler Rd. Har	32	14 87 A
Butler St. E2	57	35 82 A
Butley Ct. E3	49	36 83 C
Buttercup Cl. Rom	30	53 90 B
Butterfields. E17	38	38 88 A
Butterfly La. SE9	78	43 74 D
Butter Hill. Wall	104	28 65 C
Buttermere Cl. N.Mal	103	23 67 D
Buttermere Dri. SW15	73	24 74 B
Buttermere Wlk. E8	48	33 84 B
Butterwick. W6	62	23 78 B
Buttesland St. N1	4	32 82 B
Buttfield Cl. Dag	52	49 84 B
Buttmarsh Cl. SE18	66	43 78 D
Buttsbury Rd. Ilf	51	44 85 D
Butts Cres. Felt	82	13 72 C
Butts Green Rd. Horn	42	53 88 D
Buttsmead Nthwd	19	08 91 C
Butts Rd. Brom	89	39 71 C
Butts The. Brent	60	17 77 B
Butts The. Sun	91	11 68 A
Buxted Cl (off Middleton Rd). E8	48	33 84 D
Buxted Cl (off Richmond Rd). E8	48	33 84 D
Buxted Rd. N12	16	27 92 C
Buxton Cl. Wdf Grn	27	41 91 B
Buxton Cres. Sutt	110	24 64 A
Buxton Ct. N1	4	32 82 A
Buxton Dri. E11	27	39 89 C
Buxton Dri. N Mal	94	20 69 D
Buxton Gdns. W3	55	19 80 B
Buxton Rd. E15	49	39 85 C
Buxton Rd. E17	26	36 89 C
Buxton Rd. E4	18	38 94 B
Buxton Rd. Eri	67	50 77 D
Buxton Rd. Ilf	45	45 88 C
Buxton Rd. N19	36	29 87 D
Buxton Rd. NW2	45	22 84 B
Buxton Rd. SW14	72	21 75 A
Buxton Rd. Th Hth	105	31 67 B
Buxton St. E1	57	33 82 D
Buxton St. E1	57	34 82 C
Byam St. SW6	73	26 76 C
Byards Croft. SW16	96	29 69 B
Byatt Wlk. Hamp	92	12 70 A
Bychurch End. Tedd	83	15 71 D
Bycroft Rd. Sthl	53	13 82 C
Bycroft St. SE20	96	35 70 D
Bycullah Ave. Enf	13	31 97 D
Bycullah Rd. Enf	13	31 97 D
Byefield Rd. Islw	71	16 75 A
Bye The. W3	55	21 81 C
Byeways The. Surb	102	19 67 B
Bye Ways. Twick	82	13 72 D
Bye Way The. Har	21	15 90 B
Byeway The. SW14	72	20 75 A
Byfield Gdns. SW13	72	22 76 A
Byford Cl. E15	49	39 84 C
Bygrove Rd. SW19	95	26 70 B
Bygrove St. E14	57	37 81 D
Byland Cl. N21	16	30 94 B
Byland Cl. SE2	66	46 79 D
Byne Rd. Cars	104	27 65 A
Byne Rd. SE26	88	35 71 C
Bynes Rd. S Croy	112	32 63 D
Byng Pl. WC1	2	29 82 D
Byng Rd. Barn	11	23 96 B
Byng St. E14	64	37 79 A
Bynon Ave. Bexh	79	48 75 B
Byrne Rd. SW12	86	28 72 B
Byron Ave. E12	50	42 84 B
Byron Ave. E18	27	39 90 D
Byron Ave E. Sutt	110	26 64 B
Byron Ave. Houn	69	10 76 D
Byron Ave. N.Mal	102	22 67 A
Byron Ave. NW9	22	19 89 B
Byron Ave. Sutt	110	26 64 B
Byron Cl. E8	48	34 83 A
Byron Cl. Hamp	82	12 71 B
Byron Cl. N2	35	26 88 D
Byron Cl. Enf	13	31 97 D
Byron Gdns. Sutt	110	26 64 B
Byron Hill Rd. Har	33	15 86 A
Byron Rd. E10	38	37 87 D
Byron Rd. E17	26	37 89 A
Byron Rd. Har	33	15 88 C
Byron Rd. Har	21	15 89 B
Byron Rd. NW2	34	22 86 B
Byron Rd. S Croy	112	34 62 D
Byron Rd. W5	55	19 80 C
Byron Rd. Wem	33	17 86 C
Byron St. E14	58	38 81 C
Bysouth Cl. Ilf	28	43 90 B
Bythorn St. SW9	74	30 75 D
Byton Rd. SW17	96	27 70 B
Byward Ave. Felt	70	11 74 C
Byward St. EC3	8	33 80 A
Bywater Pl. SE16	9	37 78 D
Bywater St. SW3	9	27 78 C
Byways The. Eps	109	21 64 B
Byway The. Sutt	110	26 62 B
Bywell Pl. W1	2	29 81 A
Bywood Ave. Croy	106	35 67 D
Byworth Wlk. N19	36	30 87 C
Cabbell St. NW1	1	27 81 A
Cabinet Way. E4	26	36 91 B
Cable St. E1	57	35 80 A
Cabul Rd. SW11	74	27 76 C
Cactus Wlk. W12	55	21 81 D
Cadbury Cl. Islw	71	16 76 A
Cadbury Cl. Sun	91	09 70 C
Cadbury Rd. Sun	91	09 70 A
Cadbury Way. SE16	63	34 79 C
Caddington Cl. Barn	12	27 95 A
Caddington Rd. NW2	35	24 86 C
Cadell Cl. E2	48	33 83 D
Cade Rd. SE10	76	38 76 B
Cader Rd. SW18	73	26 74 C
Cadet Pl. E10	65	39 78 C
Cadiz Rd. Dag	52	50 84 A
Cadiz St. SE17	63	32 78 C
Cadley Terr. SE23	88	35 72 A
Cadmer Cl. N Mal	94	21 69 C
Cadmus Cl. SW4	74	29 75 B
Cadogan Cl. Beck	98	38 69 B
Cadogan Cl. E9	49	36 84 D
Cadogan Cl. Har	8	13 85 B
Cadogan Cl. Tedd	83	15 71 C
Cadogan Ct. Sutt	110	25 63 B
Cadogan Gate. SW1	9	27 78 B
Cadogan Gdns. E18	27	40 89 B
Cadogan Gdns. N21	13	31 95 A
Cadogan Gdns. N3	23	25 90 B
Cadogan Gdns. SW3	9	27 78 B
Cadogan La. SW1	6	28 79 C

Cadogan Pl. SW1 5   27 79 D
Cadogan Pl. SW1 9   28 78 A
Cadogan Rd. Surb 101   17 67 B
Cadogan Sq. SW1 9   27 78 B
Cadogan St. SW3 9   27 78 B
Cadogan Terr. E9 49   36 84 D
Cadoxton Ave. N15 37   33 88 D
Cadwallon Rd. SE9 90   44 72 A
Caedmon Rd. N7 47   30 85 B
Caernarvon Cl. Mit 96   30 68 A
Caernarvon Dri. Ilf 28   43 90 A
Caesar St. E2 4   33 82 B
Caesars Wlk. Mit 104   27 67 B
Cahill St. EC1 4   32 82 C
Cahir St. E14 64   37 78 B
Cain's La. Felt 69   09 74 A
Caird St. W10 56   24 82 B
Cairn Ave. W5 54   17 80 D
Cairndale Cl. Brom 99   39 70 D
Cairnfield Ave. NW2 34   21 86 D
Cairns Ave. Wdf Gn 27   42 91 B
Cairns Cl. Dart 80   53 74 B
Cairns Rd. SW11 74   27 74 A
Cairn Way. Stan 21   15 91 B
Cairo New Rd. Croy 105   31 65 B
Cairo Rd. E17 26   37 89 C
Caistor Mews. SW12 86   28 73 B
Caistor Park Rd. E15 50   39 83 B
Caistor Rd. SW12 86   28 73 B
Caithness Gdns. Sid 78   45 75 D
Caithness Rd. Mit 96   28 70 D
Caithness Rd. W14 62   23 79 D
Calabria Rd. N5 48   31 84 B
Calais St. SE5 75   31 76 B
Calbourne Rd. SW12 86   28 73 A
Calcott Wlk. SE9 89   41 71 B
Caldbeck Ave. Wor Pk 102   22 66 D
Caldecot Rd. SE5 75   32 76 C
Caldecott Way. E5 38   35 86 D
Calder Ave. Grnf 44   15 83 D
Calder Gdns. Edg 22   33 96 A
Calder Cl. Enf 13   19 89 A
Calderon Pl. W10 56   23 81 A
Calder Rd. Mord 103   26 67 A
Caldervale Rd. SW4 74   29 74 B
Calderwood St. SE18 66   43 78 A
Caldew St. SE5 63   32 77 D
Caldwell St. SW9 63   31 77 C
Caldy Rd. Belv 67   49 79 D
Caldy Wlk. N1 48   32 84 A
Caleb St. SE1 8   32 79 A
Caledonian Rd. N7 47   30 84 B
Caledonia St. N1 47   30 83 C
Caledon Rd. E6 50   42 83 B
Caledon Rd. Wall 111   28 64 A
Cale St. SW3 9   27 78 C
Caletock Way. E10 65   39 78 D
Calgary Ct. SE16 64   35 79 A
Calgate Cl. SW19 85   24 73 C
California Rd. N Mal 94   20 68 A
Callander Rd. SE6 88   38 72 A
Callard Ave. N13 17   31 92 B
Callcott Rd. NW6 46   24 84 D
Callcott St. W8 56   25 80 C
Callendar Rd. SW7 5   26 79 D
Callis Rd. E17 38   36 88 D
Callow St. SW3 62   26 77 B
Calmington Rd. SE5 63   33 77 A
Calmont Rd. Brom 99   39 70 A
Calne Ave. Ilf 28   43 90 B
Colonne Rd. SW19 85   23 71 B
Calshot Rd. Houn 69   07 75 B
Calshot St. N1 47   30 83 D
Calshot Way. Enf 13   13 96 B
Calshot Way. Houn 69   07 76 C
Calthorpe Gdns. Sutt 103   26 65 C
Calthorpe St. WC1 3   30 82 D
Calva Cl. Barn 12   28 96 C
Calverley Cres. Dag 41   49 86 A
Calverley Cl. Beck 98   37 70 B
Calverley Gr. N19 36   29 87 D
Calverley Rd. Eps 109   22 63 A
Calvert Ave. E2 4   33 82 B
Calvert Cl. Belv 67   49 78 A
Calverton Rd. E6 51   43 83 A
Calvert Rd. Barn 11   23 97 D
Calvert Rd. E10 65   39 78 D
Calvert's Bldgs. SE1 8   32 80 D
Calvin St. E1 4   33 82 D
Calydon Rd. SE7 65   40 78 D
Camac Rd. Twick 82   14 73 D
Cambalt Rd. SW15 73   23 74 B
Cambell Wlk. N1 47   30 83 A
Camberley Ave. Enf 13   33 96 C
Camberley Ave SW20 94   22 69 D
Camberley Rd. Houn 69   07 75 A

Cambert Way. SE3 77   40 75 D
Camberwell Church St. SE5 ...75   32 76 B
Camberwell Glebe. SE5 75   33 76 A
Camberwell Green. SE5 75   32 76 B
Camberwell Gr. SE5 75   33 76 C
Camberwell New Rd. SE5 63   31 77 D
Camberwell Pas. SE5 75   32 76 A
Camberwell Rd. SE5 63   32 77 C
Camberwell Station Rd. SE5 ..75   32 76 A
Cambeys Rd. Dag 52   50 85 C
Camborne Ave. Rom 30   54 91 C
Camborne Ave. W13 60   17 79 A
Camborne Cl. Houn 69   07 75 A
Camborne Rd. Croy 105   34 66 A
Camborne Rd. Mord 103   24 67 A
Camborne Rd. Sutt 110   25 63 D
Camborne Rd. SW18 85   25 73 A
Camborne Rd. Well 78   45 76 D
Camborne Road S. Houn 69   07 75 A
Camborne Way. Houn 69   07 75 A
Camborne Way. Houn 70   13 76 A
Camborne Way. Rom 30   54 91 C
Cambourne Ave. N9 18   35 94 B
Cambourne Mews. W11 56   24 81 C
Cambray Rd. Orp 108   45 66 B
Cambray Rd. SW12 86   29 73 C
Cambria Cl. Houn 70   13 75 C
Cambria Cl. Sid 90   44 73 D
Cambria Ct. Felt 81   10 73 B
Cambrian Ave. Ilf 40   45 88 A
Cambrian Cl. SE27 87   31 72 D
Cambrian Rd. E10 38   37 87 A
Cambrian Rd. Rich 71   18 74 D
Cambria Rd. SE5 75   32 75 A
Cambria St. SW6 62   25 77 D
Cambridge Ave. Grnf 44   15 85 D
Cambridge Ave. N Mal 94   21 69 C
Cambridge Ave. NW6 46   25 83 C
Cambridge Ave. Rom 30   53 89 A
Cambridge Ave. Well 78   45 75 D
Cambridge Circ. WC2 2   29 81 D
Cambridge Cl. Houn 70   12 75 C
Cambridge Cl. SW20 94   22 69 B
Cambridge Cottages. Rich 61   19 77 A
Cambridge Cres. E2 48   34 83 D
Cambridge Cres. Tedd 83   16 71 C
Cambridge Dri. Ruis 32   11 86 B
Cambridge Dri. SE12 77   40 74 A
Cambridge Gate Mews. NW1 ...2   28 82 D
Cambridge Gate. NW1 2   28 82 D
Cambridge Gdns. Enf 13   34 97 C
Cambridge Gdns. King 94   19 69 C
Cambridge Gdns. N17 25   32 91 D
Cambridge Gdns. N21 17   32 94 B
Cambridge Gdns. NW6 46   25 83 C
Cambridge Gdns. W10 56   24 81 C
Cambridge Green. SE9 90   43 73 D
Cambridge Grove Rd. King 94   19 68 A
Cambridge Grove Rd. King 94   19 69 C
Cambridge Gr. SE20 97   34 70 D
Cambridge Gr. W6 61   22 78 B
Cambridge Heath Rd. E1 57   35 82 C
Cambridge Park Ct. Twick 83   17 73 B
Cambridge Park. E11 39   40 88 C
Cambridge Park Rd. E11 39   39 87 B
Cambridge Park. Twick 83   17 73 B
Cambridge Park. Twick 71   17 74 C
Cambridge Pas. E9 49   35 84 C
Cambridge Pl. W8 62   25 79 B
Cambridge Rd. Ashf 91   08 70 C
Cambridge Rd. Bark 51   44 84 C
Cambridge Rd. Brom 99   40 70 C
Cambridge Rd. Cars 111   27 64 C
Cambridge Rd. E11 39   40 88 C
Cambridge Rd. E4 18   38 94 D
Cambridge Rd. Hamp 92   12 70 D
Cambridge Rd. Har 32   13 88 A
Cambridge Rd. Houn 70   12 75 C
Cambridge Rd. Ilf 40   45 87 C
Cambridge Rd. King 94   19 69 C
Cambridge Rd. Mit 96   29 68 A
Cambridge Rd. N Mal 94   21 68 C
Cambridge Rd. NW6 56   25 82 A
Cambridge Rd. NW6 46   25 83 C
Cambridge Rd. Rich 61   19 77 C
Cambridge Rd. SE20 97   34 68 B
Cambridge Rd. Sid 90   45 71 A
Cambridge Rd. Sthl 53   12 80 D
Cambridge Rd. SW11 74   27 76 B
Cambridge Rd. SW13 72   21 76 D
Cambridge Rd. SW20 94   22 69 B
Cambridge Rd. Tedd 83   16 71 C
Cambridge Rd. Twick 71   17 74 D
Cambridge Rd. W7 60   15 79 B
Cambridge Road N. W4 61   19 78 D

Cambridge Road S. W4 61   19 78 D
Cambridge Row. SE18 66   43 78 D
Cambridge Sq. W2 1   27 81 C
Cambridge St. SW1 10   29 78 C
Cambridge Terr Mews. NW1 ...2   28 82 B
Cambridge Terr. NW1 2   28 82 B
Cambridge Yd. W7 60   15 79 B
Cambus Rd. E16 58   40 81 A
Camdale Rd. SE18 66   45 77 D
Camden Ave. Felt 82   11 73 C
Camden Ave. Hay 53   11 80 B
Camden Cl. Chis 100   44 70 C
Camden Cnr. Chis 100   43 69 B
Camden Gdns. NW1 47   29 84 C
Camden Gdns. Sutt 110   25 64 D
Camden Gdns. Th Hth 97   31 68 B
Camden Gr. Chis 100   43 70 B
Camden High St. NW1 47   28 83 B
Camden Hill Rd. SE19 97   33 70 A
Camdenhurst St. E14 57   36 81 C
Camden La. N7 47   29 84 B
Camden Mews. NW1 47   29 84 B
Camden Park Rd. Chis 100   43 70 C
Camden Park Rd. NW1 47   29 84 B
Camden Pas. N1 48   31 83 B
Camden Rd. Cars 111   27 64 B
Camden Rd. E11 39   40 88 D
Camden Rd. E17 38   36 88 D
Camden Rd. N7 47   30 85 C
Camden Rd. NW1 47   29 84 C
Camden Rd. Sutt 110   25 64 D
Camden Row. SE3 77   39 76 C
Camden Sq. NW1 47   29 84 B
Camden Sq. SE15 75   33 76 B
Camden Terr. NW1 47   29 84 B
Camden Way. Chis 100   43 70 C
Camden Way. Th Hth 97   31 68 B
Camden Wlk. N1 48   31 83 B
Camelford Wlk. W11 56   24 81 C
Camellia Pl. Twick 82   13 73 B
Camellia St. SW8 10   30 77 C
Camelot Cl. SW19 85   25 71 A
Camel Rd. E16 58   41 80 D
Camera Pl. SW10 62   26 77 B
Cameron Cl. N18 .... 34 92 D
Cameron Cl. N20 15   26 93 B
Cameron Pl. E1 57   34 81 D
Cameron Rd. Brom 99   40 68 C
Cameron Row. SE6 105   31 67 D
Cameron Rd. Croy 105   31 67 D
Cameron Rd. Ilf 40   45 87 C
Cameron Rd. SE6 88   36 72 B
Camerton Cl. E8 48   33 84 B
Camilla Rd. SE16 63   34 78 B
Camlan Rd. Brom 89   39 71 B
Camlet St. E2 4   33 82 D
Camlet Way. Barn 11   25 97 B
Camley St. NW1 47   29 83 B
Camm Gdns. Surb 101   15 66 B
Camomile Ave. Mit 96   27 69 B
Camomile St. EC3 4   33 81 C
Campana Rd. SW6 73   25 76 A
Campbell Ave. Ilf 28   44 89 C
Campbell Cl. Rom 30   51 91 A
Campbell Cl. Ruis 31   10 88 C
Campbell Cl. SE18 78   43 76 A
Campbell Cl. Twick 82   14 73 D
Campbell Ct. NW9 34   20 88 C
Campbell Rd. Croy 105   31 67 D
Campbell Rd. E15 50   39 85 B
Campbell Rd. E17 26   36 89 D
Campbell Rd. E3 57   37 82 A
Campbell Rd. E6 50   42 83 A
Campbell Rd. N17 25   34 90 A
Campbell Rd. Twick 82   14 72 B
Campbell Rd. W7 54   15 80 A
Campbell St. W2 1   26 82 D
Campdale Rd. N7 36   29 86 D
Campden Cres. Dag 52   47 85 A
Campden Cres. Wem 33   16 86 D
Campden Gr. W8 56   25 79 A
Campden Hill Gdns. W8 56   25 80 C
Campden Hill Pl. W14 56   24 80 D
Campden Hill Rd. W8 56   25 79 A
Campden Hill Sq. W14 56   24 80 D
Campden Hill. W8 56   25 79 A
Campden House Cl. W8 62   25 79 A
Campden Rd. S Croy 112   33 64 C
Campden Rd. Uxb 31   07 86 C
Campden St. W8 56   25 80 C
Campen Cl. SW19 85   24 72 A
Camperdown St. E1 4   33 81 D
Campfield Rd. SE9 89   41 73 B
Campian Cl. S Croy 112   33 64 A
Campion Rd. Islw 71   15 76 B

Street	Page	Ref
Campion Rd. SW15	73	
Campion Terr. NW2	35	
Camplin Rd. Har	33	
Camplin St. SE14	64	
Camp Rd. SW19	84	
Camp Rd. SW19	85	
Campsbourne Rd. N8	24	
Campsbourne The N8	24	
Campsey Gdns. Day	51	
Campsey Rd. Dag	51	
Campsfield Rd. N8	24	
Campshill Pl. SE13	76	
Campshill Rd. SE13	76	
Campus Rd. E17	38	
Camrose Ave. Edg	21	
Camrose Ave. Edg	22	
Camrose Ave. Eri	67	
Camrose Ave. Felt	82	
Camrose Cl. Mord	95	
Camrose St. SE2	66	
Canada Ave. N18	25	
Canada Cres. W3	55	
Canada Rd. W3	55	
Canada Way. W12	55	
Canadian Ave. SE6	88	
Canal App. SE8	64	
Canal Cl. E2	57	
Canal Gr. SE15	63	
Canal Head. SE15	75	
Canal Rd. E3	57	
Canal St. SE5	63	
Canal Wlk. N1	48	
Canal Wlk. SE26	88	
Canberra Cl. Dag	52	
Canberra Cres. Dag	52	
Canberra Dri. Nthlt	53	
Canberra Rd. Bexh	67	
Canberra Rd. E6	50	
Canberra Rd. Houn	69	
Canberra Rd. SE7	65	
Canbury Ave. King	93	
Canbury Ct. King	93	
Canbury Mews. SE26	87	
Canbury Park Rd. King	93	
Canbury Pas. King	93	
Canbury Path. Orp	100	
Canbury Pl. King	93	
Cancell Rd. SW9	75	
Candahar Rd. SW11	74	
Candler St. N15	37	
Candover Rd. Horn	42	
Candover St. W1	2	
Candy St. E3	49	
Cane Cl Wall	111	
Canfield Gdns. NW6	46	
Canfield Pl. NW6	46	
Canfield Rd. Wdf Gn	27	
Canford Ave. Nthlt	43	
Canford Cl. Enf	13	
Canford Gdns. N.Mal	102	
Canford Rd. SW11	74	
Canham Rd. SE25	97	
Canham Rd. W3	61	
Canmore Gdns. SW16	96	
Cann Hall Rd. E11	39	
Canning Cres. N22	24	
Canning Cross. SE5	75	
Canning Pas. W8	5	
Canning Pl Mews. W8	5	
Canning Pl. W8	5	
Canning Rd. Croy	105	
Canning Rd. E15	50	
Canning Rd. E17	26	
Canning Rd. Har	21	
Canning Rd. N5	37	
Cannington Rd. Dag	52	
Cannizaro Rd. SW19	85	
Cannonbury Ave. Pnr	32	
Cannon Cl. Hamp	92	
Cannon Cl. SW20	95	
Cannon Dri. E14	57	
Cannon Hill La. SW20	103	
Cannon Hill La. SW20	95	
Cannon Hill. N14	16	
Cannon Hill. NW6	46	
Cannon La. NW3	35	
Cannon La. Pnr	32	
Cannon Pl. NW3	35	
Cannon Pl. SE7	65	
Cannon Rd. Bexh	79	
Cannon Rd. N14	16	
Cannon Row. SW1	7	
Cannon St. EC4	8	
Cannon Street Rd. E1	57	
Cannon Way. E Mol	92	

Street	Page	Ref
	23	74 A
	23	86 D
	18	88 A
	35	77 D
	22	71 D
	23	71 C
	30	89 C
	30	89 C
	46	84 D
	46	84 D
	30	89 A
	38	74 A
	38	74 A
	36	88 D
	18	90 B
	19	91 C
	49	77 B
	11	71 A
	25	68 C
	46	78 A
	32	91 A
	20	82 C
	20	81 A
	22	80 B
	37	73 D
	36	77 A
	36	82 C
	34	77 A
	34	76 A
	36	82 C
	32	77 B
	32	83 B
	35	71 C
	50	84 D
	50	84 D
	11	82 A
	47	77 B
	42	83 B
	07	75 A
	41	77 B
	18	69 B
	18	70 C
	34	72 C
	18	69 B
	18	69 A
	46	68 C
	18	69 A
	31	76 A
	27	76 C
	33	88 C
	52	87 D
	29	81 A
	36	83 B
	30	63 C
	26	84 C
	26	84 A
	42	91 C
	12	83 B
	31	97 D
	21	67 C
	28	74 A
	33	68 A
	21	79 A
	29	70 C
	39	86 D
	30	90 B
	33	76 C
	26	79 C
	26	79 C
	26	79 C
	33	65 B
	39	83 C
	36	89 A
	15	89 B
	31	86 D
	47	84 A
	23	71 D
	11	88 D
	13	70 B
	23	68 A
	37	80 C
	23	67 B
	24	68 A
	30	93 C
	25	85 C
	26	88 D
	12	88 C
	26	88 D
	42	78 C
	48	76 B
	30	93 C
	30	79 A
	32	80 A
	34	81 D
	13	68 D

Street	Page	Ref
Canon Ave. Rom	41	
Canon Beck Rd. SE16	64	
Canonbie Rd. SE23	88	
Canonbury Gr. N1	48	
Canonbury La. N1	48	
Canonbury Park N. N1	48	
Canonbury Park S. N1	48	
Canonbury Pl. N1	48	
Canonbury Rd. Enf	13	
Canonbury Rd. N1	48	
Canonbury Sq. N1	48	
Canonbury St. N1	48	
Canonbury Villas. N1	48	
Canon Murnane Rd. SE1	8	
Canon Rd. Brom	99	
Canons Cl. Edg	21	
Canons Cl. N2	35	
Canons Cl. Edg	21	
Canons Dri. Edg	21	
Canonsleigh Rd. Dag	51	
Canons Park Cl. Edg	21	
Canon St. N1	48	
Canon's Wlk. Croy	106	
Canrobert St. E2	57	
Canrobert St. E2	48	
Cantelowes Rd. NW1	47	
Canterbury Ave. Ilf	39	
Canterbury Ave. Sid	90	
Canterbury Cl. Beck	98	
Canterbury Cl. Grnf	53	
Canterbury Cres. SW9	75	
Canterbury Gr. SE27	87	
Canterbury Pl. SE17	63	
Canterbury Rd. Croy	105	
Canterbury Rd. E10	38	
Canterbury Rd. Felt	82	
Canterbury Rd. Har	32	
Canterbury Rd. Har	32	
Canterbury Rd. Mord	103	
Canterbury Rd. NW6	46	
Canterbury Terr. NW6	46	
Cantley Gdns. Ilf	40	
Cantley Gdns. SE19	97	
Cantley Rd. W7	60	
Canton St. E14	57	
Cantrell Rd. E3	57	
Cantwell Rd. SE18	66	
Canute Gdns. SE16	64	
Canvey St. SE1	8	
Cape Cl. Bark	51	
Capel Ave. Wall	111	
Capel Cl. Brom	107	
Capel Cl. N20	15	
Capel Gdns. Ilf	51	
Capel Gdns. Pnr	20	
Capel Rd. Barn	12	
Capel Rd. E12	50	
Capel Rd. E7	50	
Capener's Cl. SW1	6	
Cape Rd. N17	25	
Capern Rd. SW18	85	
Capitol Way. NW9	22	
Capland St. NW8	1	
Caple Rd. NW10	45	
Capper St. WC1	2	
Caprea Cl. Hay	53	
Capri Rd. Croy	105	
Capstan Ride. Enf	13	
Capstan Sq. E14	64	
Capstone Rd. Brom	89	
Capthorne Ave. Har	32	
Capworth St. E10	38	
Caradoc Cl. W2	56	
Caradoc St. E10	65	
Caradon Way. N15	25	
Caravelle Gdns. (off Javelin Way). Nthlt	53	
Caravel Mews. SE8	64	
Carberry Rd. SE19	97	
Carbery Ave. W3	61	
Carbis Rd. E14	57	
Carbuncle Pass. N17	25	
Carburton St. W1	2	
Cardale St. E14	64	
Carden Rd. SE15	75	
Cardiff Rd. Enf	13	
Cardiff Rd. W7	60	
Cardiff St. SE18	66	
Cardigan Gdns. Ilf	40	
Cardigan Rd. E3	49	
Cardigan Rd. Rich	71	
Cardigan Rd. SW13	72	
Cardigan Rd. SW19	95	
Cardigan St. SE11	63	
Cardigan Wlk. N1	48	

Street	Page	Ref
	47	88 A
	35	79 A
	35	73 A
	32	84 C
	31	84 D
	32	84 A
	32	84 A
	31	84 B
	33	97 A
	31	84 D
	31	84 D
	32	84 C
	31	84 D
	33	79 C
	41	68 B
	18	91 B
	26	87 B
	18	91 B
	18	91 B
	46	84 D
	18	91 C
	32	83 A
	35	65 D
	34	82 B
	34	83 D
	29	84 B
	42	87 A
	46	72 B
	37	69 B
	13	81 B
	31	75 A
	31	72 D
	31	78 B
	31	66 A
	38	88 C
	12	72 A
	13	88 B
	14	88 A
	26	67 C
	25	83 C
	25	83 C
	44	88 C
	33	69 B
	16	79 C
	37	81 C
	36	82 D
	43	77 D
	35	78 B
	32	80 C
	43	84 D
	30	64 D
	42	66 C
	21	83 D
	51	45 B
	12	89 D
	27	95 C
	41	85 B
	41	85 A
	28	79 A
	34	89 A
	26	73 C
	20	89 A
	26	82 D
	21	83 D
	29	82 C
	11	81 B
	33	66 B
	31	97 C
	38	79 A
	39	71 B
	12	87 D
	37	87 B
	25	81 C
	39	78 C
	32	89 D
	11	82 B
	38	77 A
	33	70 A
	10	79 A
	36	81 D
	34	90 C
	28	82 D
	38	79 C
	34	75 B
	34	96 D
	16	79 C
	45	77 C
	40	86 A
	36	83 D
	18	74 C
	22	76 C
	26	70 A
	31	78 C
	32	84 C

Street	Page	Ref
Cardinal Ave. King	83	18 71 C
Cardinal Ave. Mord	103	24 67 C
Cardinal Bourne St. SE1	8	32 79 D
Cardinal Cap Alley. SE1	8	32 80 C
Cardinal Cl. Chis	100	45 69 A
Cardinal Cl. Mord	103	24 67 C
Cardinal Cres. N Mal	94	20 69 C
Cardinal Dri. Ilt	28	44 91 A
Cardinal Pl. SW15	73	23 75 D
Cardinal Rd. Felt	81	10 73 D
Cardinal Rd. Ruis	32	11 87 D
Cardinals Way. N19	36	29 87 D
Cardinal's Wlk. Hamp	92	14 70 C
Cardinal's Wlk. Sun	91	09 70 A
Cardine Mews. SE15	63	33 79 C
Cardington Sq. Houn	70	11 75 D
Cardington St. NW1	2	29 82 A
Cardozo Rd. N7	47	30 85 C
Cardrew Ave. N12	15	26 92 D
Cardrew Cl. N12	15	26 92 D
Cardross St. W6	61	22 79 D
Cardwell Rd. N7	47	30 85 A
Cardwell Rd. SE18	66	43 78 A
Carew Cl. N7	36	30 86 B
Carew Rd. Ashf	91	08 70 A
Carew Rd. Mit	96	28 69 C
Carew Rd. N17	25	34 90 C
Carew Rd. Th Hth	97	31 68 D
Carew Rd. W13	60	17 79 A
Carew Rd. Wall	111	29 63 A
Carew St. SE5	75	32 76 C
Carey Ct. Bexh	80	49 74 B
Carey Gdns. SW8	74	29 76 B
Carey La. EC2	4	32 81 C
Carey Pl. SW1	10	29 78 B
Carey Rd. Dag	52	48 85 A
Carey St. WC2	3	30 81 D
Carfax Pl. SW4	74	29 75 D
Carfree Cl. N1	48	31 84 C
Cargill Rd. SW18	85	26 73 C
Cargreen Pl. SE25	97	33 68 D
Cargreen Rd. SE25	97	33 68 D
Carholme Rd. SE23	88	36 73 D
Carisbrook Cl. Enf	13	33 97 B
Carisbrooke Cl. Stan	21	17 90 D
Carisbrooke Rd. Brom	99	41 68 C
Carisbrooke Rd. Mit	96	30 68 C
Carisbrook Rd. E17	38	36 88 A
Carker's La. NW5	47	28 85 D
Carleton Ave. Wall	111	29 62 B
Carleton Rd. N7	47	29 85 B
Carlile Cl. E3	49	36 83 D
Carlinge Rd. NW2	46	24 84 B
Carlingford Gdns. Mit	96	28 70 C
Carlingford Rd. Mord	103	23 67 D
Carlingford Rd. N15	25	31 89 B
Carlingford Rd. NW3	46	26 85 B
Carlisle Ave. EC3	4	33 81 D
Carlisle Ave. W3	55	21 81 C
Carlisle Cl. King	94	19 69 A
Carlisle Gdns. Har	33	17 87 B
Carlisle Gdns. Ilf	39	42 88 C
Carlisle La. SE1	7	30 79 D
Carlisle Mews. King	94	19 69 A
Carlisle Pl. N11	16	28 92 B
Carlisle Pl. SW1	6	29 79 C
Carlisle Rd. E10	38	37 87 C
Carlisle Rd. Hamp	92	13 70 D
Carlisle Rd. N4	37	31 87 A
Carlisle Rd. NW6	46	24 83 A
Carlisle Rd. NW9	22	20 89 A
Carlisle Rd. Rom	42	52 88 A
Carlisle Rd. Sutt	110	24 63 D
Carlisle St. W1	2	29 81 D
Carlisle Wlk. E8	48	33 84 B
Carlos Pl. W1	6	28 80 D
Carlow St. NW1	47	29 83 C
Carlton Ave. Felt	82	11 73 A
Carlton Ave. Felt	70	11 74 C
Carlton Ave. Har	33	16 88 B
Carlton Ave. N14	12	29 95 B
Carlton Avenue E. Wem	33	18 87 C
Carlton Avenue W. Wem	33	16 86 B
Carlton Ave. S Croy	112	33 63 C
Carlton Ave. SE21	75	33 74 C
Carlton Cl. NW3	35	25 86 A
Carlton Cres. Sutt	110	24 64 A
Carlton Ct. Ilf	28	44 89 B
Carlton Ct. SW9	75	31 76 B
Carlton Dri. Ilf	28	44 89 B
Carlton Gdns. SW1		29 80 D
Carlton Gdns. W5	54	17 80 A
Carlton Gr. SE15	75	34 76 B
Carlton Hill. NW8	46	26 83 C

Carlton House Terr. SW1 ....6 .... 29 80 D
Carlton Park Ave. SW20 ....95 .... 23 69 D
Carlton Par. Orp ....108 .... 46 66 B
Carlton Rd. Barn .... 26 95 D
Carlton Rd. E11 ....39 .... 39 87 D
Carlton Rd. E12 ....50 .... 41 85 B
Carlton Rd. E17 ....36 .... 36 90 A
Carlton Rd. Eri ....67 .... 50 77 A
Carlton Rd. N11 ....19 .... 28 92 B
Carlton Rd. N15 ....25 .... 33 89 D
Carlton Rd. N4 ....37 .... 31 87 A
Carlton Rd. N Mal ....94 .... 21 69 C
Carlton Rd. Rom ....30 .... 52 89 C
Carlton Rd. S Croy ....112 .... 32 63 D
Carlton Rd. Sid ....91 .... 45 71 B
Carlton Rd. Sun ....91 .... 09 70 D
Carlton Rd. SW15 ....24 .... 24 74 A
Carlton Rd. W4 ....61 .... 20 79 B
Carlton Rd. W5 ....78 .... 17 81 C
Carlton Rd. Well ....78 .... 46 75 B
Carlton Sq. E1 .... 35 82 D
Carlton St. SW1 ....6 .... 29 79 B
Carlton Terr. E11 ....39 .... 40 88 B
Carlton Terr. N18 ....17 .... 32 92 D
Carlton Terr. N18 ....17 .... 32 92 B
Carlton Terr. SE26 ....88 .... 35 72 C
Carlton Vale. NW6 ....46 .... 25 83 C
Carluke Cl. SE7 ....65 .... 41 78 D
Carlwell St. SW17 ....86 .... 27 71 C
Carlyle Ave. Brom ....99 .... 41 68 B
Carlyle Ave. Sthl ....53 .... 12 80 B
Carlyle Cl. E Mol .... 13 69 D
Carlyle Cl. N2 ....35 .... 26 88 C
Carlyle Cl. NW10 .... 20 83 B
Carlyle Gdns. Sthl ....53 .... 12 80 B
Carlyle Rd. Croy ....105 .... 34 65 A
Carlyle Rd. E12 ....50 .... 42 85 A
Carlyle Rd. W5 ....60 .... 17 78 A
Carlyle Sq. SW3 ....62 .... 26 77 B
Carlyon Ave. Har ....87 .... 13 85 A
Carlyon Cl. Wem ....44 .... 18 83 A
Carlyon Rd. Hay ....53 .... 11 81 C
Carlyon Rd. Wem ....44 .... 18 83 A
Carmalt Gdns. SW15 ....73 .... 23 75 C
Carmarthen Pl. SE1 ....8 .... 33 79 A
*Carmel Ct. W8 ....62 .... 25 79 B
Carmelite Cl. Har ....20 .... 14 90 A
Carmelite Rd. Har ....20 .... 14 90 C
Carmelite St. EC4 ....7 .... 31 80 A
Carmelite Way. Har ....20 .... 14 90 C
Carmelite Wlk. Har ....20 .... 14 90 A
Carmen St. E14 ....57 .... 37 81 D
Carmichael Cl. SW11 ....73 .... 26 75 B
Carmichael Rd. SE25 ....97 .... 34 68 C
Carminia Rd. SW17 ....86 .... 28 72 B
Carnaby St. W1 ....6 .... 29 80 A
Carnanton Rd. E17 ....26 .... 32 72 D
Carnarvon Ave. Enf .... 38 90 B
Carnarvon Rd. Barn ....11 .... 33 97 D
Carnarvon Rd. E10 ....58 .... 24 96 A
Carnarvon Rd. E15 ....50 .... 38 88 A
Carnarvon Rd. E18 ....50 .... 39 84 B
Carnation St. SE2 ....66 .... 39 90 B
Carnbrook Rd. SE3 ....77 .... 46 78 D
Carnecke Gdns. SE9 ....77 .... 41 75 B
Carnegie Cl. Surb ....101 .... 42 74 A
Carnegie Pl. SW19 ....85 .... 18 65 B
Carnegie St. N1 .... 23 72 D
Carnforth Cl. Eps ....109 .... 30 83 B
Carnforth Rd. SW16 ....96 .... 19 63 B
Carnoustie Dri. N1 ....47 .... 29 72 D
Carnwath Rd. SW6 ....73 .... 30 84 D
Carolina Rd. Th Hth ....97 .... 25 75 B
Caroline Cl. Croy ....112 .... 32 69 A
Caroline Cl. W2 ....56 .... 33 64 A
Caroline Ct. Ashf ....91 .... 25 80 B
Caroline Gdns. E2 .... 07 70 B
Caroline Gdns. SE15 ....63 .... 33 82 A
Caroline Pl Mews. W2 ....56 .... 34 77 D
Caroline Pl. SW11 ....74 .... 25 80 B
Caroline Pl. W2 ....56 .... 28 76 C
Caroline Rd. SW19 ....95 .... 25 80 B
Caroline St. E1 .... 24 70 D
Caroline Terr. SW1 ....6 .... 35 81 D
Carol St. NW1 ....47 .... 28 78 A
Carolyn Dri. Orp ....108 .... 29 83 A
Carpenter Gdns. N21 ....47 .... 46 65 C
Carpenter's Pl. SW4 ....74 .... 31 93 B
Carpenter's Rd. E15 ....49 .... 29 75 D
Carpenter St. W1 ....6 .... 37 84 D
Carrara Wlk. SW9 ....75 .... 28 80 B
Carriage Dri E. SW11 ....9 .... 31 75 D
Carriage Dri N. SW11 ....9 .... 28 77 C
Carriage Drive S. SW11 ....74 .... 27 77 D
                                          27 76 B

Carriage Dri W. SW11 ....9 .... 27 77 D
Carrick Gdns. N17 ....25 .... 33 91 C
Carrick Mews. SE8 ....64 .... 37 77 A
Carrington Ave. Houn ....70 .... 13 74 B
Carrington Rd. Dart ....80 .... 54 74 D
Carrington Rd. Rich ....72 .... 19 75 C
Carrington St. W1 .... 28 80 D
Carrol Cl. E15 ....50 .... 39 85 D
Carrol Cl. NW5 .... 28 85 B
Carron Cl. E14 ....57 .... 37 81 D
Carroun Rd. SW8 .... 30 77 D
Carroway La. Grnf ....53 .... 14 82 B
Carrow Rd. Dag ....51 .... 46 84 D
Carr Rd. E17 ....26 .... 37 90 C
Carr Rd. Nthlt .... 14 84 C
Carrs La. N21 ....13 .... 32 95 A
Carr St. E14 .... 36 81 A
Carr St. E14 .... 36 81 C
Carshalton Gr. Sutt ....110 .... 26 64 D
Carshalton Park Rd. Cars ....111 .... 27 64 D
Carshalton Pl. Cars ....111 .... 28 64 C
Carshalton Rd. Cars ....111 .... 27 64 C
Carshalton Rd. Mit ....104 .... 28 67 A
Carshalton Rd. Sutt ....110 .... 26 64 D
Carslake Rd. SW15 ....73 .... 23 74 C
Carson Rd. Barn ....12 .... 27 96 D
Carson Rd. E16 ....58 .... 40 81 A
Carson Rd. SE21 ....87 .... 32 72 B
Carstairs Rd. SE6 ....88 .... 38 72 C
Carston Cl. SE12 .... 39 74 B
Carswell Cl. Ilf .... 41 89 D
Carswell Rd. SE6 .... 38 73 A
Carter Cl. Rom .... 49 91 D
Carter Cl. Wall ....111 .... 29 63 D
Carter Dr. Rom .... 49 91 B
Carteret St. SW1 .... 29 79 B
Carteret Way. SE8 ....64 .... 36 78 A
Carterhatch Rd. Enf .... 35 97 D
Carter La. EC4 ....3 .... 31 81 D
Carter Pl. SE17 .... 32 78 C
Carter Rd. E13 ....50 .... 40 83 B
Carter Rd. SW19 ....95 .... 26 70 B
Carters Cl. Wor Pk ....103 .... 23 66 D
Carters Hill Cl. SE9 ....88 .... 41 73 C
Carters Rd. N2 ....24 .... 27 91 C
Carter St. SE17 .... 32 78 C
Carter's Yd. SW18 ....73 .... 25 74 A
Carthew Rd. W6 ....61 .... 22 79 D
Carthew Villas. W6 ....61 .... 22 79 D
Carthusian St. EC1 ....7 .... 32 81 A
Cartins La. WC2 .... 30 80 A
Cart La. E4 ....18 .... 38 94 D
Cartmel Cl. N17 .... 34 91 D
Cartmel Gdns. Mord ....103 .... 26 67 A
Cartmel Rd. Bexh .... 49 76 A
Cartwright Gdns. WC1 ....3 .... 30 82 A
Cartwright Rd. Dag ....52 .... 48 84 D
Cartwright St. E1 .... 33 80 B
Carver Rd. SE24 ....75 .... 32 74 C
Carville Cres. Brent ....60 .... 18 78 A
Carville Pas. Brent ....60 .... 18 78 A
Cary Rd. E11 ....58 .... 39 85 A
Carysfort Rd. N16 ....48 .... 32 85 B
Carysfort Rd. N8 ....36 .... 29 88 B
Cascade Ave. N10 .... 29 89 C
Casella Rd. SE14 ....64 .... 35 77 D
Casewick Rd. SE27 .... 31 71 B
Casimir Rd. E5 ....38 .... 35 86 C
Casino Ave. SE24 ....75 .... 32 74 B
*Caslon Pl. E1 ....57 .... 34 82 D
Caspian St. SE5 ....63 .... 32 77 D
Caspian Wlk. E16 ....58 .... 41 81 D
Cassidy Rd. SW6 ....62 .... 25 77 C
Cassilda Rd. SE2 .... 46 78 A
Cassilis Rd. Twick ....71 .... 16 74 D
Cassiobury Ave. Felt .... 09 73 B
Cassiobury Rd. E17 ....38 .... 36 88 A
Cassland Rd. E9 ....49 .... 35 84 B
Cassland Rd. Th Hth ....32 .... 32 68 D
Cassleden Rd. NW10 ....45 .... 20 84 D
Casslee Rd. SE6 ....88 .... 36 73 B
Casson St. E1 .... 34 81 A
Castalia Sq. E14 ....64 .... 38 79 A
Castalia St. E14 .... 38 79 A
Castellain Rd. W9 ....46 .... 25 82 D
Castellan Ave. Rom ....30 .... 53 89 A
Castello Ave. SW15 ....73 .... 23 74 A
Castelnau Gdns. SW13 .... 22 77 B
Castelnau Row. SW13 ....61 .... 22 77 B
Castelnau. SW13 ....61 .... 22 77 B
Casterbridge Rd. SE3 ....77 .... 40 75 A
Casterton St. E8 .... 34 84 B
Castile Rd. SE18 ....68 .... 43 78 A
Castillon Rd. SE6 .... 39 72 A
Castlands Rd. SE6 ....88 .... 36 72 B

Castle Ave. E4 ....18 .... 38 92 D
Castle Ave. Eps ....109 .... 22 62 B
Castlebar Hill. W13 ....54 .... 17 81 A
Castlebar Mews. W5 ....54 .... 17 81 A
Castlebar Park. W5 ....54 .... 17 81 A
Castlebar Rd. W5 ....54 .... 17 81 A
Castle Baynard St. EC4 ....7 .... 31 80 B
Castle Baynard St. EC4 ....8 .... 32 80 A
Castle Cl. E9 ....49 .... 36 85 C
Castle Cl. Sun. ....91 .... 09 70 C
Castle Cl. SW19 ....85 .... 23 72 D
Castlecombe Dri. SW19 ....85 .... 23 73 B
Castlecombe Rd. SE9 ....89 .... 42 71 A
Castle Ct. EC3 ....4 .... 32 81 D
Castledine Rd. SE20 ....97 .... 34 70 D
Castle Dri. Ilf ....39 .... 42 88 C
Castleford Ave. SE9 ....90 .... 43 73 D
Castlegate. Rich ....71 .... 18 75 B
Castle Gdns. Dag ....51 .... 46 83 B
Castlehaven Rd. NW1 ....47 .... 28 84 D
Castle La. SW1 ....6 .... 29 79 C
Castleleigh Ct. Enf ....13 .... 32 95 B
Castlemaine Ave. Eps ....109 .... 22 62 B
Castlemaine Ave. S Croy ....112 .... 33 64 D
Castle Mews. N12 ....15 .... 26 92 C
Castle Mews. NW1 ....47 .... 28 84 B
Castle Pl. NW1 ....47 .... 28 84 B
Castle Pl. W4 ....61 .... 21 78 A
Castle Rd. Dag ....51 .... 46 83 B
Castle Rd. Enf ....14 .... 36 97 A
Castle Rd. Islw ....71 .... 15 78 D
Castle Rd. N12 ....15 .... 26 92 C
Castle Rd. Nthlt .... 43 .... 13 84 D
Castle Rd. NW1 ....47 .... 28 84 B
Castle Rd. Sthl ....59 .... 12 79 D
Castlereagh St. W1 ....1 .... 27 81 D
Castle St. E6 ....50 .... 41 83 D
Castle St. King ....93 .... 18 69 C
Castleton Ave. Bexh ....79 .... 50 76 D
Castleton Ave. Eri ....79 .... 50 76 B
Castleton Ave. Wem ....44 .... 18 85 A
Castleton Rd. E17 ....26 .... 38 90 D
Castleton Rd. Ilf ....40 .... 46 87 D
Castleton Rd. Mit ....96 .... 29 68 D
Castleton Rd. Ruis ....32 .... 11 87 D
Castleton Rd. SE9 ....89 .... 41 71 B
Castletown Rd. W14 ....62 .... 24 78 C
Castle View Gdns. Ilf ....39 .... 42 88 D
Castle Way. Eps ....109 .... 22 62 A
Castle Way. Felt ....82 .... 11 71 A
Castle Way. SW19 ....85 .... 23 72 D
Castle Wlk. Sun. ....92 .... 11 68 A
Castlewood Dri. SE9 ....77 .... 42 76 D
Castlewood Rd. N15 ....37 .... 34 88 C
Castlewood Rd. N16 ....37 .... 34 88 C
Castle Yd. N6 ....36 .... 28 87 A
Castle Yd. Rich ....71 .... 17 74 B
Castle Yd. SE1 .... 31 80 D
Caterham Ave. Ilf ....28 .... 43 90 C
Caterham Rd. SE13 ....76 .... 38 75 B
Catesby St. SE17 ....63 .... 32 78 B
Catford Bwy. SE6 ....88 .... 37 73 B
Catford Hill. SE6 ....88 .... 37 73 C
Catford Rd. SE6 ....88 .... 37 73 A
Cathall Rd. E11 ....38 .... 38 86 B
Cathay St. SE16 ....63 .... 34 79 B
Cathcart Dri. Orp ....108 .... 45 66 C
Cathcart Hill. N19 ....36 .... 29 86 C
Cathcart Rd. SW10 ....62 .... 26 77 A
Cathcart St. NW5 ....47 .... 28 84 B
Cathedral Pl. EC4 ....4 .... 32 81 C
Cathedral St. SE1 ....8 .... 32 80 D
Catherall Rd. N5 ....37 .... 32 86 C
Catherine Ct. N14 ....12 .... 29 95 A
Catherine Ct. SW19 ....85 .... 24 71 D
Catherine Dri. Ashf ....91 .... 09 70 B
Catherine Gdns. Houn ....70 .... 14 75 D
Catherine Gr. SE10 ....37 .... 37 76 B
Catherine Pl. SW1 ....6 .... 29 79 C
Catherine Rd. Rom ....42 .... 52 88 B
Catherine Rd. Surb ....101 .... 17 67 B
Catherine St. WC2 .... 30 80 B
Catherine Wheel Alley. E1 ....4 .... 33 81 A
Catherine Wheel Rd. Brent ....60 .... 17 77 D
Catherine Wheel Yd. SW1 ....6 .... 29 80 C
Cat Hill. Barn ....12 .... 27 95 B
Cathles Rd. SW12 ....74 .... 28 74 D
Cathnor Rd. W12 ....61 .... 22 79 B
Catling Cl. SE23 ....88 .... 35 72 D
Catlin's La. Pnr ....19 .... 10 89 D
Catlin St. SE16 ....63 .... 34 78 D
Caton Pas. SW16 ....86 .... 30 72 C
Cato Rd. SW4 ....74 .... 29 75 D
Cator La. Beck ....98 .... 36 69 D
Cator Rd.Cars ....111 .... 27 64 D

Cator Rd. SE26	98	35 70 B
Cator St. SE15	63	33 77 B
Cator St. SE15	63	33 77 D
Cato St. W1	1	27 81 C
Cattistock Rd. SE9	89	42 71 D
Catton St.WC1	3	30 81 B
Caulfield Rd. E6	50	42 84 D
Caulfield Rd. SE15	75	34 76 D
Causeway. Felt	69	10 75 C
Causeway. Houn	69	10 75 B
Causeway The. Cars	104	28 65 A
Causeway The. N2	24	27 89 C
Causeway The. Sutt	110	26 62 A
Causeway The. SW18	73	25 75 D
Causeway The. SW19	85	23 71 C
Causeway The. Tedd	93	15 70 B
Causeyware Rd. N9	18	35 94 A
Causton Rd. N6	36	28 87 B
Causton St. SW1	10	29 78 D
Cautley Av. SW4	74	29 74 A
Cavalier Cl. Rom	29	47 69 D
Cavalry Cres. Houn	70	11 75 D
Cavaye Pl. SW10	62	26 78 C
Cavedish Gdns. Rom	41	48 88 A
Cavell Dri. Enf	13	31 97 C
Cavell Rd. N17	25	32 91 D
Cavell St. E1	57	34 81 B
Cavendish Ave. Eri	67	50 77 A
Cavendish Ave. Har	44	15 85 A
Cavendish Ave. N3	23	25 90 C
Cavendish Ave. N Mal	94	22 68 D
Cavendish Ave. NW8	1	26 82 B
Cavendish Ave. NW8	46	26 83 D
Cavendish Ave. Sid	90	46 73 A
Cavendish Ave. W13	54	16 81 C
Cavendish Ave. Wdf Gn	27	40 91 D
Cavendish Ave. Well	78	45 75 B
Cavendish Cl. Ashf	91	09 70 B
Cavendish Cl. N18	17	34 92 D
Cavendish Cl. NW6	46	24 84 B
Cavendish Cl. NW8	1	26 82 B
Cavendish Ct. EC2	4	33 81 C
Cavendish Dri. E11	38	38 87 D
Cavendish Dri. Edg	21	18 91 B
Cavendish Gdns. Bark	51	45 85 D
Cavendish Gdns. Ilf	40	43 87 C
Cavendish Mews N. W1	2	28 81 B
Cavendish Mews S. W1	2	28 81 B
Cavendish Pl. W1	2	28 81 D
Cavendish Rd. Ashf	91	09 70 B
Cavendish Rd. Barn	11	23 96 A
Cavendish Rd. Croy	105	31 66 D
Cavendish Rd. E4	26	38 91 A
Cavendish Rd. N18	17	34 92 D
Cavendish Rd. N4	37	31 88 D
Cavendish Rd. N Mal	94	21 68 D
Cavendish Rd. NW6	46	24 84 D
Cavendish Rd. Sutt	110	26 63 A
Cavendish Rd. SW12	86	28 73 D
Cavendish Rd. SW19	96	27 70 C
Cavendish Rd. W4	72	20 76 A
Cavendish Sq. W1	2	28 81 D
Cavendish St. N1	48	32 83 D
Cavendish Terr. Felt	81	10 72 A
Cavendish Way. W Wick	106	37 66 D
Cavenham Gdns. Horn	42	44 86 D
Cavenham Gdns. Ilf	40	40 82 B
Cave Rd. E13	58	40 82 B
Cave Rd. Rich	83	17 71 A
Caverleigh Way. Wor Pk	102	22 66 A
Caverley Gdns. Har	33	17 87 B
Caversham Ave. N13	17	31 93 C
Caversham Ave. Sutt	103	24 65 A
Caversham Rd. King	93	18 69 D
Caversham Rd. N15	25	32 89 C
Caversham Rd. NW5	47	29 84 A
Caversham St. SW3	9	27 77 B
Caverswall St. W12	56	23 81 C
Cavert St. NW1	47	28 83 A
Caveside Cl. Chis	100	43 69 A
Cawdor Cres. W7	60	16 78 A
Cawnpore St. SE19	87	33 71 C
Caxton Gr. E3	57	37 82 A
Caxton Rd. N22	24	30 90 D
Caxton Rd. Sthl	59	11 79 D
Caxton Rd. SW17	85	26 71 C
Caxton Rd. W12	56	23 80 D
Caxton St. E16	58	39 80 B
Caxton Street N. E16	58	39 80 B
Caxton Street S. E16	58	39 80 B
Caxton St. SW1	6	29 79 D
Caygill Cl. Brom	99	39 68 D
Cayley Cl. SE4	76	36 75 C
Cayley Cl. Wall	111	30 63 C
Cayton Pl. EC1	4	32 82 B
Cayton Rd. Grnf	44	15 83 C
Cayton St. EC1	4	32 82 B
Cazenove Rd. E17	26	37 90 A
Cazenove Rd. N16	37	34 86 A
Cecil Ave. Bark	51	44 84 D
Cecil Ave. Enf	13	33 96 D
Cecil Ave. Horn	30	54 89 A
Cecil Ave. Wem	44	18 85 D
Cecil Cl. Ashf	91	08 70 C
Cecil Cl. W5	54	17 81 B
Cecil Ct. Barn	11	23 96 B
Cecil Ct. Croy	105	33 65 B
Cecil Ct. WC2	7	30 80 A
Cecile Park. N8	36	30 88 C
Cecilia Cl. N2	23	26 89 A
Cecilia Rd. E8	48	34 85 C
Cecil Park. Pnr	20	12 89 C
Cecil Pl. Mit	104	27 67 B
Cecil Rd. Ashf	91	08 70 A
Cecil Rd. Croy	104	30 67 D
Cecil Rd. E11	39	39 86 C
Cecil Rd. E13	50	40 83 A
Cecil Rd. E17	26	37 90 A
Cecil Rd. Enf	13	32 96 D
Cecil Rd. Har	21	15 89 A
Cecil Rd. Houn	70	14 76 C
Cecil Rd. Ilf	51	43 85 B
Cecil Rd. N10	24	28 90 D
Cecil Rd. N14	16	29 94 C
Cecil Rd. NW10	45	21 83 A
Cecil Rd. NW9	22	20 89 A
Cecil Rd. Rom	41	48 87 A
Cecil Rd. Sutt	110	24 63 B
Cecil Rd. SW19	95	25 70 D
Cecil Rd. W3	55	20 81 A
Cecil Way. Brom	107	40 66 C
Cedar Ave. Barn	16	27 94 A
Cedar Ave. Enf	14	35 97 C
Cedar Ave. Rom	41	48 88 A
Cedar Ave. Ruis	43	11 85 C
Cedar Ave. Sid	90	46 73 A
Cedar Ave. Twick	70	14 74 C
Cedar Cl. Brom	107	42 65 C
Cedar Cl. E Mol	93	15 68 C
Cedar Cl. Rom	29	50 89 C
Cedar Cl. SW15	84	20 71 B
Cedar Copse. Brom	99	42 69 D
Cedar Cres. Brom	107	42 65 C
Cedarcroft Rd. Chess	101	18 65 D
Cedar Ct. N10	24	28 90 C
Cedar Ct. SW19	85	23 72 D
Cedar Dri. N2	24	27 89 C
Cedar Dri. Pnr	20	13 91 A
Cedar Gdns. Sutt	110	26 63 A
Cedar Gr. Bex	79	47 74 D
Cedar Gr. Sthl	53	13 81 A
Cedar Gr. W5	60	17 79 B
Cedar Hts. Rich	83	18 73 C
Cedarhurst Dri. SE9	77	41 74 A
Cedar Lawn Ave. Barn	11	24 95 A
Cedar Mount. SE9	89	41 73 D
Cedarne Rd. SW6	62	25 77 D
Cedar Park Gdns. Rom	41	47 87 B
Cedar Pl. Nthwd	8	08 91 A
Cedar Pl. SE7	65	41 78 C
Cedar Rd. Brom	99	41 69 C
Cedar Rd. Croy	105	33 65 A
Cedar Rd. E Mol	93	15 68 C
Cedar Rd. Eri	81	08 73 D
Cedar Rd. Felt	81	53 66 C
Cedar Rd. Horn	42	53 89 A
Cedar Rd. Houn	70	11 76 C
Cedar Rd. N17	25	33 90 B
Cedar Rd. NW2	46	23 85 A
Cedar Rd. Rom	29	50 89 C
Cedar Rd. Sutt	110	26 63 A
Cedar Rd. Tedd	83	16 71 C
Cedar Rise. N14	16	28 94 B
Cedars Ave. E17	38	37 88 A
Cedars Ave. Mit	96	28 68 A
Cedars Cl. NW4	23	23 89 B
Cedars Ct. N9	17	33 93 A
Cedars Mews. SW4		28 75 D
Cedars Rd. Beck	98	36 69 D
Cedars Rd. Croy	105	30 64 A
Cedars Rd. E15	50	39 84 A
Cedars Rd. King	93	17 69 A
Cedars Rd. Mord	95	25 68 C
Cedars Rd. N21		31 93 B
Cedars Rd. SW13	72	22 76 C
Cedars Rd. SW4		28 75 D
Cedars Rd. W4	61	20 77 A
Cedars The. E9	49	35 84 D
Cedars The. Tedd	93	15 70 B
Cedar Terr. Rich	71	18 75 C
Cedar Tree Gr. SE27	87	31 71 D
Cedarville Gdns. SW16	96	30 70 B
Cedar Vista. Rich	60	18 77 D
Cedar Way. Sun	91	09 70 C
Cedric Ave. Rom	30	51 89 A
Cedric Rd. SE9	90	44 72 C
Celandie Way. E15	58	39 82 A
Celandine Cl. E14	57	37 81 A
Celbridge Mews. W2	56	25 81 D
Celia Rd. N19	47	29 85 B
Celtic Ave. Brom	99	39 68 A
Celtic St. E14	57	37 81 B
Cemetery La. SE7	65	42 77 A
Cemetery Rd. E7	50	39 85 B
Cemetery Rd. N17	25	33 91 C
Cenacle Cl. NW3	35	25 86 C
Centaur St. SE1	7	30 79 D
Centenary Rd. Enf	14	36 96 D
Central Ave. E11	38	38 86 B
Central Ave. E Mol	92	12 68 D
Central Ave. Enf	13	34 97 D
Central Ave. Houn	70	14 75 C
Central Ave. N2	23	25 89 B
Central Ave. N2	23	26 90 D
Central Ave. N9	17	33 93 D
Central Ave. Pnr	32	12 87 B
Central Ave. SW11	9	27 77 D
Central Ave. Wall	111	30 64 C
Central Ave. Well	78	46 76 C
Central Circ. NW4	34	22 88 B
Central Dri. Horn	42	54 86 C
Central Hill. SE19	97	33 70 A
Central Park Ave. Dag	41	50 86 C
Central Park Rd. E6	50	42 83 C
Central Pl. SE25	37	34 68 C
Central Rd. Dart	80	54 74 A
Central Rd. Mord	103	25 67 B
Central Rd. Wem	44	16 85 D
Central Rd. Wor Pk	102	22 65 A
Central Sq. E Mol	92	12 68 D
Central Sq. NW11	35	25 88 D
Central Sq. Wem	44	18 85 C
Central St. EC1	4	32 82 A
Central Way. Cars	111	27 63 C
Central Way. Felt	69	10 74 B
Central Way. Nthwd	19	09 91 C
Centre Ave. N2		27 90 C
Centre Ave. W3	55	20 80 D
Centre Common Rd. Chis	100	44 70 C
Centre Dri. E7	50	41 85 B
Centre Rd. Dag	52	49 83 D
Centre Rd. E11	39	40 86 A
Centre Rd. E7	39	40 86 C
Centre St. E2	48	34 83 D
Centre The. Felt	81	10 73 D
Centre Way. N9	18	35 93 A
Centric Cl. NW1	47	28 83 A
Centurion Cl. N7	47	30 84 D
Century Ct. Rich	83	16 71 A
Century Rd. E17	26	36 89 A
Cephas Ave. E1	57	35 82 C
Cephas St. E1	57	35 82 C
Ceres Rd. SE18	66	45 78 B
Cerise Rd. SE15	75	34 76 A
Cerne Cl. Hay	53	11 80 A
Cerne Rd. Mord	103	26 67 C
Cerney Mew. W2	5	26 80 B
Cervantes Ct. Nthwd	19	09 91 D
Ceylon Rd. W14	62	24 79 C
Chadacre Ave. Ilf	27	42 89 B
Chadacre Rd. Eps	109	22 64 D
Chadbourne St. E14	57	37 81 B
Chadbury Ct. NW7	22	22 90 A
Chadd Dri. Brom	99	42 68 A
Chadd Green. E13	50	40 83 A
Chadville Gdns. Rom	41	47 88 B
Chadway. Dag	41	47 87 C
Chadwell Ave. Rom	40	46 87 B
Chadwell Heath La. Rom	28	46 89 D
Chadwell Heath La. Rom	41	47 88 C
Chadwell St. EC1	3	31 82 A
Chadwick Ave. E4	18	38 92 B
Chadwick Cl. Tedd	93	16 70 A
Chadwick Rd. E11	39	39 88 B
Chadwick Rd. NW10	45	21 83 B
Chadwick Rd. SE15	75	33 76 D
Chadwick St. SW1	6	29 79 D
Chadwin Rd. E13	58	40 81 B
Chaffinch Ave. Croy	106	35 67 D
Chaffinch Cl. Croy	106	35 67 D
Chaffinch Rd. Beck	98	36 69 B
Chafford Way. Rom	29	47 89 C
Chagford St. NW1	1	27 82 D
Chailey Ave. Enf	13	33 97 D
Chailey St. E5	38	35 86 C

Entry	Page	Ref
Chalbury Wlk. N1	48	31 83 C
Chalcombe Rd. SE2	66	46 79 D
Chalcot Cl. Sutt	110	25 63 C
Chalcot Cres. NW1	47	27 83 B
Chalcot Gdns. NW3	47	27 84 B
Chalcot Rd. NW1	47	28 83 A
Chalcot Sq. NW1	47	27 84 D
Chalcott Gdns. Surb	101	17 66 C
Chalcroft Rd. SE13	77	39 74 A
Chaldon Path. Th Hth	97	31 68 D
Chaldon Rd. SW6	62	24 77 C
Chale Rd. SW2	74	30 74 C
Chale Wlk. Sutt	110	25 62 B
Chalfont Ave. Wem	45	19 84 B
Chalfont Ct. NW9	22	21 89 B
Chalfont Green. N9	17	33 93 C
Chalfont Rd. N9	17	33 93 D
Chalfont Rd. SE25	97	33 68 B
Chalfont Way. W13	60	16 79 D
Chalfont Wlk. Pnr	20	11 90 C
Chalford Cl. E Mol	92	13 68 C
Chalford Ct. Ilf	40	43 88 B
Chalford Gdns. Rom	30	52 89 D
Chalford Rd. SE21	87	32 71 B
Chalford Wlk. Wdf Gn	27	41 91 D
Chalgrove Ave. Mord	103	25 67 A
Chalgrove Cres. Ilf	27	42 90 C
Chalgrove Gdns. N3	23	24 89 A
Chalgrove Rd. E9	49	35 84 A
Chalgrove Rd. N17	25	34 90 B
Chalgrove Rd. Sutt	110	26 63 D
Chalice Cl. Wall	111	29 63 B
Chalkenden Cl. SE20	97	34 70 D
Chalk Farm Rd. NW1	47	28 84 C
Chalkhill Rd. Wem	34	19 86 D
Chalk Hill Rd. WL	62	23 78 B
Chalk La. Barn	12	27 96 D
Chalklands. Wem	34	20 86 C
Chalk Rd. E13	58	41 81 A
Chalkwell Park Ave. Enf	13	33 96 C
Challenge Rd. Ashf	81	08 71 B
Challice Way. SW2	86	30 73 D
Challin St. SE20	98	35 69 A
Challis Rd. Brent	60	17 78 D
Challoner Cl. N2	23	26 90 D
Challoner Cres. W14	62	24 78 D
Challoners Cl. E Mol	92	14 68 D
Challoner St. W14	62	24 78 D
Chalmers Rd. Ashf	81	07 71 D
Chalmers Road E. Ashf	81	08 71 C
Chalmer's Terr. N16	37	33 86 D
Chalmers Way. Felt	69	10 74 B
Chalmer's Wlk. SE17	63	31 77 B
Chalsey Rd. SE4	76	36 75 D
Chalthorpe St. WC1	3	30 82 D
Chalton Dri. N2	35	26 88 D
Chalton St. NW1	47	29 83 D
Chamberlain Cottages. SE5	75	32 76 B
Chamberlain Cres. W Wick	106	37 66 D
Chamberlain La. Pnr	19	10 89 C
Chamberlain Rd. N2	23	26 90 C
Chamberlain Rd. N9	17	34 93 A
Chamberlain Rd. W13	60	16 79 A
Chamberlain St. NW1	47	27 84 D
Chamberlain Way. Pnr	19	10 89 B
Chamberlain Way. Surb	101	18 66 A
Chamberlain Wlk. Felt	82	12 71 A
Chamberlayne Rd. NW10	76	23 83 D
Chambers Gdns. N2	23	26 90 B
Chambers La. NW10	46	23 84 C
Chambers Rd. N7	48	30 85 A
Chambers St. SE16	63	34 79 A
Chamber St. E1	8	33 80 B
Chamber St. E1	57	34 80 A
Chambord St. E2	4	33 82 B
Champion Cres. SE26	88	36 71 A
Champion Gr. SE5	75	32 75 B
Champion Hill. SE5	75	33 75 A
Champion Park. SE5	75	32 76 D
Champion Rd. SE26	88	36 71 A
Champneys Cl. Sutt	110	24 63 D
Chancellor Gr. SE21	87	32 72 C
Chancellors Rd. W6	62	23 78 C
Chancellors St. W6	62	23 78 C
Chancelot Rd. SE2	66	46 78 B
Chancel St. SE1	7	31 80 D
Chancery La. Beck	98	37 69 D
Chance St. E1	4	33 82 D
Chanctonbury Cl. SE9	90	43 72 D
Chanctonbury Gdns. Sutt	110	25 63 D
Chanctonbury Way. N12	15	25 92 A
Chandler Ave. E16	58	40 81 A
Chandler Cl. Hamp	92	13 69 A
Chandler St. E1	57	34 80 D
Chandlers Way. SE24	87	31 73 A
Chandos Ave. E17	26	37 90 C
Chandos Ave. N14	16	29 93 C
Chandos Ave. N20	15	26 94 D
Chandos Ave. W5	60	17 78 B
Chandos Cres. Edg	22	19 91 C
Chandos Ct. N14	16	29 93 B
Chandos Pl. WC2	7	30 80 A
Chandos Rd. E15	38	38 85 D
Chandos Rd. Har	32	14 88 A
Chandos Rd. N17	25	33 90 C
Chandos Rd. N2	24	27 90 C
Chandos Rd. NW10	55	21 82 C
Chandos Rd. NW2	46	23 85 C
Chandos Rd. Pnr	32	11 87 B
Chandos St. W1	2	28 81 B
Chandos Way. NW11	35	25 87 D
Change Alley. EC3	4	32 81 D
Channel Cl. Houn	70	13 76 A
Channelsea Rd. E15	49	38 83 B
Channing Cl. Horn	42	54 87 B
Chanton Dri. Sutt	110	23 62 C
Chantrey Rd. SW9	74	30 75 B
Chantry Cl. Har	33	18 88 B
Chantry La. Brom	107	41 67 B
Chantry Pl. Har	32	13 90 B
Chantry Rd. Chess	109	19 64 C
Chantry Rd. Har	32	13 90 B
Chantry St. N1	48	31 83 B
Chantry Way. Rain	52	50 83 D
Chant St. E15	49	38 84 D
Chapel Cl. Dart	80	51 74 A
Chapel Cl. N2	24	27 89 A
Chapel Ct. SE1	8	32 79 B
Chapel Farm Rd. SE9	89	42 72 B
Chapel Hill. Dart	80	51 74 A
Chapel Hill. N2	24	27 90 C
Chapel House St. E14	54	37 78 B
Chapel La. Houn	70	13 75 A
Chapel La. Pnr	20	11 89 B
Chapel La. Rom	41	47 87 B
Chapel Market. N1	48	31 83 C
Chapel Pl. N17	25	33 91 C
Chapel Pl. N1	48	31 83 C
Chapel Pl. W1	2	28 81 D
Chapel Rd. Bexh	79	49 75 C
Chapel Rd. Houn	70	13 75 B
Chapel Rd. SE27	87	32 71 A
Chapel Rd. Twick	83	16 73 B
Chapel Rd. W13	54	16 80 D
Chapel Side. W2	56	25 80 B
Chapel St. E15	49	38 84 D
Chapel St. Enf	13	32 96 B
Chapel St. NW1	2	27 81 A
Chapel Stones. N17	25	33 90 B
Chapel St. SW1	2	28 79 A
Chapel St. W1	2	29 81 D
Chapel Way. Brom	98	40 69 C
Chapel Way. N7	36	30 86 D
Chapel Wlk.	23	23 89 C
Chapel Wlk. Croy	105	32 65 A
Chapel Wlk. NW2	46	22 89 D
Chaplaincy Gdns. Horn	42	54 87 C
Chaplin Cres. Sun	91	09 70 A
Chaplin Rd. Dag	52	48 84 C
Chaplin Rd. E15	59	39 83 B
Chaplin Rd. N17	25	33 89 B
Chaplin Rd. NW2	46	22 84 A
Chaplin Rd. Wem	44	17 84 B
Chapman Cres. Har	33	18 88 B
Chapman Rd. Belv	67	49 78 D
Chapman Rd. Croy	105	31 66 C
Chapman Rd. E9	49	36 84 B
Chapman St. E1	57	34 81 D
Chapone Pl. W1	2	29 81 D
Chapter House St. EC4	4	32 81 C
Chapter Rd. NW2	45	22 85 D
Chapter Rd. SE17	63	31 78 D
Chapter St. SW1	10	29 78 B
Chapter Way. Hamp	82	13 71 A
Chara Pl. W4	61	20 77 B
Charcroft Cl. W14	62	23 79 B
Charcroft Gdns. Enf	14	35 96 D
Chardin Rd. W4	61	21 78 A
Chardmore Rd. N16	37	34 87 C
Chard Rd. Houn	69	07 76 D
Charecroft Way. W12	62	23 79 B
Charford Rd. E16	58	40 81 A
Chargeable La. E13	58	40 82 C
Chargeable St. E16	58	39 82 D
Charing Cross Rd. WC2	7	29 80 B
Charing Cross. SW1	7	30 80 C
Charlbert St. NW8	47	27 83 C
Charlbury Cl. Rom	30	53 91 A
Charlbury Cres. Rom	30	53 91 A
Charlbury Gdns. Ilf	40	45 86 B
Charlbury Gr. W5	54	17 81 C
Charldane Rd. SE9	90	43 72 D
Charlecote Gr. SE26	87	34 72 D
Charlecote Rd. Dag	41	48 86 C
Charles Cl. Sid	90	46 71 B
Charles Cres. Har	32	14 87 B
Charles Ct. Tedd	83	15 71 C
Charlesfield. SE9	89	41 72 C
Charles Gringling Wlk. SE18	66	43 78 A
Charles II St. SW1	6	29 80 D
Charles La. NW8	47	27 83 C
Charles Pl. NW1	2	29 82 A
Charles Rd. Dag	52	50 84 B
Charles Rd. E7	50	41 84 C
Charles Rd. Rom	41	47 88 D
Charles Rd. SW19	95	25 69 A
Charles Rd. W13	54	16 81 C
Charleston St. SE17	63	32 78 A
Charleville Circ. SE26	87	34 71 D
Charleville Rd. W14	62	24 78 D
Charleville Rd. Eri	67	50 77 C
Charlmont Rd. SW17	86	27 71 D
Charlmount Rd. SW17	96	27 70 B
Charlotte Despard Ave. SW11	74	28 76 A
Charlotte Gdns. Rom	29	49 91 B
Charlotte Mews. W1	3	29 81 A
Charlotte Pl. W1	3	29 81 A
Charlotte Rd. Dag	52	49 84 B
Charlotte Rd. EC2	4	33 82 A
Charlotte Rd. SW13	72	21 76 B
Charlotte Rd. Wall	111	29 63 A
Charlotte Row. SW4	74	29 75 A
Charlotte St. W1	3	29 81 A
Charlotte Terr. N1	47	30 83 B
Charlton Church La. SE7	65	41 78 C
Charlton Cl. Uxb	31	07 86 B
Charlton Cres. Bark	51	45 83 D
Charlton Dene. SE7	65	41 77 C
Charlton Kings Rd. NW5	47	29 85 D
Charlton La. SE7	65	41 78 D
Charlton La. Shep	91	08 68 D
Charlton Park La. SE7	65	41 77 D
Charlton Park Rd. SE7	65	41 77 B
Charlton Pl. N1	48	31 83 C
Charlton Rd. Har	21	18 89 C
Charlton Rd. N9	18	35 94 B
Charlton Rd. NW10	45	20 83 A
Charlton Rd. SE3	65	40 77 D
Charlton Rd. SE7	65	41 77 A
Charlton Rd. Shep	91	08 69 C
Charlton Rd. Wem	33	18 87 D
Charlton Way. SE10	77	39 76 A
Charlton Way. SE3	65	39 77 D
Charlwood Cl. Har	21	15 91 A
Charlwood Pl. SW1	10	29 78 A
Charlwood Rd. SW15	73	23 75 D
Charlwood St. SW1	10	29 78 C
Charlwood Terr. SW15	73	23 75 D
Charman Ave. Stan	21	17 90 D
Charminster Ave. SW19	95	25 69 D
Charminster Rd. SE9	89	41 71 B
Charminster Rd. Wor Pk	103	23 66 D
Charmouth Ct. Rich	71	18 74 B
Charmouth Rd. Well	79	47 76 A
Charnock Rd. E5	37	34 86 D
Charnwood Ave. SW19	95	25 69 D
Charnwood Cl. N Mal	94	21 68 C
Charnwood Dri. E18	27	40 89 D
Charnwood Pl. N20	15	26 93 C
Charnwood Rd. SE25	97	32 68 D
Charnwood St. E5	37	34 86 B
Charrington Rd. Croy	105	32 65 A
Charrington St. NW1	47	29 83 D
Charsley Rd. SE6	88	37 72 B
Chart Cl. Brom	99	39 69 A
Chart Cl. Croy	106	35 67 C
Charter Ave. Ilf	40	44 87 B
Charter Cres. Houn	70	12 75 C
Charter Ct. N Mal	94	21 68 A
Charter Ct. Nal	7	31 87 C
Charterhouse Ave. Wem	44	17 85 C
Charterhouse Bldgs. EC1	3	32 82 C
Charterhouse Mews. EC1	3	31 81 B
Charterhouse Rd. Orp	108	46 65 C
Charterhouse Sq. EC1	3	31 81 B
Charterhouse St. EC1	3	31 81 B
Charterhouse St. EC1	3	31 81 B
Charteris Rd. NW6	46	24 83 B

Charteris Rd. Wdf Gn....27 40 91 B
Charter Rd. King....94 19 68 B
Charter Rd The. Wdf Gn....27 39 91 B
Charters Cl. SE19....87 33 71 C
Charter Sq. King....94 19 69 D
Charter Way. N14....12 29 95 C
Charter Way. N3....23 24 89 D
Chartfield Ave. SW15....73 23 74 A
Chartfield Ave. SW15....73 23 74 A
Chartfield Sq. SW15....73 23 74 B
Chartham Gr. SE27....87 31 72 D
Chartham Rd. SE25....87 34 68 B
Chartley Ave. NW2....34 21 86 C
Chartley Ave. Stan....21 15 91 B
Charton Cl. Belv....67 48 77 B
Chart St. N1....4 32 82 B
Chartwell Cl. SE9....90 44 72 B
Chartwell Pl. Sutt....110 24 64 B
Chartwell Rd. Nthwd....19 09 91 B
Chartwell Way. SE20....97 34 69 B
Charwood. SE27....87 31 71 A
Chase Court Gdns. Enf....13 32 96 A
Chase Cross Rd. Rom....29 50 91 C
Chasefield Rd. SW17....86 27 71 B
Chase Gdns. E4....18 37 92 A
Chase Gdns. Twick....22 14 73 B
Chase Green Ave. Enf....13 32 97 C
Chase Green. Enf....13 32 96 A
Chase Hill. Enf....13 32 96 A
Chase House Gdns. Horn....42 54 86 B
Chase La (Path). Ilf....40 44 88 B
Chase La. Ilf....40 44 88 B
Chaseley St. E14....57 36 81 C
Chasemore Gdns. Croy....112 31 64 C
Chase Rd. NW10....55 20 82 D
Chase Rd. W3....55 20 81 B
Chase Ridings. Enf....13 31 97 C
Chase Side Ave. Enf....13 32 97 D
Chase Side Ave. SW20....24 69 C
Chaseside Cl. Rom....30 51 91 A
Chase Side Cres. Enf....13 32 97 A
Chase Side. Enf....13 32 97 C
Chase Side. N14....12 28 95 D
Chase Side. N14....16 29 94 A
Chase Side Pl. Enf....13 32 97 C
Chase The. Bexh....79 49 75 B
Chase The. Brom....99 40 68 B
Chase The. E12....50 41 85 B
Chase The. Edg....42 19 90 B
Chase The. Horn....42 51 86 D
Chase The. Pnr....32 11 88 C
Chase The. Pnr....20 12 89 D
Chase The. Rom....41 48 88 C
Chase The. Rom....41 50 86 D
Chase The. Rom....42 51 86 C
Chase The. Rom....30 51 89 A
Chase The. Stan....21 16 91 A
Chase THE. Sun....91 10 69 B
Chase The. SW16....97 31 70 C
Chase The. SW20....24 24 69 A
Chase The. SW4....74 28 75 B
Chase The. Wall....111 30 64 D
Chaseville Park Rd. N21....12 30 95 B
Chase Way. N14....12 29 94 C
Chasewood Ave. Enf....13 31 97 D
Chateris Rd. N4....31 87 C
Chatfield Rd. Croy....105 30 66 D
Chatfield Rd. SW11....73 26 75 A
Chatham Ave. Brom....107 40 66 A
Chatham Ave. N1....4 32 82 B
Chatham Cl. NW11....35 25 88 A
Chatham Cl. Sutt....110 24 66 B
Chatham Pl. E9....49 35 84 A
Chatham Rd. E17....26 36 89 A
Chatham Rd. King....94 19 69 C
Chatham Rd. SW11....74 27 74 B
Chatham St. SE17....63 32 78 B
Chatsfield. Eps....109 22 62 C
Chatsfield Pl. W5....54 18 81 C
Chatsworth Ave. Brom....89 40 71 B
Chatsworth Ave. NW4....23 23 90 C
Chatsworth Ave. Sid....90 46 73 C
Chatsworth Ave. SW20....24 69 C
Chatsworth Ave. Wem....44 18 85 D
Chatsworth Cl. NW4....23 23 90 C
Chatsworth Cres. Houn....70 14 75 D
Chatsworth Dri. Enf....13 34 95 C
Chatsworth Estate. E5....49 35 85 B
Chatsworth Gdns. Har....13 13 87 D
Chatsworth Gdns. N.Mal....102 21 67 B
Chatsworth Gdns. W3....55 19 80 D
Chatsworth Pl. Rich....105 16 71 A
Chatsworth Rd. Croy....105 32 65 D
Chatsworth Rd. Dart....80 53 75 C
Chatsworth Rd. E15....50 39 85 D

Chatsworth Rd. E5....49 35 85 B
Chatsworth Rd. E9....49 35 85 C
Chatsworth Rd. NW2....46 23 84 B
Chatsworth Rd. Sutt....110 23 63 A
Chatsworth Rd. W4....61 20 77 A
Chatsworth Rd. W5....54 18 82 D
Chatsworth Rise. W5....54 18 82 D
Chatsworth Way. SE27....87 32 72 C
Chatteris Ave. Rom....30 53 91 B
Chattern Hill. Ashf....07 71 B
Chattern Rd. Ashf....08 71 A
Chatterton Rd. Brom....107 41 67 B
Chatterton Rd. N4....37 31 86 D
Chatto Rd. SW11....74 27 74 B
Chaucer Ave. Houn....69 10 76 D
Chaucer Ave. Rich....72 19 76 C
Chaucer Cl. N11....29 92 D
Chaucer Gdns. Sutt....103 25 65 C
Chaucer Green. Croy....106 35 95 C
Chaucer Rd. E11....39 40 88 C
Chaucer Rd. E17....26 38 90 C
Chaucer Rd. E7....50 40 84 A
Chaucer Rd. Rom....30 52 91 D
Chaucer Rd. SE24....77 31 74 B
Chaucer Rd. Sutt....110 23 64 A
Chaucer Rd. W3....55 20 80 C
Chaucer Rd. Well....78 45 76 B
Chaucer Way. Dart....80 54 75 D
Chauncey Cl. N9....17 34 93 C
Chaundrye Cl. SE9....77 42 74 D
Chauntler Rd. E16....57 40 80 B
Cheam Common Rd. Wor Pk....103 23 65 C
Cheam Mansions. Sutt....109 24 63 C
Cheam Park Way. Sutt....110 24 63 A
Cheam Rd. Eps....109 22 62 C
Cheam Rd. Sutt....110 25 63 A
Cheam St. SE15....34 75 B
Cheapside. EC2....4 32 81 C
Cheapside. N13....17 32 92 B
Cheddar Rd. Houn....69 07 76 D
Cheddington Rd. N18....17 33 93 C
Chedworth Cl. E16....58 39 81 D
Cheeseman Cl. Hamp....12 70 A
Cheesemans Terr. W14....62 24 78 D
Chelford Rd. Brom....88 38 71 D
Chelmer Cres. Bark....51 46 83 D
Chelmer Rd. E9....36 85 D
Chelmsford Ave. Rom....29 50 91 B
Chelmsford Cl. W6....62 23 77 B
Chelmsford Dri. Rom....42 54 86 D
Chelmsford Gdns. Ilf....39 42 87 B
Chelmsford Rd. E11....39 39 87 C
Chelmsford Rd. E17....38 37 88 C
Chelmsford Rd. E18....27 39 90 B
Chelmsford Rd. N14....16 29 94 A
Chelmsford Sq. NW10....46 23 83 A
Chelsea Bridge Rd. SW1....9 28 78 C
Chelsea Bridge. SW8....9 28 77 B
Chelsea Cl. Edg....22 19 90 C
Chelsea Cl. Hamp....14 71 C
Chelsea Cl. NW10....45 21 83 A
Chelsea Emb. SW3....9 27 77 B
Chelsea Estate. SW3....9 27 77 A
Chelsea Manor Gdns. SW3....9 27 78 C
Chelsea Manor St. SW3....9 27 78 C
Chelsea Park Gdns. SW3....62 26 77 B
Chelsea Sq. SW3....62 26 78 D
Chelsfield Ave. N9....18 35 94 B
Chelsfield Gdns. SE26....88 35 72 C
Chelsfield Green. N9....18 35 94 B
Chelsham Rd. S Croy....112 32 63 B
Chelsham Rd. SW4....74 29 75 B
Chelston App. Ruis....31 10 86 A
Chelston Rd. Ruis....31 10 87 C
Chelsworth Cl. Rom....30 54 90 B
Chelsworth Dri. Rom....54 90 B
Chelsworth Dri. SE18....66 44 77 B
Cheltenham Ave. Twick....83 16 73 A
Cheltenham Gdns. E6....50 42 83 C
Cheltenham Pl. Har....21 18 89 C
Cheltenham Pl. W3....55 19 80 D
Cheltenham Rd. E10....38 38 88 C
Cheltenham Rd. Orp....108 46 65 C
Cheltenham Rd. SE13....35 74 A
Cheltenham Terr. SW3....27 78 D
Chelverton Rd. SW15....73 23 75 D
Chelwood Cl. Nthwd....19 08 91 C
Chelwood Gdns. Rich....19 76 C
Chelwood N20....15 26 93 B
Chelwood Wlk. SE4....36 75 C
Chenappa Cl. E13....58 40 82 A
Chenduit Way. Stan....15 91 B
Cheney Rd. NW1....47 30 83 C
Cheney Row. E17....26 36 90 B

Cheneys Rd. E11....39 39 86 C
Cheney St. Pnr....32 11 88 A
Chenies Mews. WC1....2 29 82 D
Chenies Pl. NW1....47 29 83 D
Chenies St. WC1....2 29 81 B
Chenies The. Orp....108 45 67 C
Cheniston Gdns. W8....62 25 79 D
Chepstow Ave. Horn....42 54 86 C
Chepstow Cl. SW15....73 24 74 B
Chepstow Cres. Ilf....40 45 88 C
Chepstow Cres. W11....56 25 80 A
Chepstow Gdns. Sthl....53 12 81 D
Chepstow Pl. W2....56 25 80 A
Chepstow Rd. Croy....105 33 65 B
Chepstow Rd. W2....56 25 81 C
Chepstow Rd. W7....60 16 79 C
Chepstow Rise. Croy....105 33 65 C
Chepstow Villas. W11....56 25 80 A
Chepstow Way. SE15....75 33 76 B
Chepstow Way. SE15....63 33 77 D
Chequers Cl. Orp....100 45 68 D
Chequers La. Dag....52 49 83 C
Chequer St. EC1....4 32 82 C
Chequers Way. N13....17 31 92 D
Cherbury St. N1....48 32 83 D
Cherimeya Gdns. E Mol....92 13 68 B
Cherington Rd. W7....54 15 80 D
Cheriton Ave. Brom....107 40 67 A
Cheriton Ave. Ilf....28 43 90 A
Cheriton Cl. W5....54 17 81 A
Cheriton Ct. SE25....105 33 67 A
Cheriton Dri. SE18....66 44 77 B
Cheriton Sq. SW17....86 28 72 B
Cherry Ave. Sthl....53 11 80 D
Cherry Cl. Cars....104 27 65 B
Cherry Cl. Mord....95 24 68 C
Cherry Cl. Ruis....31 09 86 D
Cherry Cl. SW2....87 31 73 A
Cherry Cl. W5....60 17 79 D
Cherry Cres. Brent....60 16 77 D
Cherry Croft. Pnr....20 12 91 D
Cherry Ct. Ilf....28 43 89 B
Cherrydown Ave. E4....18 37 93 C
Cherrydown Cl. E4....18 37 93 C
Cherrydown Wlk. Rom....29 49 90 D
Cherry Garth. Brent....60 17 78 D
Cherry Gdns. Dag....52 48 85 D
Cherry Gdns Rd. SE16....63 34 79 B
Cherry Hill. Barn....11 25 95 D
Cherry Hill Gdns. Croy....111 30 64 B
Cherry Laurel Wlk. SW2....74 30 74 D
Cherry Orchard Gdns. E Mol....92 12 68 B
Cherry Orchard Rd. Brom....107 42 65 A
Cherry Orchard Rd. Croy....105 32 66 D
Cherry Orchard Rd. E Mol....92 13 68 A
Cherry Orchard. SE7....65 41 77 A
Cherry St. Rom....41 50 88 B
Cherry Tree Hill. N2....36 27 88 B
Cherry Tree Rd. N2....24 27 89 D
Cherry Tree Way. Stan....21 16 91 B
Cherry Tree Wlk. Beck....98 36 68 B
Cherry Tree Wlk. EC1....4 32 82 C
Cherry Way. Eps....109 20 63 B
Cherry Way. Shep....91 09 68 C
Cherry Wlk. Brom....107 40 66 C
Cherrywood Cl. King....94 19 70 C
Cherrywood Ct. Tedd....83 16 71 C
Cherrywood Dri. SW15....73 23 74 B
Cherrywood La. Mord....95 24 68 C
Cherry Wood Way. W5....55 19 81 A
Chertsey Ct. SW14....72 19 75 B
Chertsey Dri. Sutt....103 24 55 A
Chertsey Rd. Ashf....91 08 70 B
Chertsey Rd. E11....38 38 86 B
Chertsey Rd. Felt....81 09 71 A
Chertsey Rd. Ilf....51 44 85 B
Chertsey Rd. Sun....81 09 71 C
Chertsey Rd. Twick....82 14 73 C
Chertsey St. SW17....86 28 71 C
Cherwell Ct. Eps....109 20 64 A
Cheryls Cl. SW6....73 25 76 B
Cheseman St. SE26....87 34 72 D
Chesfield Rd. King....93 18 70 C
Chesham Ave. Orp....108 43 67 D
Chesham Cl. Rom....29 50 89 D
Chesham Cl. Sutt....110 24 62 C
Chesham Cl. SW1....6 28 79 C
Chesham Cres. SE20....98 35 69 A
Chesham Mews. SW1....6 28 79 C
Chesham Pl. SW1....6 28 79 C
Chesham Pl. King....94 19 69 C
Chesham Rd. SE20....98 35 69 A
Chesham Rd. SW19....95 26 70 B
Chesham St. NW10....34 20 86 D
Chesham St. SW1....6 28 79 C

Chesham Terr. W13 ...60   16 79 B
Cheshire Cl. Mit ...96   30 68 A
Cheshire House. Mord ...103   25 66 B
Cheshire Rd. N22 ...24   30 91 B
Cheshire St. E2 ...4   33 82 D
Cheshire St. E2 ...57   34 82 C
Chesholm Rd. N16 ...37   33 86 C
Cheshunt Rd. Belv ...67   49 78 C
Cheshunt Rd. E7 ...50   40 84 B
Chesilton Rd. SW6 ...73   24 76 B
Chesney St. SW11 ...74   28 76 A
Chesnut Gr. N17 ...25   33 89 B
Chessholme Rd. Ashf ...91   08 70 A
Chessington Ave. Bexh ...67   48 77 C
Chessington Ave. N3 ...23   24 89 B
Chessington Cl. Eps ...109   20 63 A
Chessington Ct. Pnr ...20   12 89 D
Chessington Hill Park. Chess ...109   19 64 C
Chessington Rd. Eps ...109   20 63 D
Chessington Way. W Wick ...106   37 65 B
Chesson Rd. W14 ...62   24 77 B
Chesswood Way. Pnr ...20   11 90 D
Chester Ave. Rich ...71   18 74 D
Chester Ave. Twick ...82   12 73 D
Chester Cl. Ashf ...81   08 71 D
Chester Cl N. NW1 ...2   28 82 B
Chester Cl S. NW1 ...2   28 82 B
Chester Cl. Sutt ...103   25 65 A
Chester Cl. SW15 ...72   22 75 B
Chester Cl. SW1 ...6   28 79 D
Chester Ct. Har ...33   15 88 D
Chester Dri. Har ...32   13 88 C
Chesterfield Cl. SE13 ...76   38 75 A
Chesterfield Dri. Esh ...101   16 65 A
Chesterfield Gdns. N4 ...37   31 88 B
Chesterfield Gdns. W1 ...6   28 80 D
Chesterfield Gdns. SE22 ...75   33 74 B
Chesterfield Hill. W1 ...6   28 80 D
Chesterfield Rd. Barn ...11   23 95 B
Chesterfield Rd. E10 ...38   38 88 C
Chesterfield Rd. Eps ...109   20 63 D
Chesterfield Rd. N3 ...23   25 91 A
Chesterfield Rd. W4 ...61   20 77 A
Chesterfield Wlk. W1 ...6   28 80 D
Chesterfield Wlk. SE10 ...76   38 76 B
Chesterford Gdns. NW3 ...46   25 85 B
Chesterford Rd. E12 ...51   43 85 C
Chester Gate. NW1 ...2   28 82 B
Chester Gdns. Enf ...13   34 95 D
Chester Gdns. Mord ...103   26 67 A
Chester Mews. SW1 ...6   28 79 D
Chester Pl. NW1 ...2   28 82 B
Chester Rd. E11 ...39   40 88 D
Chester Rd. E16 ...58   39 82 C
Chester Rd. E17 ...38   35 88 B
Chester Rd. E7 ...50   41 84 D
Chester Rd. Houn ...69   07 75 A
Chester Rd. Houn ...69   10 75 B
Chester Rd. Ilf ...40   45 87 B
Chester Rd. N17 ...25   33 89 A
Chester Rd. N19 ...36   28 86 B
Chester Rd. N9 ...17   34 94 D
Chester Rd. Nthwd ...19   09 91 D
Chester Rd. NW1 ...2   28 82 B
Chester Rd. Sid ...78   45 74 A
Chester Rd. SW19 ...95   23 70 A
Chester Row. SW1 ...6   28 78 A
Chesters Estate The. N Mal ...94   21 69 A
Chester Sq Mews. SW1 ...6   28 79 D
Chester Sq. SW1 ...9   28 78 B
Chester St. E2 ...57   34 82 C
Chester St. SW1 ...6   28 79 D
Chester Terr. NW1 ...2   28 82 B
Chesterton Cl. Grnf ...43   13 83 D
Chesterton Cl. SW18 ...73   25 74 A
Chesterton Rd. E13 ...58   40 82 A
Chesterton Rd. W10 ...56   24 81 A
Chesterton Terr. E13 ...58   40 82 A
Chesterton Terr. King ...94   19 69 C
Chester Way. SE11 ...63   31 78 A
Chesthunte Rd. N17 ...25   32 90 C
Chestnut Alley. SW6 ...62   24 77 B
Chestnut Ave. Brent ...60   17 76 B
Chestnut Ave. E7 ...50   40 85 B
Chestnut Ave. Edg ...21   18 91 B
Chestnut Ave. E Mol ...93   15 68 B
Chestnut Ave. Eps ...109   21 64 A
Chestnut Ave. Esh ...101   15 66 C
Chestnut Ave. Hamp ...92   13 70 C
Chestnut Ave. Horn ...42   52 86 A
Chestnut Ave. N8 ...36   30 88 A
Chestnut Ave. Nthwd ...19   09 90 B
Chestnut Avenue N. E17 ...26   38 89 D
Chestnut Ave S. E17 ...38   38 88 B
Chestnut Ave. SW14 ...72   20 75 B

Chestnut Ave. Tedd ...93   15 69 B
Chestnut Ave. Wem ...44   16 85 D
Chestnut Ave. W.Wick ...107   39 65 C
Chestnut Cl. Ashf ...81   07 71 B
Chestnut Cl. Ashf ...91   09 70 B
Chestnut Cl. Cars ...104   27 66 D
Chestnut Cl. N14 ...12   29 95 B
Chestnut Cl. N16 ...37   32 86 B
Chestnut Ct. SW6 ...62   24 77 B
Chestnut Dri. Bexh ...79   48 75 A
Chestnut Dri. E11 ...39   40 88 C
Chestnut Dri. Har ...21   15 90 B
Chestnut Dri. Pnr ...32   11 88 D
Chestnut Glen. Horn ...42   52 86 A
Chestnut Gr. Barn ...12   27 95 B
Chestnut Gr. Ilf ...28   45 91 A
Chestnut Gr. Islw ...71   16 75 C
Chestnut Gr. Mit ...96   29 68 D
Chestnut Gr. N Mal ...94   20 68 B
Chestnut Gr. S Croy ...112   34 63 D
Chestnut Gr. SW12 ...86   28 73 C
Chestnut Gr. W5 ...60   17 79 D
Chestnut Gr. Wem ...44   16 85 D
Chestnut La. N20 ...15   24 94 C
Chestnut Rd. Ashf ...81   07 71 B
Chestnut Rd. King ...93   18 70 C
Chestnut Rd. N17 ...25   34 89 A
Chestnut Rd. SE27 ...87   32 72 C
Chestnut Rd. SW20 ...95   23 69 D
Chestnut Rd. Twick ...83   15 72 A
Chestnut Rise. SE18 ...66   45 78 C
Chestnut Way. Felt ...81   10 72 D
Chestnut Wlk. Shep ...91   09 68 C
Cheston Ave. Croy ...106   36 66 C
Chesworth Cl. Eri ...80   51 76 C
Chettle Cl. SE1 ...8   32 79 D
Chettle Ct. N8 ...37   31 88 C
Chetwode Rd. SW17 ...86   27 72 D
Chetwynd Ave. Barn ...16   27 94 D
Chetwynd Rd. NW5 ...36   28 86 D
Cheval Pl. SW7 ...5   27 79 C
Cheval St. E14 ...64   37 79 C
Cheveley Cl. Rom ...30   54 90 B
Cheveney Wlk. Brom ...99   40 68 A
Chevening Rd. E10 ...65   39 78 D
Chevening Rd. NW6 ...24   23 83 D
Chevening Rd. SE19 ...97   32 70 B
Cheverton Rd. N19 ...36   29 87 D
Chevet St. E9 ...49   36 85 C
Cheviot Cl. Bexh ...80   51 76 C
Cheviot Cl. Enf ...13   32 97 D
Cheviot Cl. Sutt ...110   26 62 B
Cheviot Gate. NW2 ...35   24 86 A
Cheviot Gdns. NW2 ...35   24 86 A
Cheviot Gdns. SE27 ...87   31 71 B
Cheviot Rd. Horn ...42   52 87 A
Cheviot Rd. SE27 ...87   31 71 D
Cheviot Way. Ilf ...28   45 89 C
Chewton Rd. E17 ...26   36 89 C
Cheyham Gdns. Sutt ...110   23 62 D
Cheyham Way. Sutt ...110   24 62 C
Cheyne Ave. E18 ...27   39 89 B
Cheyne Ave. Twick ...82   12 73 D
Cheyne Cl. Brom ...107   42 65 C
Cheyne Gdns. SW3 ...9   27 77 B
Cheyne Hill. Surb ...93   18 68 D
Cheyne Mews. SW3 ...9   27 77 A
Cheyne Path. W13 ...54   15 81 D
Cheyne Rd. Ashf ...91   08 70 B
Cheyne Row. SW3 ...9   27 77 A
Cheyne Wlk. NW4 ...35   23 88 C
Cheyne Wlk. Croy ...105   34 65 A
Cheyne Wlk. N21 ...13   31 95 B
Cheyne Wlk. SW10 ...9   26 77 D
Cheyne Wlk. SW3 ...9   26 77 B
Cheyne Wlk. SW3 ...9   27 77 A
Cheyneys Ave. Edg ...21   17 91 B
Chichele Gdns. Croy ...112   33 64 A
Chichele Rd. NW2 ...46   23 85 D
Chicheley Gdns. Har ...20   14 91 C
Chicheley Rd. Har ...20   14 91 C
Chicheley St. SE1 ...7   30 79 B
Chichester Ave. Ruis ...31   09 86 A
Chichester Cl. SE3 ...77   41 76 A
Chichester Ct. Eps ...109   21 62 B
Chichester Ct. Stan ...21   18 89 A
Chichester Gdns. Ilf ...39   42 87 B
Chichester Rd. Croy ...105   33 65 C
Chichester Rd. E11 ...39   39 86 C
Chichester Rd. N9 ...17   34 94 C
Chichester Rd. NW6 ...46   25 83 C
Chichester Rd. W2 ...56   25 81 B
Chichester Rents. WC2 ...3   31 81 C
Chichester St. SW1 ...10   29 78 C

Chichester Way. Felt ...82   11 73 A
Chicksand St. E1 ...4   33 81 B
Chicksand St. E1 ...57   34 81 A
Chiddingfold. N12 ...15   25 93 C
Chiddingstone Ave. Bexh ...67   48 77 D
Chiddingstone St. SW6 ...73   25 76 C
Chieveley Rd. Bexh ...79   49 75 D
Chignell Pl. W13 ...54   16 80 C
Chigwell Hill. E1 ...57   34 80 B
Chigwell Hurst Ct. Pnr ...20   11 89 B
Chigwell Rd. E18 ...27   41 90 C
Chigwell Rd. Wdf Gn ...27   42 91 A
Childebert Rd. SW17 ...86   28 72 B
Childeric Rd. SE14 ...64   36 77 C
Childerley St. SW6 ...73   24 76 A
Childers St. SE8 ...64   36 77 B
Childs Cl. Horn ...42   53 88 C
Childs Hill Wlk. NW2 ...35   24 86 D
Childs La. SE19 ...97   33 70 A
Child's Pl. SW5 ...62   25 78 A
Child's St. SW5 ...62   25 78 A
Childs Way. NW11 ...35   24 88 B
*Child's Wlk. SW5 ...62   25 78 A
Chilham Cl. Grnf ...44   16 83 C
Chilham Rd. SE9 ...89   42 71 A
Chilham Way. Brom ...107   40 66 A
Chillerton Rd. SW17 ...86   28 71 D
Chillingford Gdns. Twick ...83   15 72 D
Chillingworth Rd. N7 ...48   31 85 C
Chilmark Gdns. N.Mal ...102   22 67 C
Chilmark Rd. SW16 ...96   29 69 B
Chiltern Ave. Twick ...82   13 73 C
Chiltern Cl. Bexh ...80   51 76 A
Chiltern Cl. Uxb ...31   07 86 A
Chiltern Dene. Enf ...12   30 96 D
Chiltern Dri. Surb ...102   19 67 B
Chiltern Gdns. Brom ...99   39 68 D
Chiltern Gdns. Horn ...42   53 86 C
Chiltern Gdns. NW2 ...35   23 86 D
Chiltern Rd. E3 ...57   37 82 C
Chiltern Rd. Ilf ...40   45 88 A
Chiltern Rd. Pnr ...32   11 88 A
Chiltern Rd. Sutt ...110   26 62 C
Chilterns The. Sutt ...110   25 62 B
Chiltern St. W1 ...2   28 81 A
Chilthorne Cl. SE6 ...88   36 73 B
Chilton Ave. W5 ...60   17 78 B
Chilton Gr. SE8 ...64   36 78 A
Chiltonian Industrial Estate. SE12
...77   39 74 D
Chilton Rd. Edg ...22   19 91 A
Chilton Rd. Rich ...72   19 75 A
Chilton St. E2 ...4   33 82 D
Chilver St. E10 ...65   39 78 D
Chilworth Gdns. Sutt ...103   26 65 C
Chilworth Mews. W2 ...1   26 81 D
Chilworth St. W2 ...1   26 81 C
Chimes Ave. N13 ...17   31 92 B
Chinbrook Cres. SE12 ...89   40 72 D
Chinbrook Rd. SE12 ...89   40 72 D
Chinchilla Dri. Houn ...70   11 76 C
Chine The. N10 ...24   29 89 C
Chine The. N21 ...13   31 95 B
Chine The. Wem ...44   16 85 D
Chingford Ave. E4 ...18   37 93 D
Chingford La. Wdf Gn ...27   39 91 B
Chingford Mount Rd. E4 ...18   37 92 C
Chingford Rd. E17 ...26   37 90 D
Chingford Rd. E4 ...26   37 91 C
Chingley Cl. Brom ...99   39 70 A
Chinnor Cres. Grnf ...43   14 83 C
Chipka St. E14 ...64   38 79 A
Chipley St. SE14 ...64   36 77 A
Chipmunk Gr (off Argus Way).
  Nthlt ...53   12 82 A
Chippendale St. E5 ...38   35 86 D
Chippenham Ave. Wem ...45   19 85 D
Chippenham Ct. Pnr ...19   09 89 D
Chippenham Gdns. NW6 ...56   25 82 A
Chippenham Mews. W9 ...56   25 82 C
Chippenham Rd. Rom ...30   53 91 B
Chippenham Rd. W9 ...56   25 82 C
Chippenham Wlk. Rom ...30   53 91 B
Chipperfield Rd. Orp ...100   46 69 C
Chipstead Ave. Th Hth ...97   31 68 D
Chipstead Cl. SE19 ...97   33 70 D
Chipstead Gdns. NW2 ...34   22 86 B
Chipstead Rd. Eri ...68   51 77 C
Chipstead St. SW6 ...73   25 76 C
Chip St. SW4 ...74   29 75 D
Chisenhale Rd. E3 ...49   36 83 C
Chisholm Rd. Croy ...105   33 65 A
Chisholm Rd. Rich ...71   18 74 D
Chisledon Wlk. E9 ...49   36 84 B

Chislehurst Ave. N12 ...23   26 91 C
Chislehurst High St. Chis ...100   43 70 B
Chislehurst Rd. Brom ...99   42 69 C
Chislehurst Rd. Chis ...99   42 69 B
Chislehurst Rd. Orp ...108   45 67 A
Chislehurst Rd. Rich ...71   18 74 A
Chislehurst Rd. Sid ...90   46 71 C
Chislet Cl. Beck ...98   37 70 C
Chisley Rd. N15 ...37   33 88 C
Chiswell Sq. SE3 ...77   40 76 D
Chiswell St. EC1 ...4   32 81 B
Chiswick Cl. Croy ...104   30 65 D
Chiswick Common Rd. W4 ...61   21 78 A
Chiswick Ct. Pnr ...20   12 89 B
Chiswick High Rd. W4 ...61   20 78 D
Chiswick Lane S. W4 ...61   21 77 B
Chiswick La. W4 ...61   21 78 C
Chiswick Mall. W4 ...61   21 77 B
Chiswick Mall. W6 ...61   22 78 C
Chiswick Quay. W4 ...61   20 76 A
Chiswick Rd. N9 ...17   34 93 A
Chiswick Rd. W4 ...61   20 78 A
Chiswick Sq. W4 ...61   21 77 A
Chiswick Village. W4 ...61   19 77 B
Chitty's La. Dag ...41   47 86 B
Chitty St. W1 ...2   29 81 A
Chivalry Rd. SW11 ...74   27 74 A
Chivers Rd. E4 ...18   37 92 B
Choats Manor Way. Dag ...52   48 83 D
Chobham Gdns. SW19 ...85   23 72 B
Chobham Rd. E15 ...49   38 85 D
Cholmeley Cres. N6 ...36   28 87 B
Cholmeley Park. N6 ...36   28 87 B
Cholmley Gdns. NW6 ...46   28 85 C
Cholmley Rd. Surb ...101   16 67 D
Cholmondeley Ave. NW10 ...45   22 83 C
Cholmondeley Wlk. Rich ...71   17 74 A
Choppin's Ct. E1 ...15   34 80 D
Chorleywood Cres. Orp ...100   46 69 C
Choumert Gr. SE15 ...75   34 76 C
Choumert Rd. SE15 ...75   33 76 D
Choumert Sq. SE15 ...75   34 76 C
Chrisp St. E14 ... 37 81 D
Christ Church Ave. Tedd ...83   16 71 C
Christ Church Ave. Eri ...68   51 77 A
Christchurch Ave. Har ...21   16 89 D
Christchurch Ave. N12 ...23   26 91 A
Christchurch Ave. NW6 ...46   24 84 C
Christchurch Ave. Wem ...44   18 84 A
Christchurch Cl. SW19 ...95   24 70 D
Christchurch Gdns. Har ...21   16 89 C
Christchurch Green. Wem ...44   18 84 A
Christchurch Hill. NW3 ...35   28 86 D
Christ Church La. Barn ...11   24 97 C
Christchurch Park. Sutt ...110   26 63 C
Christchurch Pas. Barn ...11   24 96 A
Christchurch Pas. NW3 ...35   28 86 C
Christ Church Rd. Beck ...98   37 69 C
Christchurch Rd. Dart ...80   53 74 C
Christchurch Rd. Houn ...69   07 75 A
Christchurch Rd. Ilf ...40   44 87 C
Christ Church Rd. N8 ...36   30 88 C
Christchurch Rd. Pur ...112   31 62 C
Christchurch Rd. Sid ...90   45 72 D
Christ Church Rd. Surb ...101   18 67 D
Christ Church Rd. SW14 ...72   20 74 A
Christchurch Rd. SW19 ...95   26 70 D
Christchurch Rd. SW2 ...86   30 73 D
Christchurch Sq. E9 ...49   35 83 A
Christchurch St. SW3 ...9   27 77 B
Christchurch Terr. SW3 ...9   27 77 B
Christchurch Way. E10 ...65   39 78 C
Christian Fields. SW16 ...97   31 70 C
Christian St. E1 ...57   34 81 C
Christie Ct. N4 ...36   30 86 A
Christie Gdns. Rom ...40   46 87 B
Christie Rd. E9 ...49   36 84 A
Christina St. EC2 ...4   33 82 C
Christopher Ave. W7 ...60   16 79 C
Christopher Cl. Sid ...78   45 74 B
Christopher Gdns. Dag ...52   47 85 D
Christopher Mews. W11 ...56   24 80 C
Christopher St. EC2 ... 32 82 D
Chryssell Rd. SW9 ...63   31 77 C
Chubworthy St. SE14 ...64   36 77 A
Chudleigh Cres. Ilf ... 45 85 A
Chudleigh Gdns. Sutt ...103   26 65 C
Chudleigh Rd. NW6 ...46   23 84 D
Chudleigh Rd. SE4 ...76   37 74 A
Chudleigh Rd. Twick ...83   15 73 B
Chudleigh St. E1 ...57   35 81 D
Chudleigh Way. Ruis ...31   10 87 C
Chulsa Rd. SE26 ...87   34 71 D
Chumleigh St. SE5 ...63   33 77 A
Chumleigh Wlk. Surb ...93   18 68 D

Church Alley. Croy ...105   31 66 B
Church App. SE21 ...87   32 72 D
Church Ave. Beck ...98   37 69 A
Church Ave. E4 ...26   38 91 B
Church Ave. N2 ...23   26 90 D
Church Ave. Nthlt ...43   12 84 D
Church Ave. NW1 ...47   28 84 B
Church Ave. Pnr ...32   12 88 D
Church Ave. Ruis ...31   08 87 D
Church Ave. Sid ...90   46 71 D
Church Ave. Sthl ...59   12 79 C
Church Ave. SW14 ...72   20 75 B
Churchbury Cl. Enf ...13   33 97 C
Churchbury La. Enf ...13   33 97 C
Churchbury Rd. Enf ...13   33 97 C
Churchbury Rd. SE9 ...89   41 73 B
Church Cl. N20 ...16   27 93 C
Church Cl. Nthwd ... 09 81 D
Church Cres. E9 ...49   35 84 D
Church Cres. N10 ...24   28 89 D
Church Cres. N20 ...16   27 93 C
Church Cres. N3 ...23   24 90 B
Churchcroft Cl. SW12 ...86   28 73 A
Church Ct. EC4 ...3   31 81 C
Church Ct. Rich ...71   17 74 B
Churchdown. Brom ...89   39 71 A
Church Dri. Har ...32   13 88 C
Church Dri. NW9 ...34   20 87 D
Church Dri. W.Wick ...107   39 65 C
Church Elm La. Dag ...52   49 84 A
Church End. E17 ...26   37 89 D
Church End. NW4 ...22   22 89 D
Church Entry. EC4 ...3   31 81 D
Church Farm La. Sutt ...110   24 63 A
Churchfield Ave. N12 ...23   26 91 B
Churchfield Cl. Har ...20   14 89 C
Churchfield Rd. W13 ...54   17 80 C
Churchfield Rd. W3 ...55   20 80 C
Churchfield Rd. W7 ...60   15 79 A
Churchfield Rd. Well ...78   46 75 A
Churchfields Ave. Felt ...82   12 72 D
Churchfields. E18 ...27   40 90 A
Churchfields. E Mol ...92   13 68 A
Churchfields Rd. Beck ...98   36 69 C
Churchfields. SE10 ...64   38 77 A
Churchfield Way. N12 ...23   26 91 A
Church Gate. SW6 ...73   24 75 A
Church Gdns. W5 ...60   17 79 B
Church Gdns. Wem ...44   16 85 A
Church Gr. King ...93   17 69 C
Church Gr. SE13 ...76   37 74 B
Church Hill. Cars ...111   24 64 D
Church Hill. Dart ...80   51 75 C
Church Hill. E17 ...26   37 89 D
Church Hill. Har ...33   15 87 C
Church Hill. N21 ...17   31 94 A
Church Hill. Orp ...108   46 66 B
Church Hill. Pur ...111   30 62 C
Church Hill Rd. E17 ...26   37 89 D
Church Hill Rd. N20 ...16   27 94 B
Church Hill Rd. Surb ...101   18 67 A
Church Hill Rd. Sutt ...110   23 64 B
Church Hill. SE18 ...65   42 79 D
Church Hill. SE18 ...66   43 79 C
Church Hill. SW19 ...85   24 71 D
Church Hill Wood. Orp ... 45 67 B
Churchill Ave. Har ...33   16 88 D
Churchill Gdns Rd. SW1 ...10   29 77 A
Churchill Gdns. SW1 ...10   29 78 C
Churchill Gdns. W3 ...55   19 81 C
Churchill Pl. Har ...21   15 89 C
Churchill Rd. E16 ...58   41 81 C
Churchill Rd. Edg ...22   19 91 A
Churchill Rd. NW2 ...45   22 84 B
Churchill Rd. NW5 ...47   28 85 B
Churchill Rd. S Croy ...112   32 63 C
Churchill Terr. E4 ...18   37 93 C
Churchill Way. Sun ...91   10 70 A
Churchill Wlk. E9 ...49   35 85 C
Church La. Brom ...107   42 66 C
Church La. Chis ...100   44 69 A
Church La. Dag ...52   50 84 C
Church La. E11 ...39   39 87 C
Church La. E17 ...26   37 89 D
Church La. Enf ...13   32 96 B
Church La. Har ...21   15 90 B
Church La. N17 ...25   33 90 A
Church La. N2 ...23   26 89 B
Church La. N8 ...24   30 89 D
Church La. N9 ...17   34 93 A
Church La. NW9 ...34   20 87 A
Church La. Pnr ...20   12 89 C
Church La. Rom ...30   51 89 C
Church La. Surb ...101   16 67 C
Church La. SW17 ...86   28 71 C

Church La. SW19 ...95   25 69 A
Church La. Tedd ...83   15 71 D
Church La. Twick ...83   16 73 C
Church La. W5 ...60   17 79 B
Church La. Wall ...104   29 65 D
Churchley Rd. SE26 ...87   34 71 B
Church Manorway. Eri ...67   50 79 D
Church Manor Way. SE28 ...66   46 79 C
Church Manor Way. SE2 ...66   45 78 B
Churchmead Cl. Barn ...12   27 95 C
Church Meadow. Surb ...101   17 65 A
Churchmead Rd. NW10 ...45   22 84 A
Churchmore Rd. SW16 ...96   29 69 B
Church Mount. N2 ...35   26 88 B
Church Pas. Surb ...101   18 67 A
Church Path. Bark ...51   44 83 A
Church Path. Croy ...105   32 65 A
Church Path. E11 ...39   40 88 A
Church Path. E17 ...26   37 89 D
Church Path. Mit ...96   27 68 A
Church Path. Mit ...96   27 68 C
Church Path. N12 ...15   26 92 A
Church Path. N12 ...15   26 92 A
Church Path. N17 ...25   33 91 C
Church Path. N5 ...48   31 85 D
Church Path. N5 ...48   32 85 A
Church Path. N6 ...36   30 88 B
Church Path. NW10 ...45   21 84 C
Church Path. Rom ...42   51 88 A
Church Path. Sthl ...59   12 79 D
Church Path. SW14 ...72   20 75 B
Church Path. SW14 ...72   20 75 D
Church Path. SW19 ...95   24 69 D
Church Path. W3 ...61   20 79 C
Church Pl. Mit ...96   27 68 A
Church Pl. SW1 ...6   29 80 A
Church Pl. W5 ...60   17 79 B
Church Rd. Ashf ...81   07 71 C
Church Rd. Bark ...51   44 84 A
Church Rd. Bexh ...79   48 75 B
Church Rd. Brom ...99   39 68 A
Church Rd. Brom ...99   40 69 C
*Church Rd. Croy ...112   32 64 A
Church Rd. Croy ...105   32 65 C
Church Rd. E10 ...38   37 87 C
Church Rd. E12 ...50   42 85 D
Church Rd. E17 ...26   36 90 C
Church Rd. E Mol ...92   14 68 D
Church Rd. Enf ...14   35 95 C
Church Rd. Eps ...109   20 63 D
Church Rd. Eri ...67   50 78 D
Church Rd. Felt ...82   11 71 D
Church Rd. Houn ...59   13 77 C
Church Rd. Ilf ...40   45 88 C
Church Rd. Islw ...60   15 77 C
Church Rd. King ...93   18 69 D
Church Rd. Mit ...95   26 69 D
Church Rd. N17 ... 33 91 D
Church Rd. N6 ...36   28 88 C
Church Rd. N. N2 ...23   26 90 D
Church Rd. Nthlt ...43   12 83 A
Church Rd. Nthwd ...19   09 91 D
Church Rd. NW10 ...45   21 84 C
Church Rd. NW4 ...23   23 89 C
Church Rd. Pur ...111   30 62 C
Church Rd. Rich ...83   18 71 A
Church Rd. Rich ...71   18 74 A
Church Rd. Rom ...30   54 90 B
Church Rd. SE19 ...97   33 70 C
Church Rd. Sid ...90   46 71 A
Church Rd S. N2 ...24   27 90 C
Church Rd. Sthl ...59   12 79 D
Church Rd. Surb ...101   17 66 C
Church Rd. Sutt ...110   24 63 A
Church Rd. SW13 ...72   22 76 A
Church Rd. SW19 ...85   24 71 A
Church Rd. SW19 ...95   26 69 B
Church Rd. Tedd ...83   15 71 D
Church Rd. W3 ...61   20 79 A
Church Rd. W7 ...54   15 80 A
Church Rd. Wall ...104   29 65 D
Church Rd. Well ...78   46 76 D
Church Rd. Wor Pk ...102   21 66 C
Church Rise. SE23 ...88   35 72 B
Church Row. Chis ...100   44 69 A
Church Row. NW3 ...46   28 85 A
Church St. Croy ...105   32 65 A
Church St. Dag ...52   49 84 B
Church St. E15 ...50   39 83 B
Church St. Enf ...13   32 96 B
Church St. Eps ...109   22 62 A
Church St. Hamp ...92   14 69 A
Church St. Islw ...71   16 76 D
Church St. King ...93   17 69 D
Church St. N9 ...17   33 93 A

Name	Pg	Map	Ref
Church St N. E15	50	39	83 A
Church St. NW8	1	27	82 C
Church St Pas. E15	50	39	83 A
Church Stretton Rd. Houn	70	14	74 A
Church St. Sun	91	10	68 B
Church St. Sutt	110	25	64 D
Church St. Twick	83	16	73 C
Church St. W4	61	21	77 B
Church Terr. NW4	22	22	89 B
Church Terr. Rich	71	17	74 B
Church Terr. SE13	77	39	75 A
Church Vale. N2	24	27	89 B
Church Vale. SE23	88	35	72 B
Churchview Rd. Twick	82	14	72 B
Church Way. Barn	12	27	96 D
Church Way. Edg	22	19	91 A
Church Way. N20	16	27	93 C
Churchway. NW1	2	29	82 B
Church Way. S Croy	112	33	62 D
Churchwell Path. E9	49	35	85 C
Church Wlk. Brent	60	17	77 A
Church Wlk. Enf	13	32	96 B
Church Wlk. N16	48	32	85 B
Church Wlk. N16	37	32	86 D
Church Wlk. NW2	35	24	86 D
Church Wlk. NW4	23	23	89 A
Church Wlk. NW9	34	20	86 B
Church Wlk. Rich	71	17	74 B
Church Wlk. Surb	101	15	67 D
Church Wlk. SW13	72	22	76 A
Church Wlk. SW15	72	22	74 B
Church Wlk. SW16	96	29	69 C
Church Wlk. SW20	95	23	68 A
Churchyard Pas. SE5	75	32	76 B
Churchyard Row. SE11	63	31	78 B
Churnfield. N4	37	31	86 A
Churston Av. E13	50	40	83 B
Churston Cl. SW2	87	31	73 C
Churston Dri. Mord	103	24	67 A
Churston Gdns. N11	24	29	91 A
Churton Pl. SW1	10	29	78 A
Churton St. SW1	10	29	78 A
Chusan Pl. E14	57	36	81 D
Chyngton Cl. Sid	90	45	72 D
Cibber Rd. SE23	88	35	72 B
Cicada Rd. SW18	73	26	74 A
Cicely Rd. SE15	75	34	76 A
Cinderford Way. Brom	89	39	71 A
Cinnamon St. E1	57	34	80 D
Cintra Park. SE19	97	33	70 B
Circle Gdns. SW19	95	25	68 A
Circle The. NW2	34	21	86 C
Circle The. NW7	22	20	91 B
Circle The. Rich	60	18	77 D
Circuit Rd. SE28	66	45	79 B
Circuits The. Pnr	20	11	89 C
Circular Rd. N17	25	33	89 B
Circular Rd. N2	23	26	90 D
Circular Way. SE18	66	43	77 A
Circus Mews. W1	1	27	81 B
Circus Pl. EC2	4	32	81 B
Circus Rd. NW8	1	26	82 B
Circus Rd. NW8	46	26	83 D
Circus St. SE10	64	38	77 C
Cirencester St. W2	56	25	81 B
Cirencester St. W2	56	25	81 B
Cissbury Ho. SE26	87	34	72 C
Cissbury Rd. N15	37	32	88 B
Cissbury Ring N. N12	15	25	92 C
Cissbury Ring S. N12	15	24	92 D
City Garden Row. N1	48	31	83 D
City Rd. EC1	3	31	82 B
City Rd. EC1	4	32	82 D
Civic Way. Ilf	28	44	89 C
Clabon Mews. SW1	9	27	78 B
Clack La. Ruis	31	08	87 C
Clack St. SE16	64	35	79 A
Clacton Rd. E17	38	36	88 C
Clacton Rd. E6	58	41	82 B
Clacton Rd. N17	25	33	90 D
Claigmar Gdns. N3	23	25	90 B
Claire Ct. N12	15	26	93 C
Claire Ct. Pnr	20	12	91 D
Clairvale. Horn	42	54	87 A
Clairvale Rd. Houn	70	12	76 A
Clairview Rd. SW16	86	28	71 B
Clairville Gdns. W7	54	15	80 D
Clancarty Rd. SW6	73	25	76 C
Clancarty Rd. SW6	73	25	76 C
Clandon Cl. Eps	109	22	63 A
Clandon Cl. W3	61	19	79 B
Clandon Gdns. N3	23	25	89 A
Clandon Rd. Ilf	40	45	86 A
Clandon St. SE8	76	37	76 C
Clanfield Way (off Pentridge St). SE15	63	33	77 D
Clanricarde Gdns. W2	56	25	80 A
Clapham Common North Side. SW4	74	28	75 D
Clapham Common South Side. SW4	74	29	74 A
Clapham Common West Side. SW4	74	27	75 D
Clapham Cres. SW4	74	29	75 D
Clapham High St. SW4	74	29	75 D
Clapham Junction Estate. SW11	74	27	75 C
Clapham Manor Ct. SW4	74	29	75 A
Clapham Manor St. SW4	74	29	75 B
Clapham Park Rd. SW4	74	29	75 D
Clapham Rd. SW9	74	30	76 C
Clapham Rd. SW9	74	30	77 D
Clapton Common. E5	37	34	87 A
Clapton Pas. E5	49	35	85 C
Clapton Sq. E5	49	35	85 C
Clapton Terr. N16	37	34	87 C
Clapton Way. E5	37	34	86 C
Clara Pl. SE18	66	43	78 A
Clare Cl. N2	23	26	89 A
Clare Cnr. SE9	90	43	73 B
Claredale St. E2	48	34	83 D
Claredon Dri. SW15	73	23	75 C
Claredon Rd. SW19	96	27	70 C
Claredon Rd. Wall	111	28	63 D
Clare Gdns. Bark	51	46	84 C
Clare Gdns. E7	50	40	85 A
Clare Gdns. W11	56	24	81 C
Clare Hall Pl. SE16	64	35	78 A
Clare La. N1	48	32	84 C
Clare Lawn Ave. SW14	72	20	74 B
Clare Market. WC2	3	30	81 D
Claremont Ave. Har	33	18	88 A
Claremont Ave. N.Mal	102	22	67 B
Claremont Ave. Sun	91	10	69 B
Claremont Cl. N1	48	31	83 C
Claremont Cres. Dart	80	51	75 C
Claremont Gdns. Ilf	40	45	86 A
Claremont Gdns. Surb	101	18	67 A
Claremont Gr. Wdf Gn	27	41	91 A
Claremont Park. N3	23	24	90 A
Claremont Rd. Brom	99	42	68 D
Claremont Rd. Croy	105	34	66 C
Claremont Rd. E11	38	38	86 D
Claremont Rd. E17	26	36	90 C
Claremont Rd. E7	50	41	85 C
Claremont Rd. Har	21	15	90 C
Claremont Rd. Horn	42	52	88 C
Claremont Rd. N6	36	29	87 A
Claremont Rd. NW2	35	23	86 B
Claremont Rd. Surb	101	18	67 A
Claremont Rd. Tedd	83	15	71 B
Claremont Rd. Twick	71	17	74 C
Claremont Rd. W13	54	16	81 A
Claremont Rd. W9	46	24	83 D
Claremont Sq. N1	48	31	83 C
Claremont St. E16	66	43	79 A
Claremont St. N18	25	34	91 A
Claremont St. SE10	64	37	77 B
Claremont Way. NW2	35	23	87 B
Clarence Ave. Brom	99	42	68 C
Clarence Ave. Ilf	39	42	88 D
Clarence Ave. N Mal	94	20	69 D
Clarence Ave. SW4	74	29	74 D
Clarence Cres. Sid	90	46	72 D
Clarence Cres. SW4	74	29	74 D
Clarence Gdns. NW1	2	28	82 B
Clarence La. SW15	72	21	74 D
Clarence Mews. E5	48	34	85 D
Clarence Pas. NW1	47	30	83 C
Clarence Pl. E5	48	34	85 D
Clarence Rd. Bexh	79	48	75 C
Clarence Rd. Brom	99	42	68 A
Clarence Rd. Croy	105	32	66 B
Clarence Rd. E12	50	41	85 D
Clarence Rd. E16	58	39	82 C
Clarence Rd. E17	26	35	90 D
Clarence Rd. E5	48	34	85 B
Clarence Rd. Enf	14	35	95 A
Clarence Rd. N15	37	32	88 B
Clarence Rd. N22	24	30	91 C
Clarence Rd. NW6	46	24	84 D
Clarence Rd. Rich	19	19	76 A
Clarence Rd. SE9	89	42	72 A
Clarence Rd. Sid	90	46	72 D
Clarence Rd. Sutt	110	25	64 D
Clarence Rd. SW19	95	25	70 B
Clarence Rd. Tedd	93	16	70 A
Clarence Rd. W4	61	19	78 C
Clarence Rd. Wall	111	28	64 D
Clarence St. King	93	18	69 C
Clarence St. Rich	71	18	75 C
Clarence St. Sthl	53	11	79 D
Clarence Terr. Houn	70	13	75 D
Clarence Way. Wall	47	28	84 D
Clarence Wlk. SW4	74	30	76 C
Clarence Yd. SE17	63	32	78 C
Clarendon Cl. Orp	100	46	68 A
Clarendon Cl. W2	5	27	80 A
Clarendon Cres. Twick	82	14	72 D
Clarendon Cross. W11	56	24	80 A
Clarendon Gdns. Ilf	39	42	87 B
Clarendon Gdns. NW4	22	22	89 B
Clarendon Gdns. W9	1	26	82 C
Clarendon Gdns. Wem	44	18	85 A
Clarendon Green. Orp	100	46	68 C
Clarendon Gr. Mit	96	27	68 B
Clarendon Gr. NW1	2	29	82 B
Clarendon Gr. Orp	100	46	68 C
Clarendon Mews. W2	5	27	80 A
Clarendon Path. Orp	100	46	68 A
Clarendon Pl. W2	5	27	80 A
Clarendon Rd. Croy	105	31	65 B
Clarendon Rd. E11	38	38	87 D
Clarendon Rd. E17	38	37	88 D
Clarendon Rd. E18	27	40	89 A
Clarendon Rd. Har	33	15	88 C
Clarendon Rd. N15	25	32	89 C
Clarendon Rd. N18	17	34	92 C
Clarendon Rd. N22	24	30	90 D
Clarendon Rd. N8	24	30	89 B
Clarendon Rd. W11	56	24	80 A
Clarendon Rd. W5	54	18	82 C
Clarendon Rise. SE13	76	38	75 D
Clarendon St. SW1	9	28	78 D
Clarendon Terr. W9	1	26	82 C
Clarendon Way. Chis	100	45	68 B
Clarendon Way. N21	17	32	94 A
Clarendon Way. Orp	100	46	68 A
Clarendon Wlk. W11	56	24	81 C
Clarens St. SE6	88	36	72 B
Clare Rd. E11	38	38	88 D
Clare Rd. Grnf	43	14	84 B
Clare Rd. Houn	70	12	75 B
Clare Rd. NW10	45	22	84 C
Clare Rd. SE14	76	36	76 B
Clare St. E2	48	34	83 D
Claret Gdns.SE25	97	33	68 C
*Clareville Grove Mews.SW7	62	26	78 A
Clareville Gr. SW7	62	26	78 A
Clareville Rd. Orp	108	44	65 A
Clareville St. SW7	62	26	78 A
Clare Way. Bexh	79	48	76 A
Clarewood Wlk. SW9	75	31	75 D
Clarges Mews. W1	5	28	80 D
Clarges St. W1	6	28	80 D
Claribel Rd. SW9	75	31	76 D
Clarice Way. Wall	111	30	62 A
Claridge Rd. Dag	41	47	87 D
Clarissa Rd. Rom	41	47	87 B
Clarissa St. E8	48	33	83 B
Clark Cl. Eri	80	52	76 A
Clarke Path. N16	37	34	87 C
Clarkes Ave. Wor Pk	103	23	65 B
Clarkes Mews. W1	2	28	81 A
Clarkson Rd. E16	58	39	81 D
Clarkson St. E2	57	34	82 B
Clarksons The. Bark	51	44	83 C
Clark's Pl. EC3	4	33	81 C
Clark's Rd. Ilf	40	44	86 B
Clark St. E1	57	35	81 A
Clark Way. Houn	59	11	77 D
Claston Cl. Dart	80	51	75 C
Claude Rd. E10	38	38	87 C
Claude Rd. E13	50	40	83 B
Claude Rd. SE15	75	34	76 D
Claude St. E14	64	37	78 A
Claudia Pl. SW19	85	24	73 C
Claughton Rd. E13	50	41	83 C
Clauson Ave. Nthlt	43	14	85 C
Clavell St. SE10	64	38	77 A
Claverdale Rd. SW2	87	31	73 A
Clavering Ave. SW13	61	22	77 B
Clavering Cl. Twick	83	16	71 A
Clavering Rd. E12	39	41	86 B
Claverley Gr. N3	23	25	90 B
Claverley Villas. N3	23	25	91 D
Claverton St. SW1	10	29	78 C
Clave St. E1	57	35	80 C
Claxton Gr. W6	62	23	78 D
Claxton Path. SE4	76	35	75 D
Clay Ave. Mit	96	28	69 D
Claybridge Rd. SE12	89	41	71 A
Claybrook Rd. W6	62	23	77 B

Street	Pg	Ref
Claybury Bwy. Ilf.	27	42 89 A
Claybury Bwy. Ilf.	27	42 91 C
Claybury Rd. Wdf Grn	27	44 72 A
Clayfarm Rd. SE9	90	16 65 A
Claygate La. Esh	101	16 66 C
Claygate La. Surb	101	16 79 D
Claygate Rd. W13	60	42 90 C
Clayhall Ave. Ilf	27	41 71 B
Clayhill Cres. SE9	89	31 77 C
Claylands Pl. SW8	63	30 77 B
Claylands Rd. SW8	10	25 66 A
Claymore Cl. Mord	103	38 83 C
Claypole Rd. E15	49	18 78 C
Clayponds Ave. Brent	60	18 78 A
Clayponds Ave. W5	60	17 78 B
Clayponds Gdns. W5	60	18 78 C
Clayponds La. Brent	60	37 85 D
Clays La. E15	49	37 85 D
Clays Lane Cl. E15	49	27 81 B
Clay St. W1	1	18 84 C
Clayton Ave. Wem	7	17 78 D
Clayton Cres. Brent	60	21 90 A
Clayton Field. NW9	22	15 75 A
Clayton Rd. Islw	71	50 87 C
Clayton Rd. Rom	41	34 76 A
Clayton Rd. SE15	57	31 77 A
Clayton St. SE11	63	11 81 B
Clayton Terr. Hay	53	45 66 A
Clay Wood Cl. Orp	108	43 76 B
Cleanthus Cl. SE18	78	43 76 B
Cleanthus Rd. SE18	78	35 81 C
Clearbrook Way. E1	57	25 82 D
Clearwell Dri. W9	56	17 67 B
Cleaveland Rd. Surb	101	34 67 D
Cleaverholme Cl. SE25	105	31 78 C
Cleaver Sq. SE11	63	31 78 C
Cleaver St. SE11	63	34 73 D
Cleeve Hill. SE23	87	40 83 C
Clegg St. E13	50	34 80 D
Clegg St. E1	57	53 91 C
Clematis Cl. Rom	30	22 80 A
Clematis St. W12	55	24 77 B
Clem Attlee Ct. SW6	62	36 81 B
Clemence St. E14	57	29 75 D
Clement Ave. SW4	77	23 84 C
Clement Cl. NW6	46	20 78 B
Clement Cl. W4	61	47 84 A
Clementhorpe Rd. Dag	52	36 87 D
Clementina Rd. E10	33	16 79 B
Clementine Cl. W13	60	35 69 D
Clement Rd. Beck	98	24 71 C
Clement Rd. SW19	85	40 80 A
Clements Ave. E16	58	11 75 D
Clements Ct. Houn	70	30 81 D
Clements Inn Pas. WC2	3	30 81 D
Clements Inn. WC2	3	32 80 B
Clement's La. EC4	8	43 86 D
Clements La. Ilf	40	17 78 D
Clements Pl. Brent	60	42 84 D
Clements Rd. E6	50	43 86 D
Clements Rd. Ilf	40	34 79 D
Clement's Rd. SE16	63	54 86 D
Clement Way. Horn	42	44 78 B
Clendon Way. SE18	66	32 79 A
Clenham St. SE1	8	25 65 A
Clensham Ct. Sutt	103	25 65 A
Clensham La. Sutt	103	27 81 D
Clenston Mews. W1	1	32 84 A
Clephane Rd. N1	48	32 82 D
Clere Pl. EC2	4	32 82 D
Clere St. EC2	4	31 82 C
Clerkenwell Cl. EC1	3	31 82 C
Clerkenwell Green. EC1	3	31 82 D
Clerkenwell Rd. EC1	3	35 83 A
Clermont Rd. E9	49	33 86 D
Clevedon Cl. N16	33	10 76 B
Clevedon Gdns. Houn	69	33 86 B
Clevedon Pas. N16	33	19 69 C
Clevedon Rd. King	94	35 69 B
Clevedon Rd. SE20	98	17 74 D
Clevedon Rd. Twick	77	12 70 D
Cleveland Ave. Hamp	92	24 69 D
Cleveland Ave. SW20	94	21 78 B
Cleveland Ave. W4	61	32 88 A
Cleveland Gdns. N4	32	23 86 B
Cleveland Gdns. NW2	23	21 76 D
Cleveland Gdns. SW13	72	26 81 C
Cleveland Gdns. W2	1	21 65 B
Cleveland Gdns. Wor Pk	102	35 82 C
Cleveland Gr. E1	57	29 81 A
Cleveland Mews. W1	2	37 89 C
Cleveland Park Ave. E17	26	37 89 C
Cleveland Park Cres. E17	26	29 80 C
Cleveland Pl. SW1	6	40 89 A
Cleveland Rd. E18	27	43 86 D
Cleveland Rd. Ilf	40	
Cleveland Rd. Ilf	51	44 85 A
Cleveland Rd. Islw	71	16 75 C
Cleveland Rd. N1	48	32 84 D
Cleveland Rd. N9	17	34 94 B
Cleveland Rd. N Mal	109	21 68 C
Cleveland Rd. SW13	72	21 76 D
Cleveland Rd. W13	54	16 81 B
Cleveland Rd. W4	61	20 79 C
Cleveland Rd. Well	78	45 76 D
Cleveland Rd. Wor Pk	102	21 65 A
Cleveland Rise. Mord	103	23 66 B
Cleveland Row. SW1	6	29 80 C
Cleveland Sq. W2	1	26 81 C
Cleveland St. W1	2	29 81 A
Cleveland Terr. W2	1	26 81 C
Cleveland Way. E1	57	35 82 C
Cleveley Cres. W5	54	18 82 B
Cleveley Cres. W5	44	18 83 C
Cleveleys Rd. E5	34	34 86 D
Clevely Cl. SE7	65	41 78 B
Cleve Rd. NW6	46	25 84 D
Cleverly Estate. W12	55	22 80 C
Cleves Ave. Eps	109	22 62 B
Cleves Rd. E6	50	41 83 D
Cleves Rd. Rich	83	17 72 C
Cleves Way. Hamp	92	12 70 D
Cleves Way. Ruis	32	11 87 D
Cleves Wlk. Ilf	28	44 91 C
Clewer Cres. Har	20	14 90 B
Clifden Rd. Brent	60	17 77 B
Clifden Rd. E9	49	35 85 D
Clifden Rd. Twick	83	15 73 D
Cliffe Rd. S Croy	112	32 64 D
Clifford Ave. Chis	99	42 70 B
Clifford Ave. Ilf	28	43 90 D
Clifford Ave. SW14	72	20 76 C
Clifford Ave. Wall	111	29 64 A
Clifford Cl. Nthlt	45	12 83 A
Clifford Dri. SW9	75	31 75 D
Clifford Gdns. NW10	45	23 83 C
Clifford Gr. Ashf	81	07 71 A
Clifford Rd. Barn	11	25 96 B
Clifford Rd. E16	58	39 82 D
Clifford Rd. E17	27	38 90 C
Clifford Rd. Enf	14	35 95 C
Clifford Rd. Houn	70	11 75 B
Clifford Rd. Rich	83	17 72 B
Clifford Rd. SE25	97	34 68 C
Clifford Rd. Wem	44	17 83 B
Clifford's Inn Pas. EC4	3	31 81 C
Clifford St. W1	2	29 80 A
Clifford Way. NW10	23	21 85 B
Cliff Rd. NW1	47	29 84 B
Cliff Terr. SE8	76	37 76 C
Cliffview Rd. SE13	75	37 75 C
Cliff Villas. NW1	47	29 84 B
Cliff Wlk. E16	58	39 81 B
Cliftan Rd. Grnf	53	14 82 D
Clifton Ave. E17	26	35 89 B
Clifton Ave. Felt	82	11 72 C
Clifton Ave. N3	24	24 90 B
Clifton Ave. Stan	36	16 90 D
Clifton Ave. Sutt	110	25 62 D
Clifton Ave. W12	55	21 80 D
Clifton Ave. Wem	44	18 84 B
Clifton Cres. SE15	57	35 77 C
Clifton Ct. SE25	105	33 67 A
Clifton Gdns. Enf	12	30 96 C
Clifton Gdns. N15	37	33 88 D
Clifton Gdns. NW11	35	24 88 D
Clifton Gdns. W4	61	20 78 B
Clifton Gdns. W9	1	26 82 C
Clifton Gr. E8	48	34 84 A
Clifton Hill. NW8	46	25 83 D
Clifton Hill. NW8	46	26 83 A
Clifton Park Ave. SW20	93	23 69 C
Clifton Pl. W2	1	26 81 D
Clifton Rd. E16	58	39 81 A
Clifton Rd. E7	41	41 84 B
Clifton Rd. Har	21	18 89 D
Clifton Rd. Horn	42	52 88 C
Clifton Rd. Houn	70	07 75 B
Clifton Rd. Ilf	40	44 88 D
Clifton Rd. Islw	71	14 76 D
Clifton Rd. Islw	71	15 76 C
Clifton Rd. King	93	18 70 D
Clifton Rd. King	94	19 69 A
Clifton Rd. N22	24	29 90 A
Clifton Rd. N3	23	26 90 A
Clifton Rd. N8	36	29 88 D
Clifton Rd. NW10	45	22 83 C
Clifton Rd. SE25	97	33 68 C
Clifton Rd. Sid	90	45 71 A
Clifton Rd. Sthl	53	12 78 A
Clifton Rd. SW19	95	23 70 B
Clifton Rd. Tedd	83	15 71 A
Clifton Rd. W9	1	26 82 C
Clifton Rd. Wall	111	28 64 D
Clifton Rd. Well	78	47 75 A
Clifton Rise. SE14	64	36 77 C
Clifton St. EC2	4	33 82 C
Clifton Terr. N4	31	31 86 A
Clifton Villas. W9	1	26 81 A
Clifton Way. SE15	64	35 77 C
Clifton Way. Wem	44	18 83 A
Cline Rd. N11	24	29 91 A
Clinger Ct. N1	48	33 83 A
Clink St. SE1	8	32 80 D
Clinton Ave. E Mol	92	14 68 C
Clinton Ave. Well	78	46 75 C
Clinton Cres. Ilf	28	45 91 A
Clinton Rd. E3	57	36 82 A
Clinton Rd. E7	50	40 85 A
Clinton Rd. N15	25	32 89 D
Clipper Way. SE13	76	38 75 C
Clipstone Rd. Houn	70	13 75 A
Clipstone St. W1	2	29 81 A
Clissold Cl. N2	24	27 89 B
Clissold Cres. N16	48	32 85 B
Clissold Rd. N16	37	32 86 D
Clitheroe Ave. Har	32	13 87 C
Clitheroe Rd. Rom	29	50 91 A
Clitheroe Rd. SW9	74	30 76 C
Clitherow Av. W7	60	16 79 C
Clitherow Pas. Brent	60	17 78 C
Clitherow Rd. Brent	60	17 78 C
Clitterhouse Cres. NW2	23	23 87 B
Clitterhouse Rd. NW2	23	23 86 A
Clive Ave. Dart	80	51 74 D
Clive Ave. N18	25	34 91 A
Cliveden Cl. N12	15	26 92 A
Cliveden Pl. SW1	5	28 78 A
Cliveden Rd. SW19	95	24 69 B
Clivedon Ct. W13	54	16 81 B
Clive Pas. SE21	87	32 72 D
Clive Rd. Belv	67	49 78 B
Clive Rd. Enf	13	34 96 C
Clive Rd. Felt	69	10 74 C
Clive Rd. Rom	42	52 88 B
Clive Rd. SE21	87	32 72 D
Clive Rd. SW19	96	27 70 A
Clive Rd. Twick	83	16 71 A
Clive Way. Enf	13	34 96 C
Cloak La. EC4	8	32 80 B
Clock House Ave. Bark	51	44 84 C
Clockhouse La. Ashf	81	07 71 A
Clockhouse La. Felt	81	07 72 B
Clockhouse La. Rom	29	50 91 A
Clock House Rd. Beck	98	36 68 A
Clock Pl. SE17	8	31 78 B
Clock Tower Mews. N1	48	32 83 A
Clock Tower Pl. N7	47	30 84 A
Clock Tower Rd. Islw	71	15 75 B
Cloister Gdns. SE25	105	34 67 D
Cloister Rd. NW2	23	24 86 B
Cloister Rd. W3	55	20 81 A
Cloisters Ave. Brom	107	42 67 B
Clonard Way. Pnr	20	13 91 A
Clonbrock Rd. N16	48	33 85 A
Cloncurry St. SW6	73	23 76 D
Clonmel Cl. Har	32	14 87 D
Clonmel Rd. N17	25	32 89 B
Clonmel Rd. SW6	73	24 76 B
Clonmel Rd. Tedd	82	14 71 B
Clonmore St. SW18	85	25 72 A
Closemead Cl. Nthwd	19	08 91 A
Close The. Barn	12	27 95 B
Close The. Beck	98	36 68 C
Close The. Bex	79	49 74 C
Close The. Cars	111	27 62 A
Close The. E4	26	38 91 C
Close The. Ilf	40	45 88 C
Close The. Islw	70	14 76 D
Close The. Mit	96	27 68 D
Close The. N14	16	29 93 B
Close The. N20	15	24 93 B
Close The. N Mal	94	20 69 C
Close The. Orp	108	45 67 C
Close The. Pnr	32	11 87 A
Close The. Pnr	32	12 87 B
Close The. Pur	111	30 62 D
Close The. Pur	112	31 62 D
Close The. Rich	72	19 75 B
Close The. Rom	41	48 88 C
Close The. Surb	101	18 67 C
Close The. Sutt	103	24 66 B
Close The. Wem	44	18 84 A
Close The. Wem	34	20 86 C
Cloth Ct. EC1	3	31 81 B
Cloth Fair. EC1	3	31 81 B

Clothier St. E1 .... 4 33 81 C
Cloth St. EC1 .... 4 32 81 A
Cloudberry Rd. Rom .... 30 53 91 B
Cloudesdale Rd. SW17 .... 86 28 72 B
Cloudesley Pl. N1 .... 48 31 83 A
Cloudesley Rd. Bexh .... 79 48 76 B
Cloudesley Rd. Eri .... 80 51 76 B
Cloudesley Rd. N1 .... 48 31 83 A
Cloudesley Sq. N1 .... 48 31 83 A
Cloudesley St. N1 .... 48 31 83 A
Clouston Cl. Wall .... 111 30 64 C
Clova Rd. E7 .... 50 40 85 C
Clovelly Ave. NW9 .... 22 21 89 D
Clovelly Ct. Horn .... 42 54 86 B
Clovelly Gdns. Enf .... 17 33 94 A
Clovelly Gdns. Rom .... 29 49 90 B
Clovelly Rd. Bexh .... 67 48 77 A
Clovelly Rd. N8 .... 24 29 88 D
Clovelly Rd. W4 .... 61 20 79 B
Clovelly Rd. W5 .... 60 17 79 A
Clovelly Way. E1 .... 57 35 81 C
Clovelly Way. Har .... 32 12 86 B
Clovelly Way. Orp .... 108 45 67 D
Clover Cl. E11 .... 38 38 86 B
Cloverdale Gdns. Sid .... 78 45 75 D
Clover Mews. SW3 .... 9 27 77 B
Clove St. E13 .... 58 40 82 C
Clowders Rd. SE6 .... 88 36 72 D
Cloysters Green. E1 .... 57 34 80 C
Cloyster Wood. Edg .... 21 17 91 B
Club Gardens Rd. Brom .... 107 40 66 A
Club Row. E2 .... 24 33 82 D
Clumps The. Felt .... 81 08 71 B
Clunas Gdns. Rom .... 30 53 89 B
Clunbury Ave. Sthl .... 59 12 78 D
Clunbury St. N1 .... 32 83 D
Cluny Mews. SW5 .... 62 25 78 A
Cluny Pl. SE1 .... 8 33 79 C
Cluse Ct. N1 .... 48 32 83 C
Clutton St. E14 .... 57 37 81 B
Clydach Rd. Enf .... 13 33 96 D
Clyde Circ. N15 .... 33 88 C
Clyde Ct. NW1 .... 29 83 D
Clyde Pl. E10 .... 37 87 B
Clyde Rd. Croy .... 105 33 65 B
Clyde Rd. N15 .... 33 89 C
Clyde Rd. N22 .... 29 90 B
Clyde Rd. Sutt .... 110 25 64 C
Clyde Rd. Wall .... 111 29 63 A
Clydesdale Ave. Stan .... 21 17 89 B
Clydesdale. Enf .... 14 35 96 D
Clydesdale Gdns. Rich .... 72 19 75 D
Clydesdale Rd. Horn .... 51 51 87 B
Clydesdale Rd. W11 .... 68 24 81 D
Clyde St. SE8 .... 64 36 77 B
Clyde Terr. SE23 .... 88 35 72 A
Clyde Vale. SE23 .... 88 35 72 A
Clyde Way. Rom .... 30 51 90 A
Clydon Cl. Eri .... 68 51 77 A
Clymping Dene. Felt .... 81 10 73 B
Clyston St. SW8 .... 7 29 76 C
Coach and Horses Yd. W1 .... 6 29 80 A
Coach House La. SW19 .... 85 23 71 B
Coaldale Wlk. SE21 .... 87 32 73 A
Coalecroft Rd. SW15 .... 73 23 74 A
Coal Wharf Rd. W12 .... 62 23 79 B
Coates Hill Rd. Brom .... 100 43 69 C
Coate St. E2 .... 48 34 83 C
Coates Wlk (off Burford Rd). Brent
.... 60 18 78 C
Cobar Cl. Barn .... 11 26 97 B
Cobbett Rd. SE9 .... 77 42 75 A
Cobbett Rd. Twick .... 82 13 73 C
Cobbetts Ave. Ilf .... 39 41 88 B
Cobbett St. SW8 .... 10 30 77 D
Cobbler's Wlk. E mol .... 93 16 69 B
Cobbler's Wlk. Hamp .... 92 14 69 A
Cobbler's Wlk. Tedd .... 92 14 70 D
Cobbler's Wlk. Tedd .... 93 15 70 C
Cobbold Rd. E11 .... 39 39 86 D
Cobbold Rd. NW10 .... 45 21 84 B
Cobbold Rd. W12 .... 61 21 79 B
Cobb's Cl. EC4 .... 3 31 81 D
Cobb's Rd. Houn .... 70 12 75 D
Cobb St. E1 .... 4 33 81 B
Cobden Path. SE25 .... 105 34 67 B
Cobden Rd. E11 .... 39 39 86 A
Cobden Rd. SE25 .... 105 34 67 A
Cobham Ave. N.Mal .... 102 22 67 A
Cobham Cl. Brom .... 107 42 66 A
Cobham Cl. SW11 .... 74 27 74 C
Cobham Cl. Wall .... 111 30 63 A
Cobham Rd. E17 .... 26 38 90 A
Cobham Rd. Houn .... 59 11 77 C
Cobham Rd. Ilf .... 40 45 86 C

Cobham Rd. King .... 94 19 69 C
Cobham Rd. N22 .... 25 31 89 B
Cobill Cl. Horn .... 30 53 89 C
Cobland Rd. SE12 .... 89 41 71 A
Coborn Rd. E3 .... 36 82 B
Coborn Rd. E3 .... 49 36 83 D
Coborn St. E3 .... 36 82 B
Cobourg Rd. SE5 .... 63 32 78 D
Cobourg St. NW1 .... 2 29 82 A
Coburg Cres. SW2 .... 86 30 73 D
Coburg Cres. SW2 .... 27 31 73 C
Coburg Rd. N22 .... 24 30 90 D
Cochrane Mews. NW8 .... 46 26 83 D
Cochrane Rd. SW19 .... 95 24 70 D
Cochrane St. NW8 .... 46 26 83 D
Cockfosters Par. Barn .... 12 28 96 C
Cockfosters Rd. Barn .... 12 27 96 B
Cock Hill. EC2 .... 4 33 81 A
Cock La. EC1 .... 3 31 81 B
Cockpit Yd. WC1 .... 3 30 81 B
Cocks Cres. N Mal .... 94 21 68 D
Cockspur Ct. SW1 .... 6 29 80 D
Code St. E1 .... 4 33 82 D
Codling Way. Wem .... 44 17 85 B
Codrington Hill. SE23 .... 88 36 73 A
Codrington Mews. W11 .... 56 24 81 D
Cody Cl. Har .... 21 17 89 B
Cody Cl. Wall .... 111 29 63 D
Cody Rd. E16 .... 39 82 C
Coe's Alley. Barn .... 11 24 96 C
Cofers Circ. Wem .... 34 19 86 D
Cogan Ave. E17 .... 26 36 90 A
Coin St. SE1 .... 7 31 80 C
Coity Rd. NW5 .... 47 28 84 A
Cokers La. SE21 .... 87 32 73 D
Coke St. E1 .... 4 34 81 C
Colas Mews. NW6 .... 46 25 83 A
Colbeck Mews. N1 .... 48 31 84 B
Colbeck Mews. SW7 .... 62 26 78 A
Colbeck Rd. Har .... 32 14 87 A
Colberg Pl. N16 .... 37 33 87 B
Colborne Way. Wor Pk .... 23 65 A
Colburn Ave. Pnr .... 20 12 91 A
Colburn Way. Sutt .... 26 65 D
Colby Rd. SE19 .... 87 33 71 C
Colchester Ave. E12 .... 39 42 86 D
Colchester Dri. Pnr .... 32 11 88 B
Colchester Rd. E10 .... 38 38 87 A
Colchester Rd. E17 .... 38 37 88 C
Colchester Rd. Edg .... 22 20 91 C
Colchester Rd. Nthwd .... 19 10 90 C
Colchester Rd. Rom .... 30 54 90 A
Coldbath Sq. EC1 .... 3 31 82 C
Coldbath St. SE13 .... 76 37 76 B
Coldblow La. SE14 .... 64 35 77 B
Cold Blows. Mit .... 96 27 68 B
Coldershaw Rd. W13 .... 60 16 79 A
Coldershaw Rd. W13 .... 54 16 80 C
Coldfall Ave. N10 .... 24 28 90 C
Coldharbour. E14 .... 64 38 79 A
Coldharbour. E14 .... 38 80 C
Coldharbour La. Pur .... 112 31 62 C
Coldharbour La. SE5 .... 75 32 76 C
Coldharbour La. SW9 .... 75 31 75 D
Coldharbour Pl. SE5 .... 75 32 76 D
Coldharbour Rd. Croy .... 112 31 64 C
Coldharbour Way. Croy .... 112 31 64 C
Coldstream Gdns. SW18 .... 73 24 74 A
Colebert Ave. E1 .... 57 35 82 C
Colebrook Cl. SW15 .... 85 23 73 B
Colebrooke Ave. W13 .... 54 16 81 D
Colebrooke Dri. E11 .... 39 41 87 A
Colebrooke Pl. N1 .... 48 31 83 B
Colebrooke Rise. Brom .... 39 69 C
Colebrook Row. N1 .... 48 31 83 D
Colebrook Rd. E17 .... 26 37 89 C
Colebrook Rd. SW16 .... 96 30 69 A
Colebrook Way. N11 .... 16 28 92 D
Coleby Path. SE5 .... 63 32 77 D
Coledale Dri. Stan .... 21 17 90 A
Coleford Rd. SW18 .... 73 26 74 A
Colegrave Rd. E15 .... 49 38 85 B
Colegrove Rd. SE15 .... 63 33 77 B
Coleherne Ct. SW5 .... 25 78 D
Coleherne Mews. SW10 .... 62 25 78 D
Coleherne Rd. SW10 .... 62 25 78 D
Colehill Gdns. SW6 .... 73 24 76 A
Colehill La. SW6 .... 73 24 76 A
Coleman Fields. N1 .... 48 32 83 A
Coleman Rd. Belv .... 81 49 78 A
Coleman Rd. Dag .... 52 48 84 B
Coleman Rd. SE5 .... 63 33 77 C
Colemans Heath. SE9 .... 90 43 72 D
Coleman St Bldgs. EC2 .... 4 32 81 D
Coleman St. EC2 .... 32 81 D

Colenso Rd. E5 .... 49 35 85 A
Colenso Rd. Ilf .... 40 45 87 A
Cole Park Gdns. Twick .... 71 16 74 C
Cole Park Rd. Twick .... 71 16 74 C
Colepits Wood Rd. SE9 .... 78 44 74 B
Coleraine Rd. N8 .... 25 30 89 A
Coleraine Rd. SE3 .... 65 39 77 B
Cole Rd. Twick .... 71 16 74 C
Coleridge Ave. E12 .... 50 42 84 A
Coleridge Ave. Sutt .... 111 27 64 A
Coleridge Cl. SW8 .... 74 29 76 C
Coleridge Gdns. NW6 .... 46 26 84 C
Coleridge Rd. Croy .... 106 35 66 A
Coleridge Rd. E17 .... 26 36 89 B
Coleridge Rd. N12 .... 15 26 92 C
Coleridge Rd. N4 .... 37 31 86 A
Coleridge Rd. N8 .... 36 29 88 D
Coleridge Rd. Rom .... 30 52 91 D
Coleridge Way. Orp .... 108 46 67 C
Coleridge Wlk. NW11 .... 23 25 89 C
Colesburg Rd. Beck .... 98 36 69 D
Coles Cres. Har .... 32 13 86 B
Coles Green Rd. NW2 .... 34 22 86 B
Coleshill Rd. Tedd .... 93 15 70 A
Colestown St. SW11 .... 74 27 76 C
Cole St. SE1 .... 8 32 79 A
Colet Gdns. W14 .... 62 23 78 B
Coley St. WC1 .... 3 30 82 D
Colfe Rd. SE23 .... 88 36 73 C
Colina Mews. N15 .... 25 31 89 D
Colina Rd. N15 .... 37 31 88 B
Colin Cl. Croy .... 106 36 65 D
Colin Cl. NW9 .... 22 21 89 D
Colin Cl. W.Wick .... 107 39 65 D
Colin Cres. NW9 .... 22 21 89 D
Colindale Ave. NW9 .... 22 21 89 A
Colindeep Gdns. NW4 .... 22 22 89 C
Colindeep La. NW4 .... 22 22 89 C
Colindeep La. NW9 .... 22 21 89 D
Colin Dri. NW9 .... 34 21 88 B
Colinette Rd. SW15 .... 73 23 75 C
Colin Gdns. NW9 .... 22 21 89 D
Colin Park Rd. NW9 .... 22 21 89 C
Colin Rd. NW10 .... 45 22 84 A
Coliston Pas. SW18 .... 85 25 73 A
Coliston Rd. SW18 .... 85 25 73 A
Collamore Ave. SW18 .... 86 27 73 C
Collapit Cl. Har .... 32 13 88 D
College App. SE10 .... 64 38 77 A
College Av. Har .... 21 15 90 A
College Cl. E9 .... 49 35 85 C
College Cl. Har .... 21 15 91 C
College Cl. N18 .... 17 33 92 D
College Cl. Twick .... 82 14 73 D
College Cres. NW3 .... 56 26 84 A
College Cross. N1 .... 48 31 84 C
College Ct. SW3 .... 9 27 78 D
College Ct. W5 .... 54 18 80 A
College Dri. Ruis .... 31 10 87 A
College Gdns. E4 .... 18 37 94 D
College Gdns. Enf .... 13 32 97 B
College Gdns. Ilf .... 39 42 88 A
College Gdns. N18 .... 17 33 92 D
College Gdns. N.Mal .... 102 21 67 B
College Gdns. SE21 .... 87 33 73 C
College Gdns. SW17 .... 86 27 72 A
College Green. SE19 .... 97 33 70 C
College Gr. NW1 .... 47 29 83 B
College Hill. EC4 .... 4 32 80 A
College Hill Rd. Har .... 21 15 90 A
College La. NW5 .... 47 28 85 B
College Park Cl. SE13 .... 76 38 75 D
College Park Rd. N17 .... 25 33 91 B
College Pl. E17 .... 39 89 C
College Pl. NW1 .... 47 29 83 A
College Rd. Brom .... 99 40 69 A
College Rd. Croy .... 105 32 65 B
College Rd. E17 .... 38 38 88 C
College Rd. Enf .... 13 32 97 D
College Rd. Har .... 33 15 88 D
College Rd. Har .... 21 15 90 A
College Rd. Islw .... 71 15 76 B
College Rd. N17 .... 25 33 91 B
College Rd. N21 .... 11 31 93 A
College Rd. NW10 .... 46 23 83 C
College Rd. SE19 .... 87 33 71 B
College Rd. SE21 .... 87 33 72 A
College Rd. SW19 .... 95 26 70 B
College Rd. W13 .... 54 16 81 D
College Rd. Wem .... 33 17 87 D
College Slip. Brom .... 99 40 69 A
College St. EC4 .... 32 80 A
College Terr. E3 .... 57 36 82 B
College Terr. N3 .... 23 24 90 D
College View. SE9 .... 89 41 73 D

Name	Page	Ref
College Yd. NW5	47	28 85 B
Collent St. E9	49	35 84 A
Collerston Rd. E10	65	39 78 D
Colless Rd. N15	37	33 88 B
Collett Rd. SE16	63	34 79 C
Collett Way. Sthl	59	13 79 B
Collier Cl. Eps	109	19 63 B
Collier Dri. Edg	22	19 90 C
Collier Row La. Rom	29	50 90 A
Collier Row Rd. Rom	29	49 90 A
Collier St. N1	47	30 83 D
Colliers Water La. Th Hth	105	31 67 A
Collindale Ave. Eri	67	49 77 B
Collindale Ave. Sid	90	46 73 C
Collingbourne Rd. W12	55	22 80 D
Collingham Gdns. SW5	62	25 78 B
Collingham Pl. SW5	62	25 78 B
Collington St. SE10	64	38 78 D
Collingtree Rd. SE2	88	35 71 A
Collingwood Ave. N10	24	28 89 C
Collingwood Ave. Surb	102	20 66 C
Collingwood Cl. SE20	97	34 69 B
Collingwood Cl. Twick	82	13 73 A
Collingwood Rd. Mit	96	27 68 A
Collingwood Rd. N15	25	33 89 C
Collingwood Rd. Sutt	110	25 64 A
Collingwood St. E1	57	34 82 D
Collins Ave. Stan	21	18 90 C
Collins Dri. Ruis	32	11 86 A
Collins Rd. N5	48	32 79 A
Collins Sq. SE3	77	32 85 A
Collins St. SE3	77	39 76 D
Collins Yd. N1	47	39 76 C
Collinton Rd. Ilf	40	31 83 B
Collinwood Ave. Enf	14	46 86 B
Collinwood Gdns. Ilf	28	35 96 A
Collis Alley. Twick	83	43 89 C
Coll's Rd. SE15	76	15 73 C
Collyer Ave. Croy	111	35 76 A
Collyer Rd. Croy	111	30 64 A
Colman Rd. E16	58	30 64 A
Colmar Cl. E1	57	41 81 A
Colmer Pl. Har	20	35 82 D
Colmer Rd. SW16	96	14 91 D
Colmore Rd. Enf	14	30 70 C
Colnbrook St. SE1	7	35 96 C
Colne Ct. Eps	109	31 79 D
Colne Dri. Rom	30	20 64 A
Colne Rd. E5	49	54 91 B
Colne Rd. N21	17	36 85 A
Colne Rd. Twick	83	32 94 B
Colne St. E13	58	15 73 C
Colney Hatch La. N10	24	40 82 A
Colney Hatch La. N11	24	28 90 A
Colney Rd. Dart	80	27 91 B
Cologne Rd. SW11	73	54 74 D
Cologne Rd. SW11	73	26 75 D
Colombo Rd. Ilf	40	44 87 A
Colombo St. SE1	7	31 80 D
Colomb St. E10	65	39 78 C
Colonade. WC1	3	30 82 C
Colonels Wlk. Enf	13	31 96 B
Colonial Ave. Twick	82	14 74 C
Colonial Rd. Felt	81	09 73 A
Colonnades The. W2	56	25 81 D
Colson Rd. Croy	105	33 65 A
Colson Way. SW16	86	29 71 A
Colsterworth Rd. N15	25	33 89 D
Colston Ave. Cars	111	27 64 A
Colston Ct. Cars	111	27 64 B
Colston Rd. E7	50	41 84 B
Colston Rd. SW14	72	20 75 C
Coltness Cres. SE2	66	46 78 D
Colton Gdns. N17	25	32 89 A
Colton Rd. Har	33	15 88 A
Coltsfoot Path. Rom	30	53 91 C
Columbia Ave. Edg	22	19 90 B
Columbia Ave. Wor Pk	102	21 66 B
Columbia Rd. E13	58	39 82 D
Columbia Rd. E2	4	33 82 B
Columbia Rd. E2	48	34 83 C
Columbine Ave. S Croy	112	31 63 D
Columbine Way. SE13	76	38 76 C
Colva Wlk. N19	36	28 86 B
Colvestone Cres. E8	48	33 85 D
Colview Ct. SE9	89	41 73 D
Colville Gdns. W11	56	24 81 D
Colville Houses. W11	56	24 81 D
Colville Mews. W11	56	24 81 D
Colville Pl. W1	2	29 81 B
Colville Rd. E11	38	38 86 D
Colville Rd. E17	26	36 90 C
Colville Rd. N9	17	34 94 D
Colville Rd. W11	56	24 81 D
Colville Rd. W3	61	19 79 D
Colville Sq Mews. W11	56	24 81 D
Colville Sq. W11	56	24 81 D
Colville Terr. W11	56	24 81 D
Colvin Gdns. E11	27	40 89 D
Colvin Gdns. E4	18	38 93 C
Colvin Gdns. Ilf	28	44 91 C
Colvin Rd. E6	50	42 83 A
Colvin Rd. Th Hth	105	31 67 A
Colwell Rd. SE22	75	33 74 B
Colwick Cl. N6	36	29 87 B
Colwith Rd. W6	62	23 77 A
Colwood Gdns. SW19	95	26 70 D
Colworth Gr. SE17	63	32 78 A
Colworth Rd. Croy	105	34 66 C
Colworth Rd. E11	39	39 87 A
Colwyn Ave. Grnf	44	15 83 D
Colwyn Cres. Houn	70	14 76 A
Colwyn Rd. NW2	34	22 86 D
Colyer Cl. SE9	90	43 72 B
Colyers Cl. Eri	79	50 76 B
Colyers La. Eri	79	50 76 B
Colyers Wlk. Eri	80	51 76 A
Colyton Rd. Grnf	44	17 84 A
Colyton Cl. Well	79	47 76 B
Colyton Rd. SE22	75	34 74 B
Colyton Way. N18	17	34 92 C
Combe Ave. SE3	77	39 77 D
Combedale Rd. SE10	65	40 78 C
Combemartin Rd. SW18	85	24 73 C
Comber Cl. NW2	34	22 86 B
Comber Gr. SE5	63	32 77 C
Combermere Rd. Mord	103	25 67 B
Combermere Rd. SW9	74	30 75 B
Comberton Rd. E5	37	34 86 B
Combeside. SE18	66	45 77 D
Combwell Cres. SE2	66	46 79 C
Comely Bank Rd. E17	26	38 88 A
Comeragh Rd. W14	62	24 78 C
Comerford Rd. SE4	76	36 75 D
Comet Pl. SE8	64	37 77 C
Comet St. SE8	64	37 77 C
Commerce Rd. Brent	60	17 77 C
Commerce Rd. N22	24	30 90 B
Commerce Way. Croy	104	30 65 B
Commercial Dock Pas. SE16	64	36 79 D
Commercial Pl. NW1	47	28 84 D
Commercial Rd. E14	57	36 81 D
Commercial Rd. E1	57	34 81 D
Commercial Rd. N18	17	33 92 C
Commercial St. E1	4	33 81 B
Commercial Way. NW10	45	19 83 D
Commercial Way. SE15	63	34 77 C
Commerell Pl. E10	65	39 78 D
Commerell St. E10	65	39 78 C
Commodore St. E2	57	36 82 C
Commondale. SW15	73	23 75 A
Commonfield La. SW17	86	27 71 C
Common Rd. SW13	72	22 75 A
Commonside. Brom	107	41 65 C
Commonside. Brom	107	41 65 C
Commonside E. Mit	96	28 68 D
Commonside W. Mit	96	28 68 A
Common The. Sthl	59	11 78 B
Common The. W5	54	18 80 C
Commonwealth Ave. W12	55	22 80 B
Commonwealth Rd. N17	25	34 91 C
Commonwealth Way. SE2	66	47 78 C
Community Cl. Houn	69	10 76 B
Community Cl. Uxb	31	08 86 C
Community Rd. E15	49	38 85 D
Community Rd. Grnf	43	14 83 A
Como Rd. SE23	88	36 72 A
Como St. Rom	29	50 89 D
Compass Hill. Rich	71	17 74 D
Compayne Gdns. NW6	46	26 84 A
Compton Ave. E6	50	41 83 D
Compton Ave. N1	48	31 84 B
Compton Ave. N6	36	27 87 A
Compton Ave. Rom	30	53 89 A
Compton Cl. NW1	2	28 82 B
Compton Cl. W13	44	16 81 C
Compton Cres. N17	25	32 91 C
Compton Cres. Nthlt	43	11 83 B
Compton Cres. W4	61	20 77 A
Compton Pas. EC1	3	31 82 D
Compton Pl. Eri	68	51 77 B
Compton Pl. WC1	3	30 82 C
Compton Rd. Croy	105	34 66 D
Compton Rd. N1	48	31 84 B
Compton Rd. N21	17	31 94 D
Compton Rd. NW10	56	23 82 B
Compton Rd. SW19	95	24 70 B
Compton Rise. Pnr	32	12 88 B
Compton St. EC1	3	31 82 D
Compton Terr. N1	48	31 84 B
Comreddy Cl. Enf	13	31 97 B
Comus Pl. SE17	8	33 78 A
Comus Rd. N19	36	29 86 D
Comyn Rd. SW11	73	27 75 C
Comyns Cl. E16	58	39 81 B
Comyns Rd. Dag	52	49 84 C
Conaways Cl. Eps	109	22 62 C
Concanon Rd. SW2	74	30 75 D
Concert Hall App. SE1	7	30 80 D
Conchurch Cl. Sutt	110	25 63 D
Concorde Cl. Houn	70	13 76 D
Concord Rd. Enf	14	35 95 A
Concord Rd. W3	55	19 82 D
Condell Rd. SW8	74	29 76 A
Conder St. E14	57	36 81 C
Conderton Rd. SE5	75	32 75 A
Condover Cres. SE18	66	43 77 D
Conduit Ave. SE10	76	38 76 B
Conduit Ave. SE10	64	38 77 D
Conduit Ct. WC2	7	30 80 A
Conduit La. N18	17	32 92 B
Conduit Lane. S Croy	112	34 64 C
Conduit Mews. W2	1	26 81 D
Conduit Pas. W2	1	26 81 D
Conduit Pl. W2	1	26 81 D
Conduit Rd. SE18	66	43 78 D
Conduit St. W1	6	29 80 A
Conduit Way. NW10	45	20 84 A
Conduit La. Enf	14	35 95 D
Conewood St. N5	37	31 86 D
Coney Acre. SE21	87	32 73 C
Coney Hill Rd. W.Wick	107	39 65 B
Coney Way. SW8	74	30 77 B
Conference Rd. SE2	67	47 78 A
Congleton Gr. SE18	66	44 78 C
Congo Rd. SE18	66	44 78 D
Congress Rd. SE2	67	47 78 A
Congreve Rd. SE9	77	42 75 B
Congreve St. SE17	63	33 78 A
Conical Cnr. Enf	13	32 97 C
Conifer Gdns. Enf	13	33 95 C
Conifer Gdns. Sutt	103	25 65 B
Conifer Gdns. SW16	86	30 72 D
Conifers Cl. Tedd	93	17 70 C
Coniger Rd. SW6	73	25 76 C
Coningham Mews. W12	55	22 80 C
Coningham Rd. W12	61	22 79 B
Coningsby Cottages. W5	60	17 79 B
Coningsby Gdns. E4	26	37 91 B
Coningsby Rd. S Croy	112	32 62 A
Coningsby Rd. W5	60	17 79 B
Conington Rd. SE13	76	38 76 C
Conisbee Ct. N14	12	29 95 A
Conisborough Cres. SE6	88	38 72 C
Coniscliffe Rd. N13	17	32 93 C
Coniston Ave. Bark	51	45 84 C
Coniston Ave. Grnf	54	16 82 B
Coniston Ave. Well	78	45 75 A
Coniston Cl. Bark	51	45 84 C
Coniston Cl. Bexh	79	50 76 A
Coniston Cl. Eri	68	51 77 C
Coniston Cl. N20	15	26 93 C
Coniston Cl. N.Mal	103	23 67 D
Coniston Cl. W4	61	20 77 C
Coniston Ct. SE26	97	34 70 B
Conistone Way. N7	47	30 84 C
Coniston Gdns. Ilf	27	42 89 C
Coniston Gdns. N9	18	35 94 B
Coniston Gdns. NW9	34	20 88 B
Coniston Gdns. Pnr	19	13 89 C
Coniston Gdns. Sutt	110	26 63 B
Coniston Gdns. Wem	33	17 87 C
Coniston Rd. Bexh	79	50 76 A
Coniston Rd. Brom	98	38 70 B
Coniston Rd. Brom	99	39 70 A
Coniston Rd. Croy	105	34 66 A
Coniston Rd. N10	24	28 90 D
Coniston Rd. N17	25	34 91 A
Coniston Rd. Twick	70	13 74 D
Coniston Way. Chess	101	18 65 C
Coniston Wlk. E9	49	35 85 C
Conlan St. W10	56	24 82 C
Conley Rd. NW10	45	21 84 A
Conley St. SE10	65	39 78 C
Connaught Ave. Barn	16	27 94 D
Connaught Ave. E4	18	38 94 B
Connaught Ave. Enf	13	33 97 C
Connaught Ave. Houn	70	12 75 C
Connaught Cl. E10	38	36 86 A
Connaught Cl. Enf	13	33 97 C
Connaught Cl. Sutt	103	26 65 B
Connaught Cl. W2	1	27 81 C
Connaught Dri. NW11	23	25 89 C
Connaught Gdns. N10	36	28 88 B

Name	Pg	Map	Grid
Connaught Gdns. N13	17	31 92	B
Connaught House. N10	36	28 88	B
Connaught La. Ilf	40	44 86	B
Connaught Mews. W2	1	27 81	D
Connaught Pl. W2	1	27 81	D
Connaught Rd. Barn	23	95	D
Connaught Rd. E11	39	39 87	C
Connaught Rd. E16	58	41 80	B
Connaught Rd. E17	38	37 88	A
Connaught Rd. Har	21	15 90	B
Connaught Rd. Horn	42	53 86	D
Connaught Rd. Ilf	40	44 86	B
Connaught Rd. N4	37	31 87	A
Connaught Rd. N Mal	94	21 68	C
Connaught Rd. NW10	45	21 83	C
Connaught Rd. Rich	71	18 74	B
Connaught Rd. SE18	66	43 78	D
Connaught Rd. Sutt	103	26 65	B
Connaught Rd. Tedd	82	14 71	D
Connaught Rd. W13	54	16 80	B
Connaught Sq. W2	1	27 81	D
Connaught St. W2	1	27 81	C
Connaught Way. N13	17	31 92	B
Connell Cres. W5	54	18 82	D
Conningsby Rd. N4	37	31 88	D
Connington Cres. E4	18	38 93	D
Connor Rd. Dag	52	48 85	B
Connor St. E9	49	35 83	B
Conolly Rd. W7	54	15 80	C
Conrad Dri. Wor Pk	103	23 66	D
Consfield Ave. N.Mal	102	22 67	A
Consort Cl. N11	16	28 92	C
Consort Mews. Islw	70	14 74	B
Consort Rd. SE15	75	34 76	D
Cons St. SE1		31 79	A
Constable Cl. NW11	35	25 88	D
Constable Cres. N15	37	34 88	A
Constable Gdns. Edg		19 90	C
Constable Gdns. Islw	70	14 74	B
Constable Wlk. SE21	87	33 72	D
Constance Cres. Brom	107	39 66	D
Constance Rd. Croy	105	31 66	B
Constance Rd. Enf	13	33 95	C
Constance Rd. Sutt	110	26 64	A
Constance Rd. Twick	82	13 73	B
Constantine Rd. NW3	47	27 85	A
Constitution Hill. SW1	6	28 79	B
Constitution Rise. SE18	78	43 76	A
Content St. SE17	63	32 78	B
Control Tower Rd. Houn	69	07 75	B
Convair Wlk. Nthlt	53	11 82	B
Convent Gdns. W11	56	24 81	D
Convent Gdns. W5	60	17 78	A
Convent Hill. SE19	97	32 70	A
Convent Rd. Ashf	81	07 71	D
Convent Way. Sthl	59	11 78	B
Conway Cl. Stan		16 91	A
Conway Cres. Grnf	44	15 83	C
Conway Cres. Rom	41	47 88	C
Conway Dri. Ashf	81	08 70	A
Conway Dri. Sutt	110	25 63	B
Conway Gdns. Mit	96	30 68	C
Conway Gdns. Wem	33	17 87	A
Conway Gr. W3	55	20 81	B
Conway Rd. Felt	82	11 71	D
Conway Rd. Houn	69	07 75	B
Conway Rd. Houn		13 73	A
Conway Rd. Houn	70	13 74	C
Conway Rd. N14	16	30 93	C
Conway Rd. N15	37	32 88	A
Conway Rd. NW2	35	23 86	A
Conway Rd. SE18	66	45 78	A
Conway Rd. SW20	95	23 69	A
Conway St. W1	2	29 82	C
Conway Wlk. Hamp	82	12 70	B
*Conybeare. NW3	47	27 84	C
Conyers Cl. Wdf Gn	27	39 91	A
Conyer's Rd. SW16		29 70	B
Conyer's St. SW16	86	29 71	D
Conyer St. E3	49	36 83	C
Cooden Cl. Brom	99	40 70	D
Cookes Cl. E11	39	39 86	B
Cookes La. Sutt	110	24 63	A
Cookhill Rd. SE2		46 79	D
Cook's Rd. E15	49	37 83	D
Cook's Rd. SE17	63	31 77	B
Coolfin Rd. E16	58	40 81	D
Coolgardie Ave. E4	18	38 92	D
Coolgardie Rd. Ashf	81	08 71	C
Coolhurst Rd. N8		29 88	D
Cool Oak La. NW5	34	21 87	B
Coomassie Rd. W9	56	24 82	D
Coombe Ave Croy	112	33 64	A
Coombe Bank. King	94	21 69	A
Coombe Cl. Edg	21	18 90	D
Coombe Cl. Houn	70	13 75	C
Coombe Cnr. N21	17	31 94	D
Coombe Cres. Hamp	92	12 70	D
Coombe Dri. Ruis	31	10 86	D
Coombe End. King	94	20 70	D
Coombefield Cl. N.Mal	102	21 67	A
Coombe Gdns. N Mal	94	21 68	D
Coombe Gdns. SW20	94	22 69	A
Coombe Hill Glade. King	94	21 70	C
Coombe Hill Rd. King	94	21 70	C
Coombe House Chase. N Mal	94	20 69	B
Coombehurst Cl. Barn	12	29 97	D
Coombe Lane Flyover. SW20	94	21 69	B
Coombe Lane W. King	94	19 69	B
Coombe Lea. Brom	99	42 68	A
Coombe Lodge. SE7	65	41 77	A
Coombe Neville. King	94	20 70	D
Coombe Park. King	84	20 71	D
Coombe Rd. Croy	112	33 64	B
Coombe Rd. Hamp	92	12 70	D
Coombe Rd. N22	25	31 90	C
Coombe Rd. N Mal	94	21 68	A
Coombe Rd. NW10	34	20 86	D
Coombe Rd. Rom	30	54 89	B
Coombe Rd. SE26	87	34 71	B
Coombe Rd. SW20	94	19 69	A
Coombe Rd. W13	60	16 79	D
Coombe Rd. W4	61	21 78	C
Coombe Ridings. King	84	20 71	C
Coombe Rise. King	94	20 69	A
Coomber Way. Croy	104	29 66	B
Coombes Rd. Dag	52	48 83	B
Coombe Wlk. Sutt	103	25 65	D
Coombe-Wood Dri. Rom	41	48 88	D
Coombe Wood Rd. King	84	20 71	C
Coombs St. N1	48	31 83	D
Coomer Mews. SW6	62	24 77	B
Coomer Pl. SW6	62	24 77	B
Cooms Wlk. Edg	22	20 90	A
Cooperage Cl. N17		25 33 91	B
Cooper Ave. E17	26	36 90	A
Cooper Cres. Cars	104	27 65	D
Cooper Rd. Croy	112	31 64	B
Cooper Rd. NW10	45	22 85	C
Cooper Rd. NW4	35	23 88	D
Coopersale Cl. Wdf Gn	27	41 91	C
Coopersale Rd. E9	49	35 85	D
Cooper's La. E10	38	37 87	D
Coopers La. NW1	47	29 83	D
Coopers La. SE12	89	40 72	B
Cooper's Rd. SE1	63	33 78	D
Cooper's Row. EC3	8	33 80	B
Cooper St. E16	58	39 81	B
Cooper's Yd. SE19	97	33 70	A
Coote Gdns. Dag	41	48 86	D
Coote Rd. Bexh	79	48 76	B
Coote Rd. Dag	41	48 86	D
Copeland Dri. E14	38	37 88	D
Copeland Rd. E17	38	37 88	D
Copeland Rd. SE15	75	34 76	D
Copenhagen Pl. E14	57	36 81	D
Copenhagen St. N1	47	30 83	B
Cope Pl. W8	62	25 79	C
Copers Cope Rd. Beck	98	36 70	D
Cope St. SE16	64	35 78	B
Copford Cl. Wdf Gn	27	42 91	A
Copford Wlk. N1	48	32 83	A
Copinger Wlk. Edg	22	19 90	B
Copland Ave. Wem	44	17 85	D
Copland Cl. Wem	44	17 85	C
Copland Rd. Wem	44	18 84	A
Copleston Pas. SE5	75	33 75	B
Copleston Rd. SE15	75	33 75	B
Copley Cl. SE17	63	32 77	A
Copley Cl. W7	54	15 81	B
Copley Dene. Brom	99	44 69	B
Copley Park. SW16	96	30 70	B
Copley St. E1	57	35 81	B
Copnor Way (off Pentridge St). SE15	63	33 77	D
Coppelia Rd. SE3		39 75	D
Copperas St. SE8	64	37 77	B
Copper Beech Cl. Ilf	28	43 90	A
Copperbeech Cl. NW3	46	26 85	D
Copperfield App. Chig	28	44 91	B
Copperfield. Chig	28	44 91	B
Copperfield Mews. N18	17	33 92	C
Copperfield Rd. E3	57	36 81	A
Copperfield St. SE1		32 79	A
Copperfields Way. Rom	30	53 90	B
Copperfield Way. Chis	100	44 70	A
Coppermead Cl. NW2	35	23 88	C
Coppermill La. E17	30	35 88	B
Copper Mill La. SW17	85	26 71	A
Coppetts Cl. N12	24	27 91	C
Coppetts Rd. N10	24	28 90	A
Coppice Cl. Ruis	31	08 88	D
Coppice Cl. SW20	95	23 68	A
Coppice Dri. SW15	72	22 74	D
Coppice The. Enf	13	31 96	D
Coppice Way. E18	27	39 89	B
Coppice Wlk. N20	15	25 93	C
Coppies Gr. N11	16	28 92	B
Copping Cl. Croy	112	33 64	A
Coppins The. Har	21	15 91	A
Coppi The. Ashf	91	07 70	B
Coppock Cl. SW11	74	27 76	C
Coppsfield. E Mol	92	13 68	A
Copse Ave. W Wick	106	37 65	D
Copse Cl. Nthwd		19 08 90	C
Copse Glade. Surb	101	17 66	D
Copse Hill. Sutt	110	25 63	D
Copse Hill. SW20	94	22 70	C
Copse Wood Way. Nthwd	19	08 90	A
Copthall Ave. EC2		4 32 81	D
Copthall Bldgs. EC2		4 32 81	D
Copthall Cl. EC2		4 32 81	D
Copthall Dri. NW7	22	22 91	A
Copthall Gdns. NW7	22	22 91	C
Copthall Gdns. Twick	83	15 73	D
Copthall Rd E. Uxb	31	07 86	C
Copthall Rd W. Uxb	31	07 86	A
Copthorne Ave. Brom	107	42 65	B
Copthorne Ave. Ilf	28	43 91	B
Copthorne Ave. SW12	86	29 73	B
Coptic St. WC1		3 30 81	A
Coral Cl. Rom	29	47 89	A
Coralline Wlk. SE2	67	47 79	A
Coral St. SE1		7 31 79	A
Coram St. WC1		3 30 82	C
Coran Cl. N9	18	35 94	B
Corban Rd. Houn	70	13 75	A
Corbet Cl. Wall	104	28 65	A
Corbet Ct. EC3		4 32 81	D
Corbet Pl. E1		4 33 81	B
Corbet Rd. Eps	109	21 62	C
Corbett Gr. N22	24	30 91	C
Corbett Rd. E11	39	41 88	C
Corbett Rd. E17	26	38 89	A
Corbett's La. SE16	64	35 78	A
Corbetts Pas. SE16	64	35 78	A
Corbicum. E11	39	39 87	A
Corbiere Ct. SW19	95	23 70	B
Corbins La. Har	32	13 86	D
Corbridge Cres. E2	48	34 83	D
Corby Cres. Enf	12	30 96	C
Corbylands Rd. Sid	90	45 73	A
Corbyn St. N4	36	30 87	C
Corby Rd. NW10	45	20 83	D
Corby Way. E3	57	37 82	C
Cordelia St. E14	57	37 81	D
Cordingley Rd. Ruis	31	08 86	B
Cording St. E14	57	37 81	B
Cordova Rd. E3	57	36 82	A
Cordwainers Wlk. E13	50	40 83	C
Cord Way. E14	64	37 79	C
Cordwell Rd. SE13	77	39 74	A
Corelli Rd. SE3	77	42 76	A
Corfe Ave. Har	43	13 85	A
Corfield St. E2	57	34 82	B
Corfton Rd. W5	54	18 81	A
Corinium Cl. Wem	44	18 85	B
Corinne Rd. N19	47	29 85	A
Corinthian Manorway. Eri	67	50 78	B
Corinthian Rd. Eri	67	50 78	B
Corker Wlk. N7	36	30 86	B
Corkran Rd. Surb	101	18 66	A
Corkscrew Hill. W Wick	106	38 65	D
Cork St Mews. W1		6 29 80	A
Cork St. W1		6 29 80	A
Corlett St. NW1		1 27 81	A
Cormont Rd. SE5	75	31 76	B
Cornbury Rd. Edg	21	17 91	D
Cornelia Pl. Eri	68	51 77	A
Cornelia St. N7	47	30 84	B
Cornelia St. N7	48	31 84	A
Corner Green. SE3	77	40 76	C
Corner Mead. NW9	22	21 90	B
Corner Par. N18	17	34 92	C
Cornerside. Ashf	91	08 70	C
Corney Rd. W4	61	21 77	A
Cornflower Terr. SE22	75	34 74	D
Cornford Cl. Brom	107	40 67	A
Cornford Gr. SW12	86	28 72	B
Cornhill. EC3		4 32 81	D
Cornish Gr. SE20	97	34 69	B
Corn Mill Dri. Orp	108	46 66	A
Cornmill La. SE13	76	38 75	A
Cornshaw Rd. Dag	41	47 87	D
Cornthwaite Rd. E5	38	35 86	C
Cornwall Ave. E2	57	35 82	A

Street	Map	Grid
Cornwall Ave. N22	24	30 90 A
Cornwall Ave. N3	23	25 91 C
Cornwall Ave. Sthl	53	13 81 A
Cornwall Ave. Well	78	45 75 B
Cornwall Cl. Bark	51	45 84 B
Cornwall Cres. W11	56	24 81 C
Cornwall Ct. Pnr	20	12 91 D
Cornwall Gdns. NW10	45	22 84 B
Cornwall Gdns. SW7	62	25 79 D
Cornwall Gdns Wlk. SW7	62	25 79 D
Cornwall Gr. W4	21	21 78 C
Cornwallis Ave. N9	18	35 93 A
Cornwallis Gr. N9	18	44 72 D
Cornwallis Rd. Dag	52	35 93 A
Cornwallis Rd. E17	26	48 85 A
Cornwallis Rd. N19	36	35 89 D
Cornwallis Rd. N9	17	30 86 A
Cornwallis Wlk. SE9	77	34 93 B
Cornwall Mews S. SW7	5	42 75 B
Cornwall Mews W. SW7	62	26 79 C
Cornwall Rd. Croy	105	25 79 D
Cornwall Rd. Har	32	31 65 B
Cornwall Rd. N15	37	14 88 A
Cornwall Rd. N18	17	32 88 B
Cornwall Rd. N4	37	34 92 C
Cornwall Rd. Pnr	20	31 87 A
Cornwall Rd. Ruis	31	12 91 D
Cornwall Rd. SE1	7	09 86 B
Cornwall Rd. Sutt	110	31 80 C
Cornwall Rd. Twick	83	25 62 A
Cornwall St. E1	57	16 73 C
Cornwood Cl. N2	23	34 80 B
Cornwood Dri. E1	57	26 89 D
Cornworthy Rd. Dag	52	35 81 C
Corona Rd. SE12	89	47 85 C
Coronation Ave. N16	48	40 73 A
Coronation Cl. Bex	79	33 86 B
Coronation Cl. Ilf	28	47 74 D
Coronation Rd. E13	58	44 89 C
Coronation Rd. NW10	55	41 82 A
Coronation Wlk. Twick	82	19 82 D
Coronet St. N1	4	13 73 C
Corporation Ave. Houn	70	33 82 A
Corporation Row. EC1	3	12 75 C
Corporation St. E15	50	31 82 D
Corporation St. N7	47	33 83 D
Corrance Rd. SW2	74	30 75 C
Corri Pl. N14	16	29 92 B
Corringham Ct. NW11	35	25 87 A
Corringham Rd. NW11	35	25 87 A
Corringham Rd. NW11	35	25 87 B
Corringham Rd. Wem	34	19 86 A
Corringway. NW11	35	25 87 B
Corringway. W5	55	19 81 A
Corscombe Cl. King	84	20 71 C
Corsehill St. SW16	96	29 70 A
Corseley Way. E9	49	36 84 B
Corsham St. N1	4	32 82 B
Corsica St. N5	48	31 84 B
Cortayne Rd. SW6	73	24 76 D
Cortis Rd. SW15	72	22 74 D
Cortis Terr. SW15	72	22 74 D
Corunna Rd. SW8	74	29 76 A
Corunna Terr. SW8	74	29 76 A
Corvette Sq. SE10	64	38 77 B
Coryton Path. W9	56	24 82 D
Cosbycote Ave. SE24	75	32 74 A
Cosdach Ave. Wall	111	29 63 D
Cosedge Cres. Croy	112	31 64 D
Cosmo Pl. WC1	3	30 81 A
Cossall Wlk. SE15	75	34 76 B
Cosser St. SE1	7	31 79 C
Costa St. SE15	75	34 76 C
Costons Ave. Grnf	53	14 82 B
Costons La. Grnf	53	14 82 B
Coston Wlk. SE4	76	35 75 D
Cosway St. NW1	1	27 81 A
Cotall St. E14	57	37 81 A
Coteford Cl. Pnr	31	10 98 A
Coteford St. SW17	86	28 71 A
Cotelands. Croy	105	33 65 C
Cotesbach Rd. E5	38	35 86 C
Cotesmore Gdns. Dag	52	47 85 A
Cotford Rd. Th Hth	97	32 68 C
Cotham St. SE17	63	32 78 A
Cotherstone. Eps	109	20 62 B
Cotherstone Rd. SW2	86	30 73 D
Cotleigh Rd NW6	46	25 84 C
Cotleigh Rd. Rom	41	50 88 D
Cotman Cl. NW11	35	26 88 C
Cotman Cl. SW15	73	23 74 D
Cotmandene Cres. Orp	100	46 69 C
Cotman Gdns. Edg	22	19 90 C
Coton Rd. Well	78	46 75 A
Cotsford Ave. N.Mal	102	20 67 B
Cotswold Cl. Bexh	80	51 76 C
Cotswold Cl. King	94	20 70 A
Cotswold Gate. NW2	35	24 87 C
Cotswold Gdns. E6	50	41 83 D
Cotswold Gdns. Ilf	40	44 87 A
Cotswold Gdns. NW2	35	23 86 B
Cotswold Green. Enf	12	30 96 D
Cotswold Rd. Hamp	92	13 70 A
Cotswold Rd. Rom	30	54 90 D
Cotswold Rd. Sutt	110	25 62 D
Cotswold Rise. Orp	108	45 67 D
Cotswold St. SE27	87	31 71 B
Cotswold Way. Enf	12	30 96 D
Cottage Ave. Brom	107	42 66 C
Cottage Cl. Ruis	31	08 87 D
Cottage Green. SE5	63	33 77 C
Cottage Gr. Surb	101	17 67 D
Cottage Gr. SW9	74	30 75 A
Cottage Pl. SW3	5	27 79 C
Cottage Pl. Eps	109	20 63 D
Cottage St. E14	57	37 80 B
Cottage Wlk. N16	37	33 86 D
Cottage Wlk. SE15	75	33 76 B
Cottenham Dr. SW20	94	22 70 D
Cottenham Park Rd. SW20	94	22 69 B
Cottenham Pl. SW20	94	22 70 D
Cottenham Rd. E17	26	36 89 D
Cotterill Rd. Surb	101	18 66 D
Cottesbrook St. SE14	64	36 77 C
Cottesmore Ave. Ilf	28	43 90 C
Cottesmore Gdns. W8	62	25 79 D
Cottingham Chase. Ruis	31	10 86 C
Cottingham Rd. SE20	98	35 70 D
Cottingham Rd. SW8	10	30 77 D
Cottington Rd. Felt	82	11 71 B
Cottington St. SE11	63	31 78 C
Cotton Hill. Brom	88	38 71 B
Cottons App. Rom	41	50 88 B
Cotton's Gdns. E2	4	33 82 A
Cotton's La (Path). E11	39	39 87 B
Cotton St. E14	58	38 80 A
Couchmore Ave. Esh	101	15 65 A
Couchmore Ave. Ilf	27	42 90 D
Coulgate St. SE4	76	36 75 A
Coulson St. SW3	9	27 78 B
Coulter Rd. W6	61	22 79 D
Councillor St. SE5	63	32 77 C
Counter Ct. SE1	8	32 80 D
Counter St. SE1	8	33 80 C
Countess Rd. NW5	47	29 85 C
Countisbury Ave. Enf	17	33 94 B
Country Way. Felt	82	11 71 B
County Gate. Barn	11	25 95 D
County Gate. SE9	90	44 72 C
County Gr. SE5	75	32 76 A
County Rd. Th Hth	97	31 69 D
County St. SE1	8	32 79 C
Coupland Pl. SE18	66	44 78 C
Courage Cl. Horn	42	53 88 C
Courcy Rd. N8	25	31 89 A
Courland Gr. SW8	74	29 76 D
Course The. SE9	90	43 72 C
Courtauld Rd. N19	36	30 87 C
Court Ave. Belv	67	48 78 D
Court Cl. Har	21	18 89 A
Court Close Ave. Twick	82	13 72 D
Court Cl. Twick	82	13 72 D
Court Cl. Wall	111	29 63 D
Court Downs Rd. Beck	98	37 69 D
Court Dri. Croy	111	30 64 B
Court Dri. Sutt	111	27 64 A
Courtenay Ave. Har	20	14 90 A
Courtenay Ave. N6	36	27 87 A
Courtenay Gdns. Har	20	14 90 C
Courtenay Mews. E17	38	36 88 A
Courtenay Pl. E17	38	36 88 A
Courtenay Rd. E11	39	39 86 D
Courtenay Rd. E17	26	35 89 D
Courtenay Rd. SE2	98	35 70 B
Courtenay Rd. Wor Pk	103	23 65 C
Courtenay Sq. SE11	63	31 78 C
Courtenay St. SE11	63	31 78 C
Court Farm Ave. Eps	109	20 64 D
Court Farm Rd. Nthlt	43	13 84 C
Court Farm Rd. SE9	89	42 72 B
Courtfield Ave. Har	33	15 88 B
Courtfield Cres. Har	33	15 88 B
Courtfield Gdns. Ruis	31	09 86 B
Courtfield Gdns. SW5	62	25 78 B
Courtfield Gdns. W13	54	16 81 C
Courtfield Mews. SW7	62	26 78 A
Courtfield Rd. Ashf	91	07 70 B
Courtfield Rd. SW7	62	26 78 A
Courtfield Rise. W Wick	106	38 65 D
Courthill Rd. SE13	76	38 74 A
Courthope Rd. Grnf	43	14 83 D
Courthope Rd. NW3	47	27 85 B
Courthope Rd. SW19	85	24 71 C
Courthope Villas. SW19	95	24 70 C
Court House Gdns. N3	23	25 91 A
Court House Rd. N12	23	25 91 B
Courtland Ave. Ilf	39	42 86 B
Courtland Ave. SW16	96	30 70 D
Courtlands Ave. Brom	107	39 66 D
Courtlands Ave. Hamp	92	12 70 B
Courtlands Ave. Rich	72	19 76 D
Courtlands Ave. SE12	77	40 74 B
Courtlands Cl. Ruis	31	09 87 B
Courtlands Cl. S Croy	112	34 62 C
Courtlands Dri. Eps	109	21 63 B
Courtlands Rd. Surb	102	19 66 A
Courtlands. Rich	72	19 74 A
Courtlands. W5	54	17 81 A
Court Lane Gdns. SE21	87	33 73 A
Court La. SE21	87	33 73 B
Courtleet Dri. Eri	79	49 76 B
Courtleigh Gdns. NW11	23	24 89 C
Courtman Rd. N17	25	32 91 C
Courtmead Cl. SE24	75	32 74 C
Court Mead. Nthlt	53	12 82 B
Courtnell St. W2	56	25 81 C
Courtney Cl. SE19	97	33 70 A
Courtney Cres. Cars	111	27 63 D
Courtney Path. Croy	105	31 65 C
Courtney Rd. Croy	105	31 65 C
Courtney Rd. Houn	69	07 75 A
Courtney Rd. N7	48	31 85 C
Courtney Rd. SW19	96	27 70 C
Courtrai Rd. SE23	76	36 74 C
Court Rd (Orpington By Pass). Orp	108	46 66 D
Court Rd. SE25	97	33 68 B
Court Rd. SE9	89	42 73 D
Court Rd. Sthl	59	12 78 D
Court Royal. SW15	73	24 74 A
Courtside. SE26	88	35 72 C
Courtside. N8	36	29 88 D
Court St. Brom	99	40 69 C
Court St. E1	57	34 81 B
Court The. Ruis	43	12 85 A
Court Way. NW9	22	21 89 C
Court Way. Rom	30	54 90 C
Court Way. Twick	83	15 73 B
Court Way. W3	55	20 81 A
Courtyard The. N1	48	31 84 C
Court Yd. SE9	77	42 74 D
Cousin La. EC4	8	32 80 B
Couthurst Rd. SE3	65	40 77 D
Coval Gdns. SW14	72	19 75 D
Coval La. SW14	72	19 75 D
Coval Rd. SW14	72	20 75 C
Covent Gdn. WC2	7	30 80 A
Coventry Cl. NW6	46	25 83 A
Coventry Cross. E3	58	38 82 C
Coventry Rd. E1	57	34 82 D
Coventry Rd. Ilf	40	43 87 D
Coventry Rd. SE25	97	34 68 C
Coventry St. W1	6	29 80 B
Coverack Cl. Croy	106	36 66 A
Coverack Cl. N14	12	29 95 C
Coverdale Gdns. Croy	105	33 65 D
Coverdale Rd. NW2	46	24 84 C
Coverdale Rd. W12	61	22 79 B
Coverdales The. Bark	51	44 83 D
Coverley Cl. E1	57	34 81 A
Covert Rd. Chig	28	45 91 B
Covert The. Nthwd	19	08 90 A
Covert The. Orp	108	45 67 C
Covert Way. Barn	11	26 97 D
Covington Gdns. SW16	97	31 70 D
Covington Way. SW16	97	31 70 C
Cowan St. SE5	63	33 77 A
Cowbridge La. Bark	51	43 84 D
Cowbridge Rd. Har	21	18 89 D
Cowcross St. EC1	3	31 81 B
Cowdenbeath Path. N1	1	30 83 B
Cowden Rd. Orp	108	45 66 B
Cowden St. SE6	88	37 71 A
Cowdrey Cl. Enf	13	33 97 C
Cowdrey Rd. SW17	85	26 71 C
Cowen Ave. Har	32	14 86 B
Cowgate Rd. Grnf	53	14 82 B
Cowick Rd. SW17	86	27 71 B
Cowings Mead. Nthlt	43	12 84 A
Cow La. Grnf	43	14 83 D
Cowland Ave. Enf	14	35 96 C
Cowleaze Rd. King	93	18 69 A

Cowley La. E11	39	39 86 C
Cowley Rd. E11	39	40 88 B
Cowley Rd. Ilf	39	42 87 B
Cowley Rd. Rom	30	52 91 D
Cowley Rd. SW14	72	21 75 A
Cowley Rd. SW9	75	31 76 A
Cowley Rd. SW9	63	31 77 C
Cowley Rd. W3	55	21 80 D
Cowley St. SW1	7	30 79 C
Cowling Cl. W11	56	24 80 C
Cowper Ave. E6	50	42 84 C
Cowper Ave. Sutt	110	26 64 B
Cowper Cl. Brom	99	41 68 D
Cowper Cl. Well	78	46 75 A
Cowper Gdns. N14	12	29 95 C
Cowper Gdns. Wall	111	29 63 A
Cowper Rd. Belv	67	49 78 A
Cowper Rd. Brom	99	41 68 D
Cowper Rd. King	83	18 71 D
Cowper Rd. N14	16	28 94 D
Cowper Rd. N16	48	33 85 A
Cowper Rd. N18	17	34 92 C
Cowper Rd. SW19	95	26 70 A
Cowper Rd. W3	55	20 80 D
Cowper Rd. W7	54	15 80 B
Cowper's Ct. EC3	4	32 81 D
Cowper St. EC2	4	32 82 D
Cowper Terr. W10	56	23 81 B
Cowslip Rd. E18	27	40 90 D
Cowthorpe Rd. SW8	74	29 76 B
Cox La. Chess	109	19 64 A
Cox La. Eps	109	19 64 D
Cox La. Eps	109	20 64 C
Coxmount Rd. SE7	65	41 78 D
Cox's Ct. EC1	4	32 81 A
Coxson Pl. SE1	8	33 79 B
Coxs Wlk. SE21	87	34 72 A
Coxwell Rd. SE18	66	44 78 D
Crab Hill. Beck	98	38 70 D
Crabtree Ave. Rom	29	47 89 D
Crabtree Ave. Wem	44	18 83 D
Crabtree La. SW6	62	23 77 D
Crabtree Manorway. Belv	67	50 79 A
Crabtree Wlk. SE15	75	33 76 B
Craddock Rd. Enf	13	33 96 B
Craddock St. NW5	47	28 84 A
Cradley Rd. SE9	90	44 73 D
Cragmuir Park. Wem	44	18 83 B
Craigdale Rd. Horn	42	51 87 B
Craigen Ave. Croy	105	34 66 D
Craigerne Rd. SE3	65	40 77 D
Craig Gdns. E18	27	39 90 D
Craigholm. SE18	78	43 76 A
Craignair Rd. SW2	87	31 73 A
Craignish Ave. SW16	96	30 69 D
Craig Park Rd. N18	17	34 92 B
Craig Rd. Rich	83	17 71 A
Craig's Ct. SW1	7	30 80 C
Craigton Rd. SE9	77	42 75 D
Craigwell Ave. Felt	81	10 72 C
Crail Row. SE17	63	32 78 B
Cramer Ct. SW3	9	27 78 A
Cramer St. W1	2	28 81 A
Crampton Rd. SE20	98	35 70 A
Crampton St. SE17	63	32 78 C
Cranberry Cl. Nthlt	43	11 83 D
Cranberry St. E1	57	34 82 C
Cranborne Ave. Sthl	59	13 78 A
Cranborne Ave. Surb	102	19 65 C
Cranborne Rd. Bark	51	44 83 B
Cranborne Waye. Hay	53	11 80 A
Cranbourn Alley. WC2	6	29 80 B
Cranbourne Ave. E11	27	40 89 D
Cranbourne Dri. Pnr	32	11 88 B
Cranbourne Gdns. Ilf	28	44 89 A
Cranbourne Gdns. NW11	35	24 88 B
Cranbourne Rd. E12	50	42 85 C
Cranbourne Rd. E15	49	38 85 A
Cranbourne Rd. N10	24	28 90 D
Cranbourne Rd. Nthwd	19	09 89 B
*Cranbourn Pas. SE8	63	34 79 B
Cranburn St. WC2	6	29 80 B
Cranbrook Cl. Brom	107	40 67 C
Cranbrook Dri. Rom	30	53 89 C
Cranbrook Dri. Twick	82	13 73 D
Cranbrook Mews. E17	38	36 88 B
Cranbrook Park. N22	25	31 90 A
Cranbrook Rd. Barn	11	26 95 D
Cranbrook Rd. Bexh	79	48 76 B
Cranbrook Rd. Houn	70	12 75 D
Cranbrook Rd. Ilf	40	43 67 C
Cranbrook Rd. SE8	76	37 75 A
Cranbrook Rd. SW19	95	24 70 C
Cranbrook Rd. Th Hth	97	.2 69 C
Cranbrook Rd. W4	61	21 78 C

Cranbrook Rise. Ilf	39	42 87 B
Cranbrook Terr. E2	49	35 83 D
Cranbury Rd. SW6	73	25 76 D
Crane Ave. Islw	71	16 74 A
Crane Ave. W3	55	20 80 A
Cranebrook. Twick	82	14 72 A
Crane Cl. Dag	52	49 84 A
Crane Ct. EC4	3	31 81 C
Crane Ct. Eps	109	20 64 A
Craneford Cl. Twick	83	15 73 B
Craneford Way. Twick	83	15 73 B
Crane Gr. N7	48	31 84 A
Crane Mead. Ct. Twick	83	15 73 B
Crane Mead. SE16	64	35 78 B
Crane Park Rd. Twick	82	13 72 B
Crane Rd. Twick	83	15 73 C
Cranes Dr. Surb	93	18 68 D
Cranes Park Ave. Surb	93	18 68 A
Cranes Park Cres. Surb	93	18 68 A
Cranes Park. Surb	101	18 67 B
Crane St. SE10	64	38 78 D
Craneswater Park. Sthl	59	12 78 D
Crane Way. Twick	82	14 73 A
Cranfield Dri. NW7	22	21 91 C
Cranfield Rd E. Cars	111	28 62 A
Cranfield Rd. SE4	76	36 75 B
Cranfield Rd W. Cars	111	28 62 A
Cranford Ave. N13	16	30 92 C
Cranford Cl. SW20	94	22 69 B
Cranford La. Houn	69	09 75 B
Cranford La. Houn	69	09 76 B
Cranford La. Houn	59	11 77 D
Cranford St. E1	57	35 80 B
Cranford Way. N8	36	30 88 B
Cranham Rd. Horn	42	52 88 D
Cranhurst Rd. NW2	46	23 85 C
Cranleigh Cl. Bex	79	49 74 D
Cranleigh Cl. Orp	108	46 65 C
Cranleigh Cl. SE20	97	34 69 D
Cranleigh Gdns. Bark	51	44 84 B
Cranleigh Gdns. Har	33	18 88 A
Cranleigh Gdns. King	93	18 70 B
Cranleigh Gdns. N21	13	31 95 A
Cranleigh Gdns. SE25	97	33 68 A
Cranleigh Gdns. Sthl	53	12 81 D
Cranleigh Gdns. Sutt	103	25 65 B
Cranleigh Rd. Felt	81	09 71 B
Cranleigh Rd. N15	37	32 88 A
Cranleigh Rd. SW19	95	25 68 A
Cranleigh St. NW1	47	29 83 C
Cranley Dri. Ilf	40	44 87 A
Cranley Dri. Ruis	31	09 86 B
Cranley Gdns. N10	24	28 89 D
Cranley Gdns. N13	16	30 93 D
Cranley Gdns. SW7	62	26 78 D
Cranley Gdns. Wall	111	29 63 C
Cranley Mews. SW7	62	26 78 C
Cranley Pl. SW7	62	26 78 B
Cranley Rd. E13	58	40 81 B
Cranley Rd. Ilf	40	44 87 A
Cranmer Ave. W13	60	16 79 D
Cranmer Cl. Mord	103	24 67 C
Cranmer Cl. Ruis	31	11 87 D
Cranmer Cl. Stan	21	17 91 C
Cranmer Cl. Hamp	82	13 71 D
Cranmer Ct. SW4	74	30 75 A
Cranmer Farm Cl. Mit	96	27 68 D
Cranmer Gdns. Dag	52	50 85 A
Cranmer Rd. Croy	105	31 65 D
Cranmer Rd. E7	50	40 85 B
Cranmer Rd. Hamp	82	13 71 D
Cranmer Rd. King	83	18 71 C
Cranmer Rd. SW9	63	31 77 C
Cranmer Terr. SW17	85	26 71 D
Cranmore Ave. Islw	59	14 77 C
Cranmore Rd. Brom	89	39 72 D
Cranmore Rd. Chis	89	42 71 D
Cranmore Way. N10	24	29 89 C
Cranston Cl. Houn	70	12 76 C
Cranston Cl. Ruis	31	08 86 B
Cranston Gdns. E4	18	37 92 D
Cranston Rd. SE23	88	36 72 A
Cranswick Rd. SE16	63	34 78 D
Crantock Rd. SE6	88	38 72 A
Cranwell Rd. Houn	69	07 75 B
Cranwich Ave. N21	14	32 94 B
Cranwich Rd. N16	37	33 87 A
Cranwood St. EC1	4	32 82 B
Cranworth Cres. E4	18	38 94 D
Cranworth Gdns. SW9	75	31 76 A
Craster Rd. SW2	86	30 73 B
Crathie Rd. SE12	77	40 74 D
Crathorn St. SE13	76	38 75 A
Cravan Ave. Felt	81	10 72 A
Craven Ave. Sthl	53	12 81 B

Craven Ave. W5	54	17 80 A
Craven Cl. N16	37	34 87 A
Craven Gdns. Bark	51	45 83 C
Craven Gdns. Ilf	28	44 89 B
Craven Gdns. SW19	85	25 71 D
Craven Hill Gdns. W2	5	26 80 A
Craven Hill Mews. W2	5	26 80 A
Craven Hill. W2	5	26 80 A
Craven Mews. SW11	74	28 75 A
Craven Park Mews. NW10	45	20 83 A
Craven Park. NW10	45	21 83 A
Craven Park Rd. N15	37	34 88 C
Craven Park Rd. NW10	45	21 83 A
Craven Pas. WC2	7	30 80 C
Craven Rd. Croy	105	34 66 D
Craven Rd. King	93	18 69 B
Craven Rd. NW10	45	20 83 B
Craven Rd. W2	1	26 81 D
Craven Rd. W5	54	17 80 A
Craven St. WC2	7	30 80 C
Craven Terr. W2	5	26 80 A
Craven Wlk. N16	37	34 87 A
Crawford Ave. Wem	44	17 85 D
Crawford Cl. Islw	71	15 76 C
Crawford Gdns. Grnf	53	12 82 B
Crawford Gdns. N13	31	31 95 D
Crawford Mews. W1	1	27 81 B
Crawford Pas. EC1	3	31 82 C
Crawford Pl. W1	1	27 81 A
Crawford Rd. SE5	75	32 76 C
Crawford St. W1	1	27 81 B
Crawley Rd. E10	38	37 87 D
Crawley Rd. Enf	17	33 94 A
Crawley Rd. N22	25	32 90 C
Crawshaw Ct. SW9	75	31 76 A
Crawthew Gr. SE22	75	33 75 D
Cray Ave. Orp	108	46 67 B
Craybrooke Rd. Sid	90	46 71 B
Craybury End. SE9	90	44 72 A
Cray Cl. Dart	80	52 75 C
Craydene Rd. Eri	80	51 76 B
Crayford High St. Dart	80	51 74 A
Crayford Rd. Dart	80	51 74 B
Crayford Rd. N7	47	30 85 A
Crayford Way. Dart	80	51 75 C
Crayonne Cl. Sun	91	09 69 A
Cray Rd. Belv	67	49 77 A
Cray Valley Rd. Orp	100	46 68 D
Crealock Gr. Wdf Gn	27	39 91 B
Crealock St. SW18	85	26 73 A
Creasy St. SE1	8	33 79 C
Crebor St. SE22	75	34 74 C
Credenhall Dri. Brom	107	42 66 D
Credenhill St. SW16	96	29 70 A
Crediton Hill. NW6	46	25 85 D
Crediton Rd. E16	58	40 81 C
Crediton Rd. NW10	46	23 83 B
Credon Rd. E13	50	41 83 C
Credon Rd. SE16	63	34 78 D
Creechurch La. EC3	4	33 81 C
Creechurch Pl. EC3	4	33 81 C
Creed La. EC4	3	31 81 D
Creek Rd. E Mol	93	15 68 C
Creek Rd. SE8	64	37 77 A
Creekside SE8	64	37 77 D
Creeland Gr. SE6	88	36 73 D
Cree Way. Rom	30	51 91 C
Crefeld Cl. W6	62	24 77 A
Creffield Rd. W3	55	19 80 A
Creffield Rd. W5	54	18 80 B
Creighton Ave. E6	50	41 83 D
Creighton Ave. N10	24	28 90 C
Creighton Ave. N2	24	27 90 C
Creighton Rd. N17	25	33 91 C
Creighton Rd. NW6	46	23 83 D
Creighton Rd. W5	60	17 79 D
Cremer St. E2	48	33 83 D
Cremorne Gdns. Eps	109	20 62 B
Cremorne Rd. SW10	62	26 77 D
Crescent Ave. Horn	42	51 86 B
Crescent Ct. Surb	101	17 67 B
Crescent Ct. SW4	74	29 74 B
Crescent Dri. Orp	108	44 67 C
Crescent. EC3	8	33 80 B
Crescent Gdns. Ruis	31	10 87 B
Crescent Gdns. SW19	85	25 72 C
Crescent Gr. Mit	96	27 68 C
Crescent Gr. SW4	74	29 75 C
Crescent La. SW4	74	29 74 B
Crescent La. SW4	74	29 74 B
Crescent Pl. SW3	9	27 78 A
Crescent Rd. Barn	12	27 95 A
Crescent Rd. Beck	98	37 69 D
Crescent Rd. Brom	99	40 70 C
Crescent Rd. Dag	41	49 86 D

Crescent Rd. E10

Crescent Rd. E10 ....38 37 86 B
Crescent Rd. E13 ....50 40 83 A
Crescent Rd. E18 ....27 41 90 A
Crescent Rd. E6 ....50 41 83 A
Crescent Rd. Enf ....13 31 96 D
Crescent Rd. Eri ....68 51 77 B
Crescent Rd. King ....94 19 70 C
Crescent Rd. N11 ....16 27 92 B
Crescent Rd. N15 ....25 31 89 B
Crescent Rd. N22 ....24 29 90 B
Crescent Rd. N3 ....23 24 90 B
Crescent Rd. N8 ....36 29 88 D
Crescent Rd. N9 ....17 34 94 C
Crescent Rd. SE18 ....66 43 78 B
Crescent Rd. Sid ....90 45 72 D
Crescent Rd SW20 ....95 23 69 B
Crescent Rise. Barn ....12 27 95 A
Crescent Rise. N22 ....24 29 90 B
Crescent Row. EC1 ....4 32 82 C
Crescent St. N1 ....47 30 84 D
Crescent The. Barn ....11 25 97 D
Crescent The. Beck ....98 37 69 A
Crescent The. Croy ....105 32 67 D
Crescent The. E17 ....36 36 88 A
Crescent The. E Mol ....92 13 68 C
Crescent The. Har ....32 14 87 C
Crescent The. Ilf ....40 43 88 C
Crescent The. N11 ....16 28 92 A
Crescent The. N Mal ....94 20 69 C
Crescent The. NW2 ....34 22 86 D
Crescent The. Sid ....90 45 71 B
Crescent The. Sthl ....59 12 79 B
Crescent The. Surb ....101 25 62 C
Crescent The. Sutt ....110 26 64 D
Crescent The. SW13 ....72 22 76 C
Crescent The. SW19 ....85 25 72 C
Crescent The. W3 ....55 21 81 C
Crescent The. Wem ....33 16 86 B
Crescent The. W.Wick ....107 39 67 C
Crescentway. N12 ....24 27 91 A
Crescent Way. SE4 ....76 37 75 A
Crescent Way. SW16 ....97 31 70 C
Crescent Way. Barn ....11 26 97 A
Crescent Wood Rd. SE26 ....87 34 72 C
Cresford Rd. SW6 ....73 25 76 B
Crespigny Rd. NW4 ....34 22 88 D
Cressage Cl. Sthl ....53 13 82 C
Cressent St. SW4 ....74 29 75 B
Cresset Rd. E9 ....49 35 84 A
Cressfield Cl. NW5 ....47 28 85 C
Cressida Rd. N19 ....36 29 87 C
Cressingham Gr. Sutt ....110 26 64 A
Cressingham Rd. Edg ....22 20 91 D
Cressingham Rd. SE13 ....76 38 75 A
Cressington Cl. N16 ....48 33 85 C
Cresswell Gdns. SW10 ....62 26 78 C
Cresswell Park. SE3 ....77 39 75 B
Cresswell Pl. SW10 ....62 26 78 C
Cresswell Rd. Felt ....82 12 71 A
Cresswell Rd. SE25 ....97 34 68 C
Cresswell Rd. Twick ....71 17 74 D
Cresswell Way. N21 ....17 31 94 A
Cressy Ct. E1 ....57 35 81 A
Cressy Ct. W6 ....61 22 79 D
Cressy Pl. E1 ....57 35 81 A
Cressy Rd. NW3 ....47 27 85 B
Cresta Ct. W5 ....54 18 82 D
Crestbrook Ave. N13 ....17 31 93 D
Crestfield St. WC1 ....3 30 82 A
Crest Gdns. Ruis ....32 11 86 C
Creston Way. Sutt ....103 23 66 D
Crest Rd. Brom ....107 39 66 B
Crest Rd. NW2 ....34 22 86 A
Crest Rd. S Croy ....112 34 63 D
Crest The. N13 ....17 31 92 A
Crest The. NW4 ....35 23 88 A
Crest The. Surb ....102 19 67 A
Crest View Dri. Orp ....108 44 67 A
Crest View. Pnr ....20 11 89 D
Crestway. SW15 ....72 22 74 D
Creswick Rd. W3 ....55 19 80 B
Creswick Wlk. E3 ....57 37 82 A
Creswick Wlk. NW11 ....23 24 89 D
Creton St. SE18 ....66 43 79 C
Crewdson Rd. SW9 ....63 31 77 C
Crewe Pl. NW10 ....55 21 82 B
Crews St. E14 ....64 37 78 A
Crewys Rd. NW2 ....36 24 86 B
Crewys Rd. SE15 ....75 34 76 D
Crichton Ave. Wall ....111 29 64 D
Cricketers Arms Rd. Enf ....13 32 97 C
Cricketers Ct. SE11 ....63 31 78 B
Cricketfield Rd. E5 ....49 34 85 B
Cricket Green. Mit ....98 27 68 D

Cricket Ground Rd. Chis ....100 43 69 B
Cricklade Ave. Rom ....30 53 91 B
Cricklade Ave. SW2 ....86 30 72 B
Cricklade Ave. SW2 ....87 31 72 A
Cricklewood Bwy. NW2 ....46 23 85 B
Cricklewood La. NW2 ....35 24 86 D
Cridland St. E15 ....50 39 83 B
Crieff Ct. Tedd ....93 17 70 C
Crieff Rd. SW18 ....73 26 74 C
Criffel Ave. SW2 ....86 29 72 B
Crimscott. SE1 ....8 33 79 C
Crimsworth Rd. SW8 ....10 29 77 D
Crinan St. N1 ....47 30 83 C
Cringle St. SW8 ....10 29 77 C
Cripplegate St. EC2 ....4 32 81 A
Crispen Rd. Felt ....82 12 71 A
Crispin Cl. Croy ....104 30 65 A
Crispin Cres. Croy ....104 29 65 B
Crispin Rd. Edg ....22 20 91 A
Crispin St. E1 ....4 33 81 B
Crisp Rd. W6 ....62 23 78 C
Cristowe Rd. SW6 ....73 24 76 D
Criterion Mews. N19 ....36 29 86 B
Crockerton Rd. SW17 ....86 27 72 B
Crockham Way. SE9 ....90 43 71 A
Crocus Field. Barn ....11 24 95 D
Crocus Wlk. W12 ....55 21 81 D
Croft Ave. W Wick ....106 38 66 C
Croft Cl. Belv ....67 48 78 D
Croft Cl. Chis ....89 42 71 D
Croftdown Rd. NW5 ....36 22 86 D
Crofters Cl. Islw ....70 14 74 B
Croft Gdns. Ruis ....31 09 87 D
Croft Gdns. W7 ....60 16 79 A
Croft Lodge Cl. Wdf Grn ....27 40 91 B
Crofton Ave. Orp ....108 44 65 A
Crofton La. Orp ....108 44 66 B
Crofton Park Rd. SE4 ....76 36 74 D
Crofton Rd. E13 ....58 40 82 D
Crofton Rd. Orp ....108 44 65 A
Crofton Rd. SE5 ....75 33 76 C
Crofton Terr. Rich ....71 18 75 D
Crofton Way. Barn ....11 25 95 D
Crofton Way. Enf ....13 31 97 C
Croft Rd. Brom ....99 40 70 A
Croft Rd. Enf ....14 36 97 A
Croft Rd. Sutt ....111 27 64 C
Croft Rd. SW16 ....97 31 70 C
Croft Rd. SW19 ....95 26 70 C
Crofts Rd. Har ....33 16 88 A
Crofts St. E1 ....57 34 80 A
Crofts The. Shep ....91 09 66 C
Croft St. SE8 ....64 36 78 A
Croft The. Barn ....11 24 96 C
Croft The. Edg ....22 19 90 B
Croft The. Houn ....59 12 77 C
Croft The. NW10 ....45 21 83 D
Croft The. Pnr ....32 12 87 B
Croft The. Ruis ....43 11 85 A
Croft The. W5 ....54 18 81 A
Croft The. Wem ....44 17 85 C
Croftway. NW3 ....46 25 85 A
Croft Way. Sid ....90 45 72 C
Crogsland Rd. NW1 ....47 28 84 C
Croham Cl. S Croy ....112 33 63 A
Croham Manor Rd. S Croy .....112 33 63 A
Croham Mount. S Croy ....112 33 63 C
Croham Park Ave. S Croy ....112 33 64 D
Croham Rd. S Croy ....112 33 64 C
Croham Valley Rd. S Croy ......112 34 63 C
Croindene Rd. SW16 ....96 30 69 A
Cromartie Rd. N19 ....36 29 87 B
Crombie Cl. Ilf ....39 42 88 B
Crombie Mews. SW11 ....74 27 76 C
Crombie Rd. Sid ....90 44 73 D
Cromer Pl. (off Andover Rd). Orp
..................................108 45 66 A
Cromer Rd. Barn ....11 26 96 A
Cromer Rd. E10 ....38 38 87 B
Cromer Rd. Horn ....42 53 87 B
Cromer Rd. Houn ....69 07 76 C
Cromer Rd. N17 ....25 34 90 C
Cromer Rd. Rom ....41 48 88 C
Cromer Rd. Rom ....41 50 83 C
Cromer Rd. SE25 ....97 34 68 B
Cromer Rd. SW17 ....96 28 70 A
Cromer Road W. Houn ....69 07 75 A
Cromer St. WC1 ....3 30 82 A
Cromer Terr. E8 ....48 34 85 C
Cromer Villas Rd. SW18 ....73 24 74 D
Cromford Cl. Orp ....108 45 65 C
Cromford Path. E5 ....49 35 85 B
Cromford Rd. SW18 ....73 24 74 A
Cromford Way. N Mal ....94 20 69 B
Cromlix Cl. Chis ....100 43 69 D

Crompton St. W2 ....1 26 82 D
Cromwell Ave. Brom ....99 40 68 D
Cromwell Ave. N6 ....36 28 87 D
Cromwell Ave. N.Mal ....102 21 67 B
Cromwell Ave. W6 ....61 22 78 B
Cromwell Cl. Brom ....99 40 68 D
Cromwell Cl. N2 ....23 26 89 D
Cromwell Cres. SW5 ....62 25 78 A
Cromwell Ct. Wem ....44 18 83 C
Cromwell Gdns. SW7 ....5 26 79 D
Cromwell Gr. W6 ....62 23 79 C
Cromwell Mews. SW7 ....62 26 78 B
Cromwell Pl. N6 ....36 28 87 D
Cromwell Pl. SW14 ....72 20 75 A
Cromwell Pl. SW7 ....62 26 78 B
Cromwell Rd. Beck ....98 36 68 A
Cromwell Rd. Croy ....105 32 66 B
Cromwell Rd. E17 ....38 38 88 A
Cromwell Rd. E7 ....50 41 84 C
Cromwell Rd. Felt ....81 10 73 D
Cromwell Rd. Houn ....70 13 75 C
Cromwell Rd. King ....93 17 69 D
Cromwell Rd. N10 ....24 28 91 C
Cromwell Rd. N3 ....23 26 90 A
Cromwell Rd. SW19 ....85 25 71 D
Cromwell Rd. SW5 ....62 25 78 B
Cromwell Rd. SW7 ....62 26 78 A
Cromwell Rd. SW9 ....75 31 76 B
Cromwell Rd. Tedd ....93 16 70 A
Cromwell Rd. Wem ....44 18 83 C
Cromwell Rd. Wor Pk ....102 21 65 C
Cromwell St. Houn ....70 13 75 C
Crondace Rd. SW6 ....73 25 76 A
Crondall Pl. N1 ....48 33 83 C
Crondall St. N1 ....48 33 83 C
Crooked Billet Yd. E2 ....4 33 82 A
Crooked Usage. N3 ....23 24 89 A
Crooke Rd. SE8 ....64 36 78 C
Crookham Rd. SW6 ....73 24 76 B
Crook Log. Bexh ....79 47 75 B
Crookston Rd. SE9 ....78 43 75 A
Croombs Rd. E16 ....58 41 81 A
Croom's Hill Gr. SE10 ....64 38 77 C
Croom's Hill. SE10 ....64 38 77 C
Cropley St. N1 ....48 32 83 D
Croppath Rd. Dag ....52 49 85 A
Crosby Cl. Felt ....82 12 71 A
Crosby Rd. Dag ....52 49 83 B
Crosby Row. SE1 ....8 32 79 B
Crosby Wlk. E8 ....48 33 84 B
Crosby Wlk. SE24 ....87 31 73 A
Crosier Way. Ruis ....31 09 86 A
Crossbrook Rd. SE3 ....77 42 75 A
Cross Deep Gdns. Twick ....83 15 72 B
Cross Deep. Twick ....83 16 72 A
Crossfield Rd. N17 ....25 32 89 A
Crossfield Rd. NW3 ....46 26 84 B
Crossfield St. SE8 ....64 37 77 C
Crossford St. SW9 ....74 30 76 D
Crossgate. Grnf ....44 16 84 B
Cross Key Ct. EC2 ....4 32 81 D
Cross Keys Cl. W1 ....2 28 81 A
Cross Keys Sq. EC1 ....4 32 81 A
Cross La. EC3 ....8 33 80 A
Cross La. N8 ....24 30 89 D
Cross Lances Rd. Houn ....70 13 75 D
Crossland Rd. Th Hth ....105 31 67 D
Crosslands Ave. Sthl ....59 12 78 D
Crosslands Ave. W5 ....54 18 80 D
Crosslands Rd. Eps ....109 20 63 B
Crosslet St. SE17 ....63 32 78 B
Crossley St. N7 ....48 31 84 A
Crossmead Ave. Grnf ....53 13 82 B
Crossmead. SE9 ....89 42 73 D
Cross Rd. Brom ....107 42 65 A
Cross Rd. Croy ....105 32 66 D
Cross Rd. Dart ....80 53 74 C
Cross Rd. Enf ....13 33 96 C
Cross Rd. Har ....32 13 86 D
Cross Rd. Har ....32 14 88 B
Cross Rd. Har ....21 16 90 C
Cross Rd. King ....93 18 70 D
Cross Rd. N11 ....16 28 92 D
Cross Rd. N22 ....25 31 91 C
Cross Rd. N2 ....24 27 90 C
Cross Rd. Orp ....108 46 67 B
Cross Rd. Rom ....41 47 87 A
Cross Rd. Rom ....29 49 89 B
Cross Rd. SE5 ....75 33 76 C
Cross Rd. Sid ....90 46 71 B
Cross Rd. Sutt ....110 25 62 C
Cross Rd. Sutt ....110 26 64 D
Cross Rd. SW19 ....95 25 70 C

Cross Rd. Wdf Gn ...27 42 91 B
Cross St. Eri ...68 51 77 A
Cross St. Hamp ...82 14 71 C
Cross St. N18 ...17 34 92 C
Cross St. N1 ...48 31 83 B
Cross St. SW13 ...72 21 75 B
Crossthwaite Ave. SE5 ...75 32 75 D
Crosswall. EC3 ...8 33 80 B
Crossway Ct. SE4 ...76 36 76 C
Crossway. Dag ...41 47 86 C
Crossway. Enf ...17 33 94 A
Crossway. N12 ...23 26 91 B
Crossway. N16 ...48 33 85 C
Crossway. NW9 ...22 21 89 D
Crossway. NW9 ...22 21 89 D
Crossway. Orp ...100 44 68 D
Crossway. Pnr ...19 10 90 D
Crossway. Ruis ...43 11 85 A
Crossways Rd. Beck ...98 37 68 C
Crossways Rd. Mit ...96 28 68 B
Crossways. Rom ...30 52 99 B
Crossways. Sutt ...110 26 62 B
Crossways The. Houn ...59 12 77 D
Crossways The. Wem ...34 19 86 A
Crossway. SW20 ...95 23 68 C
Cross Way Rd. Har ...21 15 90 D
Crossway The. N22 ...25 31 91 D
Crossway The. SE9 ...89 41 72 B
Crossway. W3 ...54 16 82 C
Crosswell Cl. Shep ...91 08 69 C
Croston St. E8 ...48 34 83 A
Crouch Ave. Bark ...51 46 83 D
Crouch Cl. Beck ...98 37 70 A
Crouch Croft. SE9 ...90 43 72 C
Crouch End Hill. N8 ...36 29 88 D
Crouch Hall Ct. N19 ...36 30 87 C
Crouch Hall Rd. N8 ...36 29 88 D
Crouch Hill. N4 ...36 30 87 A
Crouch Hill. N8 ...36 30 88 C
Crouchmans Cl. SE26 ...87 34 72 C
Crouch Rd. NW10 ...45 20 84 D
Crowborough Rd. SW17 ...86 28 71 C
Crowder St. E1 ...57 34 80 B
Crowhurst Cl. SW9 ...75 31 76 C
Crowland Gdns. N14 ...16 29 94 A
Crowland Rd. N15 ...37 33 88 B
Crowland Rd. Th Hth ...97 32 68 D
Crowlands Ave. Rom ...41 49 88 D
Crowland Terr. N1 ...48 32 84 D
Crowland Wk. Mord ...103 26 67 C
Crow La. Rom ...41 49 87 B
Crowley Cres. Croy ...112 31 64 C
Crowline Wlk. N1 ...48 32 84 A
Crowmarsh Gdns. SE23 ...88 35 73 A
Crown Cl. E3 ...49 37 83 A
Crown Cl. NW3 ...46 25 84 B
Crown Ct. EC4 ...4 32 81 C
Crown Ct. SE12 ...77 40 74 D
Crown Ct. WC2 ...3 30 81 C
Crowndale Rd. NW1 ...7 29 83 C
Crown Dale. SE19 ...97 32 70 A
Crown Dale. SE19 ...97 32 71 C
Crownfield Ave. Ilf ...40 45 88 A
Crownfield Rd. E15 ...49 38 85 B
Crown Hill. Croy ...105 32 65 A
Crownhill Rd. NW10 ...45 21 83 B
Crownhill Rd. Wdf Gn ...27 42 91 C
Crown La. SW16 ...87 31 71 C
Crown La. Brom ...107 42 67 A
Crown La. Chis ...100 44 69 A
Crown La. Mord ...95 25 68 B
Crown La. N14 ...16 29 94 C
Crown Lane Gdns. SW16 ...87 31 71 C
Crown Lane Spur. Brom ...107 41 67 D
Crownmead Way. Rom ...49 89 D
Crown Office Row. EC4 ...7 31 80 A
Crown Pas. King ...93 17 69 D
Crown Pas. SW1 ...6 29 80 C
Crown Pl. NW5 ...47 28 84 B
Crown Rd. Enf ...13 34 96 D
Crown Rd. Ilf ...28 44 89 D
Crown Rd. Mord ...95 25 68 D
Crown Rd. N10 ...24 28 91 C
Crown Rd. N Mal ...94 20 69 A
Crown Rd. Sutt ...110 25 64 B
Crown Rd. Twick ...71 16 74 D
Crown St. Dag ...52 50 84 A
Crown St. Har ...33 15 87 C
Crownstone Rd. SW2 ...75 31 74 A
Crown St. SE5 ...63 32 77 C
Crown St. W3 ...55 19 80 D
Crown Terr. Rich ...18 75 D
Crown Wlk. Wem ...33 18 86 D
Crown Woods Way. SE9 ...78 44 74 B
Crown Works. E2 ...48 34 83 D

Crown Yd. Houn ...70 14 75 A
Crowshott Ave. Stan ...21 17 90 B
Crows Rd. E15 ...58 38 82 B
Crowther Ave. Brent ...60 18 78 A
Crowther Rd. SE25 ...97 34 68 C
Crowthorne Cl. SW18 ...85 24 73 D
Crowthorne Rd. W10 ...56 23 81 D
Croxden Cl. Edg ...22 19 89 A
Croxden Wlk. Mord ...103 26 67 C
Croxford Gdns. N22 ...25 32 91 C
Croxford Way. Rom ...41 50 87 D
Croxley Cl. Orp ...100 46 69 D
Croxley Green. Orp ...100 46 69 B
Croxley Rd. W9 ...56 24 82 B
Croxted Cl. SE21 ...87 32 73 A
Croxted Rd. SE21 ...87 32 73 D
Croyde Ave. Grnf ...53 14 82 A
Croyde Cl. Sid ...90 44 73 B
Croydon Fly The. Croy ...105 32 65 C
Croydon Gr. Croy ...105 31 66 D
Croydon Rd. Beck ...98 36 68 B
Croydon Rd. Brom ...107 41 65 D
Croydon Rd. E13 ...58 39 82 D
Croydon Rd. Houn ...69 07 75 B
Croydon Rd. Mit ...104 28 67 B
Croydon Rd. SE20 ...98 35 69 A
Croydon Rd. Wall ...104 29 65 D
Croydon Rd. W.Wick ...107 39 65 D
Croyland Rd. N9 ...34 94 C
Croylands Dri. Surb ...101 18 66 A
Croysdale Ave. Sun ...91 10 68 A
Crozier Dri. S Croy ...112 34 62 D
Crozier Terr. E9 ...49 35 85 D
Crucifix La. SE1 ...8 33 79 A
Cruden St. N1 ...48 31 83 B
Cruchton Rd. Cars ...111 27 63 D
Cruikshank St. WC1 ...3 31 82 A
Cruikshank Rd. E15 ...50 39 85 D
Crummock Gdns. NW9 ...24 21 88 A
Crumpsall St. SE2 ...67 47 78 A
Crundale Ave. NW9 ...24 19 88 A
Crunden Rd. S Croy ...112 32 63 D
Crusader Gdns. Croy ...105 33 65 C
Crusoe Rd. Eri ...67 50 78 D
Crusoe Rd. Mit ...96 27 70 D
Crutched Friars. EC3 ...8 33 80 A
Cruthchley Rd. SE6 ...89 39 72 A
Crystal Ave. Horn ...42 54 86 C
Crystal Palace Park Rd. SE26 ...87 34 70 B
Crystal Palace Park Rd. SE26 ...87 34 71 D
Crystal Palace Par. SE19 ...87 33 71 D
Crystal Palace Rd. SE22 ...75 34 74 A
Crystal Palace Station Rd. SE19
...97 34 70 A
Crystal Terr. SE19 ...97 32 70 B
Cuba Dri. Enf ...14 35 97 C
Cuba St. E14 ...64 37 79 A
Cubitt St. WC1 ...3 30 82 B
Cubitt St. Croy ...111 30 64 D
Cubitt Terr. SW4 ...74 29 75 A
Cuckoo Ave. W7 ...54 15 81 A
Cuckoo Dene. W7 ...54 15 81 A
Cuckoo Hall La. N9 ...18 35 94 A
Cuckoo Hill Dri. Pnr ...20 11 89 A
Cuckoo Hill. Pnr ...20 11 89 A
Cuckoo Hill Rd. Pnr ...20 11 89 D
Cuckoo La. W7 ...54 15 80 A
Cuda's Cl. Eps ...109 21 64 B
Cuddington Ave. Wor Pk ...102 21 65 D
Cuddington Way. Sutt ...110 24 62 C
Cudham St. SE6 ...38 73 A
Cudworth St. E1 ...57 34 82 D
Cuff Cres. SE9 ...77 41 74 D
Culford Gdns. SW3 ...9 27 78 B
Culford Gr. N1 ...48 33 84 A
Culford Mews. N1 ...48 33 84 A
Culford Rd. N1 ...48 33 84 C
Culgaith Gdns. Enf ...12 30 96 C
Cullen Way. NW10 ...55 20 82 C
Culling Rd. SE16 ...64 35 79 C
Cullington Cl. Har ...21 16 89 C
Cullingworth Rd. NW10 ...45 22 85 D
Culloden Rd. Enf ...13 31 97 D
Culloden St. E14 ...58 38 81 C
Cullum St. EC3 ...8 33 80 A
Culmington Rd. S Croy ...112 32 62 A
Culmington Rd. W13 ...54 17 80 C
Culmore Cross. SW12 ...86 28 73 D
Culmore Rd. SE15 ...64 35 77 C
Culmstock Rd. SW11 ...74 28 74 A
Culpeper Cl. Ilf ...28 43 91 B
Culpeper St. N1 ...48 31 83 C
Culross Cl. N15 ...25 32 89 C
Culross St. W1 ...6 28 80 A
Culsac Rd. Surb ...101 18 65 A

Culverden Gdns. SW12 ...86 29 72 A
Culver Gr. Stan ...21 17 90 D
Culverhouse Gdns. SW16 ...86 30 72 D
Culverley Rd. SE6 ...88 38 73 C
Culvers Ave. Cars ...104 27 65 B
Culvers Retreat. Cars ...104 27 65 B
Culverstone Cl. Brom ...107 39 67 D
Culvers Way. Cars ...104 27 65 B
Culvert Pl. SW11 ...74 28 76 C
Culvert Rd. N15 ...37 33 88 A
Culvert Rd. SW11 ...74 27 76 D
Culworth St. NW8 ...47 27 83 C
Cumberland Ave. Horn ...42 54 86 C
Cumberland Ave. NW10 ...55 19 82 B
Cumberland Ave. Well ...78 45 75 D
Cumberland Cl. Eps ...109 21 62 C
Cumberland Cl. Horn ...42 54 86 C
Cumberland Cl. SW20 ...95 23 70 D
Cumberland Cl. Twick ...71 16 74 D
Cumberland Cres. W14 ...62 24 78 A
Cumberland Dri. Bexh ...67 48 77 C
Cumberland Dri. Chess ...101 18 65 D
Cumberland Dri. Esh ...101 16 65 A
Cumberland Gate. W1 ...5 27 80 B
Cumberland Gdns. NW4 ...23 24 90 C
Cumberland Gdns. WC1 ...3 31 82 A
Cumberland Market. NW1 ...2 28 82 B
Cumberland Park. W3 ...55 20 80 A
Cumberland Pl. NW1 ...2 28 82 B
Cumberland Pl. Sun ...91 10 68 C
Cumberland Rd. Brom ...99 39 68 B
Cumberland Rd. E12 ...50 41 85 B
Cumberland Rd. E13 ...58 40 82 D
Cumberland Rd. E17 ...26 36 90 C
Cumberland Rd. Har ...32 13 88 B
Cumberland Rd. N22 ...24 30 90 D
Cumberland Rd. N9 ...18 35 94 C
Cumberland Rd. Rich ...61 19 77 C
Cumberland Rd. SE25 ...105 34 67 D
Cumberland Rd. Stan ...18 89 B
Cumberland Rd. SW13 ...72 22 76 A
Cumberland Rd. W3 ...55 20 80 A
Cumberland Rd. W7 ...60 15 79 B
Cumberland St. SW1 ...9 28 78 D
Cumberland Terrace Mews. NW1
...47 28 83 D
Cumberland Terr. NW1 ...2 28 83 D
Cumberlow Ave. SE25 ...97 34 68 A
Cumbernauld Gdns. Sun ...81 09 71 D
Cumberton Rd. N17 ...25 32 90 B
Cumbrae Gdns. Surb ...101 17 65 B
Cumbrian Ave. Bexh ...80 51 76 C
Cumbrian Gdns. NW2 ...35 24 86 A
Cumming St. N1 ...47 30 83 D
Cumnor Gdns. Eps ...109 22 63 A
Cumnor Rd. Sutt ...110 26 63 A
Cunard Rd. NW10 ...55 20 82 B
Cunard St. SE5 ...63 33 77 A
Cundy Rd. E16 ...58 41 81 C
Cundy St. SW1 ...9 28 78 A
Cunliffe Rd. Wor Pk ...109 21 64 B
Cunliffe St. SW16 ...96 29 70 A
Cunningham Cl. W Wick ...106 37 65 B
Cunningham Park. Har ...32 14 88 B
Cunningham Pl. NW8 ...1 26 82 D
Cunningham Rd. N15 ...25 34 89 C
Cunnington St. W4 ...61 20 78 A
Cupar Rd. SW11 ...74 28 76 A
Cupola Cl. Brom ...89 40 71 D
Cureton St. SW1 ...10 29 78 B
Curlew St. SE1 ...8 33 79 B
Curnick's La. SE27 ...87 32 71 A
Curran Ave. Sid ...78 45 74 B
Curran Ave. Wall ...104 28 65 C
Currey Rd. Grnf ...43 14 84 B
Curricle St. W3 ...55 21 80 C
Currie Hill Cl. SW19 ...85 24 71 B
Curry Rise. NW7 ...23 23 91 B
Cursitor St. EC4 ...3 31 81 C
Curtain Pl. EC2 ...33 82 C
Curtain Rd. EC2 ...33 82 C
Curthwaite Gdns. Enf ...12 29 95 B
Curtis Field Rd. SW16 ...87 31 71 A
Curtismill Cl. Orp ...100 46 68 B
Curtismill Way. Orp ...100 46 68 B
Curtis Rd. Eps ...109 20 64 A
Curtis Rd. Horn ...42 54 87 B
Curtis Rd. Houn ...82 12 73 B
Curtis St. SE1 ...63 33 78 B
Curtis Way. SE1 ...63 33 78 B
Curvan Cl. Eps ...109 21 62 D
Curve The. W12 ...55 22 80 A
Curwen Ave. E7 ...50 40 85 B
Curwen Rd. W12 ...61 22 79 A
Curzon Ave. Enf ...14 35 95 B

Curzon Ave. Stan ....21 16 90 A
Curzon Cres. Bark ....51 45 83 D
Curzon Cres. NW10 ....45 21 84 C
Curzon Gate. W1 ....6 28 80 C
Curzon Pl. Pnr ....32 11 88 A
Curzon Pl. W1 ....6 28 80 C
Curzon Rd. N10 ....24 28 90 D
Curzon Rd. Th Hth ....105 31 67 C
Curzon Rd. W5 ....54 16 82 D
Curzon St. W1 ....6 28 80 D
Cusack Cl. Twick ....83 15 71 B
Cutcombe Rd. SE5 ....76 37 76 C
Cuthbert Rd. Croy ....105 31 65 B
Cuthbert Rd. E17 ....26 38 89 A
Cuthbert Rd. N18 ....17 34 92 C
Cuthbert St. W2 ....1 26 82 D
Cutlers Gdns. EC2 ....4 33 81 C
Cutler St. E1 ....4 33 81 C
Cut. The SE1 ....7 31 79 A
Cuxton Cl. Bexh ....79 48 74 A
Cyclamen Way. Eps ....109 20 64 C
Cygnet Ave. Felt ....82 11 73 B
Cygnet Cl. Nthwd ....19 08 91 A
Cygnet St. E1 ....4 33 82 D
Cygnets The. Felt ....82 12 71 A
Cynthia St. N1 ....47 30 83 D
Cyntra Pl. E8 ....48 34 84 D
Cypress Ave. Twick ....82 14 73 A
Cypress Gr. Ilf ....45 45 91 A
Cypress Path. Rom ....30 53 91 D
Cypress Pl. W1 ....2 29 82 C
Cypress Rd. Har ....20 14 90 D
Cypress Rd. SE25 ....97 33 69 C
Cypress Rd. Sun ....91 09 69 A
Cyprus Ave. N3 ....23 24 90 C
Cyprus Gdns. N3 ....23 24 90 C
Cyprus Pl. E2 ....49 35 83 C
Cyprus Rd. N3 ....23 24 90 D
Cyprus Rd. N9 ....17 33 93 B
Cyprus St (off Bonner St). E2 ....49 35 83 C
Cyprus St (off Globe Rd). E2 ....49 35 83 C
Cyrena Rd. SE22 ....75 33 74 B
Cyril Rd. Bexh ....79 48 76 C
Cyril Rd. Orp ....108 44 66 A
Cyrus St. EC1 ....3 31 82 D
Czar St. SE8 ....64 37 77 A

Dabbs Hill La. Nthlt ....43 12 85 D
Dabin Cres. SE10 ....76 38 76 A
Dacca St. SE8 ....64 36 77 B
Dace Rd. E3 ....49 37 83 A
Dacre Ave. Ilf ....28 43 90 C
Dacre Cl. Grnf ....33 13 83 D
Dacre Gdns. SE13 ....77 39 75 C
Dacre Park. SE13 ....77 39 75 A
Dacre Pl. SE13 ....77 39 75 A
Dacre Rd. Croy ....104 30 66 A
Dacre Rd. E11 ....39 39 87 D
Dacre Rd. E13 ....50 40 83 B
Dacres Rd. SE23 ....88 35 72 D
Dacre St. SW1 ....6 29 79 D
Daerwood Cl. Brom ....107 42 66 D
Daffodil St. W12 ....55 21 80 B
Dafforne Rd. SW17 ....86 28 72 C
Dagenham Ave. Dag ....52 48 84 D
Dagenham Rd. E10 ....38 36 87 D
Dagenham Rd. Rain ....52 50 84 D
Dagenham Rd. Rom ....41 50 87 D
Dagmar Ave. Wem ....44 18 85 B
Dagmar Ct. E14 ....64 38 79 C
Dagmar Gdns. NW10 ....46 23 83 D
Dagmar Mews. Sthl ....59 12 79 C
Dagmar Pas. N1 ....48 31 83 B
Dagmar Rd. Dag ....52 50 84 C
Dagmar Rd. King ....93 18 69 B
Dagmar Rd. N4 ....31 31 87 A
Dagmar Rd. SE25 ....105 33 67 A
Dagmar Rd. SE5 ....33 76 A
Dagmar Rd. Sthl ....59 12 79 C
Dagmar Terr. N1 ....48 31 83 B
Dagnall Park. SE25 ....105 33 67 A
Dagnall Rd. SE25 ....105 33 67 A
Dagnall St. SW11 ....74 28 76 A
Dagnan Rd. SW12 ....86 29 73 A
Dagonet Gdns. Brom ....89 40 72 C
Dagonet Rd. Brom ....89 40 72 C
Dahlia Gdns. Mit ....96 29 68 D
Dahlia Rd. SE2 ....66 46 78 B
Dahomey Rd. SW16 ....96 29 70 A
Daimler Way. Wall ....111 30 63 C
Daines Cl. E12 ....39 42 86 D
Dainford Cl. Brom ....88 38 71 D
Dainton Cl. Brom ....89 40 69 B
Daintry Way. E9 ....49 36 84 B
Dairsie Rd. SE9 ....78 43 75 A

Dairy Wlk. SW19 ....85 24 71 A
Daisy La. SW6 ....73 25 75 A
Daisy Rd. E18 ....27 40 90 D
Dakota Gdns (off Argus Way).
  Nthlt ....53 12 82 A
Dalberg Rd. SW2 ....75 31 74 A
Dalberg Way. Belv ....67 47 79 D
Dalby Rd. SW18 ....73 26 75 C
Dalby St. NW5 ....47 28 84 B
Dalcross Rd. Houn ....70 12 76 C
Dale Ave. Edg ....21 18 90 D
Dale Ave. Houn ....70 12 75 A
Dalebury Rd. SW17 ....86 27 72 B
Dale Cl. Barn ....11 25 95 D
Dale Cl. Dart ....80 51 74 D
Dale Cl. Pnr ....19 10 90 B
Dale Cl. SE3 ....77 40 75 A
Dale Ct. King ....93 18 70 D
Dale End. Dart ....80 51 74 D
Dale Green Rd. N11 ....16 28 93 D
Dale Gr. N12 ....15 26 92 C
Daleham Gdns. NW3 ....46 26 84 B
Daleham Mews. NW3 ....46 26 84 B
Dale Park Ave. Cars ....104 27 65 B
Dale Park Rd.SE19 ....97 32 69 B
Dale Rd. Dart ....80 51 74 D
Dale Rd. E16 ....58 39 81 A
Dale Rd. Grnf ....53 -13 81 B
Dale Rd. NW5 ....47 28 85 C
Dale Rd. SE17 ....63 31 77 B
Dale Rd. Sun ....91 09 70 D
Dale Rd. Sutt ....110 24 64 B
Daleside Rd. Eps ....109 20 63 B
Daleside Rd. SW16 ....86 28 71 D
Dale St. W4 ....61 21 78 C
Dale The. Brom ....107 41 65 D
Dale View Ave. E4 ....18 38 93 A
Dale View Cres. E4 ....18 38 93 C
Dale View. Eri ....80 51 76 D
Dale View Gdns. E4 ....18 38 93 D
Daleview Rd. N15 ....37 33 88 C
Dalewood Cl. Horn ....42 54 87 A
Dalewood Gdns. Wor Pk ....102 22 65 B
Dale Wood Rd. Orp ....108 45 66 C
Daley St. E9 ....49 35 84 B
Dalgarno Gdns. W10 ....56 23 81 A
Dalgarno Way. W10 ....56 23 82 C
Dalgleish St. E14 ....57 36 81 C
Daling Way. E3 ....49 36 83 C
Dalkeith Rd. Ilf ....40 44 86 C
Dalkeith Rd. SE21 ....87 32 73 A
Dallas Rd. NW4 ....34 22 87 A
Dallas Rd. SE26 ....87 34 72 D
Dallas Rd. Sutt ....110 24 63 A
Dallas Rd. W5 ....54 18 81 B
Dallinger Rd. SE12 ....77 39 74 D
Dalling Rd. W6 ....61 22 79 D
Dallington St. EC1 ....3 31 82 D
Dallin Rd. Bexh ....79 47 75 D
Dallin Rd. SE18 ....66 43 77 D
Dalmain Rd. SE23 ....88 35 73 D
Dalmally Pas. Croy ....105 33 66 B
Dalmally Rd. Croy ....105 34 66 A
Dalmeny Ave. N7 ....47 29 85 D
Dalmeny Ave. SW16 ....97 31 69 C
Dalmeny Cl. Wem ....44 17 84 A
Dalmeny Cres. Houn ....70 14 75 D
Dalmeny Rd. Barn ....11 26 95 D
Dalmeny Rd. Bexh ....79 49 76 B
Dalmeny Rd. N7 ....47 29 85 B
Dalmeny Rd. Wor Pk ....102 22 65 D
Dalmore Rd. SE21 ....87 32 72 A
Dalrymple Rd. SE4 ....77 36 75 C
Dalston Gdns. Stan ....21 18 90 A
Dalston La. E8 ....48 34 85 C
Dalton Ave. Mit ....96 27 69 D
Dalton Cl. Dart ....80 51·75 B
Dalton Cl. Orp ....108 45 65 C
Dalton St. SE27 ....87 31 72 D
Dalwood St. SE5 ....75 33 76 A
Dalyell Rd. SW9 ....74 30 75 B
Damer Terr. SW10 ....62 26 77 C
Dames Rd. E7 ....50 40 85 A
Dame St. N1 ....48 32 83 C
Damien St. E1 ....57 34 81 D
Damon Cl. Sid ....90 46 72 D
Damsonwood Cl. Sthl ....59 13 79 C
Danbrook Rd. SW16 ....96 30 70 C
Danbury Cl. Rom ....47 89 B
Danbury Mews. Wall ....111 28 64 B
Danbury St. N1 ....48 31 83 D
Danbury Way. Wdf Gn ....27 41 91 A
Danby St. SE15 ....75 33 75 B
Dancer Rd. Rich ....72 19 75 A

Dancer Rd. SW6 ....73 24 76 B
Dando Cres. SE3 ....77 40 75 B
Danebury Ave. SW15 ....84 22 73 A
Daneby Rd. SE6 ....88 38 72 A
Danecourt Gdns. Croy ....105 33 65 D
Danecroft Rd.SE24 ....75 32 74 B
Danehill Wlk. Sid ....90 46 72 C
Danehurst Gdns. Ilf ....39 42 88 B
Danehurst St. SW6 ....73 24 76 A
Daneland. Barn ....12 27 95 D
Danemead Gr. Nthlt ....43 13 85 D
Danemere St. SW15 ....73 23 75 A
Dane Pl. E3 ....49 36 83 D
Dane Rd. Ashf ....91 08 70 B
Dane Rd. Ilf ....51 44 85 C
Dane Rd. N18 ....18 35 93 C
Dane Rd. Sthl ....53 12 80 A
Dane Rd. SW19 ....95 26 69 A
Dane Rd. W13 ....54 17 80 C
Danesbury Rd. Felt ....81 10 73 D
Danescourt Cres. Sutt ....103 26 65 A
Danescroft Ave. NW4 ....35 23 88 B
Danescroft Gdns. NW4 ....35 23 88 B
Danescroft. NW4 ....35 23 88 B
Danes Ct. Wem ....34 19 86 D
Danesdale Rd. E9 ....49 36 84 A
Danes Gate. Har ....21 15 89 A
Danesdale Rd. Rom ....41 50 87 A
Dane St. WC1 ....3 30 81 B
Daneswood Ave. SE6 ....88 38 72 C
Danethorpe Rd. Wem ....44 17 84 B
Danetree Rd. Eps ....109 20 63 D
Danette Gdns. Dag ....41 48 86 B
Daneville Rd. SE5 ....75 32 76 B
Dangan Rd. E11 ....39 40 88 C
Daniel Bolt Cl. E14 ....57 37 81 B
Daniel Pl. NW4 ....34 22 87 B
Daniel Rd. W5 ....54 18 80 B
Daniel's Rd. SE15 ....76 35 75 A
Dan Leno Wlk. SW6 ....62 25 77 D
Dansey Pl. W1 ....6 29 80 B
Dansington Rd. Well ....78 46 75 C
Danson Cres. Well ....78 46 75 B
Danson La. Well ....78 46 75 D
Danson Mead. Well ....79 47 75 A
Danson Rd. Bex ....79 47 74 B
Danson Rd. Bexh ....79 47 74 B
Danson Rd. Bex ....79 47 75 D
Danson Underpass. Sid ....79 47 74 C
Dante Rd. SE11 ....63 31 78 B
Danube St. SW3 ....9 27 78 C
Danvers Rd. N8 ....24 29 89 D
Danvers St. SW3 ....62 26 77 B
Daphne Gdns. E4 ....18 38 93 C
Daphne St. SW18 ....85 26 73 A
Daphne St. SW18 ....73 26 74 C
Daplyn St. E1 ....57 34 81 A
D'arblay St. W1 ....2 29 81 C
Darby Cres. Sun ....92 11 69 C
Darby Gdns. Sun ....92 11 69 C
Darcy Ave. Wall ....111 29 64 A
D'Arcy Dri. Har ....21 17 89 D
D'Arcy Gdns. Dag ....52 48 83 B
D'arcy Gdns. Har ....21 18 89 C
D'Arcy Rd. Sutt ....110 23 64 B
Darcy Rd. SW16 ....96 30 69 C
Dare Gdns. Dag ....41 48 86 C
Darell Rd. Rich ....72 19 75 A
Darenth Rd. N16 ....37 33 87 D
Darenth Rd. Well ....78 46 76 A
Darfield Rd. SE4 ....76 36 74 B
Darfield Way. W10 ....56 23 81 D
Darfur St. SW15 ....73 23 75 B
Dargate Cl. SE19 ....97 33 70 D
Darien Rd. SW11 ....73 26 75 D
Darke St. WC1 ....3 30 81 B
Darlan Rd. SW6 ....54 24 77 D
Darlaston Rd. SW19 ....95 23 70 D
Darley Cl. Croy ....106 36 67 C
Darley Dri. N Mal ....94 20 69 D
Darley Rd. N9 ....17 33 94 D
Darley Rd. SW11 ....74 27 74 D
Darling Rd. SE4 ....76 37 75 A
Darling Row. E1 ....57 34 82 D
Darlington Rd. SE27 ....87 31 71 D
Darnley Rd. E9 ....49 35 84 A
Darnley Rd. Wdf Gn ....27 40 90 B
Darnley Terr. W11 ....56 23 80 D
Darrell Rd. SE22 ....75 34 74 A
Darren Cl. N4 ....36 30 87 B
Darrick Wood Rd. Orp ....108 44 65 B
Darsley Dri. SW8 ....74 30 76 A
Dartfields. Rom ....30 53 91 B
Dartford Ave. Enf ....14 35 95 D
Dartford Hse. SE1 ....63 33 78 B

Dartford Rd. Dart....80 52 74 D
Dartford St. SE17....63 32 77 A
Dartmouth Cl. W11....56 24 81 D
Dartmouth Ct. SE10....76 38 76 B
Dartmouth Gr. SE10....76 38 76 A
Dartmouth Hill. SE10....76 38 76 A
Dartmouth Park Ave. NW5....36 28 86 D
Dartmouth Park Hill. N19....36 28 86 B
Dartmouth Park Hill. NW5....36 28 86 D
Dartmouth Park Rd. NW5....36 28 86 D
Dartmouth Pl. SE23....88 35 72 A
Dartmouth Pl. W4....61 21 77 A
Dartmouth Rd. Brom....107 40 66 A
Dartmouth Rd. E16....58 40 81 C
Dartmouth Rd. NW2....46 23 84 B
Dartmouth Rd. NW4....34 22 88 C
Dartmouth Rd. Ruis....31 10 86 C
Dartmouth Rd. SE23....88 35 72 A
Dartmouth Rd. SE26....88 35 72 C
Dartmouth Row. SE10....76 38 76 A
Dartmouth St. SW1....6 29 79 B
Dartmouth Terr. SE10....76 38 76 B
Dartnell Rd. Croy....105 33 66 B
Dartrey Wlk. SW10....62 26 77 C
Dart St. W10....56 24 82 B
Darville Rd. N16....37 33 86 D
Darwell Cl. E6....51 43 83 C
Darwin Ct. E13....58 40 82 B
Darwin Ct. NW1....47 28 83 A
Darwin Dri. Sthl....53 13 81 D
Darwin Rd. N22....25 31 90 D
Darwin Rd. W5....6 17 78 A
Darwin Rd. Well....78 45 75 B
Darwin St. SE17....63 32 78 B
Daryngton Dri. Grnf....44 15 83 C
Dashwood Cl. Bexh....79 49 74 A
Dashwood Rd. N8....36 30 88 D
Dassett Rd. SE27....87 31 71 D
Datchelor Pl. SE5....75 32 76 B
Datchet Rd. SE6....88 36 72 B
Date St. SE17....63 32 78 D
Daubeney Rd. E5....49 36 85 A
Daubeney Rd. N17....25 32 91 C
Dault Rd. SW18....73 26 74 C
Davenant Rd. N19....36 29 66 B
Davenant St. E1....57 34 81 A
Davenport Rd. SE6....76 38 74 C
Daventry Ave. E17....38 37 88 C
Daventry Rd. Rom....30 52 91 A
Daventry St. NW1....1 27 81 A
Davern Cl. E10....65 39 78 B
Davey Cl. N7....47 30 84 B
Davey Rd. E9....49 37 84 C
Davey St. SE15....63 33 77 B
David Ave. Grnf....54 15 82 A
David Coffer Ct. Belv....67 49 78 B
Davidge St. SE1....7 31 79 B
David Mews. W1....6 28 81 A
David Rd. Dag....41 48 86 A
Davidson Gdns. SW8....10 30 77 C
Davidson Rd. Croy....105 33 67 D
David's Rd. SE23....88 35 73 C
David St. E15....49 38 84 B
Davids Way. Ilf....28 45 91 C
Davies La. E11....39 39 86 B
Davies Mews. W1....6 28 80 B
Davies St. W1....6 28 80 B
Davington Gdns. Dag....51 46 85 D
Davington Rd. Dag....51 46 85 D
Davinia Cl. Wdf Gn....27 42 91 B
Davis Rd. Chess....109 19 64 A
Davis Rd. W3....61 21 79 B
Davis St. E13....50 41 83 C
Davisville Rd. W12....61 22 79 A
Dawes Ave. Horn....42 54 86 C
Dawes Ave. Islw....71 16 75 C
Dawes Rd. SW6....62 24 77 D
Dawes St. SE17....63 32 78 D
Dawlish Ave. Grnf....44 16 83 C
Dawlish Ave. N13....16 30 92 A
Dawlish Ave. SW18....85 25 72 B
Dawlish Dri. Ilf....51 45 85 B
Dawlish Dri. Pnr....32 12 88 C
Dawlish Dri. Ruis....31 10 86 B
Dawlish Rd. E10....38 38 86 A
Dawlish Rd. N17....25 34 89 A
Dawlish Rd. NW2....46 23 84 B
Dawlish Wlk. Rom....30 53 90 A
Dawnay Gdns. SW18....85 26 72 B
Dawnay Rd. SW18....85 26 72 B
Dawpool Rd. NW2....34 21 86 B
Daws Hill. Enf....14 38 96 A
Dawson Ave. Bark....51 45 84 D
Dawson Ave. Orp....100 46 69 D
Dawson Cl. SE18....66 44 78 A

Dawson Gdns. Bark....51 45 84 D
Dawson Pl. W2....56 25 80 A
Dawson Rd. King....93 18 68 B
Dawson Rd. NW2....46 23 85 A
Dawson St. E2....48 33 83 D
Dawson Terr. N9....18 35 94 A
Daybrook Rd. SW19....95 25 68 B
Daylesford Ave. SW15....72 22 75 C
Daymar Rd. N22....24 29 90 B
Daymer Gdns. Pnr....20 11 89 C
Day's Acre. S Croy....112 33 62 D
Daysbrook Rd. SW2....86 30 73 D
Days La. Sid....90 45 73 A
Dayton Gr. SE15....76 35 76 A
Deacon Rd. King....93 18 69 B
Deacon Rd. NW2....45 22 84 A
Deacons Cl. Pnr....19 10 90 D
Deacons Ct. Twick....83 15 72 B
Deacons Wlk. Hamp....82 13 71 A
Deacon Way. SE17....63 32 78 A
Deacon Way. Wdf Gn....27 42 91 B
Deal Rd. SW17....96 28 70 A
Deal St. E1....57 34 81 A
Dealtry Rd. SW15....73 23 75 C
Dean Bradley St. SW1....7 30 79 C
Dean Cl. E9....49 35 85 C
Deancross St. E1....57 34 81 D
Deancross St. E1....57 35 81 C
Dean Ct. Wem....33 17 86 C
Dean Dri. Stan....21 18 90 C
Deane Ave. Ruis....43 11 85 C
Deane Croft Rd. Pnr....32 11 88 C
Deane Ct. Nthwd....19 09 90 A
Deanery Mews. W1....6 28 80 C
Deanery Rd. E15....50 39 84 A
Deanery St. W1....6 28 80 C
Deane Way. Ruis....10 10 88 D
Dean Farrar St. SW1....6 29 79 D
Deanfield Gdns. Croy....112 32 64 B
Dean Gdns. E17....26 38 89 D
Deanhill Ct. SW14....72 19 75 D
Deanhill Rd. SW14....72 19 75 D
Dean La. Edg....22 20 91 A
Dean Rd. Croy....112 32 64 B
Dean Rd. Hamp....82 13 71 C
Dean Rd. Houn....70 13 74 B
Dean Rd. NW2....46 23 84 A
Dean Ryle St. SW1....10 30 78 A
Dean's Bldgs. SE17....63 32 78 B
Deansbrook Cl. Edg....22 20 91 C
Deansbrook Rd. Edg....22 20 91 A
Deans Cl. Croy....105 33 65 D
Deans Cl. Edg....22 20 91 A
Deans Cl. W4....61 19 77 B
Deanscroft Ave. NW9....34 20 87 C
Dean's Ct. EC4....3 31 81 D
Deans La. (Path). W4....61 19 77 B
Dean's Mews. W1....2 28 81 D
Dean's Pl. SW1....10 29 78 B
Deans Rd. Sutt....103 25 65 D
Dean's Rd. W7....60 15 79 B
Dean Stanley St. SW1....7 30 79 C
Dean St. E7....50 40 85 C
Dean St. W1....2 29 81 D
Dean Trench St. SW1....7 30 79 C
Dean Wlk. Edg....22 20 91 A
De Arn Gdns. Mit....96 27 68 A
Deason St. E15....49 38 83 A
Debden Cl. Wdf Gn....27 41 91 D
De Beauvoir Cres. N1....48 33 83 A
De Beauvoir Sq. N1....48 33 84 C
De Beavoir Rd. N1....48 33 84 C
Debenham Ct. E8....48 34 83 A
Debnams Rd. SE16....64 35 78 A
De Bohun Ave. N14....12 28 95 D
Deborah Cl. Islw....71 15 76 A
Debrabant Cl. Eri....67 50 77 B
Deburgh Rd. SW19....95 26 70 C
Decima St. SE1....8 33 79 C
Decoy Ave. NW11....24 23 89 C
De Crespigny Park. SE5....75 32 76 D
Deeley Rd. SW8....74 29 76 B
Deena Cl. W3....54 18 81 D
Deepdale Ave. Brom....99 39 68 D
Deepdale. SW19....85 23 71 B
Deepdene Ave. Croy....105 33 65 D
Deepdene Cl. E11....27 40 89 C
Deepdene Ct. Brom....99 39 68 A
Deepdene Ct. N21....13 31 95 D
Deepdene Gdns. SW2....86 30 73 B
Deepdene Rd. SE5....75 32 75 D
Deepdene Rd. Well....78 46 75 A

Deepwell Cl. Islw....71 16 76 A
Deepwood La. Grnf....53 14 82 B
Deerbrook Rd. SE24....87 31 73 D
Deerdale Rd. SE24....75 32 75 C
Dee Rd. Rich....71 18 75 D
Deerhurst Rd. NW2....46 23 84 B
Deerhurst Rd. SW16....86 30 71 D
Deerleap Gr. E4....14 37 95 B
Deer Park Cl. King....94 19 70 D
Deer Park Gdns. Mit....95 26 68 D
Deer Park Rd. SW19....95 26 69 C
Deeside Rd. SW17....85 26 72 D
Dee St. E14....58 38 81 C
Dee Way. Eps....109 21 62 C
Dee Way. Rom....30 51 90 A
Defiance Wlk. SE18....65 42 79 D
Defiant Way. Wall....111 30 63 C
Defoe Ave. Rich....69 19 77 C
Defoe Rd. N16....37 33 86 C
Defoe Way. Rom....29 49 91 B
De Frene Rd. SE26....88 36 72 C
Degema Rd. Chis....90 43 71 D
Dehar Cres. NW9....34 22 87 A
De Havilland Rd. Edg....22 19 90 D
De Havilland Rd. Houn....69 11 77 C
De Havilland Rd. Wall....111 30 63 C
Dekker Rd. SE21....75 33 74 C
Delacourt Rd. SE3....65 40 77 D
Delafield Rd. SE7....65 41 78 C
Delaford Rd. SE16....64 35 78 C
Delaford St. SW6....62 24 77 B
Delamare Cres. Croy....106 35 67 C
Delamere Gdns. NW7....22 20 91 B
Delamere Rd. Hay....53 11 80 B
Delamere Rd. SW20....95 23 69 B
Delamere Rd. W5....60 18 79 A
Delamere St. W2....1 27 81 A
Delamere Terr. W2....56 25 81 B
*Delancey Pas. NW1....47 29 83 A
Delancey St. NW1....47 28 83 B
De Laune St. SE17....63 31 78 D
Delaware Rd. W9....56 25 82 D
Delawyk Cres. SE24....75 32 74 D
Delcombe Ave. Wor Pk....103 23 66 C
Delft Way. SE22....75 33 74 A
Delhi Rd. Enf....17 33 94 B
Delhi St. N1....47 30 83 A
Delia St. SW18....73 26 73 B
Della Path. E5....37 34 86 D
Delibow Rd. Felt....69 10 74 B
Dell Cl. E15....49 38 83 B
Dell Cl. Wall....111 29 64 B
Dell Ct. Horn....42 54 86 A
Dell Farm Rd. Ruis....31 08 88 B
Dellfield Cl. Beck....98 38 69 A
Dell La. Eps....109 22 64 C
Dellors Cl. Barn....11 23 95 B
Dellow Cl. Ilf....40 44 87 B
Dellow St. E1....57 34 80 B
Dell Rd. Eps....109 22 63 A
Dell's Mews. SW1....10 29 78 A
Dell The. Brent....60 17 77 A
Dell The. Felt....81 10 73 B
Dell The. Pnr....20 11 90 D
Dell The. SE19....97 33 70 D
Dell The. SE2....66 46 78 C
Dell The. Wem....44 16 85 D
Dell Walk. N Mal....94 21 69 C
Dell Way. W13....54 17 81 C
Dellwood Gdns. Ilf....28 43 89 A
Delme Cres. SE3....77 40 76 D
Delmey Ct. Croy....105 33 65 D
Deloraine St. SE8....76 37 76 A
Delorme St. W6....62 23 77 B
Delta Cl. Wor Pk....102 21 65 C
Delta Gr. Nthlt....53 11 82 B
Delta Rd. Wor Pk....102 21 65 D
Delta St. E2....57 34 82 A
De Luci Rd. Eri....67 50 78 C
De Lucy St. SE2....66 46 78 B
Delvan Cl. SE18....66 43 77 C
Delvers Mead. Dag....52 50 85 A
Delverton Rd. SE17....63 31 78 D
Delvino Rd. SW6....75 25 76 A
Demesne Rd. Wall....111 29 64 D
Demeta Cl. Wem....34 20 86 C
De Montfort Rd. SW16....86 30 72 A
De Morgan Rd. SW6....73 25 75 B
Dempster Cl. Surb....101 17 66 C
Dempster Rd. SW18....73 26 74 A
Denberry Dri. Sid....90 46 72 D
Denbigh Cl. Chis....99 42 70 B
Denbigh Cl. Horn....30 54 89 D
Denbigh Cl. NW10....45 21 84 C
Denbigh Cl. Ruis....31 09 86 B

Denbigh Cl. Sutt ...110 24 64 D
Denbigh Cl. W11 ...56 24 80 B
Denbigh Gdns. Rich ...71 18 74 B
Denbigh Mews. SW1 ...10 29 78 A
Denbigh Pl. SW1 ...10 29 78 C
Denbigh Rd. E6 ...58 41 82 B
Denbigh Rd. Houn ...70 13 76 D
Denbigh Rd. Sthl ...53 12 81 D
Denbigh Rd. W11 ...56 24 80 B
Denbigh Rd. W13 ...54 16 81 D
Denbigh St. SW1 ...10 29 78 C
Denbigh Terr. W11 ...56 24 80 B
Denbridge Rd. Brom ...99 42 69 D
Den Cl. Beck ...98 38 68 C
Dendy St. SW12 ...83 28 73 C
Dene Ave. Houn ...70 12 75 B
Dene Ave. Sid ...90 46 73 B
Dene Cl. Brom ...107 39 66 D
Dene Cl SE4 ...76 33 75 A
Dene Cl. Wor Pk ...102 21 65 B
Dene Dri. Orp ...108 46 65 D
Dene Gdns. Surb ...101 16 65 A
Denehurst Gdns. NW4 ...35 23 88 C
Denehurst Gdns. Rich ...72 19 75 C
Denehurst Gdns. Twick ...82 14 73 B
Denehurst Gdns. W3 ...19 19 80 D
Dene Rd. N11 ...16 27 93 B
Dene Rd. Nthwd ...19 08 91 B
Dene The. W13 ...16 81 B
Dene The. Wem ...44 18 85 A
Denewood Cl. Barn ...11 26 95 A
Denewood Rd. N6 ...36 27 87 B
Denford St. E10 ...65 39 78 D
Dengie Wlk (off Maldon Cl). N1
...48 32 83 A
Denham Cl. Well ...79 47 75 A
Denham Cres. Mit ...96 27 68 D
Denham Dri. Ilf ...40 44 88 C
Denham Rd. Felt ...82 11 73 A
Denham Rd. N20 ...16 27 93 D
Denham St. SE10 ...65 40 78 C
Denham Way. Bark ...51 45 83 B
Denholme Rd. W9 ...56 24 82 B
Denison Cl. N2 ...23 26 89 A
Denison Rd. Felt ...81 09 71 B
Denison Rd. SW19 ...95 26 70 B
Denison Rd. W5 ...17 82 C
Denis Way. SW4 ...74 29 75 B
Denleigh Gdns. E Mol ...101 15 67 C
Denleigh Gdns. N21 ...17 31 94 A
Denman Dri. Ashf ...07 70 B
Denman Dri N. NW11 ...35 25 88 A
Denman Dri S. NW11 ...35 25 88 A
Denman Rd. SE15 ...75 33 76 D
Denman St. W1 ...6 29 80 B
Denmark Ave. SW19 ...95 24 70 C
Denmark Ct. Mord ...103 25 67 A
Denmark Gdns. Cars ...104 27 65 D
Denmark Gr. N1 ...48 31 83 C
Denmark Hill Dri. NW9 ...35 22 89 A
Denmark Hill. SE5 ...75 32 75 B
Denmark Path. SE25 ...105 34 67 B
Denmark Pl. WC2 ...2 29 81 D
Denmark Rd. Brom ...99 40 69 B
Denmark Rd. Cars ...104 27 65 D
Denmark Rd. King ...93 18 68 A
Denmark Rd. N8 ...25 31 89 C
Denmark Rd. NW6 ...46 24 83 D
Denmark Rd. SE25 ...105 34 67 B
Denmark Rd. SE5 ...75 32 76 C
Denmark Rd. SW19 ...95 23 70 B
Denmark Rd. Twick ...82 14 72 D
Denmark Rd. W13 ...54 16 80 B
Denmark St. E11 ...39 39 86 C
Denmark St. E13 ...58 40 81 B
Denmark St. E13 ...58 40 81 B
Denmark St. N17 ...25 34 91 D
Denmark St. WC2 ...2 29 81 D
Denmead Rd. Croy ...105 31 66 D
Denmead Way (off Pentridge St).
SE15 ...63 33 77 D
Dennan Rd. Surb ...101 18 66 D
Denner Rd. E4 ...18 37 93 A
Denne Terr. E8 ...33 83 B
Dennett Rd. Croy ...105 31 66 A
Dennett's Gr. SE14 ...76 35 76 D
Dennett's Rd. SE14 ...76 35 76 A
Denning Ave. Croy ...112 31 64 C
Denning Cl. Hamp ...82 12 71 D
Denning Cl. NW8 ...7 26 82 A
Denning Rd. NW3 ...46 26 85 B
Dennington Park Rd. NW6 ...46 25 84 A
Dennis Ave. Wem ...44 18 85 D
Dennis Cl. Ashf ...91 08 70 D

Dennis Park Cres. SW20 ...95 24 69 A
Dennis Rd. E Mol ...92 14 68 C
Dennis Reeve Cl. Mit ...96 27 69 B
*Denny Cres. SW11 ...63 31 78 C
Denny Gdns. Dag ...51 46 84 D
Denny Rd. N9 ...17 34 94 D
Denny St. SE11 ...63 31 78 C
Den Rd. Brom ...98 38 68 C
Densham Rd. E15 ...65 39 83 A
Densole Cl. Beck ...98 36 69 A
Densworth Gr. N9 ...18 35 93 A
Denton Cl. Barn ...11 23 95 A
Denton Rd. N18 ...17 33 92 A
Denton Rd. N8 ...36 30 88 D
Denton Rd. Twick ...71 17 74 D
Denton Rd. Well ...67 47 77 C
Denton St. SW18 ...73 25 74 D
Denton Way. E5 ...38 35 86 D
Dents Rd. SW11 ...74 27 74 D
Denver Cl. Orp ...108 45 67 C
Denver Rd. N16 ...37 33 87 A
Denyer St. SW3 ...9 29 77 C
Denzil Rd. NW10 ...45 21 85 D
Deodar Rd. SW15 ...73 24 75 C
Deodar Rd. SW15 ...73 24 75 C
Depot App. N3 ...23 25 90 B
Depot App. NW2 ...46 23 85 B
Depot Rd. Houn ...70 14 75 B
Depot St SE5 ...63 32 77 B
Deptford Bridge. SE8 ...76 37 76 A
Deptford Bwy. SE8 ...76 37 76 A
Deptford Church St. SE8 ...64 37 77 C
Deptford Ferry Rd. E14 ...64 37 78 A
Deptford Green. SE8 ...64 37 77 A
Deptford High St. SE8 ...64 37 77 C
Deptford Strand. SE8 ...64 37 78 A
De Quincey Rd. N17 ...25 32 90 B
Derby Ave. Har ...20 14 90 B
Derby Ave. N12 ...15 26 92 C
Derby Ave. Rom ...41 50 88 C
Derby Gate. SW1 ...7 30 79 A
Derby Hill Cres. SE23 ...88 35 72 A
Derby Hill. SE23 ...88 35 72 A
Derby Rd. Croy ...105 31 66 D
Derby Rd. E18 ...27 39 90 B
Derby Rd. E7 ...50 41 84 D
Derby Rd. E9 ...49 35 83 B
Derby Rd. Enf ...14 35 95 A
Derby Rd. Grnf ...43 13 83 B
Derby Rd. Houn ...70 13 75 D
Derby Rd. N18 ...18 35 92 C
Derby Rd. Surb ...102 19 66 C
Derby Rd. Sutt ...110 24 63 B
Derby Rd. SW14 ...72 19 75 D
Derby Rd. SW19 ...95 25 70 C
Derbyshire St. E2 ...57 34 82 A
Derby St. W1 ...6 28 80 C
Dereham Pl. EC2 ...4 33 82 A
Dereham Rd. Bark ...51 45 85 D
Derek Ave. Eps ...109 19 64 C
Derek Ave. Wall ...111 28 64 B
Derek Ave. Wem ...45 19 84 D
Derey Ave. Horn ...42 54 86 D
Dericote St. E8 ...48 34 83 B
Dering Pl. Croy ...112 32 64 A
Dering Rd. Croy ...112 32 64 A
Dering St. W1 ...28 81 D
Derinton Rd. SW17 ...86 28 71 A
Derley Rd. Sthl ...59 11 79 C
Dermody Gdns. SE13 ...76 38 74 B
Dermody Rd. SE13 ...76 38 74 B
Deronda Rd. SE24 ...87 31 73 D
Deroy Cl. Cars ...111 27 63 B
Derrick Ave. S Croy ...112 32 62 C
Derrick Gdns. SE7 ...65 41 78 A
Derrick Rd. Beck ...98 36 68 D
Derry Rd. Croy ...30 65 C
Derry St. W8 ...62 25 79 B
Dersingham Ave. E12 ...53 43 85 C
Dersingham Rd. NW2 ...35 24 86 C
Derwent Ave. Barn ...11 27 94 D
Derwent Ave. N18 ...17 32 92 D
Derwent Ave. NW7 ...22 20 91 B
Derwent Ave. NW9 ...34 21 88 A
Derwent Ave. Pnr ...20 12 91 A
Derwent Ave. SW15 ...84 21 71 A
Derwent Ave. Uxb ...31 07 86 C
Derwent Cres. Bexh ...59 49 76 C
Derwent Cres. N20 ...15 26 93 C
Derwent Cres. Stan ...21 17 90 C
Derwent Dri. Orp ...108 44 66 B
Derwent Gdns. Ilf ...27 42 89 C
Derwent Gdns. Wem ...33 17 87 A
Derwent Gr. SE22 ...75 33 75 D

Derwent Rd. N13 ...16 30 93 D
Derwent Rd. N.Mal ...103 23 67 D
Derwent Rd. SE20 ...97 34 69 D
Derwent Rd. Sthl ...53 13 81 C
Derwent Rd. Twick ...70 13 74 D
Derwent Rd. W5 ...60 17 79 C
Derwent Rise. NW9 ...34 21 88 C
Derwent St. E10 ...65 39 78 C
Derwentwater Rd. W3 ...55 20 80 C
Derwent Wlk. Wall ...111 28 63 D
Desborough Cl. W2 ...56 25 81 B
Desenfans Rd. SE21 ...75 33 74 C
Desford Rd. E16 ...58 39 82 C
Desmond St. SE14 ...64 36 77 A
Despard Rd. N19 ...36 29 87 C
Dethick Ct. E3 ...49 36 83 A
Detling Rd. Brom ...89 40 71 C
Detling Rd. Eri ...67 50 77 D
Detmond Rd. E5 ...38 35 86 A
Devana End. Cars ...104 27 65 D
Devas Rd. SW20 ...95 23 69 A
Devas St. E3 ...57 37 82 D
Devenay Rd. E15 ...50 39 84 D
Devenish Rd. SE2 ...66 46 79 A
Deventer Cres. SE22 ...75 33 74 A
De Vere Cotts. W8 ...5 26 79 C
De Vere Gdns. Ilf ...39 42 87 D
De Vere Gdns. W8 ...5 26 79 A
Deverell St. SE1 ...8 32 79 D
De Vere Mews. W8 ...5 26 79 C
Devereux Ct. WC2 ...3 31 81 C
Devereux Rd. SW11 ...74 27 74 D
Deveron Way. Rom ...30 51 90 A
Devizes St. N1 ...48 32 83 B
Devon Ave. Twick ...82 14 73 C
Devon Cl. Grnf ...44 17 83 A
Devoncroft Gdns. Twick ...83 16 73 A
Devon Gdns. N4 ...37 31 88 D
Devonia Gdns. N18 ...25 32 91 A
Devonia Rd. N1 ...48 31 83 D
Devonport Gdns. Ilf ...39 42 88 D
Devonport Rd. W12 ...61 22 79 B
Devonport St. E1 ...57 35 81 D
Devonport. W2 ...1 27 81 C
Devon Rd. Bark ...51 45 83 A
Devon Rd. Sutt ...110 24 62 A
Devon Rise. N2 ...23 26 89 D
Devonshire Ave. Dart ...80 52 74 D
Devonshire Ave. Sutt ...110 26 63 C
Devonshire Cl. E15 ...50 39 85 A
Devonshire Cl. W1 ...2 28 81 B
Devonshire Cres. NW7 ...23 23 91 D
Devonshire Dri. SE10 ...76 37 76 B
Devonshire Dri. Surb ...101 17 65 B
Devonshire Gdns. N17 ...25 32 91 A
Devonshire Gdns. N21 ...17 32 94 A
Devonshire Gdns. W4 ...61 20 77 C
Devonshire Gr. SE15 ...63 34 77 B
Devonshire Hill La. N17 ...25 32 91 A
Devonshire House. Sutt ...110 26 63 C
Devonshire Mews N. W1 ...2 28 81 B
Devonshire Mews S. W1 ...2 28 81 B
Devonshire Mews. W1 ...61 21 78 C
Devonshire Mews W. W1 ...2 28 81 B
Devonshire Pas. W4 ...61 21 77 A
Devonshire Pl Mews. W1 ...2 28 81 A
Devonshire Pl. NW2 ...35 25 86 C
Devonshire Pl. W1 ...2 28 82 C
Devonshire Rd. Bexh ...79 48 75 D
Devonshire Rd. Croy ...105 32 66 B
Devonshire Rd. E16 ...58 40 81 D
Devonshire Rd. E17 ...38 37 88 C
Devonshire Rd. Felt ...82 12 71 A
Devonshire Rd. Har ...32 14 88 D
Devonshire Rd. Horn ...42 53 86 B
Devonshire Rd. Ilf ...40 45 87 A
Devonshire Rd. N13 ...17 31 92 A
Devonshire Rd. N17 ...25 32 91 A
Devonshire Rd. N9 ...18 35 94 C
Devonshire Rd. NW7 ...23 23 91 D
Devonshire Rd. Orp ...108 46 66 A
Devonshire Rd. Pnr ...32 11 88 C
Devonshire Rd. Pnr ...20 12 90 B
Devonshire Rd. SE23 ...88 35 73 C
Devonshire Rd. SE9 ...89 42 72 A
Devonshire Rd. Sthl ...53 13 81 A
Devonshire Rd. Sutt ...110 26 63 C
Devonshire Rd. SW19 ...96 27 70 C
Devonshire Rd. W4 ...61 21 78 C
Devonshire Rd. W5 ...60 17 79 C
Devonshire Rd. Wall ...111 28 64 A
Devonshire Row. EC2 ...4 33 81 A
Devonshire Row Mews. W1 ...2 28 82 D
Devonshire Sq. Brom ...99 40 68 D
Devonshire Sq. EC2 ...4 33 81 C

Devonshire St. W1 ...2 — 28 81 B
Devonshire St. W4 ...61 — 21 78 C
Devonshire Terr. W2 ...1 — 26 81 C
Devonshire Way. Croy. ...106 — 36 65 B
Devons Rd. E3 ...57 — 37 82 D
Devon St. SE15 ...63 — 34 77 B
Devon Waye. Houn ...59 — 12 77 D
Devon Way. Eps. ...109 — 19 64 D
De Walden St. W1 ...2 — 28 81 A
Dewar St. SE15 ...75 — 34 75 A
Dewberry St. E14 ...58 — 38 81 A
Dewey Rd. Dag ...52 — 50 84 A
Dewey Rd. N1 ...48 — 31 83 C
Dewey St. SW17 ...86 — 27 71 D
Dewhurst Rd. W14 ...62 — 23 79 D
Dewsbury Cl. Pnr ...32 — 12 88 C
Dewsbury Cl. Rom ...30 — 54 91 A
Dewsbury Gdns. Rom ...30 — 53 91 B
Dewsbury Gdns. Wor Pk ...102 — 22 65 C
Dewsbury Rd. NW10 ...45 — 22 85 C
Dewsbury Rd. Rom ...30 — 54 91 A
Dewsbury Terr. NW1 ...47 — 28 83 B
Dexter Rd. Barn ...11 — 23 95 D
Dexter Rd. SE24 ...75 — 31 75 C
Deyncourt Rd. N17 ...25 — 32 90 B
Deyncourt Gdns. E11 ...27 — 41 89 C
D'Eynsford Rd. SE5 ...75 — 32 76 B
Dhonau Hse. SE1 ...63 — 33 78 B
Diadem Ct. W1 ...2 — 29 81 D
Dial Walk The. W8 ...62 — 25 79 B
Diameter Rd. Orp ...108 — 44 67 C
Diamond Rd. Ruis ...43 — 12 95 A
Diamond St. SE15 ...63 — 33 77 C
Diamond Terr. SE10 ...76 — 38 76 A
Diana Cl. E18 ...27 — 40 90 B
Diana Gdns. Surb ...101 — 18 65 B
Diana Rd. E17 ...26 — 36 89 B
Dianthus Cl. SE2 ...66 — 46 78 D
Diban Ave. Horn ...42 — 52 86 D
Dibden St. N1 ...48 — 32 83 A
Dibdin Cl. Sutt. ...103 — 25 65 C
Dibdin Rd. Sutt. ...103 — 25 65 A
Dicey Ave. NW2 ...46 — 23 85 A
Dickens Ave. N3 ...23 — 26 90 A
Dickens Cl. Rich ...83 — 18 72 A
Dickens Cl. Chis ...100 — 44 70 A
Dickens La. N18 ...17 — 33 92 C
Dickenson Rd. N8 ...36 — 30 87 A
Dickenson's La. SE25 ...105 — 34 67 C
Dickenson's Pl. SE25 ...105 — 34 67 C
Dickens Rd. E6 ...50 — 41 83 D
Dickens Sq. SE1 ...8 — 32 79 C
Dickens St. SW8 ...74 — 28 76 D
Dickerage La. N Mal ...94 — 20 68 A
Dickinson Rd. Felt. ...82 — 11 71 C
Dickson Fold. Pnr ...20 — 11 89 D
Dickson Rd. SE9 ...77 — 42 75 A
Dick Turpin Way. Felt. ...69 — 09 75 D
Didsbury Cl. E6 ...50 — 42 83 B
Digby Cres. N4 ...37 — 32 86 A
Digby Estate. E2 ...57 — 35 82 A
Digby Gdns. Dag ...52 — 49 83 A
Digby Pl. Croy. ...105 — 33 65 D
Digby Rd. Bark ...51 — 45 84 D
Digby Rd. E9 ...49 — 35 84 B
Digby St. E2 ...57 — 35 82 A
Diggon St. E1 ...57 — 35 81 B
Dighton Rd. SW18 ...73 — 26 75 C
Dignum St. N1 ...48 — 31 83 C
Digswell St. N7 ...48 — 31 84 A
Dilhorne Cl. SE12 ...89 — 40 72 D
Dilke St. SW3 ...9 — 27 77 B
Dillon Pl. N7 ...36 — 30 86 D
Dillwyn Cl. SE26 ...88 — 36 71 A
Dilston Cl. Nthlt ...53 — 11 82 A
Dilston Gr. SE16 ...64 — 35 78 A
Dilton Gdns. SW15 ...84 — 22 73 D
Dimes Pl. W6 ...61 — 22 78 B
Dimmock Dri. Grnf ...43 — 14 85 D
Dimond Cl. E7 ...50 — 40 85 A
Dimsdale Dri. Enf. ...13 — 34 95 C
Dimsdale Dri. NW9 ...34 — 20 87 C
Dimsdale Wlk. E13 ...50 — 40 83 C
Dingle Gdns. E14 ...57 — 37 80 A
Dingle Rd. Ashf ...81 — 07 71 D
Dingley La. SW16 ...86 — 29 72 B
Dingley Pl. EC1 ...4 — 32 82 A
Dingley Rd. EC1 ...4 — 32 82 A
Dingwall Ave. Croy ...105 — 33 65 B
Dingwall Gdns. NW11 ...35 — 25 88 C
Dingwall Rd. Cars ...111 — 27 62 B
Dingwall Rd. Croy. ...105 — 32 65 B
Dingwall Rd. SW18 ...85 — 26 73 A
Dinmont St. E2 ...48 — 34 83 D
Dinsdale Gdns. Barn ...11 — 25 95 B

Dinsdale Gdns. SE25 ...105 — 33 67 A
Dinsdale Rd. SE3 ...65 — 39 77 B
Dinsmore Rd. SW12 ...86 — 28 73 B
Dinton Rd. King ...93 — 18 70 D
Dirleton Rd. E15 ...50 — 39 83 B
Disbrowe Rd. W6 ...62 — 24 77 A
Dishforth La. NW9 ...22 — 21 90 A
Disney Pl. SE1 ...8 — 32 79 A
Disney St. SE1 ...8 — 32 79 A
Dison Cl. Enf ...14 — 35 97 B
Disraeli Cl. W4 ...61 — 20 78 B
Disraeli Rd. E7 ...50 — 40 84 A
Disraeli Rd. NW10 ...45 — 20 83 D
Disraeli Rd. SW15 ...73 — 24 75 C
Disraeli Rd. W5 ...54 — 17 80 D
Diss St. E2 ...4 — 33 82 B
Distaff La. EC4 ...8 — 32 80 A
Distillery La. W6 ...62 — 23 78 C
Distillery Rd. W6 ...62 — 23 78 C
Distillery Wlk. (off Pottery Rd). Brent ...60 — 18 77 A
Distin St. SE11 ...63 — 31 78 A
District Rd. Wem ...44 — 16 85 D
Ditch Alley. SE10 ...76 — 37 76 B
Ditchburn St. E14 ...58 — 38 80 A
Dittisham Rd. SE9 ...89 — 42 71 A
Ditton Cl. Surb. ...101 — 16 66 A
Ditton Grange Cl. Surb. ...101 — 17 66 D
Ditton Grange Dri. Surb. ...101 — 17 66 D
Ditton Hill Rd. Surb. ...101 — 17 66 C
Ditton Hill. Surb. ...101 — 17 65 B
Ditton Lawn. Surb. ...101 — 16 66 C
Ditton Rd. Bexh ...79 — 48 74 A
Ditton Rd. Sthl. ...59 — 12 78 D
Ditton Rd. Surb. ...101 — 18 66 C
Ditton Reach. Surb. ...101 — 16 67 D
Divis Way. SW15 ...72 — 22 74 D
Dixon Pl. W Wick. ...106 — 37 66 D
Dixon Rd. SE14 ...76 — 36 76 A
Dixon Rd. SE25 ...97 — 33 68 B
*Dixon's Alley. SE16 ...63 — 34 79 B
Dobbin Cl. Har ...21 — 16 90 C
Dobell Rd. SE9 ...77 — 42 74 B
Dobree Ave. NW10 ...45 — 22 84 D
Dobson Cl. NW6 ...46 — 26 84 D
Doby Ct. EC4 ...8 — 32 80 A
Dockhead. SE1 ...8 — 33 79 B
Dockley Rd. SE16 ...63 — 34 79 C
Dock Rd. Brent ...60 — 17 77 D
Dock Rd. E16 ...58 — 39 80 B
Dock St. E1 ...50 — 33 80 C
Dockwell Cl. Felt. ...69 — 10 75 C
Docwra's Blgs. N1 ...48 — 33 84 A
Dodbrooke Rd. SE27 ...87 — 31 72 D
Doddington Gr. SE17 ...63 — 31 78 D
Doddington Pl. SE17 ...63 — 31 77 B
Dodsley Pl. N9 ...18 — 35 93 C
Dodson St. SE1 ...7 — 31 79 A
Dod St. E14 ...57 — 37 81 C
Doel Cl. SW19 ...95 — 26 70 C
Doggett Rd. SE6 ...88 — 37 73 A
Doggett's Cnr. Horn ...42 — 54 86 B
Doggetts Ct. Barn ...27 — 95 A
Dog Kennel Hill. SE22 ...75 — 33 75 A
Dog La. NW10 ...45 — 21 85 A
Doherty Rd. E13 ...58 — 40 82 C
Dolben St. SE1 ...7 — 31 80 D
Dolby Rd. SW6 ...73 — 24 76 D
Dolland St. SE11 ...10 — 30 78 D
Dollis Ave. N3 ...23 — 24 90 B
Dollis Brook Wlk. Barn ...11 — 24 95 C
Dollis Cres. Ruis ...32 — 11 87 C
Dollis Hill Ave. NW2 ...34 — 22 86 D
Dollis Hill La. NW2 ...34 — 22 86 C
Dollis Park. N3 ...23 — 24 90 B
Dollis Rd. N3 ...23 — 24 91 D
Dollis Valley Way. Barn ...11 — 24 95 D
Dolman Rd. W4 ...61 — 20 78 B
Dolman St. SW4 ...74 — 30 75 D
Dolphin App. Rom ...30 — 51 89 D
Dolphin Cl. Surb. ...101 — 17 67 B
Dolphin La. E14 ...57 — 37 80 B
Dolphin Rd. Nthlt. ...43 — 13 83 C
Dolphin Rd. Sun. ...91 — 09 69 A
Dolphin Road N. Sun. ...91 — 09 69 A
Dolphin Road S. Sun. ...91 — 09 69 A
Dolphin Road W. Sun. ...91 — 09 69 A
Dombey St. WC1 ...3 — 30 81 B
Dome Hill Park. SE26 ...87 — 33 71 A
Domett Cl. SE5 ...32 — 75 D
Domingo St. EC1 ...4 — 32 82 C
Dominion Dri. Rom ...29 — 49 91 B
Dominion Rd. Croy ...105 — 33 66 B
Dominion Rd. Sthl ...59 — 12 79 C
Dominion St. EC2 ...4 — 32 81 B

Domonic Dri. SE9 ...90 — 43 72 D
Domville Gr. SE5 ...63 — 33 78 D
Donald Dri. Rom ...41 — 47 88 A
Donald Rd. Croy. ...104 — 30 67 D
Donald Rd. E13 ...50 — 40 83 B
Donaldson Rd. NW6 ...46 — 24 83 B
Donaldson Rd. SE18 ...78 — 43 76 A
Doncaster Dri. Nthlt. ...43 — 12 85 D
Doncaster Gdns. N4 ...37 — 32 88 C
Doncaster Gdns. Nthlt ...43 — 12 85 D
Doncaster Rd. N9 ...17 — 34 94 B
Doncaster Way. Horn ...42 — 54 86 D
Doncel Ct. E4 ...18 — 38 94 B
Donegal St. N1 ...47 — 30 83 D
Doneraile St. SW6 ...73 — 23 76 B
Dongola Rd. E13 ...58 — 40 82 B
Dongola Rd. N17 ...25 — 33 89 A
Dongola Road W. E13 ...58 — 40 82 B
Donington Ave. Ilf. ...40 — 44 88 A
Donkey La. Enf. ...13 — 34 97 C
Donne Ct. SE24 ...75 — 32 74 C
Donne Pl. SW3 ...9 — 27 78 A
Donnefield Ave. Edg ...21 — 18 91 C
Donne Rd. Dag ...41 — 47 86 A
Donnington Rd. Har ...33 — 17 08 D
Donnington Rd. NW10 ...45 — 22 83 B
Donnington Rd. Wor Pk ...102 — 22 65 A
Donnybrook Rd. SW16 ...96 — 29 70 D
Donovan Ave. N10 ...24 — 29 90 C
Donovan Cl. Eps. ...109 — 20 62 D
Don Phelan Cl. SE5 ...75 — 32 76 B
Don Phelan Cl. SE5 ...75 — 32 77 D
Don Way. Rom. ...30 — 51 11 C
Doone Cl. Tedd. ...93 — 16 70 A
Doon St. SE1 ...7 — 31 80 C
Doral Way. Cars. ...111 — 27 64 D
Doran Gr. SE18 ...66 — 44 77 D
Doran Wlk. E15 ...49 — 38 84 C
Dora Rd. SW19 ...85 — 25 71 A
Dora St. E14 ...57 — 36 81 D
Dorchester Ave. Har ...32 — 14 98 C
Dorchester Ave. N13 ...17 — 32 92 A
Dorchester Ct. Nthlt. ...43 — 13 85 D
Dorchester Ct. N14 ...16 — 28 94 B
Dorchester Ct. SE24 ...75 — 32 74 A
Dorchester Dri. Felt. ...69 — 74 C
Dorchester Dri. SE24 ...75 — 32 74 A
Dorchester Gdns. E4 ...18 — 37 02 A
Dorchester Gdns. NW11 ...23 — 25 89 C
Dorchester Gr. W4 ...61 — 21 78 D
Dorchester Mews. N Mal. ...94 — 20 68 D
Dorchester Rd. Mord ...103 — 26 66 A
Dorchester Rd. Nthlt. ...43 — 13 85 D
Dorchester Rd. Wor Pk ...103 — 23 66 C
Dorchester Way. Har ...33 — 18 08 D
Dorchester Way. Hay ...52 — 11 81 C
Dorcis Ave. Bexh ...79 — 48 76 C
Dordrecht Rd. W3 ...61 — 21 79 A
Dore Ave. E12 ...51 — 43 85 C
Doreen Ave. NW9 ...34 — 20 87 D
Dore Gdns. Mord ...103 — 26 66 A
Dorell Cl. Sthl. ...53 — 12 81 B
Dorian Rd. Horn. ...42 — 52 87 C
Doria Rd. SW6 ...73 — 24 76 D
Doric Way. NW1 ...2 — 29 82 B
Dorien Rd. SW20 ...95 — 23 69 D
Doris Ave. Eri ...79 — 50 76 A
Doris Rd. Ashf ...81 — 08 70 B
Doris Rd. E7 ...50 — 40 84 C
Dorking Cl. SE8 ...64 — 36 77 B
Dorking Cl. Wor Pk ...103 — 23 65 B
Dorlcote Rd. SW18 ...86 — 27 73 A
Dormans Cl. Nthwd ...19 — 08 91 D
Dorman Way. NW8 ...46 — 26 83 B
Dorman Wlk. NW10 ...45 — 20 84 B
Dormay St. SW18 ...73 — 25 74 B
Dormer Cl. Barn ...11 — 23 95 B
Dormer Cl. E15 ...50 — 39 84 B
Dormer's Ave. Sthl ...53 — 13 81 C
Dormers Rise. Sthl. ...53 — 13 81 D
Dormer's Wells La. Sthl. ...53 — 13 80 B
Dormywood. Ruis ...31 — 09 88 B
Dornberg Cl. SE3 ...65 — 40 77 C
Dornberg Rd. SE3 ...65 — 40 77 D
Dorncliffe Rd. SW6 ...73 — 24 76 C
Dorney Rise. Orp ...100 — 45 68 D
Dornfell St. NW6 ...46 — 24 85 D
Dornton Rd. S Croy ...112 — 33 64 C
Dornton Rd. SW12 ...86 — 29 72 A
Dorothy Ave. Wem ...44 — 18 84 C
Dorothy Evans Cl. Bexh ...79 — 49 75 D
Dorothy Gdns. Dag ...52 — 46 85 B
Dorothy Rd. SW11 ...74 — 27 75 B
Dorrell Pl. SW9 ...74 — 30 75 B

Dorrell Pl. SW9........................75   31 75 C
Dorrien Wlk. SW16....................86   29 72 B
Dorrington Ct. SE25..................33 69 C
Dorrington Gdns. Horn...........42   53 87 D
Dorrington St. EC1......................3   31 81 A
Dorrit Mews. N18.......................17   33 92 C
Dorrit St. SE1..............................8   32 79 A
Dorrit Way. Chis.....................100   44 70 A
Dors Cl. NW9.............................34   20 87 D
Dorset Ave. Rom.......................29   50 89 B
Dorset Ave. Sthl........................59   13 78 A
Dorset Ave. Well.......................48   45 75 D
Dorset Cl. NW1.............................1   27 81 B
Dorset Ct. N1.............................48   33 84 C
Dorset Dri. Edg..........................21   18 91 B
Dorset Gdns. Mit........................96   30 68 D
Dorset Mews. SW1.......................6   28 79 D
Dorset Pl. E15.............................9   38 84 B
Dorset Pl. SW1...........................10   29 78 D
Dorset Rd. Beck.........................35 68 B
Dorset Rd. E7.............................50   41 84 C
Dorset Rd. Har............................32   14 88 D
Dorset Rd. Mit............................95   27 69 C
Dorset Rd. N15..............................5   32 89 D
Dorset Rd. N22...........................24   30 90 A
Dorset Rd. SE9...........................42 72 A
Dorset Rd. Sutt.........................110   25 62 C
Dorset Rd. SW19........................25 69 C
Dorset Rd. SW8.........................60   30 77 D
Dorset Rd. W5................................6   17 79 C
Dorset Rise. EC4..........................3   31 81 D
Dorset Sq. Eps........................109   20 62 D
Dorset Sq. NW1.............................1   27 82 D
Dorset St. W1...............................2   28 81 A
Dorset Waye. Houn.....................59   12 77 D
Dorset Way. Twick.....................82   14 73 D
Dorville Cres. W6......................61   22 79 D
Dorville Rd. SE12.......................77   40 74 A
Douai Gr. Hamp...........................14 69 A
Doughty Ct. E1...........................57   34 80 D
Doughty Mews. WC1......................3   30 82 D
Doughty St. WC1...........................3   30 82 D
Douglas Ave. E17........................26   37 90 A
Douglas Ave. Rom.......................30   54 90 C
Douglas Ave. Wem......................96   18 84 C
Douglas Cl. Wall.......................111   30 63 A
Douglas Cres. Hay.....................53   11 82 D
Douglas Dri. Croy.....................106   37 65 C
Douglas Pl. E14..........................64   38 78 C
Douglas Pl. SW1.........................10   29 78 D
Douglas Rd. E16..........................58   40 81 A
Douglas Rd. Horn........................42   51 88 D
Douglas Rd. Houn........................55   13 75 B
Douglas Rd. Ilf...........................40   46 88 C
Douglas Rd. King.......................94   19 69 D
Douglas Rd. N1...........................48   32 84 C
Douglas Rd. N22..........................25   31 90 A
Douglas Rd. NW6.........................46   24 83 B
Douglas Rd. Surb........................18 66 D
Douglas Rd. Well........................78   46 76 B
Douglas Sq. Mord......................103   25 67 C
Douglas St. SW1.........................10   29 78 B
Douglas Terr. E17.........................6   36 90 A
Douglas Way. SE8.......................64   36 77 D
Doulton Mews. NW3....................46   25 84 B
Dounesforth Gdns. SW18...........85   25 73 D
Douro Pl. W8..............................62   25 79 D
Douro St. E3.................................5   37 83 C
Dove Cl. Nthlt............................53   11 82 D
Dovecote Ave. N22....................55   31 89 A
Dovedale Ave. Har......................33   17 88 C
Dovedale Ave. Ilf......................28   43 90 C
Dovedale Cl. Well......................78   46 76 C
Dovedale Rd. SE22......................55   34 74 D
Dovedale Rise. Mit......................96   27 70 D
Dove House Gdns. E4..................18   37 93 A
Dovehouse Mead. Bark..............51   44 83 D
Dovehouse St. SW3......................9   27 78 C
Dove Mews. SW5.........................62   26 78 C
Dove Park. Pnr...........................20   13 91 C
Dover Cl. Rom............................29   50 90 C
Dover Cotts. Surb....................101   17 67 C
Dovercourt Ave. Th Hth.............97   31 68 C
Dovercourt La. Sutt.................103   26 65 C
Dovercourt Rd. SE22.....................7   33 74 D
Dove Rd. N1................................48   32 84 B
Doverfield Rd. SW2......................86   30 73 A
Dover House Rd. SW15...............72   22 74 B
Doridge Gdns. N13.....................17   31 92 B
Dove Row. E2..............................34 83 A
Dover Park Dri. SW15................72   22 74 D
Dover Rd. E12.............................39   41 86 A
Dover Rd. N9...............................47   35 93 A
Dover Rd. Rom............................41   48 88 C
Dover Rd. SE18...........................78   43 76 A

Dover Rd. SE19...........................97   32 70 B
Dover Rd. Well...........................78   44 76 D
Dover St. W1................................29 80 C
Dover Yd. W1.................................9   29 80 C
Doves Cl. Brom.........................107   42 65 A
Dovet Ct. SW8.............................74   30 76 B
Doveton Rd. S Croy...................112   32 64 D
Doveton St. E1............................57   35 82 C
Dove Wlk. SW1..............................9   28 78 C
Dowanhill Rd. SE6......................88   38 73 D
Dowdeswell Cl. SW15................72   21 75 C
Dowding Pl. Stan........................21   16 91 A
Dower Ave. Wall.......................111   28 62 B
Dowgate Hill. EC4.........................8   32 80 B
Dowland St. W10.........................56   24 82 A
Dowlas St. SE5............................63   33 77 C
Dowman Cl. SW19........................95   25 70 D
Downage. NW4............................23   23 89 A
Downbank Ave. Bexh..................79   50 76 D
Down Barns Rd. Ruis..................32   11 86 D
Downderry Rd. Brom..................89   39 71 A
Downe Cl. Well...........................47 77 C
Downend. SE18............................66   43 77 D
Downe Rd. Mit.............................96   27 69 D
Downes Cl. Twick.......................71   16 76 A
Downes Ct. N21...........................17   31 94 C
Downfield Cl. W9.........................56   25 82 D
Downfield. Wor Pk....................102   22 66 C
Down Hall Rd. King.....................93   17 69 D
Downham Cl. Rom.......................29   49 91 C
Downham Rd. N1.........................48   33 84 C
Downham Way. Brom..................89   40 71 A
Downhills Ave. N17.....................25   32 89 B
Downhills Park Rd. N17..............25   32 89 A
Downhills Way. N17....................25   32 89 A
Downing Cl. Har..........................20   14 89 A
Downing Dri. Grnf.......................44   15 83 A
Downing Rd. Dag.........................52   48 84 D
Downing St. SW1...........................7   30 79 A
Downland Ct. N20.......................15   26 94 C
Downley Cl. SE9..........................42 72 A
Downman Rd. SE9........................77   42 75 A
Down Pl. W6................................61   22 78 D
Down Pl. W6................................62   23 78 C
Down Rd. Tedd............................93   16 70 B
Downs Ave. Chis........................89   42 71 D
Downs Ave. Pnr...........................27   12 87 B
Downs Bridge Rd. Beck..............98   33 68 A
Downsell Rd. E15........................49   38 85 B
Downsfield Rd. E17.....................38   36 89 B
Downshall Ave...........................40   45 88 C
Downs Hill. Beck........................98   33 68 A
Downshire Hill. NW3..................46   26 85 B
Downside Cl. SW19......................95   26 70 A
Downside Cres. NW3...................47   27 85 C
Downside Cres. W3.....................54   16 82 C
Downside Rd. Sutt....................111   27 63 A
Downside. Twick........................83   15 72 D
Downside Wlk. Nthlt..................53   12 82 B
Downs La. E5...............................34 85 B
Downs Park Rd. E5......................48   34 85 B
Downs Park Rd. E8......................48   34 85 C
Downs Rd. Beck..........................98   37 69 D
Downs Rd. E5...............................48   34 85 B
Downs Rd. Enf.............................13   33 96 C
Downs Rd. N16............................48   34 85 A
Downs Rd. Sutt.........................110   25 62 D
Downs Rd. Th Hth.......................97   32 69 A
Down St. E Mol...........................92   13 68 C
Downs The. SW20........................95   23 70 D
Down St Mews. W1........................6   28 80 D
Down St. W1..................................6   28 80 D
Downsview Gdns. SE19...............97   32 70 D
Downs View. Islw.......................71   16 76 A
Downsview Rd. SE19...................97   32 70 C
Downsway The. Sutt.................110   26 62 A
Downton Ave. SW2......................86   30 72 B
Downway. N12.............................24   27 91 C
Dowrey St. N1.............................48   31 83 A
Dowsett Rd. N17.........................25   33 90 D
Doyce St. SE1................................8   32 79 A
Doyle Gdns. NW10......................45   22 83 D
Doyle Rd. SE25............................34 68 C
D'Oyley St. SW1............................9   28 78 A
Doynton St. N19..........................36   28 86 B
Draco St. SE17.............................63   32 77 A
Dragon Yd. WC2.............................2   30 81 C
Dragoon Rd. SE8.........................64   36 78 D
Dragor Rd. NW10.........................50   20 82 C
Drakefell Rd. SE14......................76   35 75 B
Drakefell Rd. SE4........................76   36 75 A
Drakefield Rd. SW17...................86   28 72 C
Drakeley Ct. N5...........................31 85 B
Drake Rd. Chess........................109   19 64 C
Drake Rd. Croy..........................104   30 66 B

Drake Rd. Har..............................32   12 86 B
Drake Rd. Mit............................104   28 67 C
Drake Rd. SE4..............................76   37 75 A
Drakes Dri. Nthwd......................19   07 90 B
Drake St. Enf...............................13   32 97 B
Drakes Wlk. E6............................50   42 83 B
Drakewood Rd. SW16..................96   29 70 D
Draper Cl. Belv...........................67   48 78 B
Drapers Gdns. EC2........................4   32 81 D
Drapers Rd. E15...........................49   38 85 B
Drapers Rd. Enf...........................13   31 97 B
Drappers Way. SE16.....................63   34 78 A
Drawell Cl. SE18...........................66   45 78 C
Drax Ave. SW20...........................94   22 70 C
Draxmont. SW19..........................95   24 70 A
Draycot Rd. E11............................39   40 87 B
Draycott Ave. Har.......................33   17 88 C
Draycott Ave. SW3........................9   27 78 A
Draycott Cl. Har..........................33   16 88 D
Draycott Mews. SW6...................73   24 76 D
Draycott Pl. SW3...........................9   27 78 B
Draycott Terr. SW3.......................9   27 78 B
Drayford Cl. W9............................56   24 82 C
Dray Gdns. SW2............................74   30 74 B
Drayson Mews. W8.......................62   25 79 A
Drayton Ave. Orp.......................108   43 66 D
Drayton Ave. W13.........................54   16 80 A
Drayton Bridge Rd. W13.............54   16 81 C
Drayton Bridge Rd. W7...............54   15 80 B
Drayton Gdns. N21.......................17   31 94 B
Drayton Gdns. SW10....................62   26 78 C
Drayton Gdns. W13......................54   16 80 A
Drayton Green Rd. W13..............54   16 80 A
Drayton Green. W13.....................54   16 80 A
Drayton Gr. W13...........................54   16 80 A
Drayton Park. N5.........................48   31 85 A
Drayton Rd. Croy.......................105   31 65 B
Drayton Rd. E11...........................38   38 87 D
Drayton Rd. N17...........................25   33 90 C
Drayton Rd. NW10........................45   21 83 B
Drayton Rd. W13...........................54   16 80 B
Drayton Waye. Har.......................33   16 88 D
Dreadnought St. SE10..................65   39 79 C
Dresden Cl. NW3...........................46   25 84 B
Dresden Rd. N19...........................36   29 87 D
Dressington Ave. SE13................76   37 74 C
Drew Ave. NW7.............................23   24 91 A
Drew Gdns. Grnf..........................44   15 84 B
Drew Rd. E16................................58   41 80 D
Drewstead Rd. SW16....................86   29 72 B
Driffield Rd. E3.............................49   36 83 C
Drift The. Brom..........................107   41 65 D
Driftway The. Mit........................96   28 69 A
Drinkwater Rd. Har......................32   13 86 B
Driver's Bldgs. E1........................57   35 82 D
Drive The. Ashf............................91   08 70 D
Drive The. Bark............................51   45 84 D
Drive The. Barn............................11   24 96 A
Drive The. Barn............................11   26 95 C
Drive The. Beck............................98   37 69 A
Drive The. Bex..............................79   47 74 C
Drive The. Chis...........................100   45 68 B
Drive The. Chis...........................100   45 69 A
Drive The. E17..............................37   37 89 B
Drive The. E18..............................27   40 89 A
Drive The. E4................................18   38 94 B
Drive The. Enf..............................13   32 97 B
Drive The. Eps...........................109   21 63 B
Drive The. Eri................................67   49 77 D
Drive The. Felt..............................12   11 73 A
Drive The. Har..............................32   13 87 A
Drive The. Houn...........................70   14 76 D
Drive The. Ilf................................39   42 87 B
Drive The. Islw.............................70   14 76 D
Drive The. King.............................94   20 70 C
Drive The. Mord.........................103   26 67 B
Drive The. N11..............................24   29 91 B
Drive The. N2................................27   29 91 B
Drive The. N3................................23   25 91 C
Drive The. N7................................47   30 84 B
Drive The. Nthwd.........................19   09 90 A
Drive The. NW11..........................35   24 87 A
Drive The. Orp............................108   45 65 B
Drive The. Rom.............................29   50 91 D
Drive The. Rom.............................50   54 90 B
Drive The. Sid..............................90   46 71 B
Drive The. Surb...........................101   18 66 A
Drive The. SW20............................95   23 70 D
Drive The. Th Hth.........................97   32 68 D
Drive The. W3................................55   20 81 C
Drive The. Wall...........................111   29 62 C
Drive The. Wem.............................34   20 86 A
Drive The. W Wick......................106   38 66 B
Dr Johnsons Ave. SW17...............86   28 72 D
Droitwich Cl. SE26.......................87   34 72 C

Dromey Gdns. Har......................21 15 91 D
Dromore Rd. SW15 ....73 24 74 C
Dronfield Gdns. Dag..................52 47 85 C
Droop St. W10 ....56 23 82 B
Drover La. SE15 ....63 34 77 D
Drovers' Rd. S Croy ....112 32 64 D
Druce Rd. SE21.........................75 33 74 C
Druid St. SE1...............................8 33 79 B
Druids Way. Brom......................98 38 68 D
Drumaline Ridge. Wor Pk.........102 21 65 A
Drummond Ave. Rom ....29 50 89 D
Drummond Cres. NW1.................2 29 82 B
Drummond Rd. Croy ....105 32 65 A
Drummond Rd. E11...................39 41 88 C
Drummond Rd. Rom ....29 50 89 D
Drummond Rd. SE16 ....63 34 79 D
Drummond St. NW1 ....2 29 82 C
Drum St. E1 ....33 81 D
Drury Lane. WC2...........................3 30 81 C
Drury Rd. Har ....32 14 87 A
Dryad St. SW15..........................73 23 75 B
Dryburgh Gdns. NW9 ....22 19 89 A
Dryburgh Rd. SW15...................73 23 75 A
Dryburgh Rd. SW15...................73 23 75 C
Dryden Ave. W7.........................54 15 81 D
Dryden Cl. Ilf.............................28 45 91 B
Dryden Ct. King.........................83 17 71 B
Dryden Ct. SE11........................63 31 78 B
Dryden Rd. Enf..........................13 33 95 D
Dryden Rd. Har..........................21 15 90 B
Dryden Rd. SW19.......................95 26 70 A
Dryden Rd. Well.........................78 45 76 B
Dryden St. WC2............................3 30 81 C
Dryden Way. Orp ....108 48 66 C
Dryfield Cl. NW10......................45 20 84 A
Dryfield Rd. Edg ....22 20 91 A
Dryfield Wlk. SE8 ....64 37 77 A
Dryhill Rd. Belv ....67 48 77 B
Drylands Rd. N8 ....36 30 88 D
Drysdale Ave. E4 ....14 37 95 D
Drysdale Cl. Nthwd....................19 09 91 C
Drysdale Pl. N1 ....4 33 82 A
Drysdale St. N1 ....4 33 82 A
Du Burstow Terr. W7.................60 15 79 A
Ducal St. E2 ....4 33 82 B
Ducan Cl. Barn ....11 26 96 C
Du Cane Ct. SW12......................86 28 73 C
Du Cane Rd. W12.......................55 22 81 C
Duchess Mews. W1......................2 28 81 B
Duchess of Bedford's Wlk. W8 ...62 25 79 A
Duchess St. W1............................2 28 81 B
Duchy St. SE1...............................7 31 80 C
Ducie St. SW4 ....74 30 75 D
Duckett Rd. N4...........................37 31 88 D
Ducketts Rd. Dart......................80 51 74 B
Duckett St. E1 ....57 36 81 A
Ducking Stool Ct. Rom ....30 51 89 C
Duck La. W1..................................2 29 81 D
Duck Lees La. Enf.......................14 36 96 C
Duck's Hill Rd. Nthwd ....19 07 90 B
Ducks Hill Rd. Ruis....................19 08 89 C
Duck's Wlk. Twick......................71 17 74 A
Du Cros Dri. Stan.......................21 17 91 B
Du Cros Rd. W3 ....55 21 80 C
Dudden Hill La. NW10 ....45 21 85 D
Duddington Cl. SE9....................89 41 71 B
Dudley Ave. Har.........................21 17 89 A
Dudley Dri. Mord ....103 24 66 A
Dudley Gdns. Har ....32 14 87 D
Dudley Gdns. Rom.....................30 53 91 B
Dudley Gdns. W13......................60 16 79 B
Dudley Rd. E17...........................26 37 90 C
Dudley Rd. Felt...........................81 08 73 D
Dudley Rd. Har...........................32 14 86 A
Dudley Rd. Ilf ....51 43 85 B
Dudley Rd. King..........................93 18 68 B
Dudley Rd. N3.............................23 25 90 D
Dudley Rd. NW6 ....46 24 83 D
Dudley Rd. Rich..........................71 18 76 D
Dudley Rd. Rom..........................30 53 91 B
Dudley Rd. Sthl ....59 11 79 D
Dudley Rd. SW19........................95 25 70 A
Dudley St. W2 ....1 26 81 B
Dudlington Rd. E5 ....38 35 86 A
Dudmaston Mews. SW3 ....62 26 78 D
Dudsbury Rd. Dart.....................80 52 74 B
Dudsbury Rd. Sid ....100 46 70 B
Dudset La. Houn.........................69 10 76 A
Dufferin Ave. EC1.........................4 32 82 D
Dufferin St. EC1............................4 32 82 D
Duffield Cl. Har ....33 15 88 B
Duff St. E14................................57 37 81 D
Dufour's Pl. W1............................2 29 81 C
Duke Humphrey Rd. SE3...........77 39 76 A
Duke of Cambridge Cl. Twick ....70 14 74 D

Duke of Edinburgh Rd. Sutt .....103 26 65 B
Duke of Wellington Pl. SW1 ....6 28 79 A
Duke of York St. SW1...................6 29 80 C
Duke Rd. Ilf ....28 44 89 D
Duke Rd. W4...............................61 20 78 D
kes Ave. Edg ....21 18 91 B
Dukes Ave. Har ....32 12 88 D
Dukes Ave. Har ....21 15 89 C
Dukes Ave. Houn........................70 12 75 C
Dukes Ave. King..........................83 17 71 B
Dukes Ave. N10...........................24 29 89 A
Dukes Ave. N3 ....23 25 90 B
Dukes Ave. N Mal ....94 21 68 A
Dukes Ave. Nthlt ....43 12 84 C
Dukes Ave. Rich ....83 17 71 A
Duke's Ave. W4...........................61 20 78 D
Dukes Cl. Ashf............................87 08 71 A
Dukes Cl. Hamp..........................82 12 71 D
Dukes Ct. E6...............................51 43 83 A
Duke's Head Yd. N6 ....36 28 87 D
Dukes La. W8 ....62 25 79 B
Dukes Mews N10 ....24 28 89 B
Duke's Mews. W1 ....2 28 81 C
Duke's Pas. E17 ....26 38 89 A
Duke's Pl. EC3..............................4 33 81 C
Dukes Rd. E6 ....51 43 83 A
Dukes Rd. W3 ....55 19 82 C
Duke's Rd. WC1 ....2 29 82 B
Duke St Hill. SE1...........................8 32 80 D
Dukesthorpe Rd. SE26...............88 35 71 B
Duke St. Rich ....71 17 74 B
Duke St St James's. SW1..............6 29 80 C
Duke St. Sutt.............................110 26 64 B
Duke St. W1..................................2 28 81 C
Dukes Way. W.Wick..................107 39 65 C
Duke's Yd. W1...............................6 28 80 A
Dulas St. N4................................37 31 87 C
Dulford St. W11..........................56 24 80 A
Dulka Rd. SW11..........................74 27 74 B
Dulverton Rd. Rom.....................30 53 91 B
Dulverton Rd. Ruis.....................31 10 86 A
Dulverton Rd. SE9......................90 44 72 B
Dulwich Common. SE21.............87 33 73 D
Dulwich Rd. SE24.......................75 31 74 D
Dulwich Village. SE21.................75 33 74 C
Dulwich Wood Ave. SE19...........87 33 71 C
Dulwich Wood Park. SE19..........87 33 71 D
Dumbarton Ct. SW2....................74 30 74 D
Dumbarton Rd. SW2...................74 30 74 C
Dumbleton Cl. King....................94 19 69 B
Dumbreck Rd. SE9......................78 43 75 A
Dumont Rd. N16 ....37 33 86 C
Dumpton Pl. NW1.......................47 28 84 C
Dunbar Ave. Beck.......................98 36 68 C
Dunbar Ave. Dag ....41 49 86 C
Dunbar Ave. SW16......................97 31 69 C
Dunbar Ct. Sutt.........................110 26 64 D
Dunbar Gdns. Dag......................52 49 85 D
Dunbar Rd. E7.............................50 40 84 A
Dunbar Rd. N22..........................25 34 91 B
Dunbar Rd. N Mal ....94 20 68 C
Dunbar St. SE27.........................87 31 72 C
Dunblane Rd. SE9.......................77 42 76 C
Dunboyne Rd. NW3....................47 27 85 D
Dunbridge St. E2.........................57 34 82 D
Duncan Rd. N21..........................17 31 94 D
Duncan Gr. W3............................55 21 81 C
Duncannon St. WC2......................7 30 80 A
Duncan Rd. E8.............................48 34 83 B
Duncan Rd. Rich.........................71 18 75 C
Duncan St. N1 ....48 31 83 D
Duncan Terr. N1..........................48 31 83 D
Dunch St. E1...............................57 34 81 D
Duncombe Hill. SE23 ....88 36 73 A
Duncombe Rd. N19.....................36 29 87 D
Duncombe Rd. N19.....................36 30 87 C
Duncrievie Rd. SE13...................76 38 74 D
Duncroft. SE18............................66 45 77 C
Dundalk Rd. SE4.........................76 36 75 A
Dundas Gdns. E Mol ....92 13 68 B
Dundas Rd. SE15........................76 35 76 C
Dundee Rd. E13..........................50 40 83 D
Dundee Rd. SE25......................105 34 67 B
Dundee St. E1.............................57 34 80 D
Dundela Gdns. Eps...................109 22 64 B
Dundonald Rd. NW10.................46 23 83 B
Dundry Ho. SE26........................87 34 72 C
Dunedin Rd. E10.........................38 38 86 C
Dunedin Rd. Ilf...........................40 44 87 C
Dunedin Way. Hay.....................53 11 82 C
Dunelm Gr. SE27........................87 32 72 C
Dunelm St. E1.............................57 35 81 D
Dunfield Rd. SE6.........................88 37 71 D
Dunford Rd. N7...........................47 30 85 B
Dungarvan Ave. SW15 ....72 22 75 C

Dunheved Cl. Th Hth ....105 31 67 C
Dunheved Road N. Th Hth.......105 31 67 C
Dunheved Road S. Th Hth.......105 31 67 C
Dunheved Road W. Th Hth.......105 31 67 C
Dunholme Green. N9..................17 33 93 D
Dunholme La. N9........................17 33 93 D
Dunholme Rd. N9.......................17 33 93 D
Dunkeld Rd. Dag........................41 47 86 A
Dunkeld Rd. SE25.......................97 32 68 D
Dunkery Rd. SE9.........................89 42 72 C
Dunlace Rd. E5............................49 35 85 B
Dunleary Cl. Houn......................82 12 73 B
Dunloe Ave. N17.........................25 32 89 B
Dunloe St. E2..............................48 33 83 D
Dunlop Pl. SE16............................8 33 79 D
Dunmore Rd. NW6......................46 24 83 A
Dunmore Rd. SW20.....................95 23 69 B
Dunmow Cl. Felt.........................82 12 71 A
Dunmow Cl. Rom........................41 47 88 A
Dunmow Rd. E15.........................49 38 86 B
Dunmow Wlk. N1........................48 32 83 A
Dunmow Mead. NW9..................22 21 91 D
Dunn Mead. NW9........................22 21 91 D
Dunn's Pas. WC1..........................3 30 81 C
Dunn St. E8.................................48 33 85 D
Dunollie Pl. NW5.........................47 29 85 C
Dunollie Rd. NW5.......................47 29 85 C
Dunoon Rd. SE23.......................88 35 73 A
Dunraven Dri. Enf.......................13 31 97 C
Dunraven Rd. W12......................55 22 80 C
Draven St. W1...............................5 27 80 B
Dunsany Rd. W14........................62 23 79 D
Dunsbury Cl. Sutt.....................110 25 62 B
Dunsford Way. SW15..................72 22 74 D
Dunsmure Rd. N16......................37 33 87 C
Dunspring La. Ilf..........................28 43 90 D
Dunstable Cl. Rom......................30 53 91 B
Dunstable Mews. W1....................2 28 81 A
Dunstable Rd. E Mol ....92 12 68 D
Dunstable Rd. Rich.....................71 18 75 C
Dunstable Rd. Rom.....................30 53 91 B
Dunstall Rd. SW20......................95 23 70 A
Dunstall Way. E Mol ....92 13 68 B
Dunstall Welling Estate. Well....78 46 76 D
Dunstan Cl. N2............................23 26 89 A
Dunstan Rd. NW11.....................35 24 87 D
Dunstan's Gr. SE22.....................75 34 74 D
Dunstan's Rd. SE22....................75 34 74 D
Dunster Ave. Mord...................103 23 66 D
Dunster Cl. Barn.........................11 23 96 D
Dunster Cl. Rom..........................29 50 90 C
Dunster Ct. EC3............................8 33 80 A
Dunster Dri. NW9........................34 20 87 C
Dunster Gdns. NW6....................46 24 84 D
Dunsterville Way. SE1..................8 32 79 B
Dunster Way. Har.......................32 12 86 C
Dunston Rd. E8............................48 33 83 B
Dunston Rd. SW11......................74 28 75 A
Dunston St. E8.............................46 33 83 B
Dunton Cl. Surb........................101 18 66 C
Dunton Rd. E10...........................38 37 87 B
Dunton Rd. Rom..........................30 51 88 C
Dunton Rd. SE1...........................63 33 78 B
Duntshill Rd. SW18.....................85 25 73 D
Dunvegan Cl. E Mol....................92 13 68 D
Dunvegan Rd. SE9......................77 42 75 D
Dunwich Rd. Bexh......................79 48 76 B
Dunworth Mews. W11................56 24 81 D
Duplex Ride. SW1.........................5 27 79 B
Dupont Rd. SW20........................95 23 69 D
Dupont St. E14............................57 36 81 A
Duppas Ave. Croy.....................112 31 64 B
Duppas Hill La. Croy.................112 31 64 B
Duppas Hill Rd. Croy................112 31 64 B
Duppas Hill Terr. Croy..............105 31 65 D
Duppas Rd. Croy......................105 31 65 D
Dupree Rd. SE7...........................65 40 78 D
Dura Den Cl. Beck......................98 37 70 D
Durand Cl. Cars.........................104 27 66 D
Durand Gdns. SW9.....................74 30 76 B
Durand Way. NW10.....................45 20 84 C
Durants Park Ave. Enf................14 35 96 D
Durants Rd. Enf...........................14 35 96 D
Durant St. E2...............................57 34 82 A
Durban Gdns. Dag......................52 50 84 C
Durban Rd. Beck.........................98 36 69 D
Durban Rd. E15...........................58 39 82 A
Durban Rd. E17...........................26 38 90 B
Durban Rd. Ilf.............................40 45 87 C
Durban Rd. N17...........................25 33 91 B
Durban Rd. SE27.........................87 32 71 B
Durdans Rd. Sthl.........................53 12 81 D
Durell Gdns. Dag........................52 47 85 D
Durell Rd. Dag............................52 47 85 D
Durford Cres. SW15....................84 22 73 D
Durham Ave. Brom.....................99 39 68 D

Street	Page	Map ref
Durham Ave. Houn	59	12 78 D
Durham Ave. Rom	30	53 89 C
Durham Hill. Brom	89	39 71 B
Durham House St. WC2	7	30 80 A
Durham Pl. SW3	9	27 78 D
Durham Rd. Brom	99	39 68 B
Durham Rd. Dag	52	50 85 C
Durham Rd. E12	50	41 85 B
Durham Rd. E16	58	39 82 C
Durham Rd. Felt	82	11 73 A
Durham Rd. Har	32	13 88 B
Durham Rd. N2	24	27 89 B
Durham Rd. N7	36	30 86 B
Durham Rd. N9	17	34 93 A
Durham Rd. Sid	90	46 71 D
Durham Rd. SW20	94	22 69 B
Durham Rd. W5	60	17 79 D
Durham Rise. SE18	56	44 78 B
Durham Row. E1	57	36 81 A
Durham St. SE11	10	30 77 B
Durham Terr. W2	56	25 81 D
Durley Ave. Pnr	32	12 88 C
Durley Gdns. Mord	103	26 67 C
Durley Rd. N16	37	33 87 A
Durlston Rd. E5	37	34 86 A
Durlston St. King	93	18 70 A
Durnford St. N15	37	33 88 A
Durnford St. SE10	64	38 77 A
Durning Rd. SE19	87	32 71 D
Durnsford Ave. SW19	85	25 72 A
Durnsford Rd. N11	24	29 91 D
Durnsford Rd. SW19	85	25 72 D
Durrell Rd. SW6	73	24 76 B
Durrington Ave. SW20	95	23 70 C
Durrington Park Rd. SW20	95	23 69 A
Durrington Rd. E5	49	36 85 A
Dursley Cl. SE3	77	41 76 C
Dursley Gdns. SE3	77	41 76 B
Dursley Rd. SE3	77	41 75 D
Durward St. E1	57	34 81 B
Durweston Mews. W1	1	27 81 B
Durweston St. W1	1	27 81 B
Dury Falls Cl. Horn	42	54 87 D
Dury Rd. Barn	11	24 97 D
Dutch Yd. SW18	73	25 74 A
Duthie St. E14	58	38 80 A
Dutton St. SE10	76	38 76 A
Dye House La. E3	49	37 83 A
Dyers Hall Rd. E11	39	39 87 C
Dyer's La. SW15	72	22 75 D
Dyer's Way. Rom	30	52 91 D
Dykes Way. Brom	99	39 68 B
Dylan Rd. Belv	67	49 79 C
Dylways. SE5	75	32 75 D
Dymchurch Cl. Ilf	28	43 89 A
Dymes Path. SW19	85	23 72 B
Dymock St. SW6	73	25 75 B
Dymoke Rd. Horn	42	51 87 B
Dymond Estate. SW17	86	27 72 C
Dyneley Rd. SE12	89	41 72 C
Dyne Rd. NW6	46	24 84 D
Dynevor Rd. N16	37	33 86 C
Dynevor Rd. Rich	71	18 74 A
Dynham Rd. NW6	46	25 84 C
Dyott St. WC1	2	29 81 D
Dyott St. WC1	3	30 81 C
Dysart Ave. King	83	17 71 A
Dysart St. EC2	4	33 82 C
Dyson Rd. E11	39	39 88 C
Dyson Rd. E15	50	39 84 B
Dyson's Rd. N18	25	34 91 B
Dyson's Rd. N18	17	34 92 D
Eade Rd. N4	37	32 87 A
Eagan's Cl. N2	23	26 89 B
Eagle Ave. Rom	41	48 88 C
Eagle Cl. Enf	14	35 96 C
Eagle Ct. E11	27	40 89 C
Eagle Ct. EC1	3	31 81 B
Eagle Hill. SE19	97	32 70 B
Eagle La. E11	27	40 89 C
Eagle Lodge. NW11	35	24 87 B
Eagle Pl. SW1	6	29 80 A
Eagle Rd. Wem	44	17 84 D
Eaglesfield Rd. SE18	78	43 76 B
Eagle St. WC1	3	30 81 B
Eagle Terr. Wdf.Gn	27	40 91 D
Eaglet Pl. E1	57	35 82 C
Eagle Wharf Rd. N1	48	32 83 C
Eagling Rd. E3	57	37 82 B
Ealdham Sq. SE9	77	41 75 D
Ealing Gdns. W5	54	17 80 D
Ealing Park Gdns. W5	60	17 78 A
Ealing Rd. Brent	60	17 78 B
Ealing Rd. Nthlt	43	13 84 C
Ealing Rd. Wem	44	18 84 C
Ealing Village. W5	54	18 81 C
Eamont Rd. N Mal	94	21 68 D
Eamont Rd. NW8	47	27 83 C
Eardemont Cl. Dart	80	61 75 D
Eardley Cres. SW5	62	25 78 C
Eardley Rd. Belv	67	49 78 C
Eardley Rd. SW16	96	29 70 B
Earl Cottages. SE1	63	33 78 D
Earldom Rd. SW15	73	23 75 C
Earle Gdns. King	93	18 70 C
Earlham Gr. E7	50	40 85 C
Earlham Gr. N22	24	30 91 D
Earlham St. WC2	3	30 81 C
Earl Rd. SE1	63	33 78 D
Earl Rd. SW14	72	20 75 C
Earl Rise. SE18	66	44 78 B
Earl's Court Gdns. SW5	62	25 78 B
Earl's Court Rd. SW5	62	25 78 B
Earl's Court Rd. W8	62	25 79 C
Earl's Court Sq. SW5	62	25 78 D
Earls Cres. Har	21	15 89 C
Earlsferry Way. N1	47	30 84 D
Earlsfield Rd. SW18	85	26 73 A
Earlshall Rd. SE9	78	43 75 C
Earlsmead. Har	43	12 85 B
Earlsmead Rd. N15	37	33 88 B
Earlsmead Rd. NW10	56	23 82 A
Earl St. EC2	4	33 81 A
Earls Terr. W8	62	24 79 D
Earlsthorpe Rd. SE26	88	35 71 B
Earlstoke St. EC1	3	31 82 B
Earlston Gr. E9	48	34 83 B
Earls Wlk. Dag	51	46 85 B
Earls Wlk. W8	62	25 79 C
Earlswood Ave. Th Hth	105	31 67 A
Earlswood Cl. E10	65	39 78 C
Earlswood Gdns. Ilf	28	43 89 C
Earlswood St. E10	65	39 78 C
Early Mews. NW1	47	28 83 B
Earnshaw St. WC2	2	29 81 D
Earsby St. W14	62	24 78 A
Easby Cres. Mord	103	25 67 D
Easebourne Rd. Dag	52	47 85 C
Easleys Mews. W1	2	28 81 C
East Acton La. W3	55	21 80 A
East Arbour St. E1	57	35 81 D
East Ave. E12	50	42 84 C
East Ave. E17	38	37 88 B
East Ave. N2	23	26 89 A
East Ave. Sthl	53	12 80 B
East Ave. Wall	111	30 64 D
East Bank. N16	37	33 87 A
Eastbank Rd. Hamp	82	14 71 C
East Barnet Rd. Barn	11	26 95 B
East Boundary Rd. E12	39	42 86 D
Eastbourne Ave. W3	55	20 81 D
Eastbourne Gdns. SW14	72	20 75 A
Eastbourne Mews. W2	1	26 81 C
Eastbourne Rd. Brent	60	17 78 D
Eastbourne Rd. E15	39	39 83 A
Eastbourne Rd. Felt	82	11 72 B
Eastbourne Rd. N15	37	33 88 C
Eastbourne Rd. SW17	96	28 70 A
Eastbourne Rd. W4	61	20 77 A
Eastbourne Terr. W2	1	26 81 C
Eastbournia Ave. N9	17	34 93 D
Eastbrook Ave. Dag	52	50 85 A
Eastbrook Ave. N9	18	35 94 A
Eastbrook Dri. Rom	42	51 86 A
Eastbrook Rd. SE3	77	40 76 B
Eastbury Ave. Bark	51	45 83 A
Eastbury Ave. Enf	13	33 97 B
Eastbury Ave. Nthwd	19	10 91 A
Eastbury Gr. W4	61	21 78 C
Eastbury Rd. King	93	18 70 C
Eastbury Rd. Nthwd	19	09 91 A
Eastbury Rd. Orp	108	44 67 D
Eastbury Rd. Rom	41	50 88 D
Eastbury Sq. Bark	51	45 83 B
Eastbury Terr. E1	57	35 82 D
Eastcastle St. W1	2	29 81 C
Eastcheap. EC3	8	33 80 A
East Churchfield Rd. W3	55	20 80 D
Eastchurch Rd. Houn	69	09 75 A
East Cl. Barn	12	28 96 C
East Cl. Grnf	43	14 93 C
East Cl. W5	55	19 92 C
Eastcombe Ave. SE7	65	40 77 B
Eastcote Ave. Grnf	44	16 85 C
Eastcote Ave. Har	32	14 86 A
Eastcote La. Har	32	13 86 C
Eastcote Lane N. Nthlt	43	13 84 A
Eastcote La. Nthlt	43	12 85 D
Eastcote. Orp	108	45 66 D
Eastcote Rd. Har	32	14 86 C
Eastcote Rd. Pnr	32	11 88 B
Eastcote Rd. Ruis	31	09 87 B
Eastcote Rd. Well	78	44 76 D
Eastcote St. SW9	74	30 76 D
Eastcote View. Pnr	20	11 89 C
East Cres. Enf	13	33 95 B
East Cres. N11	16	28 93 C
Eastcroft Rd. Eps	109	21 63 C
East Cross Route. E3	49	37 83 A
East Cross Route. E9	49	36 84 B
East Ct. Wem	33	17 86 A
Eastdown Park. SE13	76	38 75 D
East Dri. Cars	111	27 62 B
East Dri. Orp	108	46 67 D
East Dulwich Gr. SE22	75	33 74 A
East Dulwich Rd.	75	34 75 C
East End Rd. N2	23	26 89 A
East End Rd. N3	23	25 90 C
East End Way. Pnr	20	12 89 A
East Entrance. Dag	52	49 83 D
Eastern Ave. E11	39	41 88 C
Eastern Ave. Ilf	40	44 88 D
Eastern Avenue E. Rom	30	51 90 B
Eastern Avenue W. Rom	29	49 89 C
Eastern Ave. Pnr	32	12 87 A
Eastern Perimeter Rd. Houn	69	10 76 C
Eastern Rd. E13	50	40 83 D
Eastern Rd. E17	38	38 88 A
Eastern Rd. N2	24	27 89 D
Eastern Rd. N22	24	30 90 A
Eastern Rd. Rom	42	51 88 B
Eastern Rd. SE4	76	38 75 C
Easternville Gdns. Ilf	40	44 88 C
East Ferry Rd. E14	64	37 79 D
Eastfield Ct. W3	55	21 80 C
Eastfield Gdns. Dag	52	49 85 A
Eastfield Rd. Dag	52	49 85 A
Eastfield Rd. E17	38	37 89 C
Eastfield Rd. N8	24	30 89 A
Eastfields. Pnr	32	11 88 A
Eastfields Rd. Mit	96	28 69 C
Eastfields W3	55	20 81 A
East Gdns. SW17	96	27 70 A
East Gdns. SW17	96	27 70 A
Eastglade. Pnr	20	12 89 B
East Harding St. EC4	3	31 81 C
East Heath Rd. NW3	35	26 86 D
East Hill. S Croy	112	33 62 C
East Hill. SW18	73	26 74 A
East Hill. Wem	34	19 87 C
East Holme. Eri	79	50 76 B
Eastholm. NW11	23	25 89 D
East India Dock Rd. E14	57	37 80 A
East India Dock Rd. E14	58	38 81 D
East India Dock Wall Rd. E14	58	38 80 B
Eastlake Rd. SE5	75	32 76 C
East La. King	93	17 68 B
Eastlands Cres. SE21	87	33 73 B
Eastlands Cres. SE22	75	33 74 D
East La. SE16	63	34 79 A
East La. Wem	33	17 86 C
Eastleigh Ave. Har	32	13 86 B
Eastleigh Cl. NW2	34	21 86 C
Eastleigh Cl. Sutt	110	25 63 D
Eastleigh Cl. Bexh	79	50 75 A
Eastleigh Rd. Houn	69	09 75 B
Eastleigh Wlk. SW15	84	22 73 A
Eastman Rd. W3	61	20 79 B
Eastmead Ave. Grnf	53	13 82 B
Eastmead Cl. Brom	99	42 69 C
East Mead. Ruis	32	11 86 D
Eastmearn Rd. SE21	87	32 72 A
Eastmoor Pl. SE7	65	41 79 D
Eastmoor St. SE7	65	41 78 B
East Mount St. E1	57	34 81 B
Eastney Rd. Croy	105	31 66 D
Eastney St. SE10	64	38 78 D
Eastnor Rd. SE9	90	44 73 C
Easton St. WC1	3	31 82 C
East Park Cl. Rom	41	48 88 A
East Pas. EC1	4	32 81 A
East Pier. E1	57	34 80 D
East Pl. SE27	87	32 71 A
East Poultry Ave. EC1	3	31 81 B
East Ramp. Houn	69	07 76 B
East Rd. Barn	12	28 94 C
East Rd. E15	50	40 83 A
East Rd. Edg	22	20 90 A
East Rd. Felt	81	08 73 B
East Rd. King	93	18 69 A
East Rd. N1	4	32 82 B
East Rd. N2	24	27 90 A
East Rd. Rom	41	48 88 A

East Rd. Rom. _41_	50 87 B
East Rd. SW19 _95_	26 70 A
East Rd. Well _78_	46 76 D
East Rochester Way. Bex. _79_	48 74 D
East Rochester Way. Sid. _78_	46 74 A
East Row. E11 _39_	40 88 C
East Row. W10 _56_	24 82 C
Eastry Ave. Brom _107_	39 67 D
Eastry Rd. Eri _67_	49 77 C
East Sheen Ave. SW14 _72_	20 75 D
Eastside Rd. NW11 _23_	24 89 D
East Smithfield. E1 _8_	33 80 B
St. Bark _51_	44 84 C
St. Bexh _79_	49 75 C
St. Brent _60_	17 77 C
St. Brom _99_	40 69 C
St. SE17 _63_	32 78 D
East Surrey Gr. SE15 _63_	33 77 D
East Tenter St. E1 _4_	33 81 D
East Towers. Pnr _32_	11 88 D
Eastview Ave. SE18 _66_	45 77 C
East View. Barn _11_	24 96 B
East View. E4 _18_	38 92 C
Eastville Ave. NW11 _35_	24 88 D
Eastway. Brom _107_	40 66 A
East Way. Croy _106_	36 65 C
Eastway. E10 _39_	37 85 A
Eastway. E11 _39_	40 88 B
Eastway. E9 _49_	36 85 D
Eastway. Mord _95_	24 68 C
Eastway Park. E9 _49_	36 84 B
East Way. Ruis _31_	10 87 C
Eastway. Wall _111_	29 64 A
Eastwell Cl. Beck _98_	36 69 A
East Wlk. Barn _16_	28 94 C
Eastwood Cl. E18 _27_	40 90 C
Eastwood Rd. E18 _27_	40 90 D
Eastwood Rd. Ilf _40_	46 87 A
Eastwood Rd. N10 _24_	28 90 C
Eastwood St. SW16 _96_	29 70 A
Eatington Rd. E10 _38_	38 88 B
Eaton Cl. SW1 _9_	28 78 A
Eaton Ct. SW1 _100_	44 70 A
Eaton Dri. SW9 _75_	31 75 D
Eaton Dr. King _94_	19 70 C
Eaton Dr. Rom _29_	49 91 D
Eaton Gate. Nthwd _19_	08 91 A
Eaton Gate. SW1 _9_	28 78 A
Eaton Gdns. Dag _52_	48 84 C
Eaton Gr. N19 _36_	29 86 D
Eaton La. Wall _6_	28 79 D
Eaton Mews N. SW1 _6_	28 79 C
Eaton Mews S. SW1 _6_	28 79 D
Eaton Mews W. SW1 _6_	28 78 A
Eaton Park Rd. N13 _17_	31 93 B
Eaton Pl. SW1 _6_	28 78 A
Eaton Pl. SW1 _6_	28 79 C
Eaton Rd. Enf _13_	33 96 C
Eaton Rd. Houn _70_	14 75 D
Eaton Rd. NW4 _35_	23 88 A
Eaton Rd. Sutt _110_	26 63 B
Eaton Rise. E11 _39_	41 88 A
Eaton Rise. W5 _54_	17 81 D
Eaton Row. SW1 _9_	28 79 D
Eatons Mead. E4 _18_	37 93 A
Eaton Sq. SW1 _6_	28 79 C
Eaton Terr Mews. SW1 _6_	28 78 A
Eaton Terr. SW1 _9_	28 78 A
Eatonville Rd. SW17 _86_	27 72 B
Eatonville Villas. SW17 _86_	27 72 B
Eaton Wlk. SE15 _75_	33 76 B
Eaton Wlk. SE15 _50_	33 77 D
Ebbisham Dr. SW8 _10_	30 77 B
Ebbisham Rd. Wor Pk _103_	23 65 A
Ebbsfleet Rd. NW2 _4_	24 85 A
Ebenezer St. N1 _4_	32 82 B
Ebenezer Wlk. SW16 _96_	29 69 A
Ebley Cl. SE15 _63_	33 77 B
Ebner St. SW18 _73_	25 74 B
Ebor St. E1 _4_	33 82 D
Ebrington Rd. Har _33_	17 88 D
Ebsworth St. SE23 _88_	35 73 B
Eburne Rd. N7 _36_	30 86 C
Ebury Bridge Rd. SW1 _9_	28 78 C
Ebury Bridge. SW1 _9_	28 78 D
Ebury Cl. Brom _107_	42 65 C
Ebury Mews E. SW1 _6_	28 79 D
Ebury Mews. SW1 _9_	28 78 B
Ebury Sq. SW1 _9_	28 78 B
Ebury St. SW1 _9_	28 78 B
Ecclesbourne Cl. N13 _17_	31 92 C
Ecclesbourne Gdns. N13 _17_	31 92 C
Ecclesbourne Rd. N1 _48_	32 84 C
Ecclesbourne Rd. Th Hth _105_	32 67 A
Eccles Rd. SW11 _74_	27 75 D
Eccleston Bridge. SW1 _9_	28 78 B
Eccleston Cl. Barn _12_	27 96 D
Eccleston Cl. Orp _108_	44 66 D
Eccleston Cres. Rom _40_	46 87 B
Ecclestone Ct. Wem _44_	18 85 C
Ecclestone Mews. Wem _44_	18 85 C
Ecclestone Pl. Wem _44_	18 85 D
Eccleston Mews. SW1 _6_	28 79 C
Eccleston Pl. SW1 _9_	28 78 B
Eccleston Rd. W13 _54_	16 80 C
Eccleston Sq Mews. SW1 _10_	29 78 A
Eccleston Sq Mews. SW1 _10_	29 78 A
Eccleston Sq. SW1 _9_	28 78 B
Eccleston Sq. SW1 _9_	28 78 B
Echelforde Dri. Ashf _81_	07 71 A
Echo Hts. E4 _18_	37 94 D
Eckersley St. E1 _4_	33 82 D
Eckford St. N1 _48_	31 83 C
Eckstein Rd. SW11 _74_	27 75 C
Eclipse Rd. E13 _58_	40 81 B
Ector Rd. SE6 _89_	39 72 A
Edbrooke Rd. W9 _56_	25 82 C
Eddisbury Ho. SE26. _87_	34 72 C
Eddiscombe Rd. SW6 _73_	24 76 D
Eddy Cl. Rom _41_	49 88 D
Eddystone Rd. SE4 _76_	36 74 A
Eden Cl. Houn _70_	12 75 B
Edenbridge Rd. E9 _49_	35 84 D
Edenbridge Rd. Enf _13_	33 95 C
Eden Cl. Wem _44_	17 83 B
Edencourt Rd. SW16. _96_	28 70 B
Edendale Rd. Bexh _79_	50 76 D
Edenfield Gdns. Wor Pk _102_	21 65 B
Eden Gr. E17 _38_	37 88 B
Eden Gr. N7 _47_	30 85 D
Edenham Way. W10 _56_	24 81 B
Edenhurst Ave. SW6 _73_	24 75 B
Eden Rd. Beck _98_	36 68 C
Eden Rd. Croy _112_	32 64 B
Eden Rd. E17 _38_	37 88 B
Eden Rd. SE27 _81_	31 71 D
Edensor Gdns. W4 _61_	21 77 C
Edensor Rd. W4 _61_	21 77 C
Eden St. King _93_	18 69 C
Edenvale St. SW6 _73_	26 76 C
Eden Way. Beck. _106_	37 67 C
Ederline Ave. SW16 _97_	31 69 C
Edgarley Terr. SW6 _73_	24 76 A
Edgar Rd. E3 _57_	37 82 B
Edgar Rd. Rom _41_	47 87 B
Edgar Rd. S Croy _112_	32 62 B
Edgeborough Way. Brom _99_	41 69 B
Edgebury . Chis. _90_	43 71 B
Edgebury Wlk. Chis. _90_	44 71 A
Edgebury Wlk. Chis. _90_	44 72 C
Edgecombe Cl. King _94_	20 70 D
Edgecombe Rd. E11 _39_	39 87 D
Edgecote Cl. W3 _55_	19 80 D
Edgefield Ave. Bark _51_	45 84 D
Edge Hill Ave. N3 _23_	25 89 C
Edge Hill Ct. SW19 _95_	23 70 D
Edgehill Gdns. Dag _52_	49 85 A
Edgehill Rd. Chis _90_	44 71 A
Edgehill Rd. Mit _96_	28 69 B
Edgehill Rd. Pur _112_	31 62 D
Edgehill Rd. W13 _54_	17 81 A
Edge Hill. SE18 _66_	43 77 B
Edge Hill. SW19 _95_	23 70 D
Edgeley La. SW4 _74_	29 75 B
Edgeley Rd. SW4 _74_	29 75 B
Edgel St. SW18 _73_	25 75 D
Edge Point Cl. SE27 _87_	31 71 D
Edge St. W8 _56_	25 80 C
Edgeware Ct. Edg _22_	19 91 A
Edgewood Green. Croy _106_	35 66 D
Edgeworth Ave. NW4 _34_	22 88 A
Edgeworth Cl. NW4 _34_	22 88 A
Edgeworth Cres. NW4 _34_	22 88 A
Edgeworth Rd. Barn _12_	27 96 C
Edgeworth Rd. SE9 _77_	41 75 C
Edgware Rd. Edg _22_	19 91 A
Edgware Rd. NW2 _34_	22 86 B
Edgware Rd. NW9 _34_	21 88 A
Edgware Rd. W2 _1_	27 81 A
Edgware Rd. W2 _1_	27 81 A
Edinburgh Ct. Mord _103_	23 67 B
Edinburgh Dri. Uxb _37_	08 80 D
Edinburgh Rd. E13 _58_	40 83 D
Edinburgh Rd. E17 _38_	37 88 A
Edinburgh Rd. N18 _17_	34 92 C
Edinburgh Rd. Sutt _110_	26 65 B
Edinburgh Rd. W7 _60_	15 79 B
Edington Rd. Enf _14_	35 97 C
Edington Rd. SE2 _66_	46 79 D
Edison Ave. Horn _42_	51 87 D
Edison Cl. Horn _42_	51 87 D
Edison Dri. Sthl _53_	13 81 D
Edison Gr. SE18 _66_	45 77 D
Edison Rd. Brom _99_	40 69 C
Edison Rd. N8 _36_	29 88 D
Edison Rd. Well _78_	45 76 B
Edis St. NW1 _47_	28 83 A
Edith Gdns. Surb _102_	19 66 B
Edith Gr. SW10 _62_	26 77 C
Edithna St. SW9 _74_	30 75 A
Edith Rd. E15 _49_	38 85 D
Edith Rd. E6 _50_	41 84 D
Edith Rd. N11 _24_	29 91 D
Edith Rd. Rom _41_	47 88 D
Edith Rd. SE25 _105_	32 67 B
Edith Rd. SW19 _95_	25 70 B
Edith Rd. W14 _62_	24 78 A
Edith Row. SW6 _73_	25 76 B
Edith St. E2 _48_	34 83 C
Edith Terr. SW10 _62_	26 77 C
Edith Villas. W14 _62_	24 78 D
Edmanson's Ct. N17 _25_	33 90 B
Edmond Ct. SE15 _76_	35 76 A
Edmonscote. W13 _54_	16 81 A
Edmonton Ct. SE16 _64_	35 79 C
Edmonton Green Shopping Centre. N9 _17_	34 93 B
Edmund Rd. Mit. _96_	27 68 A
Edmund Rd. Well _78_	46 75 A
Edmunds Cl. Hay _53_	11 81 A
Edmund St. SE5 _63_	32 77 D
Edmunds Wlk. N2 _27_	89 C
Edna Rd. SW20 _95_	23 69 D
Edna St. SW11 _74_	27 76 A
Edrick Rd. Edg _22_	20 91 A
Edrick Wlk. Edg _22_	20 91 A
Edric Rd. SE14 _64_	35 77 D
Edridge Rd. Croy _112_	32 65 D
Edward Ave. E4 _26_	87 B
Edward Ave. Mord _103_	26 67 B
Edward Cl. Hamp _82_	14 71 C
Edward Cl. N9 _17_	33 94 B
Edward Cl. Rom _30_	53 89 A
Edward Ct. E16 _58_	40 81 A
Edwardes Sq. W8 _62_	25 79 C
Edward Gr. Barn _11_	28 95 B
Edward Pl. SE8 _64_	36 77 B
Edward Rd. Barn _11_	26 95 B
Edward Rd. Brom _99_	41 70 C
Edward Rd. Chis _90_	43 71 D
Edward Rd. Croy _105_	33 66 A
Edward Rd. E17 _38_	35 88 B
Edward Rd. Felt. _69_	09 74 A
Edward Rd. Hamp _82_	14 71 C
Edward Rd. Har _32_	14 89 A
Edward Rd. Nthlt. _43_	11 83 C
Edward Rd. Rom _41_	48 88 C
Edward Rd. SE20 _98_	35 70 B
Edward's Ave. Ruis _31_	11 85 C
Edwards Cl. Wor Pk _103_	23 65 B
Edward's Cottages. N1 _48_	31 84 B
Edward's La. N16 _37_	32 86 B
Edwards Mews. W1 _2_	28 81 C
Edward Sq. N1 _47_	30 83 B
Edwards Rd. Belv _67_	49 78 A
Edward St. E13 _58_	40 82 C
Edward St. E16 _58_	40 82 C
Edward St. SE8 _64_	36 77 B
Edward Temme Ave. E15 _50_	39 84 D
Edware Ct. Edg _22_	19 91 A
Edwina Gdns. Ilf _39_	42 88 A
Edwin Ave. E6 _51_	43 83 C
Edwin Cl. Bexh _67_	48 77 B
Edwin Pl. Croy _105_	32 66 D
Edwin Rd. Edg _22_	20 91 B
Edwin Rd. Twick _83_	15 73 C
Edwin's Mead. E9 _49_	36 85 A
Edwin St. E16 _58_	40 81 A
Edwin St. E1 _57_	35 82 C
Edwyn Cl. Barn _11_	23 95 D
Effie Pl. SW6 _62_	25 77 C
Effingham Cl. Sutt _110_	25 63 D
Effingham Cl. SW19 _96_	27 70 C
Effingham Rd. Croy _104_	30 66 D
Effingham Rd. N8 _25_	31 89 D
Effingham Rd. SE12 _77_	39 74 B
Effingham Rd. Surb _101_	17 66 A
Effort St. SW17 _86_	27 71 C
Effra Par. SW2 _75_	31 74 A
Effra Rd. SW19 _95_	25 70 D
Effra Rd. SW2 _75_	31 74 A
Egan Way. SE16 _63_	34 78 D
Egbert St. NW1 _47_	28 83 A

Name	Page	Grid
Egdon Way. SE3	77	40 75 B
Egerton Cl. Pnr	19	10 89 C
Egerton Cres. SW3	9	27 78 A
Egerton Dri. SE10	76	37 76 B
Egerton Gdns. Ilf	40	45 86 D
Egerton Gdns Mews. SW3	5	27 79 C
Egerton Gdns. NW10	46	23 83 A
Egerton Gdns. NW4	22	22 89 D
Egerton Gdns. SW3	5	27 79 C
Egerton Gdns. W13	54	16 81 D
Egerton Pl. SW3	5	27 79 C
Egerton Rd. N16	37	33 87 B
Egerton Rd. N Mal	94	21 68 D
Egerton Rd. SE25	97	33 68 A
Egerton Rd. Twick	83	15 73 A
Egerton Rd. Wem	44	18 84 D
Egerton Terr. SW3	5	27 79 C
Egham Cl. Sutt	103	24 65 A
Egham Cres. Sutt	103	24 65 A
Egham Rd. E13	58	40 81 B
Eglantine Rd. SW18	73	26 74 A
Egleston Rd. Mord	93	25 67 D
Eglington Rd. E4	18	38 94 B
Eglington Rd. SE18	66	43 77 B
Eglinton Hill. SE18	66	43 77 D
Egliston Mews. SW15	73	23 75 A
Egliston Rd. SW15	73	23 75 A
Eglon Mews. NW1	47	28 84 C
Egmont Ave. Surb	102	19 66 C
Egmont Rd. Surb	102	19 66 C
Egmont Rd. Sutt	110	26 63 C
Egmont St. SE14	64	35 77 D
Egremont Rd. SE27	96	31 72 C
Eighteenth Rd. Mit	96	30 68 C
Eighth Ave. E12	50	42 85 B
Eileen Rd. SE25	105	32 67 B
Elaine Gr. NW5	47	28 85 C
Elam Cl. SE5	75	31 76 D
Elam St. SE5	75	31 76 D
Eland Pl. Croy	105	31 65 D
Eland Rd. Croy	105	31 65 D
Eland Rd. SW11	74	27 75 B
Elba Pl. SE17	63	32 78 A
Elberon Ave. Croy	104	29 67 C
Elbe St. SW6	73	26 76 C
Elborough Rd. SE25	105	34 67 A
Elborough St. SW18	85	25 73 C
Elbury Dr. E16	58	40 81 C
Elcho St. SW11	9	27 77 C
Elcot Ave. SE15	63	34 77 D
Elder Ave. N8	36	30 88 A
Elderberry Rd. W5	60	18 79 A
Elderfield Rd. E5	49	35 85 A
Elderfield Wlk. E11	39	40 88 B
Elder Oak Cl. SE20	97	34 69 B
Elder Rd. SE27	87	32 71 C
Elderslie Cl. Beck	106	37 67 D
Elderslie Rd. SE9	78	43 74 A
Elder St. E1	4	33 82 D
Elderton Rd. SE26	88	36 71 A
Eldertree Pl. Mit	96	29 69 A
Eldertree Way. Mit	96	29 69 A
Elder Wlk. N1	48	32 83 A
Eldon Ave. Croy	106	35 65 A
Eldon Gr. NW3	26	26 85 D
Eldon Park. SE25	97	34 68 D
Eldon Rd. E17	26	36 89 D
Eldon Rd. N22	25	31 90 B
Eldon Rd. N9	18	35 94 C
Eldon Rd. W8	62	25 79 D
Eldon St. EC2	4	32 81 B
Eldon Way. NW10	45	19 83 D
Eldred Rd. Bark	51	45 83 A
Eldridge Cl. Felt	81	10 73 C
Eleanor Ave. Eps	109	20 62 D
Eleanor Cres. NW7	15	23 92 B
Eleanor Gdns. Dag	41	48 86 B
Eleanor Gr. SW13	72	21 75 A
Eleanor Gr. Uxb	31	07 86 D
Eleanor Rd (off Martello St). E8	48	34 84 D
Eleanor Rd (off Richmond Rd). E8	48	34 84 B
Eleanor Rd. E15	50	39 84 B
Eleanor Rd. N11	24	30 91 A
Eleanor St. E3	52	37 82 A
Eleanor Wlk. SE18	65	42 78 B
Electric Ave. SW9	75	31 75 C
Electric La. SW9	75	31 75 C
Electric Par. Surb	101	17 67 D
Elephant and Castle. SE1	7	31 79 D
Elephant La. SE16	64	35 79 A
Elephant Rd. SE17	63	32 78 A
Elers Rd. W13	60	17 79 A
Eley Rd. N18	18	35 92 D
Elfindale Rd. SE24	75	32 74 A
Elfin Gr. Tedd	83	15 71 D
Elford Cl. SE3	77	41 75 C
Elfort Rd. N5	48	31 85 A
Elfrida Cres. SE6	88	37 71 A
Elf Row. E1	57	35 80 B
Elfwine Rd. W7	54	15 81 A
Elgar Ave. Surb	102	19 66 B
Elgar Ave. SW16	86	30 68 A
Elgar Ave. W5	60	18 79 A
Elgar Rd. Houn	82	12 73 B
Elgar St. SE16	64	36 79 C
Elgin Ave. Ashf	91	08 70 A
Elgin Ave. Har	21	16 90 D
Elgin Ave. W9	56	25 82 B
Elgin Cres. Houn	69	09 76 C
Elgin Cres. W11	56	24 80 A
Elgin Dri. Nthwd	19	09 91 C
Elgin Mews N. W9	56	25 82 B
Elgin Mews S. W9	56	25 82 B
Elgin Mews. W11	56	24 81 C
Elgin Rd. Croy	105	33 65 B
Elgin Rd. Ilf	40	45 87 A
Elgin Rd. N22	24	29 90 C
Elgin Rd. Sutt	103	26 65 C
Elgin Rd. Wall	111	29 63 A
Elgood Av. Nthwd	19	10 91 A
Elham Cl. Brom	99	41 70 D
Elia Mews. N1	48	31 83 D
Elias Pl. SW8	63	31 77 A
Elia St. N1	48	31 83 D
Elibank Rd. SE9	78	43 75 C
Elim St. SE1	8	32 79 D
Eliot Bank. SE23	87	34 72 B
Eliot Cottages. SE3	77	39 76 C
Eliot Dri. Har	32	13 86 B
Eliot Hill. SE13	76	38 76 C
Eliot Park. SE13	76	38 76 C
Eliot Pl. SE3	77	39 76 C
Eliot Rd. Dag	52	47 85 B
Eliot Vale. SE3	76	38 76 D
Elizabeth Ave. Enf	13	31 96 B
Elizabeth Ave. Ilf	40	44 86 B
Elizabeth Ave. N1	48	32 84 D
Elizabeth Bridge. SW1	6	28 78 B
Elizabeth Cl. Barn	11	23 96 B
Elizabeth Cl. Rom	29	49 90 B
Elizabeth Cl. W9	26	26 82 C
Elizabeth Clyde Cl. N15	1	33 89 C
Elizabeth Cottages. Rich	72	19 76 A
Elizabeth Cl. SW1	6	29 79 D
Elizabeth Ct. Tedd	83	15 71 C
Elizabeth Gdns. Stan	17	17 91 A
Elizabeth Gdns. Sun	91	11 68 A
Elizabeth Gdns. W3	55	21 80 D
Elizabeth Mews. NW3	47	27 84 B
Elizabeth Pl. N15	25	33 89 C
Elizabeth Rd. E6	50	41 84 D
Elizabeth Rd. N15	25	33 88 A
Elizabeth Ride. N9	18	34 94 B
Elizabeth Ride. N9	18	35 94 A
Elizabeth St. SW1	9	28 78 A
Elizabeth Terr. SE9	77	42 74 D
Elizabeth Way. Felt	82	11 71 A
Elizabeth Way. SE19	97	32 70 D
Elkington Rd. E13	58	40 82 D
Elkins The. Rom	30	51 90 C
Elkstone Rd. W10	56	24 81 B
Ellaline Rd. W6	62	22 77 B
Ellanby Cres. N18	17	34 92 D
Elland Rd. SE15	76	35 75 C
Ella Rd. N8	36	30 87 A
Ellement Cl. Pnr	32	11 88 B
Ellenborough Pl. SW15	72	22 75 C
Ellenborough Rd. N22	25	32 90 C
Ellenbridge Way. S Croy	112	33 62 B
Ellen Cl. Brom	99	41 68 B
Ellen Ct. N9	18	35 93 A
Ellen St. E1	57	34 81 C
Elleray Rd. Tedd	93	15 70 B
Ellerby St. SW6	73	23 76 B
Ellerdale Cl. NW3	26	26 85 A
Ellerdale Rd. NW3	26	26 85 C
Ellerdale St. SE13	76	37 75 B
Ellerdine Rd. Houn	70	14 75 D
Ellerker Gdns. Rich	71	18 74 C
Ellerman Ave. Twick	82	12 73 D
Ellerslie Gdns. NW10	45	22 83 A
Ellerslie Rd. W12	55	22 80 D
Ellerton Gdns. Dag	52	47 84 C
Ellerton Rd. Dag	52	47 84 C
Ellerton Rd. Surb	101	18 66 D
Ellerton Rd. SW13	72	22 76 A
Ellerton Rd. SW18	85	26 73 D
Ellerton Rd. SW20	94	22 70 C
Ellery Rd. S9	97	32 70 D
Ellery St. SE15	75	34 76 D
Ellesmere Ave. Beck	98	37 69 D
Ellesmere Cl. E11	39	39 88 B
Ellesmere Cl. Ruis	31	08 87 A
Ellesmere Gdns. Ilf	39	42 88 C
Ellesmere Gr. Barn	11	24 95 B
Ellesmere Rd. E3	49	36 83 C
Ellesmere Rd. Grnf	53	14 82 C
Ellesmere Rd. NW10	45	22 85 C
Ellesmere Rd. Twick	71	17 74 C
Ellesmere Rd. W4	61	20 77 B
Ellesmere St. E14	57	37 81 D
Ellingfort Rd. E8	48	34 84 D
Ellingham Rd. E15	49	38 85 B
Ellingham Rd. W12	61	22 79 A
Ellington Ct. N14	1	29 93 B
Ellington Rd. Felt	81	09 71 B
Ellington Rd. Houn	70	13 76 D
Ellington Rd. N10	24	28 89 D
Ellington St. N7	48	31 84 A
Elliot Cl. E15	50	39 84 C
Elliot Gdns. Rom	30	52 91 D
Elliot Gdns. Shep	91	07 68 C
Elliot Rd. NW4	34	22 88 D
Elliot Rd. Stan	21	16 91 A
Elliot Rd. SW9	63	31 77 D
Elliot Rd. W4	61	21 78 A
Elliots Ct. EC4	3	31 81 D
Elliot's Row. SE11	7	31 79 D
Elliott Cl. Wem	34	19 86 C
Elliott Rd. Brom	99	41 68 D
Elliott Rd. Th Hth	97	31 68 D
Elliott's Pl. N1	48	31 83 B
Elliott's Row. SE11	63	31 78 B
Ellis Cl. SE9	90	44 72 A
Elliscombe Rd. SE7	65	41 77 A
Ellis Ct. W7	54	15 81 B
Ellisfield Dri. SW15	84	22 73 A
Ellison Gdns. Sthl	59	12 78 B
Ellison Rd. Sid	90	44 73 D
Ellison Rd. SW16	96	30 70 C
Elliso Rd. SW13	72	21 76 D
Ellis Rd. Mit	104	27 67 D
Ellis St. SW1	9	28 78 B
Ellmore Cl. Rom	30	52 90 B
Ellora Rd. SW16	86	29 71 D
Ellsworth St. E2	57	34 82 B
Elmar Rd. N15	25	32 89 D
Elm Ave. Ruis	31	10 87 B
Elm Ave. W5	54	18 80 D
Elmbank Ave. Barn	11	23 96 C
Elm Bank Gdns. SW13	72	21 76 C
Elmbank. N14	16	29 94 A
Elmbank Way. W7	54	15 81 A
Elmbourne Dri. Belv	67	49 78 B
Elmbourne Rd. SW17	86	28 72 D
Elmbridge Ave. Surb	102	20 67 C
Elmbridge Cl. Ruis	31	10 88 D
Elmbridge Dri. Ruis	31	08 88 A
Elmbridge Rd. Ilf	28	46 91 A
Elmbridge Wlk. E8	48	34 84 C
Elmbrook Gdns. SE9	77	42 75 C
Elmbrook Rd. Sutt	110	24 64 B
Elm Cl. Cars	104	27 66 D
Elm Cl. E11	39	40 88 D
Elm Cl. Har	32	13 88 D
Elm Cl. N19	36	29 86 A
Elm Cl. NW4	35	23 88 B
Elm Cl. Rom	29	49 90 B
Elm Cl. S Croy	112	33 63 A
Elm Cl. Surb	102	20 66 A
Elm Cl. SW20	95	23 68 C
Elm Cl. Twick	82	13 72 B
Elmcourt Rd. SE27	87	31 72 B
Elm Cres. King	93	18 69 A
Elm Cres. W5	54	18 80 C
Elmcroft Ave. E11	27	40 89 D
Elmcroft Ave. N9	13	34 95 D
Elmcroft Ave. NW11	35	24 87 B
Elmcroft Ave. Sid	78	46 74 C
Elmcroft Cl. Chess	101	18 65 C
Elmcroft Cl. E11	27	40 89 D
Elmcroft Cl. Felt	69	09 74 D
Elmcroft Cl. W5	54	17 81 D
Elmcroft Cres. Har	20	13 89 A
Elmcroft Cres. NW11	35	24 87 A
Elmcroft Dri. Ashf	81	07 71 C
Elmcroft Dri. Chess	101	18 65 C
Elmcroft Gdns. NW9	22	19 89 C
Elmcroft Rd. Orp	108	46 66 A
Elmcroft St. E5	49	35 85 A
Elm Ct. EC4	3	31 80 A

Elmdale Rd. N13 ... *76* — 30 92 D
Elmdene Ave. Horn ... *42* — 54 88 B
Elmdene Cl. Beck ... *106* — 36 67 B
Elmdene Rd. SE18 ... *66* — 43 78 D
Elmdene. Surb ... *102* — 20 66 C
Elmdon Rd. Houn ... *69* — 09 75 B
Elmdon Rd. Houn ... *70* — 12 76 C
Elm Dri. Har ... *32* — 13 88 D
Elm Dri. Sun ... *92* — 11 69 C
Elmer Cl. Enf ... *12* — 30 96 B
Elmer Gdns. Edg ... *22* — 19 91 D
Elmer Gdns. Islw ... *70* — 14 75 B
Elmer Rd. SE6 ... *88* — 38 73 A
Elmer's Dr. Tedd ... *93* — 16 70 B
Elmers End Rd. Beck ... *98* — 35 68 A
Elmers End Rd. SE20 ... *98* — 35 69 C
Elmerside Rd. Beck ... *98* — 36 68 C
Elmers Rd. SE25 ... *105* — 34 66 A
Elmfield Ave. Mit ... *96* — 28 69 A
Elmfield Ave. N8 ... *36* — 30 88 A
Elmfield Ave. Tedd ... *83* — 15 71 D
Elmfield Park. Brom ... *99* — 40 68 A
Elmfield Rd. Brom ... *99* — 40 68 A
Elmfield Rd. E17 ... *38* — 35 88 D
Elmfield Rd. E4 ... *18* — 38 93 B
Elmfield Rd. N2 ... *23* — 26 89 B
Elmfield Rd. Sthl ... *59* — 12 79 C
Elmfield Rd. SW17 ... *86* — 28 72 B
Elmfield Way. S Croy ... *112* — 33 62 B
Elm Friars Wlk. NW1 ... *47* — 29 84 D
Elmgate Ave. Felt ... *82* — 11 72 C
Elm Gdns. Mit ... *96* — 29 68 D
Elm Gdns. N2 ... *23* — 26 89 A
Elm Green. W3 ... *55* — 21 81 C
Elm Gr. Eri ... *67* — 50 77 D
Elm Gr. Har ... *32* — 13 87 A
Elm Gr. Horn ... *42* — 54 88 C
Elm Gr. King ... *93* — 18 69 A
Elm Gr. N8 ... *36* — 30 88 C
Elm Gr. NW2 ... *46* — 23 85 B
Elm Gr. Orp ... *108* — 45 66 D
Elmgrove Cres. Har ... *33* — 16 88 A
Elmgrove Gdns. Har ... *33* — 16 88 A
Elm Grove Par. Wall ... *104* — 28 65 C
Elmgrove Rd. Croy ... *105* — 34 66 B
Elmgrove Rd. Har ... *33* — 15 88 B
Elm Grove Rd. SW13 ... *72* — 22 76 C
Elm Grove Rd. W5 ... *60* — 18 79 A
Elm Gr. SE15 ... *75* — 34 76 C
Elm Gr. Sutt ... *110* — 25 64 B
Elm Gr. SW19 ... *95* — 24 70 C
Elm Hall Gdns. E11 ... *39* — 40 88 D
Elmhurst Ave. Mit ... *96* — 28 70 D
Elmhurst Ave. N2 ... *23* — 26 89 B
Elmhurst. Belv ... *67* — 48 77 A
Elmhurst Dri. E18 ... *27* — 40 90 C
Elmhurst Dri. Horn ... *42* — 53 87 A
Elmhurst Lodge. Sutt ... *110* — 26 63 C
Elmhurst Rd. E7 ... *50* — 40 84 D
Elmhurst Rd. N17 ... *25* — 33 90 D
Elmhurst Rd. SE9 ... *89* — 42 72 B
Elmhurst St. SW4 ... *74* — 29 75 B
Elmington Cl. Bex ... *79* — 49 74 D
Elmington Rd. SE5 ... *63* — 32 77 D
Elmira St. SE13 ... *76* — 37 75 B
Elm La. SE6 ... *88* — 36 72 B
Elmlee Cl. Chis ... *99* — 42 70 B
Elmley St. SE18 ... *66* — 44 78 B
Elmore Rd. E11 ... *38* — 38 86 D
Elmore Rd. Enf ... *14* — 35 97 B
Elmore St. N1 ... *48* — 32 84 D
Elm Park Ave. Horn ... *42* — 52 86 D
Elm Park Ave. N15 ... *37* — 34 88 C
Elm Park Ct. Pnr ... *20* — 11 89 A
Elm Park Gdns. NW4 ... *35* — 23 88 B
Elm Park Gdns. SW10 ... *62* — 26 78 D
Elm Park La. SW3 ... *62* — 26 78 D
Elm Park Rd. E10 ... *38* — 36 87 C
Elm Park Rd. N21 ... *17* — 32 94 A
Elm Park Rd. N3 ... *23* — 24 91 D
Elm Park Rd. Pnr ... *20* — 11 89 B
Elm Park Rd. SE25 ... *97* — 33 68 B
Elm Park Rd. SW3 ... *62* — 26 77 B
Elm Park. Stan ... *21* — 17 91 A
Elm Park. SW2 ... *86* — 30 73 B
Elm Pl. SW7 ... *62* — 26 78 D
Elm Rd. Barn ... *11* — 24 96 D
Elm Rd. Beck ... *98* — 36 69 D
Elm Rd. E11 ... *38* — 38 86 B
Elm Rd. E17 ... *38* — 38 88 A
Elm Rd. E7 ... *50* — 39 84 B
Elm Rd. Eps ... *109* — 21 63 B
Elm Rd. Eri ... *80* — 52 76 A
Elm Rd. Felt ... *81* — 08 73 D
Elm Rd. King ... *93* — 18 69 B

Elm Rd. N22 ... *25* — 31 90 B
Elm Rd. N Mal ... *94* — 20 68 B
Elm Rd. Rom ... *29* — 49 90 D
Elm Rd. Sid ... *90* — 46 71 A
Elm Rd. SW14 ... *72* — 20 75 C
Elm Rd. Th Hth ... *97* — 32 68 D
Elm Rd. Wall ... *104* — 28 66 C
Elm Rd. Wem ... *44* — 18 85 C
Elm Road W. Sutt ... *103* — 24 66 B
Elm Row. NW3 ... *35* — 26 86 C
Elms Ave. N10 ... *24* — 28 89 B
Elms Ave. NW4 ... *35* — 23 88 B
Elmscott Gdns. N21 ... *13* — 32 95 C
Elmscott Rd. Brom ... *89* — 39 71 D
Elms Cres. SW4 ... *74* — 29 74 D
Elms Ct. Wem ... *44* — 16 85 A
Elmsdale Rd. E17 ... *26* — 36 89 D
Elms Gdns. Dag ... *52* — 48 85 B
Elms Gdns. Wem ... *44* — 16 85 A
Elmshaw Rd. SW15 ... *72* — 22 74 A
Elmshurst Cres. N2 ... *23* — 26 89 D
Elmside Rd. Wem ... *34* — 19 86 C
Elms La. Wem ... *44* — 16 85 A
Elmsleigh Ave. Har ... *21* — 17 89 C
Elmsleigh Ct. Sutt ... *103* — 25 65 D
Elmsleigh Rd. Twick ... *82* — 14 72 B
Elmslie Cl. Wdf Gn ... *27* — 42 91 B
Elms Mews. W2 ... *5* — 26 80 B
Elms Park Ave. Wem ... *44* — 16 85 A
Elms Rd. Har ... *21* — 15 91 C
Elms Rd. SW4 ... *74* — 29 74 A
Elmstead Ave. Chis ... *89* — 42 71 D
Elmstead Ave. Wem ... *33* — 18 86 B
Elmstead Cl. Eps ... *109* — 21 64 C
Elmstead Cl. N20 ... *15* — 25 93 A
Elmstead Gdns. Wor Pk ... *102* — 22 65 C
Elmstead Glade. Chis ... *99* — 42 70 B
Elmstead La. Chis ... *89* — 42 71 D
Elmstead Rd. Eri ... *80* — 51 76 A
Elmstead Rd. Ilf ... *40* — 45 86 B
Elmsted Cres. Well ... *67* — 47 77 A
Elms The. SW13 ... *72* — 21 75 B
Elmstone Rd. SW6 ... *73* — 25 76 A
Elm St. WC1 ... *3* — 30 82 D
Elmsway. Ashf ... *81* — 07 71 C
Elmsworth Ave. Houn ... *70* — 13 76 D
Elm Terr. Har ... *20* — 14 90 B
Elm Terr. NW2 ... *35* — 25 86 C
Elm Terr. SE9 ... *78* — 43 74 C
Elmton Way. E5 ... *37* — 34 86 C
Elm Tree Ave. Esh ... *101* — 15 66 A
Elm Tree Cl. Ashf ... *81* — 07 71 D
Elm Tree Cl. Nthlt ... *43* — 12 83 D
Elm Tree Cl. NW8 ... *1* — 26 82 B
Elm Tree Cl. NW8 ... *1* — 26 82 B
Elmtree Rd. Tedd ... *83* — 15 71 A
Elm Way. E16 ... *58* — 39 82 B
Elm Way. Eps ... *109* — 20 64 D
Elm Way. NW10 ... *45* — 21 85 A
Elm Way. NW10 ... *34* — 21 86 C
Elm Way. Wor Pk ... *103* — 23 65 C
Elm Wlk. Brom ... *107* — 42 65 D
Elm Wlk. NW3 ... *35* — 25 86 A
Elm Wlk. Rom ... *50* — 52 89 A
Elm Wlk. SW20 ... *95* — 23 68 D
Elmwood Ave. Felt ... *81* — 10 72 D
Elmwood Ave. Har ... *33* — 16 88 D
Elmwood Ave. N13 ... *16* — 30 92 C
Elmwood Cl. Eps ... *109* — 22 63 C
Elmwood Cl. Wall ... *104* — 28 65 B
Elmwood Cres. NW9 ... *22* — 20 89 C
Elmwood Ct. Wem ... *33* — 16 86 C
Elmwood Dri. Bex ... *79* — 48 74 C
Elmwood Dri. Eps ... *109* — 22 63 C
Elmwood Gdns. W7 ... *54* — 15 81 C
Elmwood Rd. Croy ... *105* — 31 66 B
Elmwood Rd. Mit ... *96* — 27 68 B
Elmwood Rd. SE24 ... *75* — 32 74 B
Elmwood Rd. W4 ... *61* — 20 77 A
Elmworth Gr. SE21 ... *87* — 32 72 B
Elnathan Mews. W9 ... *56* — 25 82 D
Elphinstone Rd. E17 ... *26* — 36 90 D
Elphinstone St. N5 ... *48* — 31 85 B
Elrick Cl. Eri ... *68* — 51 77 A
Elrington Rd. E8 ... *49* — 34 84 A
Elsa Rd. Well ... *79* — 47 76 C
Elsa St. E14 ... *54* — 36 81 A
Elsdale St. E9 ... *49* — 35 84 C
Elsden Mews. E2 ... *49* — 35 83 C
Elsden Rd. N17 ... *25* — 33 90 B
Elsenham Rd. E12 ... *51* — 43 85 C
Elsenham St. SW18 ... *85* — 24 72 B
Elsham Rd. E11 ... *50* — 39 85 A
Elsham Rd. W14 ... *62* — 24 79 A
Elsiedene Rd. N21 ... *17* — 32 94 A

Elsiemaud Rd. SE4 ... *76* — 36 74 B
Elsie Rd. SE22 ... *75* — 33 75 D
Elsinore Rd. SE23 ... *88* — 36 73 C
Elsley Rd. SW11 ... *74* — 27 75 B
Elspeth Rd. SW11 ... *74* — 27 75 B
Elspeth Rd. Wem ... *44* — 18 85 C
Elsrick Ave. Mord ... *103* — 25 67 A
Elstan Way. Croy ... *106* — 36 66 A
Elsted St. SE17 ... *63* — 32 78 B
Elstow Cl. Ruis ... *32* — 11 87 B
Elstow Gdns. Dag ... *52* — 48 83 A
Elstow Rd. Dag ... *52* — 48 83 A
Elstree Gdns. Belv ... *67* — 48 78 A
Elstree Gdns. Ilf ... *51* — 44 85 C
Elstree Gdns. N9 ... *17* — 34 94 D
Elstree Hill. Brom ... *99* — 39 70 C
Elswick Rd. SE13 ... *76* — 37 76 D
Elswick St. SW6 ... *73* — 26 76 C
Elsworthy. E Mol ... *101* — 15 67 C
Elsworthy Rd. NW3 ... *47* — 27 84 C
Elsworthy Rise. NW3 ... *47* — 27 84 C
Elsworthy Terr. NW3 ... *47* — 27 84 C
Elsynge Rd. SW18 ... *73* — 26 74 B
Eltham Green Rd. SE9 ... *77* — 41 75 C
Eltham High St. SE9 ... *78* — 43 74 C
Eltham Hill. SE9 ... *77* — 41 74 B
Eltham Palace Rd. SE9 ... *77* — 41 74 D
Eltham Park Gdns. SE9 ... *78* — 43 75 C
Eltham Rd. SE12 ... *77* — 40 74 A
Eltham Rd. SE9 ... *77* — 41 74 A
Elthiron Rd. SW6 ... *73* — 25 76 A
Elthorne Ave. W7 ... *60* — 16 79 A
Elthorne Ct. Felt ... *82* — 11 73 C
Elthorne Park Rd. W7 ... *60* — 16 79 A
Elthorne Rd. N19 ... *36* — 29 86 B
Elthorne Rd. NW9 ... *34* — 20 87 B
Elthorne Way. NW9 ... *34* — 20 88 D
Elthruda Rd. SE13 ... *76* — 38 74 D
Eltisley Rd. Ilf ... *51* — 43 85 B
Elton Ave. Barn ... *11* — 24 95 B
Elton Ave. Grnf ... *44* — 15 84 B
Elton Ave. Wem ... *44* — 16 85 D
Elton Cl. Tedd ... *93* — 17 70 C
Elton Pl. N16 ... *48* — 33 85 C
Elton Rd. King ... *94* — 19 69 A
Eltringham St. SW18 ... *73* — 26 75 C
Elvaston Mews. SW7 ... *5* — 26 79 C
Elvaston Pl. SW7 ... *5* — 26 79 C
Elveden Pl. NW10 ... *45* — 19 83 C
Elveden Rd. NW10 ... *45* — 19 83 C
Elvendon Rd. N13 ... *24* — 30 91 A
Elver Gdns. E2 ... *57* — 34 82 A
Elverson Rd. SE8 ... *76* — 37 76 D
Elverton St. SW1 ... *10* — 29 78 B
Elvet Ave. Rom ... *30* — 53 89 C
Elvin Ct. NW9 ... *34* — 20 87 A
Elvington Green. Brom ... *107* — 39 67 B
Elvington La. NW9 ... *22* — 21 90 A
Elvino Rd. SE26 ... *88* — 36 71 C
Elwill Way. Beck ... *98* — 38 68 D
Elwin St. E2 ... *57* — 34 82 A
Elwood St. N5 ... *37* — 31 86 D
Elwyn Gdns. SE12 ... *89* — 40 73 A
Ely Cl. Eri ... *80* — 51 76 D
Ely Cl. N Mal ... *94* — 21 69 C
Ely Cottages. SW8 ... *10* — 30 77 D
Ely Gdns. Dag ... *41* — 50 86 C
Ely Gdns. Ilf ... *39* — 42 87 A
Elyne Rd. N4 ... *37* — 31 88 C
Ely Pl. EC1 ... *3* — 31 81 A
Ely Pl. Wdf Gn ... *28* — 43 91 A
Ely Rd. E10 ... *38* — 38 87 A
Ely Rd. Houn ... *69* — 09 76 D
Ely Rd. Houn ... *70* — 11 75 A
Ely Rd. Th Hth ... *105* — 32 67 B
Elysian Ave. Orp ... *108* — 45 67 D
Elysium Pl. SW6 ... *73* — 24 76 D
Elysium St. SW6 ... *73* — 24 76 D
Elystan Cl. Wall ... *111* — 28 62 A
Elystan Pl. SW3 ... *9* — 27 78 D
Elystan St. SW3 ... *9* — 27 78 A
Emanuel Ave. W3 ... *55* — 20 81 C
Embankment Gdns. SW3 ... *9* — 27 77 B
Embankment Pl. WC2 ... *7* — 30 80 C
Embankment. SW15 ... *73* — 23 75 B
Embankment The. Twick ... *83* — 16 73 C
Embassey Ct. Sid ... *90* — 46 72 D
Embassy Ct. Well ... *78* — 46 75 B
Emba St. SE16 ... *63* — 34 79 A
Ember Cl. Orp ... *108* — 44 66 A
Embercourt Rd. Surb ... *101* — 15 67 C
Ember Gdns. Surb ... *101* — 15 66 A
Embleton Rd. SE13 ... *76* — 37 75 D
Embleton Wlk. Hamp ... *82* — 12 71 D

Embry Dri. Stan

Street	Page	Map Ref
Embry Dri. Stan	21	16 91 A
Emden St. SW6	73	25 76 B
Emerald Gdns. Dag	41	49 87 C
Emerald St. WC1	3	30 81 B
Emerson Dri. Horn	42	53 87 B
Emerson Gdns. Har	33	18 88 D
Emerson Rd. Ilf	40	43 87 A
Emerson St. SE1	8	32 80 C
Emery Hill St. SW1	6	29 79 C
Emery St. SE1	7	31 79 C
Emes Rd. Eri	67	50 77 C
Emily Pl. N7	48	31 85 A
Emily St. E16	58	39 81 D
Emlyn Gdns. W12	61	21 79 A
Emlyn Rd. W12	61	21 79 D
Emmanuel Rd. Nthwd	19	09 91 D
Emmanuel Rd. SW12	86	29 73 D
Emma Rd. E13	58	39 82 B
Emma St. E2	48	34 83 D
Emmett St. E14	36	36 80 B
Emmott Ave. Ilf	40	44 88 A
Emmott Cl. E2	57	36 82 C
Emmott Cl. NW11	35	28 88 C
Empire Ave. N18	25	32 91 A
Empire Ct. Wem	34	19 86 D
Empire Rd. Grnf	44	17 84 C
Empire Way. Wem	45	19 85 A
Empire Wharf Rd. E14	64	38 78 B
Empire Yd. N7	36	30 86 C
Empress Ave. E12	39	41 86 B
Empress Ave. E4	26	37 91 D
Empress Ave. Ilf	40	43 86 A
Empress Ave. Wdf Gn	27	39 91 D
Empress Dri. Chis	100	43 70 B
Empress Pl. SW6	62	25 78 C
Empress St. SE17	63	32 77 A
Empson St. E3	37	37 82 D
Emsworth Cl. N9	18	35 94 C
Emsworth Rd. Ilf	28	43 90 D
Emsworth St. SW2	86	30 72 B
Emu Rd. SW8	74	28 76 D
Ena Rd. SW16	96	30 68 A
Enbrook St. W10	56	24 82 A
Endale Cl. Cars	104	27 65 B
Endeavor Way. Bark	51	46 83 C
Endeavour Way. SW19	85	25 71 B
Endell St. WC2	3	30 81 C
Enderby St. SE10	65	39 78 C
Enderley Cl. Har	21	15 90 A
Enderley Rd. Har	21	15 90 A
Endersby Rd. Barn	11	23 95 A
Endersleigh Gdns. NW4	22	22 89 C
Endlebury Rd. E4	18	38 93 A
Endlesham Rd. SW12	86	28 73 A
Endsleigh Gdns. Ilf	39	42 87 D
Endsleigh Gdns. Surb	101	17 67 C
Endsleigh Gdns. WC1	2	29 82 D
Endsleigh Pl. WC1	2	29 82 D
Endsleigh Rd. Sthl	59	12 78 A
Endsleigh Rd. W13	54	16 80 A
Endsleigh St. WC1	2	29 82 D
Endway. Surb	102	19 66 B
Endwell Rd. SE4	76	36 75 A
Endymion Rd. N4	37	31 87 B
Endymion Rd. SW2	74	30 74 D
Enfield Rd. Brent	60	17 78 D
Enfield Rd. Enf	12	30 96 A
Enfield Rd. Houn	69	09 76 C
Enfield Rd. N1	48	33 84 C
Enfield Rd. W3	61	19 79 B
Enfield Road E. Brent	60	17 78 D
Enford St. W1	1	27 81 B
Engadine Cl. Croy	105	33 65 D
Engadine St. SW18	85	25 72 A
Engate St. SE13	76	38 75 C
Engel Park. NW7	23	23 91 A
Engineer Cl. SE18	66	43 77 A
Engineers Way. Wem	45	19 85 A
England's La. NW3	47	27 84 B
Englefield Cl. Croy	105	32 67 C
Englefield Cl. Enf	12	31 97 C
Englefield Cl. Orp	100	45 68 D
Englefield Cres. Orp	100	46 68 C
Englefield Path. Orp	100	46 68 C
Englefield Rd. N1	48	33 84 C
Engleheart Dri. Felt	69	09 74 D
Engleheart Rd. SE6	88	38 73 A
Englewood Rd. SW12	74	29 74 C
English Grounds. SE1	8	33 80 C
English St. E3	57	36 82 D
Enid St. SE16	8	33 79 D
Enkel St. N7	36	30 86 D
Enmore Ave. SE25	105	34 67 A
Enmore Gdns. SW14	72	20 74 B
Enmore Rd. SE25	105	34 67 A
Enmore Rd. Sthl	53	13 82 C
Enmore Rd. SW15	73	23 74 A
Ennerdale Ave. Stan	21	17 89 A
Ennerdale Dri. NW9	34	21 88 A
Ennerdale Gdns. Wem	33	17 87 C
Ennerdale Rd. Bexh	79	49 76 A
Ennerdale Rd. Rich	71	18 76 D
Ennersdale Rd. SE13	76	38 74 B
Ennismore Ave. Grnf	44	19 85 C
Ennismore Ave. W4	61	21 78 B
Ennismore Gdns. E Mol	101	15 67 C
Ennismore Gdns Mews. SW7	5	27 79 C
Ennismore Gdns. SW7	5	27 79 A
Ennismore Mews. SW7	5	27 79 C
Ennismore St. SW7	5	27 79 C
Ennis Rd. N4	37	31 87 C
Ennis Rd. SE18	66	44 77 B
Ensign Dri. N13	17	32 93 C
Ensign St. E1	57	34 80 A
Enslin Rd. SE9	90	43 73 A
Ensor Mews. SW7	62	26 78 D
Enstone Rd. Enf	14	36 96 A
Enterprise Way. SW18	73	25 75 C
Epirus Mews. SW6	62	25 77 C
Epirus Rd. SW6	62	25 77 D
Epping Cl. Rom	29	49 89 B
Epping Glade. E4	14	38 95 D
Epping Pl. N1	48	31 84 A
Epping Way. E4	14	37 95 D
Epple Rd. SW6	73	24 76 B
Epsom Cl. Bexh	79	49 75 B
Epsom Cl. Nthlt	43	12 85 D
Epsom Rd. Croy	105	31 65 C
Epsom Rd. E10	38	38 88 C
Epsom Rd. Eps	109	21 62 D
Epsom Rd. Ilf	40	45 88 D
Epsom Rd. Mord	103	24 67 D
Epsom Sq. Houn		09 76 D
Epsom Way. Horn	42	54 86 D
Epworth Rd. Islw	60	16 77 D
Epworth St. EC2	4	32 82 D
Erasmus St. SW1	10	29 78 B
Erconwald St. W12	55	21 81 D
Eresby Dri. W Wick	106	37 66 C
Eresby Pl. NW6	46	25 84 C
Erica Gdns. Croy	106	37 65 D
Erica St. W12	55	22 80 A
Eric Cl. E7	50	40 85 A
Ericcson Cl. SW18	73	25 74 A
Eric Rd. E7	50	40 85 A
Eric Rd. NW10	45	21 84 B
Eric Rd. Rom	41	48 87 A
Eric St. E3	57	36 82 D
Eridge Rd. W4	61	20 79 D
Erin Cl. Brom	99	39 70 C
Erindale. SE18	66	44 77 B
Erindale Terr. SE18	66	44 77 B
Erith Cres. Rom	29	50 91 C
Erith High St. Eri	68	51 78 D
Erith Rd. Belv	67	49 78 D
Erith Rd. Bexh	79	49 75 B
Erith Rd. Eri	79	50 76 A
Erlanger Rd. SE14	76	35 76 D
Erlesmere Gdns. W13	60	16 79 C
Ermine Cl. Houn		11 76 C
Ermine Rd. N15	37	33 88 D
Ermine Rd. SE13	76	37 75 D
Ermine Side. Enf	13	34 95 A
Ermington Rd. SE9	90	44 72 A
Ernald Ave. E6	50	42 83 C
Erncroft Way. Twick	71	15 74 D
Ernest Ave. SE27	87	31 71 B
Ernest Cl. Beck	106	33 65 D
Ernest Gdns. W4	61	19 77 B
Ernest Gr. Beck	106	36 67 B
Ernest Rd. Horn	42	54 88 D
Ernest Rd. King	94	19 69 D
Ernest Sq. King	94	19 69 D
Ernest St. E1	57	35 82 D
Ernle Rd. SW20	95	23 70 C
Ernshaw Pl. SW15	73	24 74 A
Erpingham Rd. SW15	73	23 75 A
Erridge Rd. SW19	95	25 69 C
Errington Rd. W9	56	24 82 D
Errol Gdns. Hay	53	11 82 C
Errol Gdns. N Mal	94	22 68 C
Erroll Rd. Rom	30	51 89 D
Errol St. EC1	4	32 82 D
Erskine Cl. Sutt	104	27 65 C
Erskine Gdns. N15	25	34 89 D
Erskine Hill. NW11	35	25 88 A
Erskine Mews. NW3	47	27 84 D
Erskine Rd. E17	26	36 89 D
Erskine Rd. NW3	47	27 84 D
Erskine Rd. Sutt	103	26 65 D
Erwood Rd. SE7	65	42 78 C
Esam Way. SW16	87	31 71 C
Escott Gdns. SE9	89	42 71 A
Escot Way. Barn	11	23 95 A
Escreet Gr. SE18	66	43 78 A
Esher Ave. Rom	41	50 88 C
Esher Ave. Sutt	103	23 65 D
Esher Cres. Houn	69	09 76 D
Esher Gdns. SW19	85	23 72 B
Esher Rd. Ilf	40	45 86 C
Eskdale Ave. Nthlt	43	12 83 B
Eskdale Cl. Wem	33	17 86 B
Eskdale Rd. Bexh	79	49 76 A
Eskmont Ridge. SE19	97	33 70 C
Esk Rd. E13	58	40 82 D
Esk Way. Rom	30	51 91 C
Esmar Cres. NW9	34	22 87 A
Esmeralda Rd. SE1	63	34 78 A
Esmond Rd. NW6	46	24 83 B
Esmond Rd. W4	61	20 79 D
Esmond St. SW15	73	24 75 C
Esparto St. SW18	85	25 73 A
Essenden Rd. Belv	67	49 78 C
Essenden Rd. S Croy	112	33 63 C
Essendine Rd. W9	56	25 82 A
Essex Ave. Islw	71	15 75 A
Essex Cl. E17	26	36 89 C
Essex Cl. Mord	103	23 66 B
Essex Cl. Rom	29	49 89 D
Essex Cl. Ruis	32	11 87 D
Essex Ct. EC4	3	31 81 C
Essex Ct. SW13	72	21 76 D
Essex Gdns. Horn	42	54 88 B
Essex Gdns. N4	37	31 89 D
Essex Gr. SE19	97	32 70 B
Essex Park Mews. W3	55	21 80 C
Essex Park. N3	23	25 91 B
Essex Place Sq. W4	61	20 78 B
Essex Pl. W4	61	20 78 B
Essex Rd. Bark	51	44 83 B
Essex Rd. Dag	52	50 85 C
Essex Rd. Dart	80	53 74 D
Essex Rd. E10	38	38 88 C
Essex Rd. E12	50	42 84 A
Essex Rd. E17	38	36 88 C
Essex Rd. E18	27	40 90 D
Essex Rd. Enf	13	32 96 D
Essex Rd. N1	48	32 84 C
Essex Rd. NW10	45	21 84 C
Essex Rd. Rom	41	47 87 A
Essex Rd S. E11	38	38 87 B
Essex Rd. W3	55	20 80 A
Essex Rd. W4	61	20 78 B
Essex St. E7	50	40 85 C
Essex St. WC2	7	31 80 A
Essex Villas. W8	62	25 79 A
Essian St. E1	57	36 81 A
Essoldo Way. Edg	21	18 89 B
Estate Way. E10	38	37 87 C
Estcourt Rd. SE25	105	34 67 D
Estcourt Rd. SW6	62	24 77 D
Estella Ave. N Mal	94	22 68 D
Estelle Rd. NW3	47	28 85 A
Esterbrooke St. SW1	10	29 78 B
Este Rd. SW11	74	27 75 A
Esther Cl. N21	17	31 94 A
Esther Rd. E11	39	39 87 A
Estreham Rd. SW16	96	29 70 B
Estridge Cl. Houn	70	13 75 C
Eswyn Rd. SW17	86	27 71 D
Etchingham Ct. N12		26 91 C
Etchingham Park Rd. N3	23	25 91 D
Etchingham Rd. E15	49	38 85 A
Eternit Wlk. SW6	73	23 76 B
Etfield Gr. Sid	90	46 71 D
Ethelbert Cl. Brom	99	40 68 A
Ethelbert Gdns. Ilf	40	43 88 A
Ethelbert Rd. Brom	99	40 68 A
Ethelbert Rd. Eri	67	50 77 C
Ethelbert Rd. SW20	95	23 69 B
Ethelbert St. SW12	86	28 73 D
Ethelburga Rd. Rom	30	54 90 B
Ethelburga St. SW11	74	27 76 A
Etheldene Ave. N10	24	29 89 C
Ethelden Rd. W12	55	22 80 D
Ethel Rd. E16	58	40 81 D
Ethel St. SE17	63	32 78 A
Etheridge Rd. NW4	35	23 87 A
Etherley Rd. N15	37	32 88 A
Etherow St. SE22	87	34 73 A
Etherstone Green. SW16	87	31 71 A
Etherstone Rd. SW16	87	31 71 A
Ethnard Rd. SE15	63	34 77 B

Street				
Ethronvi Rd. Bexh	79	48	75	A
Etloe Rd. E10	38	37	86	A
Eton Ave. Barn	12	27	95	C
Eton Ave. Houn	59	12	77	B
Eton Ave. N12	23	26	91	C
Eton Ave. N Mal	94	20	68	D
Eton Ave. NW3	47	27	84	C
Eton Ave. Wem	44	17	85	A
Eton College Rd. NW3	47	27	84	D
Eton Ct. Wem	44	17	85	A
Eton Garages. NW3	47	27	84	A
Eton Gr. NW9	22	19	89	C
Eton Gr. SE13	77	39	75	A
Eton Rd. Ilf	51	44	85	B
Eton Rd. NW3	47	27	84	D
Eton St. Rich		18	74	A
Eton Villas. NW3	47	27	84	B
Etta St. SE8	64	36	77	A
Ettrick St. E14	58	38	81	C
Etwell Pl. Surb	101	18	67	D
Eugene Cl. Rom	30	53	89	C
Eugenia Rd. SE16	64	35	78	A
Eureka Rd. King	94	19	69	C
Europa Pl. EC1	4	32	82	A
Eustace Pl. SE18	65	42	78	B
Eustace Rd. Rom	41	47	87	B
Eustace Rd. SW6	62	25	77	C
Euston Rd. Croy	105	31	66	C
Euston Rd. NW1	2	29	82	C
Euston Sq. NW1	2	29	82	B
Euston St. NW1	2	29	82	A
Evandale Rd. SW9	75	31	76	C
Evangelist Rd. NW5	47	28	85	B
Evans Cl. E8	48	33	84	B
Evans Rd. SE6	89	39	72	A
Evanston Ave. E4	26	38	91	C
Evanston Gdns. Ilf	39	42	88	C
Eva Rd. Rom	41	47	87	B
Evelina Mansions SE5	63	32	77	D
Evelina Rd. SE15	75	34	75	B
Evelina Rd. SE15	76	35	76	C
Evelina Rd. SE20	98	35	70	D
Eveline Rd. Mit	96	27	69	B
Evelyn Ave. NW9	22	20	89	D
Evelyn Ave. Ruis	31	09	88	D
Evelyn Cl. Twick	82	13	73	B
Evelyn Cres. Sun	91	09	69	B
Evelyn Ct. E8	48	34	85	A
Evelyn Ct. N1	48	32	83	D
Evelyn Dri. Pnr	20	11	91	D
Evelyn Gdns. Rich	71	18	75	C
Evelyn Gdns. SW7	62	26	78	D
Evelyn Gr. Sthl	53	12	81	D
Evelyn Gr. W5	54	18	80	D
Evelyn Rd. Barn	12	27	96	D
Evelyn Rd. E16	58	40	80	D
Evelyn Rd. E17	26	38	89	C
Evelyn Rd. Rich	83	17	72	C
Evelyn Rd. Rich	71	18	75	A
Evelyn Rd. SW19	95	25	70	B
Evelyn Rd. W4	61	20	79	D
Evelyn Sharp Cl. Rom	30	53	89	B
Evelyn St. SE8	64	36	78	D
Evelyn Terr. Rich	71	18	75	A
Evelyn Way. Sun	91	09	69	B
Evelyn Way. Wall	111	29	64	B
Evelyn Wlk. N1	48	32	83	D
Evelyn Yd. W1	2	29	81	D
Evenwood Cl. SW15	73	24	74	A
Everard Ave. Brom	107	40	66	C
Everard Way. Wem	33	18	86	C
Everatt Cl. SW18	73	24	74	B
Eve Rd. E11	50	39	85	A
Eve Rd. E15	50	39	83	C
Eve Rd. Islw	71	16	75	C
Eve Rd. N17	25	33	89	A
Everdon Rd. SW13	61	22	77	A
Everest Pl. E14	58	38	81	A
Everest Rd. SE9	77	42	74	B
Everett Cl. Pnr	19	09	89	B
Everett Wlk. Belv	67	48	78	D
Everglade Strand. NW9	22	21	90	B
Everilda St. N1		30	83	B
Evering Rd. E5	37	34	86	B
Evering Rd. N16	37	33	86	D
Everington Rd. N10	24	27	90	D
Everington St. W6	62	23	77	B
Everitt Rd. NW10	55	20	82	B
Everleigh St. N4		31	87	C
Eversfield Gdns. NW7	22	21	91	C
Eversfield Rd. Rich	71	18	76	D
Eversholt St. NW1	47	29	83	C
Evershot Rd. N4	36	30	87	D
Eversleigh Rd. Barn	71	26	95	A
Eversleigh Rd. E6	50	41	83	B
Eversleigh Rd. N3	23	24	91	D
Eversleigh Rd. SW11	74	28	76	C
Eversley Ave. Bexh	80	51	76	C
Eversley Ave. Wem	34	19	86	A
Eversley Cl. N21	12	30	95	D
Eversley Cres. Islw	70	14	76	B
Eversley Cres. N21	13	31	95	C
Eversley Cres. Ruis	31	09	86	B
Eversley Cross. Bexh	80	51	76	C
Eversley Mount. N21	12	30	95	D
Eversley Park. SW19	84	22	71	D
Eversley Rd. SE19	97	32	70	D
Eversley Rd. SE7	65	40	77	B
Eversley Rd. Surb	101	18	67	B
Eversley Way. Croy	106	37	65	C
Everthorpe Rd. SE15	75	33	75	B
Everton Dri. Stan	21	18	89	B
Everton Rd. Croy	105	34	66	C
Evesham Ave. E17	26	37	90	C
Evesham Cl. Grnf	43	13	83	D
Evesham Cl. Sutt	110	25	63	C
Evesham Green. Mord	103	25	67	D
Evesham Rd. E15	50	39	84	D
Evesham Rd. Mord	103	25	67	D
Evesham Rd. N11	16	29	92	D
Evesham St. W10	56	23	80	B
Evesham Way. Ilf	28	43	89	A
Evesham Way. SW11	74	28	75	A
Evesham Wlk. SE5	75	32	76	D
Evesham Wlk. SW9	75	31	76	A
Ewald Rd. SW6	74	24	76	D
Ewanrigg Terr. Wdf Gn	27	41	91	A
Ewart Gr. N22	25	31	90	A
Ewart Rd. SE23	88	35	73	B
Ewe Cl. N7	47	30	84	A
Ewell By-pass. Eps	109	22	62	A
Ewell Court Ave. Eps	109	21	64	C
Ewell House Gr. Eps	109	21	62	D
Ewellhurst Rd. Ilf	27	42	90	C
Ewell Park Way. Eps	109	22	63	C
Ewell Rd. Surb	101	16	66	B
Ewell Rd. Surb	101	18	66	B
Ewell Rd. Surb	102	19	66	D
Ewell Rd. Sutt	110	23	63	B
Ewelme Rd. SE23	88	35	73	C
Ewen Cres. SW12	87	31	73	A
Ewer St. SE1	8	32	80	C
Ewhurst Ave. S Croy	112	33	62	B
Ewhurst Cl. Sutt	110	23	62	A
Ewhurst Rd. SE4	76	36	74	D
Exbury Rd. SE6	88	37	72	A
Excel Ct. SW1	6	29	80	B
Excelsior Cl. King	94	19	69	C
Excelsior Gdns. SE13	76	38	76	C
Exchange Bldgs. E1	4	33	81	C
Exchange Ct. WC2	7	30	80	A
Exchange St. Rom	42	51	88	A
Exeforde Ave. Ashf	81	07	71	A
Exeter Ct. Surb	101	18	67	A
Exeter Gdns. Ilf	39	42	87	D
Exeter Mews. NW6	46	25	84	B
Exeter Rd. Croy	105	33	66	B
Exeter Rd. Dag	52	49	84	B
Exeter Rd. E16	58	40	81	A
Exeter Rd. E17	38	37	88	A
Exeter Rd. Enf	14	35	96	B
Exeter Rd. Felt	82	12	72	D
Exeter Rd. Har	32	12	86	A
Exeter Rd. N14	16	28	94	B
Exeter Rd. N9	18	35	93	A
Exeter Rd. NW2	46	24	84	A
Exeter Rd. SE15	75	33	76	B
Exeter Rd. SE15	63	33	77	D
Exeter Rd. Well	78	45	76	D
Exeter St. WC2	7	30	80	B
Exford Gdns. SE12	89	40	73	D
Exford Rd. SE12	89	40	73	D
Exhibition Cl. W12	56	23	80	A
Exhibition Rd. SW7	6	26	79	D
Exit Rd. N2	23	26	90	D
Exmoor St. W10	56	23	81	B
Exmouth Market. EC1	3	31	82	C
Exmth Pl. E8	48	34	84	D
Exmouth Rd. Brom	99	40	68	B
Exmouth Rd. E17	36	36	88	B
Exmouth Rd. Ruis	32	11	86	C
Exmouth Rd. Well	78	47	76	A
Exmouth Rd. Well	67	47	77	C
Exmouth St. E1	57	35	81	C
Exning Rd. E16	58	39	82	D
Exon St. SE17	63	33	79	A
Exton Cres. NW10	45	20	84	C
Exton Gdns. Dag	52	47	85	C
Exton St. SE1	7	31	80	C
Eyhurst Ave. Horn	42	52	86	D
Eyhurst Cl. NW2	34	22	86	B
Eylewood Rd. SE27	87	32	71	C
Eynella Rd. SE22	87	33	73	B
Eynham Rd. W12	56	23	81	C
Eynsford Cl. Orp	108	44	66	A
Eynsford Rd. Ilf	40	45	86	A
Eynsham Dri. SE2	66	46	79	D
Eynswood Dri. Sid	90	46	71	D
Eyot Gdns. W6	61	21	78	D
Eyot Green. W4	61	21	78	D
Eyre Cl. Rom	30	52	89	D
Eyre St Hill. EC1	3	31	82	C
Eythorne Rd. SW9	75	31	76	A
Ezra St. E2	4	33	82	B
Ezra St. E2	57	34	82	A
Faber Gdns. NW4	34	22	88	A
Fabian Rd. SW6	62	24	77	D
Factory La. N17	25	33	90	D
Factory Lane. Croy	105	31	65	A
Factory Pl. E14	64	38	78	C
Factory Rd. E16	65	42	79	B
Factory Rd. E16	66	43	79	A
Factory Sq. SW16	96	30	70	A
Factory Yd. W7	54	15	80	C
Fagg's Rd. Felt	69	10	74	A
Fairacre. N Mal	94	21	68	A
Fair Acres. Brom	107	40	67	A
Faacres. Ruis	31	09	87	B
Fairacres. SW15	72	22	75	C
Fairbank Ave. Orp	108	43	65	B
Fairbanks Rd. N17	25	34	89	A
Fairbourne Rd. N17	25	33	89	A
Fairbridge Rd. N19	36	29	87	D
Fairbrook Cl. N13	17	31	92	C
Fairbrook Rd. N13	25	31	91	A
Fairby Hse. SE1	63	33	78	B
Fairby Rd. SE12	77	40	74	B
Fairchild Pl. EC2	4	33	82	C
Fairchild St. EC2	4	33	82	C
Fairclough St. E1	57	34	81	C
Faircross Ave. Bark	51	44	84	A
Faircross Ave. Rom	29	50	91	D
Fair Cross. Bark	51	45	85	C
Fairdale Gdns. SW15	72	22	75	D
Fairfax Av. Eps	109	22	62	B
Fairfax Gdns. SE3	77	41	76	A
Fairfax Pl. NW6	46	26	84	C
Fairfax Rd. N8	25	31	89	C
Fairfax Rd. NW6	46	26	84	C
Fairfax Rd. Tedd	93	16	70	D
Fairfax Rd. W4	61	21	79	C
Fairfield Ave. Edg	22	19	91	D
Fairfield Ave. NW4	35	23	88	C
Fairfield Ave. Ruis	31	08	87	A
Fairfield Ave. Twick	82	13	73	D
Fairfield Cl. Enf	14	36	96	C
Fairfield Cl. Horn	42	52	87	C
Fairfield Cl. N12	15	26	92	A
Fairfield Cl. Sid	78	45	74	D
Fairfield Cres. Edg	22	19	91	B
Fairfield Cl. NW10	45	22	83	A
Fairfield Ct. Ruis	31	08	87	D
Fairfield Dri. Grnf	44	17	83	A
Fairfield Dri. Har	20	14	89	A
Fairfield Dri. SW18	73	25	74	B
Fairfield E. King	93	18	69	C
Fairfield Gdns. N8	36	30	88	A
Fairfield Gr. SE7	65	41	78	D
Fairfield N. King	93	18	69	C
Fairfield Path. Croy	112	33	64	A
Fairfield Path. Croy	105	33	65	C
Fairfield Pl. King	93	18	68	A
Fairfield Rd. Beck	98	37	69	C
Fairfield Rd. Bexh	79	48	76	D
Fairfield Rd. Brom	99	40	70	C
Fairfield Rd. Croy	105	33	65	C
Fairfield Rd. E17	26	36	90	C
Fairfield Rd. E3	49	37	83	C
Fairfield Rd. Enf	14	36	95	A
Fairfield Rd. Ilf	51	43	84	B
Fairfield Rd. King	93	18	69	C
Fairfield Rd. N18	17	34	92	C
Fairfield Rd. N8	36	30	88	A
Fairfield Rd. Orp	108	45	66	A
Fairfield Rd. Sthl	53	12	81	D
Fairfield Rd. Wdf Gn	27	40	91	A
Fairfields Cl. NW9	34	20	88	A
Fairfields Cres. NW9	34	20	88	A
Fairfields S. King	93	18	69	D
Fairfields Rd. Houn	70	14	75	A
Fairfield St. SW18	73	25	74	B
Fairfield St. SW18	73	25	75	D
Fairfield Way. Barn	11	25	95	A
Fairfield Way. Eps	109	21	64	C

Fairfield W. King ...93 — 18 69 C
Fairfoot Rd. E3 ...57 — 37 82 C
Fairford Ave. Bexh ...79 — 50 76 B
Fairford Ave. Croy ...106 — 35 67 B
Fairford Cl. Croy ...106 — 36 67 A
Fairford Gdns. Wor Pk ...102 — 21 65 D
Fairgreen. Barn ...12 — 27 96 B
Fairgreen Ct. Barn ...12 — 27 96 B
Fairgreen E. Barn ...12 — 31 67 B
Fairgreen Rd. Th Hth ...105 — 35 67 D
Fairhaven Ave. Croy ...106 — 25 84 C
Fairhazel Gdns. NW6 ...46 — 23 74 D
Fairheathe. SW15 ...73 — 52 89 D
Fairholme Ave. Rom ...30 — 24 89 C
Fairholme Cl. N3 — 09 73 A
Fairholme. Felt ● ...81 — 24 89 C
Fairholme Gdns. N3 — 31 66 A
Fairholme Rd. Croy ...105 — 15 88 B
Fairholme Rd. Har — 43 88 C
Fairholme Rd. Ilf ...40 — 24 63 B
Fairholme Rd. Sutt ...110 — 24 78 D
Fairholme Rd. W14 ...62 — 33 87 C
Fairholt Cl. N16 ...37 — 32 87 D
Fairholt Rd. N16 ...37 — 27 79 C
Fairholt St. SW7 ...5 — 53 87 D
Fairkytes Ave. Horn ...42 — 39 84 D
Fairland Rd. E15 ...50 — 25 65 A
Fairlands Ave. Sutt ...103 — 31 67 A
Fairlands Ave. Th Hth ...105 — 43 74 C
Fairlands Ct. SE9 ...78 — 47 76 D
Fairlawn Ave. Bexh ...79 — 27 89 C
Fairlawn Ave. N2 ...24 — 20 78 A
Fairlawn Ave. W4 ...61 — 12 71 B
Fairlawn Cl. Felt ...82 — 20 70 A
Fairlawn Cl. King ...94 — 29 95 D
Fairlawn Cl. N14 ...12 — 41 77 C
Fairlawn Ct. SE7 ...65 — 40 91 C
Fairlawn Dri. Wdf Gn ...27 — 28 64 D
Fairlawnes. Wall ...111 — 12 80 B
Fairlawn Gdns. Sthl ...53 — 20 78 A
Fairlawn Gr. W4 ...61 — 36 71 C
Fairlawn Park. SE26 ...88 — 24 70 D
Fairlawn Rd. SW19 ...95 — 54 87 B
Fairlawns Cl. Horn ...42 — 41 77 A
Fairlawn. SE7 ...65 — 11 90 D
Fairlawns. Pnr ...20 — 10 68 A
Fairlawns. Sun ...91 — 23 74 B
Fairlawns. SW15 ...73 — 24 74 B
Fairlawns. Twick ...71 — 17 81 B
Fairlea Pl. W5 ...54 — 35 73 A
Fairlie Gdns. SE23 ...88 — 38 93 B
Fairlight Ave. E4 ...18 — 21 83 C
Fairlight Ave. NW10 ...45 — 40 91 A
Fairlight Ave. Wdf Gn ...27 — 38 93 B
Fairlight Cl. E4 ...18 — 23 64 A
Fairlight Cl. Wor Pk ...110 — 14 83 D
Fairlight Ct. Grnf ...43 — 13 71 D
Fairlight. Hamp ...82 — 26 71 B
Fairlight Rd. SW17 ...85 — 44 91 C
Fairlop Gdns. Ilf ...28 — 39 87 A
Fairlop Rd. E11 ...51 — 44 90 C
Fairlop Rd. Ilf ...28 — 42 68 D
Fairmead. Brom ...99 — 42 68 D
Fairmead Cl. Brom ...99 — 11 77 D
Fairmead Cl. Houn ...59 — 20 68 B
Fairmead Cl. N Mal ...94 — 42 88 A
Fairmead Gdns. Ilf ...39 — 31 66 A
Fairmead Rd. Croy ...105 — 30 86 C
Fairmead Rd. N19 ...36 — 19 66 D
Fairmead. Surb ...102 — 29 71 D
Fairmile Ave. SW16 ...86 — 30 74 D
Fairmount Rd. SW2 ...74 — 43 66 B
Fairoak Cl. Orp ...108 — 54 90 C
Fairoak Dri. SE9 ...78 — 51 90 C
Fairoak Gdns. Rom ...30 — 32 83 A
Fairstead Wlk. N1 ...48 — 14 75 A
Fair St. Houn ...70 — 33 79 B
Fair St. SE1 — 40 78 C
Fairthorn Rd. SE10 ...65 — 17 84 B
Fairview Ave. Wem ...44 — 36 90 A
Fairview Cl. E17 ...26 — 13 87 C
Fairview Cres. Har ...32 — 07 71 C
Fairview. Eri ...68 — 51 77 D
Fairview Gdns. Wdf Gn ...27 — 40 90 B
Fairview Pl. SW2 ...86 — 30 73 B
Fairview Rd. Enf ...13 — 31 97 A
Fairview Rd. N15 ...37 — 33 88 D
Fairview Rd. Sutt ...111 — 27 64 C
Fairview Rd. SW16 ...96 — 30 69 B
Fairwater Ave. Well ...78 — 46 75 C
Fairway Ave. NW9 ...22 — 19 89 B
Fairway. Bexh ...79 — 48 74 A
Fairway Cl. Croy ...106 — 36 67 A
Fairway Cl. Eps ...109 — 20 64 A

Fairway Cl. NW11 ...35 — 26 87 A
Fairway Dri. Grnf ...43 — 13 84 D
Fairway Gdns. Ilf ...51 — 44 85 C
Fairway. Orp ...108 — 44 67 B
Fairways. Ashf ...91 — 07 70 B
Fairways. Islw ...71 — 15 76 A
Fairways. Stan ...21 — 18 90 C
Fairways. Tedd ...93 — 17 70 D
Fairway. SW20 ...95 — 23 68 A
Fairway The. Barn ...11 — 25 95 D
Fairway The. Brom ...107 — 42 67 B
Fairway The. E Mol ...92 — 13 68 B
Fairway The. N13 ...17 — 32 93 D
Fairway The. N14 ...12 — 28 95 D
Fairway The. N Mal ...94 — 20 69 B
Fairway The. Nthlt ...43 — 14 84 A
Fairway The. Ruis ...32 — 11 86 D
Fairway The. W3 ...55 — 21 81 C
Fairway The. Wem ...33 — 16 86 B
Fairweather Cl. N15 ...25 — 33 89 C
Fairweather Rd. N16 ...37 — 34 88 C
Fairwyn Rd. SE26 ...88 — 36 71 A
Falaize Ave. Ilf ...51 — 43 85 B
Falcon Ave. Brom ...99 — 42 68 C
Falconberg Ct. W1 ...2 — 29 81 D
Falconberg Mews. W1 ...2 — 29 81 D
Falcon Cl. Nthwd ...19 — 09 91 C
Falcon Cl. SE1 ...7 — 31 80 D
Falcon Cres. Enf ...14 — 35 95 B
Falcon Ct. E18 ...27 — 40 89 B
Falcon Ct. EC4 ...3 — 31 81 C
Falconer Wlk. N7 ...36 — 30 86 B
Falcon Gr. SW11 ...74 — 27 75 A
Falcon Rd. Enf ...14 — 35 95 B
Falcon Rd. Hamp ...92 — 12 70 D
Falcon Rd. SW11 ...74 — 27 75 A
Falconry Ct. King ...93 — 18 68 A
Falcon St. E13 ...58 — 40 82 C
Falcon Terr. SW11 ...74 — 27 75 A
Falcon Way. Har ...33 — 18 88 C
Falcon Way. Sun ...91 — 09 69 C
Falconwood Ave. Well ...78 — 45 76 C
Falconwood Par. Well ...78 — 45 75 D
Falcourt Cl. Sutt ...110 — 25 64 D
Falkirk St. N1 ...48 — 33 83 C
Falkland Ave. N11 ...16 — 28 92 B
Falkland Ave. N3 ...23 — 25 91 C
Falkland Park Ave. SE25 ...97 — 33 69 C
Falkland Pl. NW5 ...47 — 29 85 C
Falkland Rd. Barn ...11 — 24 97 C
Falkland Rd. N8 ...25 — 31 89 C
Falkland Rd. NW5 ...47 — 29 85 C
Falloden Way. NW11 ...23 — 25 89 D
Fallow Court Ave. N12 ...23 — 26 91 A
Fallowhurst Path. N3 ...23 — 26 91 C
Fallsbrook Rd. SW16 ...96 — 29 70 A
Falmer Rd. E17 ...26 — 37 89 B
Falmer Rd. Enf ...13 — 33 96 C
Falmer Rd. N15 ...37 — 32 88 B
Falmouth Ave. E4 ...18 — 38 92 D
Falmouth Cl. N22 ...24 — 39 91 A
Falmouth Cl. SE12 ...77 — 30 91 D
Falmouth Gdns. Ilf ...27 — 39 74 B
Falmouth Gdns. Ilf ...39 — 41 89 D
Falmouth Rd. SE1 ...8 — 42 88 A
Falmouth St. E15 ...49 — 32 79 C
Fambridge Cl. SE26 ...88 — 38 85 D
Fambridge Rd. Dag ...41 — 36 71 B
Fambridge Rd. SE26 ...88 — 49 87 C
Fane St. W14 ...62 — 36 71 B
Fann St. EC1 ...4 — 24 78 D
Fanshawe Ave. Bark ...51 — 32 82 C
Fanshawe Cres. Dag ...52 — 44 84 A
Fanshawe Cres. Horn ...42 — 48 85 D
Fanshawe Rd. Rich ...83 — 53 88 D
Fanshaw St. N1 ...4 — 17 71 A
Fanthorpe St. SW15 ...73 — 33 82 A
Faraday Ave. Sid ...90 — 23 75 A
Faraday Cl. N7 ...47 — 46 72 B
Faraday Rd. E15 ...50 — 30 84 B
Faraday Rd. E Mol ...92 — 39 84 B
Faraday Rd. Sthl ...53 — 13 68 C
Faraday Rd. W10 ...56 — 13 80 B
Faraday Rd. W3 ...55 — 24 81 A
Faraday Rd. Well ...78 — 20 80 A
Faraday Way. Orp ...100 — 46 75 A
Faraday Way. SE18 ...65 — 46 68 D
Fareham Rd. Felt ...82 — 41 79 D
Fareham St. W1 ...2 — 11 73 A
Farewell Pl. Mit ...96 — 29 81 D
Faringdon Ave. Brom ...108 — 27 69 A
Faringdon Ave. Rom ...30 — 43 66 A
Faringford Rd. E15 ...50 — 53 91 D
Farjeon Rd. SE3 ...77 — 39 84 C / 41 76 B

Farleigh Ave. Brom ...107 — 40 66 A
Farleigh Pl. N16 ...48 — 33 85 B
Farleigh Rd. N16 ...48 — 33 85 B
Farley Dri. Ilf ...40 — 45 87 C
Farley Rd. SE26 ...87 — 34 72 D
Farley Pl. SE25 ...97 — 34 68 C
Farley Rd. S Croy ...112 — 34 62 B
Farley Rd. SE6 ...88 — 38 73 A
Farlington Pl. SW15 ...84 — 22 73 B
Farlow Rd. SW15 ...73 — 23 75 B
Farlton Rd. SW18 ...85 — 25 73 B
Farman Gr. (off Wayfarer Rd). Nthlt ...53 — 11 82 B
Farm Ave. Har ...32 — 13 88 C
Farm Ave. NW2 ...35 — 24 86 D
Farm Ave. SW16 ...86 — 30 71 A
Farm Ave. Wem ...44 — 17 84 A
Farm Cl. Barn ...11 — 23 95 A
Farm Cl. Dag ...52 — 50 84 C
Farm Cl. Sthl ...3 — 13 80 B
Farm Cl. Sutt ...110 — 26 63 D
Farm Cl. Uxb ...31 — 07 86 B
Farm Cl. Wall ...111 — 29 62 C
Farm Cl. W.Wick ...107 — 39 65 D
Farmcote Rd. SE12 ...89 — 40 73 C
Farm Ct. NW4 ...22 — 22 89 A
Farmdale Rd. Cars ...111 — 27 63 C
Farmdale Rd. SE10 ...65 — 40 78 C
Farm Dri. Croy ...106 — 36 65 B
Farmer Rd. E10 ...38 — 37 87 D
Farmer's Rd. SE5 ...63 — 31 77 D
Farmer St. W8 ...56 — 25 80 C
Farmfield Cl. N12 ...15 — 25 93 C
Farmfield Rd. Brom ...89 — 39 71 C
Farmfield Rd. Mit ...96 — 28 69 A
Farmhouse Rd. SW16 ...96 — 29 70 C
Farmilo Rd. E17 ...38 — 37 87 A
Farmington Ave. Sutt ...103 — 26 65 D
Farm La. Croy ...106 — 36 65 B
Farm La. N14 ...12 — 28 95 D
Farmlands. Enf ...13 — 31 97 A
Farmlands. Pnr ...19 — 10 89 C
Farmlands The. Nthlt ...43 — 13 84 A
Farmland Wlk. Chis ...90 — 43 71 D
Farm La. Pur ...111 — 29 62 C
Farm La. SW6 ...62 — 25 77 C
Farmleigh. N14 ...16 — 29 94 A
Farm Pl. Dart ...80 — 52 75 C
Farm Pl. W8 ...56 — 19 91 B
Farm Rd. Edg ...22 — 12 73 C
Farm Rd. Houn ...82 — 25 67 B
Farm Rd. Mord ...103 — 32 94 B
Farm Rd. N21 ...17 — 26 63 D
Farm Rd. Sutt ...110 — 14 90 B
Farmstead Rd. Har ...20 — 38 71 B
Farmstead Rd. SE6 ...88 — 19 86 B
Farm St. W1 ...6 — 23 73 B
Farm The. SW19 ...85 — 49 74 D
Farm Vale. Bex ...79 — 47 86 C
Farmway. Dag ...41 — 23 65 C
Farm Way. Wor Pk ...103 — 25 88 A
Farm Wlk. NW11 ...35 — 39 69 A
Farnaby Rd. Brom ...99 — 41 75 C
Farnaby Rd. SE9 ...77 — 37 89 B
Farnan Ave. E17 ...26 — 30 71 C
Farnan Rd. SW16 ...86 — 36 89 A
Farnborough Ave. E17 ...26 — 19 86 B
Farnborough Cl. Wem ...34 — 42 65 D
Farnborough Common. Brom ...107
Farnborough Way (off Blake's Rd). SE15 ...63 — 33 77 D
Farncombe St. SE16 ...63 — 34 79 A
Farndale Ave. N13 ...17 — 32 93 C
Farndale Cres. Grnf ...53 — 14 82 A
Farnell Mews. SW5 ...62 — 25 78 D
Farnell Rd. Islw ...70 — 14 75 B
Farnes Dri. Rom ...30 — 53 90 C
Farnham Cl. N20 ...15 — 26 94 A
Farnham Ct. Sutt ...110 — 24 63 A
Farnham Gdns. SW20 ...94 — 22 69 D
Farnham Pl. SE1 ...7 — 31 80 D
Farnham Rd. Ilf ...40 — 45 87 B
Farnham Rd. Well ...79 — 47 76 C
Farnham Royal. SE11 ...10 — 30 78 D
Farningham Rd. N17 ...25 — 34 91 C
Farnley Rd. SE25 ...97 — 32 68 D
Faro Cl. Brom ...100 — 43 69 C
Faroe Rd. W14 ...62 — 23 79 D
Farorna Wlk. Enf ...13 — 31 97 A
Farquhar Rd. SE19 ...87 — 33 71 D
Farquhar Rd. SW19 ...85 — 32 72 C
Farquharson Rd. Croy ...105 — 52 66 C
Farrance Rd. Rom ...41 — 48 87 A
Farrance St. E14 ...57 — 37 81 C
Farrant Ave. N22 ...25 — 31 90 D

Farr Ave. Bark	51	46 83 C
Farren Rd. SE23	88	36 72 A
Farrer Rd. Har	21	18 89 C
Farrer Rd. N8	24	29 89 D
Farrier Cl. Sun	91	10 68 C
Farrier Rd. Nthlt	43	13 83 C
Farrier St. NW1	47	28 84 D
Farringdon Rd. EC1	3	31 82 C
Farringdon St. EC4	3	31 81 D
Farrington Ave. Orp	100	46 68 B
Farrins Rents. SE16	57	36 80 C
Farr Rd. Enf	13	32 97 B
Farthing Alley. SE1	63	34 79 A
Farthing Cl. Dart	80	54 75 D
Farthing Fields. E1	57	34 80 D
Farthings Cl. Pnr	31	10 88 D
Farwell Rd. Sid	90	46 71 B
Farwig La. Brom	99	40 69 A
Fashion St. E1	4	33 81 B
Fashoda Rd. Brom	99	41 68 D
Fassett Rd. E8	48	34 84 A
Fassett Rd. King	93	18 68 C
Fassett Sq. E8	48	34 84 A
Fauconberg Rd. W4	61	20 77 A
Faulkner's Alley. EC1	3	31 81 B
Faulkner St. SE14	76	35 76 A
Fauna Cl. Rom	41	47 88 C
Faunce St. SE17	63	31 78 D
Favart Rd. SW6	73	25 76 A
Faversham Ave. Enf	13	32 95 D
Faversham Rd. Beck	98	36 69 D
Faversham Rd. Mord	103	25 67 D
Faversham Rd. SE6	88	36 73 D
Fawcett Cl. SW11	73	26 76 D
Fawcett Estate. E5	37	34 87 C
Fawcett Rd. Croy	105	32 65 C
Fawcett Rd. NW10	45	21 84 D
Fawcett St. SW10	62	26 77 A
Fawe Park Rd. SW15	73	24 75 D
Fawe St. E14	57	37 81 B
Fawkham House. SE1	63	33 78 B
Fawley Rd. N17	25	34 89 C
Fawley Rd. NW6	46	25 85 D
Fawnbrake Ave. SE24	75	32 74 A
Fawn Rd. E13	50	41 83 C
Fawns Manor Rd. Felt	81	08 73 D
Fawood Ave. NW10	45	20 84 D
Faygate Cres. Bexh	79	49 74 A
Faygate Rd. SW2	86	30 72 B
Fayland Ave. SW16	86	29 71 C
Fearnley Cres. Hamp	92	12 70 B
Fearon St. SE10	65	40 78 C
Feathers Pl. SE10	64	38 77 B
Featherstone Ave. SE23	88	35 72 A
Featherstone Rd. NW7	22	22 91 B
Featherstone Rd. Sthl	59	12 79 C
Featherstone St. EC1	4	32 82 D
Featherstone Terr. Sthl	59	12 79 C
Featley Rd. SW9	75	31 75 B
Federal Rd. Grnf	44	17 83 C
Federation Rd. SE2	67	47 78 A
Feildview. SE18	85	26 73 D
Felbridge Ave. Stan	21	16 90 B
Felbridge Cl. Sutt	110	25 62 B
Felbridge Cl. SW16	87	31 71 A
Felbrigge Rd. Ilf	40	45 87 D
Felday Rd. SE13	76	37 74 D
Felden St. SW6	73	24 76 B
Feldman Cl. N16	37	34 87 C
Feldon Cl. Pnr	20	12 91 C
Felgate Mews. W6	61	22 78 B
Felhampton Rd. SE9	90	43 72 D
Felhurst Cres. Dag	52	50 85 A
Felix Ave. N8	36	30 88 C
Felix Rd. W13	54	18 80 A
Felix St. E2	48	34 83 D
Felixstowe Rd. N17	25	33 89 B
Felixstowe Rd. N9	17	34 93 C
Felixstowe Rd. NW10	55	22 82 B
Felixstowe Rd. SE2	66	46 79 D
Fellbrigg Rd. SE22	75	33 74 B
Fellbrigg St. E1	57	34 82 D
Fellbrook. Rich	83	16 72 D
Fellowes Rd. Cars	104	27 65 A
Fellows Ct. E2	48	33 83 D
Fellows Rd. NW3	47	27 84 C
Fell Rd. Croy	105	32 65 C
Felltram Way. SE7	65	40 78 C
Fell Wlk. Edg	22	19 90 B
Felmersham Cl. SW4	74	30 75 C
Felmingham Rd. SE20	98	35 69 C
Felsberg Rd. SW2	86	30 73 A
Fels Cl. Dag	41	49 86 D
Fels Farm Ave. Dag	41	50 86 C
Felsham Rd. SW15	73	23 75 A
Felsham Rd. SW15	73	23 75 B
Felspar Cl. SE18	66	45 78 D
Felstead Ave. Ilf	28	43 90 A
Felstead Rd. E11	39	40 87 B
Felstead Rd. Orp	108	46 65 B
Felstead Rd. Rom	29	50 91 C
Felstead St. E9	49	36 84 B
Felsted Rd. E16	58	41 81 D
Feltham Ave. E Mol	93	15 68 C
Felthambrook Way. Felt	81	10 71 B
Feltham Hill Rd. Ashf	81	07 71 D
Felthamhill Rd. Felt	81	10 71 B
Feltham Rd. Ashf	81	07 71 B
Feltham Rd. Mit	96	28 69 C
Felton Cl. Orp	108	43 67 D
Felton Gdns. Bark	51	45 83 C
Felton Lea. Sid	90	45 71 D
Felton Rd. Bark	51	45 83 C
Felton Rd. W13	60	17 79 A
Felton St. N1	48	32 83 B
Fencepiece Rd. Ilf	28	44 91 C
Fenchurch Ave. EC3	4	33 81 C
Fenchurch Bldgs. EC3	4	33 81 C
Fenchurch St. EC3	4	33 80 A
Fen Ct. EC3	4	33 81 C
Fendall Rd. Eps	109	20 64 C
Fendall St. SE1	8	33 79 C
Fendt Cl. E16	58	39 81 D
Fendyke Rd. Belv	67	47 78 B
Fenelon Pl. W14	62	24 78 B
Fen Gr. Sid	78	45 75 D
Fenham Rd. SE15	63	34 77 D
Fenman Ct. N17	25	34 90 B
Fenn Cl. Brom	99	40 70 A
Fennells Mead. Eps	109	21 62 B
Fennell St. SE18	66	43 77 A
Fenner Cl. SE16	63	34 78 B
Fenner Sq. SW11	73	26 75 B
Fenning St. SE1	8	33 79 A
Fenn St. E9	49	35 85 C
Fenstanton Ave. N12	23	26 91 B
Fen St. E16	58	39 80 B
Fentiman Rd. SW8	10	30 77 D
Fentiman Way. Horn	42	54 87 C
Fenton Cl. Chis	89	42 71 D
Fenton Cl. SW9	74	30 76 D
Fenton Rd. N17	25	32 91 C
Fenton's Ave. E13	50	40 83 D
Fenton St. E1	57	34 81 D
Fenwick Cl. SE18	66	43 77 A
Fenwick Gr. SE15	75	34 75 A
Fenwick Pl. SW9	74	30 75 A
Fenwick Rd. SE15	75	34 75 A
Ferdinand Pl. NW1	47	28 84 C
Ferdinand St. NW1	47	28 84 C
Ferguson Ave. Rom	30	53 90 D
Ferguson Ave. Surb	101	18 67 B
Ferguson Ct. Rom	30	53 90 D
Fergus Rd. N5	48	31 85 D
Fermain Ct. N1	48	33 83 A
Ferme Park Rd. N4	36	30 87 B
Fermor Rd. SE23	88	36 73 C
Fermoy Rd. Grnf	53	13 82 D
Fermoy Rd. W9	56	24 82 D
Fern Ave. Mit	96	29 68 D
Fernbank Ave. Wem	44	15 85 B
Fernbrook Ave. Sid	78	45 74 A
Fernbrook Dri. Har	32	13 87 B
Fernbrook Rd. SE13	77	39 74 C
Ferncliff Rd. E8	48	34 85 C
Ferncroft Ave. N12	24	27 91 B
Ferncroft Ave. NW3	46	25 85 A
Ferncroft Ave. Ruis	32	11 86 A
Ferndale Ave. E17	38	38 88 B
Ferndale Ave. Houn	70	12 75 A
Ferndale. Brom	99	41 69 C
Ferndale Ct. SW9	74	30 75 D
Ferndale Rd. E11	39	39 86 B
Ferndale Rd. E7	40	40 84 D
Ferndale Rd. N15	37	33 88 B
Ferndale Rd. Rom	29	50 90 C
Ferndale Rd. SE25	105	34 67 B
Ferndale Rd. SW4	74	30 75 C
Ferndale Terr. Har	21	15 89 D
Ferndene Rd. SE24	75	32 75 C
Fern Dene. W13	54	16 81 B
Fernden Way. Rom	41	49 88 D
Ferndown Ave. Orp	108	44 66 D
Ferndown Cl. Pnr	20	12 91 C
Ferndown Cl. Sutt	110	26 63 B
Ferndown. Horn	42	54 88 D
Ferndown. Nthwd	19	10 90 C
Ferndown Rd. SE9	89	41 73 B
Ferne Park Rd. N8	36	30 88 D
Ferney Rd. Barn	16	28 94 C
Fern Gr. Felt	81	10 73 B
Fernhall Dri. Ilf	39	41 88 B
Fernham Rd. Th Hth	97	32 68 A
Fernhead Rd. W9	56	24 82 B
Fernhill Ct. E17	26	38 90 D
Fernhill Ct. King	83	17 71 D
Fernhill Gdns. King	83	18 71 C
Fernholme Rd. SE15	76	35 74 B
Fernhurst Gdns. Edg	22	19 91 A
Fernhurst Rd. Ashf	81	08 71 A
Fernhurst Rd. Croy	105	34 66 D
Fernhurst Rd. SW6	62	24 77 D
Fern La. Houn	59	12 78 D
Fernlea Rd. Mit	96	28 69 A
Fernlea Rd. SW12	86	28 73 D
Fernleigh Cl. Croy	112	31 64 A
Fernleigh Ct. Har	20	13 90 D
Fernleigh Ct. Wem	33	18 87 C
Fernleigh Rd. N21	17	31 93 B
Fernsbury St. WC1	3	31 82 A
Ferns Cl. S Croy	112	34 62 D
Fernshaw Rd. SW10	62	26 77 A
Fernside Ave. Felt	81	10 71 B
Fernside Ct. NW4	23	23 90 D
Fernside Rd. SW12	86	28 73 A
Ferns Rd. E15	50	39 84 B
Fern St. E3	57	37 82 C
Fernthorpe Rd. SW16	96	29 70 A
Ferntower Rd. N5	48	32 85 D
Fernways. Ilf	51	43 85 B
Fernwood Ave. Grnf	44	17 84 A
Fernwood Ave. SW16	86	29 71 B
Fernwood Cl. Brom	99	41 69 C
Fernwood Cres. N20	16	27 93 D
Ferranti Cl. SE18	65	41 79 D
Ferraro Cl. Houn	59	13 77 A
Ferrers Ave. Wall	111	29 64 B
Ferrers Rd. SW16	86	29 71 D
Ferrestone Rd. N8	24	30 89 D
Ferriby Cl. N1	48	31 84 C
Ferrier St. SW18	73	25 75 D
Ferring Cl. Har	32	14 87 C
Ferrings. SE21	87	33 72 C
Ferris Ave. Croy	106	36 65 D
Ferris Rd. SE22	75	34 75 C
Ferron Rd. E5	37	34 86 D
Ferry App. SE18	66	43 79 C
Ferry La. Brent	60	18 77 A
Ferry La. N17	25	34 89 D
Ferry La. Rich	60	18 77 B
Ferry La. SW13	61	21 77 B
Ferrymead Ave. Grnf	43	13 83 D
Ferrymead Dri. Grnf	43	13 83 C
Ferrymead Gdns. Grnf	43	14 83 C
Ferrymoor. Rich	83	16 72 D
Ferry Pl. SE18	66	43 79 C
Ferry Rd. E Mol	92	13 68 A
Ferry Rd. Surb	101	16 67 D
Ferry Rd. SW13	72	22 76 A
Ferry Rd. Tedd	83	16 71 D
Ferry Rd. Twick	83	16 73 D
Ferry Sq. Brent	60	18 77 A
Ferry St. E14	64	38 78 C
Festing Rd. SW15	73	23 75 B
Festival Cl. Eri	68	51 77 D
Festival Wlk. Cars	111	27 64 B
Fetter La. EC4	3	31 81 C
Ffinch St. SE8	64	37 77 C
Field Cl. Brom	99	41 69 C
Field Cl. E4	26	37 91 B
Field Cl. Houn	69	10 76 B
Field Cl. Ruis	31	08 87 C
Field Cl. Uxb	31	07 86 B
Field Ct. WC1	3	30 81 B
Field End. Nthlt	43	11 84 B
Field End Rd. Ruis	32	11 87 D
Fieldend. SW16	96	29 69 A
Field End. Ruis	43	11 84 A
Field End. Twick	83	15 71 B
Field Gate La. Mit	96	27 69 C
Fieldgate St. E1	57	34 81 A
Fieldhouse Rd. SW12	86	29 73 C
Fielding Ave. Twick	82	14 72 C
Fielding Rd. W14	62	23 79 D
Fielding Rd. W4	61	21 79 C
Fieldings The. SE23	88	35 73 C
Fieldings Cl. SE17	63	32 77 A
Field La. Brent	60	17 77 C
Field Lane. Tedd	93	16 70 A
Field La. Tedd	83	16 71 C
Field Mead. NW9	22	21 91 D
Field Pl. EC1	48	31 83 C
Field Pl. N.Mal	102	21 67 D
Field Rd. E7	50	40 85 A
Field Rd. Felt	69	10 74 D

Name	Page	Grid
Field Rd. N17	25	33 89 A
Field Rd. W6	62	24 77 D
Fieldsend Rd. Sutt	110	24 64 C
Fields Estate. E8	48	34 84 C
Fieldside Rd. Brom	88	38 71 D
Fields Park Cres. Rom	41	47 88 B
Field St. WC1	3	30 82 B
Field View. Felt	81	08 71 B
Fieldway Cres. N5	48	31 85 C
Fieldway. Dag	52	47 85 A
Field Way. Grnf	43	13 83 B
Field Way. NW10	45	20 84 C
Fieldway. Orp	108	44 67 D
Field Way. Ruis	31	08 87 C
Fife Rd. E16	58	40 81 A
Fife Rd. King	93	18 69 C
Fife Rd. SW14	72	31 91 D
Fife Rd. N22	25	20 74 A
Fife Terr. N1	47	30 83 D
Fifield Path. SE23	88	35 72 D
Fifth Ave. E12	50	42 85 B
Fifth Ave. W10	56	24 82 A
Fifth Cross Rd. Twick	82	14 72 B
Filey Ave. N16	37	34 87 C
Filey Cl. Sutt	110	26 63 C
Filey Waye. Ruis	31	10 86 B
Fillebrook Ave. Enf	13	33 97 D
Fillebrook Rd. E11	39	39 87 A
Filmer Rd. SW6	62	24 77 D
Filston Rd. Eri	67	50 78 C
Finborough Rd. SW10	62	25 77 B
Finborough Rd. SW17	96	27 70 B
Finchale Rd. SE2	66	46 79 D
Finch Ave. SE27	87	32 71 B
Finch Cl. NW10	45	20 84 B
Finchdean Way (off Blake's Rd) SE15	63	33 77 C
Finch Dri. Felt	82	11 73 B
Finchingfield Ave. Wdf Gn	27	41 91 C
Finch La. EC3	4	32 81 D
Finchley Ct. N3	23	25 91 B
Finchley La. NW4	23	23 89 D
Finchley Park. N12	15	26 92 B
Finchley Pl. NW8	46	26 83 D
Finchley Rd. NW11	35	25 87 A
Finchley Rd. NW3	46	26 85 C
Finchley Rd. NW8	46	26 83 B
Finchley Way. N3	23	25 91 C
Finch's Ct. E14	57	37 80 B
Finck St. SE1	7	30 79 B
Finden Rd. E7	50	41 85 C
Findhorn St. E14	58	38 81 C
Findon Cl. Har	32	13 86 D
Findon Cl. SW18	73	25 74 C
Findon Rd. N9	17	34 94 D
Findon Rd. W12	61	22 79 A
Fine Bush La. Uxb	31	07 88 D
Fingal St. E10	65	39 78 D
Finland Rd. SE4	76	36 75 A
Finlays Cl. Chess	109	19 64 C
Finlay St. SW6	73	23 76 B
Finnis St. E2	57	34 82 D
Finnymore Rd. Dag	52	48 84 C
Finsbury Ave. EC2	4	32 81 B
Finsbury Circ. EC2	4	32 81 B
Finsbury Cottages. N22	24	30 91 C
Finsbury Ct. EC2	4	32 81 B
Finsbury Market. EC2	4	33 81 A
Finsbury Market. EC2	4	33 82 C
Finsbury Park Ave. N4	37	32 87 A
Finsbury Park Rd. N4	37	31 86 B
Finsbury Pavement. EC2	4	32 81 B
Finsbury Rd. N22	24	30 90 B
Finsbury Rd. N22	24	30 91 D
Finsbury Sq. EC2	4	32 81 B
Finsbury St. EC2	4	32 81 B
Finsen Rd. SE5	75	32 75 A
Finstock Rd. W10	56	23 81 D
Finucane Ct. Rich	71	18 75 B
Firbank Cl. E16	58	41 81 B
Firbank Rd. SE15	75	34 76 D
Fircroft Gdns. Har	33	15 86 C
Fircroft Rd. SW17	86	27 72 D
Fir Dene. Orp	108	43 65 C
Firdene. Surb	102	20 66 C
Fire Bell Alley. Surb	101	18 67 C
Firefly Cl. Wall	111	30 63 C
Fire Station Alley. Barn	11	24 96 A
Fir Gr. N.Mal	102	21 67 D
Firhill Rd. SE6	88	37 72 C
Firmin Rd. Dart	80	53 74 A
Fir Rd. Felt	82	11 71 C
Fir Rd. Sutt	103	24 66 D
Firs Ave. N10	24	28 89 C
Firs Ave. SW14	72	20 75 C
Firsby Ave. Croy	106	36 66 C
Firsby Rd. N16	37	34 87 C
Firs Cl. N10	24	28 89 A
Firs Cl. SE23	88	36 73 A
Firscroft. N13	17	32 93 C
Firs Dri. Houn	69	10 76 B
Firs La. N13	17	32 93 C
Firs La. N21	17	32 94 C
Firs Park Ave. N21	17	32 94 D
Firs Park Gdns. N21	17	32 94 D
First Ave. Bexh	67	47 77 C
First Ave. Dag	52	49 83 D
First Ave. E12	50	42 85 C
First Ave. E13	58	40 82 A
First Ave. E17	38	37 88 B
First Ave. E Mol	92	13 68 C
First Ave. Enf	13	33 95 B
First Ave. Eps	109	21 62 A
First Ave. N18	18	35 92 A
First Ave. NW4	23	23 89 C
First Ave. Rom	41	47 88 A
First Ave. SW14	72	21 75 A
First Ave. W10	56	24 82 D
First Ave. W3	55	21 80 D
First Ave. Wem	33	17 86 B
First Cl. E Mol	92	14 68 A
First Cross Rd. Twick	83	15 72 A
Firs The. N20	15	26 94 D
Firs The. SW20	94	22 70 C
Firs The. W5	54	17 81 B
First St. SW3	9	27 78 A
Firstway. SW20	95	22 69 C
First Way. Wem	45	19 85 B
Firs Wlk. Nthwd	19	08 91 B
Firswood Ave. Eps	109	21 64 D
Firth Gdns. SW6	73	24 76 A
Firtree Ave. Mit	96	28 69 C
Fir Tree Cl. Eps	109	21 64 B
Fir Tree Cl. Rom	29	50 89 B
Fir Tree Gr. Cars	111	27 63 D
Fir Tree Rd. Houn	70	12 75 C
Fir Trees Cl. SE16	57	36 80 C
Fir Tree Wlk. Dag	41	50 86 C
Fir Tree Wlk. Enf	13	32 96 B
Fir Wlk. Sutt	110	23 63 B
Fisher Cl. Croy	105	33 66 D
Fisher Cl. Grnf	53	13 82 A
Fisherman Cl. Rich	83	17 71 A
Fisher Rd. Har	21	15 90 D
Fishers Ct. SE14	76	35 76 B
Fisher's La. W4	61	20 78 B
Fisher St. E16	58	40 81 A
Fisher St. WC1	3	30 81 B
Fisher's Way. Belv	67	50 79 B
Fisherton St. NW8	1	26 82 D
Fishponds Rd. SW17	86	27 71 A
Fish St Hill. EC3	8	32 80 B
Fiske Ct. Bark	51	44 83 D
Fiske Ct. N17	25	34 90 A
Fisons Rd. E16	58	40 80 C
Fitzalan Rd. N3	23	24 89 B
Fitzalan St. SE11	63	31 78 A
Fitzgeorge Ave. N Mal	94	20 69 A
Fitz-George Ave. W14	62	24 78 A
Fitzgerald Ave. SW14	72	21 75 A
Fitzgerald Rd. E11	39	40 88 A
Fitzgerald Rd. Surb	101	16 67 C
Fitzgerald Rd. SW14	72	20 75 B
Fitzhardinge St. W1	2	28 81 C
Fitzhugh Gr. SW18	73	26 74 D
Fitzilian Ave. Rom	30	54 90 B
Fitzjames Ave. Croy	105	34 65 A
Fitzjames Ave. W14	62	24 78 A
Fitzjohn Ave. Barn	11	24 96 D
Fitzjohn's Ave. NW3	46	26 85 D
Fitzmaurice Pl. W1	6	28 80 D
Fitzneal St. W12	55	21 81 D
Fitzroy Cl. N6	36	27 87 D
Fitzroy Ct. W1	2	29 82 C
Fitzroy Gdns. SE19	97	33 70 C
Fitzroy Mews. W1	2	29 82 C
Fitzroy Park. N6	36	27 87 D
Fitzroy Rd. NW1	47	28 83 A
Fitzroy Sq. W1	2	29 82 C
Fitzroy St. W1	2	29 82 C
Fitzstephen Rd. Dag	52	47 85 C
Fitzwarren Gdns. N19	36	29 87 C
Fitzwilliam Ave. Rich	71	18 76 D
Fitzwilliam House. Rich	71	17 75 D
Fitzwilliam Rd. SW4	74	29 75 A
Fitz Wygram Cl. Hamp	82	14 71 C
Five Acre. NW9	22	21 90 B
Five Bell Alley. E14	57	36 80 B
Five Elms Rd. Brom	107	41 65 C
Five Elms Rd. Dag	41	48 86 D
Five Oaks La. Chig	29	48 91 A
Fives Ct. SE11	7	31 79 D
Fiveways Rd. W9	75	31 76 C
Fladbury Rd. N15	37	32 88 D
Fladgate Rd. E11	39	39 88 C
Flag Wlk. Pnr	31	10 88 C
Flambard Rd. Har	33	16 88 C
Flamborough Rd. Ruis	31	10 86 C
Flamborough St. E14	57	36 81 C
Flamborough Wlk. E14	57	36 81 C
Flamingo Gdns. (off Jetstar Way). Nthlt	53	12 82 A
Flamstead Gdns. Dag	52	47 84 C
Flamstead Rd. Dag	52	47 84 C
Flamsted Ave. Wem	45	19 84 A
Flamsted Rd. SE7	65	42 78 C
Flanchford Rd. W12	61	21 79 D
Flanders Cres. SW17	96	27 70 D
Flanders Rd. E6	51	43 83 C
Flanders Rd. W4	61	21 78 A
Flanders Way. E9	49	35 84 A
Flank St. E1	57	34 80 A
Flask Wlk. NW3	46	26 85 B
Flaxley Rd. Mord	103	25 66 B
Flaxman Ct. W1	2	29 81 D
Flaxman Rd. SE5	75	32 76 C
Flaxman Terr. WC1	2	29 82 B
Flaxton Rd. SE18	78	44 76 B
Flaxton Rd. SE18	66	45 77 C
Fleece Rd. Surb	101	17 66 C
Fleece Wlk. N7	47	30 84 A
Fleet La. EC4	3	31 81 D
Fleet Rd. NW3	47	27 85 C
Fleet Sq. WC1	3	30 82 B
Fleet St. EC4	3	31 81 C
Fleet Street Hill. E1	57	34 82 C
Fleetwood Cl. E16	58	41 81 B
Fleetwood Rd. King	94	19 68 B
Fleetwood Rd. NW10	45	22 85 C
Fleetwood Sq. King	94	19 68 B
Fleetwood St. N16	37	33 86 A
Fleming Cl. E17	26	36 90 D
Fleming Ct. Croy	112	31 64 C
Fleming Me. Mit	96	27 70 D
Fleming Rd. E17	26	36 90 D
Fleming Rd. SE17	63	31 77 B
Fleming Rd. Sthl	53	14 81 C
Fleming Way. Islw	71	15 75 D
Flempton Rd. E10	38	36 87 C
Fletcher La. E10	38	38 87 A
Fletcher Path. SE8	64	37 77 C
Fletcher Rd. W4	61	20 79 C
Fletchers Cl. Brom	99	40 68 D
Fletcher St. E1	57	34 80 A
Fletching Rd. E5	38	35 86 C
Fletching Rd. SE7	65	44 77 B
Fletton Rd. N11	24	30 91 C
Fleur Gates. SW19	85	23 73 B
Flexmere Rd. N17	25	33 90 A
Flight App. NW9	22	21 90 D
Flimwell Cl. Brom	89	39 71 C
Flintmill Cres. SE3	77	42 76 C
Flinton St. SE17	63	33 78 C
Flint St. SE17	63	32 78 B
Flitcroft St. WC2	2	29 81 D
*Flockton St. SE16	63	34 79 A
*Flockton St. SE16	63	34 79 A
Flodden Rd. SE5	75	32 76 A
Flood St. SW3	9	27 77 A
Flood Wlk. SW3	9	27 77 A
Flora Cl. E14	57	37 81 D
Flora Gdns. Rom	41	47 88 C
Flora Gdns. W6	61	22 78 B
Floral St. WC2	7	30 80 A
Flora St. Belv	67	48 78 D
Florence Ave. Enf	13	32 96 A
Florence Ave. Mord	103	26 67 A
Florence Cl. Horn	42	54 86 A
Florence Dri. Enf	13	32 96 A
Florence Gdns. W4	61	20 77 A
Florence Rd. Beck	98	36 69 C
Florence Rd. Brom	99	40 69 A
Florence Rd. E13	50	39 83 D
Florence Rd. E6	50	41 83 A
Florence Rd. Felt	81	10 73 D
Florence Rd. King	93	18 70 D
Florence Rd. N4	37	31 87 C
Florence Rd. S Croy	112	32 62 B
Florence Rd. SE14	76	35 76 B
Florence Rd. SE2	67	47 78 A
Florence Rd. Sthl	53	11 79 D
Florence Rd. SW19	95	25 70 B
Florence Rd. W4	61	20 79 D
Florence Rd. W5	54	18 80 A
Florence St. E16	58	39 82 D

Name	Page	Ref
Florence St. N1	48	31 84 D
Florence St. NW4	23	23 89 C
Florence Terr. SE14	76	36 76 B
Florfield Pas. E8	48	34 84 B
Florfield Rd. E8	48	34 84 B
Florian Ave. Sutt	110	26 64 B
Florian Rd. SW15	73	24 75 C
Florida Ct. Brom	99	39 68 D
Florida Rd. Th Hth	97	31 69 B
Florida St. E2	57	34 82 A
Floriston Cl. Stan	21	16 90 B
Floriston Gdns. Stan	21	16 90 B
Floriston Rd. Nthlt	43	13 85 D
Floss St. SW6	73	23 76 C
Flower and Dean St. E1	4	33 81 B
Flower House Cl. Brom	88	38 71 C
Flower La. NW7	22	21 91 B
Flowersmead. SW17	86	28 72 A
Flowers Mews. N19	36	29 86 A
Floyd Rd. SE7	65	41 78 C
Fludyer St. SE13	77	39 75 C
Fluer De Lis St. E1	4	33 82 D
Folair Way. SE16	63	34 78 D
Foley St. W1	2	29 81 A
Folgate St. E1	4	33 81 B
Foliot St. W12	55	21 81 D
Folkestone Rd. E17	26	37 89 D
Folkestone Rd. E6	51	43 83 C
Folkestone Rd. N18	17	34 92 A
Folkingham La. NW9	22	21 90 A
Folkington Cnr. N12	15	24 92 D
Follett St. E14	58	38 81 C
Folly La. E17	26	36 91 D
Folly La. E4	26	36 91 A
Folly Wall. E14	64	38 79 A
Fontaine Rd. SW16	96	30 70 D
Fontarabia Rd. SW11	74	28 75 C
Fontayne Ave. Rom	30	51 90 C
Fontenoy Rd. SW12	86	29 72 A
Fonteyne Gdns. Wdf Gn	27	41 90 D
Fonthill Ct. SE23	88	35 73 A
Fonthill Mews. N4	37	31 86 A
Fonthill Rd. N4	37	31 86 A
Font Hills. N2	23	26 90 C
Fontley Way. SW15	84	22 73 A
Fontmell Cl. Ashf	81	07 71 C
Fontmell Park. Ashf	81	07 71 C
Fontwell Cl. Har	21	15 91 C
Fontwell Cl. Nthlt	43	13 84 A
Fontwell Dri. Brom	108	43 67 A
Football La. Har	33	15 87 D
Footbury Hill Rd. Orp	108	46 66 A
Footpath The. SW15	72	22 74 A
Footscray Rd. SE9	78	43 74 C
Footscray Rd. SE9	78	44 73 C
Forbes St. E1	57	34 81 C
Forburg Rd. N16	37	34 87 C
Fordbridge Rd. Sun	91	10 68 C
Ford Cl. Har	32	14 87 B
Ford Cl. Shep	91	07 68 C
Ford Cl. Th Hth	105	31 67 B
Fordcroft Rd. Orp	108	46 67 B
Forde Ave. Brom	99	41 68 A
Fordel Rd. SE6	88	38 73 D
Ford End. Wdf Gn	27	40 91 B
Fordham Cl. Barn	12	27 96 A
Fordham Rd. Barn	12	27 96 A
Fordham St. E1	57	34 81 C
Fordhook Ave. W5	55	19 80 A
Fordingley Rd. W9	56	24 82 B
Fordington Ho. SE26	87	34 72 D
Fordington Rd. N6	24	27 89 D
Fordmill Rd. SE6	88	37 72 A
Ford Rd. Dag	52	49 84 C
Ford Rd. E3	49	36 83 D
Ford's Gr. N21	17	32 94 B
Fords Park Rd. E16	58	40 81 C
Ford Sq. E1	57	34 81 B
Ford St (off Old Ford Rd). E3	49	36 83 C
Ford St (off Roman Rd). E3	49	36 83 C
Ford St. E16	58	39 81 D
Fordwich Cl. Orp	108	45 66 B
Fordwych Rd. NW2	46	24 85 C
Fordyce Ave. SE13	76	38 74 C
Fordyke Rd. Dag	41	48 86 B
Foreign St. SE5	75	31 76 D
Foreland Ct. NW4	23	24 90 A
Foreland St. SE18	66	44 78 B
Foreman Ct. W6	62	23 78 A
Foremark Cl. Chig	28	45 91 B
Foreshore. SE8	64	36 78 B
Forest App. Wdf Gn	27	40 91 C
Fore St Ave. EC2	4	32 81 B
Forest Cl. E11	39	40 88 A
Forest Ct. E11	27	39 89 C
Forestdale. N11	16	29 92 B
Forest Dri. Brom	107	42 65 C
Forest Dri. E12	39	41 86 D
Forest Dri. E17	26	38 89 D
Forest Dri E. E11	38	38 87 B
Forest Dri. Sun	91	09 70 D
Forest Dri. Wdf Gn	27	39 91 C
Forest Dri W. E11	38	38 87 B
Fore St. EC2	4	32 81 B
Forester Rd. SE15	75	34 75 B
Foresters Cl. Wall	111	29 63 D
Foresters Cres. Bexh	79	49 75 D
Foresters Dri. Wall	111	29 62 B
Forest Gate. E7	50	40 85 C
Forest Gate. NW9	34	21 88 A
Forest Gdns. N17	25	33 90 D
Forest Glade. E11	39	39 88 C
Forest Gr. E8	48	33 84 D
Forest Hill Rd. SE23	76	35 74 C
Forestholme Cl. SE23	88	35 72 A
Forest La. E15	50	39 85 C
Forest Mount Rd. Wdf Gr	26	38 91 D
Fore St. N18	17	34 92 A
Fore St. N9	17	34 93 C
Fore St. Pnr	31	10 88 A
Forest Rd. E11	38	38 87 B
Forest Rd. E17	26	37 89 A
Forest Rd. E7	50	40 85 A
Forest Rd. E8	48	33 84 B
Forest Rd. Eri	80	52 76 A
Forest Rd. Felt	82	11 72 A
Forest Rd. Ilf	28	45 91 D
Forest Rd. N17	25	34 89 D
Forest Rd. N9	17	34 94 D
Forest Rd. Rich	61	19 77 C
Forest Rd. Rom	29	49 89 B
Forest Rd. Sutt	103	25 66 A
Forest Ridge. Beck	98	37 68 A
Forest Ridge. Brom	107	42 65 C
Forest Rise. E17	38	38 88 B
Forest Rise. E17	26	38 89 D
Forest Side. E7	50	40 85 B
Forest Side. Wor Pk	102	21 66 D
Forest St. E7	50	40 85 C
Forest The. E11	27	39 89 C
Forest View. E10	38	38 88 B
Forest View. E11	39	39 87 B
Forest View. E4	18	38 94 B
Forest View Rd. E12	50	42 85 A
Forest View Rd. E17	26	38 90 A
Forest Way. N19	36	29 86 A
Forest Way. Orp	108	46 67 A
Forest Way. Sid	90	44 73 B
Forfar Cl. Brom	107	40 66 C
Forfar Rd. N22	25	31 90 B
Forfar Rd. SW11	74	28 76 A
Forge Cl. Brom	107	40 66 C
Forge La. Felt	82	12 71 C
Forge La. Nthwd	19	09 91 C
Forge La. Sun	91	10 68 A
Forge La. Sutt	110	24 63 C
Forge Pl. NW1	47	28 84 A
Forman Pl. N16	48	33 85 B
Formby Ave. Stan	21	17 89 A
Formosa St. W9	56	25 82 D
Formunt Cl. E16	58	39 81 B
Forres Gdns. NW11	35	25 88 C
Forrester Path. SE26	88	35 71 A
Forrest Gdns. SW16	96	30 68 B
Forset St. W1	1	27 81 C
Forstal Cl. Brom	99	40 68 A
Forster Rd. Beck	98	36 68 A
Forster Rd. Croy	105	32 66 A
Forster Rd. E17	38	36 88 C
Forster Rd. N17	25	33 89 B
Forster Rd. SW2	86	30 73 A
Forsters Cl. Rom	41	48 88 D
Forston St. N1	48	32 83 C
Forsyte Cres. SE19	97	33 69 A
Forsyte Ct. King	94	19 69 B
Forsyth Gdns. SE17	63	31 77 B
Forsyth Pl. Enf	13	33 95 A
Forterie Gdns. Ilf	51	46 85 A
Fortescue Ave. E8	48	34 84 D
Fortescue Ave. Twick	82	14 72 C
Fortescue Rd. Edg	22	20 91 D
Fortescue Rd. SW19	95	26 70 D
Fortess Gr. NW5	47	29 85 C
Fortess Rd. NW5	47	29 85 A
Forthbridge Rd. SW11	74	28 75 C
Forth Cross Rd. Twick	82	14 72 B
Fortis Green Ave. N2	24	27 89 D
Fortis Green. N10	24	28 89 A
Fortis Green. N2	24	27 89 B
Fortis Green Rd. N10	24	28 89 A
Fortismere Ave. N10	24	28 89 C
Fortnam Rd. N19	36	29 86 B
Fortnums Acre. Stan	21	15 91 B
Fort Rd. Nthlt	43	13 84 C
Fort Rd. SE1	63	33 78 B
Fort St. E16	58	40 80 D
Fort St. E1	4	33 81 A
Fortuna Cl. N7	47	30 84 B
Fortunegate Rd. NW10	45	21 84 C
Fortune Green Rd. NW6	46	25 85 A
Fortunes Mead. Nthlt	43	12 84 A
Fortune St. EC1	4	32 82 C
Forty Acre La. E16	58	40 81 A
Forty Ave. Wem	33	18 86 B
Forty Cl. Wem	33	18 86 D
Forty Footpath. SW14	72	20 75 A
Forty La. Wem	34	19 86 B
Forumside. Edg	22	19 91 A
Forum The. E Mol	92	13 68 D
Forum Way. Edg	22	19 91 A
Forval Cl. Mit	104	27 67 B
Fosbury Mews. W2	56	25 80 B
Foscote Mews. W9	56	25 81 A
Foscote Rd. NW4	34	22 88 D
Foskett Rd. SW6	73	24 76 D
Foss Ave. Croy	112	31 64 C
Fossdene Rd. SE7	65	40 78 D
Fosse Way. W13	54	16 81 A
Fossil Rd. SE13	76	37 75 A
Fossington Rd. Belv	67	47 78 B
Fossway. Dag	41	47 86 A
Foster Ct. EC2	4	32 81 C
Foster Rd. E13	58	40 82 C
Foster Rd. W3	55	21 80 A
Foster Rd. W4	61	20 78 D
Fosters Cl. Chis	89	42 71 D
Fosters Cl. E18	27	40 90 B
Foster Wlk. NW4	23	23 89 C
Fothergill Cl. E13	50	40 83 C
Fotheringham Rd. Enf	13	33 96 D
Foubert's Pl. W1	2	29 81 C
Foulden Rd. N16	48	33 85 B
Foulden Terr. N16	48	33 85 B
Foulis Terr. SW7	62	26 78 D
Foulser Rd. SW17	86	28 72 C
Foulsham Rd. Th Hth	97	32 68 B
Founders Ct. EC2	4	32 81 D
Founders Gdns. SE19	97	32 70 C
Fountain Ct. EC4	7	31 80 A
Fountain Dri. SE19	87	33 71 B
Fountain Pl. SW9	75	31 76 A
Fountain Rd. SW17	85	26 71 B
Fountain Rd. Th Hth	97	32 69 C
Fountains Ave. Felt	82	12 72 D
Fountains Cl. Felt	82	12 72 B
Fountains Cres. N14	16	29 94 A
Fountayne Rd. N15	25	34 89 C
Fountayne Rd. N16	37	34 86 A
Fount St. SW8	10	29 77 D
Fouracres. Enf	14	36 97 A
Four Acres. N12	15	25 93 D
Fourland Wlk. Edg	22	20 91 A
Fournier St. E1	4	33 81 B
Fourth Ave. E12	50	42 85 A
Fourth Ave. Rom	41	50 87 D
Fourth Ave. W10	56	24 82 A
Fourth Way. Wem	45	20 85 A
Four Wents The. E4	18	38 93 B
Fowey Ave. Ilf	39	41 88 B
Fowler Cl. SW11	73	26 75 B
Fowler House. SW8	74	29 76 B
Fowler Rd. E7	50	40 85 A
Fowler Rd. Ilf	28	46 91 B
Fowler Rd. Mit	96	28 69 C
Fowler's Wlk. W5	54	17 82 D
Fownes St. SW11	74	27 75 A
Foxberry Rd. SE4	76	36 75 A
Foxborough Gdns.SE4	76	37 74 A
Foxbourne Rd. SW17	86	28 72 A
Foxbury Ave. Chis	100	44 70 B
Foxbury Cl. Brom	99	40 70 B
Foxbury Rd. Brom	99	40 70 B
Fox Cl. E16	58	40 81 A
Fox Cl. E1	57	35 82 C
Foxcombe Cl. E6	50	41 83 D
Foxcombe Rd. SW15	84	22 73 C
Foxcroft Rd. SE18	78	43 76 B
Foxdell. Nthwd	19	08 91 B
Foxearth Rd. S Croy	112	34 62 D
Foxes Dale. Brom	98	38 68 B
Foxes Dale. SE3	77	40 75 A
Foxfield Cl. Nthwd	19	09 91 B

Foxfield Rd. Orp	108	44 65 B
Foxglove St. W12	55	21 80 B
Foxgrove Ave. Beck	98	37 70 D
Foxgrove. N14	16	30 93 C
Foxgrove Rd. Beck	98	38 70 C
Foxham Rd. N19	36	29 86 D
Fox Hill Gdns. SE19	97	33 70 D
Fox Hill. SE19	97	33 70 D
Foxhole Rd. SE9	77	42 74 A
Foxholt Gdns. NW10	45	20 84 C
Fox House Rd. Belv	67	49 78 B
Fox & Knot St. EC1	3	31 81 B
Fox La. N13	16	30 93 D
Foxlands Cres. Dag	52	50 85 C
Foxlands Rd. Dag	52	50 85 C
Fox La. W5	54	18 82 C
Foxley Cl. E8	48	34 85 C
Foxley Ct. Sutt	110	26 63 C
Foxley La. Pur	111	30 62 C
Foxley Rd. Shep	63	31 77 D
Foxley Rd. Th Hth	97	31 68 D
Foxmore St. SW11	74	27 76 B
Fox Rd. E16	58	39 81 B
Fox's Path. Mit	96	27 69 C
Fox's Yd. E2	4	33 82 D
Foxwell St. SE4	76	36 75 A
Foxwood Cl. Felt	81	10 72 D
Foxwood Rd. SE3	77	39 75 D
Foyle Rd. N17	25	34 90 B
Foyle Rd. SE3	65	39 77 B
Framfield Rd. N5	48	31 85 D
Framfield Rd. W7	54	15 81 D
Framlingham Cl. E5	38	35 86 A
Framlingham Cres. SE9	89	42 71 B
Frampton Cl. Sutt	110	25 63 C
Frampton Park Estate. E9	49	35 84 C
Frampton Park Rd. E9	49	35 84 C
Frampton Rd. Houn	70	12 74 A
Frampton St. NW8	1	26 82 D
Francemary Rd. SE4	76	37 74 A
Frances Rd. E4	26	37 91 A
Frances St. SE18	65	42 78 B
Franche Court Rd. SW17	85	26 72 C
Francis Ave. Bexh	79	49 76 C
Francis Ave. Felt	81	10 72 C
Francis Ave. Ilf	40	44 86 B
Franciscan Rd. SW17	86	28 71 A
Francis Chichester Way. SW11	74	28 76 A
Francis Cl. Eps	109	20 64 B
Francis Cl. Shep	91	07 68 C
Francis Gr. SW19	95	24 70 B
Francis Rd. Croy	105	31 66 B
Francis Rd. Dart	80	53 74 B
Francis Rd. E10	38	38 86 A
Francis Rd. Grnf	44	17 83 A
Francis Rd. Har	33	16 88 A
Francis Rd. Houn	70	11 76 D
Francis Rd. Ilf	40	44 86 B
Francis Rd. N2	24	27 89 D
Francis Rd. Pnr	32	11 88 A
Francis Rd. Wall	111	29 63 A
Francis St. E15	50	39 85 C
Francis St. Ilf	40	44 86 B
Francis St. SW1	6	29 79 C
Francis Terr. N19	36	29 86 C
Francombe Gdns. Rom	42	52 88 C
Franconia Rd. SW4	74	29 74 B
Frank Bailey Wlk. E12	51	43 84 A
Frank Dixon Cl. SE21	87	33 73 C
Frank Dixon Way. SE21	87	33 73 C
Frankfurt Rd. SE24	75	32 74 A
Frankham St. SE8	64	37 77 C
Frankland Rd. E4	18	37 92 C
Frankland Rd. SW7	5	26 79 D
*Franklin Cl. King	94	19 68 A
Franklin Cl. N20	15	26 94 A
Franklin Cl. SE27	87	31 72 D
Franklin Cres. Mit	96	29 68 C
Franklin Pas. SE9	77	42 75 A
Franklin Rd. Bexh	79	48 76 A
Franklin Rd. SE20	98	35 69 A
Franklin Sq. SW5	45	24 78 D
Franklin's Row. SW3	9	27 78 D
Franklin St. E3	57	37 82 B
Franklin St. N15	37	33 88 C
Franklyn Gdns. Ilf	28	44 91 B
Franks Ave. N Mal	94	20 68 C
Frank St. E13	58	40 82 C
Franks Wood Ave. Orp	108	44 67 A
Franlaw Cres. N13	17	32 92 A
Franmil Rd. Horn	42	52 87 C
Fransfield Gr. SE26	87	34 72 D
Frant Cl. SE20	98	35 70 C
Franthorne Way. SE6	88	37 72 D
Frantlyn Rd. NW10	45	21 84 B
Frant Rd. Th Hth	105	31 67 B
Fraser Rd. E17	38	37 88 D
Fraser Rd. Eri	67	50 78 D
Fraser Rd. Grnf	44	17 83 A
Fraser Rd. N9	17	34 93 D
Fraser St. W4	61	21 78 C
Frating Cres. Wdf Gn	27	40 91 B
Frazer Ave. Ruis	43	11 85 C
Frazier St. SE1	7	31 79 A
Frean St. SE16	63	34 79 C
Frederica Rd. E4	18	38 94 B
Frederica St. N7	47	30 84 D
Frederick Cl. Sutt	110	24 64 D
Frederick Cl. W2	5	27 80 B
Frederick Cres. Enf	14	35 97 C
Frederick Cres. SW9	63	31 77 D
Frederick Gdns Sutt	110	24 64 D
Frederick Pl. SE18	66	43 78 D
Frederick Rd. Rain	52	50 83 D
Frederick Rd. Sutt	110	24 64 D
Frederick Row. EC1	3	31 82 B
Frederick's Pl. EC2	4	32 81 D
Frederick's Pl. N12	15	26 92 A
Frederick St. WC1	3	30 82 B
Frederick Terr. E8	48	33 84 D
Frederic Mews. SW1	6	28 79 A
Frederic St. E17	38	36 88 A
Freedom St. SW11	74	27 76 D
Freegrove Rd. N7	47	30 85 C
Freeland Park. NW4	23	24 90 C
Freeland Rd. W5	54	18 80 B
Freelands Gr. Brom	99	40 69 B
Freelands Rd. Brom	99	40 69 B
Freeling St. N1	47	30 84 D
Freeman Cl. Nthlt	43	12 84 C
Freeman Rd. Mord	103	26 67 B
Freemantle Ave. Enf	14	35 95 B
Freemantle St. SE17	63	33 78 C
Freeman Way. Horn	42	54 88 D
Freemason's Rd. Croy	105	33 66 C
Freemasons Rd. E16	58	40 81 D
Freethorpe Cl. SE19	97	33 69 A
Freke Rd. SW11	74	28 75 A
Fremantle Rd. Belv	67	49 78 A
Fremantle Rd. Ilf	28	44 90 C
Fremont St. E9	49	35 83 A
French Ordinary Ct. EC3	4	33 80 A
French Pl. EC2	4	33 82 A
French St. Sun	92	11 69 C
Frendsbury Rd. SE4	76	36 75 C
Frensham Dri. SW15	84	22 72 C
Frensham Rd. SE9	90	44 72 B
Frensham St. SE15	63	34 77 A
Frere St. SW11	74	27 76 C
Freshfield Cl. SE13	76	38 75 D
Freshfield Dri. N14	16	28 94 B
Freshfields. Croy	106	36 66 D
Freshford St. SW18	85	26 72 C
Freshwater Cl. SW17	96	28 70 A
Freshwater Cl. Sthl	53	13 82 A
Freshwater Rd. Dag	41	48 87 C
Freshwater Rd. SW17	96	28 70 A
Freshwell Ave. Rom	29	47 89 C
Fresh Wharf Rd. Bark	51	43 83 B
Freshwood Cl. Beck	98	37 69 B
Freshwood Way. Wall	111	29 62 A
Freston Gdns. Barn	12	28 95 A
Freston Park. N3	23	24 90 D
Freston Rd. W10	56	23 80 B
Freta Rd. Bexh	79	48 74 B
Frewin Rd. SW18	85	26 73 D
Friar Mews. SE27	87	31 72 D
Friar Rd. Hay	53	11 82 D
Friar Rd. Orp	108	46 67 A
Friars Ave. N20	16	27 92 A
Friars Cl. Nthlt	53	11 82 B
Friars Gdns. W3	55	20 81 D
Friars La. Rich	71	17 74 B
Friars Place La. W3	55	20 80 B
Friars Rd. E6	50	41 83 B
Friars Stile Pl. Rich	71	18 74 C
Friars Stile Rd. Rich	71	18 74 C
Friar St. EC4	3	31 81 D
Friars Way. W3	55	20 81 D
Friars Wlk. N14	16	28 94 B
Friars Wlk. SE2	67	47 78 D
Friary Cl. N12	16	27 92 C
Friary Rd. N12	16	27 92 A
Friary Rd. SE15	63	34 77 C
Friary Rd. W3	55	20 81 D
Friary Way. N12	16	27 92 A
Friday Rd. Eri	67	50 78 D
Friday Rd. Mit	96	27 70 D
Friday St. EC4	8	32 80 A
Frideswide Pl. NW5	47	29 85 C
Friendly Pl. SE10	76	37 76 B
Friendly Street Mews. SE8	76	37 76 C
Friendly St. SE8	76	37 76 A
Friendship Wlk. (off Wayfarer Rd). Nthlt	53	11 82 B
Friends' Rd. Croy	105	32 65 D
Friend St. EC1	3	31 82 B
Friern Barnet La. N11	16	27 92 D
Friern Barnet La. N20	16	27 92 A
Friern Barnet Rd. N11	16	28 92 C
Friern Ct. N20	15	26 93 D
Friern Mount Dri. N20	15	26 94 A
Friern Park. N12	15	26 92 D
Friern Rd. SE22	87	34 73 A
Friern Rd. SE22	75	34 74 C
Friern Watch Ave. N12	15	26 92 B
Frigate Mews. SE8	64	37 77 A
Frimley Ave. Wall	111	30 64 D
Frimley Gdns. Mit	96	27 68 A
Frimley Rd. Ilf	40	45 86 C
Frimley St. E1	57	35 82 D
Frimley Way. E1	57	35 82 D
Fringewood Cl. Nthwd	19	07 90 B
Frinstead Rd. Eri	68	51 77 C
Frinton Dri. Wdf Gr	26	38 91 D
Frinton Mews. Ilf	40	43 88 C
Frinton Rd. E6	58	41 82 B
Frinton Rd. N15	37	33 88 C
Frinton Rd. Rom	29	49 91 C
Frinton Rd. SW17	96	28 70 A
Friston St. SW6	73	25 76 D
Fritham Cl. N.Mal	102	21 67 C
Frith Ct. NW7	23	24 91 C
Frith La. NW7	24	24 91 A
Frith Rd. Croy	105	32 65 A
Frith Rd. E11	49	38 85 B
Frith St. W1	2	29 81 D
Frithville Gdns. W12	56	23 80 C
Frithwood Ave. Nthwd	19	09 91 B
Frizlands La. Dag	41	49 86 D
Frobisher Cl. Pnr	32	11 87 B
Frobisher Rd. N8	25	31 89 C
Frobisher St. SE10	65	39 77 A
Frogley Rd. SE22	75	33 75 D
Frogmore Cl. Sutt	103	24 65 C
Frogmore Cl. Sthl	59	13 78 A
Frogmore Gdns. Sutt	110	24 64 A
Frogmore. SW18	73	25 74 A
Frognal Ave. Har	21	15 89 D
Frognal Cl. Sid	100	46 70 A
Frognal.Cl. NW3	46	26 85 C
Frognal Cnr. Sid	100	45 70 B
Frognal Gdns. NW3	46	26 85 A
Frognal La. NW3	46	25 85 D
Frognal. NW3	46	26 85 C
Frognal Pl. Sid	90	46 71 C
Frognal Rise. NW3	46	26 85 A
Frognal Way. NW3	46	26 85 A
Froissart Rd. SE9	77	42 74 A
Frome Rd. N22	25	31 89 B
Frome St. N1	48	32 83 C
Fromondes Rd. Sutt	110	24 64 C
Frostie Wlk. E1	4	33 81 B
Froude St. SW8	74	28 76 D
Fruen Rd. Felt	81	09 73 B
Fryatt Rd. N17	25	32 91 D
Fryatt St. E14	58	39 81 C
Fry Cl. Rom	29	49 91 A
Fryent Cl. NW9	34	19 88 C
Fryent Cres. NW9	34	21 88 C
Fryent Gr. NW9	34	21 88 C
Fryent Way. NW9	34	19 88 C
Frying Pan Alley. E1	4	33 81 B
Fry Rd. E6	50	41 84 D
Fry Rd. NW10	45	21 83 B
Fryston Ave. Croy	105	34 65 A
Fuchsia St. SE2	66	46 78 D
Fulbeck Dri. NW9	22	21 90 A
Fulbeck Way. Har	20	14 90 C
Fulbourne Rd. E17	26	38 90 C
Fulbourne St. E1	57	34 81 B
Fulbrook Mews. N19	47	29 85 A
*Fulbrook Rd. N19	47	29 85 A
Fulford Rd. Eps	109	20 63 D
Fulford St. SE16	63	34 79 B
Fulham Bwy. SW6	62	25 77 C
Fulham Cl. SW6	73	25 76 A
Fulham High St. SW6	73	24 75 A
Fulham High St. SW6	73	24 76 C
Fulham Palace Rd. SW6	73	24 76 A
Fulham Palace Rd. W6	62	23 77 B
Fulham Park Gdns. SW6	73	24 76 D
Fulham Park Rd. SW6	73	24 76 D
Fulham Rd. SW10	62	24 77 A
Fulham Rd. SW6	73	24 76 B

Street	Pg	Ref
Fullbrooks Ave. Wor Pk	102	21 66 D
Fuller Rd. Dag	52	47 85 A
Fuller's Ave. E18	27	39 91 D
Fullers Ave. Surb	101	18 65 B
Fullers Cl. Rom	29	50 91 C
Fuller's La. Rom	29	50 91 C
Fuller's Rd. E18	27	39 91 D
Fuller St. E2	57	34 82 C
Fuller St. NW4	23	23 89 C
Fullers Way N. Surb	101	18 65 D
Fullers Way S. Chess	101	18 65 C
Fullerton Rd. Cars	111	27 62 A
Fullerton Rd. Croy	105	33 66 B
Fullerton Rd. SW18	73	26 74 A
Fullwood's Mews. N1	4	32 82 B
Fulmar Ct. Surb	101	18 67 D
Fulmead St. SW6	73	25 76 B
Fulmer Cl. Hamp	82	12 71 C
Fulmer Way. W13	60	16 79 D
Fulready Rd. E10	38	38 88 B
Fulstone Cl. Houn	70	12 75 D
Fulthorp Rd. SE3	77	40 76 C
Fulton Mews. W2	5	26 80 A
Fulton Rd. Wem	34	19 86 C
Fulwell Ave. Ilf	28	43 90 B
Fulwell Ct. Ilf	28	43 90 A
Fulwell Park Ave. Twick	82	14 72 A
Fulwell Rd. Tedd	82	14 71 B
Fulwich Rd. Dart	80	54 74 D
Fulwood Ave. Wem	44	18 83 D
Fulwood Gdns. Twick	71	16 74 C
Fulwood Pl. WC1	3	30 81 B
Fulwood Wlk. SW19	85	24 73 C
Furber St. W6	61	22 79 D
Furham Feild. Pnr	20	13 91 C
Furley Rd. SE15	63	34 77 C
Furlong Cl. Wall	104	28 66 C
Furlong Rd. N7	48	31 84 A
Furmage St. SW18	85	25 73 A
Furneaux Ave. SE27	87	31 71 D
Furner Cl. Dart	80	51 75 B
Furness Rd. Har	32	13 87 D
Furness Rd. Mord	103	25 67 D
Furness Rd. NW10	45	22 83 C
Furness Rd. SW6	73	25 76 D
Furnival St. EC4	3	31 81 A
Furrow La. E9	49	35 85 C
Fursby Ave. N3	23	25 91 A
Further Acre. NW9	22	21 90 D
Further Green Rd. SE6	89	39 73 C
Furzedown Dri. SW17	86	28 71 D
Furzedown Rd. Sutt	110	26 62 C
Furzedown Rd. SW17	86	28 71 D
Furzefield Cl. Chis	100	43 70 B
Furzefield Rd. SE3	65	40 77 D
Furze Fm Cl. Rom	29	48 90 C
Furze La. Pur	111	30 62 C
Furze Rd. Th Hth	97	32 68 A
Furze St. E3	57	37 81 A
Furzewood. Sun	91	10 69 A
Fyfe Way. Brom	99	40 69 C
Fyfield Rd. E17	26	38 89 B
Fyfield Rd. Enf	13	33 96 A
Fyfield Rd. SW9	75	31 75 A
Fyfield Rd. Wdf Gn	27	41 91 C
Fynes St. SW1	10	29 78 B
Gable Cl. Dart	80	52 74 A
Gable Cl. Pnr	20	13 91 C
Gabriel Cl. Felt	82	11 71 B
Gabriel Cl. Rom	29	50 91 C
Gabriel St. SE23	88	35 73 D
Gaddesden Ave. Wem	44	18 84 B
Gadesden Rd. Eps	109	20 63 A
Gage Rd. E16	58	39 81 A
Gage St. WC1	3	30 81 A
Gainford St. N1	48	31 83 A
Gainsboro Gdns. Grnf	44	15 85 C
Gainsborough Ave. Dart	80	53 74 A
Gainsborough Ave. E12	51	43 85 C
Gainsborough Cl. Beck	98	37 70 C
Gainsborough Cl. Esh	101	15 66 C
Gainsborough Ct. N12	15	25 92 D
Gainsborough Gdns. Edg	22	19 90 C
Gainsborough Gdns. Islw	70	14 74 B
Gainsborough Gdns. NW11	35	24 87 B
Gainsborough Gdns. NW3	35	26 86 D
Gainsborough Mews. SE26	87	34 72 D
Gainsborough Rd. Dag	40	46 86 D
Gainsborough Rd. E11	39	39 87 B
Gainsborough Rd. E15	58	39 82 A
Gainsborough Rd. Eps	109	20 62 C
Gainsborough Rd. N12	15	25 92 D
Gainsborough Rd. N.Mal	102	20 66 B
Gainsborough Rd. Rich	71	18 75 B
Gainsborough Rd. W4	61	21 78 B
Gainsborough Rd. Wdf Gn	27	42 91 A
Gainsborough Sq. Bexh	79	47 75 B
Gainsford Rd. E17	26	36 89 D
Gainsford St. SE1	8	33 79 B
Gairloch Rd. SE5	75	33 76 C
Gaisford St. NW5	47	29 84 A
Gaitskell Rd. SE9	90	44 73 C
Galahad Rd. Brom	89	40 71 A
Galata Rd. SW13	61	22 77 C
Galatea Sq. SE15	75	34 75 B
Galbraith St. E14	64	38 79 C
Galeborough Ave. Wdf Gn	26	38 91 D
Gale Cl. Hamp	92	12 70 A
Gale Cl. Mit	95	26 68 B
Galena Rd. W6	61	22 78 B
Galen Pl. WC1	3	30 81 A
Galesbury Rd. SW18	73	26 74 C
Gales Gdns. E2	57	34 82 B
Gale St. Dag	52	47 84 D
Gale St. E3	57	37 81 A
Gales Way. Wdf Gn	27	42 91 C
Gallants Farm Rd. Barn	16	27 94 C
Gallery Gdns. Nthlt	43	11 83 D
Gallery Rd. SE21	87	32 73 A
Galley La. Barn	11	23 96 C
Galleywall Rd. SE16	63	34 78 B
Galleywood Cres. Rom	29	50 91 B
Galliard Cl. Enf	14	35 95 C
Gallia Rd. N5	48	31 85 D
Galliard Rd. N9	13	34 95 C
Gallions Rd. SE7	65	40 78 B
Gallon Cl. SE7	65	41 78 A
Gallop The. S Croy	112	34 63 D
Gallop The. Sutt	110	26 62 B
Gallosson Rd. SE18	66	45 78 A
Galloway Rd. W12	55	22 80 C
Gallows Cnr. Rom	30	53 90 A
Gallus Cl. N21	12	30 95 D
Gallus Sq. SE3	77	40 75 B
Galpin's Rd. Th Hth	96	30 68 D
Galsworthy Ave. Rom	40	46 88 D
Galsworthy Cres. SE3	77	41 76 A
Galsworthy Rd. King	94	19 69 B
Galsworthy Rd. NW2	46	24 85 A
Galton St. W10	56	24 82 A
Galveston Rd. SW15	73	24 74 B
Galway St. EC1	4	32 82 A
Gambetta St. SW8	74	28 76 D
Gambia St. SE1	7	31 80 D
Gambole Rd. SW17	86	27 71 A
Games Rd. Barn	12	27 96 B
Gamlen Rd. SW15	73	23 75 D
Gander Green La. Sutt	110	24 64 B
Gander Green La. Sutt	103	24 65 B
Ganley Ct. SW11	73	26 75 B
Ganton St. W1	2	29 81 C
Gantshill Cres. Ilf	40	43 88 A
Gap Rd. SW19	85	25 71 D
Garage Rd. W3	55	19 81 C
Garbrand Wlk. Eps	109	21 62 B
Garbutt Pl. W1	2	28 81 A
Garden Ave. Bexh	79	49 75 A
Garden Ave. Mit	96	28 70 D
Garden City. Edg	22	19 91 A
Garden Cl. Ashf	91	08 70 A
Garden Cl. E4	18	37 92 C
Garden Cl. Hamp	82	12 71 D
Garden Cl. Nthlt	43	12 83 A
Garden Cl. Ruis	31	09 86 A
Garden Cl. SE12	89	40 72 D
Garden Cl. SW15	84	22 73 B
Garden Cl. SW9	74	30 75 B
Garden Cl. Wall	111	30 64 C
Garden Ct. EC4	7	31 80 A
Garden Ct. N12	15	25 92 A
Garden Ct. Rich	71	18 76 B
Garden Ct. SE15	75	33 76 B
Garden Ct. Wem	33	17 86 C
Gardeners La. EC4	8	32 80 A
Gardeners Rd. Croy	105	31 66 D
Gardener's Rd. E3	49	35 83 D
Gardenia Rd. Enf	13	33 95 C
Garden La. Brom	99	40 70 B
Garden Mews. W2	56	25 80 A
Garden Rd. Brom	99	40 70 B
Garden Rd. NW8	1	26 82 A
Garden Rd. Rich	72	19 75 A
Garden Rd. SE20	98	35 69 A
Garden Row. SE1	7	31 79 D
Garden St. E1	57	35 81 B
Gardens The. Beck	98	38 69 D
Gardens The. Felt	69	08 74 D
Gardens The. Har	32	14 88 C
Gardens The. N16	37	33 87 B
Gardens The. N8	24	30 89 C
Gardens The. Pnr	32	12 88 D
Gardens The. SE22	75	34 75 C
Gardens Way. E12	39	42 86 D
Garden Terr. SW1	10	29 78 D
Garden Way. NW10	45	20 84 A
Garden Wlk. EC2	4	33 82 C
Gardiner Ave. NW2	46	23 85 C
Gardner Cl. E11	39	40 88 D
Gardner Rd. E13	58	40 82 D
Gardnor Rd. NW3	46	26 85 B
Garendon Gdns. Mord	103	25 66 B
Garendon Rd. Mord	103	25 66 B
Gareth Cl. Wor Pk	103	23 65 B
Garfield Rd. E13	58	39 82 D
Garfield Rd. E4	18	38 94 D
Garfield Rd. Enf	14	35 96 C
Garfield Rd. SW11	74	28 75 A
Garfield Rd. Twick	83	16 73 C
Garford St. E14	57	37 80 A
Garibaldi St. SE18	66	45 78 A
Garland Rd. SE18	66	44 77 D
Garland Rd. Stan	21	18 90 A
Garland Way. Horn	30	54 89 C
Garlick Hill. EC4	8	32 80 A
Garlies Rd. SE23	88	36 72 C
Garman Rd. N17	26	35 91 C
Garnault Mews. EC1	3	31 82 A
Garnault Pl. EC1	3	31 82 A
Garner Rd. E17	26	38 90 A
Garner St. E2	48	34 83 C
Garnet Rd. NW10	45	21 84 A
Garnet Rd. Th Hth	97	32 68 C
Garnet St. E1	57	35 80 A
Garnett Cl. SE9	77	42 75 B
Garnett Rd. NW3	47	27 85 C
Garnham Cl. N16	37	33 86 B
Garnham St. N16	37	33 86 B
Garnies Cl. SE15	63	33 77 D
Garrad's Rd. SW16	86	29 71 B
Garrard Cl. Bexh	79	49 75 A
Garrard Cl. Chis	90	43 71 D
Garrard Wlk. NW10	45	21 84 A
Garratt Cl. Croy	111	30 64 A
Garratt La. SW17	85	26 71 B
Garratt La. SW18	85	25 73 D
Garratt Rd. Edg	22	19 91 C
Garratt Terr. SW17	86	27 71 A
Garrett St. EC1	4	32 82 C
Garrick Ave. NW11	35	24 88 C
Garrick Cl. Rich	71	17 74 B
Garrick Cl. SW18	73	26 74 A
Garrick Cl. W5	54	18 82 C
Garrick Cres. Croy	105	33 65 A
Garrick Dri. NW4	23	23 90 D
Garrick Gdns. E Mol	92	13 68 A
Garrick Park. NW4	23	23 90 D
Garrick Rd. Grnf	53	13 82 D
Garrick Rd. NW9	34	21 88 D
Garrick Rd. Rich	72	19 76 C
Garrick St. WC2	7	30 80 A
Garrick Way. NW4	23	23 89 D
Garrick Yd. WC2	7	30 80 A
Garrowsfield. Barn	11	24 95 B
Garry Cl. Rom	30	51 91 C
Garry Way. Rom	30	51 91 C
Garside Cl. Hamp	92	13 70 B
Garth Cl. King	83	18 71 D
Garth Cl. Mord	103	23 66 B
Garth Cl. Ruis	32	11 87 D
Garth Ct. W4	61	20 77 B
Garthland Dri. Barn	11	23 95 A
Garthorne Rd. SE23	88	35 73 B
Garth Rd. King	83	18 71 D
Garth Rd. Mord	103	23 66 B
Garth Rd. NW2	35	24 86 B
Garth Rd. W4	61	20 78 D
Garthside. Rich	83	18 71 C
Garth The. Hamp	92	13 70 B
Garth The. Har	33	18 88 D
Garthway. N12	24	27 91 A
Gartmoor Gdns. SW 19	85	24 73 D
Gartmore Rd. Ilf	40	45 86 B
Garton Pl. SW18	73	26 74 C
Garvary Rd. E16	58	40 81 D
Garway Rd. W2	56	25 81 D
Gascoigne Gdns. Wdf Gn	27	39 91 C
Gascoigne Pl. E2	4	33 82 B
Gascoigne Rd. Bark	51	44 83 A
Gascony Ave. NW6	46	25 84 C
Gascoyne Dri. Dart	80	51 75 B
Gascoyne Rd. E9	49	35 84 D

Gaselee St. E14 ... 58 — 38 80 A
Gasholder Pl. SE11 ... 10 — 30 78 D
Gaskarth Rd. Edg ... 22 — 20 90 C
Gaskarth Rd. SW12 ... 74 — 28 74 D
Gaskell Rd. N6 ... 36 — 27 88 D
Gaskell St. SW4 ... 74 — 30 76 C
Gaskin St. N1 ... 48 — 31 83 B
Gaspar Cl. SW7 ... 62 — 25 78 B
Gaspar Mews. SW5 ... 62 — 25 78 B
Gassiot Rd. SW17 ... 86 — 27 71 D
Gassiot Way. Sutt ... 103 — 26 65 D
Gastein Rd. W6 ... 62 — 23 77 B
Gaston Bell Cl. Rich ... 71 — 18 75 B
Gaston Rd. Mit ... 96 — 28 68 A
Gatcombe Rd. N19 ... 36 — 29 86 D
Gate End. Nthwd ... 19 — 10 91 C
Gateforth St. NW8 ... 1 — 27 82 C
Gatehill Rd. Nthwd ... 19 — 10 91 C
Gatehouse Cl. King ... 94 — 20 70 C
Gateley Rd. SW9 ... 74 — 30 75 B
Gate Mews. SW7 ... 5 — 27 79 A
Gatesborough St. EC2 ... 4 — 33 82 C
Gates Green Rd. W.Wick ... 107 — 39 65 D
Gateside Rd. SW17 ... 86 — 27 72 D
Gatestone Ct. SE19 ... 97 — 33 73 A
Gatestone Rd. SE19 ... 97 — 33 70 A
Gate St. WC2 ... 3 — 30 81 D
Gateway Arc. N1 ... 48 — 31 83 D
Gateway Cl. Nthwd ... 19 — 08 91 A
Gateway. SE17 ... 63 — 32 77 A
Gateways. Surb ... 101 — 18 67 A
Gateways. The SW3 ... 9 — 27 78 A
Gathorne Rd. N22 ... 25 — 31 90 A
Gathorne St. E2 ... 49 — 35 83 D
Gatley Ave. Eps ... 109 — 19 64 D
Gatliff Rd. SW1 ... 9 — 28 78 D
Gatling Rd. SE2 ... 82 — 46 78 C
Gaton Rd. SE2 ... 67 — 47 79 C
Gatton Cl. Sutt ... 110 — 25 62 B
Gatton Rd. SW17 ... 86 — 27 71 A
Gatward Cl. N21 ... 13 — 31 95 D
Gatward Green. N9 ... 17 — 33 93 B
Gatwick Rd. SW18 ... 85 — 24 73 B
Gatwick Way. Horn ... 42 — 54 86 D
Gauden Cl. SW4 ... 74 — 29 75 B
Gauden Rd. SW4 ... 74 — 29 75 B
Gauntlet Cl. Nthlt ... 43 — 12 84 C
Gauntlett Ct. Wem ... 44 — 16 85 D
Gauntlett Rd. Sutt ... 110 — 26 64 D
Gaunt St. SE1 ... 8 — 32 79 C
Gaunt St. SE1 ... 8 — 32 79 C
Gautrey Rd. SE15 ... 76 — 35 76 C
*Gavel St. SE17 ... 63 — 32 78 B
Gaverick St. E14 ... 64 — 37 78 A
Gavestone Cres. SE12 ... 89 — 40 73 B
Gavestone Rd. SE12 ... 89 — 40 73 B
Gavina Cl. Mord ... 104 — 27 67 A
Gawber St. E2 ... — 35 82 A
Gawsworth Cl. E15 ... 50 — 39 85 D
Gawthorne Ave. NW7 ... 15 — 24 92 C
Gay Cl. NW12 ... 45 — 22 85 D
Gaydon La. NW9 ... — 21 90 A
Gayfere Rd. Eps ... 109 — 22 64 C
Gayfere Rd. Ilf ... 27 — 42 89 B
Gayfere St. SW1 ... 7 — 30 79 C
Gayford Rd. W12 ... 61 — 21 79 B
Gay Gdns. Dag ... 52 — 50 85 C
Gayhurst Rd. E8 ... 48 — 34 84 C
Gaylor Rd. Nthlt ... 43 — 12 85 D
Gaynesford Rd. Cars ... 111 — 27 63 D
Gaynesford Rd. SE23 ... 88 — 35 72 B
Gaynes Hill Rd. Wdf Gn ... 27 — 42 91 C
Gay Rd. E15 ... 49 — 38 83 C
Gaysham Ave. Ilf ... 40 — 43 88 B
Gaysham Hall. Ilf ... 28 — 43 89 B
Gay St. SW15 ... 73 — 23 75 B
Gayton Cres. NW3 ... 46 — 26 85 B
Gayton Ct. Har ... 33 — 15 88 D
Gayton Rd. Har ... 33 — 15 88 D
Gayton Rd. NW3 ... 46 — 26 85 B
Gayville Rd. SW11 ... 74 — 27 74 D
Gaywood Cl. SW2 ... 86 — 30 73 D
Gaywood Cl. SW2 ... 87 — 31 73 C
Gaywood Rd. E17 ... 26 — 37 89 A
Gaywood St. SE1 ... 7 — 31 79 D
Gaza St. SE17 ... 63 — 30 78 B
Geariesville Gdns. ... 28 — 43 89 D
Geary Rd. NW10 ... 45 — 22 85 C
Geary St. N7 ... 47 — 30 85 D
Gedeney Rd. N17 ... 25 — 32 90 C
Gedling Pl. SE1 ... 9 — 33 79 D
Geere Rd. E15 ... 50 — 39 83 B
Gees Ct. W1 ... 2 — 28 81 C
Gee St. EC1 ... 4 — 32 82 C
Geffrye Ct. N1 ... 48 — 33 83 C

Geffrye St. E2 ... 48 — 33 83 D
Geldart Rd. SE15 ... 63 — 34 77 D
Geldeston Rd. E5 ... 37 — 34 86 A
Gelsthorpe Rd. Rom ... 29 — 49 91 D
Gemini Gr (off Javelin Way). Nthlt ...
General Gordons Pl. SE18 ... 66 — 11 82 B
General Wolfe Rd. SE10 ... 76 — 43 78 B
Genesta Rd. SE18 ... 66 — 38 76 B
Geneva Cl. Shep ... 91 — 09 69 C
Geneva Dri. SW9 ... 75 — 31 75 C
Geneva Gdns. Rom ... 41 — 48 88 A
Geneva Rd. King ... 93 — 18 68 C
Geneva Rd. Th Hth ... 96 — 32 67 A
Genever Cl. E4 ... 18 — 37 92 C
Genista Rd. N18 ... 17 — 34 92 D
Genoa Ave. SW15 ... 73 — 23 74 A
Genoa Rd. SE20 ... 98 — 35 69 A
Genotin Rd. Enf ... 13 — 32 96 B
*Genotin Terr. Enf ... 13 — 32 96 D
Gentleman's Row. Enf ... 13 — 32 96 A
Gentry Gdns. E13 ... 58 — 40 82 A
Geoffrey Cl. SE5 ... 75 — 32 76 C
Geoffrey Gdns. E6 ... 50 — 42 83 C
Geoffrey Rd. SE4 ... 76 — 36 75 B
George Comberton Wlk. E12 ... 51 — 43 85 C
George Cres. N10 ... 24 — 28 91 C
George St. WC2 ... 7 — 30 80 A
George Cl. WC2 ... — 33 86 B
George Downing Estate. N16 ... 37 — 33 86 B
George Inn Yd. SE1 ... 7 — 32 80 D
George La. Brom ... 107 — 40 66 D
George La. E18 ... 27 — 40 90 C
George La. SE13 ... 76 — 38 74 C
George Pl. N17 ... 25 — 33 89 A
George Rd. E4 ... 18 — 37 91 A
George Rd. King ... 94 — 20 70 C
George Rd. N.Mal ... 102 — 21 67 B
George Row. SE16 ... 63 — 34 79 A
George's Rd. N7 ... 47 — 30 85 D
George's Sq. SW6 ... 62 — 24 77 B
George St. Bark ... 51 — 44 84 C
George St. Croy ... 105 — 32 65 B
George St. E16 ... 58 — 39 81 D
George St. Houn ... 70 — 12 76 D
George St. Rich ... 71 — 17 74 B
George St. Rom ... 42 — 51 88 D
George St. Sthl ... 59 — 12 78 A
George St. Sutt ... 110 — 25 64 D
George St. W1 ... 1 — 27 81 D
George St. W7 ... 64 — 15 80 C
Georgette Pl. SE10 ... — 38 77 C
George V Ave. Pnr ... 20 — 13 89 A
Georgeville Gdns. Ilf ... 28 — 43 89 D
George V Way. Grnf ... 44 — 16 83 B
George Wyver Cl. SW18 ... 85 — 24 73 A
George Yd. EC3 ... 4 — 32 81 D
George Yd. W1 ... 6 — 28 80 A
Georgiana St. NW1 ... 47 — 29 83 A
Georgian Cl. Brom ... 107 — 40 66 D
Georgian Cl. Stan ... 21 — 16 91 C
Georgian Ct. Wem ... 45 — 19 84 B
Georgian Way. Har ... 32 — 14 86 B
Georgia Rd. Th Hth ... 97 — 31 69 B
Georgina Gdns. E2 ... — 33 82 B
Geraint Rd. Brom ... 89 — 40 71 A
Geraldine Rd. SW18 ... 73 — 26 74 A
Geraldine Rd. W4 ... 61 — 19 77 A
Geraldine St. SE11 ... — 31 79 D
Gerald Mews. SW1 ... 9 — 28 78 A
Gerald Rd. Dag ... 41 — 48 87 D
Gerald Rd. E16 ... 58 — 39 82 D
Gerald Rd. SW1 ... 9 — 28 78 A
Gerard Ave. Houn ... 82 — 13 73 A
Gerard Rd. Har ... 33 — 16 88 C
Gerard Rd. SW13 ... 72 — 21 76 B
Gerda Rd. SE9 ... 90 — 44 72 A
Germander Way. E15 ... 58 — 39 82 A
Gernon Rd. E3 ... 49 — 36 83 C
Geron Way. NW2 ... 34 — 22 87 D
Geron Way. NW2 ... 35 — 23 86 A
Gerrard Gdns. Pnr ... 31 — 10 88 A
Gerrard Pl. W1 ... 6 — 29 80 B
Gerrard Rd. N1 ... 48 — 31 83 D
Gerrards Cl. N14 ... 12 — 29 95 A
Gerrard's Ct. W5 ... 60 — 17 79 D
Gerrard St. W1 ... 6 — 29 80 B
Gerridge St. SE1 ... 7 — 31 79 C
Gerry Raffles Sq. E15 ... 49 — 38 84 B
Gertrude Rd. Belv ... 67 — 49 78 A
Gertrude St. SW10 ... 62 — 26 77 A
Gervase Cl. Wem ... 34 — 20 86 C
Gervase Rd. Edg ... 22 — 20 90 B
Gervase St. SE15 ... 63 — 34 77 D
Ghent St. SE6 ... 88 — 37 72 A
Gibbins Rd. E15 ... 49 — 38 84 C

Gibbon Rd. King ... 93 — 18 70 C
Gibbon Rd. SE15 ... 76 — 35 76 C
Gibbon Rd. W3 ... 55 — 21 80 A
Gibbons Rd. NW10 ... 45 — 21 84 A
Gibbon's Rents. SE1 ... 8 — 33 80 C
Gibbon Wlk. SW15 ... 72 — 22 75 C
Gibbs Cl. SE19 ... 87 — 32 71 D
Gibbs Cl. SE19 ... 87 — 32 71 D
Gibbs Green. W14 ... 62 — 24 78 D
Gibbs Rd. N18 ... 18 — 35 92 A
Gibbs Sq. SE19 ... 87 — 32 71 D
Gibraltar Cres. Eps ... 109 — 21 62 C
Gibraltar Wlk. E2 ... 4 — 33 82 B
Gibson Cl. E1 ... 57 — 35 82 C
Gibson Gdns. N16 ... 37 — 33 88 B
Gibson Rd. SE11 ... 10 — 30 78 B
Gibson Rd. Sutt ... 110 — 25 64 D
Gibson's Hill. SW16 ... 97 — 31 70 C
Gibson Sq. N1 ... 48 — 31 83 A
Gibson St. SE10 ... 65 — 39 78 C
Gidea Ave. Rom ... 30 — 52 89 A
Gidea Cl. Rom ... 30 — 52 89 A
Gideon Cl. Belv ... 67 — 49 78 B
Gideon Rd. SW11 ... 74 — 28 75 A
Giesbach Rd. N19 ... 36 — 29 86 B
Giffard Rd. N18 ... 17 — 33 92 C
Giffin St. SE8 ... 64 — 37 77 C
Gifford Gdns. W7 ... 54 — 15 81 A
Gifford St. N1 ... 47 — 30 84 C
Gift La. E15 ... 50 — 39 83 B
Giggshill Gdns. Surb ... 101 — 16 66 C
Giggs Hill. Orp ... 100 — 46 69 A
Giggs Hill Rd. Surb ... 101 — 16 66 C
Gilbert Gr. Edg ... 22 — 20 90 B
Gilbert Pl. WC1 ... 3 — 30 81 A
Gilbert Rd. Belv ... 67 — 49 79 C
Gilbert Rd. Brom ... 99 — 40 70 C
Gilbert Rd. Pnr ... 20 — 11 89 D
Gilbert Rd. Rom ... 30 — 51 89 D
Gilbert Rd. SE11 ... 63 — 31 78 A
Gilbert Rd. SW19 ... 95 — 26 70 C
Gilbert St. E15 ... 50 — 39 85 A
Gilbert St. Houn ... 70 — 14 75 A
Gilbert St. W1 ... 2 — 28 81 C
Gilbey Rd. SW17 ... 86 — 27 71 C
Gilbourne Rd. SE18 ... 66 — 45 77 B
Gilda Ave. Enf ... 14 — 36 95 A
Gilda Cres. N16 ... 37 — 34 87 C
Gilda Ct. NW7 ... 22 — 22 90 A
Gildea St. W1 ... 2 — 28 81 B
Gilden Cres. NW5 ... 47 — 28 85 C
Gildersome St. SE18 ... 66 — 43 77 A
Gilders Rd. Chess ... 109 — 19 63 A
Giles Coppice SE19 ... 87 — 33 71 B
Gilkes Cres. SE21 ... 75 — 33 74 C
Gilkes Pl. SE21 ... 75 — 33 74 C
Gill Ave. E16 ... 58 — 40 81 C
Gillender St. E3 ... 58 — 38 82 C
Gillespie Rd. N5 ... 37 — 31 86 D
Gillet Ave. E6 ... 50 — 42 83 C
Gillett Pl. N16 ... 48 — 33 85 D
Gillett Rd. Th Hth ... 97 — 32 68 D
Gillett St. N16 ... 48 — 33 85 C
Gillham Terr. N17 ... 25 — 34 91 C
Gilliam Gr. Pur ... 112 — 31 62 C
Gillian Cres. Rom ... 30 — 53 90 C
Gillian Park Rd. Sutt ... 103 — 24 66 D
Gillian St. SE13 ... 76 — 37 74 B
Gillies St. NW5 ... 47 — 28 85 C
Gillingham Mews. SW1 ... 10 — 29 78 A
Gillingham Rd. NW2 ... 35 — 24 86 C
Gillingham St. SW1 ... 10 — 29 78 A
Gillman Dri. E15 ... 50 — 39 83 B
Gillmans Rd. Orp ... 108 — 46 66 D
Gill St. E14 ... 57 — 36 80 B
Gillum Cl. Barn ... 16 — 27 94 D
Gilmore Cl. Uxb ... 31 — 07 86 C
Gilmore Cres. Ashf ... 91 — 07 70 A
Gilmore Rd. SE13 ... 76 — 38 75 D
Gilpin Ave. SW14 ... 72 — 20 75 D
Gilpin Cres. N18 ... 17 — 33 92 D
Gilpin Cres. Twick ... 82 — 13 73 B
Gilpin Rd. E5 ... 49 — 36 85 A
Gilroy Way. Orp ... 108 — 46 66 B
Gilsland Rd. Th Hth ... 97 — 32 68 D
Gilstead Rd. SW6 ... 73 — 25 76 D
Gilston Rd. SW10 ... 62 — 26 78 C
Gilton Rd. SE6 ... 89 — 39 72 C
Giltspur St. EC1 ... 3 — 31 81 B
Gilwell Cl. Enf ... 14 — 37 96 D
Gilwell La. Enf ... 14 — 38 96 D
Gipsy Hill. SE19 ... 87 — 33 71 C
Gipsy La. SW15 ... 72 — 22 75 B
Gipsy Rd. SE27 ... 87 — 32 71 B
Gipsy Rd. Well ... 79 — 47 76 D

Street	Ref
Gipsy Road Gdns. SE27	87 32 71 A
Giraud St. E14	57 37 81 D
Girdlers Rd. W4	62 23 78 B
Girdlestone Wlk. N19	36 29 86 A
Girdwood Rd. SW18	85 24 73 A
Girling Way. Felt	69 10 75 A
Gironde Rd. SW6	62 24 77 D
Girton Ave. NW9	22 19 89 A
Girton Cl. Nthlt	43 14 84 A
Girton Gdns. Croy	106 37 65 C
Girton Rd. Nthlt	43 14 84 A
Girton Rd. SE26	88 35 71 D
Gisburn Rd. N8	24 30 89 D
Gissing Wlk (Off Morland Mews). N1	48 31 84 C
Given-Wilson Wlk. E13	50 39 83 D
Gladding Rd. E12	50 41 85 B
Glade Cl. Surb	101 17 65 B
Glade Gdns. Croy	106 36 66 A
Glade La. Sthl	59 13 79 B
Glade Rd. E12	39 42 86 D
Gladeside. Croy	106 35 66 B
Gladeside. N21	16 30 94 B
Gladesmore Rd. N15	37 33 88 D
Gladeswood Rd. Belv	67 49 78 B
Glade The. Brom	99 41 69 D
Glade The. Croy	106 35 67 D
Glade The. Enf	13 31 96 A
Glade The. Eps	109 22 63 A
Glade The. Ilf	27 42 90 B
Glade The. N21	16 30 94 B
Glade The. SE7	65 41 77 C
Glade The. Sutt	110 24 62 A
Glade The. W Wick	106 37 65 D
Gladiator St. SE23	88 36 73 A
Glading Terr. N16	33 33 86 D
Gladsdale Dri. Pnr	19 10 89 D
Gladsmuir Rd. Barn	11 24 97 C
Gladsmuir Rd. N19	36 29 87 C
Gladstone Ave. E12	50 42 84 C
Gladstone Ave. Felt	81 10 73 B
Gladstone Ave. N22	25 31 90 D
Gladstone Ave. Twick	82 14 73 B
Gladstone Mews. N22	25 31 90 C
Gladstone Mews. SE20	98 35 70 C
Gladstone Park Gdns. NW2	34 22 86 D
Gladstone Rd. Croy	105 32 66 B
Gladstone Rd. Dart	80 54 74 D
Gladstone Rd. King	59 19 68 A
Gladstone Rd. Sthl	59 12 79 A
Gladstone Rd. Surb	101 18 65 A
Gladstone Rd. SW19	95 25 70 C
Gladstone Rd. W4	61 20 79 D
Gladstone St. SE1	7 31 79 D
Gladstone Terr. SW11	74 28 76 B
Gladstone Way. Har	15 89 A
Gladwell Rd. Brom	99 40 70 A
Gladwell Rd. N8	30 88 D
Gladwyn Rd. SW15	73 23 75 B
Gladys Rd. NW6	46 25 84 C
Glaisher St. SE10	64 38 77 C
Glamis Dri. Horn	42 54 87 C
Glamis Rd. E1	57 35 80 A
Glamis Pl. E1	57 35 80 A
Glamis Way. Nthlt	43 14 84 A
Glamorgan Cl. Mit	96 30 68 A
Glamorgan Rd. King	93 17 69 A
Glanfield Rd. Beck	98 36 68 D
Glanville Dri. Horn	42 54 87 D
Glanville Rd. Brom	99 40 68 B
Glanville Rd. SW2	74 30 74 A
Glasbrook Ave. Twick	82 12 73 D
Glasbrook Rd. SE9	89 41 73 B
Glaserton Rd. N16	33 33 87 A
Glasford St. SW17	96 27 70 B
Glasgow Rd. E13	50 40 83 D
Glasgow Rd. N18	17 34 92 D
Glasgow Terr. SW1	10 29 78 C
Glasshill St. SE1	7 31 79 B
Glasshouse Fields. E1	57 35 80 B
Glasshouse St. W1	6 29 80 A
Glasshouse Wlk. SE11	10 30 78 D
Glasshouse Yd. EC1	4 32 82 C
Glasslyn Rd. N8	36 29 88 B
Glassmill La. Brom	99 39 69 D
Glass St. E2	57 34 82 D
Glass Yd. SE18	66 43 79 C
Glastonbury Ave. Wdf Gn	27 41 91 B
Glastonbury Rd. Mord	103 25 66 A
Glastonbury Rd. N9	17 34 94 C
Glastonbury St. NW6	46 24 85 D
Glaucus St. E3	57 37 81 B
Glazbury Rd. W14	62 24 78 C
Glazebro Cl. SE21	87 32 72 B
Glazebrook Rd. Tedd	93 15 70 D
Glebe Ave. Enf	13 31 96 B
Glebe Ave. Har	21 18 89 A
Glebe Ave. Mit	96 27 69 C
Glebe Ave. Uxb	31 07 86 D
Glebe Ave. Wdf Gn	27 40 91 A
Glebe Cres. Har	21 18 89 A
Glebe Cres. NW4	23 23 89 C
Glebe Ct. Mit	96 27 68 B
Glebe Ct. SE3	39 75 A
Glebe Gdns. N.Mal	102 21 66 A
Glebe House Dri. Brom	100 40 66 D
Glebe Hyrst. SE19	87 33 71 B
Glebe La. Har	21 18 89 C
Glebelands Ave. E18	27 40 90 C
Glebelands Ave. Ilf	40 44 88 D
Glebelands Cl. SE5	75 33 75 A
Glebelands. Dart	80 51 75 D
Glebelands Rd. Felt	81 10 73 C
Glebe Path. Mit	96 27 68 B
Glebe Pl. SW3	9 27 77 A
Glebe Rd. Brom	99 40 69 A
Glebe Rd. Cars	111 27 63 B
Glebe Rd. Dag	52 49 84 B
Glebe Rd. E8	48 33 84 D
Glebe Rd. N3	23 26 90 C
Glebe Rd. N8	24 30 89 D
Glebe Rd. NW10	45 22 84 A
Glebe Rd. Sutt	110 24 62 A
Glebe Rd. SW13	72 22 76 C
Glebe Side. Twick	71 15 74 D
Glebe Sq. Mit	96 27 68 B
Glebe St. W4	61 21 78 C
Glebe Terr. E3	57 37 82 B
Glebe The. Chis	100 44 69 A
Glebe The. SE3	39 75 A
Glebe The. Wor Pk	102 21 66 D
Glebe Way. Eri	68 51 77 A
Glebe Way. Felt	81 13 72 C
Glebe Way. Horn	42 54 87 C
Glebe Way. W Wick	106 38 65 B
Gledhow Gdns. SW5	62 26 78 A
Gledstanes Rd. W14	62 24 78 C
Glegg Pl. SW15	73 23 75 D
Glenaffric Ave. E14	64 38 78 B
Glen Albyn Rd. SW19	85 23 72 B
Glenalla Rd. Ruis	31 09 87 B
Glenalmond Rd. Har	21 18 89 C
Glenalvon Way. SE18	65 42 78 A
Glena Mount. Sutt	110 26 64 A
Glenarm Rd. E5	49 35 85 B
Glen Ave. Ashf	81 07 71 A
Glenavon Rd. E15	50 39 84 C
Glenbarr Cl. SE9	78 43 75 B
Glenbow Rd. Brom	99 39 70 A
Glenbrow Rd. Brom	99 39 71 C
Glenbrook N. Enf	12 30 96 D
Glenbrook Rd. NW6	46 25 85 C
Glenbrook S. Enf	12 30 96 D
Glenbuck Ct. Surb	101 18 67 C
Glenbuck Rd. Surb	101 18 67 C
Glenburnie Rd. SW17	86 27 72 D
Glencairn Dri. W5	54 17 82 C
Glencairn. E16	58 41 81 B
Glencairn Rd. SW16	96 30 70 C
Glen Cl. Shep	91 07 68 C
Glencoe Ave. Ilf	40 45 87 A
Glencoe Dri. Dag	52 49 85 A
Glencoe Rd. Hay	53 11 82 D
Glen Cres. Wdf Gn	27 40 91 B
Glendale Ave. N22	25 31 91 C
Glendale Ave. Rom	41 47 87 A
Glendale Cl. SE9	78 43 75 A
Glendale Dri. SW19	85 24 71 D
Glendale Gdns. Wem	33 18 87 C
Glendale Mews. Beck	98 37 69 B
Glendale Rd. Eri	67 50 78 A
Glendall St. SW9	74 30 75 D
Glendarvon St. SW15	73 23 75 B
Glendish Rd. N17	25 34 90 B
Glendower Cres. Orp	108 46 67 C
Glendower Gdns. SW14	72 20 75 B
Glendower Pl. SW7	9 26 78 B
Glendower Rd. E4	18 34 98 A
Glendower Rd. SW14	72 20 75 B
Glendown Rd. SE2	66 46 78 C
Glendun Ct. W3	55 21 80 A
Glendun Rd. W3	55 21 80 A
Gleneagle Mews. SW16	86 29 71 D
Gleneagle Rd. SW16	86 29 71 D
Gleneagles. Stan	21 16 91 B
Gleneldon Mews. SW16	86 30 71 A
Gleneldon Rd. SW16	86 30 71 A
Glenelg Rd. SW2	74 30 74 A
Glenesk Rd. SE9	78 43 75 D
Glenfarg Rd. SE6	88 38 73 D
Glenfield Cres. Ruis	31 08 87 B
Glenfield Rd. Ashf	91 08 70 A
Glenfield Rd. SW12	86 29 73 C
Glenfield Rd. W13	60 16 79 B
Glenfield Terr. W13	54 16 80 D
Glenfinlas Way. SE5	63 31 77 D
Glenforth St. E10	65 39 78 D
Glengall Cswy. E14	64 37 79 C
Glengall Gr. E14	64 38 79 C
Glengall Pas. NW6	46 25 83 A
Glengall Rd. Bexh	79 48 75 A
Glengall Rd. NW6	46 24 83 B
Glengall Rd. SE15	63 33 77 B
Glengall Rd. Wdf Gn	27 40 91 B
Glengall Terr. SE15	63 33 77 B
Glengarnock Ave. E14	64 38 78 A
Glengarry Rd. SE 22	75 33 74 B
Glen Gdns. Croy	112 31 64 A
Glenham Dri. Ilf	40 43 88 B
Glenhead Cl. SE9	78 43 75 B
Glenhill Cl. N3	23 25 90 C
Glenhouse Rd. SE9	78 43 74 A
Glenhurst Ave. NW5	47 28 85 A
Glenhurst Ave. Ruis	31 08 87 A
Glenhurst Rd. Brent	60 17 78 C
Glenhurst Rd. N12	15 26 92 D
Glenhurst Rise. SE19	97 32 70 C
Glenilla Rd. NW3	47 27 84 A
Glenister Park Rd. SW16	96 29 70 D
Glenister Rd. E10	65 39 78 D
Glenister St. E16	66 43 79 A
Glenlea Rd. SE9	78 43 75 C
Glenloch Rd. Enf	14 35 97 C
Glenloch Rd. NW3	47 27 84 A
Glenluce Rd. SE3	65 40 77 A
Glenlyon Rd. SE9	78 43 74 A
Glenmere Ave. NW7	22 22 91 A
Glenmore Rd. NW3	47 27 84 A
Glenmore Rd. Well	78 45 76 B
Glenmore Way. Bark	51 44 83 C
Glenmount Path. SE18	66 44 78 C
Glennie Rd. SE27	87 31 72 C
Glenny Rd. Bark	51 44 84 A
Glenparke Rd. E7	50 40 84 B
Glen Rd. Chess	101 18 65 C
Glen Rd. E13	58 41 82 C
Glen Rd. E17	38 36 88 B
Glen Rise. Wdf Gn	27 40 91 B
Glen Road End. Wall	111 28 62 B
Glenrosa St. SW6	73 26 76 C
Glenroy St. W12	56 23 81 C
Glensdale Rd. SE4	76 36 75 B
Glenshiel Rd. SE9	78 43 74 A
Glenside. Chig	28 43 91 B
Glentanner Way. SW17	85 26 72 D
Glentham Gdns. SW13	61 22 77 B
Glentham Rd. SW13	61 22 77 B
Glen The. Brom	99 39 69 C
Glen The. Croy	106 35 65 D
Glen The. Enf	13 31 96 D
Glen The. Nthwd	19 08 91 D
Glen The. Orp	108 43 65 C
Glen The. Pnr	31 10 88 B
Glen The. Pnr	32 12 87 A
Glen The. Sthl	59 12 78 D
Glen The. Wem	44 17 85 B
Glenthorne Ave. Croy	106 35 66 C
Glenthorne Cl. Sutt	103 25 66 C
Glenthorne Gdns. Ilf	28 43 89 B
Glenthorne Gdns. Sutt	103 25 66 C
Glenthorne Rd. E17	38 36 88 A
Glenthorne Rd. King	93 18 68 D
Glenthorne Rd. N11	16 28 92 B
Glenthorne Rd. W6	61 22 78 B
Glenthorpe Rd. Mord	103 23 67 B
Glenton Cl. Rom	30 51 91 C
Glenton Rd. SE13	77 39 75 C
Glenton Way. Rom	30 51 91 C
Glentworth St. NW1	1 27 82 D
Glenure Rd. SE9	78 43 74 A
Glen View Rd. Brom	99 41 69 D
Glenview. SE2	67 47 77 B
Glenville Gr. SE8	64 36 77 D
Glenville Rd. King	94 19 69 A
Glen Wlk. Islw	70 14 74 B
Glenwood Ave. NW9	34 21 87 C
Glenwood Cl. Har	33 15 88 B
Glenwood Dri. Rom	30 52 89 C
Glenwood Gdns. Ilf	40 43 88 A
Glenwood Gr. NW9	34 20 87 C
Glenwood Rd. Eps	109 22 63 A

Glenwood Rd. Houn	...70	14	75 B	Goddard Cl. Shep	...91	07	68 A	Gomshall Ave. Wall	...111	30	64 C
Glenwood Rd. N15	...37	31	88 B	Goddard Rd. Beck	...98	36	68 C	Gomshall Rd. Sutt	...110	23	62 C
Glenwood Rd. SE6	...88	37	73 C	Goddington Chase. Orp	...108	46	65 D	Gondar Gdns. NW6	...46	24	85 D
Glenwood Way. Croy	...106	35	67 D	Goddington La. Orp	...108	46	65 C	Gonson St. SE8	...64	37	77 B
Glenworth Ave. E14	...64	38	78 B	Godfrey Ave. Nthlt	...43	12	83 A	Gonston Cl. SW19	...85	24	72 A
Gliddon Rd. W14	...62	24	78 C	Godfrey Ave. Twick	...82	14	73 B	Gonville Cres. Nthlt	...43	13	84 B
Glimpsing Green. Belv	...67	48	79 C	Godfrey Hill. SE18	...65	42	78 A	Gonville Rd. Th Hth	...104	30	67 B
Globe Pond Rd. SE16	...57	36	80 C	Godfrey Rd. SE18	...65	42	78 B	Gonville St. SW6	...73	24	75 A
Globe Rd. E15	...50	39	85 D	Godfrey St. E15	...49	38	83 A	Goodall Rd. E11	...38	38	86 C
Globe Rd. E1	...57	35	82 D	Godfrey St. SW3	...9	27	78 C	Gooden Ct. Har	...33	15	86 C
Globe Rd. E2	...57	35	82 A	Godfrey Way. Houn	...82	12	73 B	Goodenough Rd. SW19	...95	24	70 D
Globe Rd. Horn	...42	52	88 C	Goding St. SE11	...10	30	78 C	Goodge Pl. W1	...2	29	81 A
Globe Rd. Wdf Gn	...27	41	91 A	Godley Rd. SW18	...85	26	73 D	Goodge St. W1	...2	29	81 B
Globe Strs. SE16	...57	35	80 B	Godliman St. EC4	...4	32	81 C	Goodhall St. NW10	...55	21	82 B
Globe St. SE1	...8	32	79 B	Godman Rd. SE15	...75	34	76 D	Goodhart Way. W.Wick	...107	39	67 C
Globe Terr. E2	...57	35	82 A	Godolphin Rd. W12	...61	22	79 B	Goodinge Cl. N7	...47	30	84 A
Globe Yd. W1	...2	28	81 D	Godson Rd. Croy	...105	31	65 C	Goodinge Rd. N7	...47	30	84 A
Glossop Rd. S Croy	...112	32	62 B	Godson St. N1	...48	31	83 C	Goodman Cres. SW2	...86	29	72 B
Gloster Rd. N Mal	...94	21	68 C	Godstone Rd. Sutt	...110	26	64 A	Goodman Rd. E10	...38	38	87 A
Gloucester Ave. NW1	...47	28	83 A	Godstone Rd. Twick	...71	16	74 D	Goodman's Stile. E1	...57	34	81 C
Gloucester Ave. Sid	...90	45	72 A	Godstow Rd. SE2	...67	47	79 A	Goodman's Yd. E1	...8	33	80 B
Gloucester Ave. Well	...78	45	75 D	Godwin Cl. N1	...48	32	83 C	Goodmayes Ave. Ilf	...40	46	87 C
Gloucester Circ. SE10	...64	38	77 C	Godwin Rd. Brom	...99	41	68 A	Goodmayes La. Ilf	...40	45	86 C
Gloucester Cl. NW10	...45	20	84 D	Godwin Rd. E7	...50	40	85 B	Goodmayes Rd. Ilf	...40	45	87 C
Gloucester Cl. Surb	...101	16	66 C	Goffers Rd. SE3	...77	39	76 C	Goodmead Rd. Orp	...108	46	66 A
Gloucester Cres. NW1	...47	28	83 B	Goffs Rd. Ashf	...81	08	71 D	Goodrich Rd. SE22	...75	34	74 C
Gloucester Ct. EC3	...8	33	80 A	Goidel Cl. Wall	...111	29	64 B	Goodson House. Mord	...103	26	66 A
Gloucester Ct. Rich	...61	19	77 C	Golborne Gdns. W10	...56	24	82 D	Goodson Rd. NW10	...45	21	84 C
Gloucester Dri. N4	...37	31	86 B	Golborne Mews. W10	...56	24	81 A	Goods Way. NW1	...47	30	83 C
Gloucester Dri. NW11	...23	25	89 C	Golborne Rd. W10	...56	24	81 A	Goodway Gdns. E14	...58	38	81 D
Gloucester Gate Mews. NW1	...47	28	83 D	Golda Cl. Barn	...11	23	95 D	Goodwin Gdns. Croy	...112	31	63 B
Gloucester Gate. NW1	...47	28	83 D	Goldbeaters Gr. Edg	...22	21	91 C	Goodwin Rd. Croy	...112	31	64 D
Gloucester Gdns. Barn	...12	28	95 A	Goldbeaters Wlk. Wem	...34	19	86 D	Goodwin Rd. N9	...18	35	94 D
Gloucester Gdns. Ilf	...39	42	87 A	Goldcliff Cl. Mord	...103	25	66 A	Goodwin Rd. W12	...61	22	79 B
Gloucester Gdns. NW1	...35	24	87 B	Goldcrest Cl. E16	...58	41	81 B	Goodwins Ct. WC2	...7	30	80 A
Gloucester Gdns. Sutt	...103	25	65 B	Gold Crest Way. Pur	...111	29	62 D	Goodwin St. N4	...37	31	86 A
Gloucester Gdns. W2	...1	26	81 C	Golden Ct. Rich	...71	17	74 B	Goodwood Cl. Mord	...95	25	68 C
Gloucester Gr. Edg	...22	20	90 B	Golden La. EC1	...4	32	82 C	Goodwood Dri. Nthlt	...43	13	84 A
Gloucester Mews. W2	...1	26	81 C	Golden Manor. W7	...54	15	80 A	Goodwood Rd. SE14	...64	36	77 C
Gloucester Mews W. W2	...1	26	81 C	Golden Sq. W1	...6	29	80 A	Goodwyn's Vale. N10	...24	28	90 B
Gloucester Pl Mews. W1	...1	27	81 B	Golden Yds. NW3	...46	28	85 A	Goodyers Gdns. NW4	...35	23	88 B
Gloucester Pl. W1	...1	27	81 B	Golders Gdns. NW11	...35	24	87 B	Gooseacre La. Har	...33	17	88 B
Gloucester Rd. Barn	...11	26	95 A	Golders Green Cres. NW11	...35	25	87 A	Gooshays Dri. Rom	...30	54	91 A
Gloucester Rd. Belv	...67	48	78 D	Golders Green Rd. NW11	...35	24	87 B	Gooshays Gdns. Rom	...30	54	91 A
Gloucester Rd. Croy	...105	33	66 A	Golders Manor Dri. NW11	...35	24	88 C	Gophir La. EC4	...8	32	80 B
Gloucester Rd. E10	...38	37	87 A	Golders Park Cl. NW11	...35	25	87 C	Gopsall St. N1	...32	83 B
Gloucester Rd. E11	...39	41	88 A	Golders Rise. NW4	...35	23	88 B	Gordon Ave. E4	...27	39	91 A
Gloucester Rd. E12	...50	42	85 B	Golders Way. NW11	...35	24	87 B	Gordon Ave. Horn	...42	51	86 B
Gloucester Rd. E17	...26	35	90 D	Goldhawk Estate. W6	...61	22	79 D	Gordon Ave. S Croy	...112	32	62 C
Gloucester Rd. Felt	...82	11	73 C	Goldhawk Mews. W12	...61	22	79 B	Gordon Ave. Stan	...21	16	91 A
Gloucester Rd. Hamp	...92	13	70 D	Goldhawk Rd. W12	...61	21	79 D	Gordon Ave. SW14	...72	21	75 C
Gloucester Rd. Har	...32	13	88 B	Goldhawk Rd. W6	...61	21	78 B	Gordon Ave. Twick	...71	16	74 B
Gloucester Rd. Houn	...70	12	75 C	Gold Hill. Edg	...22	20	91 B	Gordonbrock Rd. SE4	...76	37	74 A
Gloucester Rd. King	...94	19	68 D	Goldhurst Terr. NW6	...46	26	84 C	Gordon Cl. E17	...38	37	88 C
Gloucester Rd. N17	...25	32	89 B	Golding St. E1	...57	34	81 C	Gordon Cl. N19	...36	29	87 C
Gloucester Rd. N18	...17	33	92 D	Golding Terr. E1	...57	34	81 C	Gordon Cres. Croy	...105	33	66 D
Gloucester Rd. Rich	...61	19	77 C	Goldington Cres. NW1	...47	29	83 D	Gordon Cres. Hay	...52	08	77 C
Gloucester Rd. Rom	...42	51	88 C	Goldington St. NW1	...47	29	83 D	Gordondale Rd. SW19	...85	25	72 A
Gloucester Rd. SE25	...105	33	67 C	Goldsboro Rd. SW8	...10	29	77 D	Gordon Gdns. Edg	...22	19	90 D
Gloucester Rd. SW7	...62	26	78 A	Goldsborough Cres. E4	...18	38	93 A	Gordon Gr. SE5	...75	31	76 D
Gloucester Rd. Tedd	...83	15	71 C	Goldsdown Cl. Enf	...14	36	97 C	Gordon Hill. Enf	...13	32	97 A
Gloucester Rd. Twick	...82	14	73 C	Goldsdown Rd. Enf	...14	36	97 C	Gordon House Rd. NW3	...47	28	85 A
Gloucester Rd. W3	...61	20	79 A	Goldsmid St. SE18	...66	45	78 C	Gordon Pl. W8	...62	25	79 A
Gloucester Rd. W5	...60	17	79 A	Goldsmith Ave. E12	...50	42	84 A	Gordon Rd. Bark	...51	45	83 A
Gloucester Sq. W2	...1	27	81 C	Goldsmith Ave. NW9	...34	21	88 C	Gordon Rd. Beck	...98	35	69 D
Gloucester St. SW1	...10	29	78 C	Goldsmith Ave. Rom	...41	49	87 A	Gordon Rd. Beck	...98	36	68 B
Gloucester Terr. W2	...1	26	81 C	Goldsmith Ave. W3	...55	20	80 B	Gordon Rd. Belv	...67	50	78 A
Gloucester Way. EC1	...3	31	82 A	Goldsmith Cl. Har	...32	13	87 D	Gordon Rd. Cars	...111	27	63 B
Glover Rd. Pnr	...32	25	79 A	Goldsmith La. NW9	...22	20	89 C	Gordon Rd. E11	...39	40	88 C
Gloxinia Wlk. Hamp	...92	11	88 D	Goldsmith Rd. E10	...38	37	87 D	Gordon Rd. E12	...40	43	86 C
Glycena Rd. SW11	...74	27	75 B	Goldsmith Rd. E17	...26	35	90 D	Gordon Rd. E15	...49	38	85 A
Glyde Mews SW3	...5	27	79 C	Goldsmith Rd. N11	...16	27	92 D	Gordon Rd. E18	...27	40	90 B
Glyn Ave. Barn	...11	26	96 D	Goldsmith Rd. SE15	...75	34	76 A	Gordon Rd. Enf	...13	32	97 D
Glyn Cl. Eps	...109	22	62 A	Goldsmith Rd. W3	...55	20	80 D	Gordon Rd. Har	...21	15	89 A
Glyn Cl. SE25	...97	33	69 A	Goldsmiths Cl. W3	...55	20	80 D	Gordon Rd. Houn	...71	14	75 C
Glyn Ct. SE27	...87	31	72 C	Goldsmith's Row. E2	...48	34	83 C	Gordon Rd. Ilf	...51	44	85 B
Glyndebourne Park. Orp	...108	43	65 B	Goldsmith's Sq. E2	...48	34	83 C	Gordon Rd. Ilf	...40	45	86 C
Glynde Rd. Bexh	...79	48	75 A	Goldsmith St. EC2	...4	32	81 C	Gordon Rd. King	...93	18	69 B
Glynde St. SE4	...76	36	74 D	Goldsworthy Gdns. SE16	...64	35	78 C	Gordon Rd. N11	...24	29	91 D
Glyndon Rd. SE18	...66	44	78 B	Goldwell Rd. Th Hth	...96	30	68 D	Gordon Rd. N3	...23	24	91 D
Glyn Dri. Sid	...90	46	71 B	Goldwin Cl. SE15	...76	35	76 A	Gordon Rd. N9	...17	34	93 B
Glynfield Rd. NW10	...45	21	84 C	Golf Cl. Stan	...21	17	91 C	Gordon Rd. Rich	...71	18	76 D
Glyn Rd. E5	...49	35	85 B	Golf Club Dri. King	...94	20	70 D	Gordon Rd. Rom	...41	48	88 D
Glyn Rd. Enf	...14	35	96 C	Golfe Rd. Ilf	...40	44	86 D	Gordon Rd. SE15	...75	34	76 D
Glyn Rd. Wor Pk	...103	23	65 D	Golf Rd. Brom	...100	43	68 A	Gordon Rd. Sid	...78	45	74 A
Glyn St. SE11	...10	30	78 D	Golf Rd. W5	...18	81 D	Gordon Rd. Sthl	...59	12	78 A
Glynwood Ct. SE23	...88	35	72 A	Golf Side Cl. N Mal	...94	21	69 C	Gordon Rd. Surb	...101	18	66 B
Goater's Alley. SW6	...62	24	77 D	Golf Side. Twick	...82	14	72 D	Gordon Rd. W4	...61	19	77 B
Goat Rd. Mit	...104	28	67 C	Goliath Cl. Wall	...111	30	63 C	Gordon Rd. W5	...54	17	80 A
Goat St. SE1	...8	33	79 B	Gollogly Terr. SE7	...65	41	78 C	Gordon Sq. WC1	...2	29	82 D
Gobions Ave. Rom	...29	50	91 D	Gomer Gdns. Tedd	...93	16	70 A	Gordon St. E13	...58	40	82 A
Godalming Ave. Wall	...111	30	64 D	Gomer Pl. Tedd	...93	16	70 A	Gordon St. WC1	...2	29	82 D
Godalming Rd. E14	...57	38	82 B	Gomerset Rd. Sthl	...53	13	81 A	Gordon Way. Barn	...11	24	96 D
Godbold Rd. E15	...58	39	82 A	Gomm Rd. SE16	...64	35	79 C	Gore Ct. NW9	...34	19	88 A
								Gorefield Pl. NW6	...46	25	83 C

Gore Rd. E9 ....49 .... 35 83 B
Gore Rd. SW20 ....95 .... 23 69 C
Goresbrook Rd. Dag ....52 .... 47 83 B
Gore St. SW7 ....5 .... 26 79 C
Gorham Pl. W11 ....56 .... 24 80 A
Goring Cl. Rom ....29 .... 50 90 A
Goring Gdns. Dag ....52 .... 47 85 A
Goring Rd. Dag ....52 .... 50 84 B
Goring Rd. N11 ....24 .... 30 91 A
Goring St. EC3 ....4 .... 33 81 C
Goring Way. Grnf ....43 .... 14 83 C
Gorleston Rd. N15 ....37 .... 32 68 B
Gorleston St. W14 ....60 .... 24 78 A
Gorman Rd. SE18 ....65 .... 42 78 B
Gorringe Park Ave. Mit ....96 .... 28 70 C
Gorse Rd. Croy ....106 .... 37 65 C
Gorse Rise. SW17 ....86 .... 28 71 C
Gorseway. Rom ....42 .... 51 87 C
Gorst Rd. NW10 ....55 .... 20 82 D
Gorst Rd. SW11 ....74 .... 27 74 D
Gorsuch Pl. E2 ....4 .... 33 82 B
Gosberton Rd. SW12 ....86 .... 28 73 C
Gosfield Rd. Dag ....41 .... 49 86 A
Gosfield St. W1 ....2 .... 29 81 A
Gosford Gdns. Ilf ....39 .... 42 88 B
Goslett Yd. WC2 ....2 .... 29 81 D
Gosling Cl. Grnf ....53 .... 13 82 A
Gosling Way. SW9 ....75 .... 31 76 A
Gospatrick Rd. N17 ....25 .... 32 90 C
Gosport Rd. E17 ....38 .... 36 88 B
Gosport Way (off pentridge St).
SE15 ....63 .... 33 77 D
Gosport Wlk. N15 ....25 .... 34 89 D
Gossage Rd. SE18 ....66 .... 44 78 D
Gosset St. E2 ....4 .... 33 82 B
Gosset St. E2 ....57 .... 34 82 A
Gosshill Rd. Chis ....100 .... 43 69 C
Gosterwood St. SE8 ....64 .... 36 78 C
Gostling Rd. Twick ....82 .... 13 73 C
Goston Gdns. Th Hth ....97 .... 31 68 A
Goswell Pl. EC1 ....3 .... 31 82 B
Goswell Rd. EC1 ....3 .... 31 82 B
Gothic Rd. Twick ....82 .... 14 72 B
Gottfried Mews. NW5 ....47 .... 29 85 A
Goudhurst Rd. Brom ....89 .... 39 71 D
Gough Rd. E15 ....50 .... 39 85 B
Gough Rd. Enf ....13 .... 34 97 D
Gough Sq. EC4 ....3 .... 31 81 C
Gough St. WC1 ....3 .... 30 82 D
Gough Wlk. E14 ....57 .... 37 81 C
Goulden House. SW11 ....74 .... 27 76 C
Gould Rd. Felt ....81 .... 09 73 A
Gould Rd. Twick ....83 .... 15 73 C
Gould Terr. E8 ....48 .... 34 85 D
Goulston St. E1 ....4 .... 33 81 D
Goulton Rd. E5 ....48 .... 34 85 B
Gourley Pl. N15 ....37 .... 33 68 A
Gourley St. N15 ....37 .... 33 88 A
Gourock Rd. SE9 ....88 .... 43 74 A
Govan St. E2 ....48 .... 34 83 A
Govier Cl. E15 ....50 .... 39 84 C
Gowan Ave. SW6 ....73 .... 24 76 A
Gowan Rd. NW10 ....45 .... 22 84 B
Gower Mews. WC1 ....2 .... 29 81 B
Gower Pl. WC1 ....2 .... 29 82 D
Gower Rd. E7 ....50 .... 40 84 A
Gower Rd. Islw ....60 .... 15 77 B
Gower St. WC1 ....2 .... 29 82 D
Gower's Wlk. E1 ....57 .... 34 81 C
Gowland Pl. Beck ....98 .... 36 69 D
Gowlett Rd. SE15 ....75 .... 34 75 A
Gowrie Rd. SW11 ....74 .... 28 75 A
Graburn Way. E Mol ....92 .... 14 68 B
Grace Ave. Bexh ....79 .... 48 76 D
Gracechurch St. EC3 ....8 .... 32 80 B
Gracedale Rd. SW16 ....86 .... 28 71 D
Gracefield Gdns. SW16 ....86 .... 30 72 C
Grace Path. SE26 ....88 .... 35 71 A
Grace Pl. E3 ....57 .... 37 82 B
Grace Rd. Croy ....105 .... 32 67 C
Graces Alley. E1 ....57 .... 34 80 A
Grace's Mews. SE5 ....75 .... 33 76 C
Grace's Rd. SE5 ....75 .... 33 78 C
Grace St. E3 ....57 .... 37 82 B
Gradient The. SE26 ....87 .... 34 71 A
Graeme Rd. Enf ....13 .... 33 97 C
Graemesdyke Ave. SW14 .....97 .... 19 75 D
Grafton Cl. Houn ....82 .... 12 73 C
Grafton Cl. W13 ....55 .... 16 81 C
Grafton Cl. Wor Pk ....102 .... 21 65 C
Grafton Cres. E8 ....48 .... 28 84 B
Grafton Gdns. Dag ....41 .... 48 86 A
Grafton Gdns. N4 ....37 .... 32 88 C
Grafton Mews. W1 ....2 .... 29 82 C

Grafton Park Rd. Wor Pk .....102 .... 21 65 A
Grafton Pl. NW1 ....2 .... 29 82 B
Grafton Rd. Croy ....105 .... 31 66 C
Grafton Rd. Dag ....41 .... 48 86 A
Grafton Rd. Enf ....12 .... 30 96 B
Grafton Rd. Har ....32 .... 14 88 A
Grafton Rd. N Mal ....94 .... 21 68 A
Grafton Rd. NW5 ....47 .... 28 85 C
Grafton Rd. W3 ....55 .... 20 80 A
Grafton St. Wor Pk ....102 .... 21 65 C
Grafton Sq. SW4 ....74 .... 29 75 A
Grafton St. W1 ....6 .... 28 80 B
Grafton Terr. NW5 ....47 .... 27 85 D
Grafton Way. W1 ....2 .... 29 82 C
Grafton Way. W1 ....2 .... 29 82 C
Grafton Yd. NW5 ....47 .... 28 84 B
Graham Ave. Mit ....96 .... 28 69 A
Graham Ave. W13 ....60 .... 16 79 B
Graham Cl. Croy ....106 .... 37 65 A
Graham Ct. Nthlt ....43 .... 12 85 D
Grahame Park Way. NW7 .....22 .... 21 91 B
Grahame Park Way. NW9 .....22 .... 22 90 A
Graham Gdns. Surb ....101 .... 18 66 C
Graham Rd. Bexh ....79 .... 48 75 D
Graham Rd. E13 ....58 .... 40 82 C
Graham Rd. E8 ....48 .... 34 84 A
Graham Rd. Hamp ....82 .... 13 71 A
Graham Rd. Har ....21 .... 15 89 A
Graham Rd. Mit ....96 .... 28 69 A
Graham Rd. N15 ....25 .... 31 89 B
Graham Rd. NW4 ....34 .... 22 88 D
Graham Rd. SW19 ....95 .... 24 70 D
Graham Rd. W4 ....61 .... 20 79 D
Graham St. N1 ....48 .... 31 83 D
Graham Terr. SW1 ....9 .... 28 78 A
Grainger Cl. Nthlt ....43 .... 14 85 C
Grainger Rd. Islw ....71 .... 15 76 D
Grainger Rd. N22 ....25 .... 32 90 A
Gramer Cl. E11 ....38 .... 38 86 B
Grampian Cl. Orp ....108 .... 45 67 D
Grampian Gdns. NW2 ....35 .... 24 87 C
Granada St. SW17 ....86 .... 27 71 D
Granard Ave. SW15 ....72 .... 22 74 B
Granard Rd. SW12 ....86 .... 27 73 B
Granby Bldgs. SE11 ....10 .... 30 78 B
Granby Pl. SE1 ....7 .... 31 79 A
Granby Rd. SE9 ....77 .... 42 75 B
Granby St. E2 ....4 .... 33 82 D
Granby St. E2 ....57 .... 34 82 A
Granby Terr. NW1 ....47 .... 29 83 C
Grand Arc. N12 ....15 .... 26 92 C
Grand Ave. EC1 ....3 .... 31 81 B
Grand Ave E. Wem ....45 .... 19 85 D
Grand Ave. N10 ....28 .... 89 C
Grand Ave. Surb ....102 .... 19 67 D
Grand Ave. Wem ....45 .... 19 85 D
Grand Depot Rd. SE18 ....66 .... 43 78 C
Grand Dri. SW20 ....95 .... 23 68 A
Granden Rd. SW16 ....86 .... 30 69 C
Grandison Rd. SW11 ....74 .... 27 74 B
Grandison Rd. Wor Pk ....103 .... 23 65 A
Grand Sq. SE10 ....64 .... 38 77 B
Grand Wlk. E2 ....57 .... 36 82 C
Granfield St. SW11 ....73 .... 26 76 B
Grange Ave. Barn ....16 .... 27 84 D
Grange Ave. N12 ....15 .... 26 92 C
Grange Ave. N20 ....15 .... 24 94 A
Grange Ave. SE25 ....97 .... 33 69 C
Grange Ave. Stan ....21 .... 17 90 C
Grange Ave. Twick ....83 .... 15 72 A
Grange Ave. Wdf Gn ....27 .... 40 91 C
Grange Cl. E Mol ....92 .... 13 68 D
Grange Cl. Houn ....59 .... 12 77 B
Grangecliffe Gdns. SE25 ....97 .... 33 69 C
Grange Cl. Sid ....90 .... 46 72 C
Grange Cl. Wdf Gn ....27 .... 40 91 C
Grangecourt Rd. N16 ....37 .... 33 87 C
Grange Cl. Nthlt ....43 .... 11 83 C
Grange Ct. Shep ....97 .... 07 68 C
Grange Ct. Sutt ....110 .... 25 63 D
Grange Ct. Wall ....104 .... 28 65 D
Grange Ct. WC2 ....3 .... 30 81 D
Grangedale Cl. Nthwd ....19 .... 09 90 A
Grange Dri. Chis ....99 .... 42 70 B
Grange Farm Cl. Har ....32 .... 14 86 A
Grange Gdns. N14 ....16 .... 29 94 D
Grange Gdns. Pnr ....20 .... 12 89 C
Grange Gdns. SE25 ....97 .... 33 69 C
Grange Gr. N1 ....48 .... 32 84 A
Grangehill Pl. SE9 ....77 .... 42 75 B
Grangehill Rd. SE9 ....77 .... 42 75 D
Grange Hill. SE25 ....97 .... 33 69 C
Grange La. SE21 ....87 .... 33 72 B
Grange Mansions. Eps ....109 .... 21 63 D
Grangemill Rd. SE6 ....88 .... 37 72 A

Grangemill Way. SE6 ....88 .... 37 72 A
Grange Park Ave. N21 ....13 .... 32 95 C
Grange Park Rd. E10 ....38 .... 37 87 D
Grange Park Rd. Th Hth ....97 .... 32 68 B
Grange Park. W5 ....54 .... 18 80 C
Grange Rd. Chess ....101 .... 18 65 C
Grange Rd. E10 ....38 .... 37 87 C
Grange Rd. E13 ....58 .... 40 82 A
Grange Rd. E17 ....38 .... 36 88 A
Grange Rd. Edg ....22 .... 20 91 B
Grange Rd. E Mol ....92 .... 13 68 D
Grange Rd. Har ....32 .... 14 86 B
Grange Rd. Har ....33 .... 16 88 A
Grange Rd. Ilf ....51 .... 44 85 A
Grange Rd. King ....93 .... 18 68 A
Grange Rd. N18 ....36 .... 34 91 A
Grange Rd. N6 ....36 .... 28 88 C
Grange Rd. NW10 ....45 .... 22 84 B
Grange Rd. Orp ....108 .... 44 65 A
Grange Rd. Rom ....30 .... 52 91 B
Grange Rd. S Croy ....112 .... 32 62 A
Grange Rd. SE19 ....97 .... 32 69 B
Grange Rd. SE1 ....8 .... 33 79 D
Grange Rd. SE25 ....97 .... 32 68 B
Grange Rd. Sthl ....59 .... 12 79 A
Grange Rd. Sutt ....110 .... 25 63 D
Grange Rd. SW13 ....72 .... 22 76 A
Grange Rd. Th Hth ....97 .... 32 68 D
Grange Rd. W4 ....61 .... 19 78 D
Grange Rd. W5 ....54 .... 18 80 C
Granger Way. Rom ....42 .... 52 88 C
Grange The. Croy ....106 .... 36 65 B
Grange The. E17 ....38 .... 36 88 A
Grange The. N20 ....15 .... 26 94 C
Grange The. N.Mal ....102 .... 22 67 A
Grange The. SE1 ....8 .... 33 79 D
Grange The. SW19 ....95 .... 23 70 B
Grange The. Wem ....45 .... 19 84 C
Grange The. Wor Pk ....109 .... 20 64 B
Grange Vale. Sutt ....110 .... 25 63 D
Grangeview Rd. N20 ....15 .... 26 94 C
Grange Way. Eri ....68 .... 52 77 D
Grangeway Gdns. Ilf ....39 .... 42 88 A
Grangeway. N12 ....15 .... 25 92 B
Grangeway. NW6 ....46 .... 25 84 C
Grangeway The. N21 ....13 .... 31 95 D
Grange Wlk. SE1 ....8 .... 33 79 D
Grangewood Cl. Pnr ....31 .... 10 88 A
Grangewood La. Beck ....98 .... 36 70 B
Grangewood St. E6 ....50 .... 41 83 B
Grange Yd. SE1 ....8 .... 33 79 D
Granham Gdns. N9 ....17 .... 33 93 B
Granite St. SE18 ....66 .... 45 78 D
Granleigh Rd. E11 ....39 .... 39 86 A
Gransden Ave. E8 ....48 .... 34 84 D
Gransden Rd. W12 ....61 .... 21 79 B
Grantbridge St. N1 ....48 .... 31 83 D
Grant Cl. N14 ....16 .... 29 94 A
Grantham Gdns. Rom ....41 .... 48 87 B
Grantham Pl. W1 ....6 .... 28 80 D
Grantham Rd. E12 ....51 .... 43 85 A
Grantham Rd. SW9 ....74 .... 30 76 C
Grantham Rd. W4 ....61 .... 21 77 C
Grantley Rd. Houn ....70 .... 11 76 C
Grantley St. E1 ....55 .... 35 82 D
Grantock Rd. E17 ....26 .... 38 90 B
Granton Ave. Horn ....42 .... 54 86 B
Granton Rd. Ilf ....40 .... 46 87 C
Granton Rd. SW16 ....96 .... 29 69 A
Grant Pl. Croy ....105 .... 33 66 D
Grant Rd. Croy ....105 .... 33 66 D
Grant Rd. Har ....21 .... 15 89 B
Grant Rd. SW11 ....74 .... 27 75 A
Grants Cl. NW7 ....23 .... 23 91 C
Grant St. E13 ....58 .... 40 82 A
Grant St. N1 ....48 .... 31 83 C
Grantully Rd. W9 ....56 .... 25 82 B
Granville Ave. Felt ....81 .... 10 72 A
Granville Ave. Houn ....70 .... 13 74 A
Granville Ave. N9 ....18 .... 35 93 C
Granville Cl. Croy ....105 .... 33 65 A
Granville Gdns. SW16 ....96 .... 30 70 D
Granville Gdns. W5 ....54 .... 18 80 D
Granville Gr. SE13 ....76 .... 38 75 A
Granville Park. SE13 ....76 .... 38 75 B
Granville Pl. N12 ....23 .... 26 91 C
Granville Pl. W1 ....2 .... 28 81 C
Granville Rd. Barn ....11 .... 23 96 B
Granville Rd. E17 ....38 .... 37 88 D
Granville Rd. E18 ....27 .... 40 90 D
Granville Rd. Ilf ....40 .... 43 86 B
Granville Rd. N12 ....23 .... 26 91 C
Granville Rd. N13 ....24 .... 30 91 B
Granville Rd. N22 ....25 .... 32 90 C

Name	Page	Grid
Granville Rd. N8	36	30 88 D
Granville Rd. NW2	35	24 86 B
Granville Rd. NW6	46	25 83 C
Granville Rd. Sid	90	46 71 B
Granville Rd. SW18	85	24 73 B
Granville Rd. SW19	95	25 70 C
Granville Rd. Well	79	47 75 A
Granville Sq. WC1	3	30 82 B
Granville St. WC1	3	30 82 B
Grape St. WC2	3	30 81 C
Grasdene Rd. SE18	66	46 77 C
Grasmere Ave. Houn	70	13 74 D
Grasmere Ave. Orp	108	43 65 D
Grasmere Ave. Ruis	31	08 87 A
Grasmere Ave. SW15	84	21 71 A
Grasmere Ave. SW19	95	25 68 A
Grasmere Ave. W3	55	20 80 B
Grasmere Ave. Wem	33	17 87 D
Grasmere Ct. N22	24	30 91 B
Grasmere Ct. SE26	87	34 71 C
Grasmere Gdns. Har	21	16 90 C
Grasmere Gdns. Ilf	27	42 89 D
Grasmere Gdns. Orp	108	43 65 D
Grasmere Rd. Bexh	79	50 76 C
Grasmere Rd. Brom	99	39 70 D
Grasmere Rd. E13	50	40 83 C
Grasmere Rd. N10	24	28 90 B
Grasmere Rd. N18	25	34 91 A
Grasmere Rd. Orp	108	43 65 D
Grasmere Rd. SE25	105	34 67 B
Grasmere Rd. SW16	86	30 71 D
Grassington Rd. Sid	90	46 71 A
Grassmere Rd. Horn	30	54 89 D
Grassmount. Pur	111	29 62 C
Grassmount. SE23	87	34 72 B
Grass Park. N3	23	24 90 B
Grassway. Wall	111	29 64 A
Grasvenor Ave. Barn	11	25 95 C
Grately Way (off Daniel Gdns). SE15	63	33 77 D
Gratton Rd. W14	62	24 79 C
Gratton Terr. NW2	35	23 86 D
Gravel Hill. Bex	79	49 74 B
Gravel Hill Cl. Bex	79	49 74 D
Gravel Hill Cl. Bexh	79	49 74 B
Gravel Hill. N3	23	24 90 D
Gravel La. E1	4	33 81 D
Gravelly Ride. SW19	84	22 71 A
Gravel Pit La. SE9	78	44 74 A
Gravel Rd. Brom	107	42 65 A
Gravel Rd. Twick	83	15 73 C
Gravelwood Cl. Chis	90	44 72 C
Gravenel Gdns. SW17	86	27 71 C
Graveney Gr. SE20	98	35 70 C
Graveney Rd. SW17	86	27 71 A
Gravesend Rd. W12	55	22 80 A
Graves Estate. Well	78	46 76 D
Gray Ave. Dag	41	48 87 D
Grayfriars Pas. EC1	3	31 81 D
Grayham Cres. N Mal	94	20 68 D
Grayham Rd. N Mal	94	20 68 D
Grayland Cl. Brom	99	41 69 B
Grayling Rd. N16	37	33 86 A
*Grayling Sq. E2	57	34 82 A
Grayscroft Rd. SW16	96	29 70 D
Grays Farm Rd. Orp	100	46 69 B
Grayshott Rd. SW11	74	28 75 A
Gray's Inn Pl. WC1	3	30 81 B
Gray's Inn Rd. WC1	3	30 82 D
Gray's Inn Sq. WC1	3	31 81 A
Gray St. SE1	7	31 79 A
Grayswood Gdns. SW20	94	22 69 D
Gray's Yd. W1	2	28 81 C
Grazebrook Rd. N16	37	32 86 B
Grazeley Cl. Bexh	79	50 74 A
Great Acre Ct. SW4	74	29 75 D
Great Bell Alley. EC2	4	32 81 D
Great Brownings. SE21	87	33 72 D
Great Bushey Dri. N20	15	25 94 D
Great Cambridge Rd. Enf	13	34 96 C
Great Cambridge Rd. N17	25	32 91 D
Great Cambridge Rd. N18	17	32 92 D
Great Cambridge Rd. N9	17	33 93 A
Great Cambridge Rd. N9	17	33 94 C
Great Castle St. W1	2	28 81 D
Great Central Ave. Ruis	43	11 85 C
Great Central St. NW1	1	27 81 B
Great Chapel St. W1	2	29 81 D
Great Chertsey Rd. Felt	82	13 72 C
Great Chertsey Rd. W4	61	21 77 A
Great Church La. W6	62	23 78 D
Great College St	7	30 79 C
Great Cross Ave. SE10	65	39 77 C
Great Cullings. Rom	42	51 86 A
Great Cumberland Mews. W1	1	27 81 D
Great Cumberland Pl. W1	1	27 81 D
Great Dover St. SE1	8	32 79 D
Greatdown Rd. W7	54	15 81 B
Great Eastern Rd. E15	49	38 84 B
Great Eastern St. EC2	4	33 82 C
Great Elms Rd. Brom	99	41 68 C
*Greatfield Cl. N19	47	29 85 A
Greatfield Cl. SE4	76	37 75 C
Great Field. NW9	22	21 90 A
Greatfields Rd. Bark	51	44 83 D
Great Gardens Rd. Horn	42	53 88 C
Great George St. SW1	7	30 79 A
Great Guildford St. SE1	8	32 80 C
Greatham Wlk. SW15	84	22 73 C
Great Harry Dri. SE9	90	43 72 C
Great James St. WC1	3	30 81 B
Great Marlborough St. W1	2	29 81 C
Great Maze Pond. SE1	8	32 80 D
Great Nelmes Chase. Horn	42	54 88 B
Great Newport St. WC2	3	30 80 A
Great New St. EC4	3	31 81 C
Great North Rd. Barn	11	24 96 D
Great North Rd. N12	23	26 91 A
Great North Rd. N20	15	26 94 C
Great North Rd. N20	15	26 94 C
Great North Rd. N2	24	27 89 A
Great North Way (Barnet By-Pass). NW4	23	23 90 C
Greatorex St. E1	57	34 81 A
Great Ormond St. WC1	3	30 82 D
Great Percy St. WC1	3	31 82 A
Great Peter St. SW1	6	29 79 D
Great Portland St. W1	2	28 81 B
Great Pulteney St. W1	2	29 80 A
Great Queen St. Dart	80	54 74 D
Great Queen St. WC2	3	30 81 C
Great Ross Ave. SE10	64	38 77 D
Great Russell St. WC1	2	29 81 C
Great Russell St. WC1	3	30 81 A
Great Scotland Yd. SW1	7	30 80 C
Great Smith St. SW1	6	29 79 D
Great South-West Rd. Felt	82	09 74 A
Great South West Rd. Houn	70	11 76 C
Great Spilmans. SE22	75	33 74 A
Great St Helen's. EC3	4	33 81 C
Great Strand. NW9	22	21 90 D
Great St Thomas Apostle. EC4	2	32 80 A
Grt Suffolk St. SE1	7	31 80 D
Great Suffolk St. SE1	8	32 79 A
Great Sutton St. EC1	3	31 82 D
Great Swan Alley. EC2	4	32 81 D
Great Thrift. Orp	100	44 68 C
Great Titchfield St. W1	2	29 81 A
Great Tower St. EC3	8	33 80 A
Great Trinity La. EC4	4	32 80 A
Great Turnstile. WC2	3	30 81 B
Great Western Rd. W11	56	25 81 A
Great Western Rd. W9	56	24 82 D
Great West Rd. Brent	60	17 78 D
Great West Rd. Houn	70	13 76 A
Great West Rd. Islw	60	15 77 C
Great West Rd. W6	61	22 78 C
Great West Road Chiswick. W4	61	21 78 D
Great Winchester St. EC2	4	32 81 D
Great Windmill St. W1	6	29 80 B
Greatwood. Chis	100	43 70 C
Great Woodcote Dri. Pur	111	29 62 D
Great Woodcote Park. Pur	111	30 62 C
Great Yd. SE1	8	33 79 A
Greaves Pl. SW17	86	27 71 A
Grecian Cres. SE19	97	31 70 B
Greek St. W1	2	29 81 D
Greenacre Ave. Uxb	31	07 86 C
Green Acres. Croy	105	33 65 D
Greenacres Dri. Stan	21	16 91 D
Greenacres. N3	23	24 90 C
Greenacres. SE9	78	43 74 C
Greenacre Wlk. N14	16	29 93 D
Green Arbour Ct. EC4	3	31 81 D
Green Ave. W13	60	16 79 D
Greenaway Gdns. NW3	46	25 85 B
Greenbank Ave. Wem	44	16 85 C
Greenbank Cres. NW4	24	24 89 C
Green Bank. E1	57	34 80 D
Green Bank. N12	15	25 92 B
Greenbay Rd. SE7	65	41 77 D
Greenberry St. NW8	47	27 83 C
Greenbrook Ave. Barn	11	26 97 A
Green Cl. Brom	99	39 68 A
Green Cl. Cars	104	27 65 B
Green Cl. Felt	82	12 71 C
Green Cl. NW11	35	26 87 A
Green Cl. NW9	34	20 88 C
Greencoat Pl. SW1	10	29 78 A
Greencoat Row. SW1	6	29 79 C
Green Court Ave. Croy	105	34 65 B
Greencourt Ave. Edg	22	19 90 B
Green Court Gdns. Croy	105	34 65 B
Greencourt Rd. Orp	108	45 67 A
Greencroft Ave. Ruis	32	11 86 A
Greencroft Gdns. Enf	13	33 96 A
Greencroft Gdns. NW6	46	26 84 C
Greencroft Rd. Houn	70	12 76 B
Green Dale Cl. SE22	75	33 74 A
Green Dale. SE22	75	33 75 C
Green Dragon Ct. SE1	8	32 80 D
Green Dragon La. (Path). Brent	60	18 78 C
Green Dragon La. Brent	60	18 78 D
Green Dragon La. N21	13	31 95 C
Green Dragon Yd. E1	57	34 81 A
Green Dri. Sthl	53	13 80 C
Green End. N21	17	31 93 B
Greenend Rd. W4	61	21 79 A
Greenfield Ave. Surb	102	19 67 D
Greenfield Dri. Brom	99	40 69 A
Greenfield Gdns. Dag	52	47 83 B
Greenfield Gdns. NW2	35	24 86 C
Greenfield Gdns. Orp	108	44 66 B
Greenfield Pas. Barn	11	24 96 A
Greenfield Rd. Dag	52	47 83 A
Greenfield Rd. E1	57	34 81 C
Greenfield Rd. N15	37	33 88 A
Greenfields. Sthl	53	13 80 A
Greenfield Way. Har	20	13 89 B
Greenford Ave. Sthl	53	12 80 B
Greenfrd Ave. W7	54	15 81 C
Greenford Gdns. Grnf	53	14 82 A
Greenford Rd. Grnf	43	14 83 D
Greenford Rd. Har	44	15 85 B
Greenford Rd. Sutt	110	25 64 B
Greengate. Grnf	44	16 84 B
Greengate St. E13	58	40 82 B
Green Glades. Horn	42	54 88 D
Greenhalgh Wlk. N2	23	26 89 C
Greenham Rd. N10	24	28 90 C
Greenheys Cl. Nthwd	19	09 90 A
Greenheys Dri. E18	27	39 90 D
Greenhill Cres. Har	33	15 88 C
Greenhill Gdns. Nthlt	43	12 83 D
Greenhill Gr. E12	50	42 85 A
Greenhill. NW3	46	26 85 B
Greenhill Park. Barn	11	25 95 B
Greenhill Park. NW10	45	21 83 A
Greenhill Rd. Har	33	15 88 C
Greenhill Rd. NW10	45	21 83 A
Green Hill. SE18	65	42 78 D
Greenhill's Rents. EC1	3	31 81 B
Greenhills Terr. N1	48	32 84 B
Greenhill. Sutt	103	26 65 A
Greenhill Terr. Nthlt	43	12 83 D
Greenhill Terr. SE18	65	42 78 D
Greenhill Way. Har	33	15 88 C
Greenhill Way. Har	34	19 86 B
Greenhill Way. Wem	34	19 86 B
Greenhill. Wem	34	19 86 B
Greenhithe Cl. Sid	90	45 73 A
Greenholm Rd. SE9	78	43 74 B
Green Hundred Rd. SE15	63	34 77 A
Greenhurst Rd. SE27	97	31 71 C
Greening St. SE2	67	47 78 A
Green La. Ashf	81	09 70 B
Green La. Dag	41	47 86 B
Green La. Edg	22	19 91 A
Green La. Enf	14	38 96 B
Green La. Felt	82	12 71 C
Green La. Houn	70	11 75 C
Green La. Ilf	40	45 86 B
Green La. Mord	103	23 67 C
Green La. Mord	103	25 67 D
Green La. N.Mal	102	20 67 A
Green La. Nthwd	19	09 91 C
Green La. NW4	35	23 88 B
Green La. Pur	111	29 62 D
Green La. SE20	98	35 70 D
Green La. SE9	90	43 72 A
Green La. SE9	90	43 72 D
Green La. SW16	96	30 70 D

Green La. SW16	97	31 69 A
Green La. Th Hth	97	31 69 B
Green La. W7	60	15 79 A
Greenlaw Gdns. N.Mal	102	21 66 B
Green Lawns. Ruis	32	11 87 C
Green La. Wor Pk	102	22 66 C
Greenlaw St. SE18	66	43 79 C
Greenleaf Cl. SW2	87	31 73 A
Greenleaf Rd. Ilf	28	43 89 B
Greenleaf Rd. E17	26	36 89 B
Greenleaf Rd. E6	50	41 83 A
Green Leas. Ashf	91	09 70 B
Greenleaves Ct. Ashf	91	07 70 B
Green Man Gdns. W13	54	16 80 A
Green Man La. Felt	69	10 75 C
Green Man La. W13	54	16 80 C
Green Man Pas. W13	54	16 80 D
Greenman St. N1	48	32 83 A
Green Moor Link. N21	17	31 94 B
Greenmoor Rd. Enf	14	35 97 C
Greenoak Way. SW19	85	23 71 B
Greenock Rd. SW16	96	29 69 B
Greenock Rd. W3	61	19 79 D
Greenock Way. Rom	30	51 91 C
Green Pl. Dart	80	51 74 A
Green Pond Rd. E17	26	36 89 A
Green Rd. N14	12	28 95 B
Green Rd. N20	6	26 93 C
Greenrigg Wlk. Wem	34	19 86 D
Greens Ct. W1	6	29 80 B
Greens Ct. Wem	33	17 86 D
Green's End. SE18	66	43 78 B
Greenside. Dag	41	47 87 C
Greenside Rd. Croy	105	31 66 A
Greenside Rd. W12	61	22 79 A
Green St. E13	50	41 83 A
Green St. E7	50	41 84 A
Greenstead Ave. Wdf Gn	27	41 91 A
Greenstead Cl. Wdf Gn	27	41 91 A
Greenstead Gdns. SW15	72	22 74 B
Greenstead Gdns. Wdf Gn	27	41 91 A
Greent St. Enf	14	35 97 D
Green St. Sun	91	10 69 C
Green St. W1	6	28 80 A
Green Terr. EC1	3	31 82 A
Green The. Bexh	79	49 76 A
Green The. Brom	107	40 66 A
Green The. Brom	89	40 72 C
Green The. Cars	111	28 64 A
Green The. E11	39	40 88 D
Green The. E15	50	39 84 B
Green The. E4	18	38 94 D
Green The. Houn	59	13 77 A
Green The. Mord	96	24 68 C
Green The. N14	16	29 93 D
Green The. N21	17	31 94 A
Green The. N9	17	34 93 A
Green The. N Mal	102	20 68 A
Green The. Orp	100	46 70 D
Green The. Rich	71	17 74 B
Green The. Shep	91	09 68 C
Green The. Sid	90	46 71 A
Green The. Sthl	59	12 79 B
Green The. Sutt	103	25 65 D
Green The. SW19	85	23 71 D
Green The. Twick	83	15 73 C
Green The. W3	55	21 81 C
Green The. Well	78	45 75 C
Green The. Wem	33	16 86 A
Green Vale. Bexh	79	47 74 B
Greenvale Rd. SE9	78	43 75 C
Gen Verges. Stan	21	17 91 D
Greenview Ave. Beck	106	36 67 C
Greenview Ave. Croy	106	36 67 C
Green Walk The. E4	18	38 94 D
Greenway Ave. E17	26	38 89 D
Green Way. Brom	107	42 67 C
Greenway. Chis	90	43 71 D
Greenway. Cl. N20	15	25 93 A
Greenway Cl. N4	37	32 86 A
Greenway Cl. NW9	22	20 90 D
Greenway Ct. Ilf	40	43 87 D
Greenway. Dag	41	47 87 C
Greenway Gdns. Croy	106	36 65 D
Green Way Gdns. Har	21	15 90 C
Greenway Gdns. NW9	22	20 90 D
Greenway. Har	33	18 88 A
Greenway. N14	16	30 93 A
Greenway. N20	15	25 93 A
Greenway. Pnr	19	10 90 D
Greenways. Beck	98	37 69 C
Green Way. SE9	77	41 74 B
Greenways. Esh	101	15 65 D
Greenways The. N11	24	28 91 A
Green Way. Sun	91	10 68 C
Greenway. SW20	95	23 68 C
Green Way The. Har	21	15 90 A
Greenway The. Houn	70	12 75 D
Greenway The. NW9	22	20 90 D
Greenway The. Orp	108	46 67 D
Greenway The. Pnr	32	12 88 D
Greenway The. Uxb	32	08 86 A
Greenway. Wall	111	29 64 A
Greenwell St. W1	2	28 82 D
Greenwich Church St. SE10	64	38 77 A
Greenwich High Rd. SE10	64	38 77 C
Greenwich Park St. SE10	64	38 77 B
Greenwich South St. SE10	76	38 76 A
Greenwich South St. SE10	64	38 77 C
Green Wlk. Dart	80	51 75 D
Green Wlk. Hamp	92	12 70 B
Green Wlk. NW4	23	23 88 B
Green Wlk. NW4	23	23 89 D
Green Wlk. Ruis	31	09 87 D
Green Wlk. SE1	8	33 79 C
Green Wlk. Sthl	59	13 78 C
Green Wlk. Wdf Gn	27	42 91 A
Greenwood Ave. Dag	42	50 85 A
Greenwood Ave. Enf	14	36 97 A
Greenwood Cl. Mord	95	24 68 C
Greenwood Cl. Orp	108	45 67 C
Greenwood Cl. Sid	90	46 72 A
Greenwood Cl. Surb	101	16 66 C
Greenwood Dri. E4	18	38 92 D
Greenwood Gdns. Ilf	28	44 91 C
Greenwood Gdns. N13	17	31 93 D
Greenwood Park. King	94	21 70 C
Greenwood Pl. NW5	47	28 85 D
Greenwood Rd. Croy	105	32 66 A
Greenwood Rd. E13	50	39 83 D
Greenwood Rd. E8	48	34 84 A
Greenwood Rd. Islw	71	15 75 B
Greenwood Rd. Mit	96	29 68 B
Greenwood Rd. Surb	101	16 65 A
Green Wrythe Cres. Cars	104	27 66 C
Green wrythe La. Cars	104	27 66 C
Greer Rd. Har	20	14 90 A
Greet St. SE1	7	31 79 A
Gregor Mews. SE3	65	40 77 C
Gregory Cres. SE9	89	41 73 B
Gregory Pl. W8	6	25 79 B
Gregory Rd. Rom	29	47 89 D
Gregory Rd. Sthl	59	13 79 C
Greig Cl. N8	36	30 88 A
Greig Terr. SE17	23	31 77 B
Grenaby Ave. Croy	105	32 66 B
Grenaby Rd. Croy	105	32 66 B
Grenada Rd. SE7	65	41 77 C
Grenade St. E14	57	36 80 B
Grena Gdns. Rich	71	18 75 D
Grena Rd. Rich	71	18 75 D
Grendon Gdns. Wem	34	19 86 A
Grendon St. NW8	1	27 82 C
Grenfell Ave. Horn	42	51 87 D
Grenfell Gdns. Har	33	18 87 A
Grenfell Rd. Mit	86	28 70 A
Grenfell Rd. W11	56	23 80 B
Grenfell Wlk. W11	56	23 80 B
Grennell Cl. Sutt	103	26 65 B
Grennell Rd. Sutt	103	26 65 A
Grenoble Gdns. N13	25	31 91 A
Grenville Cl. Surb	102	20 66 C
Grenville Gdns. Wdf Gn	27	41 91 C
Grenville Mews. Hamp	82	13 71 D
Grenville Mews. SW7	62	26 78 A
Grenville Pl. SW7	62	26 78 A
Grenville Rd. N19	36	30 87 C
Grenville St. WC1	3	30 82 C
Gresham Ave. N20	16	27 92 B
Gresham Cl. Bex	79	48 74 D
Gresham Cl. Enf	13	32 96 A
Gresham Dri. Rom	30	46 88 D
Gresham Gdns. NW11	35	24 87 C
Gresham Rd. Beck	98	36 69 C
Gresham Rd. E16	58	40 81 D
Gresham Rd. E6	51	42 83 D
Gresham Rd. Edg	21	18 91 B
Gresham Rd. Hamp	92	13 70 A
Gresham Rd. Houn	70	14 76 A
Gresham Rd. NW10	45	20 84 B
Gresham Rd. SE25	97	34 68 C
Gresham Rd. SW9	75	31 75 A
Gresham St. EC2	4	32 81 C
Gresham Way. SW19	85	25 72 C
Gresley Cl. N15	25	32 89 D
Gresley Rd. N19	36	30 87 A
Gressenhall Rd. SW18	73	24 74 D
Gresse St. W1	2	29 81 D
Gresswell Cl. Sid	90	46 72 C
Greswell St. SW6	73	23 76 B
Gretton Rd. N17	25	33 91 C
Greville Cl. Twick	83	16 73 B
Greville Mews. NW6	46	25 83 B
Greville Pl. NW6	46	25 83 D
Greville Rd. E17	26	38 89 C
Greville Rd. NW6	46	25 83 D
Greville Rd. Rich	71	18 74 D
Greville St. EC1	3	31 81 A
Grey Cl. NW11	35	26 88 C
Greycoat Pl. SW1	6	29 79 D
Greycoat St. SW1	6	29 79 D
Greycot Rd. Beck	88	37 71 C
Grey Eagle St. E1	4	33 82 D
Greyhound Ct. WC2	7	31 80 A
Greyhound Hill. NW4	22	22 89 B
Greyhound La. SW16	96	29 70 B
Greyhound Rd. N17	25	33 89 A
Greyhound Rd. NW10	55	22 82 B
Greyhound Rd. Sutt	110	26 64 C
Greyhound Rd. W14	62	24 77 A
Greyhound Rd. W6	62	23 77 B
Greyhound Terr. SW16	96	29 69 A
Greyladies Gdns. SE10	76	38 76 C
Greys La. Ashf	81	07 71 B
Greystead Rd. SE23	88	35 73 A
Greystoke Ave. Pnr	20	13 89 A
Greystoke Ct. W5	54	18 82 D
Greystoke Gdns. Enf	12	29 96 D
Greystoke Gdns. W5	54	18 82 D
Greystoke Park Terr. W5	54	18 82 A
Greystoke Pl. EC4	3	31 81 C
Greystone Gdns. Har	33	17 88 C
Greystone Gdns. Ilf	28	44 90 C
Greyswood St. SW16	96	28 70 B
Grey Towers Ave. Horn	42	53 87 C
Grey Towers Gdns. Horn	42	53 87 A
Grierson Rd. SE23	76	36 74 C
Griffin Manor Way. SE28	66	44 79 D
Griffin Manor Way. SE28	66	45 79 B
Griffin Rd. N17	25	33 90 C
Griffin Rd. SE18	66	44 78 D
Griffin Way. Sun	91	10 69 C
Griffiths Cl. Wor Pk	102	22 65 B
Griffiths Rd. SW19	95	25 70 D
Grigg's Pl. SE1	8	33 79 C
Griggs Rd. E10	38	38 88 C
Grimsby St. E2	4	33 82 D
Grimsby St. E2	57	34 82 C
Grimsdyke Cres. Barn	11	23 96 A
Grimsdyke Rd. Pnr	20	12 91 C
Grimsel Path. SE5	63	31 77 D
Grimstone Cl. Rom	29	49 91 B
Grimston Rd. SW6	73	24 76 D
Grimwade Ave. Croy	105	34 65 C
Grimwood Rd. Twick	83	15 73 B
Grindal St. SE1	7	31 79 A
Grinling Pl. SE8	64	37 77 A
Grinstead Rd. SE8	64	36 78 C
Grittleton Ave. Wem	45	19 84 B
Grittleton Rd. W9	56	25 82 C
Grocers' Hall Ct. EC2	4	32 81 D
Grogan Cl. Hamp	92	12 70 B
Groombridge Cl. Well	78	46 75 A
Groombridge Rd. E9	49	35 84 D
Groom Cres. SW18	85	26 73 B
Groomfield Cl. SW17	86	28 71 A
Groom Pl. SW1	6	28 79 C
Grosmont Rd. SE18	66	45 78 D
Grossall Ct. Th hth	105	31 67 C
Grosse Way. SW15	72	22 74 D
Grosvenor Ave. Cars	111	28 63 A
Grosvenor Ave. Har	32	13 88 D
Grosvenor Ave. N5	48	32 85 C
Grosvenor Ave. Rich	71	18 74 A
Grosvenor Ave. SW14	72	21 75 A
Grosvenor Bridge. SW8	9	28 77 D
Grosvenor Cottages. SW1	9	28 78 A
Grosvenor Cres. Dart	80	53 74 B
Grosvenor Cres Mews. SW1	6	28 79 A
Grosvenor Cres. NW9	22	19 89 C
Grosvenor Cres. SW1	6	28 79 A
Grosvenor Ct. N14	16	29 94 A
Grosvenor Ct. Sutt	110	26 63 A
Grosvenor Dri. Horn	42	53 87 A
Grosvenor Gdns. E6	58	41 82 B
Grosvenor Gdns. King	93	17 70 B
Grosvenor Gdns Mews E. SW1	6	28 79 D
Grosvenor Gdns Mews N. SW1	6	28 79 D
Grosvenor Gdns Mews S. SW1	6	28 79 D
Grosvenor Gdns. N10	24	29 89 A
Grosvenor Gdns. N14	12	29 95 B
Groenor Gdns. NW11	35	24 88 B
Grosvenor Gdns. NW2	46	23 85 C
Grosvenor Gdns. SW14	72	21 75 A

Street	Page	Grid
Grosvenor Gdns. SW1	6	28 79 D
Grosvenor Gdns. Wall	111	29 63 C
Grosvenor Gdns. Wdf Gn	27	40 91 B
Grosvenor Hill. SW19	95	24 70 A
Grosvenor Hill. W1	6	28 80 B
Grosvenor Park Rd. E17	38	37 88 B
Grosvenor Park. SE5	63	32 77 C
Grosvenor Pl. SW1	6	28 79 B
Grosvenor Rd. Belv	67	49 77 A
Grosvenor Rd. Bexh	79	48 74 A
Grosvenor Rd. Brent	60	17 77 B
Grosvenor Rd. Dag	41	48 87 D
Grosvenor Rd. E10	38	38 87 C
Grosvenor Rd. E11	39	40 88 B
Grosvenor Rd. E6	50	41 83 B
Grosvenor Rd. E7	50	40 84 B
Grosvenor Rd. Houn	12	12 75 B
Grosvenor Rd. Ilf	40	44 86 C
Grosvenor Rd. N10	24	28 90 B
Grosvenor Rd. N3	23	25 91 C
Grosvenor Rd. N9	17	34 94 D
Grosvenor Rd. Orp	108	45 67 C
Grosvenor Rd. Rich	18	18 74 A
Grosvenor Rd. Rom	41	50 87 B
Grosvenor Rd. SE25	97	34 68 C
Grosvenor Rd. Sthl	59	12 79 D
Grosvenor Rd. SW1	10	29 77 A
Grosvenor Rd. Twick	83	16 73 C
Grosvenor Rd. W4	54	20 78 C
Grosvenor Rd. W7	54	16 80 C
Grosvenor Rd. Wall	111	28 64 D
Grosvenor Rd. W Wick	106	37 65 B
Grosvenor Rise E. E17	38	37 88 B
Grosvenor Sq. W1	6	28 80 A
Grosvenor St. W1	6	28 80 B
Grosvenor Terr. SE5	63	32 77 A
Grosvenor Vale. Ruis	31	09 86 B
Grosvenor Wharf Rd. E14	64	38 78 B
Grote's Bldgs. SE3	77	39 76 C
Grote's Pl. SE3	77	39 76 C
Groton Rd. SW18	85	25 72 B
Grotto Ct. SE1	4	32 79 A
Grotto Pas. W1	2	28 81 A
Grotto Rd. Twick	83	15 72 B
Grove Ave. N10	24	29 90 C
Grove Ave. N3	23	25 91 C
Grove Ave. Pnr	20	12 89 C
Grove Ave. Sutt	110	25 63 A
Grove Ave. Twick	83	15 73 D
Grove Ave. W7	54	15 81 C
Grovebury Cl. Eri	67	50 77 B
Grovebury Ct. N14	16	29 94 B
Grovebury Rd. SE2	66	46 79 B
Grove Cl. Brom	107	40 65 A
Grove Cl. King	93	18 63 D
Grove Cl. N14	16	28 94 B
Grove Cl. SE23	88	36 73 C
Grove Cottages. E14	57	37 80 B
Grove Crescent Rd. E15	49	38 84 B
Grove Cres. E18	27	39 90 D
Grove Cres. Felt	82	12 71 A
Grove Cres. King	93	18 68 A
Grove Cres. NW9	22	20 89 D
Grovedale Rd. N19	36	29 86 B
Grove End. NW5	47	28 85 B
Grove End Rd. NW8	1	26 82 B
*Grove Footpath. Surb	93	18 68 C
Grove Gdns. Dag	41	50 86 C
Grove Gdns. Enf	14	35 97 B
Grove Gdns. NW4	22	22 89 C
Grove Gdns. NW8	1	27 82 A
Grove Gdns. Rich	83	16 71 A
Grove Green Rd. E11	38	38 86 B
Grovehill Ct. Brom	99	39 70 B
Grove Hill. E18	27	39 90 D
Grove Hill. Har	33	15 87 A
Grove Hill Rd. Har	33	15 87 B
Grove Hill Rd. SE5	75	33 75 A
Grove House Rd. N8	24	30 89 C
Grove La. King	93	18 68 C
Groveland Ave. SW16	96	30 70 D
Groveland Ct. EC4	4	32 81 C
Groveland Rd. Beck	98	36 68 B
Grovelands Ct. N14	16	29 94 B
Grovelands. E Mol	92	13 68 C
Grovelands Rd. N13	16	30 93 D
Grovelands Rd. N15	37	34 88 C
Grovelands Rd. Orp	100	46 70 D
Groveland Way. N.Mal	102	20 67 B
Grove La. SE5	75	32 76 D
Groveley Rd. Sun	81	09 71 D
Grove Market Pl. SE9	77	42 74 D
Grove Mews. W6	62	23 79 C
Grove Park Ave. E4	26	37 91 D
Grove Park Bridge. W4	61	20 77 C
Grove Park. E11	39	40 88 B
Grove Park Gdns. W4	61	20 77 C
Grove Park Mews. W4	61	20 77 C
Grove Park. NW9	22	20 89 C
Grove Park Rd. N15	33	33 89 C
Grove Park Rd. SE9	89	41 72 B
Grove Park Rd. W4	61	19 77 D
Grove Park. SE5	75	33 76 C
Grove Park Terr. W4	61	19 77 B
Grove Pas. E2	48	34 83 D
Grove Pl. Bark	51	44 84 C
Grove Pl. NW3	35	26 86 D
Grove Pl. W3	55	20 80 C
Grover Ct. SE13	76	37 76 D
Grove-Rd. Barn	12	27 96 A
Grove Rd. Belv	67	48 77 B
Grove Rd. Bexh	79	50 75 C
Grove Rd. Brent	60	17 78 C
Grove Rd. E11	39	39 87 B
Grove Rd. E17	38	37 88 B
Grove Rd. E18	27	39 90 D
Grove Rd. E3	36	36 82 A
Grove Rd. E4	18	38 93 C
Grove Rd. E9	49	35 83 B
Grove Rd. Edg	22	19 91 A
Grove Rd. E Mol	92	14 68 D
Grove Rd. Houn	70	13 75 C
Grove Rd. Islw	71	15 76 A
Grove Rd. Mit	96	28 69 C
Grove Rd. N11	16	28 92 D
Grove Rd. N12	15	26 92 D
Grove Rd. N15	37	33 88 A
Grove Rd. Nthwd	19	08 91 B
Grove Rd. NW2	46	23 84 A
Grove Rd. Pnr	32	12 88 B
Grove Rd. Rich	18	18 74 D
Grove Rd. Rom	41	47 88 C
Grove Rd. Surb	101	17 67 B
Grove Rd. Sutt	110	25 63 B
Grove Rd. SW13	72	21 76 D
Grove Rd. SW19	95	26 70 C
Grove Rd. Th Hth	97	31 68 C
Grove Rd. Twick	82	14 72 D
Grove Rd. W3	55	20 80 C
Grove Rd. W5	54	17 80 B
Grovestile Waye. Felt	81	08 73 B
Grove St. N18	33	33 91 B
Grove St. SE8	64	36 78 D
Grove Terrace Mews. NW5	28	28 86 D
Grove Terr. NW5	47	28 85 B
Grove Terr. Rich	18	16 71 A
Grove The. Bexh	79	47 75 D
Grove The. E15	50	39 84 A
Grove The. Enf	13	31 97 C
Grove The. Eps	109	21 62 D
Grove The. Grnf	53	14 81 C
Grove The. Islw	71	15 76 A
Grove The. N13	17	31 92 A
Grove The. N3	23	25 91 C
Grove The. N4	36	30 87 B
Grove The. N6	36	28 87 C
Grove The. N8	36	29 88 B
Grove The. NW11	34	24 87 A
Grove The. NW9	34	20 88 B
Grove The. Rich	83	16 71 A
Grove The. W5	54	18 80 A
Grove The. W Wick	106	38 65 C
Grove Vale. Chis	100	43 70 A
Grove Vale. SE22	75	33 75 D
Groveway. Dag	52	47 85 B
Groveway. SW9	75	31 76 A
Grove Way. Wem	45	20 85 C
Grummant Rd. SE15	75	33 76 B
Grundy St. E14	57	37 81 D
Gruneisen Rd. N3	23	25 91 D
Gubbins La. Rom	30	54 90 B
Gubyon Ave. SE24	75	31 74 B
Guerin Sq. E3	59	13 77 C
Guernsey Cl. Houn	69	32 73 A
Guernsey Gr. SE24	87	32 73 A
Guernsey Rd. E11	38	38 87 D
Guibal Rd. SE12	88	40 73 D
Guildersfield Rd. SW16	96	30 70 C
Guildford Ave. Felt	81	10 72 A
Guildford Gdns. Rom	30	54 91 A
Guildford Gr. SE10	76	37 76 B
Guildford Rd. Croy	105	32 67 D
Guildford Rd. E17	26	38 90 A
Guildford Rd. Ilf	40	45 86 A
Guildford Rd. Rom	30	54 91 A
Guildford Rd. SW8	74	30 76 A
Guildford Rd. Wall	111	30 64 C
Guildhall Bldgs. EC2	4	32 81 D
Guildhall Yd. EC2	4	32 81 C
Guildhouse St. SW1	10	29 78 A
Guildown Ave. N12	15	25 92 B
Guild Rd. Eri	68	51 77 D
Guild Rd. SE7	85	41 78 D
Guildsway. E17	26	36 90 B
Guilford Ave. Surb	101	18 67 B
Guilford Pl. WC1	3	30 82 D
Guilford St. WC1	3	30 82 D
Guillemot Pl. N22	24	30 90 D
Guilsborough Cl. NW10	45	21 84 C
Guiness Cl. E9	49	36 84 C
Guinness Ct. EC1	4	32 82 A
Guinness Ct. NW8	47	27 83 A
Guinness Sq. SE1	63	33 78 B
Guinness Trust Bldgs. SW3	9	27 78 B
Guinness Trust. N16	37	33 87 D
Guion Rd. SW6	73	24 76 D
Gulland Wlk. N1	48	32 84 A
Gull Cl. Wall	111	30 63 C
Gulliver Cl. Nthlt	43	12 83 B
Gulliver Rd. Sid	90	45 72 A
Gulliver St. SE16	64	36 79 D
Gumleigh Rd. W5	60	17 78 A
Gumley Gdns. Islw	71	16 75 A
Gumping Rd. Orp	108	44 65 A
Gundulf St. SE11	63	31 78 A
Gundulph Rd. Brom	99	41 68 A
Gunmakers La. E3	49	36 83 A
Gunner La. SE18	68	43 78 C
Gunnersbury Ave. W3	61	19 79 C
Gunnersbury Ave. W4	61	19 78 C
Gunnersbury Ave. W5	54	18 80 D
Gunnersbury Cl. W4	61	19 78 D
Gunnersbury Cres. W3	61	19 79 A
Gunnersbury Ct. W3	61	19 79 B
Gunnersbury Dri. W5	60	18 79 B
Gunnersbury Gdns. W3	61	19 79 A
Gunnersbury La. W3	61	19 79 A
Gunnersbury Mews. W4	61	19 78 D
Gunners Gr. E4	18	38 93 C
Gunners Rd. SW18	85	26 72 B
Gunning St. SE18	68	45 78 A
Gun St. E1	4	33 81 B
Gunstor Rd. N16	48	33 85 A
Gunter Gr. Edg	22	20 90 B
Gunter Gr. SW10	73	26 77 C
Gunterstone Rd. W14	62	24 78 C
Gunthorpe St. E1	4	33 81 D
Gunton Rd. E5	37	34 86 B
Gunton Rd. SW17	96	28 70 A
Gurdon Rd. SE7	65	40 78 C
Gurnell Gr. W13	54	15 82 D
Gurney Cl. E15	50	39 85 C
Gurney Cres. Croy	104	30 66 D
Gurney Dri. N2	23	26 89 C
Gurney Rd. Cars	111	33 64 A
Gurney Rd. E15	50	39 85 C
Gurney Rd. Nthlt	53	11 82 A
Guthrie St. SW3	9	27 78 C
Gutter La. EC2	4	32 81 C
Guyatt Gdns. Mit	28	28 69 C
Guy Rd. Wall	104	29 65 D
Guyscliff Rd. SE13	38	38 74 A
Guy St. SE1	4	32 79 B
Gwalior House. N14	12	29 95 C
Gwalior Rd. SW15	73	23 75 B
Gwendolen Ave. SW15	73	23 74 B
Gwendolen Cl. SW15	73	23 74 B
Gwendoline Ave. E13	50	40 83 B
Gwendwr Rd. W14	62	24 78 C
Gwillim Cl. Sid	58	46 75 A
Gwydor Rd. Beck	98	35 68 B
Gwydyr Rd. Brom	99	39 68 B
Gwynne Ave. Croy	106	35 66 B
Gwynne Park Ave. Wdf Gn	27	42 91 B
Gwynne Pl. WC1	3	30 82 B
Gwynne Rd. SW11	73	26 76 D
Gylcote Cl. SE5	75	32 75 D
Gyles Park. Stan	31	17 90 A
Gyllyngdune Gdns. Ilf	40	45 86 D
Haarlem Rd. W14	62	23 79 D
Haberdasher Pl. N1	4	33 82 A
Haberdasher's Ct. SE14	76	35 76 D
Haberdasher St. N1	4	32 82 B
Haccombe Rd. SW19	95	26 70 A
Hackbridge Park Gdns. Cars	104	27 65 A
Hackbridge Rd. Wall	104	28 65 A
Hackford Rd. SW9	75	31 76 A
Hackford Rd. SW9	75	31 77 C
Hackington Cres. Beck	98	37 70 A
Hackney Gr. E8	48	34 84 B
Hackney Rd. E2	48	34 83 C
Hacton La. Horn	30	54 86 D
Hadden Rd. SE28	66	45 79 C
Hadden Way. Grnf	43	14 84 B

Street	Page	Ref
Haddington Rd. Brom	88	38 71 B
Haddon Cl. Enf	13	34 95 C
Haddon Cl. N.Mal	102	21 67 B
Haddon Gr. Sid	90	45 73 B
Haddon Rd. Sutt	110	25 64 B
Haddo St. SE10	64	38 77 A
Haden Ct. N4	37	31 86 A
Hadleigh Cl. E1	57	35 82 C
Hadleigh Rd. N9	17	34 94 B
Hadleigh St. E2	57	35 82 A
Hadley Cl. N21	13	31 95 C
Hadley Gdns. Sthl	59	12 78 D
Hadley Gdns. W4	61	20 78 D
Hadley Gr. Barn	11	24 97 C
Hadley Green. Barn	11	24 97 D
Hadley Green Rd. Barn	11	24 97 D
Hadley Green W. Barn	11	24 97 D
Hadley Highstone. Barn	11	24 97 B
Hadley Rd. Barn	11	25 96 B
Hadley Rd. Belv	67	48 78 B
Hadley Rd. Enf	12	30 97 B
Hadley Rd. Mit	96	29 68 D
Hadley Ridge. Barn	11	24 96 B
Hadley St. NW1	47	28 84 B
Hadley Way. N21	13	31 95 C
Hadley Wood Rd. Barn	11	25 97 D
Hadlow Pl. SE19	97	34 70 C
Hadlow Rd. Sid	90	46 71 A
Hadlow Rd. Well	67	47 77 C
Hadrian Cl. Wall	111	30 63 C
Hadrian Estate. E2	48	34 83 C
Hadrian's Ride. Enf	13	33 95 B
Hadrian St. E10	65	39 78 C
Hadyn Park Rd. W12	61	22 79 A
Hafer Rd. SW11	74	27 75 D
Hafton Rd. SE6	89	39 73 C
Haggard Rd. Twick	83	16 73 B
Haggerston. E8	48	33 83 B
Hague St. E2	57	34 82 B
Ha-Ha Rd. SE18	65	42 77 B
Haig Homes. Mord	103	25 67 C
Haig Pl. Mord	103	25 67 C
Haig Rd. Stan	21	17 91 A
Haig Road E. E13	58	41 82 A
Haig Road W. E13	58	41 82 A
Haigville Gdns. Ilf	28	43 89 D
Hailes Cl. SW19	95	26 70 A
Haileybury Ave. Enf	13	33 95 D
Hailey Rd. Belv	67	49 79 A
Hailsham Ave. SW2	86	30 72 B
Hailsham Rd. SW17	96	28 70 A
Hailsham Terr. N18	17	32 92 D
Haimo Rd. SE9	77	41 74 B
Hainault Gore. Rom	41	48 88 A
Hainault Gore. Rom	41	48 88 A
Hainault Rd. E11	38	38 87 B
Hainault Rd. Rom	28	46 90 D
Hainault Rd. Rom	41	48 88 D
Hainault Rd. Rom	29	50 89 A
Hainault St. Ilf	40	44 86 A
Hainault St. SE9	90	43 73 D
Haines St. SW8	10	29 77 C
Hainthorpe Rd. SE27	87	31 71 B
Hainton Path. E1	57	34 81 D
Halberd Mews. E5	49	34 86 B
Halbutt St. Dag	52	48 85 D
Halbutt St. Dag	52	48 86 D
Halcomb St. N1	48	33 83 A
Halcot Ave. Bexh	79	49 74 B
Halcrow St. E1	57	34 81 B
Halcyon Way. Horn	42	54 87 D
Haldane Cl. N10	24	28 91 D
Haldane Pl. SW18	85	25 73 D
Haldane Rd. E6	58	41 82 B
Haldane Rd. Sthl	53	14 80 A
Haldane Rd. SW6	62	24 77 B
Haldan Rd. E4	73	38 91 C
Haldon Rd. SW18	73	24 74 D
Hale Cl. E4	18	38 93 C
Hale Dri. NW7	22	20 91 B
Hale End Cl. Ruis	31	10 88 C
Hale End Rd. E4	26	38 90 B
Hale End Rd. E17	26	38 91 B
Hale End Rd. Wdf Gr	26	38 91 D
Hale End. Rom	30	52 91 B
Halefield Rd. N17	25	34 90 B
Hale Gdns. N17	25	34 89 A
Hale Gdns. W3	55	19 80 C
Hale La. NW7	22	21 91 A
Hale Rd. N17	25	34 89 A
Halesowen Rd. Mord	103	25 66 B
Hales St. SE8	64	37 77 C
Hale St. E14	57	37 80 B
Halesworth Cl. E5	38	35 86 A
Halesworth Cl. Rom	30	54 91 C
Halesworth Rd. Rom	30	54 91 A
Halesworth Rd. SE13	76	37 75 B
Hale The. E4	26	38 91 D
Hale The. N17	25	34 89 A
Hale Wlk. W7	54	15 81 A
Half Acre. Brent	60	17 77 B
Half Acre Rd. W7	54	15 80 C
Half Moon Cres. N1	47	30 83 B
Half Moon Ct. EC1	4	32 81 A
Halfmoon Pas. E1	4	33 81 D
Half Moon St. W1	6	28 80 D
Halford Rd. E10	38	38 88 B
Halford Rd. Rich	71	18 74 A
Halford Rd. SW6	62	25 77 A
Halfway St. Sid	90	45 73 C
Haliburton Rd. Twick	71	16 75 C
Haliday Wlk. N1	48	32 84 B
Halidon Cl. E9	49	35 85 C
Halifax Rd. Enf	13	32 97 D
Halifax Rd. Grnf	43	13 83 B
Halifax St. SE26	87	34 72 D
Haling Gr. S Croy	112	32 63 C
Haling Park Gdns. S Croy	112	31 63 B
Haling Park Rd. S Croy	112	32 63 A
Haling Rd. S Croy	112	32 63 B
Halkin Arc. SW1	6	28 79 C
Halkin Mews. SW1	6	28 79 C
Halkin Pl. SW1	6	28 79 C
Halkin St. SW1	6	28 79 A
Halland Way. Nthwd	19	08 91 B
Hall Cl. W5	54	18 81 A
Hall Dri. SE26	88	35 71 C
Hall Dri. W7	54	15 81 C
Halley Pl. E14	57	36 81 A
Halley Rd. E12	50	41 85 D
Halley Rd. E7	50	41 84 A
Halley St. E14	57	36 81 A
Hall Farm Dri. Twick	82	14 73 B
Hallford Way. Dart	80	53 74 A
Hall Gate. NW8	1	26 82 B
Hall Gdns. E4	18	36 92 B
Halliford Cl. Shep	91	08 68 B
Halliford Rd. Sun	91	10 68 C
Halliford St. N1	48	32 84 C
Halliwell Rd. SW2	74	30 74 D
Halliwick Rd. N10	24	28 90 A
Hall La. E4	18	36 92 B
Hall La. NW4	22	22 90 C
Hallmead Rd. Sutt	103	25 65 D
Hall Oak Wlk. NW6	46	24 84 B
Hallon Gdns. E1	4	33 81 B
Hallowell Ave. Croy	111	30 64 A
Hallowell Cl. Mit	96	26 68 A
Hallowell Rd. Nthwd	19	09 91 C
Hall Place Cres. Bex	79	50 74 B
Hall Pl. W2	1	26 81 B
Hall Rd. Dart	80	54 75 D
Hall Rd. E11	49	38 85 B
Hall Rd. E15	49	38 85 B
Hall Rd. E6	50	42 83 B
Hall Rd. Islw	70	14 74 B
Hall Rd. NW8	1	26 82 A
Hall Rd. Rom	41	47 88 D
Hall Rd. Rom	30	52 89 B
Hall Rd. Wall	111	28 62 B
Hall St. EC1	3	31 82 B
Hall St. N12	15	26 92 C
Hallsville Rd. E16	58	39 81 D
Hallswelle Rd. NW11	35	24 88 B
Hall The. SE3	77	40 75 A
Hall View. SE9	89	41 72 B
Halons Rd. SE9	90	43 73 A
Halpin Pl. SE17	63	32 78 B
Halsbrook Rd. SE3	77	41 75 B
Halsbury Rd E. Nthlt	43	14 85 A
Halsbury Rd. W12	55	22 80 D
Halsbury Road W. Nthlt	43	14 85 A
Halsey St. SW3	9	27 78 B
Halsham Cl. Surb	101	17 66 B
Halsham Cres. Bark	51	45 85 D
Halsmere Rd. SE5	75	31 76 B
Halstead Ct. N1	48	32 83 D
Halstead Gdns. N21	17	32 94 D
Halstead Rd. E11	39	40 88 B
Halstead Rd. Enf	13	33 96 B
Halstead Rd. Eri	80	51 76 A
Halstead Rd. N21	17	32 94 D
Halston Cl. SW11	74	27 74 D
Halstow Rd. NW10	56	23 82 B
Halstow Rd. SE10	65	40 78 C
Halton Cross St. N1	48	31 83 B
Halton Pl. N1	48	32 83 A
Halton Rd. N1	48	31 84 D
Halt Robin La. Belv	67	49 78 B
Halt Robin Rd. Belv	67	49 78 B
Hambalt Rd. SW4	74	29 74 A
Hamble Cl. Ruis	31	09 86 A
Hambledon Gdns. SE25	97	33 68 B
Hambledon Rd. SW18	85	24 73 B
Hambledown Rd. Sid	90	45 73 A
Hamble St. SW6	73	25 75 B
Hambridge Way. SE24	87	31 73 A
Hambro Ave. Brom	107	40 66 C
Hambrook Rd. SE25	97	34 68 B
Hambro Rd. SW16	96	29 70 B
Hambro Rd. SW16	86	29 71 D
Hambrough Rd. Sthl	53	12 80 C
Ham Cl. Rich	83	17 72 C
Hamden Cres. Dag	41	49 86 D
Ham Dip. Rich	84	19 71 A
Hamelin St. E14	58	38 81 C
Ham Farm Rd. Rich	83	17 71 B
Hamfrith Rd. E15	50	39 84 B
Ham Gate Ave. Rich	83	18 71 A
Hamilton Ave. Ilf	40	44 88 A
Hamilton Ave. N9	17	34 94 A
Hamilton Ave. Rom	29	50 90 D
Hamilton Ave. Surb	102	19 65 A
Hamilton Ave. Sutt	103	24 65 A
Hamilton Cl. Barn	12	27 96 D
Hamilton Cl. Felt	81	09 71 D
Hamilton Cl. N17	25	33 89 B
Hamilton Cl. NW8	1	26 82 B
Hamilton Cres. Har	32	12 86 D
Hamilton Cres. Houn	70	13 74 B
Hamilton Cres. N13	17	31 92 A
Hamilton Ct. W5	54	18 80 B
Hamilton Dri. Rom	30	54 90 C
Hamilton Gdns. NW8	1	26 82 A
Hamilton La. N5	48	31 85 B
Hamilton Mews. W1	6	28 79 B
Hamilton Park. N5	48	31 85 B
Hamilton Park W. N5	48	31 85 B
Hamilton Pl. Sun	91	10 70 D
Hamilton Pl. W1	6	28 80 C
Hamilton Rd. Barn	12	27 96 C
Hamilton Rd. Bexh	79	48 76 C
Hamilton Rd. Brent	60	17 77 B
Hamilton Rd. E15	58	39 82 A
Hamilton Rd. E17	26	36 90 C
Hamilton Rd. Felt	81	09 71 B
Hamilton Rd. Har	33	15 88 A
Hamilton Rd. Ilf	51	43 85 B
Hamilton Rd. N2	23	26 89 A
Hamilton Rd. N9	17	34 94 A
Hamilton Rd. NW10	45	22 85 C
Hamilton Rd. NW11	35	24 87 A
Hamilton Rd. Rom	42	52 88 B
Hamilton Rd. SE27	87	32 71 B
Hamilton Rd. Sid	90	46 71 A
Hamilton Rd. Sthl	53	12 80 D
Hamilton Rd. SW19	95	25 70 D
Hamilton Rd. Th Hth	97	32 68 B
Hamilton Rd. Twick	83	15 73 C
Hamilton Rd. W4	61	21 79 A
Hamilton Rd. W5	54	18 80 A
Hamilton Sq. SE1	8	32 79 B
Hamilton St. SE8	64	37 77 A
Hamilton Terr. NW8	1	26 82 A
Hamilton Way. N13	17	31 92 B
Hamilton Way. N3	23	25 91 A
Hamilton Way. Wall	111	29 62 B
Hamish Rd. SE11	10	30 78 B
Hamlea Cl. SE12	77	40 74 A
Hamlet Cl. Rom	29	49 91 C
Hamlet Gdns. W6	61	22 78 A
Hamlet Rd. Rom	29	49 91 C
Hamlet Rd. SE19	97	34 70 C
Hamlets Way. E3	36	38 82 D
Hamlet The. SE5	75	32 75 B
Hamlin Cres. Pnr	32	11 88 A
Hamlyn Gdns. SE19	97	33 70 C
Hammelton Rd. Brom	99	40 69 A
Hammersley Ave. E16	58	39 81 D
Hammersmith Bridge Rd. W6	62	23 78 C
Hammersmith Bwy. W6	62	23 78 A
Hammersmith Fly. W6	62	23 78 C
Hammersmith Gr. W6	62	23 79 C
Hammersmith Rd. W14	62	24 78 A
Hammersmith Rd. W6	62	23 78 B
Hammett St. EC3	8	33 80 B
Hammond Ave. Mit	96	28 69 D
Hammond Cl. Grnf	43	14 85 D
Hammond Cl. Hamp	92	13 69 A

Street	Page	Ref
Hammond Rd. Enf	13	34 97 D
Hammond Rd. Sthl	59	12 79 C
Hammond St. NW5	47	29 84 A
Hamond Sq. N1	48	33 83 C
Ham Park Rd. E15	50	39 84 D
Ham Park Rd. E7	50	40 84 C
Hampden Ave. Beck	98	36 69 C
Hampden Cl. NW1	47	29 83 D
Hampden Gurney St. W1	1	27 81 D
Hampden La. N17	25	34 90 A
Hampden Rd (off Comus Rd). N19	36	29 86 D
Hampden Rd (off Holloway Rd). N19	36	29 86 B
Hampden Rd. Beck	98	36 69 C
Hampden Rd. Har	20	14 90 C
Hampden Rd. King	94	19 68 A
Hampden Rd. N10	24	28 91 C
Hampden Rd. N17	25	34 90 A
Hampden Rd. N19	36	29 86 D
Hampden Rd. N8	25	31 89 C
Hampden Rd. Rom	29	49 91 D
Hampden Way. N14	16	28 93 B
Hampshire Cl. N18	17	34 92 D
Hampshire Hog La. W6	61	22 78 B
Hampshire Rd. N22	24	30 91 D
Hampshire St. NW5	47	29 84 B
Hampson Way. SW8	74	30 76 B
Hampstead Gdns. NW11	35	25 88 C
Hampstead Green. NW3	47	27 85 C
Hampstead Gr. NW3	35	26 86 C
Hampstead High St. NW3	46	26 85 B
Hampstead Hill Gdns. NW3	47	27 85 A
Hampstead La. N6	36	27 87 B
Hampstead La. NW3	35	26 87 D
Hampstead Rd. NW1	2	29 82 A
Hampstead Sq. NW3	35	26 86 C
Hampstead Way. NW11	35	25 87 B
Hampton Cl. NW6	56	25 82 A
Hampton Cl. SW20	95	23 70 C
Hampton Court Ave. E Mol	101	15 67 A
Hampton Court Par. E Mol	93	15 68 C
Hampton Court Rd. E Mol	93	15 68 B
Hampton Court Rd. Hamp	92	14 69 C
Hampton Court Rd. King	93	17 69 C
Hampton Court Way. E Mol	101	15 67 A
Hampton Court Way. Esh	101	15 65 A
Hampton Court Way. Surb	101	16 66 B
Hampton Ct. N1	48	31 84 B
Hampton La. Felt	82	12 71 A
Hampton Rd. Croy	105	32 67 C
Hampton Rd. E11	38	38 87 D
Hampton Rd. E4	18	36 92 D
Hampton Rd. E7	50	41 85 C
Hampton Rd E. Felt	82	12 72 D
Hampton Rd. Hamp	82	14 71 D
Hampton Rd. Ilf	51	44 85 A
Hampton Rd. Tedd	83	15 71 C
Hampton Rd. Twick	82	14 72 D
Hampton Rd. Wor Pk	102	22 65 B
Hampton Rise. Har	33	18 88 C
Hampton Road W. Felt	82	12 72 C
Hampton St. SE17	63	31 76 B
Ham Ridings. Rich	83	18 71 D
Ham Shades Cl. Sid	90	46 72 C
Ham Sq. Rich	83	17 72 A
Ham St. Rich	83	17 72 A
Ham View. Croy	106	36 67 C
Ham Yd. W1	6	29 80 B
Hanameel St. E16	58	40 80 D
Hanbury Rd. N17	25	34 90 D
Hanbury Rd. W3	61	19 79 D
Hanbury St. E1	4	33 81 B
Hanbury St. E1	4	34 81 A
Hancock Rd. E3	58	38 82 A
Hancock Rd. SE19	97	32 70 B
Handa Wlk. N1	48	32 84 A
Handcroft Rd. Croy	105	31 66 B
Handcroft Rd. Croy	105	31 66 D
Hand Ct. WC1	3	30 81 B
Handel Cl. Edg	21	18 91 B
Handel St. WC1	3	30 82 C
Handel Way. Edg	22	19 91 C
Handen Rd. SE12	77	39 74 B
Handforth Rd. SW9	63	31 77 C
Handley Rd. E9	49	35 83 A
Handside Cl. Wor Pk	103	23 66 D
Hands Wlk. E16	58	40 81 C
Handsworth Ave. E4	26	38 91 B
Handsworth Rd. N17	25	32 89 B
Handtrough Way. E6	51	43 83 D
Hanford Cl. SW18	85	25 73 C
Hanger Ct. W5	55	19 82 C
Hanger Green. W5	55	19 82 C
Hanger Hill. W5	54	18 81 B
Hanger La. W5	54	18 81 B
Hanger Vale La. W5	54	18 81 D
Hanger View Way. W3	55	19 81 C
Hankey Pl. SE1	8	32 79 B
Hanley Rd. N4	36	30 87 C
Hanmer Wlk. N7	36	30 86 B
Hannay Wlk. SW16	86	29 72 B
Hannell Rd. SW6	62	24 77 C
Hannen Rd. SE27	87	31 72 D
Hannibal Rd. E1	57	35 81 A
Hannibal Way. Croy	711	30 63 B
Hannington Rd. SW4	74	28 75 B
Hanover Ave. Felt	81	10 72 A
Hanover Cl. Rich	61	19 77 C
Hanover Cl. Sutt	110	24 64 A
Hanover Gdns. Ilf	28	44 91 C
Hanover Gdns. SE11	63	31 77 A
Hanover Park. SE15	75	34 76 A
Hanover Pl. WC2	3	30 81 C
Hanover Rd. NW10	46	23 83 A
Hanover Rd. SW19	95	26 70 C
Hanover Sq. W1	2	28 81 D
Hanover St. Croy	105	31 65 D
Hanover St. W1	2	28 81 D
Hanover Terr. Islw	71	16 76 A
Hanover Terr Mews. NW1	1	27 82 B
Hanover Terr. NW1	1	27 82 B
Hanover Way. Bexh	79	47 75 B
Hanover Yd. N1	48	31 83 D
Hansard Mews. W14	62	23 79 B
Hansart Way. Enf	13	31 97 A
Hans Cres. SW1	5	27 79 D
Hanshaw Dri. Edg	22	20 90 B
Hansler Gr. E Mol	92	14 68 D
Hansler Rd. SE22	75	33 74 B
Hansol Rd. Bexh	79	48 74 A
Hanson Cl. SW12	86	28 73 B
Hanson Gdns. Sthl	59	12 79 A
Hanson St. W1	2	29 81 A
Hans Pl. SW1	5	27 79 D
Hans Rd. SW3	5	27 79 D
Hans St. SW1	5	27 79 D
Hanway Pl. W1	2	29 81 D
Hanway Rd. W7	54	15 81 C
Hanway St. W1	2	29 81 D
Hanworth Rd. Felt	81	10 73 D
Hanworth Rd. Hamp	82	13 71 C
Hanworth Rd. Houn	70	13 74 C
Hanworth Rd. Sun	91	10 70 C
Hanworth Terr. Houn	70	13 75 D
Hapgood Cl. Grnf	43	14 85 D
Harben Rd. NW6	46	26 84 C
Harberson Rd. E15	50	39 83 B
Harberson Rd. SW12	86	28 73 D
Harberton Rd. N19	36	29 87 C
Harbet Rd. E4	18	35 92 D
Harbet Rd. W2	1	27 81 A
Harbinger Rd. E14	64	37 78 B
Harbledown Rd. SW6	73	25 76 A
Harbord St. SW6	73	23 76 B
Harborough Ave. Sid	90	45 73 B
Harborough Rd. SW16	86	30 71 B
Harbour Rd. SE5	75	32 75 A
Harbridge Ave. SW15	84	22 73 A
Harbury Rd. Cars	711	27 63 C
Harbut Rd. SW11	73	26 75 D
Harbut Rd. SW11	73	26 75 D
Harcombe Rd. N16	37	33 86 C
Harcourt Ave. E12	50	42 85 D
Harcourt Ave. Sid	79	47 74 C
Harcourt Ave. Wall	711	28 64 B
Harcourt Cl. Islw	71	16 75 A
Harcourt Field. Wall	711	28 64 B
Harcourt Rd. Bexh	79	48 75 C
Harcourt Rd. E15	50	39 83 D
Harcourt Rd. N22	24	29 90 B
Harcourt Rd. SE4	76	36 75 B
Harcourt Rd. SW19	95	25 70 C
Harcourt Rd. Th Hth	105	31 67 C
Harcourt Rd. Wall	711	28 64 B
Harcourt St. W1	1	27 81 A
Harcourt Terr. SW10	62	26 78 C
Hardcourts Cl. W Wick	106	37 65 D
Hardel Rise. SW2	87	31 73 D
Hardel Wlk. SE24	87	31 73 A
Harden Ct. SE18	65	42 78 A
Hardens Manorway. SE7	65	41 79 D
Harders Rd. Mews. SE15	75	34 76 B
Harders Rd. SE15	75	34 76 D
Hardess St. SE24	75	32 75 A
Hardie Cl. NW10	45	20 85 D
Hardie Rd. Dag	41	50 86 C
Harding Cl. SE17	63	32 77 A
Hardinge Rd. N18	17	33 92 C
Hardinge Rd. NW10	46	23 83 A
Hardinge St. E1	57	35 81 C
Harding Rd. Bexh	79	48 76 D
Hardings La. SE20	90	35 70 B
Hardley Cres. Horn	30	53 89 D
Hardman Rd. King	93	18 69 C
Hardman Rd. SE7	65	40 78 D
Hardwicke Ave. Houn	70	13 76 A
Hardwicke Rd. N13	16	30 91 A
Hardwicke Rd. Rich	83	17 71 A
Hardwicke Rd. W4	61	20 78 B
Hardwick St. Bark	51	44 83 A
Hardwick Green. W13	54	16 81 B
Hardwick St. EC1	3	31 82 A
Hardwick's Way. SW18	73	25 74 A
Hardwidge St. SE1	8	33 79 A
Hardy Cl. Pnr	32	11 87 B
Hardy Pas. N22	25	31 90 C
Hardy Rd. SE3	65	39 77 B
Hardy Rd. SW19	95	25 70 D
Hardy Way. Enf	13	31 97 A
Hare and Billet Rd. SE3	76	38 76 D
Harebell Way. Rom	30	53 91 D
Harecourt Rd. N1	48	32 84 A
Hare Ct. EC4	3	31 81 C
Haredale Rd. SE24	75	32 75 C
Haredon Cl. SE23	88	35 73 B
Harefield Ave. Sutt	110	24 62 A
Harefield Cl. Enf	13	31 97 A
Harefield. Esh	101	15 65 C
Harefield Mews. SE4	76	36 75 B
Harefield Rd. N8	36	29 88 B
Harefield Rd. SE4	76	36 75 B
Harefield Rd. SW16	96	30 70 D
Hare Hall La. Rom	30	52 89 D
Hare Marsh. E2	57	34 82 C
Hare Row. E2	57	34 83 D
Haresfield Rd. Dag	52	49 84 A
Hare St. SE18	65	43 79 C
Hare Wlk. N1	48	33 83 C
Harewood Ave. Nthlt	43	12 84 D
Harewood Ave. NW1	1	27 82 C
Harewood Cl. Nthlt	43	12 84 D
Harewood Dri. Ilf	27	42 90 D
Harewood Pl. W1	2	28 81 D
Harewood Rd. Islw	71	15 76 B
Harewood Rd. S Croy	112	33 63 A
Harewood Rd. SW19	96	27 70 A
Harewood Row. NW1	1	27 81 A
Harewood Terr. Sthl	12	12 78 B
Harfield Gdns. SE5	75	33 75 A
Harfield Rd. Sun	11	11 69 D
Harford Cl. E4	18	37 94 B
Harford Rd. E4	18	37 94 B
Harford St. E2	57	36 82 C
Harford Wlk. N2	23	26 89 D
Hargood Rd. SE3	77	41 76 A
Hargrave Park. N19	36	29 86 A
Hargrave Pl. N7	47	29 85 D
Hargrave Rd. N19	36	29 86 A
Hargwyne St. SW9	74	30 75 B
Haringey Park. N8	36	30 88 C
Haringey Pas. N8	37	31 88 B
Haringey Pas. N8	25	31 89 C
Haringey Rd. N8	24	30 89 C
Harington Terr. N18	17	32 92 D
Harington Terr. N9	17	32 92 D
Harkett Cl. Har	21	15 90 D
Harland Ave. Croy	105	34 65 B
Harland Ave. Sid	90	45 72 A
Harland Rd. SE12	89	40 73 C
Harlech Gdns. Houn	59	11 77 A
Harlech Rd. N14	16	30 93 C
Harlequin Ave. Brent	60	16 77 A
Harlequin Rd. Tedd	93	16 70 D
Harlescott Rd. SE15	76	35 75 D
Harlesden Cl. Rom	30	54 91 B
Harlesden Gdns. NW10	45	21 83 B
Harlesden Rd. NW10	45	22 83 A
Harlesden Rd. Rom	30	54 91 B
Harleston Cl. E5	38	35 86 A
Harley Cl. Wem	44	17 84 B
Harley Cres. Har	20	14 89 D
Harley Ct. N12	15	26 93 C
Harleyford. Brom	99	41 69 A
Harleyford Rd. SE11	10	30 77 B
Harleyford St. SE11	63	31 77 A
Harley Gdns. SW10	62	26 78 C
Harley Gr. E3	57	36 82 B
Harley Pl. W1	2	28 81 B
Harley Rd. Har	20	14 89 D
Harley Rd. NW10	45	21 83 C
Harley Rd. NW3	47	27 84 C

Street	Page	Grid
Harley St. W1	2	28 81 B
Harlington Rd. Bexh	79	48 75 A
Harlington Road E. Felt	82	11 73 C
Harlington Road W. Felt	69	10 74 D
Harlow Gdns. Rom	29	50 91 A
Harlow Rd. N13	17	32 93 D
Harlyn Dri. Pnr	19	10 89 B
Harman Ave. Wdf Gn	27	39 91 B
Harman Cl. E4	18	38 92 B
Harman Cl. NW2	35	24 86 C
Harman Dri. Sid	78	45 75 D
Harman Rd. Enf	13	33 95 B
Harmony Cl. Wall	111	30 62 A
Harmood Gr. NW1	47	28 84 D
Harmood Pl. NW1	47	28 84 D
Harmood St. NW1	47	28 84 D
Harmsworth St. SE17	63	31 78 D
Harmsworth Way. N20	15	24 94 D
Harness Rd. SE28	66	46 79 A
Harold Ave. Belv	67	48 78 C
Harold Ct. Tedd	83	15 71 C
Harold Gibbons Ct. SE7	65	41 77 A
Harold Pl. SE11	63	31 78 C
Harold Rd. E11	39	39 87 C
Harold Rd. E13	50	40 83 B
Harold Rd. E4	18	38 93 C
Harold Rd. N15	37	33 88 B
Harold Rd. N8	24	30 89 D
Harold Rd. NW10	55	20 82 B
Harold Rd. SE19	97	33 70 C
Harold Rd. Sutt	110	26 64 B
Harold Rd. Wdf Gn	27	40 90 A
Haroldstone Rd. E17	38	36 88 A
Harold View. Rom	30	54 90 D
Harp Alley. EC4	3	31 81 D
Harpenden Rd. E12	39	41 88 A
Harpenden Rd. SE27	87	31 72 B
Harper Rd. SE1	8	32 79 C
Harper's Yd. N17	25	33 90 B
Harp La. EC3	8	33 80 A
Harp La. EC3	8	33 80 A
Harpley Sq. E1	57	35 82 D
Harpour Rd. Bark	51	44 84 A
Harp Rd. W7	54	15 81 B
Harpsden St. SW11	74	28 76 A
Harpur St. WC1	3	30 81 B
Harraden Rd. SE3	77	41 76 A
Harrap St. E14	58	38 80 B
Harriers Cl. W5	54	18 80 A
Harries Rd. Hay	53	11 82 C
Harriet Cl. E8	48	34 83 A
Harriet Gdns. Croy	105	34 65 A
Harriet St. SW1	5	27 79 B
Harriet Wlk. SW1	5	27 79 B
Harringay Gdns. N15	25	31 89 D
Harringay Rd. N15	25	31 89 D
Harrington Cl. Croy	104	30 65 A
Harrington Gdns. SW7	62	26 78 A
Harrington Hill. E5	37	34 87 D
Harrington Rd. E11	39	39 87 C
Harrington Rd. SE25	97	34 68 D
Harrington Rd. SW7	62	26 78 B
Harrington Sq. NW1	47	29 83 C
Harrington St. NW1	2	29 82 A
Harrington St. NW1	47	29 83 C
Harrington Way. SE18	65	41 79 D
Harriott Cl. E10	65	39 78 B
Harris Cl. Enf	13	31 97 B
Harris Cl. Houn	70	13 76 A
Harrison Cl. Nthwd	19	04 91 A
Harrison Rd. Dag	52	49 84 B
Harrison's Rise. Croy	105	31 65 D
Harrison St. WC1	3	30 82 A
Harris Rd. Bexh	79	48 76 B
Harris Rd. Dag	52	48 85 D
Harris St. E17	38	36 87 B
Harris St. SE5	63	32 77 D
Harris Way. Sun	91	09 69 A
Harrold Rd. Dag	51	46 85 D
Harrow Ave. Enf	13	33 95 D
Harroway Rd. SW1	73	26 76 D
Harrowby St. W1	1	27 81 C
Harrow Cres. Rom	30	52 91 D
Harrowdene Cl. Wem	44	17 85 B
Harrowdene Gdns. Tedd	93	16 70 C
Harrowdene Rd. Wem	44	17 85 B
Harrow Dri. Horn	42	53 87 A
Harrow Dri. N9	17	33 94 D
Harrowgate Rd. E9	49	36 84 C
Harrow Green. E11	39	39 86 C
Harrow La. E14	57	37 80 B
Harrow Manor Way. SE2	67	47 79 C
Harrow Park. Har	33	15 86 A
Harrow Pl. E1	4	33 81 D
Harrow Rd. Ashf	81	07 72 A
Harrow Rd. Bark	51	45 83 A
Harrow Rd. Cars	111	27 63 A
Harrow Rd. E11	39	39 86 D
Harrow Rd. E6	50	42 83 A
Harrow Rd Fly. NW1	1	27 81 A
Harrow Rd. Ilf	51	44 85 A
Harrow Rd. NW10	56	23 82 A
Harrow Rd. W10	56	24 82 C
Harrow Rd. W2	1	26 81 A
Harrow Rd. W9	56	25 82 C
Harrow Rd. Wem	44	16 85 D
Harrow Rd. Wem	45	19 84 A
Harrow View. Har	59	14 79 D
Harrow View Rd. W5	54	16 82 D
Harrow Way. Shep	91	08 69 C
Harrow Weald Park. Har	20	14 91 B
Harte Rd. Houn	70	12 76 D
Hartfield Cres. SW19	95	24 70 D
Hartfield Cres. W.Wick	107	40 65 C
Hartfield Gr. SE20	98	35 69 A
Hartfield Rd. SW19	95	24 70 D
Hartfield Terr. E3	49	37 83 C
Hartford Ave. Har	21	16 89 B
Hartford Rd. Bex	79	49 74 C
Hartford Rd. Eps	109	19 63 B
Hart Gr. Sthl	53	13 81 A
Hart Gr. W5	55	19 80 C
Hartham Cl. Islw	71	16 76 A
Hartham Cl. N7	47	30 85 C
Hartham Rd. Islw	71	16 76 A
Hartham Rd. N17	25	33 90 D
Hartham Rd. N7	47	30 85 C
Harting Rd. SE9	89	42 72 C
Hartington Cl. Har	44	15 85 A
Hartington Cl. W4	61	19 77 D
Hartington Rd. E16	58	40 81 D
Hartington Rd. E17	38	36 88 C
Hartington Rd. Sthl	59	12 79 C
Hartington Rd. SW8	10	30 77 C
Hartington Rd. Twick	71	16 74 D
Hartington Rd. W13	54	16 80 B
Hartington Rd. W4	72	20 76 A
Hartismere Rd. SW6	62	24 77 D
Hartlake Rd. E9	49	36 84 A
Hartland Dri. Ruis	31	10 86 D
Hartland Dri. Ruis	43	11 85 A
Hartland Rd. E15	50	39 84 D
Hartland Rd. Hamp	82	13 71 B
Hartland Rd. Horn	42	52 86 A
Hartland Rd. Islw	71	16 75 A
Hartland Rd. Mord	103	25 66 A
Hartland Rd. N11	16	27 92 D
Hartland Rd. NW1	47	28 84 D
Hartland Rd. NW6	46	24 83 D
Hartland Way. Croy	106	36 65 A
Hartland Way. Mord	103	24 66 B
Hartley Ave. E6	50	42 83 A
Hartley Cl. Brom	99	42 69 D
Hartley Hse.SE1	63	33 78 B
Hartley Rd. Croy	105	32 66 A
Hartley Rd. E11	39	39 87 D
Hartley Rd. Well	67	47 77 C
Hartley St. E2	57	35 82 A
Hartnoll St. N7	47	30 85 D
Harton Cl. Brom	99	41 69 B
Harton Rd. N9	17	34 93 B
Harton St. SE8	75	33 76 A
Hartshorn Alley. EC3	4	33 81 C
Harts La. Bark	51	43 84 B
Harts La. SE14	76	36 76 A
Hartslock Dri. SE2	67	47 79 B
Hartsmead Rd. SE9	89	42 72 B
Hart St. EC3	8	33 80 A
Hartsway. Enf	14	35 96 C
Hartswood Rd. W12	61	21 79 D
Hartsworth Cl. E13	50	39 83 D
Hartville Rd. SE18	66	45 78 A
Hartwell Drive. E4	26	38 91 A
Hartwell St. E8	48	33 84 B
Harvard Hill. W4	61	19 77 B
Harvard La. (Footpath). W4	61	20 78 C
Harvard Rd. Islw	71	15 76 A
Harvard Rd. SE13	76	38 74 A
Harvard Rd. W4	61	19 78 D
Harvel Cres. SE2	67	47 78 D
Harvest Bank Rd. W.Wick	107	39 65 D
Harvest Ct. Shep	91	07 68 C
Harvester Rd. Eps	109	20 62 D
Harvester's Cl. Islw	70	14 74 B
Harvest Rd. Felt	81	10 72 C
Harvey Gdns. E11	39	39 87 D
Harvey Gdns. SE7	65	41 78 D
Harvey Rd. E11	39	39 87 D
Harvey Rd. Houn	82	12 73 B
Harvey Rd. Ilf	51	43 85 D
Harvey Rd. N8	36	30 88 B
Harvey Rd. Nthlt	43	11 84 C
Harvey Rd. SE5	75	32 76 B
Harvey Rd. SE5	75	32 76 B
Harvey's Bldgs. WC2	7	30 80 A
Harvey's La. Rom	42	51 86 A
Harvey St. N1	48	32 83 B
Harvington Wlk. E8	48	34 84 C
Harvist Rd. NW6	46	24 83 C
Harwell Cl. Ruis	31	08 87 D
Harwell Pas. N2	24	27 89 D
Harwood Ave. Brom	99	40 69 D
Harwood Ave. Horn	30	54 89 A
Harwood Ave. Mit	96	27 68 A
Harwood Rd. SW6	62	25 77 C
Harwoods Yd. N21	17	31 94 A
Harwood Terr. SW6	73	25 76 B
Hascombe Terr. SE5	75	32 76 D
Haselbury Green. N9	17	33 93 C
Haselbury La. N9	17	33 93 C
Haselbury Rd. N18	17	33 92 A
Haselbury Rd. N9	17	33 93 C
Haseley End. SE23	88	35 73 A
Haselrigge Rd. SW4	74	29 75 D
Haseltine Rd. SE26	88	36 71 B
Haselwood Dri. Enf	13	31 96 D
Haskard Rd. Dag	52	47 85 B
Hasker St. SW3	9	27 78 A
Haslam Ave. Sutt	103	24 66 C
Haslam Cl. N1	48	31 84 C
Haslam Ct. Ruis	31	08 86 A
Haslemere Ave. Barn	16	27 94 D
Haslemere Ave. Houn	70	11 76 C
Haslemere Ave. Mit	95	26 69 D
Haslemere Ave. NW4	35	23 88 D
Haslemere Ave. SW18	85	25 72 B
Haslemere Ave. W13	60	16 79 C
Haslemere Ave. W7	60	16 79 C
Haslemere Cl. Hamp	82	12 71 D
Haslemere Cl. Wall	111	30 64 C
Haslemere Gdns. N3	23	24 89 D
Haslemere Rd. Bexh	79	48 76 D
Haslemere Rd. Ilf	40	45 86 B
Haslemere Rd. N21	17	31 94 D
Haslemere Rd. N8	36	30 87 A
Haslemere Rd. Th Hth	105	31 67 B
Haslett Rd. Shep	91	09 69 C
Hasluck Gdns. Barn	11	26 95 C
Hassard St. E2	48	33 83 D
Hassendean Rd. SE3	65	40 77 D
Hassett Rd. E9	49	36 84 A
Hassocks Cl. SE26	87	34 72 D
Hassocks Rd. SW16	96	29 69 B
Hassop Rd. NW2	46	23 86 B
Hassop Wlk. SE9	89	42 71 A
Hasted Rd. SE7	65	41 78 D
Hastings Ave. Ilf	28	44 89 C
Hastings Cl. Barn	11	26 96 C
Hastings Cl. SE15	63	34 77 C
Hastings Pl. Croy	105	33 66 D
Hastings Rd. Brom	107	42 65 A
Hastings Rd. Croy	105	33 66 D
Hastings Rd. N11	16	29 92 D
Hastings Rd. Rom	42	52 88 B
Hastings Rd. W13	54	16 80 B
Hastings St. WC1	3	30 82 A
Hatcham Park Mews. SE14	76	35 76 B
Hatcham Park Rd. SE14	64	35 77 D
Hatcham Rd. SE15	64	35 77 A
Hatchard Rd. N19	36	29 86 B
Hatchcroft. NW4	22	22 89 B
Hatchett Rd. Felt	81	08 73 C
Hatch Gr. Rom	29	48 89 C
Hatch La. E4	18	38 92 B
Hatch Rd. SW16	96	30 69 C
Hatcliffe Cl. SE3	77	39 75 B
Hatcliffe St. E10	65	39 78 D
Hatfield Cl. Ilf	28	43 90 D
Hatfield Cl. Mit	95	26 68 D
Hatfield Cl. SE14	64	35 77 D
Hatfield Mead. Mord	103	25 67 A
Hatfield Rd. Dag	52	48 84 C
Hatfield Rd. E15	50	39 85 C
Hatfield Rd. W13	54	16 80 C
Hatfield Rd. W4	61	20 79 B
Hatfields. SE1	7	31 80 C
Hathaway Cl. Stan	21	16 91 A
Hathaway Cres. E12	50	42 84 B
Hathaway Gdns. W13	54	16 81 A
Hathaway Rd. Croy	105	31 66 B
Hatherleigh Cl. Mord	95	25 68 C
Hatherleigh Rd. Ruis	31	10 86 A
Hatherleigh Way. Rom	30	53 90 B
Hatherley Cres. Sid	90	46 72 A

Street	Pg	Grid
Hatherley Gdns. E6	58	41 82 B
Hatherley Gdns. N8	36	30 88 C
Hatherley Gr. W2	56	25 81 D
Hatherley Mews. E17	26	37 89 C
Hatherley Rd. E17	26	37 89 C
Hatherley Rd. Rich	71	18 76 B
Hatherley Rd. Sid	90	46 72 C
Hatherley St. SW1	10	29 78 A
Hathern Gdns. SE9	90	43 71 A
Hatherop Rd. Hamp	92	12 70 D
Hathersage Ct. N5	48	32 85 D
Hathorne Cl. SE15	76	35 76 C
Hathway Gdns. Rom	41	47 88 B
Hathway St. SE15	76	35 76 D
Hatley Ave. Ilf	28	44 89 C
Hatley Cl. N11	16	27 92 D
Hatley Rd. N4	36	30 86 B
Hatteraick St. SE16	64	35 79 A
Hatton Cl. SE18	66	44 77 D
Hatton Ct. Chis	99	42 70 D
Hatton Gdn. EC1	3	31 81 A
Hatton Gdns. Mit	104	27 67 B
Hatton Green. Felt	69	10 75 C
Hatton Pl. EC1	3	31 81 A
Hatton Rd. Croy	105	31 66 C
Hatton Rd. Felt	69	09 74 A
Hatton Row. NW8	1	26 82 D
Hatton St. NW8	1	26 82 D
Hatton Wall. EC1	3	31 81 A
Haunch of Venison Yd. W1	2	28 81 D
Havana Cl. Rom	42	51 88 A
Havana Rd. SW19	85	25 72 A
Havannah St. E14	64	37 79 A
Havant Rd. E17	26	38 89 A
Havant Way (off Garnies Cl.). SE15	63	33 77 D
Havelock Pl. Har	33	15 88 C
Havelock Rd. Belv	67	48 78 B
Havelock Rd. Brom	99	41 68 C
Havelock Rd. Croy	105	33 65 B
Havelock Rd. Dart	80	52 74 D
Havelock Rd. Har	21	15 89 A
Havelock Rd. N17	25	34 90 C
Havelock Rd. Sthl	59	13 79 C
Havelock Rd. SW17	85	26 71 C
Havelock St. Ilf	40	46 86 B
Havelock St. N1	47	30 83 A
Havelock Terr. SW8	74	29 76 A
Havelock Wlk. SE23	88	35 72 A
Haven Cl. SW19	85	23 72 D
Haven Green Ct. W5	54	17 81 D
Haven Green. W5	54	17 81 D
Havenhurst Rise. Enf	13	31 97 C
Haven La. W5	54	18 81 C
Haven Mews. E3	57	36 81 B
Haven Rd. Ashf	81	07 71 B
Haven St. NW1	47	28 84 D
Haven The. Rich	72	19 75 A
Havenwood. Wem	34	19 86 D
Haverfield Gdns. Rich	61	19 77 C
Haverfield Rd. E3	57	36 82 A
Haverford Way. Edg	21	18 90 B
Haverhill Rd. E4	18	38 94 C
Haverhill Rd. SW12	86	29 73 C
Havering Dri. Rom	30	51 89 A
Havering Gdns. Rom	41	47 88 B
Havering Rd. Rom	29	50 90 D
Havering St. E1	57	35 81 D
Haversham Cl. Twick	83	17 73 B
Haverstock Hill. NW3	47	27 84 B
Haverstock Rd. NW5	47	28 85 C
Haverstock St. N1	48	31 83 D
Haverthwaite Rd. Orp	108	44 65 D
Havil St. SE5	75	33 76 A
Hawarden Gr. SE24	87	32 73 A
Hawarden Rd. E17	26	35 89 D
Hawbridge Rd. E11	38	38 87 D
Hawes Cl. Nthwd	19	09 91 D
Hawes La. W Wick	106	38 66 D
Hawes Rd. Brom	99	40 69 B
Hawes Rd. N18	25	34 91 B
Hawes St. N1	48	31 84 D
Hawgood St. E3	57	37 81 A
Hawkdene. E4	14	38 95 D
Hawke Park Rd. N22	25	31 89 B
Hawker Cl. Wall	111	30 63 C
Hawke Rd. SE19	97	33 70 A
Hawkesbury Rd. SW15	72	22 74 B
Hawkesfield Rd. SE23	88	36 72 B
Hawksley Cl. Twick	83	16 71 A
Hawkes Rd. Mit	96	27 69 B
Hawkesworth Cl. Nthwd	19	09 91 C
Hawkewood Rd. Sun	91	10 68 B
Hawkfield Ct. Islw	71	15 76 C
Hawkhurst Gdns. Rom	29	50 91 B
Hawkhurst Rd. SW16	96	29 69 B
Hawkhurst Rd. N.Mal	102	20 67 B
Hawkhurst Wa W Wick	106	37 65 B
Hawkinge Wlk. Orp	100	46 68 B
Hawkins Cl. Har	32	14 87 B
Hawkley Gdns. SE27	87	31 72 B
Hawkridge Cl. Rom	41	47 88 C
Hawkshaw Cl. SW2	86	30 73 A
Hawkshead Cl. Brom	99	39 70 C
Hawkshead Rd. NW10	45	21 84 D
Hawkshead Rd. W4	61	21 79 A
Hawkslade Rd. SE15	76	35 74 B
Hawksley Rd. N16	37	33 88 C
Hawks Mews. SE10	64	38 77 C
Hawksmoor St. W6	62	23 77 B
Hawksmouth. E4	18	38 94 A
Hawks Pas. King	93	18 69 D
Hawks Rd. King	93	18 69 D
Hawkstone Rd. SE16	64	35 78 A
Hawkwell Wlk (off Maldon Cl). N1	48	32 83 A
Hawkwood Cres. E4	14	37 95 D
Hawkwood La. Chis	100	34 87 D
Hawkwood Mount. E5	37	34 87 D
Hawlands Dri. Pnr	32	12 87 A
Hawley Cl. Hamp	92	12 70 B
Hawley Cres. NW1	47	28 84 D
Hawley Mews. NW1	47	28 84 D
Hawley Rd. NW1	47	28 84 D
Hawley St. NW1	47	28 84 D
Hawley Way. Ashf	81	07 71 D
Hawstead Rd. SE6	76	37 74 D
Hawthorn Ave. N13	16	30 92 C
Hawthorn Ave. Th Hth	97	31 69 B
Hawthorn Cl. Hamp	82	13 71 C
Hawthorn Cl. Orp	108	44 67 D
Hawthorn Cl. Rich	72	19 76 B
Hawthornden Cl. Brom	107	40 65 A
Hawthorndene Rd. Brom	107	39 65 B
Hawthorn Dri. Har	32	13 88 C
Hawthorne Ave. Cars	111	28 63 C
Hawthorne Ave. Har	33	16 88 C
Hawthorne Ave. Mit	95	26 69 D
Hawthorne Ave. Ruis	31	10 87 B
Hawthorne Cl. Brom	99	42 68 B
Hawthorne Cl. N1	48	33 84 A
Hawthorne Cl. Sutt	103	26 65 A
Hawthorne Farm Ave. Nthlt	43	12 83 A
Hawthorn Gr. NW9	34	20 87 A
Hawthorne Rd. Brom	99	42 68 B
Hawthorn Rd. E17	26	37 89 A
Hawthorn Way. N9	17	33 93 B
Hawthorn Gdns. W5	60	17 79 D
Hawthorn Gr. SE20	97	34 69 B
Hawthorn Hatch. Brent	60	16 77 D
Hawthorn Mews. NW7	23	24 90 A
Hawthorn Rd. Bexh	79	48 75 D
Hawthorn Rd. Brent	60	16 77 D
Hawthorn Rd. N18	17	33 92 D
Hawthorn Rd. N8	24	30 89 A
Hawthorn Rd. NW10	45	22 84 C
Hawthorn Rd. Sutt	111	27 63 A
Hawthorn Rd. Wall	111	28 63 D
Hawthorn Way. Shep	91	08 68 D
Hawthorn Wlk. W10	56	24 82 C
Hawtrey Ave. Nthlt	43	11 83 D
Hawtrey Dri. Ruis	31	10 87 A
Hawtrey Rd. NW3	47	27 84 C
Haxted Rd. Brom	99	40 69 B
Hayant Wlk. SW20	95	24 68 A
Hayburn Way. Horn	42	51 87 D
Hay Cl. E15	50	39 84 C
Haycroft Gdns. NW10	45	22 83 A
Haycroft Rd. Surb	101	18 65 C
Haycroft Rd. SW2	74	30 74 A
Hay Currie St. E14	57	37 81 D
Hayday Rd. E16	58	40 81 A
Hayden's Pl. W11	56	24 81 D
Hayden Way. Rom	29	50 90 C
Haydock Ave. Nthlt	43	13 84 A
Haydock Green. Nthlt	43	13 84 A
Haydon Cl. NW9	22	20 89 C
Haydon Dri. Pnr	19	10 89 C
Haydon Park Rd. SW19	85	25 71 D
Haydon Rd. Dag	41	47 86 A
Haydon's Rd. SW19	95	26 70 A
Haydon St. EC3	8	33 80 B
Haydon Wlk. EC3	4	33 81 D
Hayes Chase. W Wick	106	38 67 D
Hayes Cres. Brom	107	40 65 A
Hayes Cres. NW11	35	24 88 B
Hayes Cres. Sutt	110	23 64 B
Hayes Ct. SW2	86	30 73 C
Hayesford Park Dri. Brom	107	39 67 B
Hayes Gdn. Brom	107	40 66 C
Hayes Hill. Brom	107	39 66 C
Hayes Hill Rd. Brom	107	39 66 D
Hayes La. Beck	98	38 68 D
Hayes La. Brom	108	46 67 C
Hayes Mead Rd. Brom	107	39 66 C
Hayes Pl. NW1	1	27 82 C
Hayes Rd. Brom	99	40 68 C
Hayes Rd. Sthl	59	11 78 A
Hayes St. Brom	107	40 66 D
Hayes Way. Beck	98	38 68 D
Hayes Way. Beck	99	39 66 C
Hayes Wood Ave. Brom	107	40 66 D
Hayfield Pas. E1	57	35 82 C
Hayfield Rd. Orp	108	46 67 A
Hayfield Yd. E1	57	35 82 C
Haygarth Pl. SW19	85	23 71 D
Hay Hill. W1	6	28 80 B
Hayland Cl. NW9	22	20 89 D
Hay La. NW9	22	20 89 A
Hayles St. SE11	63	31 78 B
Hayles St. SE11	7	31 79 D
Haylett Gdns. King	93	17 68 D
Hayling Ave. Felt	81	10 72 C
Hayling Cl (off Pellerin Rd). N16	48	33 85 C
Hayling Ct. Sutt	110	23 64 A
Hayman St. N1	48	31 84 D
Haymarket Arc. SW1	6	29 80 B
Haymarket. SW1	6	29 80 B
Haymer Gdns. Wor Pk	102	22 65 C
Haymerle Rd. SE15	63	34 77 A
Hayne Rd. Beck	98	36 69 B
Haynes Cl. N17	25	34 91 D
Haynes Cl. SE3	77	39 75 A
Haynes La. SE19	97	33 70 A
Haynes Park Ct. Horn	42	53 88 A
Haynes Rd. Horn	30	53 89 D
Haynes Rd. Wem	44	18 84 C
Hayne St. EC1	3	31 81 B
Hay's La. SE1	8	33 80 C
Haysleigh Gdns. SE20	97	34 69 C
Hay's Mews. W1	6	28 80 D
Haysoms Cl. Rom	30	51 89 C
Hay St. E2	48	34 83 A
Hays Wlk. Sutt	110	23 62 D
Hayter Rd. SW2	74	30 74 B
Hayton Cl. E8	48	33 84 B
Hayward Cl. Dart	79	50 74 A
Hayward Cl. SW19	95	25 69 B
Hayward Gdns. SW15	73	23 74 C
Hayward Rd. N20	15	26 93 A
Hayward's Pl. EC1	3	31 82 D
Haywood Cl. Pnr	20	11 90 D
Haywood Rd. Brom	99	41 68 D
Hazelbank Rd. SE6	88	38 72 B
Hazelbank Rd. SE6	89	39 72 A
Hazel Bank. Surb	102	20 66 C
Hazelbourne Rd. SW12	74	29 74 C
Hazelbrouck Gdns. Ilf	28	44 91 D
Hazel Cl. Brent	60	16 77 D
Hazel Cl. Horn	42	52 86 D
Hazel Cl. Mit	96	29 68 D
Hazel Cl. N13	17	32 92 D
Hazel Cl. N19	36	29 86 A
Hazel Cl. SE15	75	34 76 C
Hazel Cl. Twick	82	14 73 A
Hazelcroft. Pnr	20	13 91 B
Hazel Cl. W5	54	18 80 A
Hazeldene Dri. Pnr	20	11 89 A
Hazeldene Rd. Ilf	40	46 86 B
Hazeldene Rd. Well	79	47 76 C
Hazeldon Rd. SE4	76	36 74 A
Hazel Dri.Eri	80	52 76 B
Hazeleigh Gdns. Wdf Gn	27	42 91 A
Hazel Gr. Enf	13	34 95 C
Hazel Gr. Orp	108	43 65 B
Hazel Gr. Rom	29	48 89 A
Hazel Gr. SE26	88	35 71 B
Hazel Gr. Wem	44	18 83 A
Hazelhurst. Beck	98	38 69 B
Hazelhurst Ct. SE6	88	38 71 C
Hazelhurst Rd. SW17	85	26 71 B
Hazel La. Rich	83	18 72 A
Hazell Cres. Rom	29	49 90 B
Hazellville Rd. N19	36	29 87 D
Hazel Mead. Eps	109	22 62 C
Hazelmere Cl. Felt	69	09 74 C
Hazelmere Cl. Nthlt	43	12 83 D
Hazelmere Gdns. Horn	42	53 88 A
Hazelmere Rd. Nthlt	43	12 83 D
Hazelmere Rd. NW6	46	25 83 A
Hazelmere Rd. Orp	100	44 68 D
Hazelmere Way. Brom	107	40 67 C
Hazelmere Wlk. Nthlt	43	12 83 D
Hazel Rd. Eri	80	52 76 A

Hazel Rd. NW10	56	23 82 A	
Hazel Rise. Horn	42	53 88 C	
Hazeltree La. Nthlt	53	12 82 A	
Hazel Way. E4	26	36 91 B	
Hazel Way. SE1	63	33 78 B	
Hazel Wlk. Brom	108	43 67 C	
Hazelwood Ave. Mord	95	25 68 D	
Hazelwood Cl. W5	60	18 79 A	
Hazelwood Cres. N13	17	31 92 A	
Hazelwood Cres. W10	56	24 82 D	
Hazelwood Ct. Surb	101	18 67 C	
Hazelwood Dri. Pnr	19	10 90 D	
Hazelwood House. N13	17	31 92 B	
Hazelwood La. N13	17	31 92 A	
Hazelwood Rd. E17	38	36 88 A	
Hazelwood Rd. Enf	13	34 95 C	
Hazlebury Rd. SW6	73	25 76 D	
Hazledean Rd. Croy	105	32 65 B	
Hazledean Rd. NW10	45	20 84 D	
Hazledene Rd. W4	61	20 77 A	
Hazlemere Gdns. Wor Pk	102	22 66 D	
Hazlewell Rd. SW15	73	23 74 A	
Hazlewood Cres. W10	56	24 82 C	
Hazlitt Mews. W14	62	24 79 C	
Hazlitt Rd. W14	62	24 79 C	
Heacham Ave. Ruis	31	08 86 A	
Headcorn Pl. Th Hth	96	30 68 B	
Headcorn Rd. Brom	85	40 71 C	
Headcorn Rd. N17	25	33 91 C	
Headcorn Rd. Th Hth	96	30 68 D	
Headfort Pl. SW1	6	28 79 A	
Headington Rd. SW18	85	26 72 A	
Headlam Rd. SW4	86	29 73 B	
Headlam St. E1	57	34 82 D	
Headley App. Ilf	40	43 88 B	
Headley Ave. Wall	111	30 64 D	
Headley Cl. Eps	109	19 63 A	
Headley Dri. Ilf	40	43 88 D	
Heads Mews. W11	56	25 81 C	
Head St. E1	57	35 81 D	
Headstone Dri. Har	21	15 89 A	
Headstone Gdns. Har	20	14 89 C	
Headstone La. Har	20	13 90 D	
Headstone Rd. Har	33	15 88 C	
Headway Cl. Rich	83	17 71 A	
Headway The. Eps	109	21 62 B	
Heald St. SE14	76	37 76 A	
Heald St. SE8	76	37 76 A	
Healey St. NW1	47	28 84 B	
Hearne Rd. W4	61	19 77 A	
Hearn Rd. Rom	42	51 88 D	
Hearn Rise. Nthlt	43	11 83 B	
Hearn St. EC2	1	33 82 C	
Hearnville Rd. SW12	86	28 73 C	
Heatham Park. Twick	83	15 73 B	
Heath Ave. Bexh	67	47 77 B	
Heath Brow. NW3	46	26 86 C	
Heath Cl. NW11	35	25 87 B	
Heath Cl. Rom	52	52 89 A	
Heath Cl. W5	54	18 82 D	
Heathcote Ave. Ilf	27	42 90 D	
Heathcote Ct. Ilf	27	42 90 D	
Heathcote Gr. E4	18	38 93 A	
Heathcote Rd. Twick	71	16 74 B	
Heathcote St. WC1	3	30 82 B	
Heathcroft Ave. Sun	91	09 70 D	
Heathcroft. NW11	35	25 87 D	
Heathcroft. W5	54	18 82 D	
Heathdale Ave. Houn	70	12 75 A	
Heathdene Dri. Belv	79	49 78 B	
Heathdene Rd. SW16	96	30 70 D	
Heathdene Rd. Wall	111	28 63 D	
Heath Dri. NW3	46	25 85 B	
Heath Dri. Rom	30	52 90 C	
Heath Dri. Sutt	110	26 62 A	
Heath Dri. SW20	95	23 68 C	
Heathedge. SE26	87	34 72 B	
Heather Ave. Rom	30	50 90 D	
Heatherbank. Chis	100	43 69 C	
Heatherbank. SE9	77	42 76 D	
Heather Cl. Hamp	92	12 69 B	
Heather Cl. Islw	70	14 74 B	
Heather Cl. Rom	29	50 90 B	
Heatherdale Cl. King	94	19 70 D	
Heatherdene Cl. Mit	96	27 68 C	
Heather Dri. Rom	30	51 90 C	
Heather Gdns. NW11	35	24 88 C	
Heather Gdns. Rom	29	50 90 D	
Heather Gdns. Sutt	110	25 63 A	
Heather Glen. Rom	29	50 90 D	
Heatherlands. Sun	91	10 70 A	
Heatherley Dri. Ilf	27	42 89 B	
Heather Park Dri. Wem	45	19 84 C	
Heather Rd. NW2	34	21 86 B	
Heather Rd. SE12	89	40 73 C	
Heatherset Gdns. SW16	96	30 70 D	
Heatherside Rd. Eps	109	20 63 D	
Heather Way. Rom	30	50 90 B	
Heather Way. Stan	21	15 91 B	
Heather Wlk. Houn	82	13 73 A	
Heather Wlk. W10	56	24 82 C	
Heatherwood Cl. E12	39	41 86 A	
Heathfield Ave. SW18	85	26 73 B	
Heathfield. Chis	100	44 70 A	
Heathfield Cl. E16	58	41 81 B	
Heathfield Ct. W4	61	20 78 D	
Heathfield. E4	18	38 93 C	
Heathfield Gdns. NW11	35	23 88 D	
Heathfield Gdns. SW18	73	26 74 D	
Heathfield Gdns. W4	61	20 78 C	
Heathfield La. Chis	100	44 70 A	
Heathfield N. Twick	83	15 73 B	
Heathfield Park. NW2	46	23 84 A	
Heathfield Rd. Bexh	79	48 75 D	
Heathfield Rd. Brom	99	39 70 D	
Heathfield Rd. Croy	112	32 64 B	
Heathfield Rd. SW18	73	26 74 D	
Heathfield Rd. W3	61	19 79 B	
Heathfield Rise. Ruis	31	08 87 A	
Heathfield Sq. SW18	85	26 73 B	
Heathfield Sq. SW18	73	26 74 D	
Heathfield S. Twick	83	15 73 B	
Heathfield Terr. SE18	66	45 77 B	
Heathfield Terr. W4	61	20 78 D	
Heathgate. NW11	35	25 88 D	
Heath Gdns. Twick	83	15 72 B	
Heath Gr. SE20	98	35 70 C	
Heath Gr. Sun	91	09 70 D	
Heath Hurst Rd. NW3	47	27 85 A	
Heathhurst Rd. S Croy	112	33 62 A	
Heathland Rd. N16	37	33 87 C	
Heathlands Cl. Sun	91	10 69 C	
Heathlands Rise. Dart	80	52 74 D	
Heath La. SE3	76	38 76 D	
Heath La. SE3	77	39 75 A	
Heathlee Rd. SE3	77	39 75 D	
Heathley End. Chis	100	44 70 A	
Heathman's Rd. SW6	73	24 76 B	
Heath Mead. SW19	85	23 72 D	
Heath Park Rd. Rom	42	52 88 B	
Heath Pas. NW3	35	25 86 B	
Heath Rd. Dart	80	51 74 D	
Heath Rd. Har	32	14 87 A	
Heath Rd. Houn	70	14 75 C	
Heath Rd. Rom	41	48 87 A	
Heath Rd. SW8	74	28 76 D	
Heath Rd. Th Hth	97	32 69 B	
Heath Rise. Brom	107	40 67 C	
Heath Rise. SW15	73	24 74 C	
Heath Royal. SW15	73	23 74 D	
Heath's Cl. Enf	13	33 97 C	
Heathside Ave. Bexh	79	48 76 C	
Heathside Cl. Esh	101	15 65 C	
Heathside. Esh	101	15 65 C	
Heathside. Houn	82	12 73 B	
Heath Side. NW3	46	26 85 B	
Heath Side. Orp	108	44 66 A	
Heathstan Rd. W12	55	22 81 C	
Heath St. Bark	51	43 83 B	
Heath St. NW3	46	26 85 A	
Heath The. W7	54	15 80 C	
Heathview Ave. Dart	80	51 74 C	
Heath View Cl. N2	23	26 89 C	
Heathview Dri. SE2	67	47 77 B	
Heathview Gdns. SW15	85	23 73 A	
Heath View. N2	23	26 89 C	
Heathview Rd. Th Hth	97	31 68 C	
Heath Villas. SE18	66	45 78 D	
Heathville Rd. N19	36	30 87 A	
Heathwall St. SW11	74	27 75 B	
Heathway. Croy	106	36 65 D	
Heathway. Dag	41	48 86 D	
Heathway. Dag	52	49 85 C	
Heath Way. Eri	79	50 76 A	
Heathway. SE3	65	40 77 C	
Heathwood Gdns. SE7	65	42 78 C	
Heaton Ave. Rom	30	52 91 C	
Heaton Cl. Rom	30	53 91 C	
Heaton Grange Rd. Rom	30	53 91 D	
Heaton Pl. E15	49	38 85 D	
Heaton Rd. Mit	96	28 70 C	
Heaton Rd. SE15	75	34 78 D	
Heaton Way. Rom	30	53 91 C	
Heaver Rd. SW11	73	26 75 B	
Heavitree Cl. SE18	66	44 78 D	
Heavitree Rd. SE18	66	44 78 D	
Hebdon Rd. SW17	86	27 72 D	
Heber Rd. NW2	46	23 85 B	
Heber Rd. SE22	75	33 74 D	
Hebron Rd. W6	62	23 79 C	
Hecham Cl. E17	26	36 90 C	
Heckfield Pl. SW6	62	25 77 C	
Heckford St. E1	57	35 80 B	
Hecron St. SE17	31 77 B	
Hector St. SE18	66	45 78 A	
Heddon Cl. Islw		16 75 C	
Heddon Court Ave. Barn	12	27 95 B	
Heddon Court Par. Barn	12	28 95 A	
Heddon Rd. Barn	12	27 95 B	
Heddon St. W1	6	29 80 A	
Hedge Hill. Enf	13	31 97 B	
Hedge La. N13	17	32 93 C	
Hedgemans Rd. Dag	52	48 84 C	
Hedgemans Way. Dag	52	48 84 A	
Hedgerley Gdns. Grnf	43	14 83 C	
Hedger's Gr. E9	49	36 84 A	
Hedge Wlk. SE6	88	37 71 D	
Hedgewood Gdns. Ilf	40	43 88 A	
Hedgley. Ilf	27	42 89 D	
Hedgley St. SE12	77	39 74 B	
Hedingham Cl. N1	48	32 84 C	
Hedingham Rd. Dag	51	46 85 D	
Hedley Rd. Houn	82	13 73 A	
Hedley Row. N5	48	32 85 D	
Heenan Cl. Bark	51	44 84 A	
Heene Rd. Enf	13	32 97 B	
Heigham Rd. E6	50	44 84 C	
Heighton Gdns. Croy	112	31 64 D	
Heights Cl. SW20	94	22 70 D	
Heights The. Beck	98	38 70 C	
Heights The. Nthlt	43	13 85 C	
Heights The. SE7	65	41 78 C	
Helby Rd. SW4	74	29 74 D	
Helder Gr SE12	89	39 73 B	
Helder St. S Croy	112	32 63 B	
Heldmann Cl. Houn	70	14 75 D	
Helena Cl. Wall	111	30 63 C	
Helena Rd. E13	50	39 83 D	
Helena Rd. E17	38	37 88 A	
Helena Rd. NW10	45	22 85 D	
Helena Rd. W5	54	17 81 B	
Helen Ave. Felt	81	10 73 B	
Helen Cl. E Mol	92	13 68 D	
Helen Cl. N2	23	26 89 A	
Helen Rd. Horn	30	53 89 B	
Helenslea Ave. NW11	35	25 87 C	
Helen's Pl. E2	57	35 82 A	
Helen St. SE18	66	43 78 B	
Helford Cl. Ruis	31	09 86 A	
Helgiford Gdns. Sun	91	09 70 C	
Heliport Estate. SW11	73	26 76 D	
Helix Gdns. SW2	74	30 74 D	
Helix Rd. SW2	75	31 74 C	
Hellings St. E1	57	34 80 C	
Helmet Row. EC1	4	32 82 C	
Helmsdale Cl. E11	39	40 88 A	
Helmsdale Cl. Rom	30	51 91 C	
Helmsdale Rd. Rom	30	51 91 C	
Helmsdale Rd. SW16	96	29 69 B	
Helmsley Pl. E8	48	34 84 D	
Helmsley St. E8	48	34 84 D	
Helston Cl. Pnr	20	12 91 D	
Helvetia St. SE6	88	36 72 B	
Hemans St Estate. SW8	10	29 77 D	
Hemans St. SW8	10	30 77 C	
Hemberton Rd. SW9	74	30 75 A	
Hemery Rd. Grnf	43	14 85 D	
Hemingford Rd. N1	47	30 84 D	
Hemingford Rd. Sutt	110	23 64 A	
Heming Rd. Edg	22	19 91 D	
Hemington Ave. N11	16	27 92 D	
Hemlock Rd. W12	55	21 80 B	
Hemming Cl. Hamp	92	13 69 A	
Hemming St. E1	57	34 82 C	
Hempstead Rd. E17	26	38 90 D	
Hemp Wlk. SE17	63	32 78 B	
Hemp Wlk. SE17	63	32 78 B	
Hemstal Rd. NW6	46	25 84 C	
Hemsted Rd. Eri	68	51 77 C	
Hemswell Dri. NW9	22	21 90 A	
Hemsworth Ct. N1	48	33 83 C	
Hemsworth St. N1	48	33 83 C	
Hemus Pl. SW3	9	27 78 C	
Henbane Path. Rom	30	53 91 D	
Henchman St. W12	55	21 81 D	
Hendale Ave. NW4	22	22 89 B	
Henderson Cl. NW10	45	20 84 A	
Henderson Dri. Dart	80	54 75 D	
Henderson Dri. NW8	1	26 82 D	
Henderson Rd. Croy	105	32 67 D	
Henderson Rd. E7	50	41 84 A	
Henderson Rd. N9	17	34 94 D	
Henderson Rd. SW18	86	27 73 A	

Name	Page	Grid
Hendham Rd. SW17	86	27 72 B
Hendon Ave. N3	23	24 90 D
Hendon Gdns. Rom	29	50 91 A
Hendon Hall Ct. NW14	23	23 89 B
Hendon La. N3	23	24 90 D
Hendon Park Row. NW11	35	24 88 D
Hendon Rd. N9	17	34 93 A
Hendon Way. NW2	35	24 87 C
Hendren Cl. Grnf	43	14 85 D
Hendre Rd. SE1	63	33 78 A
Heneage La. EC3	4	33 81 C
Heneage Pl. EC3	4	33 81 C
Heneage St. E1	4	33 81 B
Henfield Cl. Bex	79	49 74 C
Henfield Cl. N19	36	29 87 C
Henfield Rd. SW19	82	24 69 B
Hengelo Gdns. Mit	95	26 68 D
Hengist Rd. Eri	67	50 77 C
Hengist Rd. SE12	89	40 73 B
Hengist Way. Brom	99	39 68 C
Hengrave Rd. SE23	88	35 73 B
Henley Ave. Sutt	103	24 65 C
Henley Cl. Grnf	43	14 83 C
Henley Cl. Islw	71	15 76 B
Henley Dr. King	94	21 70 D
Henley Gdns. Pnr	19	10 89 B
Henley Gdns. Rom	41	48 88 A
Henley Rd. E16	65	42 79 B
Henley Rd. Ilf	51	44 85 B
Henley Rd. N18	17	33 92 A
Henley Rd. NW10	46	23 83 A
Henley St. SW11	74	28 76 C
Henley Way. Felt	82	11 71 D
Hennel Cl. SE23	88	35 72 C
Henniker Gdns. E6	58	41 82 B
Henniker Gdns. E6	50	42 83 C
Henniker Mews. SW3	62	26 77 B
Henniker Rd. E15	49	38 85 D
Henningham Rd. N17	25	32 90 B
Henning St. SW11	74	27 76 A
Henrietta Mews. WC1	3	30 82 C
Henrietta Pl. W1	2	28 81 D
Henrietta St. E15	49	38 85 C
Henrietta St. WC2	7	30 80 A
Henriques St. E1	57	34 81 C
Henry Cooper Way. SE9	89	41 72 D
Henry Darlot Dri. NW7	15	23 92 D
Henry Dickens Ct. W11	56	23 80 B
Henry Jackson Rd. SW15	73	23 75 B
Henry Prince Estate. SW18	85	25 73 D
Henry Rd. Barn	11	26 95 B
Henry Rd. E6	50	42 83 C
1Henry Rd. N4	37	32 87 C
Henry's Ave. Wdf Gn	27	39 91 B
Henryson Rd. SE4	76	37 74 A
Henry St. Brom	99	40 69 B
Henry's Wlk. Ilf	28	44 91 D
Hensford Gdns. SE26	87	34 71 B
Henshall St. N1	48	32 84 B
Henshawe Rd. Dag	41	47 86 D
Henshaw St. SE17	63	32 78 B
Henslowe Rd. SE22	75	34 74 A
Henson Ave. NW2	46	23 85 C
Henson Cl. Orp	108	43 65 B
Henson Path. Har	21	17 89 B
Henson Pl. Nthlt	43	11 83 A
Henstridge Pl. NW8	47	27 83 C
*Henty Cl. SW11	74	27 76 A
Henty Wlk. SW15	72	22 74 B
Henville Rd. Brom	99	40 69 B
Henwick Rd. SE9	77	42 75 A
Henwood Rd. SE16	64	35 79 C
Henwood Side. Wdf Gn	27	42 91 B
Hepburn Gdns. Brom	107	39 66 D
Hepple Cl. Islw	71	16 76 D
Hepplestone Cl. SW15	72	22 74 D
Hopscott Rd. E9	49	37 84 C
Hepworth Gdns. Bark	51	46 85 C
Hepworth Rd. SW16	96	30 70 C
Heracles Cl. Wall	111	30 63 C
Herald St. E2	57	34 82 D
Herbal Hill. EC1	3	31 82 C
Herbert Cres. SW1	5	27 79 D
Herbert Gdns. NW10	45	22 83 D
Herbert Gdns. Rom	41	47 87 B
Herbert Gdns. W4	61	19 77 B
Herbert Pl. SE18	66	43 77 B
Herbert Rd. Bexh	79	48 76 C
Herbert Rd. Brom	107	42 67 A
Herbert Rd. E12	50	42 85 A
Herbert Rd. E17	38	36 87 B
Herbert Rd. Horn	42	54 87 B
Herbert Rd. Ilf	40	45 86 A
Herbert Rd. King	93	18 68 B
Herbert Rd. N11	24	30 91 C
Herbert Rd. N15	37	33 88 B
Herbert Rd. NW9	34	22 88 C
Herbert Rd. SE18	66	43 77 B
Herbert Rd. Sthl	53	12 80 D
Herbert Rd. SW19	82	24 70 D
Herbert St. E13	50	40 83 C
Herbert St. NW3	47	28 84 A
Herbrand St. WC1	3	30 82 C
Hercules Pl. N7	36	30 86 C
Hercules Rd. SE1	7	31 79 C
Hercules St. N7	36	30 86 C
Hercules Yd. N7	36	30 86 C
Hereford Ave. Barn	22	27 94 D
Hereford Gdns. Ilf	39	42 87 A
Hereford Gdns. Pnr	32	12 88 A
Hereford Gdns. Twick	82	14 73 C
Hereford Mews. W2	56	25 81 C
Hereford Pl. SE14	64	36 77 D
Hereford Rd. E11	39	40 88 B
Hereford Rd. Felt	82	11 73 C
Hereford Rd. W2	56	25 81 C
Hereford Rd. W3	55	20 80 A
Hereford Rd. W5	60	17 79 C
Hereford Sq. SW7	62	26 78 A
Hereford St. E2	57	34 82 C
Herent Dri. Ilf	27	42 89 B
Hereward Ave. Pur	112	31 62 C
Hereward Gdns. N13	17	31 92 C
Hereward Rd. SW17	86	27 71 B
Herga Ct. Har	33	15 86 A
Herga Rd. Har	21	15 89 D
Heriot Ave. E4	18	37 93 A
Heriot Rd. NW4	35	23 88 A
Herlwyn Ave. Ruis	31	09 86 C
Herlwyn Gdns. SW17	86	27 71 B
Hermes St. N1	48	31 83 C
Hermes Way. Wall	111	29 63 D
Hermiston Ave. N8	36	30 88 A
Hermitage Cl. E18	27	39 89 D
Hermitage Cl. Enf	13	31 97 D
Hermitage Cl. Shep	91	07 68 C
Hermitage Cl. E18	27	40 89 C
Hermitage Gdns. NW2	35	25 86 C
Hermitage Gdns. SE19	97	32 70 C
Hermitage La. Croy	105	34 66 A
Hermitage La. N18	17	32 92 D
Hermitage La. NW2	35	25 86 C
Hermitage La. SW16	96	30 70 D
Hermitage La. N15	37	32 88 B
Hermitage Rd. N4	37	32 88 C
Hermitage Rd. SE19	97	32 70 B
Hermitage The. Rich	71	18 74 A
Hermitage The. SE23	88	35 73 C
Hermitage The. SW13	72	21 76 B
Hermitage Wall. E1	57	34 80 C
Hermitage Way. Stan	21	16 90 A
Hermitage Wlk. E18	27	39 89 D
Hermit Pl. NW6	46	25 83 B
Hermit Rd. E16	58	39 82 D
Hermit St. EC1	3	31 82 B
Hermon Hill. E11	27	40 89 C
Hermon Hill. E18	27	40 89 B
Herndon Rd. SW18	73	26 74 A
Herne Cl. NW10	45	20 85 D
Herne Hill Rd. SE24	75	32 75 C
Herne Hill. SE24	75	32 74 A
Herne Mews. N18	17	34 92 A
Herne Pl. SE24	75	31 74 B
Herne Rd. Surb	101	18 65 A
Heron Cl. E17	26	36 90 D
Heron Cl. NW10	45	21 84 A
Heron Cres. Sid	90	45 71 A
Heron Ct. Brom	99	41 68 C
Heron Ct. Rich	71	17 74 B
Herondale Ave. SW18	85	26 73 D
Herongate Rd. E12	39	41 86 A
Heron Hill. Belv	67	48 78 B
Heron Mews. Ilf	40	43 86 B
Heron Rd. Croy	105	33 65 A
Heron Rd. SE24	75	32 75 C
Heron Rd. Twick	71	16 75 C
Heronsford. W13	54	17 81 C
Herons Rise. Barn	12	27 96 C
Herrick Rd. N5	37	32 86 C
Herrick St. SW1	10	29 78 B
Herries St. W10	46	24 83 C
Herringham Rd. SE7	65	41 79 C
Herrongate Cl. Enf	13	33 97 D
Hersant Cl. NW10	45	22 83 A
Herschell Rd. SE23	88	36 73 A
Hersham Cl. SW15	84	22 73 A
Hertford Ave. SW14	72	21 75 C
Hertford Cl. Barn	11	26 96 B
Hertford Ct. N13	17	31 93 C
Hertford Pl. W1	2	29 82 C
Hertford Rd. Bark	51	43 84 D
Hertford Rd. Barn	11	26 96 B
Hertford Rd. Enf	14	35 97 C
Hertford Rd. Ilf	40	45 88 C
Hertford Rd. N1	48	33 84 C
Hertford Rd. N2	24	27 89 A
Hertford Rd. N9	17	34 94 D
Hertford St. W1	6	28 80 D
Hertford Way. Mit	96	30 68 C
Hertford Wlk. Belv	67	49 78 C
Hertley Cl. SE4	76	36 74 A
Hertslet Rd. N7	36	30 85 B
Hertslet Rd. N7	36	30 85 B
Hervey Cl. N3	23	25 90 A
Hervey Park Rd. E17	26	36 89 C
Hervey Rd. SE3	77	40 76 B
Hesketh Pl. W11	56	24 80 A
Hesketh Rd. E7	39	40 88 C
Heslop Rd. SW12	86	27 73 D
Hesper Mews. SW5	62	25 78 B
Hesperus Cres. E14	64	37 78 B
Hessel Rd. W13	60	16 79 B
Hessel St. E1	57	34 81 D
Hestercombe Ave. SW6	73	24 76 A
Hester Rd. N18	17	34 92 C
Hester Rd. SW11	9	27 77 C
Heston Ave. Houn	59	12 77 C
Heston Grange. Houn	59	12 77 B
Heston Grange La. Houn	59	12 77 B
Heston Rd. Houn	59	13 77 A
Heston St. SE8	77	37 76 A
Hetherington Rd. Shep	91	08 69 C
Hetherington Rd. SW4	74	30 75 C
Hetley Rd. W12	61	22 79 B
Hevelius Cl. E10	65	39 78 D
Hever Croft. SE9	90	43 71 A
Hever Gdns. Brom	100	43 69 C
Heverham Rd. SE18	66	49 78 A
Heversham Rd. Bexh	79	49 76 A
Hewer St. W10	56	23 81 B
Hewett Rd. Dag	52	49 85 B
Hewett St. EC2	4	33 82 C
Hewish Rd. N18	17	33 92 A
Hewitt Ave. N22	25	31 90 D
Hewitt Rd. N8	37	31 88 B
Hewlett Rd. E3	58	36 83 C
Hexagon The. N6	36	27 87 D
Hexal Rd. SE6	89	39 72 C
Hexham Gdns. Islw	60	16 77 C
Hexham Rd. Barn	11	26 96 D
Hexham Rd. Mord	103	25 66 D
Hexham Rd. SE27	87	32 72 A
Heybourne Rd. N17	25	34 91 D
Heybridge Ave. SW16	96	30 70 B
Heybridge Dri. Ilf	28	44 89 B
Heybridge Way. E10	38	36 87 D
Heyford Ave. SW20	95	24 68 B
Heyford Ave. SW8	10	30 77 D
Heyford Rd. Mit	96	27 69 C
Heygate St. SE17	63	32 78 A
Heylin Sq. E3	57	36 82 B
Heynes Rd. Dag	52	47 85 A
Heysham Rd. N15	37	32 88 D
Heythorp St. SW18	85	24 72 B
Heywood Ave. NW9	22	21 90 A
Heyworth Rd. E15	50	39 85 B
Heyworth Rd. E5	48	34 85 B
Hibbert Rd. E17	38	36 87 B
Hibbert Rd. Har	21	15 90 D
Hibbert St. SW11	73	26 75 A
Hibernia Gdns. Houn	70	13 74 A
Hibernia Rd. Houn	70	13 75 C
Hichisson Rd. SE15	76	35 74 B
Hickey's Almshouses. Rich	71	18 75 D
Hickin Cl. SE7	65	41 78 B
Hickin St. E14	64	38 79 C
Hickling Rd. Ilf	51	43 85 D
Hickman Ave. E4	26	38 91 A
Hickman Rd. Rom	41	47 87 A
Hickmore Wlk. SW4	74	29 75 A
Hicks Ave. Grnf	52	15 82 A
Hicks Cl. SW11	74	27 75 A
Hicks St. SE8	64	36 78 C
Hidcote Gdns. SW20	94	22 68 B
Hide Pl. SW1	10	29 78 B
Hide Rd. Har	20	14 89 D
Hides St. N7	47	30 84 B
Higgins Wlk. Hamp	92	12 70 A
Higham Hill Rd. E17	26	36 90 C
Higham Path. E17	26	36 89 A
Higham Pl. E17	26	36 89 A
Higham Rd. N17	25	32 89 B

Name	Page	Ref
Higham Rd. Wdf Gn.	27	40 91 A
Higham Station Ave. E4	26	37 91 B
Higham St. E17	26	36 89 A
Highbanks Cl. SE2	66	46 77 D
Highbanks Rd. Pnr	20	13 91 R
Highbarrow Rd. Croy	105	34 66 C
High Beech. S Croy	112	33 63 C
Highbridge Rd. Bark	51	43 83 B
High Bridge. SE10	64	38 78 D
Highbrook Rd. SE3	77	41 75 B
High Broom Cres. W Wick	106	37 66 B
Highbury Av. H Hth	97	31 69 D
Highbury Cl. N.Mal	102	20 67 A
Highbury Cl. W Wick	106	37 65 B
Highbury Cnr. N7	48	31 84 B
Highbury Cres. N5	48	31 85 D
Highbury Gdns. Ilf	40	45 86 A
Highbury Grange. N5	48	32 85 A
Highbury Gr. N5	48	31 85 D
Highbury Hill. N5	48	31 85 B
Highbury Mews. N5	48	31 84 A
Highbury New Park. N5	48	32 85 A
Highbury Park. N5	48	31 85 B
Highbury Pl. N5	48	31 84 B
Highbury Quadrant. N5	37	32 86 C
Highbury Rd. SW19	85	24 71 C
Highbury Station Rd. N1	48	31 84 A
Highbury Terrace Mews. N5	48	31 85 D
Highbury Terr. N5	48	31 85 D
Highclere Rd. N Mal	94	20 68 B
Highclere St. SE26	88	36 71 A
Highcliffe Dri. SW15	72	21 74 D
Highcliffe Gdns. Ilf	39	42 88 A
Highcombe Cl. SE9	89	42 73 C
Highcombe. SE7	65	40 77 B
Highcroft Ave. Wem	45	19 83 A
Highcroft Gdns. NW11	35	24 88 D
Highcroft. NW9	34	21 88 A
Highcroft Rd. N19	36	30 87 A
High Cross Rd. N17	25	34 89 A
Highcross Way. SW15	84	22 73 C
Highdaun Dr. SW16	96	30 68 D
Highdown Rd. SW15	72	22 74 D
Highdown. Wor Pk	102	21 65 B
High Dri. N Mal	94	20 69 C
High Elms Cl. Nthwd	19	08 91 B
Highfield Ave. Eri	67	49 77 B
Highfield Ave. Grnf	44	15 85 C
Highfield Ave. NW11	35	24 87 A
Highfield Ave. NW9	34	20 88 A
High field Ave. Pnr	32	12 88 B
Highfield Ave. Wem	33	18 86 D
Highfield Cl. Nthwd	19	09 90 A
Highfield Cl. NW9	34	20 88 A
Highfield Cl. Rom	29	50 91 A
Highfield Cl. Surb	101	17 66 C
Highfield Cres. Horn	42	54 86 B
Highfield Cres. Nthwd	19	09 90 A
Highfield Ct. N14	12	29 95 C
Highfield Dri. Brom	99	39 68 D
Highfield Dri. Eps	109	21 63 B
Highfield Dri. W Wick	106	38 65 C
Highfield. Felt	81	10 73 C
Highfield Gdns. NW11	35	24 88 C
Highfield Hill. SE19	97	33 70 C
Highfield Link. Rom	29	50 91 B
Highfield Rd. Bexh	79	48 74 B
Highfield Rd. Brom	99	42 68 D
Highfield Rd. Chis	100	45 68 B
Highfield Rd. Dart	80	53 74 D
Highfield Rd. Felt	81	10 73 C
Highfield Rd. Horn	42	54 86 B
Highfield Rd. Islw	71	15 76 B
Highfield Rd. N21	17	31 94 D
Highfield Rd N. Dart	80	53 74 D
Highfield Rd. Nthwd	19	09 90 A
Highfield Rd. NW11	35	24 88 C
Highfield Rd. Pur	112	31 62 C
Highfield Rd. Rom	29	50 91 A
Highfield Rd. Surb	102	20 66 A
Highfield Rd. Sutt	111	27 64 C
Highfield Rd. W3	55	20 81 A
Highfield Rd. Wdf Gn	27	42 91 C
Highfields. Sutt	103	25 65 A
Highfield Way. Horn	42	54 86 B
Highgate Ave. N6	36	28 87 B
Highgate Cl. N6	36	28 87 A
Highgate High St. N6	36	28 87 A
Highgate Hill. N19	36	29 87 C
Highgate Ho. SE26	87	34 72 C
Highgate Rd. NW5	47	28 85 B
Highgate West Hill. N6	36	28 86 A
Highgrove Rd. Dag	52	47 85 A
Highgrove Way. Ruis	31	10 87 A
High Gr. SE18	78	44 76 B
High Hill Ferry. E5	37	34 87 D
High Hill Ferry. E5	38	35 87 C
High Holborn. WC1	3	30 81 B
Highland Ave. Dag	41	50 86 C
Highland Ave. W7	54	15 81 C
Highland Croft. Beck	88	37 71 D
Highland Park. Felt	81	09 71 B
Highland Rd. Bexh	79	49 75 C
Highland Rd. Brom	99	39 69 B
Highland Rd. Nthwd	19	10 90 C
Highland Rd. SE19	97	33 70 A
Highlands Ave. W3	55	20 80 A
Highlands Cl. Houn	70	13 76 B
Highlands Ct. SE19	97	33 70 A
Highlands Gdns. Ilf	39	42 87 D
Highlands Heath. SW15	85	23 73 A
Highlands Rd. Barn	11	25 95 A
Highlands Rd. Orp	108	46 66 B
Highlands The. Edg	22	19 90 D
High La. W7	53	14 81 D
Highlea Cl. NW9	22	21 90 A
High Level Dri. SE26	87	34 71 A
Highlever Rd. W10	56	23 81 A
Highmead Cres. Wem	44	18 84 D
High Mead. Har	33	15 88 B
High Meadow Cl. Pnr	20	11 89 C
High Meadow Cres. NW9	34	20 88 B
Highmead. SE18	66	45 77 D
High Mead. W.Wick	107	39 65 A
Highmore Rd. SE3	65	39 77 C
High Mount. NW4	34	22 88 C
High Park Ave. Rich	72	19 76 A
High Park Rd. Rich	72	19 76 A
High Path. SW19	95	26 69 A
Highpoint. N6	36	28 87 A
High Point. SE9	90	43 72 D
High Rd. E10	38	37 88 D
High Rd. E18	27	40 90 A
High Rd. Har	21	15 90 A
High Rd. Ilf	40	45 86 A
High Rd. N11	16	28 92 D
High Rd. N12	23	26 91 A
High Rd. N15	37	33 88 B
High Rd. N17	25	33 90 D
High Rd. N22	24	30 90 B
High Rd. N22	25	31 89 A
High Rd. N2	24	27 89 C
High Rd. N8	24	30 89 C
High Rd. NW10	45	22 84 A
High Rd. Rom	41	47 87 B
High Rd. Wem	44	18 85 C
High Road Eastcote. Pnr	31	10 88 B
High Road Ickenham. Uxb	31	08 86 A
High Road Leyton. E10	38	37 87 D
High Road Leyton. E15	49	38 85 A
High Road Leytonstone. E11	39	39 86 A
High Road Woodford Green. Wdf Gn	27	39 91 B
Highshore Rd. SE15	75	34 76 C
High St. Barn	11	24 96 A
High St. Beck	98	37 69 C
High St. Brent	60	18 77 A
High St. Brom	99	40 69 C
High St. Cars	111	28 64 A
High St. Croy	105	32 65 C
High St. Dart	80	54 74 C
High St. E11	39	40 88 A
High St. E13	50	40 83 C
High St. E15	49	38 83 A
High St. E17	38	36 88 B
High St. E17	26	37 89 C
Highstead Cres. Eri	68	51 77 C
High St. Edg	22	19 91 A
High St. E Mol	92	13 68 C
High St. Enf	14	35 95 A
High St. Eps	109	22 62 A
High St. Felt	81	10 72 A
High St. Hamp	92	14 70 C
High St. Har	21	15 87 C
High St. Hay	69	08 76 B
High St. Horn	42	54 87 C
High St. Houn	69	10 76 A
High St. Houn	70	13 75 B
High St. Ilf	28	44 90 C
High St. King	93	17 68 B
High St. King	93	17 69 B
High St Mews. SW19	85	24 71 C
High St. N14	16	29 93 B
High St. N8	24	30 89 C
High St N. E12	50	42 84 A
High St N. E6	50	42 83 A
High St. N Mal	94	21 68 C
High St. Nthwd	19	09 90 B
Highstone Ave. E11	39	40 88 C
High St. Orp	108	46 66 C
High St. Pnr	20	12 89 A
High Street Colliers Wood. SW19	96	27 70 A
High Street Colliers Wood. SW1	95	26 70 D
High Street Harlesden. NW10	45	21 83 D
High St. Rom	42	51 88 A
High St. Ruis	31	09 87 C
High St. SE20	98	35 70 C
High St. SE25	97	34 68 C
High St. SE25	97	34 68 C
High St S. E6	50	42 83 D
High St. Sid	90	46 71 A
High St. Sthl	53	12 80 C
High St. Surb	101	16 67 C
High St. Sutt	110	24 63 A
High St. Sutt	110	25 64 B
High St. SW19	85	23 71 D
High St. Tedd	83	16 71 C
High St. Th Hth	97	32 68 D
High St. Twick	82	14 73 A
High St. W3	55	20 80 C
High St. W5	54	17 80 B
High St. Wem	44	18 85 B
High St. W Wick	106	37 66 D
High Timber St. EC4	8	32 80 A
High Trees. Barn	12	27 95 A
High Trees. Croy	106	36 66 C
Hightrees Ct. W7	54	15 80 A
High Trees. Swar	87	31 73 C
High View Ave. Wall	111	30 64 D
High View Cl. SE19	97	33 69 D
High View Ct. Har	21	15 91 C
Highview Gdns. N11	16	29 92 C
Highview Gdns. N3	23	24 89 A
High View. Pnr	20	11 89 A
High View Rd. E18	27	39 90 D
High View Rd. N2	24	27 90 B
High View Rd. SE19	97	32 70 B
Highview Rd. Sid	90	46 71 B
Highview Rd. W13	54	16 81 C
Highway The. E14	57	36 80 A
Highway The. E1	57	35 80 A
Highway The. Stan	21	16 91 C
Highway The. Sutt	110	26 62 A
Highwood Ave. N12	15	26 92 A
Highwood Cl. Orp	108	44 65 A
Highwood Dri. Orp	108	44 65 A
Highwood Gdns. Ilf	27	42 89 D
Highwood Rd. N19	36	30 86 C
High Worple. Har	32	12 87 D
Highworth Rd. N11	16	29 92 D
Hilary Ave. Mit	96	28 68 A
Hilary Cl. Eri	79	50 76 A
Hilary Cl. SW6	62	25 77 D
Hilary Rd. Sthl	59	13 79 C
Hilary Rd. Sthl	59	13 79 C
Hilary Rd. W12	55	21 80 B
Hilbert Rd. Sutt	103	23 65 D
Hilborough Cl. SW19	95	26 70 C
Hilborough Rd. E8	48	33 84 D
Hilda Rd. E16	58	39 82 C
Hilda Rd. E6	58	39 82 D
Hilda Rd. E6	58	41 84 D
Hildenborough Gdns. Brom	99	39 70 A
Hilden Dri. Eri	68	52 77 D
Hilden Lea Pl. Brom	99	39 69 C
Hildreth St. SW12	86	28 73 D
Hildyard Rd. SW6	62	25 77 A
Hiley Rd. NW10	56	23 82 A
Hilgrove Rd. NW6	46	26 84 C
Hiliary Gdns. Stan	21	17 90 C
Hillary Rise. Barn	11	25 96 C
Hillbeck Cl. SE15	64	35 77 C
Hillbeck Way. Grnf	43	14 83 B
Hillbrook Rd. SW17	86	28 71 A
Hill Brow. Brom	99	41 69 B
Hill Brow. Dart	80	51 74 D
Hillbrow. N Mal	94	21 68 A
Hillbrow Rd. Brom	99	39 70 A
Hillbury Ave. Har	33	16 88 B
Hillbury Rd. SW17	86	28 72 D
Hill Cl. Barn	11	23 95 A
Hill Cl. Chis	90	43 71 D
Hill Cl. Har	33	15 86 C
Hill Cl. NW11	35	25 88 C
Hill Cl. NW2	34	22 86 D
Hillcote Ave. SW16	97	31 70 C
Hillcourt Ave. N12	23	25 91 B
Hillcourt Rd. SE22	75	34 74 D
Hill Cres. Har	33	16 88 A
Hill Cres. Horn	42	53 88 C
Hill Cres. N20	25	25 93 B
Hill Cres. Surb	101	18 67 B

Hillcrest Ave. NW11 ...35 — 24 88 B
Hillcrest Ave. Pnr ...20 — 11 89 D
Hillcrest Cl. Beck ...106 — 36 67 D
Hillcrest Cl. SE26 ...87 — 34 71 A
Hillcrest Gdns. Esh ...101 — 15 65 D
Hillcrest Gdns. N3 ...23 — 24 89 C
Hill Crest Gdns. NW2 ...34 — 22 86 C
Hillcrest. N21 ...17 — 31 94 B
Hillcrest. N6 ...36 — 28 87 A
Hillcrest Rd. Brom ...89 — 40 71 A
Hillcrest Rd. E17 ...26 — 38 90 D
Hillcrest Rd. E18 ...27 — 40 90 C
Hillcrest Rd. Horn ...42 — 52 87 A
Hillcrest Rd. Orp ...108 — 46 85 A
Hillcrest Rd. Pur ...111 — 30 62 D
Hillcrest Rd. W3 ...55 — 19 80 D
Hillcrest Rd. W5 ...54 — 18 81 D
Hill Crest. Sid ...90 — 46 73 B
Hillcrest View. Beck ...106 — 36 67 D
Hill Cres. Wor Pk ...103 — 23 65 A
Hillcroft Ave. Pnr ...32 — 12 88 D
Hillcroft Cres. Ruis ...32 — 11 86 D
Hillcroft Cres. W5 ...54 — 18 81 C
Hillcroft Cres. Wem ...44 — 18 85 B
Hillcroome Rd. Sutt ...110 — 26 63 B
Hillcross Ave. Mord ...103 — 24 67 A
Hill Ct. Rom ...30 — 51 89 D
Hill Ct. W5 ...54 — 18 82 D
Hilldale Rd. Sutt ...110 — 24 64 B
Hilldene Ave. Rom ...30 — 53 91 A
Hilldown Rd. Brom ...107 — 39 66 D
Hilldown Rd. SW16 ...96 — 30 70 D
Hill Dri. NW9 ...34 — 20 87 C
Hilldrop Cres. N7 ...47 — 29 85 D
Hilldrop Estate. N7 ...47 — 29 85 D
Hilldrop La. N7 ...47 — 29 85 D
Hilldrop Rd. Brom ...99 — 40 70 B
Hilldrop Rd. N7 ...47 — 29 85 D
Hill Dr. SW16 ...96 — 30 68 B
Hill End. Orp ...108 — 45 65 B
Hill End. SE18 ...78 — 43 76 A
Hillersdon Ave. SW13 ...72 — 22 76 C
Hillery Cl. SE17 ...63 — 32 78 B
Hill Farm Rd. W10 ...56 — 23 81 B
Hillfield Ave. Mord ...104 — 27 67 A
Hillfield Ave. N8 ...24 — 30 89 D
Hillfield Ave. NW9 ...22 — 21 89 D
Hillfield Ave. Wem ...44 — 18 84 D
Hillfield Cl. Har ...20 — 14 89 C
Hillfield Ct. NW3 ...47 — 27 85 C
Hillfield Park Mews. N10 ...24 — 28 89 D
Hillfield Park. N10 ...24 — 28 89 D
Hillfield Park. N21 ...17 — 31 93 A
Hill Field Rd. Hamp ...92 — 12 69 B
Hillfield Rd. NW6 ...46 — 24 85 D
Hillfoot Ave. Rom ...29 — 50 90 A
Hillfoot Rd. Rom ...29 — 50 90 A
Hillgate Pl. W8 ...56 — 25 80 C
Hillgate St. W8 ...56 — 25 80 C
Hill Gr. Rom ...30 — 51 89 A
Hill House Ave. Stan ...21 — 15 91 D
Hill House Cl. N21 ...17 — 31 94 A
Hill House Rd. SW16 ...86 — 30 71 D
Hilliard Rd. Nthwd ...19 — 09 90 B
Hilliard's Ct. E1 ...57 — 35 80 C
Hillier Cl. Barn ...11 — 25 95 D
Hillier Gdns. Croy ...112 — 31 64 C
Hillier Rd. SW11 ...74 — 27 74 D
Hillier's La. Croy ...104 — 30 65 C
Hillingdon Rd. Bexh ...79 — 50 75 A
Hillingdon St. SE17 ...63 — 31 77 B
Hilngdon St. SE5 ...63 — 31 77 D
Hillington Gdns. Wdf Gn ...27 — 41 90 D
Hill La. Ruis ...31 — 08 87 C
Hillman Cl. Horn ...30 — 53 89 B
Hillman St. E8 ...48 — 34 84 B
Hillmarton Rd. N7 ...47 — 30 85 C
Hillmead Dri. SW9 ...75 — 31 75 D
Hillmont Rd. Esh ...101 — 15 65 C
Hillmore Gr. SE26 ...88 — 36 71 C
Hill Path. SW16 ...86 — 30 71 D
Hill Pl St. E14 ...57 — 37 81 C
Hill Rd. Cars ...111 — 27 63 A
Hill Rd. Har ...33 — 16 88 A
Hill Rd. Mit ...96 — 28 70 D
Hill Rd. N10 ...24 — 27 90 D
Hill Rd. Nthwd ...19 — 08 91 B
Hill Rd. NW8 ...46 — 26 83 C
Hill Rd. Pnr ...32 — 12 88 C
Hill Rd. Sutt ...110 — 25 64 D
Hill Rd. Wem ...33 — 16 86 D
Hillreach. SE18 ...65 — 42 78 D
Hill Rise. Esh ...101 — 16 65 B
Hill Rise. Grnf ...43 — 14 83 A
Hillrise Mansions. N19 ...36 — 30 87 A

Hill Rise. N9 ...13 — 34 95 D
Hill Rise. NW11 ...23 — 25 89 D
Hillrise Rd. N19 ...36 — 30 87 A
Hillrise Rd. Rom ...29 — 50 91 A
Hill Rise. Rich ...71 — 17 74 B
Hill Rise. Ruis ...31 — 08 87 D
Hill Rise. SE23 ...87 — 34 73 D
Hillsboro Rd. SE22 ...75 — 33 74 A
Hillside. NW10 ...45 — 20 83 A
Hillside Ave. N11 ...24 — 27 91 B
Hillside Ave. Wdf Gn ...27 — 41 91 A
Hillside Ave. Wem ...44 — 18 85 B
Hill Side. Barn ...11 — 26 95 A
Hillside Cl. Mord ...95 — 24 68 C
Hillside Cl. NW6 ...46 — 25 83 D
Hillside Cres. Har ...32 — 14 87 C
Hillside Cres. Nthwd ...19 — 10 90 A
Hillside Dri. Edg ...19 — 19 91 A
Hillside. Eri ...67 — 50 78 A
Hillside Gdns. Barn ...11 — 24 96 C
Hillside Gdns. E17 ...26 — 38 89 B
Hillside Gdns. Har ...33 — 18 87 A
Hillside Gdns. N6 ...36 — 28 88 D
Hillside Gdns. Nthwd ...19 — 10 91 C
Hillside Gdns. Wall ...111 — 29 63 C
Hillside Gr. N14 ...16 — 29 94 B
Hillside Gr. NW7 ...22 — 22 91 C
Hillside La. Brom ...107 — 39 65 B
Hillside La. Brom ...107 — 40 65 A
Hillside. N15 ...22 — 20 89 D
Hillside Pas. SW16 ...86 — 30 72 B
Hillside Rd. Brom ...99 — 39 88 B
Hillside Rd. Croy ...112 — 31 64 B
Hillside Rd. Dart ...80 — 52 74 C
Hillside Rd. Eps ...101 — 23 62 C
Hilide Rd. N15 ...37 — 33 88 C
Hillside Rd. Nthwd ...19 — 10 91 D
Hillside Rd. Pnr ...19 — 10 91 D
Hillside Rd. Sthl ...53 — 13 82 C
Hillside Rd. Sutt ...110 — 24 63 D
Hillside Rd. SW2 ...76 — 31 72 A
Hillside Rd. W5 ...54 — 18 81 A
Hillside Rise. Nthwd ...19 — 10 91 C
Hillside. SW19 ...95 — 23 70 B
Hill's La. Nthwd ...19 — 09 90 A
Hillsleigh Rd. W14 ...56 — 24 80 D
Hills Pl. W1 ...2 — 29 81 C
Hillstowe St. E5 ...38 — 35 86 C
Hill St. Rich ...71 — 17 74 B
Hilltop Gdns. Dart ...80 — 54 74 B
Hilltop Gdns. Orp ...108 — 45 65 A
Hill Top. Mord ...103 — 25 67 C
Hill Top. NW11 ...23 — 25 89 D
Hilltop Rd. NW6 ...46 — 25 84 C
Hill Top. Sutt ...103 — 24 66 B
Hill Top View. Wdf Gn ...27 — 42 91 B
Hillview Ave. Har ...33 — 18 88 A
Hillview Ave. Horn ...42 — 53 88 D
Hillview Cl. Pnr ...20 — 12 91 B
Hill View Cres. Ilf ...39 — 42 88 D
Hillview Cres. Orp ...108 — 45 66 D
Hill View Dri. Well ...78 — 45 76 C
Hillview Gdns. Har ...20 — 13 89 C
Hillview Gdns. NW4 ...23 — 23 89 D
Hill View Gdns. NW9 ...34 — 20 88 B
Hillview Rd. Chis ...90 — 43 71 C
Hillview Rd. NW7 ...15 — 23 92 B
Hill View Rd. Orp ...108 — 45 65 B
Hillview Rd. Pnr ...20 — 12 91 D
Hill View Rd. Sutt ...103 — 26 65 D
Hill View Rd. Twick ...71 — 16 74 C
Hillview. SW20 ...94 — 22 70 D
Hillway. N6 ...36 — 28 86 A
Hillway. NW9 ...34 — 21 87 C
Hillworth Rd. SW2 ...87 — 31 73 A
Hillyard Rd. W7 ...54 — 15 81 A
Hillyard St. SW9 ...75 — 31 76 A
Hillyfield. E17 ...26 — 36 90 C
Hilly Fields Cres. SE4 ...76 — 37 75 A
Hilsea St. E5 ...49 — 35 85 A
Hilton Ave. N12 ...23 — 26 91 B
Hilversum Cres. SE22 ...75 — 33 74 A
Himley Rd. SW17 ...96 — 27 70 B
Hinchcliffe Cl. Wall ...111 — 30 63 D
Hinchley Cl. Esh ...101 — 15 65 D
Hinchley Dri. Esh ...101 — 15 65 D
Hinchley Way. Esh ...101 — 16 65 C
Hinckley Rd. SE15 ...75 — 34 75 C
Hind Cres. Eri ...67 — 50 77 D
Hind Ct. EC4 ...2 — 31 81 C
Hinde Mews. W1 ...2 — 28 81 C
Hindes Rd. Har ...33 — 15 88 A
Hinde St. W1 ...2 — 28 81 C
Hind Gr. E14 ...57 — 37 81 C

Hindhead Gdns. Nthlt ...43 — 12 83 A
Hindhead Way. Wall ...111 — 30 64 C
Hindmans Rd. SE22 ...75 — 34 74 A
Hindmarsh Cl. E1 ...57 — 34 80 A
Hindrey Rd. E5 ...48 — 34 85 D
Hindsley's Pl. SE23 ...88 — 35 72 A
Hinkler Cl. Wall ...111 — 30 63 C
Hinkler Rd. Har ...21 — 17 89 B
Hinksey Path. SE2 ...67 — 47 79 D
Hinstock Rd. SE18 ...66 — 44 77 A
Hinton Ave. Houn ...70 — 11 75 D
Hinton Cl. SE9 ...89 — 43 73 C
Hinton Rd. N18 ...17 — 33 92 A
Hinton Rd. SE24 ...75 — 31 75 B
Hinton Rd. SE24 ...75 — 32 75 A
Hinton Rd. Wall ...111 — 29 63 A
Hippodrome Mews. W11 ...56 — 24 80 A
Hippodrome Pl. W11 ...56 — 24 80 A
Hitcham Rd. E17 ...38 — 36 87 B
Hitchin Sq. E3 ...49 — 36 83 C
Hitherfield Rd. Dag ...41 — 48 86 A
Hitherfield Rd. SW16 ...87 — 31 72 C
Hither Green La. SE13 ...76 — 38 74 D
Hitherwell Dri. Har ...20 — 14 90 B
Hitherwood Dri. SE19 ...87 — 33 71 B
Hoadly Rd. SW16 ...86 — 29 72 B
Hobart Cl. N20 ...16 — 27 93 A
Hobart Gdns. Th Hth ...97 — 32 68 B
Hobart Pl. Rich ...83 — 18 73 B
Hobart Pl. SW1 ...8 — 28 79 C
Hobart Rd. Dag ...52 — 47 85 B
Hobart Rd. Hay ...53 — 11 82 D
Hobart Rd. Ilf ...28 — 44 90 C
Hobart Rd. Wor Pk ...102 — 22 65 D
Hobbayne Rd. W7 ...53 — 14 81 D
Hobbes Wlk. SW15 ...72 — 22 74 B
Hobbs Green. N2 ...23 — 26 89 A
Hobbs Pl. N1 ...48 — 33 83 A
Hobbs' Pl. N1 ...48 — 33 83 A
Hobday St. E14 ...57 — 37 81 B
Hobill Wlk. Surb ...101 — 18 67 D
Hoblands End. Chis ...100 — 45 70 A
Hobson's Pl. E1 ...4 — 34 81 A
Hobury St. SW10 ...62 — 26 77 B
Hocker St. E2 ...4 — 33 82 B
Hockley Ave. E6 ...50 — 42 83 C
Hockley Dri. Rom ...30 — 53 90 C
Hocroft Ave. NW2 ...35 — 24 86 D
Hocroft Rd. NW2 ...46 — 24 85 B
Hocroft Wlk. NW2 ...35 — 24 86 D
Hodder Dri. Grnf ...44 — 15 83 D
Hoddesdon Rd. Belv ...67 — 49 78 C
Hodford Rd. NW11 ...35 — 24 87 D
Hodister Cl. SE5 ...63 — 32 77 C
Hodnet Gr. SE16 ...64 — 35 78 A
Hodson Cl. Har ...32 — 12 86 D
Hoe St. E17 ...26 — 37 89 C
Hofland Rd. W14 ...62 — 24 79 C
Hogan Way. E5 ...37 — 34 86 A
Hogarth Ave. Ashf ...91 — 08 70 A
Hogarth Cl. E16 ...58 — 41 81 B
Hogarth Cl. W5 ...54 — 18 81 D
Hogarth Cres. Croy ...105 — 32 66 A
Hogarth Cres. SW19 ...95 — 26 69 B
Hogarth Ct. EC3 ...8 — 33 80 A
Hogarth Ct. Houn ...59 — 12 77 C
Hogarth Ct. SE19 ...87 — 33 71 B
Hogarth Gdns. Houn ...59 — 13 77 C
Hogarth Hill. NW11 ...23 — 24 89 D
Hogarth La. W4 ...61 — 21 77 A
*Hogarth Pl. SW5 ...62 — 25 78 B
Hogarth Rd. Edg ...22 — 19 90 C
Hogarth Rd. SW5 ...62 — 25 78 B
Hogarth Roundabout. W4 ...61 — 21 77 A
Hogarth Way. Hamp ...92 — 14 69 A
Hogsmill Way. Eps ...109 — 20 64 A
Hog Hill Rd. Rom ...29 — 49 91 C
Holbeach Gdns. Sid ...78 — 45 74 D
Holbeach Rd. SE6 ...88 — 37 73 B
Holbeck Row. SE15 ...63 — 34 77 C
Holbein Mews. SW1 ...9 — 28 78 C
Holbein Pl. SW1 ...9 — 28 78 A
Holberton Gdns. NW10 ...55 — 22 82 B
Holborn. EC1 ...3 — 31 81 A
Holborn Pl. E13 ...58 — 40 81 B
Holborn Row. WC2 ...3 — 30 81 B
Holbrook Cl. N19 ...36 — 28 86 B
Holbrook Ct. N7 ...47 — 30 85 A
Holbrook La. Chis ...100 — 44 70 D
Holbrook Rd. E15 ...50 — 39 83 D
Holbrook Way. Brom ...107 — 42 67 B
Holbrook Way. Brom ...107 — 42 67 C
Holburne Cl. SE3 ...77 — 41 76 A
Holburne Gdns. SE3 ...77 — 41 76 B
Holburne Rd. SE3 ...77 — 41 76 B

Street	Page	Grid
Holburn Viaduct. EC1	3	31 81 B
Holbutt Gdns. Dag	41	48 86 D
Holcombe Rd. Ilf	40	43 87 A
Holcombe Rd. N17	25	34 89 A
Holcombe Rd. W6	61	22 78 B
Holcroft Rd. E9	49	35 84 C
Holdbrook Way. Rom	30	54 90 D
Holden Ave. N12	15	25 92 D
Holden Ave. NW9	34	20 87 C
Holdenby Rd. SE4	76	36 74 A
Holdenhurst Ave. N12	23	26 91 C
Holden Rd. N12	23	25 92 B
Holden Rd. SW11	74	28 76 C
Holdernesse Rd. SW17	86	28 72 A
Holderness Way. SE27	87	31 71 D
Holders Hill Ave. NW4	23	23 89 B
Holders Hill Cres. NW4	23	23 90 D
Holders Hill Dri. NW4	23	23 90 D
Holders Hill Gdns. NW4	23	24 90 C
Holders Hill Rd. NW7	23	24 90 A
Holdsworth Cl. Har	32	14 88 A
Holford Pl. WC1	3	30 82 B
Holford Rd. NW3	35	26 86 C
Holford St. WC1	3	31 82 A
Holgate Ave. SW11	73	26 75 B
Holgate Gdns. Dag	52	49 84 A
Holgate Rd. Dag	52	49 85 C
Holgate St. SE7	65	41 79 D
Holland Ave. Sutt	110	25 62 A
Holland Ave. SW20	94	21 69 B
Holland Cl. Barn	15	26 94 B
Holland Cl. Brom	107	39 65 B
Holland Gdns. W14	62	24 79 C
Holland Gr. SW9	63	31 77 C
Holland Park Ave. Ilf	40	45 88 B
Holland Park Ave. W11	56	24 80 C
Holland Park Gdns. W14	62	24 79 A
Holland Park Mews. W11	56	24 80 D
Holland Park Rd. W14	62	24 79 D
Holland Park. W11	56	24 80 D
Holland Pas. (off Basire St). N1	48	32 83 A
Holland Pl. W8	62	25 79 B
Holland Rd. E15	58	39 82 A
Holland Rd. E6	51	43 84 C
Holland Rd. NW10	45	22 83 D
Holland Rd. SE25	105	34 67 A
Holland Rd. W14	62	24 79 C
Holland Rd. Wem	44	17 84 B
Hollands The. Felt	82	11 71 B
Hollands The. Wor Pk	102	21 66 D
Holland St. SE1	7	31 80 D
Holland St. W8	62	25 79 A
Holland Villas Rd. W14	62	24 79 A
Holland Way. Brom	107	39 65 B
Holland Wlk. N19	36	29 87 D
Holland Wlk. W8	62	24 79 B
Hollar Rd. N16	37	33 86 D
Hollen St. W1	2	29 81 D
Holles Cl. Hamp	82	13 71 C
Holles St. W1	2	28 81 D
Hollickwood Ave. N12	24	27 91 B
Holliday Sq. SW11	73	26 75 B
Hollidge Way. Dag	52	49 84 D
Hollies Ave. Sid	90	45 73 D
Hollies Cl. Twick	83	15 72 B
Hollies Rd. W5	60	17 78 A
Hollies The. N20	15	26 94 D
Hollies The. Sid	90	46 73 C
Holligrave Rd. Brom	99	40 69 A
Hollingbourne Ave. Bexh	79	48 76 B
Hollingbourne Gdns. W13	54	16 81 D
Hollingbourne Rd. SE24	75	32 74 A
Hollingsworth Ct. Surb	101	17 66 B
Hollingsworth Rd. Croy	112	34 63 B
Hollington Cres. N Mal	102	22 67 C
Hollington Rd. N17	25	34 90 C
Hollingworth Rd. Orp	108	43 66 B
Hollman Gdns. SW16	97	31 70 B
Holloway Rd. E1	38	38 86 D
Holloway Rd. N19.	36	29 86 B
Holloway Rd. N7	47	30 85 B
Holloway St. Houn	70	13 75 B
Hollowfield La. Nthlt	43	11 84 D
Hollowfield Wlk. Nthlt	43	12 84 A
Holly Ave. N2	23	25 89 B
Holly Ave. Stan	21	18 90 C
Hollybank Cl. Hamp	82	13 71 C
Holly Berry La. NW3	46	26 85 A
Hollybrake Cl. Chis	100	44 70 D
Hollybush Cl. E11	39	40 88 A
Hollybush Gdns. E2	57	34 82 B
Hollybush Hill. E11	39	39 88 B
Hollybush Hill. NW3	46	26 85 A
Holly Bush La. Hamp	92	12 70 D
Hollybush Pl. E2	57	34 82 B
Hollybush Rd. King	93	18 70 B
Hollybush Rd. E13	58	40 82 B
Hollybush St. E13	50	40 83 D
*Hollybush Stps. NW3	46	26 85 A
Holly Bush Vale. NW3	46	26 85 A
Holly Bush Wlk. SW9	75	31 75 D
Holly Cl. Felt	82	12 71 C
Holly Cl. NW10	45	21 84 C
Holly Cres. Beck	106	36 67 B
Holly Cres. Wdf Gr	38	38 91 D
Hollycroft Ave. NW3	35	25 86 C
Hollycroft Ave. Wem	33	18 86 B
Holly Ct. SE26	88	35 71 C
Hollydale Dri. Brom	107	42 65 D
Hollydale Rd. SE15	76	35 76 C
Hollydene. SE13	76	38 74 D
Hollydown Way. E11	38	38 86 D
Hollydown Way. E11	39	39 86 C
Holly Dri. E4	18	37 94 B
Holly Farm Rd. Sthl	59	12 78 C
Hollyfield Ave. N11	16	27 92 D
Hollyfield Rd. Surb	101	18 66 B
Holly Gr. NW9	34	20 87 A
Holly Gr. SE15	75	34 76 C
Holly Hedge Terr. SE13	76	38 74 B
Holly Hill. N21	12	30 95 D
Holly Hill. NW3	46	26 85 A
Holly Hill Rd. Belv	67	49 78 D
Holly Hill Rd. Eri	67	50 78 C
Holly Lodge Gdns. N6	36	28 86 A
Hollymead. Cars	104	27 65 D
Holly Mews. SW10	62	26 78 C
Hollymoor La. Eps	109	20 62 B
Hollymount Cl. SE10	76	38 76 A
Holly Mount. NW3	46	26 85 A
Holly Park Estate. N4	36	30 87 B
Holly Park Gdns. N3	23	25 89 A
Holly Park. N3	23	24 89 B
Holly Park. N4	36	30 87 A
Holly Park Rd. N11	16	28 92 B
Holly Park Rd. W7	54	15 80 D
Holly Rd. E11	39	39 87 B
Holly Rd. Hamp	92	14 70 A
Holly Rd. Houn	70	13 75 D
Holly Rd. Twick	83	16 73 C
Holly Rd. W4	61	20 78 B
Holly St. E8	48	33 84 D
Holly Terr. N6	36	28 87 C
Hollytree Cl. SW19	85	23 73 D
Holly Way. Mit	96	29 68 B
Hollywell Row. EC2	4	33 82 C
Holly Wlk. Enf	13	32 96 B
Holly Wlk. NW3	46	26 85 A
Holly Wlk. Rich	71	18 76 C
Hollywood Mews. SW10	62	26 77 A
Hollywood Rd. E4	18	36 92 C
Hollywood Rd. SW10	62	26 77 A
Hollywood Way. Wdf Gr	26	38 91 D
Holman Rd. Eps	109	20 64 C
Holman Rd. SW11	73	26 76 D
Holmbank Dri. Shep	91	09 68 C
Holmbridge Gdns. Enf	14	35 96 D
Holmbrook Dri. NW4	35	23 88 B
Holmbrook St. E9	49	35 85 D
Holmbury Ct. SW17	86	27 72 D
Holmbury Ct. SW19	96	27 70 C
Holmbury View. E5	37	34 87 D
Holmbush Rd. SW15	73	24 74 C
Holmcote Gdns. N5	48	32 85 C
Holmcroft Way. Brom	107	42 67 B
Holmdale Gdns. NW4	35	23 88 B
Holmdale Rd. Chis	90	44 71 C
Holmdale Rd. NW6	46	25 85 C
Holmdale Terr. N15	37	33 88 C
Holmdene Ave. Har	20	13 89 B
Holmdene Ave. NW7	22	22 91 A
Holmdene Ave. SE24	75	32 74 A
Holmdene Cl. Beck	98	38 69 C
Holmdene Ct. Brom	99	42 68 A
Holmead Rd. SW6	62	25 77 D
Holmefield House. W10	56	24 82 D
Holme Lacey Rd. SE12	77	39 74 D
Holme Rd. E6	42	42 83 A
Holmes Ave. E17	26	36 89 B
Holmes Ave. NW7	15	24 92 C
Holmesdale Ave. SW14	72	19 75 D
Holmesdale Cl. SE25.	97	33 68 B
Holmesdale Rd. Bexh	79	47 76 D
Holmesdale Rd. Croy	105	32 67 B
Holmesdale Rd. N6	36	28 87 B
Holmesdale Rd. Rich	71	18 76 B
Holmesdale Rd. SE25.	97	33 68 D
Holmesdale Rd. Tedd	93	17 70 A
Holmesley Rd. SE23	77	36 74 C
Holmes Rd. NW5	47	28 85 D
Holmes Rd. SW19	95	26 70 C
Holmes Rd. Twick	83	15 72 B
Holmes Terr. SE1	7	31 79 A
Holme Way. Stan	21	15 91 B
Holmewood Gdns. SW2	86	30 73 B
Holmewood Rd. SE25	97	33 68 A
Holmewood Rd. SW2	86	30 73 B
Holmfield Rd. W4	21	21 78 D
Holmhurst Rd. Belv	67	49 78 D
Holmhurst. SE13	76	38 74 D
Holmleigh Ave. Dart	80	53 74 A
Holmleigh Rd. N16	37	33 87 C
Holmsdale Gr. Bexh	80	51 75 A
Holmshaw Cl. SE26	88	36 71 A
Holmside Ct. SW12	74	28 74 C
Holmside Rd. SW12	74	28 74 C
Holmsley Cl. N.Mal	102	21 66 B
Holms St. E2	48	34 83 C
Holmstall Ave. Edg	22	20 90 C
Holm Wlk. SE3	77	40 76 C
Holmwood Cl. Har	20	14 89 A
Holmwood Cl. Nthlt	43	13 84 B
Holmwood Cl. Sutt	110	23 63 D
Holmwood Gdns. N3	23	25 90 C
Holmwood Gdns. Wall	111	28 63 B
Holmwood Rd. Ilf	40	45 86 A
Holmwood Rd. Sutt	110	23 62 A
Holne Chase. Mord	103	25 67 C
Holne Chase. N2	35	26 88 C
Holness Rd. E15	50	39 84 B
Holroyd Rd. SW15	73	23 74 A
Holstein Way. Belv	67	48 79 C
Holsworthy Sq. WC1	3	30 82 D
Holt Cl. N10	24	28 89 C
Holton St. E1	57	35 82 D
Holt Rd. Wem	33	17 86 C
Holt The. Ilf	28	44 91 A
Holt The. Wall	111	29 64 A
Holtwhite Ave. Enf	13	32 97 C
Holtwhite's Hill. Enf	13	31 97 B
Holwell Pl. Pnr	20	12 89 C
Holwood Park Ave. Brom	107	42 65 D
Holwood Pl. SW4	74	29 75 D
Holwood Rd. Brom	99	40 69 C
Holybourne Ave. SW15	73	22 73 A
Holyhead Cl. E3	57	37 82 A
Holyoake Wlk. N2	23	26 89 A
Holyoak Rd. SE11	63	31 78 B
Holyport Rd. SW6	62	23 77 D
Holyrood Gdns. Edg	22	19 90 D
Holyrood Ave. Har	43	12 85 B
Holyrood Rd. Barn	11	26 95 D
Holyrood St. SE1	8	33 80 C
Holywell La. EC2	4	33 82 C
Home Cl. Cars	104	27 65 B
Home Cl. Nthlt	53	12 82 B
Homecroft Rd. N22	25	32 90 A
Homecroft Rd. SE26	88	35 71 C
Home Farm Cl. Shep	91	09 68 C
Home Farm Cl. Surb	101	15 66 B
Homefarm Rd. W7	54	15 81 D
Homefield Ave. Ilf	40	45 88 A
Home Field. Barn	11	24 95 B
Homefield Cl. NW10	45	20 84 A
Homefield Gdns. Mit	95	26 69 D
Homefield Gdns. N2.	23	26 89 B
Homefield Park. Sutt	110	25 63 B
Homefield Rd. Brom	99	41 69 A
Homefield Rd. Edg	22	20 91 B
Homefield Rd. SW19	85	24 71 C
Homefield Rd. Wem	44	16 85 B
Homefield Rise. Orp	108	46 66 C
Homefield St. N1	4	33 83 C
Home Gdns. Dag	41	50 86 C
Home Gdns. Dart	80	54 74 C
Homeland Dri. Sutt	110	25 62 D
Homelands Dri. SE19	97	33 70 C
Homeleigh Rd. SE15	76	35 74 B
Homemead Rd. Brom	107	42 67 B
Homemead Rd. Croy	104	29 67 C
Home Mead. Stan	21	17 90 A
Home Orchard. Dart	80	54 74 C
Home Park Rd. SW19	85	24 72 D
Home Park Wlk. King	93	17 68 D
Homer Ct. Bexh	79	50 76 A
Homer Rd. SW11	74	27 76 C
Homer Rd. Croy	106	35 67 D
Homer Rd. E9	49	36 84 A
Homer Row. W1	1	27 81 A
Homersham Rd. King	94	19 69 C
Homer St. W1	1	27 81 A
Homerton Gr. E9	49	35 85 D
Homerton High St. E9	49	35 85 D

Name	Page	Grid
Homerton Rd. E9	49	36 85 D
Homerton Row. E9	49	35 85 C
Homerton Terr. E9	49	35 84 A
Homesdale Rd. Brom	99	41 68 A
Homesdale Rd. Orp	108	45 66 A
Homesfield. NW11	35	25 88 A
Homesfield. NW11	23	25 89 C
Homestall Rd. SE22	76	35 74 A
Homestead Paddock. N14	12	28 95 B
Homestead Park. NW2	34	21 86 D
Homestead Rd. Dag	41	48 86 B
Homestead Rd. SW6	62	24 77 D
Homestead The. Dart	80	53 74 C
Homestead The. N11	16	28 92 B
Homewaters Ave. Sun	91	09 68 B
Homewood Cl. Hamp	92	12 70 B
Homewood Cres. Chis	100	45 70 A
Homfield Ave. NW4	35	23 88 B
Homildon Ho. SE26	87	34 72 C
Homington Ct. King	93	18 70 C
Honeybourne Rd. NW6	46	25 85 D
Honeybourne Way. Orp	108	44 66 D
Honeybrook Rd. SW12	86	29 73 A
Honey La. EC2	4	32 81 C
Honeypot Cl. NW9	21	18 89 D
Honeypot La. NW9	21	18 89 D
Honeypot La. Stan	21	18 90 C
Honeysett Rd. N17	25	33 90 D
Honeysuckle Cl. Rom	30	53 91 B
Honeywell Rd. SW11	74	27 74 D
Honeywood Rd. Islw	71	16 75 C
Honeywood Rd. NW10	45	21 83 D
Honeywood Wlk. Cars	111	27 64 B
Honister Cl. Stan	21	16 90 B
Honister Gdns. Stan	21	16 90 B
Honister Pl. Stan	21	16 90 B
Honiton Rd. NW6	46	24 83 D
Honiton Rd. Rom	41	50 88 D
Honiton Rd. Well	78	45 76 D
Honley Rd. SE6	88	38 73 A
Honor Oak Park. SE23	76	35 74 D
Honor Oak Rd. SE23	88	35 73 A
Honor Oak Rise. SE23	76	35 74 C
Hood Ave. N14	12	28 95 D
Hood Ave. Orp	108	46 67 B
Hood Ave. SW14	72	20 74 A
Hood Cl. Croy	105	31 66 D
Hoodcote Gdns. N21	17	31 94 B
Hood Rd. SW20	94	21 70 D
Hood Wlk. Rom	29	49 90 B
Hooke Cl. SE10	76	38 76 A
Hooker's Rd. E17	26	35 89 B
Hook Farm Rd. Brom	107	41 67 B
Hookham Ct. SW8	74	29 76 B
Hook Hill. S Croy	112	33 62 C
Hooking Green. Har	32	13 88 B
Hook La. Well	78	45 75 D
Hook Rd. Chess	101	18 65 C
Hook Rd. Eps	109	20 62 A
Hook Rd. Surb	101	18 65 A
Hook Rise N. Surb	101	18 65 A
Hook Rise N. Surb	102	19 65 C
Hook Rise S. Surb	101	18 65 D
Hook Rise S. Surb	102	19 65 C
Hooks Cl. SE15	75	34 76 B
Hooks Hall Dri. Dag	41	50 86 C
Hook The. Barn	11	26 95 D
Hook Underpass. Surb	101	18 65 C
Hook Wlk. Edg	22	20 91 A
Hooper Rd. E16	58	40 81 C
Hooper's St. E15	5	27 79 B
Hooper's Mews. W3	55	20 80 C
Hooper St. E1	57	34 81 C
Hoop La. NW11	35	25 87 A
Hope Cl. SE12	89	40 72 D
Hope Cl. Wdf Gn	27	41 91 A
Hopedale Rd. SE7	65	40 77 B
Hopefield Ave. NW6	46	24 83 C
Hope Park. Brom	99	39 70 D
Hope St. SW11	73	26 75 B
Hopetown St. E1	4	33 81 B
Hopewell St. SE5	63	32 77 D
Hop Gdns. WC2	7	30 80 A
Hopgood St. W12	56	23 80 C
Hopkins St. W1	2	29 81 D
Hoppers Rd. N21	17	31 94 C
Hopping La. N1	48	31 84 B
Hoppingwood Ave. N Mal	94	21 68 A
Hopton Gdns. N.Mal	102	22 67 C
Hopton Rd. SW16	86	30 71 C
Hopton St. SE1	7	31 80 D
Hopwood Rd. SE17	63	32 77 B
Hopwood Wlk. E8	48	34 84 C
Horace Ave. Rom	41	50 87 D
Horace Rd. E7	50	40 85 B
Horace Rd. Ilf	28	44 89 A
Horace Rd. King	93	18 68 B
Horatio St. E2	48	34 83 C
Horatius Way. Croy	111	30 64 D
Horbury Cres. W11	56	25 80 A
Horbury Mews. W11	56	24 80 B
Horder Rd. SW6	73	24 76 A
Hordle Promenade E (off Garnies Cl). SE15	63	33 77 D
Hordle Promenade N. SE15	63	33 77 D
Hordle Promenade S. SE15	63	33 77 D
Hordle Promenade W (off Blake's Rd). SE15	63	33 77 C
Horle Wlk. SW9	75	31 76 D
Horley Cl. Bexh	79	49 74 A
Horley Rd. SE9	89	42 71 A
Hormead Rd. W9	56	24 82 D
Hornbeam Cres. Brent	60	16 77 D
Hornbeam Rd. Bexh	79	50 76 C
Hornbeam Rd. Hay	53	11 81 A
Hornbeam Way. Brom	108	43 67 C
Hornbeam Wlk. Rich	83	18 72 D
Hornbuckle Cl. Har	32	14 86 B
Hornby Cl. NW3	46	26 84 D
Horncastle Cl. SE12	89	40 73 A
Horncastle Rd. SE12	89	40 73 A
Hornchurch Rd. Horn	42	52 87 D
Horndean Cl. SW15	84	22 73 C
Horndon Cl. Rom	29	50 90 A
Horndon Green. Rom	29	50 90 A
Horndon Rd. Rom	29	50 90 A
Horne Rd. Shep	91	07 68 C
Horne Way. SW6	73	23 76 C
Hornfair Rd. SE7	65	41 77 D
Hornford Way. Rom	42	51 87 A
Horniman Dri. SE23	88	35 73 A
Horning Cl. SE9	89	42 71 A
Horn La. SE10	65	40 78 A
Horn La. W3	55	20 81 C
Horn La. Wdf Gn	27	40 91 C
Horn Park Cl. SE12	77	40 74 D
Hornpark La. SE12	77	40 74 D
Hornsey La. N6	36	29 87 C
Hornsey Lane Estate. N19	36	29 87 B
Hornsey Lane Gdns. N6	36	29 87 A
Hornsey Park Rd. N8	24	30 89 B
Hornsey Rd. N19	36	30 86 A
Hornsey Rd. N7	36	30 86 D
Hornsey Rise Gdns. N19	36	30 87 A
Hornsey Rise. N19	36	30 87 A
Hornsey St. N7	47	30 85 D
Hornshay St. SE15	64	35 77 A
Horns End Pl. Ilf	40	44 88 A
Horns Rd. Ilf	40	44 88 A
Hornton Pl. W8	62	25 79 A
Hornton St. W8	62	25 79 A
Horsa Cl. Wall	111	30 63 C
Horsa Rd. Eri	67	50 77 C
Horsa Rd. SE12	89	41 73 A
Horse and Dolphin Yd. W1	6	29 80 B
Horsecroft Cl. Orp	108	46 66 D
Horsecroft Rd. Edg	22	20 91 D
Horse Fair. King	93	17 69 D
Horseferry Pl. SE10	64	38 77 A
Horseferry Rd. SW1	10	29 78 B
Horseguards Ave. SW1	7	30 80 C
Horsell Rd. N5	48	31 85 C
Horsell Rd. Orp	100	46 69 B
Horselydown La. SE1	8	33 80 D
Horsenden Ave. Grnf	44	15 85 D
Horsenden Cres. Grnf	44	15 85 D
Horsenden Lane N. Grnf	44	15 84 D
Horsenden Lane S. Grnf	44	16 83 C
Horse Shoe Alley. SE1	8	32 80 C
Horse Shoe Cres. Nthlt	43	13 83 C
Horse Shoe Green. Sutt	103	25 65 B
Horseshoe La. Enf	13	32 96 A
Horseshoe La. N20	15	23 94 D
Horse Shoe Yd. W1	6	28 80 B
Horse Yd. N1	48	31 83 B
Horsfeld Gdns. SE9	77	42 74 A
Horsfeld Rd. SE9	77	41 74 B
Horsford Rd. SW2	74	30 74 B
Horsham Ave. N12	16	27 92 C
Horsham Rd. Bexh	79	49 74 B
Horsham Rd. Felt	69	08 74 C
Horsley Rd. Brom	99	40 69 B
Horsley Rd. E4	18	38 93 A
Horsley St. SE17	63	32 77 B
Horsman St. SE5	63	32 77 A
Horsmonden Cl. Orp	108	45 68 B
Horsmonden Rd. SE4	76	36 74 D
Hortensia Rd. SW10	62	26 77 C
Horticultural Pl. W4	61	20 78 D
Horton Ave. NW2	46	24 85 A
Horton La. Eps	09	19 62 B
Horton Rd. E8	48	34 84 B
Horton St. SE13	76	37 75 B
Hortus Rd. E4	18	38 93 A
Hortus Rd. Sthl	59	12 79 B
Hosack Rd. SW17	86	28 72 A
Hoser Ave. SE12	89	40 72 A
Hosier La. EC1	3	31 81 B
Hoskin's Cl. E16	58	41 81 C
Hoskins St. SE10	64	38 78 D
Hospital Bridge Rd. Twick	82	13 73 D
Hospital La. Islw	71	15 74 B
Hospital Rd. Houn	70	13 75 A
Hotham Cl. E Mol	92	13 68 A
Hotham Rd. SW15	73	23 75 A
Hotham St. E15	50	39 83 A
Hothfield Pl. SE16	75	35 79 C
Hotspur Rd. Nthlt	43	13 83 C
Hotspur St. SE11	63	31 78 C
Houblon Rd. Rich	71	18 74 A
Houduras St. EC1	4	32 82 C
Houghton Cl (off Buttermere Wlk). E8	48	33 84 B
Houghton Cl (off Buttermere Wlk). E8	48	33 84 B
Houghton Cl. Hamp	92	12 70 A
Houghton Rd. N15	25	33 89 D
Houghton St. WC2	3	30 81 D
Houlder Cres. Croy	112	31 64 D
Houndsditch. EC3	4	33 81 C
Houndsfield Rd. N9	17	34 94 B
Hounsden Rd. N21	13	31 95 C
Hounslow Ave. Houn	70	13 74 B
Hounslow Gdns. Houn	70	13 74 B
Hounslow Rd. Felt	81	10 73 B
Hounslow Rd. Felt	82	12 72 A
Hounslow Rd. Twick	70	14 74 C
Housman Way. SE5	63	32 77 D
Houston Rd. SE23	88	36 72 C
Hove Ave. E17	38	36 88 B
Hoveden Rd. NW2	46	24 85 C
Hove Gdns. Sutt	103	25 66 D
Howard Ave. Eps	109	22 62 C
Howard Cl. Ashf	91	09 70 B
Howard Cl. Hamp	92	14 70 C
Howard Cl. N11	16	28 93 A
Howard Cl. NW2	46	24 85 A
Howard Cl. W3	55	19 81 D
Howard Mews. N5	48	31 85 B
Howard Pl. SW1	6	29 79 C
Howard Rd. Bark	51	44 83 B
Howard Rd. Brom	99	40 70 C
Howard Rd. E11	39	39 86 C
Howard Rd. E17	26	37 89 B
Howard Rd. E6	50	42 83 D
Howard Rd. Islw	71	15 75 B
Howard Rd. N15	37	33 88 C
Howard Rd. N16	48	33 85 A
Howard Rd. N Mal	94	21 68 D
Howard Rd. NW2	46	23 85 B
Howard Rd. SE20	98	35 69 A
Howard Rd. SE25	105	34 67 C
Howard Rd. Sthl	53	13 81 D
Howard Rd. Surb	101	18 67 D
Howards Cl. Pnr	19	10 90 D
Howard's La. SW15	73	23 75 C
Howard's Rd. E13	58	40 82 A
Howard St. Surb	101	16 66 B
Howard Wlk. N2	23	26 89 D
Howarth Rd. SE2	66	46 78 B
Howberry Cl. Edg	21	17 91 B
Howberry Rd. Edg	21	17 91 B
Howberry Rd. Stan	21	17 91 B
Howberry Rd. Th Hth	97	32 69 D
Howbury La. Eri	80	52 76 C
Howbury Rd. SE15	76	35 75 A
Howcroft Cres. N3	23	25 91 C
Howcroft La. Grnf	53	14 82 B
Howden Ct. SE25	97	33 69 D
Howden Rd. SE25	97	33 69 D
Howden St. SE15	75	34 75 A
Howe Cl. Rom	29	49 90 A
Howell Cl. Rom	41	47 88 B
Howell Hill Gr. Eps	110	23 62 C
Howfield Pl. N17	25	33 89 B
Howgate Rd. SW14	72	20 75 B
Howick Pl. SW1	6	29 79 C
Howie St. SW11	73	27 77 C
Howitt Rd. NW3	47	27 84 A
Howland Mews E. W1	2	29 81 A
Howland St. W1	2	29 81 A
Howletts La. Ruis	31	08 88 C
Howletts Rd. SE24	75	32 74 C

Howley Pl. W2...1, 26 81 A
Howley Rd. Croy...105, 31 65 D
Howsman Rd. SW13...61, 22 77 A
Howson Rd. SE4...76, 36 75 C
How's St. E2...48, 33 83 D
Hoxton Market. N1...4, 33 82 A
Hoxton Sq. N1...4, 33 82 A
Hoxton St. N1...4, 33 83 C
Hoylake Cres. Uxb...31, 10 86 D
Hoylake Gdns. Mit...96, 29 68 A
Hoylake Gdns. Ruis...31, 10 86 D
Hoylake Rd. W3...21, 21 81 C
Hoyle Rd. SW17...86, 27 71 C
Hoy St. E16...58, 39 81 D
Hubbard Rd. SE27...87, 32 71 A
Hubbard St. E15...50, 39 83 A
Hubert Gr. SW9...74, 30 75 A
Hubert Rd. E6...38, 41 82 B
Hucknall Cl. Rom...30, 54 91 B
Huddart St. E3...57, 36 81 B
Huddlestone Rd. E7...50, 39 85 B
Huddlestone Rd. NW2...45, 22 84 B
Huddleston Rd. N7...47, 29 85 B
Hudson Pl. SE18...38, 44 78 C
Hudson Rd. Bexh...79, 48 76 D
Hudson Rd. King...93, 18 69 A
Hudson's Pl. SW1...1, 29 78 A
Huggin Ct. EC4...8, 32 80 A
Huggin Hill. EC4...8, 32 80 A
Hughan Rd. E15...50, 39 85 C
Hughenden Ave. Har...33, 16 88 B
Hughenden Gdns. Nthlt...53, 11 82 A
Hughenden Rd. Wor Pk...102, 22 66 B
Hughes Mansions. E1...57, 34 82 C
Hughes Rd. Ashf...91, 08 70 A
Hughes Wlk. Croy...105, 32 66 A
Hugh Mews. SW1...9, 28 78 B
Hugh Pl. SW1...10, 29 78 B
Hugh St. SW1...9, 28 78 B
Hugon Rd. SW6...73, 25 75 B
Hugo Rd. N19...47, 29 85 A
Huguenot Pl. SW18...73, 26 74 A
Huguenot Sq. SE15...75, 34 75 B
Huitt Sq. SW11...1, 26 75 B
Hullbridge Mews. N1...48, 32 83 A
Hull St. EC1...8, 32 82 A
Hulme Pl. SE1...8, 32 79 A
Hulse Ave. Bark...51, 45 84 A
Hulse Ave. Rom...29, 49 90 B
Hulverston Cl. Sutt...110, 25 62 B
Humber Rd. NW2...34, 22 86 B
Humber Rd. SE3...65, 39 77 B
Humberstone Rd. E13...58, 41 82 A
Humberton Cl. E9...49, 36 85 C
Humbolt Rd. W6...62, 24 77 A
Humes Ave. W7...60, 15 79 B
Hume Way. Ruis...31, 10 88 C
Humphrey St. SE1...63, 33 78 D
Humphries Cl. Dag...52, 48 85 B
Hundred Acre. NW9...22, 21 90 D
Hungerdown. E4...18, 38 94 C
Hungerford Bridge (foot). WC2...7, 30 80 D
Hungerford La. WC2...7, 30 80 C
Hungerford Rd. N7...47, 30 85 C
Hungerford St. E1...57, 34 81 D
Hunsdon Cl. Dag...52, 48 84 A
Hunsdon Rd. SE14...64, 35 77 D
Hunslett St. E2...49, 35 83 C
Hunston Rd. Mord...103, 25 66 D
Hunter Cl. SE1...8, 32 79 D
Hunter Rd. Ilf...51, 43 85 D
Hunter Rd. SW20...95, 23 69 A
Hunter Rd. Th Hth...97, 32 68 B
Hunters Cl. SW12...86, 28 73 C
Hunters Ct. Rich...71, 17 74 B
Hunters Gr. Har...21, 17 89 C
Hunters Hall Rd. Dag...52, 49 85 D
Hunters Hill. Ruis...32, 11 88 D
Hunters Meadow. SE19...87, 33 71 A
Hunter Sq. Dag...52, 49 85 A
Hunters Rd. Chess...101, 18 65 C
Hunter St. WC1...3, 30 82 C
Hunters Way. Croy...112, 33 64 A
Hunters Way. Enf...13, 31 97 A
Hunter Wlk. E13...50, 40 83 C
Huntingdon Cl. Mit...96, 30 68 A
Huntingdon Gdns. Wor Pk...103, 23 65 C
Huntingdon Rd. N2...24, 27 89 A
Huntingdon Rd. N9...18, 34 94 C
Huntingdon St. E16...58, 39 80 B
Huntingdon St. N1...47, 30 84 D
Huntingfield Rd. SW15...72, 22 74 A
Huntings Rd. Dag...52, 49 84 A
Huntley Dri. N3...23, 25 91 A
Huntley St. WC1...2, 29 82 D

Huntley Way. SW20...94, 22 69 C
Huntly Rd. SE25...97, 33 68 C
Hunton St. E1...57, 34 82 C
Hunt Rd. Sthl...59, 13 79 C
Hunts Cl. SE3...77, 40 76 C
Hunt's Ct. WC2...7, 29 80 B
Hunt's La. E15...49, 38 83 C
Huntsman Rd. Ilf...28, 46 91 A
Huntsman St. SE17...63, 33 78 B
Hunts Mead Cl. Chis...99, 42 70 D
Hunts Mead. Enf...14, 35 96 B
Huntsmoor Rd. Eps...109, 20 64 D
Huntspill St. SW17...85, 26 72 C
Hunts Slip Rd. SE21...87, 33 72 A
Hunt St. W11...56, 23 80 D
Huntsworth Mews. NW1...1, 27 82 D
Huntsworth Mews. NW1...1, 27 82 D
Hurley Rd. Grnf...53, 13 81 B
Hurlingham Ct. SW6...73, 24 75 B
Hurlingham Gdns. SW6...73, 24 75 B
Hurlingham Rd. Bexh...67, 48 77 D
Hurlingham Rd. SW6...73, 24 76 D
Hurlock St. N5...37, 31 86 D
Hurlstone Rd. SE25...105, 33 67 A
Hurn Court Rd. Houn...70, 11 76 D
Hurnford Cl. S Croy...112, 33 62 C
Huron Rd. SW17...86, 28 72 C
Hurren Cl. SE3...77, 39 75 A
Hurry Cl. E15...50, 39 84 C
Hurst Ave. E4...18, 37 93 C
Hurst Ave. N6...36, 29 88 C
Hurstbourne Gdns. Bark...51, 45 84 A
Hurstbourne Rd. SE23...88, 36 73 C
Hurst Cl. Brom...107, 39 66 D
Hurst Cl. Chess...109, 19 64 C
Hurst Cl. E4...18, 37 93 C
Hurst Cl. Nthlt...43, 12 85 D
Hurst Cl. NW11...35, 25 88 D
Hurstcourt Rd. Sutt...103, 25 65 B
Hurstdene Ave. Brom...107, 39 66 D
Hurstdene Gdns. N16...37, 33 87 A
Hurstfield Brom...107, 40 67 A
Hurstfield Rd. E Mol...92, 13 68 A
Hurst La. E Mol...92, 14 68 A
Hurstlands Cl. Horn...42, 53 88 C
Hurst La. SE2...67, 47 78 D
Hurstleigh Gdns. Ilf...28, 43 90 A
Hurst Lodge. Wem...44, 18 84 D
Hurst ParkE Mol...92, 13 69 D
Hurst Pl. SE2...67, 47 78 D
Hurst Rd. Croy...112, 32 64 D
Hurst Rd. E17...26, 37 89 B
Hurst Rd. E Mol...92, 13 68 B
Hurst Rd. Eri...67, 50 77 C
Hurst Rd. N21...17, 31 94 C
Hurst Rd. Sid...90, 46 72 B
Hurst Rd. Walt...92, 11 68 D
Hurst Rise. Barn...11, 25 96 A
Hurst St. SE24...75, 31 74 D
Hurstview Grange. S Croy...112, 31 63 D
Hurst View Rd. S Croy...112, 33 63 C
Hurst Way. S Croy...112, 33 63 A
Hurstway Walk. W11...56, 23 80 B
Hurstwood Ave. Bexh...80, 51 76 C
Hurstwood Ave. E18...27, 40 89 D
Hurstwood Ave. Eri...80, 51 76 A
Hurstwood Dri. Brom...99, 42 68 B
Hurstwood Rd. NW11...23, 24 89 D
Huson Cl. NW3...47, 27 84 C
Husseywell Cres. Brom...107, 40 66 C
Hutching's St. E14...64, 37 79 A
Hutchings Wlk. NW11...23, 25 89 D
Hutchins Cl. E15...49, 38 84 C
Hutchinson Ct. Rom...29, 47 89 D
Hutchinson Ct. Rom...29, 47 89 D
Hutchinson Terr. Wem...33, 17 86 D
Hutton Cl. Grnf...43, 14 85 D
Hutton Cl. Wdf Gn...27, 40 91 B
Hutton Gdns. Har...20, 14 91 C
Hutton Gr. N12...15, 25 92 D
Hutton La. Har...20, 14 91 D
Hutton La. Har...20, 14 91 D
Hutton St. EC4...3, 31 81 C
Hutton Wlk. Har...20, 14 91 C
Huxbear St. SE4...76, 36 74 B
Huxley Cl. Nthlt...43, 12 83 A
Huxley Dri. Rom...40, 46 87 B
Huxley Gdns. NW10...44, 18 83 D
Huxley Pl. N13...17, 31 93 D
Huxley Rd. E10...38, 38 86 A
Huxley Rd. N18...17, 33 92 A
Huxley Rd. Well...78, 45 75 B
Huxley Sayze. N18...17, 32 92 D
Huxley St. W10...56, 24 82 A
Hyacinth Cl. Hamp...92, 13 70 A

Hyacinth Rd. SW15...84, 22 73 C
Hyde Cl. Barn...11, 24 96 B
Hyde Cl. E13...50, 40 83 C
Hyde Cres. NW9...34, 21 88 A
Hyde Estate Rd. NW9...34, 21 88 B
Hydefield Cl. N21...17, 32 94 D
Hydefield Ct. N9...17, 33 93 A
Hyde La. SW11...74, 27 76 A
Hyde Park Ave. N21...17, 32 94 D
Hyde Park Cnr. SW1...6, 28 79 A
Hyde Park Cres. W2...1, 27 81 C
Hyde Park Gate Mews. SW7...5, 26 79 A
Hyde Park Gate. SW7...5, 26 79 A
Hyde Park Gate. W8...5, 26 79 A
Hyde Park Gdns Mews. W2...5, 27 80 A
Hyde Park Gdns. N21...1, 32 94 C
Hyde Park Gdns. W2...5, 27 80 A
Hyde Park Sq Mews. W2...1, 27 81 C
Hyde Park Sq. W2...1, 27 81 C
Hyde Park St. W2...1, 27 81 C
Hyde Rd. Bexh...79, 48 76 D
Hyde Rd. N1...48, 33 83 A
Hyde Rd. Rich...71, 18 74 B
Hydeside Gdns. N9...17, 33 93 B
*Hyde's Pl. N1...48, 31 84 C
Hyde St. SE8...64, 37 77 A
Hyde Terr. Ashf...91, 09 70 A
Hyde The. Nwp...22, 21 89 C
Hydethorpe Ave. N9...17, 33 93 B
Hydethorpe Rd. SW12...86, 29 73 C
Hyde Vale. SE10...76, 38 76 B
Hyde Way. N9...17, 33 93 B
Hyde Wlk. Mord...103, 25 66 A
Hyland Cl. Horn...42, 52 87 B
Hylands Rd. E17...26, 38 90 D
Hyland Way. Horn...42, 52 87 B
Hylton St. SE18...66, 45 78 B
Hyndewood. SE23...88, 35 72 D
Hyndman St. SE15...63, 34 77 B
Hynton Rd. Dag...41, 47 86 A
Hyperion House. SW2...74, 30 74 D
Hyperion Pl. Eps...109, 20 62 B
Hyrstdene. S Croy...112, 31 64 B
Hyson Rd. SE16...63, 34 78 D
Hythe Ave. Bexh...67, 48 77 D
Hythe Cl. N18...17, 34 92 A
Hythe Path. Th Hth...97, 32 68 B
Hythe Rd. NW10...55, 22 82 C
Hythe Rd. Th Hth...97, 32 69 D
Hythe St. Dart...80, 54 74 C

Ian Ct. SE23...88, 35 72 A
Ian Sq. Enf...14, 35 97 B
Ibbotson Ave. E16...58, 39 81 D
Ibbott St. E1...57, 35 82 C
Iberian Ave. Wall...111, 30 64 A
Ibis La. W4...72, 20 76 A
Ibscott Cl. Dag...52, 50 84 A
Ibsley Gdns. SW15...84, 22 73 C
Ibsley Way. Barn...12, 27 96 C
Iceland Rd. E3...49, 37 83 A
Ickburgh Estate. E5...37, 34 86 B
Ickburgh Rd. E5...37, 34 86 D
Ickenham Cl. Ruis...31, 08 86 B
Ickenham Rd. Ruis...31, 08 87 D
Ickleton Rd. SE9...89, 42 71 A
Icknield Dri. Ilf...40, 43 88 B
Ickworth Park Rd. E17...26, 36 89 C
Ida Rd. N15...25, 32 89 D
Ida St. E14...58, 38 81 C
Iden Cl. Brom...99, 39 68 A
Idlecombe Rd. SW17...96, 28 70 A
Idmiston Rd. E15...50, 39 85 D
Idmiston Rd. SE27...87, 32 72 A
Idmiston Rd. Wor Pk...102, 21 66 B
Idmiston Sq. Wor Pk...102, 21 66 B
Idol La. EC3...8, 33 80 A
Idonia St. SE8...64, 37 77 C
Iffley Rd. W6...61, 22 79 C
Ifield Rd. SW10...62, 25 77 B
Ightham Rd. Eri...67, 49 77 C
Ilbert St. W10...56, 24 82 A
Ilchester Gdns. W2...56, 25 80 B
Ilchester Pl. W14...62, 24 79 D
Ilchester Rd. Dag...52, 47 85 C
Ildersly Gr. SE21...87, 32 72 B
Ilderton Rd. SE15...64, 35 77 A
Ilderton Rd. SE16...64, 35 78 C
Ilex Rd. NW10...45, 21 84 B
Ilex Way. SW16...87, 31 71 C
Ilford Hill. Ilf...40, 43 88 C
Ilford La. Ilf...40, 43 88 C
Ilford La. Ilf...51, 44 85 C
Ilfracombe Gdns. Rom...40, 46 87 B
Ilfracombe Rd. Brom...89, 39 72 D

Iliffe St. SE17

Iliffe St. SE17 .....63 — 31 78 D
Iliffe Yd. SE17 .....63 — 31 78 D
Ilkley Cl. SE19 .....97 — 32 70 B
Ilkley Rd. E16 .....58 — 41 81 A
Illingworth Cl. Mit. .....95 — 26 68 B
Illingworth Way. Enf .....13 — 33 95 A
Ilmington Rd. Har .....33 — 17 88 D
Ilminster Gdns. SW11 .....74 — 27 75 C
Imber Cl. N14 .....16 — 29 94 A
Imber Cross. E Mol .....101 — 15 67 D
Imber St. N1 .....48 — 32 83 B
Impact Rd. SE20 .....97 — 34 69 D
Imperial Ave. N16 .....48 — 33 85 A
Imperial Cl. Har .....32 — 13 88 C
Imperial College Rd. SW7 .....5 — 26 79 D
Imperial Ct. Har .....32 — 13 87 A
Imperial Dri. Har .....32 — 13 88 C
Imperial Gdns. Mit .....96 — 26 70 C
Imperial Mews. E6 .....50 — 41 83 D
Imperial Rd. Felt. .....81 — 09 73 A
Imperial Rd. N22 .....24 — 30 90 A
Imperial Rd. SW6 .....73 — 25 76 B
Imperial Sq. SW6 .....73 — 26 76 C
Imperial Sq. SW6 .....73 — 25 76 B
Imperial St. E3 .....58 — 38 82 A
Imperial Way. Chis .....90 — 44 72 C
Imperial Way. Croy .....112 — 31 63 A
Imperial Way. Har .....33 — 18 88 C
Inca Dri. SE9 .....90 — 43 73 B
Inchmery Rd. SE6 .....88 — 38 73 C
Independents Rd. SE3 .....77 — 39 75 B
Inderwick Rd. N8 .....36 — 30 88 D
India St. EC3 .....4 — 33 81 D
India Way. W12 .....55 — 22 80 B
Indus Rd. SE7 .....65 — 41 77 C
Ingal Rd. E13 .....58 — 40 82 C
Ingate Pl. SW8 .....74 — 28 76 B
Ingatestone Rd. E12 .....39 — 41 87 C
Ingatestone Rd. SE25 .....105 — 34 67 B
Ingatestone Rd. Wdf Gn. .....27 — 40 91 D
Ingersoll Rd. W12 .....55 — 22 80 D
Ingestre Pl. W1 .....6 — 29 80 A
Ingestre Rd. E7 .....50 — 40 85 A
Ingestre Rd. NW5 .....47 — 28 85 B
Ingham Rd. NW6 .....46 — 25 85 A
Inglebert St. EC1 .....3 — 31 82 A
Ingleborough St. SW9 .....75 — 31 76 C
Ingleby Dri. Har .....32 — 14 86 D
Ingleby Rd. Dag .....52 — 49 84 B
Ingleby Rd. Ilf. .....40 — 43 87 D
Ingleby Rd. N7 .....36 — 30 86 C
Ingleby Way. Chis .....90 — 43 71 C
Ingleby Way. Wall .....111 — 29 63 D
Ingle Cl. Pnr .....20 — 12 89 A
Ingledew Rd. SE18 .....66 — 44 78 D
Inglefield Sq. E1 .....57 — 34 80 D
Inglehurst Gdns. Ilf. .....39 — 42 88 B
Inglelow Rd. SW8 .....74 — 28 76 D
Inglemere Rd. Mit. .....96 — 27 70 D
Inglemere Rd. SE23 .....88 — 35 72 D
Inglesham Wlk. E9 .....49 — 36 84 B
Ingleside Cl. Beck. .....98 — 37 70 C
Ingleside Gr. SE3 .....65 — 39 77 B
Inglethorpe St. SW6 .....73 — 23 76 B
Ingleton Ave. Well .....78 — 46 75 A
Ingleton Rd. Cars. .....111 — 27 62 A
Ingleton Rd. N18 .....25 — 34 91 A
Ingleton St. SW9 .....75 — 31 76 C
Ingleway. N12 .....24 — 27 91 A
Inglewood. Chis .....100 — 44 70 B
Inglewood Cl. Chig. .....28 — 42 69 D
Inglewood Copse. Brom .....99 — 50 75 D
Inglewood Rd. Bexh .....79 — 25 85 C
Inglewood Rd. NW6 .....46 — 33 66 D
Inglis Rd. Croy .....105 — 18 80 B
Inglis Rd. W5 .....54 — 32 76 A
Inglis St. SE5 .....75 — 26 87 A
Ingram Ave. NW11 .....35 — 17 69 A
Ingram House. King .....93 — 27 89 C
Ingram Rd. N2 .....24 — 32 69 A
Ingram Rd. Th Hth .....97 — 14 83 B
Ingram Way. Grnf .....43 — 51 89 C
Ingrave Rd. Rom .....30 — 27 75 A
Ingrave St. SW11 .....74 — 21 78 C
Ingress St. W4 .....61 — 42 77 C
Inigo Jones Rd. SE7 .....65 — 30 80 A
Inigo Pl. WC2 .....7 — 28 84 B
Inkerman Rd. NW5 .....47 — 38 92 C
Inks Green. E4 .....18 — 21 84 C
Inman Rd. NW10 .....45 — 26 73 A
Inman Rd. SW18 .....85 — 28 82 A
Inner Circ. NW1 .....2 — 23 72 B
Inner Park Rd. SW19 .....85 — 07 75 B
Inner Ring E. Houn .....69 — 07 75 A
Inner Ring W. Houn .....69 — 20 76 A
Inner Staithe. W4 72

Inner Temple La. EC4 .....3 — 31 81 C
Innes Cl. SW20 .....95 — 24 69 C
Innes Gdns. SW15 .....72 — 22 74 D
Innes Yd. Croy .....105 — 32 65 C
Inniskilling Rd. E13 .....50 — 41 83 C
Inskip Cl. E10 .....38 — 37 86 B
Inskip Dri. Horn .....42 — 54 87 C
Inskip Rd. Dag .....41 — 47 87 D
Institute Pl. E8 .....34 — 34 85 D
Instone Cl. Wall. .....111 — 30 63 C
Insurance St. WC1 .....3 — 31 82 A
Interger Gdns. E11 .....38 — 38 87 B
International Ave. Houn .....59 — 11 78 C
Inverary Pl. SE18 .....66 — 44 77 B
Inver Cl. E5 .....38 — 35 86 A
Inverclyde Gdns. Rom .....29 — 47 89 D
Inveresk Gdns. Wor Pk. .....102 — 22 65 C
Inverforth Cl. NW3 .....35 — 26 86 A
Inverforth Rd. N11 .....16 — 28 92 D
Inverine Rd. SE7 .....65 — 40 78 D
Invermore Pl. SE18 .....66 — 44 78 A
Inverness Ave. Enf .....13 — 33 97 A
Inverness Dri. Ilf. .....28 — 45 91 A
Inverness Mews. W2 .....56 — 25 80 B
Inverness Pl. W2 .....56 — 25 80 B
Inverness Rd. Houn .....13 — 75 C
Inverness Rd. N18 .....17 — 34 92 D
Inverness Rd. Sthl .....59 — 12 78 A
Inverness Rd. Wor Pk. .....103 — 23 66 D
Inverness St. NW1 .....47 — 28 83 B
Inverness Terr. W2 .....56 — 25 80 B
Inverton Rd. SE15 .....76 — 35 75 D
Invicta Cl. Chis .....90 — 43 71 C
Invicta Gr. Ntht .....53 — 12 82 B
Invicta Rd. SE3 .....65 — 40 77 A
Inville Rd. SE17 .....63 — 32 78 D
Inville Wlk. SE17 .....63 — 32 78 D
Inwood Ave. Houn .....70 — 14 75 A
Inwood Cl. Croy .....106 — 36 65 A
Inwood Rd. Houn .....70 — 14 75 C
Inworth St. SW11 .....74 — 27 76 C
Inworth Wlk. N1 .....48 — 32 83 A
Ipswich Rd. SW17 .....96 — 28 70 A
Ireland Yd. EC4 .....3 — 31 81 D
Irongate Wharf Rd. W2 .....1 — 26 81 B
Iron Mill La. Dart .....80 — 51 75 D
Iron Mill Pl. Dart .....80 — 51 75 D
Iron Mill Pl. SW18 .....73 — 25 74 D
Iron Mill Rd. SW18 .....73 — 25 74 D
Ironmonger La. EC2 .....4 — 32 81 D
Ironmonger Pas. EC1 .....4 — 32 82 A
Ironmonger Row. EC1 .....4 — 32 82 A
Irons Way. Rom .....29 — 50 91 C
Irvine Ave. Har .....21 — 16 89 B
Irvine Cl. N20 .....16 — 27 93 A
Irvine Way. Orp .....108 — 45 66 B
Irving Ave. Ntht .....43 — 11 83 B
Irving Gr. SW9 .....74 — 30 76 D
Irving Rd. W14 .....62 — 23 79 D
Irving St. WC2 .....6 — 29 80 B
Irwell Estate. SE16 .....59 — 35 79 A
Irwin Ave. SE18 .....66 — 45 77 C
Irwin Gdns. NW10 .....45 — 22 83 B
Isabella Rd. E9 .....49 — 35 85 C
Isabella St. SE1 .....7 — 31 80 D
Isabel St. SW9 .....74 — 30 76 B
Isbell Gdns. Rom .....30 — 51 91 C
Isel Way. SE22 .....75 — 33 74 A
Isham Rd. SW16 .....96 — 30 69 C
Isia Rd. SE18 .....65 — 44 77 A
Isis St. SW18 .....85 — 26 72 A
Island Rd. Mit .....96 — 27 70 D
Island Row. E14 .....57 — 36 81 D
Islay Gdns. Houn .....70 — 11 74 B
Islay Wlk. N1 .....48 — 32 84 A
Isledon Rd. N7 .....37 — 31 86 C
Islehurst Cl. Chis .....100 — 43 69 A
Islington Green .....48 — 31 83 B
Islington High St. N1 .....48 — 31 84 C
Islington Park St. N1 .....48 — 31 84 C
Islip Gdns. Edg .....22 — 20 91 D
Islip Gdns. Ntht .....12 84 C
Islip Manor Rd. Ntht. .....43 — 12 84 C
Islip St. NW5 .....47 — 29 85 C

Ismailia Rd. E7 .....50 — 40 84 D
Isom Cl. E13 .....58 — 40 82 B
Ivanhoe Dri. Har .....21 — 16 90 D
Ivanhoe Rd. Houn .....70 — 11 75 B
Ivanhoe Rd. SE5 .....75 — 33 75 B
Ivatt Pl. W14 .....62 — 24 78 D
Ivatt Way. N15 .....25 — 32 89 A
Iveagh Ave. NW10 .....45 — 19 83 C
Iveagh Cl. E9 .....49 — 35 83 B
Iveagh Cl. Nthwd .....19 — 07 90 B
Iveagh Cl. NW10 .....45 — 19 83 C
Ivedon Rd. Well .....79 — 47 76 C
Iveley Rd. SW4 .....74 — 29 76 C
Iver Cl. N1 .....48 — 32 84 A
Ivere Dri. Barn .....11 — 25 95 D
Iverhurst Cl. Bexh .....79 — 47 74 B
Iverna Ct. W8 .....62 — 25 79 C
Iverna Gdns. Felt .....69 — 08 74 B
Iverna Gdns. W8 .....62 — 25 79 C
Iverson Rd. NW6 .....46 — 25 84 A
Ives Gdns. Rom .....30 — 51 89 D
Ives Rd. E16 .....58 — 39 81 A
Ives St. SW3 .....9 — 27 78 A
Ivestor Terr. S .....88 — 35 73 A
Ivimey St. E2 .....57 — 34 82 A
Ivinghoe Cl. Enf .....13 — 33 97 A
Ivinghoe Rd. Dag .....51 — 46 85 D
Ivor Gr. SE9 .....90 — 43 73 D
Ivor Pl. NW1 .....1 — 27 82 D
Ivor St. NW1 .....47 — 29 84 C
Ivorydown. Brom .....89 — 40 71 A
Ivybridge La. WC2 .....7 — 30 80 A
Ivychurch Cl. SE20 .....98 — 35 70 C
Ivy Church La. SE17 .....63 — 33 78 D
Ivy Cl. Har .....32 — 12 85 B
Ivy Cl. Pnr .....31 — 11 87 A
Ivy Cl. Sun .....92 — 11 69 C
Ivy Cottages. E14 .....57 — 37 80 B
Ivy Cres. W4 .....61 — 20 78 A
Ivydale Rd. Cars .....104 — 27 65 B
Ivydale Rd. SE15 .....76 — 35 75 D
Ivyday Gr. SW16 .....86 — 30 72 D
Ivydene Cl. Sutt. .....110 — 26 64 A
Ivydene Rd. E8 .....48 — 34 84 C
Ivy Gdns. Mit. .....96 — 29 68 B
Ivy Gdns. N8 .....36 — 30 88 C
Ivyhouse Rd. Dag .....52 — 48 84 A
Ivyhouse Rd. Uxb .....31 — 07 86 D
Ivy La. Houn .....70 — 12 75 D
Ivymount Rd. SE27 .....87 — 31 72 C
Ivy Rd. E16 .....58 — 40 81 C
Ivy Rd. E17 .....38 — 37 88 C
Ivy Rd. Houn .....70 — 13 75 D
Ivy Rd. N14 .....16 — 29 94 B
Ivy Rd. NW2 .....46 — 23 85 A
Ivy Rd. SE4 .....76 — 36 75 D
Ivy St. N1 .....48 — 33 83 C
Ivy Wlk. Dag .....52 — 48 84 A
Ivy Wlk. Nthwd .....19 — 09 90 A
Izane Rd. Bexh .....79 — 48 75 D

Jack Barnett Way. N22 .....24 — 30 90 D
Jack Cornwell St. E12 .....51 — 43 85 A
Jackets La. Nthwd .....19 — 07 91 D
Jackman St. E8 .....48 — 34 83 B
Jackson Rd. Bark .....51 — 44 83 B
Jackson Rd. Barn .....12 — 27 95 C
Jackson Rd. Brom .....107 — 42 66 D
Jackson Rd. N7 .....47 — 30 85 B
Jackson's La. N6 .....36 — 28 87 B
Jackson's Pl. Croy .....105 — 32 66 D
Jackson St. SE18 .....66 — 43 77 A
Jack Walker Ct. N5 .....48 — 31 85 B
Jacob St. SE1 .....63 — 34 79 A
Jacob's Well Mews. W1 .....2 — 28 81 C
Jacqueline Cl. Nthlt .....43 — 12 83 A
Jaffray Pl. SE27 .....87 — 31 71 B
Jaffray Rd. Brom .....99 — 41 68 D
Jaggard Way. SW12 .....86 — 27 73 B
Jago Cl. SE18 .....66 — 44 77 A
Jago Wlk. SE5 .....63 — 32 77 D
Jamaica Rd. SE16 .....63 — 34 79 C
Jamaica Rd. Th Hth .....105 — 31 67 D
Jamaica St. E1 .....57 — 35 81 A
James Ave. Dag .....41 — 48 87 D
James Ave. NW2 .....46 — 23 85 C
James Bedford Cl. Pnr .....20 — 11 90 C
James Boswell Cl. SW16 .....87 — 31 71 A
James Cl. E13 .....50 — 40 83 C
James Cl. Rom .....42 — 52 88 A
James Cl. N1 .....48 — 32 83 A
James Dudson Ct. NW10 .....45 — 20 84 C
James Gdns. N22 .....25 — 32 91 C

Street	No.	Map
James La. E10	38	38 87 A
James La. E11	39	39 88 C
Jameson St. W8	56	25 80 C
James Pl. N17	25	33 90 B
James Rd. Dart	80	52 74 C
James St. Bark	51	44 84 C
James St. Enf	13	33 95 B
James St. Houn	70	14 75 B
James St. W1	2	28 81 C
James St. WC2	7	30 80 A
Jamestown Rd. NW1	47	28 83 B
Jane St. E1	57	34 81 D
Janet St. E14	57	37 79 C
*Janeway Pl. SE16	63	34 79 B
Janeway St. SE16	63	34 79 A
Janice Mews. Ilf	40	43 86 D
Jansen Wlk. SW11	73	26 75 B
Janson Cl. E15	50	39 85 C
Janson Rd. E15	50	39 85 C
Jansons Rd. N15	25	33 89 A
Japan Cres. N4	36	30 87 B
Japan Rd. Rom	41	47 88 D
Jardin St. SE5	63	33 77 A
Jarrett Cl. SW2	87	31 73 D
Jarrow Cl. Mord	103	25 67 B
Jarrow Rd. N15	25	34 89 D
Jarrow Rd. Rom	41	47 88 C
Jarrow Rd. SE16	64	35 78 A
Jarrow Way. E9	49	36 85 B
Jarvis Cl. Barn	11	23 95 B
Jarvis Rd. S Croy	112	32 63 B
Jarvis Rd. SE22	75	33 75 C
Jasmine Cl. Orp	108	43 65 B
Jasmine Gdns. Croy	106	37 65 D
Jasmine Gdns. Har	32	13 86 A
Jasmine Gr. SE20	97	34 69 B
Jasmin Rd. Eps	109	20 64 D
Jason Cl. W1	2	28 81 C
Jason Wlk. SE9	90	43 71 A
Jasper Pas. SE19	97	33 70 B
Jasper Rd. SE19	97	33 70 B
Javelin Way. Nthlt	53	11 82 B
Jaycroft. Enf	13	31 97 A
Jay Mews. SW7	5	26 79 A
Jebb Ave. SW2	74	30 74 C
Jebb St. E3	49	37 83 C
Jedburgh Rd. E13	58	41 82 A
Jedburgh St. SW11	74	28 75 C
Jeddo Rd. W12	61	21 79 B
Jefferson Cl. Ilf	40	43 88 B
Jefferson Cl. W13	60	16 79 D
Jefferson Wlk. SE18	66	43 77 A
Jeffrey's Pl. NW1	47	29 84 C
Jeffrey's Rd. Enf	14	36 96 D
Jeffrey's Rd. SW4	74	30 76 C
Jeffrey's St. NW1	47	29 84 C
Jeffreys Wlk. SW4	74	30 76 C
Jeffs Rd. Sutt	110	24 64 B
Jeken Rd. SE9	77	41 75 C
Jelf Rd. SW2	75	31 74 A
Jellicoe Gdns. Stan	21	15 91 B
Jellicoe Gdns. Stan	21	16 91 A
Jellicoe Rd. N17	25	32 91 D
Jengar Cl. Sutt	110	25 64 B
Jenkins La. Bark	51	43 83 D
Jenkins Rd. E13	58	40 82 D
Jenner Pl. SW13	61	22 77 B
Jenner Rd. N16	37	34 88 A
Jennett Rd. Croy	105	31 65 C
Jennifer Rd. Brom	89	39 72 D
Jennings Rd. SE22	75	33 74 D
Jennings Way. Barn	11	23 96 A
Jenningtree Rd. Eri	68	52 77 D
Jenningtree Way. Belv	67	50 79 A
Jenny Path. Rom	30	53 91 D
Jenson Way. SE19	97	33 70 D
Jenton Ave. Bexh	79	48 76 C
Jephson Rd. E7	50	41 84 C
Jephson St. SE5	75	32 76 B
Jeppo's La. Mit	95	27 68 D
Jerdan Pl. SW6	62	25 77 C
Jeremiah St. E14	57	37 81 D
Jeremy's Green. N18	18	35 92 A
Jermyn St. SW1	6	29 80 C
Jerningham Ave. Ilf	28	43 90 D
Jerningham Rd. SE14	76	36 76 A
Jerome Cres. NW8	1	27 82 C
Jerome St. E1		33 82 D
Jerrard St. SE13	76	37 75 B
Jerrold St. N1	48	33 83 C
Jersey Ave. Stan	21	17 90 C
Jersey Dri. Orp	108	44 67 D
Jersey Rd. E11	38	38 87 D
Jersey Rd. E16	58	41 81 C
Jersey Rd. Houn	70	13 76 B
Jersey Rd. Houn	59	13 77 D
Jersey Rd. Ilf	51	43 85 B
Jersey Rd. Islw	59	14 77 D
Jersey Rd. SW17	96	28 70 B
Jersey Rd. W7	60	16 79 A
Jersey St. E2	57	34 82 B
Jerusalem Pas. EC1	3	31 82 D
Jervis Ct. W1	2	28 81 D
Jerviston Gdns. SW16	87	31 70 A
Jesmond Ave. Wem	44	18 84 B
Jesmond Rd. Croy	105	33 66 B
Jessam Ave. E5	37	34 87 D
Jessamine Rd. W7	54	15 80 D
Jesse Rd. E10	38	38 87 C
Jessica Rd. SW18	73	26 74 A
Jessop Rd. SE24	75	32 75 C
Jessops Way. Croy	104	29 67 C
Jessup Cl. SE18	66	44 78 A
Jetstar Way. Nthlt	53	12 82 A
Jewel Rd. E17	26	37 89 A
Jewry St. EC3		33 81 D
Jews Rd. SW18	73	26 75 C
Jews Wlk. SE26	87	34 71 B
Jeymer Ave. NW2	46	23 85 C
Jeymer Dri. Grnf	43	14 83 A
Jeypore Rd. SW18	73	26 74 C
Jeypore Road Pas. SW18	73	26 74 C
Jillian Cl. Hamp	92	13 70 C
Joan Cres. SE9	89	41 73 B
Joan Gdns. Dag	41	48 86 A
Joan Rd. Dag	41	48 86 A
Joan St. SE1		31 80 D
Jocelyn Rd. Rich	71	18 75 A
Jockey's Fields. WC1	3	30 81 B
Jodrell Rd. E3	49	36 84 D
Joel St. Nthwd	19	10 90 C
Joel St. Pnr	19	10 89 C
Johanna St. SE1	7	31 79 A
John Adam St. WC2	7	30 80 A
John Aird Ct. W2	1	26 81 A
John Barnes Wlk. E15	50	39 84 B
John Burns Dri. Bark	51	45 84 C
John Campbell Rd. N16	48	33 85 C
John Carpenter St. EC4		31 80 B
John Felton Rd. SE16	63	34 79 A
John Fisher St. E1	57	34 80 A
John Glynes Ct. SW15	72	22 75 D
John Islip St. SW1	10	29 78 B
*John Mc Kenna Wlk. SE16	63	34 79 C
John Newton Ct. Well	78	46 75 B
John Parker Cl. Dag	52	49 84 D
John Parker Sq. SW11	73	26 75 B
John Penn St. SE13	76	37 76 B
John Perrin Pl. Har	33	18 87 A
John Prince's St. W1	2	28 81 D
John Rennie Wlk. E1	57	34 80 D
John Roll Way. SE16	63	34 79 C
John Ruskin St. SE5	75	31 77 B
John's Ave. NW4	23	23 89 C
John's Cl. Ashf		08 71 A
Johns La. Mord	103	26 67 A
John's Mews. WC1	3	30 82 D
Johnson Cl. E8	48	34 83 A
Johnson Rd. Brom	107	41 67 B
Johnson Rd. Croy	105	32 66 B
Johnson Rd. Houn	59	11 77 C
Johnson's Cl. Cars	104	27 65 D
Johnsons Ct. EC4		31 81 C
Johnsons Dri. Hamp	92	14 69 A
Johnson's Pl. SW1	10	29 78 C
Johnson St. E1	57	35 80 A
Johnson St. Sthl	59	11 79 D
John Spencer Sq. N1	48	31 84 B
John's Pl. E1	57	34 81 D
John St. E15	50	39 83 B
John St. Enf	13	33 95 B
John's Terr. Croy	105	33 66 C
John St. Houn	70	12 76 C
Johnston Rd. Wdf Gn	27	40 91 A
Johnston Terr. NW2	35	23 86 D
John St. SE25		34 68 C
John St. WC1	3	30 82 D
John Wilson St. SE18	66	43 78 A
John Woolley Cl. SE13	77	39 75 C
Joiners Arms Yd. SE5	75	32 76 B
Joiner St. SE1	3	32 80 D
Joint Rd. N2	24	27 90 A
Jollys La. Har	32	14 87 D
Jollys La. Hay	5	12 81 A
Jonathan St. SE11	10	30 78 D
*Jones Rd. E13	58	40 82 D
Jones St. W1	2	28 80 B
Jonson Cl. Mit	96	28 68 B
Joram Way. SE16	63	34 78 D
Jordan Hill. N2	24	27 90 A
Jordan Rd. Grnf	44	17 83 A
Jordans Cl. Dag	52	49 85 B
Jordans Cl. Islw	71	15 76 C
Joseph Ct. N15		33 87 A
Josephine Ave. SW2	74	30 74 D
Joseph Powell Cl. SW12	74	29 74 C
Joseph St. E3	57	36 82 D
Joshua St. E14	58	38 81 C
Jossiline Ct. E3	49	36 83 C
Joubert St. SW11	74	27 76 D
Jowett St. SE15	63	33 77 D
Joyce Ave. N18	17	33 92 D
Joyce Green La. Dart	80	54 75 A
Joyce Green Wlk. Dart	80	54 75 D
Joyce Wlk. SW2	75	31 74 C
Joydon Dri. Rom	40	46 89 D
Jubilee Ave. E4	26	38 91 A
Jubilee Ave. Rom	41	50 88 A
Jubilee Ave. Twick	82	14 73 C
Jubilee Cl. King	93	17 69 A
Jubilee Cl. NW9	34	20 88 D
Jubilee Cl. Pnr	20	11 90 C
Jubilee Cl. Rom	41	49 88 B
Jubilee Cres. E14	64	38 79 C
Jubilee Cres. N9	17	34 94 C
Jubilee Dri. Ruis	43	12 85 A
Jubilee Gdns. Sthl	53	13 81 C
Jubilee Pl. SW3	9	27 78 C
Jubilee Rd. Grnf	44	16 83 B
Jubilee Rd. Sutt	110	23 63 D
Jubilee St. E1	57	35 81 A
Jubilee Way. Chess	102	19 65 D
Jubilee Way. Sid	90	46 72 A
Jubilee Way. SW19	95	26 69 A
Judd St. WC1	3	30 82 A
Jude St. E16	58	39 81 D
Judges' Wlk. NW3	35	26 87 A
Judith Ave. Rom	29	49 91 B
Juer St. SW11	9	27 77 A
Juglands Rd. Orp	108	46 66 C
Julia Gdns. Bark	52	47 83 D
Julian Ave. W3	55	19 80 B
Julian Cl. Barn	11	25 96 B
Julian Pl. E14	64	37 78 D
Julia St. NW5	47	28 85 C
Julien Rd. W5	60	17 79 C
Junction App. SE13	76	38 75 A
Junction Ave. W10	56	23 82 A
Junction Mews. W2	1	27 81 C
Junction Pl. W2		26 81 D
Junction Rd. Ashf	81	08 71 C
Junction Rd. Dart	80	53 74 D
Junction Rd. E13	50	40 83 D
Junction Rd. Har	33	15 88 D
Junction Rd. N17	25	34 89 A
Junction Rd. N19	36	29 86 C
Junction Rd. N9	17	34 94 C
Junction Rd. Rom	42	51 88 B
Junction Rd. S Croy	112	32 64 D
Junction Rd. W5	60	17 78 B
Juniper Gdns. SW16	96	29 69 A
Juniper Rd. Ilf	40	43 86 C
Juniper St. E1	57	35 80 A
Juniper Way. Rom	30	54 90 A
Juno Way. SE14	64	35 77 B
Jupiter Way. N7	47	30 84 B
Jupp Rd. E15	49	38 84 D
Jupp Rd W. E15	49	38 83 B
Justice Wlk. SW3	9	27 77 A
Justin Cl. Brent	17	17 77 D
Jute La. Enf	14	36 96 A
Jutland Rd. E13	58	40 82 C
Jutland Rd. SE6	88	38 73 A
Jutsums Ave. Rom	41	49 88 D
Jutsums La. Rom	41	49 88 D
Juxon Cl. Har	20	13 90 B
Juxon St. SE11	10	30 78 B
Jveington Way. SE12	89	40 73 D
Kaduna Cl. Pnr	31	10 88 B
Kale Rd. Belv	67	48 79 A
Kambala Rd. SW11	73	26 75 B
Kangley Bridge Rd. SE26	88	36 71 D
Karen Ct. Brom	99	39 69 B
Kashgar Rd. SE18	66	45 78 B
Kashmir Rd. SE7	65	41 77 D
Kassala Rd. SW11	74	27 76 B
Katharine Rd. Twick	83	16 73 C
Katherine Rd. S Croy	105	32 65 C
Katherine Gdns. Ilf	28	44 91 C
Katherine Gdns. SE9	77	41 75 D
Katherine Rd. E6	50	42 83 A
Katherine Rd. E7	50	41 84 A

Katherine Sq. W11

Katherine Sq. W11	56	24 80	C
Kathleen Ave. W3	55	20 81	A
Kathleen Ave. Wem	44	18 84	C
Kathleen Rd. SW11	74	27 75	B
Kayemoor Rd. Sutt.	111	27 63	A
Kay Rd. SW9	74	30 76	C
Kay St. E15	48	38 84	D
Kay St. E2	48	34 83	C
Kay St. Well	78	46 76	B
Kean St. WC2	3	30 81	D
Keates Estate. N16	37	33 86	B
Keats Ave. Rom	30	52 91	D
Keats Cl. Chig	28	44 91	A
Keats Gr. NW3	47	27 85	A
Keats Pl. EC2	4	32 81	B
Keats Rd. Belv	67	50 79	C
Keats Rd. Well	78	45 76	B
Keats Way. Croy	106	35 67	C
Keats Way. Grnf	53	13 81	B
Keble Cl. Nthlt	43	14 85	C
Keble Cl. Wor Pk	102	21 66	D
Keble St. SW17	85	26 71	A
Kechill Gdns. Brom	107	40 66	A
Kedleston Dri. Orp	108	45 67	B
Keeble Cl. SE18	66	43 78	B
Keedonwood Rd. Brom	89	39 71	D
Keeley Rd. Croy	105	32 65	A
Keeley St. WC2	3	30 81	D
Keeling Rd. SE9	77	41 74	B
Keemor Cl. SE18	66	43 77	C
Keen's Rd. Croy	112	32 64	A
Keen's Yd. N1	48	31 84	B
Keep The. King	93	18 70	D
Keep The. SE3	77	40 76	C
Keeton's Rd. SE16	63	34 79	D
Keevil Dri. SW19	85	24 73	A
Keighley Cl. N7	47	30 85	A
Keighley Rd. Rom	30	54 91	C
Keightley Dri. SE9	90	44 73	C
Keildon Rd. SW11	74	27 75	D
Keir Hardie Way. Bark	51	46 84	C
Keith Gr. W12	61	22 79	A
Keith Rd. Bark	51	44 83	D
Keith Rd. E17	26	36 90	B
Keith Way. Horn	42	54 87	A
Kelbrook Rd. SE3	77	42 75	A
Kelby Path. SE9	90	43 72	D
Kelceda Cl. NW2	34	22 86	A
Kelday Rd. E3	49	37 84	C
Kelfield Gdns. W10	56	23 81	D
Kelland Rd. E13	58	40 82	C
Kellaway Rd. SE3	77	41 76	D
Kellerton Rd. SE13	77	39 74	A
Kellett Rd. SW2	75	31 75	C
Kelling Gdns. Croy	105	31 66	B
Kellino St. SW17	86	27 71	B
Kellner Rd. SE28	66	45 79	D
Kell St. SE1	7	31 79	D
Kelly Cl. Shep	91	09 69	C
Kelly Rd. NW7	23	24 91	A
Kelly St. NW1	47	28 84	B
Kelly Way. Rom	41	48 88	C
Kelman Cl. SW4	74	29 76	D
Kelmore Gr. SE22	75	34 75	C
Kelmscott Cl. E17	26	36 90	B
Kelmscott Gdns. W12	61	22 79	C
Kelmscott Rd. SW11	74	27 74	B
Kelross Pas. N5	48	32 85	A
Kelross Rd. N5	48	32 85	A
Kelsall Cl. SE3	77	40 76	D
Kelsey La. Beck	98	37 68	A
Kelsey Park Ave. Beck	98	37 69	D
Kelsey Park Rd. Beck	98	37 69	C
Kelsey Rd. Orp	100	46 69	D
Kelsey Sq. Beck	98	37 69	C
Kelsey St. E2	57	34 82	C
Kelsey Way. Beck	98	37 68	A
Kelsie Way. Ilf	28	45 91	A
Kelso Pl. W8	62	25 79	D
Kelso Rd. Cars	103	26 66	A
Kelston Rd. Ilf	28	43 90	D
Kelvedon Cl. King	94	19 70	A
Kelvedon Lodge. Ilf	28	43 90	C
Kelvedon Rd. SW6	73	24 76	B
Kelvedon Way. Wdf Gn	27	42 91	B
Kelvin Ave. N13	24	30 91	B
Kelvin Ave. Tedd	93	15 70	A
Kelvinbrook. E Mol	92	13 68	B
Kelvin Cl. Eps	109	19 63	A
Kelvin Cres. Har	21	15 91	C
Kelvin Dri. Twick	71	16 74	D
Kelvin Gdns. Sthl	53	13 81	C
Kelvin Gr. Chess	101	18 65	C
Kelvin Gr. SE26	87	34 72	D
Kelvington Cl. Croy	106	36 66	A
Kelvington Rd. SE15	76	35 74	B
Kelvin Par. Orp	108	45 66	C
Kelvin Rd. N5	48	32 85	A
Kelvin Rd. Well	78	46 75	A
Kemble Dri. Brom	107	42 65	C
Kemble Rd. Croy	105	31 65	D
Kemble Rd. N17	25	34 90	A
Kemble Rd. SE23	88	35 73	D
Kemble St. WC2	3	30 81	D
Kemerton Rd. Beck	98	37 69	D
Kemerton Rd. Croy	105	33 66	B
Kemerton Rd. SE5	75	32 75	C
Kemey's St. E9	49	36 85	C
Kemnal Rd. Chis	100	44 70	A
Kemnal Rd. Chis	90	44 71	B
Kemnal Warren. Chis	100	44 70	B
Kempe Rd. NW6	46	23 83	D
Kemp Gdns. Croy		32 67	C
Kempis Way. SE22	75	33 74	A
Kemplay Rd. NW3	46	26 85	B
Kemp Rd. Dag	41	47 87	D
Kemp's Ct. W1	2	29 81	D
Kemp's Dri. E14	57	37 80	A
Kemps Dri. Nthwd	19	09 91	D
Kempsford Gdns. SW5	62	25 78	C
Kempsford Rd. SE11	63	31 78	A
Kempshott Rd. SW16	96	30 70	C
Kempson Rd. SW6	62	25 77	D
Kempthorne Rd. SE8	64	36 78	B
Kempton Ave. Horn	42	54 86	D
Kempton Ave. Nthlt	43	13 85	C
Kempton Ave. Sun	91	10 69	B
Kempton Cl. Eri	67	50 77	A
Kempton Rd. E6	50	42 83	B
Kempton Rd. Hamp	92	12 69	C
Kempton Wlk. Croy	106	36 67	C
Kempt St. SE18	66	43 77	A
Kemsing Cl. Brom	107	39 65	B
Kemsing Cl. Th Hth	97	32 68	C
Kemsing Rd. SE10	65	40 78	C
Kenbury Cl. Uxb	31	07 86	C
Kenbury St. SE5	75	32 76	C
Kenchester Cl. SW8	10	30 77	C
Kendal Ave. Bark	51	45 83	A
Kendal Ave. N18	17	32 92	B
Kendal Ave. W3	55	19 81	B
Kendale Rd. Brom	89	39 71	C
Kendal Gdns. N18	17	32 92	B
Kendal Gdns. Sutt	103	26 65	A
Kendall Ave. Beck	98	36 69	C
Kendall Ave. S. Croy	112	32 62	B
Kendall Ave S. S Croy	112	32 62	D
Kendall Pl. W1	2	28 81	A
Kendall Rd. Beck	98	36 69	C
Kendall Rd. Islw	71	16 76	C
Kendal Par. N18	17	32 92	B
Kendal Rd. NW10	45	22 85	A
Kendal St. W2	1	27 81	C
Kender St. SE14	76	35 76	A
Kendoa Rd. SW4	74	29 75	D
Kendon Cl. E11	39	40 88	B
Kendra Hall Rd. S Croy	112	31 63	D
Kendrey Gdns. Twick	83	15 73	A
Kendrick Mews. SW7	62	26 78	B
Kendrick Pl. SW7	62	26 78	B
Kenelm Cl. Har	33	16 86	C
Kenerne Dri. Barn	11	24 95	A
Keniford Rd. SW12	86	28 73	B
Kenilworth Ave. E17	26	37 89	A
Kenilworth Ave. Har	43	12 85	B
Kenilworth Ave. SW19	85	25 71	A
Kenilworth Cres. Enf	13	33 97	A
Kenilworth Ct. SW15	73	24 75	A
Kenilworth Gdns. Horn	42	53 86	D
Kenilworth Gdns. Ilf	40	45 86	B
Kenilworth Gdns. SE18	78	43 76	D
Kenilworth Gdns. Sthl	53	12 82	B
Kenilworth Rd. E3	49	36 83	C
Kenilworth Rd. Eps	109	22 64	C
Kenilworth Rd. NW6	46	24 83	B
Kenilworth Rd. Orp	108	44 67	C
Kenilworth Rd. SE20	98	35 69	B
Kenilworth Rd. W5	54	18 80	C
Kenley Ave. NW9	22	21 90	C
Kenley Cl. Chis	100	45 68	A
Kenley Gdns. Horn	42	54 86	B
Kenley Gdns. Th Hth	97	31 68	D
Kenley Rd. King	94	19 69	D
Kenley Rd. SW19	95	25 68	B
Kenley Rd. Twick	71	16 74	D
Kenley Wlk. Sutt	110	23 64	B
Kenley Wlk. W11	56	24 80	A
Kenlor Rd. SW17	85	26 71	D
Kenmare Dri. Mit	96	27 70	D
Kenmare Gdns. N13	17	32 92	A
Kenmare Rd. Th Hth	105	31 67	C
Kenmere Gdns. Wem	45	19 83	A
Kenmere Rd. Well	79	47 76	C
Kenmont Gdns. NW10	55	22 82	B
Kenmore Ave. Har	21	16 89	A
Kenmore Cl. Rich	61	19 77	C
Kenmore Gdns. Edg	22	19 90	D
Kenmore Rd. Har	21	17 89	B
Kenmore Rd. E8	48	34 85	D
Kennard Rd. E15	48	38 84	D
Kennard Rd. N11	16	27 92	D
Kennard St. SW11	74	28 76	A
Kennedy Ave. Enf	14	35 95	C
Kennedy Cl. E13	50	40 83	C
Kennedy Cl. Orp	108	44 66	D
Kennedy Cl. Pnr	20	12 91	B
Kennedy Ct. Ashf	81	08 71	C
Kennedy Path. W7	54	15 82	D
Kennedy Rd. Bark	51	45 83	A
Kennedy Rd. W7	54	15 82	C
*Kennedy Wlk. SE17	63	32 78	B
Kennet Cl. SW11	73	26 75	D
Kenneth Ave. Ilf	51	43 85	B
Kenneth Cres. NW12	45	22 85	D
Kenneth Gdns. Stan	21	16 91	A
Kenneth Rd. Rom	41	48 87	A
Kennet Rd. Dart	80	52 75	A
Kennet Rd. Islw	71	15 75	B
Kennet Rd. W9	56	24 82	D
Kennet Wharf La. EC4	8	32 80	A
Kenninghall Rd. E5	37	34 86	D
Kenninghall Rd. N18	18	35 92	C
Kenning St. SE16	64	35 79	A
Kennings Way. SE11	63	31 78	D
Kenning Terr. N1	48	33 83	A
Kennington Gr. SE11	10	30 77	B
Kennington La. SE11	10	30 78	D
Kennington La. SE11	10	31 78	C
Kennington Oval. SE11	10	30 77	B
Kennington Park Gdns. SE11	63	31 77	B
Kennington Park Pl. SE11	63	31 77	A
Kennington Park Rd. SE11	63	31 78	C
Kennington Rd. SE11	63	31 78	A
Kennington Rd. SE1	7	31 79	C
Kennoldes. SE21	87	32 72	B
Kenny Rd. NW7	15	24 92	C
Kenrick Pl. W1	2	28 81	A
Kensal Rd. W10	56	24 82	C
Kensington Ave. E12	50	42 84	B
Kensington Ave. Th Hth	97	31 69	A
Kensington Church Ct. W8	62	25 79	B
Kensington Church St. W8	62	25 79	B
Kensington Church Wlk. W8	62	25 79	B
Kensington Court Mews. W8	62	25 79	D
Kensington Court Pl. W8	62	25 79	D
Kensington Ct. W8	62	25 79	B
Kensington Dri. Wdf Gn	27	41 90	D
Kensington Gate. W8	5	26 79	C
Kensington Gdns. Ilf	39	42 87	D
Kensington Gdns. Sq. W2	56	25 81	D
Kensington Gore. SW7	5	26 79	B
Kensington High St. W14	62	24 79	D
Kensington High St. W8	62	25 79	C
Kensington Mall. W8	56	25 80	C
Kensington Mansions. SW5	62	25 78	C
Kensington Palace Gdns. W8	62	25 79	B
Kensington Palace Gdns. W8	56	25 80	D
Kensington Park Gdns. W11	56	24 80	B
Kensington Park Mews. W11	56	24 81	D
Kensington Park Rd. W11	56	24 80	B
Kensington Pl. W8	56	25 80	C
Kensington Rd. Grnf	53	13 82	A
Kensington Rd. Nthlt	43	13 83	C
Kensington Rd. Rom	41	50 88	C
Kensington Rd. SW7	5	26 79	B
Kensington Sq. W8	62	25 79	D
Kensington Terr. S Croy	112	32 63	D
Kent Ave. Dag	52	49 83	C
Kent Ave. W13	54	16 81	B
Kent Ave. Well	78	45 74	B
Kent Cl. Mit		30 68	C
Kent Ct. W3	55	19 81	C
Kent Ct. W3	55	19 81	C
Kent Dri. Barn	12	28 95	A
Kent Dri. Tedd	83	15 71	C
Kentford Way. Nthlt	11	12 83	A
Kent Gdns. Ruis	31	10 88	C
Kent Gdns. W13	54	16 81	B
Kent House La. Beck	88	36 71	C
Kent House Rd. Beck	98	36 70	C
Kent House Rd. SE26	88	36 71	C
Kentish Bldgs. SE1	8	32 80	D
Kentish Rd. Belv	67	49 78	A
Kentish Town Rd. NW1	47	28 84	D
Kentish Town Rd. NW5	47	28 85	D

Name	Map	Grid
Kentmere Rd. SE18	66	45 78 A
Kenton Ave. Har	33	15 87 B
Kenton Ave. Sthl	53	13 80 A
Kenton Ave. Sun	92	12 69 C
Kenton Ct. Har	33	16 88 D
Kenton Gdns. Har	33	17 88 A
Kenton La. Har	21	16 90 D
Kenton Park Ave. Har	21	17 89 D
Kenton Park Cl. Har	21	17 89 C
Kenton Park Cres. Har	21	17 89 D
Kenton Park Rd. Har	21	17 89 C
Kenton Rd. E9	49	35 84 B
Kenton Rd. Har	33	17 88 A
Kenton St. WC1	3	30 82 C
Kent Pas. NW1	1	27 82 B
Kent Rd. Dag	52	49 85 D
Kent Rd. Dart	80	54 74 C
Kent Rd. E Mol	92	14 68 C
Kent Rd. N21	17	32 94 B
Kent Rd. Orp	108	46 67 D
Kent Rd. Rich	61	19 77 C
Kent Rd. W4	61	20 79 C
Kent Rd. W Wick	106	37 66 D
Kent St. E13	58	40 82 B
Kent St. E2	48	33 83 D
Kent Terr. NW1	1	27 82 A
Kent View Gdns. Ilf	40	45 86 A
Kent Way. SE15	75	33 76 B
Kent Way. Surb	101	18 65 C
Kentwell Cl. SE4	76	36 75 C
Kent Wlk. SW9	75	31 75 D
Kentwode Green. SW13	61	22 77 C
Kent Yd. SW7	5	27 79 A
Kenver Ave. N12	12	26 91 B
Kenward Rd. SE9	77	41 74 B
Kenway Rd. SW5	62	25 78 B
Kenway. Rom	29	50 90 C
Ken Way. Wem	34	20 86 C
Kenwood Ave. N14	12	29 95 B
Kenwood Cl. NW3	35	26 87 D
Kenwood Dri. Beck	98	38 68 A
Kenwood Gdns. E18	27	40 89 B
Kenwood Gdns. Ilf	40	43 88 A
Kenwood Rd. N6	36	27 88 D
Kenwood Rd. N9	17	34 94 C
Kenworthy Rd. E9	49	36 84 A
Kenwyn Dri. Nw2	34	21 86 D
Kenwyn Rd. SW20	95	23 69 A
Kenwyn Rd. SW4	74	29 75 D
Kenya Rd. SE7	65	41 77 D
Kenyngton Dri. Sun	81	10 71 C
Kenyngton Pl. Har	33	17 88 A
Kenyon St. SW6	62	23 77 D
Keogh Rd. E15	50	39 84 B
Kepiel Rd. Dag	52	48 85 A
Kepler Rd. SW4	74	30 75 C
Keppel Rd. E6	50	42 83 B
Keppel Row. SE1	8	32 80 C
Keppel St. WC1	2	29 81 B
*Kerbela St. E2	57	34 82 C
Kerbey St. E14	57	37 81 D
Kerfield Pl. SE5	75	32 76 B
Kernow Ct. Horn	42	54 86 A
Kerri Cl. Barn	11	23 96 C
Kerridge Ct. N1	48	33 84 A
Kerrison Pl. W5	54	17 80 D
Kerrison Rd. E15	49	38 83 B
Kerris Rd. SW11	74	27 75 A
Kerrison Rd. W5	54	17 80 D
Kerry Cl. E16	58	40 81 D
Kerry Rd. SE14	64	36 77 B
Kersey Gdns. Rom	30	54 91 D
Kersey Gdns. SE9	89	42 71 A
Kersfield Rd. SW15	73	23 74 D
Kershaw Cl. SW18	73	26 74 D
Kershaw Rd. Dag	41	49 86 C
Kersley Mews. SW11	74	27 76 B
Kersley Rd. N16	37	33 86 C
Kersley St. SW11	74	27 76 D
Kerswell Cl. N15	37	33 88 A
Kerwick Cl. N7	47	30 84 D
Keslake Rd. NW6	46	23 83 D
Kessock Cl. N17	37	34 88 B
Kesteven Cl. Chig	28	45 91 B
Kestlake Rd. Bex	79	47 74 C
Kestlake Rd. Bex	79	47 74 C
Keston Cl. N18	17	32 92 D
Keston Cl. Well	67	47 77 C
Keston Mark. Brom	107	42 65 C
Keston Rd. N17	25	32 89 D
Keston Rd. SE15	75	34 75 A
Keston Rd. Th Hth	105	31 67 C
Kestrel Ave. SE24	75	32 74 A
Keswick Ave. Horn	42	53 87 D
Keswick Ave. SW15	84	21 71 C
Keswick Ave. SW19	95	25 69 C
Keswick Cl. Sutt	110	26 64 A
Keswick Gdns. Ilf	27	42 89 C
Keswick Gdns. Ruis	31	08 88 D
Keswick Gdns. Wem	44	18 85 A
Keswick Mews. W5	54	18 80 C
Keswick Rd. Bexh	79	49 76 A
Keswick Rd. Orp	108	46 66 A
Keswick Rd. SW15	73	24 74 A
Keswick Rd. Twick	70	14 74 C
Keswick Rd. W.Wick	107	39 65 A
Kettering Rd. Rom	30	54 91 A
Kettering St. SW16	96	29 70 A
Kett Gdns. SW2	74	30 74 B
Kettlebaston Rd. E10	38	36 87 D
Kevelioc Rd. N17	25	32 90 A
Kevin Cl. Houn	70	11 76 D
Kevington Cl. Orp	100	45 68 D
Kevington Dri. Chis	100	45 68 D
Kevington Dri. Orp	100	46 68 C
Kew Bridge Ct. W4	61	19 78 C
Kew Bridge Rd. Brent	60	18 77 B
Kew Cres. Sutt	103	24 65 D
Kewferry Dri. Nthwd	19	08 91 A
Kewferry Rd. Nthwd	19	08 91 A
Kew Foot Rd. Rich	71	18 75 A
Kew Gardens Rd. Rich	60	18 77 D
Kew Gardens Rd. Rich	61	19 77 C
Kew Green. Rich	60	18 77 B
Kew Meadow Path. Rich	72	19 76 B
Kew Rd. Brent	60	18 77 B
Kew Rd. N2	24	27 90 A
Kew Rd. Rich	71	18 76 D
Kew Rd. Rich	61	19 77 A
Key Cl. E1	57	35 82 C
Keyes Rd. Dart	80	54 75 D
Keyes Rd. NW2	46	23 85 D
Keymer Rd. SW2	86	30 72 B
Keynes Cl. N2	24	27 89 D
Keynsham Gdns. SE9	77	42 74 A
Keynsham Rd. Mord	103	25 66 D
Keynsham Rd. SE9	77	42 74 A
Keynsham Wlk. Mord	103	25 66 D
Keyse Rd. SE1	8	33 79 D
Keysham Ave. Houn	69	10 76 A
Keystone Cres. N1	47	30 83 C
Keywood Dri. Sun	91	10 70 A
Keyworth Pl. SE1	7	31 79 D
Keyworth St. SE1	7	31 79 D
Kezia St. SE8	64	36 78 C
Khama Rd. SW17	86	27 71 A
Khartoum Rd. E13	58	40 82 B
Khartoum Rd. Ilf	51	43 85 D
Khartoum Rd. SW17	85	26 71 B
Khyber Rd. SW11	74	27 76 C
Kibworth St. SW8	10	30 77 D
Kidbrooke Gdns. SE3	77	40 76 A
Kidbrooke Gr. SE3	77	40 76 B
Kidbrooke La. SE9	77	42 75 C
Kidbrooke Park Cl. SE3	77	40 76 B
Kidbrooke Park Rd. SE3	77	40 75 B
Kidbrooke Way. SE3	77	40 76 D
Kidderminster Pl. Croy	105	31 66 D
Kidderminster Rd. Croy	105	32 66 A
Kidderpore Ave. NW3	46	25 85 A
Kidderpore Gdns. NW3	46	25 85 A
Kidd Pl. SE7	65	42 78 C
Kidlington Way. NW9	22	21 90 A
Kidron Way. E9	49	35 83 A
Kielder Cl. Chig	28	45 91 B
Kiffen St. EC2	4	32 82 D
Kilburn High Rd. NW6	46	25 84 C
Kilburn La. W10	56	23 82 B
Kilburn La. W9	46	24 83 D
Kilburn Park Rd. NW6	56	25 82 A
Kilburn Pl. NW6	46	25 83 A
Kilburn Priory. NW6	46	25 83 B
Kilburn Sq. NW6	46	25 83 A
Kilburn Vale Estate. NW6	46	25 83 A
Kilburn Vale. NW6	46	25 83 B
Kildare Cl. Ruis	32	11 87 C
Kildare Gdns. W2	56	25 81 C
Kildare Rd. E16	58	40 81 A
Kildare Terr. W2	56	25 81 C
Kildare Wlk. E14	57	37 81 C
Kildoran Rd. SW2	74	30 74 A
Kildown Rd. Ilf	40	46 87 C
Kilgour Rd. SE23	76	36 74 C
Kilkie St. SW6	73	26 76 C
Killarney Rd. SW18	73	26 74 C
Killearn Rd. SE6	88	38 73 D
Killester Gdns. Wor Pk	110	23 64 A
Killick St. N1	47	30 83 D
Killieser Ave. SW2	86	30 72 A
Killip Cl. E16	58	39 81 D
Killowen Ave. Nthlt	43	14 85 C
Killowen Rd. E9	49	35 84 B
Killyon Rd. SW8	74	29 76 C
Kilmaine Rd. SW6	62	24 77 C
Kilmarsh Rd. W6	62	23 78 A
Kilmartin Ave. SW16	97	31 68 A
Kilmartin Rd. Ilf	40	46 86 A
Kilmeston Way (off Daniel Gdns). SE15	63	33 77 D
Kilmington Rd. SW13	61	22 77 A
Kilmorey Gdns. Twick	71	16 75 D
Kilmorey Rd. Twick	71	16 75 D
Kilmorie Rd. SE23	88	36 73 C
Kiln Cl. E14	57	36 80 B
Kilner St. E14	57	37 81 A
Kiln Pl. NW5	47	28 85 C
Kiln Way. Nthwd	19	09 91 A
Kilravock St. W10	56	24 82 A
Kilsby Wlk. Dag	51	46 84 B
Kimball Gdns. SW6	73	24 76 A
Kimberley Ave. E6	50	42 83 C
Kimberley Ave. Ilf	40	45 87 A
Kimberley Ave. Rom	41	50 88 C
Kimberley Ave. SE15	76	35 75 A
Kimberley Gdns. Enf	13	33 96 B
Kimberley Gdns. N4	37	31 88 B
Kimberley Rd. Beck	98	35 69 D
Kimberley Rd. E11	38	38 86 B
Kimberley Rd. E16	58	39 82 D
Kimberley Rd. E17	26	36 90 B
Kimberley Rd. N17	25	34 90 C
Kimberley Rd. N18	25	34 91 B
Kimberley Rd. NW6	46	24 83 A
Kimberley. SW9	74	30 75 A
Kimberley Rd. Th Hth	105	31 67 B
Kimber Rd. SW18	85	25 73 A
Kimble Rd. SW19	95	26 70 B
Kimbolton Cl. SE12	77	39 74 D
Kimbolton Row. SW3	9	27 78 A
Kimmeridge Gdns. SE9	89	42 71 A
Kimmeridge Rd. SE9	89	42 71 A
Kimpton Rd. SE5	75	32 76 B
Kimpton Rd. Sutt	103	24 65 B
Kinburn St. SE16	64	35 79 B
Kincaid Rd. SE15	63	34 77 D
Kinch Gr. Har	33	18 87 B
Kinder St. E1	57	34 81 D
Kinfauns Ave. Horn	42	53 88 C
Kinfauns Rd. Ilf	40	46 87 D
Kinfauns Rd. SW2	87	31 72 A
King Alfred Ave. SE6	88	37 71 A
King Alfred Rd. Rom	30	54 90 D
King and Queen St. SE17	63	32 78 C
King Arthur Cl. SE15	64	35 77 C
King Charles Cres. Surb	101	18 66 B
King Charles' Rd. Surb	101	18 67 D
King Charles St. SW1	7	30 79 A
King Charles Wlk. SW19	85	24 73 C
King David La. E1	57	35 80 A
Kingdon Rd. NW6	46	25 84 A
King Edward Ave. Dart	80	53 74 D
King Edward Dri. Chess	101	18 65 C
King Edward Rd. Barn	11	25 96 D
King Edward Rd. E10	38	38 87 C
King Edward Rd. E17	26	36 89 A
King Edward Rd. Rom	42	51 88 D
King Edward's Gdns. W3	55	19 80 C
King Edward's Gr. Tedd	93	17 70 A
King Edward's Rd. Bark	51	44 83 B
King Edward's Rd. E9	49	35 83 A
King Edward's Rd. Enf	14	35 96 D
King Edward's Rd. N9	17	34 94 B
King Edward's Rd. Ruis	31	08 87 D
King Edward St. EC1	4	32 81 C
King Edward Wlk. SE1	7	31 79 C
Kingfield Rd. W5	54	17 82 D
Kingfield St. E14	64	38 78 A
Kingfisher Ct. E Mol	93	15 68 C
Kingfisher Dri. Rich	83	16 71 B
Kingfisher Pl. N22	24	30 90 D
Kingfisher Gdns. Croy	112	31 64 D
King George Ave. E16	58	41 81 D
King George Cl. Rom	29	50 89 A
King George St. SE10	64	38 77 C
King George V1 Ave. Mit	96	27 68 D
Kingham Cl. SW18	85	26 73 A
Kingham Cl. W11	62	23 79 B
King Harolds Way. Bexh	67	48 77 C
King Henry's Rd. King	94	19 68 B
King Henry's Rd. NW3	47	27 84 C
King Henry St. N16	48	33 85 C
King Henry's Wlk. N1	48	33 84 A
Kinghorn St. EC1	4	32 81 A
King James St. SE1	7	31 79 B
King John Ct. EC2	4	33 82 C

Kingswood Rd. SW2	86	30 73 A	
Kingswood Rd. W4	61	20 79 C	
Kingswood Way. Wall	111	30 64 C	
Kingsworth Cl. Beck	106	36 67 A	
Kingthorpe Rd. NW10	45	20 84 D	
Kingwear Rd. NW5	36	28 86 D	
King William La. E10	65	39 78 C	
King William St. EC4	8	32 80 B	
King William Wlk. SE10	64	38 77 A	
Kingwood Rd. SW6	62	24 77 C	
Kinlet St. E18	78	44 76 A	
Kinloch Dri. NW9	34	21 87 A	
Kinloch St. N7	36	30 86 D	
Kinloss Gdns. N3	23	24 89 D	
Kinloss Rd. Cars	103	26 66 A	
Kinnaird Ave. Brom	99	39 70 B	
Kinnaird Ave. W4	61	20 77 C	
Kinnaird Cl. Brom	99	39 70 B	
Kinnaird Way. Wdf Gn	27	42 91 B	
Kinnear Rd. W12	61	21 79 B	
Kinnerton Pl N. SW1	5	27 79 B	
Kinnerton Pl S. SW1	5	27 79 B	
Kinnerton St. SW1	6	28 79 A	
Kinnerton Yd. SW1	6	28 79 A	
Kinnoul Rd. W6	62	24 77 A	
Kinross Ave. Wor Pk	102	22 65 A	
Kinross Cl. Har	33	18 88 B	
Kinross Cl. Sun	81	09 71 D	
Kinross Dri. Sun	81	09 71 D	
Kinsale Rd. SE15	75	34 75 A	
Kintore Way. SE1	63	33 78 B	
Kintyre Cl. SW16	96	30 68 B	
Kinveachy Gdns. SE7	65	42 78 C	
Kinver Rd. SE26	88	35 71 A	
Kipling Pl. Stan	21	15 91 B	
Kipling Rd. Bexh	79	48 76 A	
Kipling St. SE1	8	32 79 B	
Kipling Terr. N9	17	32 93 B	
Kippington Dri. SE9	89	41 73 D	
Kirby Cl. Eps	109	21 64 D	
Kirby Cl. Ilf	28	45 91 A	
Kirby Cl. Nthwd	19	09 91 B	
Kirby Estate. SE16	63	34 79 D	
Kirby Gr. SE1	8	33 79 A	
Kirby St. EC1	3	31 81 A	
Kirchen Rd. W13	54	16 80 B	
Kirkdale Rd. E11	39	39 87 A	
Kirkdale. SE26	88	35 71 A	
Kirkey Rd. SW19	95	25 69 A	
Kirkham St. SE18	66	45 77 A	
Kirkland Ave. Ilf	28	43 90 C	
Kirkland Wlk (off Crosby Wlk). E8			
	48	33 84 B	
Kirk La. SE18	66	44 77 A	
Kirklees Rd. Dag	52	47 85 C	
Kirklees Rd. Th Hth	105	31 67 A	
Kirkly Cl. S Croy	112	33 62 A	
Kirkman Pl. W1	2	29 81 B	
Kirkmichael Rd. E14	58	38 81 C	
Kirk Rd. E17	38	36 88 D	
Kirkside Rd. SE3	65	40 77 A	
Kirk's Pl. E14	57	36 81 B	
Kirkstall Ave. N17	25	32 89 D	
Kirkstall Gdns. SW2	86	30 73 C	
Kirkstall Rd. SW2	86	30 73 C	
Kirksted Rd. Mord	103	25 66 D	
Kirkstone Way. Brom	99	39 70 C	
Kirkton Rd. N15	25	33 89 C	
Kirkwall Pl. E2	57	35 82 A	
Kirkwood Rd. SE15	75	34 76 D	
Kirn Rd. W13	54	16 80 B	
Kirtley Rd. SE26	88	36 71 A	
Kirtling St. SW8	10	29 77 C	
Kirton Cl. W4	61	20 78 B	
Kirton Gdns. E2	4	33 82 B	
Kirton Rd. E13	50	41 83 C	
Kirton Wlk. Edg	22	20 91 C	
Kirwyn Way. SE5	63	31 77 D	
Kitcat Terr. E3	57	37 82 A	
Kitchener Rd. Dag	52	49 84 B	
Kitchener Rd. E17	26	37 90 B	
Kitchener Rd. E7	50	40 84 B	
Kitchener Rd. N17	25	33 89 A	
Kitchener Rd. N2	24	27 89 A	
Kitchener Rd. Th Hth	97	32 68 B	
Kitley Gdns. SE19	97	33 69 B	
Kitson Rd. SE5	63	32 77 D	
Kitson Rd. SW13	72	22 76 A	
Kittiwake Rd. Nthlt	53	11 82 B	
Kitto Rd. SE14	76	35 76 D	
Kitt's End Rd. Barn	11	24 97 B	
Kiver Rd. N19	36	30 86 A	
Klea Ave. SW4	74	29 74 C	
Knapdale Cl. SE23	87	34 72 B	
Knapmill Rd. SE6	88	37 72 B	
Knapmill Way. SE6	88	37 72 B	
Knapp Cl. NW10	45	21 84 A	
Knapp Rd. E3	57	37 82 C	
Knaresborough Pl. SW5	62	25 78 B	
Knatchbull Rd. NW10	45	20 83 B	
Knatchbull Rd. SE5	75	31 76 B	
Knebworth Ave. E17	26	37 90 A	
Knebworth Rd. N16	48	33 85 A	
Knee Hill Cres. SE2	67	47 78 A	
Knee Hill. SE2	67	47 78 C	
Kneller Gdns. Islw	70	14 74 D	
Kneller Rd. N.Mal	102	21 66 A	
Kneller Rd. SE4	76	36 75 C	
Kneller Rd. Twick	70	14 74 D	
Knightland Rd. E5	37	34 86 B	
Knighton Cl. Rom	41	50 88 D	
Knighton Cl. S Croy	112	31 62 B	
Knighton Park Rd. SE26	88	35 71 D	
Knighton Rd. E7	39	40 86 C	
Knighton Rd. Rom	41	50 88 C	
Knightrider St. EC4	7	31 80 B	
Knight's Ave. W5	60	18 79 A	
Knightsbridge Gdns. Rom	41	50 88 B	
Knightsbridge Green. SW1	5	27 79 B	
Knightsbridge. SW1	5	27 79 B	
Knightsbridge. SW7	5	27 79 A	
Knights Cl. E9	49	35 85 C	
Knight's Hill. SE21	87	31 73 D	
Knight's Hill. SE27	87	31 71 B	
Knight's Hill Sq. SE27	87	31 71 B	
Knight's La. N9	17	34 93 C	
Knight's Park. King	93	18 68 A	
Knights Rd. E16	65	40 79 A	
Knights Way. Ilf	28	44 91 A	
Knight's Wlk. SE11	63	31 78 B	
Knightwood Cres. N.Mal	102	21 67 C	
Knivett Rd. SW6	62	25 77 A	
Knobs Hill Rd. E15	49	37 83 B	
Knockholt Rd. SE9	77	41 74 B	
Knole Cl. Croy	106	35 67 C	
Knole The. SE9	90	43 71 A	
Knoll Cres. Nthwd	19	09 90 C	
Knoll Dri. N14	16	28 94 A	
Knollmead. Surb	102	20 66 C	
Knoll Rd. Bex	79	49 74 C	
Knoll Rd. Sid	90	46 71 B	
Knoll Rd. SW18	73	26 74 A	
Knoll Rise. Orp	108	45 66 D	
Knolls Cl. Wor Pk	102	22 65 D	
Knoll The. Beck	98	37 69 B	
Knoll The. Brom	107	40 66 C	
Knoll The. W13	54	17 81 A	
Knolly's Cl. SW16	87	31 72 C	
Knolly's Rd. SW16	87	31 72 C	
Knottisford St. E2	57	35 82 B	
Knotts Green Rd. E10	38	38 88 C	
Knowle Ave. Bexh	78	48 77 D	
Knowle Cl. SW9	75	31 75 A	
Knowle Rd. Brom	107	42 65 A	
Knowle Rd. Twick	83	15 73 C	
Knowles Hill Cres. SE13	76	38 74 B	
Knowles Wlk. SW4	74	29 75 A	
Knowlton Green. Brom	107	39 67 B	
Knowsley Ave. Sthl	53	13 80 D	
Knowsley Rd. SW11	74	27 76 D	
Knox Rd. E7	50	40 84 A	
Knox St. W1	1	27 81 B	
Knoyle St. SE14	64	36 77 A	
Kohat Rd. SW19	85	25 71 D	
Kosuth St. E2	10	65 39 78 C	
Kramer Mews. SW5	62	25 78 D	
Kreisel Wlk. Rich	60	18 77 B	
Kuala Gdns. SW16	96	30 69 B	
Kuhn Way. E7	50	40 85 C	
Kydbrook Cl. Orp	108	44 66 A	
Kylemore Cl. E6	50	41 83 D	
Kylemore Rd. NW6	46	25 84 C	
Kymberley Rd. Har	33	15 88 C	
Kyme Rd. Horn	42	51 88 D	
Kynaced Gdns. Stan	21	17 90 A	
Kynance Mews. SW7	5	26 79 C	
Kynance Pl. SW7	5	26 79 C	
Kynaston Ave. N16	37	33 86 D	
Kynaston Ave. Th Hth	105	32 67 A	
Kynaston Cl. Har	20	14 91 D	
Kynaston Cres. Th Hth	105	32 67 A	
Kynaston Rd. Brom	89	40 71 C	
Kynaston Rd. Enf	13	32 97 B	
Kynaston Rd. N16	37	33 86 C	
Kynaston Rd. Orp	108	46 66 B	
Kynaston Rd. Th Hth	105	32 67 A	
Kynaston Wood. Har	20	14 91 D	
Kynersley Cl. Cars	104	27 65 D	
Kynoch Rd. N18	18	35 92 B	
Kyrle Rd. SW11	74	28 74 C	
Kyverdale Rd. N16	37	33 87 D	
Laburnum Ave. Horn	42	52 86 A	
Laburnum Ave. N17	25	32 91 D	
Laburnum Gr. Houn	70	12 75 D	
Laburnum Gr. N9	17	33 93 B	
Laburnum Ave. Sutt	104	27 65 C	
Laburnum Cl. E4	26	36 91 B	
Laburnum Cl. SE15	64	35 77 C	
Laburnum Cres. Sun	91	10 69 B	
Laburnum Gdns. N21	17	32 93 A	
Laburnum Gr. N21	17	32 93 A	
Laburnum Gr. N Mal	94	20 69 D	
Laburnum Gr. NW9	34	20 87 A	
Laburnum Gr. Ruis	31	08 86 D	
Laburnum Gr. Sthl	53	12 82 D	
Laburnum Rd. Mit	96	28 69 C	
Laburnum Rd. SW19	95	26 70 C	
Laburnum St. E2	48	33 83 B	
Laburnum Way. Brom	108	43 66 B	
Lacey Wlk. E3	49	37 83 C	
Lackington St. EC2	4	32 81 B	
Lacock Cl. SW19	95	26 70 A	
Lacon Rd. SE22	75	34 74 A	
Lacy Dri. Hamp	92	12 69 B	
Lacy Rd. SW15	73	23 75 D	
Ladas Rd. SE27	87	32 71 C	
Ladbroke Cres. W11	56	24 81 C	
Ladbroke Gdns. W11	56	24 80 B	
Ladbroke Gr. W10	56	24 81 A	
Ladbroke Gr. W11	56	24 80 B	
Ladbroke Mews. W11	56	24 80 C	
Ladbroke Rd. Enf	13	33 95 D	
Ladbroke Sq. W11	56	24 80 D	
Ladbroke Terr. W11	56	24 80 D	
Ladbroke Wlk. W11	56	24 80 D	
Ladbrook Cl. Pnr	32	12 88 B	
Ladbrook Rd. SE25	97	32 68 D	
Ladderstile Ride. King	84	20 71 C	
Ladderswood Way. N11	16	29 92 C	
Ladycroft Rd. SE13	76	37 75 B	
Ladycroft Wlk. Stan	21	17 90 D	
Ladygate La. Ruis	31	08 88 C	
Lady Hay. Wor Pk	102	21 65 B	
Lady Margaret Rd. N19	47	29 85 A	
Lady Margaret Rd. Sthl	53	12 81 B	
Ladysmith Ave. E6	50	42 83 C	
Ladysmith Ave. Ilf	40	45 87 A	
Ladysmith Rd. E16	58	39 82 B	
Ladysmith Rd. Enf	13	33 97 D	
Ladysmith Rd. Har	21	15 90 C	
Ladysmith Rd. N17	25	34 90 C	
Ladysmith Rd. N18	17	34 92 D	
Ladysmith Rd. SE9	78	43 74 C	
Lady Somerset Rd. NW5	47	28 85 B	
Ladywell Rd. SE13	76	37 74 B	
Ladywell St. E15	50	39 83 B	
Ladywood Ave. Orp	108	45 67 A	
Ladywood Rd. Surb	102	19 65 A	
Lafone Ave. Felt	82	11 72 A	
Lafone St. SE1	8	33 79 B	
Lagonda Ave. Ilf	28	45 91 B	
Laing Cl. Ilf	28	44 91 B	
Laing Dean. Nthlt	43	11 83 A	
Laing's Ave. Mit	96	27 69 D	
Lainson St. SW18	85	25 73 A	
Lairdale Cl. SE21	87	32 73 A	
Lairs Cl. N7	47	30 84 A	
Laitwood Rd. SW12	86	28 73 D	
Lake Ave. Brom	99	40 70 A	
Lake Cl. SW19	85	24 71 D	
Lakedale Rd. SE18	66	45 78 C	
Lakefield Rd. N22	25	31 90 D	
Lake Gdns. Dag	52	49 85 C	
Lake Gdns. Rich	83	16 72 B	
Lake Gdns. Wall	104	28 65 D	
Lakehall Gdns. Th Hth	105	31 67 B	
Lakehall Rd. Th Hth	105	31 67 B	
Lake House Rd. E11	39	40 86 A	
Lakehurst Rd. Eps	109	21 64 C	
Lakeland Cl. Har	20	14 91 B	
Lakenheath. N14	12	29 95 B	
Lake Rd. Croy	106	36 65 B	
Lake Rd. Rom	29	47 89 D	
Lake Rd. SW19	85	24 71 D	
Lake Rise. Rom	30	51 89 B	
Lakeside Ave. Ilf	27	41 89 D	
Lakeside. Beck	98	37 68 B	
Lakeside Cl. Ruis	19	08 89 D	
Lakeside Cl. SE25	97	34 69 C	
Lakeside Cl. Sid	79	47 74 C	
Lakeside Cres. Barn	12	27 95 B	
Lakeside Dri. Brom	107	42 65 C	
Lakeside. Enf	12	29 96 D	

Lakeside Rd. N13

Lakeside Rd. N13 ....16 30 93 D
Lakeside Rd. W14 ....62 23 79 D
Lakeside. W13 ....54 17 81 C
Lakeside. Wall ....111 28 64 B
Lakeside Way. Wem ....45 19 85 A
Lakeswood Rd. Orp ....108 44 67 C
Lake View. Edg ....21 18 91 B
Lakeview Rd. SE27 ....87 31 71 D
Lakeview Rd. Well ....78 46 75 D
Lakis Cl. NW3 ....46 26 85 A
Laleham Rd. SE6 ....88 38 73 A
Laleham Rd. Shep ....91 07 68 C
Lalor St. SW6 ....73 24 76 C
Lambarde Ave. SE9 ....90 43 71 A
Lamberhurst Rd. Dag ....41 48 87 D
Lamberhurst Rd. SE27 ....87 31 71 C
Lambert Ave. Rich ....72 19 75 B
Lambert Rd. E16 ....58 40 81 D
Lambert Rd. N12 ....15 26 92 D
Lambert Rd. SW2 ....74 30 74 B
Lambert's Pl. Croy ....105 32 66 D
Lambert's Rd. Surb ....101 18 67 B
Lambert St. N1 ....48 31 84 C
Lambert Way. N12 ....23 26 91 A
Lambert Way. N12 ....23 26 91 A
Lambert Way. N12 ....15 26 92 C
Lambert Way. N12 ....15 26 92 C
Lambert Wlk. Wem ....33 17 86 D
Lambeth Bridge. SW1 ....10 30 78 A
Lambeth High St. SE1 ....10 30 78 B
Lambeth Hill. EC4 ....8 32 80 A
Lambeth Mews. SE11 ....10 30 78 B
Lambeth Palace Rd. SE1 ....7 30 79 D
Lambeth Rd. Croy ....105 31 66 D
Lambeth Rd. SE1 ....7 31 79 C
Lambeth Wlk. SE11 ....10 30 78 B
Lamb La. E8 ....48 34 84 D
Lamble St. NW5 ....47 28 85 C
Lambley Rd. Dag ....51 46 84 B
Lamb Mews. N1 ....48 31 83 B
Lambolle Pl. NW3 ....47 27 84 A
Lambolle Rd. NW3 ....47 27 84 A
Lambourn Cl. NW5 ....47 29 85 A
Lambourn Cl. W7 ....60 15 79 B
Lambourne Ave. SW19 ....85 24 71 B
Lambourne Gdns. Bark ....51 45 84 D
Lambourne Gdns. E4 ....13 37 93 A
Lambourne Gdns. Enf ....13 33 97 D
Lambourne Gdns. Horn ....42 53 86 B
Lambourne Gr. King ....94 19 69 D
Lambourne Pl. SE3 ....77 40 76 B
Lambourne Rd. Bark ....51 45 84 D
Lambourne Rd. E11 ....38 38 87 A
Lambourne Rd. Ilf ....40 35 86 A
Lambrook Terr. SW6 ....73 24 76 A
Lamb's Bldgs. EC1 ....4 32 82 D
Lamb's Conduit Pas. WC1 ....3 30 81 B
Lamb's Conduit St. WC1 ....3 30 82 D
Lambscroft Ave. SE9 ....89 41 72 D
Lambs Meadow. Wdf Gn ....27 41 90 D
Lamb's Pas. EC1 ....4 32 82 D
Lamb St. E1 ....5 33 81 B
Lamb's Terr. N9 ....17 33 93 A
Lambs Wlk. Enf ....13 32 97 C
Lambton Pl. W11 ....56 24 81 D
Lambton Rd. N19 ....36 30 87 D
Lambton Rd. SW20 ....95 23 69 A
Lamb Wlk. SE1 ....8 33 79 A
Lamerock Rd. Brom ....89 39 71 B
Lamerton St. SE8 ....64 37 77 A
Lamford Cl. N17 ....25 43 90 D
Lamington St. W6 ....61 32 91 D
Lammas Ave. Mit ....96 22 78 B
Lammas Green. SE26 ....87 28 69 C
Lammas Park Gdns. W5 ....54 34 72 D
Lammas Park Rd. W5 ....60 17 80 C
Lammas Rd. E10 ....38 17 79 B
Lammas Rd. E9 ....49 36 87 C
Lammas Rd. Rich ....83 35 84 D
Lammermoor Rd. SW12 ....86 17 71 A
Lamont Rd. Pas. SW10 ....62 28 73 B
Lamont Rd. SW10 ....62 26 77 B
Lamorbey Cl. Sid ....90 45 73 D
Lamorna Cl. Orp ....108 46 66 A
Lamorna Gr. Stan ....21 17 90 D
Lampard Gr. N16 ....37 33 87 D
Lampern Sq. E2 ....57 34 82 A
Lampeter Sq. W6 ....62 24 77 A
Lampmead Rd. SE12 ....77 39 75 D
Lamport Cl. SE18 ....65 42 78 B
Lampton Ave. Houn ....70 13 76 D
Lampton House Cl. SW19 ....85 23 71 B

Lampton Park Rd. Houn ....70 13 76 D
Lampton Rd. Houn ....70 13 76 D
Lanacre Ave. NW9 ....22 21 90 A
Lanark Cl. W5 ....54 17 81 A
Lanark Pl. W9 ....26 82 C
Lanark Rd. W9 ....46 25 83 D
Lanark Rd. W9 ....26 82 A
Lanata Wlk. Hay ....53 11 82 D
Lanbury Rd. SE15 ....76 35 75 D
Lancashire Ct. W1 ....6 28 80 B
Lancaster Ave. Bark ....51 45 84 C
Lancaster Ave. E18 ....27 40 89 D
Lancaster Ave. Mit ....104 30 67 A
Lancaster Ave. SE27 ....87 32 72 A
Lancaster Ave. SW19 ....85 23 71 D
Lancaster Cl. Brom ....99 39 68 D
Lancaster Cl. King ....83 17 71 D
Lancaster Cottages. Rich ....71 18 74 C
Lancaster Ct. Sutt ....110 25 63 C
Lancaster Ct. SW6 ....25 77 C
Lancaster Dri. NW3 ....47 27 84 A
Lancaster Garages. NW3 ....47 27 84 A
Lancaster Gate. W2 ....5 26 80 A
Lancaster Gdns. King ....83 17 71 D
Lancaster Gdns. SW19 ....85 24 71 C
Lancaster Gdns. W13 ....60 16 79 B
Lancaster Gr. NW3 ....47 27 84 A
Lancaster Mews. Rich ....71 18 74 C
Lancaster Mews. W2 ....5 26 80 A
Lancaster Park. Rich ....71 18 74 A
Lancaster Pl. Houn ....11 76 C
Lancaster Pl. SW19 ....85 23 71 D
Lancaster Pl. Twick ....16 73 A
Lancaster Pl. WC2 ....7 30 80 B
Lancaster Rd. Barn ....11 26 95 B
Lancaster Rd. E11 ....39 39 86 A
Lancaster Rd. E17 ....26 35 90 D
Lancaster Rd. E7 ....50 40 84 D
Lancaster Rd. Enf ....13 32 97 B
Lancaster Rd. Har ....32 13 88 A
Lancaster Rd. N11 ....29 31 93 B
Lancaster Rd. N18 ....17 33 92 D
Lancaster Rd. N4 ....31 30 87 A
Lancaster Rd. Nthlt ....43 14 84 A
Lancaster Rd. NW10 ....45 22 85 C
Lancaster Rd. SE25 ....97 34 68 A
Lancaster Rd. Sthl ....53 12 80 A
Lancaster Rd. SW19 ....85 24 71 C
Lancaster Rd. W11 ....46 24 81 C
Lancaster St. SE1 ....7 31 79 B
Lancaster Terr. W2 ....5 26 80 B
Lancaster Terr. W2 ....5 26 80 B
Lancefield St. W10 ....56 24 82 B
Lancell St. N16 ....37 33 86 A
Lancelot Ave. Wem ....44 17 85 B
Lancelot Cres. Wem ....44 17 85 B
Lancelot Gdns. Barn ....16 28 94 A
Lancelot Pl. SW7 ....5 27 79 B
Lancelot Rd. Ilf ....28 45 91 C
Lancelot Rd. Well ....78 46 75 C
Lancelot Rd. Wem ....44 17 85 D
Lance Rd. Har ....32 14 87 A
Lancey Cl. SE7 ....65 41 78 B
Lanchester Rd. N6 ....36 27 88 B
Lancing Gdns. N9 ....17 33 94 D
Lancing Rd. Croy ....104 30 66 B
Lancing Rd. Felt ....81 09 72 B
Lancing Rd. Ilf ....40 44 88 D
Lancing Rd. Orp ....108 46 65 B
Lancing Rd. Rom ....30 54 91 C
Lancing Rd. W13 ....54 16 80 B
Lancing St. NW1 ....2 29 82 B
Landcroft Rd. SE22 ....75 33 74 D
Landells Rd. SE22 ....75 34 74 C
Landford Rd. SW15 ....73 23 75 A
Landgrove Rd. SW19 ....85 25 71 C
Landmann Way. SE14 ....64 35 78 D
Landon Pl. SW1 ....5 27 79 D
Landon Way. Ashf ....07 70 B
Landon Wlk. E14 ....57 37 80 B
Landor Rd. SW9 ....74 30 75 A
Landor Wlk. W12 ....61 22 79 A
Landport Way. (off Garnies Cl.) SE15 ....63 33 77 D
Landra Gdns. N21 ....13 31 95 D
Landridge Rd. SW6 ....73 24 76 D
Landrock Rd. N8 ....36 30 88 D
Landscape Rd. Wdf Gn ....27 40 91 D
Landsdowne Ave. Bexh ....67 47 77 D
Landseer Ave. E12 ....51 43 85 C
Landseer Cl. Edg ....22 19 90 C
Landseer Cl. SW19 ....95 26 69 B
Landseer Rd. Enf ....13 34 95 A
Landseer Rd. N19 ....36 30 86 A
Landseer Rd. N.Mal ....102 20 66 B
Landseer Rd. Sutt ....110 25 63 A

Landstead Rd. SE18 ....66 44 77 D
Lane App. NW7 ....15 24 92 C
Lane Cl. NW2 ....34 22 88 D
Lane End. Bexh ....79 49 75 B
Lanercost Cl. SW2 ....87 31 72 A
Lanercost Gdns. N14 ....16 29 94 A
Lanercost Rd. SW2 ....87 31 72 A
Laneside Ave. Dag ....41 48 87 B
Laneside. Chis ....90 44 71 C
Lane The. NW8 ....46 26 83 C
Lane The. SE3 ....77 40 75 A
Laneway. SW15 ....22 74 B
Lanfranc Rd. E3 ....49 36 83 C
Lanfranc St. SE1 ....7 31 79 C
Lanfrey Pl. W14 ....62 24 78 D
Langbourne Ave. N6 ....36 28 86 A
Langbrook Rd. SE3 ....77 41 76 D
Langcroft Cl. Cars ....104 27 65 D
Langdale Ave. Mit ....96 27 68 B
Langdale Ave. Orp ....108 43 65 D
Langdale Cl. SE17 ....63 32 77 A
Langdale Cres. Bexh ....79 49 76 A
Langdale Rd. SE10 ....64 38 77 C
Langdale Rd. Th Hth ....97 31 68 C
Langdale St. E1 ....57 34 81 D
Langdon Dri. NW9 ....34 20 87 C
Langdon Park Rd. N6 ....36 29 87 A
Langdon Pl. SW14 ....72 20 75 A
Langdon Rd. Brom ....99 40 68 B
Langdon Rd. E6 ....51 43 83 A
Langdon Rd. Mord ....103 26 67 A
Langdon Shaw. Sid ....90 45 71 D
Langdon Wlk. Mord ....103 26 67 A
Langford Cl. E8 ....48 34 85 C
Langford Cl. N15 ....25 33 88 C
Langford Cl. NW8 ....46 26 83 C
Langford Cres. Barn ....12 27 96 D
Langford Green. SE5 ....75 33 75 A
Langford Rd. NW8 ....46 26 83 C
Langford Pl. Sid ....90 46 72 C
Langford Rd. Barn ....12 27 96 D
Langford Rd. SW6 ....73 25 76 D
Langford Rd. Wdf Gn ....27 41 91 A
Langham Cl. N15 ....25 31 89 B
Langham Ct. Horn ....42 53 87 B
Langham Dri. Rom ....40 46 88 D
Langham Gdns. Edg ....22 20 91 C
Langham Gdns. N21 ....13 31 95 B
Langham Gdns. Rich ....83 17 71 A
Langham Gdns. W13 ....54 16 80 B
Langham Gdns. Wem ....33 17 86 A
Langham House Cl. Rich ....83 17 71 B
Langham Pl. N15 ....25 31 89 B
Langham Pl. W1 ....2 28 81 B
Langham Rd. Edg ....22 20 91 A
Langham Rd. N15 ....25 32 89 A
Langham Rd. SW20 ....95 23 69 A
Langham Rd. Tedd ....93 16 70 B
Langham St. W1 ....2 28 81 B
Langhedge Cl. N18 ....25 33 91 B
Langhedge La. N18 ....25 33 91 B
Langholm Cl. SW12 ....86 29 73 B
Langhorne Rd. Dag ....52 49 84 C
Langland Cres. Stan ....21 17 90 D
Langland Ct. Nthwd ....19 08 91 C
Langland Dri. Pnr ....20 12 91 C
Langland Gdns. Croy ....106 36 65 B
Langland Gdns. NW3 ....46 25 85 D
Langler Rd. NW10 ....46 23 83 C
Langley Ave. Ruis ....31 10 86 B
Langley Ave. Surb ....101 18 66 C
Langley Ave. Wor Pk ....103 23 65 B
Langley Cl. Rom ....30 53 91 D
Langley Cres. Dag ....52 47 84 D
Langley Cres. E11 ....39 41 87 A
Langley Ct. WC2 ....3 30 80 A
Langley Dri. E11 ....39 40 87 B
Langley Dri. W3 ....61 19 79 B
Langley Gdns. Dag ....52 47 84 D
Langley Gdns. Orp ....108 43 67 D
Langley Gr. N Mal ....94 21 66 C
Langley La. SW8 ....10 30 77 B
Langley Oaks Ave. S Croy ....112 34 62 C
Langley Park. NW7 ....22 21 91 A
Langley Park Rd. Sutt ....110 26 63 A
Langley Rd. Beck ....98 36 68 C
Langley Rd. Islw ....71 15 76 D
Langley Rd. Surb ....101 18 66 A
Langley Rd. SW19 ....95 25 69 A
Langley Rd. Well ....47 47 77 A
Langley St. WC2 ....3 30 81 C
Langley Way. W.Wick ....107 39 66 A

Langmore Ct. Bexh ...79 47 75 B
Langroyd Rd. SW17 ...86 27 72 B
Langside Ave. SW15 ...72 22 75 C
Langside Cres. N14. ...16 29 93 D
Lang St. E1 ...57 35 82 C
Langthorn Ct. EC2 ...4 32 81 D
Langthorne Rd. E11 ...49 38 85 B
Langthorne Rd. E11 ...38 38 86 C
Langthorne St. SW6 ...62 23 77 D
Langton Ave. N20 ...15 26 94 B
Langton Cl. WC1 ...3 30 82 D
Langton Rd. E Mol ...92 14 68 C
Langton Rd. Har ...20 14 91 C
Langton Rd. NW2 ...35 23 86 C
Langton Rd. SW9 ...63 31 77 D
Langton Rise. SE23 ...87 34 73 B
Langton St. SW10 ...62 26 77 A
Langton Way. Croy ...112 33 64 A
Langton Way. SE3 ...77 40 76 A
Langtry Rd. Nthlt ...43 11 83 D
Langtry Rd. NW8 ...46 25 83 B
Langtry Wlk. NW8 ...46 26 83 A
Langwood Chase. Tedd ...93 17 70 A
Lanhill Rd. W9 ...56 25 82 C
Lanier Rd. SE13 ...76 38 74 D
Lankaster Gdns. N2 ...23 26 90 B
Lankers Dri. Har ...32 12 88 D
Lankton Cl. Beck ...98 38 69 A
Lannoy Rd. SE9 ...90 44 73 C
Lanrick Rd. E14 ...58 39 81 C
Lanridge Rd. Belv ...67 47 79 D
Lansbury Ave. Bark ...51 46 84 C
Lansbury Ave. Felt ...69 10 74 D
Lansbury Ave. N18 ...17 33 92 C
Lansbury Ave. Rom ...41 48 88 A
Lansbury Cl. NW10 ...45 20 85 C
Lansbury Gdns. E14 ...58 38 81 D
Lansbury Rd. Enf ...14 35 97 B
Lansbury Way. N18 ...17 33 92 C
Lanscombe Wlk. SW8 ...10 30 77 C
Lansdell Rd. Mit ...96 28 69 C
Lansdowne Ave. Orp ...108 43 66 D
Lansdowne Cl. SW20 ...95 23 70 D
Lansdowne Cl. Twick ...83 15 73 D
Lansdowne Cres. W11 ...56 24 80 A
Lansdowne Ct. Pur ...112 31 62 D
Lansdowne Ct. Wor Pk ...102 22 65 A
Lansdowne Dri. E8 ...48 34 84 C
Lansdowne Gdns. SW8 ...74 30 76 A
Lansdowne Gr. NW10 ...45 21 85 A
Lansdowne Hill. SE27 ...87 31 72 D
Lansdowne La. SE7 ...65 41 78 D
Lansdowne Mews. SE7 ...65 41 78 D
Lansdowne Mews. W11 ...56 24 80 D
Lansdowne Pl. SE19 ...97 33 70 D
Lansdowne Pl. SE1 ...8 32 79 D
Lansdowne Rd. Brom ...99 40 70 D
Lansdowne Rd. Croy ...105 32 66 D
Lansdowne Rd. E11 ...39 39 86 B
Lansdowne Rd. E17 ...38 37 88 C
Lansdowne Rd. E18 ...27 40 89 A
Lansdowne Rd. E4 ...18 37 93 A
Lansdowne Rd. Eps ...109 20 63 D
Lansdowne Rd. Har ...33 15 87 A
Lansdowne Rd. Houn ...70 13 75 B
Lansdowne Rd. Ilf ...40 45 87 B
Lansdowne Rd. N10 ...24 29 90 C
Lansdowne Rd. N3 ...23 25 91 C
Lansdowne Rd. N7 ...25 34 90 A
Lansdowne Rd. Stan ...21 17 91 A
Lansdowne Rd. SW20 ...95 23 70 C
Lansdowne Rd. W11 ...56 24 80 A
Lansdowne Rd. W1 ...6 28 80 D
Lansdowne Rise. W11 ...56 24 80 A
Lansdowne Terr. WC1 ...3 30 82 C
Lansdowne Way. SW8 ...74 30 76 A
Lansdowne Wlk. W11 ...56 24 80 D
Lansdown Rd. E7 ...50 41 84 C
Lansdown Rd. Sid ...90 46 72 D
Lansfield Ave. N18 ...17 34 92 A
Lantern Cl. SW15 ...72 22 75 C
Lantern Cl. Wem ...44 17 85 D
Lant St. SE1 ...8 32 79 A
Lanvanor Rd. SE15 ...76 35 76 C
Lapford Cl. W9 ...56 24 82 D
Lapponum Wlk. Hay ...53 11 82 D
Lapse Wood Wlk. SE23 ...87 34 73 D
Lapstone Gdns. Har ...33 17 88 C
Larbert Rd. SW16 ...96 29 70 C
Larby Pl. Eps ...9 21 62 C
Larch Ave. W3 ...55 21 80 C
Larch Cl. N19 ...36 29 86 A
Larch Cl. SW12 ...86 28 72 B
Larch Cres. Eps ...109 19 63 B
Larch Cres. Hay ...53 11 81 B

Larch Dene. Orp ...108 43 65 A
Larches Ave. SW14 ...72 20 75 D
Larches The. N13 ...17 32 93 C
Larch Green. NW9 ...22 21 90 A
Larch Rd. NW2 ...46 23 85 A
Larch Tree Way. Croy ...106 37 65 C
Larch Way. Brom ...108 43 66 A
Larchwood Ave. Rom ...29 49 91 B
Larchwood Cl. Rom ...29 50 91 A
Larchwood Rd. SE9 ...90 43 72 B
Larcom St. SE17 ...63 32 78 A
Larden Rd. W3 ...61 21 79 A
Largewood Ave. Surb ...102 19 65 A
Larissa St. SE17 ...63 32 78 D
Larkbere Rd. SE26 ...88 36 71 A
Larkfield Ave. Har ...21 16 89 B
Larkfield Cl. Brom ...107 40 65 A
Larkfield Rd. Rich ...71 18 75 C
Larkfield Rd. Sid ...90 45 72 D
Larkhall La. SW4 ...74 30 76 C
Larkhall Rise. SW4 ...74 29 76 D
Lark Row. E2 ...49 35 83 A
Larksfield Gr. Enf ...13 34 97 B
Larkshall Cres. E4 ...18 38 92 A
Larkshall Rd. E4 ...18 38 93 D
Larkspur Cl. N17 ...25 32 91 D
Larkspur Ct. Wall ...111 28 63 B
Larkspur Way. Eps ...109 20 64 C
Larkswood Cl. E4 ...18 38 92 D
Larkswood Rd. E4 ...18 37 92 B
Larkswood Rise. Pnr ...20 11 89 C
Larkway Cl. NW9 ...22 20 89 D
Larnach Rd. W6 ...62 23 77 B
Larne Rd. Ruis ...31 09 87 B
Larner Rd. Eri ...68 51 77 C
Larpent Ave. SW15 ...73 23 74 A
Larwood Cl. Grnf ...43 14 85 D
Lascelles Ave. Har ...32 14 87 B
Lascelles Cl. E11 ...38 38 86 B
Lascott's Rd. N22 ...24 30 91 B
Lassa Rd. SE9 ...77 42 74 B
Lassell St. SE10 ...64 38 78 D
Latchett Rd. E18 ...27 40 90 B
Latchingdon Gdns. Wdf Gn ...27 42 91 A
Latchmere Cl. Rich ...83 18 71 C
Latchmere La. King ...93 18 70 B
Latchmere La. King ...83 18 71 D
Latchmere Pas. SW11 ...74 27 76 D
Latchmere Rd. King ...93 18 70 B
Latchmere Rd. SW11 ...74 27 76 D
Latchmere St. SW11 ...74 27 76 D
Lateward Rd. Brent ...60 17 77 B
Latham Cl. Twick ...83 16 73 A
Latham Cl. Bexh ...79 49 74 A
Latham Rd. Twick ...83 15 73 B
Lathkill Cl. Enf ...17 34 94 A
Lathom Rd. E6 ...50 42 84 D
Latimer Ave. E6 ...50 42 83 B
Latimer Cl. Pnr ...20 11 90 A
Latimer Cl. Wor Pk ...109 22 64 B
Latimer Gdns. Pnr ...20 11 90 A
Latimer Pl. W10 ...56 23 81 C
Latimer Rd. Barn ...11 25 96 B
Latimer Rd. Croy ...105 31 65 D
Latimer Rd. E7 ...50 40 85 B
Latimer Rd. N15 ...37 33 88 C
Latimer Rd. SW19 ...95 25 70 B
Latimer Rd. Tedd ...83 15 71 D
Latimer Rd. W10 ...56 23 81 C
Latimer. SE17 ...63 33 78 C
Latimer St. E1 ...57 35 81 B
Latona Rd. SE15 ...63 34 77 A
La Tourne Gdns. Orp ...108 44 65 C
Latymer Ct. W6 ...62 23 78 B
Latymer Rd. N9 ...17 33 94 D
Latymer Way. N9 ...17 33 93 A
Lauder Cl. Nthlt ...43 11 83 D
Lauderdale Dri. Rich ...83 17 72 D
Lauderdale Rd. W9 ...56 25 82 B
Laud St. Croy ...105 32 65 C
Laud St. SE11 ...10 30 78 D
Laughton Rd. Nthlt ...43 11 83 B
Launcelot Rd. Brom ...89 40 71 A
Launcelot St. SE1 ...7 31 79 A
Launceston Cl. Rom ...30 50 90 A
Launceston Ct. Th Hth ...105 31 67 C
Launceston Gdns. Grnf ...44 17 84 C
Launceston Pl. W8 ...5 26 79 C
Launceston Rd. Grnf ...44 17 83 A
Launch St. E14 ...64 38 79 C
Laundry Rd. W6 ...62 24 77 A
Laura Cl. E11 ...39 41 88 A
Laura Cl. Enf ...13 33 95 A
Lauradale Rd. N2 ...24 27 89 D
Laura Pl. E5 ...49 35 85 A

Laurel Ave. Twick ...83 15 73 D
Laurel Bank Rd. Enf ...13 32 97 B
Laurel Cl. Ilf ...28 44 91 B
Laurel Cl. N19 ...36 29 86 A
Laurel Cl. Sid ...90 46 72 C
Laurel Cres. Croy ...106 37 65 C
Laurel Cres. Rom ...42 51 97 C
Laurel Ct. SE25 ...105 33 67 A
Laurel Dri. N21 ...17 31 94 A
Laurel Gdns. E4 ...18 37 94 B
Laurel Gdns. Houn ...70 12 75 C
Laurel Gdns. W7 ...54 15 80 C
Laurel Gr. SE20 ...98 35 70 C
Laurel Gr. SE26 ...88 36 71 A
Laurel Manor. Sutt ...110 26 63 C
Laurel Park. Har ...21 15 91 D
Laurel Rd. Hamp ...82 14 71 D
Laurel Rd. SW13 ...72 22 76 C
Laurel Rd. SW20 ...94 22 69 B
Laurel St. E8 ...48 33 84 B
Laurel View. N12 ...15 25 93 D
Laurel Way. E18 ...27 39 89 D
Laurel Way. N20 ...15 25 93 C
Laurence Pountney Hill. EC4 ...8 32 80 B
Laurence Pountney La. EC4 ...8 32 80 B
Laurie Gr. SE14 ...76 36 76 A
Laurie Rd. W7 ...54 15 81 A
Laurier Rd. Croy ...105 33 66 B
Laurier Rd. NW5 ...36 28 86 D
Laurie Wlk. Rom ...42 51 98 A
Lauriston Rd. E9 ...49 35 84 D
Lauriston Rd. SW19 ...95 23 70 B
Lausanne Rd. N8 ...25 31 89 C
Lausanne Rd. SE15 ...76 35 76 C
Lavell St. N16 ...48 32 85 B
Lavender Ave. Mit ...96 27 69 B
Lavender Ave. NW9 ...34 20 87 C
Lavender Ave. Wor Pk ...103 23 65 C
Lavender Cl. Rom ...30 53 91 D
Lavender Cl. SW3 ...62 26 77 B
Lavender Cl. Wall ...111 28 64 B
Lavender Ct. E Mol ...92 13 68 B
Lavender Gdns. Enf ...13 31 97 B
Lavender Gdns. SW11 ...74 27 75 D
Lavender Gr. E8 ...48 34 84 C
Lavender Gr. Mit ...96 27 69 A
Lavender Hill. Enf ...13 31 97 B
Lavender Hill. SW11 ...74 27 75 B
Lavender Rd. Croy ...104 30 67 D
Lavender Rd. Enf ...13 32 97 B
Lavender Rd. Eps ...109 19 64 D
Lavender Rd. Sutt ...110 26 64 B
Lavender Rd. SW11 ...73 26 75 B
Lavender Rd. Wall ...111 28 64 A
Lavender St. E15 ...50 39 84 A
Lavender Sweep. SW11 ...74 27 75 D
Lavender Terr. SW11 ...74 27 75 A
Lavender Vale. Wall ...111 29 63 B
Lavender Way. Croy ...106 35 67 D
Lavender Wlk. Mit ...96 28 68 A
Lavender Wlk. SW11 ...74 27 75 D
Lavengro Rd. SE27 ...87 32 72 A
Lavenham Rd. SW18 ...85 25 73 C
Lavernock Rd. Bexh ...79 49 76 C
Lavers Rd. N16 ...37 33 86 C
Laverstoke Gdns. SW15 ...84 22 73 A
Laverton Mews. SW5 ...62 25 78 B
Laverton Pl. SW5 ...62 25 78 B
Lavidge Rd. SE9 ...89 42 72 B
Lavina Gr. N1 ...47 30 83 D
Lavington Rd. Croy ...111 30 64 B
Lavington Rd. W13 ...54 16 80 D
Lavington St. SE1 ...7 31 80 D
Lavinia Rd. Dart ...80 54 74 D
Lawdon Gdns. Croy ...112 31 64 B
Lawford Cl. Wall ...111 30 62 A
Lawford Gdns. Dart ...80 53 74 A
Lawford Rd. NW5 ...47 29 84 A
Lawford Rd. W4 ...61 20 77 C
Lawless St. E14 ...57 37 80 B
Lawley Rd. N14 ...16 28 94 B
Lawley St. E5 ...49 35 85 A
Lawn Cl. Brom ...99 40 70 D
Lawn Cl. N9 ...17 33 94 B
Lawn Cl. N Mal ...94 21 69 C
Lawn Cl. Ruis ...31 09 86 D
Lawn Cres. Rich ...71 18 76 D
Lawn Dri. E7 ...50 41 85 B
Lawn Farm Gr. Rom ...29 48 89 A
Lawn Gdns. W7 ...54 15 80 C
Lawn La. SW8 ...10 30 77 B
Lawn Park Gr. Rom ...29 48 89 C
Lawn Pl. SE15 ...75 33 76 B
Lawn Rd. SE15 ...63 33 77 D
Lawn Rd. Beck ...98 36 70 D

Lawn Rd. NW3	47	27 85 D	Leaf Cl. E Mol	101	15 67 A
Lawns Ct. Wem	33	18 86 B	Leaf Cl. Nthwd	19	08 91 D
Lawns Ct. Wem	34	19 86 A	Leaf Gr. SE27	87	31 71 C
Lawnside. SE3	77	39 75 D	Leafield Cl. SW16	97	31 70 B
Lawns The. E4	18	37 92 C	Leafield Rd. Sutt	103	25 65 A
Lawns The. Pnr	20	13 91 C	Leafield Rd. SW20	95	24 68 B
Lawns The. SE19	97	32 69 B	Leafy Oak Rd. SE12	89	41 72 C
Lawns The. SE3	77	39 75 B	Leafy Way. Croy	105	33 65 B
Lawns The. Sid	90	46 71 B	Lea Gdns. Wem	44	18 85 B
Lawns The. Sutt	110	24 63 C	Leagrave St. E5	38	35 86 C
Lawns Way. Rom	29	50 91 C	Lea Hall Rd. E10	38	37 87 C
Lawn Terr. SE3	77	39 75 A	Leaholme Waye. Ruis	31	08 88 C
Lawn Vale. Pnr	20	12 90 C	Leahurst Rd. SE13	76	38 74 B
Lawrence Ave. E12	51	43 85 A	Leahurst Rd. SE13	77	39 74 C
Lawrence Ave. E17	26	36 90 A	Leake Ct. SE1	7	30 79 B
Lawrence Ave. N13	17	31 92 B	Leake St. SE1	7	30 79 B
Lawrence Ave. N.Mal	102	21 66 A	Lealand Rd. N15	37	33 88 D
Lawrence Cl. E3	49	37 83 C	Leamington Ave. Brom	89	41 71 C
Lawrence Cl. N15	25	33 89 C	Leamington Ave. E17	38	37 88 A
Lawrence Cres. Dag	41	49 86 D	Leamington Ave. Mord	95	24 68 D
Lawrence Cres. Edg	22	19 90 C	Leamington Ave. Orp	108	45 65 C
Lawrence Hill. E4	18	37 93 A	Leamington Cl. Brom	89	41 71 C
Lawrence Hill Gdns. Dart	80	53 74 C	Leamington Cl. E12	50	42 85 C
Lawrence Hill Rd. Dart	80	53 74 C	Leamington Cl. Houn	70	14 74 A
Lawrence La. EC2	4	32 81 C	Leamington Cres. Har	32	12 86 D
Lawrence Pl. N1	47	30 83 A	Leamington Gdns. Ilf	40	45 86 B
Lawrence Rd. E13	50	40 83 B	Leamington Park. W3	55	20 81 B
Lawrence Rd. E6	50	42 83 A	Leamington Rd. Sthl	59	11 78 B
Lawrence Rd. Hamp	92	12 70 D	Leamington Rd Villas. W11	56	24 81 B
Lawrence Rd. Houn	70	11 75 C	Leamouth Rd. E14	58	38 80 B
Lawrence Rd. N15	25	33 89 C	Leander Rd. Nthlt	43	13 83 C
Lawrence Rd. N18	17	34 92 B	Leander Rd. SW2	75	31 74 C
Lawrence Rd. Pnr	32	11 88 B	Leander Rd. Th Hth	96	30 68 D
Lawrence Rd. Rich	83	17 71 A	Lea Rd. Beck	98	37 69 C
Lawrence Rd. Rom	42	52 88 B	Lea Rd. Enf	13	32 97 B
Lawrence Rd. SE25	97	33 68 D	Lea Rd. Sthl	59	12 78 A
Lawrence Rd. W5	60	17 78 B	Leas Dale. SE9	90	43 72 C
Lawrence's Bldgs. N16	37	33 86 D	Leas Green. Chis	100	45 70 B
Lawrence St. E16	58	39 81 B	Leaside Ave. N10	24	28 89 C
Lawrence St. SW3	9	27 77 A	Leaside Rd. E5	38	35 87 C
Lawrence Weaver Cl. Mord	103	25 67 C	Leasowes Rd. E10	38	37 87 C
Lawrence Yd. N15	25	33 89 C	Leather Bottle Green. Belv	67	48 79 D
Lawrie Park Ave. SE26	87	34 71 D	Leather Cl. Mit	96	28 69 C
Lawrie Park Cres. SE26	87	34 71 D	Leatherdale St. E1	57	35 82 B
*Lawrie Park Gdns. SE26	87	34 71 D	*Leatherdale St. E1	57	35 82 C
Lawrie Park Rd. SE6	88	35 71 C	Leather Gdns. E15	50	39 83 A
Lawson Cl. E16	58	41 81 A	Leatherhead Cl. N16	37	33 87 C
Lawson Cl. SW19	85	23 72 D	Leather La. EC1	3	31 81 A
Lawson Rd. Dart	80	53 75 D	Leathermarket St. SE1	8	33 79 A
Lawson Rd. Enf	14	35 97 A	Leathersellers Cl. Barn	11	24 96 A
Lawson Rd. Sthl	53	13 82 C	Leathsale Rd. Har	32	13 86 D
Law St. SE1	8	32 79 D	Leathwaite Rd. SW11	74	27 74 B
Lawton Rd. Barn	11	26 96 B	Leathwell Rd. SE8	76	37 76 D
Lawton Rd. E10	38	38 87 C	Lea Vale. Bexh	79	50 75 D
Lawton Rd. E3	57	36 82 A	Lea Valley Rd. E4	14	37 95 C
Laxfield Ct. E8	48	34 83 A	Lea Valley Rd. Enf	14	36 95 A
Laxley Cl. SE5	63	31 77 D	Leaveland Cl. Beck	98	37 68 C
Laxton Pl. NW1	2	28 82 D	Leaver Gdns. Grnf	44	15 83 C
Layard Rd. Enf	13	33 97 B	Leavesden Rd. Stan	21	16 91 A
Layard Rd. SE16	63	34 78 B	Lea View House. E5	37	34 87 D
Layard Sq. SE16	63	34 78 B	Lebanon Ave. Felt	82	11 71 C
Laycock St. N1	48	31 84 A	Lebanon Ct. Twick	83	16 73 B
Layer Gdns. W3	55	19 80 A	Lebanon Gds. SW18	73	25 74 C
Layfield Cl. NW4	34	22 87 B	Lebanon Park. Twick	83	16 73 B
Layfield Cres. NW4	34	22 87 B	Lebanon Rd. Croy	105	33 65 A
Layfield Rd. NW4	34	22 87 B	Lebanon Rd. SW18	73	25 74 A
Layhams Rd. W Wick	106	38 65 D	Lebrun Sq. SE3	77	40 75 B
Laymead Cl. Nthlt	43	12 84 A	Lechmere App. Wdf Gn	27	41 90 C
Laystall St. EC1	3	31 82 C	Lechmere Ave. Wdf Gn	27	41 90 D
Layton Cres. Croy	112	31 64 D	Lechmere Rd. NW2	45	22 84 B
Layton Rd. Brent	60	17 78 D	Leckford Rd. SW18	85	26 73 C
Layton Rd. Brent	60	17 78 D	Leckwith Ave. Bexh	67	48 77 A
Layton Rd. Houn	70	13 75 D	Lecky St. SW7	62	26 78 D
Layton Rd. N1	48	31 83 C	Leconfield Ave. SW13	72	21 75 B
Layton's La. Sun	91	09 69 D	Leconfield Rd. N5	48	32 85 B
Lazar Wlk. N7	36	30 86 B	Leda e. Enf	14	35 97 B
Lazell Wlk. SE9	89	41 73 D	Leda Rd. SE18	65	42 79 D
Lazenby Ct. WC2	7	30 80 A	Ledbury Mews N. W11	56	25 81 C
Leabank Cl. Har	33	15 86 C	Ledbury Mews W. W11	56	25 80 A
Leabank View N15	37	34 88 C	Ledbury Pl. Croy	112	32 64 A
Leabourne Rd. N16	37	34 87 A	Ledbury Rd. Croy	112	32 64 B
Lea Bridge Rd. E10	38	36 87 B	Ledbury Rd. W11	56	25 81 C
Lea Bridge Rd. E5	38	35 86 C	Ledbury St. SE15	63	34 77 C
Leacroft Ave. SW12	86	27 73 B	Ledrington Rd. SE19	97	34 70 A
Leadale Ave. E4	18	37 93 A	Ledway Dri. Wem	33	18 87 B
Leadale Rd. N15	37	34 88 C	Lee Ave. Rom	41	48 88 C
Leadale Rd. N16	37	34 88 C	Leechcroft Ave. Sid	78	45 74 B
Leadenhall St. EC3	4	33 81 C	Leechcroft Rd. Wall	104	28 65 C
Leadenhall Market. EC3	4	33 81 C	Lee Church St. SE13	77	39 75 C
Leadenhall Pl. EC3	4	33 81 C	Lee Cl. E17	26	35 90 A
Leadenhall St. EC3	4	33 81 C	Lee Conservancy Rd. E9	49	36 85 D
Leadenham Ct. E3	57	37 82 C	Leecroft Rd. Barn	24 36 C
Leader Ave. E12	51	43 85 C	Leeds Pl. N4	36	30 87 D
Leadings The. Wem	34	20 86 C	Leeds Rd. Ilf	40	44 87 D
			Leeds St. N18	17	34 92 C
Leegate. SE12	77	39 74 B			
Lee Green. Orp	108	46 67 A			
Lee Green. SE12	77	39 74 B			
Lee High Rd. SE12	77	39 75 D			
Lee High Rd. SE13	77	38 75 D			
Leeke St. WC1	3	30 82 B			
Leeland Rd. W13	54	16 80 C			
Leeland Terr. W13	54	16 80 C			
Leeland Way. NW10	45	21 85 B			
Leemount Cl. NW4	23	23 89 D			
Lee Park. SE3	77	39 75 B			
Lee Park Way. N18	18	35 92 B			
Lee Park Way. N9	18	36 93 C			
Lee Rd. Enf	13	34 95 C			
Lee Rd. Grnf	44	17 83 A			
Lee Rd. NW7	23	23 91 D			
Lee Rd. SE3	77	39 75 D			
Lee Rd. SW19	95	25 69 B			
Lees Ave. Nthwd	19	09 90 B			
Leeside. Barn	11	24 95 C			
Leesiders. NW11	35	24 88 D			
Leeside Rd. N17	37	35 91 A			
Leesness Ave. Bexh	67	47 77 D			
Leeson Rd. SE24	75	31 75 C			
Leesons Hill. Chis	100	45 68 B			
Leesons Hill. Orp	100	46 68 B			
Leesons Way. Orp	100	45 69 D			
Lees Pl. W1	6	28 80 A			
Lees Pl. E8	48	33 83 B			
Lees The. Croy	106	36 65 B			
Lee Terr. SE3	77	39 75 A			
Lee View. Enf	13	31 97 B			
Leeward Gdns. SW19	95	24 70 A			
Leeway. SE8	64	36 78 D			
Lefevre Wlk. E3	37 83 A			
Leffern Rd. W12	61	22 79 A			
Lefroy Rd. W12	61	21 79 B			
Legard Rd. N5	37	31 86 D			
Legatt Rd. SE9	77	41 74 B			
Leggatt Rd. E15	49	38 83 C			
Legge St. SE13	76	38 74 A			
Leghorn Rd. NW10	45	22 83 C			
Leghorn Rd. SE18	66	44 78 D			
Legion Cl. N1	48	31 84 C			
Legion Ct. Mord	103	25 67 C			
Legion Rd. Grnf	43	14 83 C			
Legon Ave. Rom	41	50 87 C			
Legrace Ave. Houn	70	11 76 D			
Leicester Ave. Mit	96	30 68 C			
Leicester Cl. Wor Pk	110	23 64 A			
Leicester Ct. WC2	6	29 80 B			
Leicester Gdns. Ilf	40	45 87 A			
Leicester Pl. WC2	6	29 80 B			
Leicester Rd. Barn	11	25 96 D			
Leicester Rd. Croy	105	33 66 A			
Leicester Rd. E11	39	40 88 B			
Leicester Rd. N2	27	28 89 A			
Leicester Rd. NW10	45	20 84 D			
Leicester Sq. WC2	6	29 80 B			
Leicester St. WC2	6	29 80 B			
Leigham Ave. SW16	86	30 72 C			
Leigham Court Rd. SW16	86	30 72 D			
Leigham Dri. Islw	60	15 77 C			
Leigham Vale. SW16	87	31 72 A			
Leigh Ave. Ilf	27	41 89 D			
Leigh Cl. N Mal	94	20 68 D			
Leigh Ct. Har	33	15 87 C			
Leigh Gdns. NW10	46	23 83 C			
Leigh Orchard Cl. SW16	86	30 72 D			
Leigh Pl. EC1	3	31 81 A			
Leigh Pl. Well	78	46 76 C			
Leigh Rd. E10	38	38 87 A			
Leigh Rd. E6	51	43 84 C			
Leigh Rd. Houn	70	14 75 D			
Leigh Rd. N5	48	31 85 B			
Leigh St. WC1	3	30 82 A			
Leighton Ave. E12	51	43 85 C			
Leighton Ave. Pnr	20	12 89 A			
Leighton Cl. Edg	22	19 90 C			
Leighton Cres. NW5	47	29 85 C			
Leighton Gdns. NW10	46	23 83 C			
Leighton Gr. NW5	47	29 85 C			
Leighton Pl. NW5	47	29 85 C			
Leighton Rd. Enf	13	34 95 A			
Leighton Rd. Har	20	14 90 D			
Leighton Rd. NW5	47	29 85 C			
Leighton Rd. W13	60	16 79 A			
Leighton St. Croy	105	31 66 D			
Leinster Gdns. W2	1	26 81 C			
Leinster Mews. W2	5	26 80 A			
Leinster Pl. W2	1	26 81 C			
Leinster Rd. N10	24	28 89 D			
Leinster Rd. NW6	45	25 82 A			
Leinster Sq. W2	56	25 81 D			
Leinster Terr. W2	5	26 80 A			

Leith Cl. NW9 ...34 | 20 87 D
Leithcote Gdns. SW16 ...86 | 30 71 B
Leithcote Path. SW16 ...86 | 30 72 D
Leith Hill Green. Orp ...100 | 46 69 A
Leith Hill. Orp ...100 | 46 69 A
Leith Rd. N22 ...25 | 31 90 B
Leith Yd. NW6 ...46 | 25 83 A
Lela Ave. Houn ...70 | 11 76 C
Lelitia Cl. E8 ...48 | 34 83 A
Leman Pas. E1 ...57 | 34 81 C
Leman St. E1 ...57 | 34 81 C
Lemark Cl. Stan ...21 | 17 91 A
Le May Ave. SE12 ...89 | 40 72 D
Lemna Rd. E11 ...39 | 39 87 A
Lemon St. E1 ...4 | 33 81 D
Lemonwell Dri. SE9 ...78 | 44 74 A
Lemsford Cl. N15 ...37 | 34 88 A
Lena Gdns. W6 ...62 | 23 79 C
Lenham Rd. Bexh ...67 | 48 77 B
Lenham Rd. SE12 ...77 | 39 75 D
Lenham Rd. Sutt ...110 | 26 64 C
Lenham Rd. Th Hth ...97 | 32 69 D
Lennard Ave. W.Wick ...107 | 39 65 C
Lennard Cl. W.Wick ...107 | 39 65 A
Lennard Rd. Beck ...98 | 36 70 C
Lennard Rd. Brom ...107 | 42 66 D
Lennard Rd. Croy ...105 | 32 66 C
Lennard Rd. SE20 ...98 | 35 70 B
Lennox Cl. Rom ...42 | 51 88 D
Lennox Gdns. Croy ...112 | 31 64 B
Lennox Gdns. Ilf ...39 | 42 87 D
Lennox Gdns Mews. SW1 ...9 | 27 78 B
Lennox Gdns. NW10 ...45 | 21 85 B
Lennox Gdns. SW1 ...5 | 27 79 D
Lennox Rd. E17 ...38 | 37 88 C
Lennox Rd. N4 ...37 | 31 86 A
Lenor Cl. Bexh ...79 | 48 75 C
Lensbury Way. SE2 ...67 | 47 79 D
Lens Rd. E7 ...50 | 41 84 C
Lenthall Rd. E8 ...48 | 34 84 C
Lenthal Pl. SW7 ...62 | 26 78 A
Lenthorp Rd. E10 ...65 | 39 78 B
Lentmead Rd. Brom ...89 | 39 72 D
Lenton Rise. Rich ...71 | 18 75 A
Lenton St. SE18 ...66 | 44 78 B
Lenton Terr. N4 ...37 | 31 86 A
Lenville Way. SE16 ...63 | 34 78 C
Leo Ct. Brent ...60 | 17 77 D
Leof Cres. SE6 ...88 | 37 71 D
Leominster Rd. Mord ...103 | 26 67 C
Leominster Wlk. Mord ...103 | 26 67 C
Leonard Ave. Mord ...103 | 26 67 A
Leonard Ave. Rom ...41 | 50 87 D
Leonard Ct. Har ...21 | 15 90 A
Leonard Pl. N16 ...48 | 33 85 A
Leonard Rd. E4 ...26 | 37 91 A
Leonard Rd. E7 ...50 | 40 85 A
Leonard Rd. N9 ...17 | 34 93 C
Leonard Rd. Sthl ...59 | 11 79 D
Leonard Rd. SW16 ...96 | 29 69 A
Leonard St. EC2 ...4 | 33 82 C
Leontine Cl. SE15 ...63 | 34 77 C
Leopards Ct. EC1 ...3 | 31 81 A
Leopold Ave. SW19 ...85 | 24 71 D
Leopold Rd. E17 ...38 | 37 88 A
Leopold Rd. N18 ...18 | 35 92 C
Leopold Rd. N18 ...18 | 35 92 C
Leopold Rd. N2 ...23 | 26 89 B
Leopold Rd. NW10 ...45 | 21 84 C
Leopold Rd. SW19 ...85 | 24 71 D
Leopold Rd. W5 ...54 | 18 80 D
Leopold St. E3 ...57 | 36 81 B
Leopold Wlk. SE11 ...10 | 30 78 D
Leo St. SE15 ...63 | 34 77 D
Leppoc Rd. SW4 ...74 | 29 74 B
Leroy St. SE1 ...8 | 33 79 C
Lescombe Cl. SE23 ...88 | 36 72 C
Lescombe Rd. SE23 ...88 | 36 72 C
Leslie Gdns. Sutt ...110 | 25 63 C
Leslie Gr. Croy ...105 | 33 66 C
Leslie Grove Pl. Croy ...105 | 33 66 C
Leslie Park Rd. Croy ...105 | 33 66 C
Leslie Prince Ct. SE5 ...63 | 32 77 D
Leslie Rd. E11 ...49 | 38 85 B
Leslie Rd. E16 ...58 | 40 81 D
Leslie Rd. N2 ...23 | 26 89 B
Leslie Smith Sq. SE18 ...66 | 43 77 A
Lesney Park. Eri ...67 | 50 77 B
Lesney Park Rd. Eri ...67 | 50 77 B
Lessada St. E3 ...49 | 35 83 D
Lessar Ave. SW4 ...74 | 29 74 C
Lessingham Ave. Ilf ...28 | 43 89 A
Lessingham Ave SW17 ...86 | 28 71 A
Lessing St. SE23 ...88 | 35 73 D
Lessington Ave. Rom ...41 | 50 88 C

Lessness Park. Belv ...67 | 49 78 C
Lessness Rd. Belv ...67 | 49 78 C
Lessness Rd. Mord ...103 | 26 67 A
Lester Ave. E15 ...58 | 39 82 C
Leswin Pl. N16 ...37 | 33 86 D
Leswin Rd. N16 ...37 | 33 86 D
Letchford Gdns. NW10 ...55 | 22 82 A
Letchford Mews. NW10 ...55 | 22 82 A
Letchworth Ave. Felt ...81 | 09 73 B
Letchworth Cl. Brom ...107 | 40 67 A
Letchworth Dri. Brom ...107 | 40 67 A
Letchworth St. SW17 ...86 | 27 71 B
Lethbridge Cl. SE10 ...76 | 38 76 A
Letterstone Rd. SW6 ...62 | 24 77 D
Lettice St. SW6 ...73 | 24 76 B
Lett Rd. E15 ...49 | 38 84 D
Lettsom St. SE5 ...75 | 33 76 C
Lettsom Wlk. E13 ...50 | 40 83 C
Leucha Rd. E17 ...38 | 36 88 A
Levana Cl. SW 19 ...85 | 24 73 C
Levehurst Way. SW4 ...74 | 30 76 C
Levendale Rd. SE23 ...88 | 36 72 B
Leven Rd. E14 ...58 | 38 81 D
Leverett St. SW3 ...9 | 27 78 A
Leverholme Gdns. SE9 ...90 | 43 71 A
Leverington Pl. N1 ...4 | 32 82 B
Leverson St. SW16 ...96 | 29 70 A
Lever St. EC1 ...4 | 32 82 A
Leverton Pl. NW5 ...47 | 29 85 C
Leverton St. NW5 ...47 | 29 85 C
Levett Gdns. Ilf ...40 | 46 86 C
Levett Rd. Bark ...51 | 45 84 A
Levine Gdns. Bark ...52 | 47 83 D
Levison Way. N19 ...36 | 29 86 B
Lewes Cl. Nthlt ...43 | 13 84 A
Lewesdon Cl. SW19 ...85 | 23 73 D
Lewes Rd. Brom ...99 | 41 69 D
Lewes Rd. N12 ...16 | 27 92 C
Leweston Pl. N16 ...37 | 33 87 B
Lewgars Ave. NW9 ...34 | 20 88 C
Lewin Rd. Bexh ...79 | 48 75 C
Lewin Rd. SW16 ...96 | 29 70 B
Lewis Ave. E17 ...26 | 37 90 A
Lewis Cres. NW10 ...45 | 20 85 D
Lewis Gdns. N2 ...23 | 26 90 D
Lewis Gr. SE13 ...76 | 38 75 A
Lewisham Centre. SE13 ...76 | 38 75 A
Lewisham High St. SE13 ...76 | 38 75 C
Lewisham Hill. SE13 ...76 | 38 76 C
Lewisham Park. SE13 ...76 | 38 74 A
Lewisham Rd. SE13 ...76 | 38 76 C
Lewisham St. SW1 ...6 | 29 79 B
Lewisham Way. SE14 ...76 | 36 76 B
Lewisham Way. SE4 ...76 | 37 76 C
Lewis Rd. Horn ...42 | 53 88 C
Lewis Rd. Mit ...96 | 27 69 C
Lewis Rd. Rich ...71 | 17 74 B
Lewis Rd. Sthl ...59 | 12 79 A
Lewis Rd. Sutt ...110 | 25 64 B
Lewis Rd. Well ...79 | 47 75 A
Lewis St. NW1 ...47 | 28 84 D
Lexden Dri. Rom ...40 | 46 88 D
Lexden Rd. Mit ...96 | 29 68 D
Lexden Rd. W3 ...53 | 19 80 D
Lexham Gardens Mews. W8 ...62 | 25 79 D
Lexham Gdns. W8 ...62 | 25 78 D
Lexham Mews. W8 ...62 | 25 79 C
Lexham Wlk. W8 ...62 | 25 79 D
Lexington Ct. Pur ...112 | 32 62 C
Lexington St. W1 ...6 | 29 80 A
Lexington Way. Barn ...11 | 23 96 D
Lexton Gdns. SW12 ...86 | 29 73 D
Leyborne Ave. W13 ...60 | 16 79 A
Leyborne Park. Rich ...72 | 19 76 A
Leybourne Cl. Brom ...107 | 40 67 C
Leybourne Rd. E11 ...39 | 39 87 D
Leybourne Rd. NW1 ...47 | 28 84 D
Leybourne Rd. NW9 ...34 | 19 88 A
*Leybourne St. NW1 ...47 | 28 84 D
Leybridge Ct. SE12 ...77 | 40 74 A
Leyburn Cl. E17 ...26 | 37 89 D
Leyburn Cres. Rom ...30 | 54 91 C
Leyburn Gdns. Croy ...105 | 33 65 A
Leyburn Gr. N18 ...25 | 34 91 A
Leyburn Rd. N18 ...25 | 34 91 B
Leyburn Rd. Rom ...30 | 54 91 C
Leycroft Gdns. Eri ...80 | 52 76 B
Leyden Mansions. N19 ...36 | 30 87 A
Leyden St. E1 ...4 | 33 81 B
Leyes Rd. E16 ...58 | 41 81 D
Leyfield. Wor Pk ...102 | 21 66 D
Leyland Ave. Enf ...14 | 36 97 C
Leyland Rd. SE12 ...77 | 40 74 A
Leylands. SW18 ...73 | 24 74 D
Leyland Rd. SE14 ...64 | 35 77 D

Leys Ave. Dag ...52 | 50 84 C
Leys Cl. Dag ...52 | 50 84 D
Leys Cl. Har ...32 | 14 88 B
Leysdown Ave. Bexh ...79 | 50 75 C
Leysdown Rd. SE9 ...89 | 42 72 B
Leysfield Rd. W12 ...62 | 22 79 C
Leys Gdns. Barn ...12 | 28 95 A
Leyspring Rd. E11 ...39 | 39 87 D
Leys Rd E. Enf ...14 | 36 97 A
Leys Rd W. Enf ...14 | 36 97 A
Leys The. Har ...33 | 18 88 D
Leys The. N2 ...23 | 26 89 C
Ley St. Ilf ...40 | 44 87 D
Leyswood Dri. Ilf ...40 | 45 88 A
Leyswood Dri. Ilf ...28 | 45 89 C
Leythe Rd. W3 ...61 | 20 79 A
Leyton Grange. E10 ...38 | 37 86 A
Leyton Green Rd. E10 ...38 | 38 88 C
Leyton Park Rd. E10 ...38 | 38 86 C
Leyton Rd. E15 ...49 | 38 85 D
Leyton Rd. SW19 ...95 | 26 70 C
Leyton Way. E11 ...39 | 39 87 B
Leytonstone Rd. E15 ...50 | 39 85 C
Leywick St. E15 ...50 | 39 83 C
Liardet St. SE14 ...64 | 36 77 A
Liberia Rd. N5 ...48 | 31 84 B
Liberty Ave. SW19 ...95 | 26 69 B
Liberty St. SW9 ...74 | 30 76 B
Liberty The. Rom ...42 | 51 88 A
Libra Rd. E13 ...50 | 40 83 C
Libra Rd. E3 ...49 | 36 83 D
Library Pl. E1 ...57 | 34 80 B
Library St. SE1 ...7 | 31 79 B
Lichen Ct. Ilf ...28 | 43 89 B
Lichfield Ct. Surb ...101 | 18 67 A
Lichfield Gdns. Rich ...71 | 18 74 A
Lichfield Gr. N3 ...23 | 25 90 C
Lichfield Rd. Dag ...67 | 47 86 C
Lichfield Rd. E3 ...57 | 36 82 A
Lichfield Rd. E6 ...58 | 41 82 B
Lichfield Rd. Houn ...70 | 11 75 A
Lichfield Rd. N9 ...17 | 34 93 A
Lichfield Rd. Nthwd ...19 | 10 89 A
Lichfield Rd. NW2 ...46 | 24 85 A
Lichfield Rd. Rich ...71 | 18 76 B
Lidbury Rd. NW7 ...15 | 24 92 C
Liddell Cl. Har ...21 | 17 89 B
Liddell Gdns. NW10 ...46 | 23 83 C
Lidding Rd. Har ...33 | 17 88 B
Liddington Rd. E15 ...50 | 39 83 B
Liddon Rd. Brom ...99 | 41 68 B
Liddon Rd. E13 ...58 | 40 82 B
Lidfield Rd. N16 ...48 | 32 85 B
Lidiard Rd. SW18 ...85 | 26 72 B
Lidlington Pl. NW1 ...47 | 29 83 C
Lidyard Rd. N19 ...36 | 29 87 C
Liffler Rd. SE18 ...66 | 45 78 C
Liffords Pl. SW13 ...72 | 21 76 D
Lifford St. SW15 ...73 | 23 75 D
Lightcliffe Rd. N13 ...17 | 31 93 C
Lightfoot Rd. N8 ...24 | 30 89 C
Lightley Cl. Wem ...44 | 18 83 B
Ligonier St. E2 ...4 | 33 82 D
Lilac Cl. E4 ...26 | 36 91 B
Lilac Gdns. Croy ...106 | 37 65 C
Lilac Gdns. Rom ...42 | 51 87 C
Lilac Gdns. W5 ...60 | 17 79 D
Lilac Pl. SE11 ...10 | 30 78 B
Lilac St. W12 ...55 | 22 80 A
Lilburne Gdns. SE9 ...77 | 42 74 A
Lilburne Rd. SE9 ...77 | 42 74 A
Lilburne Wlk. NW10 ...45 | 20 84 A
Lile Cres. W7 ...54 | 15 81 A
Lilestone St. NW8 ...1 | 27 82 C
Liford Rd. SE5 ...75 | 31 76 D
Lilian Ave. W3 ...61 | 19 79 A
Lilian Board Way. Grnf ...43 | 14 85 D
Lilian Gdns. Wdf Gn ...27 | 40 90 B
Lilian Rd. SW13 ...61 | 22 77 B
Lilian Rd. SW16 ...96 | 29 69 A
Lillechurch Rd. Dag ...52 | 47 85 C
Lilleshall Rd. Mord ...103 | 26 67 D
Lillie Rd. SW6 ...62 | 24 77 B
Lilleshall Rd. SW4 ...74 | 29 75 A
Lillie Yd. SW6 ...62 | 25 77 A
Lilliput Ave. Nthlt ...43 | 12 83 B
Lilliput Rd. Rom ...41 | 50 87 B
Lily Cl. W14 ...62 | 24 78 A
Lily Gdns. Wem ...44 | 17 83 C
Lily Pl. EC1 ...3 | 31 81 A
Lily Rd. E17 ...38 | 37 88 C
Lilyville Rd. SW6 ...73 | 24 76 B
Limbourne Ave. Dag ...41 | 48 87 B
Limburg Rd. SW11 ...74 | 27 75 C

Lime Cl. Cars

Lime Cl. Cars ...104 — 27 65 B
Lime Cres. Sun ...92 — 11 69 C
Limecroft Cl. Eps ...109 — 20 63 D
Lime Ct. Horn ...42 — 53 87 A
Limedene Cl. Pnr ...20 — 11 90 B
Lime Gr. Ilf ...28 — 45 91 B
Lime Gr. N20 ...15 — 24 94 B
Lime Gr. N Mal ...94 — 20 88 B
Lime Gr. Orp ...108 — 43 65 B
Lime Gr. Ruis ...31 — 10 87 B
Lime Gr. Sid ...78 — 45 74 D
Lime Gr. Twick ...71 — 16 74 C
Lime Gr. W12 ...62 — 23 79 A
Limehouse Cswy. E14 ...57 — 36 80 B
Limehouse Fields Estate. E14 ...57 — 36 81 A
Limerick Cl. SW12 ...86 — 29 73 A
Lime Row. Belv ...67 — 48 79 D
Limerston St. SW10 ...62 — 26 77 B
Limes Ave. Cars ...104 — 27 66 D
Limes Ave. Chig ...28 — 44 91 B
Limes Ave. Croy ...105 — 31 65 C
Limes Ave. E11 ...27 — 40 89 D
Limes Ave. E12 ...39 — 42 86 D
Limes Ave. N12 ...15 — 26 92 A
Limes Ave. NW11 ...35 — 24 87 A
Limes Ave. NW7 ...22 — 21 91 A
Limes Ave. SE20 ...97 — 34 70 D
Limes Ave. SW13 ...72 — 21 76 D
Limes Ave The. N11 ...16 — 29 92 C
Limes Cl. Ashf ...81 — 07 71 C
Limesdale Gdns. Edg ...22 — 20 90 C
Limes Field Rd. SW14 ...72 — 21 75 A
Limesford Rd. SE15 ...76 — 35 75 D
Limes Gdns. SW18 ...73 — 25 74 C
Limes Gr. SE13 ...76 — 38 75 C
Limes Pl. Croy ...105 — 32 66 B
Limes Rd. Beck ...98 — 37 69 D
Limes Rd. Croy ...105 — 32 66 B
Lime St. E17 ...26 — 36 89 C
Lime St. EC3 ...4 — 33 81 C
Limes The. Brom ...107 — 42 65 A
Limestone Wlk. Belv ...4 — 47 79 B
Lime St Pas. EC3 ...4 — 33 81 C
Lime St. Rom ...29 — 50 89 C
Limes Wlk. SE15 ...75 — 34 75 D
Limes Wlk. SE15 ...76 — 35 75 C
Limes Wlk. W5 ...60 — 17 79 B
Lime Tree Ave. Esh ...101 — 15 66 C
Lime Tree Ave. SE20 ...97 — 34 69 B
Lime Tree Ave. Surb ...101 — 15 66 C
Lime Tree Ave. W8 ...62 — 24 79 B
Limetree Cl. SW2 ...86 — 30 73 D
Lime Tree Gr. Croy ...106 — 36 65 D
Limetree Pl. Mit ...96 — 28 69 B
Lime Tree Rd. Houn ...70 — 13 76 B
Lime Wlk. E Mol ...93 — 15 68 D
Limewood Cl. W13 ...54 — 17 81 C
Limewood Rd. Eri ...67 — 50 77 C
Limpsfield Ave. SW19 ...85 — 23 72 B
Limpsfield Ave. Th Hth ...104 — 30 67 B
Linacre Rd. NW2 ...45 — 22 84 B
Linchmere Rd. SE12 ...89 — 39 73 B
Lincoln Ave. N14 ...16 — 29 93 A
Lincoln Ave. Rom ...42 — 51 87 C
Lincoln Ave. SW19 ...85 — 23 72 D
Lincoln Ave. Twick ...82 — 14 72 A
Lincoln Cl. Eri ...80 — 51 76 D
Lincoln Cl. Grnf ...53 — 14 83 A
Lincoln Cl. Har ...32 — 12 88 B
Lincoln Cres. Enf ...13 — 33 95 A
Lincoln Ct. Enf ...13 — 32 96 D
Lincoln Ct. N16 ...37 — 32 87 B
Lincoln Gdns. Ilf ...39 — 42 87 A
Lincoln Green Rd. Orp ...108 — 45 67 B
Lincoln Mews. NW6 ...46 — 24 83 B
Lincoln Rd. E13 ...58 — 40 82 D
Lincoln Rd. E18 ...27 — 40 90 A
Lincoln Rd. E7 ...50 — 41 84 B
Lincoln Rd. Enf ...13 — 34 95 A
Lincoln Rd. Eri ...80 — 51 76 D
Lincoln Rd. Felt ...82 — 12 72 D
Lincoln Rd. Har ...32 — 12 88 B
Lincoln Rd. Mit ...104 — 30 67 A
Lincoln Rd. N2 ...24 — 27 89 A
Lincoln Rd. N Mal ...94 — 20 68 A
Lincoln Rd. Nthwd ...19 — 09 89 B
Lincoln Rd. SE25 ...97 — 32 87 B
Lincoln Rd. Sid ...90 — 46 71 D
Lincoln Rd. Wem ...44 — 17 84 B
Lincoln Rd. Wor Pk ...102 — 22 66 D
Lincoln's Inn Fields. WC2 ...3 — 30 81 D
Lincoln St. E11 ...39 — 39 86 A
Lincoln St. SW3 ...9 — 27 78 B
Lincoln Way. Enf ...13 — 34 95 B
Lincoln Way. Sun ...91 — 09 69 A

Lincoln Wlk. Eps ...109 — 20 62 D
Lincombe Rd. Brom ...89 — 39 72 D
Lindal Cres. Enf ...12 — 30 96 D
Lindales The. N17 ...25 — 33 91 B
Lindal Rd. SE4 ...76 — 36 74 B
Lindbergh Rd. Wall ...111 — 30 63 C
Linden Ave. Enf ...13 — 34 97 A
Linden Ave. Houn ...70 — 13 74 B
Linden Ave. NW10 ...46 — 23 83 D
Linden Ave. Ruis ...31 — 10 86 D
Linden Ave. Th Hth ...97 — 31 68 D
Linden Ave. Wem ...44 — 18 85 D
Linden Cl. N14 ...12 — 29 95 C
Linden Cl. Ruis ...31 — 10 87 C
Linden Cl. Surb ...101 — 15 66 B
Linden Cres. Grnf ...44 — 15 84 B
Linden Cres. King ...93 — 18 69 D
Linden Cres. Wdf Gn ...27 — 40 91 B
Lindenfield. Chis ...100 — 43 69 D
Linden Gdns. Enf ...13 — 34 97 A
Linden Gdns. W2 ...56 — 25 80 A
Linden Gdns. W4 ...61 — 20 78 D
Linden Gr. N Mal ...94 — 21 68 A
Linden Gr. SE15 ...76 — 35 75 A
Linden Gr. SE26 ...98 — 35 70 A
Linden Gr. Tedd ...83 — 15 71 D
Linden Lawns. Wem ...35 — 18 85 B
Linden La. N2 ... — 26 88 A
Linden Leas. W Wick ...106 — 38 65 B
Linden Mews. W2 ...56 — 25 80 A
Linden Pas. W4 ...61 — 20 78 D
Linden Rd. Hamp ...92 — 13 69 A
Linden Rd. N10 ...24 — 28 89 D
Linden Rd. N11 ...16 — 28 93 A
Linden Rd. N15 ...25 — 32 89 C
Lindens The. N12 ...15 — 26 92 D
Lindens The. W4 ...72 — 20 76 A
Linden St. Rom ...29 — 50 89 D
Linden Way. N14 ...12 — 29 95 C
Linden Way. Pur ...111 — 29 62 C
Lindeth Cl. Stan ...21 — 16 91 B
Lindfield Gdns. NW3 ...46 — 26 85 C
Lindfield Rd. Croy ...105 — 33 67 D
Lindfield Rd. W5 ...54 — 17 82 C
Lindfield St. E14 ...57 — 37 81 C
Lindisfarne Rd. Dag ...41 — 47 86 C
Lindisfarne Way. SW20 ...94 — 22 70 C
Lindley Ct. King ...93 — 36 85 A
Lindley Rd. E10 ...38 — 17 70 C
Lindley St. E1 ...57 — 38 86 A
Lindley St. E1 ...74 — 35 81 A
Lindore Rd. SW11 ...74 — 27 75 D
Lindores Rd. Cars ...103 — 26 66 A
Lindo St. SE15 ...76 — 35 76 C
Lind Rd. Sutt ...110 — 26 64 C
Lindrop St. SW6 ...73 — 26 76 C
Lindsay Dri. Har ...33 — 18 88 B
Lindsay Rd. Hamp ...82 — 13 71 B
Lindsay Rd. Wor Pk ...102 — 22 65 B
Lindsell Rd. Bark ...51 — 44 83 A
Lindsell St. SE10 ...76 — 38 76 A
Lindsey Cl. Brom ...99 — 42 68 A
Lindsey Cl. Mit ...96 — 30 68 C
Lindsey Ct. N13 ...17 — 31 93 C
Lindsey Rd. Dag ...41 — 47 86 C
Lindsey St. EC1 ...3 — 31 81 B
Lindsey Way. Horn ...42 — 53 88 A
Lind St. SE8 ...76 — 37 76 D
Lindum Rd. Tedd ...93 — 17 70 C
Lindway. SE27 ...87 — 31 71 D
Linford Rd. E17 ...26 — 38 89 A
Linford St. SW8 ...74 — 29 76 A
Lingards Rd. SE13 ...90 — 38 75 C
Lingey Cl. Sid ... — 45 72 B
Lingfield Ave. Horn ...42 — 54 86 D
Lingfield Ave. King ...93 — 18 68 D
Lingfield Cl. Enf ...13 — 33 95 C
Lingfield Cl. Nthwd ...19 — 09 91 C
Lingfield Cres. SE9 ...78 — 44 75 D
Lingfield Gdns. N9 ...17 — 34 94 B
Lingfield Rd. SW19 ...95 — 23 70 B
Lingfield Rd. Wor Pk ...103 — 23 65 C
Lingham St. SW9 ...74 — 30 76 C
Lingholm Way. Barn ...11 — 23 95 B
Ling Rd. E16 ...58 — 40 81 A
Ling Rd. Eri ...67 — 50 77 A
Ling's Coppice. SE21 ...87 — 32 72 B
Lingwell Rd. SW17 ...86 — 27 72 C
Lingwood. Bexh ...79 — 49 76 D
Lingwood Gdns. Islw ...60 — 15 77 C
Lingwood Rd. E5 ...37 — 34 87 A
Linhope St. NW1 ...1 — 27 82 D
Linkfield. Brom ...107 — 40 67 C
Linkfield. E Mol ...92 — 13 68 B
Linkfield Rd. Islw ...71 — 15 76 D

Link La. Wall ...111 — 30 63 A
Linklea Cl. NW9 ...22 — 21 91 C
Link Rd. Dag ...52 — 49 83 D
Link Rd. Felt ...81 — 09 73 B
Link Rd. N11 ...16 — 28 92 A
Link Rd. Wall ...104 — 28 66 C
Links Ave. Mord ...95 — 25 68 C
Links Ave. Rom ...30 — 52 90 C
Linkscroft Ave. Ashf ...91 — 07 70 B
Links Dri. N20 ...15 — 25 94 D
Links Gdns. SW16 ...97 — 31 70 C
Linkside. Enf ...13 — 31 96 A
Linkside Gdns. Enf ... — 28 91 B
Linkside. N12 ...23 — 21 69 C
Linkside. N Mal ...94 — 21 86 B
Links Rd. NW2 ...34 — 28 76 A
Links Rd. SW17 ...96 — 19 81 C
Links Rd. W3 ...55 — 38 66 C
Links Rd. W Wick ...106 — 35 85 C
Link St. E9 ...49 — 36 89 C
Links View Cl. Stan ...21 — 16 91 A
Links View. N3 ...23 — 24 91 D
Links View Rd. Croy ...106 — 37 65 C
Links View Rd. Hamp ...82 — 14 71 A
Links Way. Beck ...106 — 37 67 C
Linksway. Nthwd ...19 — 08 90 A
Linksway. NW4 ...23 — 23 90 D
Link The. Enf ...14 — 36 97 A
Link The. Nthlt ...43 — 12 85 D
Link The. Pnr ...32 — 11 87 A
Link The. W3 ...55 — 19 81 D
Link The. Wem ...33 — 17 87 C
Linkway. Barn ...11 — 25 95 D
Link Way. Brom ...52 — 42 66 A
Linkway. Dag ... — 47 85 A
Link Way. Horn ...42 — 54 87 C
Linkway. N4 ...37 — 32 87 A
Linkway. Pnr ...20 — 11 90 B
Link Way. Rich ...83 — 16 72 B
Linkway. SW20 ...94 — 22 68 B
Linkway The. Sutt ...110 — 26 62 B
Linkwood Wlk. N7 ...47 — 29 84 D
Linley Cres. Rom ...29 — 50 89 A
Linley Ct. Sutt ...110 — 26 64 A
Linley Rd. N17 ...25 — 33 90 C
Linnell Cl. NW11 ...35 — 25 88 D
Linnell Dr. NW11 ...35 — 25 88 D
Linnell Rd. N18 ...17 — 34 92 C
Linnell Rd. SE5 ...75 — 33 76 C
Linnet Mews. SW12 ...86 — 28 73 A
Linnett Cl. E4 ...18 — 38 92 A
Linom Rd. SW4 ...74 — 30 75 C
Linscott Rd. E5 ...49 — 35 85 A
Linsey St. SE16 ...63 — 34 78 A
Linsey St. SE16 ...63 — 34 79 C
Linstead St. NW6 ...46 — 25 84 C
Linstead Way. SW18 ...85 — 24 73 A
Linsted Ct. SE9 ... — 45 74 C
Linthorpe Ave. Wem ...44 — 17 84 A
Linthorpe Rd. Barn ...12 — 27 96 A
Linthorpe Rd. N16 ...37 — 33 87 A
Linton Cl. Well ...78 — 46 76 B
Linton Ct. Rom ...30 — 51 90 C
Linton Gr. SE27 ...87 — 32 71 C
Linton Rd. Bark ...51 — 44 84 C
Lintons The. Bark ...51 — 44 84 C
Linton St. N1 ...48 — 32 83 A
Linver Rd. SW6 ...73 — 25 76 C
Linwood Way (off Daniel Gdns). SE15 ...63 — 33 77 D
Linzee Rd. N8 ...24 — 30 89 C
Lion Ave. Twick ...83 — 15 73 D
Lionel Gdns. SE9 ...77 — 41 74 B
Lionel Mews. W10 ...56 — 24 81 A
Lionel Rd. Brent ...60 — 18 78 A
Lionel Rd. SE9 ...77 — 41 74 B
Lion Gate Gdns. Rich ...71 — 18 75 B
Lion Rd. Bexh ...79 — 48 75 D
Lion Rd. Croy ...105 — 32 67 A
Lion Rd. N9 ...17 — 34 93 A
Lion Rd. Twick ...83 — 15 73 D
Lions Cl. SE9 ...89 — 41 72 D
Lion Way. Brent ...60 — 17 77 D
Liphook Cres. SE23 ...88 — 35 73 A
Lipton Rd. E1 ...57 — 35 81 D
Lisbon Ave. Twick ...82 — 14 72 A
Lisburne Rd. NW3 ...47 — 27 85 B
Lisford St. SE15 ...75 — 33 76 B
Lisgar Terr. W14 ...62 — 24 78 B
Liskeard Cl. Chis ...100 — 44 70 A
Liskeard Gdns. SE3 ...77 — 24 86 C
Lisle Ct. NW2 ...35 — 29 80 B
Lisle St. WC2 ...6 — 16 76 C
Lismore Cl. Islw ...71 — 16 76 C

Lismore Rd. N17 ....25 33 89 B
Lismore Rd. S Croy ....112 33 63 A
Lismore Wlk. N1 ....48 32 84 A
Lissenden Gdns. NW5 ....47 28 85 A
Lisson Gr. NW8 ....1 27 82 C
Lisson St. NW1 ....1 27 81 A
Liss Way (off Cator St). SE15 ....63 33 77 D
Lister Gdns. N18 ....17 30 85 B
Lister Mews. N7 ....47 39 87 D
Lister Rd. E11 ....39 34 90 A
Liston Rd. N17 ....25 29 75 A
Liston Rd. SW4 ....74 41 91 C
Listowel Rd. Dag ....41 49 86 C
Listria Park. N16 ....37 33 86 A
Litchfield Ave. E15 ....50 39 84 A
Litchfield Ave. Mord ....103 24 66 B
Litchfield Gdns. NW10 ....45 22 84 A
Litchfield Rd. Sutt ....110 26 64 A
Litchfield St. WC2 ....6 29 80 B
Litchfield Way. NW11 ....35 26 88 A
Lithgow's Rd. Houn ....69 09 75 D
Lithos Rd. NW3 ....46 26 84 A
Litlington St. SE16 ....63 34 78 B
Little Acre. Beck ....98 37 68 A
Little Albany St. NW1 ....2 28 82 D
Little Argyll St. W1 ....2 29 81 C
Little Aston Rd. Rom ....30 54 91 D
Little Birches. Sid ....90 45 72 A
Little Boltons The. SW10 ....62 26 78 C
Little Bornes. SE21 ....87 33 71 A
Little Britain. EC1 ....4 32 81 A
Little Brownings. SE23 ....87 34 72 B
Littlebury Rd. SW4 ....74 29 75 B
Little Bury St. N9 ....17 33 94 A
Little Cedars. N12 ....15 26 92 A
Little Chester St. SW1 ....6 28 79 D
Little College La. EC4 ....8 32 80 B
Little College St. SW1 ....7 30 79 C
Little Combe Cl. SW15 ....73 23 74 D
Littlecombe. SE7 ....65 40 77 B
Littlecote Cl. SW19 ....85 24 73 A
Littlecroft. SE9 ....78 43 75 A
Little Ct. W.Wick ....107 39 65 A
Littledale. SE2 ....66 46 77 A
Little Dimocks. SW12 ....86 28 72 B
Little Dorrit Ct. SE1 ....8 32 79 A
Little Ealing La. W5 ....60 17 79 C
Little Edward St. NW1 ....47 28 83 D
Little Essex St. WC2 ....7 31 80 A
Little Ferry Rd. Twick ....83 16 73 D
*Littlefield Cl. N19 ....47 29 85 A
Littlefield Rd. Edg ....22 20 91 C
Little Gearies. Ilf ....28 43 89 D
Little George St. SW1 ....7 30 79 A
Little Green. Rich ....71 17 75 D
Little Green St. NW5 ....47 28 85 B
Littlegrove. Barn ....12 27 95 C
Little Haven. SE19 ....97 32 70 C
Little Heath Rd. Bexh ....67 34 77 D
Littleheath Rd. S Croy ....112 34 62 B
Little Heath. Rom ....28 46 89 D
Little Heath. SE7 ....65 42 78 C
Little Ilford La. E12 ....50 42 85 B
Littlejohn Rd. Orp ....108 46 67 B
Littlejohn Rd. W7 ....54 15 81 D
Little Marlborough St. W1 ....2 29 81 C
Littlemede. SE9 ....89 42 72 D
Littlemoor Rd. Ilf ....40 44 86 D
Littlemore Rd. SE2 ....66 46 79 A
Little Moss La. Pnr ....20 12 90 C
Little Newport St. WC2 ....9 29 80 B
Little New St. EC4 ....3 31 81 C
Little Orchard Cl. Pnr ....20 12 90 C
Little Park Dri. Felt ....82 12 72 A
Little Park Gdns. Enf ....13 32 96 B
Little Portland St. W1 ....2 29 81 C
Little Queen's Rd. Tedd ....93 15 70 B
Little Rd. Croy ....105 33 66 C
Little Redlands. Brom ....99 42 69 C
Littlers Cl. SW19 ....95 26 69 B
Little Russell St. WC1 ....3 30 81 A
Little Sanctuary. SW1 ....7 30 79 A
Little Smith St. SW1 ....6 29 79 D
Little Somerset St. E1 ....4 33 81 D
Little St James's St. SW1 ....6 29 80 C
Little St Leonards. SW14 ....72 20 75 A
Littlestone Cl. Beck ....98 37 70 A
Little Strand. NW9 ....22 21 90 D
Little Thrift. Orp ....100 44 68 C
Little Titchfield St. W1 ....2 29 81 A
Littleton Cres. Har ....33 15 86 B
Littleton Rd. Ashf ....91 08 70 C
Littleton Rd. Har ....33 16 86 C
Littleton St. SW18 ....85 26 72 A

Little Trinity La. EC4 ....8 32 80 A
Littlewood Cl. W13 ....60 16 79 D
Littlewood. SE13 ....76 38 74 C
Littleworth Rd. Esh ....101 15 65 C
Livermere Rd. E8 ....48 33 83 B
Liverpool Gr. SE17 ....63 32 78 D
Liverpool Rd. E10 ....38 38 88 C
Liverpool Rd. E16 ....58 39 81 A
Liverpool Rd. King ....94 19 70 C
Liverpool Rd. N1 ....48 31 84 C
Liverpool Rd. N7 ....48 31 84 A
Liverpool Rd. Th Hth ....97 32 68 A
Liverpool Rd. W5 ....60 17 79 B
Liverpool St. EC2 ....33 81 A
Livesey Pl. SE15 ....63 34 77 A
Livingstone Ct. E10 ....38 38 88 C
Livingstone Pl. E14 ....64 38 78 C
Livingstone Rd. E15 ....49 38 83 A
Livingstone Rd. E17 ....38 37 88 D
Livingstone Rd. Houn ....14 75 C
Livingstone Rd. N13 ....24 30 91 A
Livingstone Rd. Sthl ....53 11 80 B
Livingstone Rd. SW11 ....73 26 75 B
Livingstone Rd. Th Hth ....97 32 69 D
Livingstone Wlk. SW11 ....73 26 75 B
Livonia St. W1 ....2 29 81 C
Lizard St. EC1 ....4 32 82 A
Lizhan St. SE3 ....65 40 77 D
Llanelly Rd. NW2 ....35 24 86 B
Llanover Rd. SE18 ....66 43 77 C
Llanover Rd. Wem ....33 17 86 D
Llanthony Rd. Mord ....103 26 67 D
Llanvanor Rd. NW2 ....35 24 86 B
Llewellyn St. SE16 ....63 34 79 A
Lloyd Ave. SW16 ....96 30 69 A
Lloyd Baker St. WC1 ....3 31 82 A
Lloyd Ct. Pnr ....32 11 88 B
Lloyd Park Ave. Croy ....112 33 64 B
Lloyd Rd. Dag ....52 48 84 D
Lloyd Rd. E17 ....26 35 89 D
Lloyd Rd. E6 ....50 42 83 B
Lloyd Rd. Wor Pk ....103 23 65 D
Lloyd's Ave. EC3 ....8 33 80 A
Lloyd's Pl. SE3 ....77 39 76 C
Lloyd Sq. WC1 ....3 31 82 A
Lloyd's Row. EC1 ....3 31 82 B
Lloyd St. WC1 ....3 31 82 A
Lloyds Way. Beck ....106 36 67 B
Loampit Hill. SE13 ....76 37 76 D
Loampit Vale. SE13 ....76 37 75 B
Loats Rd. SW4 ....74 30 74 C
Lobby Rd. SE28 ....66 45 79 A
Locarno Rd. Grnf ....53 14 82 D
Locarno Rd. W3 ....55 20 80 C
Lochaber Rd. SE13 ....77 39 75 C
Lochaline St. W6 ....62 23 77 A
Lochinvar Estate. SW12 ....86 28 73 B
Lochinvar St. SW12 ....86 28 73 B
Lochmere Cl. Eri ....67 49 77 B
Lochnagar St. E14 ....58 38 81 A
Lock Chase. SE3 ....77 39 75 A
Locksley Dri. Orp ....108 46 67 C
Locket Rd. Har ....21 15 90 D
Lockfield Ave. Enf ....14 36 97 B
Lockhart Cl. N7 ....47 30 84 B
Lockhart St. E3 ....57 36 82 D
Lockhurst St. E5 ....49 35 85 B
Lockier Wlk. Wem ....33 17 86 D
Lockington Rd. SW8 ....74 28 76 B
Lockmead Rd. N15 ....37 34 88 C
Lockmead Rd. SE13 ....76 38 75 A
Lock Rd. Rich ....83 17 71 A
Lock's La. Mit ....96 28 69 C
Locksley Sq. Surb ....101 17 67 D
Locksley St. E14 ....57 36 81 B
Locksmeade Rd. Rich ....83 17 71 A
Lockwood Rd. Ilf ....40 44 86 A
Lockwood Sq. SE16 ....63 34 79 D
Lockwood Way. Chess ....109 19 64 C
Lockwood Wlk. Rom ....42 51 88 A
Lockyer St. SE1 ....8 32 79 B
Loddiges Rd. E9 ....49 35 84 C
Loder St. SE15 ....64 35 77 C
Lodge Ave. Croy ....105 31 65 C
Lodge Ave. Dag ....51 46 84 B
Lodge Ave. Dart ....80 53 74 C
Lodge Ave. Har ....21 18 89 C
Lodge Ave. Rom ....30 52 89 C
Lodge Ave. SW14 ....72 21 75 A
Lodge Cl. Edg ....21 18 91 B
Lodge Cl. Islw ....71 16 76 B
Lodge Cl. N18 ....17 32 92 C
Lodge Cl. Orp ....108 46 66 D
Lodge Cl. Wall ....104 28 66 C

Lodge Cres. Orp ....108 46 66 D
Lodge Ct. Horn ....42 54 86 A
Lodge Dri. N13 ....17 31 92 A
Lodge Gdns. Beck ....106 36 67 B
Lodge Hill. Ilf ....27 42 89 C
Lodge Hill. Well ....47 47 77 A
Lodge La. Bex ....79 47 74 D
Lodge La. N12 ....15 26 92 C
Lodge La. Rom ....29 49 91 C
Lodge Path. N2 ....23 26 90 D
Lodge Pl. Sutt ....110 25 64 D
Lodge Rd. Brom ....99 41 70 C
Lodge Rd. Croy ....105 31 66 B
Lodge Rd. NW4 ....23 23 89 C
Lodge Rd. NW8 ....1 27 82 A
Lodge Rd. Sutt ....110 25 64 D
Lodge Rd. Wall ....111 28 64 D
Lodge The. Tedd ....93 15 70 B
Lodge Villas. Wdf Gn ....27 39 91 D
Lodge Way. Shep ....91 08 69 C
Lodore Gdns. NW9 ....34 21 88 A
Lodore St. E14 ....58 38 81 C
Loftie St. SE16 ....63 34 79 A
Lofting Rd. N1 ....48 31 84 C
Loftus Rd. W12 ....55 22 80 D
Logan Cl. Enf ....14 35 97 B
Logan Cl. Houn ....12 75 B
Logan Mew. W8 ....62 25 78 A
Logan Pl. W8 ....62 25 78 A
Logan Rd. N9 ....17 34 93 B
Logan Rd. Wem ....33 18 86 A
Logs Hill. Chis ....99 42 69 A
Logs Hill Cl. Chis ....99 42 69 A
Lollard Pl. SE11 ....63 31 78 A
Lollard St. SE11 ....10 30 78 B
Lollard St. SE11 ....63 31 78 A
Loman St. SE1 ....7 31 79 B
Lomas St. E1 ....57 34 81 A
Lombard Ave. Enf ....14 35 97 A
Lombard Ave. Ilf ....40 45 87 C
Lombard Ct. EC4 ....8 32 80 B
Lombard La. EC4 ....3 31 81 C
Lombard Rd. N11 ....16 29 92 C
Lombard Rd. SW11 ....73 26 76 D
Lombard Rd. SW19 ....95 26 69 C
Lombard St. EC3 ....8 32 81 D
Lombard Wall. SE7 ....65 40 78 B
Lombardy Pl. W2 ....56 25 80 B
Lomond Cl. N15 ....25 33 89 C
Lomond Cl. Wem ....18 84 D
Lomond Gr. SE5 ....63 32 77 D
Lona Cl. SE6 ....88 37 73 A
Loncroft Rd. SE5 ....33 77 A
Londesborough Rd. N16 ....33 85 A
London Bridge. EC4 ....8 32 80 B
London Bridge St. SE1 ....8 32 80 D
London Fields East Side. E8 ......48 34 84 A
London Fields West Side. E8 .....48 34 84 C
London La. Brom ....99 39 70 D
London La. E8 ....48 34 84 D
London Mews. W2 ....1 26 81 D
London Rd. Ashf ....81 07 73 C
London Rd. Bark ....57 43 84 D
London Rd. Brent ....60 17 77 C
London Rd. Brom ....99 39 69 B
London Rd. Croy ....105 31 66 B
London Rd. Dart ....50 74 B
London Rd. E13 ....50 40 83 C
London Rd. Enf ....13 32 96 D
London Rd. Eps ....109 22 63 D
London Rd. Har ....33 15 86 A
London Rd. Houn ....70 14 75 B
London Rd. Islw ....71 15 76 D
London Rd. King ....93 18 69 D
London Rd. Mit ....96 27 69 D
London Rd. Mit ....104 28 66 A
London Rd. Mord ....103 25 67 A
London Rd. Mord ....95 25 68 D
London Rd. Rom ....41 49 88 D
London Rd. SE1 ....7 31 79 D
London Rd. SE23 ....35 73 C
London Rd. S Ock ....68 54 79 B
London Rd. Sutt ....103 23 65 D
London Rd. SW17 ....96 27 70 B
London Rd. Th Hth ....105 31 67 A
London Rd. Twick ....83 16 73 A
London Rd. Twick ....71 16 74 C
London Rd. Wall ....104 28 65 C
London Rd. Wem ....44 18 84 A
London St. EC3 ....8 33 80 A
London St. W2 ....1 26 81 D
London Wall. EC2 ....4 32 81 A
Longacre Pl. Cars ....111 28 63 A
Longacre Rd. E17 ....26 38 90 B
Long Acre. WC2 ....3 30 81 C

Longbeach Rd. SW11

Street	Page	Grid
Longbeach Rd. SW11	74	28 75 A
Longberrys. NW2	35	24 86 D
Longbridge Rd. Bark.	51	45 84 A
Longbridge Rd. Dag.	51	46 85 B
Longbridge Way. SE13	76	38 74 A
Longbury Dri. Orp	100	46 69 D
Longcrofte Rd. Edg	21	17 91 D
Longcroft. SE9	90	43 72 C
Longdon Wood. Brom.	107	42 65 C
Longdown Rd. SE6	88	37 71 A
Long Dri. Grnf.	43	13 83 B
Long Dri. Ruis	43	11 85 B
Long Dri. W3	55	21 81 C
Long Elmes. Har	20	14 90 A
Longfellow Rd. E17	38	36 88 D
Longfellow Rd. Wor Pk.	102	22 66 D
Longfield Ave. E17	26	36 89 C
Longfield Ave. Horn.	42	51 87 B
Longfield Ave. NW7	22	22 91 C
Longfield Ave. W5	54	17 80 A
Longfield Ave. Wall	104	28 66 C
Longfield Ave. Wem	33	18 87 C
Longfield. Brom	99	39 69 B
Longfield Cres. SE26	88	35 72 C
Longfield Dri. SW14	72	19 74 B
Long Field. NW9	22	21 91 D
Longfield Rd. W5	54	17 81 C
Longfield St. SW18	85	25 73 A
Longfield Wlk. W5	54	17 81 C
Longford Av. Felt.	69	13 80 B
Longford Ave. Sthl	53	13 71 A
Longford Cl. Hamp	82	11 80 B
Longford Cl. Hay	53	20 64 A
Longford Ct. Eps.	109	11 80 B
Longford Gdns. Hay	53	26 65 A
Longford Rd. Twick	82	13 73 D
Longford St. NW1	2	28 82 D
Longford Wlk. SE24	87	31 73 A
Long Grove Rd. Eps	109	19 62 D
Longhayes Ave. Rom	29	47 89 D
Longhayes Ct. Rom	29	47 89 D
Longhayes Ct. Rom	29	47 89 D
Longheath Gdns. Croy	106	35 67 B
Longhedge St. SW11	74	28 76 C
1Longhill Rd. SE6	88	38 72 D
Longhope Cl. SE15	63	33 77 B
Longhurst Rd. Croy	105	34 67 D
Longhurst Rd. Croy	106	35 67 C
Longhurst Rd. SE13	77	39 74 A
Long La. Bexh	79	48 76 B
Long La. Croy.	106	35 67 C
Long La. EC1	3	31 81 B
Long La. N3	23	25 90 B
Longland Ct. SE1	63	34 78 C
Longland Dri. N20.	15	25 93 B
Longlands Park Cres. Sid	90	45 72 A
Longlands Rd. Sid.	90	45 72 D
Longlands Rd. SE1	8	32 79 B
Long La. Uxb	31	07 86 D
Longleat Rd. Enf.	13	33 95 A
Longleat Way. Felt.	81	08 73 B
Longleigh La. Bexh	67	47 77 A
Longleigh La. SE2.	67	47 77 A
Longley Ave. Wem	44	18 83 B
Longley Rd. Croy	105	31 66 B
Longley Rd. Har.	20	14 89 D
Longley Rd. SW17	96	27 70 A
Long Leys. E4	26	37 91 B
Longley St. SE1	63	34 78 A
Longmead. Chis	100	43 69 C
Long Mead. NW9	22	21 90 B
Longmeadow Rd. Sid	90	45 73 C
Longmead Rd. Eps.	109	21 62 C
Longmead Rd. Surb.	101	15 66 B
Longmead Rd. SW17	86	27 71 B
Longmore Av. Barn	11	26 95 D
Longmore St. SW1	10	29 78 A
Longnor Rd. E1	57	35 82 B
Long Pond Rd. SE3	77	39 76 A
Longport Cl. Ilf	28	46 91 A
Long Rd. SW4	74	29 75 C
Longreach Ct. Bark.	51	44 83 D
Longreach Rd. Eri	68	52 77 D
Longridge La. Sthl	53	13 81 D
Longridge Rd. SW5	62	25 78 A
Long's Ct. WC2	6	29 80 B
Longshaw Rd. E4	18	38 93 D
Longshore. SE8	64	36 78 B
Longstaff Cres. SW18	85	25 73 A
Longstaff Rd. SW18	85	25 73 A
Longstaff Rd. SW18	73	25 74 C
Long St. E2	4	33 82 B
Long St. E2	48	33 83 D
Longstone Ave. NW10	45	21 83 B
Longstone Rd. SW17	86	28 71 D
Longthornton Rd. SW16	96	29 69 D
Longton Ave. SE26	87	34 71 A
Longton Gr. SE26	87	34 71 B
Longview Way. Rom	29	50 90 B
Longville Rd. SE11	63	31 78 B
Long Walk. N Mal	94	20 68 A
Long Wlk. SE18	66	43 77 B
Long Wlk. SE1	8	33 79 C
Long Wlk. SW13	72	21 76 D
Longwood Dri. SW15	72	22 74 C
Longwood Gdn. Ilf	28	43 89 A
Long Yd. WC1	3	30 82 D
Loning The. NW9	22	21 89 D
Lonsdale Ave. E6	58	41 82 D
Lonsdale Ave. Rom	41	50 88 C
Lonsdale Ave. Wem	44	18 84 A
Lonsdale Cl. Pnr	20	12 91 C
Lonsdale Cl. SE9	89	41 72 D
Lonsdale Cres. Ilf	40	43 88 D
Lonsdale Dri. Enf	12	30 95 A
Lonsdale Drive N. Enf	12	30 96 C
Lonsdale Gdns. Th Hth	96	30 68 D
Lonsdale Mews. Rich.	72	19 76 A
Lonsdale Mews. W11	56	24 81 D
Lonsdale Pl. N1	48	31 84 C
Lonsdale Rd. Bexh	79	48 76 D
Lonsdale Rd. E11	39	39 87 B
Lonsdale Rd. NW6	46	24 83 B
Lonsdale Rd. SE25	97	34 68 D
Lonsdale Rd. Sthl	59	11 79 D
Lonsdale Rd. SW13	61	22 77 A
Lonsdale Rd. W11	56	24 81 D
Lonsdale Rd. W4	61	21 78 B
Lonsdale Sq. N1	48	31 84 C
Lon Sq. E2	48	34 83 C
Loobert Rd. N15	25	33 89 A
Looe Gdns. Ilf	28	43 90 D
Loop Rd. Chis	100	44 70 A
Lopen Rd. N18	17	33 92 A
Loraine Cl. Enf	14	35 95 A
Loraine Rd. N7	47	30 85 B
Loraine Rd. W4	61	19 77 B
Lord Ave. Ilf	27	42 89 B
Lord Chancellor Wlk. King	94	20 69 A
Lorden Wlk. E2	57	34 82 A
Lord Gdns. Ilf	27	42 89 D
Lord Hills Rd. W2	56	25 81 B
Lord Holland La. SW9	75	31 76 C
Lord Napier Pl. W6	61	22 78 C
Lord North St. SW1	7	30 79 C
Lord Roberts Mews. SW6	62	25 77 D
Lord Roberts Terr. SE18	66	43 78 C
Lordsbury Field. Wall.	711	29 62 C
Lords Cl. Felt.	82	12 72 A
Lords Cl. SE21	87	32 72 A
Lordship Gr. N16	37	32 86 B
Lordship La. N17	25	32 90 B
Lordship La. N22	25	31 90 A
Lordship La. SE22	75	33 74 D
Lordship Park Mews. N16.	37	32 86 A
Lordship Pk. N16	37	32 86 B
Lordship Pl. SW3	9	27 77 A
Lordship Rd. N16	37	32 87 D
Lordship Rd. Nthlt	43	12 84 C
Lordship Terr. N16	37	33 86 A
Lordsmead Rd. N17	25	33 90 C
Lord Warwick St. SE18	65	42 79 D
Lorenzo St. N1	47	30 83 D
Lorenzo St. WC1	3	30 82 B
Loretto Gdns. Har	21	18 89 C
Lorian Cl. N12	15	25 92 B
Loring Rd. Islw	71	15 76 D
Loring Rd. N20	16	16 80 A
Loris Rd. W6	62	27 93 A
Lorne Ave. Croy	106	23 79 C
Lorne Cl. NW8	1	35 66 B
Lorne Gdns. Croy	106	27 82 A
Lorne Gdns. E11	27	35 66 B
Lorne Gdns. W11	62	41 89 C
Lorne Rd. E17	38	23 79 B
Lorne Rd. E7	50	37 88 A
Lorne Rd. Har	21	41 85 A
Lorne Rd. N4	36	15 90 D
Lorne Rd. Rich.	71	30 87 D
Lorn Rd. SW9	75	18 74 B
Lorraine Park. Har	21	31 76 C
Lorrimore Rd. SE17	63	15 91 C
Lorrimore Sq. SE17	63	31 77 B
Losberne Way. SE16	63	31 77 B
Lothair Rd. W5	60	34 78 C
Lothair Road. N4	37	17 79 B
Lothair Road S. N4	37	31 88 D
Lothbury. EC2	4	31 87 B
Lothian Mews. SW9	63	32 81 D
		31 77 D
Lothian Rd. SW9	75	31 76 B
Lothian Rd. SW9	63	31 77 D
Lothrop St. W10	56	24 82 A
Lots Rd. SW10	62	26 77 C
Loubet St. SW17	96	27 70 B
Loudoun Ave. Ilf	40	43 88 B
Loudoun Rd. NW8.	46	26 83 A
Loudwater Cl. Sun	91	10 68 B
Loudwater Rd. Sun	91	10 68 C
Loughborough Park. SW9	75	31 75 D
Loughborough Rd. SW9	75	31 76 C
Loughborough St. SE11	10	30 78 D
Lough Rd. N7	47	30 84 B
Louisa Gdns. E1	57	35 82 D
Louisa St. E1	57	35 82 D
Louise Rd. E15	50	39 84 A
Louisville Rd. SW17	86	28 72 C
Louvaine Rd. SW11	73	26 75 D
Lovat Cl. NW2	34	21 86 D
Lovat La. EC3	8	33 80 A
Lovatt Cl. Edg	22	19 91 B
Lovatt Dri. Ruis	31	09 88 B
Lovat Wlk. Houn	59	12 77 C
Loveday Rd. W13	54	16 80 D
Lovegrove St. SE1	63	34 77 A
Lovekyn Cl. King.	93	18 69 D
Love La. Bex	79	49 74 C
Love La. Brom	99	40 69 C
Lovelace Ave. Brom	108	43 67 C
Lovelace Gdns. Bark	51	46 85 C
Lovelace Gdns. Surb	101	17 66 B
Lovelace Green. SE9	77	42 75 B
Lovelace Rd. Barn	16	27 94 A
Lovelace Rd. SE21	87	32 73 C
Lovelace Rd. Surb.	101	17 66 B
Love La. EC2	4	32 81 C
Love La. Mit.	96	27 68 A
Love La. Mord	103	25 66 B
Love La. N17	25	33 91 C
Love La. Pnr	20	12 89 A
Love La. SE18	66	43 78 B
Love La. SE25	97	34 68 B
Love La. Surb	101	17 65 B
Love La. Sutt.	110	24 63 B
Lovel Ave. Well	78	46 76 C
Love La. Wdf Gn	27	42 91 B
Lovelinch Cl. SE15	64	35 77 A
Lovell Pl. SE16	64	17 72 C
Lovell Rd. Rich.	83	13 81 D
Lovell Rd. Sthl.	53	46 84 B
Loveridge Mews. NW6	46	46 84 B
Loveridge Rd. NW6	46	25 91 C
Lovers' Wlk. N3	23	24 91 B
Lovers' Wlk. NW7	23	39 77 C
Lovers' Wlk. SE10	65	26 66 B
Lovett Dri. Cars	103	25 75 D
Lovett's Pl. SW18	73	20 85 C
Lovett Way. NW10	45	32 76 D
Love Wlk. SE5	75	44 65 C
Lovibonds Ave. Orp	108	43 85 B
Lowbrook Rd. Ilf.	51	33 72 D
Low Cross Wood La. SE21	87	34 94 D
Lowden Rd. N9	17	32 75 C
Lowden Rd. SE24	75	12 80 A
Lowden Rd. Sthl	53	40 81 A
Lowe Ave. E16	58	36 81 C
Lowell St. E14	57	50 83 D
Lowen Rd. Rain	52	34 66 C
Lower Addiscombe Rd. Croy	105	51 91 B
Lower Bedfords Rd. Rom	30	28 79 D
Lower Belgrave St. SW1	6	15 79 A
Lower Boston Rd. W7	60	49 83 A
Lower Broad St. Dag	52	42 69 B
Lower Camden. Chis	99	31 65 B
Lower Church St. Croy	105	34 85 B
Lower Clapton Rd. E5	48	22 75 B
Lower Common S. SW15	72	32 64 A
Lower Coombe St. Croy	112	23 69 B
Lower Downs Rd. SW20	95	31 65 B
Lower Drayton Pl. Croy.	105	17 74 B
Lower George St. Rich.	71	42 66 D
Lower Gravel Rd. Brom	107	27 68 A
Lower Green W. Mit.	96	28 79 D
Lower Grosvenor Pl. SW1	6	36 92 C
Lower Hall La. E4	18	11 69 D
Lower Hampton Rd. Sun	92	17 70 D
Lower Ham Rd. King	93	17 71 D
Lower Ham Rd. King	83	29 80 A
Lower James St. W1	6	29 80 A
Lower John St. W1	6	30 95 A
Lower Kendal Ave. Enf	12	29 91 A
Lower Maidstone Rd. N11	24	22 78 D
Lower Mall. W6	61	23 78 C
Lower Mall. W6	61	50 83 C
Lower Mardyke Ave. Rain.	52	19 68 B
Lower Marsh La. King	94	

Street	Pg	Grid
Lower Marsh. SE1	7	31 79 A
Lower Merton Rise. NW3	47	27 84 C
Lower Morden La. Mord	103	24 67 C
Lower Mortlake Rd. Rich	71	18 75 D
Lower Moss La. Rom	42	51 88 D
Lower Park Rd. Belv	67	49 78 A
Lower Park Rd. N11	16	29 92 C
Lower Rd. Belv	67	49 79 D
Lower Rd. Eri	67	50 78 B
Lower Rd. Har	32	14 87 D
Lower Rd. N2	24	27 90 A
Lower Rd. Orp	108	46 67 D
Lower Rd. SE16	64	35 79 C
Lower Rd. SE8	64	35 78 B
Lowerd. Sutt	110	26 64 A
Lower Richmond Rd. Rich	72	19 75 A
Lower Richmond Rd. SW14	72	20 75 A
Lower Richmond Rd. SW15	73	23 75 B
Lower Sloane St. SW1	9	28 78 C
Lower Sq. Islw	71	16 75 B
Lower Staithe. W4	72	20 76 A
Lower Station Rd. Dart	80	51 74 C
Lower Strand. NW9	22	21 90 D
Lower Sunbury Rd. Hamp	92	13 69 C
Lower Teddington Rd. King	93	17 69 B
Lower Terr. NW3	35	26 86 C
Lower Thames St. EC3	8	33 80 A
Lowestoft Cl. E5	38	35 86 A
Loweswater Cl. Wem	33	17 86 B
Lowfield Rd. NW6	46	25 84 C
Lowfield Rd. W3	55	20 81 C
Lowfield St. Dart	80	54 74 C
Low Hall Cl. E4	18	37 94 B
Low Hall La. E17	38	36 88 C
Lowick Rd. Har	33	15 88 A
Lowland Gdns. Rom	41	49 88 D
Lowlands Rd. Har	33	15 87 A
Lowlands Rd. Pnr	32	11 88 C
Lowman Rd. N7	47	30 85 B
Lowndes Cl. SW1	6	28 79 C
Lowndes Pl. SW1	6	28 79 C
Lowndes Sq. SW1	5	27 79 B
Lowndes St. SW1	6	28 79 C
Lownds Ave. Brom	99	40 69 C
Lowood St. E1	57	35 80 A
Lowshoe La. Rom	29	49 90 B
Lowswood Cl. Nthwd	19	08 90 A
Lowther Dri. Enf	12	30 96 C
Lowther Hill. SE23	88	36 73 A
Lowther Rd. E17	26	36 90 C
Lowther Rd. King	93	18 69 B
Lowther Rd. N7	48	31 85 C
Lowther Rd. Stan	21	18 89 B
Lowther Rd. SW13	72	21 76 B
Lowth Rd. SE5	75	32 76 C
Loxford Ave. E6	50	41 83 D
Loxford La. Ilf	51	44 85 D
Loxford Rd. Bark	51	43 84 B
Loxham Rd. E4	26	37 91 D
Loxham St. WC1	3	30 82 A
Loxley Cl. SE26	88	35 71 D
Loxley Rd. Hamp	82	12 71 B
Loxley Rd. SW18	85	26 73 D
Loxton Rd. SE23	88	36 73 C
Loxwood Rd. N17	25	33 89 A
Lubbock Rd. Chis	99	42 70 D
Lubbock St. SE14	64	35 77 C
Lucan Pl. SW3	9	27 78 A
Lucan Rd. Barn	11	24 96 A
Lucas Ave. E13	50	40 83 B
Lucas Ave. Har	32	13 86 A
Lucas Ct. SE26	88	36 71 D
Lucas Rd. SE20	98	35 70 A
Lucas Sq. NW11	35	25 88 C
Lucas St. SE8	76	37 76 A
Lucerne Cl. N13	16	30 93 C
Lucerne Ct. Beck	98	37 70 C
Lucerne Gr. E17	26	38 89 D
Lucerne Mews. W8	56	25 80 C
Lucerne Rd. N5	48	31 85 B
Lucerne Rd. Orp	108	45 66 D
Lucerne Rd. Th Hth	97	32 68 C
Lucerne Way. Rom	30	53 91 B
Lucey Rd. SE16	63	34 79 C
Lucey Way. SE16	63	34 79 C
Lucie Ave. Ashf	91	07 70 B
Lucien Rd. SW17	86	28 71 A
Lucien Rd. SW19	85	25 72 B
Lucknow St. SE18	66	45 77 C
Lucorn Cl. SE12	77	39 74 D
Lucy Cres. W3	55	20 81 A
Lucy Gdns. Dag	41	48 86 C
Luddesdon Rd. Eri	67	49 77 C
Ludford Cl. NW9	22	21 90 C
Ludgate Bwy. EC4	3	31 81 D
Ludgate Circ. EC4	3	31 81 D
Ludgate Ct. EC4	3	31 81 D
Ludgate Hill. EC4	3	31 81 D
Ludgate Sq. EC4	3	31 81 D
Ludham. NW5	47	27 85 D
Ludlow Cl. Har	43	12 85 B
Ludlow Rd. Felt	81	10 71 A
Ludlow Rd. W5	54	17 82 C
Ludlow St. EC1	4	32 82 C
Ludlow Way. N2	23	26 89 C
Ludovick Wlk. SW15	72	21 75 D
Ludwick Mews. SE14	64	36 77 C
Ludwigshafen Pl. Rom	30	51 89 C
Luffield Rd. SE2	66	46 79 D
Luffman Rd. SE12	88	40 72 D
Lugard Rd. SE15	75	34 76 B
Luke St. EC2	4	33 82 C
Lukin Cres. E4	18	38 93 D
Lukin St. E1	57	35 81 C
Lullingstone Cl. Orp	100	46 70 D
Lullingstone Cres. Orp	100	46 70 D
Lullingstone Rd. Belv	67	48 77 B
Lullington Garth. N12	15	24 92 D
Lullington Rd. Dag	52	48 84 C
Lullington Rd. SE20	97	34 70 C
Lulot Gdns. N6	36	28 86 B
Lulworth Ave. Houn	59	14 77 C
Lulworth Ave. Wem	33	17 87 A
Lulworth Cl. Har	32	12 86 D
Lulworth Dri. Pnr	32	12 87 A
Lulworth Gdns. Har	32	12 86 B
Lulworth Rd. SE15	75	34 76 D
Lulworth Rd. SE9	89	42 72 A
Lulworth Rd. Well	78	45 76 D
Lulworth Waye. Hay	53	11 81 C
Lumley Cl. Belv	67	49 78 C
Lumley Ct. WC2	7	30 80 A
Lumley Gdns. Sutt	110	24 64 C
Lumley Rd. Sutt	110	24 64 C
Lumley St. W1	2	28 81 C
Luna Rd. Th Hth	97	32 68 A
Lundy Wlk. N1	48	32 84 A
Lunham Rd. SE19	97	33 70 A
Luntley Pl. E1	57	34 81 A
Lupin Cl. SW2	87	31 72 B
Lupton Cl. SE12	89	40 71 B
Lupton St. NW5	47	29 85 A
Lupus St. SW1	10	29 78 C
Lurgan Ave. W6	62	23 77 B
Lurline Gdns. SW11	74	28 76 A
Luscombe Way. SW8	10	30 77 C
Lushington Rd. NW10	45	22 83 D
Lushington Rd. SE6	88	37 71 D
Luther Rd. Tedd	93	15 71 D
Luton Pl. SE10	64	38 77 C
Luton Rd. E13	58	40 82 C
Luton Rd. E17	26	36 89 B
Luton St. NW8	1	26 82 D
Lutton Terr. NW3	46	26 85 A
Luttrell Ave. SW15	72	22 74 B
Lutwyche Rd. SE6	88	36 72 B
Luxborough St. W1	2	28 81 A
Luxemburg Gdns. W6	62	23 78 B
Luxfield Rd. SE9	89	42 73 C
Luxford St. SE16	64	35 78 B
Luxmore St. SE4	76	36 76 B
Luxor St. SE5	75	32 76 C
Lxworth Pl. SW3	9	27 78 A
Lyall Ave. SE21	87	33 71 B
Lyall Mews. SW1	6	28 79 C
Lyall Mews W. SW1	6	28 79 C
Lyall St. SW1	6	28 79 C
Lyal Rd. E3	49	36 83 C
Lycett Pl. W12	61	22 79 A
Lych Gate Rd. Orp	108	46 66 C
Lyconby Gdns. Croy	106	36 66 A
Lydd Cl. Sid	90	45 72 C
Lydden Ct. SE9	78	45 74 C
Lydden Gr. SW18	85	25 73 A
Lydden Rd. SW18	85	25 73 A
Lydd Rd. Bexh	79	48 77 D
Lydeard Rd. E6	50	42 84 D
Lydford Cl (off Truman's Rd) N16	48	33 85 C
Lydford Rd. N15	37	32 88 B
Lydford Rd. NW2	46	23 84 B
Lydford Rd. W9	56	24 82 D
Lydhurst Ave. SW2	87	30 72 B
Lydhurst Rd. Grnf	53	13 82 D
Lydia Rd. Eri	68	51 77 B
Lydney Cl. SE15	63	33 77 C
Lydney Cl. SW19	85	24 72 A
Lydon Rd. SW4	74	29 75 A
Lydstep Rd. Chis	90	43 71 A
Lyford Rd. SW18	86	27 73 C
Lyford St. SE18	65	42 78 A
Lygoe Rd. N2	23	26 90 B
Lygon Pl. SW1	6	28 79 D
Lyham Cl. SW2	74	30 74 C
Lyham Rd. SW2	74	30 74 A
Lymbourne Cl. Sutt	110	25 62 C
Lyme Farm Rd. SE12	77	40 75 C
Lyme Gr. E9	49	35 84 C
Lymer Ave. SE19	87	33 71 D
Lyme Rd. Well	78	46 76 B
Lymescote Gdns. Sutt	103	25 65 A
Lyme St. NW1	47	29 84 C
Lyminge Cl. Sid	90	45 71 B
Lyminge Gdns. SW18	86	27 73 C
Lymington Ave. N22	25	31 90 D
Lymington Cl. SW16	96	29 69 D
Lymington Dri. Ruis	31	08 86 B
Lymington Gdns. Eps	109	21 64 D
Lymington Rd. Dag	41	47 87 D
Lymington Rd. NW6	46	25 84 B
Lympstone Gdns. SE15	63	34 77 C
Lynbridge Gdns. N13	17	31 92 B
Lynbrook Cl. Rain	52	50 83 D
Lynbrook Cl. SE15	63	33 77 C
Lynchen Cl. Houn	69	10 76 B
Lynch Wlk. SE8	64	36 77 B
Lyncott Cres. SW4	74	28 75 D
Lyncroft Ave. Pnr	32	12 88 A
Lyncroft Gdns. Eps	109	21 62 B
Lyncroft Gdns. Houn	70	14 74 A
Lyncroft Gdns. NW6	46	25 85 C
Lyncroft Gdns. W13	54	17 80 C
Lyndale Ave. NW2	35	24 86 D
Lyndale Cl. SE3	65	39 77 B
Lyndale. NW2	46	24 85 B
Lynden Hyrst. Croy	105	33 65 B
Lyndhurst Ave. N12	24	27 91 B
Lyndhurst Ave. NW7	22	21 91 A
Lyndhurst Ave. Pnr	19	10 90 B
Lyndhurst Ave. Sthl	53	13 80 D
Lyndhurst Ave. Sun	91	10 68 A
Lyndhurst Ave. Surb	102	19 66 D
Lyndhurst Ave. SW16	96	29 69 D
Lyndhurst Ave. Twick	82	13 73 C
Lyndhurst Cl. Bexh	79	49 75 B
Lyndhurst Cl. Croy	105	33 65 D
Lyndhurst Cl. NW10	34	20 86 D
Lyndhurst Ct. Sutt	110	25 63 C
Lyndhurst Dri. E10	38	38 87 A
Lyndhurst Dri. Horn	42	53 87 A
Lyndhurst Dri. N.Mal	102	21 66 B
Lyndhurst Gdns. Bark	51	45 84 A
Lyndhurst Gdns. Enf	13	33 96 C
Lyndhurst Gdns. Ilf	40	44 88 D
Lyndhurst Gdns. N3	23	24 90 A
Lyndhurst Gdns. NW3	46	26 85 D
Lyndhurst Gdns. Pnr	19	10 90 B
Lyndhurst Gr. SE15	75	33 76 D
Lyndhurst Rd. Bexh	79	49 75 B
Lyndhurst Rd. E4	26	38 91 C
Lyndhurst Rd. N18	17	34 92 A
Lyndhurst Rd. N22	25	31 91 A
Lyndhurst Rd. NW3	46	26 85 D
Lyndhurst Rd. Th Hth	97	31 68 C
Lyndhurst Sq. SE15	75	33 76 B
Lyndhurst Way. SE15	75	33 76 D
Lyndhurst Way. Sutt	110	25 62 A
Lyndon Ave. Pnr	20	12 91 A
Lyndon Ave. Sid	78	45 74 B
Lyndon Ave. Wall	104	28 65 C
Lyndon Rd. Belv	67	49 78 A
Lyne Cres. E17	26	36 90 B
Lynegrove Ave. Ashf	81	08 71 C
Lyneham Wlk. E5	49	36 85 C
Lynette Ave. SW4	74	29 74 C
Lynford Gdns. Ilf	40	45 86 B
Lynford Rd. Well	48	46 76 D
Lynmouth Ave. Enf	13	33 95 D
Lynmouth Ave. Mord	103	23 66 B
Lynmouth Dri. Ruis	31	10 86 D
Lynmouth Gdns. Grnf	54	17 84 C
Lynmouth Gdns. Houn	70	11 76 B
Lynmouth Rd. E17	38	36 88 A
Lynmouth Rd. Grnf	44	16 83 B
Lynmouth Rd. N16	37	33 87 D
Lynmouth Rd. N2	24	27 89 D
Lynmouth Rise. Orp	100	46 68 D
Lynn Cl. Ashf	81	08 71 D
Lynn Cl. Har	20	14 90 D
Lynnett Rd. Dag	41	47 86 B
Lynne Way. Nthlt	43	11 83 D
Lynne Way. NW10	45	21 84 A
Lynn Rd. E11	39	39 86 C
Lynn Rd. Ilf	40	44 87 B
Lynn Rd. SW12	86	28 73 B

Entry		Ref
Lynn Rd. SW12	74	28 74 D
Lynn St. Enf.	13	32 97 B
Lynross Cl. Rom.	30	54 90 D
Lynstead Cl. Bexh.	79	49 74 B
Lynstead Cl. Brom.	99	41 69 C
Lynsted Ct. Beck.	98	41 75 D
Lynsted Gdns. SE9	77	26 92 B
Lynton Ave. N12	15	21 89 D
Lynton Ave. NW9	22	21 89 D
Lynton Ave. Orp.	100	46 68 D
Lynton Ave. Rom.	29	49 90 B
Lynton Ave. W13	55	16 81 C
Lynton Cl. Islw.	71	15 75 D
Lynton Cres. Ilf.	40	43 88 D
Lynton Gdns. Enf.	17	33 94 A
Lynton Gdns. N11	24	29 91 B
Lynton Mead. N20	15	25 93 B
Lynton Rd. Croy.	105	31 67 C
Lynton Rd. E4	18	37 92 D
Lynton Rd. Har.	32	12 86 A
Lynton Rd. N8	36	28 83 B
Lynton Rd. N.Mal.	102	20 67 B
Lynton Rd. NW6	46	24 83 D
Lynton Rd. SE1	63	34 78 A
Lynton Rd. W3	55	19 80 B
Lynwood Cl. E18	27	41 90 A
Lynwood Cl. Har.	32	12 86 C
Lynwood Cl. Rom.	29	49 91 B
Lynwood Ct. King.	94	19 69 D
Lynwood Dri. Nthwd.	19	09 90 B
Lynwood Dri. Wor Pk.	102	22 65 A
Lynwood Dr. Rom.	29	49 91 D
Lynwood Gdns. Croy.	111	30 64 B
Lynwood Gdns. Sthl.	53	12 81 D
Lynwood Rd. N21	17	31 94 C
Lynwood Rd. Orp.	108	45 66 C
Lynwood Rd. Surb.	101	15 65 B
Lynwood Rd. SW17	86	27 71 B
Lynwood Rd. W5	54	18 82 C
Lyon Meade. Stan.	21	17 90 A
Lyon Park Ave. Wem.	44	18 84 B
Lyon Rd. Har.	33	15 88 D
Lyon Rd. Rom.	42	51 87 B
Lyon Rd. SW19	95	26 69 A
Lyonsdown Ave. Barn.	11	26 95 C
Lyonsdown Rd. Barn.	11	26 95 D
Lyons Pl. NW8	1	26 82 D
Lyon St. N1	47	30 84 D
Lyon Way. Grnf.	44	15 83 A
Lyoth Rd. Orp.	108	44 65 A
Lyric Rd. SW13	72	21 76 B
Lysander Gr. N19	36	29 87 D
Lysander Rd. Croy.	111	30 63 B
Lysander Rd. Ruis.	31	08 86 B
Lysander Way. Orp.	108	44 65 C
Lysias Rd. SW12	74	28 74 D
Lysia St. SW6	62	23 77 D
Lysons Wlk. SW15	72	22 74 A
Lytchet Rd. Brom.	99	44 70 D
Lytchet Way. Enf.	14	35 97 A
Lytchgate Cl. S Croy.	112	33 63 C
Lytcott Gr. SE22	75	33 74 B
Lytham Gr. W5	54	18 82 B
Lytham St. SE17	63	32 78 D
Lyttleton Cl. NW3	47	27 84 C
Lyttleton Rd. E10	38	38 86 C
Lyttleton Rd. N8	25	31 89 A
Lytltlon Ct. NW2	35	31 93 A
Lytton Ave. N13	17	26 88 B
Lytton Cl. N2	35	12 84 D
Lytton Cl. Nthlt.	43	29 64 B
Lytton Gdns. Wall.	111	24 74 C
Lytton Gr. SW15	73	26 96 C
Lytton Rd. Barn.	11	39 87 A
Lytton Rd. E11	39	12 91 C
Lytton Rd. Pnr.	20	52 88 B
Lytton Rd. Rom.	42	40 77 D
Lyveden Rd. SE3	65	27 70 B
Lyveden Rd. SW17	96	
Maberley Cres. SE19	97	34 70 C
Maberley Rd. Beck.	98	35 68 B
Maberley Rd. SE19	97	34 69 A
Mabledon Pl. WC1	2	29 82 B
Mablethorpe Rd. SW6	62	24 77 C
Mabley St. E9	49	36 84 A
Mabley St. E9	49	36 85 C
Macaret Cl. N20	15	26 94 A
Macaulay Ave. Esh.	101	15 65 A
Macaulay Rd. E6	50	41 83 D
Macaulay Rd. SW4	74	28 75 B
Macaulay Sq. SW4	74	28 75 B
Macbean St. SE18	66	43 79 D
Macbeth St. W6	61	22 78 D
Macclesfield Rd. EC1	4	32 82 A
Macclesfield Rd. SE25	106	35 67 A
Macclesfield St. W1	6	29 80 B
Macdonald Ave. Dag.	41	49 86 D
Macdonald Ave. Horn.	30	54 90 D
Macdonald Rd. E17	26	38 90 C
Macdonald Rd. E7	50	40 85 A
Macdonald Rd. N11	24	27 92 D
Macdonald Rd. N19	36	29 86 A
Macdonald Way. Horn.	30	54 89 C
Macduff Rd. SW11	74	28 76 A
Mace St. E2	49	35 83 D
Macfarlane Rd. W12	66	23 80 C
Mac Farren Pl. NW1	2	28 82 C
Macgregor Rd. E16	58	41 81 A
Machell Rd. SE15	76	35 75 A
Mackay Rd. SW4	74	28 75 B
Mackennal St. NW8	47	27 83 C
Mackenzie Rd. Beck.	98	35 69 D
Mackenzie Rd. N7	47	30 84 B
Mackeson Rd. NW3	47	27 85 B
Mackie Rd. SW2	87	31 73 A
Mackintosh La. E9	49	35 85 D
Macklin St. WC2	3	30 81 C
Mackrow Wlk. E14	58	38 80 A
Macks Rd. SE16	63	34 78 B
Mackworth St. NW1	2	29 82 A
Maclean Rd. SE23	76	36 74 C
Macleod St. SE17	63	32 78 C
Maclise Rd. W14	62	24 79 C
Macoma Rd. SE18	66	44 77 B
Macoma Terr. SE18	66	44 77 B
Macquarie Way. E14	64	37 78 B
Macready Pl. N7	47	30 85 A
Macroom Rd. W9	56	24 82 B
Mada Rd. Orp.	108	43 65 D
Maddams St. E3	57	37 82 D
Maddison Cl. Tedd.	93	15 70 B
Maddock Way. SE17	63	31 77 B
Maddox St. W1	6	29 80 A
Madeira Ave. Brom.	99	39 70 C
Madeira Gr. Wdf Gn.	27	41 91 A
Madeira Rd. E11	39	39 87 C
Madeira Rd. Mit.	96	27 68 D
Madeira Rd. N13	13	31 95 D
Madeley Rd. W5	54	18 81 C
Madeline Rd. SE20	97	34 70 C
Maderira Rd. SW16	86	30 71 C
Madison Cres. Bexh.	67	47 77 C
Madison Gdns. Bexh.	67	47 77 C
Madison Gdns. Brom.	99	39 68 B
Madras Pl. N7	48	31 84 A
Madras Rd. Ilf.	51	43 85 B
Madrid Rd. SW13	61	22 77 C
Madron St. SE17	63	33 78 C
Mafeking Ave. Brent.	60	18 77 A
Mafeking Ave. E6	50	42 83 C
Mafeking Ave. Ilf.	40	44 87 B
Mafeking Rd. E16	58	39 82 D
Mafeking Rd. Enf.	13	33 96 B
Mafeking Rd. N17	25	29 86 A
Magdala Rd. N19	36	16 75 A
Magdala Rd. Islw.	71	32 63 D
Magdala Rd. S Croy.	112	34 76 D
Magdalene Cl. SE15	75	33 80 B
Magdalen Pas. E1	7	07 68 A
Magdalen Rd. Shep.	91	26 73 D
Magdalen Rd. SW18	85	33 80 C
Magdalen St. SE1	8	31 77 A
Magee St. SE11	63	34 83 A
Magnin Cl. E8	48	19 70 B
Magnolia Cl. King.	94	18 87 B
Magnolia Cl. Har.	33	19 76 B
Magnolia Ct. Rich.	72	25 63 D
Magnolia Ct. Sutt.	110	30 75 C
Magnolia Ct. SW4	74	19 77 B
Magnolia Rd. W4	61	20 64 C
Magnolia Way. Eps.	109	19 77 B
Magnolia Wharf. W4	61	31 81 C
Magpie Alley. EC4	3	42 67 C
Magpie Hall Cl. Brom.	107	42 67 D
Magpie Hall La. Brom.	107	17 71 A
Maguire Dri. Rich.	83	33 79 B
Maguire St. SE1	8	11 84 A
Mahlon Ave. Ruis.	57	36 80 C
Mahogany Cl. SE16	64	37 94 B
Maida Ave. E4	18	26 82 C
Maida Ave. W2	1	49 79 C
Maida Rd. Belv.	67	52 74 A
Maida Vale Rd. Dart.	80	26 82 A
Maida Vale. W9	1	37 94 B
Maida Way. E4	18	52 75 C
Maiden La. Dart.	80	29 84 D
Maiden La. N7	47	30 80 A
Maiden La. WC2	7	
Maiden Rd. E15	50	39 84 C
Maidstone Ave. Rom.	29	50 90 C
Maidstone Bldgs. SE1	8	32 80 D
Maidstone Hill. SE10	76	38 76 A
Maidstone Rd. N11	24	29 91 B
Maidstone St. E2	48	34 83 C
Mail Coach Yd. E2	4	33 82 A
Main Ave. Enf.	13	33 95 B
Main Rd. Rom.	30	52 89 A
Main Rd. Sid.	90	45 71 B
Mainridge Rd. Chis.	90	43 71 A
Main St. Felt.	82	11 71 D
Maismore St. SE15	63	34 77 A
Maitland Cl. Houn.	70	12 75 B
Maitland Cl. SE10	64	37 77 D
Maitland Park Estate. NW3	47	27 84 B
Maitland Park Rd. NW3	47	27 84 B
Maitland Park Villas. NW3	47	27 84 B
Maitland Rd. E15	50	39 84 B
Maitland Rd. SE26	44	35 70 B
Maize Row. E14	57	36 81 D
Majendie Rd. SE18	66	44 78 D
Major Rd. E15	49	38 85 D
Major Rd. SE16	63	34 79 C
Makepeace Ave. N6	36	28 86 A
Makepeace Rd. Nthlt.	43	12 83 A
Makins St. SW3	9	27 78 A
Malabar St. E14	64	37 79 A
Malam Gdns. E14	57	37 80 B
Malbrook Rd. SW15	72	22 75 D
Malcolm Cres. NW4	34	22 88 C
Malcolm Rd. E7	50	39 84 B
Malcolm Rd. Surb.	101	18 66 C
Malcolm Pl. E2	57	35 82 C
Malcolm Rd. E1	57	35 82 C
Malcolm Rd. SE20	98	35 70 C
Malcolm Rd. SE25	105	34 67 C
Malcolm Rd. SW19	95	24 70 A
Malcolm Way. E11	27	40 89 C
Malden Ave. Grnf.	44	15 84 A
Malden Ave. SE25	97	34 68 B
Malden Cres. NW1	47	28 84 A
Malden Ct. N Mal.	94	22 68 B
Malden Ct. N Mal.	94	22 68 D
Malden Green Ave. Wor Pk.	102	22 66 C
Malden Hill Gdns. N Mal.	94	21 68 A
Malden Hill. N Mal.	94	21 68 A
Malden Park. N.Mal.	102	21 67 D
Malden Pl. NW5	47	28 85 C
Malden Rd. N.Mal.	102	21 67 D
Malden Rd. NW3	47	28 84 A
Malden Rd. Ilf.	110	23 64 A
Malden Rd. Wor Pk.	102	22 66 C
Malden Way. N.Mal.	102	21 67 A
Maldon Cl. N1	48	32 83 A
Maldon Cl. SE5	75	33 75 A
Maldon Cl. N9	17	33 93 D
Maldon Rd. Rom.	41	50 87 A
Maldon Rd. W3	55	20 80 A
Maldon Rd. Wall.	111	28 64 D
Maldon Wlk. Wdf Gn.	27	41 91 A
Malet St. WC1	2	29 81 B
Maley Ave. SE27	87	31 72 B
Maley Pl. WC1	2	29 82 C
Malford Ct. E18	27	40 90 C
Malford Gr. E18	27	39 89 B
Malfort Rd. SE5	75	33 75 A
Malham Rd. SE23	76	35 73 D
Mallams Mews. SW9	75	31 75 B
Mallard Cl. Barn.	11	26 94 B
Mallard Cl. Barn.	11	26 95 D
Mallard Cl. E9	49	36 84 B
Mallard Cl. Houn.	82	13 73 A
Mallard Pl. N22	24	30 90 D
Mallard Pl. Twick.	83	16 72 C
Mallards Rd. Wdf Gn.	27	40 91 D
Mallard Way. Nthwd.	20	08 91 C
Mallard Way. NW9	34	20 87 A
Mallet Dri. Nthlt.	43	12 85 D
Mallet Rd. SE13	76	38 74 D
Malling Cl. Croy.	106	35 67 C
Malling Gdns. Mord.	103	26 67 C
Malling Way. Brom.	107	39 66 B
Mallinson Rd. Croy.	104	29 65 D
Mallinson Rd. SW11	74	27 74 B
Mallord St. SW3	62	26 77 B
Mallory Cl. SE4	76	36 75 C
Mallory Gdns. Barn.	16	28 94 A
Mallory St. NW8	1	27 82 C
Mallow Mead. NW7	23	24 91 C
Mallow St. EC1	4	32 82 D
Mallows The. Uxb.	31	07 86 D
Mall Rd. W6	61	22 78 D
Mall The. Brent.	60	17 77 B
Mall The. Brom.	99	40 68 A

Mall The. Croy	105	
Mall The. Dag	52	32 65 A
Mall The. E15	49	49 84 A
Mall The. Har	33	38 84 D
Mall The. N14	16	18 88 D
Mall The. Surb	101	30 93 C
Mall The. SW14	72	17 67 B
Mall. The SW1	6	20 74 A
Mall The. W5	54	29 80 D
Malmains Cl. Beck	98	18 80 A
Malmains Way. Beck	98	38 68 D
Malmesbury Cl. Pnr	19	38 68 D
Malmesbury Rd. E16	58	10 89 C
Malmesbury Rd. E18	27	39 81 A
Malmesbury Rd. E3	49	39 90 B
Malmesbury Rd. Mord	103	37 83 C
Malmesbury Terr. E16	58	26 67 C
Malpas Dri. Pnr	32	39 81 B
Malpas Rd. Dag	52	11 88 B
Malpas Rd. E8	48	47 84 B
Malpas Rd. SE4	76	34 85 D
Malta Rd. E10	38	36 76 D
Malta St. EC1	3	37 87 A
Maltby Cl. Orp	108	31 82 D
Maltby Rd. Chess	109	46 66 C
Maltby St. SE1	8	19 63 A
Malthouse Dri. Felt	82	33 79 D
Maltings Cl. SW13	72	11 71 D
Maltings The. Orp	108	21 76 C
Malton Rd. W10	56	45 66 D
Malton St. SE18	66	24 81 C
Maltravers St. WC2	7	45 77 A
Malt St. SE1	63	31 80 A
Malva Cl. SW18	73	34 77 A
Malva Rd. SW18	73	25 74 D
Malvern Ave. Bexh	67	25 74 B
Malvern Ave. E4	26	48 77 C
Malvern Ave. Har	32	38 91 D
Malvern Cl. Mit	96	12 86 D
Malvern Cl. Surb	101	29 68 A
Malvern Cl. Uxb	31	18 66 C
Malvern Cl. W10	56	07 86 A
Malvern Dri. Felt	82	24 81 B
Malvern Dri. Ilf	51	11 71 D
Malvern Gdns. Har	21	45 85 B
Malvern Gdns. NW2	35	18 89 C
Malvern Mews. NW6	56	24 86 A
Malvern Pl. W9	56	25 82 A
Malvern Rd. E11	39	24 82 B
Malvern Rd. E6	50	39 86 B
Malvern Rd. E8	48	42 83 A
Malvern Rd. Hamp	92	34 84 C
Malvern Rd. Horn	42	13 69 A
Malvern Rd. N17	25	52 88 C
Malvern Rd. N8	25	34 89 A
Malvern Rd. NW6	56	31 89 A
Malvern Rd. Surb	101	25 82 A
Malvern Rd. Th Hth	97	18 66 C
Malvern Terr. N1	48	31 68 C
Malvern Terr. N9	17	31 83 A
Malvern Way. W13	54	33 94 D
Malwood Rd. SW12	74	16 81 B
Malyons Rd. SE13	76	28 74 D
Malyons Terr. SE13	76	37 74 B
Managers St. E14	58	37 74 B
Manaton Cl. SE15	75	38 80 C
Manaton Cres. Sthl	53	34 75 B
Manbey Gr. E15	50	13 81 C
Manbey Park Rd. E15	50	39 84 A
Manbey Rd. E15	50	39 84 A
Manbey St. E15	50	39 84 A
Manchester Dri. W10	56	39 84 A
Manchester Gr. E14	64	24 82 C
Manchester Rd. E14	64	38 78 C
Manchester Rd. N15	37	38 79 C
Manchester Rd. Th Hth	97	32 88 D
Manchester Sq. W1	2	32 68 A
Manchester St. W1	2	28 81 C
Manchester Way. Dag	52	28 81 A
Manchuria Rd. SW11	74	49 85 B
Manciple St. SE1	8	28 74 C
Mandalay Rd. SW4	74	32 79 B
Mandarin St. E14	57	29 74 A
Mandela Cl. NW10	45	37 80 A
Mandeville Cl. SE3	65	20 84 C
Mandeville Dri. Surb	101	40 77 C
Mandeville Pl. W1	2	17 66 D
Mandeville Rd. Islw	71	28 81 C
Mandeville Rd. N14	16	16 76 C
Mandeville Rd. Nthlt	43	29 93 A
Mandeville St. E5	49	13 84 A
Mandrake Rd. SW17	86	36 85 A
Mandrell Rd. SW2	74	27 72 D
Manette St. W1	2	30 74 A
Manfred Rd. SW15	73	29 81 D
		24 74 B
Manger Rd. N7	47	30 84 A
Mangold Way. Belv	67	48 79 C
Manilla St. E14	64	37 79 A
Maniloba Ct. SE16	64	35 79 A
Manister Rd. SE2	66	46 79 C
Manley Ct. N16	37	33 86 D
Manley St. NW1	47	28 83 A
Manmouth Ave. King	93	17 70 C
Manningford Cl. EC1	3	31 82 B
Manning Gdns. Har	33	17 87 B
Manning Rd. Dag	52	49 84 C
Manning Rd. E17	38	36 88 A
Manningtree Cl. SW18	85	24 73 C
*Manningtree St. E1	57	34 81 C
Mannin Rd. Rom	40	46 88 D
Mannock Rd. N22	25	31 89 B
Mann's Cl. Islw	71	15 74 B
Manns Rd. Edg	22	19 91 A
Manoel Rd. Twick	82	14 72 A
Manor Alley. W4	61	21 78 C
Manor Ave. Horn	42	53 88 A
Manor Ave. Houn	70	11 76 D
Manor Ave. Nthlt	43	12 84 D
Manor Ave. SE4	76	36 76 D
Manorbrook. SE3	77	40 75 C
Manor Cl. Barn	11	24 96 C
Manor Cl. Dag	52	50 84 B
Manor Cl. Dart	80	51 75 C
Manor Cl. E17	26	36 90 C
Manor Cl. NW9	34	19 88 B
Manor Cl. Rom	42	52 88 A
Manor Cl. Ruis	31	09 87 D
Manor Cl. Wor Pk	102	21 66 C
Manor Cottages App. N2	23	26 90 C
Manor Cottages. Nthwd	19	09 90 B
Manor Court Rd. W7	54	15 80 A
Manor Cres. Horn	42	53 88 A
Manor Cres. Surb	102	19 67 C
Manor Ct. N14	16	29 93 B
Manor Ct. SW16	86	30 72 C
Manor Ct. Twick	82	14 72 A
Manordene Cl. Surb	101	16 66 C
Manor Dri. Eps	109	21 63 A
Manor Dri. Esh	101	16 65 C
Manor Dri. Felt	82	11 71 C
Manor Dri. N14	16	28 94 D
Manor Dri. N20	16	27 93 D
Manor Dri. Sun	91	10 69 C
Manor Dri. Surb	102	19 67 C
Manor Drive N. N.Mal	102	20 66 B
Manor Drive N. Wor Pk	102	21 66 C
Manor Drive The. Wor Pk	102	21 66 C
Manor Dri. Wem	44	18 85 B
Manor Farm Rd. Th Hth	97	31 69 C
Manor Farm Rd. Wem	44	17 83 D
*Manorfield Cl. N19	47	29 85 A
Manor Fields. SW15	73	23 74 D
Manor Gate. Nthlt	43	12 84 C
Manorgate Rd. King	94	19 69 A
Manor Gdns. Hamp	92	14 70 C
Manor Gdns. N7	36	30 86 C
Manor Gdns. Rich	71	18 75 D
Manor Gdns. Ruis	43	11 85 C
Manor Gdns. S Croy	112	33 63 B
Manor Gdns. Sun	91	10 69 C
Manor Gdns. SW20	95	24 69 D
Manor Gdns. W3	61	19 78 A
Manor Gr. Beck	98	37 69 D
Manor Gr. Rich	72	19 75 A
Manor Gr. SE15	64	35 77 A
Manor Hall Ave. NW4	23	23 90 D
Manor Hall Dri. NW4	23	23 90 D
Manor Hall Gdns. E10	38	37 87 C
Manor House Dri. NW6	46	23 84 D
Manor House Estate. Stan	21	16 91 B
Manor La. Felt	81	10 72 A
Manor Lane Terr. SE13	77	39 74 A
Manor La. SE12	77	39 74 C
Manor La. SE13	77	39 74 A
Manor La. Sun	91	10 69 D
Manor La. Sutt	110	26 64 C
Manor Mews. NW6	46	25 83 C
Manor Mews. SE4	76	36 76 D
Manor Mount. SE23	88	35 73 C
Manor Pk. Chis	100	44 69 B
Manor Park Cl. W Wick	106	37 66 D
Manor Park Cres. Edg	22	19 91 A
Manor Park Dri. Har	20	13 89 B
Manor Park Gdns. Edg	22	19 91 A
Manor Park Rd. Chis	100	44 69 B
Manor Park Rd. E12	50	41 85 B
Manor Park Rd. N2	23	26 89 A
Manor Park Rd. NW10	45	21 83 B
Manor Park Rd. Sutt	110	26 64 C
Manor Park Rd. W Wick	106	37 66 D
Manor Park. Rich	71	18 75 D
Manor Park. SE13	77	39 74 A
Manor Pl. Chis	100	44 69 D
Manor Pl. Felt	81	10 73 C
Manor Pl. Mit	96	29 68 A
Manor Pl. SE17	63	32 78 C
Manor Pl. Sutt	110	25 64 B
Manor Rd. Ashf	81	07 71 C
Manor Rd. Bark	51	45 84 B
Manor Rd. Barn	11	24 96 C
Manor Rd. Beck	98	37 69 D
Manor Rd. Chig	28	43 91 A
Manor Rd. Dag	52	50 84 B
Manor Rd. Dart	80	51 75 C
Manor Rd. E10	38	37 87 A
Manor Rd. E15	58	39 82 A
Manor Rd. E17	26	36 90 C
Manor Rd. E Mol	92	14 68 D
Manor Rd. Enf	13	32 97 D
Manor Rd. Eri	68	52 77 A
Manor Rd. Har	33	16 88 C
Manor Rd. Mit	96	29 68 A
Manor Rd. N16	37	33 87 C
Manor Rd. N17	25	34 90 B
Manor Rd. N22	24	30 91 A
Manor Rd. N. Esh	101	15 65 B
Manor Rd. N. Surb	101	16 66 C
Manor Rd. N. Wall	111	28 64 B
Manor Rd. Rich	71	18 75 D
Manor Rd. Rom	41	47 88 D
Manor Rd. Rom	42	52 88 A
Manor Rd. Ruis	31	08 87 D
Manor Rd. SE25	9	34 68 A
Manor Rd. S. Esh	101	15 65 D
Manor Rd. Sid	90	46 72 C
Manor Rd. Sutt	110	24 63 D
Manor Rd. SW20	95	24 69 D
Manor Rd. Tedd	83	16 71 D
Manor Rd. Twick	82	14 72 B
Manor Rd. W13	54	16 80 A
Manor Rd. Wall	111	28 64 D
Manor Rd. Wdf Gn	27	42 91 B
Manor Rd. W Wick	106	37 65 B
Manorside. Barn	11	24 96 C
Manor Sq. Dag	41	47 86 B
Manor St Estate. SW3	9	27 77 A
Manor Vale. Brent	60	17 78 C
Manor Way. N3	23	25 90 D
Manor Way. Beck	98	37 68 B
Manor Way. Bexh	79	50 75 B
Manor Way. Brom	107	42 67 C
Manor Way. E4	18	38 92 B
Manorway. Enf	17	33 94 A
Manor Way. Har	20	13 89 D
Manor Way. Mit	96	29 68 A
Manor Way. NW9	22	21 89 C
Manor Way. Orp	100	44 68 C
Manor Way. Ruis	31	09 87 D
Manor Way. S Croy	112	33 63 B
Manor Way. SE3	77	40 75 C
Manor Way. Sthl	59	11 78 B
Manor Way The. Wall	111	28 64 B
Manor Way. Wor Pk	102	21 66 D
Manresa Rd. SW3	9	27 78 C
Mansard Cl. Pnr	20	11 89 B
Mansel Gr. E17	26	37 90 A
Mansell Rd. Grnf	53	13 81 B
Mansell Rd. W3	61	20 79 B
Mansell St. E1	8	33 80 B
Mansell St. E1	4	33 81 D
Mansel Rd. SW19	95	24 70 A
Manse Rd. N16	37	33 86 D
Mansergh Cl. SE18	65	42 77 C
Mansfield Ave. Barn	12	28 95 C
Mansfield Ave. N15	25	32 89 D
Mansfield Cl. N9	13	34 95 C
Mansfield Gdns. Horn	42	53 86 B
Mansfield Hill. E4	18	37 94 D
Mansfield Hts. N2	36	27 88 B
Mansfield Mews. W1	2	28 81 B
Mansfield Pl. NW3	46	26 85 A
Mansfield Pl. S Croy	112	32 63 B
Mansfield Rd. E11	39	40 88 D
Mansfield Rd. E17	26	36 89 D
Mansfield Rd. Ilf	40	43 86 A
Mansfield Rd. NW3	47	28 85 A
Mansfield Rd. S Croy	112	32 63 B
Mansfield Rd. W3	55	19 82 D
Mansfield St. W1	2	28 81 B
Mansford St. E2	48	34 83 C
Manship Rd. Mit	96	28 69 A
Mansion House Pl. EC4	4	32 81 D
Mansion House St. EC2	4	32 81 D
Manson Mews. SW7	62	26 78 B
Manson Pl. SW7	62	26 78 B

Manstead Gdns. Rom ...41 — 47 87 A
Manston Ave. Sthl ...59 — 13 78 A
Manstone Rd. NW2 ...46 — 24 85 C
Mantell St. N1 ...48 — 31 83 C
Manthorpe Rd. SE18 ...66 — 44 78 C
Mantilla Rd. SW17 ...86 — 28 71 A
Mantle Rd. SE4 ...76 — 36 75 A
Manton Ave. W7 ...60 — 16 79 A
Manton Rd. SE2 ...66 — 46 78 A
Mantua St. SW11 ...73 — 26 75 B
Mantus Cl. E1 ...57 — 35 82 C
Mantus Rd. E1 ...57 — 35 82 C
Manus Way. N20 ...15 — 26 94 C
Manville Gdns. SW17 ...86 — 28 72 D
Manville Rd. SW17 ...86 — 28 72 D
Manwood Rd. SE4 ...76 — 36 74 D
Many Gates. SW12 ...86 — 28 72 B
Mapesbury Rd. NW2 ...46 — 24 84 A
Mape St. E2 ...26 — 34 82 D
Maple Ave. E4 ... — 36 91 B
Maple Ave. Har ...32 — 13 86 B
Maple Ave. W3 ...55 — 21 80 C
Maple Cl. Horn ...42 — 52 86 D
Maple Cl. Mit ...96 — 28 59 B
Maple Cl. N16 ...37 — 34 88 C
Maple Cl. Nthlt ...53 — 11 82 B
Maple Cl. Orp ...108 — 44 67 B
Maple Cl. Ruis ...31 — 10 88 D
Maple Cl. SW4 ...74 — 29 74 D
Maple Cres. Sid ...78 — 46 74 C
Maple Ct. N Mal ...94 — 21 68 A
Mapledale Ave. Croy ...105 — 34 65 D
Mapledene Estate. E8 ...48 — 34 84 C
Mapledene Rd. E8 ...48 — 34 84 C
Maple Gdns. Edg ...22 — 21 91 C
Maple Gr. Brent ...60 — 16 77 D
Maple Gr. NW9 ...34 — 20 87 A
Maple Gr. Sthl ...53 — 12 81 B
Maple Gr. W5 ...60 — 17 79 D
Mapleleafe Gdns. Ilf ...28 — 43 89 B
Maple Pl. W1 ...2 — 29 81 A
Maple Rd. E11 ...39 — 39 88 C
Maple Rd. Hay ...53 — 11 82 D
Maple Rd. Nthlt ...53 — 11 82 A
Maple Rd. SE20 ...98 — 35 70 C
Maple Rd. Surb ...101 — 17 67 B
Maples Pl. E1 ...57 — 34 81 B
Maplestead Rd. Dag ...51 — 46 83 B
Maplestead Rd. SW2 ...86 — 30 73 B
Maple St. Rom ...29 — 50 89 C
Maple St. W1 ...2 — 29 82 C
Maplethorpe Rd. Th Hth ...97 — 31 68 D
Mapleton Cl. Brom ...107 — 40 67 C
Mapleton Cres. SW18 ...73 — 25 74 D
Mapleton Rd. Enf ...13 — 34 97 D
Mapleton Rd. SW18 ...73 — 25 74 C
Mapleton Rd. SW18 ...73 — 25 74 D
Maple Way. Felt ...81 — 10 72 C
Maple Wlk. Sutt ...110 — 25 62 D
Maple Wlk. W10 ...56 — 23 82 D
Maplin Cl. N21 ...12 — 30 95 D
Maplin Rd. E16 ...58 — 40 81 C
Maplin St. E3 ...57 — 36 82 B
Mapperley Dri. Wdf Gn ...67 — 39 91 C
Maran Way. Belv ...56 — 47 79 D
Marban Rd. W9 ...56 — 24 82 B
Marble Arch. W1 ...5 — 27 80 B
Marble Cl. W3 ...55 — 19 80 D
Marble Hill Cl. Twick ...83 — 16 73 B
Marble Hill Gdns. Twick ...83 — 16 73 B
Marbrook Ct. SE12 ...89 — 41 72 C
Marcellina Way. Orp ...108 — 45 65 D
Marcet Rd. Dart ...80 — 53 74 A
Marchant Rd. E11 ...38 — 38 86 B
Marchbank Rd. SW5 ...62 — 24 77 B
March Ct. SW15 ...72 — 22 75 D
Marchmont Rd. Rich ...71 — 18 74 B
Marchmont Rd. Wall ...111 — 29 63 C
Marchmont St. WC1 ...3 — 30 82 C
March Rd. Twick ...83 — 16 73 A
March's Pl. SW15 ...73 — 23 75 B
Marchwood Cl. SE5 ...63 — 33 77 C
Marchwood Cres. W5 ...54 — 17 81 D
Marcia Rd. SE1 ...63 — 33 78 A
Marcilly Rd. SW18 ...73 — 26 74 B
Marco Way. Sthl ...53 — 13 81 D
Marcon Pl. E8 ...48 — 34 85 D
Marco Rd. W6 ...62 — 23 79 C
Marcus Ct. E15 ...50 — 39 83 A
Marcus St. E15 ...50 — 39 83 B
Marcus St. SW18 ...73 — 25 74 D
Marcus Terr. SW18 ...73 — 25 74 D
Mardale Dri. NW9 ...34 — 20 88 B
Mardell Rd. Croy ...106 — 35 67 B
Marden Ave. Brom ...107 — 40 67 C

Marden Cres. Bex ...79 — 50 74 A
Marden Cres. Croy ...104 — 30 67 D
Marden Rd. Croy ...104 — 30 67 D
Marden Rd. N17 ...25 — 33 90 C
Marden Rd. Rom ...42 — 51 88 C
Marden Sq. SE16 ...63 — 34 79 D
Marder Rd. W13 ...60 — 16 79 A
Marechal Neil Ave. Sid ...90 — 44 72 D
Maresfield. Croy ...105 — 33 65 C
Maresfield Gdns. NW3 ...46 — 26 84 A
Mare St. E8 ...48 — 34 84 D
Margaret Ave. E4 ...14 — 37 95 D
Margaret Bondfield Ave. Bark ...51 — 46 84 C
Margaret Cl. Rom ...42 — 52 88 B
Margaret Ct. W1 ...2 — 29 81 C
Margaret Dri. Horn ...42 — 54 87 B
Margaret Rd. Barn ...11 — 26 96 D
Margaret Rd. Bex ...79 — 47 74 D
Margaret Rd. N16 ...37 — 33 87 D
Margaret Rd. Rom ...42 — 52 88 B
Margaret Rd. W1 ...2 — 29 81 C
Margaretta Terr. SW3 ...9 — 27 77 A
Margaretting Rd. E12 ...39 — 41 87 C
Margaret Way. Ilf ...39 — 42 88 C
Margate Rd. SW2 ...74 — 30 74 A
Margery Park Rd. E7 ...50 — 40 84 A
Margery Rd. Dag ...41 — 47 86 D
Margery St. WC1 ...3 — 31 82 A
Margin Dri. SW19 ...85 — 23 71 B
Margravine Gdns. W6 ...62 — 23 78 D
Margravine Rd. W6 ...62 — 23 77 B
Marham Gdns. Mord ...103 — 26 67 C
Marham Gdns. SW18 ...86 — 27 73 C
Maria Cl. SE1 ...63 — 34 78 A
Mariam Gdns. Horn ...42 — 54 86 B
Marian Cl. E9 ...49 — 35 85 C
Marian Ct. Sutt ...110 — 25 64 D
Marian Pl. E2 ...48 — 34 83 D
Marian Rd. SW16 ...96 — 29 69 A
Marian Sq. E2 ...48 — 34 83 C
Marian St. E2 ...48 — 34 83 D
Marian Way. NW10 ...45 — 21 84 D
Maria Terr. E1 ...57 — 35 82 D
Maria Theresa Cl. N.Mal ...102 — 20 67 B
Maribor. SE10 ...64 — 38 77 C
Maricas Ave. Har ...20 — 14 90 B
Mariette Way. Wall ...111 — 30 62 A
Marigold Rd. SE16 ...63 — 34 79 B
Marigold Way. E4 ...26 — 36 91 B
Marina Ave. N.Mal ...102 — 22 67 B
Marina Cl. Brom ...99 — 40 68 A
Marina Dri. Well ...78 — 45 76 C
Marina Gdns. Rom ...41 — 49 88 B
Marina Way. Tedd ...93 — 17 70 D
Marinefield Rd. SW6 ...73 — 25 76 D
Mariner Gdns. Rich ...83 — 17 72 C
Mariner Rd. E12 ...51 — 43 85 A
Marine St. SE16 ...63 — 34 79 C
Marion Cl. Ilf ...28 — 44 91 D
Marion Cres. Orp ...108 — 46 67 A
Marion Rd. Th Hth ...105 — 32 67 B
Marion Rd. SE13 ...76 — 38 75 B
Marischal Rd. SE13 ...76 — 36 82 D
Marius Rd. SW17 ...86 — 28 72 A
Marjorie Cr. SW11 ...74 — 28 75 C
Mark Ave. E4 ...14 — 37 95 D
Mark Cl. Bexh ...79 — 48 76 A
Market Ct. W1 ...2 — 29 81 C
Market Hill. SE18 ...66 — 43 79 C
Market La. Edg ...22 — 20 90 A
Market Link. Rom ...6 — 51 89 C
Market Mews. W1 ...2 — 28 80 D
Market Pl. Bexh ...79 — 49 75 C
Market Pl. Brent ...60 — 17 77 D
Market Pl. Enf ...13 — 32 96 B
Market Pl. King ...93 — 17 69 D
Market Pl. N2 ...26 — 26 89 B
Market Pl. N2 ...24 — 27 89 A
Market Pl. Rom ...42 — 51 88 A
Market Pl. SE16 ...63 — 34 78 B
Market Pl. SE18 ...66 — 43 78 B
Market Pl. W1 ...2 — 29 81 C
Market Pl. W3 ...55 — 20 80 C
Market Rd. N7 ...47 — 30 84 A
Market Rd. Rich ...72 — 19 75 A
Market Sq. Brom ...99 — 40 69 C
Market Sq The. N9 ...17 — 37 81 D
Market St. E6 ...51 — 43 83 C
Market St. SE18 ...66 — 43 78 A
Market Way. E14 ...57 — 37 81 D
Market Way. Wem ...44 — 18 85 C
Markfield Gdns. E4 ...18 — 37 94 B
Markfield Rd. N15 ...37 — 34 88 A
Markham Pl. SW3 ...9 — 27 78 D

Markham Sq. SW3 ...9 — 27 78 D
Markham St. SW3 ...9 — 27 78 C
Markhole Cl. Hamp ...92 — 12 70 D
Markhouse Ave. E17 ...38 — 36 88 C
Markhouse Pas. E17 ...38 — 36 88 D
Markhouse Rd. E17 ...38 — 36 88 D
Mark La. EC3 ...3 — 33 80 A
Markmanor Ave. E17 ...25 — 36 87 B
Mark Rd. N22 ...24 — 31 90 D
Marksbury Ave. Rich ...72 — 19 75 A
Marks Rd. Rom ...41 — 50 88 B
Mark St. E15 ...50 — 39 84 C
Mark St. EC2 ...4 — 33 82 C
Mark St. EC2 ...4 — 33 82 C
Markway. Sun ...92 — 11 69 C
Markway The. Sun ...92 — 11 69 C
Markwell Cl. SE26 ...87 — 34 71 B
Markyate Rd. Dag ...51 — 46 85 D
Marlan Cl. Hay ...53 — 11 82 D
Marlands Rd. Ilf ...27 — 42 89 B
Marlborough Ave. E8 ...48 — 34 83 A
Marlborough Ave. N14 ...16 — 29 93 C
Marlborough Ave. Ruis ...31 — 08 88 D
Marlborough Bldgs. SW3 ...9 — 27 78 A
Marlborough Cl. N20 ...16 — 27 93 D
Marlborough Cl. Orp ...108 — 45 67 D
Marlborough Cl. SE17 ...63 — 32 78 A
Marlborough Cl. SW19 ...96 — 27 70 A
Marlborough Cres. W4 ...61 — 21 79 C
Marlborough Dri. Ilf ...27 — 42 89 A
Marlborough Gdns. N20 ...16 — 27 93 D
Marlborough Gdns. Surb ...101 — 17 66 B
Marlborough Gr. SE1 ...63 — 34 78 C
Marlborough Hill. Har ...21 — 15 89 C
Marlborough Hill. NW8 ...46 — 26 83 A
Marlborough La. SE7 ...65 — 41 77 C
Marlborough Park Ave. Sid ...90 — 46 73 C
Marlborough Pl. NW8 ...46 — 26 83 C
Marlborough Rd. Bexh ...79 — 47 75 B
Marlborough Rd. Brom ...99 — 41 68 C
Marlborough Rd. Dag ...52 — 47 85 C
Marlborough Rd. Dart ...80 — 53 74 C
Marlborough Rd. E15 ...50 — 39 85 A
Marlborough Rd. E18 ...27 — 40 89 A
Marlborough Rd. E4 ...26 — 37 91 B
Marlborough Rd. E7 ...50 — 41 84 C
Marlborough Rd. Felt ...82 — 11 72 B
Marlborough Rd. Hamp ...92 — 13 70 A
Marlborough Rd. Islw ...60 — 16 77 D
Marlborough Rd. N19 ...36 — 30 86 A
Marlborough Rd. N22 ...24 — 30 91 B
Marlborough Rd. N9 ...17 — 33 94 D
Marlborough Rd. Rich ...71 — 18 74 D
Marlborough Rd. Rom ...29 — 49 89 D
Marlborough Rd. S Croy ...112 — 32 63 C
Marlborough Rd. Sthl ...59 — 11 79 C
Marlborough Rd. Sutt ...103 — 25 65 A
Marlborough Rd. SW19 ...95 — 26 70 B
Marlborough Rd. SW19 ...96 — 27 70 A
Marlborough Rd. SW1 ...6 — 29 80 C
Marlborough Rd. W4 ...61 — 20 78 B
Marlborough Rd. W5 ...61 — 17 79 B
Marlborough St. SW3 ...9 — 27 78 A
Marlborough Yd. N19 ...36 — 29 86 B
Marler Rd. SE23 ...88 — 36 73 D
Marley Ave. Bexh ...67 — 47 77 B
Marley Cl. Grnf ...53 — 13 82 A
Marley Wlk. NW2 ...46 — 23 84 A
Marlingdene Cl. Hamp ...92 — 13 70 A
Marlings Cl. Chis ...100 — 45 68 C
Marlings Park Ave. Chis ...100 — 45 68 A
Marloes Cl. Wem ...44 — 17 85 B
Marloes Rd. W8 ...62 — 25 79 D
Marlow Cl. Ilf ...28 — 44 90 A
Marlow Cl. SE20 ...97 — 34 68 B
Marlow Cres. Twick ...71 — 15 74 D
Marlow Dri. Sutt ...103 — 23 65 D
Marlowe Cl. Chis ...100 — 44 70 B
Marlowe Gdns. Rom ...30 — 53 90 A
Marlowe Gdns. SE9 ...78 — 43 74 C
Marlowe Rd. E17 ...26 — 38 89 C
Marlowe Sq. Mit ...96 — 29 68 C
Marlowes The. Bexh ...79 — 50 75 D
Marlowes The. NW8 ...46 — 26 83 B
Marlow Rd. SE20 ...97 — 34 68 B
Marlow Rd. Sthl ...59 — 12 79 D
Marl St. SW18 ...73 — 26 75 C
Marlton St. E10 ...65 — 39 78 D
Marmion App. E4 ...18 — 37 92 A
Marmion Ave. E4 ...18 — 36 92 B
Marmion Cl. E4 ...18 — 37 92 A
Marmion Mews. SW11 ...74 — 28 75 A
Marmion Rd. SW11 ...74 — 28 75 C
Marmont Rd. SE15 ...75 — 34 76 A
Marmora Rd. SE22 ...76 — 35 74 C

Name	Page	Grid
Marmot Rd. Houn	70	11 75 B
Marnadon Rd. SE18	66	45 78 B
Marne Ave. N11	16	28 92 B
Marne Ave. Well	78	46 75 A
Marnell Way. Houn	70	11 75 B
Marne St. W10	56	24 82 A
Marney Rd. SW11	74	28 75 C
Marnham Ave. NW2	46	24 85 A
Marnham Cres. Grnf	43	13 83 D
Marnock Rd. SE4	76	36 74 B
Maroon St. E14	57	36 81 A
Marquess Rd. N1	48	32 84 B
Marquis Cl. Wem	44	18 84 D
Marquis Rd. N22	24	30 91 B
Marquis Rd. N4	36	30 87 D
Marquis Rd. NW1	47	29 84 B
Marrick Cl. SW15	72	22 75 C
Marriott Cl. Felt	69	08 74 D
Marriott Rd. Barn	11	23 96 B
Marriott Rd. E15	50	39 83 A
Marriott Rd. N10	24	27 90 B
Marriott Rd. N4	36	30 87 D
Marriotts Cl. NW9	34	21 88 D
Marryat Pl. SW19	85	24 71 A
Marryat Rd. SW19	85	24 71 A
Marryatt Ct. W5	54	18 81 D
Marsala Rd. SE13	76	37 75 D
Marsden Rd. N9	17	34 93 B
Marsden Rd. SE15	75	33 75 B
Marsden St. NW5	47	28 84 A
Marshall Cl. Har	32	14 87 B
Marshall Cl. Houn	70	12 74 B
Marshall Gdns. SE1	7	31 79 D
Marshall Rd. N17	25	32 90 B
Marshalls Dri. Rom	30	51 89 A
Marshalls Gr. SE18	65	42 78 A
Marshalls Rd. Rom	29	50 89 D
Marshall St. W1	2	25 64 B
Marshalsea Rd. SE1	8	32 79 A
Marsham Cl. Chis	90	43 71 D
Marsham St. SW1	10	29 78 B
Marsh Ave. Eps	109	21 62 C
Marsh Ave. Mit	96	28 69 C
Marshbrook Cl. SE3	77	41 75 B
Marsh Dri. NW9	34	21 88 D
Marsh Farm Rd. Twick	83	15 73 D
Marshfield St. E14	64	38 79 C
Marshgate La. E15	49	37 83 B
Marshgate Path. SE18	66	44 79 C
Marsh Green Rd. Dag	52	49 83 A
Marsh Hill. E9	49	36 85 C
Marsh La. E10	38	36 88 A
Marsh La. N17	25	34 90 B
Marsh La. Stan	21	17 91 B
Marsh Rd. Pnr	20	12 89 C
Marsh Rd. Wem	44	17 83 D
Marsh St. Dart	80	54 74 B
Marsh St. E14	64	37 78 B
Marsland Cl. SE17	63	31 78 D
Marston Ave. Dag	41	49 86 C
Marston Cl. Dag	41	49 88 C
Marston Cl. NW6	46	26 84 C
Marston Rd. Ilf	27	42 90 C
Marston Rd. Tedd	83	16 71 D
Marston Way. SW19	97	32 70 C
Marsworth Ave. Pnr	20	11 90 B
Martaban Rd. N16	37	33 86 B
Martello St. E8	48	34 84 D
Martello Terr. E8	48	34 84 D
Martell Rd. SE21	87	32 72 D
Martel Pl. E8	48	33 84 B
Marten Rd. E17	26	37 90 C
Martens Ave. Bexh	79	50 75 C
Martens Cl. Bexh	79	50 75 C
Martha Ct. E2	48	34 83 D
Martha Rd. E15	50	39 84 A
Martha St. E1	57	35 81 C
Marthorne Cres. Har	20	14 90 D
Martin Bowes Rd. SE9	77	42 75 B
Martin Cres. Croy	105	31 66 C
Martindale Rd. Houn	70	12 75 A
Martindale Rd. SW12	86	28 73 B
Martindale. SW14	72	20 74 A
Martin Dene. Bexh	79	48 74 B
Martin Dri. Nthlt	43	12 85 D
Martineau Rd. N5	48	31 85 B
Martineau St. E1	57	35 80 A
Martingale Cl. Sun	91	10 68 C
Martingales Cl. Rich	83	17 72 D
Martins. Gdns. Dag	52	47 85 B
Martin Gr. Mord	95	25 68 A
Martin La. EC4	8	32 80 B
Martin Rd. Dag	52	47 85 B
Martin Rise. Bexh	79	48 74 B
Martins Cl. W Wick	106	38 66 D
Martins Mount. Barn	11	25 96 D
Martin's Rd. Brom	99	39 69 D
Martins Slip. Brom	99	39 69 D
Martins Wlk. N10	24	28 90 A
Martin Way. Mord	95	24 68 B
Martin Way. SW20	95	24 68 A
Martlet Gr. Nthlt	53	11 82 B
Martley Dri. Ilf	40	43 88 B
Marton Cl. SE6	88	37 72 C
Marton Rd. N16	37	33 86 A
Marvels Cl. SE12	89	40 72 B
Marvels La. SE12	89	41 72 C
Marville Rd. SW6	62	24 77 D
Marvin St. E8	48	34 84 B
Marwood Cl. Well	78	46 75 B
Marwood Way. SE16	63	34 78 D
Mary Adelaide Cl. SW15	84	21 72 C
Mary Ann Buildings. SE8	64	37 77 A
Maryatt Ave. Har	32	13 86 B
Marybank. SE18	65	42 78 B
Mary Cl. Har	21	18 89 D
Mary Datchelor Cl. SE5	75	32 76 B
Maryland Park. E15	50	39 85 C
Maryland Point. E15	50	39 84 A
Maryland Rd. E15	49	38 85 D
Maryland Rd. N22	25	31 91 A
Maryland Rd. Th Hth	97	31 69 B
Maryland Sq. E15	50	39 85 C
Marylands Rd. W9	56	25 82 C
Maryland St. E15	50	39 85 C
Maryland Way. Sun	91	10 69 C
Marylebone High St. W1	2	28 81 A
Marylebone La. W1	2	28 81 C
Marylebone Mews. W1	2	28 81 B
Marylebone Pas. W1	2	29 81 C
Marylebone Rd. NW1	1	27 81 B
Marylebone St. W1	2	28 81 A
Marylee Way. SE11	10	30 78 B
Maryon Gr. SE7	65	42 78 A
Maryon Mews. NW3	47	27 85 A
Maryon Rd. SE18	65	42 78 A
Maryon Rd. SE7	65	42 78 A
Mary Peters Dri. Grnf	43	14 85 D
Mary Pl. W11	56	24 80 A
Mary Rose Cl. Hamp	92	13 69 A
Mary St. E16	58	39 81 B
Mary's Terr. Twick	83	16 73 A
Mary St. N1	48	32 83 A
Mary Terr. NW1	47	29 83 A
Masbro Rd. W14	62	23 79 D
Mascalls Ct. SE7	65	41 77 A
Mascalls Rd. SE7	65	41 77 A
Mascotte Rd. SW15	73	23 75 D
Mascotts Cl. NW2	34	22 86 D
Masefield Ave. Stan	21	15 91 B
Masefield Ave. Sthl	53	13 80 A
Masefield Cl. Eri	80	51 76 B
Masefield Cl. Rom	30	53 90 A
Masefield Cres. N14	12	29 95 C
Masefield Cres. Rom	30	53 90 A
Masefield La. Hay	53	11 82 C
Masefield Rd. Hamp	82	12 71 B
Masefield View. Orp	108	44 65 C
Mashie Rd. W3	55	21 81 C
Mashiters Hill. Rom	29	50 90 B
Mashiters Wlk. Rom	30	51 89 A
Maskall Cl. SW2	87	31 73 C
Maskell Rd. SW17	85	26 72 C
Maskelyne Cl. SW11	74	27 76 A
Mason Cl. Bexh	79	49 75 B
Mason Cl. E16	58	40 80 A
Mason Cl. Hamp	92	12 69 B
Mason Cl. SW20	95	23 69 B
Mason's Arms Mews. W1	6	28 80 B
Mason's Ave. Croy	105	32 65 C
Mason's Ave. EC2	4	32 81 D
Masons Ave. Har	21	15 89 D
Mason's Green La. W3	55	19 81 A
Mason's Hill. Brom	99	40 68 D
Masons Hill. SE18	66	43 78 B
Mason's Pl. EC1	4	32 82 A
Mason's Pl. Mit	96	27 69 B
Mason St. SE17	63	32 78 B
Mason's Yd. SW19	85	23 71 D
Mason's Yd. SW1	6	29 80 C
Massey Cl. N11	16	28 92 D
Massie Rd. E8	48	34 84 A
Massinger St. SE17	63	33 78 A
Massingham St. E1	57	35 82 D
Masson Ave. Ruis	43	11 84 A
Master Gunners' Pl. SE18	65	42 77 C
Master Gunners' Pl. SE18	77	42 76 A
Master's St. E1	57	35 81 B
Mast House Terr. E14	64	37 78 A
Maswell Park Cres. Houn	70	14 74 A
Maswell Park Rd. Houn	70	13 74 B
Matcham Rd. E11	39	39 86 D
Matfield Cl. Brom	107	40 67 A
Matfield Rd. Belv	67	49 77 A
Matham Gr. SE22	75	33 75 D
Matheson Rd. W14	62	24 78 B
Mathews Ave. E6	51	43 83 C
Mathews Park Ave. E15	50	39 84 B
Matilda St. N1	47	30 83 B
Matlock Cres. Sutt	110	24 64 A
Matlock Gdns. Horn	42	54 86 C
Matlock Gdns. Sutt	110	24 64 A
Matlock Pl. Sutt	110	24 64 A
Matlock Rd. E10	38	38 88 C
Matlock St. E14	57	36 81 C
Matlock Way. N Mal	94	20 69 B
Matlow Ct. NW9	22	21 89 B
Matrimony Pl. SW8	74	29 76 C
Matthew Cl. W10	56	23 82 D
Matthew Parker St. SW1	6	29 79 B
Matthews Cl. Rom	30	54 90 D
Matthews Rd. Grnf	43	14 85 D
Matthews St. SW11	74	27 76 D
Matthias Rd. N16	48	33 85 C
Mattingly Way (off Daniel Gdns.). SE15	63	33 77 D
Mattison Rd. N4	37	31 88 D
Mattock La. W13	54	16 80 D
Mattock La. W5	54	17 80 A
Maude Rd. E17	38	36 88 A
Maude Rd. SE5	75	33 76 A
Maudesville Cottages. W7	54	15 80 C
Maude Terr. E17	26	36 89 C
Maud Gdns. Bark	51	45 83 D
Maud Gdns. E13	50	39 83 D
Maudlins Green. E1	57	34 80 C
Maud Rd. E10	38	38 86 C
Maud Rd. E13	50	39 83 B
Maudslay Rd. SE9	77	42 75 B
Maud St. E16	58	39 81 B
Mauleverer Rd. SW2	74	30 74 A
Maundeby Wlk. NW10	45	21 84 A
Maunder Rd. W7	54	15 80 D
Maunsel St. SW1	10	29 78 B
Maurice Ave. N22	25	31 90 D
Maurice Browne Cl. NW7	23	23 91 B
Maurice Ct. Brent	60	17 77 D
Maurice St. W12	55	22 81 D
Maurice Wlk. NW11	23	26 89 C
Maurier Cl. Nthlt	43	11 83 A
Mauritius Rd. E10	38	39 78 A
Maury Rd. N16	37	34 86 C
Mavelstone Cl. Brom	99	42 69 A
Mavelstone Rd. Brom	99	42 69 A
Maverton Rd. E3	49	37 83 A
Mavis Ave. Eps	109	21 64 C
Mavis Cl. Eps	109	21 64 C
Mavis Gr. Horn	42	54 86 A
Mawbey Pl. SE1	63	33 78 D
Mawbey Rd. SE1	63	33 78 D
Mawbey St. SW8	10	30 77 C
Mawney Cl. Rom	29	49 90 D
Mawney Rd. Rom	29	49 89 B
Mawson Cl. SW20	95	24 69 C
Mawson La. W4	61	21 77 B
Maxey Gdns. Dag	52	48 85 A
Maxey Rd. Dag	52	48 85 A
Maxey Rd. SE18	66	44 78 A
Maxilla Gdns. W10	56	23 81 D
Maxilla Wlk. W10	56	23 81 D
Maximfeldt Rd. Eri	68	51 78 C
Maxim Rd. Dart	80	51 74 A
Maxim Rd. Eri	68	51 78 A
Maxim Rd. N21	13	31 95 C
Maxted Park. Har	33	15 87 A
Maxted Rd. SE15	75	34 75 A
Maxwell Gdns. Orp	108	45 65 D
Maxwell Rd. Ashf	91	08 70 A
Maxwell Rd. Nthwd	19	08 91 D
Maxwell Rd. SW6	62	25 77 D
Maxwell Rd. Well	78	46 75 A
Mayall Rd. SE24	75	31 74 B
May Ave. Orp	108	46 67 B
Maybank Ave. E18	27	40 90 D
Maybank Ave. Wem	44	16 85 C
Maybank Gdns. Pnr	31	10 88 A
Maybank Rd. E18	27	41 90 A
Mayberry Pl. Surb	101	18 66 B
Maybourne Cl. SE26	87	34 71 D
Maybrick Rd. Horn	42	53 88 C
Maybury Cl. Orp	108	43 67 B
Maybury Gdns. NW10	45	22 84 B

Name	Page	Grid
Maybury Rd. Bark	51	46 83 C
Maybury Rd. E13	58	41 82 C
Maybury St. SW17	86	27 71 C
Maybush Rd. Horn	42	54 87 A
Maychurch Cl. Stan	21	17 91 D
Maycock Gr. Nthwd	19	09 91 B
Maycroft. Pnr	19	10 90 D
Maycross Ave. Mord	95	25 68 C
Mayday Gdns. Dag	42	76 C
Mayday Rd. Croy	105	31 67 D
Mayerne Rd. SE9	77	41 74 B
Mayesbrook Rd. Bark	51	45 83 B
Mayesbrook Rd. Dag	40	46 86 D
Mayesford Rd. Rom	41	47 87 A
Mayes Rd. N22	24	30 90 D
Mayeswood Rd. SE12	89	41 71 A
Mayfair Ave. Bexh	79	47 76 B
Mayfair Ave. Ilf	40	43 86 A
Mayfair Ave. Rom	41	47 88 D
Mayfair Ave. Twick	82	14 73 A
Mayfair Ave. Wor Pk	102	22 66 C
Mayfair Cl. Beck	98	37 69 B
Mayfair Cl. Surb	101	18 66 C
Mayfair Gdns. N17	25	32 91 B
Mayfair Gdns. Wdf Gn	27	40 91 C
Mayfair Pl. W1	6	28 80 D
Mayfair Rd. Dart	80	53 74 B
Mayfair Terr. N14	16	29 94 B
Mayfield Ave. Har	33	16 88 B
Mayfield Ave. N12	15	26 92 B
Mayfield Ave. N14	16	29 93 B
Mayfield Ave. Orp	108	45 66 B
Mayfield Ave. W13	60	16 79 B
Mayfield Ave. W4	61	21 78 A
Mayfield Ave. Wdf Gn	27	40 91 A
Mayfield. Bexh	79	07 70 B
Mayfield Cl. Ashf	91	33 84 B
Mayfield Cl. E8	48	33 84 B
Mayfield Cl. SE20	97	34 69 B
Mayfield Cl. Surb	101	16 66 D
Mayfield Cres. N9	13	34 95 D
Mayfield Cres. Th Hth	96	30 68 D
Mayfield Dri. Pnr	20	12 89 D
Mayfield Gdns. NW4	35	23 88 D
Mayfield Gdns. W7	54	15 81 A
Mayfield Rd. Belv	67	50 78 A
Mayfield Rd. Brom	107	42 67 A
Mayfield Rd. Dag	41	47 87 C
Mayfield Rd. E13	58	39 82 D
Mayfield Rd. E17	26	36 90 C
Mayfield Rd. E4	18	38 93 B
Mayfield Rd. E8	48	33 84 D
Mayfield Rd. Enf	14	35 97 D
Mayfield Rd. N8	36	30 88 D
Mayfield Rd. S Croy	112	32 62 B
Mayfield Rd. Sutt	110	26 63 B
Mayfield Rd. SW19	94	24 69 B
Mayfield Rd. Th Hth	104	30 67 B
Mayfield Rd. W3	55	19 80 A
Mayfields Cl. Wem	34	19 86 A
Mayfields. Wem	34	19 86 A
Mayflower Cl. Ruis	31	08 88 C
Mayflower Rd. SW9	88	30 75 A
Mayflower St. SE16	64	35 79 A
Mayfly Gdns (off Seaspite Cl). Nthlt	53	11 82 B
Mayford Cl. SW12	86	27 73 B
Mayford. NW1	47	29 83 C
Mayford Rd. SW12	86	28 73 A
May Gdns. Wem	54	17 82 A
Maygood St. N1	48	31 83 C
Maygreen Cres. Horn	42	52 87 A
Maygrove Rd. NW6	46	24 84 B
Mayhew Cl. E4	18	37 93 C
Mayhill Rd. Barn	11	24 95 C
Mayhill Rd. SE7	65	37 77 B
Maynard Cl. Eri	68	51 77 D
Maynard Rd. E17	38	38 88 A
Maynards. Horn	42	54 87 A
Mayola Rd. E5	49	35 85 A
Mayo Rd. NW10	45	21 84 A
Mayo Rd. SE25	105	32 67 B
Mayow Rd. SE23	88	35 72 D
Mayow Rd. SE26	88	35 71 B
Mayplace Ave. Dart	80	52 75 C
Mayplace Cl. Bexh	79	49 75 B
Mayplace La. SE18	66	43 77 B
Mayplace Rd E. Bexh	79	50 75 B
Mayplace Rd E. Dart	80	51 75 C
Mayplace Rd W. Bexh	79	49 75 C
Maypole Cres. Eri	68	53 77 B
Maypole Cres. Ilf	28	44 91 D
May Rd. E13	50	40 83 C
May Rd. E4	26	37 91 A
May Rd. Twick	83	15 73 C
Mayroyd Ave. Surb	102	19 65 A
May's Buildings Mews. SE10	64	38 77 D
Mays Ct. WC2	7	30 80 A
May's Hill Rd. Brom	99	39 68 A
Mays La. Barn	11	24 95 A
Maysoule Rd. SW11	73	26 75 D
Mays Rd. Tedd	82	14 71 D
May St. W14	62	24 78 D
Mayswood Gdns. Dag	52	50 84 B
Mayton St. N7	36	30 86 D
Maytree Ct. Nthlt	53	12 82 A
Maytree Wlk. SW2	87	31 72 A
Mayville Rd. E11	39	39 86 A
Mayville Rd. E11	39	39 86 C
Mayville Rd. Ilf	51	43 85 B
Maywin Dri. Horn	42	54 87 D
Maywood Cl. Beck	98	37 70 D
Maze Hill SE10	65	39 77 A
Maze Hill. SE3	65	39 77 C
Mazenod Ave. NW6	46	25 84 C
Maze Rd. Rich	61	19 77 C
Mcadam Dri. Enf	13	31 97 D
McAuley Cl. SE1	7	31 79 C
McCall Cl. SW4	74	30 76 C
Mc Call Cres. SE7	65	42 78 C
Mc Carthy Rd. Felt	82	11 71 C
Mc Crone Mews. NW3	46	26 84 B
McCullum Rd. E3	49	36 83 D
Mc Dermott Cl. SW11	74	27 75 A
Mc Dermott Rd. SE15	75	34 75 A
McDougall Ct. Rich	72	19 76 C
Mcdowall Rd. SE5	75	40 81 A
Mc Dowall Rd. SE5	75	32 76 A
McEntee Ave. E17	26	36 90 A
McEwen Way. E15	49	38 83 B
McGrath Rd. E15	50	39 84 B
McGregor Rd. W11	56	24 81 B
Mcintosh Cl. Rom	30	51 89 A
Mcintosh Cl. Wall	111	30 63 C
Mcintosh Rd. Rom	30	51 89 A
McKay Rd. SW20	94	22 70 D
McKerrell Rd. SE15	75	34 76 A
Mckiernan Ct. SW11	73	26 76 D
Mc Leod Rd. SE2	66	46 78 A
McLeod Rd. SE2	67	47 78 A
McLeod's Mews. SW7	62	25 78 B
Mcmillan St. SE8	64	37 77 A
Mc Neil Rd. SE5	75	33 76 C
Meadbrook SW20	95	23 68 C
Mead Cl. Har	20	14 90 B
Mead Cl. Rom	30	52 90 C
Mead Cres. E4	18	38 92 A
Mead Cres. Sutt	111	27 64 A
Meadcroft Rd. SE11	63	31 77 B
Mead Ct. NW9	34	20 88 B
Meade Cl. W4	61	19 77 A
Mead Field. Har	32	12 86 D
Meadfoot Rd. SW16	96	29 69 A
Mead Gr. Rom	29	48 89 A
Meadlands Dri. Rich	83	17 72 B
Meadow Ave. Croy	106	35 67 D
Meadowbank SW6	62	23 77 C
Meadowbank Gdns. Houn	69	10 76 B
Meadowbank. N21	12	30 95 D
Meadowbank. NW3	47	27 84 D
Meadowbank Rd. NW9	34	20 87 B
Meadowbank. SE3	77	39 75 B
Meadowbank. Surb	101	18 67 D
Meadow Cl. Barn	11	24 95 D
Meadow Cl. Chis	90	43 71 D
Meadow Cl. E4	18	37 94 D
Meadow Cl. Enf	14	36 97 A
Meadow Cl. Esh	101	15 65 D
Meadow Cl. Houn		13 73 A
Meadow Cl. Nthlt	43	13 83 C
Meadow Cl. Rich	83	18 73 C
Meadow Cl. Ruis	31	09 88 D
Meadow Cl. SE6	89	37 71 C
Meadow Cl. SW20	95	23 68 C
Meadowcourt Rd. SE3	77	39 75 D
Meadow Croft. Brom	99	42 68 B
Meadowcroft Rd. N13	17	31 93 A
Meadow Dri. N10	24	28 89 B
Meadow Dri. NW4	23	23 90 C
Meadow Garth. NW10	45	20 84 A
Meadow Hill. N.Mal	102	21 67 C
Meadowlands. Horn	42	54 87 A
Meadow Mews. SW8	10	30 77 B
Meadow Pl. SW8	10	30 77 C
Meadow Rd. Ashf	81	08 71 D
Meadow Rd. Bark	51	46 84 C
Meadow Rd. Brom	99	39 69 C
Meadow Rd. Dag	52	48 84 B
Meadow Rd. Felt	82	12 72 A
Meadow Rd. Pnr	20	12 89 C
Meadow Rd. Rom	41	50 87 C
Meadow Rd. Sthl	53	12 80 B
Meadow Rd. Sutt	111	27 64 C
Meadow Rd. SW19	95	26 70 C
Meadow Rd. SW8	10	30 77 D
Meadow Row. SE1	8	32 79 C
Meadows End. Sun	91	10 69 A
Meadows Gdns. Edg	22	20 91 A
Meadowside Rd. Sutt	110	24 62 A
Meadowside. SE9	77	41 75 C
Meadowside. Twick	83	17 73 B
Meadow Stile. Croy	105	32 65 C
Meadow The. Chis	100	44 70 A
Meadowview Rd. Bex	79	48 74 D
Meadowview Rd. Eps	109	21 62 A
Meadowview Rd. SE6	88	37 71 C
Meadow View Rd. Th Hth	105	31 67 B
Meadow View. Sid	90	46 73 B
Meadow Waye. Houn	59	12 77 C
Meadow Way. NW9	34	20 88 B
Meadow Way. Orp	108	43 65 C
Meadow Way. Ruis	31	10 88 D
Meadow Way The. Har	21	15 90 A
Meadow Way. Wem	44	17 85 B
Meadow Wlk. Dag	52	48 84 B
Meadow Wlk. E18	27	40 89 C
Meadow Wlk. Eps	109	21 63 B
Meadow Wlk. Wall	104	28 65 D
Mead Path. SW17	85	26 71 D
Mead Path. SW19	95	26 70 B
Mead Plat. NW10	45	20 84 A
Mead Pl. Croy	105	32 66 C
Mead Pl. E9	49	35 84 A
Mead Rd. Chis	100	44 70 A
Mead Rd. Edg	22	19 91 A
Mead Rd. Rich	83	17 72 C
Mead Row. SE1	7	31 79 C
Meads La. Ilf	40	45 87 B
Meads Rd. Enf	14	36 97 A
Meads The. N22	25	31 90 D
Meads The. Edg	22	20 91 B
Meads The. Sutt	103	24 65 C
Mead The. Beck	98	38 69 A
Mead The. N2	23	26 90 C
Mead The. Uxb	31	07 86 A
Mead The. W13	54	16 81 B
Mead The. Wall	111	29 63 B
Mead The. W Wick	106	38 66 D
Meadvale Rd. Croy	105	33 67 D
Meadvale Rd. W5	54	17 82 C
Meadway. Ashf	81	07 71 A
Meadway. Barn	11	25 96 C
Meadway. Beck	98	38 69 A
Mead Way. Brom	107	39 67 D
Meadway Cl. Barn	11	25 96 C
Meadway Cl. NW11	35	25 88 D
Meadway Ct. Pnr	20	13 91 B
Mead Way. Croy	106	36 65 A
Meadway Ct. NW11	35	25 88 D
Meadway Ct. W5	54	18 82 D
Meadway Gate. NW11	35	25 88 C
Meadway Gdns. Ruis	31	08 88 D
Meadway. Ilf	51	45 85 A
Meadway. N14	16	30 93 A
Meadway. NW11	25	88 D
Meadway. Rom	30	52 90 C
Mead Way. Ruis	31	08 88 D
Meadway. Surb	102	20 66 C
Meadway. SW20	95	23 68 C
Meadway The. SE3	76	38 76 D
Meadway. Twick	82	14 73 D
Meaford Way. SE20	97	34 70 D
Meaford Way. SE20	98	35 70 C
Meanley Rd. E12	50	42 85 C
Meard St. W1	2	29 81 D
Meath Cl. Orp	108	46 67 B
Meath Rd. E15	50	39 83 D
Meath Rd. Ilf	40	44 86 C
Meath St. SW11	74	28 76 B
Mechanic's Path. SE8	64	37 77 C
Mecklenburgh Pl. WC1	3	30 82 D
Mecklenburgh Sq. WC1	3	30 82 D
Medburn St. NW1	47	29 83 D
Medcroft Gdns. SW14	72	20 75 C
Medebourne Cl. SE3	77	40 75 A
Medesenge Way. N13	25	31 91 B
Medfield St. SW15	84	22 73 B
Medhurst Rd. E3	49	36 83 C
Median Rd. E5	49	35 85 C
Medina Ave. Esh	101	15 65 C
Medina Gr. N7	37	31 86 C
Medina Rd. N7	37	31 86 C
Medland Cl. Cars	104	28 66 C
Medlar Cl. Nthlt	43	11 83 D

Medlar St. SE5 .....75 32 76 A
Medley Rd. NW6 .....46 25 84 A
Medora Rd. Rom .....29 50 89 D
Medora Rd. SW2 .....86 30 73 B
Medusa Rd. SE6 .....79 37 74 D
Medway Bldgs. S3 .....49 38 83 C
Medway Cl. Croy .....106 35 67 C
Medway Cl. Ilf .....51 44 85 C
Medway Dri. Grnf .....44 15 83 D
Medway Gdns. Wem .....44 16 85 A
Medway Par. Grnf .....44 15 83 D
Medway Rd. Dart .....80 52 75 A
Medway Rd. E3 .....49 36 83 C
Medway St. SW1 .....6 29 79 D
Medwin St. SW4 .....74 30 75 D
Meerbrook Rd. SE3 .....77 41 75 A
Meeson Rd. E15 .....50 39 84 D
Meeson St. E5 .....49 36 85 A
Meeting Field Path. E9 .....49 35 84 A
Meetinghouse Alley. E1 .....57 34 80 D
Meeting House La. SE15 .....63 34 77 D
Mehetabel Rd. E9 .....49 35 85 C
Melanda Cl. Chis .....89 42 71 D
Melanie Cl. Bexh .....79 48 76 A
Melba Way. SE13 .....76 37 76 B
Melbourne Ave. N13 .....24 30 91 B
Melbourne Ave. Pnr .....20 13 89 B
Melbourne Ave. W13 .....54 16 80 C
Melbourne Cl. Orp .....108 45 66 A
Melbourne Cl. Wall .....111 29 64 C
Melbourne Ct. SE20 .....97 34 70 C
Melbourne Gdns. Rom .....41 44 88 A
Melbourne Gr. SE22 .....75 33 75 D
Melbourne Mews. SW9 .....75 31 76 A
Melbourne Pl. WC2 .....3 30 81 D
Melbourne Rd. E10 .....38 37 87 B
Melbourne Rd. E17 .....26 36 89 C
Melbourne Rd. E6 .....50 42 83 D
Melbourne Rd. Ilf .....40 43 87 D
Melbourne Rd. SW19 .....95 25 69 A
Melbourne Rd. Tedd .....93 17 70 A
Melbourne Rd. Wall .....111 29 64 C
Melbourne Sq. SW9 .....75 31 76 A
Melbourne Way. Enf .....13 13 79 D
Melbury Ave. Sthl .....59 13 79 D
Melbury Cl. Chis .....99 42 70 B
Melbury Ct. W8 .....62 25 79 C
Melbury Dri. SE5 .....63 33 77 C
Melbury Gdns. SW20 .....94 22 69 B
Melbury Rd. Har .....33 18 88 B
Melbury Rd. W14 .....24 79 D
Melbury Ter. NW1 .....1 27 82 C
Melcombe Gdns. Har .....33 18 88 D
Melcombe Pl. NW1 .....1 27 81 B
Melcombe St. NW1 .....27 82 D
Meldon Cl. SW6 .....73 25 76 B
Meldrum Rd. Ilf .....40 46 86 A
Melfield Gdns. SE6 .....88 38 71 D
Melford Ave. Bark .....51 45 84 B
Melford Ct. SE22 .....87 34 73 A
Melford Rd. E11 .....39 38 86 A
Melford Rd. E17 .....26 36 89 D
Melford Rd. Ilf .....40 44 86 B
Melford Rd. SE22 .....87 34 73 C
Melfort Ave. Th Hth .....97 31 68 B
Melfort Rd. Th Hth .....97 31 68 B
Melgund Rd. N5 .....48 33 85 C
Melina Pl. NW8 .....1 26 82 B
Melina Rd. W12 .....61 22 79 B
Melior Pl. SE1 .....8 33 79 A
Melior St. SE1 .....8 33 79 A
Meliot Rd. SE6 .....88 38 72 B
Melksham Cl. Rom .....30 54 91 D
Melksham Dri. Rom .....30 54 91 D
Melksham Gdns. Rom .....30 54 91 D
Melksham Green. Rom .....30 54 91 D
Meller Cl. Croy .....104 30 67 B
Melling St. SE18 .....66 45 77 A
Mellish Cl. Bark .....51 45 83 B
Mellish Ct. Surb .....101 18 67 C
Mellish St. E14 .....64 37 79 C
Mellison Rd. SW17 .....86 27 71 C
Mellitus St. W12 .....55 21 81 B
Mellows Rd. Ilf .....27 42 89 B
Mellows Rd. Wall .....111 29 64 D
Mells Cres. SE9 .....89 42 71 B
Mell St. E10 .....65 39 78 C
Melody Rd. SW18 .....73 26 74 A
Melody Rd. SW18 .....73 26 74 C
Melon Pl. W8 .....62 25 79 A
Melon Rd. SE15 .....75 34 76 A
Melrose Ave. Grnf .....43 13 83 D
Melrose Ave. Mit .....96 28 70 D
Melrose Ave. N22 .....25 31 90 B
Melrose Ave. NW2 .....46 23 85 C

Melrose Ave. SW16 .....97 31 68 A
Melrose Ave. SW19 .....85 25 72 C
Melrose Ave. Twick .....82 13 73 B
Melrose Cl. Grnf .....43 13 83 D
Melrose Dri. Sthl .....53 13 80 C
Melrose Gdns. Edg .....22 19 90 D
Melrose Gdns. N Mal .....94 20 68 B
Melrose Gdns. W6 .....62 23 79 C
Melrose Rd. Har .....20 12 89 D
Melrose Rd. SW13 .....72 21 76 D
Melrose Rd. SW18 .....73 24 74 D
Melrose Rd. SW19 .....95 25 69 A
Melrose Rd. W3 .....61 20 79 C
Melrose Ter. W6 .....62 23 79 C
Melsa Rd. Mord .....103 26 67 C
Meltham Way. SE16 .....63 34 78 D
Melthorne Dri. Ruis .....32 11 86 C
Melthorpe Gdns. SE3 .....77 42 76 A
Melton Cl. Ruis .....32 11 87 C
Melton Ct. SW7 .....62 26 78 B
Melton Gdns. Rom .....42 51 87 B
Melton Pl. Eps .....109 20 62 B
Melton St. NW1 .....2 29 82 B
Melville Ave. Grnf .....44 15 85 D
Melville Ave. S Croy .....112 33 64 D
Melville Ave. SW20 .....94 22 70 C
Melville Cl. W4 .....61 19 78 C
Melville Gdns. N13 .....17 31 92 D
Melville Rd. E17 .....26 36 89 B
Melville Rd. NW10 .....45 20 84 D
Melville Rd. Rom .....29 49 90 B
Melville Rd. SW13 .....72 22 76 A
Melville St. N1 .....48 32 84 C
Melville Villas Rd. W3 .....55 20 80 D
Melvin Rd. SE20 .....98 35 69 A
Melyn Cl. NW19 .....47 29 85 A
Memel Ct. EC1 .....4 32 82 C
Memel St. EC1 .....4 32 82 C
Memorial Ave. E15 .....58 39 82 A
Memorial Cl. Houn .....59 12 77 B
Mendip Cl. SE26 .....88 35 71 A
Mendip Cres. SW11 .....73 26 75 A
Mendip Dri. NW2 .....35 24 86 A
Mendip Rd. Bexh .....80 51 76 A
Mendip Rd. Horn .....42 52 87 A
Mendip Rd. Ilf .....40 45 88 A
Mendip Rd. SW11 .....73 26 75 A
Mendora Rd. SW6 .....62 24 77 D
Mendoza Cl. Horn .....42 54 88 A
Menelik Rd. NW2 .....46 24 85 B
Meness Path. SE18 .....66 43 77 A
Menlo Gdns. SE19 .....97 32 70 D
Menotti St. E2 .....57 34 82 C
Menthone Pl. Horn .....42 53 87 B
Mentmore Cl. Har .....33 17 88 C
Mentmore Ter. E8 .....48 34 84 D
Meon Rd. W3 .....61 20 79 A
Meopham Rd. Mit .....96 29 69 A
Mepham Cres. Har .....20 14 91 C
Mepham Gdns. Har .....20 14 91 C
Mepham St. SE1 .....7 31 80 C
Mera Dri. Bexh .....79 49 75 C
Mercator Rd. SE13 .....76 38 75 D
Merccia Gr. SE13 .....76 38 75 C
Mercer Cl. Surb .....101 15 66 B
Merceron St. E1 .....57 34 82 D
Mercer Pl. Pnr .....20 11 90 C
Mercers Cl. E10 .....65 39 78 B
Mercers Rd. N19 .....36 29 86 D
Mercer St. WC2 .....3 30 81 C
Merchant St. E3 .....57 36 82 B
Merchiston Rd. SE6 .....88 38 72 B
Merchland Rd. SE9 .....90 44 73 C
Mercier Rd. SW15 .....73 24 74 A
Mercury Gdns. Rom .....42 51 88 B
Mercury Way. SE14 .....64 35 77 B
Mercy Terr. SE13 .....76 37 74 B
Merebank La. Croy .....111 30 64 D
Mere Cl. Orp .....108 43 65 B
Mere Cl. SW15 .....85 23 73 B
Meredith Ave. NW2 .....46 23 85 C
Meredith Cl. Pnr .....20 11 91 D
Meredith St. E13 .....58 40 82 A
Meredith St. EC1 .....3 31 82 B
Meredyth Rd. SW13 .....72 22 76 C
Mere End. Croy .....106 35 66 B
Mereside. Orp .....108 43 65 A
Meretone Cl. SE4 .....76 36 75 C
Meretune Ct. Mord .....95 24 68 B
Merevale Cres. Mord .....103 26 67 C
Mereway Rd. Twick .....83 15 73 C
Merewood Cl. Brom .....100 43 69 C
Merewood Rd. Bexh .....79 50 76 C
Mereworth Cl. Brom .....107 39 67 B
Mereworth Dri. SE18 .....66 44 77 C

Merhsam Rd. Th Hth .....97 32 69 D
Meridan Rd. SE7 .....65 41 77 D
Meriden Cl. Brom .....99 41 70 D
Meriden Cl. Ilf .....28 44 90 A
Meridian Wlk. N17 .....25 33 91 A
Merifield Rd. SE9 .....87 41 75 C
Merino Pl. Sid .....78 46 74 C
Merivale Rd. Har .....32 14 87 A
Merivale Rd. SW15 .....73 24 75 C
Merlewood Dri. Chis .....99 42 69 B
Merley Ct. NW9 .....34 20 87 C
Merlin Cl. Croy .....112 33 64 A
Merlin Cl. Nthlt .....53 11 82 A
Merlin Cl. Rom .....29 50 91 B
Merlin Cres. Edg .....21 18 90 B
Merlin Gdns. Brom .....89 40 72 C
Merlin Gdns. Rom .....29 50 91 B
Merlin Gr. Beck .....106 37 67 A
Merlin Gr. Ilf .....28 44 91 C
Merlin Rd. E12 .....39 41 86 B
Merlin Rd. Rom .....29 50 91 B
Merlin Rd. Well .....78 46 75 C
Merlins Ave. Har .....32 12 86 D
Merlin St. WC1 .....3 31 82 A
Mermaid Ct. SE1 .....8 32 79 B
Merredene St. SW2 .....74 30 74 D
Merrick Rd. Sthl .....59 12 79 B
Merrick Rd. Sthl .....59 12 79 D
Merrick Sq. SE1 .....8 32 79 D
Merridene. N21 .....13 31 95 D
Merrielands Cres. Dag .....52 48 83 D
Merrilands Rd. Wor Pk .....103 23 68 C
Merrilees Rd. Sid .....90 45 73 A
Merriman Rd. SE3 .....77 41 76 A
Merrington Rd. SW6 .....62 25 77 A
Merritt Rd. SE4 .....76 36 74 B
Merrivale Ave. Ilf .....27 41 89 D
Merrivale. N14 .....12 29 95 D
Merrow Rd. Sutt .....110 23 62 B
Merrows Cl. Nthwd .....19 08 91 A
Merrow St. SE17 .....63 32 78 D
Merrow Wlk. SE17 .....63 32 78 D
Merrydown Way. Chis .....99 42 69 A
Merryfield. SE3 .....77 39 76 D
Merryhill Cl. E4 .....18 37 94 B
Merryhills Ct. N14 .....12 29 95 A
Merryhills Dri. Enf .....12 29 96 D
Merryweather Ct. N.Mal .....102 21 67 A
Mersey Rd. E17 .....26 36 89 B
Mersham Dri. NW9 .....34 19 88 B
Merten Rd. Rom .....41 48 87 A
Merthyr Terr. SW13 .....61 22 77 B
Merton Ave. Nthlt .....43 14 85 C
Merton Ave. W4 .....61 21 78 B
Merton Gdns. Orp .....108 43 67 B
Merton Hall Gdns. SW20 .....95 24 69 A
Merton Hall Rd. SW19 .....95 24 69 A
Merton High St. SW19 .....95 26 70 C
Merton La. N6 .....36 27 86 B
Merton Mansions. SW20 .....95 23 69 D
Merton Rd. Bark .....51 45 84 D
Merton Rd. E17 .....38 38 88 C
Merton Rd. Har .....32 14 87 C
Merton Rd. Ilf .....40 45 87 B
Merton Rd. SE25 .....105 34 67 A
Merton Rd. SW18 .....85 25 73 C
Merton Rd. SW19 .....95 25 70 D
Merton Rise. NW3 .....47 27 84 C
Merton Way. E Mol .....92 14 68 A
Mertins Rd. SE15 .....76 35 74 B
Mervan Rd. SW2 .....75 31 75 C
Mervyn Ave. SE9 .....90 44 72 A
Mervyn Rd. W13 .....60 16 79 C
Messaline Ave. W3 .....55 20 80 A
Messent Rd. SE9 .....88 41 74 A
Messeter Pl. SE9 .....78 43 74 C
Messina Ave. NW6 .....46 25 84 C
Metcalf Rd. Ashf .....81 07 71 D
Metcalf Wlk. Felt .....82 12 71 A
Meteor St. SW11 .....74 28 75 C
Meteor Way. Wall .....111 30 63 C
Methering Way. NW9 .....22 21 90 A
Methley St. SE11 .....63 31 78 C
Methuen Cl. Edg .....22 19 91 C
Methuen Park. N10 .....24 28 89 B
Methuen Rd. Belv .....67 49 78 B
Methuen Rd. Bexh .....79 48 75 D
Methuen Rd. Edg .....22 19 91 C
Methwold Rd. W10 .....56 23 81 B
Mews The. Ilf .....39 41 88 B
Mews The. N1 .....48 32 83 A
Mews The. Rom .....30 51 89 C
Mews The. Sid .....90 46 71 A
Mexfield Rd. SW15 .....73 24 74 B
Meyer Rd. Eri .....67 50 77 B

Meymott St. SE1

Street	Page	Grid
Meymott St. SE1	7	31 80 D
Meynell Cres. E9	49	35 84 D
Meynell Gdns. E9	49	35 84 D
Meynell Rd. E9	49	35 84 D
Meynell Rd. Rom	30	52 91 D
Meyrick Rd. NW10	45	22 84 A
Meyrick Rd. SW11	74	27 75 A
Miall Wlk. SE26	88	36 71 A
Micawber St. N1	4	32 82 A
Michael Gaynor Cl. W7	54	15 80 D
Michael Gdns. Horn	30	53 89 D
Michael Rd. E11	39	39 87 D
Michael Rd. SE25	97	33 68 A
Michael Rd. SW6	73	25 76 B
Michaels Cl. SE13	77	39 75 A
Micheldever Rd. SE12	77	39 74 D
Michelham Gdns. Twick	83	15 72 D
Michel's Row. Rich	71	18 75 C
Michigan Ave. E12	50	42 85 B
Michleham Down. N12	15	24 92 B
Mickleham Cl. Orp	100	46 69 C
Mickleham Gdns. Sutt	110	24 63 A
Mickleham Rd. Orp	100	46 69 C
Micklethwaite Rd. SW6	62	25 77 A
Midcroft. Ruis	31	09 87 C
Middle Dartrey Wlk. SW10	62	26 77 D
Middlefielde. W13	54	16 81 B
Middlefield Gdns. Ilf	40	43 88 D
Middle Field. NW8	46	26 83 B
Middleham Gdns. N18	25	34 91 A
Middleham Rd. N18	25	34 91 B
Middle La. N8	36	30 88 A
Middle Lane Mews. N8	36	30 88 A
Middle La. Tedd	89	15 70 B
Middle Park Ave. SE9	78	42 73 C
Middle Path. Har	32	14 87 D
Middle Rd. Barn	12	27 95 C
Middle Rd. E13	50	40 83 C
Middle Rd. Har	32	14 87 D
Middle Rd. N2	24	27 90 A
Middle Rd. SW16	96	29 69 D
Middle Row. W10	56	24 82 C
Middlesborough Rd. N18	17	34 92 C
Middlesex Pas. EC1	3	31 81 B
Middlesex Pl. E9	49	35 84 A
Middlesex Rd. Mit	104	30 67 A
Middlesex St. E1	4	33 81 D
Middle St. Croy	105	32 65 C
Middle St. EC1	4	32 81 A
Middle Temple La. EC4	7	31 80 A
Middleton Ave. E4	18	36 93 D
Middleton Ave. Grnf	43	14 83 D
Middleton Ave. Sid	100	46 70 B
Middleton Bldgs. W1	2	29 81 A
Middleton Cl. E4	18	36 93 D
Middleton Dri. Pnr	19	10 69 A
Middleton Gdns. Ilf	40	43 88 D
Middleton Gr. N7	47	30 85 C
Middleton Mews. N7	47	30 85 C
Middleton Rd. Cars	104	27 66 A
Middleton Rd. E8	48	33 84 D
Middleton Rd. Eps	109	20 62 D
Middleton Rd. Mord	103	26 67 C
Middleton Rd. NW11	35	25 87 A
Middleton St. E2	57	34 82 B
Middleton Way. SE13	76	38 75 D
Middle Way. Hay	53	11 82 C
Middleway. NW11	35	25 88 B
Middle Way. SW16	96	29 69 D
Middle Yd. SE1	8	15 90 D
Midfield Ave. Bexh	79	50 75 A
Midfield Par. Bexh	79	50 75 A
Midfield Way. Orp	100	45 69 B
Midford Pl. W1	2	29 82 C
Midholm Cl. NW11	23	25 89 D
Midholm. NW11	23	25 89 D
Midholm Rd. Croy	106	36 65 A
Midhope. Wem	34	19 87 C
Midhope St. WC1	3	30 82 A
Midhurst Ave. Croy	105	31 66 A
Midhurst Ave. N10	24	28 89 A
Midhurst Hill. Bexh	79	49 74 A
Midhurst Rd. W13	60	16 79 C
Midland Pl. E14	64	38 78 C
Midland Rd. E10	38	38 87 A
Midland Rd. NW1	3	30 82 A
Midland Rd. NW1	47	30 83 C
Midland Terr. NW10	55	21 82 C
Midland Terr. NW2	35	23 86 D
Midleton Rd. N Mal	94	20 69 C
Midlothian Rd. E3	57	36 82 D
Midmoor Rd. SW12	86	29 73 C
Midmoor Rd. SW19	95	24 69 A
Midstrath Rd. NW10	45	21 85 A
Midsummer Ave. Houn	70	12 75 D
Midway. Sutt	103	24 66 B
Midwood Cl. NW2	34	22 86 D
Miers Cl. E6	51	43 83 A
Mighell Ave. Ilf	39	41 88 B
Milborne Gr. SW10	62	26 78 C
Milborne St. E9	49	35 84 A
Milborough Cres. SE12	77	39 74 C
Milcote St. SE1	7	31 79 B
Mildenhall Rd. E5		35 86 C
Mildmay Ave. N1	48	32 84 B
Mildmay Gr. N1	48	32 85 D
Mildmay Park. N1	48	32 85 D
Mildmay Rd. Ilf	40	43 86 D
Mildmay Rd. N1	48	33 85 C
Mildmay Rd. Rom	41	50 88 A
Mildmay St. N1	48	32 84 B
Mildred Ave. NthIt	43	13 85 D
Mildred Rd. Eri	68	51 78 C
Mile End Pl. E1	57	35 82 D
Mile End Rd. E1	57	35 82 D
Mile End Rd. E3	57	36 82 B
Mile End The. E17	26	35 90 A
Mile Rd. Croy	104	29 66 D
Mile Rd. Wall	104	29 66 C
Milespit Hill. NW7	23	23 91 A
Miles Pl. NW8	1	26 81 B
Miles Pl. Surb	93	18 68 D
Miles Rd. Mit	96	27 68 A
Miles Rd. N8	24	30 89 A
Miles St. SW8	10	30 77 A
Milestone Cl. Sutt	110	26 63 D
Milestone Rd. SE19	97	33 70 B
Miles Way. N20	16	27 93 A
Milfoil St. W12	55	22 80 A
Milford Cl. SE2	67	48 77 A
Milford Gdns. Edg	22	19 91 C
Milford Gdns. Wem	44	17 85 D
Milford Gr. Sutt	110	26 64 A
Milford La. WC2	7	31 80 A
Milford La. WC2	7	31 80 A
Milford Rd. Sthl	53	13 80 A
Milford Rd. W13	54	16 80 D
Milford St. SW8	74	28 75 B
Milford Way. SE15	75	33 76 B
Milk St. Brom	99	40 70 B
Milk St. EC2	4	32 81 C
Milkwell Gdns. Wdf Gn	27	40 91 D
Milkwood Rd. SE24	75	31 75 D
Milk Yd. E1	57	35 80 A
Millais Ave. E12	51	43 85 C
Millais Gdns. Edg	22	19 90 C
Millais Rd. E11	49	38 85 B
Millais Rd. Enf	13	33 95 B
Millais Rd. N.Mal	102	21 66 A
Millais Way. Eps	109	20 64 A
Millard Cl (off Boleyn Rd). N16	48	33 85 C
Millard Terr. Dag	52	49 84 A
Millbank. SW1	10	30 78 A
Millbank Way. SE12	77	40 74 A
Milbourne La. Felt	82	12 71 A
Mill Bridge. Barn	11	24 95 B
Millbrook Ave. Well	78	44 75 D
Millbrook Gdns. Rom	41	48 88 C
Millbrook Gdns. Rom	30	51 90 A
Millbrook Pas. SW9	75	31 75 B
Millbrook Rd. N9	75	34 94 D
Millbrook Rd. SW9	75	31 75 B
Mill Cl. Cars	104	28 65 A
Mill Cnr. Barn	11	24 97 B
Millender Wlk. SE16	64	35 78 A
Miller Cl. Pnr	20	11 90 C
Miller Rd. Croy	105	31 66 C
Miller Rd. SW19	95	26 70 B
Miller's Ave. E8	48	33 85 D
Miller's Ct. W6	61	21 78 D
Miller's Terr. E8	48	33 85 D
Miller St. NW1	47	29 83 C
Millers Yd. N3	23	25 91 D
Millet Rd. Grnf	43	13 83 D
Mill Farm Ave. Sun	91	09 70 C
Mill Farm Cl. Pnr	20	11 90 C
Mill Farm Cres. Houn	82	12 73 C
Millfield Ave. E17	26	36 90 A
Mill Field Cres. Houn	82	12 73 D
Millfield. King	93	16 68 B
Millfield La. N6	36	27 86 B
Millfield Pl. N6	36	28 86 A
Millfield Rd. Edg	22	20 90 C
Millfields Cl. Orp	100	46 68 D
Millfields Rd. E5	38	35 86 D
Millfield. Sun	91	08 69 B
Mill Footpath. Rom	42	51 88 D
Mill Gdns. SE26	87	34 72 D
Mill Green. Mit	104	28 66 A
Mill Green Rd. Mit	104	28 66 A
Millgrove St. SW11	74	28 76 C
Mill Hill Gr. W3	55	19 80 D
Mill Hill Rd. SW13	72	22 76 C
Mill Hill Rd. W3	61	19 79 B
Mill Hill. SW13	72	22 75 A
Mill Hill Terr. W3	55	19 80 D
Millhouse Pl. SE27	87	31 71 C
Millicent Fawcett Ct. N17	25	33 90 B
Millicent Rd. E10	38	36 87 D
Milligan St. E14	57	36 80 B
Milling Rd. Edg	22	20 91 D
Mill La. Cars	111	28 64 A
Mill La. Croy	104	30 65 D
Mill La. Enf	14	37 96 B
Mill La. Eps	109	21 62 B
Mill La. NW6	46	24 85 D
Mill La. Rom	41	48 88 C
Mill La. SE18	66	43 78 C
Millman Mews. WC1	3	30 82 D
Millman St. WC1	3	30 82 D
Millmark Gr. SE14	76	36 76 C
Millmarsh La. Enf	14	36 97 D
Mill Mead Rd. N17	25	34 89 A
Mill Park Ave. Horn	42	54 86 A
Mill Plat Ave. Islw	71	16 76 C
Mill Plat. Islw	71	16 76 C
Mill Pl. Chis	100	43 69 B
Mill Pl. Dart	80	52 75 C
Mill Pl. E14	57	36 81 C
Mill Pl. King	93	18 68 B
Mill Pond Rd. Dart	80	54 74 C
Mill Rd. E16	58	40 80 D
Mill Rd. Eri	67	50 77 C
Mill Rd. Ilf	40	43 86 C
Mill Rd. SE13	76	38 75 A
Mill Rd. SW19	95	26 70 C
Mill Rd. Twick	82	14 72 A
Mill Row. N1	48	33 83 A
Mills Ct. EC2	4	33 82 A
Mills Gr. NW4	23	23 89 B
Millshot Cl. SW6	73	23 76 A
Millside. Cars	104	27 65 B
Mills Row. W4	61	20 78 B
Mill St. King	93	18 68 A
Millstream Rd. SE1	8	33 79 B
Mill St. SE1	8	33 79 B
Mill St. W1	6	29 80 A
Mill Vale. Brom	99	39 69 D
Mill View Gdns. Croy	106	35 65 D
Millwall Dock Rd. E14	64	37 79 C
Millwall Wlk. SE18	69	10 74 B
Mill Way. Felt	69	12 84 B
Millway Gdns. NthIt	43	14 74 A
Millwood St. W10	56	24 81 A
Mill Yd. E1	57	34 80 A
Milman Cl. Pnr	20	11 89 B
Milman Rd. NW6	46	24 83 C
Milman's St. SW10	62	26 77 B
Milne Feild. Pnr	20	13 91 C
Milne Gdns. SE9	77	42 74 A
Milner Dri. Twick	82	14 73 B
Milner Pl. Cars	111	28 64 A
Milner Pl. N1	48	31 83 A
Milner Rd. Dag	41	47 86 A
Milner Rd. E15	58	39 82 A
Milner Rd. King	93	17 68 B
Milner Rd. Mord	103	26 67 B
Milner Rd. SW19	95	25 69 B
Milner Rd. Th Hth	97	32 68 B
Milner Sq. N1	48	31 84 C
Milner St. SW3	9	27 78 B
Milnthorpe Rd. W4	61	20 77 B
Milo Rd. SE22	7	33 74 D
Milroy Wlk. SE1	7	31 80 D
Milson Rd. W14	62	24 79 C
Milton Ave. Barn	11	24 95 B
Milton Ave. Croy	105	32 66 B
Milton Ave. E6	50	42 84 C
Milton Ave. Horn	51	86 B
Milton Ave. N6	36	29 87 A
Milton Ave. NW10	45	20 83 B
Milton Ave. NW9	22	20 89 A
Milton Ave. Sutt	111	27 64 A
Milton Cl . N2	35	26 88 C
Milton Cl. Sutt	103	26 65 D
Milton Court Rd. SE14	64	36 77 A
Milton Cres. Ilf	40	44 88 C
Milton Ct. EC2	4	32 81 B
Milton Ct. King	83	18 71 A
Milton Ct. Uxb	31	07 86 D
Milton Gr. N11	16	29 92 D
Milton Gr. N16	48	33 85 A
Milton Park. N6	36	29 87 A

Milton Pl. N7....48 — 31 85 C
Milton Rd. Belv....67 — 49 78 A
Milton Rd. Croy....105 — 32 66 B
Milton Rd. E17....26 — 37 89 C
Milton Rd. Hamp....92 — 13 70 C
Milton Rd. Har....21 — 15 89 C
Milton Rd. Mit....96 — 28 70 C
Milton Rd. N15....25 — 31 89 D
Milton Rd. N6....36 — 29 87 A
Milton Rd. NW9....34 — 22 87 A
Milton Rd. Rom....42 — 52 88 C
Milton Rd. SE24....75 — 31 74 B
Milton Rd. Sutt....103 — 25 65 C
Milton Rd. SW14....72 — 20 75 B
Milton Rd. SW19....95 — 26 70 A
Milton Rd. W3....55 — 20 80 D
Milton Rd. W7....54 — 15 80 B
Milton Rd. Wall....111 — 29 63 B
Milton Rd. Well....78 — 45 76 B
Milton St. EC2....4 — 32 81 B
Milverton Rd. Ilf....40 — 45 86 B
Milverton Rd. NW6....46 — 23 84 C
Milverton St. SE11....63 — 31 78 C
Milverton Way. SE9....90 — 43 71 A
Milward St. E1....57 — 34 81 B
Mimosa Cl. Rom....30 — 53 91 C
Mimosa Rd. Hay....53 — 11 81 A
Mimosa St. SW6....73 — 24 76 B
Minard Rd. SE6....89 — 39 73 C
Mina Rd. SE17....63 — 33 78 C
Mina Rd. SW19....95 — 25 69 A
Minchenden Cres. N14....16 — 29 93 D
Minchenden Ct. N14....16 — 29 93 B
Mincing La. EC3....8 — 33 80 A
Minden Rd. SE20....97 — 34 69 B
Minehead Rd. Har....32 — 13 86 C
Minehead Rd. SW16....86 — 30 71 D
Minera St. SE18....66 — 45 78 A
Minera Mews. SW1....9 — 28 78 A
Minerva Cl. Sid....... — 45 71 A
Minerva Rd. E4....26 — 37 91 D
Minerva Rd. King....93 — 18 69 D
Minerva Rd. NW10....55 — 20 82 B
Minerva St. E2....48 — 34 83 D
Minet Ave. NW10....45 — 21 83 C
Minet Gdns. NW10....45 — 21 83 C
Minet Rd. SW9....75 — 31 76 D
Minford Gdns. W14....62 — 23 79 B
Mingard Wlk. N7....36 — 30 86 B
Ming St. E14....57 — 37 80 A
Mink Ct. Houn....70 — 11 76 C
Minniedale. Surb....101 — 18 67 B
Minnow St. SE17....63 — 33 78 A
Minories. EC3....8 — 33 80 B
Minshull St. SW8....74 — 29 76 B
Minson Rd. E9....49 — 35 83 B
Minstead Gdns. SW15....84 — 21 73 B
Minstead Way. N.Mal....102 — 21 67 C
Minster Ave. Sutt....103 — 25 65 A
Minster Ct. W5....54 — 18 82 D
Minster Dri. Croy....112 — 33 64 A
Minster Gdns. E Mol....92 — 12 68 D
Minsterley Ave. Shep....92 — 09 68 C
Mintern Cl. N13....13 — 31 95 D
Minterne Ave. Sthl....59 — 13 78 A
Minterne Rd. Har....33 — 18 88 B
Minterne Waye. Hay....53 — 11 81 C
Mintern St. N1....48 — 32 83 D
Minton Mews. NW3....46 — 25 84 B
Mint Rd. Wall....111 — 28 64 B
Mint St. SE1....8 — 32 79 A
Mint Wlk. Croy....105 — 32 65 C
Mirabel Rd. SW6....62 — 24 77 D
Miranda Rd. N19....36 — 29 87 C
Mirfield St. SE7....65 — 41 79 D
Miriam Rd. SE18....66 — 45 78 C
Mirro Path. SE9....89 — 41 72 C
Missenden Gdns. Mord....103 — 26 67 C
Mission Gr. E17....38 — 36 88 A
Mission Pl. SE15....75 — 34 76 A
Mission Sq (off Pottery Rd). Brent....60 — 18 77 A
Mitcham Garden Village. Mit....104 — 28 67 A
Mitcham La. SW16....86 — 29 71 D
Mitcham Park. Mit....96 — 27 68 C
Mitcham Rd. Croy....104 — 30 66 B
Mitcham Rd. Ilf....40 — 45 87 B
Mitcham Rd. SW17....86 — 27 71 D
Mitcham Rd. SW17....96 — 28 70 A
Mitchell Cl. SE2....67 — 47 78 A

Mitchell Rd. N13....17 — 32 92 C
Mitchell Rd. Orp....108 — 45 65 D
Mitchell St. EC1....4 — 32 82 C
Mitchell Way. Brom....99 — 40 69 A
Mitchell Way. NW10....45 — 20 84 A
Mitchison Rd. N1....48 — 32 84 B
Mitchley Rd. N17....25 — 34 89 A
Mitford Rd. N19....36 — 30 86 A
Mitre Cl. Sutt....110 — 26 63 D
Mitre Ct. EC2....... — 32 81 C
Mitre Ct. EC4....3 — 31 81 C
Mitre Rd. SE1....7 — 31 79 A
Mitre Sq. EC3....... — 33 81 C
Mitre St. EC3....... — 33 81 C
Mitre The. E14....57 — 36 80 B
Moat Cres. N3....25 — 25 89 B
Moat Dri. Har....34 — 19 88 A
Moat Dri. E13....50 — 41 83 C
Moat Dri. Har....20 — 14 89 D
Moat Dri. Ruis....31 — 09 87 A
Moat Farm Rd. Nthlt....43 — 12 84 D
Moat La. E Mol....93 — 15 68 B
Moat La. Eri....80 — 52 76 A
Moat Pl. SW9....74 — 30 75 B
Moat Pl. W3....55 — 19 81 D
Moat Side Enf....... — 14 93 C
Moat Side. Felt....82 — 11 71 A
Moat The. N Mal....... — 21 69 A
Moberly Rd. SW4....86 — 29 73 B
Modbury Gdns. NW5....47 — 28 84 A
Modder Pl. SW15....73 — 23 75 D
Model Cottages. SW14....72 — 20 75 A
Model Farm Cl. SE9....89 — 42 72 C
Modern Ct. EC4....3 — 31 81 D
Moffat Ct. SW19....95 — 25 71 C
Moffat Gdns. Mit....96 — 27 68 A
Moffat Rd. N13....22 — 30 91 A
Moffat Rd. SW17....86 — 27 71 B
Moffat Rd. Th Hth....97 — 32 69 D
Mogden La. Islw....71 — 15 74 B
Mohan Cl. N14....12 — 28 95 D
Moiety Rd. E14....64 — 37 79 A
Moira Cl. N17....25 — 33 90 C
Moira Rd. SE9....77 — 42 75 D
Moir Cl. S Croy....112 — 34 62 A
Moland Mead. SE16....64 — 35 78 D
Mole Abbey Gdns. E Mol....93 — 13 68 B
Mole Ct. Eps....109 — 20 64 A
Molember Rd. E Mol....101 — 15 67 A
Molescroft. SE9....90 — 44 72 C
Molesey Ave. E Mol....92 — 12 68 D
Molesey Dri. Sutt....103 — 24 65 C
Molesford Rd. SW6....73 — 25 76 A
Molesham Cl. E Mol....92 — 13 68 B
Molesham Way. E Mol....92 — 13 68 B
Molesworth St. SE13....76 — 37 75 A
Moliner Ct. Beck....98 — 37 70 C
Mollison Ave. Enf....14 — 36 96 A
Mollison Ave. Enf....14 — 36 97 B
Mollison Dri. Wall....111 — 30 63 C
Mollison Way. Edg....22 — 19 90 C
Molyneux St. W1....... — 27 81 A
Monarch Cl. Felt....81 — 09 73 A
Monarch Cl. N2....35 — 26 88 B
Monarch Rd. Belv....67 — 49 79 C
Monarch's Way. Ruis....31 — 09 87 C
Mona Rd. SE15....76 — 35 76 C
Mona St. E16....58 — 39 81 B
Monastery Gdns. Enf....13 — 32 97 D
Monaveen Gdns. E Mol....92 — 13 68 B
Monck St. SW1....6 — 29 79 D
Monclar Rd. SE5....75 — 33 75 C
Moncorvo Pl. SW7....5 — 27 79 A
Moncrieff St. SE15....75 — 34 76 C
Monega Rd. E12....50 — 41 84 B
Monega Rd. E7....50 — 41 84 A
Mongers La. Eps....109 — 22 62 C
Monier Rd. E3....49 — 37 84 C
Monivea Rd. Beck....98 — 36 70 D
Monk Dri. E16....58 — 40 80 A
Monkfrith Ave. N14....12 — 28 95 D
Monkfrith Cl. N14....16 — 28 94 B
Monkfrith Way. N14....16 — 28 94 B
Monkham's Ave. Wdf Gn....27 — 40 91 B
Monkleigh Rd. Mord....95 — 24 68 C
Monks Ave. Barn....11 — 26 95 C
Monks Cl. Enf....13 — 32 97 C
Monks Cl. Ruis....43 — 11 85 B
Monks Cl. SE2....67 — 47 78 B
Monksdene Gdns. Sutt....103 — 25 65 D
Monks Dri. W3....55 — 19 81 C
Monks Orchard Rd. Beck....106 — 37 66 A
Monks Park Gdns. Wem....45 — 19 84 D
Monks Park. Wem....45 — 20 84 A
Monks Rd. Enf....13 — 32 97 C

Monk St. SE18....66 — 43 78 A
Monks Way. Beck....106 — 37 67 C
Monks Way. Orp....108 — 44 66 D
Monkswood Gdns. Ilf....28 — 43 89 A
Monkton Rd. Well....78 — 45 76 D
Monkton St. SE11....63 — 31 78 A
Monkville Ave. NW11....24 — 24 89 D
Monkwell Sq. EC2....... — 32 81 A
Monmouth Ave. E18....27 — 40 89 B
Monmouth Cl. Mit....96 — 30 68 C
Monmouth Cl. Well....78 — 46 75 C
Monmouth Pl. W2....56 — 25 81 D
Monmouth Rd. Dag....52 — 48 85 D
Monmouth Rd. N9....17 — 34 93 B
Monmouth Rd. N9....18 — 35 93 A
Monmouth Rd. W2....56 — 25 81 C
Monmouth St. WC2....4 — 30 81 C
Monnery Rd. N19....36 — 29 86 C
Monnow Rd. SE1....63 — 34 78 A
Monoux Gr. E17....26 — 37 90 A
Monroe Cres. Enf....13 — 34 97 B
Monroe Dri. SW14....72 — 19 74 B
Monro Gdns. Har....21 — 15 91 C
Monsell Rd. N4....37 — 31 86 D
Monson Rd. NW10....45 — 22 83 D
Monson Rd. SE14....64 — 35 77 D
Mons Way. Brom....107 — 42 67 C
Montacute Rd. Mord....103 — 26 67 D
Montacute Rd. SE6....88 — 36 73 B
Montagu Cres. N18....17 — 34 92 B
Montague Ave. SE4....... — 37 75 C
Montague Ave. W7....54 — 15 80 D
Montague Cl. SE1....8 — 32 80 D
Montague Gdns. W5....55 — 19 80 A
Montague Pl. E14....58 — 38 80 A
Montague Pl. WC1....... — 29 81 B
Montague Rd. Croy....105 — 31 66 D
Montague Rd. E11....39 — 39 86 B
Montague Rd. E8....... — 34 85 C
Montague Rd. Houn....70 — 13 75 B
Montague Rd. N15....25 — 34 89 C
Montague Rd. N8....36 — 30 88 B
Montague Rd. Rich....71 — 18 74 C
Montague Rd. Sthl....59 — 12 78 A
Montague Rd. SW19....95 — 25 70 D
Montague Rd. W13....54 — 16 81 D
Montague Rd. W7....60 — 15 79 B
Montague Sq. SE14....... — 35 77 C
Montague St. WC1....3 — 30 81 A
Montague Waye. Sthl....59 — 12 79 C
Montagu Gdns. N18....17 — 34 92 B
Montagu Gdns. Wall....111 — 29 64 A
Montagu Mansions. W1....1 — 27 81 B
Montagu Mews N. W1....1 — 27 81 B
Montagu Mews S. W1....1 — 27 81 D
Montagu Mews W. W1....1 — 27 81 D
Montagu Pl. W1....1 — 27 81 B
Montagu Rd. N18....18 — 35 92 A
Montagu Rd. N9....18 — 35 93 A
Montagu Rd. NW4....34 — 22 88 C
Montagu Row. W1....1 — 27 81 B
Montagu Sq. W1....1 — 27 81 D
Montagu St. W1....1 — 27 81 D
Montana Cl. S Croy....112 — 32 62 D
Montana Rd. SW17....86 — 28 72 C
Montana Rd. SW20....95 — 23 69 A
Montbelle Rd. SE9....90 — 43 72 D
Montcalm Cl. Brom....107 — 40 67 C
Montcalm Rd. SE7....65 — 41 77 D
Montclare St. E2....... — 33 82 D
Monteagle Ave. Bark....51 — 44 84 A
Monteagle Way. E5....... — 34 86 C
Monteagle Way. SE15....75 — 34 75 B
Montefiore Ct. N16....37 — 33 87 D
Montefiore St. SW8....74 — 28 76 D
Monteith Rd. E3....49 — 36 83 B
Montem Rd. N Mal....94 — 21 68 C
Montem Rd. SE23....88 — 36 73 B
Montem St. N4....36 — 30 87 D
Montenotte Rd. N8....36 — 29 88 A
Montesole Ct. Pnr....20 — 11 90 C
Montford Pl. SE11....63 — 31 78 C
Montford Rd. Sun....91 — 10 68 C
Montfort Gdns. Ilf....28 — 44 91 A
Montfort Pl. SW19....85 — 23 73 D

Montgolfier Wlk (off Argus Way). Nthlt....53 — 12 82 A
Montgomery Ave. Esh....101 — 15 65 A
Montgomery Cl. Mit....96 — 30 68 C
Montgomery Cl. Sid....78 — 45 74 D
Montgomery Rd. Edg....22 — 18 91 B
Montgomery Rd. W4....61 — 20 78 A
Montholme Rd. SW11....74 — 27 74 D
Monthope Rd. E1....... — 34 81 A
Montolieu Gdns. SW15....73 — 23 74 A

Street	Page	Grid
Montpelier Ave. W5	54	17 81 A
Montpelier Ct. W5	54	17 81 B
Montpelier Gdns. E6	58	41 82 B
Montpelier Gdns. E6	50	42 83 C
Montpelier Gdns. Rom	41	47 87 A
Montpelier Gr. NW5	47	29 85 C
Montpelier Mew. SW7	5	27 79 C
Montpelier Pl. SW7	5	27 79 C
Montpelier Rd. N3	23	26 90 A
Montpelier Rd. Pur	112	31 62 D
Montpelier Rd. SE15	75	34 76 B
Montpelier Rd. Sutt	110	26 64 A
Montpelier Rd. W5	54	17 81 B
Montpelier Rise. Wem	33	17 87 D
Montpelier Row. SE3	77	39 76 D
Montpelier Row. Twick	83	17 73 A
Montpelier Sq. SW7	5	27 79 A
Montpelier St. SW7	5	27 79 C
Montpelier Terr. SW7	5	27 79 A
Montpelier Vale. SE3	77	39 76 D
Montpelier Wlk. SW7	5	27 79 C
Montpellier Rise. NW11	35	24 87 A
Montpellier Way. NW11	35	24 87 A
Montrave Rd. SE20	98	35 70 C
Montreal Pl. WC2	7	30 80 B
Montreal Rd. Ilf	40	44 87 A
Montrell Rd. SW2	86	30 73 C
Montrose Ave. Edg	22	20 90 B
Montrose Ave. NW6	46	24 83 C
Montrose Ave. Rom	30	53 90 C
Montrose Ave. Sid	90	46 73 A
Montrose Ave. Twick	82	13 73 B
Montrose Ave. Well	78	45 75 A
Montrose Cl. Ashf	81	08 71 C
Montrose Cl. Well	78	45 75 B
Montrose Cres. N12	23	26 91 A
Montrose Cres. Wem	44	18 84 A
Montrose Gdns. Mit	96	27 69 D
Montrose Gdns. Sutt	103	25 65 B
Montrose Pl. SW1	6	28 79 A
Montrose Rd. Felt	69	08 74 D
Montrose Rd. Har	21	15 90 D
Montrose Way. SE23	88	35 73 D
Montserrat Ave. Wdf Gr	26	38 91 D
Montserrat Rd. SW15	73	24 75 C
Monument St. EC3	8	32 80 B
Monza St. E1	57	35 80 C
Moodkee St. SE16	64	35 79 C
Moody St. E1	57	35 82 B
Moon La. Barn	11	24 96 B
Moon St. N1	48	31 83 B
Moorcroft Rd. SW16	86	30 72 C
Moorcroft Way. Pnr	32	12 88 A
Moordown. SE18	78	43 76 B
Moore Cl. Mit	96	28 69 D
Moore Cl. SW14	72	20 75 A
Moore Cl. Wall	111	30 63 C
Moorefield Rd. N17	25	33 90 D
Moorehead Way. SE3	77	40 75 A
Mooreland Rd. Brom	99	39 70 D
Moore Park Rd. SW6	62	25 77 D
Moore Rd. SE19	97	32 70 A
Moore St. SW3	9	27 78 B
Moore Wlk. E7	50	40 85 A
Moorey Cl. E15	50	39 83 B
Moorfield Ave. W5	54	17 82 D
Moorfield Rd. Enf	14	35 97 A
Moorfield Rd. Orp	108	46 66 A
Moorfields. EC2	4	32 81 B
Moorfields Highwalk. EC2	4	32 81 B
Moorgate. EC2	4	32 81 B
Moorgate Pl. EC2	4	32 81 D
Moorhouse Rd. Har	21	17 89 B
Moorhouse Rd. W2	56	25 81 C
Moorings The. E16	58	41 81 A
Moor La. Chess	109	19 63 A
Moor La. EC2	4	32 81 B
Moor La. EC2	4	32 81 B
Moorland Cl. Houn	82	13 73 A
Moorland Cl. Rom	29	49 90 B
Moorland Rd. SW9	75	31 75 D
Moorlands Ave. NW7	22	22 91 B
Moormead Dri. Eps	109	21 64 C
Moor Mead Rd. Twick	71	16 74 C
Moor Park Rd. Nthwd	19	08 91 B
Moor Pl. EC2	4	32 81 B
Moorside Rd. Brom	89	39 71 B
Moor St. W1	2	29 81 D
Morant St. E14	57	37 80 A
Mora Rd. NW2	46	23 85 A
Mora St. EC1	4	32 82 A
Morat St. SW9	74	30 76 B
Moravian Cl. SW3	62	26 77 B
Moravian Pl. SW10	62	26 77 B
Moravian St. E2	57	35 82 A
Moray Cl. Rom	30	51 91 C
Moray Mews. N4	36	30 86 B
Moray Rd. N4	36	30 86 B
Moray Rd. N4	37	31 87 C
Moray Way. Rom	30	51 91 C
Mordaunt Gdns. Dag	52	48 84 C
Mordaunt Rd. NW10	45	20 83 B
Mordaunt St. SW9	74	30 75 B
Morden Ct. Mord	95	25 68 D
Morden Gdns. Grnf	44	15 85 D
Morden Gdns. Mit	95	26 68 D
Morden Hall Rd. Mord	95	26 68 C
Morden Hill. SE13	76	38 76 C
Morden La. SE13	76	38 76 A
Morden Rd. Mord	95	26 68 D
Morden Rd. SE3	77	40 76 C
Morden Rd. SW19	95	25 69 C
Morden Road Mews. SE3	77	40 76 C
Morden St. SE13	76	37 76 B
Morden Way. Sutt	103	25 66 A
Morden Wharf Rd. SE10	65	39 79 C
Morder Rd. Rom	41	48 87 A
Mordon Rd. Ilf	40	45 87 B
Morecambe St. SE17	63	32 78 C
Morecambe Terr. N18	17	32 92 B
More Cl. E16	58	39 81 D
More Cl. W14	62	24 78 A
Morecoombe Cl. King	94	19 70 D
Moredred Rd. SE6	89	39 72 A
Moree Way. N18	17	34 92 A
Moreland Ct. NW2	35	25 86 C
Moreland St. EC1	3	31 82 B
Moreland Way. E4	18	38 93 C
Morella Rd. SW12	86	27 73 B
Moremead Rd. SE6	88	37 71 A
Morena St. SE6	88	37 73 B
Moresbury Wlk. SW8	74	29 76 C
Moresby Ave. Surb	102	19 66 B
Moresby Rd. E5	37	34 87 D
Moreton Ave. Islw	71	15 76 A
Moreton Cl. E5	38	35 86 A
Moreton Cl. N15	37	32 88 D
Moreton Cl. NW7	23	23 91 A
Moreton Pl. SW1	10	29 78 C
Moreton Rd. N15	37	32 88 D
Moreton Rd. S Croy	112	32 64 D
Moreton Rd. Wor Pk	102	22 65 B
Moreton St. SW1	10	29 78 D
Moreton Terr Mews N. SW1	10	29 78 C
Moreton Terr Mews S. SW1	10	29 78 C
Moreton Terr. SW1	10	29 78 C
Morford Cl. Ruis	31	10 87 B
Morford Way. Ruis	31	10 87 B
Morgan Ave. E17	26	38 89 D
Morgan Cl. Dag	52	49 84 C
Morgan Cl. Nthwd	19	09 91 B
Morgan Ct. Ashf	81	07 71 D
Morgan Rd. Brom	99	40 70 C
Morgan Rd. N7	48	31 85 C
Morgan Rd. W10	56	24 81 B
Morgans La. SE1	8	33 80 C
Morgan St. E16	58	39 81 B
Morgan St. E3	57	36 82 A
Morgan St. E3	57	36 82 B
Morgan's Wlk. SW11	9	27 77 C
Morgan Way. Wdf Gn	27	42 91 B
Morie St. SW18	73	25 74 B
Morieux Rd. E10	38	36 87 D
Moring Rd. SW17	86	28 71 A
Morkyns Wlk. SE21	87	33 72 C
Morland Ave. Croy	105	33 66 C
Morland Ave. Dart	80	52 74 B
Morland Cl. Hamp	82	12 71 D
Morland Cl. NW11	35	25 87 D
Morland Estate. E8	48	34 84 C
Morland Gdns. Sthl	53	13 80 D
Morland Mews. N1	48	31 84 C
Morland Rd. Croy	105	33 66 B
Morland Rd. Dag	52	49 84 C
Morland Rd. E17	38	35 88 B
Morland Rd. Har	21	18 89 C
Morland Rd. Ilf	40	43 86 B
Morland Rd. SE20	98	35 70 B
Morland Rd. Sutt	110	26 64 C
Morley Ave. E4	26	38 91 D
Morley Ave. N18	17	34 92 A
Morley Ave. N22	25	31 90 D
Morley Cl. Orp	108	43 65 B
Morley Crescent E. Stan	21	17 89 B
Morley Crescent W. Stan	21	17 89 A
Morley Cres. Ruis	32	11 86 A
Morley House. E5	37	34 86 A
Morley Rd. Bark	51	44 83 B
Morley Rd. Chis	100	44 69 A
Morley Rd. E10	38	38 87 C
Morley Rd. E15	50	39 83 D
Morley Rd. Rom	41	48 88 A
Morley Rd. S Croy	112	33 62 D
Morley Rd. SE13	76	38 75 C
Morley Rd. Sutt	103	24 66 D
Morley Rd. Twick	71	17 74 D
Morley St. SE1	7	31 79 A
Morna Rd. SE5	75	32 76 C
Morning La. E9	49	35 84 A
Morningside Rd. Wor Pk	103	23 65 A
Mornington Ave. Brom	99	41 68 B
Mornington Ave. Ilf	40	43 87 A
Mornington Ave. W14	62	24 78 B
Mornington Cres. Houn	69	10 76 B
Mornington Cres. NW1	47	29 83 C
Mornington Gr. E3	57	37 82 A
Mornington Mews. SE5	75	32 76 A
Mornington Pl. NW1	47	29 83 C
Mornington Rd. Ashf	81	08 71 C
Mornington Rd. E11	39	39 87 D
Mornington Rd. E4	18	38 94 B
Mornington Rd. SE8	64	36 77 D
Mornington St. NW1	47	28 83 D
Mornington Terr. NW1	47	28 83 D
Mornington Wlk. Rich	83	17 71 A
Morninston Rd. Grnf	53	13 82 D
Morocco St. SE1	8	33 79 A
Morpeth Gr. E9	49	35 83 B
Morpeth Rd. E9	49	35 83 B
Morpeth St. E2	57	35 82 B
Morpeth Terr. SW1	10	29 78 A
Morpeth Wlk. N17	25	34 91 D
Morrab Gdns. Ilf	40	45 86 D
Morris Ave. E12	50	42 85 D
Morris Cl. Orp	108	45 65 C
Morris Gdns. SW18	85	25 73 A
Morrish Rd. SW2	86	30 73 A
Morrison Ave. N17	25	33 89 A
Morrison Rd. Bark	52	48 83 C
Morrison St. SW11	74	28 75 A
Morris Pl. N4	37	31 86 A
Morris Rd. Dag	41	48 86 B
Morris Rd. E14	57	37 81 B
Morris Rd. E15	50	39 85 A
Morris Rd. Islw	71	15 75 B
Morris Rd. Rom	30	52 91 D
Morris St. E1	57	34 81 D
Morse Cl. E13	58	40 82 A
Morshead Rd. W9	56	25 82 B
Morston Gdns. SE9	89	42 71 B
Morten Cl. SW4	74	29 74 D
Morteyne Rd. N17	25	32 90 B
Mortgramit Sq. SE18	66	43 79 C
Mortham St. E15	50	39 83 A
Mortimer Cl. NW2	35	24 86 D
Mortimer Cl. SW16	86	29 72 B
Mortimer Cres. NW6	46	25 83 B
Mortimer Cres. Wor Pk	102	20 65 D
Mortimer Estate. NW6	46	25 83 B
Mortimer Market. WC1	2	29 82 C
Mortimer Pl. NW6	46	25 83 B
Mortimer Rd. Eri	67	50 77 B
Mortimer Rd. Mit	96	27 69 D
Mortimer Rd. N1	48	33 84 C
Mortimer Rd. NW10	56	23 82 A
Mortimer Rd. Orp	108	46 66 C
Mortimer Rd. W13	54	17 81 C
Mortimer Sq. W11	56	23 80 B
Mortimer St. W1	2	29 81 A
Mortimer Terr. NW5	47	28 85 B
Mortlake Cl. Croy	104	30 65 C
Mortlake High St. SW14	72	20 75 B
Mortlake Rd. E16	58	40 81 D
Mortlake Rd. Ilf	51	44 85 B
Mortlake Rd. Rich	72	19 76 D
Mortlock Cl. SE15	75	34 76 B
Mortlock Ct. E12	50	41 85 B
Morton Cres. N14	16	29 92 B
Morton Ct. Nthlt	43	14 85 C
Morton Gdns. Wall	111	29 64 C
Morton Mews. SW5	62	25 78 B
Morton Rd. E15	50	39 84 D
Morton Rd. Mord	103	26 67 B
Morton Rd. N1	48	32 84 C
Morton Way. N14	16	29 92 B
Morvale Cl. Belv	67	48 78 B
Morval Rd. SW2	75	31 74 A
Morven Rd. SW17	86	27 72 D
Morville St. E3	49	37 83 C
Morwell St. WC1	2	29 81 B
Moscow Pl. W2	56	25 80 B
Moscow Rd. W2	56	25 80 B
Moselle Ave. N22	25	31 90 D
Moselle Cl. N8	24	30 89 B
Moselle Pl. N17	25	33 91 C

Street	Page	Ref
Moselle St. N17	25	33 91 C
Moslyn Mews. Har	33	16 88 A
Mossborough Cl. N12	23	25 91 B
Mossbury Rd. SW11	74	27 75 A
Moss Cl. Pnr	20	12 90 D
Mossdown Cl. Belv	67	49 78 A
Mossford Ct. Ilf	28	43 90 D
Mossford Green. Ilf	28	44 89 A
Mossford La. Ilf	28	44 90 C
Mossford St. E3	57	36 82 D
Mossington Rd. SE16	64	35 78 A
Moss La. Pnr	20	12 90 D
Moss La. Rom	42	51 88 D
Mosslea Rd. Brom	107	41 67 B
Mosslea Rd. Orp	108	44 65 C
Mosslea Rd. SE20	98	35 70 A
Mossop St. SW3	9	27 78 A
Moss Rd. Dag	52	49 84 C
Mossville Gdns. Mord	95	24 68 D
Mostyn Ave. Wem	44	18 85 D
Mostyn Gdns. NW10	46	23 83 D
Mostyn Gr. E3	49	37 83 C
Mostyn Rd. Edg	22	21 91 C
Mostyn Rd. SW19	95	24 69 D
Mostyn Rd. SW9	75	31 76 A
Mosul Way. Brom	107	42 67 C
Motcomb St. SW1	6	28 79 C
Motley St. SW8	74	29 76 C
Motspur Park. N.Mal	102	22 67 C
Mottingham Gdns. SE9	89	41 73 D
Mottingham La. SE12	89	41 73 A
Mottingham La. SE9	89	41 73 D
Mottingham Rd. N9	18	35 94 B
Mottingham Rd. SE9	89	42 72 D
Mottisfont Rd. SE2	66	46 79 D
Moulins Rd. E9	49	35 84 D
Moulton Ave. Houn	70	12 76 C
Moundfield Rd. N16	37	34 88 C
Mound The. SE9	90	43 72 C
Mountacre Cl. SE28	87	34 71 A
Mount Adon Park. SE22	87	34 73 A
Mount Angelus Rd. SW15	84	21 73 B
Mount Ararat Rd. Rich	71	18 74 A
Mount Ash Rd. SE26	87	34 72 D
Mount Ave. E4	18	37 93 D
Mount Ave. Sthl	53	13 81 C
Mount Ave. W5	54	17 81 B
Mountbatten Cl. SE18	66	45 77 A
Mountbatten Cl. SE19	87	33 71 C
Mountbel Rd. Stan	21	16 90 C
Mount Cl. Barn	12	28 96 C
Mount Cl. Brom	99	42 69 A
Mount Cl. Cars	111	28 62 A
Mount Cl. W5	54	17 81 A
Mountcombe Cl. Surb	101	18 66 A
Mount Ct. W.Wick	107	39 65 A
Mount Dri. Bexh	79	48 74 A
Mount Dri. Har	32	12 88 B
Mount Dri. Wem	33	20 86 A
Mountearl Gdns. SW16	86	30 72 D
Mount Echo Ave. E4	18	37 94 D
Mount Echo Dri. E4	18	37 94 D
Mount Ephraim La. SW16	86	29 72 D
Mount Ephraim Rd. SW16	86	29 72 D
Mountfield Rd. E6	51	43 83 C
Mountfield Rd. N3	23	25 89 A
Mountfield Rd. W5	54	18 81 C
Mountford Rd. E8	48	34 85 C
Mountford St. E1	57	34 81 C
Mountford Terr. N1	48	31 84 C
Mountfort Cres. N1	48	31 84 C
Mount Gdns. SE26	87	34 72 D
Mountgrove Rd. N5	37	32 86 C
Mounthurst Rd. Brom	107	39 66 B
Mountjoy Cl. SE2	66	46 79 B
Mount Mills. EC1	3	31 82 B
Mount Nod Rd. SW16	86	30 72 D
Mount Park Ave. Har	33	15 86 A
Mount Park Ave. S Croy	112	31 62 B
Mount Park. Cars	111	28 62 A
Mount Park Cres. W5	54	17 81 D
Mount Park Rd. Har	32	14 86 D
Mount Park Rd. Pnr	31	10 88 A
Mount Park Rd. W5	54	17 81 D
Mount Pleasant. Barn	12	27 96 D
Mount Pleasant Cres. N4	36	30 87 B
Mount Pleasant. Eps	109	21 62 D
Mount Pleasant Hill. E5	38	35 86 A
Mount Pleasant. Ilf	51	44 85 C
Mount Pleasant Rd. Dart	80	54 74 D
Mount Pleasant Rd. E17	26	36 90 C
Mount Pleasant Rd. N17	25	33 90 C
Mount Pleasant Rd. N Mal	94	20 68 A
Mount Pleasant Rd. NW10	46	23 83 A
Mount Pleasant Rd. Rom	29	50 91 B
Mount Pleasant Rd. SE13	76	38 74 C
Mount Pleasant Rd. W5	54	17 82 C
Mount Pleasant. Ruis	32	11 86 B
Mount Pleasant. SE27	86	32 71 A
Mount Pleasant Villas. N4	36	30 87 B
Mount Pleasant. WC1	3	31 82 C
Mount Pleasant. Wem	44	18 83 B
Mount Pleasant Wlk. Bex	79	50 74 A
Mount Pleasant Wlk. Bex	79	50 74 A
Mount Pl. W3	55	19 80 D
Mount Rd. Barn	12	27 95 A
Mount Rd. Bexh	79	48 74 A
Mount Rd. Chess	109	19 64 A
Mount Rd. Dag	41	48 87 D
Mount Rd. Dart	80	51 74 D
Mount Rd. Felt	82	12 72 C
Mount Rd. Ilf	51	43 85 D
Mount Rd. Mit	96	27 69 C
Mount Rd. Mit	96	27 69 C
Mount Rd. N Mal	94	20 68 B
Mount Rd. NW2	35	23 86 C
Mount Rd. NW4	34	22 88 C
Mount.Rd. SE19	97	33 70 A
Mount Rd. SW9	85	25 72 A
Mount Row. W1	6	28 80 B
Mountsfield Ct. SE13	76	38 74 D
Mountside. Stan	21	16 90 A
Mounts Pond Rd. SE13	76	38 76 D
Mounts Pond Rd. SE3	77	39 76 C
Mount Sq The. NW3	35	26 86 C
Mount Stewart Ave. Har	33	17 87 B
Mount St. W1	6	28 80 A
Mount Terr. E1	57	34 81 B
Mount The. E5	37	34 86 B
Mount The. Eps	109	21 62 D
Mount The. Eps	109	22 64 B
Mount The. N20	15	26 93 A
Mount The. N Mal	94	21 68 A
Mount The. NW3	35	26 86 C
Mount The. Wem	44	20 86 A
Mount Vernon. NW3	46	26 85 A
Mountview Ct. N15	25	31 89 D
Mountview. Nthwd	19	09 91 B
Mount View Rd. E4	18	38 94 B
Mount View Rd. N4	36	30 87 B
Mount View Rd. NW9	34	20 88 B
Mountview Rd. Orp	108	46 66 A
Mount. View. W5	54	17 81 B
Mount Villas. SE27	86	31 72 D
Mount Way. Cars	111	28 62 A
Mountwood Cl. S Croy	112	34 62 D
Mountwood. E Mol	92	13 68 B
Movers La. Bark	57	45 83 A
Mowatt Cl. N19	36	29 87 D
Mowbray Rd. Barn	11	26 95 A
Mowbray Rd. NW6	46	24 84 C
Mowbray Rd. Rich	83	17 72 C
Mowbray Rd. SE19	97	33 69 B
Mowbrays Cl. Rom	29	50 90 A
Mowbrays Rd. Rom	29	50 90 C
Mowlem St. E2	48	34 83 D
Mowll St. SW9	63	31 77 C
Moxon Cl. E13	50	39 83 D
Moxon St. Barn	11	24 96 B
Moxon St. W1	2	28 81 A
Moye Cl. E2	48	34 83 C
Moyers Rd. E10	38	38 87 A
Moylan Rd. W6	62	24 77 A
Moyne Pl. NW10	45	19 83 C
Moyser Rd. SW16	86	28 71 D
Moyser Rd. SW16	86	29 70 A
Mozart St. W10	56	24 82 B
Muchelney Rd. Mord	103	26 67 D
Muggeridge Rd. Dag	52	49 85 B
Muirdown Ave. SW14	72	20 75 D
Muirfield. W3	55	21 81 C
Muirkirk Rd. SE6	88	38 73 C
Muir Rd. E5	37	34 86 C
Mulberry Cl. E4	18	37 93 A
Mulberry Cl. Nthlt	43	12 83 C
Mulberry Cl. NW3	46	26 85 B
Mulberry Cl. NW4	23	23 89 A
Mulberry Cl. Rom	30	53 89 C
Mulberry Cl. SW16	86	29 71 A
Mulberry Cres. Brent	60	17 77 C
Mulberry Ct. Bark	51	45 84 D
Mulberry Ct. Surb	101	17 66 B
Mulberry La. Croy	105	33 66 D
Mulberry Pl. W6	61	22 78 C
Mulberry St. E1	57	34 81 C
Mulberry Way. Belv	67	50 79 A
Mulberry Way. E18	27	40 90 D
Mulberry Way. Ilf	28	44 89 C
Mulberry Wlk. SW3	82	26 77 B
Mulgrave Rd. Croy	105	32 65 D
Mulgrave Rd. Har	33	16 86 A
Mulgrave Rd. NW10	45	21 85 B
Mulgrave Rd. Sutt	110	25 63 A
Mulgrave Rd. SW6	62	24 77 B
Mulgrave Rd. W5	54	17 82 D
Mulholland Cl. Mit	96	28 69 D
Mulkern Rd. N19	36	29 87 D
Mullberry Mews. Wall	111	29 63 A
Muller Rd. SW4	74	29 74 D
*Mullet Gdns. E2	57	34 82 A
Mullins Path. SW14	72	20 75 B
Mullion Cl. Har	20	13 90 B
Mull Wlk. N1	48	32 84 B
Mulready St. NW8	1	27 82 C
Multi Way. W3	61	21 79 A
Multon Rd. SW18	85	26 73 D
Mumford Ct. EC2	4	32 81 C
Mumford Rd. SE24	75	31 74 B
Muncaster Cl. Ashf	81	07 71 A
Muncaster Rd. Ashf	81	07 71 D
Muncaster Rd. SW11	74	28 74 A
Mundania Rd. SE22	76	35 74 A
Munday Rd. E16	58	40 80 A
Munden St. W14	62	24 78 A
Mundford Rd. E5	38	35 86 A
Mund St. W14	62	24 78 D
Mundy St. N1	4	33 82 A
Munnings Gdns. Islw	70	14 74 B
Munro Mews. W10	56	24 81 A
Munster Ave. Houn	70	12 74 A
Munster Ct. Tedd	93	17 70 A
Munster Gdns. N13	17	32 92 A
Munster Rd. SW6	73	24 76 B
Munster Sq. NW1	2	28 82 D
Munton Rd. SE17	63	32 78 A
Murchison Rd. E10	38	38 86 A
Murdock St. SE15	63	34 77 B
Murfett Cl. SW19	85	24 72 A
Muriel St. N1	47	30 83 B
Murillo Rd. SE13	76	38 75 D
Murphy St. SE1	7	31 79 A
Murray Ave. Brom	99	40 69 D
Murray Ave. Houn	70	13 74 B
Murray Cres. Pnr	20	11 90 B
Murray Gr. N1	4	32 83 D
Murray Mews. NW1	47	29 84 D
Murray Rd. Nthwd	19	09 91 C
Murray Rd. Orp	100	46 68 B
Murray Rd. Rich	83	17 72 A
Murray Rd. SW19	95	23 70 B
Murray Rd. W5	60	17 78 A
Murray Sq. E16	58	40 81 D
Murray St. NW1	47	29 84 D
Murrays Yd. SE18	66	43 78 B
Murray Terr. NW3	46	26 85 B
Murtwell Dri. Chig	28	44 91 A
Musard Rd. W6	62	24 77 A
Musbury St. E1	57	35 81 C
Muscatel Pl. SE5	75	33 76 A
Muschamp Rd. Cars	104	27 65 A
Muschamp Rd. SE15	75	33 75 B
Muscovy St. EC3		33 80 A
Museum Pas. E2	57	35 82 A
Museum St. WC1		30 81 C
Musgrave Cres. SW6	73	25 76 A
Musgrave Cl. SW11	74	27 76 A
Musgrave Rd. Islw	71	15 76 B
Musgrove Cl. Barn	11	26 97 A
Musgrove Rd. SE14	76	36 76 A
Musjid Rd. SW11	73	26 76 D
Musquash Way. Houn	70	11 76 C
Muston Rd. E5	37	34 86 B
Muswell Ave. N10	24	28 90 D
Muswell Hill Bwy. N10	24	28 89 B
Muswell Hill. N10	24	28 89 C
Muswell Hill Pl. N10	24	28 89 D
Muswell Hill Rd. N10	24	28 89 D
Muswell Hill Rd. N6	36	28 88 C
Muswell Mews. N10	24	28 89 B
Muswell Rd. N10	24	28 90 D
Mutrix Rd. NW6	46	25 83 A
Mutton Pl. NW1	47	28 84 A
Muybridge Rd. N Mal	94	20 69 C
Myatt Rd. SW9	75	31 76 B
Mycenae Rd. SE3	85	40 77 A
Myddelton Ave. Enf	13	33 97 B
Myddelton Cl. Enf	13	33 97 B
Myddelton Gdns. N21	17	32 94 A
Myddelton Park. N20	15	26 93 B
Myddelton Pas. EC1	3	31 82 A
Myddelton Sq. EC1	3	31 82 A

Street	Pg	Ref
Myddelton St. EC1	3	31 82 A
Myddelton Rd. N22	24	30 91 D
Myddelton Rd. N8	24	30 89 C
Mylis Cl. SE26	87	34 71 B
Mylne Cl. W6	61	22 78 C
Mylne Cl. EC1	3	31 82 A
Mylne St. EC1	3	31 83 C
Mynster Rd. Tedd	93	17 70 A
Myra St. SE2	46	46 78 A
Myrdle St. E1	57	34 81 C
Myron Pl. SE13		38 75 A
Myrtle Alley. SE18	66	43 79 C
Myrtle Ave. Felt	69	09 74 A
Myrtle Ave. Ruis	31	10 87 B
Myrtleberry Cl. E8		33 84 B
Myrtle Cl. Barn	16	27 94 D
Myrtle Cl. Eri		51 76 A
Myrtledene Rd. SE2	66	15 80 C
Myrtle Gdns. W7	54	20 69 C
Myrtle Gr. N Mal	94	37 65 C
Myrtle Rd. Croy	106	36 88 C
Myrtle Rd. E17	38	42 83 A
Myrtle Rd. E6	50	14 70 A
Myrtle Rd. Hamp	92	14 76 C
Myrtle Rd. Houn	70	43 86 B
Myrtle Rd. Ilf	40	32 93 C
Myrtle Rd. N13	17	53 91 A
Myrtle Rd. Rom	55	26 64 C
Myrtle Rd. Sutt	110	20 80 C
Myrtle Rd. W3		08 91 D
Myrtleside Cl. Nthwd	19	33 83 C
Myrtle Wlk. N1		27 75 D
Mysore Rd. SW11	74	32 72 D
Myton Rd. SE21		
Nadine St. SE7	65	41 78 C
Nagle Cl. E17	26	38 90 D
Nag's Head La. Well		46 75 B
Nags Head Rd. Enf	14	36 96 D
Nairne Gr. SE24	75	32 74 B
Nairn Rd. Ruis	43	11 84 A
Nairn St. E14	58	38 81 A
Naish Ct. N1	47	30 83 A
Nallhead Rd. Felt	82	11 71 C
Namton Dr. Th Hth	96	30 68 D
Nanescombe. SE12	89	40 73 C
Nankin St. E14	57	37 81 C
Nansen Rd. SW11	74	28 75 A
Nansen Village. N12	15	25 92 B
Nantes Cl. SW18	73	26 75 C
Nantes Pas. E1	4	33 81 B
Nant Rd. NW2	35	24 86 B
Nant St. E2		34 82 B
Napier Ave. SW6	73	24 75 B
Napier Cl. SE8		36 77 D
Napier Cl. W14	62	24 79 D
Napier Cl. SW6	73	24 75 B
Napier Gr. N1	48	32 83 C
Napier Pl. W14	62	24 79 D
Napier Rd. Ashf	91	08 70 D
Napier Rd. Belv	67	48 78 B
Napier Rd. Brom	99	40 68 D
Napier Rd. E11	39	39 86 C
Napier Rd. E15	50	39 83 C
Napier Rd. E6	51	43 83 C
Napier Rd. Enf	14	35 95 B
Napier Rd. Islw	71	16 75 C
Napier Rd. N17	25	33 89 A
Napier Rd. NW10	55	22 82 B
Napier Rd. S Croy	112	32 63 D
Napier Rd. SE25	97	34 68 D
Napier Rd. W14	62	24 79 D
Napier Rd. Wem	44	17 84 B
Napier St. SE8	64	36 77 D
Napier Terr. N1	48	31 84 D
Napoleon Rd. E5	55	34 85 B
Napoleon Rd. E5	37	34 86 D
Napoleon Rd. Twick		36 73 B
Narbonne Ave. SW4	74	29 74 A
Narboro Ct. Rom		52 88 C
Narborough St. SW6	73	25 76 D
Narcissus Rd. NW6		25 85 C
Narford Rd. E5	37	34 86 A
Narrow St. E14	57	36 80 A
Narrow St. W3	55	19 80 D
Narrow Way. Brom	107	42 67 C
Nascot St. W12	56	23 81 C
Naseby Cl. Islw	71	15 76 A
Naseby Cl. NW6	46	26 84 C
Naseby Rd. Dag	41	49 86 C
Naseby Rd. Ilf	27	42 90 B
Naseby Rd. SE19	97	32 70 B
Nash Green. Brom	99	40 70 A
Nash Rd. N9	18	35 93 A
Nash Rd. Rom	29	47 89 D
Nash Rd. SE4	76	36 74 A
Nasmyth St. W6	61	22 79 D
Nassau Rd. SW13	72	21 76 B
Nassau St. W1	2	29 81 A
Nassington Rd. NW3	47	27 85 A
Natalie Cl. Felt	81	08 73 B
Natal Rd. Ilf	51	43 85 B
Natal Rd. N11	24	30 91 A
Natal Rd. SW16	96	29 70 B
Natal Rd. Th Hth	97	32 68 B
Nathans Rd. Wem	93	17 86 A
Nathan Way. SE28	66	45 79 D
Nation Way. E4		38 94 C
Naval Row. E14	58	38 80 A
Navarino Gr. E8		34 84 A
Navarino Rd. E8		34 84 A
Navarre Gdns. Rom		49 91 B
Navarre Rd. E6	50	42 83 C
Navarre St. E2	4	33 82 D
Navenby Wlk. E3	57	37 82 C
Navestock Cres. Wdf Gn	27	41 90 A
Navy St. SW4	74	29 75 B
Naylor Cl. Enf		35 95 B
Naylor Rd. N20	15	26 93 A
Naylor Rd. SE15	63	34 77 D
Neal Ave. Sthl	53	12 82 D
Neal Cl. Nthwd	19	10 90 A
Nealden St. SW9		30 75 B
Neale Cl. N2	3	26 89 A
Neal St. WC2		30 81 C
Neal's Yd. Eri	67	30 81 C
Neal's Yd. WC2		21 90 B
Near Acre. NW9		21 85 C
Neasden Cl. NW10	45	20 86 D
Neasden La. NW10	34	21 85 A
Neasden La. NW10	45	46 85 D
Neasham Rd. Dag	51	33 77 A
Neate St. SE5	63	29 78 A
Neath Gdns. Mord	103	26 67 C
Neathouse Pl. SW1	10	53 90 B
Neats Acre. Ruis	31	32 79 B
Neave Cres. Rom	30	33 79 D
Nebraska St. SE1	8	37 76 D
Neckinger Estate. SE16	8	25 81 C
Neckinger St. SE1	8	23 86 D
Nectarine Way. SE13	76	19 85 C
Needham Rd. W11	56	08 71 C
Needham Terr. NW2	35	37 73 A
Neeld Cres. NW4	34	23 77 A
Neeld Cres. Wem	45	37 73 A
Neil Cl. Ashf	81	35 78 A
Nelgarde Rd. SE6	88	23 77 B
Nella Rd. W6	62	54 88 B
Nelldale Rd. SE16	64	54 88 C
Nelmes Cl. Horn	42	54 88 B
Nelmes Cres. Horn	30	54 88 C
Nelmes Rd. Horn	54	54 88 C
Nelmes Way. Horn	30	54 88 C
Nelson Cl. Croy	105	20 69 B
Nelson Cl. Rom	29	49 90 B
Nelson Gdns. E2	57	34 82 A
Nelson Gdns. Houn	70	13 74 C
Nelson Grove Rd. SW19	95	32 82 A
Nelson Pas. EC1	4	31 83 B
Nelson Pl. N1	48	31 83 B
Nelson Pl. Sid	90	46 71 A
Nelson Pl. W3	55	19 80 D
Nelson Rd. Belv	67	48 78 B
Nelson Rd. Brom	99	43 54 C
Nelson Rd. Dart	80	53 74 C
Nelson Rd. E11	27	40 89 D
Nelson Rd. E4	26	37 91 B
Nelson Rd. Enf	14	35 95 B
Nelson Rd. Har	33	13 74 B
Nelson Rd. Houn	70	13 74 C
Nelson Rd. N15	25	33 89 C
Nelson Rd. N8	36	30 88 D
Nelson Rd. N9	17	34 93 B
Nelson Rd. N.Mal	102	20 67 B
Nelson Rd. SE10	64	38 77 A
Nelson Rd. Sid	90	46 71 A
Nelson Rd. Stan	21	17 91 A
Nelson Rd. SW19	95	26 70 C
Nelson Rd. Twick	82	13 73 B
Nelson Sq. SE1	7	31 79 B
Nelsons Row. SW4	74	29 75 D
Nelson St. E16	58	39 80 B
Nelson St. E1	57	34 81 C
Nelson St. E6	50	43 83 A
Nelson St. E6	51	43 83 A
Nelson Terr. N1	48	31 83 D
Nelson Wlk. SE16	57	36 80 C
Nelwyn Ave. Horn	42	54 88 B
Nemoure Rd. W3	55	20 80 A
Nene Rd. Houn	69	07 76 B
Nepaul Rd. SW11	74	27 76 C
Nepean St. SW15	84	22 73 A
Neptune Rd. Har	32	14 88 D
Neptune Rd. Houn	69	08 76 B
Neptune St. SE16	64	35 79 C
Nero Ct. Brent	60	17 77 D
Nesbit Cl. SE3	77	39 76 C
Nesbit Rd. SE9	77	41 75 D
Nesbitts Alley. Barn	11	24 96 B
Ness Rd. Eri	68	53 77 B
Ness St. SE16	63	34 79 C
*Nesta Rd. Wdf Gn	27	39 91 B
Nestor Ave. N21	13	31 95 D
Netheravon Rd. W4	61	21 78 D
Netheravon Rd. W7	54	15 80 D
Netheravon Road S. W4	61	21 78 D
Netherbury Rd. W5	60	17 79 D
Netherby Gdns. Enf	12	30 96 C
Netherby Rd. SE23	88	35 73 A
Nether Cl. N3	23	25 91 C
Nethercourt Ave. N3	23	25 91 C
Netherfield Gdns. Bark	51	44 84 D
Netherfield Rd. N12	15	25 92 D
Netherfield Rd. SW17	86	28 72 C
Netherford Rd. SW4	74	29 76 C
Netherhall Gdns. NW3	46	26 85 C
Netherhall Way. NW3	46	26 85 C
Netherlands Rd. Barn	11	26 95 D
Netherleight Cl. N6	36	28 87 D
Netherpark Dri. Rom	30	51 90 D
Nether St. N12	15	25 92 D
Nether St. N3	23	25 91 C
Netherton Gr. SW10	62	26 77 A
Netherton Rd. N15	37	32 88 D
Netherton Rd. Twick	71	16 74 B
Netherwood Rd. W14	62	23 79 B
Netherwood St. NW6	46	24 84 B
Netley Cl. Sutt	110	23 64 D
Netley Gdns. Mord	103	26 66 A
Netley Rd (West). Houn	69	08 76 B
Netley Rd. Brent	60	18 77 A
Netley Rd. E17	38	36 88 B
Netley Rd. Houn	69	08 76 B
Netley Rd. Ilf	40	44 88 B
Netley Rd. Mord	103	26 66 A
Netley St. NW1	2	29 82 A
Nettlecombe Cl. Sutt	110	25 62 B
Nettleden Ave. Wem	45	19 84 A
Nettlefold Pl. SE27	87	31 72 D
Nettlestead Cl. Beck	98	36 70 D
Nettleton Rd. Houn	69	07 76 B
Nettleton Rd. SE14	76	35 76 B
Nettlewood Rd. SW16	96	29 70 D
Neuchatel Rd. SE6	88	36 72 B
Nevada St. SE10	64	38 77 A
Nevern Pl. SW5	62	25 78 A
Nevern Rd. SW5	62	25 78 A
Nevern Sq. SW5	62	25 78 A
Neville Ave. N Mal	94	20 69 B
Neville Cl. E11	39	39 86 D
Neville Cl. Houn	70	13 76 D
Neville Cl. NW1	47	29 83 D
Neville Cl. NW6	46	24 83 D
Neville Cl. SE15	75	34 76 A
Neville Cl. Sid	61	45 71 B
Neville Cl. W3	61	20 79 A
Neville Dri. N2	35	26 88 C
Neville Gdns. Dag	41	47 86 D
Neville Gill Cl. SW18	73	25 74 D
Neville Rd. Croy	105	32 68 B
Neville Rd. Dag	41	47 86 D
Neville Rd. E7	50	40 84 D
Neville Rd. Ilf	28	44 90 A
Neville Rd. King	94	19 69 C
Neville Rd. NW6	46	24 83 D
Neville Rd. Rich	83	17 72 A
Neville's Ct. NW2	34	22 86 C
Neville's Ct. NW2	34	22 85 C
Neville's Ct. SW7	62	26 78 D
Neville Terr. SW7	62	26 78 D
Neville Wlk. Cars	104	27 66 A
Nevill Pl. N22		30 90 B
Nevill Rd. N16	48	33 85 A
Nevill Rd. N16	37	33 86 C
Nevin Dri. E4	18	37 94 D
Nevis Cl. Rom		51 91 A
Nevis Rd. SW17	86	28 72 A
Newall Rd. Houn	69	08 76 A
Newark Cres. NW10	55	20 82 B
Newark Rd. S Croy	112	32 63 B
Newark St. E1	57	34 81 B
Newark Way. NW4	22	22 89 A
New Barns Ave. Mit	96	29 68 D

Name	Page	Grid
New Barn St. E13	58	40 82 D
Newbery Rd. Eri	80	51 76 B
Newbolt Ave. Sutt	110	23 64 D
Newbolt Rd. Stan	21	15 91 B
New Bond St. W1	6	28 80 B
Newborough Green. N Mal	94	20 68 D
New Brent St. NW4	35	23 88 A
New Bridge St. EC4	3	31 81 D
New Broad St. EC2	4	33 81 A
New Broadway. W5	54	17 80 B
Newburgh Rd. W3	55	20 80 C
Newburgh St. W1	2	29 81 C
New Burlington Mews. W1	6	29 80 A
New Burlington Pl. W1	6	29 80 A
New Burlington St. W1	6	29 80 A
Newburn St. SE11	10	30 78 D
Newbury Cl. Nthlt	43	12 84 B
Newbury Cl. Rom	30	53 91 B
Newbury Gdns. Eps	109	21 64 B
Newbury Gdns. Horn	42	54 86 D
Newbury Gdns. Rom	30	53 91 B
Newbury Mews. NW5	4	28 84 A
Newbury Rd. Brom	99	40 68 A
Newbury Rd. Houn	69	07 76 A
Newbury Rd. Ilf	40	45 88 C
Newbury Rd. Rom	30	53 91 B
Newbury St. EC1	4	32 81 A
Newbury Way. Nthlt	43	12 84 B
Newby Cl. Enf	13	33 97 C
Newby Pl. E14	58	38 80 A
Newby St. SW8	74	28 75 B
Newcastle Ave. Ilf	28	46 91 A
Newcastle Cl. EC4	3	31 81 D
Newcastle Ct. EC4	4	32 80 A
Newcastle Pl. W2	1	26 81 B
Newcastle Row. EC1	3	31 82 C
New Cavendish St. W1	2	28 81 B
New Change. EC4	4	32 81 C
New Chapel Sq. Felt	81	10 73 D
New Charles St. EC1	3	31 82 B
New Church Rd. SE5	63	32 77 B
New Church Rd. SE5	63	32 77 C
New City Rd. E13	58	41 82 A
New Cl. Felt	81	12 71 C
New Cl. SW19	95	26 68 A
New Colebrooke Ct. Cars	111	28 63 C
New College Mews. N1	48	31 84 C
Newcombe Park. Wem	44	18 83 B
Newcombe St. W8	56	25 80 C
Newcome Gdns. SW16	86	30 71 A
Newcomen Rd. E11	39	39 86 D
Newcomen Rd. SW11	73	26 75 B
Newcomen St. SE1	8	32 79 B
New Compton St. WC2	3	30 81 C
Newcourt St. NW8	47	27 83 C
New Coventry St. W1	6	29 80 B
New Cross Gate. SE14	76	35 76 B
New Cross Rd. SE14	76	35 76 B
New Ct. Dart :	80	54 74 C
New Ct. EC4	3	31 80 A
New Ct. Nthlt	43	13 85 D
Newdales Cl. N9	17	34 93 A
Newdene Ave. Nthlt	43	11 83 D
Newell St. E14	57	36 80 B
New End. NW3	3	26 86 C
New End Sq. NW3	46	26 85 B
Newent Cl. Cars	104	27 66 D
Newent Cl. SE15	63	33 77 C
New Farm Ave. Brom	99	40 68 C
New Farm La. Nthwd	19	09 90 A
New Fetter La. EC4	4	31 81 C
Newfield Cl. Hamp	92	13 69 A
Newfield Rise. NW2	29	22 86 D
New Forest La. Chig	28	43 91 A
Newgale Gdns. Edg	21	18 90 B
Newgate Cl. Felt	82	12 72 C
Newgate. Croy	105	32 66 C
Newgate St. EC1	3	31 81 D
New Goulston St. E1	4	33 81 D
New Hall Dri. Rom	30	54 90 A
New Ham Rd. Houn	69	08 76 A
Newham's Row. SE1	8	33 79 A
Newham Way. E16	58	40 81 B
Newhaven Cres. Ashf	81	08 71 D
Newhaven Gdns. SE9	77	41 75 D
Newhaven Rd. SE25	105	32 67 B
New Heston Rd. Houn	59	12 77 D
Newhouse Ave. Rom	29	47 89 B
Newhouse Cl. N.Mal	102	21 66 A
Newhouse Wlk. Mord	103	26 66 A
Newick Cl. Bex	79	49 74 D
Newick Rd. E5	4	34 85 B
Newick Rd. E5	38	35 86 C
Newing Green. Brom	99	41 70 D
Newington Barrow Way. N7	36	30 86 D
Newington Butts. SE11	63	31 78 B
Newington Cswy. SE1		32 79 C
Newington Green. N5	48	32 85 D
Newington Green Rd. N1	48	32 85 D
New Inn Bwy. EC2	4	33 82 C
New Inn Pas. WC2	3	30 81 D
New Inn Sq. EC2	4	33 82 C
New Inn St. EC2	4	33 82 C
New Inn Yd. EC2	4	33 82 C
New Kent Rd. SE1	63	32 78 B
New King's Rd. SW6	73	25 76 C
New King St. SE8	64	37 77 A
Newland Cl. Pnr	20	12 91 B
Newland Ct. Wem	34	19 86 A
Newland Dri. Enf	13	34 97 B
Newland Gdns. W13	60	16 79 A
Newland Rd. N8	24	30 89 A
Newlands Ave. Surb	101	15 66 C
Newlands Cl. Sthl	59	12 78 C
Newlands Cl. Wem	44	17 84 A
Newlands Ct. SE9	77	43 74 C
Newlands Park. SE26	88	35 71 D
Newlands Pl. Barn	11	23 95 B
Newlands Rd. SW16	90	30 69 C
Newlands The. Wall	111	29 63 D
New London St. EC3		33 80 A
New Lydenburg St. SE7	65	41 79 C
Newlyn Gdns. Har	32	12 87 B
Newlyn Rd. Barn	11	24 96 D
Newlyn Rd. N17	25	33 90 B
Newlyn Rd. Well	78	45 76 D
Newman Cl. Horn	54	88 A
Newman Pas. W1	2	29 81 A
Newman Rd. Brom	29	40 69 A
Newman Rd. Croy	104	30 66 D
Newman Rd. E13	58	40 82 B
Newman Rd. E17	38	35 88 B
Newman Rd. Houn	69	07 76 A
Newman's Ct. EC3	4	32 81 D
Newman's Row. WC2	3	30 81 B
Newman St. W1	2	29 81 A
Newman's Way. Barn	11	26 97 A
Newmarket Ave. Nthlt	43	13 85 D
Newmarket Green. SE9		41 73 B
Newminster Rd. Mord	103	26 67 C
New Mount St. E15		38 84 D
Newnes Path. SW15	72	22 75 D
Newnham Ave. Ruis	23	11 87 C
Newnham Cl. Nthlt	43	14 84 A
Newnham Gdns. Nthlt	43	14 84 A
Newnham Rd. N22	24	30 90 B
Newnhams Cl. Brom	99	42 68 B
Newnham Terr. SE1		31 79 C
Newnham Way. Har	33	18 88 A
New North Pl. EC2		33 82 C
New North Rd. Ilf	28	45 91 B
New North Rd. N1	48	32 83 B
New North St. WC1	3	30 81 B
Newton Cl. N4	37	32 87 B
New Oak Rd. N2	23	26 90 C
New Orleans Wlk. N19	36	29 87 B
New Oxford St. WC1	3	30 81 C
New Park Ave. N13	17	32 92 D
New Park Cl. Nthlt	43	12 84 A
New Park Estate. N18		35 92 C
New Park Rd. Ashf	81	08 71 C
New Park Rd. SW2	86	30 73 A
New Place Sq. SE16	63	34 79 D
New Plaistow Rd. E15	58	39 83 A
Newport Ave. E13	58	40 82 D
Newport Cl. Enf		29 80 B
Newport Pl. WC2	6	29 80 B
Newport Rd. E10	58	38 86 B
Newport Rd. E17	26	36 89 C
Newport Rd. Houn	69	07 76 A
Newport Rd. SW13	72	22 76 A
Newport St. SE11	10	30 78 B
Newquay Cres. Har	32	12 86 A
Newquay Rd. SE6	88	38 72 A
New Quebec St. W1	1	27 81 D
New Rd. Brent	60	17 77 B
New Rd. Dag	52	49 83 D
New Rd. E1	57	34 81 B
New Rd. E4	18	37 92 B
New Rd. E Mol	92	13 68 A
New Rd. Felt	81	09 74 D
New Rd. Felt	81	10 73 D
New Rd. Felt	81	12 71 C
New Rd. Har	44	15 85 B
New Rd. Hay	68	08 76 A
New Rd. Houn	70	13 75 D
New Rd. Ilf	40	45 86 A
New Rd. King	94	19 70 C
New Rd. Mit	104	28 66 C
New Rd. N17	25	33 90 B
New Rd. N2	24	27 90 A
New Rd. N8	36	30 88 A
New Rd. N9	17	34 93 A
New Rd. NW7		24 91 C
New Rd. Orp	108	46 66 A
New Rd. Rain	52	50 83 C
New Rd. Rich	67	17 71 A
New Rd. SE2	67	47 78 D
New Rd. Shep	91	07 68 B
New Rd. Well	78	46 76 D
New River Cres. N13		31 92 B
New River Wlk. N1	48	32 84 C
New Row. WC2	7	30 80 A
Newry Rd. Twick	71	16 74 A
Newsam Ave. N15	37	32 88 B
New Spring Gdns Wlk. SE11	10	30 78 C
New Sq. WC2	3	30 81 D
Newstead Ave. Orp	108	46 65 A
Newstead Rd. SE12	89	39 73 B
Newstead Way. SW19	85	24 71 A
Newstead Wlk. Cars	103	26 66 A
New St. EC2	4	33 81 A
New Street Hill. Brom	89	41 71 C
New Street Hill. SE12	89	41 71 D
New Street Sq. EC4	3	31 81 C
Newton Ave. N10	24	28 90 B
Newton Ave. W3	71	20 79 A
Newton Gr. W4	61	21 78 A
Newton Rd. E15	49	38 85 D
Newton Rd. Har	21	15 90 C
Newton Rd. Islw	71	15 76 D
Newton Rd. N15	37	34 88 A
Newton Rd. NW2	35	23 86 C
Newton Rd. SW19	95	24 70 C
Newton Rd. W2	56	25 81 D
Newton Rd. Well	78	46 75 A
Newton Rd. Wem	44	18 84 D
Newton St. WC2	3	30 81 C
Newton's Yd. SW18	73	25 74 A
Newton Way. N18	17	32 92 C
Newton Wlk. Edg	22	19 90 B
Newton Wlk. Edg	22	20 90 A
Newtown St. SW11	74	28 76 B
New Trinity Rd. N2	23	26 90 D
New Turnstile. WC2	3	30 81 B
New Union Cl. E14	64	38 79 C
New Union St. EC2	4	32 81 B
New Wanstead. E11	39	40 88 C
New Way Rd. NW9	22	21 89 C
New Wharf Rd. N1	47	30 83 C
Newyears Green La. Uxb	31	07 88 C
New Zealand Way. W12	55	22 80 B
Niagara Ave. W5	60	17 78 A
Niagara Cl. SE16	64	35 79 C
Nibthwaite Rd. Har	33	15 88 A
Nicholas Cl. Grnf	43	13 83 D
Nicholas Gdns. W5	60	17 79 B
Nicholas La. EC4	4	32 80 B
Nicholas Rd. Croy	111	30 64 A
Nicholas Rd. Dag	41	48 86 D
Nicholas Rd. E1	57	35 82 C
Nicholas Way. Nthwd	19	08 90 A
Nicholay Rd. N19	36	29 86 B
Nicholay Rd. N19	36	29 87 D
Nichol Cl. N14	16	29 94 D
Nicholes Rd. Houn	70	13 75 C
Nichol La. Brom	99	40 70 D
Nicholl St. E2	48	34 83 A
Nicholsfield Wlk. N7	47	30 85 D
Nichols Green. W5	54	18 81 D
Nicholson Rd. Croy	105	33 66 D
Nicholson St. SE1	7	31 80 D
Nicola Cl. Har	20	14 90 D
Nicola Cl. S Croy	112	32 63 A
Nicoll Pl. NW4	34	22 88 D
Nicoll Rd. NW10	45	21 83 A
Nicosia Rd. SW18	86	27 73 A
Niederwald Rd. SE26	88	36 71 A
Nigel Cl. Nthlt	43	12 83 A
Nigel Mews. Ilf	61	43 85 B
Nigel Playfair Ave. W6	61	22 78 D
Nigel Rd. E7	50	41 85 C
Nigel Rd. SE15	75	34 75 A
Nigeria Rd. SE7	65	41 77 D
Nightingale Cl. Car	104	28 65 A
Nightingale Cl. W4	61	20 77 A
Nightingale Dri. Eps	109	19 63 B
Nightingale Gr. SE13	76	38 74 B
Nightingale La. Brom	99	41 69 D
Nightingale La. E11	39	40 88 D
Nightingale La. N8	24	30 89 A
Nightingale La. Rich	83	18 73 A
Nightingale La. SW12	74	28 74 C

Nightingale Pl. SE18 ....66 ... 43 77 A
Nightingale Rd. Cars. ...104 ... 27 65 D
Nightingale Rd. E5. ....37 ... 34 86 D
Nightingale Rd. Hamp ...92 ... 13 70 A
Nightingale Rd. N22 ...24 ... 30 91 D
Nightingale Rd. N9. ....18 ... 35 94 D
Nightingale Rd. NW10 ...45 ... 21 83 D
Nightingale Rd. Orp ...108 ... 44 67 C
Nightingale Rd. W7 ....54 ... 15 80 D
Nightingale Sq. SW12 ...86 ... 28 73 A
Nightingale Vale. SE18 ...66 ... 43 77 A
Nightingale Wlk. SW4 ...74 ... 28 74 D
Nile Path. SE18 ....66 ... 43 77 A
Nile Rd. E13 ....50 ... 41 83 C
Nile St. N1 ....4 ... 32 82 B
Nile Terr. SE15 ....63 ... 33 78 D
Nimbus Rd. Eps ...109 ... 20 62 D
Nimegen Way. SE22 ...75 ... 33 74 A
Nimrod Pas. N1 ....48 ... 33 84 A
Nimrod Rd. Houn ...69 ... 07 76 A
Nimrod Rd. SW16 ....96 ... 28 71 D
Nimrod Way. Houn ...69 ... 07 76 A
Nine Acres Cl. E12 ....52 ... 42 85 C
Nine Elms La. SW8 ....70 ... 29 77 B
Nineteenth Rd. Mit. ...96 ... 30 68 C
Nisbet House. E9 ....49 ... 35 85 D
Nithdale Rd. SE18 ....66 ... 43 77 D
Nithsdale Gr. Ruis ....31 ... 08 86 C
Niton Cl. Barn ....11 ... 23 95 A
Niton Rd. Rich ....72 ... 19 75 A
Niton St. SW6 ....62 ... 23 77 D
Nobel Rd. N18 ....18 ... 35 92 A
Noble Cnr. Houn ....70 ... 13 76 A
Noble St EC2 ....4 ... 32 81 C
Noel Park Rd. N22 ....25 ... 31 90 C
Noel Rd. N1 ....48 ... 31 83 D
Noel Rd. W3 ....55 ... 19 81 D
Noel Sq. Dag ....52 ... 47 85 A
Noel St. W1 ....2 ... 29 81 C
Nolan Way. E5. ....48 ... 34 85 A
Nolton Pl. Edg ....21 ... 18 90 B
Nonsuch Cl. Ilf ....28 ... 43 91 B
Nonsuch Court Ave. ...109 ... 22 62 D
Nonsuch Wlk. Sutt. ...110 ... 23 62 D
Nora Gdns. NW4 ....23 ... 23 89 D
Norbiton Ave. King ....94 ... 19 69 C
Norbiton Common Rd. King ...94 ... 19 68 B
Norbiton Hall. King. ...93 ... 18 69 D
Norbiton Rd. E14 ....57 ... 36 81 D
Norbroke St. W12 ....55 ... 21 80 B
Norburn St. W10 ....2 ... 24 81 A
Norbury Ave. Houn ....70 ... 14 75 D
Norbury Ave. SW16 ....96 ... 30 69 B
Norbury Ave. Th Hth. ...97 ... 31 69 D
Norbury Brook. Th Hth ...105 ... 32 67 A
Norbury Cl. SW16 ....96 ... 31 69 A
Norbury Court Rd. SW16 ...96 ... 30 69 C
Norbury Cres. SW16 ....97 ... 31 69 C
Norbury Cross. SW16 ....96 ... 30 68 A
Norbury Gdns. Rom ....41 ... 47 88 B
Norbury Hill. SW16 ....96 ... 31 70 D
Norbury Rd. E4 ....18 ... 37 92 C
Norbury Rd. Th Hth ....97 ... 32 69 C
Norbury Rise. SW16 ....96 ... 30 68 A
Norcombe Gdns. Har ....33 ... 10 88 A
Norcott Cl. Hay ....53 ... 11 82 C
Norcott Rd. N16 ....37 ... 34 86 C
Norcroft Gdns. SE22 ....87 ... 34 73 A
Norcutt Rd. Twick ....83 ... 15 73 C
Nordenfeldt Rd. Eri ....67 ... 50 78 D
Norfolk Ave. N13 ....25 ... 31 91 B
Norfolk Ave. N15 ....37 ... 33 88 D
Norfolk Ave. S Croy ...112 ... 34 62 C
Norfolk Cl. Barn ....12 ... 28 96 C
Norfolk Cl. N13 ....25 ... 31 91 B
Norfolk Cl. N2 ....23 ... 27 89 A
Norfolk Cl. Twick ....71 ... 16 74 D
Norfolk Cres. Sid ....90 ... 45 73 A
Norfolk Cres. W2 ....1 ... 27 81 C
Norfolk Gdns. Bexh. ...79 ... 48 76 B
Norfolk House Rd. SW16 ...86 ... 30 72 C
Norfolk Pl. W2. ....1 ... 26 81 D
Norfolk Pl. Well. ....78 ... 46 76 C
Norfolk Rd. Bark ....51 ... 45 84 C
Norfolk Rd. Barn ....11 ... 25 96 A
Norfolk Rd. Dag ....52 ... 49 85 D
Norfolk Rd. E17 ....26 ... 35 90 D
Norfolk Rd. E6. ....51 ... 43 83 A
Norfolk Rd. Enf ....13 ... 34 95 B
Norfolk Rd. Felt ....82 ... 11 73 C
Norfolk Rd. Har ....32 ... 13 88 B
Norfolk Rd. Ilf ....40 ... 45 87 A
Norfolk Rd. NW10 ....45 ... 21 84 C
Norfolk Rd. NW8 ....26 ... 26 83 B
Norfolk Rd. Rom ....41 ... 50 88 C

Norfolk Rd. SW19 ....96 ... 27 70 A
Norfolk Rd. Th Hth ....97 ... 32 68 A
Norfolk Row. SE11 ....10 ... 30 78 B
Norfolk Sq. Mews. W2 ....1 ... 26 81 D
Norfolk Sq. W2. ....1 ... 26 81 D
Norfolk St. E7 ....50 ... 40 85 C
Norgrove St. SW12 ....86 ... 28 73 A
Norhyrst Ave. SE25 ....97 ... 33 68 B
Norland Pl. W11 ....56 ... 24 80 C
Norland Rd. W11 ....56 ... 23 80 D
Norlands Cres. Chis ...100 ... 43 69 B
Norland Sq. W11 ....56 ... 24 80 C
Norley Vale. SW15 ....84 ... 22 73 C
Norlington Rd. E10 ....38 ... 38 87 C
Norlington Rd. E11 ....38 ... 38 87 D
Norman Ave. Felt. ....82 ... 12 72 B
Norman Ave. N22 ....25 ... 32 90 A
Norman Ave. S Croy ...112 ... 32 62 C
Norman Ave. Sthl ....53 ... 12 80 A
Norman Ave. Twick ....83 ... 17 73 A
Normanby Cl. SW15 ....73 ... 24 74 B
Normanby Rd. NW10 ....45 ... 21 85 B
Normandy Rd. SW9 ....75 ... 31 76 A
Normandy Terr. E16 ....58 ... 40 81 D
Normandy Way. Eri ....80 ... 51 76 A
Norman Gr. E3 ....49 ... 36 83 C
Normanhurst. Ashf ....81 ... 07 71 C
Normanhurst Ave. Bexh ...79 ... 47 76 B
Normanhurst Ave. Well ...79 ... 47 76 B
Normanhurst Dri. Twick ...71 ... 16 74 B
Normanhurst Rd. Orp ...100 ... 46 69 D
Normanhurst Rd. SW2 ....86 ... 30 72 B
Norman Rd. Ashf ....91 ... 08 70 B
Norman Rd. Belv ....67 ... 49 79 B
Norman Rd. E11. ....39 ... 39 86 A
Norman Rd. Horn ....42 ... 52 87 B
Norman Rd. Ilf ....51 ... 43 85 D
Norman Rd. N15 ....37 ... 33 88 B
Norman Rd. SE10 ....64 ... 37 77 D
Norman Rd. Sutt. ...110 ... 25 64 C
Norman Rd. SW19 ....95 ... 26 70 C
Norman Rd. Th Hth ...105 ... 31 67 B
Normans Cl. NW10 ....45 ... 20 84 B
Normansfield Ave. Tedd ...93 ... 17 70 C
Normanshire Dri. E4. ...18 ... 37 92 B
Normans Mead. NW10 ....45 ... 20 84 B
Norman St. EC1 ....4 ... 32 82 A
Normanton Ave. SW19 ....85 ... 25 72 A
Normanton Rd. S Croy ...112 ... 33 63 A
Normanton St. SE23 ....88 ... 35 72 B
Norman Way. N14 ....16 ... 30 93 A
Norman Way. W3 ....55 ... 19 81 B
Normington Cl. SW16 ....87 ... 31 71 C
Norrice Lea. N2 ....23 ... 26 88 B
Norris St. SW1 ....6 ... 29 80 B
Norris Way. Dart. ....80 ... 51 75 B
Norroy Rd. SW15 ....73 ... 23 75 D
Norrys Cl. Barn ....12 ... 27 96 D
Norrys Rd. Barn ....12 ... 27 96 D
Norseman Way. Grnf. ...43 ... 13 83 B
Norstead Pl. SW15 ....84 ... 22 72 C
North Access Rd. E17 ....38 ... 35 88 D
North Acre. NW9 ....22 ... 21 90 A
North Acton Rd. NW. ...55 ... 20 82 B
Northall Rd. Bexh ....79 ... 50 76 C
Northampton Bldgs. EC1 ...3 ... 31 82 C
Northampton Gr. N1 ....48 ... 32 85 D
Northampton Park. N1 ....48 ... 32 84 B
Northampton Rd. Croy ...105 ... 34 65 A
Northampton Rd. EC1 ....3 ... 31 82 C
Northampton Rd. Enf ....14 ... 36 96 C
Northampton Sq. EC1 ....3 ... 31 82 B
Northampton St. N1. ...48 ... 32 84 C
Northanger Rd. SW16 ....96 ... 30 70 A
North Audley St. W1 ....6 ... 28 80 A
North Ave. Cars ...111 ... 24 63 C
North Ave. Har ....32 ... 13 88 D
North Ave. N18 ....17 ... 34 92 A
North Ave. Rich ....72 ... 19 76 A
North Ave. Sthl ....53 ... 12 80 B
North Ave. W10 ....56 ... 23 82 A
North Ave. W13 ....54 ... 16 81 B
North Bank. NW8 ....1 ... 27 82 A
Northbank Rd. E17 ....26 ... 38 90 C
North Birkbeck Rd. E11 ...38 ... 38 86 D
Northborough Rd. SW16 ...96 ... 30 69 C
Northbourne. Brom ...107 ... 40 66 A
Northbourne Rd. SW4 ....74 ... 29 74 B

Northbrook Dri. Nthwd ...19 ... 09 91 C
Northbrook Rd. Barn ....11 ... 24 95 C
Northbrook Rd. Croy ...105 ... 32 67 B
Northbrook Rd. Ilf. ....40 ... 43 86 A
Northbrook Rd. N22 ....24 ... 30 91 C
Northbrook Rd. SE13 ....77 ... 38 74 A
Northburgh St. EC1 ....3 ... 31 82 D
North Carriage Dri. W2 ....5 ... 27 80 A
Northchurch Rd. N1 ....48 ... 32 84 D
Northchurch Rd. Wem ....45 ... 19 84 A
Northchurch Terr. N1 ....48 ... 33 84 C
North Circular Rd. E17 ....26 ... 38 90 A
North Circular Rd. E18 ....27 ... 40 90 A
North Circular Rd. E4. ....26 ... 36 91 B
North Circular Rd. Ilf ....27 ... 42 89 D
North Circular Rd. N11 ....24 ... 29 91 A
North Circular Rd. N12 ....23 ... 26 90 B
North Circular Rd. N12 ....24 ... 27 91 C
North Circular Rd. N13 ....17 ... 31 92 C
North Circular Rd. N18 ....17 ... 34 92 C
North Circular Rd. N3 ....23 ... 25 89 B
North Circular Rd. N3 ....23 ... 25 89 B
North Circular Rd. NW10 ...45 ... 19 84 D
North Circular Rd. NW11 ...35 ... 24 88 A
North Circular Rd. NW2 ....34 ... 22 87 C
North Circular Rd. NW2 ....34 ... 22 87 C
North Circular Rd. W3 ....61 ... 19 79 C
North Circular Rd. Wem ....61 ... 19 78 A
North Circular Rd. Wdf Gn ...27 ... 41 90 D
North Cl. Barn ....11 ... 23 95 A
North Cl. Bexh ....79 ... 47 75 D
North Cl. Dag ....52 ... 49 83 A
North Cl. Felt ....69 ... 08 74 D
Northcliffe Cl. Wor Pk ...102 ... 21 65 C
Northcliffe Dri. N20 ....15 ... 24 94 D
North Cl. Mord ....95 ... 24 68 C
North Common Rd. W5 ....54 ... 18 80 A
Northcote Ave. Islw ....71 ... 16 74 A
Northcote Ave. Sthl ....53 ... 12 80 A
Northcote Ave. Surb ...102 ... 19 66 B
Northcote Ave. W5 ....54 ... 18 80 A
Northcote. Pnr ....20 ... 11 90 C
Northcote Rd. Croy ...105 ... 32 67 D
Northcote Rd. N Mal ....94 ... 20 68 B
Northcote Rd. NW10 ....45 ... 21 84 C
Northcote Rd. Sid ....90 ... 45 71 A
Northcote Rd. SW11 ....74 ... 27 74 B
Northcote Rd. Twick ....71 ... 16 74 A
Northcott Ave. N22 ....24 ... 30 90 A
North Countess Rd. E17 ....26 ... 36 90 B
Northcourt. W1 ....2 ... 29 81 A
North Cres. N3 ....23 ... 24 90 D
North Cres. WC1 ....2 ... 29 81 B
Northcroft Rd. Eps ...109 ... 21 63 C
Northcroft Rd. W13 ....60 ... 16 79 D
North Crofts. SE23 ....87 ... 34 73 D
North Cross Rd. Ilf ....28 ... 44 89 C
North Cross Rd. SE22 ....75 ... 33 74 B
Northdene Gdns. N15 ....37 ... 33 88 D
North Dene. Houn ....70 ... 13 76 B
Northdown Cl. Ruis. ....31 ... 09 86 D
Northdown Gdns. Ilf ....40 ... 45 88 A
Northdown Rd. Horn ....42 ... 52 87 B
Northdown Rd. Sutt. ...110 ... 25 62 C
Northdown Rd. Well ....79 ... 47 76 C
Northdown St. N1 ....47 ... 30 83 D
North Dri. Houn ....70 ... 14 76 C
North Dri. Rom ....30 ... 53 89 A
North Dri. Ruis ....31 ... 09 87 A
North Dri. SW16 ....86 ... 29 71 A
North End Ave. NW3 ....35 ... 26 86 A
North End Cre. W14 ....62 ... 24 78 B
North End. Croy ...105 ... 32 65 A
North End. NW3 ....35 ... 26 86 A
Northend Rd. Eri ....80 ... 51 76 B
North End Rd. NW11 ....35 ... 25 87 D
North End Rd. SW6 ....62 ... 25 77 A
North End Rd. W14 ....62 ... 24 78 D
North End Rd. Wem ....34 ... 19 86 C
North End Way. NW3 ....35 ... 26 86 A
Northern Ave. N9 ....17 ... 33 93 B
Northernhay Wlk. Mord ....95 ... 24 68 C
Northern Perimeter Rd (West).
   Houn ....69 ... 07 76 A
Northern Perimeter Rd. Houn ...69 ... 08 76 B
Northern Rd. E13 ....50 ... 40 83 D
Northey Ave. Sutt. ...110 ... 24 62 C
North Eyot Gdns. W6 ....61 ... 21 78 D
Northey St. E14 ....57 ... 36 80 A
Northfield Ave. Pnr. ....20 ... 11 89 D
Northfield Ave. W13 ....60 ... 16 79 B
Northfield Ave. W5 ....60 ... 17 79 C
Northfield Cres. Sutt. ...110 ... 24 64 A

Name	Page	Ref
Northfield Gdns. Dag	52	48 85 B
Northfield Path. Dag	52	48 85 B
Northfield Rd. Barn	12	27 96 A
Northfield Rd. Dag	52	48 85 B
Northfield Rd. E6	50	42 84 D
Northfield Rd. Enf	13	34 95 B
North Field Rd.Houn	59	11 77 B
Northfield Rd. N16	37	33 87 A
Northfield Rd. W13	60	16 79 B
Northfields W3	55	20 81 A
Northfields SW18	73	25 75 C
North Folgate. E1	4	33 81 A
Northgate. Nthwd	19	08 91 C
North Gdns SW19	95	26 70 D
North Gower St. NW1	7	29 82 A
North Green. NW9	22	21 91 C
North. N15	57	32 88 B
North. Gr. N6	36	28 87 A
North Hatton Rd. Houn	69	08 76 B
North Hill Ave. N6	36	27 88 D
North Hill. N6	36	28 88 C
North Hyde La. Houn	59	12 77 A
North Hyde La. Sthl	59	12 78 C
Northiam. N12	15	25 93 C
Northiam St. E2	48	34 83 B
Northiam St. E9	49	35 83 A
Northington St. WC1	3	30 82 D
Northlands St. SE5	75	32 76 C
North La. Tedd	93	15 70 B
North Lodge Cl. SW15	73	23 74 B
North Mall. N9	17	34 93 B
North Mews. WC1	3	30 82 D
Northolme Gdns. Edg	22	19 90 A
Northolme Rd. N5	48	32 85 A
Northolme Rise. Orp	108	45 65 A
Northolt Ave. Ruis	43	11 85 C
Northolt Gdns. Grnf	44	15 85 D
Northolt Rd. Har	56	14 86 C
Northover. Brom	89	39 72 D
North Park. SE9	78	43 74 C
North Pas. SW18	73	25 75 C
North Pl. Mit	96	27 70 D
North Pl. Tedd	93	15 70 B
North Pole Rd. W10	56	23 81 A
Northport St. N1	48	33 83 A
North Rd. Belv	81	49 79 D
North Rd. Brent	60	18 77 A
North Rd. Brom	99	40 69 B
North Rd. Dart	80	52 74 C
North Rd. Edg	22	19 90 B
North Rd. Felt	69	08 74 D
North Rd. Ilf	37	45 86 A
North Rd. N6	24	27 90 A
North Rd. N6	36	28 87 A
North Rd. N7	47	30 84 A
North Rd. N9	17	34 94 D
North Rd. Rich	72	19 76 C
North Rd. Rom	41	48 88 A
North Rd. SE18	66	45 78 A
North Rd. Sthl	53	13 80 A
North Rd. Surb	101	17 67 D
North Rd. SW19	95	26 70 A
North Rd. W5	60	17 79 D
North Rd. W Wick	106	37 66 D
Northrop Rd. Houn	69	09 76 A
North Row. W1	6	28 80 A
Northside Rd. Brom	99	40 69 A
North Side Wandsworth Common.		
SW18	73	26 74 B
Northspur Rd. Sutt	103	25 65 C
North Sq. N9	17	34 93 B
North Sq. NW11	35	25 88 A
North St. Bark	51	44 84 C
North St. Bexh	79	49 75 C
North St. Brom	99	40 69 A
North St. Cars	111	22 64 B
North St. E13	50	40 83 D
Northstead Rd. SW2	87	31 72 A
North St. Horn	42	53 87 D
North St. Islw	71	16 75 A
North St. NW4	35	23 88 A
North St Pas. E13	50	40 83 D
North St. Rom	29	50 89 D
North St. Rom	29	50 89 D
North St. Rom	42	51 88 A
North St. SW4	74	29 75 A
North Tenter St. E1	4	33 81 D
North Terr. SW3	5	27 79 C
Northumberland Alley. EC3	4	33 81 C
Northumberland Ave. E12	39	41 87 C
Northumberland Ave. Enf	13	34 97 B
Northumberland Ave. Horn	42	53 88 A
Northumberland Ave. Islw	60	16 77 C
Northumberland Ave. WC2	7	30 80 C
Northumberland Ave. Well	78	45 75 A
Northumberland Cl. Eri	67	50 77 C
Northumberland Cres. Felt	69	09 74 C
Northumberland Gdns. Mit	104	29 67 B
Northumberland Gdns. N9	17	33 93 D
Northumberland Gr. N17	25	34 91 D
Northumberland Park. Eri	67	50 77 C
Northumberland Park. N17	25	34 91 C
Northumberland Pl. Rich	71	17 74 B
Northumberland Pl. W2	56	25 81 C
Northumberland Rd. Barn	15	26 94 A
Northumberland Rd. E17	38	37 87 A
Northumberland Rd. Har	32	13 88 A
Northumberland St. WC2	7	30 80 C
Northumberland Way. Eri	79	50 76 B
Northumbria St. E14	57	37 81 C
North Verbena Gdns. W6	61	22 78 C
Northview Cres. NW10	15	21 85 B
Northview Dri. Wdf Gn	27	41 90 D
North View. Pnr	32	11 87 A
North View Rd. N8	24	29 89 B
North View. SW19	85	23 71 C
North View. W5	54	17 82 C
North Villas. NW1	47	29 84 B
Northway. Mord	95	24 68 C
North Way. N11	24	29 91 A
North Way. N9	18	35 93 B
Northway NW11	35	25 88 B
North Way. NW9	22	19 89 B
North Way. Pnr	20	11 89 D
Northway Rd. Croy	105	33 66 B
Northway Rd. SE5	75	32 75 A
Northway. Wall	111	29 64 A
North West Pier. E1	57	34 80 D
Northwest Pl. N1	48	31 83 C
North Wharf Rd. W2	1	24 82 D
Northwick Ave. Har	33	16 88 D
Northwick Circ. Har	33	17 88 C
Northwick Cl. NW8	1	26 82 D
Northwick Park Rd. Har	33	15 88 D
Northwick Rd. Wem	44	17 83 B
Northwick Terr. NW8	1	26 82 D
Northwold Dri. Pnr	20	11 89 A
Northwold Rd. E5	34	36 86 A
Northwold Rd. N16	37	33 86 B
Northwood Gdns. Grnf	44	15 85 D
Northwood Gdns. Ilf	28	43 89 C
Northwood Gdns. N12	15	26 92 D
Northwood Hills Circ. Nthwd	19	10 90 A
Northwood Pl. Belv	67	48 79 D
Northwood Rd. Cars	111	28 63 A
Northwood Rd. N6	36	28 87 B
Northwood Rd. SE23	88	36 73 D
North Wd. Rd. Th Hth	97	32 69 A
Northwood Way. Nthwd	19	10 91 C
Northwood Way. SE19	97	33 70 A
North Woolwich Rd. E16	58	40 80 D
North Worple Way. SW14	72	20 75 B
Norton Ave. Surb	102	19 66 B
Norton Cl. E4	18	37 92 C
Norton Gdns. SW16	96	30 69 C
Norton Rd. Dag	52	50 84 B
Norton Rd. E10	38	36 87 D
Norton Rd. Wem	44	17 84 B
Norval Rd. Wem	33	16 87 D
Norway Pl. E14	57	36 81 D
Norway St. SE10	64	37 77 B
Norwich Rd. E7	50	40 85 C
Norwich Rd. Grnf	43	13 83 B
Norwich Rd. Nthwd	19	09 89 B
Norwich Rd. Th Hth	97	32 68 A
Norwich St. EC4	3	31 81 C
Norwich Wlk. Edg	22	20 91 C
Norwood Ave. Rom	42	51 87 A
Norwood Ave. Wem	44	18 83 D
Norwood Cl. Sthl	59	13 78 A
Norwood Cres. Houn	69	08 76 A
Norwood Dri. Har	32	13 88 C
Norwood Gdns. Hay	53	11 82 C
Norwood Gdns. Sthl	59	12 78 B
Norwood Green Rd. Sthl	59	13 78 A
Norwood High St. SE27	87	32 71 A
Norwood Park Rd. SE27	87	32 71 C
Norwood Rd. SE24	87	31 73 B
Norwood Rd. SE27	87	31 72 B
Norwood Rd. Sthl	59	12 78 B
Notley St. SE5	63	32 77 D
Notson Rd. SE25	97	34 68 D
Notting Barn Rd. W10	56	23 82 D
Nottingdale Sq. W11	56	24 80 C
Nottingham Ave. E16	58	41 81 C
Nottingham Ct. WC2	3	30 81 C
Nottingham Pl. W1	2	28 81 A
Nottingham Rd. E10	38	38 88 C
Nottingham Rd. Islw	71	15 76 D
Nottingham Rd. S Croy	112	32 64 C
Nottingham Rd. SW17	86	27 73 D
Nottingham St. W1	2	28 81 A
Notting Hill Gate. W11	56	25 80 C
Nova Mews. Mord	103	24 66 A
Novar Cl. Orp	108	45 66 B
Nova Rd. Croy	105	32 66 A
Novar Rd. SE9	90	44 73 C
Novello St. SW6	73	25 76 A
Nowell Rd. SW13	61	22 77 A
Nower Hill. Pnr	20	12 89 D
Noyna Rd. SW17	86	27 72 D
Nuding Cl. SE13	76	37 75 A
Nugent Rd. N19	36	30 87 C
Nugent Rd. SE25	97	33 68 B
Nugent's Park. Pnr	20	12 90 C
Nugent Terr. NW8	46	26 83 C
Nun Ct. EC2	4	32 81 D
Nuneaton Rd. Dag	52	48 84 C
Nunhead Cres. SE15	75	34 75 B
Nunhead Gr. SE15	75	35 75 A
Nunhead La. SE15	75	34 75 B
Nunhead Pas. SE15	75	34 75 B
Nunnington Cl. SE9	89	42 72 C
Nunn's Rd. Enf	13	32 97 C
Nupton Dri. Barn	11	23 95 C
Nursery Ave. Bexh	79	48 75 B
Nursery Ave. Croy	106	35 65 B
Nursery Ave. N3	23	26 90 C
Nursery Cl. Croy	106	35 65 B
Nursery Cl. Enf	14	35 97 B
Nursery Cl. Eps	109	21 62 C
Nursery Cl. Felt	81	10 73 B
Nursery Cl. Orp	108	46 66 A
Nursery Cl. Rom	41	47 88 D
Nursery Cl. SW15	73	23 75 D
Nursery Cl. N17	25	33 91 D
Nursery Gdns. Enf	14	35 97 B
Nursery Gdns. Sun	91	09 69 D
Nursery La. E7	50	40 84 B
Nursery La. W10	56	23 81 A
Nursery Rd. E9	49	35 84 A
Nursery Rd. Mit	96	27 68 A
Nursery Rd. N14	16	29 94 A
Nursery Rd. N2	23	26 90 B
Nursery Rd. Pnr	20	11 89 A
Nursery Rd. Sun	91	09 69 D
Nursery Rd. Sutt	110	26 64 A
Nursery Rd. SW19	95	24 70 C
Nursery Rd. SW19	95	25 69 D
Nursery Rd. SW9	74	30 75 D
Nursery Row. Th Hth	97	32 68 D
Nursery Row. Barn	11	24 96 A
Nursery St. N17	25	33 91 D
Nursery The. Eri	68	51 77 D
Nursery Wlk. NW4	23	23 89 A
Nursery Wlk. Rom	41	50 88 D
Nurstead Rd. Eri	67	49 77 C
Nutbourne St. W10	56	24 82 A
Nutbrook St. SE15	75	34 75 A
Nutbrowne Rd. Dag	52	48 83 B
Nutcroft Rd. SE15	63	34 77 D
Nutfield Cl. N18	25	34 91 A
Nutfield Gdns. Ilf	40	46 86 A
Nutfield Gdns. Nthlt	43	11 83 C
Nutfield Pas. Th Hth	97	31 68 D
Nutfield Pl. Th Hth	97	31 68 D
Nutfield Rd. E15	49	38 85 A
Nutfield Rd. NW2	34	22 86 C
Nutfield Rd. SE22	75	33 75 D
Nutfield Rd. Th Hth	97	31 68 D
Nutfield Way. Orp	108	43 65 B
Nutford Pl. W1	1	27 81 D
Nuthurst Ave. SW2	86	30 72 B
Nutley Terr. NW3	46	26 84 B
Nuttall St. N1	48	33 83 C
Nutter La. E11	39	41 88 A
Nutt St. SE15	63	33 77 D
Nutty La. Shep	91	08 68 A
Nutwell St. SW17	86	27 71 C
Nuxley Rd. Belv	67	49 78 B
Nyanza St. SE18	66	44 77 B
Nye Bevan Estate. E5	38	35 86 D
Nylands Ave. Rich	72	19 76 C
Nymans Gdns. SW20	94	22 68 B
Nynehead St. SE14	64	36 77 C
Nyon Gr. SE6	88	36 72 B
Nyssa Cl. Wdf Gn	27	42 91 B
Nyton Cl. N19	36	30 87 C
Oak Ave. Croy	106	37 65 B
Oak Ave. Enf	12	30 97 B
Oak Ave. Hamp	92	12 70 B
Oak Ave. Houn	59	12 77 C
Oak Ave. N10	24	28 91 D

Oak Ave. N17 .....25 33 91 C
Oak Ave. N8 .....24 30 89 C
Oak Ave. Uxb .....31 07 86 B
Oakbank Gr. SE24 .....75 32 75 C
Oakbrook Cl. SE12 .....89 40 71 B
Oakbury Rd. SW6 .....73 25 76 D
Oak Cl. N14 .....16 28 94 B
Oak Cl. Sutt .....103 26 65 A
Oakcombe Cl. N Mal .....94 21 69 A
Oak Cottage Cl. SE6 .....89 39 73 D
Oak Cres. E16 .....58 39 81 A
Oakcroft Cl. Pnr .....19 10 90 D
Oakcroft Rd. Chess .....101 18 65 D
Oakcroft Rd. SE13 .....76 38 76 D
*Oakcroft Villas. Chess .....101 18 65 D
Oakdale Ave. Har .....33 18 88 A
Oakdale Ave. Nthwd .....19 10 90 C
Oakdale. Beck .....98 38 69 A
Oakdale. N14 .....16 28 94 D
Oakdale Rd. E11 .....38 38 86 B
Oakdale Rd. E18 .....27 40 90 D
Oakdale Rd. E7 .....50 40 84 D
Oakdale Rd. Eps .....109 20 62 B
Oakdale Rd. N4 .....37 32 88 D
Oakdale Rd. SE15 .....86 35 75 A
Oakdale Rd. SW16 .....86 30 71 C
Oakdene Ave. Chis .....90 43 71 A
Oakdene Ave. Chis .....90 43 71 C
Oakdene Ave. Eri .....67 50 77 A
Oakdene Ave. Surb .....101 16 66 C
Oak Dene Cl. Horn .....? 52 88 D
Oakdene Cl. Pnr .....20 12 91 D
Oakdene Dri. Surb .....102 20 66 C
Oakdene Park. N3 .....23 24 91 D
Oakdene Rd. Orp .....108 46 67 C
Oak Dene. W13 .....54 16 81 B
Oakden St. SE11 .....73 31 78 A
Oake Ct. SW15 .....? 24 74 A
Oakenshaw Cl. Surb .....101 18 66 A
Oakeshott Av. N6 .....36 28 86 A
Oakey La. SE1 .....? 31 79 C
Oakfield Ave. Har .....21 16 89 B
Oakfield Cl. N8 .....36 30 87 A
Oakfield Cl. N.Mal .....102 21 67 B
Oakfield. E4 .....? 18 92 D
Oakfield Gdns. Beck .....106 37 67 A
Oakfield Gdns. Cars .....104 27 66 D
Oakfield Gdns. Grnf .....53 14 82 B
Oakfield Gdns. N18 .....17 33 92 A
Oakfield Gdns. SE19 .....? 33 71 D
Oakfield Rd. Ashf .....81 07 71 D
Oakfield Rd. Croy .....105 32 66 C
Oakfield Rd. E17 .....26 36 90 C
Oakfield Rd. E6 .....50 42 83 A
Oakfield Rd. Ilf .....? 43 86 D
Oakfield Rd. N14 .....16 30 93 A
Oakfield Rd. N3 .....23 25 90 B
Oakfield Rd. N4 .....37 31 87 A
Oakfield Rd. N8 .....37 31 88 C
Oakfield Rd. Orp .....108 46 66 A
Oakfield Rd. SE20 .....97 34 70 D
Oakfield Rd. SW19 .....85 23 72 D
Oakfields Rd. NW11 .....35 24 88 C
Oakfield St. SW10 .....62 26 77 A
Oakford Rd. NW5 .....47 29 85 A
Oak Gdns. Croy .....106 37 65 A
Oak Gdns. Edg .....22 20 90 C
Oak Glade. Nthwd .....19 07 90 B
Oak Glen. Horn .....30 54 89 A
Oak Gr. NW2 .....46 24 85 A
Oak Grove Rd. SE20 .....98 35 69 C
Oak Gr. Ruis .....31 10 86 D
Oak Gr. Sun .....91 10 70 D
Oak Gr. W Wick .....106 38 66 C
Oakhall Ct. E11 .....39 40 88 D
Oakhall Ct. Sun .....81 09 71 D
Oakhall Dri. Sun .....81 09 71 D
Oak Hall Rd. E11 .....39 40 88 D
Oakham Cl. SE6 .....88 36 72 B
Oakham Dri. Brom .....99 39 68 D
Oakhampton Cl. N12 .....15 26 92 D
Oakhampton Rd. NW7 .....23 23 91 D
Oakhill Ave. NW3 .....46 25 85 B
Oakhill Ave. Pnr .....20 12 90 C
Oak Hill Cl. Wdf Gr .....26 38 91 D
Oak Hill Cres. Surb .....101 18 66 A
Oak Hill Cres. Wdf Gn .....27 39 91 C
Oakhill Ct. SW19 .....95 23 70 D
Oakhill Dri. Surb .....101 18 66 A
Oak Hill Gdns. Wdf Gn .....27 39 90 A
Oak Hill Gr. Surb .....101 18 67 C
Oak Hill Park Mews. NW3 .....46 26 85 A
Oak Hill Pk. NW3 .....46 25 85 B
Oak Hill Path. Surb .....101 18 67 C
Oakhill Pl. SW15 .....73 25 74 A

Oakhill Rd. Beck .....98 38 69 C
Oakhill Rd. Orp .....108 45 65 B
Oak Hill Rd. Surb .....101 18 67 C
Oakhill Rd. Sutt .....? 26 65 C
Oakhill Rd. SW15 .....73 24 74 B
Oakhill Rd. SW15 .....73 25 74 A
Oakhill Rd. SW16 .....96 30 69 B
Oak Hill. Surb .....101 18 66 A
Oak Hill Way. NW3 .....46 25 85 B
Oak Hill. Wdf Gn .....27 39 91 C
Oakhouse Rd. Bexh .....79 49 74 A
Oakhurst Av. Barn .....16 27 94 A
Oakhurst Ave. Bexh .....67 48 77 C
Oakhurst Cl. E17 .....27 39 89 C
Oakhurst Gdns. Bexh .....67 48 77 C
Oakhurst Gdns. E17 .....27 39 89 C
Oakhurst Gr. SE22 .....? 34 75 C
Oakhurst Rise. Cars .....? 27 62 B
Oakington Ave. Har .....32 13 87 A
Oakington Ave. Wem .....33 18 86 D
Oakington Dri. Sun .....92 11 69 C
Oakington Manor Dri. Wem .....45 19 85 C
Oakington Rd. W9 .....56 23 82 B
Oakington Way. N8 .....36 30 87 A
Oak La. E14 .....57 36 80 B
Oak La. Islw .....71 15 75 C
Oak La. N11 .....24 29 91 B
Oak La. N2 .....? 26 90 D
Oaklands Ave. Islw .....60 15 77 B
Oaklands Ave. N9 .....? 34 95 D
Oaklands Ave. Rom .....30 51 89 D
Oaklands Ave. Sid .....? 45 73 B
Oaklands Ave. Th Hth .....97 31 68 C
Oaklands Ave. W Wick .....106 37 65 D
Oaklands Cl. Bexh .....79 48 74 B
Oaklands Cl. Orp .....108 45 67 C
Oaklands Cl. Wem .....44 17 85 D
Oaklands Gate. Nthwd .....19 09 91 A
Oaklands Gr. W12 .....55 22 80 C
Oaklands La. Barn .....? 23 96 C
Oaklands Mews. NW2 .....? 23 85 B
Oaklands. N21 .....16 30 93 B
Oaklands Park Ave. Ilf .....40 44 86 A
Oaklands Pas. NW2 .....46 23 85 B
Oaklands Pl. SW4 .....? 29 75 D
Oaklands Rd. Bexh .....79 48 75 D
Oaklands Rd. Brom .....? 39 70 C
Oaklands Rd. N20 .....15 24 94 B
Oaklands Rd. NW2 .....46 23 85 B
Oaklands Rd. SW14 .....72 20 75 B
Oaklands Rd. W7 .....60 16 79 A
Oaklands. Twick .....82 14 73 A
Oaklands. W13 .....? 16 81 A
Oakland Way. Eps .....109 21 63 A
Oak La. Twick .....83 16 73 A
Oakleafe Gdns. Ilf .....28 43 89 B
Oaklea Pas. King .....93 17 68 B
Oakleigh Ave. Edg .....22 19 90 D
Oakleigh Ave. N20 .....16 27 94 C
Oakleigh Ave. Surb .....102 19 65 A
Oakleigh Cl. N20 .....16 27 93 D
Oakleigh Cres. N20 .....? 27 93 C
Oakleigh Ct. Barn .....12 27 95 C
Oakleigh Ct. Edg .....? 20 90 C
Oakleigh Gdns. N20 .....15 26 94 C
Oakleigh Park Ave. Chis .....100 43 69 A
Oakleigh Park N. N20 .....15 26 94 D
Oakleigh Park S. N20 .....? 27 94 C
Oakleigh Rd. Pnr .....20 12 91 B
Oakleigh Road N. N20 .....15 27 93 A
Oakleigh Road S. N11 .....? 28 92 A
Oakleigh Way. Mit .....96 28 69 B
Oakleigh Way. Surb .....102 19 66 D
Oakley Ave. Bark .....51 45 84 D
Oakley Ave. Croy .....111 30 64 B
Oakley Ave. W5 .....? 19 80 A
Oakley Cl. Islw .....70 14 76 B
Oakley Cl. W7 .....54 15 80 A
Oakley Cres. EC1 .....48 31 83 D
Oakley Dri. Brom .....107 42 65 C
Oakley Dri. SE9 .....? 44 73 D
Oakley Gdns. N8 .....36 30 88 B
Oakley Gdns. SW3 .....? 27 77 A
Oakley Pl. SE1 .....? 33 78 D
Oakley Rd. Brom .....107 42 65 A
Oakleyd. Har .....? 15 88 C
Oakley Rd. N1 .....48 32 84 D
Oakley Rd. SE25 .....105 34 67 B
Oakley Sq. NW1 .....47 29 83 A
Oakley St. SW3 .....? 27 77 A
Oakley Wlk. W6 .....? 23 77 B
Oak Lodge Dri. W Wick .....106 37 66 B
Oakmead Ave. Brom .....107 40 67 C
Oakmeade. Pnr .....? 20 13 91 A

Oakmead Rd. Croy .....104 29 67 D
Oakmead Rd. SW12 .....86 28 73 D
Oakmere Rd. SE2 .....66 46 77 A
Oakmont Pl. Orp .....108 44 66 D
Oak Pl. SW18 .....73 25 74 B
Oak Rd. Eri .....67 50 77 C
Oak Rd. Eri .....80 52 76 C
Oak Rd. N Mal .....94 20 69 D
Oak Rd. Rom .....30 54 90 B
Oakridge Rd. Brom .....89 39 71 A
Oaks Ave. Felt .....82 12 72 A
Oaks Ave. Rom .....29 50 90 C
Oaks Ave. SE19 .....87 33 71 C
Oaks Ave. Wor Pk .....109 22 64 B
Oaksford Ave. SE26 .....87 34 72 D
Oakshade Rd. Brom .....88 38 71 B
Oakshaw Rd. SW18 .....85 25 73 B
Oaks La. Croy .....106 35 65 C
Oaks La. Ilf .....40 45 88 A
Oaks La. Ilf .....28 45 89 C
Oaks The. N12 .....15 25 92 B
Oaks The. Ruis .....31 09 87 A
Oaks The. SE18 .....66 44 78 C
Oaks The. Wdf Gn .....27 39 91 C
Oaks Track. Cars .....111 28 62 C
Oaks Track. Wall .....111 28 62 D
Oak St. Rom .....41 50 88 A
Oak St. Rom .....29 50 89 C
Oaks Way. Cars .....111 27 63 D
Oaks Way. Surb .....101 17 66 B
Oakthorpe Rd. N13 .....17 31 92 C
Oaktree Ave. N13 .....17 31 93 D
Oak Tree Ave. N2 .....23 25 89 B
Oak Tree Cl. Stan .....21 17 91 C
Oak Tree Cl. W5 .....54 17 81 C
Oak Tree Cl. W3 .....55 19 80 B
Oak Tree Dell. NW9 .....34 20 88 B
Oak Tree Dri. N20 .....15 25 94 D
Oak Tree Gdns. Brom .....89 40 71 D
Oak Tree Rd. NW8 .....1 27 82 A
Oakview Gdns. N2 .....23 26 89 D
Oakview Gr. Croy .....106 36 66 C
Oakview Rd. SE6 .....88 37 71 D
Oak Village. NW5 .....? 28 85 A
Oakway. Brom .....98 38 69 D
Oakway Cl. Bex .....? 48 74 C
Oak Way. Croy .....106 35 67 D
Oak Way. Felt .....? 09 73 C
Oak Way. N14 .....16 28 94 B
Oakways. SE9 .....? 43 74 D
Oakway. SW20 .....95 23 68 C
Oak Way. W3 .....55 21 80 C
Oakwood Ave. Beck .....98 38 69 C
Oakwood Ave. Brom .....99 40 68 B
Oakwood Ave. Mit .....95 26 69 D
Oakwood Ave. N14 .....16 29 94 B
Oakwood Ave. Sthl .....53 13 80 A
Oakwood Chase. Horn .....42 54 88 D
Oakwood Cl. Chis .....99 42 70 B
Oakwood Cl. N14 .....12 29 95 C
Oakwood Cl. Wdf Gn .....27 42 91 A
Oakwood Cres. Grnf .....44 16 84 B
Oakwood Cres. N21 .....12 30 95 D
Oakwood Ct. W14 .....62 24 79 D
Oakwood Dri. Bexh .....79 50 75 C
Oakwood Dri. SE19 .....? 33 70 A
Oakwood Gdns. Ilf .....40 45 86 B
Oakwood Gdns. Orp .....108 44 65 A
Oakwood Gdns. Sutt .....103 25 65 A
Oakwood La. W14 .....? 24 79 D
Oakwood Park Rd. N14 .....12 30 95 C
Oakwood Pl. Croy .....105 31 67 C
Oakwood Rd. Croy .....105 31 67 C
Oakwood Rd. NW11 .....35 25 88 B
Oakwood Rd. Orp .....108 44 65 A
Oakwood Rd. Pnr .....19 10 90 D
Oakwood Rd. SW20 .....94 21 68 C
Oakwood. Surb .....101 18 67 D
Oakwood View. N14 .....16 29 94 B
Oakwood. Wall .....111 28 62 B
Oakworth Rd. W10 .....56 23 81 B
Oast House Way. Orp .....108 46 68 D
Oatfield Rd. Orp .....108 45 66 D
Oat La. EC2 .....? 32 81 C
Oatland Rise. E17 .....26 36 90 C
Oatlands Rd. Enf .....14 35 97 A
Oban Rd. E13 .....58 41 82 A
Oban Rd. SE25 .....? 32 68 D
Oban St. E14 .....58 38 81 D
Oberstein Rd. SW11 .....73 26 75 D
Oborne Cl. SE24 .....? 32 74 A
Observatory Gdns. W8 .....62 25 79 A
Observatory Rd. SW14 .....72 20 75 C
Occupation La. SE18 .....78 43 76 B

Name	Page	Grid
Occupation La. W5	60	17 78 B
Occupation Rd. SE17	63	32 78 C
Ocean St. E1	57	35 81 B
Ockendon Rd. N1	48	32 84 B
Ockham Dri. Orp	100	46 70 C
Ockley Ct. Sutt	110	26 64 A
Ockley Rd. Croy	104	30 66 B
Ockley Rd. SW16	86	30 72 C
Octavia Cl. Mit	104	27 67 A
Octavia Rd. Islw	71	15 75 B
Octavia St. SW11	74	27 76 A
Octavius St. SE8	64	37 77 C
Odard Rd. E Mol	92	13 68 C
Odessa Rd. E7	50	40 85 A
Odessa Rd. NW10	45	22 83 C
Odessa St. SE16	74	36 79 D
Odger St. SW11	74	27 76 D
Odhams Wlk. WC2	3	30 81 C
Offa's Mead. E9	89	36 85 A
Offenham Rd. SE9	89	42 71 B
Offerton Rd. SW4	74	29 75 A
Offham Slope. N12	15	24 92 D
Offley Rd. SW9	63	31 77 C
Offord Cl. N1	25	34 91 A
Offord Rd. N1	48	31 84 C
Ogilby St. SE18	65	42 78 B
Oglander Rd. SE15	86	33 75 B
Ogle St. W1	2	29 81 A
Oglethorpe Rd. Dag	41	49 86 C
Ohio Rd. E13	58	39 82 D
Oil Mill La. W6	61	22 78 C
Okeburn Rd. SW17	86	28 71 C
Okehampton Cres. Well	78	46 76 B
Okehampton Rd. NW10	46	23 83 B
Okehampton Rd. Rom	30	53 91 A
Olaf St. W11	61	23 80 B
Old Bailey. EC4	3	31 81 D
Old Barn Cl. Sutt	110	24 63 C
Old Barn Way. Bexh	79	50 75 B
Old Barrack Yd. SW1	6	28 79 A
Old Barrowfield. E15	50	39 83 A
Oldberry Rd. Edg	22	20 91 B
Old Bethnal Green Rd. E2	57	34 82 B
Old Bldgs. WC2	3	31 81 C
Old Bond St. W1	6	29 80 A
Oldborough Rd. Wem	33	17 86 A
Old Brewery Mews. NW3	46	26 85 B
Old Bridge Cl. Nthlt	43	13 83 C
Old Bridge St. King	93	17 69 D
Old Broad St. EC3	4	32 81 C
Old Bromley Rd. Brom	88	38 71 D
Old Brompton Rd. SW5	62	25 78 D
Old Brompton Rd. SW7	62	26 78 B
Old Burlington St. W1	6	29 80 A
Oldbury Pl. W1	2	28 81 A
Oldbury Rd. Enf	13	34 97 C
Old Castle St. E1	4	33 81 D
Old Cavendish St. W1	2	28 81 D
Old Change Ct. EC4	4	32 81 C
Old Charlton Rd. Shep	91	08 68 C
Oldchurch Gdns. Rom	41	50 87 B
Old Church La. NW9	44	20 86 B
Old Church La. Stan	21	17 91 A
Old Church La. Stan	21	17 91 C
Old Church Rd. E1	57	35 81 D
Old Church Rd. E4	18	37 93 A
Oldchurch Rd. Rom	42	51 88 C
Oldchurch Rise. Rom	42	51 87 A
Old Church St. SW3	62	26 78 D
Old Clem Sq. SE18	66	43 77 A
Old Compton St. W1	2	29 81 D
Old Cote Dri. Houn	70	13 77 A
Old Court Pl. W8	62	25 79 B
Old Deer Park Gdns. Rich	71	18 75 A
Old Devonshire Rd. SW12	86	28 73 B
Old Dock Cl. Rich	61	19 77 A
Old Dover Rd. SE3	65	40 77 D
Old Farm Ave. N14	16	29 94 A
Old Farm Ave. Sid	90	45 72 B
Old Farm Cl. Houn	70	12 75 D
Old Farm Pas. Hamp	92	14 69 A
Old Farm Rd E. Sid	90	46 72 A
Old Farm Rd. Hamp	92	12 70 B
Old Farm Rd. N2	23	26 90 B
Old Farm Rd W. Sid	90	45 72 B
Oldfield Cl. Brom	99	42 68 D
Oldfield Cl. Grnf	44	15 84 A
Oldfield Farm Gdns. Grnf	43	14 83 B
Oldfield Gr. SE16	86	35 78 B
Oldfield La. Grnf	53	14 82 A
Oldfield La. Grnf	43	14 83 B
Oldfield Mews. N6	36	29 87 A
Oldfield Rd. Bexh	79	48 76 C
Oldfield Rd. Brom	99	42 68 D
Oldfield Rd. Hamp	92	12 69 B
Oldfield Rd. N16	37	33 86 C
Oldfield Rd. NW10	45	21 84 D
Oldfield Rd. SW19	95	24 70 A
Oldfield Rd. W3	61	21 79 B
Oldfields Circ. Nthlt	43	14 84 A
Oldfields Rd. Sutt	103	25 65 A
Old Fish St Hill. EC4	8	32 80 A
Old Fold Cl. Barn	11	24 97 B
Old Fold La. Barn	11	24 97 B
Old Fold View. Barn	11	23 96 A
Old Ford Rd. E2	49	35 83 C
Old Ford Rd. E2	49	36 83 A
Old Forge Way. Sid	90	46 71 B
Old Fox Footpath. S Croy	112	33 62 A
Old Gloucester St. WC1	3	30 81 A
Old Hall Cl. Pnr	20	12 90 A
Old Hall Dri. Pnr	20	12 90 A
Oldham Terr. W3	61	20 79 A
Old Hatch Manor. Ruis	31	10 87 A
Old Hill. Chis	43	43 69 A
Oldhill St. N16	37	34 87 C
Old Homestead Rd. Brom	99	41 68 C
Old House Cl. Eps	109	21 67 D
Old House Cl. SW19	85	24 71 C
Old Howlett's La. Ruis	31	08 88 D
Old Jamaica Rd. SE16	63	34 79 C
Old James St. SE15	75	34 75 B
Old Jewry. EC2	4	32 81 D
Old Kenton La. NW9	34	19 88 B
Old Kent Rd. SE15	63	34 77 B
Old Kent Rd. SE1	63	33 78 D
Old Kingston Rd. Wor Pk	102	20 65 C
Old Malden La. Wor Pk	102	21 65 A
Old Manor Dri. Islw	70	14 74 C
Old Manor Way. Bexh	79	50 76 D
Old Manor Yd. SW5	62	25 78 B
Old Market Sq. E2	4	33 82 B
Old Marylebone Rd. NW1	1	27 81 A
Old Mill Ct. E18	27	41 89 A
Old Mill Rd. SE18	66	44 77 B
Old Montague St. E1	57	34 81 A
Old Nichol St. E2	4	33 82 D
Old North St. WC1	3	30 81 B
Old Oak Common La. NW10	55	21 82 C
Old Oak Common La. W3	55	21 81 D
Old Oak La. NW10	55	21 82 B
Old Oak Rd. W12	65	21 80 B
Old Orchard. Sun	92	11 69 C
Old Palace La. Rich	71	17 74 A
Old Palace Rd. Croy	105	32 65 C
Old Palace Yd. Rich	71	17 74 B
Old Paradise St. SE11	10	30 78 B
Old Park Ave. Enf	13	32 96 C
Old Park Ave. SW12	74	28 74 C
Old Park Gr. Enf	13	32 96 C
Old Park La. W1	6	28 80 D
Old Park Mews. Houn	59	12 77 D
Old Park Rd. Enf	13	31 96 D
Old Park Rd. N13	16	30 92 B
Old Park Rd. SE2	66	46 78 C
Old Park Ridings. N21	13	32 95 A
Old Park Vw. Enf	13	31 96 B
Old Perry St. Chis	100	45 70 C
Old Pye St. SW1	6	29 79 D
Old Quebec St. W1	1	27 81 D
Old Queen St. SW1	6	29 79 B
Old Rd. Bexh	79	50 75 D
Old Rd. Enf	14	35 97 A
Old Rd. SE13	77	39 75 C
Old Rectory Gdns. Edg	22	19 91 A
Oldridge Rd. SW12	86	28 73 B
Old Rope Wlk. Sun	91	10 68 B
Old Rope Wlk. Sun	9	11 68 A
Old Ruislip Rd. Nthlt	43	11 83 C
Old Schools La. Eps	109	21 62 B
Old Seacoal La. EC4	3	31 81 D
Old South Lambeth Rd. SW8	10	30 77 C
Old Sq. WC2	3	31 81 C
Old St. E13	50	41 83 C
Oldstead Rd. Brom	88	38 71 B
Old St. EC1	4	32 82 D
Old Swan Yd. Cars	111	27 64 B
Old Town. Croy	105	31 65 B
Old Town. SW4	74	29 75 A
Old Tranyard. SE18	66	45 78 A
Old Woolwich Rd. SE10	64	38 78 D
O'Leary Pl. E1	57	35 81 A
Oley Pl. E1		35 81 B
Olga St. E3	49	36 83 C
Olinda Rd. N16	37	33 88 D
Oliphant St. W10	56	23 82 B
Oliver Ave. SE25	97	33 68 B
Oliver Cl. E10	38	37 86 B
Oliver Ct. SE18	66	44 78 A
Olive Rd. E13	58	41 82 A
Olive Rd. NW2	46	23 85 A
Olive Rd. SW19	95	26 70 C
Olive Rd. W5	60	17 79 D
Oliver Gr. SE25	97	33 68 D
Oliver Rd. E10	38	37 86 D
Oliver Rd. E17	38	38 88 A
Oliver Rd. N Mal	94	20 69 C
Oliver Rd. Sutt	110	26 64 B
Oliver's Yd. EC2	4	32 82 D
Olive St. Rom	41	50 88 B
Olivette St. SW15	73	23 75 B
Ollerton Green. E3	49	36 83 B
Ollerton Rd. N11	16	29 92 D
Olley Cl. Wall	111	30 63 C
Ollgar Cl. W12	55	21 80 D
Olliffe St. E14	64	38 79 C
Olmar St. SE1	63	34 77 A
Olney Rd. SE17	63	32 77 A
Olorane Gdns. NW3	35	25 86 C
Olron Cres. Bexh	79	48 74 A
Olven Rd. SE18	66	44 77 A
Olveston Wlk. Cars	103	26 67 D
Olyffe Ave. Well	78	46 76 C
Olyffe Dri. Beck	98	38 69 A
Olympia Wy. W14	62	24 79 C
Olympia Yd. W2	56	25 80 B
Olympic Way. Grnf	43	13 83 B
Olympic Way. Wem	45	19 85 A
Omeara St. SE1	8	32 80 C
Omega Pl. N1	47	30 83 C
Omega St. SE14	76	37 76 A
Ommaney Rd. SE14	76	36 76 A
Ondine Rd. SE15	75	33 75 D
O'Neill Path. SE18	66	43 77 A
One Tree Cl. SE23	76	35 74 C
Ongar Cl. Rom	41	47 88 A
Ongar Rd. SW6	62	25 77 A
Onra Rd. E17	38	37 87 A
Onslow Ave. Rich	71	18 74 A
Onslow Ave. Sutt	110	24 62 D
Onslow Cl. E4	18	38 93 B
Onslow Cl. Surb	101	15 66 C
Onslow Cres. Chis	100	43 69 B
Onslow Gdns. E18	27	41 89 A
Onslow Gdns. N10	36	28 88 B
Onslow Gdns. N21	13	31 95 A
Onslow Gdns. Surb	101	15 66 C
Onslow Gdns. Wall	111	29 63 C
Onslow Mews E. SW7	62	26 78 B
Onslow Mews. SW7	62	26 78 B
Onslow Rd. Croy	105	31 66 A
Onslow Rd. N Mal	94	22 68 C
Onslow Rd. Rich	71	18 74 C
Onslow Sq. SW7	62	26 78 B
Onslow St. EC1	3	31 82 C
Onslow Way. Surb	101	15 66 C
Onslow Gdns. SW7	62	26 78 D
Ontario St. SE1	7	31 79 D
Opal Mews. Ilf	40	43 86 B
Opal St. SE11	63	31 78 D
Openshaw Rd. SE2	66	46 78 B
Openview. SW18	85	26 72 B
Ophir Terr. SE15	75	34 76 A
Opossum Dri. Houn	70	11 75 A
Oppidans Rd. NW3	47	27 84 D
Orange Ct. E1	57	34 80 C
Orange Hill Rd. Edg	22	20 91 C
Orange Pl. SE16	64	35 79 C
Orange Row. E1	57	34 81 A
Orangery La. SE9	77	42 74 B
Orange St. WC2	6	29 80 B
Orange Yd. W1	2	29 81 D
Oratory La. SW3	9	27 78 C
Orbain Rd. SW6	62	24 77 C
Orbel St. SW11	74	27 76 A
Orb St. SE17	63	32 78 B
Orchard Ave. Ashf	91	08 70 A
Orchard Ave. Belv	67	48 77 B
Orchard Ave. Croy	106	33 66 C
Orchard Ave. Felt	69	08 74 B
Orchard Ave. Houn	59	12 77 C
Orchard Ave. Mit	104	28 66 C
Orchard Ave. N14	16	29 94 A
Orchard Ave. N20	15	26 93 B
Orchard Ave. N3	23	25 89 A
Orchard Ave. N Mal	94	21 68 A
Orchard Ave. Sthl	53	12 80 D
Orchard Ave. Surb	101	16 65 A
Orchard Cl. Ashf	91	08 70 A
Orchard Cl. Bexh	79	48 76 A
Orchard Cl. Edg	21	18 91 A
Orchard Cl. Ruis	31	08 87 A
Orchard Cl. Surb	101	16 66 B
Orchard Cl. SW20	95	23 68 C

Orchard Cl. Wem ... 44 18 83 A
Orchard Cres. Enf ... 13 33 97 B
Orchard Ct. Wor Pk ... 102 22 66 C
Orchard Dri. SE3 ... 77 39 76 C
Orchard Gate. Grnf ... 44 16 84 B
Orchard Gate. NW9 ... 22 21 89 C
Orchard Gr. Croy ... 106 36 66 A
Orchard Gr. Edg ... 22 19 90 B
Orchard Green. Orp ... 108 45 65 A
Orchard Gr. Har ... 33 18 88 B
Orchard Gr. Orp ... 108 45 66 D
Orchard Hill. Dart ... 80 51 74 A
Orchard Hill. SE13 ... 76 37 76 B
Orchard La. SW20 ... 94 22 69 B
Orchardleigh Ave. Enf ... 14 35 97 C
Orchardmede. N21 ... 7 32 95 D
Orchard Pl. E14 ... 58 39 81 C
Orchard Pl. N17 ... 25 33 91 D
Orchard Rd. Barn ... 11 24 96 D
Orchard Rd. Belv ... 67 49 78 A
Orchard Rd. Brent ... 60 17 77 A
Orchard Rd. Brom ... 99 41 69 A
Orchard Rd. Dag ... 52 49 83 A
Orchard Rd. Enf ... 14 35 95 A
Orchard Rd. Hamp ... 92 13 70 C
Orchard Rd. Houn ... 70 12 74 B
Orchard Rd. King ... 93 18 69 C
Orchard Rd. Mit ... 104 28 66 C
Orchard Rd. N6 ... 36 28 87 B
Orchard Rd. Rich ... 72 19 75 A
Orchard Rd. Rom ... 29 49 90 D
Orchard Rd. Sid ... 90 45 71 A
Orchard Rd. Sun ... 91 10 70 D
Orchard Rd. Sutt ... 110 25 64 A
Orchard Rd. Twick ... 71 16 74 B
Orchard Rd. Well ... 78 46 75 B
Orchard Rise. Croy ... 106 36 66 D
Orchard Rise E. Sid ... 78 45 74 B
Orchard Rise. King ... 94 20 69 A
Orchard Rise. Rich ... 72 19 75 D
Orchard Rise W. Sid ... 78 45 74 A
Orchardson St. NW8 ... 1 26 82 D
Orchard Sq. W14 ... 62 24 78 D
Orchard St. Dart ... 80 54 74 C
Orchard St. E17 ... 26 36 89 C
Orchard St. W1 ... 2 28 81 C
Orchard The. Eps ... 109 21 63 D
Orchard The. Houn ... 70 14 76 C
Orchard The. N21 ... 7 32 95 D
Orchard The. NW11 ... 35 25 88 A
Orchard The. SE3 ... 76 38 76 D
Orchard The. W4 ... 61 20 78 B
Orchard Way. Beck ... 106 36 67 B
Orchard Way. Croy ... 106 36 66 A
Orchard Way. Enf ... 13 33 96 A
Orchard Way. Sutt ... 110 26 64 B
Orchid Rd. N14 ... 16 29 94 A
Orchid St. W12 ... 55 22 80 A
Orchis Way. Rom ... 30 54 91 B
Orde Hall St. WC1 ... 3 30 81 B
Ordell Rd. E3 ... 49 36 83 D
Ordnance Cl. Felt ... 81 10 72 A
Ordnance Cres. SE10 ... 65 39 79 A
Ordnance Hill. NW8 ... 46 26 83 D
*Ordnance Mews. NW8 ... 46 26 83 D
Ordnance Rd. E16 ... 58 39 81 B
Ordnance Rd. SE18 ... 66 43 77 A
Oregon Ave. E12 ... 50 42 85 B
Oregon Sq. Orp ... 108 44 66 D
Orford Gdns. Twick ... 83 15 72 B
Orford Rd. E17 ... 38 37 88 B
Orford Rd. E17 ... 26 37 89 D
Orford Rd. E18 ... 27 40 89 B
Organ La. E4 ... 18 38 93 A
Oriel Ct. NW3 ... 46 26 85 A
Oriel Gdns. Ilf ... 27 42 89 B
Oriel Pl. NW3 ... 46 26 85 A
Oriel Rd. E9 ... 49 36 84 A
Oriel Way. Nthlt ... 43 13 84 D
Oriental Rd. E16 ... 58 41 80 D
Oriental St. E14 ... 57 37 80 A
Orient St. SE11 ... 63 31 78 B
Orient Way E5 ... 38 35 86 D
Orissa Rd. SE18 ... 66 45 78 C
Orkney St. SW11 ... 74 28 76 C
Orlando Gdns. Eps ... 109 20 62 D
Orlando Rd. SW4 ... 74 29 75 A
Orleans Ct. Twick ... 83 16 73 B
Orleans Rd. SE19 ... 97 32 70 B
Orleans Rd. Twick ... 83 17 73 A
Orleston Mews. N7 ... 48 31 84 A
Orleston Rd. N7 ... 48 31 84 A
Orley Farm Rd. Har ... 33 15 86 C
Orlop St. E10 ... 65 39 78 C
Ormanton Rd. SE26 ... 87 34 71 A

Orme Ct Mews. W2 ... 56 25 80 B
Orme Ct. W2 ... 56 25 80 B
Orme La. W2 ... 56 25 80 B
Ormeley Rd. SW12 ... 86 28 73 D
Orme Rd. King ... 94 19 69 D
Ormerod Gdns. Mit ... 96 28 69 A
Ormesby Way. Har ... 33 18 88 B
Orme Sq. W2 ... 56 25 80 B
Ormiston Gr. W12 ... 55 22 80 D
Ormiston Rd. SE10 ... 65 40 78 C
Ormond Ave. Hamp ... 92 13 69 B
*Ormond Ave. Rich ... 71 17 74 B
Ormond Cl. WC1 ... 3 30 81 A
Ormond Cres. Hamp ... 92 13 69 B
Ormond Dri. Hamp ... 92 13 70 D
Ormonde Ave. Eps ... 109 20 62 D
Ormonde Ave. Orp ... 108 44 65 A
Ormonde Gate. SW3 ... 9 27 78 D
Ormonde Pl. SW1 ... 9 28 78 A
Ormonde Rd. SW14 ... 72 20 75 A
Ormonde Terr. NW8 ... 47 27 83 B
Ormond Mews. WC1 ... 3 30 82 C
Ormond Rd. N19 ... 36 30 87 C
Ormond Rd. Rich ... 71 17 74 B
Ormond Yd. SW1 ... 9 29 80 C
Ormsby Gdns. Grnf ... 43 14 83 C
Ormsby Pl. N16 ... 37 33 86 D
Ormsby St. E2 ... 48 33 83 D
Ormsby. Sutt ... 110 25 63 D
Ormside St. SE15 ... 64 35 77 A
Ornan Rd. NW3 ... 47 27 85 C
Oronsay Wlk. N1 ... 48 32 84 B
Orpen Wlk. N16 ... 37 33 86 C
Orpheus St. SE5 ... 75 32 76 B
Orpington Gdns. N18 ... 17 33 93 C
Orpington Rd. Chis ... 100 45 68 A
Orpington Rd. N21 ... 7 31 94 D
Orpwood Cl. Hamp ... 92 12 70 B
Orsett St. SE11 ... 10 30 78 D
Orsett Terr. W2 ... 1 26 81 C
Orsett Terr. Wdf Gn ... 27 41 91 C
Orsman Rd. N1 ... 48 33 83 A
Orton St. E1 ... 57 34 80 C
Orville Rd. SW11 ... 73 26 76 D
Orwell Ct. E8 ... 48 34 83 A
Osbaldeston Rd. N16 ... 37 34 87 C
Osberton Rd. SE12 ... 77 40 74 A
Osbert St. SW1 ... 10 29 78 B
Osborn Cl. E8 ... 48 34 83 A
Osborne Cl. Beck ... 98 36 68 C
Osborne Cl. Felt ... 82 11 71 C
Osborne Cl. Horn ... 42 52 88 D
Osborne Cl. Surb ... 101 18 67 C
Osborne Cl. W5 ... 54 18 81 A
Osborne Gdns. NW7 ... 23 23 91 D
Osborne Gdns. Th Hth ... 97 32 69 C
Osborne Gr. E17 ... 26 36 89 D
Osborne Pl. Sutt ... 110 26 64 D
Osborne Rd. Belv ... 67 48 77 B
Osborne Rd. Dag ... 52 48 85 D
Osborne Rd. E10 ... 38 37 86 B
Osborne Rd. E7 ... 40 40 85 D
Osborne Rd. E9 ... 49 36 84 B
Osborne Rd. Enf ... 14 36 97 C
Osborne Rd. Horn ... 42 53 88 C
Osborne Rd. Houn ... 70 12 75 B
Osborne Rd. King ... 93 18 70 C
Osborne Rd. N13 ... 7 31 93 C
Osborne Rd. N4 ... 37 31 87 C
Osborne Rd. NW2 ... 45 22 84 B
Osborne Rd. Sthl ... 53 14 81 C
Osborne Rd. Th Hth ... 97 32 69 C
Osborne Rd. W3 ... 61 19 79 B
Osborne Sq. Dag ... 52 48 85 B
Osborn La. SE23 ... 88 36 73 A
Osborn St. E1 ... 57 33 81 B
Osborn St. E1 ... 57 34 81 C
Osborn Terr. SE3 ... 76 39 75 D
Oscar St. SE8 ... 76 37 76 A
Oscar St. SE8 ... 76 37 76 C
Oseney Cres. NW5 ... 47 29 84 B
O'Shea Gr. E3 ... 49 36 83 B
Osidge La. N14 ... 16 28 94 D
Osiers Rd. SW18 ... 73 25 75 C
Osier St. E1 ... 57 35 82 C
Osier Way. E10 ... 38 37 86 D
Osier Way. Mit ... 104 27 67 B
Oslac Rd. SE6 ... 88 37 71 D
Osman Cl. N15 ... 37 32 88 D
Osman Rd. N9 ... 17 34 93 C
Osman Rd. W6 ... 62 23 79 C
Osmond Cl. Har ... 32 14 86 A
Osmond Gdns. Wall ... 111 29 64 C
Osmund St. W12 ... 55 21 81 B
Osnaburgh St. NW1 ... 2 28 82 D

Osnaburgh Terr. NW1 ... 2 28 82 D
Osney Wlk. Cars ... 103 26 67 D
Ospringe Cl. SE9 ... 78 44 74 D
Ospringe Rd. NW5 ... 47 29 85 A
Osric Path. N1 ... 48 33 83 C
Ossian Rd. N4 ... 36 30 87 B
Ossington Bldgs. W1 ... 2 28 81 A
Ossington Cl. W2 ... 56 25 80 A
Ossington St. W2 ... 56 25 80 B
Ossory Rd. SE15 ... 63 34 77 A
Ossulston St. NW1 ... 2 29 82 B
Ossulston St. NW1 ... 2 29 82 B
Ostade Rd. SW2 ... 86 30 73 B
Ostend Pl. SE17 ... 63 32 78 A
Osten Mews. SW7 ... 62 25 79 D
Osterberg Rd. Dart ... 80 54 75 D
Osterley Ave. Islw ... 59 14 77 D
Osterley Cres. Islw ... 71 15 76 B
Osterley Ct. Islw ... 70 14 76 B
Osterley Ct. Islw ... 59 14 77 D
Osterley La. Islw ... 59 14 78 A
Osterley La. Sthl ... 53 13 78 D
Osterley Park Rd. Sthl ... 59 12 79 D
Osterley Park View Rd. W7 ... 60 15 79 A
Osterley Rd. Islw ... 59 15 77 C
Osterley Rd. N16 ... 48 33 85 A
Osterly Gdns. Th Hth ... 97 32 69 C
Oswald's Mead. E9 ... 49 36 85 A
Oswald St. E5 ... 38 35 86 D
Oswald Pl. N9 ... 17 34 93 B
Osward Rd. SW17 ... 85 27 72 B
Oswin St. SE11 ... 63 31 78 B
Oswin St. SE11 ... 7 31 79 D
Oswyth Rd. SE5 ... 75 33 76 C
Otford Cl. Bex ... 79 49 74 D
Otford Cl. Brom ... 100 43 68 A
Otford Cres. SE4 ... 76 36 74 D
Othello Cl. SE11 ... 63 31 78 D
Otho Ct. Brent ... 60 17 77 D
Otis St. E3 ... 50 38 82 A
Otley App. Ilf ... 40 43 88 D
Otley Dri. Ilf ... 40 43 88 D
Otley Rd. E16 ... 58 41 81 C
Otley Terr. E5 ... 38 35 86 D
Ottawa Gdns. Dag ... 52 50 84 D
Ottaway St. E5 ... 38 34 86 C
Otterbourne Rd. Croy ... 105 32 65 A
Otterbourne Rd. E4 ... 18 38 93 D
Otterburn Gdns. Islw ... 60 16 77 C
Otterburn St. SW17 ... 96 27 70 B
Otterden St. SE6 ... 88 37 71 A
Otter Rd. Grnf ... 53 14 82 C
Otto Cl. SE26 ... 87 34 72 D
Otto St. SE17 ... 63 31 77 B
Oulton Cl. E5 ... 38 35 86 A
Oulton Cres. Bark ... 51 45 85 D
Oulton Rd. N15 ... 37 32 88 B
Ouseley Rd. SW12 ... 86 27 73 D
Outer Circ. NW1 ... 1 27 82 D
Outgate Rd. NW10 ... 45 21 84 D
Outram Pl. N1 ... 47 30 83 A
Outram Rd. Croy ... 106 33 65 B
Outram Rd. E6 ... 50 42 83 A
Outram Rd. N22 ... 24 29 90 B
Outwich St. EC3 ... 4 33 81 C
Oval Pl. SW8 ... 10 30 77 D
Oval Rd. Croy ... 105 33 66 C
Oval Rd. NW1 ... 47 28 83 B
Oval Road N. Dag ... 52 49 83 B
Oval Road S. Dag ... 52 49 83 D
Oval The. E2 ... 48 34 83 D
Oval The. Sid ... 90 46 73 A
Oval Way. SE11 ... 10 30 77 B
Overbrae. Beck ... 88 37 71 C
Overbrook Wlk. Edg ... 22 19 91 C
Overbury Ave. Beck ... 98 38 68 A
Overbury Rd. N15 ... 37 32 88 D
Overbury St. E5 ... 49 35 85 B
Overcliff Rd. SE13 ... 76 35 75 A
Overcourt Cl. Sid ... 78 46 74 D
Overdale Ave. N Mal ... 94 20 69 D
Overdale Rd. W5 ... 60 17 79 C
Overdown Rd. SE6 ... 88 37 71 B
Overhill Rd. Pur ... 112 31 62 C
Overhill Rd. SE22 ... 87 34 73 A
Overhill Way. Beck ... 106 38 67 B
Overlea Rd. E5 ... 37 34 87 A
Overmead. Sid ... 90 44 73 B
Overstand Cl. Beck ... 106 37 67 A
Overstone Gdns. Croy ... 106 36 66 B
Overstone Rd. W6 ... 62 23 78 A
Over Strand. NW9 ... 22 21 90 B
Overton Cl. Islw ... 71 15 76 B

Overton Cl. NW10	45	20 84 A	Padbury Ct. E2	4	33 82 B	Palamos Rd. E10	38	37 87 C
Overton Dri. E11	39	40 87 B	Paddenswick Rd. W6	61	22 79 C	Palatine Ave. N16	48	33 85 B
Overton Dri. Rom	41	47 87 A	Paddington Green. W2	1	26 81 B	Palatine Rd. N16	48	33 85 A
Overton Rd. E10	38	36 87 C	Paddington St. W1	2	28 81 A	Palemo Rd. NW10	44	22 83 C
Overton Rd. N14	12	30 95 A	Paddock Cl. Nthlt	43	13 83 C	Palestine Gr. SW19	95	26 69 B
Overton Rd. SE2	67	47 79 D	Paddock Cl. SE26	88	35 71 B	Palewell Cl. Orp	100	46 69 D
Overton Rd. Sutt	110	25 63 C	Paddock Gdns. SE19	88	33 70 A	Palewell Common Dri. SW14	72	20 74 B
Overton Rd. SW9	75	31 76 C	Paddock Rd. NW2	34	22 86 A	Palewell Park. SW14	72	20 75 D
Overton's Yd. Croy	105	32 65 C	Paddock Rd. Ruis	32	11 86 D	Palfrey Pl. SW8	10	30 77 D
Overy St. Dart	80	54 74 C	Paddocks Cl. Har	43	13 85 B	Palfrey Pl. SW8	63	31 77 C
Ovesdon Ave. Har	32	12 87 D	Paddocks The. Barn	12	27 96 B	Palgrave Ave. Sthl	53	13 80 A
Ovett Cl. SE19	97	33 70 A	Paddocks The. Wem	34	19 86 B	Palgrave Rd. W12	61	21 79 D
Ovex Cl. E14	64	38 79 A	Paddock Way. Chis	100	44 70 D			
Ovington Gdns. SW3	5	27 79 C	Paddock Rd. Bexh	79	48 75 C	Palissy St. E2	4	33 82 B
Ovington Mews. SW3	5	27 79 C	Padfield Rd. SE5	75	32 75 A	Pallant Way. Orp	108	43 65 C
Ovington Sq. SW3	5	27 79 C	Padnall Ct. Rom	29	47 89 B	Pallet Way. SE18	77	42 76 A
Ovington St. SW3	9	27 78 B	Padnall Rd. Rom	29	47 89 B	Palliser Rd. W14	62	24 78 C
Owen Gdns. Wdf Gn	27	42 91 A	Padnall Rd. Rom	29	47 89 D	Pall Mall E. SW1	3	29 80 D
Owenite St. SE2	66	46 78 B	Padstow Rd. Enf	13	31 97 B	Pall Mall Pl. SW1	6	29 80 C
Owen Rd. Hay	53	11 82 A	Padua Rd. SE20	98	35 69 A	Pall Mall. SW1	6	29 80 D
Owen Rd. N13	17	32 92 C	Pagden St. SW8	74	28 76 B	Palmar Cres. Bexh	79	49 76 C
Owen's Ct. EC1	3	31 82 B	Pageant Strs. SE16	57	36 80 C	Palmar Rd. Bexh	79	49 76 C
Owen's Row. EC1	3	31 82 B	Pageant Wlk. Croy	105	33 65 C	Palmeira Rd. Bexh	79	47 75 B
Owen St. EC1	48	31 83 D	Page Cl. Hamp	92	12 70 A	Palmer Ave. Sutt	110	23 64 A
Owens Way. SE23	88	36 73 A	Page Cl. Har	33	18 88 D	Palmer Cl. Houn	70	13 76 A
Owen Way. NW10	45	20 84 A	Page Cres. Croy	112	31 64 D	Palmer Cres. King	93	18 68 A
Owgan Cl. SE5	63	32 77 D	Page Cres. Eri	68	51 77 D	Palmer Pl. N5	48	31 85 C
Owlets Hall Cl. Horn	30	54 89 B	Page Green Rd. N15	37	34 88 A	Palmer Rd. E13	58	40 82 D
Oxberry Ave. SW6	73	24 76 C	Page Green Terr. N15	37	33 88 B	Palmers Dri. & E Mol	92	13 68 C
Oxendon St. SW1	6	29 80 B	Page Heath La. Brom	99	41 68 B	Palmers La. Enf	14	35 97 A
Oxenford St. SE15	75	33 75 B	Page Heath Villas	99	41 68 B	Palmers Pas. SW14	72	20 75 A
Oxenpark Ave. Wem	33	18 87 A	Page High. N22	25	31 89 A	Palmer's Rd. E2	49	35 83 D
Oxestalls Rd. SE8	64	36 78 C	Pagehurst Rd. Croy	105	34 66 B	Palmer's Rd. N11	16	29 92 C
Oxford Ave. Hay	69	09 76 B	Page Rd. Felt	81	08 73 B	Palmers Rd. SW14	72	20 75 A
Oxford Ave. Houn	69	13 78 C	Page's Hill. N10	24	28 90 C	Palmerston Cres. N13	16	30 92 D
Oxford Ave. SW20	24	24 69 C	Page's La. N10	24	28 90 C	Palmerston Cres. SE18	66	44 77 A
Oxford Ave. W10	56	23 82 A	Pages La. N10	24	28 90 C	Palmerston Ct. Surb	101	17 66 B
Oxford Circus Ave. W1	2	29 81 C	Pages St. NW7	22	22 91 C	Palmerston Gr. SW19	95	25 70 C
Oxford Circ. W1	2	29 81 C	Page's Wlk. SE1	63	33 78 A	Palmerston Rd (off Hemstal Rd)		
Oxford Cl. Ashf	91	08 70 C	Page's Yd. W4	61	21 77 A	NW6	46	25 84 C
Oxford Cl. Mit	96	29 68 A	Paget Ave. Sutt	103	26 65 D	Palmerston Rd (off Kilburn High		
Oxford Cl. N9	17	34 93 B	Paget Cl. Hamp	82	14 71 B	Rd). NW6	46	24 84 D
Oxford Cres. N.Mal	102	20 67 D	Paget Gdns. Chis	100	43 69 B	Palmerston Rd. Cars	111	27 64 B
Oxford Ct. EC4	8	32 80 B	Paget Rd. Ilf	51	43 85 B	Palmerston Rd. E17	26	36 89 D
Oxford Ct. W3	55	19 81 C	Paget Rd. N16	37	32 87 D	Palmerston Rd. E7	50	40 84 B
Oxford Dri. Ruis	32	11 86 B	Paget Rise. SE18	66	43 77 C	Palmerston Rd. Har	21	15 89 B
Oxford Gdns. N20	15	26 94 D	Paget St. EC1	3	31 82 B	Palmerston Rd. N22	25	30 91 B
Oxford Gdns. N21	17	32 94 A	Paget Terr. SE18	66	43 77 A	Palmerston Rd. Sutt	110	26 64 C
Oxford Gdns. W10	56	23 81 D	Pagnell St. SE14	64	36 77 D	Palmerston Rd. SW14	72	20 75 A
Oxford Gdns. W4	61	19 77 B	Pagoda Ave. Rich	71	18 75 B	Palmerston Rd. SW19	95	25 70 C
Oxford Rd. Cars	111	27 64 C	Pagoda Gdns. Chis	100	38 76 D	Palmerston Rd. Th Hth	105	32 67 B
Oxford Rd. E15	49	38 84 B	Paignton Rd. N15	37	33 88 C	Palmerston Rd. W3	61	20 79 C
Oxford Rd. Enf	13	34 95 B	Paignton Rd. Ruis	31	10 86 C	Palmerston Way. SW8	9	28 77 D
Oxford Rd. Har	32	14 88 C	Paine Ct. SE3	65	39 77 B	Palmer St. SW1	6	29 79 D
Oxford Rd. Har	21	15 89 B	Paines Brook Rd. Rom	30	54 91 B	Palm Gr. W5	60	18 79 C
Oxford Rd. Ilf	51	44 85 C	Paines Brook Way. Rom	30	54 91 B	Palm Rd. Rom	41	50 88 A
Oxford Rd. N4	31	31 87 C	Paines Cl. Pnr	20	12 89 A	Palm St. E3	57	36 82 A
Oxford Rd. N9	17	34 93 B	Paine's La. Pnr	20	12 90 C	Pamber St. W10	56	23 81 D
Oxford Rd. NW6	46	25 83 C	Pain's Cl. Mit	96	28 69 D	Pamela Gdns. Pnr	31	10 88 B
Oxford Rd. Rom	30	54 91 B	*Painsthorpe Rd. N16	37	33 86 C	Pampisford Rd. Pur	112	31 62 D
Oxford Rd. SE19	97	32 70 B	Painters Rd. Ilf	28	46 89 A	Pampisford Rd. S Croy	112	31 62 B
Oxford Rd. Sid	90	46 71 D	Paisley Rd. Cars	103	26 66 C	Pams Way. Eps	19	20 64 D
Oxford Rd. SW15	73	24 75 C	Paisley Rd. N22	25	31 90 B	Pancras La. EC4	4	32 81 D
Oxford Rd. Tedd	82	14 71 D	Pakeman St. N7	36	30 86 D	Pancras Rd. NW1	47	29 83 D
Oxford Rd. W5	54	17 80 B	Pakenham Cl. SW12	86	28 73 C	Pandora Ct. Surb	101	18 67 C
Oxford Rd. Wall	111	29 64 C	Pakenham St. WC1	3	30 82 D	Pandora Rd. NW6	46	25 84 A
Oxford Road N. W4	61	19 78 D	Palace Ave. W8	62	25 79 B	Panfield Mews. Ilf	40	43 88 C
Oxford Road S. W4	61	19 78 D	Palace Ct. Har	33	18 88 C	Panfield Rd. SE2	66	46 79 C
Oxford Sq. W2	1	27 81 C	Palace Ct. W2	56	25 80 B	Pangbourne Ave. W10	56	23 81 A
Oxford St. W1	2	28 81 D	Palace Court Gdns. N10	24	29 89 A	Panhard Pl. Sthl	53	13 80 B
Oxford Way. Felt	82	11 71 B	Palace Gates Rd. N22	24	29 90 B	Pank Ave. Barn	11	26 95 A
Oxford Wlk. Sthl	53	12 80 D	Palace Gate. W8	5	26 79 A	Panmure Rd. SE26	87	34 72 D
Oxgate Gdns. NW2	34	22 86 B	Palace Gdn Mews. W8	56	25 80 C	Pansy Gdns. W12	55	22 80 A
Oxgate La. NW2	34	22 86 B	Palace Gdns. Enf	13	32 96 D	Pantiles The. Bexh	67	48 77 D
Oxhawth Cres. Brom	108	43 67 D	Palace Gdns Terr. W8	56	25 80 D	Pantiles The. Brom	99	42 68 A
Oxhey Dri. Nthwd	19	10 91 B	Palace Gr. Brom	99	40 69 B	Panton St. SW1	6	29 80 B
Oxhey La. Pnr	20	13 91 B	Palace Green. W8	56	25 80 D	Panyer Alley. EC4	4	32 81 C
Ox La. Eps	109	22 62 A	Palace Gr. SE19	97	33 70 D	Papillons Wlk. SE3	87	40 76 C
Oxleas Cl. Well	78	44 76 D	Palace Mews. SW1	9	28 78 A	Papworth Way. SE24	87	31 73 A
Oxleay Rd. Har	32	13 87 C	Palace Pl. SW1	6	29 79 C	Parade Mews. SE27	87	31 72 B
Oxleigh Cl. N.Mal	102	21 67 A	Palace Rd. Brom	99	40 69 B	Parade The. Sun	91	09 70 D
Oxley Cl. Rom	30	53 90 C	Palace Rd. E Mol	92	14 68 B	Parade. The SW11	9	27 77 D
Oxleys Rd. NW2	34	22 86 D	Palace Rd. King	93	17 68 D	Paradise Pas. N7	48	31 84 A
Oxlow La. Dag	52	49 85 A	Palace Rd. N11	24	30 91 C	Paradise Rd. Rich	71	18 74 A
Oxonian St. SE22	75	33 75 D	Palace Rd. N8	36	29 88 B	Paradise Rd. SW4	74	30 76 C
Oxted Cl. Mit	95	26 68 B	Palace Rd. Ruis	43	12 85 A	Paradise Row. E2	57	34 82 B
Oxtoby Way. SW16	96	29 69 B	Palace Rd. SE19	97	33 70 D	Paradise St. SE16	63	34 79 B
Ozins Way. E16	58	40 81 C	Palace Rd. SW2	87	31 72 A	Paradise Wlk. SW3	9	27 77 B
			Palace Rd. SW19	97	33 70 D	*Paragon Mews. SE1	63	32 78 B
Pace Pl. E1	57	34 81 D	Palace St. SW1	6	29 79 C	Paragon Pl. SE3	77	39 76 D
Pacific Rd. E16	58	40 81 C	Palace View. Brom	99	40 68 B	Paragon Pl. Surb	101	18 67 D
Packham Ct. Wor Pk	103	23 65 C	Palace View. Croy	106	36 65 D	Paragon Rd. E9	49	35 84 A
Packington Sq. N1	48	32 83 A	Palace View. E4	18	37 92 D	Paragon The. SE3	77	40 76 C
Packington St. N1	48	32 83 A	Palace View. SE12	89	40 72 A	Parbury Rd. SE23	76	36 74 C
Packmores Rd. SE9	78	44 74 B						

Parchmore Rd. Th Hth

Parchmore Rd. Th Hth ...97 32 68 A
Parchmore Way. Th Hth ...97 32 69 C
Pardoner St. SE1 ...8 32 79 D
Pardon St. EC1 ...3 31 82 D
Parfett St. E1 ...57 34 81 C
Parfrey St. W6 ...62 23 77 B
Parham Dri. Ilf ...40 43 88 B
Paris Gdn. SE1 ...7 31 80 D
Parish La. SE20 ...98 35 70 D
Park App. Well ...46 75 D
Park Ave. E15 ...50 39 84 A
Park Ave. Bark ...51 44 84 A
Park Ave. Brom ...99 39 70 B
Park Ave. Cars ...111 28 63 A
Park Ave. E6 ...51 43 83 C
Park Ave. Enf ...13 33 95 C
Park Ave. Houn ...70 13 74 D
Park Ave. Ilf ...40 43 87 C
Park Ave. Mit ...96 28 70 D
Park Ave. N13 ...17 31 93 C
Park Ave. N18 ...17 34 92 A
Park Ave. N22 ...24 30 90 B
Park Ave. N3 ...23 25 90 B
Park Ave N. N8 ...24 29 89 D
Park Avenue East. Eps ...109 22 63 A
Park Avenue Mews. Mit ...96 28 70 D
Park Avenue N. NW10 ...54 22 85 D
Park Avenue Rd. N17 ...25 34 91 D
Park Avenue West. Eps ...109 22 63 A
Park Ave. NW10 ...54 18 82 B
Park Ave. NW10 ...54 18 83 D
Park Ave. NW11 ...35 25 87 D
Park Ave. NW2 ...45 22 84 B
Park Ave. Orp ...108 43 65 A
Park Ave. Orp ...108 46 65 C
Park Ave. Ruis ...31 09 88 C
Park Ave S. N8 ...24 29 89 D
Park Ave. Sthl ...53 13 80 C
Park Ave. SW14 ...72 20 75 D
Park Ave. W Wick ...106 38 65 A
Park Bvd. Rom ...50 51 90 B
Park Chase. Wem ...44 18 85 B
Park Cl. Cars ...111 27 63 B
Park Cl. E9 ...49 35 83 A
Park Cl. Hamp ...21 14 69 A
Park Cl. Har ...21 15 90 A
Park Cl. Houn ...70 14 74 A
Park Cl. N20 ...15 26 92 B
Park Cl. NW10 ...54 18 82 B
Park Cl. NW2 ...34 22 86 D
Park Cl. SW1 ...5 27 79 B
Park Cl. W14 ...62 24 79 D
Park Cottages. Twick ...71 16 74 D
Park Crescent. Eri ...67 50 77 B
Park Cres. Enf ...13 32 96 D
Park Cres. Eri ...67 50 77 B
Park Cres. Har ...21 15 90 A
Park Cres. Horn ...42 52 87 A
Park Cres Mews E. W1 ...2 28 82 D
Park Cres Mews W. W1 ...2 28 82 D
Park Cres. N3 ...23 26 91 C
Park Cres. Twick ...14 73 D
Park Cres. W1 ...2 28 82 D
Park Croft. Edg ...22 20 90 A
Parkcroft Rd. SE12 ...89 39 73 B
Park Ct. E17 ...37 88 B
Park Ct. King ...93 17 69 A
Park Ct. N12 ...15 26 92 D
Park Ct. N Mal ...94 20 68 D
Park Ct. Wem ...44 18 85 C
Parkdale Cres. Wor Pk ...102 20 65 D
Parkdale Rd. SE18 ...68 45 78 C
Park Dri. Dag ...50 86 C
Park Dri. Har ...32 13 87 A
Park Dri. Har ...21 15 91 A
Park Dri. N21 ...13 32 95 C
Park Dri. NW11 ...35 25 87 D
Park Dri. SE7 ...65 42 77 A
Park Dri. SW14 ...72 20 75 D
Park Dri. W3 ...61 19 79 C
Park Dri. Rom ...29 50 89 D
Park End. Brom ...99 39 69 B
Park End. NW3 ...47 27 85 A
Park End Rd. Rom ...30 51 89 C
Parke Rd. Sun ...10 68 C
Parke Rd. SW13 ...61 22 77 C
Parker Mews. WC2 ...3 30 81 C
Parker Rd. Croy ...112 32 64 A
Parker's Bldgs. SE16 ...8 33 79 D
Parkers Rd. N2 ...27 90 A
Parker's Row. SE1 ...8 33 79 B
Parker St. WC2 ...3 30 81 C
Park Farm Cl. N2 ...23 26 89 A
Park Farm Cl. Pnr ...31 10 88 B
Park Farm Rd. Brom ...99 41 69 B

Park Farm Rd. King ...93 18 70 C
Parkfield Ave. Felt ...81 10 72 C
Parkfield Ave. Har ...20 12 83 C
Parkfield Ave. Nthlt ...43 21 75 C
Parkfield Ave. SW14 ...72 19 91 B
Parkfield Cl. Edg ...12 12 83 C
Parkfield Cl. Nthlt ...43 10 72 C
Parkfield Cres. Felt ...81 14 90 C
Parkfield Cres. Har ...20 12 86 A
Parkfield Cres. Ruis ...32 11 83 D
Parkfield Dri. Nthlt ...43 13 89 B
Parkfield Gdns. Har ...20 15 76 A
Parkfield. Islw ...10 72 C
Parkfield Rd. Felt ...81 14 86 C
Parkfield Rd. Har ...32 12 83 C
Parkfield Rd. Nthlt ...43 22 84 D
Parkfield Rd. NW10 ...54 36 76 B
Parkfield Rd. SE14 ...76 07 86 B
Parkfield Rd. Uxb ...21 87 C
Parkfields Ave. NW9 ...34 22 69 D
Parkfields Ave. SW20 ...94 18 71 D
Parkfields. Croy ...106 23 75 C
Parkfields Rd. King ...83 31 83 C
Parkfields. SW15 ...73 42 67 B
Parkfield St N1 ...48 26 97 A
Parkfield Way. Brom ...107 19 70 B
Parkgate Ave. Barn ...16 26 97 A
Parkgate Cl. King ...94 20 74 B
Parkgate Cres. Barn ...16 30 94 B
Parkgate Gdns. SW14 ...72 26 89 B
Park Gate. N21 ...16 27 77 C
Park Gate. N2 ...23 28 64 D
Parkgate Rd. SW11 ...9 39 75 B
Parkgate Rd. Wall ...111 17 81 B
Parkgate. SE3 ...77 50 78 B
Park Gate. W5 ...54 17 81 B
Park Gdns. Eri ...67 19 88 B
Park Gdns. King ...83 50 75 C
Park Gdns. NW9 ...79 40 83 A
Park Gr. Bexh ...79 29 91 D
Park Gr. Brom ...99 40 69 B
Park Gr. E15 ...50 40 83 A
Park Gr. N11 ...24 39 86 A
Park Grove Rd. E11 ...27 89 C
Park Hall Rd. N2 ...24 32 72 D
Park Hall Rd. SE21 ...27 96 A
Parkham St. SW11 ...74 42 68 D
Park Hill. Brom ...99 27 63 B
Park Hill. Cars ...111 27 64 C
Park Hill Cl. Cars ...111 53 86 A
Parkhill Cl. Horn ...42 27 72 C
Park Hill Ct. SW17 ...86 39 60 C
Park Hill Rd. Brom ...99 33 65 C
Park Hill Rd. Croy ...105 38 94 A
Parkhill Rd. E4 ...18 27 85 D
Parkhill Rd. NW3 ...47 45 72 C
Parkhill Rd. Sid ...90 28 63 D
Park Hill Rd. Wall ...111 18 74 D
Park Hill. Rich ...71 33 65 C
Park Hill Rise. Croy ...105 34 73 D
Park Hill. SE23 ...87 29 74 B
Park Hill. SW4 ...74 17 81 B
Park Hill. W5 ...54 27 85 D
Park Hill Wlk. NW3 ...47 34 84 A
Parkholme Rd. E8 ...48 17 74 A
Park House Gdns. Twick ...71 28 87 A
Park House Pas. N6 ...36 32 77 D
Parkhouse St. SE5 ...63 20 62 C
Parkhurst. Eps ...109 49 74 C
Parkhurst Rd. Bex ...79 43 85 A
Parkhurst Rd. E12 ...51 36 39 C
Parkhurst Rd. E17 ...26 28 92 B
Parkhurst Rd. N11 ...16 34 90 C
Parkhurst Rd. N17 ...25 30 91 B
Parkhurst Rd. N22 ...24 30 85 A
Parkhurst Rd. N7 ...26 64 B
Parkhurst Rd. Sutt ...110 28 64 C
Park La. Cars ...111 32 65 D
Park La. Croy ...105 38 83 B
Park La. E15 ...49 13 86 D
Park La. Har ...32 52 87 A
Park La. Horn ...42 10 76 A
Park La. Houn ...69 34 91 C
Park La. N17 ...25 33 93 C
Park La. N18 ...17 33 93 D
Park La. N9 ...17 26 64 B
Parkland Ave. Rom ...51 28 64 C
Parkland Gr. Ashf ...81 07 71 A
Parkland Rd. Ashf ...81 07 71 A
Parkland Rd. N22 ...24 30 90 D
Parkland Rd. Wdf Grn ...27 40 91 D
Parklands Ct. Houn ...70 11 76 D
Parklands Dri. N3 ...24 24 49 A
Parklands Rd. SW16 ...86 28 71 D
Parklands. Surb ...101 18 67 B

Parklands Way. Wor Pk ...102 21 65 A
Park Lane Cl. N17 ...25 34 91 C
Park La. Rich ...71 17 75 D
Park La. Rom ...41 47 88 D
Park La. Sutt ...110 24 63 A
Park La. Tedd ...93 15 70 B
Park La. W1 ...6 28 80 A
Park La. Wem ...44 18 85 A
Park Lawn. Th Hth ...97 32 69 C
Parklea Cl. NW9 ...22 21 90 A
Parkleigh Rd. SW19 ...95 25 69 D
Parkleys. King ...83 18 71 A
Parkleys. Rich ...83 17 71 B
Park Mansions Arc. SW1 ...5 27 79 B
Parkmead Gdns. NW7 ...22 21 91 B
Park Mead. Har ...32 13 86 D
Park Mead. Sid ...90 46 74 B
Park Mead. SW15 ...79 47 74 C
Parkmead. SW15 ...73 22 74 D
Park Par. NW10 ...45 21 83 D
Park Pl. Hamp ...92 14 70 A
Park Pl. SW1 ...6 29 80 C
Park Pl Villas. W2 ...1 26 81 A
Park Pl. W3 ...61 19 78 A
Park Pl. W5 ...54 17 80 D
Park Pl. Wem ...44 18 85 B
Park Rd. Ashf ...81 07 71 D
Park Rd. Barn ...11 24 96 D
Park Rd. Barn ...12 27 96 C
Park Rd. Beck ...98 37 70 C
Park Rd. Brom ...99 40 69 B
Park Rd. Chis ...100 43 70 B
Park Rd. E10 ...38 37 87 C
Park Rd. E12 ...39 40 87 D
Park Rd. E15 ...50 40 83 A
Park Rd. E17 ...36 88 B
Park Rd. E6 ...50 41 83 A
Park Rd. E Mol ...92 14 68 C
Park Rd. Felt ...82 11 71 B
Park Rd. Hamp ...92 14 71 C
Park Rd. Houn ...70 14 74 A
Park Rd. Ilf ...40 44 86 D
Park Rd. Islw ...71 16 76 D
Park Rd. King ...93 17 69 A
Park Rd. King ...94 19 70 A
Park Rd. N11 ...30 91 C
Park Rd. N14 ...16 29 94 D
Park Rd. N15 ...25 31 89 D
Park Rd. N18 ...17 34 92 A
Park Rd. N2 ...23 26 89 B
Park Rd. N8 ...36 29 88 B
Park Rd. N Mal ...94 20 68 D
Park Rd. NW10 ...45 20 83 A
Park Rd. NW4 ...22 87 B
Park Rd. NW9 ...34 20 87 B
Park Rd. Rich ...71 18 74 D
Park Rd. SE25 ...97 33 68 C
Park Rd. Sun ...10 70 D
Park Rd. Surb ...101 18 67 B
Park Rd. Sutt ...110 24 63 A
Park Rd. SW19 ...95 26 70 B
Park Rd. Tedd ...93 15 70 B
Park Rd. Twick ...71 17 74 C
Park Rd. W4 ...61 20 77 B
Park Rd. W7 ...54 15 80 B
Park Rd. Wall ...111 21 64 D
Park Rd. Wem ...44 18 84 A
Park Ridings. N8 ...25 31 89 A
Park Rise. Har ...21 15 90 A
Park Rise Rd. SE23 ...88 36 73 C
Park Rise. SE23 ...88 36 73 C
Park Road E. W3 ...20 79 A
Park Road. NW1 ...1 27 82 C
Park Road N. W3 ...61 19 79 B
Park Road N. W4 ...20 78 D
Park Row. SE10 ...64 38 77 B
Park Royal Rd. NW10 ...55 20 82 C
Parkshot. Rich ...71 17 75 D
Parkside Ave. Bexh ...80 51 76 C
Parkside Ave. Brom ...99 42 68 C
Parkside Ave. Rom ...29 50 89 B
Parkside Ave. Rom ...50 51 90 C
Parkside Ave. SW19 ...85 23 71 D
Parkside Cres. Surb ...102 20 67 C
Parkside Cross. Bexh ...51 76 C
Parkside Estate. E9 ...49 35 83 A
Parkside Gdns. Barn ...16 28 94 A
Parkside Gdns. SW19 ...85 23 71 B
Parkside. Hamp ...21 14 71 D
Parkside. N3 ...25 91 D
Park Side. NW2 ...45 22 85 B
Parkside. NW7 ...22 91 A
Parkside Rd. Belv ...67 50 78 A
Parkside Rd. Houn ...70 13 74 B

Name	Pg	Grid
Parkside. SE3	65	39 77 D
Parkside. Sid	90	46 72 B
Parkside St. SW11	74	28 76 A
Parkside. Sutt.	110	24 63 A
Parkside. SW19	85	23 71 B
Parkside Way. Har	20	14 89 C
Park Sq E. NW1	2	28 82 D
Park Sq Mews. NW1	2	28 82 D
Park Sq W. NW1	2	28 82 D
Park St. Croy	105	32 65 A
Parkstead Rd. SW15	72	22 74 B
Parkstone Ave. Horn.	42	54 88 C
Parkstone Ave. N18	17	33 92 D
Parkstone Rd. E17	26	38 89 A
Parkstone Rd. SE15	75	34 76 C
Park St. SE1	8	32 80 C
Park St. Tedd	93	15 70 A
Park St. W1	6	28 80 A
Park Terr. Wor Pk	102	22 66 C
Park The. Cars.	111	27 64 D
Park The. N6	36	28 88 C
Park The. NW11	35	25 87 D
Park The. SE19	97	33 70 D
Park The. Sid	90	46 71 A
Park The. W5	54	17 80 D
Parkthorne Cl. Har	32	13 88 D
Parkthorne Dri. Har	32	13 88 D
Parkthorne Rd. SW12	86	29 73 B
Park View Cres. N11	16	28 92 B
Park View Gdns. Ilf.	27	42 89 D
Park View Gdns. NW4	35	23 88 A
Park View. N21	16	30 94 B
Park View. N5	48	32 85 A
Park View. N Mal	94	21 68 A
Park View. Pnr	20	12 90 B
Park View Rd. Bexh	79	47 75 B
Parkview Rd. Croy	105	34 66 C
Park View Rd. N17	25	34 90 C
Park View Rd. N3	23	25 90 B
Park View Rd. NW10	45	21 85 B
Park View Rd. Pnr	19	10 91 D
Park View Rd. SE9	90	43 72 B
Park View Rd. Sthl	53	13 80 C
Park View Rd. W5	54	18 81 A
Park View Rd. Well	79	47 75 A
Park View. W3	55	20 81 A
Park View. Wem	45	19 85 D
Park Village E. NW1	47	28 83 D
Park Village W. NW1	47	28 83 D
Park Villas. Rom	41	47 88 D
Parkville Rd. SW6	62	24 77 D
Park Vista. SE10	64	38 77 B
Parkway. Belv.	67	48 79 C
Park Way Ct. Ruis	31	09 87 D
Park Way. Edg	22	19 90 B
Park Way. E Mol	92	13 68 B
Park Way. Enf.	13	31 97 C
Park Way. Felt.	81	10 73 B
Parkway. Ilf.	40	45 86 D
Parkway. N14	16	30 93 A
Park Way. N20	16	27 92 B
Park Way. NW11	35	24 88 A
Parkway. NW1	47	28 83 B
Parkway. Rom.	30	51 90 D
Park Way. Ruis	31	10 87 C
Parkway. SW20	95	23 68 D
Parkway The. Houn	69	10 76 B
Park West Pl. W2	1	27 81 C
Park West. W2	1	27 81 C
Park Wlk. N6	36	28 87 A
Park Wlk. SW10	62	26 77 B
Parkwood. Beck.	98	37 70 C
Parkwood Gr. Sun	91	10 68 A
Parkwood. N11	24	28 91 A
Parkwood. N20	16	27 93 D
Parkwood Rd. Islw.	71	16 76 A
Parkwood Rd. SW19	85	24 71 D
Parliament Hill. NW3	47	27 85 A
Parliament St. SW1	7	30 79 A
Parma Cres. SW11	74	27 75 D
Parmiter Pl. E2	49	35 83 C
Parmiter St. E2	48	34 83 D
Parmuir Rd. SW20	94	22 69 B
Parnell Rd. E3	49	36 83 B
Parnham St. E14	57	36 81 C
Parolles Rd. N19	36	29 87 C
Paroma Rd. Belv.	67	49 79 C
Parr Ave. Eps.	109	22 62 B
Parr Ct. Felt.	82	11 71 A
Parr Rd. E6	50	41 83 B
Parr Rd. Stan.	21	18 90 A
Parrs Cl. S Croy	112	32 62 B
Parr's Pl. Hamp.	92	13 70 C
Parr St. N1	48	32 83 D
Parry Cl. Eps.	109	22 63 C
Parry Pl. SE18	66	43 78 B
Parry Rd. SE25	97	33 68 A
Parry St. SW8	10	30 77 A
Parsifal Rd. NW6	46	25 85 C
Parsloes Ave. Dag	52	48 85 D
Parsonage Gdns. Enf.	13	32 97 C
Parsonage La. Enf.	13	32 97 D
Parsonage Manorway. Belv.	67	49 77 A
Parsonage St. E14	64	38 78 A
Parsons Green La. SW6	73	25 76 A
Parsons Green. SW6	73	25 76 A
Parson's Mead. Croy.	105	31 66 D
Parsons Mead. E Mol	92	14 68 A
Parsons Rd. E13	50	41 83 C
Parson St. NW4	23	23 89 A
Parthenia Rd. SW6	73	25 76 A
Partingdale La. NW7	15	23 92 D
Partington Cl. N19	36	29 87 D
Partridge Dri. Orp	108	44 65 C
Partridge Green. SE9	90	43 72 C
Partridge Rd. Sid	90	45 71 A
Partridge Way. N22	24	30 90 A
Pascal St. SW8	10	29 77 D
Pascoe Rd. SE13	76	38 74 B
Pasley Cl. SE17	63	32 78 C
Pasquier Rd. E17	26	36 89 A
Passage The. Rich	71	17 74 B
Passey Pl. SE9	90	42 74 D
Passfield Dri. E14	57	37 81 B
Passfields. SE6	88	38 72 C
Passing Alley. EC1	3	31 82 D
Passmore Gdns. N11	24	29 91 B
Passmore St. SW1	9	28 78 C
Pasteur Gdns. N18	17	32 92 C
Paston Cl. E5	38	35 86 D
Paston Cres. SE12	89	40 73 B
Pastor St. SE11	63	31 78 B
Pasture Cl. Wem	33	16 86 D
Pasture Rd. Dag	52	48 85 D
Pasture Rd. SE6	89	39 73 D
Pasture Rd. Wem	33	16 86 D
Pastures The. N20	15	24 94 D
Patcham Terr. SW11	74	28 76 B
Paternoster Row. EC4	4	32 81 C
Paternoster Sq. EC4	3	31 81 D
Pater St. W8	62	25 79 C
Pates Manor Dri. Felt	81	08 73 B
Pathfield Rd. SW16	96	29 70 B
Path The. SW19	95	25 69 B
Patience Rd. SW11	74	27 76 C
Patio Cl. SW4	74	29 74 D
Patmore St. SW8	74	29 76 A
Patmos Rd. SW9	75	31 76 B
Paton Cl. E3	57	37 82 A
Paton St. EC1	4	32 82 A
Patricia Ct. SE2	66	46 77 D
Patricia Dri. Horn	42	54 87 C
Patrick Connolly Gdns. E3	57	37 82 B
Patrick Pas. SW11	74	27 76 C
Patrick Rd. E13	58	41 82 A
Patriot Sq. E2	48	34 83 D
Patrol Pl. SE6	76	37 74 D
Patshull Pl. NW5	47	29 84 A
Patshull Rd. NW5	47	29 84 A
Patten Alley. Rich	71	17 74 B
Pattenden Rd. SE6	88	36 73 D
Patten Rd. SW18	86	27 73 A
Patterdale Cl. Brom	99	39 70 A
Patterdale Rd. SE15	64	35 77 C
Patterson Rd. SE19	97	33 70 B
Pattison Rd. NW2	35	25 86 C
Pattison Wlk. SE18	66	44 78 C
Paul Cl. E15	50	39 84 C
Paulet Rd. SE5	75	31 76 B
Paul Gdns. Croy	105	33 65 B
Paulhan Rd. Har	33	17 89 D
Paulin Dri. N21	17	31 94 A
Pauline Cres. Twick	82	14 73 C
Paul St. E15	50	39 83 A
Paul St. EC2	4	33 82 C
Paultons Sq. SW3	62	26 77 B
Paultons St. SW3	62	26 77 B
Pauntley St. N19	36	29 87 C
Paved Ct. Rich	71	17 74 B
Paveley Dri. SW11	9	27 82 C
Paveley St. NW8	1	27 82 A
Pavement Mews. Rom	41	47 87 B
Pavement Sq. Croy	105	34 66 C
Pavement The. SW4	74	29 75 C
Pavet Cl. Dag	52	49 84 B
Pavilion Rd. Ilf.	39	42 87 B
Pavilion Rd. SW1	5	27 79 D
Pavilion St. SW1	5	27 79 D
Pavilion Terr.	101	16 67 A
Pavilion Way. Ruis	32	11 86 A
Pawleyne Cl. SE20	98	35 70 C
Pawsey Cl. E13	50	40 83 A
Pawson's Rd. Croy	105	32 67 A
Paxford Rd. Wem	33	16 86 B
Paxton Cl. Rich	71	18 76 D
Paxton Pl. SE27	97	33 71 A
Paxton Rd. Brom	99	40 70 C
Paxton Rd. N17	25	34 91 C
Paxton Rd. W4	61	21 77 A
Paynell Ct. SE3	65	39 75 A
Payne Rd. E3	49	37 83 D
Payne St. SE8	64	36 77 D
Peabody Ave. SW1	9	28 78 D
* Peabody Bldgs. SE17	63	32 78 B
* Peabody Bldgs. SE5	75	32 76 B
Peabody Cl. SE10	76	37 76 B
Peabody Cottages. N17	25	33 90 A
Peabody Estate. E1	57	34 80 A
Peabody Estate. E1	57	35 80 B
Peabody Estate. E2	48	34 83 D
Peabody Estate. N1	48	32 83 A
Peabody Estate. SE1	8	32 80 C
Peabody Estate. SE24	87	31 73 B
Peabody Estate. SW1	10	29 78 A
Peabody Estate. SW6	62	24 77 B
Peabody Estate. W10	56	23 82 C
Peabody Estate. W6	61	23 78 C
Peabody Hill. SE21	87	31 73 D
Peabody Yd. N1	48	32 83 A
Peace Gr. Wem	34	19 86 B
Peace St. E1	57	34 82 C
Peaches Cl. Sutt.	110	24 63 C
Peachum Rd. SE3	65	39 77 B
Peacock Ave. Felt.	81	08 73 D
Peacock Cl. Horn	30	54 89 C
Peacock St. SE17	63	31 78 B
Peacock Wlk. N6	36	28 87 B
Peacock Wlk. SE17	63	31 78 B
Peakes Pl. SE18	66	43 78 B
Peak Hill Ave. SE26	88	35 71 A
Peak Hill Gdns. SE26	88	35 71 A
Peak Hill. SE26	88	35 71 A
Peaks Hill. Pur	111	30 62 C
Peaks Hill Rise. Pur	111	30 62 C
Peak The. SE26	88	35 72 C
Peal Gdns. W3	54	16 82 C
Peall Rd. Croy	104	30 67 D
Pearcefield Ave. SE23	88	35 73 C
Pear Cl. NW9	23	20 89 D
Pearcroft Rd. E11	38	38 86 B
Peardon St. SW8	74	28 76 D
Peareswood Gdns. Stan	21	17 90 B
Pearfield Rd. SE23	88	36 72 C
Pearl Rd. E17	26	37 89 A
Pearl St. E1	57	34 80 D
Pearman St. SE1	8	31 79 A
Pearscroft Ct. SW6	73	25 76 B
Pearscroft Rd. SW6	73	25 76 B
Pearson's Ave. SE14	64	37 76 A
Pearson St. E2	48	33 83 D
Pears Rd. Houn	70	13 75 D
Pear Tree Cl. Eri	79	50 76 B
Pear Tree Cl. Mit.	96	27 69 C
Pear Tree Ct. EC1	3	31 82 C
Peartree Gdns. Dag	51	46 85 B
Peartree Gdns. Rom	29	49 90 D
Pear Tree Rd. Ashf	81	08 71 C
Peartree Rd. Enf	13	33 96 A
Pear Tree St. EC1	4	32 82 C
Peary Pl. E2	57	35 82 A
Pebworth Rd. Har	33	18 86 A
Peckarmans Wood. SE26	87	34 72 C
Peckett Sq. N5	48	32 85 A
Peckford Pl. SW9	75	31 76 C
Peckham Gr. SE15	63	33 77 C
Peckham High St. SE15	75	34 76 A
Peckham Hill St. SE15	63	34 77 C
Peckham Park Rd. SE15	63	34 77 A
Peckham Rd. SE15	75	33 76 B
Peckham Rd. SE5	75	33 76 A
Peckham Rye. SE15	75	34 75 D
Peckwater St. NW5	47	29 85 C
Pedlars Wlk. N7	47	30 85 C
Pedley St. E1	49	33 82 D
Pedley St. E1	49	34 82 C
Pedro St. E5	49	35 85 B
Pedworth Rd. SE16	64	35 78 A
Peek Cres. SW19	85	23 71 D
Peel Dri. Ilf.	27	42 90 C
Peel Gr. E2	49	35 83 C
Peel Pass. W8	56	25 80 C
Peel Prec. NW6	46	25 83 C
Peel Rd. E18	27	39 90 B

Name	Page	Grid
Peel Rd. Har	21	15 89 B
Peel Rd. NW6	46	25 83 C
Peel Rd. Wem	33	17 86 D
Peel St. W8	56	25 80 C
Peel Way. Rom	30	54 90 D
Peerage Way. Horn	42	54 87 B
Peerless St. EC1	4	32 82 B
Pegamoid Rd. N18	18	35 92 A
Pegamoid Rd. N18	18	35 93 C
Pegasus Pl. SE11	63	31 77 A
Pegasus Rd. Croy	112	31 63 A
Pegelm Gdns. Horn	42	54 87 B
Pegg Rd. Houn	59	11 77 D
Pegley Gdns. SE12	89	40 72 A
Pegwell St. SE18	66	45 77 C
Pekin St. E14	57	37 81 C
Peldon Ct. Rich	71	18 74 B
Peldon Pas. Rich	71	18 75 D
Peldon Wlk. N1	4	31 83 B
Pelham Ave. Bark	51	45 83 B
Pelham Cl. SE5	75	33 75 A
Pelham Cres. SW7	9	27 78 A
Pelham Pl. SW7	9	27 78 A
Pelham Rd. Beck	98	35 69 C
Pelham Rd. Bexh	79	49 75 A
Pelham Rd. E18	27	40 89 B
Pelham Rd. Ilf	40	44 86 B
Pelham Rd. N15	23	33 89 D
Pelham Rd. N22	25	31 90 C
Pelham Rd. SW19	95	25 70 C
Pelham Rd. SW7	9	27 78 A
*Pelican Pas. E1	57	35 82 C
Pelican Wlk. SW9	75	31 75 D
Pelier St. SE17	63	32 77 A
Pelinore Rd. SE6	89	39 72 A
Pellant Rd. SW6	62	24 77 C
Pellatt Gr. N22	25	31 90 A
Pellatt Rd. SE22	75	33 74 B
Pellerin Rd. N16	48	33 85 C
Pelling St. E14	57	37 81 C
Pellipar Cl. N13	17	31 93 C
Pellipar Gdns. SE18	65	42 78 D
Pelly Rd. E13	50	40 83 A
Pelton Ave. Sutt	110	25 62 D
Pelton Rd. E10	65	39 78 C
Pembar Ave. E17	26	36 89 A
Pember Rd. NW10	56	23 82 B
Pemberton Ave. Rom	30	52 89 B
Pemberton Gdns. N19	36	29 86 C
Pemberton Gdns. Rom	41	48 88 A
Pemberton Pl. E8	49	35 84 C
Pemberton Rd. E Mol	92	14 68 C
Pemberton Rd. N4	37	31 88 B
Pemberton Row. EC4	3	31 81 C
Pemberton Terr. N19	36	29 86 C
Pembridge Ave. Twick	82	12 73 D
Pembridge Cres. W11	56	25 80 A
Pembridge Gdns. W2	56	25 80 A
Pembridge Mews. W11	56	25 80 A
Pembridge Pl. W2	56	25 80 A
Pembridge Rd. W11	56	25 80 A
Pembridge Sq. W2	56	25 80 A
Pembridge Villas. W11	56	25 80 A
Pembroke Ave. Enf	13	34 97 B
Pembroke Ave. Har	21	16 89 B
Pembroke Ave. Surb	102	19 67 B
Pembroke Cl. SW1	6	28 79 A
Pembroke Gdns. Cl. W8	62	25 79 C
Pembroke Gdns. Dag	41	49 86 D
Pembroke Gdns. W8	62	25 78 A
Pembroke Mews. W8	62	25 79 C
Pembroke Pl. Edg	22	19 91 C
Pembroke Pl. Islw	71	15 76 C
Pembroke Pl. W8	62	25 79 C
Pembroke Rd. Brom	99	41 69 C
Pembroke Rd. E17	38	37 88 B
Pembroke Rd. Eri	67	50 78 B
Pembroke Rd. Grnf	53	13 82 D
Pembroke Rd. Ilf	40	45 87 B
Pembroke Rd. Mit	96	28 69 C
Pembroke Rd. N10	24	28 91 C
Pembroke Rd. N13	17	32 93 C
Pembroke Rd. N15	23	33 88 B
Pembroke Rd. N8	24	30 89 C
Pembroke Rd. Ruis	31	09 87 D
Pembroke Rd. SE25	97	33 68 C
Pembroke Rd. W8	62	25 78 A
Pembroke Rd. Wem	33	17 86 D
Pembroke Sq. W8	62	25 79 C
Pembroke St. N1	47	30 84 C
Pembroke Studios. W8	62	24 79 D
Pembroke Villas. Rich	71	17 75 D
Pembroke Villas. W8	62	25 78 A
Pembroke Wlk. W8	62	25 78 A
Pembury Ave. Wor Pk	102	22 66 A
Pembury Cl. Brom	107	39 66 B
Pembury Cl. E5	48	34 85 D
Pembury Pl. E5	48	34 85 D
Pembury Rd. Bexh	67	48 77 A
Pembury Rd. E5	48	34 85 D
Pembury Rd. N17	25	33 90 B
Pembury Rd. SE25	97	34 68 C
Pemdevon Rd. Croy	105	31 66 A
Pemell Cl. E1	57	35 82 C
Penally Pl. N1	48	32 83 B
Penang St. E1	57	34 80 D
Penarth Cl. Sutt	110	26 63 C
Penarth St. SE15	6	35 77 A
Penberth Rd. SE6	88	38 73 C
Penbury Rd. Sthl	59	12 78 D
Pencraig Way SE15	63	34 77 B
Penda Rd. Eri	67	49 77 D
Pendarves Rd. SW20	95	23 69 A
Penda's Mead. E9	49	36 85 A
Pendennis Rd. N17	25	32 89 B
Pendennis Rd. SW16	86	30 71 A
Penderel Rd. Houn	70	13 74 A
Penderry Rise. SE6	88	38 72 B
Penderyn Way. N7	47	29 85 B
Pendle Ho. SE26	87	34 72 C
Pendle Rd. SW16	86	29 71 C
Pendlestone Rd. E17	38	37 88 B
Pendragon Rd. Brom	89	40 72 C
Pendrell Rd. SE4	76	36 76 C
Pendrell St. SE18	66	44 77 B
Pendula Dri. Hay	53	11 81 B
Penerley Rd. SE6	88	38 73 C
Penfold Pl. NW1	1	27 81 A
Penfold Rd. N9	19	35 94 D
Penfold St. NW1	1	27 81 A
Penfold St. NW8	1	26 82 D
Penford Gdns. SE9	77	41 75 B
Penford St. SE5	75	31 76 D
Pengarth Rd. Bex	79	47 74 D
Penge La. SE20	98	35 70 D
Penge Rd. SE20	97	34 68 A
Penge Rd. SE25	97	34 68 A
Penhall Rd. SE7	65	41 78 B
Penhill Rd. Bex	79	47 74 C
Penhurst Rd. Ilf	28	44 91 C
Penhurst Wlk. Brom	107	39 67 B
Penifather La. Grnf	53	14 82 B
Peninsular Cl. Felt	69	09 74 C
Penistone Rd. SW16	96	30 70 C
Penistone Wlk. Rom	30	53 91 A
Penketh Dri. Har	32	14 86 D
Penmon Rd. SE2	66	46 79 C
Pennack Rd. SE15	63	33 77 B
Pennant Terr. E17	26	36 90 D
Pennard Rd. W12	62	23 79 A
Pennards The. Sun	92	11 68 A
Pennant Mews. W8	62	25 78 B
Penn Cl. Grnf	43	13 83 D
Penn Cl. Har	21	17 89 C
Penner Cl. SW19	85	24 72 A
Pennethorne Cl. E9	49	35 83 A
Pennethorne Rd. SE15	63	34 77 D
Penn Gdns. Chis	100	43 69 D
Penn Gdns. Rom	29	49 91 C
Pennine Dri. NW2	35	23 86 B
Pennine La. NW2	35	24 86 A
Pennine Way. Bexh	80	51 76 A
Pennington Cl. Rom	29	49 91 A
Pennington St. E1	57	34 80 B
Penn La. Bex	79	48 74 C
Penn Rd. N7	47	30 85 C
Penn St. N1	48	32 83 B
Pennyfields. E14	57	37 80 A
Pennymore Wlk. W9	56	24 82 D
Penny Rd. NW10	55	19 82 B
Penpoll Rd. E8	48	34 84 B
Penpool La. Well	68	46 75 B
Penrhyn Ave. E17	26	37 90 A
Penrhyn Cres. E17	26	37 90 A
Penrhyn Cres. SW14	72	20 75 C
Penrhyn Gdns. King	93	17 68 D
Penrhyn Gr. E17	26	37 90 A
Penrhyn Rd. King	93	18 68 A
Penrith Cl. Beck	98	37 69 B
Penrith Cl. SW15	73	24 74 A
Penrith Pl. SE27	87	31 72 B
Penrith Rd. Ilf	28	45 91 B
Penrith Rd. N15	23	32 88 B
Penrith Rd. N Mal	94	20 68 D
Penrith Rd. Th Hth	97	32 69 C
Penrith St. SW16	96	29 70 A
Penrose Gr. SE17	63	32 78 C
Penrose St. SE17	63	32 78 C
Penryn St. NW1	47	29 83 D
Penry St. SE1	63	33 78 A
Pensbury Pl. SW8	74	29 76 C
Pensbury St. SW8	74	29 76 C
Pensford Ave. Rich	72	19 76 C
Penshurst Ave. Sid	78	46 74 C
Penshurst Green. Brom	107	39 67 B
Penshurst Rd. Bexh	79	48 76 B
Penshurst Rd. E9	49	35 84 D
Penshurst Rd. N17	25	33 91 C
Penshurst Rd. Th Hth	105	31 67 B
Penshurst Way. Sutt	110	25 63 C
Penstock Path. N22	24	30 89 B
Pentelow Gdns. Felt	69	10 74 C
Pentire Rd. E17	26	38 90 B
Pentland Cl. NW11	35	24 86 A
Pentlands Cl. Mit	96	28 68 B
Pentland St. SW18	73	26 74 C
Pentland Way. Ruis	31	08 86 C
Pentlow St. SW15	73	23 75 A
Pentney Rd. E4	18	38 94 D
Pentney Rd. SW12	86	29 73 C
Pentney Rd. SW19	95	24 69 A
Penton Gr. N1	48	31 83 C
Penton Pl. SE17	63	31 78 D
Penton Rise. WC1	3	30 82 B
Penton St. N1	48	31 83 C
Pentonville Rd. N1	47	30 83 D
Pentridge St. SE15	63	33 77 D
Pentyre Ave. N18	17	32 92 D
Penwerris Ave. Islw	59	14 77 C
Penwith Rd. SW18	85	25 72 B
Penwortham Rd. S Croy	112	32 62 D
Penwortham Rd. SW16	96	29 70 A
Penylan Pl. Edg	22	19 91 C
Penywern Rd. SW5	62	25 78 C
Penzance Pl. W11	56	24 80 C
Penzance St. W11	56	24 80 C
Peony Gdns. W12	55	22 80 A
Peploe Rd. NW6	46	23 83 D
Pepper St. SE1	8	32 79 A
Peptha Rd. SW18	73	25 74 C
Pepys Cres. Barn	11	23 95 A
Pepys Rd. SE14	76	35 76 D
Pepys Rd. SW20	95	23 69 A
Pepys Rise. Orp	108	45 66 D
Pepys St. EC3	8	33 80 A
Perceval Ave. NW3	47	27 85 C
Perch St. E8	48	33 85 B
Percival Cl. N17	25	33 91 D
Percival Gdns. Rom	41	47 88 D
Percival Rd. Felt	69	09 72 B
Percival Rd. Horn	42	53 88 C
Percival Rd. Orp	108	44 65 A
Percival Rd. SW14	72	20 75 C
Percival St. EC1	3	31 82 B
Percival Way. Eps	109	20 64 B
Percy Ave. Ashf	81	07 71 C
Percy Bryant Rd. Sun	91	09 70 C
Percy Circ. WC1	3	30 82 B
Percy Gdns. Enf	14	35 95 B
Percy Gdns. Islw	71	16 75 A
Percy Gdns. Wor Pk	102	21 66 C
Percy Mews. W1	2	29 81 B
Percy Pl. W12	55	22 80 C
Percy Rd. Bexh	79	48 76 C
Percy Rd. E11	39	39 87 A
Percy Rd. E16	58	39 81 A
Percy Rd. Hamp	92	13 70 C
Percy Rd. Ilf	40	46 87 A
Percy Rd. Islw	71	16 75 C
Percy Rd. Mit	104	28 66 A
Percy Rd. N12	15	26 92 C
Percy Rd. N21	17	32 94 A
Percy Rd. Rom	29	49 89 B
Percy Rd. SE20	98	35 69 B
Percy Rd. SE25	105	34 67 A
Percy Rd. Twick	82	13 73 D
Percy Rd. W12	71	22 79 A
Percy St. W1	2	29 81 B
Percy Way. Twick	82	14 73 C
Peregrine Rd. Sun	91	09 69 D
Peregrine Way. SW19	95	23 70 C
Perham Rd. W14	62	24 78 D
Perifield. SE21	87	32 73 C
Perimeade Rd. Grnf	44	17 83 C
Periton Rd. SE9	77	41 75 D
Perivale Gdns. W13	54	16 82 D
Perivale Grange. Grnf	54	16 82 A
Perivale La. Grnf	54	16 82 A
Perkin Cl. Wem	34	16 85 D
Perkins Rd. Ilf	40	44 88 B
Perkins Rents. SW1	6	29 79 D
Perks Cl. SE3	77	39 76 C
Perlock Ave. Har	32	14 87 C
Perpins Rd. SE9	78	45 74 C

Name	Map	Grid
Perran Rd. SW2	87	31 72 B
Perran Wlk (off Clayponds La). Brent	60	18 78 C
Perren St. NW5	47	28 84 B
Perrers Rd. W6	61	22 78 B
Perring Estate. E3	57	37 81 A
Perrin Rd. Wem	44	16 85 B
Perrin's Ct. NW3	46	26 85 A
Perrin's La. NW3	46	26 85 A
Perrins Wlk. NW3	46	26 85 A
Perrott St. SE18	66	44 78 A
Perry Cl. Rain	52	50 83 D
Perry Ct. N15	37	33 88 C
Perryfield Way. NW9	34	21 87 B
Perryfield Way. Rich	83	16 72 D
Perry Garth. Nthlt	43	11 83 A
Perry Gdns. N9		33 93 C
Perry Hall Cl. Orp	108	46 66 A
Perry Hall Rd. Orp	108	46 66 A
Perry Hill. SE6	88	35 72 D
Perry How. Wor Pk	102	21 66 D
Perrymans Farm Rd. Ilf	40	44 88 B
Perry Mead. Enf	13	31 97 D
Perrymead St. SW6	73	25 76 D
Perryn Rd. SE16	63	34 79 D
Perryn Rd. W3	55	20 80 B
Perry Rise. SE23	88	36 72 C
Perry's Pl. W1	2	29 81 D
Perry St. Chis	100	45 70 A
Perry St. Dart	80	51 75 A
Perry Vale. SE23	88	35 72 B
Perseverance Pl. Rich	71	18 75 C
Persfield Cl. Eps	109	22 62 C
Persfield Mews. Eps	109	21 62 D
Pershore Cl. Ilf	40	43 88 B
Pershore Gr. Cars	103	26 67 D
Pert Cl. N11	24	28 91 B
Perth Ave. Hay	53	11 82 C
Perth Ave. NW9	34	21 87 A
Perth Cl. SW20	94	22 69 C
Perth Rd. Bark	51	44 83 B
Perth Rd. Beck	98	38 69 C
Perth Rd. E10	38	36 87 D
Perth Rd. E13	50	40 83 D
Perth Rd. Ilf	40	43 87 B
Perth Rd. N22	25	31 90 B
Perth Rd. N4	37	31 87 C
Perth Terr. Ilf	40	44 87 A
Perwell Ave.	32	12 87 D
Peter Ave. NW10	45	22 84 D
Peterborough Gdns. Ilf	39	42 87 A
Peterborough Mews. SW6	73	25 76 C
Peterborough Rd. Cars	104	27 66 B
Peterborough Rd. E10	38	38 88 D
Peterborough Rd. E17	38	38 88 A
Peterborough Rd. Har	33	15 87 B
Peterborough Rd. SW6	73	25 75 A
Peterborough Villas. SW6	73	25 76 B
Petergate. SW11	73	26 75 C
Peters Cl. Stan	21	17 91 B
Petersfield Ave. Rom	30	54 91 B
Petersfield Cl. N18	17	32 92 C
Petersfield Rd. W3	61	20 79 A
Petersfield Rise. SW15	84	22 73 D
Petersham Cl. Rich	83	17 72 B
Petersham Cl. Sutt	110	25 64 C
Petersham Dri. Orp	100	46 68 A
Petersham Gdns. Orp	100	45 69 D
Petersham La. SW7	5	26 79 C
Petersham Mews. SW7	5	26 79 C
Petersham Pl. SW7	5	26 79 C
Petersham Rd. Rich	83	18 73 C
Peter's Hill. EC4	8	32 80 A
Peter's La. EC1	3	31 81 B
Peters Path. SE26	87	34 71 B
Peter St. E2	4	33 82 B
Peterstone Rd. SE2	66	46 79 B
Peterstow Cl. SW19	85	24 72 A
Peter St. W1	6	29 80 B
Petherton Ct. Har	33	15 88 D
Petherton Rd. N5	48	32 85 D
Petley Rd. W6	62	23 77 D
Peto Pl. NW1	2	28 82 D
Peto Street N. E16	58	39 80 B
Peto Street S. E16	58	39 80 B
Petrie Cl. NW2	46	24 84 A
Pettits Bvd. Rom	30	51 90 C
Pettits Cl. Rom	30	51 90 C
Pettits Lane N. Rom	30	51 90 C
Pettits La. Rom	30	51 89 A
Pettit's Pl. Dag	52	49 85 C
Pettit's Rd. Dag	52	49 85 C
Pettiward Cl. SW15	73	23 75 C
Pettley Gdns. Rom	41	50 88 B
Pettman Cres. SE28	66	44 79 D
Pettsgrove Ave. Wem	44	17 85 C
Pett's Hill. Nthlt	43	13 85 D
Petts La. Shep	91	07 68 C
Petts St. SE18	65	42 78 A
Petts Wood Rd. Orp	108	44 67 B
Petty France. SW1	6	29 79 C
Petworth Gdns. SW20	94	22 68 B
Petworth Rd. Bexh	79	49 74 A
Petworth Rd. N12	16	27 92 C
Petworth St. SW11	74	27 76 A
Petyt Pl. SW3	9	27 77 A
Petyward. SW3	9	27 78 A
Pevensey Ave. Enf	13	33 97 C
Pevensey Ave. N11	16	29 92 D
Pevensey Cl. Islw	59	14 77 C
Pevensey Rd. E7	50	40 85 A
Pevensey Rd. Felt	82	12 73 C
Pevensey Rd. SW17	85	26 71 B
Peveril Dri. Tedd	82	14 71 D
Pewsey Cl. E4	18	37 92 C
Peyton Pl. SE10	64	38 77 C
Phelp St. SE17	63	32 77 A
Phene St. SW3	9	27 77 A
Philan Way. Rom	29	50 91 B
Philbeach Gdns. SW5	62	25 78 C
Philchurch Pl. E1	57	34 81 C
Philip Ave. Rom	41	50 87 D
Philip Gdns. Croy	106	36 65 B
Philip La. N15	25	33 89 A
Philipot Path. SE9	77	42 74 D
Philipot Path. SE9	78	43 74 C
Philippa Gdns. SE9	77	41 74 B
Philip Rd. SE15	75	34 75 A
Philip St. E13	58	40 82 C
Philip Wlk. SE15	75	34 75 B
Phillimore Gardens Cl. W8	62	25 79 C
Phillimore Gdns. NW10	46	23 83 A
Phillimore Gdns. W8	62	25 79 A
Phillimore Pl. W8	62	25 79 A
Phillimore Wlk. W8	62	25 79 C
Phillipp St. N1	48	33 83 A
Phillips Cl. Dart	80	52 74 D
Phillips Way. Brom	99	40 69 C
Philpot La. EC3	8	33 80 A
Philpot St. E1	57	34 81 D
Phineas Pett Rd. SE9	77	42 75 A
Phipp's Bridge Rd. Mit	95	26 68 B
Phipp's Bridge Rd. SW19	95	26 69 C
Phipp St. EC2	4	33 82 C
Phoebeth Rd. SE4	76	37 74 A
Phoenix Dri. Brom	107	41 65 D
Phoenix Rd. NW1	47	29 83 D
Phoenix Rd. SE20	98	35 70 A
Phoenix St. WC2	2	29 81 D
Phoenix Way. Houn	59	11 77 B
Phoenix Way. WC1	3	30 82 D
Phyllis Ave. N.Mal	102	22 67 B
Picardy Manorway. Belv	67	49 79 D
Picardy Rd. Belv	67	49 78 A
Picardy St. Belv	67	49 79 C
Piccadilly Arc. SW1	6	29 80 C
Piccadilly Circ. W1	6	29 80 B
Piccadilly Pl. W1	6	29 80 A
Piccadilly. W1	6	29 80 C
Pickard St. EC1	3	31 82 B
Pickering Ave. E6	51	43 83 C
Pickering Mews. W2	56	25 81 D
Pickering Pl. SW1	6	29 80 C
Pickering St. N1	48	32 83 A
Pickets St. SW12	86	28 73 B
Pickett Croft. Stan	21	17 90 B
Pickett's Lock La. N9	18	35 93 B
Pickford Cl. Bexh	79	48 76 C
Pickford La. Bexh	79	48 76 C
Pickford Rd. Bexh	79	48 75 A
Pickhurst Green. Brom	107	39 66 B
Pickhurst La. Brom	107	39 66 D
Pickhurst La. W.Wick	107	39 67 C
Pickhurst Mead. Brom	107	39 66 B
Pickhurst Park. Brom	107	39 67 A
Pickhurst Rise. W.Wick	107	39 66 C
Pickle Herring St. SE1	8	33 80 C
Pickwick Cl. SE9	89	42 73 C
Pickwick Mews. N18	17	33 92 C
Pickwick Pl. Har	33	15 87 A
Pickwick Rd. SE21	87	32 78 A
Pickwick St. SE1	8	32 79 A
Pickwick Way. Chis	100	44 70 A
Pickworth Cl. SW8	9	30 77 C
Picton Pl. W1	2	28 81 C
Picton St. SE5	63	32 77 D
Piedmont Rd. SE18	66	44 78 D
Piermont Rd. SE22	75	34 74 B
Pier Rd. E16	65	42 79 B
Pier Rd. E16	66	43 79 A
Pier Rd. Eri	68	51 77 A
Pier Rd. Felt	69	10 74 B
Pierrepoint Rd. W3	55	19 80 B
Pierrepont Arc. N1	48	31 83 D
Pierrepont Row. N1	48	31 83 D
Pier St. E14	64	38 78 A
Pier Terr. SW18	73	26 75 C
Pigeon La. Hamp	82	13 71 A
Pigott St. E14	57	37 81 C
Pike Cl. Brom	89	40 71 D
Pike's End. Pnr	19	10 89 D
Pilgrimage St. SE1	8	32 79 B
Pilgrim Hill. SE27	87	32 71 A
Pilgrim's La. NW3	46	26 85 D
Pilgrim's Pl. NW3	46	26 85 D
Pilgrim's Rise. Barn	12	27 95 A
Pilgrim St. EC4	3	31 81 D
Pilgrims Way. N19	36	29 87 D
Pilgrims Way. Wem	34	19 87 D
Pilgrim's Way. S Croy	112	33 64 D
Pilkington Rd. Orp	108	44 65 A
Pilkington Rd. SE15	75	34 76 D
Pillmans Cl. Sid	100	46 70 B
Pilsden Cl. SW19	85	23 73 D
Pilton Estate The. Croy	105	31 65 B
Pilton Rd. SE17	63	32 78 C
Pimlico Rd. SW1	9	28 78 C
Pimlico Wlk. N1	4	33 82 A
Pimpernel Way. Rom	30	53 91 B
Pinchin St. E1	57	34 80 A
Pincott Rd. Bexh	79	49 75 C
Pincott Rd. SW19	95	26 69 A
Pindar St. EC2	4	33 81 A
Pindock Mews. W9	56	25 82 D
Pine Apple Ct. SW1	6	29 79 C
Pine Ave. W.Wick	106	37 66 D
Pine Cl. N14	16	29 94 A
Pine Cl. N19	36	29 86 C
Pine Cl. Nthwd	19	09 91 A
Pinefield Cl. E14	57	37 80 A
Pine Gdns. Ruis	31	10 86 D
Pine Gdns. Surb	102	19 67 C
Pine Gr. N20	15	25 94 C
Pine Gr. N4	36	30 86 B
Pine Gr. SW19	85	24 71 D
Pinehurst Wlk (off Andover Rd). Orp	108	45 66 C
Pine Rd. N11	16	28 93 A
Pine Rd. NW2	46	23 85 B
Pine Ridge. Cars	111	28 62 A
Pines Rd. Brom	99	42 69 C
Pine St. EC1	3	31 82 C
Pines The. Sun	91	10 68 A
Pine Tree Cl. Houn	69	10 76 B
Pine Wlk. Cars	110	26 62 D
Pine Wlk. Surb	102	19 67 C
Pinewood Ave. Pnr	20	13 91 B
Pinewood Ave. Sid	90	45 73 C
Pinewood Cl. Croy	106	36 65 C
Pinewood Cl. Orp	108	44 66 D
Pinewood Cl. Pnr	20	13 91 B
Pinewood Gr. SW4	74	29 74 D
Pinewood Gr. W5	54	17 81 C
Pinewood Pl. Eps	109	20 64 B
Pinewood Rd. Felt	81	10 72 D
Pinewood Rd. SE2	67	47 77 B
Pine Wood. Sun	91	10 69 A
Pinfold Rd. SW16	86	30 71 A
Pinkham Way. N11	24	28 91 C
Pinley Gdns. Dag	51	46 83 B
Pinnacle Hill. Bexh	79	49 75 D
Pinnell Rd. SE9	77	41 75 D
Pinner Ct. Pnr	20	13 89 C
Pinner Green. Pnr	20	11 90 C
Pinner Gr. Pnr	20	12 88 A
Pinner Hill. Pnr	19	10 91 D
Pinner Hill Rd. Pnr	20	11 90 C
Pinner Park Ave. Har	20	14 90 C
Pinner Park Gdns. Har	20	14 90 C
Pinner Rd. Har	32	14 88 D
Pinner Rd. Nthwd	19	10 90 A
Pinner Rd. Pnr	20	13 89 C
Pinner Rd. Pnr	20	13 89 C
Pinner View. Har	32	14 88 A
Pinn Way. Ruis	31	09 87 A
Pintail Rd. Wdf Gn	27	40 91 D
Pinto Way. SE3	77	40 75 D
Piper Cl. N7	47	30 84 B
Piper Rd. King	94	19 68 A
Pipers Green. NW9	34	20 88 A
Pipewell Rd. Cars	104	27 67 C
Pippin Cl. Croy	106	36 66 D
Pippins Ct. Ashf	91	07 70 B
Piquet Rd. SE20	98	35 69 C

Name	Page	Ref
Pirbright Rd. SW18	85	25 73 C
Pirie St. E16	58	40 80 D
Pitcairn Cl. Rom	29	49 89 C
Pitcairn Rd. Mit	96	27 70 D
Pitcairn St. SW8	74	28 75 B
Pitchford St. E15	50	39 84 C
Pitfield St. N1	4	33 82 A
Pitfield St. N1	48	33 83 C
Pitfield Way. Enf	14	35 97 A
Pitfield Way. NW10	45	20 84 A
Pitfold Cl. SE12	77	40 74 D
Pitfold Rd. SE12	77	40 74 C
Pitlake. Croy	105	31 65 B
Pitman St. SE5	63	32 77 C
Pitsea Pl. E1	57	35 81 D
Pitsea St. E1	57	35 81 D
Pitshanger La. W5	54	17 82 C
Pitsmead Ave. Brom	107	40 66 A
Pitt Cres. SW19	85	25 71 B
Pitt Rd. Th Hth	105	32 67 A
Pitt's Ct. SE1	8	33 80 C
Pitt's Head Mews. W1	6	28 80 C
Pitt St. SE15	75	33 76 B
Pitt St. SE15	63	33 77 D
Pitt St. W8	62	25 79 A
Pittville Gdns. SE25	97	34 68 A
Pixfield Ct. Brom	99	33 69 D
Pixley St. E14	57	36 81 D
Place Farm Ave. Orp	108	44 66 D
Plaistow Gr. Brom	99	40 70 D
Plaistow Gr. E15	50	39 83 B
Plaistow La. Brom	99	41 69 A
Plaistow Park Rd. E13	50	40 83 D
Plaistow Rd. E15	50	39 83 D
Plane St. SE26	87	34 72 D
Plane Tree Cres. Felt	81	10 72 D
Plane Tree Wlk. SE19	97	33 70 A
Plantagenet Cl. Wor Pk	109	20 64 B
Plantagenet Gdns. Rom	41	47 87 B
Plantagenet Pl. Rom	41	47 87 B
Plantagenet Rd. Barn	11	26 96 C
Plantain Pl. SE1	8	32 79 B
Plantation Rd. Eri	80	52 76 A
Plantation The. SE3	77	40 76 C
Plashet Gr. E6	50	41 84 D
Plashet Rd. E13	50	40 84 D
Plassy Rd. SE6	88	37 73 B
Platford Green. Horn	30	54 89 C
Platina St. EC2	4	32 82 D
Plato Rd. SW2	74	30 75 C
Platt's La. NW3	35	25 86 C
Platts Rd. Enf	14	35 97 A
Platt St. NW1	47	29 83 D
Platt The. SW15	73	23 75 B
Plawsfield Rd. Beck	98	35 68 B
Plaxtol Cl. Brom	99	41 69 A
Plaxtol Rd. Eri	67	49 77 C
Playfair St. W6	62	23 78 C
Playfield Ave. Rom	29	50 90 A
Playfield Cres. SE22	76	33 74 B
Playfield Rd. Edg	22	20 90 C
Playford Rd. N4	36	30 86 B
Playford Rd. N4	37	31 86 A
Playgreen Way. SE6	88	37 71 A
Playhouse Yd. EC4	3	31 80 D
Pleasance Rd. Orp	100	46 68 B
Pleasance Rd. SW15	72	22 74 B
Pleasance The. SW15	72	22 75 D
Pleasant Gr. Croy	106	36 65 D
Pleasant Pl. N1	48	31 84 D
Pleasant Row. NW1	47	28 83 B
Pleasant View. Eri	68	51 78 C
Pleasant Way. Wem	44	17 83 C
Plender Pl. NW1	47	29 83 A
Plender St. NW1	47	29 83 A
Pleshey Rd. N7	47	29 85 B
Plesman Way. Wall	111	30 62 A
Plevna Cres. N15	37	33 88 C
Plevna Rd. Hamp	92	13 69 B
Plevna Rd. N9	17	34 93 D
Plevna St. E14	64	38 79 C
Pleydell Ave. SE19	97	33 70 D
Pleydell Ave. W6	61	21 78 B
Pleydell St. EC4	3	31 81 C
Plimsoll Cl. E14	57	37 81 D
Plimsoll Rd. N4	37	31 86 D
Plimsoll Rd. N5	37	31 86 D
Plough Alley. E1	57	34 80 C
Plough Ct. EC4	8	32 80 B
Plough La. Cl. Wall	111	30 64 C
Plough La. Pur	111	30 62 D
Plough La. SE22	75	33 74 D
Plough La. SW17	85	26 71 A
Plough La. SW19	85	25 71 D
Plough La. Wall	111	30 64 B
Ploughmans End. Islw	70	14 74 B
Ploughmans Way. SW11	73	26 75 D
Plough Pl. EC4	3	31 81 C
Plough Rd. Eps	109	20 63 D
Plough Rd. SW11	73	26 75 D
Plough St. E1	57	34 81 C
Plough Ter. SW11	73	26 75 D
Ploughway. SE16	64	36 78 A
Plough Yd. EC2	4	33 82 C
Plough Yd. EC2	4	33 82 C
Plumber's Pl. EC1	3	31 82 C
Plumbers Row. E1	57	34 81 C
Plumbridge St. SE10	76	38 76 A
Plum Garth. Brent	60	17 78 B
Plum La. SE18	66	44 77 C
Plummer La. Mit	96	27 69 D
Plummer Rd. SW4	86	29 73 B
Plumpton Ave. Horn	42	54 86 D
Plumpton Cl. Nthlt	43	13 84 A
Plumstead Common Rd. SE18	66	44 77 A
Plumstead High St. SE18	66	45 78 A
Plumstead Rd. SE18	66	44 78 A
Plumtree Ct. EC4	3	31 81 D
Plymouth Rd. Brom	99	40 69 B
Plymouth Rd. E16	58	40 81 A
Plympton Ave. NW6	46	24 84 D
Plympton Pl. NW8	1	27 82 C
Plympton Rd. NW6	46	24 84 D
Plympton St. NW8	1	27 82 C
Plymstock Rd. Well	67	47 77 C
Pocklington Cl. NW9	22	21 90 C
Pocklington Ct. SW15	84	22 73 C
Pocock St. SE1	7	31 79 B
Podmore Rd. SW18	73	26 75 C
Poets Corner. SW1	7	30 79 C
Poet's Rd. N5	48	32 85 D
Pointalls Cl. N3	23	26 90 C
Point Cl. SE10	76	38 76 A
Point Hill. SE10	76	38 76 A
Point Pleasant. SW18	73	25 75 C
Poland St. W1	2	29 81 C
Polebrook Rd. SE3	77	41 75 A
Pole Cat Alley. Brom	107	39 65 B
Polecroft La. SE6	88	36 72 B
Pole Hill Rd. E4	18	38 94 A
Polesden Gdns. SW20	94	22 69 D
Polesworth Rd. Dag	52	47 84 D
Pollard Cl. E16	58	40 80 A
Pollard Cl. N7	47	30 85 B
Pollard Rd. Mord	103	26 67 B
Pollard Rd. N20	16	27 93 A
Pollard Row. E2	57	34 82 A
Pollards Cres. SW16	96	30 68 A
Pollards Hill E. SW16	96	30 68 B
Pollards Hill N. SW16	96	30 68 B
Pollards Hill S. SW16	96	30 68 B
Pollards Hill W. SW16	96	30 68 B
Pollard St. E2	57	34 82 A
Pollards Wood Rd. SW16	96	30 68 A
Pollen St. W1	2	29 81 C
Pollitt Dr. NW8	1	26 82 D
Polperro Cl. Orp	108	45 67 D
Polsted Rd. SE6	88	36 73 B
Polthorne Gr. SE18	66	44 78 B
Polworth Rd. SW16	86	30 71 C
Polygon Rd. NW1	47	29 83 D
Polygon The. SW4	74	29 75 C
Polytechnic St. SE18	66	43 78 A
Pomell Way. E1	4	33 81 D
Pomeroy St. SE14	76	35 76 A
Pomfret Rd. SE5	75	32 75 A
Pond Cl. SE3	77	39 76 D
Pond Cottage La. W Wick	106	37 66 C
Pond Cottages. SE21	87	33 73 C
Ponder St. N7	47	30 84 D
Pondfield Rd. Brom	107	39 66 C
Pondfield Rd. Dag	52	49 85 D
Pondfield Rd. Orp	108	43 65 D
Pond Green. Ruis	31	09 86 A
Pond Hill Gdns. Sutt	110	24 63 A
Pond Mead. SE21	75	32 74 D
Pond Pl. SW3	9	27 78 C
Pond Rd. E15	50	39 83 C
Pond Rd. SE3	77	39 76 D
Pond St. NW3	47	27 85 B
Pond Way. Tedd	93	17 70 A
Ponler St. E1	57	34 81 D
Ponsard Rd. NW10	55	22 82 B
Ponsford St. E9	49	35 84 A
Ponsonby Pl. SW1	10	29 78 D
Ponsonby Rd. SW15	84	22 73 B
Ponsonby Terr. SW1	10	29 78 D
Pontefract Rd. Brom	89	39 71 D
Ponton Rd. SW8	10	29 77 D
Pont St Mews. SW1	5	27 79 D
Pont St. SW1	5	27 79 D
Pontypool Pl. SE1	7	31 79 B
Pontypool Wlk. Rom	30	53 91 A
Pool Cl. Beck	88	37 71 C
Poole Cl. Ruis	31	09 86 A
Poole Court Rd. Houn	70	12 76 C
Poole Rd. E9	49	35 84 B
Poole Rd. Eps	109	20 63 B
Poole Rd. Horn	42	54 87 B
Pooles Bldgs. EC1	3	31 82 C
Pooles La. Dag	52	48 83 C
Pooles La. SW10	62	26 77 C
Pooles Park. N4	37	31 86 A
Poole St. N1	48	32 83 B
Poolsford Rd. NW9	22	21 89 C
Poonah St. E1	57	35 81 C
Pope Rd. Brom	107	41 67 B
Pope's Ave. Twick	83	15 72 A
Popes Dri. N3	23	25 90 A
Popes Gr. Croy	106	36 65 D
Pope's Gr. Twick	83	15 72 B
Pope's Head Alley. EC3	4	32 81 D
Pope's La. W5	60	18 79 C
Pope's La. W5	61	19 79 C
Pope's Rd. SW9	75	31 75 A
Pope St. SE1	8	33 79 A
Popham Cl. Felt	82	12 72 D
Popham Rd (off Brittania Row). N1	48	32 83 A
Popham Rd (off New North Rd). N1	48	32 83 A
Popham St. N1	48	32 83 A
Poplar Ave. Mit	96	27 69 D
Poplar Ave. Orp	108	43 65 B
Poplar Ave. Sthl	59	13 79 D
Poplar Bath St. E14	57	37 80 B
Poplar Cl. Pnr	20	11 90 B
Poplar Cres. Eps	109	20 63 A
Poplar Ct. Nthlt	43	11 83 C
Poplar Ct. SW19	85	25 71 C
Poplar Farm Cl. Eps	109	20 63 A
Poplar Gdns. N Mal	94	20 69 D
Poplar Gr. N Mal	94	20 68 B
Poplar Gr. W6	62	23 79 A
Poplar Gr. Wem	34	20 86 C
Poplar High St. E14	57	37 80 B
Poplar Mews. W12	56	23 80 C
Poplar Pl. W2	56	25 80 B
Poplar Rd. Ashf	81	08 71 C
Poplar Rd. SE24	75	32 75 C
Poplar Rd. Sutt	103	24 66 D
Poplar Rd. SW19	95	25 69 C
Poplar Road S. SW19	95	25 68 A
Poplars Ave. NW2	46	23 84 A
Poplars Cl. Ruis	31	09 87 C
Poplars Rd. E17	38	37 88 D
Poplars The. N14	12	28 95 B
Poplar St. Rom	29	50 89 C
Poplar Way. Felt	81	10 72 D
Poplar Way. Ilf	28	44 89 C
Poplar Wlk. Croy	105	32 66 C
Poplar Wlk. SE24	75	32 75 A
Poplar Wlk. SE24	75	32 75 C
Poppins Ct. EC4	3	31 81 D
Poppleton Rd. E11	39	39 88 C
Popular Mount. Belv	67	50 78 A
Porchester Gdn Mews. W2	56	25 81 D
Porchester Gdns. W2	56	25 80 B
Porchester Mead. Beck	98	37 70 B
Porchester Mews. W2	56	25 81 D
Porchester Pl. W2	1	27 81 C
Porchester Rd. King	94	19 69 D
Porchester Rd. W2	56	25 81 D
Porchester Sq. W2	56	25 81 D
Porchester Terr N. W2	56	25 81 D
Porchester Terr. W2	5	26 80 A
Porchfield Cl. Sutt	110	25 62 D
Porch Way. N20	16	27 93 D
Porcupine Cl. SE9	89	42 72 A
Porden Rd. SW2	74	30 75 D
Porlock Ho. SE26	87	34 72 C
Porlock Rd. Enf	17	33 94 B
Porlock St. SE1	8	32 79 B
Porrington Cl. Chis	100	43 69 A
Portal Cl. SE27	87	31 72 C
Portbury Cl. SE15	75	34 76 A
Portchester Cl. Horn	42	54 88 C
Port Cres. E13	58	40 82 D
Portelet Rd. E1	57	35 82 D
Porten Rd. W14	62	24 79 C
Porters Ave. Dag	52	47 85 C
Porter St. W1	1	27 81 B
Porteus Rd. W2	56	26 81 A
Portgate Cl. W9	56	24 82 D
Porthcawe Rd. SE26	88	36 71 B

Porthkerry Ave. Well. ...78 46 75 C
Portia Ct. Bark ...51 46 84 C
Portia Way. E3 ...57 36 82 D
Portinscale Rd. SW15 ...73 24 74 B
Portland Ave. N16 ...37 33 87 B
Portland Ave. N.Mal ...102 21 66 B
Portland Ave. Sid ...78 46 74 C
Portland Crescent W. Stan. ...21 17 89 B
Portland Cres. Felt. ...81 08 71 B
Portland Cres. Grnf ...53 14 81 A
Portland Cres. SE9 ...89 42 72 A
Portland Cres. Stan. ...21 18 90 C
Portland Gdns. N4 ...37 31 89 D
Portland Gdns. Rom ...41 47 88 B
Portland Gr. SW8 ...74 30 76 B
Portland Mews. W1 ...2 29 81 C
Portland Pl. SE25 ...97 34 68 C
Portland Pl. W1 ...2 28 81 D
Portland Rd. Brom ...89 41 71 C
Portland Rd. King ...93 18 68 B
Portland Rd. Mit ...96 27 69 C
Portland Rd. N15 ...25 33 89 D
Portland Rd. SE25 ...105 34 67 B
Portland Rd. SE9 ...89 42 72 A
Portland Rd. Sthl ...59 12 79 D
Portland Rd. W11 ...56 24 80 C
Portland Rise. N4 ...37 32 87 C
Portland Ter. SE17 ...63 32 78 D
Portland Terr. Rich ...71 17 75 D
Portland Wlk. SE17 ...63 32 77 B
Portman Bldgs. NW1 ...1 27 82 C
Portman Cl. Bexh. ...79 47 75 B
Portman Cl. W1 ...2 28 81 C
Portman Dri. Wdf Gn ...27 41 90 D
Portman Gdns. NW9 ...22 20 90 D
Portman Mews S. W1 ...2 28 81 C
Portman Pl. E2 ...57 35 82 A
Portman Rd. King ...93 18 69 D
Portman Sq. W1 ...2 28 81 C
Portman St. W1 ...2 28 81 C
Portman Towers. W1 ...1 27 81 D
Portmeadow Wlk. SE2 ...67 47 79 B
Portmeers Cl. E17 ...38 36 88 D
Portnall Rd. W9 ...56 24 82 B
Portnoi Cl. Rom ...29 50 90 D
Portobello Ct Estate. W11 ...56 24 81 D
Portobello Mews. W11 ...56 25 80 A
Portobello Rd. W10 ...56 24 81 A
Portobello Rd. W11 ...56 24 81 D
Porton Ct. Surb ...101 17 67 C
Portpool La. EC1 ...3 31 81 A
Portree Cl. N22 ...24 30 91 D
Portree St. E14 ...58 38 81 D
Portsdown Mews. NW11 ...35 24 88 D
Portsea Mews. W2 ...1 27 81 C
Portsea Pl. W2 ...1 27 81 C
Portslade Rd. SW8 ...74 29 76 C
Portsmouth Ave. Surb ...101 16 66 A
Portsmouth Rd. Esh ...101 15 65 A
Portsmouth Rd. Surb ...101 16 66 B
Portsmouth Rd. SW15 ...85 23 73 A
Portsmouth St. WC2 ...3 30 81 D
Portsoken St. E1 ...8 33 80 B
Portswood Pl. SW15 ...84 21 73 B
Portswood Pl. SW15 ...72 21 74 D
Portugal Gdns. Twick ...82 14 72 A
Portugal St. WC2 ...3 30 81 D
Portway Cres. Eps ...109 22 62 A
Portway. E15 ...50 39 83 B
Portway. Eps ...109 22 62 A
Portway Gdns. SE18 ...65 41 77 D
Postern Green. Enf ...13 31 96 A
Post La. Twick ...82 14 73 C
Post Office Alley. W4 ...61 19 77 B
Post Office App. E7 ...50 40 85 D
Post Office Ct. EC4 ...4 32 81 D
Postway Mews. Ilf ...40 43 86 D
Potier St. SE1 ...8 32 79 D
Potter Cl. Mit ...96 28 69 D
Potter Heights Cl. Pnr ...19 10 91 D
Potterne Cl. SW19 ...85 23 73 B
Potters Fields. SE1 ...8 33 80 C
Potters Gr. N Mal ...94 20 68 C
Potter's La. Barn ...11 25 96 C
Potter's La. SW16 ...96 29 70 B
Potter's Rd. Barn ...11 25 96 D
Potter St. Nthwd ...19 10 90 B
Potter St. Pnr ...19 10 90 B
Potter Street Hill. Pnr ...19 10 91 D
Pottery La. W11 ...56 24 80 C
Pottery Rd. Brent ...60 18 77 A
Pottery St. SE16 ...63 34 79 B
Pott St. E2 ...57 34 82 B
Poulett Gdns. Twick ...83 16 73 C
Poulett Rd. E6 ...50 42 83 D

Poulner Way. SE15 ...63 33 77 D
Poulton Ave. Sutt ...103 26 65 D
Poulton Ave. Sutt ...104 27 65 C
Poulton Cl. E8 ...48 34 85 D
Poultry. EC2 ...4 32 81 D
Pound Cl. Orp ...108 44 65 B
Pound Cl. Surb ...101 17 66 C
Pound Court Dr. Orp ...108 45 66 B
Pound La. NW10 ...45 22 84 A
Pound Park Rd. SE7 ...65 41 78 B
Pound Pl. SE9 ...78 43 74 C
Pound St. Cars ...111 27 64 D
Pountney Rd. SW11 ...74 28 75 A
Poverest Rd. Orp ...108 46 67 A
Powder Mill La. Twick ...82 13 73 C
Powell Cl. Edg ...21 18 91 B
Powell Cl. Wall ...111 30 63 C
Powell Gdns. Dag ...52 49 85 A
Powell Rd. E5 ...37 34 86 D
Powell's Wlk. W4 ...61 21 77 A
Power Rd. W4 ...61 19 78 B
Powerscroft Rd. E5 ...49 35 85 A
Powers Ct. Twick ...83 17 73 B
Powis Gdns. NW11 ...35 24 87 D
Powis Gdns. W11 ...56 24 81 D
Powis Mews. W11 ...56 24 81 D
Powis Pl. WC1 ...3 30 82 C
Powis Rd. E3 ...57 37 82 B
Powis Sq. W11 ...56 24 81 D
Powis St. SE18 ...66 43 79 C
Powis Terr. W11 ...56 24 81 D
Powlett Pl. NW1 ...47 28 84 D
Pownall Gdns. Houn ...70 13 75 D
Pownall Rd. E8 ...48 34 83 A
Pownall Rd. Houn ...70 13 75 D
Powster Rd. Brom ...89 40 71 D
Powys Cl. Bexh. ...67 47 77 B
Powys La. N13 ...16 30 92 A
Powys La. N14 ...16 30 92 A
Poynders Ct. SW4 ...74 29 74 C
Poynders Gdns. SW4 ...86 29 73 A
Poynders Rd. SW4 ...86 29 73 B
Poynings Rd. N19 ...36 29 86 C
Poynings Way. N12 ...15 25 92 C
Poynings Way. Rom ...30 54 90 A
Poyntell Cres. Chis ...100 44 69 B
Poynter Rd. Enf ...13 34 95 A
Poynton Rd. N17 ...25 34 90 C
Poyntz Rd. SW11 ...74 27 76 D
Poyser St. E2 ...48 34 83 D
Praed Mews. W2 ...1 26 81 D
Praed St. W2 ...1 26 81 D
Pragel St. E13 ...50 41 83 C
Pragnell Rd. SE12 ...89 40 72 B
Prague Pl. SW2 ...74 30 74 A
Prah Rd. N4 ...37 31 86 A
Prairie St. SW8 ...74 28 76 D
Pratt Mews. NW1 ...47 29 83 A
Pratt St. NW1 ...47 29 83 A
Pratt Wlk. SE11 ...10 30 78 B
Prayle Gr. NW2 ...35 23 87 B
Prayle Gr. NW2 ...35 23 87 D
Prebend Gdns. W6 ...61 21 78 B
Prebend St. N1 ...48 32 83 A
Precincts The. Mord ...103 25 67 C
Premier Pl. SW15 ...73 23 75 D
Prendergast Rd. SE3 ...77 39 75 A
Prentice Ct. SW19 ...85 24 71 D
Prentis Rd. SW16 ...86 29 71 B
Prentiss Ct. SE7 ...65 41 78 B
Presburg Rd. N.Mal ...102 21 67 A
Prescelly Pl. Edg ...21 18 90 B
Prescot St. E1 ...8 33 80 B
Prescott Ave. Orp ...108 43 67 D
Prescott Pl. SW4 ...74 29 75 D
President. EC1 ...4 32 82 A
Press Rd. NW10 ...34 20 86 D
Prestbury Rd. E7 ...50 41 84 C
Prestbury Sq. SE9 ...89 42 71 B
Prested Rd. SW11 ...74 27 75 C
Preston Ave. E4 ...26 38 91 B
Preston Cl. SE1 ...63 33 78 A
Preston Cl. Twick ...83 15 72 C
Preston Dri. Bexh ...79 47 76 B
Preston Dri. E11 ...39 41 88 A
Preston Dri. Eps ...109 21 63 B
Preston Gdns. Ilf ...39 42 88 D
Preston Gdns. NW10 ...45 21 84 A
Preston Hill. Har ...33 18 88 D
Preston Pl. NW2 ...45 22 84 A
Preston Pl. Rich ...71 18 74 A
Preston Rd. Brom ...107 40 65 A
Preston Rd. E11 ...39 39 88 C
Preston Rd. Har ...33 18 87 A
Preston Rd. SE19 ...97 31 70 B

Preston Rd. SW20 ...94 22 70 C
Preston Rd. Wem ...33 18 86 A
Preston's Rd. E14 ...58 38 80 C
Preston Waye. Har ...33 18 87 C
Prestwick Cl. Sthl ...59 12 78 C
Prestwood Ave. Har ...21 16 89 D
Prestwood Cl. Har ...21 16 89 D
Prestwood Gdns. Croy ...105 32 66 A
Pretoria Ave. E17 ...38 36 89 C
Pretoria Cres. E4 ...18 38 94 C
Pretoria Rd. E11 ...38 38 87 D
Pretoria Rd. E16 ...58 39 82 D
Pretoria Rd. E4 ...18 38 94 D
Pretoria Rd. Ilf ...51 43 85 D
Pretoria Rd. N17 ...25 33 91 B
Pretoria Rd. Rom ...41 50 88 A
Pretoria Rd. SW16 ...86 29 71 C
Pretoria Road N. N18 ...25 33 91 B
Prevost Rd. N11 ...16 28 93 A
Price Cl. NW7 ...23 24 91 A
Price's St. SE1 ...7 31 80 D
Price's Yd. N1 ...47 30 83 B
Price Way. Hamp ...92 12 70 A
Pricklers Hill. Barn ...11 25 95 B
Prickley Wood. Brom ...107 39 66 D
Priddy's Yd. Croy ...105 32 65 A
Prideaux Pl. W3 ...55 20 80 B
Prideaux Pl. WC1 ...3 30 82 B
Prideaux Rd. SW9 ...74 30 75 A
Pridham Rd E. Th Hth. ...97 32 68 D
Priestfield Rd. SE23 ...88 36 72 C
Priestlands Park Rd. Sid. ...90 45 72 D
Priestley Cl. N16 ...37 33 87 B
Priestley Gdns. Rom ...40 46 88 D
Priestley Way. E17 ...26 35 89 B
Priestley Way. NW2 ...34 22 87 C
Priestley Way. NW9 ...34 22 87 C
Priestly Rd. Mit ...96 28 69 C
Priests Ave. Rom ...29 50 90 D
Priests Bridge. SW14 ...72 21 75 A
Priests Bridge. SW15 ...72 21 75 B
Priest's Ct. EC2 ...4 32 81 C
Prima Rd. SW 9 ...63 31 77 C
Primrose Ave. Enf ...13 33 97 A
Primrose Ave. Rom ...40 46 87 B
Primrose Cl. Har ...32 12 86 D
Primrose Gdns. NW3 ...47 27 84 A
Primrose Gdns. Ruis ...43 11 85 C
Primrose Glen. Horn ...30 54 89 C
Primrose Hill. NW3 ...47 27 84 D
Primrose Hill. EC4 ...3 31 81 C
Primrose Hill Rd. NW3 ...47 27 84 D
Primrose Hill Studios. NW1 ...47 28 83 A
Primrose Rd. E10 ...38 37 87 D
Primrose Rd. E18 ...27 40 90 D
Primrose St. EC2 ...4 33 81 A
Primrose Way. Wem ...44 17 83 D
Primula St. W12 ...55 22 81 C
Prince Albert Rd. NW1 ...47 28 83 A
Prince Albert Rd. NW8 ...47 27 83 C
Prince Arthur Mews. NW3 ...46 26 85 A
Prince Arthur Rd. NW3 ...46 26 85 C
Prince Charles Dri. NW4 ...35 23 87 A
Prince Charles Rd. SE3 ...77 39 76 B
Prince Charles Way. Wall ...104 28 65 D
Prince Cl. SW17 ...86 27 72 D
Prince Consort Dri. Chis ...100 44 69 B
Prince Consort Rd. SW7 ...5 26 79 D
Princedale Rd. W11 ...56 24 80 C
Prince Edward Rd. E9 ...49 36 84 B
Prince George Ave. N14 ...12 29 95 B
Prince George Rd. N16 ...48 33 85 A
Prince George's Ave. SW20 ...95 23 69 C
Prince George's Rd. SW19 ...95 26 69 B
Prince Henry Rd. SE7 ...65 41 77 D
Prince Imperial Rd. Chis ...100 43 70 D
Prince Imperial Rd. SE18 ...78 43 76 A
Prince John Rd. SE9 ...77 42 74 A
Prince of Orange La. SE10 ...64 38 77 C
Prince of Wales Cl. NW4 ...22 22 89 D
Prince of Wales Dri. SW11 ...74 28 76 A
Prince of Wales Dri. SW11 ...2 28 77 D
Prince of Wales Rd. E16 ...58 41 81 C
Prince of Wales Rd. NW5 ...47 28 84 A
Prince of Wales Rd. SE3 ...77 39 76 B
Prince Of Wales Rd. Sutt. ...103 26 65 B
Prince of Wales Terr. W4 ...61 21 78 C
Prince of Wales Terr. W8 ...62 25 79 B
Prince Rd. Croy ...112 31 64 D
Prince Rd. SE25 ...105 33 67 A
Prince Rd. SE25 ...97 33 68 C
Prince Regent La. E13 ...58 41 82 C

Prince Regent La. E16 ...58 | 41 81 C
Prince Regent Rd. Houn ...70 | 14 75 A
Prince Rupert Rd. SE9 ...77 | 42 75 B
Princes Arc. SW1 ...6 | 29 80 C
Princes Ave. Cars ...111 | 27 62 B
Prince's Ave. Grnf ...53 | 13 81 D
Princes Ave. N10 ...24 | 28 89 B
Princes Ave. N13 ...17 | 31 92 C
Princes Ave. N22 ...24 | 29 90 B
Princes Ave. N3 ...23 | 25 90 B
Princes Ave. NW9 ...22 | 19 89 D
Princes Ave. Orp ...108 | 45 67 A
Princes Ave. Surb ...102 | 19 65 A
Princes Ave. W3 ...61 | 19 78 C
Prince's Cl. NW9 ...22 | 19 89 C
Prince's Cl. Tedd ...82 | 14 71 B
Princes Ct. Wem ...44 | 18 85 C
Princes Dri. Har ...21 | 15 89 A
Princes Gate Mews. SW7 ...5 | 26 79 D
Princes Gdns. SW7 ...5 | 26 79 D
Princes Gdns. W3 ...55 | 19 81 C
Princes Gdns. W5 ...54 | 17 82 C
Princes La. N10 ...24 | 28 89 B
Prince's Mews. W2 ...56 | 25 80 B
Princes Park Ave. NW11 ...35 | 24 88 A
Prince's Plain. Brom ...107 | 42 66 D
Princes Pl. W11 ...56 | 24 80 C
Princes Rd. Dart ...80 | 52 74 C
Princes Rd. Felt ...81 | 09 72 D
Princes Rd. Ilf ...28 | 44 89 D
Princes Rd. King ...94 | 19 70 C
Princes Rd. N18 ...18 | 35 92 A
Princes Rd. Rich ...71 | 18 74 B
Princes Rd. Rich ...71 | 18 76 B
Princes Rd. Rom ...42 | 52 88 A
Princes Rd. SE20 ...98 | 35 70 B
Prince's Rd. SW14 ...72 | 20 75 B
Prince's Rd. SW19 ...95 | 25 70 A
Prince's Rd. Tedd ...82 | 14 71 B
Prince's Rd. W13 ...54 | 16 80 D
Princes Rise. SE13 ...76 | 38 76 C
Princess Ave. Wem ...33 | 18 86 A
Princess Cres. N4 ...37 | 31 86 B
Princess May Rd. N16 ...48 | 33 85 A
Princess Mews. NW3 ...46 | 26 84 B
Princess Par. Orp ...108 | 43 65 C
Prince's Sq. W2 ...56 | 25 80 B
Princess Rd. Croy ...105 | 32 67 C
Princess Rd. NW1 ...47 | 28 83 A
Princess Rd. NW6 ...46 | 25 83 C
Princess St. SE1 ...7 | 31 79 D
Princess's Wlk. Rich ...60 | 18 77 C
Princes St. Bexh ...79 | 48 75 B
Prince's St. EC2 ...4 | 32 81 D
Princes St. N17 ...25 | 33 91 A
Princes St. Rich ...71 | 18 74 A
Princes St. Sutt ...110 | 26 64 B
Princes St. W1 ...2 | 28 81 D
Prince's Terr. E13 ...50 | 40 83 B
Prince St. SE8 ...64 | 37 77 A
Princes Way. Croy ...111 | 30 64 D
Princes Way. Ruis ...43 | 12 85 A
Princes Way. SW19 ...85 | 24 73 C
Princes Way. W.Wick ...107 | 39 65 D
Princes Yd. W11 ...56 | 24 80 C
Princethorpe Rd. SE26 ...88 | 35 71 B
Princeton St. WC1 ...3 | 30 81 B
Pringle Gdns. SW16 ...86 | 29 71 A
Pring St. W10 ...56 | 23 80 B
Printer St. EC4 ...3 | 31 81 C
Printing House Yd. E2 ...4 | 33 82 A
Priolo Rd. SE7 ...65 | 41 78 C
Prior Ave. Sutt ...111 | 27 63 C
Prior Bolton St. N1 ...48 | 31 84 B
Prioress St. SE1 ...8 | 33 79 C
Prioress Wlk. SE27 ...87 | 31 72 D
Priors Croft. E17 ...26 | 36 90 D
Priors Field. Nthlt ...43 | 12 84 A
Priorsford Ave. Orp ...100 | 46 68 D
Priors Gdns. Ruis ...43 | 11 85 C
Priors Mead. Enf ...13 | 33 97 A
Priors Park. Horn ...42 | 53 86 C
Prior St. SE10 ...64 | 38 77 C
Priory Ave. E17 ...38 | 37 88 A
Priory Ave. E4 ...18 | 37 93 C
Priory Ave. N8 ...24 | 29 89 D
Priory Ave. Orp ...108 | 44 67 D
Priory Ave. Sutt ...110 | 23 64 B
Priory Ave. W4 ...61 | 21 79 C
Priory Ave. Wem ...44 | 15 85 B
Priory Cl. Beck ...98 | 36 68 A
Priory Cl. Chis ...99 | 42 69 B
Priory Cl. Dart ...80 | 53 74 B
Priory Cl. E18 ...27 | 40 90 A
Priory Cl. E4 ...18 | 36 93 D

Priory Cl. Hamp ...92 | 12 69 B
Priory Cl. N14 ...12 | 28 95 B
Priory Cl. N20 ...15 | 24 94 B
Priory Cl. N3 ...23 | 24 90 B
Priory Cl. Ruis ...31 | 09 87 D
Priory Cl. Sun ...91 | 10 70 C
Priory Cl. SW19 ...95 | 25 69 B
Priory Cl. Wem ...44 | 15 85 B
Priory Cres. SE19 ...97 | 32 70 C
Priory Cres. Sutt ...110 | 23 64 B
Priory Cres. Wem ...33 | 16 86 C
Priory Ct. E17 ...26 | 36 90 D
Priory Ct. E6 ...50 | 41 83 B
Priory Ct. SE15 ...76 | 35 75 C
Priory Ct. SW8 ...74 | 29 76 B
Priory Dri. SE2 ...67 | 47 78 D
Priory Gdns. Dart ...80 | 53 74 B
Priory Gdns. Hamp ...92 | 12 69 B
Priory Gdns. N6 ...36 | 28 88 D
Priory Gdns. SW13 ...72 | 21 75 B
Priory Gdns. W4 ...61 | 21 78 A
Priory Gdns. Wem ...44 | 16 85 A
Priory Gr. SW8 ...74 | 30 76 A
Priory Hill. Dart ...80 | 53 74 D
Priory Hill. Wem ...44 | 16 85 A
Priory Lane. E.Mol ...92 | 13 68 D
Priory La. SW15 ...72 | 21 74 B
Priory Mews. SW8 ...74 | 29 76 B
Priory Park Rd. NW6 ...46 | 24 83 B
Priory Park Rd. Wem ...44 | 16 85 A
Priory Pl. Dart ...80 | 53 74 D
Priory Rd. Bark ...51 | 44 84 D
Priory Rd. Chess ...101 | 18 65 C
Priory Rd. Croy ...105 | 31 66 A
Priory Rd. Dart ...80 | 53 74 D
Priory Rd. E6 ...50 | 41 83 B
Priory Rd. Hamp ...92 | 13 70 C
Priory Rd. Houn ...70 | 14 74 A
Priory Rd. N8 ...24 | 29 89 D
Priory Rd. NW6 ...46 | 25 84 D
Priory Rd. Rich ...61 | 19 77 C
Priory Rd. Sutt ...110 | 23 64 B
Priory Rd. SW19 ...95 | 26 70 D
Priory Rd. W4 ...61 | 20 79 D
Priory St. E3 ...57 | 37 82 B
Priory Terr. NW6 ...46 | 25 83 B
Priory The. SE3 ...77 | 39 75 D
Priory Way. Har ...20 | 13 89 D
Priory Way. Sthl ...59 | 11 79 D
Priory Wlk. SW10 ...62 | 26 78 C
Priscilla Rd. E3 ...57 | 37 82 A
Pritchard's Rd. E2 ...48 | 34 83 C
Priter Rd. SE16 ...63 | 34 79 C
Priter Way. SE16 ...63 | 34 79 C
Private Rd. Enf ...13 | 33 95 A
Probert Rd. SW2 ...75 | 31 74 A
Probyn Rd. SW2 ...87 | 31 72 B
Procter St. WC1 ...3 | 30 81 B
Proctors Cl. Felt ...81 | 10 73 C
Progress Way. Croy ...104 | 30 65 B
Progress Way. Enf ...13 | 34 95 A
Progress Way. N22 ...25 | 31 90 A
Promenade Approach Rd. W4 ...61 | 21 77 C
Promenade The. W4 ...72 | 21 76 A
Proof Butts Rd. SE28 ...66 | 45 79 A
Prospect Cl. Belv ...67 | 49 78 A
Prospect Cl. Houn ...70 | 12 76 B
Prospect Cl. Ruis ...32 | 11 87 B
Prospect Cl. SE26 ...87 | 34 71 B
Prospect Cottages. SW18 ...73 | 25 75 C
Prospect Cres. Twick ...70 | 14 74 C
Prospect Hill. E17 ...26 | 37 89 D
Prospect Pl. Brom ...99 | 40 68 B
Prospect Pl. N17 ...25 | 33 91 C
Prospect Pl. N2 ...23 | 26 89 D
Prospect Pl. NW2 ...35 | 24 86 D
Prospect Pl. Rom ...29 | 50 90 C
Prospect Pl. W4 ...61 | 20 78 D
Prospect Rd. Barn ...11 | 25 96 D
Prospect Rd. Horn ...30 | 54 89 B
Prospect Rd. N2 ...24 | 27 89 A
Prospect Rd. NW2 ...35 | 25 86 C
Prospect Rd. Surb ...101 | 17 67 C
Prospect Rd. Wdf Gn ...27 | 41 91 A
Prospect Ring. N2 ...24 | 27 89 A
Prospect St. SE16 ...64 | 34 79 B
Prospect Vale. SE18 ...65 | 42 78 A
Prospect Wlk. E2 ...57 | 35 82 B
Prospero Rd. N19 ...36 | 29 87 D
Prothero Gdns. NW4 ...34 | 22 88 B
Prothero Rd. SW6 ...62 | 24 77 D
Prout Gr. NW10 ...45 | 21 85 B
Prout Rd. E5 ...37 | 34 86 D
Provence St. N1 ...48 | 32 83 C

Providence Ct. W1 ...6 | 28 80 A
Providence Pl. N1 ...48 | 31 83 B
Providence Row. N1 ...47 | 30 83 D
*Providence Yd. E2 ...57 | 34 82 A
Provost Rd. NW3 ...47 | 27 84 D
Provost St. N1 ...4 | 32 82 B
Prowse Pl. NW1 ...47 | 29 84 C
Pruden Cl. N14 ...16 | 29 93 A
Prudent Pas. EC2 ...4 | 32 81 C
Prusom St. E1 ...8 | 34 80 D
Pryors The. NW3 ...35 | 26 86 D
Pudding La. EC3 ...8 | 32 80 B
Pudding Mill La. E15 ...49 | 37 83 B
Puddle Dock. EC4 ...7 | 31 80 B
Pugh's Pl. W1 ...2 | 29 81 C
Pulborough Rd. SW18 ...85 | 24 73 B
Pulborough Way. Houn ...70 | 11 75 C
Pulford Rd. N15 ...37 | 32 88 D
Pulham Ave. N2 ...23 | 26 89 D
Puller Rd. Barn ...11 | 24 96 A
Pullman Cl. SW2 ...86 | 30 73 D
Pullman Gdns. SW15 ...73 | 23 74 C
Pulross Rd. SW9 ...74 | 30 75 B
Pulteney Cl. E3 ...49 | 36 83 B
Pulteney Rd. E18 ...27 | 40 89 B
Pulteney Terr. N1 ...47 | 30 83 B
Pulton Pl. SW6 ...62 | 25 77 C
Puma Ct. E1 ...4 | 33 81 B
Pump Alley. Brent ...60 | 17 77 D
Pump Cl. Nthlt ...43 | 13 83 C
Pump Ct. EC4 ...3 | 31 81 C
Pumping Station Rd. W4 ...61 | 21 77 C
Pump Pail N. Croy ...105 | 32 65 C
Pump Pail S. Croy ...105 | 32 65 C
Punderson's Gdns. E2 ...57 | 34 82 B
Purbeck Ave. N.Mal ...102 | 21 67 D
Purbeck Dri. NW2 ...35 | 23 86 B
Purbeck Dri. NW2 ...35 | 24 86 A
Purbeck Rd. Horn ...42 | 52 87 A
Purberry Gr. Eps ...109 | 21 62 D
Purbrook St. SE1 ...8 | 33 79 C
Purcell Cres. SW6 ...62 | 24 77 C
Purcell Rd. Grnf ...53 | 13 81 B
Purcell St. N1 ...48 | 33 83 C
Purchese St. NW1 ...47 | 29 83 D
Purdy St. E3 ...57 | 37 82 D
Purland Cl. Dag ...41 | 48 87 D
Purland Rd. SE28 ...66 | 46 79 A
Purleigh Ave. Wdf Gn ...27 | 42 91 A
Purley Ave. NW2 ...35 | 24 86 A
Purley Bury Ave. Pur ...112 | 32 62 C
Purley Cl. Ilf ...28 | 43 90 C
Purley Ct. Pur ...112 | 31 62 D
Purley Downs Rd. Pur ...112 | 32 62 C
Purley Oaks Rd. S.Croy ...112 | 32 62 D
Purley Park Rd. Pur ...112 | 31 62 D
Purley Pl. N1 ...48 | 31 84 D
Purley Rd. N9 ...17 | 33 93 C
Purley Rd. S.Croy ...112 | 32 63 D
Purley Way. Croy ...112 | 31 64 A
Purley Way. Pur ...112 | 31 62 C
Purnell Pl. SE16 ...57 | 35 80 D
Purneys Rd. SE9 ...77 | 41 75 D
Pursers Cross Rd. SW6 ...73 | 24 76 B
Pursley Rd. NW7 ...22 | 22 91 B
Purves Rd. NW10 ...55 | 22 82 B
Purves Rd. NW10 ...46 | 23 83 C
Putney Bridge App. SW6 ...73 | 24 75 A
Putney Bridge Rd. SW15 ...73 | 24 75 D
Putney Common. SW15 ...73 | 23 75 A
Putney Heath. SW15 ...73 | 23 74 C
Putney Heath. SW15 ...73 | 23 74 C
Putney High St. SW15 ...73 | 24 75 C
Putney Hill. SW15 ...85 | 23 73 B
Putney Hill. SW15 ...73 | 23 74 B
Putney Park Ave. SW15 ...72 | 22 75 C
Putney Park La. SW15 ...72 | 22 74 B
Pycombe Cnr. N12 ...15 | 24 92 B
Pylbrook Rd. Sutt ...103 | 25 65 D
Pym Cl. Barn ...11 | 26 95 B
Pymers Mead. SE21 ...87 | 32 73 C
Pymmes Cl. N13 ...16 | 30 92 D
Pymmes gardens N. N9 ...17 | 33 93 D
Pymmes Gardens S. N9 ...17 | 33 93 D
Pymmes Green Rd. N11 ...16 | 29 93 C
Pymmes Rd. N13 ...16 | 30 91 A
Pymms Brook Dri. Barn ...12 | 27 96 C
Pynchester Cl. Uxb ...31 | 07 86 A
*Pynfolds. SE16 ...63 | 34 79 B
Pynham Cl. SE2 ...66 | 46 79 D
Pyrland Rd. N5 ...48 | 32 85 D
Pyrland Rd. Rich ...71 | 18 74 D
Pyrmont Gr. SE27 ...87 | 31 72 D
Pyrmont Rd. Ilf ...40 | 44 86 A

Pyrmont Rd. W4.....61 19 77 A
Pytchley Cres. SE19.....97 32 70 A
Pytchley Rd. SE22.....75 33 75 A

Quadrangle The. E17.....26 36 90 D
Quadrangle The. W2.....1 27 81 C
Quadrant Arc. Rom.....42 51 88 A
Quadrant Arc. W1.....6 29 80 A
Quadrant Cl. NW4.....34 22 88 B
Quadrant Gr. NW5.....47 27 85 D
Quadrant Rd. N2.....24 27 90 A
Quadrant Rd. Rich.....71 17 75 D
Quadrant Rd. Th Hth.....97 31 68 D
Quadrant The. Bexh.....67 47 77 D
Quadrant The. Rich.....71 17 75 D
Quadrant The. Sutt.....110 26 63 A
Quadrant The. SW20.....95 24 69 A
Quaggy Wlk. SE3.....77 40 75 C
Quainton St. NW10.....34 20 86 D
Quaker La. Sthl.....59 13 79 C
Quakers Course. NW9.....22 21 90 B
Quakers La. Ilf.....71 16 76 A
Quaker St. E1.....4 33 82 D
Quality Ct. WC2.....3 31 81 C
Quantock Ct. Grnf.....44 15 85 C
Quantock Gdns. NW2.....35 23 86 B
Quantock Rd. Bexh.....80 51 76 C
Quarles Cl. Rom.....29 49 91 C
Quarley Way (off Pentridge St). SE15.....63 33 77 D
Quarrendon St. SW6.....73 25 76 C
Quarr Rd. Cars.....104 27 67 C
Quarry Park Rd. Sutt.....110 24 63 B
Quarry Rd. SW18.....73 26 74 C
Quarry Rise. Sutt.....110 24 63 B
Quarterdeck The. E14.....64 37 79 A
Quartermile La. E10.....49 37 85 B
Quartermile La. E15.....49 37 85 B
Quebec Mews. W1.....1 27 81 D
Quebec Rd. Hay.....53 11 81 C
Quebec Rd. Ilf.....40 44 87 A
Quebec Way. SE16.....64 36 79 C
Queen Adelaide Rd. SE20.....98 35 70 C
Queen Alexandra's Ct. SW19.....85 24 71 D
Queen Anne Ave. Brom.....99 39 68 B
Queen Anne Gate. Bexh.....79 47 75 B
Queen Anne Mews. W1.....2 28 81 B
Queen Anne Rd. E9.....49 35 84 B
Queen Annes Cl. Twick.....82 14 72 D
Queen Anne's Gate. SW1.....6 29 79 B
Queen Anne's Gdns. Enf.....13 33 95 C
Queen Anne's Gdns. Mit.....96 27 68 B
Queen Anne's Gdns. W4.....61 21 79 C
Queen Anne's Gdns. W5.....60 18 79 A
Queen Anne's Gr. Enf.....13 33 95 C
Queen Anne's Gr. W4.....61 21 79 C
Queen Anne's Gr. W5.....60 18 79 A
Queen Anne's Pl. Enf.....13 33 95 D
Queen Anne St. W1.....2 28 81 B
Queenborough Gdns. Ilf.....28 43 89 C
Queen Caroline St. W6.....62 23 78 C
Queen Elizabeth Gdns. Mord.....95 25 68 C
Queen Elizabeth Rd. E17.....26 36 89 A
Queen Elizabeth Rd. King.....93 18 69 D
Queen Elizabeth's Cl. N16.....37 32 86 B
Queen Elizabeth's Dri. N14.....16 30 94 C
Queen Elizabeth St. SE1.....8 33 79 B
Queen Elizabeth's Wlk. N16.....37 32 86 B
Queen Elizabeth's Wlk. Wall.....111 29 64 B
Queen Elizabeth Wlk. SW13.....72 22 76 B
Queenhill Rd. S Croy.....112 34 62 D
Queenhithe. EC4.....8 32 80 A
Queen Margaret's Gr. N1.....48 33 85 C
Queen Mary Ave. Mord.....103 23 67 B
Queen Mary Rd. SE19.....97 31 70 B
Queen Mary Rd. Shep.....91 08 69 C
Queen Mary's Ave. Cars.....111 27 63 D
Queens Acre. Sutt.....110 24 63 C
Queens Ave. Felt.....82 11 71 A
Queen's Ave. Grnf.....53 14 81 C
Queens Ave. N10.....24 28 89 B
Queens Ave. N20.....15 26 93 B
Queen's Ave. N21.....17 31 94 D
Queen's Ave. N3.....23 26 90 A
Queens Ave. Stan.....21 17 89 A
Queensberry House. Rich.....71 17 74 B
Queensberry Mews W. SW7.....62 26 78 B
Queensberry Pl. SW7.....62 26 78 B
Queensberry Way. SW7.....62 26 78 B
Queensborough Mews. W2.....5 26 80 A
Queensborough Pas. W2.....5 26 80 A
Queensborough Terr. W2.....5 26 80 A
Queensbridge Ct. E2.....48 33 83 D
Queensbridge Park. Islw.....71 15 74 A

Queensbridge Rd. E2.....48 33 83 B
Queensbridge Rd. E8.....48 33 84 D
Queensbury Ct. Th Hth.....97 32 69 C
Queensbury Rd. NW9.....34 20 87 B
Queensbury Rd. Wem.....44 18 83 D
Queensbury Station Par. Edg.....21 18 89 B
Queensbury St. N1.....48 32 84 C
Queen's Circ. SW11.....9 28 77 D
Queen's Club Gdns. W14.....62 24 77 A
Queen's Cl. Wall.....111 28 64 D
Queenscourt. Wem.....44 18 85 A
Queen's Cres. NW5.....47 28 84 A
Queens Cres. Rich.....71 18 74 B
Queenscroft Rd. SE9.....77 41 74 D
Queen's Ct. King.....94 19 70 C
Queen's Ct. Rich.....71 18 74 D
Queensdale Cres. W11.....56 23 80 D
Queensdale Pl. W11.....56 24 80 C
Queensdale Rd. W11.....56 24 80 C
Queensdale Wlk. W11.....56 24 80 C
Queensdown Rd. E5.....48 34 85 B
Queens Dri. E10.....38 37 87 A
Queen's Dri. N4.....37 31 86 B
Queen's Dri. Surb.....101 16 67 C
Queens Dri. Surb.....102 19 67 C
Queen's Dri. W3.....55 19 81 C
Queen's Elm Sq. SW3.....62 26 78 D
Queensferry Wlk. N15.....25 34 89 D
Queensfield Ct. Sutt.....110 23 64 A
Queensgate Gdns. Chis.....100 44 69 B
Queen's Gate Gdns. SW7.....5 26 79 C
Queen's Gate Mews. SW7.....5 26 79 C
Queen's Gate Pl Mews. SW7.....5 26 79 C
Queensgate Pl. NW6.....46 25 84 C
Queen's Gate Pl. SW7.....5 26 79 C
Queen's Gate. SW7.....5 26 79 C
Queen's Gate Terr. SW7.....5 26 79 C
Queen's Gdns. Houn.....70 12 76 A
Queen's Gdns. NW4.....35 23 88 A
Queens Gdns. Rain.....52 50 83 D
Queen's Gdns. W2.....5 26 80 A
Queen's Gdns. W5.....54 17 82 C
Queen's Grove. NW8.....46 26 83 B
Queen's Grove Rd. E4.....18 38 94 D
Queen's Head St. N1.....48 31 83 B
Queen's Head Yd. SE1.....8 32 80 D
Queens La. N10.....24 28 89 B
Queensland Ave. N18.....25 32 91 A
Queensland Ave. SW19.....95 25 69 B
Queensland Pl. N7.....48 31 85 A
Queensland Rd. N7.....48 31 85 A
Queen's Market. E13.....50 41 83 A
Queensmead Ave.....109 22 62 D
Queensmead. NW8.....46 26 83 B
Queen's Mead Rd. Brom.....99 39 69 D
Queensmere Cl. SW19.....85 23 72 B
Queensmere Rd. SW19.....85 23 72 B
Queen's Mews. W2.....56 25 80 B
Queensmill Rd. SW6.....62 23 77 D
Queens Parade Cl. N11.....16 27 92 D
Queens Park Ct. W10.....56 23 82 B
Queens Park Gdns. Felt.....81 09 72 D
Queens Park Rd. Rom.....30 54 90 B
Queens Pas. Chis.....100 43 70 B
Queen's Pl. Mord.....95 25 68 C
Queen's Prom. King.....93 17 68 D
Queen Sq Pl. WC1.....3 30 82 C
Queen Sq. WC1.....3 30 81 A
Queen's Rd. Bark.....51 44 84 C
Queen's Rd. Barn.....11 23 96 B
Queens Rd. Beck.....98 36 69 C
Queen's Rd. Brom.....99 40 69 C
Queen's Rd. Chis.....100 43 70 B
Queen's Rd. Croy.....105 32 67 C
Queen's Rd. E11.....39 39 87 A
Queen's Rd. E17.....38 36 88 D
Queen's Rd. Enf.....13 33 96 C
Queen's Rd. Eri.....68 51 77 A
Queen's Rd. Felt.....81 10 73 D
Queen's Rd. Hamp.....82 13 71 B
Queen's Rd. Houn.....70 13 75 B
Queen's Rd. Ilf.....40 44 86 A
Queen's Rd. Mit.....95 26 68 B
Queens Rd. Mord.....95 25 68 C
Queen's Rd. N11.....24 30 91 A
Queen's Rd. N3.....23 26 90 A
Queen's Rd. N9.....17 34 93 B
Queen's Rd. N.Mal.....102 21 67 B
Queen's Rd. NW4.....35 23 88 A
Queens Rd. Rich.....71 18 74 D
Queen's Rd. SE15.....76 35 76 A
Queen's Rd. Sthl.....59 12 79 A
Queen's Rd. Surb.....101 15 67 B
Queens Rd. Sutt.....110 25 62 C

Queen's Rd. SW14.....72 20 75 B
Queen's Rd. SW19.....95 25 70 A
Queen's Rd. Tedd.....93 15 70 B
Queen's Rd. Twick.....83 16 73 C
Queen's Rd. W5.....54 18 81 C
Queen's Rd. Wall.....111 28 64 D
Queen's Rd. Well.....78 46 76 D
Queen's Ride. Rich.....60 18 77 C
Queen's Ride. Rich.....84 20 73 C
Queen's Ride. SW13.....72 22 75 A
Queen's Ride. SW15.....72 22 75 B
Queen's Rise. Rich.....71 18 74 D
Queen's Row. SE17.....63 32 77 B
Queen St. Bexh.....79 48 75 B
Queen St. Croy.....105 32 65 C
Queen St. EC4.....8 32 80 A
Queen St. Eri.....68 51 77 A
Queens Terr. E13.....50 40 83 B
Queen's Terr. Islw.....71 16 75 C
Queens Terr. NW8.....46 26 83 D
Queensthorpe Rd. SE26.....88 35 71 B
Queen St. N17.....25 33 91 A
Queenstown Rd. SW11.....74 27 76 B
Queenstown Rd. SW8.....9 28 77 D
Queen St Pl. EC4.....8 32 80 A
Queen St. Rom.....41 50 88 D
Queen St. W1.....6 28 80 D
Queensville Rd. SW12.....86 29 73 B
Queensway. Croy.....112 31 64 C
Queensway. Enf.....14 35 96 C
Queens Way. Felt.....82 11 71 A
Queens Way. NW4.....35 23 88 A
Queensway. Orp.....108 44 67 C
Queensway. Sun.....91 10 69 D
Queensway. W2.....56 25 80 B
Queensway. W.Wick.....107 39 65 C
Queens Well Ave. N20.....16 27 92 A
Queens Wlk. E4.....18 38 94 D
Queens Wlk. Har.....21 15 89 C
Queens Wlk. NW9.....34 20 86 A
Queens Wlk. Ruis.....43 11 85 B
Queen's Wlk. SW1.....6 29 80 C
Queen's Wlk. W5.....54 17 81 A
Queenswood Ave. E17.....26 38 90 A
Queenswood Ave. Hamp.....92 13 70 B
Queenswood Ave. Houn.....70 12 76 D
Queenswood Ave. Th Hth.....105 31 67 A
Queenswood Ave. Wall.....111 29 64 B
Queenswood Ct. SE27.....87 32 71 A
Queenswood Gdns. E11.....39 40 86 B
Queenswood Park. N3.....23 24 90 C
Queen's Wood Rd. N10.....36 28 88 D
Queenswood Rd. SE23.....88 36 72 C
Queenswood Rd. Sid.....78 45 74 D
Queen Victoria Ave. Wem.....44 17 84 D
Queen Victoria St. EC4.....8 32 80 A
Quemerford Rd. N7.....47 30 85 D
Quentin Pl. SE13.....77 39 75 A
Quentin Rd. SE13.....77 39 75 A
Quernmore Cl. Brom.....99 40 70 A
Quernmore Rd. Brom.....99 40 70 A
Quernmore Rd. N4.....37 31 88 C
Querrin St. SW6.....73 26 76 C
Quex Mews. NW6.....46 25 83 A
Quex Rd. NW6.....46 25 83 A
Quick Pl. N1.....48 31 83 B
Quick Rd. W4.....61 21 78 C
Quicksilver Pl. N22.....24 30 90 D
Quicks Rd. SW19.....95 25 70 D
Quick St. N1.....48 31 83 D
Quickswood. NW3.....47 27 84 C
Quiet Nook. Brom.....107 41 65 D
Quill La. SW15.....73 23 75 D
Quill St. SE1.....8 32 79 A
Quilter St. E2.....57 34 82 A
Quinta Dri. Barn.....11 23 95 A
Quintin Ave. SW20.....95 24 69 B
Quintin Cl. Beck.....98 38 68 A
Quinton Cl. Wall.....111 28 64 B
Quinton Rd. Surb.....101 16 66 C
Quinton St. SW18.....85 26 72 A
Quixley St. E14.....58 38 80 B
Quorn Rd. SE22.....75 33 75 A

Rabbit Row. W8.....56 25 80 C
Rabbits Rd. E12.....50 42 85 A
Raby Rd. N Mal.....94 20 68 D
Raby St. E14.....54 36 81 C
Raccoon Way. Houn.....70 11 76 C
Racton Rd. SW6.....62 25 77 A
Radbourne Ave. W5.....60 17 78 A
Radbourne Cl. E5.....49 35 85 B
Radbourne Cres. E17.....26 38 89 B

Radbourne Rd. SW12	*86*	29 73 D
Radcliffe Ave. Enf.	*13*	32 97 A
Radcliffe Ave. NW10	*45*	22 83 C
Radcliffe Gdns. Cars.	*111*	27 63 C
Radcliffe Path. SW8	*74*	29 76 C
Radcliffe Rd. Croy.	*105*	33 65 D
Radcliffe Rd. Har.	*21*	16 90 C
Radcliffe Rd. N21	*17*	31 94 D
Radcliffe Sq. SW15	*73*	23 74 D
Radcliffe Way. Nthl.	*53*	11 82 B
*Radcot St. SE11	*63*	31 78 C
Raddington Rd. W10	*56*	24 81 A
Radfield Way. Sid.	*90*	44 73 B
Radford Rd. SE13	*76*	38 74 C
Radipole Rd. SW6	*73*	24 76 B
Radland Rd. E16	*58*	40 81 C
Radlet Ave. SE26	*87*	34 72 B
Radlett Cl. E7	*50*	39 84 B
Radlett Pl. NW8	*47*	27 83 A
Radley Ave. Ilf.	*51*	46 85 A
Radley Gdns. Har.	*21*	18 89 C
Radley Mews. W8	*62*	25 79 D
Radley Rd. N17	*25*	33 90 C
Radley's La. E18	*27*	40 90 C
Radleys Mead. Dag.	*52*	49 84 B
Radley Sq. E5	*38*	35 86 A
Radlix Rd. E10	*38*	37 87 C
Radnor Ave. Har.	*33*	15 88 A
Radnor Ave. Well.	*78*	46 74 B
Radnor Cl. Chis.	*100*	45 70 A
Radnor Cl. Mit.	*96*	30 68 C
Radnor Cres. Ilf.	*39*	42 88 B
Radnor Gdns. Enf.	*13*	33 97 A
Radnor Gdns. Twick.	*83*	15 72 B
Radnor Mews. W2	*1*	26 81 D
Radnor Pl. W2	*1*	27 81 C
Radnor Rd. Har.	*33*	15 88 A
Radnor Rd. NW6	*46*	24 83 A
Radnor Rd. SE15	*63*	34 77 C
Radnor Rd. Twick.	*83*	15 72 B
Radnor St. EC1	*4*	32 82 A
Radnor Wlk. Croy.	*106*	36 67 D
Radnor Wlk. SW3	*9*	27 78 D
Radstock Ave. Har.	*21*	16 89 B
Radstock St. SW11	*9*	27 77 C
Raeburn Ave. Dart.	*80*	52 74 B
Raeburn Ave. Surb.	*102*	19 67 D
Raeburn Cl. King.	*93*	17 70 D
Raeburn Cl. NW11	*35*	26 88 C
Raeburn Rd. Edg.	*22*	19 90 A
Raeburn Rd. Sid.	*78*	45 74 C
Raeburn St. SW2	*74*	30 75 C
Rafford Way. Brom.	*99*	40 68 B
Raggleswood. Chis.	*100*	43 69 A
Raglan Ct. S Croy.	*112*	31 64 D
Raglan Ct. Wem.	*44*	18 85 B
Raglan Rd. Belv.	*67*	48 78 B
Raglan Rd. Brom.	*99*	41 68 C
Raglan Rd. E17	*38*	38 88 B
Raglan Rd. Enf.	*17*	33 94 B
Raglan Rd. SE18	*66*	44 78 C
Raglan St. NW5	*47*	28 84 B
Raglan Way. Nthlt.	*43*	14 84 A
Ragley Cl. W3	*61*	20 79 A
Raider Cl. Rom.	*29*	49 90 B
Railey Mews. NW5	*47*	29 85 B
Railshead Rd. Islw.	*71*	16 75 D
Railton Rd. SE24	*75*	31 74 B
Railway App. Har.	*21*	15 89 D
Railway App. SE1	*8*	32 80 D
Railway App. Twick.	*83*	16 73 A
Railway Ave. SE16	*64*	35 79 A
Railway Pas. Tedd.	*93*	16 70 A
Railway Pl. Belv.	*67*	49 79 C
Railway Pl. EC3	*8*	33 80 A
Railway Pl. SW19	*95*	24 70 B
Railway Rd. Tedd.	*83*	15 71 B
Railway Rise. SE22	*75*	33 75 C
Railway Side. SW13	*72*	21 75 A
Railway St. N1	*47*	30 83 C
Railway St. Rom.	*41*	47 87 A
Railway Terr. E17	*26*	38 90 A
Railway Terr. Felt.	*81*	10 73 C
Railway Terr. SE13	*76*	37 74 B
Rainborough Cl. NW10	*45*	20 84 A
*Rainbow St. SE5	*63*	33 77 C
Raine St. E1	*57*	34 80 D
Rainham Cl. SW11	*74*	27 74 C
Rainham Rd. NW10	*56*	23 82 B
Rainham Road N. Dag.	*41*	49 86 D
Rainham Road S. Dag.	*52*	50 84 A
Rainhill Way. E3	*57*	37 82 A
Rainsborough Ave. SE8	*64*	36 78 A
Rainsford Rd. NW10	*45*	19 83 D

Rainsford St. W2	*1*	27 81 C
Rainsford Way. Horn.	*42*	52 87 C
Rainton Rd. SE7	*65*	40 78 C
Rainville Rd. W6	*62*	23 77 A
Raisins Hill. Pnr.	*19*	10 89 B
Raith Ave. N14	*16*	29 93 D
Raleana Rd. E14	*58*	38 80 C
Raleigh Ave. Wall.	*111*	29 64 B
Raleigh Cl. NW4	*35*	23 88 A
Raleigh Cl. Pnr.	*31*	11 87 B
Raleigh Cl. Ruis.	*31*	09 86 B
Raleigh Cl. Wat.	*111*	28 63 B
Raleigh Dri. N20	*16*	27 93 C
Raleigh Dri. Surb.	*102*	20 66 C
Raleigh Gdns. Mit.	*96*	27 68 B
Raleigh Gdns. SW2	*74*	30 74 D
Raleigh Mews. N1	*48*	31 83 B
Raleigh Rd. Enf.	*13*	32 96 D
Raleigh Rd. Felt.	*81*	09 72 B
Raleigh Rd. N2	*24*	27 90 C
Raleigh Rd. N8	*25*	31 89 C
Raleigh Rd. Rich.	*71*	18 75 B
Raleigh Rd. SE20	*98*	35 70 D
Raleigh Rd. Sthl.	*59*	12 78 C
Raleigh St. N1	*48*	31 83 B
Raleigh Way. Felt.	*82*	11 71 C
Raleigh Way. N14	*16*	29 94 D
Ralston St. SW3	*9*	27 78 D
Rama Ct. Har.	*33*	15 86 A
Rambler Cl. SW16	*86*	29 71 A
Ramelagh Gdns. E11	*39*	41 88 A
Ramilles Cl. SW2	*74*	30 74 C
Ramillies Pl. W1	*2*	29 81 C
Ramillies Rd. Sid.	*78*	46 74 D
Ramillies Rd. W4	*61*	20 79 D
Ramillies St. W1	*2*	29 81 C
Ramily Ct. SW6	*73*	24 76 D
Rampart St. E1	*57*	34 81 D
Rampayne St. SW1	*10*	29 78 D
Ram Pl. E9	*49*	35 84 A
Rampton Cl. E4	*18*	37 93 C
Ramsay Gdns. Rom.	*30*	53 90 A
Ramsay Rd. E7	*39*	39 86 D
Ramsay Rd. W3	*61*	20 79 A
Ramscroft Cl. N9	*17*	33 94 A
Ramsdale Rd. SW17	*86*	28 71 D
Ramsden Dr. Rom.	*29*	49 91 C
Ramsden Rd. Eri.	*80*	50 77 D
Ramsden Rd. N11	*16*	27 92 D
Ramsden Rd. Orp.	*108*	46 66 D
Ramsden Rd. SW12	*86*	28 73 A
Ramsey Rd. NW9	*34*	22 87 B
Ramsey Rd. Th Hth.	*104*	30 67 D
Ramsey St. E2	*57*	34 82 C
Ramsey Way. N14	*16*	29 94 A
Ramsey Wlk. N1	*48*	32 84 B
Ramsgate St. E8	*48*	33 84 B
Ramsgill App. Ilf.	*28*	45 89 D
Ramsgill Dri. Ilf.	*28*	45 89 D
Rams Gr. Rom.	*29*	48 89 C
Ramulis Dri. Hay.	*53*	11 82 D
Rancliffe Gdns. SE9	*77*	42 75 C
Rancliffe Rd. E6	*50*	42 83 C
Randall Ave. NW2	*34*	21 86 D
Randall Cl. Eri.	*67*	50 77 A
Randall Cl. SW11	*74*	27 76 A
Randall Cl. NW7	*22*	22 91 C
Randall Dri. Horn.	*42*	53 86 D
Randall Pl. SE10	*64*	38 77 C
Randall Rd. Rom.	*42*	51 88 D
Randall Rd. SE11	*10*	30 78 B
Randall Row. SE11	*10*	30 78 B
Randell's Rd. N1	*47*	30 83 A
Randle Rd. Rich.	*83*	17 71 A
Randlesdown Rd. SE6	*88*	37 72 D
Randolph App. E16.	*58*	41 81 C
Randolph Ave. W9	*1*	26 82 A
Randolph Cl. Bexh.	*79*	50 75 A
Randolph Cl. King.	*84*	20 71 C
Randolph Cres. W9	*1*	26 82 C
Randolph Gdns. NW6	*46*	25 83 D
Randolph Mews. W9	*1*	26 82 C
Randolph Rd. E17	*38*	37 88 B
Randolph Rd. Sthl.	*59*	12 79 B
Randolph Rd. W9	*1*	26 82 C
Randolph St. NW1	*47*	29 84 C
Randon Cl. Har.	*20*	13 90 D
Ranelagh Ave. SW13	*72*	22 76 C
Ranelagh Ave. SW6	*73*	24 75 B
Ranelagh Dri. Twick.	*71*	16 74 B
Ranelagh Gdns. Ilf.	*40*	43 87 A
Ranelagh Gdns. SW6	*73*	24 75 B
Ranelagh Gdns. W4	*61*	20 77 C
Ranelagh Gr. SW1	*9*	28 78 C
Ranelagh Mews. W5	*60*	17 79 B

Ranelagh Pl. N.Mal.	*102*	21 67 A
Ranelagh Rd. E11	*50*	39 85 A
Ranelaghd. E15	*50*	39 83 C
Ranelagh Rd. E6	*51*	43 83 C
Ranelagh Rd. N17	*25*	33 89 A
Ranelagh Rd. N22	*24*	30 90 B
Ranelagh Rd. NW10	*45*	21 83 D
Ranelagh Rd. SW1	*10*	29 78 C
Ranelagh Rd. W5	*60*	17 79 B
Ranelagh Rd. Wem.	*44*	17 84 B
Raneleagh Rd. Sthl.	*53*	11 80 D
Ranfurly Rd. Sutt.	*103*	25 65 A
Rangefield Rd. Brom.	*89*	39 71 D
Rangemoor Rd. 15	*37*	33 88 B
Rangers Sq. SE10	*76*	38 76 B
Rangoon St. EC3	*4*	33 81 D
Rankin Cl. NW9	*22*	21 89 A
Ranleigh Gdns. Bexh.	*67*	48 77 D
Ranmere St. SW12	*86*	28 73 D
Ranmoor Cl. Har.	*20*	14 89 D
Ranmoor Gdns. Har.	*20*	14 89 D
Ranmore Ave. Croy.	*105*	33 65 D
Ranmore Path. Orp.	*100*	46 68 C
Ranmore Rd. Sutt.	*110*	23 62 B
Rannoch Rd. W6	*62*	23 77 B
Rannock Ave. NW9	*34*	21 87 A
Ransom Rd. SE7	*65*	41 78 A
Ranston St. NW1	*1*	27 81 A
Ranulf Rd. NW2	*46*	24 85 B
Ranwell Cl. E3	*49*	36 83 B
Ranworth Rd. N9	*18*	35 93 A
Raphael Ave. Rom.	*30*	51 89 B
Raphael St. SW7	*2*	27 79 B
Rashleigh St. SW8	*74*	28 76 D
Rasper Rd. N20	*15*	26 93 A
Rastell Ave. SW2	*86*	29 73 D
Ratcliffe Cross St. E1	*57*	35 81 D
Ratcliffe La. E14.	*57*	36 81 C
Ratcliffe Orchard. E1	*57*	35 80 B
Ratcliff Rd. E7	*50*	41 85 C
Rathbone Pl. W1	*2*	29 81 D
Rathbone St. E16	*58*	39 81 D
Rathbone St. W1	*2*	29 81 A
Rathcoole Ave. N8	*36*	30 88 B
Rathcoole Gdns. N8	*36*	30 88 B
Rathfern Rd. SE6	*88*	36 73 D
Rathgar Ave. W13	*54*	17 80 C
Rathgar Cl. N3	*23*	24 90 D
Rathgar Rd. SW9	*75*	31 75 B
Rathlin Wlk. N1	*48*	32 84 A
Rathmell Dri. SW4	*74*	29 74 D
Rathmore Rd. SE7	*65*	40 78 D
Rattray Rd. SW2	*75*	31 74 A
Raul Rd. SE15	*75*	34 76 A
Raveley St. NW5	*47*	29 85 A
Ravendale Rd. Sun.	*91*	09 69 D
Ravenet St. SW11	*74*	28 76 B
Ravenfield Rd. SW17	*86*	27 72 D
Ravenhill Rd. E13	*50*	41 83 C
Ravenna Rd. SW15	*73*	23 75 D
Ravenor Ct. Grnf.	*53*	13 82 D
Ravenor Park Rd. Grnf.	*53*	13 82 B
Raven Rd. E18	*27*	41 90 C
Raven Rd. SE11	*10*	30 78 B
Raven Row. E1	*57*	34 81 B
Ravensbourne Ave. Brom.	*98*	38 69 B
Ravensbourne Cres. Rom.	*30*	54 89 B
Ravensbourne Gdns. Ilf.	*28*	43 90 B
Ravensbourne Gdns. W13	*54*	16 81 B
Ravensbourne Park Cres. SE6	*88*	36 73 B
Ravensbourne Park. SE6	*88*	37 73 A
Ravensbourne Pl. SE13	*76*	37 76 D
Ravensbourne Rd. Brom.	*99*	40 68 A
Ravensbourne Rd. Dart.	*80*	52 75 A
Ravensbourne Rd. SE6	*88*	36 73 D
Ravensbourne Rd. Twick.	*71*	17 74 C
Ravensbury Ave. Mord.	*103*	26 67 A
Ravensbury Gr. Mit.	*95*	26 68 D
Ravensbury La. Mit.	*95*	26 68 D
Ravensbury Path. Mit.	*95*	26 68 D
Ravensbury Path. Mit.	*95*	27 68 A
Ravensbury Rd. Orp.	*100*	46 68 C
Ravensbury Terr. SW18	*85*	25 72 B
Ravenscar Rd. Brom.	*89*	39 71 A
Ravenscar Rd. Surb.	*101*	18 65 B
Ravens Cl. Brom.	*99*	39 69 D
Ravens Cl. Enf.	*13*	33 97 C
Ravenscourt Cl. Horn.	*42*	54 86 C
Ravenscourt Cl. Ruis.	*31*	08 87 A
Ravenscourt Dri. Horn.	*42*	54 86 A
Ravenscourt Gdns. W6	*61*	22 78 A
Ravenscourt Gr. Horn.	*42*	54 86 A

Street	Page	Ref
Ravenscourt Park. W6	61	22 78 A
Ravenscourt Pl. W6	61	22 78 B
Ravenscourt Rd. Orp	100	46 69 D
Ravenscourt Rd. W6	61	22 78 B
Ravenscourt Sq. W6	61	22 79 C
Ravenscourt. Sun	91	09 69 B
Ravenscraig Rd. N11	16	29 92 A
Ravenscroft Ave. NW11	35	24 87 B
Ravenscroft Ave. W6	61	22 78 A
Ravenscroft Ave. Wem	33	18 87 B
Ravenscroft Cl. E16	58	40 81 A
Ravenscroft. E2	4	33 82 B
Ravenscroft Park. Barn	11	23 96 B
Ravenscroft Rd. Beck	98	35 69 D
Ravenscroft Rd. E16	58	40 81 A
Ravenscroft Rd. W4	61	20 78 A
Ravensdale Ave. N12	15	26 92 B
Ravensdale Gdns. SE19	97	32 70 D
Ravensdale Rd. Houn	70	12 75 A
Ravensdale Rd. N16	37	33 88 D
Ravensdon St. SE11	63	31 78 C
Ravensfield. Dag	52	47 85 B
Ravensfield Gdns. Eps	109	21 64 A
Ravenshaw St. NW6	46	24 85 D
Ravenshill. Chis	100	43 69 B
Ravenshurst Ave. NW4	23	23 89 C
Ravenslea Rd. SW12	86	27 73 D
Ravensmead Rd. Brom	98	38 70 D
Ravensmede Way. W4	61	21 78 B
Ravens Mews. SE12	77	40 74 A
Ravenstone Rd. N8	25	31 89 A
Ravenstone Rd. NW9	34	21 88 D
Ravenstone St. SW12	86	28 73 C
Ravens Way. SE12	77	40 74 A
Ravenswood Ave. Surb	102	19 65 A
Ravenswood Ave. W Wick	106	38 66 C
Ravenswood Cres. Har	32	12 86 B
Ravenswood Cres. W Wick	106	38 66 C
Ravenswood Ct. King	94	19 70 B
Ravenswood Gdns. Islw	71	15 76 A
Ravenswood Park. Nthwd	19	10 91 A
Ravenswood Rd. Croy	105	31 65 D
Ravenswood Rd. E17	38	38 88 A
Ravenswood Rd. E17	26	38 89 C
Ravenswood Rd. SW12	86	28 73 B
Ravensworth Rd. NW10	55	22 82 B
Ravensworth Rd. SE9	89	42 71 B
Ravent Rd. SE11	10	30 78 B
Ravey St. EC2	4	33 82 C
Ravine Gro. SE18	66	45 77 A
Ravleigh Ave. Tedd	93	15 70 A
Rawlings St. SW3	9	27 78 B
Rawlins Cl. N3	23	24 89 A
Rawnsley Ave. Mit	95	27 67 A
Rawreth Wlk (off Basire St). N1	48	32 83 A
Rawson St. SW11	74	28 76 B
Rawsthorne Pl. EC1	3	31 82 B
Rawstone Wlk. E13	50	40 83 C
Rawstorne St. EC1	3	31 82 B
Raydean Rd. Barn	11	25 95 B
Raydons Gdns. Dag	52	48 85 C
Raydons Rd. Dag	52	48 85 C
Raydon St. N19	36	28 86 B
Rayfield Cl. Brom	107	42 67 C
Rayford Ave. SE12	89	39 73 B
Rayford Cl. Dart	80	53 74 A
Ray Gdns. Bark	51	46 83 C
Rayleas Cl. SE18	78	43 76 B
Rayleigh Cl. N13	17	32 93 D
Rayleigh Ct.King	93	18 69 D
Rayleigh Rd. N13	17	32 93 D
Rayleigh Rd. SW19	95	24 69 B
Rayleigh Rise. S Croy	112	33 63 A
Ray Lodge Rd. Wdf Gn	27	41 91 B
Raymead Ave. Th Hth	105	31 67 A
Raymead Pas. Th Hth	105	31 67 A
Raymere Gdns. SE18	66	45 77 C
Raymond Ave. E18	27	39 90 D
Raymond Ave. W13	60	16 79 C
Raymond Cl. SE26	88	35 71 C
Raymond Rd. Beck	98	36 68 C
Raymond Rd. Ilf	40	44 87 B
Raymond Rd. SW19	95	24 70 A
Raymouth Rd. SE16	63	34 78 B
Rayne Ct. E18	27	39 89 D
Rayners Cl. Wem	44	17 85 D
Rayners La. Har	32	13 86 B
Rayners La. Pnr	32	12 88 D
Rayner's Rd. SW15	73	24 74 A
Raynes Ave. E11	39	41 87 A
Raynesfield. SW20	95	23 68 A
Raynham Ave. N18	17	34 92 C
Raynham Rd. N18	17	34 92 C
Raynham Rd. W6	61	22 78 B
Raynham Terr. N18	17	34 92 C
Raynham. W2	1	27 81 C
Raynor Cl. Sthl	53	12 80 D
Raynor Pl. N1	48	32 83 A
Raynton Cl. Har	32	12 87 A
Rays Ave. N18	18	35 92 A
Rays Rd. N18	18	35 92 A
Ray St. EC1	3	31 82 C
Ray Wlk. N7	36	30 86 B
Reade Wlk. NW10	45	21 84 C
Reading La. E8	48	34 84 B
Reading Rd. Nthlt	43	14 85 C
Reading Rd. Sutt	110	26 64 C
Reading Way. NW7	15	24 92 C
Reapers Way. Islw	70	14 74 B
Reardon Path. E1	57	34 80 D
Reardon St. E1	57	34 80 D
Reaston St. SE14	64	35 77 D
Rebecca Terr. SE16	64	35 79 C
Reckitt Rd. W4	61	21 78 C
Record St. SE15	64	35 77 A
Recovery St. SW17	86	27 71 C
Recreation Ave. Rom	41	50 88 A
Recreation Ave. Rom	30	54 90 D
Recreation Rd. Brom	99	39 69 D
Recreation Rd. SE26	88	35 71 B
Recreation Rd. Sthl	59	12 78 A
Recreation Way. Mit	96	30 68 A
Rector St. N1	48	32 83 A
Rectory Cl. Dart	80	51 75 C
Rectory Cl. E4	18	37 93 C
Rectory Cl. N3	23	24 90 B
Rectory Cl. Shep	91	07 68 A
Rectory Cl. Sid	90	46 71 B
Rectory Cl. Surb	101	17 66 C
Rectory Cl. SW20	95	23 68 A
Rectory Cres. E11	39	41 88 C
Rectory Field Cres. SE7	65	41 77 C
Rectory Gdns. N8	24	30 89 C
Rectory Gdns. Nthlt	43	12 83 B
Rectory Gdns. SW4	74	29 75 A
Rectory Gr. Croy	105	31 65 B
Rectory Green. Beck	98	36 69 B
Rectory Gr. Hamp	82	12 71 B
Rectory Gr. SW4	74	29 75 A
Rectory La. Edg	22	19 91 A
Rectory La. Sid	90	46 71 B
Rectory La. Surb	101	17 66 C
Rectory La. SW17	96	28 70 A
Rectory La. SW17	86	28 71 C
Rectory La. Wall	111	29 64 A
Rectory Orchard The. SW19	85	24 71 A
Rectory Park Ave. Nthlt	53	12 82 B
Rectory Pl. SE18	66	43 78 A
Rectory Rd. Beck	98	37 69 A
Rectory Rd. Dag	52	49 84 D
Rectory Rd. E12	50	42 85 D
Rectory Rd. E17	26	37 89 D
Rectory Rd. E8	48	34 85 A
Rectory Rd. Houn	70	11 76 C
Rectory Rd. N16	37	33 86 D
Rectory Rd. Sthl	59	12 79 D
Rectory Rd. Sutt	103	25 65 D
Rectory Rd. SW13	72	22 76 C
Rectory Rd. W3	45	19 80 D
Rectory Sq. E1	57	35 81 B
Rectory Way. Uxb	31	07 86 B
Reculver Mews. N18	17	34 92 A
Reculver Rd. SE16	64	35 78 D
Redanchof Cl. SW3	9	27 77 A
Redan Pl. W2	1	25 81 D
Redan St. W14	62	23 79 D
Redan Terr. SE5	75	32 76 C
Redberry Gr. SE26	88	35 72 C
Redbourne Ave. N3	23	25 90 A
Redbridge Gdns. SE5	63	33 77 C
Redbridge Lane E. Ilf	39	42 88 A
Redbridge Lane W. E11	39	41 88 C
Redburn St. SW3	9	27 77 B
Redcar Cl. Nthlt	43	13 84 B
Redcar St. SE5	63	32 77 C
Redcastle Cl. E1	57	35 80 A
Red Cedars Rd. Orp	108	45 66 A
Redchurch St. E2	4	33 82 D
Redcliffe Gdns. Ilf	40	43 87 C
Redcliffe Gdns. SW10	62	25 77 B
Redcliffe Mews. SW10	62	25 78 D
Redcliffe Pl. SW10	62	26 77 A
Redcliffe Rd. SW10	62	26 77 A
Redcliffe Sq. SW10	62	25 78 D
Redcliffe St. SW10	62	25 77 B
Redcliffe Wlk. Wem	34	19 86 D
Redclose Ave. Mord	103	25 67 A
Redclyffe Rd. E6	50	41 83 A
Redcroft Rd. Sthl	53	14 81 C
Redcross Way. SE1	8	32 80 C
Redden Court Rd. Horn	30	54 89 B
Redden Court Rd. Rom	30	54 89 A
Reddington Cl. S Croy	112	33 62 A
Reddins Rd. SE15	63	34 77 A
Reddons Rd. Beck	98	36 70 C
Reddy Rd. Eri	68	51 77 B
Rede Pl. W2	56	25 80 A
Redesdale Gdns. Islw	60	16 77 C
Redesdale St. SW3	9	27 78 D
Redfern Ave. Houn	82	13 73 A
Redfern Gdns. Rom	30	53 90 D
Redfern Rd. NW10	45	21 84 C
Redfern Rd. SE6	88	38 73 A
Redfield La. SW5	62	25 78 B
Redfield Mews. SW5	62	25 78 A
Redford Ave. Th Hth	96	30 68 D
Redford Ave. Wall	111	30 63 A
Redford Wlk. N1	48	32 83 A
Redgates Dri. Brom	107	40 65 B
Redgate Terr. SW15	73	23 74 D
Redgrave Rd. SW15	73	23 75 B
Red Hill. Chis	90	43 71 D
Redhill Dri. Edg	22	20 90 C
Redhill St. NW1	2	28 82 B
Red House La. Bexh	79	48 75 C
Red House Rd. Croy	104	29 67 D
Redington Gdns. NW3	46	25 85 B
Redington Rd. NW3	46	25 85 B
Redland Gdns. E Mol	92	12 68 D
Redlands. N15	25	32 89 D
Redlands Rd. Enf	14	36 97 A
Redlands Way. SW2	86	30 73 B
Redlaw Way. SE16	63	34 78 C
Redleaf Cl. Belv	67	49 77 A
Redleaves Ave. Ashf	91	07 70 B
Redlees Cl. Islw	71	16 75 C
Red Lion Cl. SE17	63	32 77 B
Red Lion Ct. EC4	3	31 81 C
Red Lion Hill. N2	23	26 90 D
Red Lion La. SE18	78	43 76 A
Red Lion Pl. SE18	78	43 76 A
Red Lion Rd. Surb	102	19 66 C
Red Lion Row. SE17	63	32 77 A
Red Lion Sq. WC1	3	30 81 B
Red Lion St. Rich	71	17 74 B
Red Lion St. WC1	3	30 81 B
Red Lion Yd. W1	6	28 80 C
Red Lodge Rd. W Wick	106	38 66 B
Redman's Rd. E1	57	35 81 A
Redmead La. E1	57	34 80 C
Redmore Rd. W6	61	22 78 B
Red Oak Cl. Orp	108	43 65 B
Red Path. E9	49	36 84 B
Red Pl. W1	6	28 80 A
Redpoll Way. Belv	67	47 79 D
Red Post Hill. SE24	75	32 74 B
Redriffe Rd. E13	50	39 83 B
Redriff Rd. Rom	29	49 90 D
Redriff Rd. SE16	64	35 79 D
Redruth Cl. N22	24	30 91 D
Redruth House. Sutt	110	25 63 D
Redruth Rd. E9	49	35 83 A
Redston Rd. N8	24	29 89 D
Redvers Rd. N22	25	31 90 C
Redvers St. E2	4	33 82 A
Redwald Rd. E5	49	36 85 A
Redway Dri. Twick	82	14 73 A
Redwing Path. SE18	66	44 79 B
Redwood Cl. SE16	64	36 80 C
Redwood Ct. Surb	101	17 66 B
Redwoods. SW15	84	22 73 C
Reece Mews. SW7	62	26 78 B
Reed Ave. Orp	108	45 65 C
Reed Cl. E16	58	40 81 A
Reed Cl. SE12	77	40 74 A
Reede Gdns. Dag	52	49 84 D
Reede Rd. Dag	52	49 84 B
Reede Way. Dag	52	49 84 B
Reedham St. N15	25	34 89 D
Reedham St. SE15	75	34 75 A
Reedholm Villas. N16	48	32 85 B
Reed Pond Wlk. Rom	30	51 90 D
Reed Rd. N17	25	33 90 D
Reedsfield Rd. Ashf	81	07 71 B
Reed's Pl. NW1	47	29 84 B
Reedworth St. SE11	63	31 78 A
Rees Gdns. Croy	105	33 67 D
Reesland Cl. E12	51	43 84 A
Rees St. N1	48	32 83 A
Reets Farm Cl. NW9	34	21 88 C
Reeves Ave. NW9	34	20 87 B
Reeves Cnr. Croy	105	31 65 B
Reeves Mews. W1	6	28 80 A

Street	Pg	Grid
Reeves Pl. N1	48	33 83 C
Reeves Rd. E3	57	37 82 D
Reform Row. N17	25	33 90 D
Reform St. SW11	74	27 76 D
Regal Cl. W5	54	17 81 B
Regal Cres. Wall	104	28 65 D
Regal Ct. N18	17	33 92 D
Regal Ct. Wem	44	17 85 B
Regal La. NW1	47	28 83 A
Regal Way. Har	33	18 88 C
Regan Way. N1	48	33 83 C
Regarth Ave. Rom	42	51 88 C
Regency Cl. Hamp	82	12 71 D
Regency Cl. W5	54	18 81 C
Regency Ct. Sutt	110	25 64 B
Regency Ct. Tedd	93	16 70 B
Regency Dri. Ruis	31	09 87 C
Regency Mews. Islw	71	15 74 A
Regency Mews. NW10	45	22 84 A
Regency St. SW1	10	29 78 B
Regency Way. Bexh	79	47 75 B
Regency Wlk. Croy	106	36 67 D
Regent Cl. Har	33	18 88 C
Regent Cl. N12	15	26 92 C
Regent Pl. Croy	105	33 66 D
Regent Pl. W1	6	29 80 A
Regent Rd. SE24	75	31 74 B
Regent Rd. Surb	102	19 67 A
Regents Ave. N13	17	31 92 C
Regents Cl. S Croy	112	33 63 A
Regents Ct. E8	48	34 83 A
Regents Mews. NW8	46	26 83 C
Regent's Park Barracks. NW1	47	28 83 D
Regent's Park Rd. N3	23	24 90 D
Regent's Park Rd. NW1	47	27 83 B
Regent's Park Rd. NW1	47	28 84 C
Regent's Park Terr. NW1	47	28 83 B
Regent's Pl. SE3	77	40 76 C
Regent's Row. E8	48	34 83 A
Regent Sq. Belv	67	49 78 B
Regent Sq. E3	57	37 82 B
Regent Sq. WC1	3	30 82 A
Regent's Row. E8	48	34 83 A
Regent St. NW10	56	23 82 B
Regent St. SW1	6	29 80 B
Regent St. W1	6	29 80 A
Regent St. W4	61	19 78 C
Regina Cl. Barn	11	23 96 B
Reginald Rd. E7	50	40 84 A
Reginald Rd. Nthwd	19	09 91 D
Reginald Rd. SE8	64	37 77 C
Reginald Sq. SE8	64	37 77 C
Regina Rd. N4	36	30 87 D
Regina Rd. SE25	97	34 68 A
Regina Rd. Sthl	59	11 78 A
Regina Rd. W13	54	16 80 C
Regina Terr. W13	54	16 80 D
Regis Ct. Felt	69	08 74 D
Regnart Bldgs. NW1	2	29 82 C
Reid Ct. Pnr	19	10 89 C
Reidhaven Rd. SE18	66	45 78 A
Reigate Ave. Sutt	103	25 66 D
Reigate Rd. Brom	89	40 72 C
Reigate Rd. Eps	109	22 62 C
Reigate Rd. Ilf	40	45 86 B
Reigate Rd. Wall	111	30 64 C
Reighton Rd. E5	37	34 86 A
Relay Rd. W12	56	23 80 C
Relf Rd. SE15	75	34 75 A
Relko Ct. Eps	109	20 62 D
Relko Gdns. Sutt	110	26 64 D
Relton Mews. SW7	5	27 79 C
Rembrandt Cl. SW1	9	28 78 C
Rembrandt Rd. Edg	22	19 90 C
Rembrandt Rd. SE13	77	39 75 C
Remembrance Ave. N2	25	89 B
Remington Rd. N15	37	32 88 D
Remington St. N1	48	31 83 D
Remnant St. WC2	3	30 81 D
Rempstone Mews. N1	48	32 83 D
Remus Rd. E3	49	37 84 C
Rendlesham Rd. E5	37	34 86 C
Rendlesham Rd. Enf	13	31 97 B
Renforth St. SE16	64	35 79 A
Renfrew Rd. Houn	70	12 76 C
Renfrew Rd. King	94	20 70 C
Renfrew Rd. SE11	63	31 78 B
Renmuir St. SW17	96	27 70 B
Rennell St. SE13	76	38 75 A
Renness Rd. E17	26	36 89 A
Rennets Cl. Sid	78	45 74 A
Rennets Wood Rd. SE9	78	44 74 B
Rennie St. SE1	7	31 80 D
Renown Cl. Croy	105	31 66 D
Renown Cl. Rom	29	49 90 B
Rensburg Rd. E17	38	35 88 D
Renshaw Cl. Belv	67	48 77 B
Renters Ave. NW4	35	23 88 C
Renton Cl. SW2	74	30 74 D
Renwick Rd. Bark	51	46 83 D
Repens Way. Hay	53	11 82 D
Rephidim St. SE1	8	33 79 C
Replingham Rd. SW18	85	25 73 C
Reporton Rd. SW6	62	24 77 C
Repository Rd. SE18	65	42 78 D
Repton Ave. Rom	30	52 89 A
Repton Ave. Wem	44	17 85 A
Repton Cl. Cars	111	27 64 C
Repton Ct. Beck	98	37 69 B
Repton Dri. Rom	30	52 89 C
Repton Gdns. Rom	30	52 89 A
Repton Gr. Ilf	27	42 90 B
Repton Rd. Har	21	18 89 D
Repton Rd. Orp	108	46 65 C
Repton St. E14	57	36 81 C
Repulse Cl. Rom	29	49 90 B
Reservoir Rd. N14	12	29 95 A
Reservoir Rd. Ruis	19	08 89 D
Reservoir Rd. SE4	76	36 76 C
Resolution Wlk. SE18	65	42 79 D
Restell Cl. SE3	65	39 77 A
Restmor Way. Wall	104	28 65 A
Reston Pl. SW7	5	26 79 A
Restons Cres. SE9	78	45 74 C
Retcar Cl. N6	36	28 86 B
Retford Rd. Rom	30	54 91 B
Retford St. N1	48	33 83 C
Retingham Way. E4	18	37 93 B
Retreat Cl. Har	33	17 88 A
Retreat Pl. E9	49	35 84 A
Retreat Rd. Rich	71	17 74 B
Retreat The. Har	32	13 87 A
Retreat The. NW9	34	20 88 B
Retreat The. Surb	101	18 67 D
Retreat The. SW14	72	21 75 A
Retreat The. Th Hth	97	32 68 D
Retreat The. Wor Pk	102	22 65 B
Revell Rd. King	94	19 69 B
Revell Rd. Sutt	110	24 63 B
Revelon Rd. SE4	76	35 75 A
Revelstoke Rd. SW18	85	25 72 A
Reventlow Rd. SE9	90	44 73 C
Reverdy Rd. SE1	63	34 78 A
Revesby Rd. Cars	104	27 67 C
Review Rd. Dag	52	49 83 B
Review Rd. NW2	34	21 86 B
Rewell St. SW6	62	26 77 C
Rewley Rd. Cars	103	26 67 D
Rex Ave. Ashf	81	07 71 C
Reydon Ave. E11	39	41 88 C
Reynard Cl. Brom	100	43 68 A
Reynard Dri. SE19	97	33 70 D
Reynardson Rd. N17	25	32 91 C
Reynolds Ave. E12	51	43 85 C
Reynolds Ave. Rom	41	47 87 A
Reynolds Cl. Cars	104	27 66 D
Reynolds Cl. NW11	35	25 87 B
Reynolds Cl. E11	39	39 86 D
Reynolds Ct. Rom	29	47 89 B
Reynolds Ct. Rom	29	47 89 B
Reynolds Dri. Eng	22	19 89 A
Reynolds Pl. Rich	71	18 74 D
Reynolds Rd. SE3	65	40 77 D
Reynolds Rd. Hay	53	11 82 C
Reynolds Rd. N.Mal	102	20 66 B
Reynolds Rd. SE15	76	35 74 A
Reynolds Rd. W4	61	20 79 C
Reynolds Way. Croy	112	33 64 A
Rheidol Mew. N1	48	32 83 C
Rheidol Terr. N1	48	32 83 A
Rheola Cl. N17	25	33 90 B
Rhoda St. E2	4	33 82 D
Rhodes Ave. N22	24	29 90 A
Rhodesia Rd. E11	38	38 86 B
Rhodesia Rd. SW9	74	30 76 C
Rhodes-moorhouse Ct. Mord	103	25 67 C
Rhodes St. N7	47	30 85 D
Rhodeswell Rd. E14	57	36 81 B
Rhododendron Dell. Rich	71	18 76 A
Rhododendron Dell. Rich	60	18 77 C
Rhondda Gr. E3	57	36 82 A
Rhyl Rd. Grnf	44	15 83 D
Rhyl St. NW5	47	28 84 A
Rhys Ave. N11	24	29 91 D
Ribble Cl. Wdf Gn	27	41 91 A
Ribblesdale Ave. Nthlt	43	13 84 B
Ribblesdale Rd. N8	24	30 89 D
Ribblesdale Rd. SW16	86	28 71 D
Ribchester Ave. Grnf	54	15 82 B
Ribston Cl. Brom	107	42 66 D
Ricardo St. E14	57	37 81 D
Ricards Rd. SW19	85	24 71 D
Richards Ave. Rom	41	50 88 C
Richards Cl. Har	33	16 88 A
Richardson Rd. E15	50	39 83 C
Richardson's Mews. W1	2	29 82 C
Richards Pl. E17	26	37 89 A
Richard's Pl. SW3	9	27 78 A
Richard St. E1	57	34 81 D
Richbell Pl. WC1	3	30 81 B
Richborne Terr. SW8	10	30 77 D
Richborough Rd. NW2	46	24 85 A
Richford Rd. E15	50	39 83 B
Richford St. W6	62	23 79 C
Richlands Ave. Eps	109	22 64 C
Rich La. SW5	62	25 78 D
Richmer Rd. Eri	68	52 77 C
Richmond Ave. E4	18	38 92 D
Richmond Ave. Felt	69	09 74 C
Richmond Ave. N1	48	31 83 A
Richmond Ave. NW10	46	23 84 A
Richmond Ave. SW20	95	24 69 A
Richmond Bldgs. W1	2	29 81 D
Richmond Cl. E17	38	36 88 D
Richmond Cres. E4	18	38 92 D
Richmond Cres. N1	48	31 83 A
Richmond Cres. N9	17	34 94 C
Richmond Ct. Mit	95	26 68 B
Richmond Gdns. Har	21	15 91 B
Richmond Gdns. NW4	22	22 89 C
Richmond Green. Croy	104	30 65 C
Richmond Green. Rich	71	17 74 B
Richmond Gr. N1	48	31 84 D
Richmond Gr. Surb	101	18 67 D
Richmond Hill. Rich	71	18 74 C
Richmond Hill. Rich	71	18 74 C
Richmond Ho. SE26	87	34 72 C
Richmond Mews. W1	2	29 81 D
Richmond Park Rd. King	93	18 70 C
Richmond Park Rd. SW14	72	20 75 D
Richmond Pl. SE18	66	44 78 A
Richmond Rd. Barn	11	26 95 A
Richmond Rd. Croy	104	30 65 C
Richmond Rd. E11	38	38 86 B
Richmond Rd. E4	18	38 94 D
Richmond Rd. E7	50	40 85 D
Richmond Rd. E8	48	34 84 C
Richmond Rd. Ilf	40	44 86 C
Richmond Rd. Islw	71	16 75 A
Richmond Rd. King	93	18 70 C
Richmond Rd. N11	24	30 91 A
Richmond Rd. N15	37	33 88 C
Richmond Rd. N2	23	26 90 C
Richmond Rd. Rom	42	51 88 D
Richmond Rd. SW20	94	22 69 B
Richmond Rd. Th Hth	97	31 68 D
Richmond Rd. Twick	83	16 73 B
Richmond Rd. W5	60	18 79 A
Richmond St. E13	50	40 83 C
Richmond Terr Mews. SW1	7	30 79 A
Richmond Terr. SW1	7	30 79 A
Richmond Way. E11	39	40 86 A
Richmond Way. W12	62	23 79 B
Richmond Way. W14	62	23 79 B
Richmount Gdns. SE3	77	40 75 A
Rich St. E14	57	36 80 B
Rickard Cl. SW2	87	31 73 C
Rickards Cl. Surb	101	18 65 A
Rickards Cl. Sthl	53	14 80 C
Rickett St. SW6	62	25 77 A
Rickman St. E1	57	35 82 C
Rickmansworth Rd. Nthwd	19	08 91 D
Rickmansworth Rd. Pnr	20	11 90 C
Rickthorne Rd. N19	36	30 86 A
Rickyard Path. SE9	77	42 75 C
Ridding La. Grnf	44	15 85 D
Riddlesdown Rd. Pur	112	32 62 C
Riddons Rd. SE12	89	41 71 A
Rideout St. SE18	65	42 78 B
Ride The. Brent	60	17 78 C
Ride The. Enf	14	35 96 A
Ridgdale St. E3	49	37 83 D
Ridge Ave. Dart	80	51 74 D
Ridge Ave. N21	17	32 94 B
Ridgebrook Rd. SE3	77	41 75 B
Ridge Cl. NW4	23	23 90 D
Ridge Cl. NW9	22	20 89 D
Ridge Crest. Enf	12	30 97 B
Ridge Hill. NW11	35	24 87 C
Ridge Langley. S Croy	112	34 62 A
Ridgemount Ave. Croy	106	35 65 B
Ridgemount Cl. SE20	97	34 70 D
Ridgemount Gdns. Enf	13	31 97 D
Ridge Park. Pur	111	29 62 D

Ridge Rd. Mit	96	28 70 D	Ringmore Rise. SE23	87	34 73 B
Ridge Rd. N21	17	32 94 B	Ringshall Rd. Orp	100	46 68 A
Ridge Rd. N8	36	30 88 D	Ringslade Rd. N22	24	30 90 D
Ridge Rd. NW2	35	24 86 D	Ringstead Rd. SE6	88	37 73 B
Ridge Rd. Sutt	103	24 66 D	Ringstead Rd. Sutt	110	26 64 D
Ridge's Yd. Croy	105	31 65 D	Ring Way. N11	24	29 91 A
Ridge The. Barn	11	24 95 B	Ringway. Sthl	59	12 78 C
Ridge The. Orp	108	44 65 B	Ringwold Cl. Beck	98	36 70 C
Ridge The. Pur	111	29 62 D	Ringwood Ave. Croy	104	30 66 A
Ridge The. Surb	102	19 67 A	Ringwood Ave. Horn	42	53 86 B
Ridge The. Twick	82	14 73 B	Ringwood Ave. N2	24	27 89 B
Ridgeview Cl. Barn	11	23 95 D	Ringwood Cl. Pnr	20	11 89 A
Ridgeview Rd. N20	15	26 93 C	Ringwood Gdns. SW15	84	22 73 C
Ridgeway Ave. Barn	12	27 95 D	Ringwood Rd. E17	38	36 88 D
Ridgeway. Brom	107	40 65 A	Ringwood Way. Hamp	82	13 71 A
Ridgeway Cres Gdns. Orp	108	45 65 C	Ringwood Way. N21	17	31 94 B
Ridgeway Cres. Orp	108	45 65 C	Ripley Gdns. Sutt	110	26 64 A
Ridge Way. Dart	80	51 74 D	Ripley Gdns. SW14	72	20 75 B
Ridgeway Dri. Brom	89	40 71 B	Ripley Rd. Belv	67	49 78 A
Ridgeway E. Sid	78	45 74 B	Ripley Rd. E16	58	41 81 C
Ridge Way. Felt	82	12 72 C	Ripley Rd. Enf	13	32 97 A
Ridgeway Gdns. Ilf	39	42 88 A	Ripley Rd. Hamp	92	13 70 C
Ridgeway Gdns. SW19	95	23 70 D	Ripley Rd. Ilf	40	45 86 B
Ridgeway Pl. SW19	95	24 70 A	Ripley Villas. W5	54	17 81 C
Ridgeway Rd. Islw	71	15 76 A	Ripon Cl. Nthlt	43	13 84 B
Ridgeway Road N. Islw	60	15 77 C	Ripon Gdns. Ilf	39	42 87 A
Ridge Way. SE19	97	33 70 A	Ripon Rd. N17	25	32 89 B
Ridgeway. SW19	95	23 70 B	Ripon Rd. N9	17	34 94 B
Ridgeway The. Croy	104	30 65 D	Ripon Rd. SE18	66	43 78 B
Ridgeway The. E4	18	38 94 C	Rippersley Rd. Well	78	46 76 A
Ridgeway The. Enf	13	31 97 C	Ripple Rd. Bark	45	45 83 A
Ridgeway The. Har	32	12 88 B	Ripple Rd. Dag	52	48 83 A
Ridgeway The. Har	33	17 88 C	Ripplevale Gr. N1	48	31 84 C
Ridgeway The. N11	16	27 92 B	Rippolson Rd. SE18	66	45 78 D
Ridgeway The. N14	16	30 93 A	Ripston Rd. Ashf	81	08 71 D
Ridgeway The. N3	23	25 91 D	Risborough Dri. Wor Pk	102	22 66 B
Ridgeway The. NW11	35	24 87 D	Risborough St. SE1	7	31 79 B
Ridgeway The. NW7	15	23 92 C	Risdon St. SE16	79	35 79 A
Ridgeway The. NW9	22	20 89 D	Risebridge Chase. Rom	30	51 91 B
Ridgeway The. Rom	30	52 89 C	Risebridge Rd. Rom	30	52 90 A
Ridgeway The. Rom	30	54 90 B	Risedale Rd. Bexh	79	50 75 A
Ridgeway The. Ruis	31	10 87 A	Riseholme St. E9	49	36 84 B
Ridge Way The. S Croy	112	33 62 C	Riseldine Rd. SE23	76	36 74 C
Ridgeway The. Stan	21	17 91 A	Rise Park Bvd. Rom	30	51 90 B
Ridgeway The. W3	61	19 79 C	Rise Park Par. Rom	30	51 90 C
Ridgeway W. Sid	78	45 74 A	Rise The. Dart	80	51 75 D
Ridgewell Cl. Dag	52	49 83 B	Rise The. E11	39	40 88 A
Ridgewell Cl. N1	48	32 83 A	Rise The. Eps	109	21 62 D
Ridgewell Rd. E16	58	41 81 A	Rise The. Grnf	44	16 85 C
Ridgmount Gdns. WC1	2	29 81 B	Rise The. N13	17	31 92 A
Ridgmount Pl. WC1	2	29 81 B	Rise The. NW7	21	21 91 B
Ridgmount Rd. SW18	73	25 74 B	Rise The. Wem	45	21 85 A
Ridgmount St. WC1	2	29 81 B	Rising Hill Cl. Nthwd	19	08 91 A
Ridgway Rd. SW9	75	31 75 B	Risinghill St. N1	48	31 83 C
Ridgway The. Sutt	110	26 63 D	Risingholme Cl. Har	21	15 90 A
Riding House St. W1	2	29 81 A	Risingholme Rd. Har	21	15 90 C
Ridings Ave. N21	13	32 95 A	Risings The. E17	26	38 89 D
Ridings The. Barn	15	26 94 B	Rising Sun Ct. EC1	3	31 81 B
Ridings The. Sun	91	10 69 A	Risley Ave. N17	25	32 90 B
Ridings The. Surb	102	19 67 A	Rita Rd. SW8	10	30 77 D
Ridings The. W5	54	18 82 D	Ritches Rd. N15	25	32 88 A
Riding The. NW11	35	24 87 B	Ritchie Rd. Croy	105	34 67 D
Ridley Ave. W13	60	16 79 D	Ritchie St. N1	48	31 83 C
Ridley Cl. Rom	30	52 90 B	Ritchings Ave. E17	26	36 89 C
Ridley Rd. Brom	99	39 68 B	Ritherdon Rd. SW17	86	28 72 B
Ridley Rd. E7	50	41 85 A	Ritson Rd. E8	48	34 84 A
Ridley Rd. E8	48	33 85 D	Ritter St. SE18	66	43 77 A
Ridley Rd. NW10	45	22 83 C	Rivenhall Gdns. E18	27	39 89 D
Ridley Rd. SW19	95	25 70 D	River Ave. N13	17	31 93 D
Ridley Rd. Well	78	46 76 B	River Ave. Surb	101	16 66 A
Ridsdale Rd. SE20	78	34 69 B	River Bank. E Mol	92	13 68 A
Riefield Rd. SE9	78	44 75 C	Riverbank. E Mol	93	15 68 C
Riffel Rd. NW2	46	23 85 C	River Bank. N21	17	32 94 A
Rifle Ct. SE11	63	31 77 A	River Bank. Surb	101	15 67 B
Rifle Pl. W11	52	23 80 D	River Barge Cl. E14	64	38 79 A
Rifle St. E14	57	37 81 B	River Cl. E11	39	41 88 C
Rigault Rd. SW6	73	24 76 C	River Cl. Ruis	31	09 88 D
Rigby Cl. Croy	105	31 65 C	Rivercourt Rd. W6	67	22 78 D
Rigby Mews. Ilf	40	43 86 B	River Ct. Surb	101	17 67 B
Rigden St. E14	57	37 81 D	Riverdale Gdns. Twick	71	17 74 A
Rigeley Rd. NW10	55	22 82 A	Riverdale Rd. Belv	67	49 78 D
Rigg App. E10	38	36 87 C	Riverdale Rd. Bex	79	48 74 D
Rigge Pl. SW4	74	29 75 D	Riverdale Rd. Eri	67	50 78 C
Riggindale Rd. SW16	86	29 71 B	Riverdale Rd. Felt	82	12 71 B
Riley Rd. SE1	8	33 79 B	Riverdale Rd. SE18	66	45 78 D
Riley St. SW10	62	26 77 D	Riverdale Rd. Twick	71	17 74 C
Ring Cl. Brom	99	40 70 D	Riverdene Rd. Ilf	40	43 86 D
Ringcroft St. N7	48	31 85 C	River Front. Enf	13	33 96 A
Ringer's Rd. Brom	99	40 68 A	River Gdns. Cars	104	28 65 C
Ringford Rd. SW18	73	25 74 C	River Gdns. Felt	65	10 74 B
Ringles Ct. E6	51	43 83 B	River Grove Park. Beck	98	36 69 B
Ringmer Ave. SW6	73	24 76 A	Riverhead Cl. E17	26	35 90 D
Ringmer Gdns. N19	36	30 86 A	Riverholme Dri. Eps	109	21 62 A
Ringmer Pl. N21	13	32 95 B	River Ho. SE26	87	34 72 D
Ringmer Way. Brom	107	42 67 B	River La. Rich	83	17 73 D

Rivermead Cl. Tedd	83	16 71 D
Rivermead Ct. SW6	73	24 75 B
River Meads Ave. Twick	82	13 72 D
Rivermead. Surb	101	17 67 B
River Park Gdns. Brom	98	38 70 D
River Park Rd. N22	24	30 90 D
River Pl. N1	48	32 84 C
River Rd. Bark	51	45 83 C
River Reach. Tedd	83	17 71 C
Riversdale Rd. N5	37	32 86 C
Riversdale Rd. Rom	29	49 91 D
Riversdale Rd. Surb	101	16 67 C
Riversfield Rd. Enf	13	33 96 A
River Side Ave. Rich	71	18 76 A
Riverside Cl. King	93	17 68 D
Riverside Cl. W7	54	15 82 C
Riverside Cl. Wall	104	28 65 D
Riverside Dri. Mit	104	27 67 A
Riverside Dri. Rich	83	17 72 A
Riverside Dri. W4	72	21 76 A
Riverside Gdns. Enf	13	32 97 D
Riverside Gdns. W6	61	22 78 D
Riverside Gdns. Wem	44	18 83 C
Riverside Mansions. E1	57	35 80 C
Riverside. NW4	34	22 87 B
Riverside Rd. E15	49	38 83 C
Riverside Rd. N15	37	34 88 C
Riverside Rd. SW17	85	26 72 C
Riverside. SE7	65	41 79 C
Riverside. Twick	83	16 73 D
Riverside Way. Dart	80	54 74 A
Riverside Wlk. E10	65	39 78 A
Riverside Wlk. Islw	71	15 75 A
River St. EC1	3	31 82 A
River Terr. W6	62	23 78 C
Riverton Cl. W9	56	24 82 B
River View. Enf	13	32 96 A
Riverview Gdns. SW13	61	22 77 B
River View Gdns. Twick	83	15 72 B
Riverview Gr. W4	61	19 77 B
Riverview Park. SE6	88	37 72 A
Riverview Rd. Eps	109	20 64 B
Riverview Rd. W4	61	19 77 B
River Way. Eps	109	20 64 D
Riverway. N13	17	31 92 A
River Way. SE10	65	39 79 D
River Way. Twick	82	13 72 B
River Wlk. SW6	62	23 77 C
River Wlk. SW6	73	24 75 A
River Wlk. SW6	73	24 75 A
River Wlk. W6	62	23 77 A
Riverwood La. Chis	100	44 69 D
Rivington Ave. Wdf Gn	27	41 90 D
Rivington Cres. NW9	22	21 91 D
Rivington Pl. EC2	4	33 82 A
Rivington St. EC2	4	33 82 A
Rivington Wlk. E8	48	34 83 A
Rivulet Rd. N17	25	32 91 C
Rixsen Rd. E12	50	42 85 C
Roach Rd. E3	49	37 84 C
Roads Pl. N19	36	30 86 A
Roan St. SE10	64	38 77 A
Robb Rd. Stan	21	16 91 A
Robert Adam St. W1	2	28 81 C
Roberta St. E2	57	34 82 A
Robert Cl. W9	1	26 82 C
Robert Keen Cl. SE15	75	34 76 A
Robert Lowe Cl. SE14	64	35 77 D
Roberton Dri. Brom	99	41 69 A
Robert's Alley. W5	60	17 79 B
Robertsbridge Rd. Cars	103	26 66 B
Roberts Cl. Rom	30	52 90 B
Roberts Cl. Sutt	110	23 63 D
Roberts Ct. SE20	98	35 69 A
Roberts Mews. SW1	6	28 79 C
Robertson St. SW8	74	28 76 D
Roberts Rd. Belv	67	49 78 C
Roberts Rd. E17	26	37 90 B
Roberts Rd. NW7	23	24 91 A
Robert St. Croy	105	32 65 C
Robert St. E16	66	43 79 B
Robert St. NW1	2	29 82 A
Robert St. SE18	68	44 78 B
Robert St. WC2	7	30 80 A
Robeson St. E3	57	36 81 B
Robina Cl. Bexh	79	47 75 D
Robina Cl. Ilf	28	45 91 A
Robin Cl. Rom	29	50 91 D
Robin Cl. Wall	19	29 64 C
Robin Gr. Har	33	18 88 D
Robin Gr. N6	36	28 86 A
Robin Grove Church Wlk. Brent	60	17 77 A
Robin Hill Dri. Chis	99	42 70 A
Robinhood Cl. Mit	96	29 68 A

Street	Ref	Grid
Robin Hood Dri. Har	21	15 91 D
Robin Hood Gdns. E14	58	38 80 A
Robin Hood Green. Orp	108	46 67 A
Robin Hood La. Bexh	79	48 74 A
Robin Hood La. E14	58	38 80 A
Robinhood La. Mit	96	29 68 A
Robin Hood La. Sutt	110	25 64 C
Robin Hood Rd. SW15	84	21 71 A
Robin Hood Rd. SW19	94	22 71 C
Robin Hood Way	44	15 84 B
Robin Hood Way. SW15	84	21 71 A
Robin Hood Way. SW20	94	21 70 B
Robins Ct. SE12	89	41 72 C
Robins Gr. W.Wick	107	40 65 C
Robinson Rd. Dag	52	49 85 A
Robinson Rd. E2	49	35 83 C
Robinson Rd. SW17	96	27 70 A
Robinson Rd. SW17	96	27 70 B
Robinson's Cl. SW13	54	16 81 A
Robinson St. SW3	9	27 77 B
Robin Way. Orp	100	46 68 B
Robinwood Pl. SW15	84	20 71 B
Robsart St. SW9	75	31 76 C
Robson Ave. NW10	45	22 84 C
Robson Cl. Enf	13	31 97 D
Robson Rd. SE27	97	32 72 C
Roch Ave. Edg	21	18 90 D
Rochdale Rd. E17	38	37 87 A
Rochdale Rd. SE2	66	46 78 B
Rochelle Cl. SW11	73	26 75 D
Rochelle St. E2	4	33 82 B
Rochemont Wlk. E8	48	34 83 A
Roche Rd. SW16	96	30 69 B
Rochester Ave. Brom	99	40 69 D
Rochester Ave. Felt	81	09 72 B
Rochester Cl. Enf	13	33 97 A
Rochester Cl. Sid	78	46 74 B
Rochester Cl. SW16	96	30 70 C
Rochester Dri. Bex	79	49 74 C
Rochester Dri. Pnr	32	11 88 B
Rochester Gdns. Croy	105	33 65 C
Rochester Gdns. Ilf	39	42 87 B
Rochester Mews. NW1	47	29 84 C
Rochester Pl. NW1	47	29 84 C
Rochester Rd. Cars	111	27 64 B
Rochester Rd. Nthwd	19	09 89 B
Rochester Rd. NW1	47	29 84 A
Rochester Row. SW1	10	29 78 A
Rochester Sq. NW1	47	29 84 C
Rochester St. SW1	6	29 79 D
Rochester Terr. NW1	47	29 84 A
Rochester Way. SE3	77	41 76 C
Rochester Way. SE9	77	42 75 C
Rochester Wlk. SE1	8	32 80 D
Roche Wlk. Cars	103	26 67 D
Rochford Ave. Rom	41	47 88 A
Rochford Cl. E6	41	83 D
Rochford Way. Croy	104	30 67 C
Rochford Wlk. E8	48	34 84 C
Rock Ave. SW14	72	20 75 B
Rockbourne Mews. SE23	88	35 73 D
Rockbourne Rd. SE23	88	35 73 D
Rockchase Gdns. Horn	42	54 88 C
Rockford Ave. Grnf	44	16 83 D
Rock Gdns. Dag	52	49 85 D
Rock Grove Way. SE16	78	34 78 A
Rockhall Rd. NW2	46	23 85 B
Rockhampton Cl. SE27	87	31 71 A
Rockhampton Rd. S Croy	112	33 63 A
Rockhampton Rd. SE27	87	31 71 A
Rock Hill. SE26	87	33 71 B
Rockingham Ave. Horn	42	52 88 D
Rockingham Cl. SW15	72	21 75 D
Rockingham St. SE1	8	32 79 C
Rockland Rd. SW15	73	24 75 C
Rocklands Dri. Stan	29	17 90 C
Rockley Rd. W14	62	23 79 C
Rockmount Rd. SE18	66	45 78 D
Rockmount Rd. SE19	97	32 70 B
Rocks La. SW13	72	22 76 D
Rock St. N4	37	31 86 A
Rockware Ave. Grnf	44	14 83 B
Rockware Ave. Grnf	44	15 83 A
Rockwell Gdns. SE19	87	33 71 A
Rockwell Rd. Dag	52	49 85 D
Rockwood Pl. W12	62	23 79 A
Rocliffe St. N1	48	31 83 D
Rocombe Cres. SE23	88	35 73 A
Rocque La. SE3	77	39 75 B
Rodborough Rd. NW11	35	25 87 C
Roden Ct. N6		29 87 B
Roden Gdns. SE25	105	33 67 C
Rodenhurst Rd. SW4		29 74 D
Roden St. Ilf	40	43 86 C
Roden St. N7	36	30 86 D
Roden Way. Ilf	40	43 86 C
Roderick Rd. NW3	47	27 85 B
Roding Ave. Bark	51	43 84 D
Roding Ave. Wdf Gn	27	42 91 A
Roding Lane N. Wdf Gn	27	42 90 A
Roding Lane S. Ilf	27	41 89 D
Roding Lodge. Ilf	39	41 88 D
Roding Rd. E5	49	36 85 C
Rodings The. Wdf Gn	27	41 91 A
Rodmarton St. W1	1	27 81 B
Rodmel Slope. N12	15	24 92 D
Rodmere St. E10	65	39 78 C
Rodmill La. SW2	86	30 73 A
Rodney Cl. Croy	105	31 66 D
Rodney Cl. N.Mal	102	21 67 A
Rodney Gdns. Pnr	32	12 87 A
Rodney Pl. E17	26	36 90 D
Rodney Pl. SE17	63	32 78 A
Rodney Pl. SW19	95	26 69 A
Rodney Rd. E11	27	40 89 D
Rodney Rd. Mit	96	27 68 A
Rodney Rd. N.Mal	102	21 67 A
Rodney Rd. SE17	63	32 78 B
Rodney Rd. Twick	82	13 73 A
Rodney St. N1	47	30 83 D
Rodney Way. Rom	29	49 90 B
Rodsley St. SE1	63	34 77 A
Rodway Rd. Brom	99	40 69 B
Rodway Rd. SW15	84	22 73 A
Rodwell Rd. SE22	75	33 74 D
Roebourne Way. E16	66	43 79 A
Roebuck Cl. Felt	81	10 71 B
Roebuck Rd. N17	25	33 91 B
Roebuck Rd. Chess	109	19 64 A
Roebuck Rd. Ilf	28	46 91 B
Roedean Ave. Enf	14	35 97 A
Roedean Cl. Enf	14	35 97 A
Roedean Cres. SW15	72	21 74 C
Roe End. NW9	22	20 89 C
Roe Green. NW9	34	20 88 A
Roehampton Cl. SW15	72	22 75 C
Roehampton Dri. Chis	100	44 70 A
Roehampton Gate. SW15	72	21 74 C
Roehampton High St. SW15	84	22 73 A
Roehampton La. SW15	72	22 74 A
Roehampton Vale. SW15	84	21 72 B
Roe La. NW9	22	20 89 C
Roe Way. Wall	111	30 63 A
Rofant Rd. Nthwd	19	09 91 A
Roffey St. E14	64	38 79 A
Roger Reede's Almshouses. Rom	30	
Rogers Estate. E2	57	35 82 A
Rogers Rd. Dag	52	49 85 C
Rogers Rd. E16	57	39 81 D
Rogers Rd. SW17	86	27 71 A
Rogers Ruff. Nthwd	19	08 90 A
Roger St. WC1	3	30 82 D
Rogers Wlk. N12	15	25 93 D
Rojack Rd. SE23	88	35 73 D
Rokeby Gdns. Wdf Gn	27	40 90 A
Rokeby Pl. SW20	94	22 70 D
Rokeby Rd. SE4	76	36 76 D
Rokeby St. E15	50	39 83 A
Rokesby Cl. Well	78	44 76 D
Rokesby Pl. Wem		17 85 D
Rokesly Ave. N8	36	30 88 A
Roland Gdns. SW10		26 78 C
Roland Gdns. SW7	62	26 78 C
Roland Rd. E17	26	38 89 D
Roland Way. SE17	63	32 78 D
Roland Way. SW7		26 78 C
Roland Way. Wor Pk	102	21 65 B
Roles Gr. Rom	29	48 89 C
Rolfe Cl. Barn	12	27 96 C
Rollesby Rd. Chess	109	19 63 A
Rolleston Ave. Orp	108	43 67 D
Rolleston Cl. Orp	108	43 66 B
Rolleston Rd. S Croy	112	32 63 D
Roll Gdns. Ilf	40	43 88 A
Rollins St. SE15	64	35 77 A
Rollit Cres. Houn		13 74 A
Rollit St. N7	48	31 85 C
Rolls Bldgs. EC4	3	31 81 C
Rollscourt Ave. SE24	75	32 74 A
Rolls Park Ave. E4	18	37 92 D
Rolls Park Rd. E4	18	37 92 D
Rolls Pas. EC4	3	31 81 C
Rolls Rd. SE1	63	33 78 D
Rolt St. SE14	64	36 77 A
Rolvenden Gdns. Brom	41	70 D
Roman Cl. Felt	70	11 74 A
Roman Cl. Rain	52	50 83 D
Romanhurst Ave. Brom	99	39 68 C
Romanhurst Gdns. Brom	99	39 68 C
Roman Rd. E2	57	35 82 A
Roman Rd. E3	49	36 83 C
Roman Rd. Ilf	51	43 84 B
Roman Rd. N10	24	28 91 D
Roman Rd. N2	24	27 90 A
Roman Rd. W4	61	21 78 B
Roman Rise. SE19	97	32 70 B
Roman Way. Croy	105	31 65 B
Roman Way. Enf	13	33 95 B
Roman Way. N7	47	30 84 B
Roman Way. SE15	64	35 77 C
Romany Gdns. E17	26	36 90 A
Romany Gdns. Sutt	103	25 66 A
Romany Rise. Orp	108	44 66 C
Roma Rd. E17	26	36 89 A
Romberg Rd. SW17	86	28 72 C
Romborough Gdns. SE13	76	38 74 A
Romborough Way. SE13	76	38 74 A
Rom Cres. Rom	42	51 87 B
Romero Sq. SE3	77	41 75 C
Romeyn Rd. SW16	86	30 72 D
Romford Rd. Chig	29	48 91 C
Romford Rd. E12	50	42 85 B
Romford Rd. E15	50	39 84 A
Romford Rd. E7	50	40 85 D
Romford Rd. Rom	29	48 91 D
Romford St. E1	57	34 81 B
Romilly Rd. N4	37	31 86 D
Romilly St. W1	2	29 81 D
Rommany Rd. SE27	87	32 71 B
Romney Chase. Horn	42	54 88 D
Romney Cl. Ashf	81	08 71 C
Romney Cl. Har	13	87 A
Romney Cl. N17	25	34 90 B
Romney Cl. NW11	35	26 87 C
Romney Cl. SE14	64	35 77 C
Romney Dri. Brom	99	41 70 D
Romney Dri. Har	32	13 87 A
Romney Gdns. Bexh	79	48 76 B
Romney Rd. N.Mal	102	20 67 D
Romney Rd. SE10	64	38 77 B
Romney St. SW1	7	30 79 C
Romola Rd. SE24	87	31 73 D
Romsey Gdns. Dag	52	47 83 B
Romsey Rd. Dag	52	47 83 B
Romsey Rd. W13	54	16 80 A
Ronald Ave. E15	58	39 82 A
Ronald Cl. Beck	106	36 67 B
Ronalds Rd. Brom	99	40 69 A
Ronalds Rd. N5	48	31 85 C
Ronald St. E1	57	35 81 C
Ronaldstone Rd. Sid	78	45 74 C
Rona Rd. NW3	47	28 85 A
Rona Wlk. N1	48	32 84 B
Rondu Rd. NW2	46	24 85 C
Ronelaan Rd. Surb	101	18 65 D
Roneo Cnr. Horn	42	51 87 D
Ronver Rd. SE12	89	39 73 D
Rood La. EC3	8	33 80 A
Rookby Ct. N21	17	31 93 B
Rookeries Cl. Felt	82	11 72 C
Rookery Cl. NW9	34	21 88 B
Rookery Cres. Dag	52	49 84 D
Rookery La. Brom	107	41 67 D
Rookery Rd. SW4		29 75 C
Rookery Way. NW9	34	21 88 B
Rooke Way. E10	65	39 78 D
Rookfield Ave. N10	24	29 89 C
Rookfield Cl. N10	24	29 89 C
Rookley Cl. Sutt	110	25 62 D
Rooksmead Rd. Sun	91	10 69 C
Rookstone Rd. SW17	86	27 71 D
Rookwood Ave. N Mal	94	22 68 C
Rookwood Ave. Wall	111	29 64 B
Rookwood Rd. N16	37	33 87 B
Roosevelt Way. Dag	52	50 84 B
Ropemakers Fields. E14	57	36 80 B
Ropemaker St. EC2	4	32 81 B
Roper La. SE1	8	33 79 A
Ropers Ave. E4	18	38 92 C
Roper St. SE9	78	43 74 C
Ropers Wlk. SE24	87	31 73 A
Roper Way. Mit	96	28 69 C
Ropery St. E3	57	36 82 D
Rope Walk Gdns. E1	57	34 81 C
Rope Yard Rails. SE18	66	43 79 D
Ropley St. E2	48	34 83 C
Rosa Alba Mews. N5	48	32 85 A
Rosa Ave. Ashf		07 71 A
Rosaline Rd. SW6	62	24 77 C
Rosamond St. SE26	87	34 72 D
Rosary Cl. Houn	70	12 76 C
Rosary Gdns. Ashf	81	07 71 B

Street	Pg	Grid			Street	Pg	Grid		
Rosary Gdns. SW7	62	26	78	A	Rose Hill. Sutt	103	25	66	D
Rosaville Rd. SW6	62	24	77	D	Roseland Cl. N17	25	32	91	D
Roscoe St. EC1	4	32	82	C	Rose La. Rom	29	48	89	C
Roscoff Cl. Edg	22	20	90	A	Roseleigh Ave. N5	48	31	85	B
Roseacre Cl. Horn	42	54	87	B	Rosemary Ave. E Mol	92	13	68	C
Roseacre Cl. W13	54	16	81	B	Rosemary Ave. Enf	13	33	97	A
Roseacre Rd. Well	78	46	75	B	Rosemary Ave. Houn	70	11	76	D
Roseacre Rd. Well	79	47	75	A	Rosemary Ave. N2	23	25	89	D
Rose Alley. SE1	8	32	80	C	Rosemary Ave. N3	23	25	89	D
Rose and Crown Ct. EC2	4	32	81	C	Rosemary Ave. N9	17	34	94	D
Rose and Crown Yd. SW1	6	29	80	C	Rosemary Ave. Rom	30	51	89	B
Rose Ave. E18	27	40	90	D	Rosemary Dri. Ilf	39	41	88	B
Rose Ave. Mit	96	27	69	B	Rosemary Gdns. Dag	41	48	87	D
Rose Ave. Mord	103	26	67	A	Rosemary La. SW14	72	20	75	A
Rosebank Ave. Wem	44	15	85	B	Rosemary Rd. SE15	63	33	77	D
Rose Bank Cl. N12	16	27	92	C	Rosemary Rd. SE15	63	33	77	D
Rosebank Gdns. E3	49	36	83	D	Rosemary Rd. Well	78	45	76	B
Rosebank Gr. E17	26	36	89	B	Rosemary St. N1	48	32	83	B
Rosebank Rd. E17	38	37	88	D	Rosemead Ave. Felt	81	09	72	B
Rosebank Rd. W7	60	15	79	A	Rosemead Ave. Mit	96	29	68	A
Rosebank. SE20	97	34	70	D	Rosemead Ave. Wem	44	18	85	C
Rosebank. SW6	62	23	77	C	Rosemead. NW9	34	22	87	A
Rosebank Villas. E17	26	37	89	C	Rosemont Rd. N12	23	26	91	A
Rosebank Way. W3	55	20	81	D	Rosemont Rd. NW3	46	26	84	A
Rosebank Wlk. N7	47	29	84	D	Rosemont Rd. Rich	71	18	74	C
Roseberry Gdns. N4	37	32	88	C	Rosemont Rd. W3	55	19	80	B
Roseberry Gdns. Orp	108	45	65	C	Rosemont Rd. Wem	44	18	83	A
Roseberry Pl. E8	48	33	84	B	Rosemoor St. SW3	9	27	78	B
Roseberry Sq. EC1	3	31	82	C	Rosemount Dri. Brom	99	42	68	D
Roseberry St. SE16	63	34	78	B	Rosemount Rd. N Mal	94	20	68	A
Rosebery Ave. E12	50	42	84	B	Rosemount Rd. W13	54	16	81	C
Rosebery Ave. EC1	3	31	82	C	Rosenau Cres. SW11	74	27	76	B
Rosebery Ave. Har	43	12	85	B	Rosenau Rd. SW11	74	27	76	B
Rosebery Ave. N17	25	34	90	C	Rosendale Rd. SE21	87	32	72	A
Rosebery Ave. N Mal	94	21	69	C	Roseneath Ave. N21	17	31	94	D
Rosebery Ave. Sid	90	45	73	A	Roseneath Rd. SW11	74	28	74	C
Rosebery Ave. Th Hth	97	32	69	C	Roseneath Wlk. Enf	13	33	96	C
Rosebery Cl. Mord	103	23	67	D	Rosenthal Rd. SE6	76	38	74	C
Rosebery Gdns. N8	36	30	88	A	Rosenthorpe Rd. SE15	76	35	74	B
Rosebery Gdns. Sutt	110	25	64	B	Roserton St. E14	64	38	79	A
Rosebery Gdns. W13	54	16	81	C	Rosery The. Croy	106	35	67	D
Rosebery Mews. N10	24	29	90	C	Roses The. Wdf Gn	27	39	91	D
Rosebery Rd. Houn	70	14	74	A	Rose St. WC2	7	30	80	A
Rosebery Rd. King	94	19	69	D	Rosetta Cl. SW8	10	30	77	C
Rosebery Rd. N10	24	29	90	C	Roseveare Rd. SE12	89	41	71	A
Rosebery Rd. N9	17	34	93	A	Roseville Ave. Houn	70	13	74	A
Rosebery Rd. Sutt	110	24	63	B	Rosevine Rd. SW20	95	23	69	A
Rosebery Rd. SW2	74	30	74	C	Rose Way. SE12	77	40	74	A
Rosebery Sq. King	94	19	69	D	Roseway. SE21	75	32	74	D
Rosebine Ave. Twick	82	14	73	B	Rose Wlk. Surb	102	19	67	B
Roseburg Rd. SW6	73	25	76	D	Rose Wlk. W Wick	106	38	65	B
Rosebury Vale. Ruis	31	10	86	A	Rosewood Ave. Grnf	44	16	84	A
Rosecourt Rd. Croy	104	30	67	D	Rosewood Ct. Brom	99	41	69	B
Rosecroft Ave. NW3	35	25	86	C	Rosewood Ct. King	94	19	70	C
Rosecroft Gdns. Twick	82	14	73	D	Rosewood Gr. Sutt	103	26	65	A
Rosecroft Gdns. Sthl	53	13	82	C	Rosher Cl. E15	49	38	84	D
Rosecroft Wlk. Pnr	32	11	88	B	Rosina St. E9	49	35	84	B
Rosecroft Wlk. Wem	44	17	85	D	Roskeen Ct. SW20	95	23	70	C
Rosedale Cl. SE2	66	46	79	D	Roskell Rd. SW15	73	23	75	B
Rosedale Cl. Stan	21	16	91	B	Roskild Ct. Wem	44	18	85	B
Rosedale Cl. W7	60	15	79	B	Roslin Rd. W3	59	19	79	D
Rosedale Gdns. Dag	51	46	84	D	Roslin Way. Brom	89	40	71	C
Rose Dale. Orp	108	43	65	B	Roslyn Cl. Mit	95	26	69	D
Rosedale Rd. Dag	51	46	84	D	Roslyn Gdns. Rom	30	51	90	D
Rosedale Rd. E7	50	41	85	C	Roslyn Rd. N15	33	33	88	A
Rosedale Rd. Eps	109	22	64	C	Rosmead Rd. W11	56	24	80	A
Rosedale Rd. Rich	71	18	75	C	Rosoman Pl. EC1	3	31	82	C
Rosedale Rd. Rom	29	50	89	A	Rosoman St. EC1	3	31	82	C
Rosene Ave. Croy	104	30	66	B	Rossall Cl. Horn	42	52	88	C
Rosedene Ave. Grnf	53	13	82	A	Rossall Cres. NW10	54	18	82	B
Rosedene Ave. Mord	103	25	67	A	Ross Ave. Dag	41	48	87	D
Rosedene Ave. SW16	86	30	72	D	Ross Ave. NW7	15	24	92	C
Rosedene Gdns. Ilf	28	43	89	C	Ross Cl. Har	20	14	91	C
Rosedene. NW6	46	23	83	B	Ross Ct. SW15	85	23	73	B
Rosedene Terr. E10	38	37	86	B	Rossdale Dri. Enf	14	35	95	C
Rosedew Rd. W6	62	23	77	B	Rossdale Dri. NW9	34	20	87	C
Rose End. Wor Pk	103	23	66	D	Rossdale Rd. SW15	73	23	75	C
Rosefield Gdns. E14	57	37	80	A	Rossdale. Sutt	111	27	64	C
Rose Garden Cl. Edg	21	18	91	A	Rosse Mews. SE3	77	40	76	B
Rose Gdns. Felt	81	10	72	A	Rossendale St. E5	37	34	86	B
Rose Gdns. Sthl	53	13	82	C	Rossindel Rd. Houn	70	13	74	A
Rose Gdns. W5	60	17	79	D	Rossington St. E5	37	34	86	A
Rose Glen. NW9	22	20	89	D	Rossiter Rd. SW12	86	28	73	D
Rose Glen. Rom	42	51	87	C	Rossland Cl. Bexh	79	49	74	B
Rosehart Mews. W11	56	25	81	C	Rosslyn Ave. Barn	12	27	95	C
Rosehatch Ave. Rom	29	47	89	B	Rosslyn Ave. Dag	41	48	87	B
Roseheath Rd. Houn	70	12	74	B	Rosslyn Ave. Felt	69	10	74	C
Rosehill Ave. Sutt	103	26	66	C	Rosslyn Ave. Rom	54	50	90	D
Rosehill Ct. Mord	103	26	66	A	Rosslyn Ave. SW13	72	21	75	B
Rosehill Gdns. Grnf	44	15	85	D	Rosslyn Cl. W.Wick	107	39	65	D
Rosehill Gdns. Sutt	103	26	65	A	Rosslyn Cres. Har	21	15	89	D
Rosehill. Hamp	92	13	69	A	Rosslyn Cres. Wem	44	18	86	C
Rose Hill Park W. Sutt	103	26	65	A	Rosslyn Hill. NW3	46	26	85	D
Rosehill Rd. SW18	73	26	74	A	Rosslyn Mews. NW3	46	26	85	B

Street	Pg	Grid		
Rosslyn Park Mews. NW3	46	26	85	D
Rosslyn Rd. Bark	51	44	84	D
Rosslyn Rd. E17	26	38	89	C
Rosslyn Rd. Twick	71	17	74	C
Rossmore Rd. NW1	1	27	82	C
Ross Par. Wall	111	28	63	B
Ross Rd. Dart	80	52	74	C
Ross Rd. SE25	97	33	68	A
Ross Rd. Twick	82	14	73	C
Ross Rd. Wall	111	29	64	C
Rosswood Gdns. Wall	111	29	63	A
Rostella Rd. SW17	85	26	71	B
Rostrevor Ave. N15	37	33	88	D
Rostrevor Gdns. Sthl	59	12	78	C
Rostrevor Rd. SW6	73	24	76	B
Rotary St. SE1	7	31	79	D
Rothbury Gdns. Islw	60	16	77	C
Rothbury Rd. E9	49	36	84	D
Rothbury Wlk. N17	25	34	91	D
Rotherfield Rd. Cars	111	28	64	C
Rotherfield St. N1	48	32	84	C
Rotherham Wlk. SE1	7	31	80	D
Rotherhill Ave. SW16	96	29	70	B
Rotherhithe New Rd. SE16	63	34	78	D
Rotherhithe Old Rd. SE16	64	35	78	B
Rotherhithe St. SE16	64	35	79	A
Rotherhithe St. SE16	57	36	80	C
Rotherhithe Tunnel. E1	57	35	80	B
Rothermere Rd. Croy	111	30	64	D
Rotherwick Hill. W5	55	19	82	C
Rotherwick Rd. NW11	35	25	87	A
Rotherwood Rd. SW15	73	23	75	B
Rothery St. N1	48	31	83	B
Rothesay Ave. Grnf	43	14	84	B
Rothesay Ave. Rich	72	19	75	D
Rothesay Ave. SW20	95	24	69	C
Rothesay Rd. SE25	97	33	68	C
Rothsay Rd. E7	50	41	84	A
Rothsay St. SE1	8	33	79	C
Rothsay Wlk. E14	64	38	79	D
Rothschild Rd. W4	61	20	79	C
Rothschild St. SE27	87	31	71	B
Rothwell Gdns. Dag	52	47	83	A
Rothwell Rd. Dag	52	47	83	A
Rothwell St. NW1	47	27	83	B
Roth Wlk. N7	36	30	86	B
Rouel Rd. SE16	63	34	78	A
Rouel Rd. SE16	63	34	79	C
Rougemont Ave. Mord	103	25	67	C
Roundacre. SW19	85	23	72	B
Round Gr. Croy	106	35	66	B
Roundhay Cl. SE23	88	35	72	B
Roundhill Dri. Enf	12	30	96	D
Round Hill. SE26	88	35	72	C
Roundtable Rd. Brom	89	39	72	D
Roundtree Rd. Wem	44	16	85	D
Roundway Rd. Ilf	27	42	90	D
Roundways. Ruis	31	09	86	D
Roundway The. N17	25	32	91	D
Roundwood. Chis	100	43	69	D
Roundwood Cl. Ruis	31	08	87	B
Roundwood Rd. NW10	45	21	84	D
Rounton Rd. E3	57	37	82	C
Roupell Rd. SW2	86	30	73	D
Roupell St. SE1	7	31	80	C
Rouse Gdns. SE21	87	33	71	A
Routh Rd. SW18	86	27	73	A
Rover Ave. Ilf	28	45	91	B
Rowallan Rd. SW6	62	24	77	C
Rowan Ave. E4	26	36	91	B
Rowan Cl. N Mal	94	21	69	C
Rowan Cl. SW16	96	29	69	A
Rowan Cl. W5	60	18	79	A
Rowan Cl. Wem	33	16	86	C
Rowan Cres. SW16	96	29	69	A
Rowan Dri. NW9	22	22	89	A
Rowan Gdns. Croy	105	33	65	D
Rowan Rd. Bexh	79	48	75	A
Rowan Rd. Brent	60	16	77	D
Rowan Rd. SW16	96	29	69	C
Rowan Rd. W6	62	23	78	B
Rowans The. N13	17	32	93	C
Rowans The. Sun	91	09	71	D
Rowan Terr. W6	62	23	78	B
Rowantree Cl. N21	17	32	94	D
Rowantree Rd. Enf	13	31	97	D
Rowantree Rd. N21	17	32	94	D
Rowan Way. Rom	29	47	89	A
Rowan Wlk. Brom	107	42	65	D
Rowan Wlk. Horn	30	53	89	D
Rowan Wlk. N19	36	29	86	A
Rowan Wlk. N2	35	26	88	A
Rowan Wlk. W10	56	24	82	C
Rowben Cl. N20	15	25	94	D
Rowberry Cl. SW6	62	23	77	D

Name	Page	Grid
Rowcross Pl. SE1	63	33 78 D
Rowcross St. SE1	63	33 78 D
Rowdell Rd. Nthlt	43	13 83 A
Rowden Rd. Beck	98	36 69 B
Rowden Rd. E4	37	37 91 B
Rowden Rd. Eps	109	20 64 A
Rowditch La. SW11	84	28 76 C
Rowdon Ave. NW10	45	22 84 D
Rowdowns Rd. Dag	52	48 84 D
Rowe Gdns. Bark	51	46 83 C
Rowe La. E9	35	35 85 C
Rowena Cres. SW11	74	27 76 C
Rowe Wlk. Har	32	13 86 C
Rowfant Rd. SW17	86	28 72 A
Rowhill Rd. E5	35	34 85 B
Rowington Cl. W2	56	25 81 B
Rowland Ave. Har	21	17 89 A
Rowland Ct. E16	58	39 82 D
Rowland Gr. SE26	92	34 72 D
Rowland Hill Ave. N17	25	32 91 B
Rowland Hill St. NW3	47	27 85 C
Rowlands Ave. Pnr	20	13 91 B
Rowlands Cl. NW7	24	22 91 C
Rowlands Rd. Dag	41	48 86 B
Rowland Way. Ashf	91	08 70 D
Rowland Way. SW19	95	25 69 B
Rowley Ave. Sid	90	46 73 B
Rowley Cl. Wem	44	18 84 D
Rowley Gdns. N4	37	32 87 A
Rowley Rd. N15	37	32 88 A
Rowley Way. NW8	46	26 83 A
Rowlls Rd. King	93	18 68 B
Rowney Gdns. Dag	52	47 84 A
Rowney Rd. Dag	51	46 84 B
Rowntree Clifford Cl. E13	58	40 82 B
Rowntree Rd. Twick	83	15 73 C
Rowse Cl. E15	49	38 83 A
Rowsley Ave. NW4	23	23 89 A
Rowstock Gdns. N7	47	29 85 D
Rowton Rd. SE18	66	44 77 C
Roxborough Ave. Har	33	15 87 A
Roxborough Ave. Islw	60	15 77 D
Roxborough Park. Har	33	15 87 A
Roxborough Rd. Har	32	14 88 D
Roxbourne Cl. Nthlt	43	11 84 B
Roxburgh Rd. SE27	87	31 71 D
Roxburn Way. Ruis	31	09 86 D
Roxby Pl. SW6	62	25 77 A
Roxeth Green Ave. Har	32	14 86 A
Roxeth Gr. Har	43	13 85 B
Roxeth Hill. Har	32	14 86 B
Roxley Rd. SE13	76	37 74 D
Roxwell Rd. Bark	52	46 83 C
Roxll Rd. W12	61	22 79 A
Roxwell Way. Wdf Gn	22	41 91 C
Roxy Ave. Rom	41	47 87 A
Royal Arc. W1	6	29 80 A
Royal Ave. SW3	7	27 78 D
Royal Ave. Wor Pk	102	21 65 A
Royal Circ. SE27	87	31 72 C
Royal Cl. Wor Pk	102	21 65 A
Royal College St. NW1	47	29 83 A
Royal Cres. Mews. W11	56	23 80 D
Royal Cres. Ruis	32	12 86 C
Royal Cres. W11	56	24 80 C
Royal Exchange Ave. EC3	4	32 81 D
Royal Exchange Bldgs. EC3	4	32 81 D
Royal Hill. SE10	64	38 77 C
Royal Hospital Rd. SW3	7	27 78 D
Royal Jubilee Ct. Rom	30	52 89 A
Royal Mint St. E1	8	33 80 B
Royal Naval Pl. SE14	64	36 77 D
Royal Oak Ct. SE22	75	34 75 D
Royal Oak Rd. Bexh	79	48 75 D
Royal Oak Rd. E8	48	34 84 B
Royal Opera Arc. SW1	6	29 80 D
Royal Par. Chis	100	44 70 C
Royal Par. SE3	65	39 76 D
Royal Pl. SE10	64	38 77 C
Royal Rd. E16	58	41 81 D
Royal Rd. SE17	63	31 77 B
Royal Rd. Tedd	82	14 71 D
Royal St. SE1	7	30 79 D
Royal Victor Pl. E3	49	35 84 D
Royal Wlk. Wall	104	29 56 C
Roycraft Ave. Bark	51	45 83 D
Roycroft Cl. E18	27	40 90 B
Roycroft Cl. SW2	87	31 73 C
Roydene Rd. SE18	66	45 76 C
Roydon Cl. SW11	74	27 76 D
Roy Gdns. Ilf	40	45 88 B
Roy Gr. Hamp	92	13 70 B
Royle Cl. Rom	42	52 88 B
Royle Cres. W3	54	16 82 C
Roy Rd. Nthwd	19	09 91 D
Roysden St. NW1	47	29 84 C
Royston Ave. E4	18	37 92 D
Royston Ave. Sutt	103	26 65 D
Royston Ave. Wall	111	29 64 B
Royston Cl. Houn	69	10 76 B
Royston Gdns. Ilf	39	41 88 D
Royston Gr. Pnr	20	13 91 A
Royston Park Rd. Pnr	20	12 91 B
Royston Rd. Dart	80	51 74 D
Royston Rd. Rich	71	18 74 A
Royston Rd. SE20	98	35 69 B
Royston St. E2	49	34 83 A
Roystons The. Surb	102	19 67 B
Rozel Rd. SW4	74	29 75 A
Rubastic Rd. Sthl	59	11 79 C
Rubens Rd. Nthlt	43	11 83 D
Rubens St. SE6	88	36 72 B
Ruby Rd. E17	26	37 89 A
Ruby St. SE15	63	34 77 B
Ruby Triangle. SE15	63	34 77 B
Ruckholt Cl. E10	38	37 86 D
Ruckholt Rd. E10	38	37 86 D
Rucklidge Ave. NW10	45	22 83 C
Rucklidge Pas. NW10	45	21 83 D
Rudall Cres. NW3	46	26 85 B
Ruddstreet Cl. SE18	66	43 78 B
Rudland Rd. Bexh	79	49 75 B
Rudloe Rd. SW12	86	29 73 A
Rudolph Rd. E13	50	39 83 D
Rudolph Rd. NW6	46	25 83 C
Rudyard Gr. NW7	22	20 91 A
Ruffetts Cl. S Croy	112	34 63 D
Ruffetts The. S Croy	112	34 63 D
Rufford Cl. Har	33	16 88 C
Rufford St. N1	47	30 83 A
Rufus Cl. Ruis	32	12 86 C
Rufus St. N1	4	33 82 A
Rugby Ave. Grnf	43	14 84 B
Rugby Ave. N9	17	33 94 D
Rugby Ave. Wem	44	17 85 A
Rugby Cl. Har	21	15 89 C
Rugby Gdns. Dag	52	47 84 A
Rugby Lane. Sutt	110	23 62 B
Rugby Rd. Dag	52	47 84 A
Rugby Rd. Islw	71	15 74 A
Rugby Rd. NW9	22	19 89 D
Rugby Rd. Twick	71	15 74 C
Rugby Rd. W4	61	21 79 A
Rugby St. WC1	3	30 82 D
Rugg St. E14	57	37 80 A
Ruislip Cl. Grnf	53	13 82 D
Ruislip Ct. Ruis	31	09 86 B
Ruislip Rd. Grnf	53	13 82 A
Ruislip Rd. Nthlt	43	11 83 D
Ruislip Road E. Grnf	53	14 82 C
Ruislip Road E. W13	54	16 82 C
Ruislip Road E. W7	54	15 82 C
Ruislip St. SW17	86	27 71 B
Rumbold Rd. SW6	62	25 77 D
Rum Cl. E1	57	35 80 A
Rumsey Cl. Hamp	92	12 70 B
Rumsey Rd. SW9	74	30 75 B
Runbury Circ. NW9	34	20 86 B
Runcorn Cl. N15	25	34 89 D
Runcorn Pl. W11	56	24 80 A
Rundell Cres. NW4	34	22 88 B
Runham St. SE17	63	32 78 D
Runnelfield. Har	33	15 86 C
Running Horse Yd. Brent	60	18 77 A
Runnymede Cl. Twick	82	13 73 B
Runnymede Cres. SW16	96	30 69 A
Runnymede Gdns. Grnf	44	15 83 C
Runnymede Gdns. Twick	82	13 73 B
Runnymede Rd. Twick	82	13 74 D
Runnymede. SW19	95	26 69 B
Runway The. Ruis	43	11 85 C
Rupack St. SE16	64	35 79 A
Rupert Ave. Wem	44	18 85 C
Rupert Ct. W1	6	29 80 B
Rupert Gdns. SW9	75	31 76 D
Rupert Rd (off Holloway Rd). N19	36	29 86 B
Rupert Rd (off Yerbury Rd). N19	36	29 86 D
Rupert Rd. N19	36	29 86 D
Rupert Rd. NW6	46	24 83 D
Rupert Rd. W4	61	21 79 C
Rupert St. W1	6	29 80 B
Rural Way. SW16	96	29 70 C
Ruscoe Rd. E16	58	39 81 D
Ruscombe Way. Felt	81	09 73 B
Rusham Rd. SW12	86	27 73 B
Rushbrook Cres. E17	26	36 90 B
Rushbrook Rd. SE9	90	44 72 A
Rushcroft Rd. E4	26	37 91 D
Rushcroft Rd. SW2	75	31 75 C
Rushden Cl. SE19	97	32 70 D
Rushdene Ave. Barn	16	27 94 A
Rushdene Cl. Nthlt	43	11 83 C
Rushdene Cres. Nthlt	53	11 82 A
Rushdene Rd. Pnr	32	11 88 D
Rushdene. SE2	67	47 79 D
Rushden Gdns. Ilf	28	43 89 A
Rushden Gdns. NW7	23	23 91 A
Rushen Wlk. Cars	103	26 66 D
Rushet Rd. Orp	100	46 69 C
Rushett Cl. Surb	101	16 66 C
Rushett Rd. Surb	101	16 66 B
Rushey Cl. N Mal	94	20 68 D
Rushey Green. SE6	88	37 73 B
Rushey Hill. Enf	12	30 96 D
Rushey Mead. SE13	76	37 74 A
Rushford Rd. SE4	76	36 74 D
Rush Green Gdns. Rom	41	50 87 C
Rush Green Rd. Rom	41	49 87 D
Rushgrove Ave. NW9	22	21 89 D
Rush Grove St. SE18	65	42 78 B
Rush Hill Mews. SW11	74	28 75 A
Rush Hill Rd. SW11	74	28 75 A
Rushmead Cl. Croy	112	33 64 B
Rushmead. E2	57	34 82 B
Rushmead. Rich	83	16 72 D
Rushmere Ct. Wor Pk	102	22 65 A
Rushmoor Cl. Pnr	19	10 88 D
Rushmore Cl. Brom	99	42 68 A
Rushmore Cres. E5	49	35 85 B
Rushmore Rd. E5	49	35 85 B
Rusholme Ave. Dag	41	49 86 C
Rusholme Gr. SE19	87	33 71 C
Rusholme Rd. SW15	73	24 74 C
Rushout Ave. Har	33	16 88 D
Rush The. SW19	95	24 69 B
Rushton St. N1	48	32 83 D
Rushworth St. SE1	7	31 79 B
Ruskin Ave. E12	50	42 84 A
Ruskin Ave. Felt	69	09 74 D
Ruskin Ave. Rich	61	19 77 C
Ruskin Ave. Well	78	46 76 C
Ruskin Cl. NW11	35	25 88 D
Ruskin Ct. SE9	77	42 74 D
Ruskin Dri. Orp	108	45 65 C
Ruskin Dri. Well	78	46 75 A
Ruskin Dri. Wor Pk	103	23 65 A
Ruskin Gdns. Har	21	18 89 D
Ruskin Gdns. Rom	30	52 91 D
Ruskin Gdns. W5	54	17 82 D
Ruskin Gr. Well	78	46 76 C
Ruskin Rd. Belv	67	49 78 A
Ruskin Rd. Cars	111	28 64 C
Ruskin Rd. Croy	105	31 65 B
Ruskin Rd. Islw	71	15 75 B
Ruskin Rd. N17	25	33 90 B
Ruskin Rd. Sthl	53	12 80 A
Ruskin Wlk. Brom	107	42 67 D
Ruskin Wlk. N9	17	34 93 A
Ruskin Wlk. SE24	75	32 74 A
Rusland Ave. Orp	108	44 65 D
Rusland Park Rd. Har	21	15 89 C
Rusper Cl. Dag	52	47 84 A
Rusper Rd. N22	25	32 89 A
Russell Ave. N22	25	31 90 D
Russell Cl. Beck	98	38 68 A
Russell Cl. Bexh	79	49 75 C
Russell Cl. Dart	80	52 75 C
Russell Cl. NW10	45	20 84 C
Russell Cl. Ruis	32	11 86 A
Russell Ct. Brom	99	39 70 D
Russell Ct. Surb	101	18 66 A
Russell Ct. SW1	6	29 80 C
Russell Ct. Wall	111	29 64 C
Russell Gdns Mews. W14	62	24 79 C
Russell Gdns. N20	16	27 93 A
Russell Gdns. NW11	35	24 88 C
Russell Gdns. Rich	83	17 72 A
Russell Gdns. SW1	62	24 79 C
Russell Green Cl. Pur	112	31 62 C
Russell Gr. SW9	63	31 77 C
Russell Hill. Pur	111	30 62 D
Russell Hill Rd. Pur	112	31 62 C
Russell La. N20	16	27 93 B
Russell Pl. SW1	10	29 78 D
Russell Rd. E10	38	37 88 D
Russell Rd. E16	58	40 81 D
Russell Rd. E17	26	36 89 B
Russell Rd. E4	18	36 92 B
Russell Rd. Mit	96	27 68 A
Russell Rd. N13	24	30 91 B
Russell Rd. N15	37	33 88 A
Russell Rd. N20	16	27 93 A

Russell Rd. N8 ... 36 | 29 88 D
Russell Rd. Nthlt ... 43 | 14 85 C
Russell Rd. NW9 ... 34 | 21 88 D
Russell Rd. SW19 ... 95 | 25 70 C
Russell Rd. Twick ... 71 | 15 74 D
Russell Rd. W14 ... 62 | 24 79 C
Russell's Footpath. SW16 ... 86 | 30 71 C
Russell Sq. WC1 ... 3 | 30 81 A
Russell St. WC2 ... 7 | 30 80 A
Russell Yd. SW15 ... 73 | 24 75 C
Russel Rd. N 13 ... 24 | 30 91 B
Russet Cres. N7 ... 47 | 30 85 D
Russets Cl. E4 ... 18 | 38 93 D
Russet Way. SE13 ... 76 | 37 76 D
Russia Ct. EC2 ... 4 | 32 81 C
Russia Dock Rd. SE16 ... 57 | 36 80 C
Russia La. E2 ... 49 | 35 83 C
Russia Row. EC2 ... 4 | 32 81 C
Rusthall Ave. W4 ... 61 | 20 79 D
Rusthall Cl. Croy ... 106 | 35 67 C
Rustic Ave. SW16 ... 96 | 28 70 D
Rustic Pl. Wem ... 44 | 17 85 B
Rustington Wlk. Mord ... 103 | 24 66 B
Ruston Ave. Surb ... 102 | 19 66 B
Ruston Mews. W11 ... 56 | 24 81 C
Ruston St. E3 ... 49 | 36 83 B
Rust Sq. SE5 ... 63 | 32 77 D
Rutford Rd. SW16 ... 86 | 30 71 C
Ruth Cl. Har ... 21 | 18 89 D
Rutherford Cl. Sutt ... 110 | 26 63 B
Rutherford St. SW1 ... 10 | 29 78 B
Rutherford Way. Wem ... 45 | 19 85 A
Rutherglen Rd. SE2 ... 66 | 46 77 A
Rutherwyke Cl. Eps ... 109 | 22 63 A
Ruthin Rd. SE3 ... 65 | 40 77 A
Ruthven St. E9 ... 49 | 35 83 B
Rutland Ave. Sid ... 90 | 46 73 A
Rutland Cl. Eps ... 109 | 20 62 D
Rutland Cl. SW14 ... 72 | 20 75 A
Rutland Ct. W3 ... 55 | 19 81 C
Rutland Dri. Mord ... 103 | 25 66 A
Rutland Dri. Rich ... 83 | 17 73 D
Rutland Gate. Belv ... 67 | 49 78 D
Rutland Gate. Brom ... 99 | 39 68 D
Rutland Gate Mews. SW7 ... 5 | 27 79 A
Rutland Gate. SW7 ... 5 | 27 79 A
Rutland Gdns. Croy ... 112 | 33 64 A
Rutland Gdns. Dag ... 52 | 47 85 C
Rutland Gdns Mews. SW7 ... 5 | 27 79 A
Rutland Gdns. N4 ... 37 | 32 88 C
Rutland Gdns. SW7 ... 5 | 27 79 A
Rutland Gdns. W13 ... 54 | 16 81 A
Rutland Gr. W6 ... 61 | 22 78 D
Rutland Mews E. SW7 ... 5 | 27 79 C
Rutland Mews S. SW7 ... 5 | 27 79 C
Rutland Mews W. SW7 ... 5 | 27 79 C
Rutland Park. NW2 ... 46 | 23 84 A
Rutland Park. SE6 ... 88 | 36 72 B
Rutland Pl. EC1 ... 3 | 31 81 B
Rutland Rd. E11 ... 39 | 40 88 B
Rutland Rd. E17 ... 38 | 37 88 C
Rutland Rd. E7 ... 50 | 41 84 D
Rutland Rd. E9 ... 49 | 35 83 B
Rutland Rd. Har ... 32 | 14 88 C
Rutland Rd. Ilf ... 40 | 43 86 D
Rutland Rd. Sthl ... 53 | 13 81 A
Rutland Rd. SW19 ... 96 | 27 70 C
Rutland Rd. Twick ... 82 | 14 72 B
Rutland St. SW7 ... 5 | 27 79 C
Rutland Wlk. SE6 ... 88 | 36 72 B
Rutley Cl. SE11 ... 63 | 31 77 B
Rutlish Rd. SW19 ... 95 | 25 69 A
Rutter Gdns. Mit ... 95 | 26 68 D
Rutt's Terr. SE14 ... 76 | 35 76 B
Ruvigny Gdns. SW15 ... 73 | 23 75 B
Ruxley Cl. Eps ... 109 | 19 64 D
Ruxley La. Eps ... 109 | 20 64 C
Ryan Cl. SE3 ... 77 | 41 75 C
Rycroft Way. N17 ... 25 | 33 89 B
Ryculff Sq. SE3 ... 77 | 39 76 D
Rydal Cl. NW4 ... 23 | 24 90 A
Rydal Cres. Grnf ... 54 | 17 82 A
Rydal Dri. Bexh ... 79 | 49 76 A
Rydal Gdns. NW9 ... 34 | 21 88 A
Rydal Gdns. SW15 ... 84 | 21 71 C
Rydal Gdns. Twick ... 70 | 13 74 D
Rydal Gdns. Wem ... 33 | 17 87 C
Rydal Rd. SW16 ... 86 | 29 71 B
Rydal Way. Enf ... 14 | 35 95 C
Rydal Way. Ruis ... 43 | 11 85 A
Ryde Pl. Twick ... 71 | 17 74 D
Ryder Cl. Brom ... 89 | 40 71 D
Ryder Ct. SW1 ... 6 | 29 80 C
Ryder's Terr. NW8 ... 46 | 26 83 C
Ryder St. SW1 ... 6 | 29 80 C

Ryder Yd. SW1 ... 6 | 29 80 C
Ryde Vale Rd. SW17 ... 86 | 29 72 A
Rydons Cl. SE9 ... 77 | 42 75 A
Rydon St. N1 ... 48 | 32 83 A
Rydston Cl. N7 ... 47 | 30 84 D
Rye Cl. Bex ... 79 | 49 74 D
Ryecotes Mead. SE21 ... 87 | 33 73 C
Ryecroft Ave. Ilf ... 28 | 43 90 D
Ryecroft Ave. Twick ... 82 | 13 73 D
Ryecroft Cres. Barn ... 11 | 23 95 A
Ryecroft Rd. Orp ... 108 | 44 67 D
Ryecroft Rd. SE13 ... 76 | 38 74 A
Ryecroft Rd. SW16 ... 97 | 31 70 A
Ryecroft St. SW6 ... 73 | 25 76 B
Ryedale. SE22 ... 75 | 34 74 D
Ryefield Cres. Nthwd ... 19 | 10 90 C
Ryefield Path. SW15 ... 84 | 22 73 C
Ryefield Rd. SE19 ... 97 | 32 70 A
Rye Hill Park. SE15 ... 76 | 35 75 C
Ryelands Cres. SE9 ... 77 | 41 74 C
Rye La. SE15 ... 75 | 34 76 C
Rye Pas. SE15 ... 75 | 34 75 A
Rye Rd. SE15 ... 76 | 35 75 D
Rye The. N14 ... 16 | 29 94 A
Rye Way. Edg ... 21 | 18 91 B
Rye Wlk. SW15 ... 73 | 23 74 B
Ryfold Rd. SW19 ... 85 | 25 72 C
Ryhope Rd. N11 ... 16 | 28 92 B
Ryland Cl. Felt ... 81 | 09 71 B
Rylandes Rd. NW2 ... 34 | 22 86 C
Rylandes Rd. S Croy ... 112 | 34 62 D
Ryland Rd. NW5 ... 47 | 28 84 B
Rylett Cres. W12 ... 61 | 21 79 D
Rylett Rd. W12 ... 61 | 21 79 D
Rylston Rd. N13 ... 17 | 32 92 D
Rylston Rd. SW6 ... 62 | 24 77 D
Rymer Rd. Croy ... 105 | 33 66 A
Rymer Rd. SW18 ... 73 | 26 74 A
Rymer St. SE24 ... 75 | 31 74 D
Rysbrack St. SW3 ... 5 | 27 79 D
Rythe Ct. Surb ... 101 | 16 66 A

Sabbarton St. E16 ... 58 | 39 81 D
Sabella Ct. E3 ... 49 | 36 83 D
Sabine Rd. SW11 ... 74 | 28 75 A
Sable Cl. Houn ... 70 | 11 75 A
Sable St. N1 ... 48 | 31 84 D
Sach Rd. E5 ... 37 | 34 86 B
Sackville Ave. Brom ... 107 | 40 66 C
Sackville Cl. Har ... 32 | 14 86 D
Sackville Cres. Rom ... 30 | 54 90 A
Sackville Gdns. Ilf ... 39 | 42 87 D
Sackville Rd. Sutt ... 110 | 25 63 C
Sackville St. W1 ... 6 | 29 80 A
Saddlecombe Way. N12 ... 15 | 25 92 C
Saddlers Cl. Pnr ... 20 | 13 91 A
Saddlers Ride. E Mol ... 92 | 14 69 C
Saddlescombe Way. N12 ... 15 | 25 92 C
Saddleworth Rd. Rom ... 30 | 53 91 A
Sadler Cl. Mit ... 96 | 27 69 D
Saffron Cl. NW11 ... 35 | 24 88 D
Saffron Hill. EC1 ... 3 | 31 81 A
Saffron Rd. Rom ... 29 | 50 90 D
Saffron St. EC1 ... 3 | 31 81 A
Saffron Way. Surb ... 101 | 17 66 D
Sage Way. WC1 ... 3 | 30 82 B
Saigasso Cl. E16 ... 58 | 41 81 D
Sail St. SE11 ... 7 | 30 79 D
Sainfoin Rd. SW17 ... 86 | 28 72 A
Sainsbury Rd. SE19 ... 87 | 33 71 C
St Agatha's Dr. King ... 93 | 18 70 B
St Agatha's Gr. Cars ... 104 | 27 66 D
St Agnes Cl. E9 ... 49 | 35 83 A
St. Agnes Pl. SE11 ... 63 | 31 77 B
St Aidan's Rd. SE22 ... 75 | 34 74 D
St Aidan's Rd. W13 ... 60 | 16 79 B
St Albans Ave. Felt ... 82 | 11 71 D
St Albans Ave. W4 ... 61 | 20 79 D
St Albans Cres. N22 ... 25 | 31 90 A
St Alban's Cres. Wdf Gn ... 27 | 40 90 A
St Alban's Gdns. Tedd ... 83 | 16 71 C
St Alban's Gr. Cars ... 104 | 27 66 A
St Alban's Gr. W8 ... 62 | 25 79 D
St Alban's Mews. W2 ... 1 | 26 81 B
St Alban's Pl. N1 ... 48 | 31 83 B
St Alban's Rd. N5 ... 45 | 20 83 A
St Albans Rd. Barn ... 11 | 24 97 C
St Alban's Rd. Dart ... 80 | 54 74 D
St Albans Rd. Ilf ... 40 | 45 87 B
St Alban's Rd. King ... 93 | 18 70 A
St Alban's Rd. NW5 ... 36 | 28 86 D
St Albans Rd. Sutt ... 110 | 24 64 B
St Alban's Rd. Wdf Gn ... 27 | 40 91 C
St Alban's St. SW1 ... 6 | 29 80 B
St Albans Terr. W6 ... 62 | 24 77 A

St Albans Terr. W6 ... 62 | 24 77 A
St Alfege Pas. SE10 ... 64 | 38 77 A
St Alfege Rd. SE7 ... 65 | 41 77 B
St Alphage Gdn. EC2 ... 4 | 32 81 A
St Alphage Highwalk. EC2 ... 4 | 32 81 A
St Alphage Wlk. Edg ... 22 | 20 90 C
St Alphege Rd. N9 ... 18 | 35 94 A
St Alphonsus Rd. SW4 ... 74 | 29 75 D
St Amunds Cl. SE6 ... 88 | 37 71 A
St Andrews Ave. Wem ... 44 | 16 85 A
St Andrew's Cl. Islw ... 71 | 15 76 A
St Andrew's Cl. N12 ... 15 | 26 92 A
St Andrew's Cl. NW2 ... 34 | 22 86 D
St Andrews Cl. Ruis ... 32 | 11 86 B
St Andrew's Cl. Shep ... 91 | 08 68 D
St Andrew's Cl. Stan ... 21 | 17 90 C
St Andrew's Ct. SW18 ... 85 | 26 72 A
St Andrews Dri. Orp ... 108 | 46 66 B
St Andrew's Dri. Stan ... 21 | 17 90 A
St Andrew's Gr. N16 ... 37 | 32 87 D
St Andrew's Hill. EC4 ... 3 | 31 81 D
St Andrew's Mews. N16 ... 37 | 33 87 C
St Andrew's Pl. NW1 ... 2 | 28 82 D
St Andrew's Rd. Cars ... 104 | 27 65 C
St Andrew's Rd. Croy ... 112 | 32 64 A
St Andrew's Rd. E11 ... 39 | 38 88 C
St Andrew's Rd. E13 ... 58 | 40 82 B
St Andrews Rd. E17 ... 26 | 36 90 C
St Andrew's Rd. Enf ... 13 | 32 96 B
St Andrew's Rd. Ilf ... 39 | 42 87 B
St Andrews Rd. N9 ... 18 | 35 94 A
St Andrew's Rd. NW10 ... 45 | 22 84 B
St Andrews Rd. NW11 ... 35 | 24 88 D
St Andrews Rd. NW9 ... 34 | 20 87 D
St Andrew's Rd. Rom ... 41 | 50 88 D
St Andrew's Rd. Surb ... 101 | 17 67 D
St Andrew's Rd. W14 ... 62 | 24 77 A
St Andrew's Rd. W3 ... 55 | 21 81 C
St Andrew's Rd. W7 ... 60 | 15 79 A
St Andrew's Sq. Surb ... 101 | 17 67 D
St Andrew's Sq. W11 ... 56 | 24 81 C
St Andrew St. EC4 ... 3 | 31 81 A
St Anne's Cl. N6 ... 36 | 28 86 C
St Anne's Ct. W1 ... 2 | 29 81 D
St Annes Gdns. NW10 ... 54 | 18 82 B
St Anne's Pas. E14 ... 57 | 36 81 D
St Annes Rd. E11 ... 38 | 38 86 B
St Anne's Rd. Wem ... 44 | 17 85 D
St Anne's Row. E14 ... 57 | 36 81 D
St Anne St. E14 ... 57 | 36 81 D
St Ann's Bark ... 51 | 44 83 A
St Ann's Cres. SW18 ... 73 | 26 74 C
St Ann's Gdns. NW5 ... 47 | 28 84 A
St Ann's Hill. SW18 ... 73 | 26 74 C
St Ann's La. SW1 ... 6 | 29 79 D
St Ann's Park Rd. SW18 ... 73 | 26 74 C
St Ann's Pas. SW13 ... 72 | 21 75 A
St Ann's Rd. Bark ... 51 | 44 83 A
St Ann's Rd. Har ... 33 | 15 88 C
St Ann's Rd. N15 ... 37 | 32 88 B
St Ann's Rd. N9 ... 17 | 33 94 D
St Anns Rd. SW13 ... 72 | 21 76 D
St Ann's Rd. W11 ... 56 | 23 80 D
St Ann's St. SW1 ... 6 | 29 79 D
St Ann's Terr. NW8 ... 46 | 26 83 D
St Ann's Villas Rd. W11 ... 56 | 23 80 D
St Ann's Way. S Croy ... 112 | 31 63 B
St Anselm's Pl. W1 ... 6 | 28 80 B
St Anthony's Ave. Wdf Gn ... 27 | 41 91 C
St Anthony's Cl. E1 ... 57 | 34 80 C
St Anthonys Cl. SW17 ... 86 | 27 72 A
St Anthony's Ct. Orp ... 108 | 43 65 B
St Anthony's Way. Felt ... 69 | 09 75 D
St Antony's Rd. E7 ... 50 | 40 84 D
St Arvans Cl. Croy ... 105 | 33 65 C
St Asaph Rd. SE4 ... 76 | 35 75 B
St Aubyn's Ave. Houn ... 70 | 13 74 A
St Aubyn's Ave. SW19 ... 85 | 24 71 D
St Aubyns Cl. Orp ... 108 | 45 65 D
St Aubyns Gdns. Orp ... 108 | 45 65 D
St Aubyn's Rd. SE19 ... 97 | 33 70 B
St Audrey Ave. Bexh ... 79 | 49 76 C
St Augustine's Ave. Brom ... 107 | 42 67 A
St Augustine's Ave. S Croy ... 112 | 32 63 C
St Augustine's Ave. W5 ... 44 | 18 83 C
St Augustine's Ave. Wem ... 33 | 18 86 C
1St Augustine's Ct. E11 ... 39 | 39 87 D
St Augustine's Rd. Belv ... 67 | 48 78 B
St Augustine's Rd. NW1 ... 47 | 29 84 D
St Austell Cl. Edg ... 21 | 18 90 D
St Austell Rd. SE13 ... 76 | 38 76 D
St Awdry's Rd. Bark ... 51 | 44 84 D
St Awdry's Wlk. Bark ... 51 | 44 84 D
St Barnabas Rd. E17 ... 38 | 37 88 C
St Barnabas Rd. Mit ... 96 | 28 70 C

St Barnabas' Rd. Sutt....*110* 26 64 D
St Barnabas Rd. Wdf Gn....*27* 41 91 C
St Barnabas St. SW1....*9* 28 78 C
St Barnabas Terr. E9....*49* 35 85 D
St Barnabas Villas. SW8....*74* 30 76 A
St Bartholemew's Rd. E6....*50* 42 83 D
St Benedict's Cl. SW17....*86* 28 71 C
St Benets Cl. SW17....*86* 27 72 A
St Benet's Gr. Cars....*103* 26 66 A
St Benet's Pl. EC3....*8* 32 80 B
St Bernards Cl. SE27....*87* 32 71 B
St Bernards. Croy....*105* 33 65 C
St Bernard's Rd. E6....*50* 42 83 A
St Blaise Ave. Brom....*99* 40 69 D
St Botolph St. EC3....*4* 33 81 D
St Bride's Ave. EC4....*3* 31 81 D
St Bride's Ave. Edg....*21* 18 90 B
St Brides Cl. Belv....*67* 47 79 B
St Bride's Pas. EC4....*3* 31 81 D
St Bride St. EC4....*3* 31 81 D
St Catherines Cl. SW17....*86* 27 72 A
St Catherine's Ct. W4....*61* 21 79 C
St Catherine's Dri. SE14....*76* 35 76 D
St Catherines Farm Ct. Ruis....*31* 08 88 C
St Catherines Rd. E4....*18* 37 93 A
St Catherines Rd. Ruis....*31* 08 88 D
St Chad's Gdns. Rom....*41* 48 87 A
St Chad's Pl. WC1....*3* 30 82 B
St Chad's Rd. Rom....*41* 48 87 A
St Chad's St. WC1....*3* 30 82 A
St Charles Pl. W10....*56* 24 81 A
St Charles Sq. W10....*56* 24 81 A
St Christopher's Cl. Islw....*71* 15 76 A
St Christopher's Pl. W1....*2* 28 81 C
St Clair Cl. Ilf....*27* 42 90 D
St Clair Rd. E13....*50* 40 83 D
St Clair's Rd. Croy....*105* 33 65 A
St Clare St. EC3....*4* 33 81 D
St Clement Danes. SW17....*85* 26 71 B
St Clement's Ct. EC4....*8* 32 80 B
St Clement's Hts. SE26....*87* 34 72 C
St Clement's La. WC2....*3* 30 81 D
St Clements Rd. N1....*48* 31 84 C
St Cloud Rd. SE27....*87* 32 71 B
St Crispin's Cl. Sthl....*53* 12 81 D
St Cross St. EC1....*3* 31 81 A
St Cuthberts Gdns. Pnr....*20* 12 91 D
St Cuthbert's Rd. NW2....*46* 24 84 B
St Cyprian's St. SW17....*86* 27 71 B
St Davids Cl. Wem....*34* 20 86 C
St David's Cl. W Wick....*106* 37 66 B
St David's Dri. Edg....*21* 18 90 B
St David's Rd. NW4....*34* 22 87 B
St Denis Rd. SE27....*87* 32 71 B
St Dionis Rd. SW6....*73* 24 76 D
St Donatt's Rd. SE14....*76* 36 76 B
St Dunstan's Alley. EC3....*8* 33 80 A
St Dunstan's Ave. W3....*55* 20 80 B
St Dunstan's Ct. EC4....*3* 31 81 C
St Dunstan's Gdns. W3....*55* 20 80 B
St Dunstan's Hill. EC3....*8* 33 80 A
St Dunstan's Hill. Sutt....*110* 24 64 A
St Dunstan's La. Beck....*106* 38 67 A
St Dunstan's La. EC3....*8* 33 80 A
St Dunstan's Rd. E7....*50* 41 84 A
St Dunstan's Rd. Felt....*81* 09 72 D
St Dunstan's Rd. Houn....*70* 11 76 C
St Dunstan's Rd. SE25....*97* 33 68 D
St Dunstan's Rd. W6....*62* 23 78 D
St Dunstan's Rd. W7....*60* 15 79 A
St Edmunds Ave. Ruis....*31* 08 88 D
St Edmunds Cl. Belv....*67* 47 79 B
St Edmund's Cl. NW8....*47* 27 83 B
St Edmunds Cl. SW17....*86* 27 72 A
St Edmunds Dri. Stan....*21* 16 90 A
St Edmund's La. Twick....*82* 13 73 B
St Edmunds Rd. Dart....*80* 54 75 D
St Edmund's Rd. Ilf....*39* 42 88 D
St Edmunds Rd. N9....*17* 34 94 A
St Edmund's Terr. NW8....*47* 27 83 B
St Edward's Cl. NW11....*35* 25 88 C
St Edwards Way. Rom....*30* 51 89 C
St Egberts Way. E4....*18* 38 94 C
St Elmo Rd. W12....*61* 21 79 B
St Erkenwald Rd. Bark....*51* 44 83 B
St Ermin's Hill. SW1....*6* 29 79 D
St Ervan's Rd. W10....*56* 24 81 A
St Faith's Cl. Enf....*13* 32 97 A
St Faith's Rd. SE21....*87* 31 73 D
St Fidelis' Rd. Eri....*67* 50 78 B
St Fillans Rd. SE6....*88* 38 73 C
St Francis Cl. Orp....*108* 45 67 C
St Francis' Rd. Eri....*67* 50 78 B
St Francis Rd. SE22....*75* 33 75 C

St Gabriel's Rd. NW2....*46* 23 85 D
St George's Ave. E7....*50* 40 84 D
St George's Ave. Horn....*42* 54 87 B
St George's Ave. N7....*47* 29 85 B
St George's Ave. NW9....*22* 20 89 D
St George's Ave. Sthl....*53* 12 80 B
St George's Ave. W5....*60* 17 79 B
St George's Circ. SE1....*7* 31 79 D
St George's Cl. NW11....*35* 24 88 D
St Georges Cl. Wem....*33* 16 86 C
St George's Dri. SW1....*10* 29 78 C
St George's Dri. Uxb....*31* 07 86 A
St Georges Field. W2....*1* 27 81 C
St George's Gdns. Surb....*102* 19 65 B
St George's Gr. SW17....*85* 26 72 D
St George's La. EC3....*3* 32 80 B
St George's Mews. NW1....*47* 27 84 D
St George's Rd. Beck....*98* 37 69 B
St Georges Rd. Brom....*99* 42 68 B
St Georges Rd. Dag....*52* 48 85 A
St George's Rd. E10....*38* 38 86 C
St George's Rd. E7....*50* 40 84 B
St George's Rd. Felt....*82* 11 71 B
St George's Rd. Ilf....*39* 42 87 B
St George's Rd. King....*94* 19 70 C
St George's Rd. Mit....*96* 28 68 B
St George's Rd. N13....*16* 30 93 B
St George's Rd. N9....*17* 34 93 C
St George's Rd. NW11....*35* 24 88 D
St George's Rd. Orp....*108* 44 67 D
St George's Rd. Rich....*71* 18 75 B
St George's Rd. SE1....*7* 31 79 D
St George's Rd. SW19....*95* 24 70 B
St George's Rd. Twick....*71* 16 74 B
St Georges Rd. W4....*61* 20 79 B
St George's Rd. W7....*54* 15 80 D
St George's Rd. Wall....*111* 28 64 D
St Georges Rd W. Brom....*99* 42 69 C
St George's Sq. E7....*50* 40 84 D
St George's Sq. N Mal....*94* 21 68 A
St George's Sq. SW1....*10* 29 78 D
St George's Terr. NW1....*47* 27 84 D
St George St. W1....*6* 28 80 B
St George's Way. SE15....*63* 33 77 A
St George's Wlk. Croy....*105* 32 65 C
St Gerards Cl. SW4....*74* 29 74 A
St German's Pl. SE3....*77* 40 76 A
St German's Rd. SE23....*88* 36 73 C
St Giles Ave. Dag....*52* 49 84 D
St Giles Circ. W1....*2* 29 81 D
St Giles Cl. Dag....*52* 49 84 D
St Giles High St. WC2....*2* 29 81 D
St Giles Pl. WC2....*2* 29 81 D
St Giles Rd. SE5....*75* 33 76 A
St Gothard Rd. SE27....*87* 32 71 B
St Helena Rd. SE16....*64* 35 78 B
St Helena St. WC1....*3* 31 82 A
St Helen's Cres. SW16....*96* 30 69 B
St Helen's Gdns. W10....*56* 23 81 D
St Helen's Pl. EC3....*4* 33 81 C
St Helens Rd. Belv....*67* 47 79 B
St Helen's Rd. Ilf....*39* 42 88 D
St Helen's Rd. SW16....*96* 30 69 B
St Helen's Rd. W13....*54* 17 80 C
St Helier Ave. Mord....*103* 26 67 A
St Heliers Ave. Houn....*70* 13 74 A
St Helier's Rd. E10....*38* 38 88 C
St Hilda's Cl. NW6....*46* 23 83 B
St Hildas Cl. SW17....*86* 27 72 A
St Hilda's Rd. SW13....*61* 22 77 B
St Hughes Cl. SW17....*86* 27 72 A
St Hugh's Rd. SE20....*97* 34 69 B
St Ivians Dri. Rom....*30* 52 89 A
St James Rd. N20....*16* 27 93 C
St James Ave. Eps....*109* 22 62 C
St James' Ave. Sutt....*110* 25 64 C
St James' Ave. W13....*54* 16 80 C
St James Cl. N20....*16* 27 93 C
St James' Cl. N.Mal....*102* 21 67 B
St James Cl. Ruis....*32* 11 86 A
St James Cottages. Rich....*71* 17 74 B
St James's Ct. Croy....*105* 31 66 B
St James' Ct. SW1....*6* 29 79 C
St James' Gdns. Wem....*44* 18 84 C
St James' Gr. SW11....*74* 27 76 D
St James Pl. Dart....*80* 53 74 D
St James Rd. Cars....*104* 27 65 C
St James Rd. E15....*50* 39 85 D
St James' Rd. Mit....*96* 28 70 C
St James' Rd. N9....*17* 34 93 B
St James' Rd. Surb....*101* 17 67 D
St James' Rd. Sutt....*110* 25 64 C
St James's App. EC2....*4* 33 82 C
St James's Ave. Beck....*98* 36 68 A
St James's Ave. E2....*49* 35 83 C

St James's Ave. Hamp....*82* 14 71 C
St James's Cl. SE18....*66* 44 78 C
St James's Cl. SW17....*86* 27 72 B
St James's Cres. SW9....*75* 31 75 A
St James's Dri. SW17....*86* 27 73 D
St James's Gdns. W11....*56* 24 80 C
St James's La. N10....*24* 28 89 D
St James's Market. SW1....*6* 29 80 B
St James's Park. Croy....*105* 32 66 A
St James's Pas. EC3....*4* 33 81 C
St James's Path. E17....*38* 36 88 B
St James's Pl. SW1....*6* 29 80 C
St James's Rd. Croy....*105* 32 66 A
St James's Rd. Hamp....*82* 13 71 D
St James's Rd. King....*93* 17 68 A
St James's Rd. SE16....*63* 34 79 C
St James's Rd. SE1....*63* 34 78 C
St James's Row. EC1....*3* 31 82 D
St James's. SE14....*76* 36 76 A
St James's Sq. SW1....*6* 29 80 D
St James's St. E17....*38* 36 88 A
St James's Terrace Mews, NW8
........*47* 27 83 B
St James's Terr. NW8....*47* 27 83 D
St James St. W6....*62* 23 78 C
St James's Wlk. EC1....*3* 31 82 D
St James Wlk. SE15....*63* 33 77 D
St Joan's Rd. N9....*17* 33 94 D
St John's Ave. N11....*16* 27 92 D
St John's Ave. NW10....*45* 21 83 B
St John's Ave. SW15....*73* 23 74 B
St John's Church Rd. E9....*49* 35 85 C
St John's Cl. Wem....*44* 18 85 C
St John's Cres. SW9....*75* 31 75 A
St John's Ct. Islw....*71* 15 76 D
St John's Ct. N4....*37* 31 86 B
St Johns Estate. SW11....*73* 26 76 B
St John's Gdns. W11....*56* 24 80 B
St John's Gr. N19....*36* 29 86 A
St John's Gr. Rich....*71* 18 75 C
St John's Gr. SW13....*72* 21 76 D
St John's Hill Gr. SW11....*73* 26 75 D
St John's Hill. SW11....*73* 26 75 D
St John's Hill. SW18....*73* 26 74 B
St John's La. EC1....*3* 31 81 B
St John's Park. SE3....*65* 40 77 C
St John's Pas. SW19....*95* 24 70 A
St John's Path. EC1....*3* 31 82 D
St John's Pl. EC1....*3* 31 82 D
St John's Rd. Bark....*51* 45 83 A
St John's Rd. Cars....*104* 27 65 C
St John's Rd. Croy....*105* 31 65 D
St John's Rd. E16....*58* 40 81 C
St John's Rd. E17....*26* 38 90 C
St John's Rd. E4....*18* 37 92 B
St John's Rd. E6....*50* 42 83 A
St John's Rd. E Mol....*92* 14 68 D
St John's Rd. Eri....*67* 50 78 D
St John's Rd. Felt....*82* 12 71 B
St John's Rd. Har....*33* 15 88 D
St Johns Rd. Ilf....*40* 45 87 A
St John's Rd. Islw....*71* 15 76 D
St John's Rd. King....*93* 17 69 A
St John's Rd. N15....*37* 33 88 C
St Johns Rd. N Mal....*94* 20 68 A
St John's Rd. NW11....*35* 24 88 D
St John's Rd. Orp....*108* 45 67 C
St John's Rd. Rich....*71* 18 75 C
St John's Rd. SE20....*98* 35 70 A
St John's Rd. Sid....*90* 46 71 B
St John's Rd. Sthl....*59* 12 79 C
St John's Rd. Sutt....*103* 25 65 B
St John's Rd. SW11....*74* 27 75 C
St John's Rd. SW19....*95* 24 70 A
St John's Rd. Well....*78* 46 75 B
St John's Rd. Wem....*44* 18 85 C
St John's Sq. EC1....*3* 31 82 D
St John St. EC1....*3* 31 82 D
St John St. EC1....*48* 31 83 C
St John's Terr. E7....*50* 40 84 B
St John's Terr. SE18....*66* 44 77 B
St John's Terr. W10....*56* 23 82 D
St John's Vale. SE8....*76* 37 76 C
St John's Villas. N19....*36* 29 86 B
St John's Way. N19....*36* 29 87 D
St John's Wood High St. NW8....*47* 27 83 C
St John's Wood Park. NW8....*46* 26 83 B
St John's Wood Rd. NW8....*1* 26 82 B
St John's Wood Terr. NW8....*47* 27 83 C
St Joseph's Dri. Sthl....*53* 12 80 C
St Joseph's Rd. N9....*18* 35 94 A
St Joseph's St. SW8....*74* 28 76 B
St Judes Ct. Wdf Gn....*27* 42 91 C
St Jude's Rd. E2....*48* 34 83 D

Name	Page	Grid
St Jude St. N1	48	33 85 C
St Julian's Cl. SW16	87	31 71 A
St Julian's Farm Rd. SE27	87	31 71 B
St Julian's Rd. NW6	46	25 83 A
St Katharine's Way. E1	8	33 80 B
St Katherine's Prec. NW1	47	28 83 D
St Katherines Rd. Belv	67	47 79 B
St Katherine's Row. EC3	8	33 80 A
St Keverne Rd. SE9	89	42 71 A
St Kilda Rd. Orp	108	45 66 D
St Kilda Rd. W13	60	16 79 A
St Kilda's Rd. Har	33	15 88 C
St Kilda's Rd. N16	37	33 87 C
St Laurence's Cl. NW6	46	23 83 B
St Lawrence Cl. Edg	21	18 91 D
St Lawrence Dri. Pnr	31	10 88 B
St Lawrence St. E14	58	38 80 C
St Lawrence Terr. W10	56	24 81 A
St Lawrence Way. SW9	75	31 76 C
St Leonard's Ave. E4	26	38 91 B
St Leonards Ave. Har	33	17 88 A
St Leonards Cl. Well	78	46 75 A
St Leonards Gdns. Houn	70	12 76 A
St Leonards Gdns Ilf	51	44 85 C
St Leonard's Rd. Croy	105	31 65 D
St Leonards Rd. E14	58	38 81 A
St Leonard's Rd. E14	58	38 81 C
St Leonard's Rd. NW10	55	20 82 D
St Leonard's Rd. Surb	101	10 66 A
St Leonard's Rd. Surb	101	17 67 B
St Leonards Rd. SW14	72	20 75 A
St Leonard's Rd. W13	54	17 80 A
St Leonard's Sq. NW5	47	28 84 A
St Leonard's Sq. Surb	101	17 67 B
St Leonard's St. E3	57	37 82 B
St Leonard's Terr. SW3	9	27 78 D
St Leonards Wlk. SW16	96	30 70 D
St Loo Ave. SW3	9	27 77 A
St Louis Rd. SE27	87	32 71 B
St Loy's Rd. N17	25	33 89 B
St Luke's Ave. Ilf	51	43 85 D
St Luke's Ave. SW4	74	29 75 D
St Lukes Cl. SE25	105	34 67 D
St Luke's Mews. W11	56	24 81 D
St Luke's Rd. W11	56	24 81 B
St Luke's Sq. E16	58	39 81 D
St Luke's St. SW3	9	27 78 C
St Luke's Yd. W9	46	24 83 D
St Malo Ave. N9	18	35 93 C
St Margarets Ave. Ashf	81	07 71 D
St Margaret's Ave. Har	32	14 86 C
St Margaret's Ave. N15	25	31 89 D
St Margarets Ave. N20	15	26 94 C
St Margarets Ave. Sid	90	44 72 D
St Margaret's Ave. Sutt	103	24 65 C
St Margarets. Bark	51	44 83 B
St Margaret's Cres. SW15	72	22 74 B
St Margaret's Ct. SE1	8	32 80 D
St Margaret's Dri. Twick	71	16 74 B
St Margaret's Gr. E11	39	39 86 D
St Margaret's Gr. SE18	66	44 78 C
St Margaret's Gr. Twick	71	16 74 C
St Margaret's Pas. SE13	66	39 75 A
St Margaret's Path. SE18	66	44 78 C
St Margaret's Rd. Beck	98	35 68 D
St Margaret's Rd. E12	39	41 86 A
St Margaret's Rd. Islw	71	16 75 D
St Margaret's Rd. N17	25	33 89 A
St Margarets Rd. NW10	56	23 82 A
St Margarets Rd. Ruis	31	08 88 D
St Margaret's Rd. SE4	76	36 75 D
St Margaret's Rd. Twick	71	16 74 D
St Margaret's Rd. W7	60	15 79 A
St Margaret's Terr. SE18	66	44 78 C
St Margaret St. SW1	7	30 79 A
St Mark's Cl. Barn	11	25 96 B
St Mark's Cres. NW1	47	28 83 A
St Marks Gate. E9	49	36 84 D
St Mark's Gr. SW10	62	25 77 D
St Mark's Hill. Surb	101	18 67 A
St Mark's Pl. SW19	95	24 70 B
St Mark's Pl. W11	56	24 81 C
St Mark's Rd. Brom	99	40 68 B
St Mark's Rd. Enf	13	33 95 B
St Mark's Rd. Mit	88	28 69 C
St Mark's Rd. SE25	97	34 68 C
St Mark's Rd. Tedd	93	16 70 D
St Mark's Rd. W10	56	23 81 D
St Mark's Rd. W5	54	18 80 C
St Mark's Rd. W7	60	15 79 A
St Mark's Rise. E8	48	33 85 D
St Mark's Sq. NW1	47	28 83 A
St Mark St. E1	4	33 81 D
St Martin's App. Ruis	31	09 87 A
St Martin's Ave. E6	50	41 83 D
St Martins Cl. Belv	67	47 79 B
St Martin's Cl. Enf	13	34 97 B
St Martin's Cl. NW1	47	29 83 A
St Martin's Cl. WC2	7	30 80 A
St Martin's La. WC2	7	30 80 A
St Martin's Le Grand. EC1	4	32 81 C
St Martin's Pl. WC2	7	30 80 A
St Martin's Rd. Dart	54	74 D
St Martin's Rd. N2	23	26 90 B
St Martin's Rd. N9	17	34 93 B
St Martin's Rd. SW9	74	30 76 D
St Martin's St. WC2	7	29 80 B
St Martin's Way. SW17	85	26 72 C
St Mary Abbot's Pl. W8	62	24 79 D
St Mary Abbots Terr. W14	62	24 79 D
St Mary at Hill. EC3	8	33 80 A
St Mary Ave. Wall	104	28 65 D
St Mary Axe. EC3	4	33 81 C
St Marychurch St. SE16	64	35 79 A
St Mary Rd. E17	26	37 89 D
St Mary' Rd. N9	18	35 94 C
St Mary's App. E12	50	42 85 D
St Mary's Ave. Brom	99	39 68 A
St Mary's Ave. E11	39	40 87 B
St Mary's Ave. N3	23	24 90 C
St Marys Ave. Sthl	59	13 78 B
St Mary's Ave. Tedd	93	15 70 B
St Marys. Bark	51	44 83 B
St Mary's Cl. Eps	109	21 62 B
St Mary's Cl. N17	25	34 90 A
St Mary's Cl. Orp	100	46 69 D
St Mary's Cl. Sun	91	10 68 C
St Mary's Cres. Islw	60	15 77 C
St Mary's Cres. NW4	22	22 89 B
St Mary's Dri. Felt	83	08 73 A
St Mary's Gdns. SE11	63	31 78 A
St Mary's Green. N2	23	26 89 A
St Mary's Gr. N1	48	31 84 B
St Mary's Gr. Rich	71	18 75 D
St Mary's Gr. SW13	72	22 75 B
St Mary's Gr. W4	61	19 77 B
St Mary's Mansions. W2	1	26 81 B
St Mary's Path. N1	48	31 83 B
St Mary's Pl. W5	60	17 79 B
St Mary's Rd. Barn	16	27 94 B
St Mary's Rd. E10	38	38 86 A
St Mary's Rd. E13	50	40 83 D
St Marys Rd. Ilf	40	44 86 B
St Mary's Rd. N2	23	26 90 B
St Mary's Rd. N8	24	30 89 C
St Mary's Rd. NW10	45	20 83 A
St Mary's Rd. N11	35	24 87 A
St Mary's Rd. S Croy	112	32 62 B
St Mary's Rd. SE15	76	35 76 C
St Mary's Rd. SE25	97	33 68 A
St Mary's Rd. Surb	101	17 66 C
St Mary's Rd. Surb	101	17 67 D
St Mary's Rd. SW19	85	24 71 C
St Mary's Rd. W5	60	17 79 B
St Mary's Rd. Wor Pk	102	21 65 A
St Mary's Sq. W2	1	26 81 B
St Mary's Sq. W5	60	17 79 B
St Mary's Terr. W2	1	26 81 B
St Mary St. SE18	66	43 79 C
St Mary's Wlk. SE11	63	31 78 A
St Matthew's Ave. Surb	101	18 66 D
St Matthews Dri. Brom	99	42 68 B
St Matthew's Rd. SW2	74	30 74 B
St Matthews Rd. SW2	74	30 75 D
St Matthew's Rd. W5	54	18 80 C
St Matthew's Row. E2	57	34 82 C
St Matthew St. SW1	6	29 79 D
St Matthias Cl. NW9	34	21 88 B
St Maur Rd. SW6	73	24 76 B
St Merryn Cl. SE18	66	44 77 D
St Merryn Ct. Beck	98	37 70 C
St Michael's Alley. EC3	4	32 81 D
St Michaels Ave. N9	18	35 94 A
St Michaels Ave. Wem	49	19 85 C
St Michaels Cl. Brom	99	42 68 A
St Michael's Cl. N12	16	27 92 C
St Michael's Cl. N3	23	24 90 D
St Michael's Cres. Pnr	32	12 88 C
St Michael's Gdns. W10	56	24 81 A
St Michaels Rd. Ashf	81	07 71 C
St Michael's Rd. Croy	105	32 66 C
St Michael's Rd. NW2	46	23 85 A
St Michael's Rd. SW9	74	30 76 D
St Michael's Rd. Wall	111	29 63 A
St Michael's Rd. Well	78	46 75 B
St Michael's St. W2	1	27 81 C
St Michael's Terr. N22	24	30 90 A
St Mildred's Ct. EC2	4	32 81 D
St Mildreds Rd. SE12	89	39 73 B
St Neot's Rd. Rom	30	54 91 D
St Nicholas Ave. Horn	42	52 86 C
St Nicholas Rd. SE18	66	45 78 B
St Nicholas Rd. Surb	101	15 67 D
St Nicholas Rd. Sutt	110	25 64 D
St Nicholas St. SE8	76	36 76 B
St Nicholas Way. Sutt	110	25 64 D
St Nicolas La. Chis	99	42 69 A
St Norbert Green. SE4	76	36 75 C
St Norbert Rd. SE4	76	36 75 C
St Normans Way. Eps	109	22 62 C
St Olaf's Rd. SW6	60	24 77 C
St Olave's Ct. EC2	4	32 81 D
St Olave's Gdns. SE11	63	31 78 A
St Olave's Rd. E6	51	43 83 A
St Olaves Wlk. SW16	96	29 69 D
St Oswald's Pl. SE11	10	30 78 D
St Oswald's Rd. SW16	97	31 69 D
St Oswulf St. SW1	10	29 78 D
St Pancras Ct. N2	23	26 90 D
St Pancras Way. NW1	47	29 83 A
St Paul's Alley. EC4	3	31 81 D
St Paul's Ave. Har	21	18 89 D
St Paul's Ave. NW2	46	23 84 A
St Paul's Ave. SE16	57	35 80 D
St Paul's Church Yd. EC4	4	32 81 C
St Paul's Church Yd. EC4	4	32 81 C
St Paul's Cl. Ashf	81	08 71 C
St Paul's Cl. Houn	70	12 76 C
St Pauls Cl. SE7	65	41 78 D
St Pauls Cl. W5	60	18 79 B
St Paul's Cray Rd. Chis	100	44 69 B
St Paul's Cres. NW1	47	29 84 D
St Paul's Dri. E15	49	38 85 D
St Paul's Pl. N1	48	32 84 B
St Pauls Rd. Bark	51	44 83 A
St Paul's Rd. Brent	66	17 77 B
St Paul's Rd. Eri	67	50 77 C
St Paul's Rd. N11		28 92 D
St Paul's Rd. N17	25	34 90 A
St Paul's Rd. N1	48	32 84 A
St Pauls Rd. Rich	71	18 75 B
St Paul's Rd. Th Hth	97	32 68 A
St Paul's Sq. Brom	99	40 69 C
St Paul Sq. N1	48	32 83 A
St Paul's Way. E3	57	36 81 B
St Paul's Way. N3	23	25 91 D
St Paul's Wood Hill. Orp	100	45 69 D
St Peter's Alley. EC3	4	32 81 D
St Peters Ave. E17	27	39 89 C
St Peter's Ave. E2	48	34 83 C
St Peter's Ave. N18	17	34 92 A
St Petersburgh Mews. W2	56	25 80 B
St Petersburgh Pl. W2	56	25 80 B
St Peters Cl. Chis	100	44 70 D
St Peter's Cl. E2	48	34 83 C
St Peter's Cl. Ilf	28	45 89 D
St Peters Cl. Ruis	32	11 86 B
St Peter's Cl. SW17	85	27 72 A
St Peter's Ct. NW4	35	23 88 A
St Peter's Gdns. SE27	87	31 71 A
St Peter's Gr. W6	61	22 78 A
St Peter's Rd. Croy	112	32 64 B
St Peter's Rd. E Mol		13 68 C
St Peters Rd. King	94	19 69 C
St Peter's Rd. N9	18	35 94 D
St Peter's Rd. Sthl	53	13 81 A
St Peter's Rd. Twick	71	16 74 B
St Peter's Rd. W6	61	22 78 C
St Peter's Sq. E2	48	34 83 C
St Peter's Sq. W6	61	21 78 D
St Peter's St. N1	48	31 83 D
St Peter's Street Mews. N1	48	32 83 C
St Peter's Ter. S Croy	112	32 64 D
St Peter's Terr. SW6	62	24 77 D
St Peter's Villas. W6	61	22 78 A
St Peters Way. W5	54	17 81 B
St Philips Ave. E2	48	33 84 C
St Philip's Ave. Wor Pk	102	22 65 B
St Philip Sq. SW8	74	28 76 D
St Philip's Rd. E8	48	34 84 A
St Philip's Rd. Surb	101	17 67 D
St Philip St. SW8	74	28 76 D
St Philip's Way. N1	48	32 83 A
St Quentin Rd. Well	78	45 75 B
St Quintin Ave. W10	56	23 81 B
St Quintin Gdns. W10	56	23 81 A
St Quintin Rd. E13	58	40 82 B
St Raphael's Way. NW10	45	20 85 C
St Regis Cl. N10		28 90 D
St Ronans Cres. Wdf Gn	27	40 91 C
St Rule St. SW8	74	29 76 C

St Saviors Cl. E17....38 — 37 88 C
St Saviour's Rd. Croy....105 — 32 67 C
St Saviour's Rd. SW2....74 — 30 74 B
Saints Dri. E7....50 — 41 85 D
St Silas Pl. NW5....47 — 28 84 A
St Simon's Ave. SW15....73 — 23 74 A
St Stephen's Ave. E17....38 — 38 88 A
St Stephen's Ave. W12....61 — 22 79 B
St Stephen's Ave. W13....54 — 16 81 D
St Stephen's Cl. E17....38 — 37 88 B
St Stephen's Cl. NW8....47 — 27 83 A
St Stephen's Cl. Sthl....53 — 13 81 A
St Stephen's Cres. Th Hth....97 — 31 68 A
St Stephen's Cres. W2....56 — 25 81 C
St Stephen's Gdns. Twick....71 — 17 74 C
St Stephen's Gdns. W2....56 — 25 81 C
St Stephen's Gr. SE13....76 — 38 75 A
St Stephen's Mews. W2....56 — 25 81 A
St Stephen's Pas. Twick....71 — 17 74 C
St Stephens Rd. Barn....11 — 23 95 B
St Stephen's Rd. E17....38 — 37 88 B
St Stephen's Rd. E3....49 — 36 83 D
St Stephens Rd. E6....50 — 41 84 C
St Stephen's Rd. Houn....70 — 13 74 B
St Stephen's Rd. W13....54 — 16 81 D
St Stephen's Row. EC4....4 — 32 81 D
St Stephen's Terr. SW8....10 — 30 77 D
St Swithin's La. EC4....8 — 32 80 B
St Swithun's Rd. SE13....76 — 38 74 D
St Theresa's Rd. Felt....69 — 09 75 D
St Thomas' Dri. Orp....108 — 44 66 C
St Thomas Dri. Pnr....20 — 12 90 A
St Thomas Gdns. Ilf....51 — 44 84 A
St Thomas' Gdns. NW5....47 — 28 84 A
St Thomas Rd. Belv....67 — 50 79 A
St Thomas Rd. E16....58 — 40 81 C
St Thomas Rd. N14....16 — 29 94 B
St Thomas' Rd. W4....61 — 20 77 C
St Thomas's Pl. E9....49 — 35 84 C
St Thomas's Rd. N4....37 — 31 86 C
St Thomas's Rd. NW10....45 — 20 83 A
St Thomas's Sq. E9....49 — 35 84 C
St Thomas St. SE1....8 — 32 80 D
St Thomas's Way. SW6....62 — 24 77 D
St Ursula Gr. Pnr....32 — 12 88 A
St Ursula Rd. Sthl....53 — 13 81 C
St Vincent Rd. Twick....70 — 14 74 C
St Vincent St. W1....2 — 28 81 A
St Wilfrid's Cl. Barn....12 — 27 95 A
St Wilfrid's Rd. Barn....12 — 27 95 A
St Winefride's Ave. E12....50 — 42 85 D
St Winifred's Rd. Tedd....93 — 16 70 B
Salamanca Pl. SE1....10 — 30 78 B
Salamanca St. SE11....10 — 30 78 B
Salamanca St. SE1....10 — 30 78 B
Salcombe Dri. Mord....103 — 23 66 D
Salcombe Dri. Rom....41 — 48 88 D
Salcombe Gdns. NW7....23 — 23 91 A
Salcombe Rd. E17....38 — 36 87 B
Salcombe Rd. N16....48 — 33 85 C
Salcombe Way. Ruis....31 — 10 86 A
Salcott Rd. Croy....111 — 30 64 B
Salcott Rd. SW11....74 — 27 74 B
Salehurst Cl. Har....33 — 18 88 A
Salehurst Rd. SE4....76 — 36 74 D
Salem Pl. Croy....105 — 32 65 C
Salem Rd. W2....56 — 25 80 B
Sale Pl. W2....1 — 27 81 C
Sale St. E2....57 — 34 82 C
Salford Rd. SW2....86 — 29 73 D
Salisbury Ave. Bark....51 — 45 84 C
Salisbury Ave. N3....23 — 24 89 B
Salisbury Ave. Sutt....110 — 24 63 B
Salisbury Cl. SE17....63 — 32 78 B
Salisbury Cl. Wor Pk....102 — 21 65 D
Salisbury Ct. EC4....3 — 31 81 D
Salisbury Ct. N3....23 — 24 90 D
Salisbury Gdns. SW19....95 — 24 70 C
Salisbury Mews. SW6....62 — 24 77 D
Salisbury Plain. NW4....35 — 23 88 B
Salisbury Pl. W1....1 — 27 81 B
Salisbury Rd. Barn....11 — 24 96 A
Salisbury Rd. Brom....107 — 42 67 A
Salisbury Rd. Cars....111 — 27 63 B
Salisbury Rd. Dag....52 — 49 84 B
Salisbury Rd. E10....38 — 38 86 A
Salisbury Rd. E12....50 — 42 85 C
Salisbury Rd. E17....38 — 38 88 A
Salisbury Rd. E4....18 — 37 93 C
Salisbury Rd. E7....50 — 40 84 A
Salisbury Rd. Felt....82 — 11 73 C
Salisbury Rd. Har....32 — 14 88 B
Salisbury Rd. Houn....70 — 11 75 A
Salisbury Rd. Ilf....40 — 45 86 A
Salisbury Rd. N22....25 — 31 90 D

Salisbury Rd. N4....37 — 31 88 B
Salisbury Rd. N9....17 — 34 93 C
Salisbury Rd. N Mal....94 — 20 68 B
Salisbury Rd. Pnr....19 — 10 89 C
Salisbury Rd. Rich....71 — 18 75 C
Salisbury Rd. Rom....42 — 52 88 B
Salisbury Rd. SE25....105 — 34 67 C
Salisbury Rd. Sthl....59 — 12 78 A
Salisbury Rd. SW19....95 — 24 70 C
Salisbury Rd. W13....60 — 16 79 B
Salisbury Rd. Wor Pk....102 — 21 65 D
Salisbury Sq. EC4....3 — 31 81 D
Salisbury St. NW8....1 — 27 82 C
Salisbury St. W3....61 — 20 79 A
Salisbury Terr. SE15....76 — 35 75 A
Salisbury Wlk. N19....36 — 29 86 A
Salix Cl. Sun....91 — 10 70 D
Salman Rd. E13....50 — 39 83 D
Salmen Cl. Stan....21 — 16 91 A
Salmon La. E14....57 — 36 81 C
Salmon Rd. Belv....67 — 49 78 C
Salmons Rd. N9....17 — 34 94 C
Salmon St. E14....57 — 36 81 D
Salmon St. NW9....34 — 20 87 A
Salomons Rd. E13....58 — 41 81 A
Salop Rd. E17....38 — 35 88 D
Saltash Cl. Sutt....110 — 24 64 B
Saltash Rd. Ilf....28 — 44 91 D
Saltash Rd. Well....79 — 47 76 A
Saltcoats Rd. W4....61 — 21 79 A
Saltcroft Cl. NW9....34 — 19 87 D
Salterford Rd. SW17....96 — 28 70 A
Salter Rd. SE16....57 — 36 80 C
Salters Hall Ct. EC4....8 — 32 80 B
Salter's Hill. SE19....87 — 32 71 D
Salters Rd. E17....26 — 38 89 D
Salters Rd. W10....56 — 23 82 D
Salter St. E14....57 — 37 80 A
Salter St. NW10....55 — 22 82 A
Salterton Rd. N7....36 — 30 86 D
Saltford Cl. Eri....68 — 51 78 C
Saltoun Rd. SW2....75 — 31 75 C
Saltram Cl. N15....25 — 33 89 D
Saltram Cres. W9....56 — 25 82 A
Saltwell St. E14....57 — 37 80 A
Saltwood Gr. SE17....63 — 32 78 D
Salusbury Rd. NW6....46 — 24 83 A
Salvador. SW17....86 — 27 71 D
Salvia Gdns. Grnf....44 — 16 83 C
Salvin Rd. SW15....73 — 23 75 B
Salway Cl. Wdf Gn....27 — 40 91 C
Salway Pl. E15....49 — 38 84 B
Salway Rd. E15....49 — 38 84 B
Samantha Cl. E17....38 — 36 87 B
Sam Bartram Cl. SE7....65 — 41 78 C
Samels Ct. W6....61 — 22 78 C
Samford St. NW8....1 — 27 82 C
Samos Cl. SE3....65 — 39 77 D
Samos Rd. SE20....97 — 34 69 D
Sampson Ave. Barn....11 — 23 95 B
Sampson St. E1....57 — 34 80 C
Samson St. E13....50 — 41 83 C
Samuel Johnson Cl. SW16....87 — 31 71 A
Samuel Lewis Buildings. N1....48 — 31 84 C
Samuel Lewis Trust Dwellings.9 — 27 78 A
Samuel Lewis Trust Dwellings (off Dalston La). E8....48 — 34 85 C
Samuel Lewis Trust Dwellings (off Downs Park Rd). E8....48 — 34 85 C
Samuel Lewis Trust Dwellings. SW6....62 — 25 77 C
Samuel Lewis Trust Dwellings. W14....62 — 24 78 A
Samuel Lewis Trust Estate. N15....37 — 33 88 C
Samuel St. SE18....65 — 42 78 B
Sancroft Cl. NW2....34 — 22 86 D
Sancroft Rd. Har....21 — 16 90 C
Sancroft St. SE11....63 — 31 78 C
Sanctuary Cl. Dart....80 — 53 74 D
Sanctuary St. SE1....8 — 32 79 A
Sanctuary. The. SW1....6 — 29 79 D
Sanctuary. The. Bex....79 — 47 74 D
Sanctuary The. Mord....103 — 25 67 C
Sandall Cl. W5....54 — 18 82 C
Sandall Rd. NW5....47 — 29 84 A
Sandall Rd. W5....54 — 18 82 C
Sandal Rd. N18....17 — 34 92 C
Sandal Rd. N Mal....94 — 21 68 C
Sandal St. E15....50 — 39 83 A
Sandalwood Cl. E2....57 — 36 82 C
Sandalwood Rd. Felt....81 — 10 72 D
Sandbach Pl. SE18....66 — 44 78 C
Sandbourne Ave. SW19....95 — 25 69 D
Sandbourne Rd. SE4....76 — 36 76 C

Sandbrook Cl. NW7....22 — 20 91 B
Sandbrook Rd. N16....37 — 33 86 C
Sandby Green. SE9....77 — 42 75 A
Sandcliff Rd. Eri....67 — 50 78 D
Sanddown Ct. Sutt....110 — 25 63 D
Sandell's Ave. Ashf....81 — 08 71 C
Sandell St. SE1....7 — 31 79 A
Sanders Cl. Hamp....82 — 14 71 C
Sanders La. NW7....23 — 23 91 D
Sanderson Cl. NW5....47 — 28 85 B
Sanderstead Ave. NW2....35 — 24 86 A
Sanderstead Cl. SW4....86 — 29 73 A
Sanderstead Rd. E10....38 — 36 87 C
Sanderstead Rd. Orp....108 — 46 67 D
Sanderstead Rd. S Croy....112 — 32 62 B
Sandfield Gdns. Th Hth....97 — 31 68 B
Sandfield Pas. Th Hth....97 — 32 69 C
Sandfield Pl. Th Hth....97 — 32 68 A
Sandfield Rd. Th Hth....97 — 31 68 B
Sandford Ave. N22....25 — 32 90 A
Sandford Ct. N16....37 — 33 87 C
Sandford Rd. Bexh....79 — 48 75 A
Sandford Rd. Brom....99 — 40 68 D
Sandford Row. SE17....63 — 32 78 D
Sandford St. SW6....62 — 25 77 D
Sandgate Rd. Well....67 — 47 77 C
Sandgate St. SE15....63 — 34 77 B
Sandhills. Wall....111 — 29 64 B
Sandhurst Ave. Har....32 — 13 88 D
Sandhurst Ave. Surb....102 — 19 66 B
Sandhurst Cl. NW9....22 — 19 89 A
Sandhurst Cl. S Croy....112 — 33 62 A
Sandhurst Dri. Ilf....51 — 45 85 B
Sandhurst Rd. Bexh....79 — 47 74 B
Sandhurst Rd. Enf....14 — 35 95 D
Sandhurst Rd. NW9....22 — 19 89 A
Sandhurst Rd. Orp....108 — 46 65 C
Sandhurst Rd. SE6....88 — 38 73 C
Sandhurst Rd. Sid....90 — 46 72 C
Sandhurst Way. S Croy....112 — 33 63 D
Sandiford Rd. Sutt....103 — 24 65 B
Sandiland Cres. Brom....107 — 39 65 B
Sandilands. Croy....105 — 34 65 B
Sandilands Rd. SW6....73 — 25 76 B
Sandison St. SE15....75 — 34 75 A
Sandland St. WC1....3 — 30 81 B
Sandling Rise. SE9....90 — 43 72 C
Sandlings The. N22....25 — 31 89 B
Sandmere Rd. SW4....74 — 30 75 C
Sandown Ave. Dag....52 — 50 84 A
Sandown Ave. Horn....42 — 53 86 B
Sandown Cl. Houn....69 — 10 76 A
Sandown Dri. Cars....111 — 28 62 A
Sandown Rd. SE25....105 — 34 67 B
Sandown Way. Nthlt....43 — 12 85 C
Sandpit Pl. SE7....65 — 42 78 C
Sandpit Rd. Brom....89 — 39 71 C
Sandpit Rd. Dart....80 — 53 75 C
Sandpits Rd. Rich....83 — 17 72 B
Sandra Cl. Houn....70 — 13 74 B
Sandra Cl. N22....25 — 32 90 C
Sandridge Cl. Har....21 — 15 89 C
Sandridge St. N19....36 — 29 86 A
Sandringham Ave. SW20....95 — 24 69 C
Sandringham Cl. Enf....13 — 33 97 C
Sandringham Cl. Ilf....28 — 44 89 A
Sandringham Cres. Har....32 — 13 86 D
Sandringham Dri. Well....78 — 45 76 C
Sandringham Gdns. Houn....60 — 10 76 A
Sandringham Gdns. Ilf....28 — 44 89 A
Sandringham Gdns. N12....23 — 26 91 B
Sandringham Gdns. N8....36 — 30 88 C
Sandringham Mews. W5....54 — 17 80 B
Sandringham Rd. Th Hth....105 — 32 67 A
Sandringham Rd. Bark....51 — 45 84 B
Sandringham Rd. Brom....89 — 40 71 C
Sandringham Rd. E10....238 — 38 88 D
Sandringham Rd. E7....50 — 41 85 C
Sandringham Rd. E8....48 — 33 85 D
Sandringham Rd. N22....25 — 32 90 C
Sandringham Rd. Nthlt....43 — 13 84 C
Sandringham Rd. NW11....35 — 24 87 A
Sandringham Rd. NW2....45 — 22 84 B
Sandringham Rd. Wor Pk....102 — 22 65 D
Sandrock Rd. SE13....76 — 37 75 A
Sands End La. SW6....73 — 25 76 B
Sandstone Pl. N6....36 — 28 86 B
Sandstone Rd. SE12....89 — 40 72 B
Sands Way. Wdf Gn....27 — 42 91 B
Sandtoft Rd. SE7....65 — 40 77 B
Sandwell Cres. NW6....46 — 25 84 A
Sandwich St. WC1....3 — 30 82 A
Sandy Bury. Orp....108 — 44 65 D
Sandycombe Rd. Felt....81 — 10 73 C

Sandycombe Rd. Rich ....*72* 19 76 C
Sandycoombe Rd. Twick ....*71* 17 74 C
Sandycroft. SE2 ....*66* 46 77 A
Sandy Dri. Felt ....*81* 09 73 C
Sandy Hill Ave. SE18 ....*66* 43 78 D
Sandyhill Rd. Ilf ....*51* 43 85 B
Sandy Hill Rd. SE18 ....*66* 43 78 D
Sandy Hill Rd. Wall ....*111* 29 62 A
Sandy La. King ....*93* 17 69 A
Sandy La. Mar ....*96* 28 69 A
Sandy La. Nthwd ....*19* 10 91 B
Sandy La N. Wall ....*111* 29 64 D
Sandy La. Orp ....*108* 46 66 A
Sandy La. Rich ....*83* 17 72 B
Sandy La. Sutt ....*110* 24 62 A
Sandy La S. Wall ....*111* 29 63 C
Sandy La. Tedd ....*93* 16 70 D
Sandy Lodge Way. Nthwd ....*19* 09 91 A
Sandymount Ave. Stan ....*21* 17 91 B
Sandy Rd. NW3 ....*35* 25 86 B
Sandy Ridge. Chis ....*100* 43 70 A
Sandy's Row. E1 ....*4* 33 81 A
Sandy Way. Croy ....*106* 36 65 D
Sanford St. SE14 ....*64* 36 77 A
Sanford Terr. N16 ....*37* 33 86 D
Sanford Wlk. N16 ....*37* 33 86 B
Sanford Wlk. SE14 ....*64* 36 77 A
Sangley Rd SE25 ....*97* 33 68 C
Sangley Rd. SE6 ....*88* 38 73 C
Sangora Rd. SW11 ....*73* 26 75 D
Sansom Rd. E11 ....*39* 39 86 B
Sansom St. SE5 ....*75* 32 76 B
Sansom St. SE5 ....*63* 32 77 D
Sans Wlk. EC1 ....*3* 31 82 D
Santley St. SW4 ....*74* 30 75 D
Santos Rd. SW18 ....*73* 25 74 A
Sapphire Rd. SE8 ....*64* 36 78 A
Saracen Ct. ....*105* 32 67 D
Saracen's Head Yd. EC3 ....*4* 33 81 D
Saracen St. E14 ....*57* 37 81 C
Sarah St. N1 ....*4* 33 82 A
Saratoga Rd. E5 ....*49* 35 85 A
Sardinia St. WC2 ....*3* 30 81 D
Sark Cl. Houn ....*59* 13 77 C
Sark Wlk. E16 ....*58* 40 81 D
*Sarnesfield Rd. Enf ....*13* 32 96 B
Sarre Rd. NW2 ....*46* 24 85 D
Sarsen Ave. Houn ....*70* 12 76 D
Sarsfeld Rd. SW12 ....*86* 27 73 D
Sarsfield Rd. Grnf ....*44* 17 83 C
Sartor Rd. SE15 ....*76* 35 75 D
Satchell Mead. NW9 ....*22* 21 90 B
Satchwell Rd. E2 ....*57* 34 82 A
Sauls Green. E11 ....*39* 39 86 C
Saunders Ness Rd. E14 ....*64* 38 78 B
Saunders Rd. SE18 ....*66* 45 78 D
Saunders St. SE11 ....*63* 31 78 A
Saunderton Rd. Wem ....*44* 16 85 D
Saunton Rd. Horn ....*42* 52 86 A
Savage Gdns. EC3 ....*8* 33 80 A
Savernake Rd. N9 ....*13* 34 95 C
Savernake Rd. NW3 ....*47* 27 85 B
Savile Cl. N.Mal ....*102* 21 67 A
Savile Gdns. Croy ....*105* 33 65 B
Saville Cres. Ashf ....*91* 08 70 B
Saville Rd. Rom ....*41* 48 87 B
Saville Rd. Twick ....*83* 15 73 D
Saville Rd. W4 ....*61* 20 79 D
Saville Row. Enf ....*14* 35 97 D
Saville Row. W1 ....*6* 29 80 A
Savill Gdns. SW20 ....*94* 22 68 A
Savill Row. Wdf Grn ....*27* 39 91 B
Savona Cl. SW19 ....*95* 23 70 D
Savona St. SW8 ....*10* 29 77 C
Savoy Bldgs. WC2 ....*7* 30 80 B
Savoy Cl. E15 ....*50* 39 83 A
Savoy Ct. WC2 ....*7* 30 80 A
Savoy Hill. WC2 ....*7* 30 80 B
Savoy Pl. WC2 ....*7* 30 80 B
Savoy Rd. Dart ....*80* 53 74 B
Savoy Row. WC2 ....*7* 30 80 B
Savoy Steps. WC2 ....*7* 30 80 B
Savoy St. WC2 ....*7* 30 80 B
Savoy Way. WC2 ....*7* 30 80 B
Sawkins Cl. SW19 ....*85* 24 72 A
Sawley Rd. W12 ....*55* 22 80 C
Sawtry Cl. Cars ....*104* 27 66 A
Sawyer's Hill. Rich ....*84* 19 73 A
Sawyers Lawn. W13 ....*54* 16 81 C
Sawyer St. SE1 ....*8* 32 79 A
Saxby Rd. SW2 ....*86* 30 73 A
Saxham Rd. Bark ....*51* 45 83 D
Saxlingham Rd. E4 ....*18* 38 93 D
Saxon Ave. Felt ....*82* 12 72 B

Saxonbury Ave. Sun ....*92* 11 68 A
Saxonbury Cl. Mit ....*95* 26 68 B
Saxonbury Gdns. Surb ....*101* 17 66 C
Saxon Cl. Rom ....*30* 54 90 D
Saxon Dr. W3 ....*55* 19 81 B
Saxon Gdns. Sthl ....*53* 12 80 A
Saxon Rd. Ashf ....*91* 08 70 B
Saxon Rd. Brom ....*99* 39 70 D
Saxon Rd. E3 ....*49* 36 83 D
Saxon Rd. Ilf ....*51* 43 85 D
Saxon Rd. N22 ....*25* 31 90 B
Saxon Rd. SE25 ....*105* 32 67 B
Saxon Rd. Sthl ....*53* 12 80 A
Saxon Rd. Wem ....*34* 20 86 C
Saxon Way. N14 ....*12* 29 95 C
Saxton Cl. SE13 ....*76* 38 75 B
Saxville Rd. Orp ....*100* 46 69 D
Sayer St. SE17 ....*63* 32 78 A
Sayes Court Rd. Orp ....*100* 46 68 D
Sayes Court St. SE8 ....*64* 36 77 B
Scads Hill Cl. Orp ....*108* 45 67 D
Scala St. W1 ....*2* 29 81 A
Scales Rd. N17 ....*25* 34 89 A
Scampston Mews. W10 ....*56* 23 81 D
Scandrett St. E1 ....*57* 34 80 D
Scarba Wlk. N1 ....*48* 32 84 B
Scarborough Rd. E11 ....*38* 38 87 D
Scarborough Rd. N4 ....*37* 31 87 C
Scarborough Rd. N9 ....*18* 35 94 A
Scarborough St. E1 ....*4* 33 81 D
Scarbrook Rd. Croy ....*105* 32 65 C
Scarle Rd. Wem ....*44* 17 84 B
Scarlet Rd. SE6 ....*89* 39 72 C
Scarlette Manor Way. SE24 ....*87* 31 73 A
Scarsbrook Rd. SE3 ....*77* 41 75 B
Scarsdale Pl. W8 ....*62* 25 79 D
Scarsdale Rd. Har ....*32* 14 86 C
Scarsdale Villas. W8 ....*62* 25 79 C
Scarth Rd. SW13 ....*72* 22 75 A
Scawen Rd. SE8 ....*64* 36 78 C
Scawfell St. E2 ....*48* 33 83 D
Scaynes Link. N12 ....*15* 25 92 A
Sceaux Gdns. SE5 ....*75* 33 76 A
Sceptre Rd. E2 ....*57* 35 82 A
Schofield Wlk. SE3 ....*65* 40 77 D
Scholars Rd. E4 ....*18* 38 94 D
Scholars Rd. SW12 ....*86* 29 73 C
Scholefield Rd. N19 ....*36* 29 86 B
Scholefield Rd. N19 ....*36* 29 87 D
School App. E2 ....*4* 33 82 A
Schoolhouse La. E1 ....*57* 35 80 B
School House La. Tedd ....*93* 17 70 C
School La. King ....*93* 17 69 A
School La. Pnr ....*20* 12 89 C
School La. Surb ....*101* 18 66 D
School La. Well ....*78* 46 75 B
School Pas. King ....*93* 18 69 D
School Pas. Sthl ....*53* 12 80 B
School Rd. Ashf ....*91* 07 70 B
School Rd. Chis ....*100* 44 70 C
School Rd. Dag ....*52* 49 83 A
School Rd. E12 ....*50* 42 85 B
School Rd. E Mol ....*92* 14 68 D
School Rd. Hamp ....*92* 14 70 A
School Rd. Houn ....*70* 14 75 A
School Rd. King ....*93* 17 69 A
School Rd. NW10 ....*55* 20 82 D
School Road Ave. Hamp ....*92* 14 70 A
School Way. Dag ....*41* 47 86 C
Schoolway. N12 ....*23* 26 91 B
School Wlk. Sun ....*91* 10 68 A
Schubert Rd. SW15 ....*73* 24 74 B
Sclater St. E1 ....*4* 33 82 D
Scoble Pl. N16 ....*48* 33 85 B
Scoles Cres. SW2 ....*87* 31 73 C
Scoresby St. SE1 ....*7* 31 80 D
Scorton Ave. Grnf ....*44* 16 83 C
Scotch Common W13 ....*54* 16 81 B
Scoter Cl. Wdf Grn ....*27* 40 91 D
Scot Gr. Pnr ....*20* 11 91 D
Scotia Ct. SE16 ....*64* 35 79 C
Scotland Green. N17 ....*25* 33 90 D
Scotland Green Rd. Enf ....*14* 35 95 B
Scotland Green Rd N. Enf ....*14* 36 96 C
Scotland Pl. SW1 ....*7* 30 80 C
Scotsdale Cl. Orp ....*100* 45 68 C
Scotsdale Cl. Sutt ....*110* 24 63 C
Scotsdale Rd. SE12 ....*77* 40 74 D
Scotswood St. EC1 ....*3* 31 82 C
Scotswood Wlk. N17 ....*25* 34 91 C
Scott Cl. Eps ....*109* 20 64 C
Scott Cl. SW16 ....*96* 30 69 B
Scott Cres. Eri ....*80* 51 76 B
Scott Cres. Har ....*32* 13 87 D
Scott Ellis Gdns. NW8 ....*1* 26 82 B

Scottes Rd. Dag ....*41* 47 87 D
Scott Gdns. Houn ....*59* 11 77 D
Scott Lidgett Cres. SE16 ....*63* 34 79 A
Scott's Ave. Brom ....*98* 38 69 D
Scott's Ave. Sun ....*91* 09 70 A
Scotts Dri. Hamp ....*92* 13 70 D
Scotts Farm Rd. Eps ....*109* 20 63 A
Scott's La. Brom ....*98* 38 69 D
Scottsas SE18 ....*66* 43 78 B
Scotts Rd. Brom ....*99* 40 70 C
Scotts Rd. E10 ....*38* 38 87 C
Scotts Rd. Sthl ....*59* 11 79 D
Scott's Rd. W12 ....*61* 22 79 B
Scott St. E1 ....*57* 34 82 D
Scott's Way. Sun ....*91* 09 70 C
Scott's Yd. EC4 ....*8* 32 80 B
Scoulding Rd. E16 ....*58* 40 81 C
Scouler St. E14 ....*58* 38 80 B
Scout La. SW4 ....*74* 29 75 A
Scovell Cres. SE1 ....*8* 32 79 A
Scovell Rd. SE1 ....*8* 32 79 A
Scrafton Rd. Ilf ....*40* 43 86 D
Scrattons Terr. Bark ....*52* 47 83 B
Scriven St. E8 ....*48* 33 83 B
Scrooby St. SE6 ....*76* 37 74 D
Scrubs La. NW10 ....*55* 22 82 D
Scrubs La. W10 ....*56* 23 81 A
Scrutton Cl. SW12 ....*86* 29 73 B
Scrutton St. EC2 ....*4* 33 82 C
Scudamore La. NW9 ....*22* 20 89 C
Scutari Rd. SE22 ....*76* 35 74 A
Scylla Cres. Felt ....*81* 07 73 B
Scylla Rd. Felt ....*69* 07 74 D
Scylla Rd. SE15 ....*75* 34 75 B
Seabright St. E2 ....*57* 34 82 B
Seabrook Dri. W.Wick ....*107* 39 65 A
Seabrook Gdns. Rom ....*41* 49 87 A
Seabrook Rd. Dag ....*41* 47 86 D
Seacoal La. EC4 ....*3* 31 81 D
Seacourt Rd. SE2 ....*67* 47 79 B
Seafield Rd. N11 ....*16* 29 92 B
Seaford Cl. Ruis ....*31* 08 86 B
Seaford Rd. E17 ....*26* 37 89 B
Seaford Rd. Enf ....*13* 33 96 C
Seaford Rd. N15 ....*37* 33 88 A
Seaford Rd. W13 ....*54* 16 80 D
Seaford St. WC1 ....*3* 30 82 A
Seaforth Ave. N Mal ....*94* 22 68 D
Seaforth Cl. Rom ....*30* 51 91 C
Seaforth Cres. N5 ....*48* 32 85 C
Seaforth Gdns. Eps ....*109* 21 64 D
Seaforth Gdns. N21 ....*17* 31 94 C
Seaforth Pl. SW1 ....*6* 29 79 C
Seager Pl. E3 ....*57* 36 81 B
Seagrave Cl. E1 ....*57* 35 81 B
Seagrave Rd. SW6 ....*62* 25 77 A
Seagry Rd. E11 ....*39* 40 87 B
Sealand Rd. Houn ....*69* 07 74 C
Sealand Wlk. Nthlt ....*53* 12 82 A
Seal St. E8 ....*48* 33 85 B
Searle Ct. N4 ....*36* 30 87 D
Searles Cl. SW11 ....*9* 27 77 C
Searles Rd. SE1 ....*63* 32 78 B
Sears St. SE5 ....*63* 32 77 D
Seasprite Cl. Nthlt ....*53* 11 82 B
Seaton Ave. Ilf ....*51* 45 85 D
Seaton Cl. E13 ....*58* 40 82 C
Seaton Cl. SE11 ....*63* 31 78 D
Seaton Cl. Twick ....*70* 14 74 D
Seaton Gdns. Ruis ....*31* 10 86 A
Seaton Pl. NW1 ....*2* 29 82 C
Seaton Rd. Mit ....*96* 27 69 C
Seaton Rd. Twick ....*70* 14 74 C
Seaton Rd. Well ....*67* 47 77 C
Seaton Rd. Wem ....*44* 18 83 C
Seaton St. N18 ....*17* 34 92 C
Sebastion St. EC1 ....*3* 31 82 B
Sebastopol Rd. N9 ....*17* 34 93 C
Sebbon St. N1 ....*48* 31 84 D
Sebert Rd. E7 ....*50* 40 85 B
Sebright Pas. E2 ....*48* 34 83 C
Sebright Rd. Barn ....*11* 23 96 B
Secker Cres. Har ....*7* 14 90 A
Secker St. SE1 ....*7* 31 80 C
Second Ave. Dag ....*52* 49 83 D
Second Ave. E12 ....*50* 42 85 C
Second Ave. E13 ....*58* 40 82 A
Second Ave. E17 ....*38* 37 88 A
Second Ave. Enf ....*13* 33 95 B
Second Ave. N18 ....*18* 35 92 A
Second Ave. NW4 ....*23* 23 89 D
Second Ave. Rom ....*41* 47 88 A
Second Ave. SW14 ....*72* 21 75 A
Second Ave. W10 ....*56* 24 82 C
Second Ave. W3 ....*55* 21 80 D

Second Ave. Wem

Second Ave. Wem	*33*	17 86 B
Second Cl. E Mol	*92*	14 68 C
Second Cross Rd. Twick	*83*	15 72 A
Second Way. Wem	*45*	19 85 B
Sedan Way. SE17	*63*	33 78 C
Sedcote Rd. Enf	*14*	35 95 B
Sedding St. SW1	*9*	28 78 A
Seddon Rd. Mord	*103*	26 67 B
Seddon St. WC1	*3*	30 82 B
Sedgebrook Rd. SE3	*77*	41 75 B
Sedgecombe Ave. Har	*33*	17 88 A
Sedgeford Rd. W3	*55*	21 80 D
Sedgehill Rd. SE6	*88*	37 71 D
Sedgemere Ave. N2	*23*	26 89 A
Sedgemoor Dri. Dag	*52*	49 85 A
Sedgeway. SE6	*89*	39 73 D
Sedgewood Cl. Brom	*107*	39 66 B
Sedgmoor Pl. SE5	*63*	33 77 C
Sedgwick Rd. E10	*38*	38 86 A
Sedgwick St. E9	*49*	35 85 D
Sedleigh Rd. SW18	*73*	24 74 D
Sedlescombe Rd. SW6	*62*	25 77 A
Sedley Pl. W1	*2*	28 81 D
Seeley Dri. SE21	*87*	33 71 B
Seelig Ave. NW9	*34*	22 87 A
Seely Rd. SW17	*96*	28 70 A
Seething La. EC3	*8*	33 80 A
Seething Wells La. Surb	*101*	17 67 C
Sefton Ave. Har	*20*	14 90 B
Sefton Ave. NW7	*22*	20 91 B
Sefton Cl. Orp	*100*	45 68 D
Sefton Ct. Houn	*70*	13 76 B
Sefton Rd. Croy	*105*	34 66 C
Sefton Rd. Eps	*109*	20 62 D
Sefton Rd. Orp	*100*	45 68 D
Sefton St. SW15	*73*	23 75 A
Sekforde St EC1	*3*	31 82 D
Selbie Ave. NW10	*45*	21 85 D
Selborne Ave. E12	*51*	43 85 A
Selborne Ave. E17	*38*	36 88 B
Selborne Gdns. Grnf	*44*	16 83 C
Selborne Gdns. NW4	*22*	22 89 C
Selborne Rd. Croy	*105*	33 65 D
Selborne Rd. E17	*38*	37 88 A
Selborne Rd. Ilf	*40*	43 86 A
Selborne Rd. N14	*16*	30 93 C
Selborne Rd. N22	*24*	30 90 B
Selborne Rd. SE5	*75*	32 76 D
Selborne Rd. Sid	*90*	46 71 B
Selbourne Ave. Surb	*102*	19 65 C
Selbourne Rd. N Mal	*94*	21 69 C
Selby Chase. Ruis	*31*	10 86 B
Selby Cl. Chis	*100*	43 70 A
Selby Gdns. Sthl	*53*	13 82 C
Selby Green. Cars	*104*	27 66 A
Selby Rd. Ashf	*91*	08 70 A
Selby Rd. Cars	*104*	27 66 A
Selby Rd. E11	*39*	39 86 C
Selby Rd. E13	*58*	40 81 B
Selby Rd. N17	*25*	33 91 A
Selby Rd. SE20	*97*	34 69 C
Selby Rd. W5	*54*	17 82 C
Selby St. E1	*57*	34 82 C
Selcroft Rd. E10	*65*	39 78 D
Selden Rd. SE15	*76*	35 76 C
Seldon Wlk. N7	*36*	30 86 B
Selhurst New Rd. SE25	*105*	33 67 C
Selhurst Pl. SE25	*105*	33 67 C
Selhurst Rd. N9	*17*	33 93 C
Selhurst Rd. SE25	*105*	33 67 A
Selinas La. Dag	*41*	48 87 B
Selkirk Rd. SW17	*86*	27 71 A
Selkirk Rd. Twick	*82*	14 73 C
Sellers Hall Cl. N3	*23*	25 91 C
Sellincourt Rd. SW17	*96*	27 70 B
Sellindge Cl. Beck	*98*	36 70 D
Sellon Mews. SE11	*10*	30 78 B
Sellons Ave. NW10	*45*	21 83 B
Selous St. NW1	*47*	29 83 A
Selsdon Ave. S Croy	*112*	32 63 B
Selsdon Cl. Rom	*29*	50 90 A
Selsdon Cl. Surb	*101*	18 67 A
Selsdon Rd. E11	*39*	40 87 A
Selsdon Rd. E13	*50*	41 83 C
Selsdon Rd. N Mal	*94*	21 86 B
Selsdon Rd. S Croy	*112*	32 63 B
Selsdon Rd. SE27	*87*	31 71 B
Selsea Pl. N16	*48*	33 85 C
Selsey Cres. Well	*79*	47 76 B
Selsey St. E14	*57*	37 81 A
Selway Cl. Pnr	*19*	10 89 B
Selwood Dri. Barn	*11*	23 95 B
Selwood Pl. SW7	*62*	26 78 D
Selwood Rd. Croy	*105*	34 66 D
Selwood Rd. Sutt	*103*	24 66 D
Selwood Terr. SW7	*62*	26 78 D
Selworthy Cl. E11	*39*	40 88 A
Selworthy Rd. SE6	*88*	36 72 D
Selwyn Ave. E4	*26*	38 91 A
Selwyn Ave. Ilf	*40*	45 88 D
Selwyn Ave. Rich	*71*	18 75 B
Selwyn Cl. Houn	*70*	12 75 C
Selwyn Cres. Well	*78*	46 75 D
Selwyn Ct. Edg	*22*	19 91 D
Selwyn Pl. Orp	*100*	46 68 B
Selwyn Rd. E13	*50*	40 83 B
Selwyn Rd. E3	*49*	36 83 D
Selwyn Rd. N.Mal	*102*	20 67 B
Selwyn Rd. NW10	*45*	21 84 C
Semley Pl. SW1	*9*	28 78 B
Semley Rd. SW16	*96*	30 69 C
Senate St. SE15	*76*	35 76 C
Seneca Rd. W4	*74*	30 75 C
Seneca Rd. Th Hth	*97*	32 68 C
Senga Rd. Wall	*104*	28 66 C
Senhouse Rd. Sutt	*103*	23 65 D
Senior St. W2	*56*	25 81 B
Senior St. W2	*56*	25 81 B
Senlac Rd. SE12	*89*	40 73 D
Sennen Rd. Enf	*17*	33 94 B
Sennen Wlk. SE9	*89*	42 72 C
Senrab St. E1	*57*	35 81 D
Sentinel Sq. NW4	*23*	23 89 C
September Way. Stan	*21*	16 91 B
Sequoia Gdns. Orp	*108*	45 66 B
Sequoia Park. Pnr	*20*	13 91 B
Serbin Cl. E10	*38*	38 87 A
Serjeants' Inn. EC4	*3*	31 81 C
Serle St. WC2	*3*	30 81 D
Sermon La. EC4	*4*	32 81 C
Serpentine Rd. W2	*5*	27 80 D
Serviden Dri. Brom	*99*	41 69 B
Servius Ct. Brent	*60*	17 77 D
Setchell Rd. SE1	*63*	33 78 B
Setchell Way. SE1	*63*	33 78 B
Seth St. SE16	*64*	35 79 A
Seton Gdns. Dag	*52*	47 84 C
Settle Rd. E13	*50*	40 83 C
Settles St. E1	*57*	34 81 C
Settrington Rd. SW6	*73*	25 76 D
Seven Kings Rd. Ilf	*40*	44 86 B
Sevenoaks Cl. Bexh	*79*	49 75 D
Sevenoaks Ct. Nthwd	*19*	08 91 C
Sevenoaks Rd. Orp	*108*	46 65 C
Sevenoaks Rd. SE4	*76*	36 74 D
Seven Sisters Rd. N15	*37*	33 88 A
Seven Sisters Rd. N4	*37*	32 87 A
Seventh Ave. E12	*50*	42 85 B
Severn Ave. Rom	*30*	52 89 B
Severn Dri. Esh	*101*	16 65 A
Severn Way. NW10	*45*	21 85 D
Severus Rd. SW11	*74*	27 75 C
Seville St. SW1	*5*	27 79 B
Sevington Rd. NW4	*34*	22 88 D
Sevington St. W9	*56*	25 82 D
Seward Rd. Beck	*98*	35 69 D
Seward Rd. W7	*60*	16 79 A
Seward St. EC1	*4*	32 82 A
Sewardstone Gdns. E4	*14*	37 95 B
Sewardstone Rd. E2	*49*	35 83 C
Sewardstone Rd. E4	*18*	37 94 B
Sewardstone Rd. Enf	*14*	37 96 B
Sewdley St. E5	*49*	35 85 B
Sewell Rd. SE2	*66*	46 79 B
Sewell St. E13	*58*	40 82 A
Seymer Dri. Grnf	*43*	13 83 B
Seymer Rd. Rom	*29*	50 89 B
Seymour Ave. Eps	*109*	22 62 B
Seymour Ave. Mord	*103*	23 66 B
Seymour Ave. N17	*25*	34 90 C
Seymour Cl. Pnr	*20*	12 90 B
Seymour Cl. SW20	*94*	22 70 D
Seymour Ct. N10	*24*	28 90 C
Seymour Ct. N21	*12*	30 95 D
Seymour Gdns. Felt	*82*	11 71 A
Seymour Gdns. Ilf	*39*	42 87 D
Seymour Gdns. Ruis	*32*	11 87 D
Seymour Gdns. Surb	*101*	18 67 B
Seymour Gdns. Twick	*83*	16 73 B
Seymour Mews. W1	*2*	28 81 C
Seymour Pl. SE25	*97*	34 68 D
Seymour Pl. W1	*1*	27 81 D
Seymour Rd. Cars	*111*	28 64 C
Seymour Rd. E10	*38*	36 87 D
Seymour Rd. E4	*18*	37 94 D
Seymour Rd. E6	*50*	41 83 D
Seymour Rd. E Mol	*92*	14 68 C
Seymour Rd. Hamp	*82*	14 71 C
Seymour Rd. King	*93*	17 69 B
Seymour Rd. Mit	*104*	28 66 A
Seymour Rd. N3	*23*	25 91 B
Seymour Rd. N8	*37*	31 88 B
Seymour Rd. N9	*17*	34 93 B
Seymour Rd. SW18	*73*	24 74 D
Seymour Rd. SW19	*85*	23 72 D
Seymour Rd. W4	*61*	20 78 A
Seymour St. W1	*1*	27 81 D
Seymour Terr. SE20	*97*	34 69 B
Seymour Villas. SE20	*97*	34 69 B
Seymour Way. Sun	*91*	09 70 A
Seymour Wlk. SW10	*62*	26 77 A
Seyssel St. E14	*64*	38 78 A
Shaa Rd. W3	*55*	20 80 B
Shacklegate La. Tedd	*83*	15 71 A
Shackleton Cl. SE23	*87*	34 72 B
Shackleton Cl. SE23	*88*	35 72 A
Shackleton Ct. W12	*61*	22 79 B
Shackleton Rd. Sthl	*53*	12 80 B
Shacklewell La. E8	*48*	33 85 D
Shacklewell Rd. N16	*48*	33 85 B
Shacklewell Row. E8	*48*	33 85 D
Shacklewell St. E2	*4*	33 82 B
Shadbolt Cl. Wor Pk	*102*	21 65 B
Shad Thames. SE1	*8*	33 79 B
Shadwell Ct. Nthlt	*43*	12 93 D
Shadwell Dri. Nthlt	*53*	12 82 B
Shadwell Gdns. E1	*57*	35 80 A
Shadwell Pierhead. E1	*57*	35 80 A
Shadwell Pl. E1	*57*	35 80 A
Shaef Way. Tedd	*93*	16 70 C
Shafter Rd. Dag	*52*	50 84 A
Shaftesbury Ave.	*32*	14 87 C
Shaftesbury Ave. Barn	*11*	26 96 C
Shaftesbury Ave. Enf	*14*	35 97 D
Shaftesbury Ave. Har	*81*	10 73 A
Shaftesbury Ave. Har	*33*	18 88 C
Shaftesbury Ave. Sthl	*53*	13 79 C
Shaftesbury Ave. W1	*6*	29 80 B
Shaftesbury Circ. Har	*32*	14 87 C
Shaftesbury Mews. W8	*62*	25 79 C
Shaftesbury Rd. Beck	*98*	36 69 D
Shaftesbury Rd. Cars	*104*	27 66 A
Shaftesbury Rd. E10	*38*	37 87 C
Shaftesbury Rd. E17	*38*	37 88 D
Shaftesbury Rd. E4	*18*	38 94 D
Shaftesbury Rd. E7	*50*	41 84 C
Shaftesbury Rd. N18	*25*	33 91 B
Shaftesbury Rd. N19	*36*	30 87 D
Shaftesbury Rd. Rich	*71*	18 75 A
Shaftesbury Rd. Rom	*42*	51 88 D
Shaftesburys The. Bark	*51*	44 83 A
Shaftesbury St. N1	*48*	32 83 D
Shaftesbury Waye. Hay	*53*	11 81 C
Shaftesbury Way. Twick	*82*	14 72 D
Shafto Mews. SW1	*5*	27 79 D
Shafton Rd. E9	*49*	35 83 B
Shafts Ct. EC3	*4*	33 81 C
Shakespeare Ave. Felt	*69*	10 74 C
Shakespeare Ave. Hay	*53*	11 82 C
Shakespeare Ave. N11	*16*	29 92 C
Shakespeare Ave. NW10	*45*	20 83 B
Shakespeare Cres. E12	*50*	42 84 B
Shakespeare Cres. NW10	*45*	20 83 B
Shakespeare Dri. Har	*33*	18 88 D
Shakespeare Gdns. N2	*24*	27 89 D
Shakespeare Mews. N16	*48*	33 85 A
Shakespeare Rd. Bexh	*79*	48 76 A
Shakespeare Rd. E17	*26*	35 90 D
Shakespeare Rd. N3	*23*	25 90 A
Shakespeare Rd. Rom	*42*	51 88 D
Shakespeare Rd. W3	*55*	20 80 C
Shakespeare Rd. W7	*54*	15 80 B
Shakespeare Sq. Ilf	*28*	44 91 A
Shakespeare Way. Felt	*82*	11 71 A
Shakspeare Wlk. N16	*48*	33 85 A
Shalcomb St. SW10	*62*	26 77 A
Shaldon Dri. Mord	*103*	24 67 A
Shaldon Dri. Ruis	*32*	11 86 C
Shaldon Rd. Edg	*21*	18 90 D
Shalfleet Dri. W10	*56*	23 80 B
Shalford Ct. N1	*48*	31 83 C
Shalimar Gdns. W3	*55*	20 80 A
Shalimar Rd. W3	*55*	20 80 A
Shallons Rd. SE9	*90*	43 71 B
Shalstone Rd. SW14	*72*	19 75 B
Shalston Villas. Surb	*101*	18 67 D
Shamrock Rd. Croy	*104*	30 67 D
Shamrock St. SW4	*74*	29 75 B
Shamrock Way. N14	*16*	28 94 D
Shandon Rd. SW4	*74*	29 74 C
Shand St. SE1	*8*	33 79 A
Shand St. SE1	*8*	33 80 C
Shandy St. E2	*57*	36 82 C
Shanklin Rd. N15	*25*	34 89 C
Shanklin Rd. N8	*36*	29 88 B

Name	Pg	Grid
Shanklin Way. SE15	63	33 77 D
Shannon Cl. Sthl	59	11 78 D
Shannon Corner. N Mal	94	22 68 C
Shannon Gr. SW9	74	30 75 D
Shannon Pl. NW8	47	27 83 C
Shap Cres. Cars	104	27 66 D
Shap St. E2	48	33 83 D
Shardcroft Ave. SE24	75	31 74 B
Shardeloes Rd. SE14	76	36 76 D
Shard's Sq. SE15	63	34 77 A
Sharman St. Sid	90	46 71 A
Sharnbrooke Cl. Well	79	47 75 A
Sharon Cl. Surb	101	17 66 C
Sharon Gdns. E9	49	35 83 A
Sharon Rd. Enf	14	36 97 C
Sharon Rd. W4	61	20 78 D
Sharples Hall St. NW1	47	27 83 B
Sharps La. Ruis	31	08 87 D
Sharp Way. Dart	80	54 75 B
Sharratt St. SE15	64	35 77 A
Sharstead St. SE17	63	31 78 D
Sharvel La. Nthlt	43	11 83 A
Shaver's Pl. SW1	6	29 80 B
Shaw Ave. Bark	52	48 83 C
Shawbrooke Rd. SE9	77	41 75 D
Shawbury Rd. SE22	75	33 74 B
Shawfield Park. Brom	99	41 69 D
Shawfield St. SW3	9	27 78 C
Shawford Rd. Eps	109	20 63 B
Shaw Gdns. Bark	52	48 83 C
Shaw Path. Brom	89	39 72 D
Shaw Rd. Brom	89	39 72 D
Shaw Rd. Enf	14	35 97 B
Shaw Sq. E17	26	36 90 A
Shaw Way. Wall	111	30 63 C
Shearing Dri. Cars	103	26 66 A
Shearling Way. N7	47	30 84 A
Shearman Rd. SE3	77	39 75 D
Shears Ct. Sun	91	09 70 C
Shearwood Cres. Dart	80	52 75 A
Sheaveshill Ave. NW9	22	21 89 C
Sheaveshill Ct. NW9	22	21 89 C
Sheba St. E1	4	33 82 D
Sheen Common Dri. Rich	72	19 75 C
Sheen Court Rd. Rich	72	19 75 C
Sheendale Rd. Rich	71	18 75 D
Sheenewood. SE26	87	34 71 B
Sheen Gate Gdns. SW14	72	20 75 C
Sheen Gr. N1	48	31 83 A
Sheen La. SW14	72	20 75 C
Sheen Park. Rich	71	18 75 C
Sheen Rd. Orp	100	45 68 D
Sheen Rd. Rich	71	18 75 D
Sheen Way. Wall	111	30 64 D
Sheen Wood. SW14	72	20 74 A
Sheepcote La. SW11	74	27 76 D
Sheepcote Rd. Har	33	15 88 D
Sheepcotes Rd. Rom	29	48 89 C
Sheephouse Way. N.Mal	102	21 66 A
Sheep La. E8	48	34 83 B
Sheerwater Rd. E16	58	41 81 B
Sheffield Sq. E3	32	36 82 B
Sheffield Terr. W8	56	25 80 C
Shefton Rise. Nthwd	19	10 91 C
Sheila Cl. Rom	29	49 91 D
Sheila Rd. Rom	29	49 91 D
Sheilings The. Horn	42	54 88 B
Shelbourne Cl. Pnr	20	12 89 B
Shelbourne Rd. N17	25	34 90 B
Shelburne Rd. N7	47	30 85 B
Shelbury Cl. Sid	90	46 72 C
Shelbury Rd. SE22	75	34 74 B
Sheldon Ave. Ilf	28	43 90 D
Sheldon Ave. N6	36	27 88 D
Sheldon Cl. SE20	97	34 69 B
Sheldon Rd. Bexh	79	48 76 B
Sheldon Rd. Dag	52	48 84 C
Sheldon Rd. N18	17	33 92 A
Sheldon Rd. NW2	46	23 85 B
Sheldon St. Croy	105	32 65 C
Sheldrake Pl. W8	62	25 79 A
Sheldrick Cl. SW19	95	26 69 D
Shelford Pl. N16	37	32 86 D
Shelford Rd. Barn	11	23 95 C
Shelford Rise. SE19	97	33 70 D
Shelgate Rd. SW11	74	27 74 B
Shell Cl. Brom	107	42 67 C
Shelley Ave. E12	50	42 84 A
Shelley Ave. Grnf	53	14 82 B
Shelley Ave. Horn	42	51 87 D
Shelley Cl. Grnf	53	14 82 B
Shelley Cl. Orp	108	45 65 C
Shelley Cres. Houn	70	11 76 B
Shelley Cres. Sthl	53	12 81 D
Shelley Dri. Well	78	45 76 A
Shelley Gdns. Wem	33	17 86 A
Shellness Rd. E5	48	34 85 D
Shell Rd. SE13	76	37 75 B
Shellwood Rd. SW11	74	27 76 D
Shelmerdine Cl. E3	57	37 81 A
Shelson Ave. Felt	81	09 71 B
Shelton Rd. SW19	95	25 69 A
Shelton St. WC2	3	30 81 C
Shenfield Rd. Wdf Gn	27	40 91 D
Shenfield St. N1	48	33 83 C
Shenley Ave. Ruis	31	09 86 B
Shenley Rd. Houn	70	12 76 A
Shenley Rd. SE5	75	33 76 A
Shenstone Cl. Bexh	79	50 75 D
Shenstone Gdns. Ilf	28	46 89 C
Shenstone Gdns. Rom	30	53 90 A
Shepherd Cl. W1	2	28 80 A
Shepherdess Pl. N1	4	32 82 B
Shepherdess Wlk. N1	48	32 83 C
Shepherd Market. W1	2	28 80 D
Shepherd's Bush Green. W12	62	23 79 A
Shepherd's Bush Market. W12	62	23 79 A
Shepherd's Bush Pl. W12	62	23 79 B
Shepherd's Bush Rd. W6	62	23 79 C
Shepherds Cl. N6	36	28 88 D
Shepherds Cl. Orp	108	45 65 D
Shepherds Cl. Rom	41	47 88 B
Shepherd's Hill. N6	36	29 88 C
Shepherds La. Dart	80	53 74 C
Shepherd's La. E9	48	35 84 A
Shepherd's Path. NW3	46	26 85 D
Shepherds Pl. W1	6	28 80 A
Shepherd St. W1	6	28 80 D
Shepherd's Wlk. NW3	46	26 85 D
Shepley Cl. Cars	104	28 65 C
Sheppard Cl. Surb	93	18 68 C
Sheppard's Ct. Har	33	15 87 A
Sheppard St. E16	58	39 82 D
Shepperd St. E3	57	37 82 D
Shepperton Rd. N1	48	32 83 B
Shepperton Rd. Orp	108	44 67 C
Sheppey Cl. Eri	68	52 77 D
Sheppey Gdns. Dag	52	47 84 C
Sheppey Rd. Dag	52	47 84 C
Sheppey Wlk. N1	48	32 84 A
Sherard Rd. SE9	77	42 74 A
Sheraton St. W1	2	29 81 D
Sherborne Ave. Enf	14	35 97 C
Sherborne Ave. Sthl	59	13 78 A
Sherborne Cres. Cars	104	27 66 A
Sherborne Gdns. NW9	22	19 89 A
Sherborne Gdns. W13	54	16 81 B
Sherborne La. EC4	8	32 80 B
Sherborne Rd. Felt	81	08 73 D
Sherborne Rd. Orp	108	45 67 B
Sherborne Rd. Sutt	103	25 66 C
Sherborne St. N1	48	32 83 B
Sherboro Rd. N15	37	33 88 D
Sherbrooke Cl. Bexh	79	49 75 C
Sherbrooke Rd. SW6	62	24 77 C
Sherbrook Gdns. N21	17	31 94 B
Shere Ave. Sutt	110	23 62 C
Sheredan Rd. E4	18	38 92 D
Shere Rd. Ilf	40	43 88 A
Sherfield Gdns. SW15	72	21 74 D
Sheridan Cl. Rom	30	53 91 C
Sheridan Cres. Chis	100	43 69 D
Sheridan Gdns. Har	33	17 88 D
Sheridan Pl. Har	33	15 87 A
Sheridan Rd. Belv	67	49 78 A
Sheridan Rd. Bexh	79	48 75 A
Sheridan Rd. E12	50	42 85 D
Sheridan Rd. E7	39	39 86 D
Sheridan Rd. Rich	83	17 72 C
Sheridan Rd. SW19	95	24 69 B
Sheridan St. E1	57	35 81 C
Sheridan Wlk. Cars	111	27 64 D
Sheridan Wlk. NW11	35	25 88 C
Sheringham Ave. E12	50	42 85 B
Sheringham Ave. N14	12	29 95 D
Sheringham Ave. Rom	41	50 88 C
Sheringham Ave. Twick	82	13 73 C
Sheringham Dri. Bark	51	46 85 C
Sheringham Rd. N7	48	31 84 A
Sheringham Rd. SE20	98	35 68 A
Sherington Avenue. Pnr	20	13 91 C
Sherington Rd. SE7	65	40 77 B
Sherland Rd. Twick	83	15 73 D
Sherlies Ave. Orp	108	45 65 A
Sherlock Mews. W1	2	28 81 A
Shermanbury Pl. Eri	68	51 77 D
Sherman Rd. Brom	99	40 69 A
Shernhall St. E17	38	38 88 A
Shernhall St. E17	26	38 89 C
Sherrard Rd. E12	50	41 85 D
Sherrard Rd. E7	50	41 84 A
Sherrards Way. Barn	11	25 95 D
Sherrick Green Rd. NW10	45	22 85 D
Sherriff Rd. NW6	46	25 84 A
Sherringham Ave. Felt	81	10 72 C
Sherringham Ave. N17	25	34 90 C
Sherrock Gdns. NW4	22	22 89 C
Shert Path. SE18	66	43 77 B
Sherwin Rd. SE14	76	35 76 B
Sherwood Ave. E18	27	40 89 B
Sherwood Ave. Grnf	44	15 85 C
Sherwood Ave. Ruis	31	09 88 C
Sherwood Ave. SW16	96	29 70 D
Sherwood Cl. Bex	79	47 74 C
Sherwood Cl. SW15	72	22 75 B
Sherwood Cl. W13	54	16 80 D
Sherwood Gdns. Bark	51	44 84 D
Sherwood Park Ave. Sid	78	46 74 D
Sherwood Park Rd. Mit	96	29 68 D
Sherwood Park Rd. Sutt	110	25 64 C
Sherwood Rd. Croy	105	34 66 D
Sherwood Rd. Hamp	82	14 71 C
Sherwood Rd. Har	32	14 86 A
Sherwood Rd. Ilf	28	44 89 D
Sherwood Rd. NW4	22	23 89 A
Sherwood Rd. SW19	95	24 70 D
Sherwood Rd. Well	78	45 75 A
Sherwood St. N20	15	26 93 D
Sherwood St. W1	6	29 80 A
Sherwood. Surb	101	17 65 B
Sherwood Terr. N20	15	26 93 D
Sherwood Way. W Wick	106	38 65 A
Shetland Rd. E3	49	36 83 D
Shield Dri. Brent	60	16 77 B
Shieldhall St. SE2	67	47 78 A
Shield Rd. Ashf	81	08 71 B
Shifford Path. SE23	88	35 72 D
Shillibeer Pl. W1	1	27 81 A
Shillingford St. N1	48	31 84 D
Shillington St. SW11	74	27 76 C
Shillitoe Rd. N13	17	32 92 C
Shinfield St. W12	56	23 81 C
Shinglewell Rd. Eri	67	49 77 C
Ship Alley. W4	61	19 77 A
Ship and Mermaid Row. SE1	8	33 79 A
Shipka Rd. SW12	86	28 73 D
Ship Lane Pas. SW14	72	20 76 C
Ship La. SW14	72	20 76 C
Shipman Rd. E16	58	41 81 C
Shipman Rd. SE23	88	35 72 B
Ship St. SE8	76	37 76 A
Ship Tavern Pas. EC3	8	33 80 A
Shipton Cl. Dag	41	47 86 D
Shipton St. E2	4	33 82 B
Shipwright Yd. SE1	8	33 80 C
Shirburn Cl. SE23	88	35 73 A
Shirbutt St. E14	57	37 80 B
Shirebrook Rd. SE3	77	41 75 B
Shire Ct. Well	67	47 79 D
Shirehall Cl. NW4	35	23 88 D
Shirehall Gdns. NW4	35	23 88 D
Shirehall La. NW4	35	23 88 D
Shirehall Park. NW4	35	23 88 D
Shires The. Rich	83	18 71 A
Shirland Mews. W9	56	24 82 B
Shirland Rd. W9	56	25 82 C
Shirley Ave. Croy	106	35 66 C
Shirley Ave. Sutt	110	24 62 D
Shirley Ave. Sutt	111	27 64 A
Shirley Church Rd. Croy	106	36 65 C
Shirley Cl. Dart	80	53 75 C
Shirley Cl. Houn	70	14 74 A
Shirley Cres. Beck	98	36 68 C
Shirley Dri. Houn	70	14 74 A
Shirley Gdns. Bark	51	45 84 A
Shirley Gdns. Horn	42	53 86 A
Shirley Gdns. W7	54	16 80 C
Shirley Gr. N9	18	35 94 B
Shirley Gr. SW11	74	28 75 A
Shirley House Dri. SE7	65	41 77 C
Shirley Hts. Wall	111	29 62 A
Shirley Oaks. Croy	106	35 66 D
Shirley Park Rd. Croy	106	35 66 C
Shirley Rd. Croy	105	34 66 D
Shirley Rd. E15	50	39 84 C
Shirley Rd. Enf	13	32 96 A
Shirley Rd. Sid	90	45 72 C
Shirley Rd. W4	61	20 79 B
Shirley Rd. Wall	111	29 62 A
Shirley St. E16	58	39 81 D
Shirley St. N1	47	30 83 B
Shirley Way. Croy	106	36 65 D
Shirlock Rd. NW3	47	27 85 B
Shobden Rd. N17	25	32 90 B

Street	Page	Grid
Shoebury Rd. E6	50	42 84 D
Shoe La. EC4	3	31 81 C
Sholto Rd. Houn	69	07 74 A
Shooters Ave. Har	21	17 89 C
Shooters Hill Rd. SE10	76	38 76 B
Shooters Hill Rd. SE18	77	42 76 A
Shooters Hill Rd. SE3	77	39 76 B
Shooters Hill. SE18	78	43 76 A
Shooters Hill. Well	78	44 76 C
Shooters Rd. Enf	13	31 97 B
Shoot-up Hill. NW2	46	24 84 A
Shore Cl. Felt	81	10 73 A
Shore Cl. Hamp	82	12 71 C
Shoreditch High St. E1	4	33 82 C
Shore Gr. Felt	82	13 72 A
Shoreham Cl. Croy	106	35 67 C
Shoreham Rd. SW18	73	25 74 B
Shoreham Rd. Orp	100	46 69 D
Shoreham Way. Brom	107	40 67 C
Shore Pl. E9	49	35 84 C
Shore Rd. E9	49	35 84 C
Shorncliffe Rd. SE1	63	33 78 D
Shorndean St. SE6	88	38 73 C
Shorne Cl. Sid	78	46 74 D
Shornefield Cl. Brom	100	43 68 A
Shornells Way. SE2	67	47 78 C
Shorrolds Rd. SW6	62	25 77 C
Shortcroft Rd. Eps	109	21 63 D
Shortcrofts Rd. Dag	52	48 84 B
Shorter St. E1	8	33 80 B
Shortfield. Wall	111	28 63 B
Shortgate. N12	15	24 92 B
Shortlands Cl. N18	17	32 93 D
Shortlands Gdns. Brom	99	39 69 C
Shortlands Gr. Brom	98	38 68 B
Shortlands Rd. Brom	99	39 69 C
Shortlands Rd. E10	38	37 87 B
Shortlands Rd. King	93	18 70 D
Shortlands. W6	62	23 78 B
Short Rd. E11	39	39 86 A
Short Rd. E15	49	38 83 B
Short Rd. W4	61	21 77 A
Shorts Croft. NW9	22	19 89 D
Shorts Rd. WC2	3	30 81 C
Shorts Rd. Cars	111	27 64 C
Short St. SE1	7	31 79 A
Short Way. N12	24	27 91 A
Shortway. SE9	77	42 75 A
Short Way. Twick	82	14 73 A
Shotfield. Wall	111	28 63 B
Shottendane Rd. SW6	73	25 76 A
Shottery Cl. SE9	89	42 72 C
Shottfield Ave. SW14	72	21 75 C
Shoulder of Mutton Alley. E14	57	36 80 A
Shouldham St. W1	1	27 81 A
Shrapnel Cl. SE18	65	42 77 C
Shrapnel Rd. SE9	77	42 75 B
Shrewsbury Ave. Har	21	18 89 C
Shrewsbury Ave. SW14	72	20 75 D
Shrewsbury Cl. Surb	101	18 65 A
Shrewsbury Cres. NW10	45	20 83 B
Shrewsbury La. SE18	78	43 76 B
Shrewsbury Mews. W2	56	25 81 A
Shrewsbury Rd. Beck	98	36 68 A
Shrewsbury Rd. Cars	104	27 66 A
Shrewsbury Rd. E7	50	41 84 B
Shrewsbury Rd. N11	24	29 91 B
Shrewsbury Rd. W2	56	25 81 C
Shrewsbury Wlk. Islw	71	16 75 A
Shrewton Rd. SW17	96	27 70 D
Shroffold Rd. Brom	89	39 72 D
Shropshire Cl. Mit	96	30 68 C
Shropshire Pl. WC1	2	29 82 D
Shropshire Rd. N22	24	30 91 D
Shroton St. NW1	1	27 81 A
Shrubberies The. E18	27	40 90 C
Shrubbery Gdns. N21	17	31 94 B
Shrubbery Rd. N9	17	34 93 C
Shrubbery Rd. Sthl	53	13 80 C
Shrubbery Rd. SW16	86	30 71 A
Shrubbery The. E11	39	40 88 B
Shrubland Gr. Wor Pk	103	23 65 C
Shrubland Rd. E10	38	37 87 A
Shrubland Rd. E17	38	37 88 A
Shrubland Rd. E8	48	34 83 A
Shrublands Ave. Croy	106	37 65 C
Shrublands Cl. Chig	28	44 91 A
Shrublands Cl. N20	15	26 93 B
Shuna Wlk. N1	48	32 84 B
Shurland Ave. Barn	11	26 95 D
Shuttle Cl. Sid	90	45 73 B
Shuttlemead. Bex	79	48 74 D
Shuttle Rd. Dart	80	52 75 A
Shuttle St. E1	57	34 82 C
Shuttleworth Rd. SW11	74	27 76 C
Sibella Rd. SW4	74	29 76 D
Sibley Cl. Bexh	79	48 74 A
Sibley Gr. E12	50	42 84 D
Sibthorpe Rd. SE12	89	41 73 A
Sibthorp Rd. Mit	96	27 69 D
Sibton Rd. Cars	104	26 64 A
Sicilian Ave. WC1	3	30 81 A
Sickert Ct (off Canonbury St). N1	48	32 84 C
Sickert Ct (off Northampton St). N1	48	32 84 C
Sidbury St. SW6	73	24 76 A
Sidcup By Pass Rd. Sid	100	46 70 A
Sidcup Hill. Sid	90	46 71 D
Sidcup Rd. SE9	77	41 74 C
Sidcup Rd. SE9	89	42 73 D
Siddon La. NW1	1	27 82 D
Siddons Rd. Croy	105	31 65 C
Siddons Rd. N17	25	34 90 A
Siddons Rd. SE23	88	36 72 A
Side Rd. E17	38	36 88 B
Sidewood Rd. SE9	90	44 73 D
Sidford Pl. SE1	7	30 79 D
Sidings The. E11	38	38 87 D
Sidmouth Ave. Islw	71	15 76 C
Sidmouth Dri. Ruis	31	10 86 B
Sidmouth Rd. E10	38	38 86 C
Sidmouth Rd. NW2	46	23 84 C
Sidmouth Rd. Orp	100	46 68 D
Sidmouth Rd. SE15	75	33 76 B
Sidmouth Rd. Well	67	47 77 C
Sidmouth St. WC1	3	30 82 B
Sidney Ave. N13	16	30 92 D
Sidney Gdns. Brent	60	17 77 B
Sidney Gr. EC1	3	31 82 B
Sidney Gr. EC1	48	31 83 D
Sidney Rd. Beck	98	36 69 C
Sidney Rd. E7	39	40 86 C
Sidney Rd. Har	20	14 89 A
Sidney Rd. N22	24	30 91 D
Sidney Rd. SE25	105	34 67 A
Sidney Rd. SW9	74	30 76 D
Sidney Rd. Twick	71	16 74 D
Sidney Sq. E1	57	35 81 A
Sidney St. E1	57	35 81 A
Sidworth St. E8	48	34 84 D
Siebert Rd. SE3	65	40 77 A
Siemens Rd. SE18	65	41 79 D
Sigdon Pas. E8	48	34 85 C
Sigdon Rd. E8	48	34 85 C
Sigs The. Pnr	31	10 88 D
Silbury Ho. SE26	87	34 72 C
Silbury St. N1	4	32 82 B
Silchester Rd. W10	56	23 81 D
Silecroft Rd. Bexh	79	49 76 A
Silesia Bldgs. E8	48	34 84 D
Silex St. SE1	7	31 79 B
Silk Cl. SE12	77	40 74 A
Silkfield Rd. NW9	34	21 88 B
Silk Mills Rd. SE13	76	37 76 D
Silk Mills Path. SE13	76	38 76 C
Silksteam Rd. Edg	22	20 90 A
Silk St. EC2	4	32 81 A
Silsoe Rd. N22	24	30 89 B
Silver Birch Ave. E4	26	36 91 B
Silver Cl. Har	20	14 91 D
Silvercliffe.Gdns. Barn	12	27 96 C
Silver Cres. W4	61	19 78 B
Silverdale Ave. Ilf	40	45 88 B
Silverdale Cl. Nthlt	43	12 85 D
Silverdale Cl. Sutt	110	24 64 B
Silverdale Cl. W7	54	15 80 D
Silverdale Dri. Sun	91	10 69 D
Silverdale. Enf	12	30 96 C
Silverdale Rd. Bexh	79	49 76 D
Silverdale Rd. E4	26	38 91 B
Silverdale Rd. Orp	100	44 68 C
Silverdale Rd. Orp	100	46 68 A
Silverdale.SE26	88	35 71 A
Silverhall St. Islw	71	16 75 A
Silverholme Cl. Har	33	18 87 A
Silver Jubilee Way. Houn	69	10 76 D
Silver La. W Wick	106	38 65 B
Silverleigh Rd. Th Hth	105	31 67 A
Silvermere Ave. Rom	29	49 91 B
Silvermere Rd. SE6	76	37 74 D
Silver Pl. W1	6	29 80 A
Silver Rd. W12	56	23 80 B
Silver Spring Cl. Eri	67	49 77 B
Silver St. Enf	13	32 96 B
Silver St. N18	17	33 92 A
Silverston Way. Stan	21	17 91 A
Silverthorne Rd. SW8	74	28 76 D
Silverthorn Gdns. E4	18	37 93 A
Silverton Rd. W6	62	23 77 B
Silvertown By-Pass. E16	58	41 80 D
Silvertown Way. E16	58	39 80 B
Silvertree La. Grnf	53	14 82 B
Silver Way. Rom	29	49 89 B
Silver Wlk. SE16	57	36 80 D
Silverwood Cl. Beck	98	37 70 C
Silverwood Cl. Nthwd	19	08 90 A
Silvester Rd. SE22	75	34 74 A
Silvester St. SE1	8	32 79 B
Silwood St. SE16	64	35 78 C
Simla Cl. SE14	64	36 77 A
Simmons Cl. N20	16	27 93 A
Simmons La. E4	18	38 93 B
Simmons Rd. SE18	66	43 78 D
Simmons Way. N20	16	27 93 A
Simms Cl. Cars	104	27 65 A
Simms Rd. SE1	63	34 78 A
Simnel Rd. SE12	89	40 73 B
Simon Cl. W11	56	25 80 A
Simonds Rd. E10	38	37 86 A
Simone Cl. Brom	99	41 69 B
Simons Wlk. E15	49	38 85 D
Simpson Rd. Houn	70	12 74 D
Simpson Rd. Rich	83	17 71 A
Simpson's Rd. Brom	99	40 68 A
Simpson's Rd. E14	57	37 80 B
Simrose Ct. SW18	73	25 74 A
Sims Cl. Rom	30	51 89 D
Sims Wlk. SE3	77	39 75 D
Sinclair Ct. Beck	98	37 70 C
Sinclair Gdns. W14	62	23 79 B
Sinclair Gr. NW11	35	23 88 D
Sinclair Rd. E4	18	36 92 D
Sinclair Rd. W14	62	24 79 C
Sinclare Cl. Enf	13	33 97 B
Singapore Rd. W13	54	16 80 C
Singer St. EC2	4	32 82 B
Singleton Cl. Croy	105	32 66 A
Singleton Cl. SW17	96	27 70 D
Singleton Rd. Dag	52	48 85 D
Singleton Scarp. N12	15	25 92 C
Sinnott Rd. E17	26	35 90 A
Sion Ct. Twick	83	16 73 D
Sion Rd. Twick	83	16 73 D
Sipson Rd. W.Dray	69	07 76 B
Sipson Way. W.Dray	69	07 76 A
Sir Alexander Cl. W3	55	21 80 D
Sir Alexander Rd. W3	55	21 80 D
Sirdar Rd. Mit	96	28 70 A
Sirdar Rd. N22	25	32 90 C
Sirdar Rd. W11	56	24 80 A
Sir Thomas More Estate. SW3	62	26 77 B
Sise La. EC4	4	32 81 D
Sisley Rd. Bark	51	45 83 B
Sispara Gdns. SW18	73	24 74 D
Sissinghurst Rd. Croy	105	34 66 A
Sisters Ave. SW11	74	27 75 D
Sistova Rd. SW12	86	28 73 D
Sittingbourne Ave. Enf	13	32 95 D
Siverst Cl. Nthlt	43	13 84 B
Siviter Way. Dag	52	49 84 D
Siward Rd. Brom	99	41 68 A
Siward Rd. N17	25	32 90 B
Siward Rd. SW17	95	26 72 C
Sixth Ave. E12	50	42 85 B
Sixth Ave. W10	56	24 82 A
Sixth Cross Rd. Twick	82	14 72 C
Skardu Rd. NW2	46	24 85 C
Skeena Hill SW18	85	24 73 A
Skeffington Rd. E6	50	42 83 B
Skelbrook St. SW18	85	26 72 A
Skelgill Rd. SW15	73	24 75 D
Skelley Rd. E15	50	39 84 D
Skelton Cl. E8	48	33 84 B
Skelton Rd. E7	50	40 84 A
Skelton's La. E10	38	37 87 B
Skelwith Rd. W6	62	23 77 A
Sketchley Gdns. SE16	64	35 78 D
Sketty Rd. Enf	13	33 96 B
Skiers St. E15	50	39 83 A
Skiffington Cl. SW2	87	31 73 C
Skin Market Pl. SE1	8	32 80 C
Skinner Ct. E2	4	34 83 D
Skinner Pl. SW1	9	28 78 A
Skinners La. EC4	8	32 80 A
Skinner St. EC1	3	31 82 C
Skipton St. SE1	7	31 79 D
Skipworth Rd. E9	49	35 83 A
Skomer Wlk. N1	48	32 84 C
Sky Peals Rd. Wdf Gr	26	38 90 D
Sladebrook Rd. SE3	77	41 75 B
Sladedale Rd. SE18	66	45 78 C
Slade Gdns. Eri	80	51 76 B
Slade Green Rd. Eri	68	52 77 C
Sladen Pl. E5	48	34 85 B

Slades Cl. Enf....13 31 96 A
Slades Dri. Chis....90 44 72 C
Slades Dri. SE9....90 44 71 A
Slades Gdns. Enf....13 31 96 A
Slades Hill. Enf....13 31 96 A
Slades Rise. Enf....13 31 96 A
Slade The. SE18....66 44 77 A
Slade Wlk. SE17....63 32 77 A
Slagrove Pl. SE13....76 37 74 B
Slaidburn St. SW10....62 26 77 A
Slaithwaite Rd. SE13....76 38 75 C
Slaney Pl. N7....48 31 85 C
Sleaford St. SW8....10 29 77 C
Slewins Cl. Horn....42 53 88 A
Slewins La. Horn....42 53 88 A
Slindon Ct. N16....37 33 86 D
Slingsby Pl. WC2....7 30 80 A
Slippers Pl. SE16....63 34 79 D
Sloane Ave. SW3....9 27 78 A
Sloane Ct E. SW3....9 28 78 C
Sloane Ct W. SW3....9 28 78 C
Sloane Gdns. Orp....108 44 65 C
Sloane Gdns. SW1....9 28 78 A
Sloane Sq. SW1....9 28 78 A
Sloane St. SW1....5 27 79 D
Sloane Terr. SW1....9 28 78 A
Sloane Wlk. Croy....106 36 67 D
Slough La. NW9....34 20 88 C
Sly St. E1....57 34 81 D
Smallberry Ave. Islw....71 15 76 D
Smallbrook Mews. W2....1 26 81 D
Smalley Cl. N16....37 33 86 D
Smallwood Rd. SW17....85 26 71 B
Smardale Rd. SW18....73 26 74 A
Smarden Cl. Belv....67 49 78 C
Smarden Gr. SE9....89 42 71 B
Smart Cl. Rom....30 52 90 B
Smart's Pl. N18....17 34 92 C
Smart's Pl. WC2....3 30 81 C
Smart St. E2....57 35 82 B
Smeaton Rd. SW18....85 25 73 A
Smedley St. SW8....74 29 76 D
Smeed Rd. E3....43 37 84 C
Smithfield St. EC1....3 31 81 B
Smith Hill. Brent....60 18 77 A
Smithies Rd. SE2....66 46 78 B
Smith's Ct. W1....6 29 80 A
Smith's Ct. W1....6 29 80 B
Smithson Rd. N17....25 32 90 B
Smith Sq. SW1....7 30 79 C
Smith St. Surb....101 18 67 D
Smith St. SW3....9 27 78 D
Smith's Yd. Croy....105 32 65 C
Smith Terr. SW3....9 27 78 D
Smithwood Cl. SW19....85 24 72 A
Smithy St. E1....57 35 81 A
Smock Wlk. Croy....105 32 67 C
Smoothfield. Houn....70 13 75 C
Smyrk's Rd. SE17....63 33 78 C
Smyrna Rd. NW6....46 25 84 C
Smythe St. E14....57 37 80 B
Snakes La. Barn....12 29 96 A
Snakes La. Wdf Gn....27 40 91 B
Snaresbrook Rd. E11....27 39 89 D
Snarsgate St. W10....56 23 81 A
Sneath Ave. NW11....35 24 87 A
Snell's Park. N18....25 33 91 B
Sneyd Rd. NW2....46 23 85 A
Snowbury Rd. SW6....73 25 76 D
Snowbury Rd. SW6....73 25 76 D
Snowden St. EC2....4 33 82 C
Snowdon Ct. Rom....30 53 89 C
Snowdrop Cl. Hamp....92 13 70 A
Snowdrop Path. Rom....30 53 91 D
Snowfields. SE1....8 32 79 B
Snow Hill. EC1....3 31 81 B
Snowshill Rd. E12....50 42 85 C
Soames St. SE15....75 33 75 B
Soames Wlk. N Mal....94 21 69 A
Socket La. Brom....107 40 67 D
Soho Sq. W1....2 29 81 D
Soho St. W1....2 29 81 D
Solebay St. E2....57 36 82 C
Solent Rd. NW6....46 25 85 C
Soley Mews. WC1....3 31 82 A
Solna Ave. SW15....73 23 74 A
Solna Rd. N21....17 32 94 B
Solomon's Pas. SE15....75 34 75 D
Solon New Rd. SW4....74 30 75 C
Solon Rd. SW2....74 30 75 C
Solway Cl. E8....48 33 84 B
Solway Cl. Houn....70 12 75 A
Solway Rd. N22....25 31 90 B
Solway Rd. SE22....75 34 75 C
Somaford Gr. Barn....11 26 95 D

Somali Rd. NW2....46 24 85 D
Somerby Rd. Bark....51 44 84 D
Somerfield Rd. N4....37 31 86 B
Somerford Cl. Pnr....19 10 89 C
Somerford Gr. N16....48 33 85 B
Somerford Gr. N17....25 34 91 C
Somerford Grove Estate. N16....48 33 85 B
Somerford St. E1....57 34 82 D
Somerhill Ave. Sid....90 46 73 B
Somerhill Rd. Well....78 46 76 D
Somerleyton Pas. SW9....75 31 75 D
Somerleyton Rd. SW9....75 31 75 C
Somersby Gdns. Ilf....39 42 88 B
Somers Cl. NW1....47 29 83 D
Somers Cres. W2....1 27 81 C
Somerset Ave. SW20....94 22 69 D
Somerset Ave. Well....78 45 75 D
Somerset Cl. Eps....109 21 62 A
Somerset Cl. N.Mal....102 21 67 C
Somerset Cl. Wdf Gn....27 40 90 A
Somerset Estate. SW11....73 26 76 B
Somerset Estate. SW11....74 27 76 A
Somerset Gdns. N6....36 28 87 A
Somerset Gdns. SE13....76 37 76 D
Somerset Gdns. SW16....96 30 68 B
Somerset Gdns. Tedd....83 15 71 C
Somerset Rd. Barn....11 26 95 A
Somerset Rd. Brent....60 17 77 B
Somerset Rd. Dart....80 52 74 D
Somerset Rd. E17....38 37 88 C
Somerset Rd. Har....32 14 88 A
Somerset Rd. King....93 18 69 D
Somerset Rd. N17....25 33 89 B
Somerset Rd. N18....17 33 92 D
Somerset Rd. NW4....23 23 89 C
Somerset Rd. Orp....108 46 66 A
Somerset Rd. SW19....85 23 72 D
Somerset Rd. Tedd....83 15 71 C
Somerset Rd. W13....54 17 80 C
Somerset Rd. W4....61 20 79 D
Somerset Sq. W14....62 24 79 B
Somerset Waye. Houn....59 12 77 C
Somersham Rd. Bexh....79 48 76 C
Somers Pl. SW2....86 30 73 B
Somers Rd. E17....26 36 89 D
Somers Rd. SW2....74 30 74 D
Somers Town Estate. NW1....47 29 83 C
Somerton Ave. Rich....72 19 75 B
Somerton Rd. NW2....35 24 86 C
Somerton Rd. SE15....75 34 75 D
Somertrees Ave. SE12....89 40 72 B
Somervell Rd. Har....43 13 85 C
Somerville Rd. Dart....80 54 74 D
Somerville Rd. Rom....41 47 88 A
Somerville Rd. SE20....98 35 70 D
Sonderburg Rd. N7....36 30 86 D
Sondes St. SE17....63 32 77 B
Sonia Ct. Har....33 15 88 D
Sonia Gdns. Houn....59 13 77 C
Sonia Gdns. N12....15 26 92 A
Sonia Gdns. NW10....45 21 85 B
Sonning Rd. SE25....105 34 67 C
Sophia Cl. N7....47 30 84 B
Sophia Rd. E10....38 37 87 D
Sophia Rd. E16....58 40 81 D
Sopwith Rd. Houn....59 11 77 C
Sorrel Wlk. Rom....30 51 89 B
Sorrento Rd. Sutt....103 25 65 D
Sotheby Rd. N5....37 32 86 C
Sotheran Cl. E8....48 34 83 A
Sotheron Rd. SW6....62 25 77 D
Soudan Rd. SW11....74 27 76 B
Souldern Rd. W14....62 23 79 D
Sounding's Alley. E3....49 37 83 A
South Access Rd. E17....38 36 88 C
South Acre. NW9....22 21 90 D
South Africa Rd. W12....55 22 80 B
Southall Ct. Sthl....53 12 80 B
Southall La. Sthl....59 11 78 A
Southall Pl. SE1....8 32 79 B
Southampton Bldgs. WC2....3 31 81 A
Southampton Gdns. Mit....104 30 67 A
Southampton Pl. WC1....3 30 81 A
Southampton Rd. Houn....69 07 74 C
Southampton Rd. NW5....47 27 85 D
Southampton Row. WC1....3 30 81 A
Southampton St. WC2....7 30 80 A
Southampton Way. SE5....75 33 76 B
Southampton Way. SE5....63 33 77 C
Southam St. W10....56 24 82 C
South Audley Sq. W1....6 28 80 C
South Ave. Cars....111 28 63 C
South Ave. E4....18 37 94 B
South Ave. N2....23 25 89 D
South Avenue Gdns. Sthl....53 12 80 B

South Ave. Rich....72 19 76 C
South Ave. Sthl....53 12 80 B
South Ave. W10....56 23 82 A
South Bank Lodge. Surb....101 18 67 C
Southbank. Surb....101 16 66 B
South Bank. Surb....101 18 67 C
South Bank Terr. Surb....101 18 67 C
South Birkbeck Rd. E11....38 38 86 D
South Black Lion La. W6....61 22 78 C
South Bolton Gdns. SW10....62 25 78 D
South Border The. Pur....111 30 62 C
Southborough Cl. Surb....101 17 66 D
Southborough La. Brom....107 42 67 B
Southborough Rd. Brom....99 42 68 C
Southborough Rd. E9....49 35 83 B
Southborough Rd. Surb....101 18 66 C
South Boundary Rd. E12....39 42 86 D
Southbourne Ave. NW9....22 20 90 D
Southbourne. Brom....107 40 66 A
Southbourne Cl. Pnr....32 12 87 A
Southbourne Cres. NW4....23 24 89 C
Southbourne Gdns. Ilf....51 44 85 C
Southbourne Gdns. Ruis....31 10 86 D
Southbourne Gdns. Ruis....32 11 87 C
Southbourne Gdns. SE12....77 40 74 B
Southbridge Pl. Croy....112 32 64 A
Southbridge Rd. Croy....112 32 64 A
Southbridge Way. Sthl....59 12 79 A
Southbrook Rd. SE12....77 39 74 D
Southbrook Rd. SW16....96 30 69 A
Southbury Ave. Enf....13 34 96 C
Southbury Rd. Enf....13 33 96 D
South Carriage Dri. SW1....5 27 79 B
South Carriage Dri. SW7....5 27 79 A
Southchurch Rd. E6....50 42 83 D
South Cl. Barn....11 24 96 B
South Cl. Bexh....79 47 75 D
South Cl. Dag....52 49 83 A
South Cl. Mord....103 25 67 C
South Cl. N6....36 28 88 D
South Cl. Pnr....20 11 90 B
South Cl. Pnr....32 12 87 B
South Cl. Twick....82 13 72 C
Southcombe St. W14....62 24 78 A
Southcote Ave. Felt....81 10 72 A
Southcote Ave. Surb....102 19 66 B
Southcote Rd. E17....38 35 88 B
Southcote Rd. N19....47 29 85 A
Southcote Rd. S Croy....112 33 62 D
Southcote Rd. SE25....105 34 67 D
South Countess Rd. E17....26 36 89 B
South Cres. WC1....2 29 81 B
Southcroft Ave. Well....78 46 75 A
Southcroft Ave. W Wick....106 38 65 A
Southcroft Rd. Orp....108 45 65 C
Southcroft Rd. SW17....96 28 70 A
South Cross Rd. Ilf....28 44 89 C
South Croxted Rd. SE21....87 32 72 D
Southdale. Chig....28 44 91 B
Southdean Gdns. SW19....85 24 72 B
Southdene. Ct. N11....16 29 93 C
Southdown Ave. W7....60 16 78 A
Southdown Cres. Har....32 14 87 C
Southdown Cres. Ilf....40 45 88 A
Southdown Dri. SW20....95 23 70 D
Southdown Rd. Cars....111 28 62 A
Southdown Rd. Horn....42 52 87 B
Southdown Rd. SW20....95 23 69 B
South Dri. E12....39 42 86 D
South Dri. Rom....30 53 89 A
South Dri. Ruis....31 09 87 C
South Dri. Sutt....110 24 62 A
South Ealing Rd. W5....60 17 79 D
South Eastern Ave. N9....7 33 93 D
South Eaton Pl. SW1....9 28 78 A
South Eden Park Rd. Beck....106 37 67 B
South Edwardes Sq. W8....62 25 79 C
Southend Arterial Rd Horn....30 54 89 B
Southend Arterial Rd. Rom....30 53 90 D
South End Cl. NW3....47 27 85 A
Southend Cl. SE9....78 43 74 D
Southend Cres. SE9....78 43 74 D
South End Green. NW3....47 27 85 A
Southend La. SE26....88 36 71 B
Southend La. SE6....88 37 71 B
Southend Rd. Beck....98 37 70 C
Southend Rd. E18....27 40 90 A
Southend Rd. E6....50 42 84 D
South End Rd. NW3....47 27 85 A
South End Row. W8....62 25 79 D
South End. W8....62 25 79 D
Southern Ave. Felt....81 10 73 C
Southern Ave. SE25....97 33 68 B

Entry	Page	Ref
Southern Gr. E3	57	36 82 D
Southern Perimeter Rd. Houn	69	08 74 A
Southern Rd. E13	50	40 83 D
Southern Rd. N2	24	27 89 D
Southern Row. W10	56	24 82 C
Southern St. N1	47	30 83 D
Southern Way. Rom	41	49 88 C
Southern Way. Rom	41	49 88 C
Southerton Rd. W6	62	23 78 A
South Esk Rd. E7	50	41 84 A
Southey Rd. N15	37	33 88 A
Southey Rd. SW19	95	25 70 C
Southey Rd. SW9	37	31 76 A
Southey St. SE20	98	35 70 D
Southfield. Barn	71	23 95 D
Southfield Cottages. W7	60	15 79 B
Southfield Gdns. Twick	72	15 71 B
Southfield Park. Har	18	13 89 D
Southfield Rd. Chis	100	46 68 A
Southfield Rd. Enf	14	35 95 C
Southfield Rd. N17	37	20 79 B
Southfield Rd. W4	61	21 79 C
Southfields Ave. Ashf	91	07 70 B
Southfields. E Mol	101	15 67 C
Southfields. NW4	22	22 89 B
Southfields Rd. SW18	73	25 74 C
Southfields. Sutt	103	25 65 A
Southfleet Rd. Orp	108	45 65 C
South Gate Ave. Felt	81	08 71 B
Southgate Gr. N1	48	32 84 D
Southgate Rd. N1	48	32 84 D
Southgate Way. N2	27	27 90 A
South Gdns. SW19	95	26 70 D
South Gr. E17	24	36 88 B
South Gr. N15	37	32 88 B
South Gr. N6	24	28 87 C
South Hill Ave. Har	32	14 86 D
South Hill. Chis		42 70 B
South Hill Gr. Har	44	15 85 A
South Hill Park. NW3	27	27 85 A
South Hill Rd. Brom	99	39 68 C
Southill La. Pnr	19	10 89 D
Southill Rd. Chis	99	42 70 D
South Island Pl. SW9	93	31 77 C
South La. King	93	17 68 B
South Lambeth Pl. SW8	10	30 77 A
South Lambeth Rd. SW8	10	30 77 C
Southland Rd. SE18	66	45 77 D
Southlands Gr. Brom	99	42 68 A
Southlands Rd. Brom	99	41 68 D
Southland Way. Houn		14 74 B
South Lane W. N.Mal	102	20 68 D
South Lodge Ave.	96	30 68 C
South Lodge Cres. Enf	12	29 96 D
South Lodge Dri. N14	12	29 95 B
South Mall. N9	17	34 93 C
South Mead. Eps	109	21 63 D
South Mead. NW9		21 90 B
Southmead Rd. SW19	85	24 73 C
South Molton La. W1		28 81 D
South Molton Rd. E16	58	40 81 C
South Molton St. W1		28 81 D
Southmont Rd. Esh	101	15 65 C
Southmoor Way. E9	49	36 85 D
South Norwood Hill. SE25	97	33 68 B
Southold Rise. SE9		43 72 C
Southolm St. SW11	74	28 76 B
Southover. Brom	99	40 70 A
Southover. Brom	99	40 71 C
Southover. N12	15	25 92 A
South Parade. SW3	62	26 78 D
South Park Cres. Ilf	40	45 86 C
South Park Cres. SE6		39 73 D
South Park Dri. Bark	51	45 85 C
South Park Dri. Ilf	40	45 86 C
South Park Gr. N.Mal	94	20 68 C
South Park Hill Rd. S Croy	112	32 64 B
South Park Rd. Ilf	40	45 86 D
South Park Rd. SW19	95	25 70 A
South Park Terr. Ilf		45 86 C
South Park Way. Ruis	43	11 85 C
Southpar. W4	61	20 78 B
South Pl. EC2	4	32 81 B
South Pl. Mews. EC2	4	32 81 B
South Pl. Surb	101	18 66 B
Southport Rd. SE18	66	44 78 B
South Rd. Edg		19 90 B
South Rd. Eri	68	51 77 D
South Rd. Felt		11 71 C
South Rd. Hamp	92	12 70 B
South Rd. N9	17	34 94 C
South Rd. Rom	41	47 88 A
South Rd. Rom	41	48 88 C
South Rd. SE23	88	35 72 B
South Rd. Sthl	53	12 80 D
South Rd. SW19	95	26 70 A
South Rd. Twick	82	14 72 D
South Rd. W5	60	17 78 B
South Rise. Cars	111	27 62 A
South Row. SE3	77	39 76 D
Southsea Rd. King	93	18 68 C
Southside Common. SW19	95	23 70 B
South Side. W6		21 79 D
Southspring. Sid	90	44 73 B
South Sq. NW11		25 88 D
South Sq. WC1	3	31 81 C
South St. Brom	99	40 69 C
South St. Enf	14	35 95 B
South St. Islw	71	16 75 A
South St. Rain	52	50 83 D
South St. Rom	51	48 88 C
South St. W1	6	28 80 C
South Tenter St. EC4		33 80 B
South Terr. N22	24	29 90 D
South Terr. Surb	101	18 67 C
South Terr. SW7	9	27 78 A
South Vale. Har	44	15 85 A
Southvale Rd. SE3	77	39 76 C
South Vale. SE19	97	33 70 A
Southview Ave. NW10	45	21 85 D
South View. Brom	99	41 69 C
South View Cl. Bex		48 74 D
South View Cres. Ilf	40	43 88 D
Southview Dri. E18		40 89 B
Southview Gdns. Wall	111	29 63 C
Southview Rd. Brom	88	38 71 B
South View Rd. N8	24	30 89 A
South View Rd. Pnr	19	10 91 B
South Villas. NW1		29 84 B
Southville Cl. Eps	109	20 62 B
Southville Cl. Felt	81	09 73 C
Southville Cres. Felt		09 73 C
Southville Rd. Felt	81	09 73 C
Southville Rd. Surb	101	16 66 B
Southville. SW8		29 78 B
Southwark Bridge. EC4		32 80 A
Southwark Bridge Rd. SE1	8	32 80 A
Southwark Park Rd. SE16	63	34 78 A
Southwark Pl. Brom	99	42 68 B
Southwark St. SE1	8	32 80 C
Southwater Cl. E14	57	36 81 D
Southway. Brom		40 66 A
Southway. Cars	110	26 62 D
Southway Cl. W12	61	22 79 B
South Way. Croy		36 65 C
South Way. Har	20	13 89 C
South Way. N11		29 91 A
Southway. N20	15	25 93 A
South Way. N9		35 93 A
Southway. NW11	35	25 88 B
Southway. SW20	95	23 68 D
Southway. Wall	111	29 63 C
South Way. Wem	45	19 85 D
Southwell Ave. Nthlt	43	13 84 A
Southwell Gdns. SW7	62	26 78 A
Southwell Grove Rd. E11	39	39 86 A
Southwell Rd. Har	33	17 88 D
Southwell Rd. SE5	75	32 75 A
Southwell Rd. Th Hth	105	31 67 C
South Western Rd. Twick	71	16 74 D
South West India Dock Entrance. E14	64	38 79 A
Southwest Rd. E11	38	38 87 D
South Wharf Rd. W2	1	26 81 D
Southwick Mews. W2	1	26 81 D
Southwick Pl. W2	1	27 81 C
Southwick St. W2	1	27 81 C
South Wlk. W.Wick	107	39 65 C
Southwold Dri. Bark	51	46 85 C
Southwold Rd. Bex		49 74 D
Southwold Rd. E5	38	35 86 A
Southwood Ave. King	94	20 69 A
Southwood Ave. N6	36	28 87 B
Southwood Cl. Brom	99	42 68 D
Southwood Cl. Wor Pk	103	23 66 D
Southwood Dri. Surb	102	20 66 C
Southwood Gdns. Esh	101	16 65 C
Southwood Gdns. Ilf	28	43 89 D
Southwood La. N6	36	28 87 A
Southwood Lawn Rd. N6	36	28 87 B
Southwood Park. N6	36	28 87 B
Southwood Rd. SE9	90	43 72 B
South Worple Ave. SW14	72	21 75 A
South Worple Way. SW14	72	20 75 B
South Yd. EC2	4	32 81 B
Sovereign Cl. Ruis		09 87 C
Sovereign Cl. W5	54	17 81 A
Sowerby Cl. SE9	77	42 74 B
Space Waye. Felt	69	10 74 A
Spa Cl. SE25	97	33 69 A
Spafield St. EC1	3	31 82 C
Spa Hill. SE19	97	32 69 B
Spalding Rd. NW4	35	23 87 A
Spalding Rd. SW17	86	28 71 D
Spanby Rd. E3	57	37 82 C
Spaniards Cl. NW11		26 87 D
Spaniards End. NW3	35	26 87 D
Spaniard's Rd. NW3	35	26 86 A
Spanish Pl. W1	2	28 81 C
Spanish Rd. SW18	73	26 74 A
Spa Rd. SE16	8	33 79 D
Spa Rd. SE16	8	33 79 D
Sparkbridge Rd. Har	21	15 89 C
Sparks Cl. Hamp	92	12 70 A
Sparrow Dri. Orp	108	44 66 D
Sparrow Farm Dri. Felt	82	11 73 B
Sparrow Farm Rd. Eps	109	22 64 B
Sparrow Green. Dag	41	49 86 D
Sparrows La. SE9	90	44 73 C
Sparsholt Rd. Bark	51	45 83 A
Sparsholt Rd. N19	36	30 87 D
Sparta St. SE10	76	38 76 A
Spearman St. SE18	66	43 77 A
Spear Mews. SW5	62	25 78 A
Spears Rd. N19	36	30 87 C
Speart La. Houn	59	12 77 C
Spedan Cl. NW3	35	26 86 C
Speedwell St. SE8	64	37 77 C
Speedy Pl. WC1	3	30 82 A
Speer Rd. Surb	101	15 67 D
Speirs Cl. N.Mal	102	21 67 D
Spekehill SE9		42 72 D
Speke Rd. Th Hth	97	32 69 D
Speldhurst Cl. Brom	107	39 67 B
Speldhurst Rd. E9	49	35 84 D
Speldhurst Rd. W4	61	20 79 D
Spellbrook Wlk (off Basire St). N1	48	32 83 A
Spelman St. E1	57	34 81 A
Spelthorne Gr. Sun	91	09 70 D
Spelthorne La. Ashf	91	08 70 C
Spencer Ave. N13	24	30 90 A
Spencer Cl. NW10	54	18 82 B
Spencer Cl. Orp	108	45 65 B
Spencer Dri. N2	35	26 88 C
Spencer Gdns. SW14	72	20 74 A
Spencer Hill Rd. SW19	95	24 70 C
Spencer Hill. SW19	95	24 70 B
Spencer Mews. W6	62	24 77 A
Spencer Park. SW18	73	26 74 B
Spencer Pas. E2	48	34 83 D
Spencer Pl. Croy	105	32 66 B
Spencer Rd. Brom	99	39 70 D
Spencer Rd. E17	26	38 90 C
Spencer Rd. E6	50	41 83 B
Spencer Rd. E Mol	92	14 68 C
Spencer Rd. Har	21	15 90 C
Spencer Rd. Ilf	40	45 87 C
Spencer Rd. Islw	70	14 76 A
Spencer Rd. Mit	104	28 66 A
Spencer Rd. Mit	96	28 68 A
Spencer Rd. N11	16	28 92 B
Spencer Rd. N17	25	34 90 A
Spencer Rd. N8	36	30 88 B
Spencer Rd. Rain	52	50 83 D
Spencer Rd. S Croy	112	33 64 C
Spencer Rd. SW18	73	26 74 B
Spencer Rd. SW20	94	22 69 B
Spencer Rd. Twick	83	15 72 A
Spencer Rd. W3	55	20 80 C
Spencer Rd. W4	61	20 77 C
Spencer Rd. Wem	33	17 66 A
Spencer Rise. NW5	36	28 86 D
Spencer St. EC1	3	31 82 B
Spencer St. Sthl	59	11 79 B
Spencer Wlk. SW15	73	23 75 D
Spenser Rd. N16	48	33 85 A
Spenser Rd. SE24	75	31 74 B
Spenser St. SW1	6	29 79 C
Spensley Wlk. N16	37	32 86 D
Speranza St. SE18	66	45 78 D
Sperling Rd. N17	25	33 90 D
Spert St. E14	57	36 80 A
Speyside. N14	12	29 95 C
Spey St. E14	58	38 81 A
Spey Way. Rom	30	51 91 C
Spezia Rd. NW10	45	22 83 C
Spicer Cl. SE5	75	31 76 D
Spices Yd. Croy	112	32 64 A
Spielman Rd. Dart	80	54 75 D
Spigurnell Rd. N17	25	32 90 B
Spikes Bridge Rd. Sthl	53	12 80 A
Spilsby Cl. NW9	22	21 90 C
Spilsby Rd. Rom	30	54 91 C

Spindlewood Gdns. Croy ...112	33 64 A	
Spinel Cl. SE18...66	45 78 D	
Springfield Mount. NW9...34	21 88 A	
Spinnells Rd. Har...32	12 87 D	
Spinney Cl. N.Mal...102	21 67 A	
Spinney Dri. Felt...81	08 73 A	
Spinney Gdns. Dag...52	48 85 C	
Spinney Oak. Brom...99	42 69 C	
Spinneys The. Brom...99	42 69 D	
Spinney The. Barn...11	25 97 D	
Spinney The. N21...17	31 94 A	
Spinney The. Sun...91	10 69 A	
Spinney The. Sutt...110	23 64 A	
Spinney The. SW16...86	29 72 D	
Spinney The. Wem...33	16 86 C	
Spital Sq. E1...8	33 81 A	
Spital St. Dart...80	53 74 D	
Spital St. E1...57	34 82 C	
Spital Yd. E1...4	33 81 A	
Spitfire Way. Houn...59	11 97 A	
Spode Wlk. NW6...46	25 85 D	
Spondon Rd. N15...25	34 89 C	
Spooner's Mews. W3...55	20 80 D	
Spooner Wlk. Wall...111	29 64 D	
Sportsbank St. SE6...88	38 73 A	
Spottons Gr. N17...25	32 90 C	
Spratt Hall Rd. E11...39	40 88 C	
Spray St. SE18...66	43 78 B	
Spreighton Rd. E Mol...92	13 68 D	
Sprimont Pl. SW3...9	27 78 D	
Springall St. SE15...63	34 77 D	
Springbank. N21...12	30 95 D	
Springbank Rd. SE13...77	39 74 C	
Springbank Wlk. N7...29	84 D	
Springbourne Ct. Beck...98	38 69 A	
Spring Bridge Rd.W5...54	17 80 B	
Springclose La. Sutt...110	24 63 A	
Spring Cottages. Surb...101	17 67 B	
Springcroft Ave. N2...24	27 89 D	
Spring Ct. Eps...109	21 62 B	
Springdale Rd. N16...48	32 85 B	
Spring Dri. Pnr...31	10 88 C	
Springfield Ave. Hamp...92	13 70 B	
Springfield Ave. N10...24	29 89 A	
Springfield Ave. SW20...95	24 68 B	
Springfield Cl. N12...15	25 92 D	
Springfield Ct. King...93	18 68 A	
Springfield Dri. Ilf...40	44 88 C	
Springfield. E5...37	34 87 D	
Springfield Gdns. Brom...99	42 68 D	
Springfield Gdns. E5...37	34 87 D	
Springfield Gdns. NW9...34	20 88 B	
Springfield Gdns. Ruis...31	10 86 D	
Springfield Gdns. W Wick...106	41 91 C	
Springfield Gr. SE7...65	37 65 B	
Springfield Gr. Sun...91	10 69 A	
Springfield La. NW6...46	25 83 B	
Springfield Rd. Bexh...79	49 75 D	
Springfield Rd. Brom...99	42 68 D	
Springfield Rd. E15...58	39 82 A	
Springfield Rd. E17...38	36 88 D	
Springfield Rd. E6...50	42 84 D	
Springfield Rd. Eps...110	23 62 C	
Springfield Rd. Har...33	15 88 C	
Springfield Rd. Hay...53	11 80 C	
Springfield Rd. King...93	18 68 A	
Springfield Rd. N11...16	29 92 C	
Springfield Rd. N15...25	34 89 C	
Springfield Rd. NW8...46	26 83 A	
Springfield Rd. SE26...87	34 71 D	
Springfield Rd. SW19...85	25 71 C	
Springfield Rd. Tedd...83	16 71 C	
Springfield Rd. Th Hth...97	32 69 A	
Springfield Rd. Twick...82	13 73 C	
Springfield Rd. W7...54	15 80 C	
Springfield Rd. Il...111	28 64 D	
Springfield Rd. Well...78	46 75 B	
Springfield Rise. SE26...87	34 72 D	
Springfield Wlk (off Andover Rd).		
Orp...108	44 66 D	
Springfield Wlk. NW6...46	25 83 B	
Spring Gdns. E Mol...92	14 68 C	
Spring Gdns. N5...48	32 85 C	
Spring Gdns. Rom...41	50 88 C	
Spring Gdns. SW1...6	29 80 D	
Spring Gdns. Wall...111	29 64 C	
Spring Gdns. Wdf Gn...27	41 91 C	
Spring Gr. Hamp...92	13 69 B	
Spring Grove Cres. Houn...70	14 76 A	
Spring Grove Rd. Houn...70	14 76 A	
Spring Grove Rd. Islw...70	14 76 B	
Spring Grove Rd. Rich...71	18 74 B	
Spring Gr. W4...61	19 77 A	
Springhead Rd. Eri...68	51 77 B	
Springhill Cl. SE5...75	32 75 B	
Spring Hill. E5...37	34 87 A	
Spring Hill. SE26...88	35 71 A	
Spring La. Croy...105	34 67 D	
Spring La. E5...37	34 67 D	
Spring La. SE25...105	34 67 D	
Spring Mews. W1...1	27 81 B	
Spring Park Ave. Croy...106	35 65 B	
Springpark Dri. Beck...98	38 68 A	
Springpark Dri. N4...37	32 87 C	
Spring Park Rd. Croy...106	35 65 B	
Spring Pas. SW15...73	23 75 B	
Spring Path. NW3...46	26 85 D	
Spring Pl. NW5...47	28 85 D	
Springpond Rd. Dag...52	48 85 C	
Spring Rd. Felt...81	09 72 D	
Springrice Rd. SE13...77	38 74 D	
Spring St. Eps...109	21 62 B	
Spring St. W2...1	26 81 D	
Spring Val. Bexh...79	49 75 D	
Springvale Ave. Brent...60	18 78 C	
Spring Vale. Dart...80	53 74 D	
Spring Vale Terr. W14...62	23 79 D	
Spring Villa Rd. Edg...22	19 91 C	
Springwater Cl. SE18...78	43 76 A	
Springway. Har...32	14 87 B	
Springwell Ave. NW10...45	22 83 A	
Springwell Cl. SW16...87	31 71 A	
Springwell Rd. Houn...	11 76 B	
Springwell Rd. SW16...87	31 71 A	
Spring Wlk. E1...57	34 81 A	
Springwood Way. Rom...42	52 88 A	
Sprowston Mews. E7...50	40 85 C	
Sprowston Rd. E7...50	40 85 C	
Sprucedale Gdns. Wall...111	30 62 A	
Spruce Hills Rd. E17...26	38 90 C	
Sprules Rd. SE4...76	36 76 C	
Spurfield. E Mol...92	13 68 B	
Spurgeon Ave. SE19...97	32 69 B	
Spurgeon Rd. SE19...97	32 70 D	
Spurgeon St. SE1...8	32 79 D	
Spurling Rd. Dag...52	48 84 B	
Spurling Rd. SE22...75	33 75 D	
Spur Rd. Bark...51	44 83 C	
Spur Rd. Felt...69	10 75 D	
Spur Rd. Islw...60	16 77 D	
Spur Rd. N15...25	32 89 D	
Spur Rd. Orp...108	46 65 A	
Spurstowe Rd. E8...48	34 84 B	
Spurstowe Terr. E8...48	34 85 D	
Square The. Cars...111	28 64 C	
Square The. Ilf...40	43 87 A	
Square The. Rich...71	17 74 B	
Square The. W6...62	23 78 C	
Squaray St. SW17...85	26 72 C	
Squire's Bridge Rd. Shep...91	07 68 A	
Squires La. N3...23	26 90 A	
Squire's Mount. NW3...35	26 86 D	
Squire's Rd. Shep...91	07 68 C	
Squires Wood Dri. Chis...99	42 70 D	
Squirrel Cl. Houn...70	11 75 A	
Squirrels Cl. N12...15	26 92 A	
Squirrels Green. Wor Pk...102	22 65 A	
Squirrel's Heath Ave. Rom...30	52 89 B	
Squirrels Heath La. Horn...30	53 89 C	
Squirrels Heath La. Rom...30	53 89 C	
Squirrels Heath Rd. Rom...30	54 90 D	
Squirrels The. Pnr...20	12 89 B	
Squirrel's The. SE13...76	38 75 B	
Squirries St. E2...57	34 82 A	
Stable Cl. Nthlt...43	13 83 C	
Stables End. Orp...108	44 65 C	
Stables Way. SE11...63	31 78 C	
Stable Way. W10...56	23 81 D	
Stable Way. W12...56	23 81 C	
Stable Wlk. N2...23	26 90 B	
Stable Yd Rd. SW1...6	29 79 A	
Stacey Ave. N18...18	35 92 A	
Stacey Cl. E10...38	38 88 B	
Stacey St. WC2...2	29 81 D	
Stackhouse St. SW1...5	27 79 D	
Stacy Path. SE5...63	33 77 C	
Staddon Ct. Beck...98	36 68 C	
Stadium Rd. Dart...80	51 74 B	
Stadium Rd. SE18...65	42 77 B	
Stadium St. SW10...62	26 77 C	
Stadium Way. Wem...45	19 85 A	
Staffa Rd. E10...38	36 87 C	
Stafford Ave. Horn...30	53 89 B	
Stafford Cl. N14...12	29 95 A	
Stafford Cl. NW6...56	25 82 A	
Stafford Cl. Sutt...110	24 63 A	
Stafford Cripps House. SW6...62	24 77 B	
Stafford Gdns. Croy...111	30 64 D	
Stafford Pl. Rich...83	18 73 B	
Stafford Pl. SW1...	29 79 C	
Stafford Rd. Croy...111	30 64 D	
Stafford Rd. E3...49	36 83 D	
Stafford Rd. E7...50	41 84 B	
Stafford Rd. Har...20	14 91 C	
Stafford Rd. N Mal...94	20 68 A	
Stafford Rd. NW6...56	25 82 A	
Stafford Rd. Sid...90	45 71 A	
Stafford Rd. Wall...111	29 63 B	
Staffordshire St. SE15...75	34 76 A	
Stafford St. W1...6	29 80 C	
Stafford Terr. W8...62	25 79 A	
Stafford Wlk. Rich...71	18 76 A	
Staff St. EC1...4	32 82 B	
Stag Cl. Edg...22	19 90 D	
Staggart Green. Chig...28	46 91 A	
Stag La. Edg...22	19 90 D	
Stag La. NW9...22	20 89 A	
Stag La. SW15...84	21 72 B	
Stag Pl. SW1...6	29 79 C	
Stag Ride. SW19...84	22 72 C	
Stainbank Rd. Mit...96	28 68 D	
Stainby Rd. N15...25	33 89 D	
Stainer St. SE1...8	32 80 D	
Staines Ave. Sutt...103	24 65 A	
Staines Rd. Felt...81	09 73 A	
Staines Rd. Houn...70	12 75 C	
Staines Rd. Ilf...51	44 85 B	
Staines Rd. Twick...82	14 72 C	
Staines Road E. Sun...92	11 69 D	
Staines Road W. Ashf...91	08 70 C	
Staines Road W. Sun...91	09 70 D	
Stainford Cl. Ashf...81	08 71 D	
Stainforth Rd. E17...26	37 89 C	
Stainforth Rd. Ilf...40	44 88 D	
Staining La. EC2...4	32 81 C	
Stainmore Cl. Chis...100	44 69 B	
Stainsbury St. E2...49	35 83 C	
Stainsby Pl. E14...57	37 81 C	
Stainsby Rd. E14...57	37 81 C	
Stainton Rd. Enf...14	35 97 A	
Stainton Rd. SE6...88	38 73 B	
Stainton Rd. SE6...76	38 74 D	
Stalbridge St. NW1...1	27 81 A	
Stalham St. SE16...63	34 79 D	
Stambourne Way. SE19...97	33 70 D	
Stambourne Way. W Wick...106	38 65 C	
Stamford Brook Ave. W6...61	21 78 B	
Stamford Brook Gdns. W6...61	21 79 D	
Stamford Brook Rd. W6...61	21 79 D	
Stamford Cl. Har...21	15 91 C	
Stamford Cl. N15...25	34 89 C	
Stamford Cl. NW3...35	26 86 C	
Stamford Cl. Sthl...53	13 80 A	
Stamford Ct. W6...61	21 78 B	
Stamford Dri. Brom...99	39 68 D	
Stamford Gdns. Dag...52	47 84 C	
Stamford Grove E. N16...37	34 87 C	
Stamford Grove W. N16...37	34 87 C	
Stamford Hill. N16...37	33 87 D	
Stamford Rd. Dag...52	47 84 C	
Stamford Rd. E6...50	42 83 A	
Stamford Rd. N15...37	34 88 A	
Stamford Rd. N1...48	33 84 A	
Stamford St. SE1...7	31 80 C	
Stamp Pl. E2...48	33 83 D	
Stanard Cl. N16...37	33 87 A	
Stanborough Cl. Hamp...92	12 70 B	
Stanborough Pas. E8...48	33 84 B	
Stanborough Rd. Islw...70	14 75 B	
Stanbridge Rd. SW15...73	23 75 A	
Stanbrook Ct. W1...6	29 80 C	
Stanbrook Rd. SE2...66	46 79 B	
Stanbury Ct. NW3...47	27 84 B	
Stanbury Rd. SE15...75	34 76 D	
Stanbury Rd. SE15...75	35 76 C	
Stancroft. NW9...34	21 88 A	
Standale Gr. Ruis...31	08 88 A	
Standard Pl. EC2...4	33 82 A	
Standard Rd. Belv...67	49 78 C	
Standard Rd. Bexh...79	48 75 C	
Standard Rd. Houn...70	12 75 A	
Standard Rd. NW10...55	20 82 D	
Standen Ave. Horn...42	54 86 C	
Standfield Gdns. Dag...52	49 84 A	
Standfield Rd. Dag...52	49 85 C	
Standish Rd. W6...61	22 78 A	
Stane Cl. SW19...95	25 70 D	
Stane Way. Eps...109	22 62 C	
Stane Way. SE18...65	42 77 C	
Stanfield Rd. E3...49	36 83 C	
Stanford Cl. Hamp...92	12 70 B	
Stanford Cl. Rom...41	49 88 D	
Stanford Cl. Ruis...31	08 88 C	
Stanford Cl. Wdf Gn...	42 91 A	

Stanford Pl. SE17 ....63 33 78 A
Stanford Rd. N11 ....16 27 92 D
Stanford Rd. SW16 ....96 30 69 C
Stanford Rd. W8 ....62 25 79 D
Stanford Way. SW16 ....96 29 69 D
Stanger Rd. SE25 ....97 34 68 C
Stanham Pl. Dart ....80 52 75 C
Stanham Rd. Dart ....80 53 74 A
Stanhope Ave. Brom ....107 40 66 C
Stanhope Ave. Har ....20 14 90 B
Stanhope Ave. N3 ....23 24 89 B
Stanhope Gate. W1 ....6 28 80 C
Stanhope Gdns. Dag ....41 48 86 D
Stanhope Gdns. Ilf ....39 42 87 D
Stanhope Gdns. N4 ....37 32 88 C
Stanhope Gdns. N6 ....36 29 88 C
Stanhope Gdns. SW7 ....62 26 78 A
Stanhope Gr. Beck ....98 36 68 D
Stanhope Mews E. SW7 ....62 26 78 A
Stanhope Mews S. SW7 ....62 26 78 A
Stanhope Mews W. SW7 ....62 26 78 A
Stanhope Park Rd. Grnf ....53 14 82 C
Stanhope Pl. W2 ....5 27 80 B
Stanhope Rd. Barn ....11 23 95 D
Stanhope Rd. Bexh ....79 48 76 C
Stanhope Rd. Cars ....111 28 63 C
Stanhope Rd. Croy ....105 33 65 C
Stanhope Rd. Dag ....41 48 86 D
Stanhope Rd. E17 ....38 37 88 B
Stanhope Rd. Grnf ....53 14 81 A
Stanhope Rd. N12 ....15 26 92 C
Stanhope Rd. N6 ....36 29 87 A
Stanhope Rd. Sid ....90 46 71 A
Stanhope Row. W1 ....6 28 80 D
Stanhope St. NW1 ....2 29 82 A
Stanhope Terr. W2 ....5 26 80 B
Stanier Cl. SW5 ....62 24 78 D
Stanlake Mews. W12 ....56 23 80 C
Stanlake Rd. W12 ....56 23 80 C
Stanlake Villas. W12 ....56 23 80 C
Stanley Ave. Bark ....51 45 83 D
Stanley Ave. Beck ....98 38 68 A
Stanley Ave. Dag ....41 48 87 B
Stanley Ave. Grnf ....43 14 83 A
Stanley Ave. N.Mal ....102 22 67 A
Stanley Ave. Rom ....30 52 89 C
Stanley Ave. Wem ....44 18 84 C
Stanley Cl. Horn ....42 53 86 A
Stanley Cl. Rom ....30 52 89 C
Stanley Cl. SW8 ....10 30 77 B
Stanley Cl. Wem ....44 18 84 C
Stanley Cres. W11 ....56 24 80 B
Stanleycroft Cl. Islw ....71 15 76 A
Stanley Ct. Sutt ....110 25 63 D
Stanley Ct. W5 ....54 17 81 A
Stanley Gardens Rd. Tedd ....83 15 71 C
Stanley Gdns. Mit ....96 28 70 A
Stanley Gdns. NW2 ....46 23 85 C
Stanley Gdns. W11 ....56 24 80 B
Stanley Gdns. W3 ....61 21 79 A
Stanley Gdns. Wall ....111 29 63 A
Stanley Gr. Croy ....105 31 67 C
Stanley Gr. SW8 ....74 28 76 C
Stanley Park Dri. Wem ....44 18 83 B
Stanley Park Rd. Cars ....111 27 63 D
Stanley Park Rd. Wall ....111 28 63 B
Stanley Park Rd. Wall ....111 28 63 B
Stanley Pas. NW1 ....47 30 83 C
Stanley Rd. Brom ....99 41 68 C
Stanley Rd. Cars ....111 28 63 C
Stanley Rd. Croy ....105 31 87 C
Stanley Rd. E10 ....50 37 88 D
Stanley Rd. E12 ....50 42 85 C
Stanley Rd. E15 ....49 38 83 B
Stanley Rd. E18 ....27 39 90 B
Stanley Rd. E4 ....18 38 94 D
Stanley Rd. Enf ....13 33 96 A
Stanley Rd. Har ....32 14 86 A
Stanley Rd. Horn ....42 53 86 B
Stanley Rd. Houn ....70 14 75 C
Stanley Rd. Ilf ....40 44 86 B
Stanley Rd. Mit ....96 28 70 C
Stanley Rd. Mord ....95 25 68 C
Stanley Rd. N10 ....24 28 91 D
Stanley Rd. N11 ....16 29 92 D
Stanley Rd. N15 ....25 31 89 D
Stanley Rd. N2 ....23 26 89 B
Stanley Rd. N9 ....17 33 93 B
Stanley Rd. Nthwd ....19 10 90 A
Stanley Rd. NW9 ....34 22 87 A
Stanley Rd. Orp ....108 45 66 D
Stanley Rd. Sid ....90 46 72 C
Stanley Rd. Sthl ....53 12 80 A
Stanley Rd. Sutt ....110 25 63 D
Stanley Rd. SW14 ....72 19 75 D

Stanley Rd. SW19 ....95 25 70 A
Stanley Rd. Tedd ....83 15 71 C
Stanley Rd. Twick ....82 14 72 D
Stanley Rd. W3 ....61 20 79 C
Stanley Rd. Wem ....44 18 84 B
Stanley Sq. Cars ....111 27 62 B
Stanley St. SE8 ....64 36 77 D
Stanley Terr. N19 ....36 30 86 A
Stanley Way. Orp ....108 46 67 B
Stanmer St. SW11 ....74 27 76 C
Stanmore Gdns. Rich ....71 18 75 B
Stanmore Gdns. Sutt ....103 26 65 C
Stanmore Pl. NW1 ....28 83 B
Stanmore Rd. Belv ....67 50 78 A
Stanmore Rd. E11 ....39 39 87 D
Stanmore Rd. N15 ....25 31 89 D
Stanmore Rd. Rich ....71 18 75 B
Stanmore St. N1 ....47 30 83 B
Stanmore Terr. Beck ....37 69 C
Stannard Rd. E8 ....48 34 84 A
Stannary Pl. SE11 ....77 31 78 C
Stannary St. SE11 ....63 31 78 C
Stansden Rd. SW18 ....85 25 73 A
Stansfeld Hse. SE1 ....63 33 78 B
Stansfeld Rd. E16 ....58 41 81 B
Stansfield Rd. Houn ....69 10 76 D
Stansfield Rd. SW9 ....74 30 75 B
Stansgate Rd. Dag ....41 49 86 C
Stanstead Cl. Brom ....107 39 67 D
Stanstead Gr. SE6 ....88 36 73 D
Stanstead Manor. Sutt ....110 25 63 A
Stanstead Rd. E11 ....39 40 88 B
Stanstead Rd. SE23 ....88 38 73 C
Stanstead Rd. SE6 ....88 36 73 D
Stanswood Gdns. SE5 ....63 33 77 C
Stanthorpe Cl. SW16 ....86 30 71 C
Stanthorpe Rd. SW16 ....86 30 71 A
Stanton Ave. Tedd ....93 15 70 A
Stanton Ave. Tedd ....83 15 71 C
Stanton Cl. Eps ....109 19 64 D
Stanton Cl. Wor Pk ....103 23 66 D
Stanton Cl. Croy ....105 32 66 A
Stanton Rd. SW20 ....92 23 69 B
Stanton St. SE15 ....75 34 76 A
Stanton. SW13 ....72 21 76 D
Stanton Way. SE26 ....88 36 71 B
Stanway Gdns. Edg ....20 91 A
Stanway Gdns. W3 ....55 19 80 C
Stanway St. N1 ....48 33 83 C
Stanwell Rd. Felt ....81 07 73 B
Stanwick Rd. W14 ....62 24 78 B
Stapenhill Rd. Wem ....33 16 86 D
Staplefield Cl. Pnr ....20 12 91 C
Staplefield Cl. SW2 ....86 30 73 C
Stapleford Ave. Ilf ....40 45 88 A
Stapleford Cl. King ....94 19 68 A
Stapleford Cl. SW19 ....85 24 73 A
Stapleford Gdns. Rom ....29 49 91 A
Stapleford Rd. Wem ....44 17 84 D
Staplehurst Rd. Cars ....111 27 63 C
Staplehurst Rd. SE13 ....77 39 74 A
Staple Inn Bldgs. WC2 ....3 31 81 A
Staples Cl. SE16 ....57 36 80 C
Staple St. SE1 ....8 32 79 B
Stapleton Gdns. Croy ....112 31 64 C
Stapleton Hall Rd. N4 ....36 30 87 B
Stapleton Rd. Bexh ....67 48 77 D
Stapleton Rd. Orp ....108 45 65 D
Stapley Rd. Belv ....67 49 78 C
Stapylton Rd. Barn ....11 24 96 A
Star Alley. EC3 ....8 33 80 A
Starboard Way. E14 ....64 37 79 C
Starch House La. Ilf ....28 44 90 D
Starcross St. NW1 ....2 29 82 A
Starfield Rd. W12 ....61 22 79 A
Star & Garter Hill. Rich ....83 18 73 A
Star Hill. Dart ....80 51 74 A
Starkleigh Way. SE16 ....63 34 78 D
Star La. E16 ....58 39 82 D
Starling Cl. Pnr ....20 11 89 A
Star Rd. Islw ....70 14 76 D
Star Rd. W14 ....62 24 78 D
Star St. W2 ....1 27 81 C
Starts Cl. Orp ....108 43 65 C
Starts Hill Rd. Orp ....108 43 65 D
Star Yd. WC2 ....3 31 81 C
Statham Gr. N16 ....37 32 86 D
Statham Gr. N18 ....17 33 92 C
Station App. Barn ....11 26 96 C
Station App. Beck ....98 37 69 A
Station App. Bexh ....79 48 76 C
Station App. Bexh ....79 50 76 C
Station App. Brom ....107 40 66 C
Station App. Chis ....99 42 70 A

Station App. Chis ....100 43 69 C
Station App. Dart ....80 54 74 C
Station App. E11 ....39 40 88 A
Station App. Eps ....109 22 64 C
Station App. Esh ....101 15 65 D
Station App. Hamp ....92 13 69 A
Station App. King ....94 19 69 A
Station App. N11 ....16 28 92 D
Station App. Nthwd ....19 09 91 C
Station App. NW10 ....55 21 82 B
Station App. Orp ....100 45 65 B
Station App. Orp ....100 46 68 D
Station App. Pnr ....20 12 89 C
Station App. Ruis ....72 19 76 C
Station App. Ruis ....31 09 87 C
Station App. Ruis ....11 85 C
Station App. S Croy ....112 32 62 B
Station App. S Croy ....112 32 62 B
Station App. SE26 ....88 36 71 D
Station App. SE3 ....77 40 75 B
Station App. SE9 ....89 42 73 D
Station App. SE9 ....77 42 74 A
Station App. Sun ....91 10 69 A
Station App. Sutt ....110 24 63 C
Station App. SW16 ....86 30 71 C
Station App. SW6 ....73 24 75 A
Station App. Well ....48 46 76 C
Station App. Wem ....44 16 84 B
Station App. Wor Pk ....102 22 66 C
Station Ave. Eps ....109 21 62 A
Station Ave. N Mal ....94 21 68 A
Station Ave. Rich ....72 19 76 A
Station Ave. SW9 ....75 31 75 B
Station Cl. Hamp ....92 13 69 B
Station Cl. N12 ....15 25 92 B
Station Cl. N3 ....23 25 90 A
Station Cres. N15 ....25 32 89 D
Station Cres. SE3 ....65 40 78 C
Station Cres. Wem ....44 16 84 B
Stationers Hall Ct. EC4 ....3 31 81 D
Station Estate. Beck ....35 68 D
Station Estate Rd. Felt ....81 10 73 D
Station Garage Mews. SW16 ....96 29 70 D
Station Gdns. W4 ....61 20 77 C
Station Gr. Wem ....44 18 84 A
Station Hill. Brom ....107 40 65 A
Station La. Horn ....42 54 86 A
Station Par. Bark ....51 44 84 C
Station Par. Barn ....12 28 96 C
Station Par. N14 ....16 29 94 D
Station Par. NW2 ....46 23 84 A
Station Par. Rich ....72 19 76 A
Station Pas. E18 ....27 40 90 D
Station Pas. SE15 ....75 35 76 A
Station Path. SW6 ....73 24 75 B
Station Pl. N4 ....36 31 88 A
Station Rd. Barn ....11 25 95 B
Station Rd. Belv ....67 49 79 C
Station Rd. Bexh ....79 48 75 A
Station Rd. Brom ....99 39 69 C
Station Rd. Brom ....99 40 69 A
Station Rd. Cars ....111 27 64 B
Station Rd. Croy ....105 32 66 C
Station Rd. Dag ....80 47 87 B
Station Rd. Dart ....80 51 74 D
Station Rd. E10 ....50 38 86 C
Station Rd. E12 ....50 42 85 A
Station Rd. E17 ....38 36 88 A
Station Rd. E4 ....18 38 94 B
Station Rd. E7 ....50 40 85 A
Station Rd. Edg ....22 19 91 A
Station Rd. Hamp ....92 13 69 B
Station Rd. Har ....32 13 88 B
Station Rd. Har ....31 15 88 B
Station Rd. Houn ....70 13 75 D
Station Rd. Ilf ....40 43 86 D
Station Rd. King ....93 17 69 B
Station Rd. King ....94 19 69 A
Station Rd. N11 ....16 27 92 D
Station Rd. N17 ....25 34 89 A
Station Rd. N21 ....17 31 94 D
Station Rd. N22 ....24 30 90 D
Station Rd. N22 ....24 30 91 C
Station Rd. N3 ....25 25 90 C
Station Rd. N. Belv ....67 49 79 D
Station Rd. N.Mal ....102 22 67 B
Station Rd. NW10 ....45 21 83 D
Station Rd. NW4 ....34 22 88 C
Station Rd. NW7 ....22 21 91 A
Station Rd. Orp ....108 45 65 B
Station Rd. Rom ....30 52 89 D
Station Rd. Rom ....30 54 90 B
Station Rd. SE20 ....98 35 70 A

Name	Page	Ref
Station Rd. SE25	97	33 68 D
Station Rd. Sid	90	46 72 C
Station Rd. Sun	91	10 70 C
Station Rd. Surb	101	15 66 B
Station Rd. Sutt.	110	25 62 C
Station Rd. SW13	72	22 76 C
Station Rd. SW19	95	26 69 B
Station Rd. Tedd	83	15 71 D
Station Rd. Tedd	93	16 70 A
Station Rd. Twick	83	15 73 D
Station Rd. W5	54	18 81 D
Station Rd. W7	54	15 80 C
Station Rd. W Wick	106	38 66 C
Station Rise. SE27	87	31 72 B
Station Sq. Orp	108	44 67 A
Station Sq. Orp	100	46 68 D
Station St. E15	49	38 84 D
Station Terr. NW10	46	23 83 D
Station Terr. SE5	75	32 76 A
Station View. Grnf	43	14 83 B
Station Way SE15	75	34 76 C
Station Way. Sutt	110	24 63 C
Station Yd. Twick	83	16 73 A
Stauford St. SW1	10	29 78 B
Staunton Rd. King	93	18 70 D
Staunton St. SE8	64	36 77 B
Staveley Cl. E9	49	35 85 C
Staveley Cl. N7	47	30 85 A
Staveley Cl. SE15	76	35 76 A
Staveley Ct. E11	39	40 88 A
Staveley Gdns. W4	72	20 76 B
Staveley Gdns. W4	61	20 77 D
Staveley Rd. Ashf	91	08 70 B
Staveley Rd. W4	61	20 77 D
Staverton Rd. Horn	42	53 88 D
Staverton Rd. NW2	46	23 84 C
Stavordale Rd. Cars	103	26 66 A
Stavordale Rd. N5	48	31 85 B
Stayner's Rd. E1	57	35 82 D
Stayton Rd. Sutt	103	25 65 C
Stead St. SE17	63	32 78 B
Steam Farm La. Felt	69	09 75 D
Stean St. E8	48	33 83 B
Stebbing Way. Bark	51	46 83 C
Stebondale St. E14	64	38 78 A
Stedham Pl. WC1	3	30 81 C
Stedman Cl. Uxb	31	07 86 C
Steedman St. SE17	63	32 78 A
Steeds Rd. N10	24	27 90 D
Steele Rd. E11	50	39 84 A
Steele Rd. Islw	71	16 75 C
Steele Rd. N17	25	33 89 B
Steele Rd. NW10	45	20 83 C
Steele Rd. W4	61	20 79 C
Steele's Mews N. NW3	47	27 84 B
Steele's Mews S. NW3	47	27 84 B
Steele's Rd. NW3	47	27 84 B
Steel's La. E1	57	35 81 C
Steen Way. SE22	75	33 74 A
Steep Hill. SW16	86	29 72 D
Steeple Cl. SW19	85	24 71 C
Steeple Cl. SW6	73	24 76 C
Steeplestone Cl. N18	17	32 92 C
Steeple Wlk (off Maldon Cl). N1	48	
Steerforth St. SW18	85	32 83 A
Steers Mead. Mit	96	26 72 A
Stella Rd. SW17	96	27 70 B
Stelling Rd. Eri	67	50 77 D
Stellman Cl. E5	37	34 86 C
Stembridge Rd. SE20	97	34 69 D
Stephen Cl. E8	48	34 83 A
Stephen Cl. Orp	108	45 65 D
Stephendale Rd. SW6	73	26 76 C
Stephen Mews. W1	2	29 81 B
Stephen Rd. Bexh	79	50 75 A
Stephenson Rd. Houn	82	13 73 A
Stephenson Rd. W7		15 81 D
Stephenson St. E16	58	39 81 A
Stephenson St. NW10	55	21 82 B
Stephenson Way. NW1	2	29 82 C
Stephen's Rd. E15	50	39 83 C
Stephen St. W1	2	29 81 B
Stepney Cswy. E1	57	35 81 D
Stepney Green. E1	57	35 81 B
Stepney High St. E1	57	35 81 B
Stepney Way. E1	57	35 81 A
Sterling Rd. Enf	13	32 97 B
Sterling St. SW7	5	27 79 C
Sterling Way. N18	17	33 92 C
Sterndale Rd. W14	62	23 79 D
Sterne St. W12	62	23 79 B
Sternhall La. SE15	75	34 75 A
Sternhold Ave. SW2	86	29 72 B
Sterry Cres. Dag	52	49 85 C
Sterry Dri. E Mol	101	15 67 C
Sterry Dri. Eps	109	21 64 A
Sterry Gdns. Dag	52	49 84 A
Sterry Rd. Bark	51	45 83 B
Sterry Rd. Dag	52	49 85 C
Sterry St. SE1	8	32 79 B
Steucers La. SE23	88	36 73 C
Stevedale Rd. Well	79	47 76 C
Stevenage Rd. E6	51	43 84 A
Stevenage Rd. SW6	73	23 76 B
Stevens Ave. E9	49	35 84 A
Stevens Cl. Beck	98	37 70 A
Stevens Cl. Hamp	92	12 70 B
Stevens Cl. Pnr	32	11 88 A
Stevenson Cl. Eri	68	52 77 D
Stevens Rd. Dag	41	47 86 C
Stevens St. SE1	8	33 79 C
Steventon Rd. W12	55	21 80 B
Stewards Holte Wlk. N11	16	28 92 B
Steward St. E1	4	33 81 A
Stewards Wlk. Rom	42	51 88 A
Stewart Ave. Shep	91	07 68 C
Stewart Cl. Hamp	92	12 70 A
Stewart Cl. NW9	34	20 88 C
Stewart Rd. E15	49	38 85 B
Stewartsby Cl. N18	17	32 93 C
Stewart's Gr. SW3	9	27 78 C
Stewart's Rd. SW8	74	29 76 A
Stewart St. E14	64	38 79 A
Stew La. EC4	8	32 80 A
Steyne Rd. W3	55	19 80 D
Steyning Gr. SE9	89	42 71 B
Steynings Way. N12	15	25 92 C
Steyning Way. Houn	70	11 75 C
Stickland Rd. Belv	67	49 78 A
Stickleton Cl. Grnf	53	13 82 B
Stilecroft Gdns. Wem	33	16 86 D
Stile Hall Gdns. W4	61	19 78 C
Stile Path. Sun	91	10 68 A
Stiles Cl. Brom	107	42 67 D
Stillingfleet Rd. SW13	61	22 77 A
Stillington St. SW1	10	29 78 A
Stillness Rd. SE23	76	36 74 D
Stilton Cres. NW10	45	20 84 C
Stipularis Dri. Hay	53	11 82 D
Stirling Rd. E13	50	40 83 D
Stirling Rd. E17	26	36 89 A
Stirling Rd. Har	21	15 89 B
Stirling Rd. N17	25	34 90 A
Stirling Rd. N22	25	31 90 B
Stirling Rd. SW9	74	30 76 C
Stirling Rd. Twick	82	13 73 B
Stirling Rd. W3	61	19 79 D
Stirling Road Path. E17	26	36 89 A
Stiven Cres. Har	32	12 86 D
Stockbury Rd. Croy	106	35 67 C
Stockdale Rd. Dag	48	48 86 B
Stockdove Way. Grnf	54	15 82 B
Stockfield Rd. SW16	86	30 72 D
Stockholm Rd. SE16	64	34 78 C
Stockhurst Cl. SW6	73	23 76 B
Stockingswater La. Enf	74	36 96 B
Stockland Rd. Rom	41	50 88 D
Stock Orchard Cres. N7	47	30 85 D
Stock Orchard St. N7	47	30 85 D
Stockport Rd. SW16	96	29 69 B
Stocksfield Rd. E17	26	38 89 A
Stocks Pl. E14	57	36 80 B
Stock St. E13	50	40 83 C
Stockton Gdns. N17	25	32 91 C
Stockton Rd. N17	25	32 91 C
Stockton Rd. N18	25	34 91 B
Stockwell Ave. SW9	74	30 75 B
Stockwell Ave. SW9	75	31 75 A
Stockwell Gdns. SW9	74	30 76 B
Stockwell Green. SW9	74	30 76 D
Stockwell La. SW9	74	30 76 D
Stockwell Mews. SW9	74	30 76 D
Stockwell Park Cres. SW9	74	30 76 D
Stockwell Park Rd. SW9	74	30 76 D
Stockwell Park Wlk. SW9	75	31 75 A
Stockwell Rd. SW9	74	30 75 B
Stockwell St. SE10	64	38 77 A
Stockwell Terr. SW9	74	30 76 B
Stodart Rd. SE20	98	35 69 A
Stofield Gdns. SE9	89	41 72 D
Stoford Cl. SW19	85	24 73 A
Stoke Ave. Ilf	28	46 91 A
Stokenchurch St. SW6	73	25 76 B
Stoke Newington Church St. N16	37	
Stoke Newington Common N16	37	33 86 C
Stoke Newington Rd. N16	48	33 86 B
Stoke Newington Rd. N16	48	33 85 B
Stoke Pl. NW10	55	21 82 B
Stoke Rd. King	94	20 70 C
Stokesley St. W12	55	21 81 D
Stokes Rd. Croy	106	36 67 D
Stonard Rd. Dag	51	46 85 B
Stonard Rd. N13	17	31 93 C
Stondon Park. SE23	76	36 74 C
Stondon Wlk. E6	50	41 83 D
Stone Bldgs. WC2	3	30 81 B
Stonebridge Common. E8	4	33 84 D
Stonebridge Park. NW10	45	20 84 D
Stonebridge Rd. N15	37	33 88 B
Stonebridge Way. Wem	45	19 84 B
Stone Cl. Dag	41	48 86 B
Stonecot Cl. Sutt	103	24 66 C
Stonecot Hill. Sutt	103	24 66 A
Stonecroft Rd. Eri	67	50 77 C
Stonecroft Way. Croy	104	30 66 A
Stonecutter St. EC4	3	31 81 D
Stonefield Cl. Bexh	79	49 75 A
Stonefield Cl. Ruis	43	12 85 C
Stonefield St. N1	48	31 83 A
Stonefield Way. Ruis	43	12 85 C
Stonefield Way. SE7	65	41 77 D
Stonehall Ave. Ilf	39	42 88 C
Stoneham Rd. N11	16	29 92 C
Stonehill Cl. SW14	72	20 74 B
Stonehill Rd. SW14	72	20 74 B
Stonehill Rd. W4	61	19 78 C
Stonehills Ct. SE21	87	33 72 C
Stonehorse Rd. Enf	14	35 95 A
Stonehouse Ct. EC2	4	33 81 C
Stoneleigh Ave. Enf	13	34 97 B
Stoneleigh Ave. Wor Pk	102	22 65 C
Stoneleigh Cres. Eps	109	22 64 A
Stoneleigh Par. Eps	109	21 63 B
Stoneleigh Park Ave. Croy	106	35 67 D
Stoneleigh Park Rd. Eps	109	22 64 D
Stoneleigh Pl. W11	56	23 80 B
Stoneleigh Rd. Cars	104	27 66 A
Stoneleigh Rd. Ilf	27	42 89 D
Stoneleigh Rd. N17	25	33 89 B
Stoneleigh Rd. SW11	56	23 80 D
Stoneleigh Terr. N6	36	28 86 B
Stonell's Rd. SW11	74	27 74 D
Stonenest St. N4	36	30 87 D
Stone Park Ave. Beck	98	37 68 D
Stone Pl. Wor Pk	102	22 65 A
Stone Rd. Brom	107	39 67 B
Stones End St. SE1	8	32 79 A
Stone St. Croy	112	31 64 C
Stone Strs. E1	57	35 80 B
Stonewood Rd. Eri	68	51 78 C
Stoney Alley. SE18	78	43 76 C
Stoneyard La. E14	57	37 80 B
Stoneycroft Cl. SE12	89	39 73 B
Stoneycroft Rd. Wdf Grn	27	42 91 A
Stoneydown Ave. E17	26	36 89 C
Stoneydown House. E17	26	36 89 C
Stoney La. EC3	4	33 81 D
Stoney La. SE19	97	33 70 B
Stoney St. SE1	8	32 80 D
Stonhouse St. SW4	74	29 75 B
Stonor Rd. W14	62	24 78 B
Stopford Rd. E13	50	40 83 A
Stopford Rd. SE17	63	31 78 D
Store Rd. E16	66	43 79 A
Store St. E15	49	38 85 D
Store St. WC1	2	29 81 B
Storey Rd. E17	26	36 89 D
Storey Rd. N6	36	27 88 D
Storey's Gate. SW1	6	29 79 B
Storey St. E16	66	43 79 A
Stories Rd. SE5	75	33 75 A
Stork Rd. E7	50	40 84 A
Storksmead Rd. Edg.	22	19 91 C
Stork's Rd. SE16	63	34 79 C
Stormont Rd. N6	36	27 87 B
Stormont Rd. SW11	74	28 75 C
Storrington Rd. Croy	105	33 66 D
Story St. N1	47	30 84 D
Stothard Pl. E1	4	33 81 A
Stothard St. E1	57	35 82 C
Stoughton Ave. Sutt	110	24 64 C
Stoughton Cl. SW15	84	22 73 C
Stour Ave. Sthl	59	13 78 C
Stourcliffe St. W1	1	27 81 D
Stourhead Cl. SW19	85	23 73 B
Stourhead Gdns. SW20.	94	22 68 A
Stour Rd. Dag	41	49 86 A
Stour Rd. Dart	80	52 75 A
Stour Rd. E3	49	37 84 C
Stourton Ave. Felt	82	12 71 B
Stowage. SE8	64	37 77 A
Stow Cres. E17	26	36 91 C

Stowe Cres. Ruis

Stowe Cres. Ruis....31 08 88 C
Stowe Gdns. N9....17 33 94 D
Stowe Pl. N15....25 33 89 A
Stowe Rd. W12....61 22 79 B
Stox Mead. Har....20 14 90 B
Stracey Rd. E7....50 40 85 A
Stracey Rd. NW10....45 20 83 B
Strachan Pl. SW19....95 23 70 A
Stradbroke Dri. Chig....28 43 91 B
Stradbroke Gr. Ilf....27 42 90 D
Stradbroke Rd. N5....48 32 85 A
Stradella Rd. SE24....75 32 74 C
Strafford Ave. Ilf....28 43 90 C
Strafford Rd. Barn....11 24 96 A
Strafford Rd. Houn....70 12 75 B
Strafford Rd. Twick....83 16 73 A
Strafford Rd. W3....61 20 79 A
Strafford St. E14....64 37 79 A
Strahan Rd. E3....57 36 82 A
Straight Rd. Rom....30 53 91 C
Straightsmouth. SE10....64 38 77 C
Straight The. Sthl....59 12 79 A
Straker's Rd. SE15....75 34 75 D
Straker's Rd. SE22....75 34 74 B
Strandfield Cl. SE18....66 45 78 C
Strand La. WC2....7 30 80 B
Strand-on-the-Green. W4....61 19 77 A
Strand-on-the-Green. W4....61 19 77 B
Strand Pl. N18....17 33 92 A
Strand. WC2....7 30 80 B
Strangways Terr. W14....62 24 79 D
Stranraer Way. N1....47 30 84 D
Stratford Ave. W8....62 25 79 D
Stratford Cl. Bark....51 46 84 C
Stratford Cl. Dag....52 50 84 C
Stratford Ct. N Mal....94 20 68 D
Stratford Gr. SW15....73 23 75 D
Stratford Pl. W1....2 28 81 D
Stratford Rd. E13....50 40 83 A
Stratford Rd. Hay....53 11 82 C
Stratford Rd. Sthl....59 12 78 A
Stratford Rd. Th Hth....97 31 68 B
Stratford Rd. W8....62 25 79 C
Stratford Villas. NW1....47 29 84 D
Strathan Cl. SW18....73 24 74 D
Strathaven Rd. SE12....77 40 74 D
Strathblaine Rd. SW11....73 26 75 D
Strathblaine Rd. SW11....74 27 75 C
Strathbrook Rd. SW16....96 30 70 D
Strathcona Rd. Wem....33 17 86 B
Strathdale. SW16....86 30 71 D
Strathdon Dri. SW17....85 26 72 D
Strathearn Ave. Twick....82 14 73 C
Strathearn Pl. W2....5 27 80 A
Strathearn Rd. Sutt....110 25 64 C
Strathearn Rd. SW19....85 25 71 A
Strathede Rd. SE3....65 40 77 C
Strathfield Gdns. Bark....51 44 84 A
Strathleven Rd. SW2....74 30 74 A
Strathmore Gdns. Edg....22 19 90 D
Strathmore Gdns. Horn....42 51 87 D
Strathmore Gdns. N3....23 25 90 B
Strathmore Gdns. W8....56 25 80 C
Strathmore Rd. Croy....105 32 66 B
Strathmore Rd. SW19....85 25 72 C
Strathmore Rd. Tedd....83 15 71 A
Strathnairn St. SE1....63 34 78 A
Strathray Gdns. NW3....47 27 84 A
Strath Terr. SW11....74 27 75 C
Strathville Rd. SW18....85 25 73 D
Strathyre Ave. SW16....97 31 68 A
Stratton Ave. Wall....111 29 62 B
Stratton Cl. Bexh....79 48 75 A
Stratton Cl. Edg....21 18 91 B
Stratton Cl. Houn....70 13 76 A
Stratton Cl. SW19....95 25 69 C
Strattondale St. E14....64 38 79 C
Stratton Dri. Bark....51 45 84 B
Stratton Gdns. Sthl....53 13 81 C
Stratton Rd. Bexh....79 48 75 A
Stratton Rd. Sun....91 09 69 D
Stratton Rd. SW19....95 25 69 C
Stratton St. W1....6 28 80 D
Strauss Rd. W4....61 20 79 B
Strawberry Hill Cl. Twick....83 15 72 D
Strawberry Hill Rd. Twick....83 15 72 D
Strawberry La. Cars....104 28 65 C
Strawberry Vale. N2....23 26 90 B
Strawberry Vale. Twick....83 16 72 C
Streamdale. SE2....66 46 77 B
Streamside Cl. Brom....99 40 68 C
Stream Way. Belv....67 49 77 A
Streatfield Rd. E6....50 42 83 B
Streatfield Rd. Har....21 17 89 B
Streatham Common N. SW16....86 30 71 D

Streatham Common S. SW16....96 30 70 B
Streatham Ct. SW16....86 30 72 C
Streatham High Rd. SW16....96 30 70 C
Streatham High Rd. SW16....96 30 71 A
Streatham Hill SW2....86 30 73 C
Streatham Pl. SW2....86 30 73 A
Streatham Rd. Mit....96 28 69 A
Streatham Rd. SW16....96 28 70 D
Streatham St. WC1....3 30 81 C
Streatham Vale. SW16....96 29 70 C
Streathbourne Rd. SW17....86 28 72 C
Streatley Pl. NW3....46 26 85 A
Streatley Rd. NW6....46 24 84 D
Streimer Rd. E15....49 38 83 C
Strelley Way. W3....55 21 80 A
Stretton Rd. Croy....105 33 66 A
Stretton Rd. Rich....83 17 72 A
Strickland Ave. (off Joyce Green La). Dart....80 54 75 B
Strickland Ave. (off Sharp Way). Dart....80 54 75 B
Strickland Row. SW18....85 26 73 B
Strickland St. SE8....76 37 76 A
Stride Rd. E13....50 39 83 D
Stride Cl. N10....24 28 91 C
Strode Rd. E7....50 40 85 A
Strode Rd. N17....25 33 90 C
Strode Rd. NW10....45 22 84 A
Strode Rd. SW6....62 24 77 C
Strode Rd. E12....50 41 84 B
Strone Rd. E7....50 41 84 A
Strongbow Cres. SE9....77 42 74 B
Strongbow Rd. SE9....77 42 74 B
Strongbridge Cl. Har....32 13 87 C
Stronsa Rd. W12....61 21 79 B
Strood Ave. Rom....41 50 87 D
Stroud Cres. SW15....84 22 72 C
Stroud Field. Nthlt....43 12 84 A
Stroud Gate. Har....43 13 85 B
Stroud Green Gdns. Croy....106 35 66 A
Stroud Green Rd. N4....36 30 87 D
Stroud Green Rd. N4....37 31 87 C
Stroud Green Way. Croy....106 35 67 C
Stroudley Wlk. E3....57 37 82 B
Stroud Rd. SE25....105 34 67 C
Stroud Rd. SW19....85 25 72 C
Stroud Way. Ashf....91 07 70 B
Stroughton Cl. SE11....10 30 78 B
Strout's Pl. E2....4 33 82 B
Strutton Ground. SW1....9 29 79 D
Strype St. E1....4 33 81 B
Stuart Ave. Brom....107 40 66 C
Stuart Ave. Har....32 12 86 D
Stuart Ave. NW9....34 22 87 A
Stuart Ave. W5....60 18 79 B
Stuart Cres. Croy....106 36 65 D
Stuart Cres. N22....24 30 90 B
Stuart Gr. Tedd....83 15 71 C
Stuart Mantle Way. Eri....68 51 77 C
Stuart Pl. Mit....96 27 69 B
Stuart Rd. Bark....51 45 84 D
Stuart Rd. Barn....16 27 94 B
Stuart Rd. Har....21 15 89 B
Stuart Rd. NW6....56 25 82 B
Stuart Rd. Rich....83 16 72 D
Stuart Rd. SE15....76 35 75 C
Stuart Rd. SW19....85 25 72 C
Stuart Rd. Th Hth....97 32 68 C
Stuart Rd. W3....55 20 80 C
Stuart Rd. Well....78 46 76 B
Stuat Evans Cl. Well....79 47 75 A
Stubbs Way. SW19....95 26 69 B
Stucley Pl. NW1....47 28 84 D
Stucley Rd. Houn....59 14 77 C
Studdridge St. SW6....73 25 76 C
Studd St. N1....48 31 83 B
Studholme Ct. NW3....46 25 85 A
Studholme St. SE15....63 34 77 D
Studio Pl. SW1....5 27 79 B
Studios Rd. Shep....91 07 68 A
Studland Cl. Sid....90 45 72 D
Studland Rd. King....93 18 70 A
Studland Rd. SE26....88 35 71 D
Studland Rd. W7....54 15 81 C
Studland St. W6....61 22 78 B
Studley Ave. E4....26 38 91 D
Studley Cl. E5....49 36 85 C
Studley Ct. Sid....90 46 71 D
Studley Dri. Ilf....39 41 88 D
Studley Grange Rd. W7....60 15 79 B
Studley Rd. Dag....52 47 84 D
Studley Rd. E7....50 40 84 B
Studley Rd. SW4....74 30 76 C
Stukeley Rd. E7....50 40 84 D

Stukeley St. WC2....3 30 81 C
Stumps Hill La. Beck....98 37 70 A
Sturdy Rd. SE15....75 34 76 D
Sturge Ave. E17....27 37 90 D
Sturgeon Rd. SE17....63 32 78 C
Sturges Field. Chis....100 44 70 B
Sturgess Ave. NW4....34 22 87 B
Sturge St. SE1....8 32 79 A
Sturmer Way. N7....47 30 85 D
Sturrock Cl. N15....25 32 89 D
Sturry St. E14....57 37 81 D
Sturt St. N1....4 32 83 C
Stutfield St. E1....57 34 81 C
Styles Gdns. SW9....75 31 75 B
Styles Way. Beck....98 38 68 C
Sudbourne Rd. SW2....74 30 74 B
Sudbrooke Rd. SW12....74 28 74 C
Sudbrook Gdns. Rich....83 18 72 C
Sudbrook La. Rich....83 18 72 A
Sudbury Ave. Wem....44 17 85 B
Sudbury Court Dri. Har....33 16 86 C
Sudbury Court Rd. Har....33 16 86 C
Sudbury Cres. Brom....89 40 70 A
Sudbury Cres. Brom....89 40 71 C
Sudbury Cres. Wem....44 16 85 D
Sudbury Croft. Wem....44 15 85 B
Sudbury Gdns. Croy....112 33 64 A
Sudbury Heights Ave. Grnf....44 16 85 C
Sudbury Hill Cl. Wem....33 15 86 D
Sudbury Hill. Har....33 15 86 C
Sudbury Rd. Bark....51 45 85 D
Sudeley St. N1....48 31 83 D
Sudlow Rd. SW18....73 25 74 A
Sudrey St. SE1....8 32 79 A
Suez Ave. Grnf....44 15 83 D
Suez Rd. Enf....14 36 96 C
Suffield Rd. E4....18 37 92 B
Suffield Rd. N15....37 33 88 B
Suffield Rd. SE20....98 35 69 C
Suffolk Ct. Ilf....40 45 88 C
Suffolk La. EC4....4 32 80 B
Suffolk Park Rd. E17....26 36 89 C
Suffolk Pl. SW1....6 29 80 D
Suffolk Rd. Bark....51 45 84 C
Suffolk Rd. Dag....52 50 85 C
Suffolk Rd. Dart....80 54 74 C
Suffolk Rd. E13....58 39 82 B
Suffolk Rd. Enf....13 34 95 B
Suffolk Rd. Har....32 13 88 A
Suffolk Rd. Ilf....40 45 88 C
Suffolk Rd. N15....37 32 88 B
Suffolk Rd. NW10....45 21 84 C
Suffolk Rd. SE25....97 33 68 D
Suffolk Rd. SW13....61 22 77 C
Suffolk Rd. Wor Pk....102 21 65 B
Suffolk Rd. E7....54 40 85 A
Suffolk St. SW1....6 29 80 D
Sugar Bakers Ct. EC3....4 33 81 C
Sugar House La. E15....49 38 83 C
Sugar Loaf Ct. EC4....8 32 80 A
Sugar Loaf Wlk. E2....57 35 82 A
Sugden Rd. Surb....101 16 66 D
Sugden Rd. SW11....74 28 75 C
Sugden Rd. Bark....51 45 83 D
Sulgrave Gdns. W12....62 23 79 A
Sulgrave Rd. W6....62 23 79 C
Sulina Rd. SW2....86 30 73 A
Sulivan Ct. SW6....73 25 76 C
Sulivan Rd. SW6....73 25 75 A
Sullivan Ave. E16....58 41 81 B
Sullivan Cl. E Mol....92 13 68 B
Sullivan Cl. SW11....74 27 75 A
Sullivan Rd. SE11....63 31 78 A
Sultan Rd. E11....27 40 89 D
Sultan St. Beck....98 35 69 D
Sultan St. SE5....63 32 77 C
Sumatra Rd. NW6....46 25 84 A
Sumburgh Rd. SW12....74 28 74 C
Summer Ave. E Mol....101 15 67 A
Summercourt Rd. E1....57 35 81 C
Summerfield Ave. NW6....46 24 83 C
Summerfield La. Surb....101 17 65 B
Summerfield Rd. W5....54 16 82 D
Summerfield St. SE12....89 39 73 B
Summer Gdns. E Mol....101 15 67 A
Summer Hill. Chis....100 43 69 C
Summerhill Cl. Orp....108 46 65 C
Summerhill Gr. Enf....13 33 95 C
Summerhill Rd. Dart....80 53 74 D
Summerhill Rd. N15....25 32 89 D
Summerhouse Ave. Houn....70 12 76 A
Summerhouse Rd. N16....37 33 86 A
Summerland Gdns. N10....24 28 89 B
Summerlands Ave. W3....55 20 80 A
Summerlee Ave. N2....24 27 89 D

Summerlee Gdns. N2 24
Summerley St. SW18 85
Summerley St. SW18 85
Summer Rd. E Mol 101
Summer Rd. Sutt 101
Summersby Rd. N6 36
Summers Cl. NW9 34
Summers Cl. Sutt 110
Summers La. N12 24
Summers Row. N12 24
Summers St. EC1 3
Summerstown. SW17 85
Summer Trees. Sun 91
Summerville Gdns. Sutt..............110
Summerwood Rd. Islw 71
Summit Ave. NW9 34
Summit Cl. Edg 22
Summit Cl. N14 16
Summit Cl. NW9 22
Summit Ct. NW2 46
Summit Ct. NW2 46
Summit Dri. Wdf Gn 27
Summit Estate. N16 37
Summit Rd. E17 26
Summit Rd. Nthlt 43
Summit Way. N14 16
Summit Way. SE19 97
Sumner Ave. SE15 75
Sumner Bldgs. SE1 8
Sumner Gdns. Croy 105
Sumner Place Mews. SW7 62
Sumner Pl. SW7 62
Sumner Rd. Croy 105
Sumner Rd. Har 32
Sumner Rd. SE15 63
Sumner Rd. SE15 75
Sumner Road S. Croy 105
Sumner St. SE1 6
Sumpter Cl. NW3 46
Sun Alley. Rich 71
Sunbeam Rd. NW10 55
Sunbury Ave. SW14 72
Sunbury Court Rd. Sun 92
Sunbury Cres. Felt 81
Sunbury Cross Centre. Sun 91
Sunbury La. SW11 73
Sunbury Rd. Felt 81
Sunbury Rd. Sutt 103
Sunbury St. SE18 65
Sunbury Way. Felt 82
Suncroft Pl. SE26 88
Sun Ct. EC3 4
Sun Ct. Eri 80
Sunderland Ct. SE22 87
Sunderland Rd. SE23 88
Sunderland Rd. W5 60
Sunderland Terr. W2 56
Sunderland Way. E12 39
Sundew Ave. W12 55
Sundial Ave. SE25 97
Sundorne Rd. SE7 65
Sundown Rd. Ashf 81
Sundra Wlk. E1 57
Sundridge Ave. Brom 99
Sundridge Ave. Chis 99
Sundridge Ave. Well 78
Sundridge Pl. Croy 105
Sundridge Rd. Croy 105
Sunfields Pl. SE3 65
Sunflower Way. Rom 30
Sunkist Way. Wall 111
Sunland Ave. Bexh 79
Sun La. SE3 65
Sunleigh Rd. Wem 44
Sunley Gdns. Grnf 44
Sunmead Rd. Sun 91
Sunna Gdns. Sun 91
Sunningdale Ave. Bark 51
Sunningdale Ave. Felt 82
Sunningdale Ave. Ruis 32
Sunningdale Ave. W3 55
Sunningdale Cl. Stan 21
*Sunningdale Gdns. NW9 34
Sunningdale Gdns. W8 62
Sunningdale. N14 16
Sunningdale Rd. Brom 99
Sunningdale Rd. Sutt 110
Sunningdale. Sthl 53
Sunningfields Cres. NW4 22
Sunningfields Rd. NW4 22
Sunninghill Gdns. 28
Sunninghill Rd. SE13 76
Sunny Bank. SE25 97
Sunny Cres. NW10 45
Sunnycroft Rd. Houn 70

Sunnycroft Rd. SE25 97
Sunnycroft Rd. Sthl 53
Sunnydale Gdns. NW7 22
Sunnydale. Orp 108
Sunnydale Rd. SE12 77
Sunnydene Ave. E4 18
Sunnydene Ave. Ruis 31
Sunnydene Cl. Rom 30
Sunnydene Gdns. Wem 44
Sunnydene St. SE26 88
Sunnyfield Rd. Chis 100
Sunny Gardens Rd. NW4 23
Sunny Hill Ct. NW4 22
Sunny Hill. NW4 22
Sunnyhill Rd. SW16 86
Sunnyhurst Cl. Sutt 103
Sunnymead Ave. Mit 96
Sunnymead Rd. NW9 34
Sunnymead Rd. SW15 72
Sunnymede Ave. Eps 109
Sunnymede Dri. Ilf 28
Sunny Nook Gdns. S Croy 112
Sunnyside Dri. E4 18
Sunnyside. NW2 35
Sunnyside Pas. SW19 95
Sunnyside Pl. SW19 95
Sunnyside Rd. E10 38
Sunnyside Rd. Ilf 40
Sunnyside Rd. N19 36
Sunnyside Rd. Tedd 82
Sunnyside Rd. W5 54
Sunnyside Road E. N9 17
Sunnyside Road N. N9 17
Sunnyside Road S. N9 17
Sunnyside. SW19 95
Sunny View. NW9 34
Sunny Way. N12 24
*Sun Pas. SE16 63
Sunray Ave. Brom 107
Sunray Ave. SE24 75
Sunray Ave. SE5 75
Sunray Ave. Surb 102
Sun Rd. W14 62
Sunrise Ave. Horn 42
Sunrise Cl. Felt 82
Sunrise Lodge. Horn 42
Sunset Ave. E4 18
Sunset Gdns. SE25 97
Sunset Rd. SE5 75
Sunset View. Barn 11
Sunshine Way. Mit 96
Sun St. EC2 4
Sun St Pas. EC2 4
Sunwell Cl. SE15 75
Surbiton Cres. King 93
Surbiton Ct. Surb 101
Surbiton Hall Cl. King 93
Surbiton Hill Park. Surb 102
Surbiton Hill Rd. Surb 101
Surbiton Rd. King 93
Surgeon St. SE18 66
Surrendale Pl. W9 56
Surrey Canal Rd. SE14 64
Surrey Gr. SE17 63
Surrey Gr. Sutt 103
Surrey Lane Estate. SW11 74
Surrey La. SW11 74
Surrey Mews. SE27 87
Surrey Rd. Bark 51
Surrey Rd. Dag 52
Surrey Rd. Har 32
Surrey Rd. SE15 76
Surrey Rd. W Wick 106
Surrey Row. SE1 7
Surrey Sq. SE17 63
Surrey St. Croy 105
Surrey St. E13 58
Surrey St. WC2 7
Surrey Terr. SE17 63
Surridge Gdns. SE19 97
Surr St. N7 47
Surry Mount. SE23 87
Susan Cl. Rom 29
Susannah St. E14 58
Susan Rd. SE3 77
Susan Wood. Chis 100
Sussex Ave. Islw 71
Sussex Ave. Rom 30
Sussex Cl. Ilf 39
Sussex Cl. N19 36
Sussex Cl. N Mal 94
Sussex Cl. Twick 71
Sussex Cres. Nthlt 43

Sussex Gdns. N4 37
Sussex Gdns. N6 36
Sussex Gdns. W2 1
Sussex Mews E. W2 1
Sussex Mews W. W2 5
Sussex Pl. EC3 4
Sussex Pl. N Mal 94
Sussex Pl. NW1 1
Sussex Pl. W2 1
Sussex Rd. Cars 111
Sussex Rd. E6 51
Sussex Rd. Eri 67
Sussex Rd. Har 32
Sussex Rd. Mit 104
Sussex Rd. N Mal 94
Sussex Rd. S Croy 112
Sussex Rd. Sid 90
Sussex Rd. Sthl 59
Sussex Rd. W Wick 106
Sussex Ring. N12 15
Sussex Sq. W2 5
Sussex St. E13 58
Sussex St. SW1 9
Sussex Way. Barn 12
Sussex Way. N19 36
Sussex Wlk. SW9 75
Sutcliffe Cl. NW11 35
Sutcliffe Rd. SE18 66
Sutcliffe Rd. Well 79
Sutherland Ave. Orp 108
Sutherland Ave. Sun 91
Sutherland Ave. W13 54
Sutherland Ave. W9 56
Sutherland Ave. Well 78
Sutherland Cl. Barn 11
Sutherland Ct. NW9 34
Sutherland Dri. SW19 95
Sutherland Gdns. Sun 91
Sutherland Gdns. SW14 72
Sutherland Gdns. Wor Pk 102
Sutherland Gr. SW18 85
Sutherland Gr. Tedd 83
Sutherland Pl. W2 56
Sutherland Rd. Belv 67
Sutherland Rd. Croy 105
Sutherland Rd. E17 35
Sutherland Rd. E3 49
Sutherland Rd. End 14
Sutherland Rd. N17 25
Sutherland Rd. N9 17
Sutherland Rd. Sthl 53
Sutherland Rd. W13 54
Sutherland Rd. W4 61
Sutherland Row. SW1 9
Sutherland Sq. SE17 63
Sutherland St. SW1 9
Sutherland Wlk. SE17 63
Sutlej Rd. SE7 65
Sutterton St. N7 47
Sutton Arc. Sutt 110
Sutton Cl. Beck 98
Sutton Cl. Pnr 31
Sutton Cl. Sutt 110
Sutton Cl. W4 61
Sutton Common Rd. Sutt 103
Sutton Court Rd. E13 58
Sutton Court Rd. Sutt 110
Sutton Court Rd. W4 61
Sutton Court Roundabout. W4 61
Sutton Cres. Barn 11
Sutton Ct. SE19 97
Sutton Ct. Sutt 110
Sutton Ct. W4 61
Sutton Dene. Houn 70
Sutton Dwellings. N1 48
Sutton Dwellings. SW3 9
Sutton Estate The. W10 56
Sutton Gdns. Bark 51
Sutton Gdns. Croy 51
Sutton Green. Bark 51
Sutton Gr. Sutt 110
Sutton Hall Rd. Houn 59
Sutton La. Houn 70
Sutton La. W4 61
Sutton Park Rd. Sutt 110
Sutton Pl. E9 49
Sutton Rd. Bark 51
Sutton Rd. E13 58
Sutton Rd. E17 35
Sutton Rd. Houn 70
Sutton Rd. N10 24
Sutton Row. W1 2
Suttons Ave. Horn 42
Suttons Gdns. Horn 42
Suttons La. Horn 42

Name				Name				Name			
Sutton Sq. Houn	70	12 76 B		Sycamore Gr. NW9	34	20 87 A		Talbot Ct. EC3	8	32 80 B
Sutton St. E1	57	35 81 C		Sycamore Rd. SW19	95	23 70 A		Talbot Gdns. Ilf	40	46 86 A
Sutton Way. Houn	70	12 76 B		Sycamore St. EC1	4	32 82 C		Talbot Pl. SE3	77	39 76 C
Sutton Way. W10	56	23 82 C		Sycamore Way. Th Hth	105	31 67 A		Talbot Rd. Brom	99	40 68 B
Swaby Rd. SW18	85	26 72 A		Sycamore Wlk. Ilf	28	44 89 C		Talbot Rd. Cars	111	28 64 C
Swaffham Way. N22	25	31 91 D		Sycamore Wlk. W10	56	24 82 C		Talbot Rd. Dag	52	48 84 D
Swaffield Rd SW18	85	26 73 A		Sydenham Av. SE26	87	34 71 D		Talbot Rd. E6	51	43 83 C
Swain Rd. Th Hth	105	32 67 A		Sydenham Hill. SE26	87	34 72 C		Talbot Rd. E7	50	40 85 A
Swain's La. N6	36	28 86 B		Sydenham Park Rd. SE26	88	35 72 C		Talbot Rd. Har	21	15 90 D
Swainson Rd. W3	61	21 79 B		Sydenham Park. SE26	88	35 72 C		Talbot Rd. Islw	71	16 75 C
Swains Rd. SW17	96	27 70 D		Sydenham Pl. SE27	87	31 72 D		Talbot Rd. N15	25	33 89 D
Swaisland Rd. Dart	80	52 74 D		Sydenham Rd. Croy	105	32 66 B		Talbot Rd. N22	24	29 90 A
Swaislands Dri. Dart	80	51 74 B		Sydenham Rd. SE26	88	35 71 D		Talbot Rd. N6	36	28 88 C
Swakeleys Rd. Uxb	31	07 86 D		Sydenham Rise. SE23	87	34 72 B		Talbot Rd. Sthl	59	12 78 A
Swale Rd. Dart	80	52 75 C		Sydenham Station App. SE26	88	35 71 A		Talbot Rd. Th Hth	97	32 68 D
Swallands Rd. SE6	88	37 72 C		Sydmons Ct. SE23	88	35 73 A		Talbot Rd. Twick	83	15 73 D
Swallow Cl. SE14	76	35 76 A		Sydner Mews. N16	48	33 85 B		Talbot Rd. W11	56	24 81 D
Swallow Dri. Nthlt	43	13 83 C		Sydner Rd. N16	48	33 85 B		Talbot Rd. W13	54	16 80 A
Swallowfield Rd. SE7	65	40 78 D		Sydney Cl. SW3	62	26 78 B		Talbot Rd. W2	56	25 81 C
Swallow Pas Pl. W1	2	28 81 D		Sydney Cres. Ashf	91	07 70 B		Talbot Rd. Wem	44	17 84 B
Swallow St. W1	6	29 80 A		Sydney Elson Way. E6	51	43 83 C		Talbot Sq. W2	1	26 81 D
Swanage Rd. E4	26	38 91 C		Sydney Gr. NW4	35	23 88 A		Talbot Wlk (off Heron Cl). NW10		
Swanage Rd. SW18	73	26 74 C		Sydney Mews. SW3	62	26 78 B			45	21 84 A
Swanage Waye. Hay	53	11 81 C		Sydney Pl. SW7		27 78 A		Talbot Wlk. W11	56	24 81 C
Swanbridge Rd. Bexh	79	49 76 B		Sydney Rd. Bexh	79	47 75 D		Talbot Yd. SE1	8	32 80 D
Swan Cl. Felt	82	12 71 A		Sydney Rd. E11	40	88 D		Talcott Path. SW2	87	31 73 C
Swan Cl. Orp	100	46 68 A		Sydney Rd. Enf	13	32 96 D		Talfourd Pl. SE15		33 76 B
Swan Ct. SW3		27 78 C		Sydney Rd. Felt	81	10 73 C		Talfourd Rd. SE15	75	33 76 B
Swanfield St. E2	4	33 82 B		Sydney Rd. Ilf	28	44 90 C		Talgarth Rd. W14	62	24 78 C
Swan La. EC4	3	32 80 B		Sydney Rd. N10	24	28 91 D		Talgarth Rd. W6	62	23 78 D
Swan La. N20	15	26 93 C		Sydney Rd. N8	25	31 89 C		Talisman Sq. SE26	87	34 71 A
Swanley Rd. Well	79	47 76 A		Sydney Rd. Rich	71	18 75 C		Talisman Way. Wem	33	18 86 D
Swan Mead. SE1	8	33 79 C		Sydney Rd. SE2	67	47 79 D		Tallack Cl. Har	21	15 91 C
Swan Mews. SW9	74	30 76 D		Sydney Rd. Sid	90	45 71 A		Tallack Rd. E10	38	36 87 D
Swan Pas. E1	57	34 80 A		Sydney Rd. Sutt	110	25 64 A		Tall Elms Cl. Brom	107	39 67 B
Swan Pl. SW13	72	21 76 D		Sydney Rd. SW20	95	23 69 D		Tall Elms Cl. Brom	99	39 68 D
Swan Rd. Felt	82	12 71 A		Sydney Rd. Tedd	83	15 71 D		Tallis Gr. SE7	65	40 77 B
Swan Rd. SE16	64	35 79 A		Sydney Rd. W13	60	16 79 A		Tallis St. EC4	7	31 80 A
Swan Rd. SE18	65	41 79 D		Sydney St. SW3	62	27 78 C		Talma Gdns. Twick	83	15 73 A
Swanscombe Rd. W11	56	23 80 D		Sylvan Ave. Horn	42	54 88 D		Talmage Cl. SE23	88	35 73 A
Swanscombe Rd. W4	61	21 78 C		Sylvan Ave. N22	25	31 91 C		Talman Gr. Stan	21	17 91 B
Swansea Rd. Enf	14	35 96 C		Sylvan Ave. N3	23	25 90 C		Talma Rd. SW2	75	31 75 C
Swan St. Islw	71	16 75 B		Sylvan Ave. NW7	22	21 91 A		Talwin St. E3	57	37 82 B
Swan St. SE1	8	32 79 A		Sylvan Ave. Rom	41	48 88 D		Tamarisk Sq. W12	55	21 80 B
Swanton Gdns. SW19	85	23 73 D		Sylvan Cl. S Croy	112	34 62 D		Tamar Sq. Wdf Gn	27	40 91 B
Swanton Rd. Eri	67	49 77 D		Sylvan Gdns. Surb	101	17 66 B		Tamar St. SE7	65	42 79 C
Swan Way. Enf	14	35 97 D		Sylvan Gr. SE15	63	34 77 B		Tamar Way. N17	26	34 89 A
Swanwick Cl. SW15	84	21 73 B		Sylvan Hill. SE19	97	33 69 A		Tamian Way. Houn	70	11 75 C
Swan Wlk. Rom	42	51 88 A		Sylvan Rd. E11	39	40 88 A		Tamworth Ave. Wdf Gn	27	39 91 A
Swan Wlk. SW3	9	27 77 B		Sylvan Rd. E17	38	37 88 A		Tamworth La. Mit	96	28 68 B
Swan Yd. N1	48	31 84 B		Sylvan Rd. E7	50	40 84 B		Tamworth Park. Mit	96	28 68 B
Sward Rd. Orp	108	46 67 C		Sylvan Rd. Ilf	44	46 88 A		Tamworth Pl. Croy	105	32 65 A
Swaton Rd. E3	57	37 82 C		Sylvan Rd. SE19	97	33 69 B		Tamworth Rd. Croy	105	32 65 A
Swaylands Rd. Belv	67	49 77 A		Sylvan Way. Dag	51	46 85 B		Tamworth St. SW6	62	25 77 A
Swedenborg Gdns. E1	57	34 80 B		Sylverdale Rd. Croy	105	31 65 D		Tancred Rd. N4	37	31 88 D
Sweeney Cres. SE1	8	33 79 B		Sylvester Ave. Chis	99	42 70 B		Tandridge Dri. Orp	108	44 66 D
Sweet Briar Green. N9	17	33 93 D		Sylvester Path. E8	48	34 84 B		Tandridge Pl. Orp	108	44 66 D
Sweet Briar Gr. N9	17	33 93 D		Sylvester Rd. E17	38	36 87 B		Tanfield Ave. NW2	34	21 86 D
Sweet Briar Wlk. N18	17	33 92 B		Sylvester Rd. E8	48	34 84 B		Tanfield Rd. Croy	112	32 64 A
Sweetmans Ave. Pnr	20	11 89 B		Sylvester Rd. N2	23	26 90 D		Tangent Rd. Rom	30	53 90 B
Sweets Way. N20	15	26 93 B		Sylvester Rd. Wem	44	17 85 C		Tangier Rd. Rich	72	19 75 B
Swetenham Wlk. SE18	66	44 78 C		Sylvia Ave. Pnr	20	12 91 B		Tanglewood Cl. Croy	106	35 65 C
Swete St. E13	50	40 83 C		Sylvia Gdns. Wem	45	19 84 D		Tangley Gr. SW15	84	21 73 B
Sweyn Pl. SE3	77	40 76 C		Symes Mews. NW1	47	29 83 C		Tangley Park Rd. Hamp	92	12 70 B
Swift Cl. Har	32	13 86 B		Symons St. SW3	9	27 78 B		Tangley Park Rd. Hamp	82	12 71 D
Swift Rd. Felt	82	12 71 A		Syon La. Islw	60	15 77 D		Tangmere Gdns. Nthlt	43	11 83 D
Swift Rd. Sthl	59	13 79 C		Syon Park Gdns. Islw	60	15 77 D		Tangmere Way. NW9	22	21 90 C
Swiftsden Way. Brom	99	39 70 A		Tabard St. SE1	8	32 79 D		Tanhurst Wlk. Belv	67	47 79 D
Swift St. SW6	73	24 76 A		Taber Gr. SW19	95	24 70 D		Tankerton Rd. Surb	101	18 65 B
Swift St. SW6	73	24 76 B		*Tabernacle Ave. E13	58	40 82 C		Tankerton St. WC1	3	30 82 A
Swinbrook Rd. W10	56	24 81 A		Tabernacle St. EC2	4	32 82 D		Tankerville Rd. SW16	96	29 70 D
Swinburne Cres. Croy	106	35 67 C		Tableer Ave. SW4	74	29 74 B		Tank Hill Rd. Grays	68	54 78 D
Swinburne Rd. SW15	72	22 75 C		Tabley Rd. N7	47	30 85 A		Tankridge Rd. NW2	34	22 86 B
Swinderby Rd. Wem	44	18 84 A		Tabor Ct. Sutt	110	24 63 A		Tanners End La. N18	17	33 92 C
Swindon Cl. Ilf	40	45 87 C		Tabor Gdns. Sutt	110	24 63 A		Tanner's Hill. SE8	76	37 76 A
Swindon St. W12	56	23 80 C		Tabor Rd. W6	61	22 79 D		Tanners La. Ilf	28	44 89 A
Swinfield Cl. Felt	82	12 71 A		Tachbrook Mews. SW1	10	29 78 A		Tanner St. Bark	54	44 84 A
Swinford Gdns. SW9	75	31 75 B		Tachbrook Rd. Felt	81	09 73 B		Tanner St. SE1	8	33 79 B
Swingate La. SE18	66	45 77 C		Tachbrook Rd. Sthl	59	11 78 B		Tannery Cl. Dag	41	49 86 D
Swinnerton St. E9	49	36 85 C		Tachbrook St. SW1	10	29 78 A		Tannington Terr. N4	37	31 86 C
Swinton Cl. Wem	34	19 87 D		Tadema Rd. SW10	62	26 77 C		Tannsfeld Rd. SE26	88	35 71 D
Swinton Pl. WC1	3	30 82 B		Tadmor Cl. Sun	91	09 68 D		Tansley Cl. N7	47	29 85 D
Swinton St. WC1	3	30 82 B		Tadmor St. W12	56	23 80 D		Tanswell St. SE1	7	31 79 A
Swithland Gdns. SE9	90	43 71 A		Tadworth Ave. N.Mal	102	21 67 B		Tansy Cl. Rom	30	54 91 A
Swyncombe Ave. W5	60	16 78 B		Tadworth Rd. NW2	34	22 86 A		Tantallon Rd. SW12	86	28 73 C
Sybourn St. E17	38	36 87 B		Taffey's How. Mit	96	27 68 A		Tant Ave. E16	58	39 81 D
Sycamore Ave. Sid	78	45 74 D		Taft Way. E3	57	37 82 B		Tantony Gr. Rom	29	47 89 B
Sycamore Ave. W5	60	17 79 D		Tailworth St. E1	57	34 81 A		Tanworth Gdns. Pnr	20	11 90 C
Sycamore Cl. Cars	111	27 64 B		Tait Rd. Croy	105	33 66 A		Tanza Rd. NW3	47	27 85 A
Sycamore Cl. E16	58	39 82 C		Takeley Cl. Rom	29	50 90 D		Tapestry Cl. Sutt	110	25 63 D
Sycamore Cl. Nthlt	43	12 83 A		Talacre Rd. NW5	47	28 84 A		Taplow St. N1	4	32 83 C
Sycamore Gdns. Mit	95	26 69 D		Talbot Cl. N15	25	33 89 D		Tappesfield Rd. SE15	76	35 75 A
Sycamore Gdns. W6	61	22 79 D		Talbot Ave. N2	23	26 89 B		Tapping Cl. King	94	19 70 C
Sycamore Gr. N Mal	94	21 68 A		Talbot Cres. NW4	34	22 88 A		Tapp St. E1	57	34 82 D
								Tapster St. Barn	11	24 96 B

Taransay Wlk. N1	48	32	84 B
Tarbert Rd. SE22	75	33	74 A
Tarbert Wlk. E1	57	35	80 A
Target Cl. Felt	69	09	74 C
Tariff Rd. N17	25	34	91 A
Tarleton Gdns. SE23	87	34	73 D
Tarling Cl. Sid	90	46	72 D
Tarling Rd. E16	58	39	81 D
Tarling Rd. N2	23	26	90 C
Tarling St. E1	57	35	81 C
Tarnbank. Enf	12	30	95 A
Tarn St. SE1	8	32	79 C
Tarnwood Park. SE9	89	42	73 D
Tarrington Cl. SW16	86	29	72 D
Tarver Rd. SE17	63	31	78 D
Tarves Way. SE10	64	37	77 D
Tash Pl. N11	16	28	92 D
Tasker Rd. NW3	47	27	85 D
Tasmania Terr. N18	25	32	91 A
Tasman Rd. SW9	74	30	75 A
Tasman Wlk. E16	58	41	81 D
Tasso Rd. W6	62	24	77 A
Tatam Rd. NW10	45	20	84 D
Tate Rd. Sutt	110	25	64 C
Tatnell Rd. SE23	76	36	74 C
Tattersall Cl. SE9	77	42	74 A
Tatton Cres. N16	37	33	87 B
Tatum St. SE17	63	33	78 A
Taunton Ave. Houn	70	14	76 C
Taunton Ave. SW20	94	22	69 D
Taunton Cl. Bexh	79	50	76 D
Taunton Cl. Sutt	103	25	66 C
Taunton Dri. Enf	13	31	96 A
Taunton Mews. NW1	1	27	82 D
Taunton Pl. NW1	1	27	82 D
Taunton Rd. Grnf	43	13	83 B
Taunton Rd. SE12	77	39	74 B
Taunton Way. Stan	21	18	90 C
Taverners Cl. W11	56	24	80 C
Taverner Sq. N5	48	32	85 A
Tavern La. SW9	75	31	76 C
Tavistock Ave. E17	26	36	89 A
Tavistock Ave. Grnf	43	16	83 C
Tavistock Cl (off Crossway). N16			
	48	33	85 C
Tavistock Cl. Rom	30	53	90 B
Tavistock Cres. Mit	96	30	68 C
Tavistock Cres. W11	56	24	81 B
Tavistock Gdns. Ilf	51	45	85 A
Tavistock Gr. Croy	105	32	66 B
Tavistock Mews. W11	56	24	81 D
Tavistock Pl. N14	16	28	94 B
Tavistock Pl. WC1	3	30	82 C
Tavistock Rd. Brom	99	40	68 C
Tavistock Rd. Cars	103	26	66 D
Tavistock Rd. Croy	105	32	66 D
Tavistock Rd. E15	50	39	84 B
Tavistock Rd. E18	27	40	89 A
Tavistock Rd. E7	50	39	85 B
Tavistock Rd. Edg	22	19	90 A
Tavistock Rd. N4	37	32	88 D
Tavistock Rd. NW10	45	21	83 D
Tavistock Rd. W11	56	24	81 B
Tavistock Rd. Well	79	47	76 A
Tavistock Sq. WC1	2	29	82 D
Tavistock St. WC2	7	30	80 A
Tavistock St. WC2	3	30	81 D
Tavistock Terr. N19	36	29	86 D
Tavistock Wlk. Cars	103	26	66 D
Taviton St. WC1	2	29	82 D
Tavy Bridge. SE2	67	47	79 A
Tavy Cl. SE11	63	31	78 C
Tawkesbury Gdns. NW9	22	19	89 B
Tawny Way. SE16	64	35	78 B
Tayben Ave. Twick	71	15	74 C
Tay Bldgs. SE1	8	33	79 C
Taybridge Rd. SW11	74	28	75 A
Tayburn Cl. E14	58	38	81 C
Taylor Ave. Rich	61	19	79 D
Taylor Cl. Hamp	82	14	71 C
Taylor Cl. N17	25	34	91 C
Taylor Cl. Rom	29	49	91 C
Taylor Rd. Mit	96	27	70 D
Taylor Rd. Wall	111	28	64 D
Taylor's Bldgs. SE18	66	43	78 B
Taylor's Cl. Sid	90	45	72 D
Taylor's Green. W3	55	21	81 C
Taylor's La. Barn	11	24	97 B
Taylor's La. NW10	45	21	84 C
Taylor's La. SE26	87	34	71 B
Taylor St. SE18	66	43	78 B
Taymount Rise. SE23	88	35	72 A
Tayport Cl. N1	47	30	84 C
Tay Way. Rom	30	51	90 B
Taywood Rd. Nthlt	53	12	82 B
Teak Cl. SE16	57	36	80 C
Teal Ct. Wall	111	29	64 C
Teale St. E2	48	34	83 C
Tealing Dri. Eps	109	20	64 B
Teasel Way. E15	58	39	82 A
Teather St. SE5	63	33	77 C
Tebworth Rd. N17	25	33	91 D
Teddington Cl. Eps	109	20	62 D
Teddington Park Rd. Tedd	83	15	71 B
Teddington Park. Tedd	83	15	71 D
Tedworth Gdns. SW3	9	27	78 D
Tedworth Sq. SW3	9	27	78 D
Tees Ave. Grnf	44	15	83 D
Teesdale Ave. Islw	71	16	76 A
Teesdale Cl. E2	48	34	83 D
Teesdale Gdns. Islw	71	16	76 A
Teesdale Gdns. SE25	97	33	69 C
Teesdale Rd. E11	39	39	87 B
Teesdale St. E2	48	34	83 D
Teesdale Yd. E2	48	34	83 D
Teeswater Ct. Belv	67	47	79 D
Tee The. W3	55	21	81 C
Teevan Cl. Croy	105	34	66 A
Teevan Rd. Croy	105	34	66 A
Teignmouth Cl. Edg	21	18	90 D
Teignmouth Cl. SW4	74	29	75 D
Teignmouth Gdns. Grnf	54	16	82 A
Teignmouth Rd. NW2	46	23	84 B
Teignmouth Rd. Well	79	47	76 C
Telcote Way. Ruis	32	11	87 A
Telegraph Hill. NW3	35	25	86 D
Telegraph Mews. Ilf	40	46	87 C
Telegraph Rd. SW15	85	23	73 A
Telegraph St. EC2	4	32	81 D
Telegraph Track. Cars	111	28	62 C
Telemann Sq. SE3	77	40	75 B
Telephone Pl. W14	62	24	77 B
Telferscot Rd. SW12	86	29	73 D
Telford Ave. SW2	86	30	73 C
Telford Cl. SE19	97	33	70 B
Telford Rd. Houn	82	13	73 A
Telford Rd. N11	16	29	92 C
Telford Rd. NW9	34	22	88 C
Telford Rd. SE9	90	44	72 B
Telford Rd. Sthl	53	13	81 D
Telford Rd. W10	56	24	81 A
Telford Way. W3	55	21	81 A
Telham Rd. E6	51	43	83 C
Tell Gr. SE22	75	33	75 D
Tellson Ave. SE18	77	41	76 B
Telscombe Cl. Orp	108	45	65 A
Temeraire St. SE16	64	35	79 A
Tempelhof Ave. NW4	35	23	87 A
Temperley Rd. SW12	86	28	73 A
Templar Pl. Hamp	92	13	70 C
Templars Ave. NW11	35	24	88 D
Templars Cres. N3	23	25	90 C
Templars Dri. Har	20	14	91 B
Templar St. SW9	75	31	76 D
Temple Ave. Croy	106	36	65 D
Temple Ave. Dag	41	49	87 C
Temple Ave. EC4	7	31	80 A
Temple Ave. N20	15	26	94 B
Temple Cl. N3	23	24	90 D
Templecombe Rd. E9	49	35	83 A
Templecombe Way. Mord	103	24	67 A
Templecroft. Ashf	91	08	70 B
Temple Fortune Hill. NW11	35	25	88 A
Temple Fortune La. NW11	35	25	88 C
Temple Gdns. Dag	41	47	86 D
Temple Gdns. NW11	35	24	88 D
Temple Gr. Enf	13	31	96 B
Temple Gr. NW11	35	25	88 C
Temple Hill. Dart	80	54	74 B
Temple Hill Sq. Dart	80	54	74 B
Temple La. EC4	3	31	81 C
Templeman Rd. W7	54	15	81 B
Templemead Cl. W3	55	21	81 C
Temple Mead Cl. Stan	21	16	91 B
Temple Mills La. E15	49	38	85 A
Temple Mills Rd. E15	49	38	85 A
Temple Pl. WC2	7	30	80 B
Temple Rd. Croy	112	32	64 B
Temple Rd. E6	50	42	83 A
Temple Rd. Houn	70	14	75 C
Temple Rd. N8	24	30	89 D
Temple Rd. NW2	46	23	85 A
Temple Rd. Rich	71	18	76 D
Temple Rd. W4	61	20	79 C
Temple Rd. W5	60	17	79 D
Temple Sheen Rd. SW14	72	20	75 C
Temple Sheen. SW14	72	20	74 A
Temple St. E2	48	34	83 D
Templeton Ave. E4	18	37	93 C
Templeton Cl (off Crossway). N16			
	48	33	85 C
Templeton Cl. SE19	97	32	69 B
Templeton Pl. SW5	62	25	78 A
Templeton Rd. N15	37	32	88 D
Temple Way. Sutt	103	26	65 D
Templewood Ave. NW3	35	25	86 D
Templewood Gdns. NW3	35	25	86 D
Templewood. W13	54	16	81 B
Temple Yd. E2	48	34	83 D
Tempsford Ct. Har	33	15	88 D
Temsford Cl. Har	20	14	90 C
Tenbury Cl. E7	50	41	85 D
Tenbury Ct. SW2	86	30	73 C
Tenby Ave. Har	21	16	90 D
Tenby Cl. N15	25	33	89 D
Tenby Cl. Rom	41	48	88 C
Tenby Cl. Rom	41	48	88 C
Tenby Ct. E17	38	36	88 A
Tenby Gdns. Nthlt	43	13	84 A
Tenby Rd. E17	38	36	88 A
Tenby Rd. Edg	21	18	90 D
Tenby Rd. Enf	14	35	96 C
Tenby Rd. Rom	41	48	88 C
Tenby Rd. Well	79	47	76 B
Tench St. E1	57	34	80 D
Tenda Rd. SE16	63	34	78 B
Tendring Way. Rom	41	47	88 A
Tenham Ave. SW2	86	29	72 B
Tenison Ct. W1	6	29	80 A
Tenison Way. SE1	7	31	80 C
Tenniel Cl. W2	56	25	80 B
Tennis Court La. E Mol	93	15	68 B
Tennison Rd. SE25	105	33	67 B
Tennis St. SE1	8	32	79 B
Tenniswood Rd. Enf	13	33	97 A
Tennyson Ave. E11	39	40	87 A
Tennyson Ave. E12	50	42	84 C
Tennyson Ave. N. Mal	102	22	67 B
Tennyson Ave. NW9	22	20	89 A
Tennyson Ave. Twick	83	15	72 B
Tennyson Cl. Felt	69	10	74 C
Tennyson Cl. Well	78	45	76 B
Tennyson Rd. E10	38	37	86 B
Tennyson Rd. E15	50	39	84 C
Tennyson Rd. E17	38	36	88 D
Tennyson Rd. Houn	70	14	76 C
Tennyson Rd. NW6	46	24	83 B
Tennyson Rd. Rom	30	53	91 C
Tennyson Rd. SE20	98	35	70 D
Tennyson Rd. W7	54	15	80 B
Tennyson St. SW8	74	28	76 D
Tennyson Way. Horn	42	51	86 B
Tensing Rd. Sthl	59	13	79 C
Tentelow La. Sthl	59	13	79 D
Tenterden Cl. NW4	23	23	89 B
Tenterden Dri. NW4	23	23	89 B
Tenterden Gdns. Croy	105	34	66 A
Tenterden Gdns. NW4	23	23	89 B
Tenterden Rd. Croy	105	34	66 A
Tenterden Rd. Dag	41	48	86 B
Tenterden Rd. N17	25	33	91 C
Tenterden St. W1	2	28	81 D
Tenter Ground. E1	4	33	81 B
Tent St. E1	57	34	82 D
Terborch Way. SE22	75	33	74 A
Teresa Wlk. N10	36	28	88 B
Terling Cl. E11	39	39	86 D
Terling Rd. Dag	41	49	86 A
Terling Wlk. N1	48	32	83 A
Terminus Pl. SW1	6	28	79 D
Terrace Ave. W10	56	23	82 A
Terrace Gdns. SW13	72	21	76 D
Terrace Hill. Croy	105	31	65 D
Terrace La. Rich	71	18	74 C
Terrace Rd. E13	50	40	83 A
Terrace Rd. E9	49	35	84 D
Terrace The. E12	39	42	86 A
Terrace The. EC4	3	31	81 C
Terrace The. NW6	46	25	83 A
Terrace The. SW13	72	21	76 C
Terrace Wlk. Dag	52	48	85 C
Terrapin Rd. SW17	86	28	72 D
Terrick Rd. N22	24	30	90 A
Terrick St. W12	55	22	81 D
Terrilands. Pnr	20	12	89 B
Terront Rd. N15	25	32	89 C
Testerton Wlk. W11	56	23	80 B
Testwood Ct. W7	54	15	80 A
Tetbury Pl. N1	48	31	83 B
Tetcott Rd. SW10	62	26	77 C
Tetherdown. N10	24	28	89 A
Tetterby Way. SE16	63	34	78 D
Tetty Way. Brom	99	40	69 C

Name	Map	Ref
Teversham La. SW8	74	30 76 B
Teviot Cl. Well	78	46 76 B
Teviot St. E14	58	38 81 A
Tewkesbury Ave. Pnr	32	12 88 A
Tewkesbury Ave. SE23	87	34 73 B
*Tewkesbury Cl. N15	37	32 88 D
Tewkesbury Rd. Cars	103	22 66 D
Tewkesbury Rd. N15	37	32 88 D
Tewkesbury Rd. W13	16	80 A
Tewkesbury Terr. N11	24	29 91 B
Tewson Rd. SE18	66	45 78 C
Teynham Ave. Enf	13	32 95 D
Teynham Green. Brom	107	40 67 A
Teynton Terr. N17	25	32 90 C
Thackeray Ave. N17	25	34 90 C
Thackeray Cl. Har	32	13 87 C
Thackeray Cl. SW19	95	23 70 D
Thackeray Ct. W5	54	18 81 D
Thackeray Gdns. Rom	40	46 87 B
Thackeray Rd. SW8	74	28 76 D
Thackeray St. W8	62	25 79 D
Thakeham Cl. SE26	87	34 71 D
Thakeray Rd. E6	50	41 83 D
Thalias St. SE10	64	38 77 B
Thames Ave. Dag	52	50 83 C
Thames Ave. Grnf	44	15 83 D
Thames Bank. SW14	72	20 76 C
Thames Cl. Hamp	92	13 69 D
Thames Dri. Ruis	31	08 88 C
Thames Eyot. Twick	83	16 73 C
Thamesgate Cl. Rich	83	16 71 B
Thameshill Ave. Rom	29	50 90 C
Thameside. Tedd	93	17 70 D
Thames Meadow. E Mol	92	13 68 A
Thames Pl. E14	57	36 80 B
Thamespoint. Tedd	93	17 70 D
Thames Rd. Dart	80	52 75 A
Thames Rd. E16	58	41 80 D
Thames Rd. W4	61	19 77 B
Thames Side. King	93	17 69 B
Thames Side. Surb	101	16 67 D
Thames St. Hamp	92	13 69 D
Thames St. King	93	17 69 C
Thames St. SE10	64	38 77 A
Thames St. Sun	92	11 68 A
Thamesvale Cl. Houn	70	13 76 C
Thames Village. W4	72	20 76 A
Thanescroft Gdns. Croy	105	33 65 C
Thanet Ct. W3	55	19 81 C
Thanet Dri. Brom	107	41 65 D
Thanet Pl. Croy	112	32 64 A
Thanet Rd. Eri	68	51 77 C
Thanet St. WC1	3	30 82 A
Thane Villas. N7	36	30 86 D
Thanington Ct. SE9	78	45 74 C
Tharp Rd. Wall	111	29 64 D
Thatcham Gdns. N20	15	26 94 A
Thatchers Way. Islw	70	14 74 B
Thathes Gr. Rom	29	48 89 C
Thavie's Inn. EC4	3	31 81 C
Thaxted Pl. SW20	95	23 70 D
Thaxted Rd. SE9	90	44 72 A
Thaxton Rd. W14	62	24 77 B
Thayers Farm Rd. Beck	98	36 69 A
Thayer St. W1	2	28 81 C
Theatre St. SW11	74	27 75 B
Theberton St. N1	48	31 83 B
The Cedars. E9	49	35 84 D
The Chevenings. Sid	90	46 72 D
The Curve. W12	55	22 80 A
Theed St. SE1	7	31 80 C
The Hatch. Enf	14	35 97 B
The Link. W3	55	19 81 D
Thelma Gdns. SE3	77	42 76 A
Thelma Gr. Tedd	93	16 70 A
Theobald Cres. Har	20	14 90 A
Theobald Rd. Croy	105	31 65 B
Theobald Rd. E17	38	37 87 A
Theobald's Ave. N12	15	26 92 A
Theobald's Rd. WC1	3	30 81 B
Theobald St. SE1	8	32 79 D
Theodore Rd. SE13	76	38 74 D
Therapia La. Croy	104	29 66 B
Therapia Rd. SE22	76	35 74 C
Theresa Rd. W6	61	22 78 A
Theresa's Wlk. S Croy	112	32 63 B
Thermopylae Gate. E14	64	37 78 B
Theseus Wlk. N1	48	31 83 D
Thesiger Rd. SE20	87	35 70 D
The Sir Oswald Stoll Foundation. SW6	62	25 77 D
The Sunny Rd. Enf	14	35 97 B
Thetford Cl. N22	25	31 91 B
Thetford Gdns. Dag	52	47 83 B
Thetford Rd. Dag	52	47 84 D
Thetford Rd. N.Mal	102	21 67 A
Theydon Gr. Wdf Gn	27	41 91 A
Theydon Rd. E5	38	35 86 A
Theydon St. E17	38	36 87 B
Thicket Cres. Sutt	110	26 64 A
Thicket Gr. Dag	52	47 84 A
Thicket Gr. SE20	97	34 70 C
Thicket Rd. SE20	97	34 70 D
Thicket Rd. Sutt	110	26 64 A
Third Ave. Dag	52	49 83 D
Third Ave. E12	50	42 85 B
Third Ave. E13	58	40 82 A
Third Ave. E17	38	37 88 A
Third Ave. Enf	13	33 95 B
Third Ave. Rom	41	47 88 A
Third Ave. W10	56	24 82 A
Third Ave. W3	55	21 80 D
Third Ave. Wem	33	17 86 B
Third Cl. E Mol	92	14 68 C
Third Cross Rd. Twick	82	14 72 B
Thirleby Rd. Edg	22	20 90 B
Thirleby Rd. SW1	6	29 79 C
Thirlmere Ave. Grnf	54	17 82 A
Thirlmere Gdns. Nthwd	19	08 91 A
Thirlmere Gdns. Wem	33	17 87 D
Thirlmere Rd. Bexh	79	50 76 A
Thirlmere Rd. N10	24	28 90 B
Thirlmere Rd. SW16	86	29 71 B
Thirlmere Rise. Brom	99	39 70 B
Thirsk Cl. Nthlt	43	13 84 A
Thirsk Rd. Mit	96	28 70 C
Thirsk Rd. SW11	74	28 75 A
Thirza Rd. Dart	80	54 74 D
Thistlebrook. SE2	67	47 79 C
Thistlecroft Gdns. Stan	21	17 90 D
Thistledene Ave. Har	32	12 86 C
Thistledene. E Mol	101	15 67 C
Thistle Gr. SW10	62	26 78 C
Thistle Gr. SW10	62	26 78 C
Thistlemead. Chis	100	43 69 D
Thistlewaite Rd. E5	37	34 86 D
Thistlewood Cl. N7	36	30 86 B
Thistleworth Cl. Islw	59	14 77 D
Thomas A' Beckett Cl. Wem	44	15 85 B
Thomas Baines Rd. SW11	73	26 75 B
Thomas Doyle St. SE1	7	31 79 D
Thomas La. SE6	88	37 73 A
Thomas More St. E1	57	34 80 C
Thomas More Way. N2	23	26 89 A
Thomas Rd. E14	57	37 81 A
Thomas St. SE18	66	43 78 B
Thompson Ave. Rich	72	19 75 A
Thompson Rd. Dag	41	48 86 D
Thompson Rd. SE22	75	33 74 D
Thompson's Ave. SE5	63	32 77 C
Thomson Cres. Croy	105	31 66 C
Thomson Rd. Har	21	15 89 A
Thorburn Way. SW19	95	26 69 B
Thoresby St. N1	4	32 82 A
Thorkhill Gdns. Surb	101	16 66 C
Thorkhill Rd. Surb	101	16 66 B
Thornaby Gdns. N18	17	34 92 C
Thornbury Cl. N16	48	34 78 A
Thornbury Sq. SE1	63	34 78 A
Thornbury Av. Islw	59	14 77 D
Thornbury Cl (off Boleyn Rd). N16	48	33 85 C
Thornbury Rd. Islw	70	14 76 B
Thornbury Rd. SW2	74	30 74 C
Thornby Rd. E5	38	35 86 C
Thorn Cl. Brom	108	43 67 C
Thorncliffe Rd. Sthl	53	12 78 D
Thorncliffe Rd. SW4	74	30 74 C
Thorn Cl. Nthlt	53	12 82 B
Thorncombe Rd. SE22	75	33 74 A
Thorncroft. Horn	42	52 88 D
Thorncroft Rd. Sutt	110	25 64 D
Thorncroft St. SW8	10	30 77 C
Thorndean St. SW18	85	26 72 A
Thorndene Ave. N11	16	28 94 C
Thorndike Ave. Nthlt	43	11 83 D
Thorndike Cl. SW10	62	26 77 C
Thorndike Rd. SW1	10	29 78 B
Thorndon Cl. Orp	100	45 69 D
Thorndon Gdns. Eps	109	21 64 A
Thorndon Rd. Orp	100	45 69 D
Thorndyke Ct. Pnr	20	12 91 D
Thorne Cl. Ashf	91	08 70 C
Thorne Cl. E11	50	39 85 A
Thorne Cl. E16	58	40 81 C
Thorne Cl. Eri	67	49 77 B
Thorne Cl. N Mal	94	20 68 C
Thorneloe Gdns. Croy	112	31 64 D
Thorne Pas. SW13	72	21 76 C
Thorne Rd. N Mal	94	20 68 C
Thorne Rd. SW8	10	30 77 C
Thorne's Cl. Beck	98	38 68 A
Thorne St. E16	58	39 81 D
Thorne St. SW13	72	21 75 A
Thornet Wood Rd. Brom	100	43 68 A
Thorney Hedge Rd. W4	61	19 78 B
Thorney St. SW1	10	30 78 A
Thornfield Ave. NW7	23	24 90 A
Thornfield Rd. W12	61	22 79 B
Thornford Rd. SE13	76	38 74 A
Thorngate Rd. W9	56	25 82 C
Thorngrove Rd. E13	50	40 83 B
Thornham Gr. E15	49	38 85 D
Thornham St. SE10	64	37 77 B
Thornhaugh Mews. WC1	2	29 82 D
Thornhaugh St. WC1	2	29 82 D
Thornhill Ave. SE18	66	45 77 C
Thornhill Ave. Surb	101	18 65 A
Thornhill Cres. N1	47	30 84 D
Thornhill Gdns. Bark	51	45 84 C
Thornhill Gdns. E10	37	38 86 B
Thornhill Gr. N1	48	31 84 C
Thornhill Rd. Croy	105	32 66 A
Thornhill Rd. E10	38	37 86 B
Thornhill Rd. N1	48	31 84 C
Thornhill Rd. Surb	101	18 65 B
Thornhill Rd. Uxb	31	07 86 C
Thornhill Sq. N1	47	30 84 D
Thornlaw Rd. SE27	87	31 71 B
Thornley Cl. N17	25	34 91 C
Thornley Dri. Har	32	13 86 B
Thornley Pl. E10	65	39 78 C
Thornsbeach Rd. SE6	88	38 72 A
Thornsett Pl. SE20	97	34 69 D
Thornsett Rd. SE20	97	34 69 D
Thornsett Rd. SW18	85	25 73 D
Thornton Ave. Croy	104	30 67 D
Thornton Ave. SW2	86	29 73 D
Thornton Ave. W4	61	21 78 A
Thornton Dene. Beck	98	37 69 C
Thornton Gdns. SW12	86	29 73 D
Thornton Gr. Pnr	20	13 91 A
Thornton Hill. SW19	95	24 70 C
Thornton Pl. W1	2	27 81 B
Thornton Rd. Barn	11	24 96 A
Thornton Rd. Belv	67	49 78 B
Thornton Rd. Brom	89	40 71 C
Thornton Rd. Cars	103	26 66 D
Thornton Rd. Croy	104	30 67 D
Thornton Rd. E11	38	38 86 B
Thornton Rd. Ilf	51	43 85 B
Thornton Rd. SW12	86	29 73 D
Thornton Rd. SW14	72	20 75 B
Thornton Rd. SW19	95	23 70 B
Thornton Rd. Th Hth	105	31 67 A
Thornton Row. Th Hth	105	31 67 A
Thorntons Farm Ave. Rom	41	50 86 B
Thornton St. SW9	75	31 76 C
Thornton Way. NW11	35	25 88 B
Thorntree Rd. SE7	65	41 78 D
Thornville St. SE8	76	37 76 A
Thornwood Cl. E18	27	40 90 D
Thornwood Rd. SE13	77	39 74 A
Thorogood Gdns. E15	50	39 85 C
Thorold Rd. Ilf	40	44 87 C
Thorold Rd. N22	24	30 91 C
Thorpebank Rd. W12	55	22 80 C
Thorpe Cl. Horn	42	53 87 B
Thorpe Cl. Orp	108	45 65 A
Thorpe Cl. SE26	88	35 71 B
Thorpe Cl. W10	56	24 81 C
Thorpe Cres. E17	28	36 90 B
Thorpedale Gdns. Ilf	28	43 89 D
Thorpedale Rd. N4	36	30 87 D
Thorpe Hall Rd. E17	26	38 90 A
Thorpe Rd. Bark	51	44 84 D
Thorpe Rd. E17	26	38 90 C
Thorpe Rd. E6	50	42 83 B
Thorpe Rd. E7	50	39 85 B
Thorpe Rd. King	93	18 70 C
Thorpe Rd. N15	33	33 88 C
Thorpewood Ave. SE26	87	34 72 B
Thorpewood Ave. SE26	88	35 72 A
Thorsden Way. SE19	87	33 71 C
Thorverton Rd. NW2	35	24 86 C
Thoydon Rd. E3	49	36 83 C
Thrale Rd. SW16	86	29 71 C
Thrale St. SE1	8	32 80 C
Thrawl St. E1	4	33 81 B
Threadneedle St. EC2	4	32 81 D
Three Colt Cnr. E2	57	34 82 C
Three Colts La. E2	57	34 82 D
Three Colt St. E14	57	36 80 B

Name		Grid
Three Corners. Bexh ...79	50 76 C
Three Kings Rd. Mit ...96	28 68 A
Three Kings Yd. W1 ...6	28 80 B
Three Mill La. E3 ...58	38 82 A
Three Nun Ct. EC2 ...4	32 81 C
Three Oak La. SE1 ...8	33 79 B
Threshers Pl. W11 ...56	24 80 A
Thriftwood. SE23 ...88	35 72 D
Throckmorten Rd. E16 ...58	40 81 D
Throgmorton Ave. EC2 ...4	32 81 D
Throgmorton St. EC2 ...4	32 81 D
Throwley Cl. SE2 ...67	47 79 C
Throwley Rd. Sutt ...110	25 64 D
Throwley Way. Sutt ...110	25 64 D
Thrupp Cl. Mit ...96	28 69 D
Thrush St. SE17 ...63	32 78 C
Thruxton Way. (OFF Garnies Cl).	
SE15 ...63	33 77 D
Thurbarn Rd. SE6 ...87	37 71 D
Thurland Rd. SE16 ...63	34 79 C
Thurlby Cl. Har ...33	16 88 C
Thurlby Cl. Wdf Gn ...27	42 91 B
Thurlby Rd. SE27 ...87	31 71 B
Thurlby Rd. Wem ...44	17 84 B
Thurleigh Ave. SW12 ...74	28 74 C
Thurleigh Rd. SW12 ...74	28 74 C
Thurleigh Rd. SW12 ...74	28 74 C
Thurleston Ave. Mord ...103	24 67 A
Thurlestone Av. Ilf ...51	45 85 B
Thurlestone Ave. N12 ...24	27 91 B
Thurlestone Rd. SE27 ...87	31 71 A
Thurloe Cl. SW7 ...9	27 78 A
Thurloe Gdns. Rom ...42	51 88 D
Thurloe Place Mews. SW7 ...62	26 78 B
Thurloe Pl. SW7 ...62	26 78 B
Thurloe Pl. SW7 ...5	27 79 C
Thurloe Sq. SW7 ...9	27 78 A
Thurloe St. SW7 ...62	26 78 B
Thuow Gdns. Ilf ...28	44 91 B
Thurlow Gdns. Wem ...44	17 85 D
Thurlow Hill. SE21 ...87	32 72 A
Thurlow Park Rd. SE21 ...87	32 72 A
Thurlow Rd. NW3 ...46	26 85 D
Thurlow Rd. W7 ...60	16 79 A
Thurlow St. SE17 ...63	33 78 C
Thurlow Terr. NW5 ...47	28 85 C
Thurlow Wlk. SE17 ...63	33 78 C
Thurlston Rd. Ruis ...31	10 86 C
Thurnby Ct. Twick ...83	15 72 C
Thursley Gdns. SW19 ...85	23 72 B
Thursley Rd. SE9 ...89	42 72 D
Thurso St. SW17 ...85	26 71 B
Thurstan Rd. SW20 ...94	22 70 D
Thurston Rd. SE13 ...76	37 75 B
Thurston Rd. Sthl ...53	13 81 C
Thurtle Rd. E2 ...48	33 83 D
Thwaite Cl. Eri ...37	50 77 A
Thyra Gr. N12 ...23	25 91 B
Tibbat's Rd. E3 ...57	37 82 D
Tibbenham Wlk. E13 ...50	39 83 D
Tibberton Sq. N1 ...48	32 84 C
Tibbets Cl. SW19 ...85	23 73 D
Tibbet's Cnr. SW15 ...85	23 73 B
Tibbet's Ride. SW15 ...85	23 73 B
Ticehurst Rd. SE23 ...88	36 72 A
Tichmarsh. Eps ...109	20 62 C
Tickford Cl. SE2 ...67	47 79 A
Tidal Basin Rd. E16 ...58	39 80 B
Tidenham Gdns. Croy ...105	33 65 C
Tideswell Rd. Croy ...106	37 65 C
Tideswell Rd. SW15 ...73	23 74 A
Tideway Cl. Rich ...83	17 71 A
Tidey St. E3 ...57	37 81 A
Tidford Rd. Well ...78	45 76 D
Tidworth Rd. E3 ...57	37 82 C
Tiepigs La. Brom ...107	39 66 D
Tiepigs La. W.Wick ...107	39 65 B
Tierney Rd. SW2 ...86	30 73 C
Tiger La. Brom ...99	40 68 B
Tiger Way. E5 ...48	34 85 B
Tilbrook Rd. SE3 ...77	41 75 B
Tilbury Cl. Orp ...100	46 69 D
Tilbury Rd. E10 ...38	38 87 A
Tilbury Rd. E6 ...52	42 83 D
Tildesley Rd. SW15 ...73	23 74 A
Tile Farm Rd. Orp ...108	44 65 D
Tilehurst Rd. Sutt ...110	24 64 A
Tilehurst Rd. SW18 ...85	26 73 D
Tile Kiln La. N13 ...17	32 92 C
Tile Kiln La. N6 ...36	29 87 C
Tile Kilns La. Uxb ...31	07 87 B
Tileyard Rd. N7 ...47	30 84 C
Tile Yd. E14 ...57	36 81 D
Tilford Gdns. SW19 ...85	23 73 D
Tiller Rd. E14 ...64	37 79 C
Tillett Cl. NW10 ...45	20 84 A
Tillet Way. E2 ...57	34 82 A
Tillingbourne Gdns. N3 ...23	24 89 B
Tillingbourne Green. Orp ...100	46 68 C
Tillingbourne Way. N3 ...23	24 89 D
Tillingham Way. N12 ...15	25 92 A
Tilling Rd. NW2 ...22	22 87 D
Tilling Rd. NW2 ...35	23 87 A
Tillman St. E1 ...57	34 81 D
Tilloch St. N1 ...47	30 84 D
Tillotson Rd. Har ...20	13 91 C
Tillotson Rd. Ilf ...40	43 87 A
Tillotson Rd. N9 ...17	33 93 B
Tillotson St. E1 ...57	35 81 B
Tilney Ct. EC1 ...4	32 82 C
Tilney Gdns. N1 ...48	32 84 B
Tilney Rd. Dag ...52	48 84 B
Tilney Rd. Sthl ...59	11 78 A
Tilney St. W1 ...6	28 80 C
Tilson Gdns. SW2 ...86	30 73 A
Tilson Rd. N17 ...25	34 90 A
Tilton St. SW6 ...62	24 77 A
Tiltwood The. W3 ...55	20 80 A
Tilt Yard App. SE9 ...77	42 74 D
Timber Cl. Chis ...100	43 69 C
Timber Cl. Eps ...109	21 64 A
Timbercroft La. SE18 ...66	45 77 C
Timberland Rd. E1 ...57	34 81 D
Timberling Gdns. S Croy ...112	32 62 D
Timber Mill Way. SW4 ...74	29 75 B
Timberslip Dri. Wall ...111	29 62 B
Timber St. EC1 ...4	32 82 C
Timberwharf Rd. N16 ...37	34 88 C
Timothy Rd. E3 ...57	36 81 B
Timsbury Wlk. SW15 ...84	22 73 C
Tindall Cl. Rom ...30	54 90 D
Tindal St. SW9 ...75	31 76 B
Tinderbox Alley. SW14 ...72	20 75 B
Tinsley Rd. E1 ...57	35 81 A
Tintagel Cres. SE22 ...75	33 75 D
Tintagel Gdns. SE22 ...75	33 75 D
Tintern Ave. NW9 ...19	19 89 B
Tintern Cl. SW15 ...73	24 74 A
Tintern Cl. SW19 ...95	26 70 A
Tintern Gdns. N14 ...16	29 94 A
Tintern Rd. Cars ...103	26 66 D
Tintern Rd. N22 ...25	32 90 A
Tintern St. SW4 ...74	30 75 C
Tintern Way. Har ...32	13 87 D
Tinto Rd. E16 ...58	40 82 C
Tinworth St. SE11 ...7	30 78 D
Tippetts Cl. Enf ...13	32 97 A
Tipthorpe Rd. SW11 ...74	28 75 A
Tipton Dri. Croy ...112	33 64 A
Tiptree Cres. Ilf ...28	43 89 A
Tiptree Dri. Enf ...13	32 96 D
Tirlemont Rd. S Croy ...112	32 63 C
Tirrell Rd. Croy ...105	32 67 C
Tisbury Ct. W1 ...6	29 80 B
Tisbury Rd. SW16 ...96	30 69 C
Tisdall Pl. SE17 ...63	32 78 B
Titchborne Row. W2 ...1	27 81 C
Titchfield Rd. Cars ...103	26 66 D
Titchfield Rd. NW8 ...47	27 83 B
Titchfield Wlk. Cars ...103	26 66 B
Titchwell Rd. SW18 ...85	26 73 D
Tite St. SW3 ...9	27 77 B
Tithe Barn Cl. King ...93	18 69 B
Tithe Cl. NW7 ...22	22 90 A
Tithe Farm Ave. Har ...32	13 86 C
Tithe Farm Cl. Har ...32	13 86 C
Tithe Wlk. NW7 ...22	22 90 A
Titley Cl. E4 ...18	37 92 C
Titmus St. W12 ...61	22 79 B
Tivendale. N8 ...24	30 89 A
Tiverton Ave. Ilf ...28	43 89 A
Tiverton Dri. SE9 ...90	44 73 C
Tiverton Rd. Edg ...21	18 90 D
Tiverton Rd. Houn ...70	14 76 C
Tiverton Rd. N15 ...237	32 88 D
Tiverton Rd. N18 ...17	33 92 C
Tiverton Rd. NW10 ...46	23 83 B
Tiverton Rd. Ruis ...31	10 86 C
Tiverton Rd. Wem ...44	18 83 C
Tiverton St. SE1 ...8	32 79 C
Tivoli Gdns. SE18 ...65	42 78 A
Tivoli Rd. Houn ...70	12 75 C
Tivoli Rd. N8 ...36	29 88 B
Tivoli Rd. SE27 ...87	32 71 C
Tobago St. E14 ...64	37 79 A
Tobin Cl. NW3 ...47	27 84 C
Toby La. E2 ...57	36 82 C
Todds Wlk. N7 ...36	30 86 B
Tokenhouse Yd. EC2 ...4	32 81 D
Token Yd. SW15 ...73	24 75 C
Tokyngton Ave. Wem ...45	19 84 A
Toland Sq. SW15 ...72	22 74 A
Tolbut Ct. Rom ...42	51 88 D
Tolcarne Dri. Pnr ...19	10 89 B
Toley Ave. Wem ...33	18 87 A
Tollesbury Gdns. Ilf ...28	44 89 B
Tollet St. E1 ...57	35 82 D
Tollgate Dri. SE21 ...87	33 72 C
Tollgate Rd. E16 ...58	41 81 B
Tollhouse Way. N19 ...36	29 86 A
Tollington Park. N4 ...36	30 86 B
Tollington Pl. N4 ...36	30 86 B
Tollington Rd. N7 ...47	30 85 B
Tollington Way. N7 ...36	30 86 A
Tolmers Sq. NW1 ...2	29 82 C
Tolsford Rd. E5 ...48	34 85 D
Tolson Rd. Islw ...71	16 75 A
Tolverne Rd. SW20 ...95	23 69 A
Tolworth Cl. Surb ...119	19 66 D
Tolworth Gdns. Rom ...41	47 88 B
Tolworth Park Rd. Surb ...101	18 65 B
Tolworth Rd. Surb ...101	18 65 A
Tolworth Rise N. Surb ...102	20 66 C
Tolworth Rise S. Surb ...102	20 66 C
Tolworth Underpass. Surb ...102	19 65 B
Tomahawk Gdns (off Javelin Way).	
Nthlt ...53	11 82 B
Tom Coombs Cl. SE9 ...77	42 75 C
Tom Cribb Rd. SE28 ...66	44 79 D
Tomlin's Gr. E3 ...57	37 82 A
Tomlinson Cl. E2 ...4	33 82 B
Tomlins Orchard. Bark ...51	44 83 A
Tomlins Terr. E14 ...57	36 81 B
Tomlins Wlk. N7 ...36	30 86 B
Tom Mann Cl. Bark ...51	45 83 A
Tompion St. EC1 ...3	31 82 B
Tomswood Cl. Wfd ...28	44 90 A
Tomswood Hill. Ilf ...28	44 91 C
Tomswood Rd. Chig ...28	43 91 A
Tonbridge Cres. Har ...21	18 89 C
Tonbridge Rd. E Mol ...92	12 68 D
Tonbridge Rd. Rom ...30	53 91 D
Tonbridge St. WC1 ...3	30 82 A
Tonfield Rd. Sutt ...103	24 66 D
Tonge Cl. Beck ...106	37 67 A
Tonsley Hill. SW18 ...73	25 74 B
Tonsley Pl. SW18 ...73	25 74 B
Tonsley Rd. SW18 ...73	25 74 B
Tonsley St. SW18 ...73	25 74 B
Tonstall Rd. Eps ...109	20 62 D
Tonstall Rd. Mit ...96	28 68 C
Tooke Cl. Pnr ...20	12 90 A
Tooley St. SE1 ...8	33 80 C
Toorack Rd. Har ...20	14 90 D
Tooting Bec Gdns. SW16 ...86	29 71 B
Tooting Bec.Rd. SW12 ...86	28 72 C
Tooting Bec Rd. SW16 ...86	29 71 A
Tooting Bwy. SW17 ...86	27 71 C
Tooting Gr. SW17 ...86	27 71 C
Tooting High St. SW17 ...86	27 70 A
Tooting High St. SW17 ...86	27 71 C
Tootswood Rd. Brom ...99	39 68 C
Topaz St. SE11 ...10	30 78 B
Topham Sq. N17 ...25	32 90 C
Topham St. EC1 ...3	31 82 C
Top House Rise. E4 ...18	38 94 A
Topiary Sq. Rich ...71	18 75 B
Topley St. SE9 ...77	41 75 D
Top Park. Beck ...107	39 67 A
Topp Wlk. NW2 ...35	23 86 A
Topsfield Rd. N8 ...36	30 88 A
Topsham Rd. SW17 ...86	28 71 A
Torbay Rd. Har ...32	12 86 A
Torbay Rd. NW6 ...46	24 84 D
Torbay St. NW1 ...47	28 84 D
Torbridge Cl. Edg ...21	18 91 C
Torcross Dri. SE23 ...88	35 72 A
Torcross Rd. Ruis ...32	11 86 C
Tor Gdns. W8 ...62	25 79 A
Tormead Cl. Sutt ...110	25 63 A
Tormount Rd. SE18 ...66	45 78 C
Toronto Ave. E12 ...50	42 85 B
Toronto Rd. E11 ...49	38 85 B
Toronto Rd. Ilf ...40	44 87 C
Torquay Gdns. Ilf ...27	41 89 D
Torquay St. W2 ...56	25 81 B
Torrance Cl. Horn ...42	53 87 B
Tor Rd. Well ...79	47 76 A
Torrens Rd. E15 ...50	39 84 B
Torrens Rd. SW2 ...74	30 74 B
Torrens Sq. E15 ...50	39 84 B
Torrens St. N1 ...48	31 83 D
Torre Wlk. Cars ...104	27 66 C
Torriano Ave. NW5 ...47	29 85 D
Torriano Cottages. NW5 ...47	29 85 D

Torridge Gdns. SE15

Name		Grid
Torridge Gdns. SE15	76	35 75 C
Torridge Rd. Th Hth	105	31 67 B
Torridon Rd. SE13	89	39 73 A
Torridon Rd. SE6	88	38 73 D
Torrington Ave. N12	15	26 92 D
Torrington Ct. SE26	87	34 71 C
Torrington Dri. Har	32	13 86 D
Torrington Gdns. Grnf	44	17 84 C
Torrington Gdns. N11	24	29 91 A
Torrington Gr. N12	15	27 92 C
Torrington Park N12	15	26 92 B
Torrington Pl. WC1	3	29 82 D
Torrington Rd. Dag	41	48 87 D
Torrington Rd. E18	27	40 89 A
Torrington Rd. Grnf	44	17 83 A
Torrington Rd. Ruis	31	10 86 C
Torrington Sq. WC1	3	29 82 D
Torrington Way. Mord	103	25 67 C
Torr Rd. SE20	98	35 70 D
Torver Rd. Har	21	15 89 C
Torver Way. Orp	108	44 65 B
Torwood Rd. SW15	72	22 74 A
Tothill St. SW1	4	29 79 B
Totnes Rd. Well	67	47 77 C
Totnes Wlk. N2	23	26 89 D
Tottenhall Rd. N13	17	31 92 D
Tottenham Ct Rd. W1	2	29 81 B
Tottenham Green East South Side.		
N15	25	33 89 D
Tottenham Green E. N15	25	33 89 D
Tottenham La. N8	36	30 88 A
Tottenham La. N8	24	30 89 D
Tottenham Mews. W1	2	29 81 A
Tottenham Rd. N1	48	33 84 A
Tottenham St. W1	2	29 81 A
Totterdown St. SW17	86	27 71 D
Totteridge Common. N20	15	23 94 D
Totteridge La. N20	15	25 94 D
Totteridge Village. N20	15	24 94 D
Totternhoe Cl. Har	33	17 88 A
Totton Rd. Th Hth	104	31 68 A
Totty St. E3	49	36 83 C
Toulmin St. SE1	8	32 79 A
Toulon St. SE5	63	32 77 C
Tournay Rd. SW6	63	24 77 D
*Toussaint Wlk. SE16	63	34 79 C
Tovil Cl. SE20	97	34 69 D
Towcester Rd. E3	58	38 82 C
Tower Bridge App. E1	8	33 80 B
Tower Bridge. E1	8	33 80 D
Tower Bridge Rd. SE1	8	33 79 A
Tower Cl. Ilf	28	43 91 B
Tower Cl. Orp	108	45 65 D
Tower Cl. SE20	97	34 70 D
Tower Ct. N16	37	33 87 B
Tower Ct. W2	3	30 81 C
Tower Gardens Rd. N17	25	32 90 B
Tower Hamlets Rd. E17	26	37 89 A
Tower Hamlets Rd. E7	50	39 85 D
Tower Hill. EC3	8	33 80 B
Tower Mews. E17	26	37 89 C
Tower Rd. Belv	67	50 78 A
Tower Rd. Bexh	79	49 75 C
Tower Rd. Dart	80	53 74 D
Tower Rd. NW10	45	22 84 C
Tower Rd. Orp	108	45 65 D
Tower Rd. Twick	83	15 72 D
Tower Rise. Rich	71	18 75 A
Tower Royal. EC4	8	32 80 A
Towers Pl. Rich	71	18 74 A
Towers Rd. Pnr	20	12 90 A
Towers Rd. Sthl	53	13 82 C
Tower St. WC2	3	30 81 C
Tower Terr. N22	24	30 90 D
Tower View. Croy	106	36 66 A
Towfield Rd. Felt	82	12 72 B
Towncourt Cres. Orp	100	44 68 D
Town Court La. Orp	108	44 66 B
Towncourt Path. N4	37	32 87 C
Towney Mead Ct. Nthlt	43	12 83 D
Towney Mead Ct. Nthlt	43	12 83 D
Towney Mead. Nthlt	43	12 83 D
Towney Mead. Nthlt	43	12 83 D
Town Hall App. N16	48	33 85 A
Town Hall App. N16	48	33 85 A
Town Hall Ave. W4	61	20 78 D
Town Hall Rd. SW11	74	27 75 B
Townholm Cres. W7	60	15 79 D
Townley Ct. E15	50	39 84 B
Townley Rd. Bexh	79	48 74 B
Townley Rd. SE22	75	33 74 A
Townley St. SE17	63	32 78 D
Town Meadow Rd. Brent	60	17 77 D
Townmead Rd. Rich	72	19 76 D
Townmead Rd. SW6	73	26 76 C

Name		Grid
Townmead. SW6	73	25 75 B
Town Quay. Bark	51	43 83 B
Town Rd. N9	17	34 93 B
Townsend Ave. N14	16	29 92 B
Townsend La. NW9	34	20 87 B
Townsend Rd. N15	37	33 88 B
Townsend Rd. Sthl	53	12 80 C
Townsend St. SE17	63	33 78 A
Townsend's Yd. N6		28 87 D
Townsend Way. Nthwd	19	09 91 D
Townshend Estate. NW8	47	27 83 C
Townshend Rd. Chis	90	43 71 D
Townshend Rd. NW8	47	27 83 A
Townshend Rd. Rich	71	18 75 D
Townshend Terr. Rich	71	18 75 D
Town Sq. Enf	68	51 77 A
Town Tree Rd. Ashf	81	07 71 C
Towton Rd. SE27	87	32 72 A
Toynbee Rd. SW20	95	24 69 A
Toynbee St. E1		33 81 B
Toyne Way. N6	36	27 88 D
Tracey Ave. NW2		23 85 C
Tracy Ct. Stan		17 91 C
Tradescant Rd. SW8	10	30 77 C
Trading Estate Rd. NW1	55	20 82 C
Trafalar Ct. E6	51	43 83 A
Trafalgar Ave. N17	25	33 91 A
Trafalgar Ave. SE15	63	33 77 B
Trafalgar Ave. Wor Pk	103	23 66 D
Trafalgar Gdns. E1	57	35 81 B
Trafalgar Gr. SE10	64	38 77 B
Trafalgar Pl. N18	17	34 92 C
Trafalgar Rd. SW19	95	26 70 C
Trafalgar Rd. Twick	82	14 72 B
Trafalgar Sq. SW1		29 80 D
Trafalgar Sq. WC2		30 80 C
Trafalgar St. SE17	63	32 78 D
Trafford Cl. E15	49	37 85 D
Trafford Rd. Th Hth	104	30 67 B
Traherne Lodge. Tedd	83	15 71 D
Tramway Ave. E15		38 84 D
Tramway Ave. N9	18	35 94 A
Tramway Path. Mit	104	27 68 C
Tramway Path. Mit	104	28 67 C
Tranmere Rd. N9	17	33 94 B
Tranmere Rd. SW18	85	26 72 A
Tranmere Rd. Twick	82	13 73 B
Tranquil Pas. SE3	77	39 76 D
Tranquil Rise. Eri	68	51 78 C
Tranquil Vale. SE3	77	39 76 C
Transept St. NW1		27 81 A
Transmere Cl. Orp	108	44 67 C
Transmere Rd. Orp	108	44 67 C
Transport Ave. Brent	60	16 77 B
Tranton Rd. SE16	63	34 79 C
Traps La. N Mal	94	21 69 A
Travellers Way. Houn	70	11 76 C
Travers Rd. N7	37	31 86 C
Treadgold St. W11	56	23 80 B
Treadway St. E2	48	34 83 D
Treaty Rd. Houn	70	13 75 B
Treaty St. N1	47	30 83 B
Trebeck St. W1		28 80 D
Trebovir Rd. SW5	62	25 78 A
Treby St. E3	57	36 82 D
Trecastle Way. N7	47	29 85 B
Tredegar Rd. E3	49	36 83 D
Tredegar Rd. N11	24	29 91 D
Tredegar Sq. E3	57	36 82 B
Tredegar Terr. E3	57	36 82 B
Trederwen Rd. E8	48	34 83 A
Tredown Rd. SE26	88	35 71 C
Tredwell Cl. Brom	99	42 68 C
Tree Cl. Rich	83	17 73 D
Treen Ave. SW13	72	21 75 B
Tree Rd. E16	58	41 81 C
Treetops Cl. SE2	67	48 78 C
Treewall Gdns. Brom	89	40 71 B
Trefgarne Rd. Dag	41	49 86 A
Trefoil Rd. SW18	73	26 74 A
Tregaron Ave. N8	36	30 88 C
Tregaron Gdns. N Mal		21 68 C
Tregarvon Rd. SW11	74	28 75 C
Tregenna Ave. Har	43	13 85 A
Tregenna Cl. N14		29 95 A
Trego Rd. E9		37 84 C
Tregothnan Rd. SW9	74	30 75 A
Tregunter Rd. SW10	62	26 78 C
Trehearn Rd. Ilf		28 44 91 D
Treherne Ct. SW9	71	31 76 B
Trehern Rd. SW14	72	20 75 B
Trehurst St. E5		36 85 C
Trelawney Estate. E9	49	35 84 A
Trelawney Rd. Ilf	28	44 91 D

Name		Grid
Trelawn Rd. E11	38	38 86 C
Trelawn Rd. SW2	75	31 74 A
Trellis Sq. E3	57	36 82 B
Treloar Gdns. SE19	97	32 70 B
Tremadoc Rd. SW4	74	29 75 D
Tremaine Cl. SE4	76	37 76 C
Tremaine Rd. SE20	97	34 69 D
Tremlett Gr. N19	36	29 86 C
Tremlett Mews. N19		29 86 C
Trenance Gdns. Ilf	41	46 86 C
Trenchard Cl. Stan		16 91 A
Trenchard Ct. Mord	103	25 67 C
Trenchard Cl. SE10	64	38 78 D
Trenchold St. SW8	10	30 77 A
Trenholme Cl. SE20	97	34 70 D
Trenholme Rd. SE20	97	34 70 D
Trenholme Terr. SE20	97	34 70 D
Trenmar Gdns. NW10	55	22 82 B
Trent Ave. W5	60	17 79 C
Trent Gdns. N14	12	28 95 D
Trentham Dri. Orp	108	46 67 A
Trentham St. SW18	85	25 73 C
Trent Rd. SW2	74	30 74 B
Trent Way. Wor Pk	103	23 65 C
Trentwood Side. Enf	12	30 96 B
Treport St. SW18	85	25 73 B
Tresco Cl. Brom	99	39 70 A
Trescoe Gdns. Har	32	12 87 A
Tresco Gdns. Ilf	40	46 86 A
Tresco Rd. SE15	75	34 75 D
Tresham Cres. NW8	1	27 82 C
Tresham Rd. Bark	51	45 84 D
Tresham Wlk. E9	49	35 85 C
Tressillian Cres. SE4		37 75 A
Tressillian Rd. SE4	76	37 75 A
Trestis Cl. Hay		11 81 B
Treswell Rd. Dag	52	48 83 B
Trevanion Rd. W14	62	24 78 C
Treve Ave. Har	32	14 87 B
Trevelyan Ave. E12		42 85 B
Trevelyan Cl. Dart	80	54 75 D
Trevelyan Cres. Har		17 87 B
Trevelyan Gdns. NW10	46	23 83 A
Trevelyan Rd. E15		39 85 B
Trevelyan Rd. SW17	96	27 70 B
Treveris St. SE1		31 80 D
Treverton St. W10	56	23 82 D
Treville St. SW15	84	22 73 B
Treviso Rd. SE23	88	35 72 B
Trevithick Dri. Dart	80	54 75 D
Trevithick St. SE8	64	37 77 A
Trevone Gdns. Pnr	32	12 88 C
Trevor Cl. Barn	11	26 95 D
Trevor Cl. Brom	107	40 66 A
Trevor Cl. Islw	71	15 74 B
Trevor Cl. Nthlt	43	11 83 C
Trevor Cl. Stan		15 91 D
Trevor Gdns. Edg	22	20 90 B
Trevor Gdns. Nthlt		11 83 C
Trevor Pl. SW7	5	27 79 A
Trevor Rd. Edg	22	20 90 B
Trevor Rd. SW19	95	24 70 C
Trevor Rd. Wdf Gn	27	40 91 C
Trevor Sq. SW7	5	27 79 A
Trevor St. SW7	5	27 79 A
Trevose Rd. E17	26	38 90 B
Trewince Rd. SW20	95	23 69 A
Trewint St. SW18	85	26 72 A
Trewsbury Rd. SE26	88	35 71 D
Triandra Way. Hay	53	11 81 B
Triangle Ct. E16	58	41 81 A
Triangle Pl. SW4	74	29 75 D
Triangle Rd. E8	48	34 83 B
Triangle The. E8	48	34 83 B
Triangle The. King	94	20 69 C
Trident Gdns. (off Jetstar Way).		
Nthlt	53	11 82 B
Trident St. SE16	64	35 78 B
Trident Way. Sthl	59	11 79 C
Trigon Rd. SW8	10	30 77 D
Trilby Rd. SE23	88	35 72 B
Trimmer Wlk. (off Netley Rd).		
Brent	60	18 77 A
Trinder Gdns. N19	36	30 87 C
Trinder Rd. Barn	11	23 95 A
Trinder Rd. N19	36	30 87 C
Tring Ave. Sthl	53	12 81 D
Tring Ave. W5	54	18 80 D
Tring Ave. Wem	45	19 84 A
Tring Cl. Ilf	40	44 88 B
Tring Ct. Twick	83	16 71 A
Trinidad Gdns. Dag	52	50 84 D
Trinidad St. E14	57	36 80 B
Trinity Ave. Enf	13	33 95 D
Trinity Ave. N2	23	26 89 B

Street	Page	Ref
Trinity Church Rd. SW13	61	22 77 B
Trinity Church Sq. SE1	8	32 79 C
Trinity Cl. Brom	107	42 66 C
Trinity Cl. E11	39	39 86 A
Trinity Cl. Houn	70	12 75 C
Trinity Cl. Nthwd	19	09 91 A
Trinity Cl. NW3	46	26 85 B
Trinity Cl. S Croy	112	33 62 B
Trinity Cl. SE13	76	38 75 D
Trinity Cres. SW17	86	28 72 A
Trinity Estate. SE8	64	36 78 D
Trinity Gdns. E16	58	39 81 B
Trinity Gdns. SW9	74	30 75 D
Trinity Green. E1	57	35 81 A
Trinity Gr. SE10	76	38 76 A
Trinity Pl. EC3	8	33 80 B
Trinity Rd. Ilf	28	44 89 A
Trinity Rd. N22	24	30 90 B
Trinity Rd. N22	24	30 91 C
Trinity Rd. N2	23	26 89 B
Trinity Rd. Rich	71	18 75 B
Trinity Rd. Sthl	53	12 80 C
Trinity Rd. SW17	86	27 72 B
Trinity Rd. SW18	73	26 74 B
Trinity Rd. SW19	95	25 70 A
Trinity Rise. SW2	87	31 73 B
Trinity Sq. EC3	8	33 80 B
Trinity St. E16	58	39 81 B
Trinity St. Enf	13	32 97 C
Trinity St. SE1	8	32 79 A
Trinity St. SE1	8	32 79 D
Trinity Way. W13	55	21 80 B
Trio Pl. SE1	8	32 79 A
Tristan Sq. SE3	77	39 75 A
Tristram Cl. E17	26	38 89 B
Tristram Rd. Brom	89	39 71 B
Triton Sq. NW1	2	29 82 C
Tritton Ave. Croy	111	30 64 A
Tritton Rd. SE21	87	32 72 D
Triumph Cl. Hay	69	08 76 A
Trojan Way. Croy	105	31 65 C
Troon St. E1	57	36 81 C
Trosley Rd. Belv	67	49 77 A
Trossachs Rd. SE22	75	33 74 A
Trothy Rd. SE1	63	34 78 A
Trott Rd. N10	24	28 91 C
Trott St. SW11	74	27 76 A
Troughton Rd. SE7	65	40 78 D
Troutbeck Rd. SE14	76	36 76 A
Trouville Rd. SW4	74	29 74 C
Trowbridge Rd. E9	49	36 84 B
Trowbridge Rd. Rom	30	53 91 B
Trowlock Ave. Tedd	93	17 70 A
Trowlock Way. Tedd	93	17 70 B
Troy Rd. SE19	97	32 70 B
Troy St. SE18	66	43 78 B
Troy Town. SE15	75	34 75 A
Trulook Rd. N17	25	34 91 C
Truman's Rd. N16	48	33 85 D
Trumpers Way. W7	60	15 79 D
Trumpington Rd. E7	50	39 85 B
Trump St. EC2	4	32 81 C
Trundle St. SE1	8	32 79 A
Trundley's Rd. SE8	64	35 78 D
Trundley's Terr. SE8	64	35 78 B
Truro Gdns. Ilf	39	42 87 A
Truro Rd. E17	26	38 89 D
Truro Rd. N22	24	30 91 D
Truro St. NW5	47	28 84 A
Truro Wlk. Rom	30	53 91 A
Truslove Rd. SE27	87	31 71 D
Trussley Rd. W6	62	23 79 C
Trustons Gdns. Horn	42	52 87 A
Trust Wlk. SE21	87	31 73 D
Tryfan Cl. Ilf	39	41 88 B
Tryon St. SW3	9	27 78 D
Tuam Rd. SE18	66	44 77 B
Tubbenden Cl. Orp	108	45 65 C
Tubbenden La. Orp	108	45 65 C
Tubbs Rd. NW10	45	21 83 D
Tuck's Ct. EC4	3	31 81 C
Tudor Ave. Hamp	92	13 70 C
Tudor Ave. Rom	30	52 89 A
Tudor Ave. Wor Pk	109	22 64 B
Tudor Cl. Chis	99	42 69 B
Tudor Cl. Dart	80	52 74 D
Tudor Cl. NW3	47	27 85 C
Tudor Cl. NW7	22	22 91 A
Tudor Cl. NW9	34	20 86 A
Tudor Cl. Pnr	31	10 88 A
Tudor Cl. Sutt	110	23 64 D
Tudor Cl. Sutt	110	24 63 A
Tudor Cl. SW2	74	30 74 D
Tudor Cl. Wall	111	29 63 C
Tudor Court N. Wem	45	19 85 C
Tudor Court S. Wem	45	19 85 C
Tudor Cres. Enf	13	32 97 A
Tudor Cres. Ilf	28	44 91 A
Tudor Ct. E17	38	36 87 B
Tudor Ct. Felt	82	11 71 A
Tudor Ct. N1	48	33 84 A
Tudor Ct. Tedd	93	15 70 B
Tudor Dri. King	83	18 71 C
Tudor Dri. Mord	103	24 66 A
Tudor Dri. Rom	30	52 89 C
Tudor Gdns. NW9	34	20 86 A
Tudor Gdns. Rom	30	52 89 C
Tudor Gdns. SW13	72	21 75 A
Tudor Gdns. Twick	83	15 73 D
Tudor Gdns. W3	55	19 81 C
Tudor Gdns. W Wick	106	38 65 C
Tudor Gr. E9	49	35 84 C
Tudor Pl. Mit	96	27 70 C
Tudor Rd. Ashf	91	08 70 B
Tudor Rd. Bark	51	45 83 B
Tudor Rd. Barn	11	25 96 B
Tudor Rd. Beck	98	38 68 A
Tudor Rd. E4	26	37 91 B
Tudor Rd. E6	50	41 83 A
Tudor Rd. E9	49	35 83 A
Tudor Rd. Hamp	92	13 70 C
Tudor Rd. Har	20	14 90 D
Tudor Rd. Houn	70	14 75 D
Tudor Rd. King	94	19 70 C
Tudor Rd. N9	18	35 94 A
Tudor Rd. Pnr	20	11 90 C
Tudor Rd. SE19	97	33 70 D
Tudor Rd. SE25	105	34 67 B
Tudor Rd. Sthl	53	12 80 A
Tudor St. EC4	7	31 80 A
Tudor Way. N14	16	29 94 D
Tudor Way. Orp	108	44 67 B
Tudor Way. W3	61	19 79 A
Tudway Rd. SE3	77	41 75 C
Tufnail Rd. Dart	80	54 74 D
Tufnell Park Rd. N19	47	29 85 A
Tufnell Park Rd. N7	47	29 85 B
Tufton Gdns. E Mol	92	13 69 D
Tufton Rd. E4	18	37 92 A
Tufton St. SW1	7	30 79 C
Tugela Rd. Croy	105	32 67 D
Tugela St. SE6	88	36 72 B
Tuilerie St. E2	48	34 83 C
Tulip Cl. Rom	30	53 91 B
Tuliptree Ave. Rich	60	18 77 C
Tulse Cl. Beck	98	38 68 A
Tulse Hill. SW2	87	31 73 C
Tulsemere Rd. SE27	87	32 72 A
Tuncombe Rd. N18	17	33 92 A
Tunley Rd. NW10	45	20 83 A
Tunley Rd. SW17	86	28 72 A
Tunmarsh La. E13	58	41 82 A
Tunnel Ave. SE10	65	39 79 C
Tunnel Gdns. N11	24	29 91 C
Tunnel Rd. SE16	64	35 79 A
Tunstall Ave. Ilf	28	46 91 A
Tunstall Rd. Croy	105	33 66 C
Tunstall Rd. SW9	74	30 75 D
Tunstall Wlk (off Ealing Rd). Brent		18 77 A
Tunworth Cl. NW9	34	20 88 C
Tunworth Cres. SW15	72	21 74 D
Turenne Cl. SW18	73	26 75 C
Turin Rd. N9	18	35 94 A
Turin St. E2	48	34 82 A
Turkey Oak Cl. SE19	97	33 70 C
Turks Row. SW3	9	27 78 D
Turle Rd. N4	36	30 86 B
Turley Cl. E15	50	39 83 A
Turnagain La. EC4	3	31 81 D
Turnage Rd. Dag	41	48 87 C
Turnant Rd. N17	25	32 90 A
Turnberry Way. Orp	108	44 66 D
Turnchapel Mews. SW4	74	28 75 B
Turner Ave. Mit	96	27 69 B
Turner Ave. N15	25	33 89 C
Turner Ave. Twick	82	14 72 C
Turner Cl. NW11	35	25 88 D
Turner Dri. NW11	35	25 88 D
Turner Rd. E17	26	38 89 A
Turner Rd. Edg	21	18 90 D
Turner Rd. N.Mal	102	20 66 B
Turner's Rd. E3	57	36 81 B
Turner St. E16	57	39 81 D
Turner St. E1	57	34 81 B
Turner's Wood. NW11	35	26 87 C
Turneville Rd. W14	62	24 77 B
Turney Rd. SE21	87	32 73 B
Turney Rd. SE21	87	33 74 C
Turnham Green Terr. W4	61	21 78 A
Turnham Rd. SE4	76	36 74 A
Turnmill St. EC1	3	31 81 B
Turnpike Cl. SE8	64	36 77 D
Turnpike Ct. Bexh	79	47 75 D
Turnpike La. N8	25	31 89 A
Turnpike Link. Croy	105	33 65 A
Turnpin La. SE10	64	38 77 A
Turpentine La. SW1	9	28 78 D
Turpin Ave. Rom	29	49 91 B
Turpington Cl. Brom	107	42 66 A
Turpington La. Brom	107	42 67 C
Turpin Rd. Felt	69	09 74 D
Turpin's La. Wdf	28	43 91 A
Turpin Way. N19	36	29 86 B
Turpin Way. Wall	111	28 63 D
Turquand St. SE17	63	32 78 A
Turret Gr. SW4	74	29 75 A
Turtle Rd. SW16	96	30 69 C
Turton Rd. Wem	44	18 85 C
Turville St. E2	4	33 82 D
Tuscan Rd. SE18	66	44 78 D
Tuskar St. E10	65	39 78 C
T Watson Cott Homes. Barn	11	24 95 A
Tweedale Gr. Ruis	31	08 86 C
Tweeddale Rd. Cars	103	26 66 B
Tweed Glen. Rom	29	50 91 D
Tweed Glen. Rom	29	50 91 D
Tweed Green. Rom	29	50 91 D
Tweed Green. Rom	29	50 91 D
Tweedmouth Rd. E13	50	40 83 D
Tweed Way. Rom	29	50 91 D
Tweedy Rd. Brom	99	40 69 A
Tweezer's Alley. WC2	7	31 80 A
Twelvetrees Cres. E3	58	38 82 C
Twickenham Cl. Croy	104	30 65 D
Twickenham Gdns. Grnf	44	16 85 C
Twickenham Gdns. Har	21	15 91 C
Twickenham Rd. E11	38	38 86 B
Twickenham Rd. Felt	82	13 72 C
Twickenham Rd. Islw	71	16 75 C
Twickenham Rd. Rich	83	16 71 A
Twickenham Rd. Rich	71	17 75 D
Twigg Cl. Eri	68	51 77 C
Twilley St. SW18	85	25 73 A
Twine Ct. E1	57	35 80 A
Twineham Green. N12	15	25 92 A
Twining Ave. Twick	82	14 72 D
Twinn Rd. NW7	23	24 91 A
Twisden Rd. NW5	47	28 85 B
Twybridge Way. NW10	45	20 84 C
Twyford Ave. N2	24	27 89 B
Twyford Ave. W3	55	19 80 A
Twyford Cres. W3	55	19 80 C
Twyford Pl. WC2	3	30 81 D
Twyford Rd. Cars	103	26 66 D
Twyford Rd. Har	32	13 87 B
Twyford Rd. Ilf	51	44 85 C
Twyford St. N1	47	30 83 B
Tyas Rd. E16	58	39 82 D
Tybenham Rd. SW19	95	25 68 A
Tyberry Rd. Enf	14	35 96 A
Tyburn La. Har	33	15 87 B
Tyburn Way. W1	5	27 80 B
Tyers Gate. SE1	8	33 79 A
Tyers St. SE11	10	30 78 D
Tyers Terr. SE11	10	30 78 D
Tyeshurst Cl. SE2	67	48 78 C
Tylecroft Rd. SW16	96	30 69 C
Tyle Green. Horn	30	54 89 D
Tylehurst Gdns. Ilf	51	44 85 C
Tyler Gr. Dart	80	54 75 D
Tylers Gate. Har	33	18 88 C
Tylers Path. Cars	111	27 64 B
Tyler St. E10	65	39 78 C
Tylia Rd. E5	48	34 85 B
Tylney Ave. SE19	87	33 71 D
Tylney Rd. Brom	99	41 69 D
Tylney Rd. E7	50	41 85 A
Tynan Cl. Felt	81	10 73 C
Tyndale La. N1	48	31 84 D
Tyndale Terr. N1	48	31 84 D
Tyndall Rd. E10	38	38 86 A
Tyndall Rd. Well	78	45 75 B
Tynedale Mansions. N1	48	31 84 D
Tyneham Cl. SW11	74	28 75 A
Tyneham Rd. SW11	74	28 75 A
Tynemouth Rd. Mit	96	28 70 C
Tynemouth Rd. N15	25	33 89 D
Tynemouth Rd. SW6	73	26 76 C
Tyne St. E1	4	33 81 D
Tynwald Ho. SE26	87	34 72 D
Tyrawley Rd. SW6	73	25 76 B
Tyrell Cl. Har	44	15 85 A
Tyrell Ct. Cars	111	27 64 B
Tyrone Rd. E6	50	42 83 D

Tyron Way. Sid 90
Tyrrell Ave. Well 78
Tyrrell Rd. SE22 75
Tyrrel Way. NW9 34
Tyrwhitt Rd. SE4 76
Tysoe St. EC1 3
Tyson Rd. SE23 88
Tyssen Pas. E8 48
Tyssen Rd. N16 37
Tyssen St. E8 48
Tyssen St. N1 48
Tytherton Rd. N19 36

Uamvar St. E14 57
Uckfield Gr. Mit. 96
Udall Gdns. Rom. 29
Udall St. SW1 10
Udney Park Rd. Tedd 93
Uffington Rd. NW10 45
Uffington Rd. SE27 87
Ufford Cl. Har. 20
Ufford Rd. Har. 20
Ufford St. SE1 7
Ufton Gr. N1 48
Ufton Rd. N1 48
Ullathorne Rd. SW16 86
Ulleswater Rd. N14 16
Ullin St. E14 58
Ullswater Cl. Brom 99
Ullswater Cl. SW15 84
Ullswater Cres. SW15 84
Ullswater Rd. SE27 87
Ullswater Rd. SW13 61
Ulster Gdns. N13 17
Ulster Pl. NW1 2
Ulundi Rd. SE3 65
Ulva Rd. SW15 73
Ulverscroft Rd. SE22 75
Ulverstone Rd. SE27 87
Ulverston Rd. E17 26
Ulysses Rd. NW6 46
Umberston St. E1 57
Umbria St. SW15 72
Umfreville Rd. N4 37
Underbridge Way. Enf 14
Undercliff Rd. SE13 76
Underhill. Barn 11
Underhill Pas. NW1 47
Underhill Rd. SE22 88
Underhill St. NW1 47
Underne Ave. N14 16
Undershaft. EC3 4
Undershaw Rd. Brom 89
Underwood Rd. E1 19
Underwood Rd. E4 18
Underwood Row. N1 4
Underwood St. N1 4
Underwood The. SE9 89
Undine St. SW17 86
Uneeda Dri. Grnf. 43
Unicorn Pas. SE1 8
Union Ct. EC2 4
Union Dri. E2 57
Union Gr. SW8 74
Union Mews. SW4 74
Union Rd. Brom 107
Union Rd. Croy 105
Union Rd. N11 24
Union Rd. Nthlt 43
Union Rd. SW8 74
Union Rd. Wem 18
Union St. Barn 11
Union St. E15 49
Union St. King 93
Union St. N1 48
Union St. SE1 32
Union Wlk. E2 4
Unity Way. SE18 32
University Cl. NW9 22
University Pl. Eri. 21
University Rd. SW19 95
University St. WC1 2
Unwin Ave. Felt. 69
Unwin Cl. SE15 63
Unwin Rd. Islw 71
Unwin Rd. SW7 26
Upbrook Mews. W2 1
Upcerne Rd. SW10 62
Updale Rd. Sid 90
Upfield. Croy 105
Upfield Rd. W7 54
Upgrove Manor Way. SE24 87
Uphall Rd. Ilf 31
Upham Park Rd. W4 61
Uphill Dri. NW9 34

45 71 D
46 74 B
34 75 C
22 87 A
37 75 A
31 82 A
35 73 A
33 84 B
33 86 D
33 84 B
33 83 C
29 86 D

37 81 B
28 69 A
49 91 A
29 78 A
16 70 A
22 83 B
31 71 A
13 91 C
13 91 C
31 79 B
33 84 C
33 84 C
29 71 A
30 93 D
38 81 A
39 70 C
20 71 B
20 71 B
31 72 B
22 77 C
32 92 A
28 82 D
39 77 A
23 75 D
34 74 A
31 72 B
38 90 D
24 85 C
34 81 D
22 74 C
31 88 D
36 96 A
37 75 B
25 95 A
28 83 B
34 74 C
28 83 B
28 93 B
33 81 C
39 72 D
34 82 C
37 92 D
32 82 A
32 82 A
42 72 B
27 71 D
14 83 B
33 80 C
33 81 C
36 82 C
29 76 D
30 76 C
32 66 A
29 91 B
13 63 C
29 76 D
18 64 A
24 96 A
38 83 B
17 69 D
32 83 A
32 80 C
33 82 B
41 79 D
21 91 D
50 77 C
26 70 B
29 82 C
08 74 B
34 77 A
15 75 A
26 79 D
26 81 C
26 77 C
45 71 B
34 65 B
15 81 B
31 73 A
43 85 D
21 78 A
20 88 A

Upland Court Rd. Rom 30
Upland Rd. Bexh 79
Upland Rd. E13 58
Upland Rd. S Croy 112
Upland Rd. SE22 75
Upland Rd. Sutt. 110
Uplands Ave. E17 26
Uplands. Beck. 98
Uplands Cl. SW14 72
Uplands Park Rd. Enf. 13
Uplands Rd. Barn. 16
Uplands Rd. N8 37
Uplands Rd. Orp 108
Uplands Rd. Rom 29
Uplands Rd. Wdf Grn 27
Uplands The. Ruis. 31
Uplands Way. N21 13
Upminster Rd. Horn 42
Upney La. Bark. 51
Upnor Way. SE17 63
Uppark Dri. Ilf 40
Upper Abbey Rd. Belv. 67
Upper Addison Gdns. W14 62
Upper Bardsey Wlk. N1 48
Upper Belgrave St. SW1 6
Upper Berenger Wlk. SW10 62
Upper Berkeley St. W1 1
Upper Beulah Hill. SE19 97
Upper Blantyre Wlk. SW10 62
Upper Brentwood Rd. Rom 30
Upper Brighton Rd. Surb. 101
Upper Brockley Rd. SE4 76
Upper Brockley Rd. SE4 76
Upper Brook St. W1 6
Upper Butts. Brent. 60
Upper Caldy Wlk. N1 48
Upper Camelford Wlk. W11 56
Upper Cavendish Ave. N3 23
Upper Cheyne Row. SW3 9
Upper Clapton Rd. E5 37
Upper Clarendon Wlk. W11 56
Upper Dartrey Wlk. SW10 62
Upper Dengie Wlk (off Maldon Cl).
N1 48
Upper Elmers End Rd. Beck ..106
Upper Farm Rd. E Mol 92
Upper Green E. Mit. 96
Upper Green W. Mit 96
Upper Grenfell Wlk. W11 56
Upper Grosvenor St. W1 6
Upper Grotto Rd. Twick 83
Upper Ground. SE1 7
Upper Grove Rd. Belv 67
Upper Gr. SE25 97
Upper Gulland Wlk. N1 48
Upper Halliford Rd. Shep 91
Upper Ham Rd. Rich 83
Upper Handa Wlk. N1 48
Upper Harley St. NW1 2
Upper Hawkwell Wlk (off Maldon
Cl). N1 48
Upper Holly Hill Rd. Belv 67
Upper James St. W1 6
Upper John St. W1 6
Upper Lismore Wlk. N1 48
Upper Mall. W6 61
Upper Marsh. SE1 7
Upper Montague St. W1 1
Upper Mulgrave Rd. Sutt 110
Upper North St. E14 57
Upper Park Rd. Belv 67
Upper Park Rd. Brom 99
Upper Park Rd. King 94
Upper Park Rd. N11 16
Upper Park Rd. NW3 47
Upper Phillimore Gdns. W8 62
Upper Rainham Rd. Horn 42
Upper Ramsey Wlk. N1 48
Upper Rawreth Wlk (off Basire
St). N1 48
Upper Rd. E13 58
Upper Rd. N2 24
Upper Rd. Wall 111
Upper Richmond Rd. SW1K 73
Upper Richmond Rd. W. Rich...72
Upper Richmond Rd. W14 72
Upper Richmond Rd. W15 72
Upper Selsdon Rd. S Croy 112
Upper Sheppey Wlk. N1 48
Upper Sheridan Rd. Belv. 67
Upper Shirley Rd. Croy 106
Upper Sq. Islw 71
Upper Staithe. W4 72
Upper St Martin's La. WC2 7
Upper St. N1 48

54 90 D
48 75 B
40 82 C
32 64 D
34 74 B
26 63 D
35 90 D
37 69 C
19 74 B
31 97 C
28 94 C
31 88 C
46 66 D
47 89 B
42 91 C
10 87 A
31 95 A
54 86 B
45 84 B
33 78 C
44 88 C
49 78 A
24 79 A
32 84 A
28 79 C
26 77 D
27 81 D
33 69 A
26 77 D
53 89 A
18 66 A
36 76 D
36 76 D
28 80 A
17 77 A
32 84 A
24 81 C
25 89 A
27 77 A
34 86 B
24 81 C
26 77 D

32 83 A
36 67 B
12 68 D
27 68 B
27 69 D
23 80 B
28 80 A
15 72 B
31 80 C
48 77 B
33 68 D
32 84 A
09 68 A
17 71 B
32 84 A
28 82 C

32 83 A
49 78 D
29 80 A
29 80 A
32 84 A
22 78 C
30 79 B
27 81 B
24 63 C
37 81 C
49 78 B
41 69 A
19 70 A
29 92 C
27 85 D
25 79 A
51 86 B
32 84 B

32 83 A
40 82 A
29 64 D
23 75 D
19 75 D
20 75 D
21 75 D
34 62 A
32 84 A
49 78 A
35 65 D
16 75 A
20 76 A
30 80 A
31 83 B

Upper Sunbury Rd. Hamp 92
Upper Sutton La. Houn 70
Upper Tachbrook St. SW1 10
Upper Talbot Wlk. W11 56
Upper Teddington Rd. King 93
Upper Teddington Rd. Tedd 93
Upper Terr. NW3 35
Upper Thames St. EC4 2
Upper Tollington Park. N4 37
Upperton Rd. Sid 90
Upperton Road E. E13 58
Upperton Road W. E13 58
Upper Tooting Park. SW17 86
Upper Tooting Rd. SW17 86
Upper Town Rd. Grnf 53
Upper Tulse Hill. SW2 86
Upper Vernon Rd. Sutt 110
Upper Walthamstow Rd. E17 ...26
Upper Whistler Wlk. SW10 62
Upper Wickham La. Well 78
Upper Wimpole St. W1 2
Upper Woburn Pl. WC1 2
Uppingham Ave. Stan. 21
Upsdell Ave. N13 25
Upstall St. SE5 75
Upton Ave. E7 50
Upton Cl. Bex 79
Upton Cross. E13 50
Upton Dene. Sutt 110
Upton Gdns. Har 33
Upton La. E7 50
Upton Park Rd. E7 50
Upton Rd. Bex 79
Upton Rd. Bexh 79
Upton Rd. Houn 70
Upton Rd. N18 17
Upton Rd S. Bex 79
Upton Rd. SE18 66
Upton Rd. Th Hth 97
Upway. N12 24
Upwood Rd. SE12 77
Upwood Rd. SW16 96
Urban Ave. Horn 42
Urlwin St. SE5 63
Urlwin Wlk. SW9 75
Urmston Dri. SW19 85
Urquhart Ct. Beck. 98
Ursula St. SW11 74
Urswick Gdns. Dag 52
Urswick Rd. Dag. 52
Urswick Rd. E5 49
Usher Rd. E3 49
Usher Rd. E3 49
Usk Rd. SW11 73
Usk St. E16 58
Usk St. E2 57
Uvedale Rd. Dag 41
Uvedale Rd. Enf 13
Uverdale Rd. SW10 62
Uxbridge Rd. Hamp 82
Uxbridge Rd. Har. 20
Uxbridge Rd. King. 101
Uxbridge Rd. Pnr 20
Uxbridge Rd. Stan. 21
Uxbridge Rd. Sthl 53
Uxbridge Rd. Twick 82
Uxbridge Rd. W12 55
Uxbridge Rd. W13 54
Uxbridge Rd. W3 55
Uxbridge Rd. W5 54
Uxbridge Rd. W7 54
Uxbridge St. W8 56
Uxendon Cres. Wem 33
Uxendon Hill. Wem 33

Valan Leas. Brom 99
Vale Cl. Twick 83
Vale Cl. W9 1
Vale Cottages. Brom 99
Vale Cres. SW15 84
Vale Croft Pnr 32
Vale Ct. Wem 33
Vale Dri. Barn 11
Vale End. SE22 75
Vale Estate The. W3 55
Vale Gr. N4 37
Vale Gr. W3 55
Vale La. W3 55
Vale-Lodge. SE23 88
Valence Ave. Dag 41
Valence Circ. Dag 41
Valence Rd. Eri. 67
Valence Wood Rd. Dag 41
Valentia Pl. SW9 75
Valentine Ct. SE23 88

13 69 A
13 76 A
29 78 A
24 81 C
17 69 A
17 70 C
26 86 C
32 80 A
31 87 C
45 71 D
41 82 A
41 82 A
28 72 A
27 72 D
13 82 D
30 73 B
22 64 D
38 89 B
26 77 D
46 76 D
28 81 A
29 82 B
17 90 C
31 91 A
31 76 B
40 84 C
48 74 D
40 83 A
25 63 D
17 88 C
40 84 D
40 84 D
48 74 D
48 74 A
13 75 A
34 92 D
48 74 D
44 77 A
32 69 D
27 91 A
40 74 C
30 69 A
53 86 C
32 77 A
31 76 A
24 73 C
36 70 D
27 76 A
48 84 C
48 84 C
35 85 C
36 83 B
36 83 D
26 75 C
39 80 B
35 82 B
49 86 C
32 95 B
26 77 C
13 71 B
14 91 D
17 67 B
12 91 D
15 91 B
13 80 C
11 72 B
22 80 D
16 80 D
20 80 D
18 80 A
15 80 D
15 80 D
25 80 C
18 87 C
18 87 B

39 68 A
16 72 C
26 82 A
40 68 A
21 71 A
12 88 A
17 86 C
25 95 A
33 75 D
21 80 C
32 87 A
20 80 D
19 81 A
35 72 A
47 86 B
48 86 C
50 77 D
48 86 C
31 75 C
35 72 B

Valentine Pl. SE1 ...7 31 79 B
Valentine Rd. E9 ...49 35 84 B
Valentine Rd. Har ...32 14 86 C
Valentine Row. SE1 ...7 31 79 B
Valentines Rd. Ilf ...40 43 87 D
Valentines Way. Rom ...42 51 86 A
Vale of Health. NW3 ...35 26 86 D
Vale Rd. Brom ...100 43 69 C
Vale Rd. E7 ...50 40 84 B
Vale Rd. Mit ...96 29 68 D
Vale Rd. N4 ...37 32 88 C
Vale Rd N. Surb ...101 18 65 A
Vale Rd S. Surb ...101 18 65 A
Vale Rd. Sutt ...110 25 64 B
Vale Rd. Wor Pk ...102 21 65 D
Valerian Way. E15 ...58 39 82 A
Valerie Ct. Sutt ...110 25 63 D
Vale Rise. NW11 ...35 24 87 D
Vale Row. N5 ...37 31 86 D
Vale Royal. N7 ...47 30 84 C
Valeswood Rd. Brom ...89 39 71 D
Vale Terr. N4 ...37 32 87 A
Vale The. Croy ...106 35 65 B
Vale The. Felt ...69 10 74 D
Vale The. Houn ...59 12 77 A
Vale The. N10 ...24 28 90 A
Vale The. N14 ...16 29 94 A
Vale The. NW11 ...35 24 86 A
Vale The. Ruis ...43 11 85 A
Vale The. Sun ...91 10 70 A
Vale The. SW3 ...62 26 77 B
Vale The. W3 ...55 21 80 C
Vale The. Wdf Gn ...27 40 91 C
Valetta Gr. E13 ...50 40 83 C
Valetta Rd. W3 ...61 21 79 B
Valette St. E9 ...49 35 84 A
Valiant Cl. Nthlt ...53 11 82 B
Valiant Cl. Rom ...29 49 90 D
Vallance Rd. E1 ...57 34 82 C
Vallance Rd. E2 ...57 34 82 C
Vallance Rd. N22 ...24 29 90 C
Vallentin Rd. E17 ...26 38 89 C
Valley Ave. N12 ...15 26 92 B
Valley Cl. Dart ...80 51 74 D
Valley Cl. Pnr ...19 10 90 D
Valley Dri. NW9 ...34 19 88 B
Valleyfield Rd. SW16 ...86 30 71 D
Valley Fields Cres. Enf ...13 31 97 C
Valley Gdns. SW19 ...95 26 70 D
Valley Gdns. Wem ...44 18 84 D
Valley Gr. SE7 ...65 41 78 C
Valley Mews. Twick ...83 16 72 A
Valley Rd. Belv ...67 50 78 A
Valley Rd. Brom ...99 39 69 C
Valley Rd. Dart ...80 51 74 D
Valley Rd. Eri ...67 50 78 B
Valley Rd. Orp ...100 46 70 D
Valley Rd. SW16 ...86 30 71 B
Valley Side. E4 ...18 37 94 C
Valley View. Barn ...11 24 95 C
Valley Wlk. Croy ...106 35 65 A
Valliere Rd. NW10 ...55 22 82 A
Valliers Wood Rd. Sid ...90 45 73 C
Vallis Way. W13 ...54 16 81 A
Valmar Rd. SE5 ...75 32 76 A
Valnay St. SW17 ...86 27 71 D
Valognes Ave. E17 ...26 36 90 A
Valonia Gdns. SW18 ...73 24 74 D
Vambery Rd. SE18 ...66 44 77 A
Vanbrough Cres. Nthlt ...43 11 83 A
Vanbrugh Fields. SE3 ...65 39 77 D
Vanbrugh Hill. E10 ...65 39 78 D
Vanbrugh Hill. SE3 ...65 39 77 B
Vanbrugh Park Rd. SE3 ...65 39 77 D
Vanbrugh Park Rd W. SE3 ...65 39 77 D
Vanbrugh Park. SE3 ...65 39 77 D
Vanbrugh Rd. W4 ...61 20 79 D
Vanbrugh Terr. SE3 ...77 39 76 B
Vanburgh Cl. Orp ...108 45 66 C
Vancouver Rd. Edg ...22 19 90 B
Vancouver Rd. Rich ...83 17 71 A
Vancouver Rd. SE23 ...88 36 72 A
Vanderbilt Rd. SW18 ...85 26 73 C
Vandome Cl. E16 ...58 40 81 D
Vandon Pas. SW1 ...6 29 79 C
Vandon St. SW1 ...6 29 79 C
Van Dyck Ave. N.Mal ...102 20 66 B
Vandyke Cl. SW15 ...73 23 74 D
Vandyke Cross. SE9 ...77 42 74 A
Vandy St. EC2 ...4 33 82 C
Vane Cl. Har ...33 18 88 D
Vane Cl. NW3 ...46 26 85 B
Vanessa Cl. Belv ...67 49 78 C
Vane St. SW1 ...10 29 78 A
Vanguard Cl. Croy ...105 31 66 D

Vanguard Cl. Rom ...29 49 90 D
Vanguard St. SE8 ...76 37 76 A
Vanguard Way. Wall ...111 30 63 C
Vanoc Gdns. Brom ...89 40 71 A
Vansittart Rd. E7 ...50 40 85 A
Vansittart St. SE14 ...64 36 77 C
Vanston Pl. SW6 ...62 25 77 C
Vant Rd. SW17 ...86 27 71 D
Varcoe Rd. SE16 ...64 35 78 C
Vardens Rd. SW11 ...73 26 75 D
Varden St. E1 ...57 34 81 D
Varley Rd. E16 ...58 40 81 D
Varna Rd. Hamp ...92 13 69 B
Varna Rd. SW6 ...62 24 77 D
Varndell St. NW1 ...2 29 82 A
Vartry Rd. N15 ...37 33 88 C
Vassall Rd. SW9 ...63 31 77 C
Vauban St. SE16 ...8 33 79 D
Vaughan Ave. NW4 ...34 22 88 A
Vaughan Ave. W6 ...61 21 78 B
Vaughan Cl. Hamp ...92 12 70 A
Vaughan Gdns. Ilf ...39 42 87 B
Vaughan Rd. E15 ...50 39 84 B
Vaughan Rd. Har ...32 14 86 D
Vaughan Rd. SE5 ...75 32 75 A
Vaughan Rd. Surb ...101 16 66 B
Vaughan Rd. Well ...78 45 76 D
Vaughan Williams Cl. SE8 ...64 37 77 C
Vauxhall Bridge Rd. SW1 ...10 29 78 A
Vauxhall Bridge. SE1 ...10 30 78 C
Vauxhall Cross. SE1 ...10 30 78 C
Vauxhall Gdns. S Croy ...112 32 63 A
Vauxhall Gr. SW8 ...10 30 77 B
Vauxhall St. SE11 ...10 30 78 D
Vauxhall Wlk. SE11 ...10 30 78 D
Vawdrey Cl. E1 ...57 35 82 C
Vectis Gdns. SW17 ...96 28 70 B
Vectis Rd. SW17 ...96 28 70 B
Veda Rd. SE13 ...76 37 75 C
Veldt Way. SE22 ...75 33 74 A
Venables St. NW8 ...1 26 81 B
Vencourt Pl. W6 ...61 22 78 A
Venetian Rd. SE5 ...75 32 76 C
Venetia Rd. N4 ...37 31 88 D
Venetia Rd. W5 ...60 17 79 B
Venner Rd. SE26 ...88 35 71 C
Venners Cl. Bexh ...80 51 76 C
Venn St. SW4 ...74 29 75 C
Ventnor Ave. Stan ...21 16 90 B
Ventnor Dri. N20 ...15 25 93 D
Ventnor Gdns. Bark ...51 45 84 A
Ventnor Rd. SE14 ...64 35 77 D
Ventnor Rd. Sutt ...110 25 63 D
Venue St. E14 ...58 38 81 A
Venus Rd. SE18 ...65 42 79 D
Vera Ave. N21 ...13 31 95 A
Vera Rd. SW6 ...73 24 76 A
Verbena Gdns. W6 ...61 22 78 C
Verdant La. SE6 ...89 39 73 C
Verdayne Ave. Croy ...106 35 65 B
Verdun Rd. SE18 ...66 46 77 A
Verdun Rd. SW13 ...61 22 77 C
Vereker Dri. Sun ...91 10 69 C
Vereker Rd. W14 ...62 24 78 C
Vere St. W1 ...2 28 81 D
Vermont Rd. SE19 ...97 33 70 A
Vermont Rd. Sutt ...103 25 65 D
Vermont Rd. SW18 ...73 25 74 D
Verney Gdns. Dag ...52 48 85 A
Verney Rd. Dag ...52 48 85 A
Verney Rd. SE16 ...63 34 78 D
Verney St. NW10 ...34 20 86 D
Verney Way. SE16 ...63 34 78 D
Vernham Rd. SE18 ...66 44 77 A
Vernon Ave. E12 ...50 42 85 B
Vernon Ave. SW20 ...95 23 69 D
Vernon Ave. Wdf Gn ...27 40 91 D
Vernon Cl. Eps ...109 20 63 A
Vernon Cl. Orp ...100 46 68 B
Vernon Cres. Barn ...12 28 95 C
Vernon Ct. Stan ...21 16 90 B
Vernon Dri. Stan ...21 16 90 A
Vernon Pl. WC1 ...3 30 81 A
Vernon Rd. E11 ...39 39 87 C
Vernon Rd. E15 ...50 39 84 C
Vernon Rd. E17 ...38 36 88 B
Vernon Rd. E3 ...49 36 83 D
Vernon Rd. Felt ...81 09 72 B
Vernon Rd. Ilf ...40 45 87 D
Vernon Rd. N8 ...25 31 89 A
Vernon Rd. Sutt ...110 26 64 C
Vernon Rd. SW14 ...72 20 75 B
Vernon Rise. Grnf ...43 14 85 D
Vernon Rise. WC1 ...3 30 82 B
Vernon Sq. WC1 ...3 30 82 B

Vernon St. W14 ...62 24 78 A
Vernon Yd. W11 ...56 24 80 B
Veroan Rd. Bexh ...79 48 76 C
Verona Dri. Surb ...101 18 65 A
Verona Rd. E7 ...50 40 84 C
Veronica Cl. Rom ...30 53 91 C
Veronica Rd. SW17 ...86 28 72 B
Veronique Gdns. Ilf ...40 44 88 A
Verran Rd. SW12 ...86 28 73 B
Versailles Rd. SE20 ...97 34 70 C
Verulam Ave. E17 ...38 36 87 B
Verulam Rd. Sthl ...53 13 82 C
Verulam St. WC1 ...3 31 81 A
Verwood Rd. Har ...20 14 90 C
Vesey Path. E14 ...57 37 81 D
Vespan Rd. W12 ...61 22 79 A
Vesta Rd. SE4 ...76 36 76 C
Vestris Rd. SE23 ...88 35 72 B
Vestry Mews. SE5 ...75 33 76 A
Vestry Rd. E17 ...26 37 89 D
Vestry Rd. SE5 ...75 33 76 A
Vestry St. N1 ...4 32 82 B
Vevey St. SE6 ...88 36 72 B
Veysey Gdns. Dag ...41 49 86 C
Viaduct Pl. E2 ...57 34 82 B
Viaduct Rd. N2 ...24 27 90 C
Viaduct St. E2 ...57 34 82 B
Viaduct The. Wem ...44 18 83 A
Viaduct Yd. EC1 ...3 31 81 A
Vian St. SE13 ...76 37 75 B
Vibart Gdns. SW2 ...86 30 73 B
Vibart Wlk. N1 ...47 30 83 A
Vicarage Ave. SE3 ...65 40 77 C
Vicarage Cl. Eri ...67 50 77 A
Vicarage Cl. Nthlt ...43 12 84 D
Vicarage Cl. Ruis ...31 08 87 B
Vicarage Cres. SW11 ...73 26 76 B
Vicarage Ct. Felt ...81 08 73 A
Vicarage Dri. Bark ...51 44 84 C
Vicarage Dri. SW14 ...72 20 74 B
Vicarage Farm Rd. Houn ...70 12 76 A
Vicarage Gate. W8 ...62 25 79 B
Vicarage Gate. W8 ...56 25 80 D
Vicarage Gdns. Mit ...96 27 68 A
Vicarage Gdns. W8 ...56 25 80 C
Vicarage Gr. SE5 ...75 32 76 B
Vicarage La. E15 ...50 39 84 D
Vicarage La. Eps ...109 22 62 A
Vicarage La. Ilf ...40 44 87 D
Vicarage Park. SE18 ...66 44 78 C
Vicarage Path. N8 ...36 30 87 A
Vicarage Rd. Croy ...105 31 65 C
Vicarage Rd. Dag ...52 49 84 D
Vicarage Rd. E10 ...38 37 87 D
Vicarage Rd. E15 ...50 39 84 D
Vicarage Rd. Horn ...42 52 87 C
Vicarage Rd. King ...93 17 69 A
Vicarage Rd. N17 ...25 34 90 A
Vicarage Rd. NW4 ...34 22 88 C
Vicarage Rd. SE18 ...66 44 78 C
Vicarage Rd. Sun ...91 10 70 A
Vicarage Rd. Sutt ...103 25 65 D
Vicarage Rd. SW14 ...72 20 74 B
Vicarage Rd. Tedd ...83 16 71 C
Vicarage Rd. Twick ...70 14 74 C
Vicarage Rd. Twick ...83 15 72 A
Vicarage Wdf Gn ...27 42 91 C
Vicarage Way. Har ...32 13 87 A
Vicarage Way. NW10 ...34 20 86 D
Vicarage Wlk. SW6 ...73 26 76 B
Vicar's Cl. E15 ...50 40 83 A
Vicar's Cl. E9 ...49 35 83 A
Vicar's Cl. Enf ...13 33 97 C
Vicars Hill. SE13 ...76 37 75 D
Vicar's Moor La. N21 ...17 31 94 B
Vicars Oak Rd. SE19 ...97 33 70 A
Vicar's Rd. NW5 ...47 28 85 C
Vicar's Wlk. Dag ...40 46 86 D
Viceroy Cl. N2 ...24 27 89 C
Viceroy Rd. SW8 ...74 30 76 A
Vickers Rd. Eri ...67 50 78 D
Victor App. Horn ...42 53 87 D
Victor Cl. Horn ...42 53 87 D
Victor Gdns. Horn ...42 53 87 D
Victor Gr. Wem ...44 18 84 C
Victoria Arc. SW1 ...6 28 79 D
Victoria Ave. Barn ...11 26 96 D
Victoria Ave. E6 ...50 41 83 B
Victoria Ave. EC2 ...4 33 81 A
Victoria Ave. E Mol ...92 13 68 B
Victoria Ave. Houn ...70 13 74 A
Victoria Ave. N3 ...23 24 90 B
Victoria Ave. Rom ...29 49 91 B
Victoria Ave. S Croy ...112 32 62 C
Victoria Ave. Surb ...101 17 67 D

Victoria Ave. Wall................104   28 65 C
Victoria Ave. Wem................45   19 84 B
Victoria Cl. E Mol................92   13 68 A
Victoria Cl. Har................33   15 88 D
Victoria Cottages. Rich................72   19 76 A
Victoria Cres. N15................37   33 88 A
Victoria Cres. SE19................97   33 70 A
Victoria Cres. SW19................95   24 70 D
Victoria Ct. W3................61   19 79 A
Victoria Ct. Wem................45   19 84 A
Victoria Dock Rd. E16................58   40 80 A
Victoria Dri. SW19................85   23 73 D
Victoria Emb. EC4................7   31 80 A
Victoria Emb. SW1................7   30 79 A
Victoria Emb. WC2................7   30 80 B
Victoria Gdns. Houn................70   12 76 A
Victoria Gdns. W11................56   25 80 C
Victoria Gr Mews. W2................56   25 80 B
Victoria Gr. N12................15   26 92 D
Victoria Gr. W8................5   26 79 C
Victoria La. Barn................11   24 96 D
Victoria Mews. NW6................46   25 83 A
Victoria Mews. SW4................74   28 75 D
Victorian Gr. N16................37   33 86 C
Victorian Rd. N16................37   33 86 D
Victoria Park Rd. E9................49   36 84 C
Victoria Park Sq. E2................57   35 82 A
Victoria Pl. Rich................71   17 74 B
Victoria Rd. Bark................51   43 84 B
Victoria Rd. Barn................11   26 96 D
Victoria Rd. Bexh................79   49 75 C
Victoria Rd. Brom................107   41 67 B
Victoria Rd. Chis................90   43 71 C
Victoria Rd. Dag................52   50 85 C
Victoria Rd. Dart................90   54 74 A
Victoria Rd. E11................50   39 85 A
Victoria Rd. E13................50   40 83 C
Victoria Rd. E17................26   38 90 C
Victoria Rd. E18................27   40 89 B
Victoria Rd. Eri................68   51 77 A
Victoria Rd. Felt................81   10 73 D
Victoria Rd. King................93   18 69 D
Victoria Rd. Mit................96   27 70 D
Victoria Rd. N15................25   34 89 C
Victoria Rd. N18................17   33 92 B
Victoria Rd. N22................24   29 90 B
Victoria Rd. N4................36   30 87 B
Victoria Rd. N4................37   31 87 C
Victoria Rd. N9................17   33 93 D
Victoria Rd. NW10................55   21 82 C
Victoria Rd. NW4................23   23 89 D
Victoria Rd. Rom................42   51 88 B
Victoria Rd. Ruis................31   10 86 A
Victoria Rd. Ruis................43   11 85 D
Victoria Rd. Sid................90   46 72 C
Victoria Rd. Sthl................59   12 79 D
Victoria Rd. Surb................101   17 67 D
Victoria Rd. Sutt................110   26 64 D
Victoria Rd. SW14................72   20 75 B
Victoria Rd. Tedd................93   16 70 A
Victoria Rd. Twick................83   16 73 B
Victoria Rd. W3................55   20 81 C
Victoria Rd. W5................54   16 81 B
Victoria Rd. W8................5   26 79 C
Victoria Rise. SW4................74   28 75 B
Victoria Scott Ct. Dart................80   51 75 A
Victoria Sq. SW1................6   28 79 D
Victoria St. Belv................67   48 78 D
Victoria St. E15................50   39 84 C
Victoria St. SW1................6   29 79 C
Victoria Terr. Har................33   15 87 C
Victoria Terr. N4................37   31 87 C
Victoria Vils. N9................17   32 92 D
Victoria Villas. Rich................71   18 75 D
Victoria Way. SE7................65   40 78 D
Victor Rd. Har................20   14 89 A
Victor Rd. NW10................55   22 82 B
Victor Rd. SE20................98   35 70 D
Victor Rd. Tedd................83   15 71 A
Victors Dri. Hamp................92   12 70 A
Victor Wlk. Horn................42   53 87 D
Victory Ave. Mord................103   26 67 A
Victory Pl. SE17................63   32 78 B
Victory Pl. SE19................97   33 70 A
Victory Rd. SW19................95   26 70 C
Victory Sq. SE5................63   32 77 D
Victory Way. Rom................29   49 90 B
Victory Wlk. SE8................76   37 76 A
View Cl. Har................20   14 89 D
View Cl. N6................36   27 87 B
Viewfield Rd. SW18................73   24 74 D
Viewland Rd. SE18................66   45 78 D
View Rd. N6................36   27 88 D
View The. SE2................67   48 78 C
Viga Rd. N21................13   31 95 C

Vigilant Cl. SE26................87   34 71 A
Vignoles Rd. Rom................41   49 87 A
Vigo St. W1................6   29 80 A
Viking Rd. Sthl................53   12 80 A
Villacourt Rd. SE18................66   46 77 A
Village Cl. E4................18   38 92 C
Village Green Rd. Dart................80   52 75 C
Village Home The. Ilf................28   44 89 A
Village Rd. Enf................13   33 95 C
Village Rd. N3................23   24 90 C
Village Row. Sutt................110   25 63 C
Village The. SE7................65   41 77 B
Village Way. Ashf................81   07 71 A
Village Way. Beck................98   37 68 A
Village Way E. Har................32   13 87 A
Village Way. NW10................45   20 85 B
Village Way. Pnr................32   12 87 B
Village Way. SE21................75   32 74 D
Villa Rd. SW9................75   31 75 A
Villas Rd. SE18................66   44 78 A
Villa St. SE17................63   32 78 D
Villa St. SE17................63   32 78 D
Villa Wlk. SE17................63   32 78 D
Villers Cl. E10................38   37 86 A
Villiers Ave. Surb................101   18 67 B
Villiers Ave. Twick................82   12 73 D
Villiers Cl. King................93   18 68 D
Villiers Rd. Beck................98   35 69 D
Villiers Rd. Islw................71   15 76 C
Villiers Rd. King................93   18 68 B
Villiers Rd. NW2................45   22 84 A
Villiers Rd. Sthl................53   12 80 D
Villiers St. WC2................7   30 80 C
Vincam Cl. Twick................82   13 73 A
Vincent Ave. Surb................102   19 65 B
Vincent Cl. Barn................11   25 96 B
Vincent Cl. Brom................99   40 68 D
Vincent Cl. Ilf................28   44 91 A
Vincent Cl. Sid................90   45 73 C
Vincent Dri. Shep................91   09 68 A
Vincent Gdns. NW2................34   21 86 D
Vincent Rd. Croy................105   33 66 A
Vincent Rd. Dag................52   48 84 C
Vincent Rd. E4................26   38 91 B
Vincent Rd. Houn................70   11 75 B
Vincent Rd. Islw................70   14 76 B
Vincent Rd. King................94   19 68 A
Vincent Rd. N15................25   32 89 C
Vincent Rd. N22................25   31 90 C
Vincent Rd. SE18................66   43 78 B
Vincent Rd. W3................61   20 79 C
Vincent Rd. Wem................44   18 84 D
Vincent Row. Hamp................14   71 C
Vincent Sq. N22................25   31 90 C
Vincent Sq. SW1................29   78 B
Vincent St. E16................58   39 81 B
Vincent Sq. SW1................29   78 B
Vincent Terr. N1................48   31 83 D
Vince St. EC1................4   32 82 B
Vine Cl. Surb................101   18 67 D
Vine Cl. Sutt................103   26 65 C
Vine Ct. E1................57   34 81 A
Vine Ct. Har................33   18 88 C
Vinegar Yd. SE1................8   33 79 A
Vine Gdns. Ilf................51   44 85 C
Vine Hill. EC1................3   31 82 C
Vine La. SE1................8   33 80 C
Vine Pl. Houn................70   13 75 D
Vine Rd. E15................50   39 84 D
Vine Rd. E Mol................92   14 68 C
Vine Rd. SW13................72   21 75 B
Vineries Cl. Dag................52   48 84 B
Vineries Gdns. Grnf................33   96 A
Vineries The. Enf................13   33 96 A
Vineries The. N14................12   29 95 C
Vinery Villas. NW8................1   27 82 A
Vines Ave. N3................3   25 90 B
Vine St. EC3................8   33 80 B
Vine St. EC3................3   33 81 D
Vine St. Rom................29   50 89 C
Vine St. W1................8   29 80 A
Vineyard Ave. NW7................23   24 91 C
Vineyard Cl. SE6................88   37 73 C
Vineyard Hill Rd. SW19................85   25 71 A
Vineyard Pas. Rich................71   18 74 A
Vineyard Path. SW14................72   20 75 B
Vineyard Rd. Felt................81   10 72 C
Vineyard Row. King................93   17 69 A
Vineyard The. Rich................71   18 74 A
Vineyard Wlk. EC1................3   31 82 C
Vine Yd. SE1................8   32 79 A
Viney Rd. SE13................75   37 75 B
Vining St. SW9................75   31 75 C
Vinlake Ave. Uxb................31   07 86 C
Vinson Cl. Orp................108   46 66 C

Vintners Pl. EC4................8   32 80 A
Viola Ave. Felt................70   11 74 C
Viola Ave. SE2................66   46 78 D
Viola Sq. W12................55   21 80 B
Violet Gdns. Croy................112   31 64 D
Violet Hill. NW8................46   26 83 C
Violet La. Croy................112   31 64 D
Violet Rd. E14................57   37 81 B
Violet Rd. E17................38   37 88 C
Violet Rd. E18................27   40 90 D
Violet Rd. E3................57   37 82 D
Violet St. E2................57   34 82 D
Virgil Pl. W1................1   27 81 B
Virgil St. SE1................7   30 79 D
Virginia Gdns. Ilf................28   44 90 D
Virginia Rd. E2................4   33 82 B
Virginia Rd. Th Hth................97   31 69 B
Virginia St. E1................57   34 80 A
Virginia Wlk. SW2................74   30 74 D
Viscount Gr. Nthlt................53   11 82 B
Viscount St. EC1................4   32 81 A
Viscount Way. Houn................69   09 75 C
Vista Ave. Enf................14   35 97 D
Vista Dri. Ilf................39   41 88 B
Vista The. SE9................89   41 73 B
Vista Way. Har................33   18 88 C
Vivian Ave. NW4................34   22 88 B
Vivian Ave. Wem................45   19 84 B
Vivian Gdns. Wem................45   19 85 C
Vivian Rd. E3................49   36 83 C
Vivian Sq. SE15................75   34 75 B
Vivian Way. N2................35   26 88 B
Vivian Way. N2................24   27 89 C
Vivienne Cl. Twick................71   17 74 D
Voce Rd. SE18................66   44 77 D
Voewood Cl. N.Mal................102   21 67 D
Voltaire Rd. SW4................74   29 75 B
Voluntary Pl. E11................39   40 88 C
Vorley Rd. N19................36   29 86 A
Voss Ct. SW16................96   30 70 A
Voss St. E2................57   34 82 A
Vrow Wlk. E Mol................93   15 68 B
Vulcan Cl. Wall................111   30 63 D
Vulcan Gate. Enf................13   31 97 C
Vulcan Rd. SE4................76   36 76 D
Vulcan Terr. SE4................76   36 76 D
Vulcan Way. N7................47   30 84 B
Vyner Rd. W3................55   20 80 B
Vyner St. E2................48   34 83 B
Vyne The. Bexh................79   49 75 B
Vyse Cl. Barn................11   23 96 C

Wadding St. SE17................63   32 78 B
Waddington Rd. E15................49   38 84 B
Waddington St. E15................49   38 84 B
Waddington Way. SE19................97   32 69 A
Waddon Cl. Croy................105   31 65 C
Waddon Court Rd. Croy................105   31 65 C
Waddon Marsh Way. Croy................104   30 66 D
Waddon New Rd. Croy................105   31 65 B
Waddon Park Ave. Croy................105   31 65 C
Waddon Rd. Croy................105   31 65 D
Waddon Way. Croy................112   31 63 B
Wade Rd. E16................68   41 81 C
Wade's Gr. N21................17   31 94 A
Wade's Hill. N21................17   31 94 A
Wade's La. Tedd................83   16 71 C
Wadeson St. E2................48   34 83 D
Wadeville Cl. Belv................67   49 78 C
Wadham Ave. E17................26   37 91 D
Wadham Gdns. Grnf................44   14 84 B
Wadham Gdns. NW3................47   27 84 C
Wadham Rd. E17................26   38 90 A
Wadham Rd. SW15................73   24 75 C
Wadhurst Cl. SE20................97   34 69 D
Wadhurst Rd. W4................61   20 79 D
Wadley Rd. E11................39   39 87 A
Wadsworth Cl. Enf................14   35 95 B
Wadsworth Cl. Grnf................44   17 83 C
Wadsworth Rd. Grnf................44   17 83 C
Wager St. E3................57   36 82 D
Waggon La. N18................25   34 91 A
Waghorn Rd. Har................21   17 89 B
Waghorn St. SE15................75   34 75 A
Wagner St. SE15................64   35 77 C
Waid Cl. Dart................80   54 74 D
Waights Ct. King................93   18 69 A
Wainfleet Ave. Rom................29   50 90 C
Wainford Cl. SW19................85   23 73 D
Waite Davies Rd. SE12................89   39 73 B
Waite St. SE15................63   33 77 B
Waithman St. EC4................3   31 81 D
Wakefield Gdns. Ilf................39   42 88 C

Wakefield Gdns. SE19	97	33 70	C
Wakefield Rd. N15	37	33 88	B
Wakefield Rd. N11	16	29 92	D
Wakefield Rd. Rich	71	17 74	B
Wakefield St. E6	50	41 83	B
Wakefield St. E6	50	42 83	A
Wakefield St. N18	17	34 92	C
Wakefield St. WC1	3	30 82	A
Wakehams Hill. Pnr	20	12 89	B
Wakeham St. N1	48	32 84	B
Wakehurst Rd. SW11	74	27 74	B
Wakeling Rd. W7	54	15 81	B
Wakeling St. E14	57	36 81	C
Wakelin Rd. E15	50	39 83	C
Wakeman Rd. NW10	56	23 82	B
Wakemans Hill Ave. NW9	34	20 88	B
Wakerfield Cl. Horn	42	54 88	B
Wakering Rd. Bark	51	44 84	C
Wakley St. EC1	3	31 82	B
Walberswick St. SW8	10	30 77	C
Walbrook. EC4	4	32 81	D
Walburgh St. E1	57	34 81	D
Walcorde Ave. SE17	63	32 78	A
Walcot Rd. Enf	14	36 97	D
Walcot Sq. SE11	63	31 78	A
Waldeck Gr. SE27	87	31 72	D
Waldeck Rd. Dart	80	54 74	D
Waldeck Rd. N15	25	31 89	D
Waldeck Rd. SW14	72	20 75	A
Waldeck Rd. W13	54	16 81	D
Waldeck Rd. W4	61	19 77	A
Waldegrave Ave. Tedd	83	15 71	D
Waldegrave Gdns. Twick	83	15 72	D
Waldegrave Park. Twick	83	15 71	B
Waldegrave Rd. Brom	99	42 68	D
Waldegrave Rd. Dag	41	47 86	A
Waldegrave Rd. N8	25	31 89	A
Waldegrave Rd. SE19	97	33 70	D
Waldegrave Rd. Tedd	83	15 71	D
Waldegrave Rd. Twick	83	15 72	D
Waldegrave Rd. W5	54	18 80	B
Waldegrove. Croy	105	33 65	D
Waldemar Ave. SW6	73	24 76	C
Waldemar Ave. W13	54	17 80	C
Waldemar Rd. SW19	85	25 71	C
Walden Ave. N13	17	32 92	A
Walden Ave. Rain	52	50 83	D
Walden Ave. Ser	89	42 71	B
Walden Cl. Belv	67	48 78	D
Walden Gdns. Th Hth	96	30 68	D
Walden Rd. Chis	99	42 70	B
Walden Rd. Horn	42	53 88	D
Walden Rd. N17	25	32 90	B
Waldenshaw Rd. SE23	88	35 73	C
Walden St. E1	57	34 81	D
Walden Way. Horn	42	53 88	D
Walden Way. Ilf	28	45 91	C
Walden Way. NW7	23	23 91	B
Waldo Pl. Mit	96	27 70	C
Waldo Rd. Brom	99	41 68	B
Waldo Rd. NW10	55	22 82	B
Waldorf Cl. S Croy	112	31 62	B
Waldram Cres. SE23	88	35 73	C
Waldram Park Rd. SE23	88	35 73	D
Waldram Pl. SE23	88	35 73	C
Waldron Gdns. Brom	98	38 68	C
Waldronhyrst. S Croy	112	31 64	B
Waldron Mews. SW3	62	26 77	B
Waldron Rd. Har	33	15 87	C
Waldron Rd. SW18	85	26 72	A
Waldrons Path. S Croy	112	32 64	A
Waldrons. S Croy	112	32 64	A
Waldrons The. Croy	112	32 64	A
Waldron's Yd. Har	32	14 86	B
Waleran Cl. Stan	21	15 91	B
Walerand Rd. SE13	76	38 76	C
Wales Ave. Cars	111	27 64	C
Wales Farm Rd. W3	55	20 81	B
Waleton Acres. Wall	111	29 63	B
Waley St. E1	57	35 81	B
Walfield Ave. N20	15	25 94	B
Walford Rd. N16	48	33 85	A
Walfrey Gdns. Dag	52	48 84	C
Walham Green Arc. SW6	62	25 77	C
Walham Gr. SW6	62	25 77	C
Walham Rise. SW19	95	24 70	A
Walham Yd. SW6	62	25 77	C
Walkden Rd. Chis	90	43 71	C
Walker Cl. Dart	80	51 75	B
Walker Cl. Hamp	92	12 70	B
Walker Cl. SE18	66	44 78	A
Walkerscroft Mead. SE21	87	32 73	D
Walker's Ct. W1	6	29 80	B
Walkford Way. SE15	63	33 77	D
Walkley Rd. Dart	80	52 74	B
Walk Pl. E2	57	36 82	C
Walks The. N2	23	26 89	B
Walk The. Horn	42	54 86	B
Walk The. Sun	91	09 70	D
Wallace Cl. Shep	91	08 68	D
Wallace Cres. Cars	111	27 64	D
Wallace Rd. N1	48	32 84	A
Wallasey Cres. Uxb	31	07 86	C
Wallbutton Rd. SE4	76	36 76	C
Wallcote Ave. NW2	35	23 87	D
Wall End Rd. E6	51	43 83	A
Wallenger Ave. Rom	30	52 89	B
Waller Dri. Nthwd	19	10 90	A
Waller Rd. SE14	76	35 76	D
Wallers Cl. Wdf Gn	27	42 91	B
Wallflower St. W12	55	21 80	B
Wallgrave Rd. SW5	62	25 78	B
Wallhouse Rd. Eri	68	53 77	C
Wallingford Ave. W10	56	23 81	D
Wallington Cl. Ruis	31	08 88	C
Wallington Rd. Ilf	40	45 87	B
Wallington Sq. Wall	111	29 63	A
Wallis Alley. SE1	8	32 79	A
Wallis Cl. SW11	73	26 75	B
Wallis Rd. E9	49	37 84	A
Wallis Rd. Sthl	53	13 81	D
Wallorton Gdns. SW14	72	20 75	D
Wall St. N1	48	32 84	B
Wallwood Rd. E11	38	38 87	B
Wallwood St. E14	57	36 81	B
Walmar Cl. Barn	11	26 97	B
Walmer Cl. Rom	29	49 90	D
Walmer Gdns. W13	60	16 79	A
Walmer Pl. W1	1	27 81	B
Walmer Rd. W10	56	23 81	C
Walmer Rd. W11	56	24 80	A
Walmer St. W1	1	27 81	B
Walmer Terr. SE18	66	44 78	B
Walmgate Rd. Grnf	44	16 83	B
Walmington Fold. N12	15	25 92	C
Walm La. NW2	46	23 84	B
Walney Wlk. N1	48	32 84	A
Walnut Cl. Cars	111	27 64	D
Walnut Cl. Ilf	28	44 89	C
Walnut Gr. Enf	13	32 95	B
Walnut Mews. Sutt	110	26 63	C
Walnuts Rd. Orp	108	46 66	D
Walnut Tree Ave. Mit	96	27 68	A
Walnut Tree Cl. Chis	100	44 69	A
Walnut Tree Cl. SW13	61	21 77	D
Walnut Tree Cotts. SW19	85	24 71	C
Walnut Tree Rd. Brent	60	18 77	A
Walnut Tree Rd. Dag	41	47 86	D
Walnut Tree Rd. E10	65	39 78	C
Walnut Tree Rd. Eri	68	51 78	C
Walnut Tree Rd. Houn	59	12 77	B
Walnut Tree Rd. Shep	91	08 69	C
Walnut Tree Wlk. SE11	63	31 78	A
Walnut Way. Ruis	43	11 84	A
Walpole Ave. Rich	71	18 76	D
Walpole Cl. Pnr	20	13 91	A
Walpole Cl. W13	60	17 79	A
Walpole Cres. Tedd	83	15 71	D
Walpole Gdns. Twick	83	15 72	C
Walpole Gdns. W4	61	20 78	B
Walpole Pl. Tedd	83	15 71	D
Walpole Rd. Brom	107	41 67	B
Walpole Rd. Croy	105	32 65	B
Walpole Rd. E17	26	36 89	C
Walpole Rd. E18	27	39 90	B
Walpole Rd. E6	50	41 84	C
Walpole Rd. N17	25	32 90	C
Walpole Rd. Surb	101	18 67	C
Walpole Rd. SW19	95	26 70	B
Walpole Rd. Tedd	83	15 71	D
Walpole Rd. Twick	83	15 72	A
Walpole St. SW3	9	27 78	D
Walrond Ave. Wem	44	18 85	C
Walsham Cl. N16	37	34 87	C
Walsham Rd. Felt	81	10 73	B
Walsham Rd. SE14	76	35 76	D
Walsingham Gdns. Eps	109	21 64	D
Walsingham Park. Chis	100	44 69	D
Walsingham Rd. E5	37	34 86	D
Walsingham Rd. Enf	13	32 95	B
Walsingham Rd. Mit	104	27 67	B
Walsingham Rd. Orp	100	46 69	B
Walsingham Rd. W13	54	16 80	C
Walters Rd. Enf	14	35 96	C
Walter's Rd. SE25	97	33 68	C
Walter St. E2	57	35 82	B
Walter St. King	93	18 69	A
Walters Yd. Brom	99	40 69	C
Walter Terr. E1	57	35 81	D
Walterton Rd. W9	56	25 82	C
Walter Wlk. Edg	22	20 91	A
Waltham Ave. NW9	34	19 88	C
Waltham Cl. Dart	80	52 74	C
Waltham Dri. Edg	22	19 90	C
Waltham Green Ct. SW6	62	25 77	D
Waltham Park. E17	26	37 90	A
Waltham Park Way. E17	26	37 91	C
Waltham Rd. Cars	104	27 66	C
Waltham Rd. Sthl	59	12 79	C
Waltham Rd. Wdf Gn	27	42 91	A
Walthamstow Ave. E4	26	37 91	C
Waltham Way. E4	18	36 93	B
Waltheof Ave. N17	25	32 90	B
Waltheof Gdns. N17	25	32 90	B
Walton Ave. Har	43	12 85	B
Walton Ave. N Mal	94	21 68	D
Walton Ave. Sutt	103	24 65	D
Walton Cl. E5	38	35 86	D
Walton Cl. Har	20	14 89	D
Walton Cl. NW2	34	22 86	B
Walton Cl. SW8	10	30 77	D
Walton Dri. Har	20	14 89	D
Walton Gdns. Felt	81	09 71	B
Walton Gdns. W3	55	19 81	B
Walton Gdns. Wem	33	18 86	A
Walton Pl. SW3	5	27 79	D
Walton Rd. E12	51	43 85	A
Walton Rd. E13	50	41 83	C
Walton Rd. E Mol	92	13 68	D
Walton Rd. Har	20	14 89	D
Walton Rd. N15	25	33 89	D
Walton Rd. Rom	29	48 91	D
Walton Rd. Sid	90	46 72	D
Walton St. Enf	13	32 97	B
Walton St. SW3	5	27 79	C
Walton Way. W3	55	19 81	B
Walworth Pl. SE17	63	32 78	C
Walworth Rd. SE17	63	32 78	C
Walwyn Ave. Brom	99	41 68	D
Wanborough Dri. SW15	84	22 73	D
Wandle Bank. Croy	104	30 65	C
Wandle Bank. SW19	95	26 70	D
Wandle Court Gdns. Croy	104	30 65	C
Wandle Ct. Eps	109	20 64	A
Wandle Rd. Croy	104	30 65	C
Wandle Rd. Croy	105	32 65	C
Wandle Rd. Mord	103	26 67	B
Wandle Rd. SW17	86	27 72	A
Wandle Rd. Wall	104	28 65	B
Wandle Side. Croy	104	30 65	D
Wandle Side. Wall	104	28 65	D
Wandle Way. Mit	104	27 67	B
Wandon Rd. SW6	62	25 77	D
Wandsworth Bridge Rd. SW6	73	25 76	D
Wandsworth Common West Side. SW18	73	26 74	B
Wandsworth High St. SW18	73	25 74	B
Wandsworth Plain. SW18	73	25 74	B
Wandsworth Rd. SW8	74	29 76	D
Wandsworth Rd. SW8	10	30 77	D
Wangey Rd. Rom	41	47 87	B
Wanless Rd. SE24	75	32 75	A
Wanley Rd. SE5	75	32 75	D
Wanlip Rd. E13	58	40 82	D
Wannock Gdns. Ilf	28	43 91	D
Wansbeck Rd. E9	49	36 84	D
Wansdown Pl. SW6	62	25 77	D
Wansey St. SE17	63	32 78	A
Wansford Rd. Wdf Gn	27	41 90	A
Wanstead Cl. Brom	99	41 69	C
Wanstead Gdns. Ilf	39	41 88	D
Wanstead La. Ilf	39	42 88	C
Wanstead Park Ave. E12	39	41 86	B
Wanstead Park Rd. Ilf	39	42 87	D
Wanstead Pl. E11	39	40 88	A
Wanstead Rd. Brom	99	41 69	C
Wantage Rd. SE12	77	39 74	B
Wantz Rd. Dag	52	49 85	B
Wapping Dock St. E1	57	34 80	D
Wapping High St. E1	57	34 80	D
Wapping La. E1	57	34 80	D
Wapping Wall. E1	57	35 80	C
Warbank La. King	94	21 70	D
Warbeck Rd. W12	61	22 79	B
Warberry Rd. N22	24	30 90	D
Warboys App. King	94	19 70	B
Warboys Cres. E4	18	38 92	C
Warboys Rd. King	94	19 70	B
Warboys Rd. King	84	20 71	C
Warburton Cl. Har	20	14 91	B
Warburton Rd. E8	48	34 83	B
Warburton Rd. Twick	82	13 73	D
Warburton St. E8	48	34 83	B
Warburton Terr. E17	26	37 90	D
Wardale Cl. SE16	64	35 78	A

Name	Page	Grid
Ward Cl. Eri	67	50 77 B
Wardell Cl. NW9	22	21 91 C
Warden Ave. Har	32	12 87 D
Warden Rd. NW5	47	28 84 A
Wardens Gr. SE1	8	32 80 C
Wardle St. E9	49	35 85 D
Wardley St. SW18	85	25 73 A
Wardo Ave. SW6	73	24 76 A
Wardour Mews. W1	2	29 81 C
Wardour St. W1	2	29 81 D
Ward Rd. E15	49	33 83 B
Ward Rd. N19	36	29 86 C
Wardrobe Pl. EC4	3	31 81 D
Wardrobe Terr. EC4	7	31 80 B
Wardrobe The. Rich	71	17 74 B
Wards Rd. Ilf	40	44 87 B
Wareham Cl. Houn	70	13 75 D
Waremead Rd. Ilf	40	43 88 B
Warfield Rd. Felt	81	09 73 A
Warfield Rd. Hamp	92	13 69 B
Warfield Rd. NW10	56	23 82 B
Wargrave Ave. N15	37	33 88 D
Wargrave Rd. Har	32	14 86 C
Warham Rd. Har	21	15 90 D
Warham Rd. N4	37	31 88 B
Warham Rd. S Croy	112	32 64 C
Warham St. SE5	63	31 77 D
Waring St. SE27	87	32 71 A
Warkworth Gdns. Islw	60	16 77 C
Warkworth Rd. N17	25	32 91 D
Warland Rd. SE18	66	44 77 D
Warley Ave. Dag	41	48 87 B
Warley Rd. Ilf	28	43 90 A
Warley Rd. N9	18	35 93 A
Warley Rd. Wdf Gn	27	40 91 D
Warley St. E2	57	35 82 B
Warlingham Rd. Th Hth	97	31 68 D
Warlock Rd. W9	56	24 82 D
Warlock Rd. W9	56	25 82 C
Warlters Cl. N7	47	30 85 A
Warlters Rd. N7	47	30 85 A
Warltersville Mansions. N19	36	30 87 A
Warltersville Rd. N19	36	30 87 B
Warming Cl. E5	38	35 86 D
*Warmington St. E13	58	40 82 C
Warminster Gdns. SE25	97	34 69 C
Warminster Rd. SE25	97	34 69 C
Warminster Sq. SE25	97	34 69 C
Warminster Way. Mit	96	28 69 D
Warndon St. SE16	64	35 78 B
Warneford Rd. Har	21	18 89 A
Warneford St. E9	48	34 83 B
Warner Ave. Sutt	103	24 65 A
Warner Cl. E15	50	39 85 C
Warner Cl. NW9	34	22 87 A
Warner Pl. E2	57	34 82 A
Warner Rd. Brom	99	39 70 D
Warner Rd. E17	26	36 89 C
Warner Rd. N8	24	29 89 D
Warner Rd. SE5	75	32 76 A
Warner St. EC1	3	31 82 C
Warner Yd. EC1	3	31 82 C
Warnham Ct. Rd. Cars	111	27 63 D
Warnham Rd. N12	16	27 92 C
Warple Rd. SW18	73	25 75 D
Warple Way. W3	61	21 79 A
Warren Ave. Brom	99	39 70 C
Warren Ave. E10	38	38 86 D
Warren Ave. Rich	72	19 75 D
Warren Ave. Sutt	110	24 62 D
Warren Cl. Bexh	79	49 74 A
Warren Cl. N9	18	35 94 B
Warren Cl. SE21	87	32 73 A
Warren Cl. Wem	33	17 86 B
Warren Cres. N9	17	33 94 B
Warren Ct. Beck	98	37 70 C
Warren Ct. N1	48	31 83 C
Warren Cutting. King	94	20 70 D
Warrender Rd. N19	47	29 85 A
Warrender Way. Ruis	31	10 87 A
Warren Dri. Grnf	53	14 82 C
Warren Dri. Horn	42	52 86 D
Warren Dri. Ruis	32	11 87 B
Warren Drive N. Surb	102	19 66 D
Warren Drive S. Surb	102	20 66 C
Warren Drive The. E11	39	41 87 A
Warren Footpath. Twick	83	17 73 B
Warren Footpath. Twick	71	17 74 D
Warren Gdns. E15	49	38 85 D
Warren La. SE18	66	43 79 D
Warren Mews. W1	2	29 82 C
Warren Park. King	94	20 70 A
Warren Park Rd. Sutt	111	27 63 A
Warren Rd. Ashf	91	09 70 C
Warren Rd. Bexh	79	49 74 A
Warren Rd. Brom	107	39 65 B
Warren Rd. Brom	107	40 65 A
Warren Rd. Croy	105	33 66 D
Warren Rd. E10	38	38 86 C
Warren Rd. E11	39	41 87 A
Warren Rd. E4	18	38 93 A
Warren Rd. Ilf	40	44 88 B
Warren Rd. King	94	20 70 A
Warren Rd. NW2	34	21 86 B
Warren Rd. SW19	96	27 70 A
Warren Rd. Twick	70	14 74 D
Warren Rise. N Mal	94	20 69 B
Warren St. W1	2	29 82 C
Warren Terr. Rom	29	47 89 D
Warren The. Cars	111	27 62 A
Warren The. E12	50	42 85 A
Warren The. Houn	59	12 77 D
Warren The. Wor Pk	102	20 65 D
Warren Way. NW7	23	24 91 A
Warren Wlk. SE7	65	41 77 A
Warren Wood Cl. Brom	107	40 65 A
Warriner Ave. Horn	42	53 86 B
Warriner Gdns. SW11	74	28 76 A
Warrington Cres. W9	1	26 82 C
Warrington Gdns. Horn	42	53 88 C
Warrington Gdns. W9	1	26 82 C
Warrington Pl. E14	58	38 80 C
Warrington Rd. Croy	105	31 65 D
Warrington Rd. Dag	41	48 86 A
Warrington Rd. Har	33	15 88 A
Warrington Rd. Rich	71	17 74 B
Warrington Sq. Dag	41	47 86 B
Warrior Sq. E12	51	43 85 A
Warspite Rd. SE18	65	42 79 C
Warton Rd. E15	49	38 83 A
Warwick Ave. Har	43	12 85 B
Warwick Ave. W9	56	25 82 D
Warwick Ave. W9	1	26 82 C
Warwick Cl. Barn	11	26 95 B
Warwick Cl. Hamp	92	14 70 C
Warwick Cl. Orp	108	46 65 C
Warwick Cres. W2	1	27 81 A
Warwick Ct. SE15	75	34 76 C
Warwick Ct. WC1	3	30 81 B
Warwick Dene. W5	54	18 80 C
Warwick Dri. SW15	72	22 75 B
Warwick Gdns. Ilf	40	43 87 D
Warwick Gdns. N4	37	32 88 C
Warwick Gdns. Rom	30	53 89 A
Warwick Gdns. Surb	101	15 67 B
Warwick Gdns. W14	62	24 78 A
Warwick Gr. E5	37	34 87 D
Warwick Gr. Surb	101	18 66 B
Warwick House St. SW1	6	29 80 D
Warwick La. EC4	3	31 81 D
Warwick Pl. N. SW1	10	29 78 A
Warwick Pl. W5	60	17 79 B
Warwick Pl. W9	1	26 81 A
Warwick Rd. Barn	11	25 96 D
Warwick Rd. E11	39	40 88 B
Warwick Rd. E12	50	42 85 C
Warwick Rd. E15	50	39 84 B
Warwick Rd. E17	26	36 90 D
Warwick Rd. E4	18	37 92 C
Warwick Rd. Houn	69	10 75 B
Warwick Rd. King	93	17 69 A
Warwick Rd. N11	24	29 91 B
Warwick Rd. N18	17	33 92 B
Warwick Rd. N Mal	94	20 68 A
Warwick Rd. SE20	97	34 68 B
Warwick Rd. Sid	90	46 71 D
Warwick Rd. Sthl	59	12 79 D
Warwick Rd. Surb	101	15 67 B
Warwick Rd. Sutt	110	26 64 C
Warwick Rd. SW5	62	25 78 C
Warwick Rd. Th Hth	97	31 68 A
Warwick Rd. Twick	83	15 73 C
Warwick Rd. W14	62	24 78 B
Warwick Rd. W5	54	18 80 C
Warwick Rd. Well	79	47 75 A
Warwick Row. SW1	10	28 79 D
Warwickshire Path. SE8	64	36 77 D
Warwickshire Rd. N16	48	33 85 A
Warwick Sq. EC4	3	31 81 D
Warwick Sq Mews. SW1	10	29 78 A
Warwick Sq. SW1	10	29 78 A
Warwick St. W1	2	29 80 A
Warwick Terr. SE18	66	44 77 B
Warwick Way. SW1	10	29 78 A
Warwick Yd. EC1	4	32 82 C
Washington Ave. E12	50	42 85 B
Washington Rd. E18	27	39 90 D
Washington Rd. E6	50	41 84 C
Washington Rd. King	94	19 69
Washington Rd. SW13	61	22 77
Washington Rd. Wor Pk	102	22 66
Wastdale Mews. SE23	88	35 73
Wastdale Rd. SE23	88	35 73
Watchfield Ct. W4	61	20 78
Watcombe Cottages. Rich	61	19 77
Watcombe Pl. SE25	97	34 68
Watcombe Rd. SE25	105	34 67
Waterbank Rd. SE6	88	38 71
Waterbeach Dri. NW9	22	21 90
Waterbeach Rd. Dag	52	47 84
Waterbrook La. NW4	35	23 88
Waterdale Rd. SE2	86	46 77
Waterden Rd. E15	49	37 84
Waterer Rise. Wall	111	29 63
Waterfall Cl. N14	16	29 93
Waterfall Rd. N11	16	29 92
Waterfall Rd. N14	16	29 93
Waterfall Rd. SW19	96	27 70
Waterford Rd. SW6	62	25 77
Watergate. EC4	7	31 80
Watergate St. SE8	64	37 77
Watergate Wlk. WC2	7	30 80
Water Gdns. The W2	1	27 81
Waterhead Cl. Eri	68	51 77
Waterhouse Cl. E16	58	41 81
Waterhouse Cl. NW3	46	26 85
Waterhouse Cl. W6	62	23 78
Water La. E15	50	39 84
Water La. Ilf	40	45 86
Water La. King	93	17 69
Water La. Rich	71	17 74
Water La. Twick	83	16 73
Waterloo Bridge. WC2	7	30 80
Waterloo Cl. E9	49	35 85
Waterloo Gdns. E2	49	35 83
Waterloo Gdns. Rom	41	50 88
Waterloo Pas. NW6	46	24 84
Waterloo Pl. Rich	71	18 75
Waterloo Pl. Rich	61	19 77
Waterloo Pl. SW1	6	29 80
Waterloo Rd. E10	38	37 87
Waterloo Rd. E6	50	41 84
Waterloo Rd. E7	50	39 85
Waterloo Rd. Ilf	28	44 90
Waterloo Rd. NW2	34	22 86
Waterloo Rd. Rom	42	51 88
Waterloo Rd. SE1	7	31 79
Waterloo Rd. SE1	7	31 80
Waterloo Rd. Sutt	110	26 64
Waterloo Terr. N1	48	31 84
Waterlow Ct. NW11	35	25 87
Waterlow Rd. N19	36	29 87
Waterman St. SW15	73	23 75
Watermans Wlk. SE16	57	36 80
Watermead. Felt	81	09 73
Watermead La. Cars	104	27 66
Watermead Rd. SE6	88	38 71
Watermen's Sq. SE20	98	35 70
Watermill Cl. Rich	83	17 72
Watermill La. N18	17	33 92
Water Mill Way. Felt	82	13 72
Waters Rd. Wem	44	18 83
Watersedge. Eps	109	20 64
Watersfield Way. Edg	21	17 91
Waters Gdns. Dag	52	49 85
Watersid Beck	98	36 69
*Waterside Cl. SE16	63	34 79
Waterside. Dart	80	51 74
Waterside Pl. NW1	47	28 83
Waterside Rd. Sthl	59	13 79
Waterson St. E2	4	33 82
Watersplash Rd. Shep	91	07 68
Waters Rd. King	94	19 69
Waters Rd. SE6	89	39 72
Waters Sq. King	94	19 68
Water St. WC2	7	31 80
Water Tower Hill. Croy	112	33 64
Waterworks La. E5	38	35 86
Waterworks Rd. SW2	74	30 74
Waterworks Yd. Croy	105	32 65
Watery La. Nthlt	43	11 83
Watery La. Sid	100	46 70
Watery La. SW20	95	24 69
Wates Way. Mit	104	27 67
Wateville Rd. N17	25	32 90
Watford Cl. SW11	74	27 76
Watford Rd. E16	58	40 81
Watford Rd. Har	33	16 87
Watford Rd. Nthwd	19	09 91
Watford Rd. Wem	44	16 85
Watford Way. NW4	22	22 89
Watford Way. NW7	22	21 91
Watkin Rd. Wem	34	19 86

Name	Page	Ref
Watkinson Rd. N7	47	30 84 B
Watling Ave. Edg	22	20 90 B
Watling Ct. EC4	4	32 81 C
Watling Gdns. NW2	46	24 84 B
Watling St. Bexh	79	50 75 C
Watling St. EC4	4	32 81 C
Watlington Gr. SE26	88	36 71 C
Watney Market. E1	57	34 81 D
Watney Rd. SW14	72	20 75 A
Watneys Rd. Mit.	104	29 67 B
Watney St. E1	57	34 81 D
Watson Ave. E6	51	43 84 C
Watson Ave. Sutt.	103	24 65 A
Watson Cl. N16	48	32 85 D
Watson Cl. SW19	96	27 70 C
Watson's Mews. W1	1	27 81 A
Watsons Rd. N22	24	30 90 D
Watson's St. SE8	64	37 77 C
Watson St. E13	50	40 83 D
Watsons Yd. NW2	34	21 86 B
Wattcsfield Rd. E5	38	35 86 C
Watts Bridge Rd. Eri.	68	51 77 B
Watts Gr. E3	57	37 81 B
Watt's La. Chis.	100	44 69 A
Watt's La. Tedd.	83	16 71 C
Watts Rd. Surb	101	16 66 A
Watts St. E1	57	34 80 D
Wat Tyler Rd. SE3	76	38 76 D
Wauthier Cl. N13	17	31 92 D
Wavell Dri. Sid	78	45 74 C
Wavel Mews. NW6	46	26 84 A
Wavendon Ave. W4	61	20 78 D
Waveney Ave. SE15	75	34 75 D
Waverley Ave. E4	18	36 92 B
Waverley Ave. Surb	102	20 67 C
Waverley Ave. Sutt.	103	26 65 A
Waverley Ave. Twick	82	13 73 C
Waverley Ave. Wem	44	18 85 D
Waverley Cl. Brom	107	41 67 B
Waverley Cl. E18	27	41 90 C
Waverley Cres. Rom	30	53 91 C
Waverley Cres. SE18	66	44 78 D
Waverley Gdns. Bark	51	45 83 C
Waverley Gdns. Ilf	28	44 90 C
Waverley Gdns. Nthwd	19	10 90 A
Waverley Gr. N3	23	24 89 A
Waverley Pl. N4.	31	31 87 D
Waverley Pl. NW8.	46	26 83 D
Waverley Rd. E17	26	38 89 A
Waverley Rd. E18	27	41 90 A
Waverley Rd. Enf	13	31 96 B
Waverley Rd. Eps.	109	22 64 D
Waverley Rd. Har	32	12 87 C
Waverley Rd. N17.	25	34 91 D
Waverley Rd. N8.	36	30 87 A
Waverley Rd. SE18	66	44 78 D
Waverley Rd. SE25	97	34 68 B
Waverley Rd. Sthl.	53	13 80 A
Waverley Way. Cars.	111	27 63 A
Waverton Rd. SW18.	85	26 73 A
Waverton St. W1.	6	28 80 D
Wavertree Rd. E18.	27	40 90 C
Wavertree Rd. SW2	86	30 73 D
Waxham. NW5	47	27 85 D
Waxlow Cres. Sthl	53	13 81 C
Waxlow Rd. NW10.	45	20 83 D
Waxwell Cl. Pnr	20	11 90 D
Waxwell La. Pnr	20	11 90 D
Wayborne Gr. Ruis.	31	08 88 C
Waye Ave. Houn	69	10 76 A
Wayfarer Rd. Nthlt	53	12 82 A
Wayford St. SW11	74	27 76 C
Wayland Ave. E8	48	34 85 C
Wayland Cl. E8	48	34 85 C
Waylett Pl. SE27	87	31 72 D
Waylett Pl. Wem	44	17 85 B
Wayne Cl. Orp	108	45 65 D
Waynflete Ave. Croy	105	31 65 D
Waynflete Sq. W10	56	23 80 B
Waynflete Sq. W10	56	23 81 D
Waynflete St. SW18.	85	26 72 A
Wayside Ave. Horn	42	53 86 B
Wayside Cl. N14.	12	29 95 C
Wayside Cl. Rom	30	51 89 B
Wayside Ct. Twick.	71	17 74 C
Wayside Ct. Wem	34	19 86 C
Wayside Gdns. Dag	52	49 85 C
Wayside Gr. SE9	89	42 71 B
Wayside. NW11	35	24 87 C
Wayside. SW14.	72	20 74 A
Weald Cl. Brom	107	42 65 A
Weald La. Har	20	14 90 D
Weald Rise. Har	21	15 90 B
Weald Sq. E5.	37	34 86 B
Wealdstone Rd. Sutt.	103	24 65 B
Weald The. Chis	99	42 70 B
Weald Way. Rom	41	49 88 D
Wealdwood Gdns. Pnr	20	13 91 B
Weale Rd. E4	18	38 93 D
Weardale Gdns. Enf	13	32 97 B
Weardale Rd. SE13	76	38 75 D
Wear Pl. E2	57	34 82 B
Wearside Rd. SE13	76	37 75 D
Weatherley Cl. E3	57	36 81 B
Weavers House. E11	39	40 88 C
Weaver's La. SE1	8	33 80 C
Weaver St. E1	57	34 82 C
Weaver Wlk SE27	87	31 71 A
Webber Cl. Eri	68	52 77 D
Webber Row. SE1	7	31 79 A
Webber St. SE1	7	31 79 B
Webb Estate. E5	37	34 87 C
*Webb Gdns. E13	58	40 82 C
Webb Rd. SE3	65	39 77 B
Webb's Rd. SW11	74	27 74 B
Webb St. SE1	8	33 79 C
Weber Row. SE1	7	31 79 C
Webster Gdns. W5	54	17 80 D
Webster Rd. E11	38	38 86 C
Webster Rd. SE16	63	34 79 C
Wedderburn Rd. Bark	51	45 83 A
Wedderburn Rd. NW3	46	26 85 D
Wedgewood Wlk. NW6	46	25 85 D
Wedgwood Cl. Nthwd	19	08 91 A
Wedgwood Way. SE19	97	32 70 A
Wedlake Cl. Horn	42	54 87 C
Wedlake St. W10	56	24 82 C
Wedmore Ave. Ilf	28	43 90 A
Wedmore Gdns. N19	36	29 86 B
Wedmore Mews. N19	36	29 86 D
Wedmore Rd. Grnf	53	14 82 B
Wedmore St. N19	36	29 86 D
Weech Rd. NW6	46	25 85 A
Weedington Rd. NW5	47	28 85 C
Weekley Sq. SW11	73	26 75 B
Weigall Rd. SE12	77	40 75 C
Weighhouse St. W1	2	28 81 C
Weighton Rd. Har	20	14 90 B
Weighton Rd. SE20	97	34 69 D
Weihurst Gdns. Sutt.	110	26 64 D
Weimar St. SW15	73	24 75 A
Weirdale Rd. N20.	16	27 93 B
Weir Hall Ave. N18	25	32 91 B
Weir Hall Gdns. N18	17	32 92 D
Weir Hall Rd. N17	25	32 91 D
Weir Hall Rd. N18	25	32 91 B
Weir Rd. SW12	86	29 73 A
Weir Rd. SW19	85	25 72 D
Weir's Pas. NW1	2	29 82 B
Weiss Rd. SW15	73	23 75 B
Welbeck Ave. Brom	89	40 71 B
Welbeck Ave. Sid	90	46 73 C
Welbeck Cl. Eps.	109	22 63 C
Welbeck Cl. N12	15	26 92 D
Welbeck Cl. N.Mal.	102	21 67 B
Welbeck Rd. Barn	12	27 95 C
Welbeck Rd. Cars	104	27 66 C
Welbeck Rd. E6	58	41 82 B
Welbeck Rd. Har	32	13 87 D
Welbeck Rd. Sutt.	103	26 65 B
Welbeck St. W1	2	28 81 D
Welbeck Way. W1	2	28 81 D
Welbeck Wlk. Cars	104	27 66 C
Welby St. SE5	75	31 76 B
Welch Pl. Pnr	20	11 90 A
Weld Pl. N11	16	28 92 D
Welfare Rd. E15	50	39 84 C
Welford Cl. E5	38	35 86 D
Welham Rd. SW16	96	28 70 B
Welhouse Rd. Cars	104	27 65 A
Wellacre Rd. Har	33	16 88 D
Wellan Cl. Well	78	46 74 B
Wellands Cl. Brom	99	42 69 D
Welland St. SE10	64	38 77 A
Well App. Barn	11	23 95 A
Wellbrook Rd. Orp	108	43 65 D
Wellclose Sq. E1	57	34 80 A
Wellclose St. E1	57	34 80 A
Well Cl. Ruis	32	12 86 C
Wellcome Ave. Dart	80	54 75 C
Well Cottage Cl. E11	39	41 87 A
Well Ct. EC4	4	32 81 C
Well Ct. EC4	4	32 81 C
Welldon Cres. Har	33	15 88 C
Wellers Ct. NW1	47	30 83 C
Weller St. SE1	7	32 79 A
Wellesley Ave. W6	61	22 79 D
Wellesley Court Rd. Croy	105	32 65 B
Wellesley Cres. Twick	83	15 72 C
Wellesley Ct. Sutt.	103	24 66 C
Wellesley Ct. Twick	83	15 72 C
Wellesley Gr. Croy	105	32 65 B
Wellesley Pl. NW5	47	28 85 C
Wellesley Rd. Croy	105	32 66 C
Wellesley Rd. E11	39	40 88 A
Wellesley Rd. E17	38	37 88 C
Wellesley Rd. Har	33	15 88 A
Wellesley Rd. Ilf	40	44 87 C
Wellesley Rd. N22	25	31 90 C
Wellesley Rd. NW5	47	28 85 C
Wellesley Rd. Sutt.	110	26 63 A
Wellesley Rd. Twick	83	15 72 C
Wellesley Rd. W4	61	19 78 D
Wellesley St. E1	57	35 81 B
Wellesley Terr. N1	4	32 82 A
Wellfield Ave. N10	24	28 89 B
Wellfield Rd. SW16	86	30 71 B
Wellfield Wlk. SW16	86	30 71 D
Wellfield Wlk. SW16	87	31 71 A
Welford Pl. SW19	85	24 71 A
Wellgarth. Grnf	44	16 84 B
Wellgarth Rd. NW11	35	25 87 D
Well Hall Par. SE9	77	42 75 D
Well Hall Rd. SE9	77	42 75 C
Wellhouse La. Barn	11	23 96 D
Wellhouse Rd. Beck.	98	37 68 C
Welling High St. Well	78	46 75 B
Wellington Ave. E4	18	37 93 B
Wellington Ave. Houn	70	13 74 A
Wellington Av. N15.	37	34 88 C
Wellington Ave. N9.	17	34 93 B
Wellington Ave. Pnr	20	12 90 B
Wellington Ave. Pnr	20	12 90 B
Wellington Ave. Sid	78	46 74 C
Wellington Ave. Wor Pk	103	23 65 C
Wellington Bldgs. SW1	9	28 78 C
Wellington Cl. Dag.	52	50 84 C
Wellington Cl. SE14	76	35 76 B
Wellington Cl. W11	56	25 81 C
Wellington Cres. N Mal	94	20 68 A
Wellington Dri. Dag.	52	50 84 C
Wellington Gdns. Hamp	82	14 71 B
Wellington Gdns. SE7	65	41 78 C
Wellington Gr. SE10.	64	38 77 D
Wellington Pas. E11.	39	40 88 A
Wellington Pl. NW8	1	26 82 B
Wellington Rd. Belv	67	48 78 D
Wellington Rd. Bex.	79	47 74 B
Wellington Rd. Brom	99	41 68 C
Wellington Rd. Croy	105	31 66 B
Wellington Rd. Dart	80	53 74 C
Wellington Rd. E10	38	36 87 C
Wellington Rd. E11	239	40 88 A
Wellington Rd. E17	26	36 89 C
Wellington Rd. E6.	50	42 83 D
Wellington Rd. E7	50	39 85 D
Wellington Rd. Enf	17	33 94 A
Wellington Rd. Enf.	13	33 95 C
Wellington Rd. Felt.	69	09 74 A
Wellington Rd. Hamp	82	14 71 B
Wellington Rd. Har	21	15 89 A
Wellington Rd N. Houn	70	12 75 B
Wellington Rd. NW10	56	23 82 B
Wellington Rd. NW8	1	27 82 A
Wellington Rd. Orp	108	46 67 D
Wellington Rd. Pnr	20	12 90 B
Wellington Rd S. Houn	70	12 74 B
Wellington Rd. SW19	85	25 72 A
Wellington Rd. W5.	60	17 79 C
Wellington Row. E2	4	33 82 B
Wellington Row. E2	57	34 82 A
Wellington Sq. SW3	9	27 78 D
Wellington St. Bark	51	44 83 A
Wellington St. SE18	66	43 78 A
Wellington St. WC2	7	30 80 B
Wellington Terr. Har	32	14 87 D
Wellington Way. E3	57	37 82 A
Wellington Yd. Rich	71	17 74 B
Welling Way. SE9	78	44 75 B
Welling Way. Well	78	45 75 A
Well La. SW14	72	20 74 A
Wellmeadow Rd. SE13	77	39 74 C
Wellmeadow Rd. SE6	89	39 73 C
Wellmeadow Rd. W7	60	16 78 A
Wellow Wlk. Cars	103	26 66 D
Wells Pas. NW3	35	26 86 D
Well Rd. Barn	11	23 95 A
Well Rd. NW3.	35	26 86 D
Wells Cl. Nthlt	53	11 92 A
Wells Dri. NW9	34	20 87 D
Wells Gdns. Dag	52	49 85 D
Wells Gdns. Ilf.	39	42 87 A

Wells House Rd. NW10 55   21 81 A
Wellside Cl. Barn...11   23 96 C
Wellside Gdns. SW14...72   20 74 A
Wells Mews. W1...2   29 81 C
Wellsmoor Gdns. Brom...100   43 68 A
Wells Park Rd. SE26...87   34 71 B
Wellsprings Cres. Wem...34   19 86 D
Wells Rd. Brom...99   42 69 D
Wells Rd. W12...62   23 79 A
Wells Rise. NW8...47   27 83 B
Wells Sq. WC1...3   30 82 B
Wells St. W1...2   29 81 C
Well St. E15...50   39 84 A
Well St. E9...49   35 84 C
Wellstead Ave. N9...18   35 94 B
Wellstead Rd. E6...51   43 83 C
Wells Terr. N4...37   31 86 A
Wells Way. SE5...63   33 77 A
Wells Way. SW7...5   26 79 D
Wells Yd. N7...48   31 85 C
Well Wlk. NW3...35   26 86 D
Wellwood Rd. Ilf...40   46 87 A
Welsby Ct. W5...54   17 81 A
Welsford St. SE1...63   34 78 A
Welsh Cl. E13...58   40 82 A
Welshpool St. E8...48   34 83 A
Weltje Rd. W6...61   22 78 A
Welton Rd. SE18...66   45 77 C
Welwyn Ave. Felt...69   09 74 D
Welwyn St. E2...57   35 82 A
Wembley Hill Rd. Wem...44   18 85 B
Wembley Park Dri. Wem...33   18 86 D
Wembley Rd. Hamp...92   13 69 A
Wembley Way. Wem...45   19 84 B
Wemborough Rd. Stan...21   17 91 C
Wembury Rd. N6...36   28 87 B
Wemyss Rd. SE3...77   39 76 D
Wendela Ct. Har...33   15 86 A
Wendell Rd. W12...61   21 79 B
Wendling. NW5...47   27 85 D
Wendling Rd. Sutt...103   26 65 B
Wendon St. E3...49   36 83 B
Wendover Dri. N.Mal...102   21 67 D
Wendover Rd. Brom...99   40 68 B
Wendover Rd. NW10...45   21 83 D
Wendover Rd. SE9...77   41 75 B
Wendover Way. Orp...108   46 67 C
Wendover Way. Well...78   46 75 C
Wendy Cl. Enf...13   33 95 D
Wendy Way. Wem...44   18 83 A
Wenlock Ct. N1...48   32 83 D
Wenlock Rd. Edg...22   19 91 B
Wenlock Rd. N1...48   32 83 C
Wenlock St. N1...48   32 83 D
Wennington Rd. E3...49   35 83 D
Wensley Ave. Wdf Gn...27   40 91 C
Wensleydale Ave. Ilf...27   42 90 C
Wensleydale Gdns. Hamp...92   13 70 D
Wensleydale Rd. Hamp...92   13 70 D
Wensley Rd. N18...25   34 91 B
Wentland Cl. SE6...88   38 72 B
Wentland Rd. SE6...88   38 72 B
Wentworth Ave. N3...23   25 91 D
Wentworth Cl. Ashf...81   07 71 B
Wentworth Cl. Mord...103   25 66 A
Wentworth Cl. N3...23   25 91 D
Wentworth Cl. Surb...101   17 65 B
Wentworth Cres. SE15...63   34 77 C
Wentworth Dri. Dart...80   52 74 C
Wentworth Dri. Pnr...31   10 88 A
Wentworth Dwellings. E1...4   33 81 D
Wentworth Gdns. N13...13   31 95 D
Wentworth Hill. Wem...33   18 87 D
Wentworth Mews. E3...57   36 82 B
Wentworth Mews. E3...57   36 82 C
Wentworth Park. N3...23   25 91 D
Wentworth Rd. Barn...11   23 96 B
Wentworth Rd. Croy...105   31 66 A
Wentworth Rd. E12...50   41 85 B
Wentworth Rd. NW11...35   24 87 B
Wentworth Rd. Sthl...59   11 78 B
Wentworth St. E1...4   33 81 B
Wentworth Way. Pnr...20   11 89 D
Wenvoe Ave. Bexh...79   49 76 D
Wernbrook St. SE18...66   44 77 A
Werndee Rd. SE25...97   34 68 C
Werneth Hall Rd. Ilf...28   43 89 A
Wern St. WC1...3   30 82 D
Werrington St. NW1...47   29 83 D
Werter Rd. SW15...73   24 75 C
Wesleyan Pl. NW5...47   28 85 B
Wesley Ave. Houn...70   12 76 D
Wesley Ave. NW10...55   20 82 B
Wesley Cl. Har...32   14 86 A
Wesley Cl. N7...36   30 86 B

Wesley Cl. SE17...63   31 78 B
Wesley Rd. E10...38   38 87 A
Wesley Rd. N2...24   27 90 A
Wesley Rd. NW10...45   20 83 A
Wesley Sq. W11...56   24 81 C
Wesley St. W1...2   28 81 A
Wessex Ave. SW19...95   25 68 A
Wessex Cl. Ilf...40   45 88 C
Wessex Cl. King...94   19 69 B
Wessex Cl. SW15...73   23 74 B
Wessex Dri. Eri...80   51 76 C
Wessex Dri. Pnr...20   12 91 C
Wessex Gdns. NW11...35   24 87 C
Wessex La. Grnf...43   14 83 D
Wessex St. E2...57   35 82 A
Wessex Way. NW11...35   24 87 C
Westacott Cl. N19...36   29 87 D
West App. Orp...108   44 67 A
West Arbour St. E1...57   35 81 D
West Ave. E17...38   37 88 B
West Ave. N2...23   25 89 B
West Ave. N3...23   25 91 A
West Avenue Rd. E17...26   37 89 C
West Ave. NW4...35   23 88 B
West Ave. Pnr...32   12 87 B
West Ave. Sthl...53   12 80 B
West Ave. Wall...111   30 64 C
West Bank. Enf...13   32 97 C
West Bank. N16...37   33 87 A
Westbank Rd. Hamp...92   14 70 A
West Barnes La. N.Mal...102   22 67 B
West Barnes La. N Mal...94   22 68 B
West Barnes La. SW20...94   22 69 D
Westbeech Rd. N22...25   31 89 A
Westbere Rd. NW2...46   24 85 C
Westbourne Ave. Sutt...103   24 65 A
Westbourne Ave. W3...55   20 81 D
Westbourne Cl. Hay...53   11 82 C
Westbourne Cres. W2...5   26 80 B
Westbourne Dri. SE23...88   35 72 B
Westbourne Gdns. W2...56   25 81 D
Westbourne Gr. Bexh...79   49 75 D
Westbourne Gr Mews. W11...56   25 81 C
Westbourne Gr Terr. W2...56   25 81 D
Westbourne Gr. W11...56   25 81 C
Westbourne Park Pas. W2...56   25 81 D
Westbourne Park Rd. W2...56   25 81 A
Westbourne Park Villas. W2...56   25 81 B
Westbourne Pl. N9...17   34 93 D
Westbourne Rd. Bexh...67   48 77 C
Westbourne Rd. Croy...105   33 67 D
Westbourne Rd. Felt...81   09 72 D
Westbourne Rd. N7...47   30 84 B
Westbourne Rd. N7...48   31 84 A
Westbourne Rd. SE26...98   35 70 B
Westbourne St. W2...5   26 80 B
Westbourne Terr Mews W2...1   26 81 C
Westbourne Terr Rd. W2...1   27 81 A
Westbourne Terr. W2...1   26 81 C
Westbridge Rd. SW11...74   27 76 A
Westbrook Ave. Hamp...92   12 70 D
Westbrook Cl. Barn...11   26 96 B
Westbrook Cres. Barn...11   26 96 B
Westbrooke Cres. Well...79   47 75 A
Westbrooke Rd. SE9...90   44 72 B
Westbrooke Rd. Well...79   47 75 A
Westbrook Rd. Houn...59   12 77 D
Westbrook Rd. SE3...77   40 76 B
Westbrook Rd. Th Hth...97   32 69 D
Westbrook Sq. Barn...11   26 96 B
Westbury Ave. N22...25   31 90 D
Westbury Ave. Sthl...53   13 82 C
Westbury Ave. Wem...44   18 84 C
Westbury Cl. Ruis...31   10 87 A
Westbury Gr. N12...23   25 91 A
Westbury Lodge Cl. Pnr...20   11 89 B
Westbury Pl. Brent...60   17 77 B
Westbury Rd. Bark...51   44 83 B
Westbury Rd. Beck...98   36 68 A
Westbury Rd. Brom...99   41 69 B
Westbury Rd. Croy...105   32 67 D
Westbury Rd. E17...26   37 89 C
Westbury Rd. E7...50   40 84 B
Westbury Rd. Felt...82   11 72 B
Westbury Rd. Ilf...40   43 86 A
Westbury Rd. N11...24   30 91 A
Westbury Rd. N12...15   25 92 D
Westbury Rd. N13...24   30 91 A
Westbury Rd. N.Mal...102   20 67 B
Westbury Rd. SE20...98   35 69 B
Westbury Rd. W5...54   18 81 C
Westbury Rd. Wem...44   18 84 C
Westbury Terr. E7...50   40 84 B
West Carriage Dri. W2...5   27 80 C

West Central St. WC1...3   30 81 C
West Centre Ave. W10...56   23 82 A
West Chantry. Har...20   13 90 B
Westchester Dri. NW4...23   23 89 B
West Cl. Barn...12   28 96 C
West Cl. Grnf...43   14 83 C
West Cl. Hamp...92   12 70 A
West Cl. N9...17   33 93 D
West Cl. Wem...33   18 87 D
Westcombe Ave. Croy...104   30 66 B
Westcombe Dri. Barn...11   25 95 A
Westcombe Hill. SE10...65   40 78 C
Westcombe Hill. SE3...65   40 77 A
Westcombe Park Rd. SE3...65   39 77 D
West Common Rd. Brom...107   40 65 D
Westcoombe Ave. SW20...94   21 69 B
Westcote Rd. SW16...96   29 70 A
Westcote Rd. SW16...86   29 71 C
Westcote Rise. Ruis...31   08 87 A
Westcott Cl. N15...37   33 88 D
Westcott Cres. W7...54   15 81 A
Westcott Rd. SE17...63   31 77 B
Westcott Way. Sutt...110   23 62 C
Westcroft Cl. NW2...46   24 85 A
Westcroft Cl. NW9...34   19 88 B
Westcroft Estate. NW2...46   24 85 A
Westcroft Gdns. Mord...95   24 68 D
Westcroft Rd. Cars...111   28 64 A
Westcroft Rd. Wall...111   28 64 B
Westcroft Sq. 6...61   22 78 A
Westcroft Way. NW2...46   24 85 A
West Cromwell Rd. SW5...62   25 78 A
West Cromwell Rd. W14...62   24 78 D
West Cross Route. W10...56   23 80 B
West Cross Route. W11...56   23 80 D
West Cross Way. Brent...60   16 77 B
West Ct. Islw...59   14 77 C
West Ct. Wem...33   17 86 A
Westdale Pas. SE18...66   43 77 B
Westdale Rd. SE18...66   43 77 B
Westdean Ave. SE12...89   41 73 C
Westdean Cl. SW18...73   25 74 D
Westdown Rd. E15...49   38 85 A
Westdown Rd. SE6...88   37 73 A
West Dri. Cars...110   26 62 D
West Dri. Har...20   14 91 B
West Dri. Sutt...110   24 62 A
West Dri. SW16...86   29 71 A
West Drive Gdns. Har...20   14 91 B
West Eaton Pl Mews. SW1...9   28 78 A
West Eaton Pl. SW1...9   28 78 A
West Ella Rd. NW10...45   21 84 C
West End Ave. E10...38   38 88 B
West End Ave. Pnr...20   11 89 D
West End Ct. Pnr...20   11 89 D
West End Gdns. Nthlt...53   11 82 A
West End La. Barn...11   23 96 D
West End La. NW6...46   25 84 B
West End La. Pnr...20   11 89 D
West End Rd. Nthlt...43   11 84 C
West End Rd. Ruis...31   09 86 B
West End Rd. Sthl...53   12 80 C
Westerdale Rd. SE10...65   40 78 C
Westerfield Rd. N15...37   33 88 B
Westergate Rd. SE2...67   48 77 A
Westerham Ave. N9...17   33 93 C
Westerham Dri. Sid...79   47 74 C
Westerham Rd. Brom...107   42 65 C
Westerham Rd. E10...38   37 87 B
Westerley Cres. SE26...88   36 71 D
Western Ave. Dag...52   50 84 B
Western Ave. Grnf...44   15 83 C
Western Ave. Grnf...54   16 82 B
Western Ave. Nthlt...43   12 83 B
Western Ave. NW11...35   23 88 D
Western Ave. Rom...30   53 90 C
Western Ave. W3...55   20 82 C
Western Ave. W5...54   18 82 A
Western Ct. N3...23   25 91 A
Western Gdns. W5...55   19 80 A
Western La. SW12...86   28 73 A
Western Mews. W9...56   24 82 D
Western Par. Barn...11   25 95 B
Western Rd. E13...50   41 83 C
Western Rd. E17...38   38 88 A
Western Rd. Mit...96   27 69 C
Western Rd. N22...24   30 90 D
Western Rd. N2...24   27 89 D
Western Rd. NW10...55   20 82 C
Western Rd. Rom...42   51 88 B
Western Rd. Sthl...59   11 79 D
Western Rd. Sutt...110   25 64 C
Western Rd. SW19...95   26 69 B
Western Rd. SW9...75   31 75 A
Western Rd. W5...54   17 80 B

Westernville Gdns. Ilf	40	44 87 A
Western Way. Barn	11	25 95 D
Western Way. SE28	66	45 79 A
Westferry Rd. E14	64	37 79 A
Westfield Cl. Enf	14	36 96 A
Westfield Cl. Sutt	110	24 64 B
Westfield Dri. Har	21	17 89 D
Westfield Gdns. Har	21	17 89 D
Westfield La. Har	21	17 89 D
Westfield Park. Pnr	20	12 91 D
Westfield Rd. Beck	98	36 69 D
Westfield Rd. Bexh	79	50 75 A
Westfield Rd. Croy	105	31 65 B
Westfield Rd. Dag	52	48 85 B
Westfield Rd. Mit	96	27 69 D
Westfield Rd. Surb	101	17 67 B
Westfield Rd. Sutt	110	24 64 B
Westfield Rd. W13	54	16 80 C
Westfields Ave. SW13	72	21 75 A
Westfields Rd. W3	55	19 81 B
Westfields. SW13	72	21 75 B
Westfield St. SE18	65	41 79 D
Westfield Way. Ruis	31	09 86 D
Westgate Mews. W10	56	24 82 C
Westgate Rd. Beck	98	38 69 A
Westgate Rd. Dart	80	53 74 D
Westgate Rd. SE25	97	34 68 D
Westgate St. E8	48	34 83 B
Westgate Terr. SW10	62	25 77 B
West Gate. W5	54	18 82 A
West Gdns. E1	57	34 80 B
West Gdns. Eps	109	21 62 C
West Gdns. SW17	96	27 70 A
West Gdns. SW17	96	27 70 A
Westglade Ct. Har	33	17 88 B
West Green Rd. N	25	32 89 D
Westgrove La. SE10	76	38 76 A
West Gr. SE10	76	38 76 A
West Gr. Wdf Gn	27	41 91 A
West Halkin St. SW1	6	28 79 C
West Hallowes. SE9	89	42 73 C
West Hall Rd. Rich	72	19 76 B
Westhall Rd. SE5	63	31 77 D
West Ham La. E15	50	39 84 C
West Hampstead Mews. NW6	46	25 84 B
West Harding St. EC4	3	31 81 C
West Hatch Manor. Ruis	31	09 87 D
Westhay Gdns. SW14	72	19 74 B
West Heath Ave. NW11	35	25 87 C
West Heath Cl. Dart	80	51 74 D
West Heath Cl. NW3	35	25 86 C
West Heath Dri. NW11	35	25 87 C
West Heath Gdns. NW3	35	25 86 C
West Heath Rd. Dart	80	51 74 D
West Heath Rd. NW3	35	25 86 D
West Heath Rd. SE2	67	47 77 B
West Hendon Bwy. NW9	34	22 87 A
West Hill Ct. N6	36	28 86 C
West Hill. Dart	80	53 74 D
West Hill Dri. Dart	80	53 74 D
West Hill. Har	33	15 86 A
Westhill Park. N6	36	27 86 B
West Hill Rd. SW18	73	24 74 D
West Hill Rise. Dart	80	53 74 D
West Hill. S Croy	112	33 62 A
West Hill. SW15	85	23 73 B
West Hill. SW15	73	24 74 C
West Hill Way. N20	15	25 94 D
West Hill. Wem	33	18 87 D
West Holme. Eri	79	50 76 A
Westholme Gdns. Ruis	31	10 87 C
Westholme. Orp	108	45 66 B
Westholm. NW11	23	25 89 D
Westhorne Ave. SE12	77	40 74 D
Westhorne Ave. SE9	77	41 74 B
Westhorpe Gdns. NW4	23	23 89 B
Westhorpe Rd. SW15	73	23 75 A
West House Cl. SW19	85	24 73 C
Westhurst Dri. Chis	90	43 71 D
West India Dock Rd. E14	57	37 80 A
Westlake Cl. N13	17	31 93 C
Westlake. SE16	64	35 78 A
Westland Ave. Horn	42	54 87 C
Westland Dri. Brom	107	39 65 B
Westland Pl. N1	4	32 82 B
Westlands Terr. SW12	74	29 74 C
West La. SE16	63	34 79 B
Westlea Rd. W7	60	16 79 C
Westleigh Ave. SW15	73	23 74 A
Westleigh Dri. Brom	99	42 69 A
Westleigh Gdns. Edg	22	19 90 A
West Lodge Ave. W3	55	19 80 C
West Mall. W8	56	25 80 C
West Mead. Eps	109	21 63 A
Westmead Rd. Sutt	110	26 64 B
West Mead. Ruis	43	11 85 A
Westmead. SW15	72	22 74 D
Westmede. Chig	28	44 91 A
West Mews. SW1	10	29 78 A
Westminster Ave. Th Hth	97	31 69 D
Westminster Bridge Rd. SE1	7	31 79 C
Westminster Bridge. SW1	7	30 79 A
Westminster Cl. Ilf	28	44 90 D
Westminster Dri. N13	16	30 92 C
Westminster Gdns. Bark	51	45 83 C
Westminster Gdns. Ilf	28	44 90 D
Westminster Rd. N9	17	34 94 D
Westminster Rd. Sutt	103	26 65 B
Westminster Rd. W7	54	15 80 C
Westmoat Cl. Beck	98	38 70 C
Westmont Rd. Esh	101	15 65 A
Westmoor Gdns. nf	14	35 97 D
Westmoor Rd. Enf	14	35 97 D
Westmoor St. SE7	65	41 79 D
Westmoreland Ave. Horn	30	53 89 C
Westmoreland Ave. Well	78	45 75 C
Westmoreland Bldgs. EC1	4	32 81 A
Westmoreland Dri. Sutt	110	25 62 B
Westmoreland Pl. Brom	99	40 68 A
Westmoreland Pl. SW1	9	28 78 D
Westmoreland Pl. W5	54	17 81 B
Westmoreland Rd. Brom	99	39 68 D
Westmoreland Rd. NW9	21	18 89 B
Westmoreland Rd. SE17	63	32 77 B
Westmoreland Rd. SW13	72	22 76 A
Westmoreland St. W1	2	28 81 A
Westmoreland Wlk. SE17	63	33 78 C
Westmorland Cl. E12	39	41 86 B
Westmorland Cl. Eps	109	21 62 A
Westmorland Cl. Twick	71	16 74 D
Westmorland. Mit	104	30 67 A
Westmorland Rd. E17	38	37 88 C
Westmorland Rd. Har	32	13 88 B
Westmount Rd. SE9	78	43 75 C
West Oak. Beck	98	38 69 B
Westoe Rd. N9	17	34 93 B
Weston Ave. E Mol	92	12 68 D
Weston Ave. Surb	101	15 66 A
Weston Dri. Stan	21	16 90 B
Weston Gdns. Islw	71	15 76 A
Weston Gr. Brom	99	39 69 B
Weston Green. Dag	52	48 85 B
Weston Green Rd. Esh	101	15 66 C
Weston Green Rd. Surb	101	15 66 A
Weston Green. Surb	101	15 66 C
Weston Park Cl. Surb	101	15 66 C
Weston Park. N8	36	30 88 C
Weston Park. Surb	101	15 66 C
Weston Pk. King	93	18 69 C
Weston Rd. Brom	99	39 70 D
Weston Rd. Dag	52	48 85 A
Weston Rd. Enf	13	32 97 D
Weston Rd. Surb	101	15 66 C
Weston Rd. W4	61	20 79 C
Weston Rise. WC1	3	30 82 B
Weston St. SE1	8	32 79 B
Weston St. SE1	8	33 80 C
Westover Cl. Sutt	110	25 62 B
Westover Rd. SW18	73	26 74 C
Westow Hill. SE19	97	33 70 B
Westow St. SE19	97	33 70 A
West Park Ave. Rich	72	19 76 B
West Park Cl. Rom	41	47 88 B
West Park Rd. Rich	72	19 76 A
West Park. SE9	89	42 73 C
West Pier. E1	57	34 80 D
West Pl. SW19	85	23 71 C
Westpole Ave. Barn	12	28 96 D
Westport Rd. E13	58	40 82 D
Westport St. E1	57	35 81 D
West Poultry Ave. EC1	3	31 81 B
West Quarters. W12	55	22 81 C
West Ramp. Houn	69	07 76 A
West Rd. Barn	16	28 94 C
West Rd. E15	50	39 83 B
West Rd. Felt	81	08 73 B
West Rd. King	94	20 69 A
West Rd. N17	25	34 91 B
West Rd. N2	23	26 90 D
West Rd. Rom	41	47 88 D
West Rd. Rom	41	50 87 B
West Rd. SW3	9	27 77 B
West Rd. SW4	74	29 74 B
West Rd. W5	54	18 81 A
West Ridge Gdns. Grnf	43	14 83 C
Westrow Dri. Bark	51	46 84 A
Westrow Gdns. Ilf	40	45 86 D
West Row. W10	56	24 82 C
West Sheen Vale. Rich	71	18 75 D
West Side Common. SW19	95	23 70 A
Westside. NW4	22	22 90 D
West Smithfield. EC1	3	31 81 B
West Sq. SE11	7	31 79 D
West St. Bexh	79	48 75 B
West St. Brom	99	40 69 C
West St. Cars	111	27 64 B
West St. Croy	112	32 64 A
West St. E11	39	39 86 C
West St. E17	38	37 88 B
West St. E2	48	34 83 D
West St. Eps	109	21 62 D
West St. Eri	68	51 78 C
West St. Har	33	15 87 C
West St La. Cars	111	27 64 B
West Street Pl. Croy	112	32 64 A
West St. Sutt	110	25 64 D
West St. WC2	2	29 81 D
West Temple Sheen. SW14	72	19 74 B
West Tenter St. E1	4	33 81 D
West Towers. Pnr	32	11 88 D
Westview Cl. NW10	45	21 85 D
Westview Cres. N9	17	33 94 A
Westview Dri. Wdf Gn	27	41 90 D
West View. Felt	81	08 73 A
West View. NW4	22	22 89 D
West View. NW4	35	23 88 A
West View. NW4	23	23 89 C
West View Rd. Dart	80	54 74 D
Westville Rd. Surb	101	16 66 A
Westville Rd. W12	61	22 79 A
Westward Rd. E4	18	36 92 D
Westward Way. Har	33	18 88 C
West Warwick Pl. SW1	10	29 78 A
West Way. Cars	110	26 62 D
Westway Cl. SW20	94	22 68 B
West Way. Croy	106	36 65 C
West Way. Edg	22	20 91 A
West Way Gdns. Croy	106	35 65 B
West Way. Houn	70	12 76 B
West Way. N18	17	32 92 B
West Way. NW10	34	20 86 D
West Way. Orp	108	44 67 B
West Way. Pnr	20	11 89 D
West Way. Ruis	31	09 87 D
Westways. Eps	109	21 64 B
Westway. SW20	94	23 68 C
Westway. W10	56	24 81 C
Westway. W12	55	22 80 A
Westway. W2	1	26 81 A
Westway. W3	56	25 81 A
West Way. W Wick	106	38 67 D
Westwell Rd. SW16	96	30 70 A
Westwell Road App. SW16	96	30 70 A
Westwick Gdns. Houn	69	10 76 D
Westwick Gdns. W14	62	23 79 B
Westwood Ave. Har	43	13 85 B
Westwood Ave. SE19	97	32 69 A
Westwood Cl. Ruis	31	08 88 C
Westwood Gdns. SW13	72	21 75 B
Westwood Hill. SE26	87	34 71 C
Westwood La. Sid	78	46 74 A
Westwood La. Well	78	45 75 D
Westwood Park. SE23	87	34 73 B
Westwood Rd. E16	58	40 80 D
Westwood Rd. Ilf	40	46 87 A
Westwood Rd. SW13	72	21 75 B
Wetheral Dri. Stan	21	17 90 A
Wetherby Cl. Nthlt	43	13 84 B
Wetherby Gdns. SW5	62	26 78 A
Wetherby Mews. SW5	62	25 78 D
Wetherby Pl. SW7	62	26 78 A
Wetherby Rd. Enf	13	32 97 A
Wetherden St. E17	38	36 87 B
Wetherell Rd. E9	49	35 83 B
Wetherill Rd. N10	24	28 90 A
Wettern Cl. S Croy	112	33 62 C
Wexford Rd. SW12	86	27 73 B
Weybourne St. SW18	85	26 72 A
Weybridge Point. SW11	74	27 76 D
Weybridge Rd. Th Hth	97	31 68 C
Wey Ct. Eps	109	20 64 A
Weydown Cl. SW19	85	24 73 C
Weyhill Rd. E1	57	34 81 C
Weyland Rd. Dag	41	48 86 D
Weyman Rd. SE3	77	41 76 A
Weymarks The. N17	25	32 91 B
Weymouth Ave. W5	60	17 79 C
Weymouth Ct. Sutt	110	25 63 C
Weymouth Mews. W1	2	28 81 B
Weymouth St. W1	2	28 81 B
Weymouth Terr. E2	48	33 83 D

Wickham Mews. SE4 ....76 — 36 76 D
Wickham Rd. Beck ....98 — 37 68 B
Wickham Rd. Croy ....106 — 36 65 A
Wickham Rd. E4 ....26 — 38 91 C
Wickham Rd. Har ....20 — 14 90 D
Wickham Rd. SE4 ....76 — 35 75 B
Wickham St. SE11 ....10 — 30 78 D
Wickham St. Well ....78 — 45 76 C
Wickham St. Well ....78 — 46 76 C
Wickham Way. Beck ....106 — 38 67 A
Wick La. E3 ....49 — 37 83 A
Wickliffe Ave. N3 ....23 — 24 90 C
Wickliffe Gdns. Wem ....34 — 19 86 B
Wicklow St. WC1 ....3 — 30 82 B
Wick Rd. E9 ....49 — 35 84 B
Wick Rd. Tedd ....93 — 17 70 C
Wicks Cl. SE9 ....89 — 41 71 B
Wick Sq. E9 ....49 — 36 84 B
Wickwood St. SE5 ....75 — 31 76 D
Widdenham Rd. N7 ....47 — 30 85 B
Widdicombe Ave. Har ....32 — 12 86 A
Widdin St. E15 ....45 — 39 84 C
Widecombe Cl. Rom ....30 — 53 90 B
Widecombe Gdns. Ilf ....27 — 42 89 C
Widecombe Rd. SE9 ....89 — 42 72 C
Widecombe Way. N2 ....23 — 26 89 D
Widegate St. E1 ....4 — 33 81 A
Widenham Cl. Pnr ....32 — 11 88 A
Wide Way. Mit ....96 — 29 68 B
Widley Rd. W9 ....56 — 25 82 C
Widmore Lodge Rd. Brom ....99 — 41 69 D
Widmore Rd. Brom ....99 — 41 69 C
Wieland Rd. Nthwd ....19 — 10 91 C
Wigeon Path. SE28 ....66 — 44 79 D
Wiggins Mead. NW9 ....22 — 21 91 D
Wigginton Ave. Wem ....45 — 19 84 B
Wightman Rd. N4 ....37 — 31 88 C
Wightman Rd. N8 ....25 — 31 89 C
Wigley Rd. Felt ....82 — 11 73 D
Wigmore Pl. W1 ....2 — 28 81 D
Wigmore Rd. Cars ....104 — 27 66 C
Wigmore St. W1 ....2 — 28 81 C
Wigmore Wlk. Cars ....103 — 26 65 B
Wigram Rd. E11 ....39 — 41 88 C
Wigram Sq. E17 ....26 — 38 89 A
Wigston Rd. E13 ....58 — 40 82 D
Wigton Gdns. Stan ....21 — 18 90 A
*Wigton Pl. SE11 ....63 — 31 78 C
Wilberforce Rd. E17 ....26 — 36 90 B
Wilberforce Rd. N4 ....37 — 31 86 B
Wilberforce Rd. NW9 ....34 — 22 88 C
Wilberforce Way. SW19 ....95 — 23 70 B
Wilbraham Pl. SW1 ....9 — 28 78 A
Wilbury Ave. Sutt ....110 — 24 62 D
Wilbury Way. N13 ....17 — 32 92 D
Wilby Mews. W11 ....56 — 24 80 D
Wilcox Pl. SW1 ....6 — 29 79 C
Wilcox Rd. Sutt ....110 — 25 64 B
Wilcox Rd. SW8 ....10 — 30 77 C
Wilcox Rd. Tedd ....82 — 14 71 B
Wildcroft Gdns. Edg ....21 — 17 91 B
Wildcroft Manor. SW15 ....85 — 23 73 A
Wildcroft Rd. SW15 ....85 — 23 73 A
Wild Ct. WC2 ....3 — 30 81 D
Wilde Cl. E8 ....48 — 34 83 A
Wilde Pl. N13 ....25 — 31 91 B
Wilderness Rd. Chis ....100 — 43 70 D
Wilderness The. Hamp ....82 — 13 71 B
Wilderton Rd. N16 ....19 — 33 87 A
Wildfell Rd. SE6 ....68 — 37 73 B
Wild Goose Dri. SE14 ....76 — 35 76 A
Wild Hatch. NW11 ....35 — 25 88 C
Wild Oaks Cl. Nthwd ....19 — 09 91 B
Wild's Rents. SE1 ....8 — 33 79 C
Wild St. WC2 ....3 — 30 81 D
Wildwood Cl. SE12 ....89 — 39 73 B
Wildwood Gr. NW3 ....35 — 26 87 C
Wildwood. Nthwd ....19 — 08 91 B
Wildwood Rd. NW11 ....35 — 26 87 A
Wildwood Rise. NW11 ....35 — 26 87 C
*Wilford Cl. Enf ....13 — 32 96 B
Wilford Cl. Nthwd ....19 — 08 91 D
Wilford Rd. Croy ....105 — 32 66 A
Wilfred St. SW1 ....6 — 29 79 C
Wilfrid Gdns. W3 ....55 — 20 81 A
Wilkes St. E1 ....4 — 33 81 B
Wilkes St. E1 ....4 — 33 82 D
Wilkinson Cl. Dart ....80 — 54 75 D
Wilkinson Rd. E16 ....58 — 41 81 C
Wilkinson St. SW8 ....10 — 30 77 D
Wilkinson Way. W4 ....61 — 20 79 B
Wilkin St. NW5 ....47 — 28 84 B
Wilkin Street Mews. NW5 ....47 — 28 84 B
Wilks Pl. N1 ....48 — 33 83 C
Willan Rd. N17 ....25 — 33 90 C

Willan Wall. E16 ....58 — 39 80 B
Willard St. SW8 ....74 — 28 75 B
Willcocks Cl. Chess ....101 — 18 65 C
Willcott Rd. W3 ....55 — 19 80 D
Will Crooks Gdns. SE9 ....77 — 41 75 D
Willenhall Ave. Barn ....11 — 26 95 C
Willenhall Rd. SE18 ....66 — 43 78 D
Willersley Ave. Orp ....108 — 44 65 D
Willersley Ave. Sid ....90 — 45 73 B
Willersley Cl. Sid ....90 — 45 73 D
Willesden La. NW2 ....46 — 23 84 A
Willesden La. NW6 ....46 — 24 84 C
Willes Rd. NW5 ....47 — 28 84 B
Willett Cl. Nthlt ....53 — 11 82 A
Willett Cl. Orp ....108 — 45 67 C
Willett Pl. Th Hth ....105 — 31 67 A
Willett Rd. Th Hth ....105 — 31 67 A
Willett Way. Orp ....108 — 45 67 A
Willet Way. SE16 ....63 — 34 78 D
William Barefoot Dr. SE9 ....90 — 43 72 C
William Bonney Estate. SW4 ....74 — 29 75 D
William Booth Rd. SE20 ....97 — 34 69 A
William Cl. Rom ....29 — 50 90 B
William Dromey Ct. NW6 ....46 — 24 84 D
William Ellis Way. SE16 ....63 — 34 79 C
William Guy Gdns. E3 ....57 — 37 82 B
William IV St. WC2 ....7 — 30 80 A
William Margrie Cl. SE15 ....75 — 34 76 C
William Mews. SW1 ....5 — 27 79 B
William Morley Cl. E6 ....50 — 41 83 B
William Morris Cl. E17 ....26 — 36 89 B
William Rd. NW1 ....2 — 29 82 A
William Rd. Sutt ....110 — 26 64 C
William Rd. SW19 ....95 — 24 70 C
Williams Ave. E17 ....26 — 36 90 B
William's Bldgs. E2 ....57 — 35 82 C
Williams Gr. N22 ....25 — 31 90 A
Williams La. Mord ....103 — 26 67 A
Williams La. SW14 ....72 — 20 76 C
Williamson Cl. E10 ....65 — 39 78 D
Williamson St. N7 ....47 — 30 85 A
Williamson Way. NW7 ....23 — 24 91 A
Williams Rd. Sthl ....53 — 12 78 A
William's Rd. W13 ....54 — 16 80 C
William St. Bark ....51 — 44 84 C
William St. Cars ....104 — 27 65 D
William St. E10 ....38 — 37 88 D
Williams Terr. Croy ....112 — 31 63 A
William St. N17 ....25 — 33 91 C
William St. W1 ....5 — 27 79 B
Willifield Way. NW11 ....35 — 25 88 A
Willingale Cl. Wdf Gn ....27 — 41 91 A
Willingdon Rd. N22 ....25 — 31 90 D
Willingham Terr. NW5 ....47 — 29 85 C
Willingham Way. King ....94 — 19 68 A
Willington Rd. SW9 ....74 — 30 75 A
Willis Ave. Sutt ....111 — 27 63 A
Willis Rd. Croy ....105 — 32 66 A
Willis Rd. E15 ....50 — 39 83 D
Willis Rd. Eri ....67 — 50 78 B
Willis St. E14 ....57 — 37 81 D
Willmore End. SW19 ....95 — 25 69 D
Willoughby Ave. Croy ....111 — 30 64 B
Willoughby Gr. N17 ....25 — 34 91 D
Willoughby La. N17 ....25 — 34 91 D
Willoughby Park Rd. N17 ....25 — 34 91 D
Willoughby Rd. King ....108 — 18 69 B
Willoughby Rd. N8 ....25 — 31 89 C
Willoughby Rd. NW3 ....46 — 26 85 B
Willoughby Rd. Twick ....71 — 17 74 B
Willoughby St. WC1 ....3 — 30 81 A
Willow Ave. Sid ....78 — 46 74 C
Willow Ave. SW13 ....72 — 21 76 D
Willow Bank. Rich ....83 — 16 72 D
Willow Bank. SW6 ....73 — 24 75 A
Willow Bridge Rd. N1 ....48 — 32 84 A
Willowbrook Rd. SE15 ....63 — 33 77 D
Willowbrook Rd. Sthl ....59 — 13 79 C
Willow Cl. Bex ....78 — 48 74 D
Willow Cl. Brent ....60 — 17 77 A
Willow Cl. Brom ....107 — 42 67 B
Willow Cl. Horn ....42 — 52 86 D
Willow Cl. Orp ....108 — 46 66 B
Willowcourt Ave. Har ....33 — 16 88 B
Willow Ct. Wall ....111 — 28 63 D
Willowdene Cl. Twick ....82 — 14 73 A
Willow Dene. Pnr ....21 — 11 90 D
Willow Dri. Barn ....11 — 24 96 C
Willow End. N20 ....15 — 25 93 A
Willow End. Surb ....101 — 18 66 C
Willow Gdns. Houn ....13 — 13 76 A
Willow Gdns. Ruis ....31 — 09 86 B
Willow Gr. Chis ....100 — 43 70 B
Willow Gr. E13 ....50 — 40 83 C
Willow Green. NW9 ....22 — 21 90 A

Willow Gr. Ruis ....31 — 09 87 D
Willowhayne Gdns. Wor Pk ....110 — 23 64 A
Willowherb Wlk. Rom ....30 — 53 91 C
Willow La. Mit ....104 — 27 67 D
Willowmead Cl. W5 ....54 — 17 81 B
Willow Mount. Croy ....105 — 33 65 C
Willow Pl. SW1 ....10 — 29 78 A
Willow Rd. E12 ....39 — 42 86 D
Willow Rd. Enf ....13 — 33 97 C
Willow Rd. Eri ....80 — 52 76 A
Willow Rd. N.Mal ....94 — 20 68 C
Willow Rd. NW3 ....46 — 26 85 B
Willow Rd. Rom ....41 — 48 88 C
Willow Rd. W5 ....60 — 18 79 A
Willows Ave. Mord ....103 — 25 67 B
Willows Cl. Pnr ....21 — 11 90 C
Willow St. E4 ....18 — 38 94 B
Willow St. EC2 ....4 — 33 82 C
Willow St. Rom ....29 — 50 89 C
Willow Tree Cl. Hay ....53 — 11 82 C
Willow Tree Cl. SW18 ....85 — 25 73 D
Willowtree Cl. Uxb ....31 — 08 86 C
Willow Tree La. Hay ....53 — 11 82 D
Willow Vale. Chis ....100 — 43 70 B
Willow Vale. W12 ....55 — 22 80 C
Willow View. SW19 ....95 — 26 69 B
Willow Way. Eps ....109 — 20 63 B
Willow Way. N3 ....23 — 25 91 D
Willow Way. SE26 ....88 — 35 72 C
Willow Way. Sun ....91 — 10 68 C
Willow Way. Twick ....82 — 13 72 B
Willow Way. Wem ....33 — 16 86 C
Willow Wlk. E17 ....37 — 36 88 B
Willow Wlk. Ilf ....40 — 43 86 B
Willow Wlk. N15 ....25 — 31 89 D
Willow Wlk. N21 ....12 — 30 95 D
Willow Wlk. N2 ....23 — 26 90 D
Willow Wlk. Orp ....8 — 43 65 D
Willow Wlk. SE1 ....63 — 33 78 B
Willow Wlk. Sutt ....103 — 24 65 D
Willow Wood Cres. SE25 ....105 — 33 67 C
Willrose Cres. SE2 ....66 — 46 78 D
Wills Cres. Houn ....70 — 13 74 D
Willshaw St. SE14 ....76 — 36 76 D
Wilman Gr. E8 ....48 — 34 84 C
Wilmar Gdns. W Wick ....106 — 37 66 D
Wilmer Cl. King ....83 — 18 71 D
Wilmer Cres. King ....83 — 18 71 D
Wilmer Gdns (off Hoxton St). N1
....48 — 33 83 A
Wilmer Gdns (off Kingsland Rd).
E8 ....48 — 33 83 A
Wilmer Lea Cl. E15 ....49 — 38 84 D
Wilmer Pl. N16 ....37 — 33 86 B
Wilmer Way. N14 ....16 — 29 92 B
Wilmington Ave. W4 ....61 — 20 77 D
Wilmington Gdns. Bark ....51 — 45 84 C
Wilmington Sq. WC1 ....3 — 31 82 A
Wilmington St. WC1 ....3 — 31 82 A
Wilmot Cl. N2 ....23 — 26 90 C
Wilmot Cl. SE15 ....63 — 34 77 C
Wilmot Pl. NW1 ....47 — 29 84 C
Wilmot Pl. W7 ....54 — 15 80 C
Wilmot Rd. Cars ....111 — 27 64 D
Wilmot Rd. Dart ....80 — 52 74 B
Wilmot Rd. E10 ....38 — 37 86 B
Wilmot Rd. N17 ....25 — 32 89 B
Wilmot St. E2 ....57 — 34 82 B
Wilmount St. SE18 ....66 — 43 78 B
Wilna Rd. SW18 ....85 — 26 73 A
Wisham St. W11 ....56 — 24 80 C
Wilsmere Dri. Har ....21 — 15 91 C
Wilsmere Dri. Nthlt ....43 — 12 85 C
Wilson Ave. Mit ....96 — 27 69 A
Wilson Gdns. Har ....32 — 14 87 A
Wilson Gr. SE16 ....63 — 34 79 B
Wilson Rd. E6 ....58 — 41 82 B
Wilson Rd. Har ....32 — 14 87 A
Wilson Rd. Ilf ....39 — 42 87 B
Wilson Rd. SE5 ....75 — 33 76 A
Wilson's Ave. N17 ....25 — 33 90 D
Wilson's Pl. E14 ....57 — 36 81 D
Wilson Sq. EC2 ....2 — 32 81 B
Wilson's Rd. W6 ....62 — 23 78 D
Wilson St. E17 ....38 — 38 88 A
Wilson St. N21 ....17 — 31 94 A
Wilthorne Gdns. Dag ....52 — 49 84 D
Wilton Ave. W4 ....61 — 21 78 C
Wilton Cres. SW19 ....19 — 24 69 B
Wilton Cres. SW1 ....6 — 28 79 A
Wilton Dr. Rom ....29 — 50 91 D
Wilton Estate. E8 ....48 — 34 84 A
Wilton Gdns. E Mol ....92 — 13 68 A
Wilton Gr. N.Mal ....102 — 21 67 D

Street	Page	Grid
Wilton Mews. SW1	6	28 79 D
Wilton Pl. Har	33	15 88 D
Wilton Pl. SW1	6	28 79 A
Wilton Rd. Barn	12	27 96 D
Wilton Rd. Houn	70	11 75 B
Wilton Rd. N10	24	28 90 C
Wilton Rd. SE2	67	47 78 A
Wilton Rd. SW19	96	27 70 C
Wilton Rd. SW1	10	29 78 A
Wilton Row. SW1	6	28 79 A
Wilton Row. SW1	6	28 79 A
Wilton Sq. N1	48	32 83 B
Wilton St. SW1	6	28 79 D
Wilton Terr. SW1	6	28 79 C
Wilton Villas. N1	48	32 83 B
Wilton Way. E8	48	34 84 B
Wiltshire Ave. Horn	30	54 89 D
Wiltshire Cl. SW3	9	27 78 B
Wiltshire Gdns. Twick	82	14 73 C
Wiltshire La. Pnr	19	09 89 B
Wiltshire Rd. Orp	108	46 66 A
Wiltshire Rd. SW9	75	31 75 A
Wiltshire Rd. Th Hth	97	31 68 A
Wiltshire Row. N1	48	32 83 B
Wilverley Cres. N.Mal	102	21 67 C
Wimbart Rd. SW2	86	30 73 B
Wimbledon Bridge. SW19	95	24 70 B
Wimbledon Hill Rd. SW19	95	24 70 A
Wimbledon Park Rd. SW18	85	24 73 B
Wimbledon Park Side. SW19	85	23 73 D
Wimbledon Rd. SW17	85	26 71 A
Wimbolt St. E2	57	34 82 A
Wimborne Ave. Hay	53	11 81 C
Wimborne Ave. Orp	100	45 68 B
Wimborne Ave. Sthl	59	13 78 A
Wimborne Cl. SE12	77	39 74 B
Wimborne Cl. Wor Pk	103	23 66 C
Wimborne Dri. NW9	22	19 89 A
Wimborne Dri. Pnr	32	12 87 A
Wimborne Gdns. W13	54	16 81 B
Wimborne Rd. N17	25	33 90 C
Wimborne Rd. N9	17	34 93 A
Wimborne Way. Beck	98	36 68 C
Wimbourne St. N1	48	32 83 D
Wimpole Cl. King	94	19 69 C
Wimpole Mews. W1	2	28 81 B
Wimpole St. W1	2	28 81 B
Winans Wlk. SW9	75	31 76 C
Wincanton Cres. Nthlt	43	13 85 D
Wincanton Gdns. Ilf	28	43 90 D
Wincanton Rd. SW18	85	24 73 B
Winchcombe Rd. Cars	104	27 66 C
Winchcomb Gdns. SE9	77	41 75 B
Winchelsea Ave. Bexh	67	48 77 D
Winchelsea Cl. SW15	73	23 74 B
Winchelsea Rd. E7	50	40 85 A
Winchelsea Rd. N17	25	33 89 A
Winchelsea Rd. NW10	45	20 83 B
Winchelsey Rise. S Croy	112	33 63 B
Winchendon Rd. SW6	73	24 76 B
Winchendon Rd. Tedd	82	14 71 B
Winchester Ave. Houn	69	12 77 B
Winchester Ave. NW6	46	24 83 A
Winchester Ave. NW9	22	19 89 A
Winchester Cl. Brom	88	39 68 B
Winchester Cl. Enf	13	33 95 A
Winchester Cl. King	94	19 70 D
Winchester Cl. SE17	63	31 78 B
Winchester Dri. Pnr	32	11 88 B
Winchester Mews. NW3	46	26 84 D
Winchester Mews. W1	2	28 81 A
Winchester Park. Brom	99	39 68 B
Winchester Pl. E8	48	33 85 D
Winchester Pl. N6	36	28 87 D
Winchester Rd. Bexh	79	47 76 D
Winchester Rd. Brom	99	39 68 B
Winchester Rd. E4	26	38 91 C
Winchester Rd. Felt	82	12 72 D
Winchester Rd. Har	21	18 89 C
Winchester Rd. Ilf	40	44 86 D
Winchester Rd. N6	36	28 87 B
Winchester Rd. N9	17	34 94 C
Winchester Rd. Nthwd	19	10 89 A
Winchester Rd. NW3	46	26 84 D
Winchester Rd. Twick	71	16 74 D
Winchester Sq. SE1	32	32 80 D
Winchester St. SW1	6	28 78 D
Winchester St. W3	61	20 79 A
Winchester Wlk. SE1	32	32 80 D
Winchet Wlk. Croy	106	35 67 C
Winchfield Cl. Har	33	17 88 C
Winchfield Rd. SE26	88	36 71 C
Winchilsea Cres. E Mol	92	14 69 C
Winchmore Hill Rd. N14	16	30 94 A
Winchmore Hill Rd. N21	16	30 94 B
Winckley Cl. Har	33	18 88 B
Wincott St. SE11	63	31 78 A
Wincrofts Dri. SE9	78	44 75 D
Windborough Rd. Cars	111	28 63 C
Windermere Ave. Har	33	17 87 A
Windermere Ave. N3	23	25 89 A
Windermere Ave. NW6	46	24 83 A
Windermere Ave. Ruis	32	11 87 D
Windermere Ave. SW19	95	25 68 B
Windermere Ave. Wem	33	17 87 C
Windermere Cl. Orp	108	43 65 D
Windermere Cl. SW13	61	21 77 B
Windermere Gdns. Ilf	39	42 88 A
Windermere Gr. Wem	33	17 87 C
Windermere House. E3	57	36 82 D
Windermere Rd. Bexh	80	50 76 C
Windermere Rd. Croy	105	33 66 D
Windermere Rd. N10	24	28 90 B
Windermere Rd. N19	36	29 86 A
Windermere Rd. Sthl	53	13 81 A
Windermere Rd. SW15	84	21 71 C
Windermere Rd. SW16	86	29 69 D
Windermere Rd. W5	60	17 79 C
Windermere Rd. W.Wick	107	39 65 C
Winders Rd. SW11	74	27 76 C
Windfield Cl. SE26	88	35 71 B
Windham Rd. Rich	72	18 75 B
Winding Way. Dag	41	47 86 C
Windlass Pl. SE8	64	36 78 A
Windlesham Gr. SW19	85	23 73 D
Windley Cl. SE23	87	35 72 A
Windmill Alley. W4	61	21 78 A
Windmill Cl. SE1	63	34 78 A
Windmill Cl. Sun	91	09 70 C
Windmill Cl. Surb	101	17 66 A
Windmill Cl. NW2	46	24 84 A
Windmill Dri. SW4	75	28 74 B
Windmill Gdns. Enf	13	31 96 A
Windmill Gr. Croy	105	32 66 A
Windmill Gr. Croy	105	32 67 C
Windmill Hill. Enf	13	31 96 B
Windmill Hill. NW3	46	26 88 C
Windmill Hill Ruis	31	09 87 B
Windmill La. E15	49	38 84 B
Windmill La. Grnf	53	14 81 A
Windmill La. Islw	71	15 78 C
Windmill La. Sthl	53	14 79 D
Windmill La. Surb	101	16 66 B
Windmill Pas. W4	61	21 78 A
Windmill Rd. Brent	60	17 77 B
Windmill Rd. Croy	105	32 66 A
Windmill Rd. Hamp	83	14 71 C
Windmill Rd. Mit	96	29 68 C
Windmill Rd. N18	17	32 93 A
Windmill Rd. Sun	91	09 69 A
Windmill Rd. SW18	73	26 74 D
Windmill Rd. SW19	84	22 71 B
Windmill Rd. W4	61	21 78 A
Windmill Rd. W5	60	17 78 C
Windmill Road W. Sun	91	09 69 A
Windmill Row. SE11	63	31 78 C
Windmill St. W1	2	29 81 B
Windmill St. W1	7	29 81 B
Windmill Way. Ruis	31	09 87 D
Windmill Wlk. SE1	7	31 80 B
Windmill Wlk. SE1	7	31 80 C
Windover Ave. NW9	22	20 89 D
Windrush Cl. SW11	73	26 75 D
Windrush Cl. W4	61	20 77 C
Windrush La. SE23	88	35 72 D
Windsor Ave. E17	26	36 90 C
Windsor Ave. E Mol	92	13 68 A
Windsor Ave. N Mal	102	20 67 A
Windsor Ave. Sutt	103	24 65 C
Windsor Ave. SW19	95	26 69 A
Windsor Cl. Brent	60	16 77 B
Windsor Cl. Har	33	13 86 C
Windsor Cl. N3	23	24 90 C
Windsor Cl. Nthwd	19	10 90 C
Windsor Cl. SE27	87	32 71 A
Windsor Cres. Har	34	13 86 C
Windsor Cres. Wem	34	19 86 D
Windsor Ct. N14	16	29 94 A
Windsor Ct. NW11	35	24 88 C
Windsor Ct. Sun	91	10 70 C
Windsor Dri. Barn	12	27 95 D
Windsor Dri. Dart	80	52 74 C
Windsor Gdns. W9	55	25 82 C
Windsor Gr. SE27	87	32 71 A
Windsor Pl. SW1	10	29 78 A
Windsor Rd. Barn	11	24 95 C
Windsor Rd. Bexh	79	48 75 C
Windsor Rd. Dag	41	48 86 C
Windsor Rd. E10	39	37 86 B
Windsor Rd. E11	39	40 86 A
Windsor Rd. E4	18	37 92 B
Windsor Rd. E7	50	41 85 C
Windsor Rd. Har	20	14 90 B
Windsor Rd. Horn	42	53 87 A
Windsor Rd. Houn	70	11 76 C
Windsor Rd. Ilf	40	44 85 A
Windsor Rd. Ilf	40	44 86 D
Windsor Rd. King	93	18 70 C
Windsor Rd. N13	17	31 93 C
Windsor Rd. N17	25	34 90 C
Windsor Rd. N3	23	24 90 C
Windsor Rd. N7	36	30 86 C
Windsor Rd. NW2	45	22 84 B
Windsor Rd. Rich	71	18 76 D
Windsor Rd. Sid	100	46 70 B
Windsor Rd. Sthl	59	12 79 D
Windsor Rd. Sun	91	10 70 A
Windsor Rd. Tedd	82	14 71 D
Windsor Rd. Th Hth	91	31 69 D
Windsor Rd. W5	54	18 80 A
Windsor Rd. Wor Pk	102	22 65 A
Windsor St. N1	48	31 83 B
Windsor Terr. N1	48	32 82 A
Windsor Wlk. SE5	75	32 76 D
Windspoint Dri. SE15	63	34 77 B
Windus Rd. N16	37	33 87 D
Windus Wlk. N16	37	33 87 D
Windy Ridge. Brom	99	42 69 A
Windy Ridge Cl. SW19	85	23 71 D
Wine Cl. E1	57	35 80 A
Wine Office Ct. EC4	3	31 81 C
Winforton St. SE10	76	38 76 A
Winfrith Rd. SW18	85	26 73 C
Wingate Cres. Croy	104	30 67 C
Wingate Rd. Ilf	51	43 85 D
Wingate Rd. W6	61	22 79 D
Wingfield Mews. SE15	75	34 75 A
Wingfield Rd. E15	50	39 85 C
Wingfield Rd. E17	38	37 88 B
Wingfield Rd. King	94	19 70 A
Wingfield Rd. SE15	75	34 75 A
Wingford Rd. SW2	74	30 74 C
Wingletye La. Horn	42	54 87 D
Wingletye La. Horn	30	54 89 D
Wingmore Rd. SE24	62	32 75 A
Wingrave Rd. W6	62	23 77 A
*Wingrave. SE17	63	32 78 B
Wingrove Rd. SE6	89	39 72 A
Winifred Pl. N12	15	26 92 C
Winifred Rd. Dag	41	48 87 C
Winifred Rd. Dart	80	52 74 B
Winifred Rd. Eri	68	51 78 C
Winifred Rd. Hamp	82	13 71 A
Winifred Rd. SW19	95	25 69 A
Winifred Terr. E13	50	40 83 C
Winifred Terr. N9	17	33 94 B
Winkfield Rd. E13	50	40 83 D
Winkfield Rd. N22	25	31 90 A
Winkley Ct. Har	32	13 86 C
Winkley St. E2	48	34 83 D
Winlaton Rd. Brom	88	38 71 B
Winmill Rd. Dag	41	48 86 D
Winn Common Rd. SE18	66	45 78 D
Winnett St. W1	3	29 80 B
Winnington Cl. N2	35	26 88 D
Winnington Rd. N2	35	26 88 D
Winn Rd. SE12	89	40 73 D
Winns Ave. E17	26	36 89 B
Winns Mews. N15	25	33 89 C
Winns Terr. E17	26	37 89 A
Winsbeach. E17	26	38 90 D
Winscombe Cres. W5	54	17 82 D
Winscombe St. N19	36	28 86 B
Winsford Rd. SE6	88	36 72 D
Winsford Terr. N18	17	32 92 D
Winsham Gr. SW11	74	26 74 A
Winslade Rd. SW2	74	30 74 A
Winslade Way. SE6	88	37 73 B
Winsland Mews. W2	1	26 81 D
Winsland St. W2	1	26 81 D
Winsley St. W1	2	29 81 C
Winslow Cl. Pnr	31	10 88 D
Winslow Rd. W6	62	23 77 A
Winslow Way. Felt	82	12 72 C
Winstanley Rd. SW11	73	26 75 B
Winstead Gdns. Dag	52	50 85 C
Winston Ave. NW9	34	21 87 A
Winston Cl. Har	21	15 91 B
Winston Ct. Rom	29	49 89 D
Winston Ct. Har	20	13 91 C
Winston Rd. N16	48	32 85 B
Winston Wlk. W4	61	20 78 B
Winter Ave. E6	52	42 83 A
Winterborne Ave. Orp	108	44 65 D
Winterbourne Rd. Dag	41	47 86 A

Winterbourne Rd. SE6	88	36 73 D
Winterbourne Rd. Th Hth	97	31 68 B
Winter Box Wlk. Rich	71	18 74 B
Winterbrook Rd. SE24	75	32 74 C
Winterfold Cl. SW19	85	24 72 A
Winters Rd. Surb	101	16 66 B
Winterstoke Rd. SE6	88	36 73 D
Winterton Pl. SW10	62	26 77 A
Winterwell Rd. SW2	54	30 74 A
Winthorpe Rd. SW15	73	24 75 C
Winthrop St. E1	57	34 81 B
Winthrop Wlk. Wem	33	18 86 C
Winton Ave. N11	54	29 91 C
Winton Cl. N9	18	35 94 B
Winton Gdns. Edg	18	18 91 D
Winton Way. SW16	87	31 71 C
Wirral Ho. SE26	87	34 72 C
Wisbeach Rd. Croy	105	32 67 B
Wisborough Rd. S Croy	112	33 62 B
Wisdons Cl. Dag	41	49 87 D
Wise La. NW7		22 91 A
Wiseman Rd. E10	38	37 86 A
Wise Rd. E15		38 83 B
Wiseton Rd. SW17	86	27 73 D
Wishart Rd. SE3		41 76 D
Wisley Rd. Orp	100	46 70 D
Wisley Rd. SW11	74	28 74 A
Wistaria Cl. Orp	108	43 65 B
Wisteria Rd. SE13	76	38 75 D
Witan St. E2		34 82 B
Witcher Pl. NW1	47	29 84 A
Witham Rd. Dag	82	49 85 C
Witham Rd. Islw	70	14 76 B
Witham Rd. Rom	82	52 88 B
Witham Rd. SE20	98	35 68 A
Witham Rd. W13	64	16 80 C
Witherby Cl. Croy	112	33 64 A
Witherfield Way. SE16		34 78 D
Witherings The. Horn	42	54 88 B
Witherington Rd. N5		31 85 C
Withers Mead. NW9	22	21 90 B
Witherston Way. SE9	87	43 72 A
Withington Rd. N2	24	27 90 A
Withycombe Rd. SW19	85	23 73 B
Withy La. Ruis	31	08 88 A
Withy Mead. E4	18	38 93 D
Witley Gdns. Sthl	59	12 78 B
Witley Rd. N19	36	29 86 A
Witney Cl. Pnr	20	12 91 B
Witney Path. SE23	88	35 72 D
Wittenham Way. E4	18	38 93 D
Wittersham Rd. Brom	89	39 71 D
Wivenhoe Cl. SE15	51	34 75 B
Wivenhoe Ct. Houn	70	12 75 D
Wivenhoe Rd. Bark	54	46 83 D
Wiverton Rd. SE26	88	35 71 C
Wix Rd. Dag	52	47 83 B
Wix's La. SW4	74	28 75 D
Woburn Cl. SW19	95	26 70 A
Woburn Ct. Croy	105	32 66 C
Woburn Mews. WC1	2	29 82 D
Woburn Pl. WC1	3	30 82 C
Woburn Rd. Cars	104	27 66 C
Woburn Rd. Croy	105	32 66 C
Woburn Sq. WC1	2	29 82 D
Woburn Wlk. WC1	2	29 82 B
Woffington Cl. King	93	17 69 A
Woking Cl. SW15	72	21 75 D
Woldham Rd. Brom	99	41 68 C
Wolfe Cl. Brom	107	40 67 C
Wolfe Cres. SE7	65	41 78 D
Wolferton Rd. E12	50	42 85 B
Wolfington Rd. SE27	87	31 71 B
Wolfram Cl. SE13	77	39 74 A
Wolftencroft Cl. SW11	74	27 75 A
Wolseley Ave. SW19	85	25 72 A
Wolseley Gdns. W4	61	19 77 B
Wolseley Rd. Cars	104	28 66 A
Wolseley Rd. E7	57	40 84 D
Wolseley Rd. Har	21	15 89 A
Wolseley Rd. N22	24	30 90 B
Wolseley Rd. N8	35	29 88 B
Wolseley Rd. Rom	41	50 87 B
Wolseley Rd. W4	61	20 78 A
Wolseley St. SE1	63	34 79 A
Wolsey Ave. E17	26	36 89 B
Wolsey Ave. Surb	101	15 67 B
Wolsey Cl. Houn	57	14 75 C
Wolsey Cl. King	94	19 69 B
Wolsey Cl. Sthl	59	14 79 C
Wolsey Cl. Wor Pk	109	22 64 A
Wolsey Cres. Mord	93	24 66 B
Wolsey Dr. King	93	18 70 A
Wolsey Gdns. Ilf		44 91 A
Wolsey Gr. Edg	22	20 91 D
Wolsey Mews. NW5	47	29 84 A
Wolsey Rd. Ashf	91	09 70 B
Wolsey Rd. E Mol	92	14 68 D
Wolsey Rd. Enf	13	34 97 D
Wolsey Rd. Hamp	92	14 71 C
Wolsey Rd. N1	48	33 85 C
Wolsey St. E1	57	35 81 A
Wolsey Way. Chess	109	19 64 C
Wolsley Cl. Dart	80	51 74 A
Wolstonbury Rd	12	25 92 C
Wolvercote Rd. SE2	57	47 79 B
Wolverley St. E2	57	34 82 B
Wolverton Ave. King	94	19 69 A
Wolverton Gdns. W5	54	18 80 B
Wolverton Gdns. W6	62	23 78 B
Wolverton Rd. Stan	21	17 91 C
Wolverton. SE17	57	33 78 C
Wolverton Way. N14	12	29 95 A
Wolves La. N13	25	31 91 A
Wolves La. N22	25	31 91 C
Womersley Rd. N8	36	30 88 D
Wonersh Way. Sutt	110	23 62 B
Wonford Cl. King	94	21 69 A
Wontner Rd. SW17	84	22 72 B
Woodall Rd. Enf	14	35 95 D
Woodbank Rd. Brom	89	39 72 D
Woodbastwick Rd. SE26	88	36 71 C
Woodberry Ave. Har	26	14 89 C
Woodberry Ave. N21	17	31 93 B
Woodberry Cl. Sun	91	10 70 A
Woodberry Cres. N10	24	28 89 B
Woodberry Down. N4		32 87 A
Woodberry Gdns. N12	23	26 91 A
Woodberry Gr. N12	23	26 91 A
Woodberry Gr. N4	37	32 87 A
Woodberry Way. E4	18	38 94 A
Woodberry Way. N12	23	26 91 A
Woodbine Cl. Twick	82	14 72 B
Woodbine Gr. SE20	87	34 70 D
Woodbine La. Wor Pk	103	23 65 C
Woodbine Pl. E11	39	40 88 D
Woodbine Rd. Sid	90	45 73 C
Woodbines Ave. King	93	17 68 B
Woodbine Terr. E9	49	35 84 A
Woodborough Rd. SW15	72	22 75 D
Woodbourne Ave. SW16	86	29 72 D
Woodbourne Gdns. Wall	111	28 63 D
Woodbridge Cl. N7	36	30 86 B
Woodbridge Cl. NW2	34	22 86 C
Woodbridge Ct. Wdf Gn	27	42 91 C
Woodbridge Rd. Bark	51	45 85 D
Woodbridge St. EC1	3	31 82 D
Woodbrook Rd. SE2	66	46 77 A
Woodburn Cl. NW4	35	23 88 B
Woodbury Cl. Croy	53	33 65 B
Woodbury Cl. E11	27	40 89 D
Woodbury Dri. Sutt	110	26 62 C
Woodbury Ho. SE26	87	34 72 D
Woodbury Park Rd. W13	54	16 82 D
Woodbury Rd. E17	26	37 89 D
Woodbury St. SW17	87	27 71 C
Woodchester Sq. W2	56	25 81 B
Woodchurch Cl. Sid	90	45 72 C
Woodchurch Dri. Brom	99	41 70 D
Woodchurch Rd. NW6		26 84 A
Wood Cl. E2	57	34 82 C
Wood Cl. Har	32	14 87 B
Wood Cl. NW9	34	20 87 B
Woodclyffe Dri. Chis	100	43 69 C
Woodcock Dell Ave. Har	33	17 87 B
Woodcock Hill. Har	33	17 87 A
Woodcombe Cres. SE23	88	35 73 C
Woodcote Ave. Horn	42	52 86 C
Woodcote Ave. NW7	23	23 91 A
Woodcote Ave. Th Hth		31 68 D
Woodcote Ave. Wall	111	28 62 B
Woodcote Cl. Enf	14	35 95 C
Woodcote Cl. King	83	18 71 D
Woodcote Dri. Orp	108	44 66 D
Woodcote Dri. Pur		29 62 D
Woodcote Green. Wall	111	29 62 A
Woodcote Mews. Wall	111	28 63 B
Woodcote Pl. SE27	87	31 71 C
Woodcote Rd. E11	27	40 87 A
Woodcote Rd. Wall	111	29 63 C
Woodcroft Ave. NW7	23	21 91 A
Woodcroft Ave. Stan	21	16 90 A
Woodcroft Grnf		44 16 84 A
Woodcroft. N21		31 94 C
Woodcroft Rd. Th Hth	105	31 67 D
Woodcroft. SE9	89	42 72 D
Wood Dri. Chis	99	42 70 A
Wood End Ave. Har	43	14 85 A
Wood End Cl. Nthlt		14 85 D
Woodend Gdns. Enf	12	30 96 C
Wood End Gdns. Nthlt	43	14 85 D
Wood End La. Nthlt	43	14 85 C
Woodend Rd. E17	26	38 90 C
Wood End Rd. Har	44	15 85 B
Woodend. SE19	97	32 70 A
Woodend. Sutt	103	26 65 A
Wood End The. Wall	111	28 62 B
Wood End Way. Nthlt	43	14 85 C
Wooder Gdns. E7	50	40 85 A
Woodfall Ave. Barn	11	24 95 B
Woodfall Rd. N4		31 86 A
Woodfall St. SW3	9	27 78 D
Woodfarrs. SE5	75	32 75 D
Woodfield Ave. Cars	111	28 63 A
Woodfield Ave. NW9	22	21 89 C
Woodfield Ave. SW16	86	29 72 D
Woodfield Ave. W5	54	17 82 C
Woodfield Ave. Wem	33	17 86 C
Woodfield Cl. SE19	97	32 70 C
Woodfield Cres. W5	54	17 82 D
Woodfield Dri. Barn	16	28 94 C
Woodfield Dri. Rom	30	52 89 C
Woodfield Gdns. N.Mal	102	21 67 B
Woodfield Gr. SW16	86	29 72 D
Woodfield La. SW16	86	29 72 D
Woodfield Pl. W9	56	24 82 D
Woodfield Rd. Houn	69	10 76 D
Woodfield Rd. Surb	101	15 65 B
Woodfield Rd. W5	54	17 82 C
Woodfield Rd. W9	56	25 81 A
Woodfield Way. Horn	42	53 87 D
Woodfield Way. N11	24	29 91 D
Woodfines The. Horn	42	53 88 D
Woodford Ave. Ilf	27	42 89 D
Woodford Bridge Rd. Ilf	27	42 89 C
Woodford Cres. Pnr	19	10 90 D
Woodford New Rd. E17	27	39 89 A
Woodford New Rd. E18	27	39 90 A
Woodford New Rd. Wdf Gn	27	39 91 D
Woodford Pl. Wem	33	18 87 C
Woodford Rd. E18	27	40 89 A
Woodford Rd. E7	50	40 85 B
Woodgate Cres. Nthwd	19	10 91 A
Woodger Rd. W12	62	23 79 A
Woodgrange Ave. Enf	13	34 95 C
Woodgrange Ave. Har	33	17 88 B
Woodgrange Ave. N12	23	26 91 B
Woodgrange Ave. W5	55	19 80 C
Woodgrange Cl. Har	33	17 88 B
Woodgrange Gdns. Enf	13	34 95 C
Woodgrange Rd. E7	50	40 85 B
Woodhall Ave. Pnr	20	12 90 A
Woodhall Ave. SE21	87	33 72 D
Woodhall Cres. Horn	42	54 87 D
Woodhall Dri. Pnr	20	12 90 A
Woodhall Dri. SE21	87	33 72 D
Woodhall Gate. Pnr	20	11 90 B
Woodham Ct. E18	27	39 89 D
Woodham Rd. SE6	88	38 72 C
Woodhaven Gdns. Ilf	28	44 89 C
Woodhayes. Chis	100	43 70 B
Woodhead Dri. Orp	108	45 65 A
Woodheyes Rd. NW10	45	21 85 C
Woodhill Cres. Har	33	17 88 D
Woodhill. SE18	65	42 78 A
Woodhouse Ave. Grnf	44	15 83 D
Woodhouse Cl. Grnf	44	15 83 D
Woodhouse Gr. E12	50	42 84 A
Woodhouse Rd. E11	39	39 86 D
Woodhouse Rd. N12	24	27 91 A
Woodhurst Ave. Orp		44 67 C
Woodhurst Rd. SE2	66	46 78 A
Woodhurst Rd. W3	55	20 80 A
Woodington Cl. SE9	78	43 74 C
Woodison St. E3	57	36 82 C
Woodknoll Dri. Chis	99	42 69 B
Wood La. Dag	41	49 86 D
Wood La. Islw	60	15 77 D
Wood La. N6	36	28 88 D
Woodland App. Grnf	44	16 84 A
Woodland Cl. Eps	109	21 63 A
Woodland Cl. NW9	34	20 88 C
Woodland Cl. SE19	97	33 70 A
Woodland Cl. Uxb	31	07 86 B
Woodland Cres. SE10	65	39 77 A
Woodland Gdns. Islw	71	15 75 A
Woodland Gdns. N10	36	28 88 A
Woodland Hill. SE19	97	33 70 A
Woodland Rd. E4	18	38 94 C
Woodland Rd. N11	16	28 92 D
Woodland Rd. SE19	97	33 70 B
Woodland Rd. Th Hth	97	31 68 C
Woodland Rise. N10	24	28 89 D
Woodlands Ave. E11	39	40 87 D
Woodlands Ave. Horn	42	54 88 A

Woodlands Ave. N3

Woodlands Ave. N3 .....23 | 26 90 A
Woodlands Ave. N Mal .....94 | 20 69 B
Woodlands Ave. Rom .....41 | 48 87 A
Woodlands Ave. Ruis .....32 | 11 87 B
Woodlands Ave. Sid .....90 | 45 73 C
Woodlands Ave. W3 .....55 | 19 80 D
Woodlands Ave. Wor Pk .....102 | 22 65 A
Woodlands. Bexh .....79 | 49 74 B
Woodlands Cl. Brom .....99 | 42 69 D
Woodlands Cl. NW11 .....35 | 24 88 A
Woodlands Dri. Stan .....21 | 15 91 B
Woodlands Dri. Sun .....92 | 11 69 C
Woodlands Gr. E10 .....65 | 39 78 C
Woodlands Gr. Islw .....71 | 15 76 C
Woodlands. Har .....20 | 13 89 C
Woodlands. N12 .....23 | 26 91 A
Woodlands. NW11 .....35 | 24 88 A
Woodlands Par. Ashf .....91 | 08 70 A
Woodlands Park Rd. N15 .....37 | 32 88 A
Woodlands Park Rd. SE10 .....65 | 39 77 A
Woodlands Rd. Bexh .....79 | 48 75 A
Woodlands Rd. Brom .....99 | 42 69 D
Woodlands Rd. E11 .....39 | 39 86 A
Woodlands Rd. E17 .....26 | 38 89 A
Woodlands Rd. Enf .....13 | 32 97 B
Woodlands Rd. Har .....33 | 15 88 B
Woodlands Rd. Ilf .....51 | 44 85 A
Woodlands Rd. Ilf .....40 | 44 86 C
Woodlands Rd. Islw .....71 | 14 75 B
Woodlands Rd. Islw .....71 | 15 75 A
Woodlands Rd. Islw .....71 | 15 76 D
Woodlands Rd. N9 .....18 | 35 94 C
Woodlands Rd. Rom .....30 | 51 89 B
Woodlands Rd. Sthl .....53 | 11 80 D
Woodlands Rd. Surb .....101 | 17 66 B
Woodlands Rd. SW13 .....72 | 21 75 B
Woodlands Rise. Grnf .....44 | 16 84 A
Woodlands. SE19 .....97 | 32 70 C
Woodlands St. SE13 .....88 | 38 73 B
Woodlands. SW20 .....95 | 23 68 D
Woodland St (off Dalston La). E8 .....48 | 33 84 B
Woodland St (off Forest Rd). E8 .....48 | 33 84 B
Woodlands The. Islw .....71 | 15 76 D
Woodlands The. N14 .....15 | 28 94 D
Woodlands The. SE13 .....88 | 38 73 B
Woodlands The. Wall .....111 | 28 62 B
Woodlands Way. SW15 .....73 | 24 74 B
Woodland Terr. SE7 .....65 | 42 78 A
Woodland Way. Croy .....106 | 36 66 C
Woodland Way. Mit .....95 | 28 70 C
Woodland Way. Mord .....95 | 24 68 D
Woodland Way. N21 .....17 | 31 93 A
Woodland Way. NW7 .....22 | 21 91 B
Woodland Way. Orp .....108 | 44 67 A
Woodland Way. SE2 .....67 | 47 78 B
Woodland Way. Surb .....102 | 19 65 B
Woodland Way. W Wick .....106 | 38 65 C
Woodland Wlk. Brom .....89 | 39 71 A
Woodland Wlk. E10 .....65 | 39 78 C
Wood La. NW9 .....34 | 20 87 B
Wood La. Ruis .....31 | 09 86 A
Wood La. W12 .....56 | 23 80 A
Woodlawn Cres. Twick .....82 | 13 72 B
Woodlawn Dri. Felt .....82 | 11 72 B
Woodlawn Rd. SW6 .....73 | 23 76 B
Woodlawn Rd. SW6 .....62 | 23 77 D
Woodlea Dri. Brom .....107 | 39 67 A
Woodlea Gr. Nthwd .....19 | 08 91 A
Woodlea Rd. N16 .....37 | 33 86 C
Woodleigh Ave. N12 .....24 | 27 91 A
Woodleigh Gdns. SW16 .....96 | 30 72 C
Woodley Cl. SW17 .....96 | 27 70 D
Wood Lodge Gdns. Brom .....99 | 42 70 C
Wood Lodge La. W Wick .....106 | 38 65 C
Woodlodge. SW19 .....85 | 24 71 D
Woodman Mews. W10 .....55 | 22 81 B
Woodman Path. Ilf .....28 | 45 91 A
Woodmansterne La. Wall .....111 | 28 62 D
Woodmansterne Rd. Cars .....111 | 27 62 C
Woodmansterne Rd. SW16 .....96 | 29 69 B
Woodmere Ave. Croy .....106 | 35 66 B
Woodmere Cl. Croy .....106 | 35 66 B
Woodmere Gdns. Croy .....106 | 35 66 B
Woodmere. SE9 .....89 | 42 73 B
Woodmere Way. Beck .....106 | 38 67 B
Woodneigh St. SW6 .....73 | 25 76 A
Woodnook Rd. SW16 .....86 | 28 71 D
Woodpecker Cl. N9 .....13 | 34 95 D
Woodpecker Rd. SE14 .....64 | 36 77 A
Wooduquest Ave. SE24 .....75 | 32 74 A
Wood Rd. Shep .....91 | 07 68 C
Wood Ride. Barn .....11 | 26 97 B
Wood Ride. Orp .....100 | 45 68 C

Wooridge Way. Nthwd .....19 | 09 91 A
Wooridings Ave. Pnr .....20 | 12 90 B
Woodridings Cl. Pnr .....20 | 12 91 D
Woodriffe Rd. E11 .....38 | 38 87 B
Wood Rise. Pnr .....31 | 10 88 A
Woodrow Cl. Grnf .....44 | 16 84 D
Woodrow Ct. N17 .....25 | 34 91 D
Woodrow. SE18 .....65 | 42 78 B
Woodrush Way. Rom .....29 | 47 89 D
Wood's Bldgs. E1 .....57 | 34 81 B
Woodseer St. E1 .....4 | 33 81 B
Woodseer St. E1 .....57 | 34 81 A
Woodsford Sq. W14 .....62 | 24 79 A
Woodshire Rd. Dag .....41 | 49 86 D
Woodside Ave. Chis .....90 | 44 71 C
Woodside Ave. Esh .....101 | 15 66 A
Woodside Ave. N10 .....24 | 28 89 C
Woodside Ave. N12 .....15 | 26 92 A
Woodside Ave. N6 .....36 | 27 88 B
Woodside Ave. SE25 .....105 | 34 67 B
Woodside Ave. Wem .....44 | 18 83 A
Woodside Cl. Bexh .....79 | 50 75 D
Woodside Cl. Surb .....102 | 20 66 A
Woodside Cl. Wem .....44 | 18 83 A
Woodside Court Rd. Croy .....105 | 34 66 A
Woodside Cres. Sid .....90 | 45 72 C
Woodside Ct. N12 .....15 | 25 92 B
Woodside Ct. W5 .....54 | 18 80 C
Woodside End. Wem .....44 | 18 83 A
Woodside Gdns. E4 .....26 | 37 91 B
Woodside Gdns. N17 .....25 | 33 90 D
Woodside Grange Rd. N12 .....15 | 25 92 B
Woodside Green. SE25 .....105 | 34 67 C
Woodside Gr. N12 .....15 | 26 93 C
Woodside La. Bex .....79 | 47 74 D
Woodside La. N12 .....15 | 26 93 C
Woodside. NW11 .....35 | 25 88 A
Woodside Park Ave. E17 .....26 | 38 89 D
Woodside Park Rd. N12 .....15 | 26 92 A
Woodside Park. SE25 .....105 | 34 67 D
Woodside Pl. Wem .....44 | 18 83 A
Woodside Rd. Bexh .....79 | 50 75 D
Woodside Rd. Brom .....107 | 42 67 A
Woodside Rd. E13 .....58 | 41 82 C
Woodside Rd. King .....93 | 18 70 C
Woodside Rd. N22 .....25 | 31 91 C
Woodside Rd. N Mal .....94 | 21 69 C
Woodside Rd. Nthwd .....19 | 09 91 D
Woodside Rd. Sid .....90 | 45 72 C
Woodside Rd. Sutt .....103 | 26 65 C
Woodside. SW19 .....85 | 24 71 D
Woodside Way. Croy .....106 | 35 67 C
Woodside Way. SW16 .....96 | 29 69 A
Woods Mews. W1 .....6 | 28 80 A
Woodsome Rd. NW5 .....36 | 28 86 D
Wood's Pl. SE1 .....8 | 33 79 C
Woodspring Rd. SW19 .....85 | 24 72 A
Wood's Rd. SE15 .....75 | 34 76 B
Wood St. Barn .....11 | 23 96 D
Wood St. Cars .....111 | 28 66 A
Wood St. E16 .....58 | 40 80 B
Wood St. E17 .....26 | 38 89 C
Woodstead Gr. Edg .....21 | 18 91 A
Wood St. EC2 .....4 | 32 81 C
Wood St. King .....93 | 17 69 D
Woodstock Ave. Islw .....71 | 16 74 A
Woodstock Ave. NW11 .....35 | 24 87 A
Woodstock Ave. Sthl .....53 | 12 82 B
Woodstock Ave. Sutt .....103 | 24 66 B
Woodstock Ave. W13 .....60 | 16 79 C
Woodstock Cl. Stan .....21 | 18 90 C
Woodstock Cres. N9 .....13 | 34 95 D
Woodstock Ct. SE12 .....77 | 40 74 C
Woodstock Gdns. Beck .....98 | 37 69 B
Woodstock Gdns. Ilf .....40 | 46 86 A
Woodstock Gr. W12 .....62 | 23 79 B
Woodstock La N. Surb .....101 | 17 65 A
Woodstock La S. Chess .....101 | 17 65 C
Woodstock Mews. W1 .....2 | 28 81 A
Woodstock Rd. Cars .....111 | 28 64 C
Woodstock Rd. Croy .....105 | 32 65 D
Woodstock Rd. E17 .....26 | 38 90 D
Woodstock Rd. E7 .....50 | 41 84 C
Woodstock Rd. N4 .....37 | 31 87 C
Woodstock Rd. NW11 .....35 | 24 87 D
Woodstock Rd. W4 .....61 | 21 79 C
Woodstock Rd. Wem .....44 | 18 84 D
Woodstock Rise. Sutt .....103 | 24 66 B
Woodstock St. E16 .....58 | 39 81 D
Woodstock St. W1 .....2 | 28 81 D
Woodstock Terr. E14 .....57 | 37 80 B
Woodstock Way. Mit .....96 | 28 69 D
Woodstone Ave. Eps .....109 | 22 64 C
Wood St. W4 .....61 | 21 78 C

Woodsyre. SE26 .....87 | 33 71 B
Woodthorpe Rd. SW15 .....72 | 22 75 D
Woodvale Ave. SE25 .....97 | 33 69 D
Wood Vale. N10 .....36 | 29 88 A
Wood Vale. SE23 .....87 | 34 73 B
Woodvale Wlk. SE27 .....97 | 32 71 C
Woodview Ave. E4 .....18 | 38 92 A
Woodville Cl. Rich .....83 | 16 71 A
Woodville Cl. SE12 .....77 | 40 74 A
Woodville Gdns. Ilf .....28 | 43 89 D
Woodville Gdns. NW11 .....35 | 23 87 B
Woodville Gdns. Ruis .....31 | 08 87 A
Woodville Gdns. W5 .....54 | 18 81 C
Woodville Rd. Barn .....11 | 25 96 B
Woodville Rd. E11 .....39 | 39 87 D
Woodville Rd. E17 .....26 | 36 89 D
Woodville Rd. E18 .....27 | 40 90 D
Woodville Rd. Mord .....95 | 25 68 C
Woodville Rd. N16 .....48 | 33 85 C
Woodville Rd. NW11 .....35 | 24 87 A
Woodville Rd. NW6 .....46 | 24 83 D
Woodville Rd. Rich .....83 | 17 72 C
Woodville Rd. Th Hth .....97 | 32 68 B
Woodville Rd. W5 .....54 | 17 81 D
Woodville. SE18 .....65 | 42 78 A
Woodward Ave. NW4 .....34 | 22 88 A
Woodwarde Rd. SE22 .....75 | 33 74 D
Woodward Gdns. Dag .....52 | 47 84 C
Woodward Rd. Dag .....52 | 47 84 C
Woodway Cres. Har .....33 | 16 88 C
Wood Way. Orp .....108 | 43 65 A
Woodwell St. SW18 .....73 | 26 74 A
Wood Wharf SE10 .....64 | 37 77 B
Woodyard Cl. NW5 .....47 | 28 85 C
Woodyard La. SE21 .....87 | 33 73 A
Woodyates Rd. SE12 .....89 | 40 73 B
Woodyates Rd. SE12 .....77 | 40 74 C
Woolacombe Rd. SE3 .....77 | 41 76 C
Wooler St. SE17 .....63 | 32 78 D
Woollaston Rd. N4 .....37 | 31 88 D
Woolmead Ave. NW9 .....34 | 22 87 A
Woolmer Gdns. N18 .....17 | 34 92 C
Woolmer Rd. N18 .....17 | 34 92 C
Woolmore St. E14 .....58 | 38 80 A
Wool Rd. SW20 .....94 | 22 70 B
Woolstaplers Way. SE16 .....63 | 34 79 C
Woolston Cl. E17 .....26 | 35 90 D
Woolstone Rd. SE23 .....88 | 36 72 A
Woolwich Church St. SE18 .....65 | 42 79 D
Woolwich Common. SE18 .....66 | 43 77 A
Woolwich High St. SE18 .....66 | 43 79 C
Woolwich Manorway. E16 .....66 | 43 79 B
Woolwich New Rd. SE18 .....66 | 43 78 B
Woolwich Rd. Belv .....67 | 48 78 D
Woolwich Rd. Bexh .....79 | 49 75 A
Woolwich Rd. E10 .....65 | 39 78 D
Woolwich Rd. E7 .....65 | 41 78 A
Woolwich Rd. SE2 .....67 | 48 77 A
Wooster Gdns. E14 .....58 | 38 81 D
Wootton Cl. Horn .....42 | 53 88 B
Wootton Gr. N3 .....23 | 25 90 A
Wootton St. SE1 .....7 | 31 80 C
Worbeck Rd. SE20 .....98 | 35 69 C
Worcester Ave. N17 .....25 | 34 91 C
Worcester Cl. Croy .....106 | 37 65 A
Worcester Cl. Mit .....96 | 28 69 C
Worcester Gdns. Grnf .....43 | 14 84 B
Worcester Gdns. Ilf .....39 | 42 87 A
Worcester Gdns. Wor Pk .....102 | 21 65 C
Worcester Mews. NW3 .....46 | 25 84 B
Worcester Park Rd. Wor Pk .....102 | 20 65 D
Worcester Pl. EC4 .....4 | 32 80 A
Worcester Rd. E12 .....50 | 42 85 B
Worcester Rd. E17 .....26 | 35 90 D
Worcester Rd. Sutt .....110 | 25 63 D
Worcester Rd. SW19 .....85 | 24 71 D
Worcester Rd. W12 .....62 | 42 84 C
Wordsworth Ave. E12 .....50 | 42 84 C
Wordsworth Ave. E18 .....27 | 39 90 D
Wordsworth Ave. Grnf .....53 | 14 82 B
Wordsworth Cl. Rom .....30 | 53 90 A
Wordsworth Dri. Sutt .....110 | 23 64 A
Wordsworth Par. N15 .....25 | 31 89 D
Wordsworth Rd. Hamp .....82 | 12 71 B
Wordsworth Rd. N16 .....48 | 33 85 A
Wordsworth Rd. SE20 .....98 | 35 70 D
Wordsworth Rd. Wall .....111 | 29 63 A
Wordsworth Rd. Well .....78 | 45 76 A
Wordsworth Wlk. NW11 .....23 | 25 89 C
Worfield St. SW11 .....74 | 27 78 A
Worfield St. SW11 .....9 | 27 77 C
Worgan St. SE11 .....10 | 30 78 D
Worland Rd. E15 .....50 | 39 84 C
World's End La. N21 .....12 | 30 96 D
World's End Pas. SW10 .....62 | 26 77 D
World's End Pl. SW10 .....62 | 26 77 C

Worlidge St. W6 62
Worlingham Rd. SE22 75
Wormholt Rd. W12 55
Wormwood St. EC3 4
Wornington Rd. W10 56
Woronzow Rd. NW8 47
Worple Ave. Islw. 71
Worple Ave. SW19 95
Worple Cl. Har. 32
Worple Rd. Islw. 71
Worple Rd. SW19 95
Worple Rd. SW20 95
Worple Road Mews. SW19 ...95
Worple Way. SW14 72
Worple Way. Har. 32
Worple Way. Rich. 71
Worship St. EC2 4
Worslade Rd. SW17 85
Worsley Bridge Rd. Beck. 88
Worsley Rd. E11 50
Worsopp Dri. SW4 74
Worthfield Cl. Eps. 109
Worthing Cl. E15 50
Worthing Rd. Houn. 59
Worthington Rd. Surb. 101
Wortley Rd. Croy. 105
Wortley Rd. E6 50
Worton Gdns. Islw. 74
Worton Rd. Islw. 71
Worton Rd. Islw. 70
Worton Rd. Islw. 71
Worton Way. Houn. 70
Worton Way. Islw. 70
Wotton Rd. NW2 35
Wotton Rd. SE8 64
Wotton Way. Sutt. 110
Wouldham Rd. E16. 58
Wragby Rd. E11 39
Wrampling Pl. N9 17
Wrangthorn Wlk. Croy. 112
Wray Ave. Ilf. 28
Wray Cl. Horn. 42
Wray Cres. N4 36
Wrayfield Rd. Sutt. 110
Wray Rd. Sutt. 110
Wrekin Rd. SE18. 66
Wren Ave. NW2 46
Wren Ave. Sthl. 59
Wren Gdns. Dag. 52
Wren Gdns. Horn 42
Wren Path. SE28 66
Wren Rd. Dag. 52
Wren Rd. SE5 57
Wren's Ave. Ashf. 81
Wren's Park House. E5 37
Wren St. WC1 3
Wrentham Ave. NW10. 46
Wrenthorpe Rd. Brom. 89
Wrenwood Way. Pnr 19
Wrexham Rd. E3 43
Wricklemarsh Rd. SE3. 77
Wrigglesworth St. SE14 62
Wright Cl. SE13 76
Wright Rd. Houn. 59
Wright Rd. N1 48
Wright's Green. SW4 74
Wright's La. W8 62
Wrights Pl. NW10 45
Wright's Rd. E3 49
Wrights Rd. SE25 97
Wright's Row. Wall 111
Wrights Wlk. SW14 72
Wrigley Cl. E4 18
Wrotham Rd. Barn 11
Wrotham Rd. NW1 47
Wrotham Rd. W13. 54
Wrotham Rd. Well 79
Wrottesley Rd. NW10 56
Wrottesley Rd. SE18 66
Wroughton Rd. SW11 74
Wroughton Terr. NW4 22
Wroxall Rd. Dag. 52
Wroxham Gdns. N11 24
Wroxton Rd. SE15 76
Wrythe Green Rd. Cars 104
Wrythe La. Cars. 103
Wulfstan St. W12 55
Wyatt Ct. Wem 44
Wyatt Park Rd. SW2 86
Wyatt Rd. Dart. 80
Wyatt Rd. E7 50
Wyatt Rd. N5. 37
Wyatt's La. E17 26
Wybert St. NW1 2
Wyborne House. NW10 45
Wyborne Way. NW10 45

23 78 C
33 75 D
22 80 C
33 81 C
24 81 A
27 83 A
16 74 A
23 70 D
12 87 D
16 75 C
24 70 B
23 69 B
24 70 B
20 75 B
12 87 D
18 75 D
33 82 C
26 71 B
37 71 C
39 85 A
29 74 A
20 63 D
32 78 D
50 83 A
12 77 B
18 66 D
31 66 A
41 84 D
14 76 D
14 75 D
15 75 A
14 76 D
14 76 D
23 86 C
36 77 B
23 62 C
39 81 D
39 86 C
34 94 C
31 64 A
43 89 A
53 87 A
30 86 B
23 64 B
24 62 B
44 77 C
23 85 A
12 78 B
47 85 D
51 87 D
44 79 D
47 85 D
32 76 B
08 71 A
34 86 B
30 82 D
23 83 D
39 71 A
10 89 D
37 83 C
41 76 A
35 77 D
38 75 D
11 77 C
33 84 A
29 75 D
20 84 A
36 83 D
33 68 A
28 64 B
20 75 B
38 92 D
24 97 C
29 84 C
17 80 C
47 76 A
22 83 C
44 77 A
27 74 D
22 89 D
47 85 C
29 91 D
35 76 C
27 65 D
26 66 D
21 81 D
18 83 A
30 72 B
51 75 B
40 84 A
32 86 C
38 89 A
29 82 C
20 84 C
20 84 C

Wyburn Ave. Barn. 11
Wycham Ave. Sid. 90
Wyche Gr. S Croy. 112
Wych End. Beck. 98
Wycherley Cres. Barn 11
Wychwood Ave. Edg. 21
Wychwood Ave. Th Hth. 97
Wychwood Cl. Edg. 21
Wychwood End. N6 36
Wychwood Gdns. Ilf 27
Wychwood Way. Nthwd 19
Wychwood Way. SE19 97
Wycliffe Cl. Well 78
Wycliffe Rd. SW11 74
Wycliffe Rd. SW11 74
Wycliffe Rd. SW19 95
Wyclif St. EC1 3
Wycombe Gdns. NW11 35
Wycombe Rd. Ilf 39
Wycombe Rd. N17 25
Wycombe Rd. Wem 45
Wydehurst Rd. Croy. 103
Wydell Cl. Mord. 103
Wydeville Manor Rd. SE12 89
Wye Cl. Ashf 81
Wye Cl. Orp. 108
Wye Cl. Ruis. 26
Wye St. SW11 73
Wyevale Cl. Pnr 19
Wyfields. Ilf. 28
Wyfold Rd. SW6 62
Wyhill Wlk. Dag. 52
Wyke Gdns. W7 60
Wykeham Ave. Dag. 52
Wykeham Ave. Horn 42
Wykeham Green. Dag 52
Wykeham Hill. Wem 33
Wykeham Rd. Har. 16
Wykeham Rd. NW4 35
Wykeham Rise. N20. 15
Wyke Rd. E3. 49
Wyke Rd. SW20 95
Wylchin Cl. Pnr 19
Wyldes Cl. NW11 15
Wyldfield Gdns. N9 17
Wyld Way. Wem 45
Wyleu St. SE23 88
Wylie Rd. Sthl 55
Wyllen Cl. E1 57
Wymering Rd. W9 56
Wymond St. SW15 73
Wynan Rd. E14 63
Wynash Gdns. Cars 111
Wynaud Cr. N22 24
Wynchgate. Har. 21
Wynchgate. N14 16
Wynchgate. N21 16
Wyncroft Cl. Brom 99
Wyndale Ave. NW9 34
Wyndcliff Rd. SE7. 65
Wyndcroft Cl. Enf. 13
Wyndham Cl. Orp. 108
Wyndham Cl. Sutt. 110
Wyndham Cres. Houn. 70
Wyndham Cres. N19. 36
Wyndham Mews. W1 1
Wyndham Pl. W1 1
Wyndham Rd. Barn 11
Wyndham Rd. E6. 50
Wyndham Rd. King. 63
Wyndham Rd. SE5. 63
Wyndham Rd. W13. 60
Wyndham St. W1 1
Wyndham Yd. W1 1
Wyneham Rd. SE24 75
Wynell Rd. SE23 88
Wynford Gr. Orp. 100
Wynford Rd. N1 47
Wynford Way. SE9 89
Wynlie Gdns. Pnr 19
Wynndale Rd. E18. 26
Wynne Rd. SW9 75
Wynn's Ave. Sid 78
Wynnstay Gdns. W8 62
Wynter St. SW11 73
Wynton Gdns. SE25 105
Wynton Gdns. SE25 97
Wynton Pl. W3 55
Wynyard Terr. SE11 10
Wynyatt St. EC1 3
Wyresdale Cres. Grnf 51
Wyteleaf Cl. Ruis. 31
Wythburn Pl. W1 1
Wythenshawe Rd. Dag. 41
Wythens Wlk. SE9 78

24 96 B
45 73 C
32 63 D
36 70 D
25 95 D
17 91 B
32 68 A
17 91 B
29 87 A
42 89 D
09 91 D
33 70 A
45 76 B
28 75 A
28 76 C
25 70 B
31 82 B
25 86 A
42 88 B
34 90 A
19 83 A
34 66 A
23 67 D
40 71 B
07 71 B
45 66 B
08 88 C
26 75 B
10 89 A
43 90 B
24 77 C
50 84 A
16 79 C
47 84 A
53 88 D
47 84 A
18 87 D
16 89 D
23 88 A
24 94 C
37 84 C
23 69 C
09 89 B
26 87 C
33 93 B
19 84 B
35 73 D
13 79 C
35 82 C
25 82 A
23 75 A
30 78 D
27 64 C
30 91 B
15 91 C
30 94 C
30 94 A
42 68 B
19 88 C
40 77 B
31 96 B
44 66 C
25 63 C
13 74 C
29 86 C
27 81 B
27 81 B
29 94 D
41 84 D
18 70 D
32 77 C
16 79 D
27 81 B
27 81 B
32 74 B
35 72 D
46 68 B
30 83 D
43 72 D
10 90 D
40 90 B
31 76 C
46 74 A
25 79 C
26 75 C
33 67 B
33 68 D
19 81 D
10 78 D
31 82 B
15 82 B
08 88 C
27 81 D
49 86 C
43 74 D

Wythes Cl. Brom. 99
Wythfield Rd. SE9 77
Wyvenhoe Rd. Har. 43
Wyvern Cl. Orp. 108
Wyvern Estate The. N Mal. 94
Wyvern Rd. Pur. 112
Wyvil Rd. SW8. 30
Wyvis St. E14 57

Yabsley St. E14 58
Yalding Rd. SE16 63
Yarborough Rd. SW19 95
Yardbridge Cl. Sutt. 10
Yardley Cl. E4 14
Yardley Ct. Sutt. 10
Yardley La. E4 14
Yardley St. WC1 3
Yarmouth Cres. N17 37
Yarmouth Pl. W1 6
Yarnton Way. Belv. 67
Yarnton Way. SE2 67
Yateley St. SE18. 65
Yeading Ave. Har. 32
Yeading Fork. Hay 53
Yeading La. Hay 53
Yeading La. Nthlt 53
Yeate St. N1 48
Yeatman Rd. N6 30
Yeldham Rd. W6. 62
Yelverton Cl. Rom. 30
Yelverton Lodge. Twick. 83
Yelverton Rd. SW11 73
Yenston Cl. Mord. 103
Yeoman Cl. SE27 31
Yeoman Rd. Nthlt 43
Yeomans Acre. Ruis. 31
Yeoman's Row. SW3. 5
Yeoman Rd. SE8 64
Yeomans Way. Enf 14
Yeoman's Yd. E1. 9
Yeomen Way. Ilf 28
Yeo St. E3 57
Yeovil Cl. Orp. 108
Yerbury Rd. N19 36
Yester Dri. Chis 99
Yester Park. Chis. 99
Yester Rd. Chis. 99
Yevele Way. Horn 42
Yewdale Cl. Brom 99
Yewfield Rd. NW10 45
Yew Gr. NW2 17
Yew Tree Cl. N21 17
Yew Tree Cl. Well 102
Yew Tree Cl. Wor Pk 102
Yew Tree Gdns. Rom 41
Yew Tree Gdns. Rom 41
Yewtree Rd. Beck. 98
Yew Tree Rd. W12 55
Yew Tree Wlk. Houn 70
Yew Tree Wlk. Pur. 112
Yew Wlk. Har. 33
Yoakley Rd. N16. 37
Yoke Cl. N7 47
Yolande Gdns. SE9. 77
Yonge Park. N4 47
York Ave. SE17 63
York Ave. Sid. 90
York Ave. Stan. 21
York Ave. SW14 72
York Ave. W7 54
York Bldgs. WC2 7
York Bridge. NW1 2
York Cl. Mord. 95
York Cl. W7 54
York Gate. N14. 16
York Gate. NW1 2
York Gdns. SE15 76
York Hill. SE27 87
York House Pl. W8 62
Yorkland Ave. Well 78
York Mews. Ilf. 40
York Mews. NW5. 47
York Par. Brent. 60
York Pl. Ilf. 40
York Pl. SW11 73
York Pl. WC2 7
York Rd. Barn. 11
York Rd. Brent. 60
York Rd. Croy. 105
York Rd. E10 38
York Rd. E17 38
York Rd. E4. 18
York Rd. E7 50
York Rd. Houn. 70
York Rd. Ilf. 40

42 69 D
42 74 D
14 85 A
46 65 D
22 68 C
31 62 D
30 77 B
37 81 B

38 80 C
34 79 C
26 69 B
25 62 D
37 95 B
23 64 A
37 95 B
31 82 A
34 88 B
28 80 D
47 79 D
48 79 B
41 79 D
12 87 C
11 82 C
11 82 C
11 82 A
32 84 D
27 88 D
23 78 D
53 90 B
17 73 A
24 76 D
25 67 C
31 72 D
12 84 C
10 88 C
27 79 C
36 78 A
35 97 C
33 80 B
44 91 A
37 81 B
46 65 D
29 86 D
42 70 B
42 70 B
42 70 D
54 87 A
39 70 A
21 84 B
23 85 B
31 94 A
46 76 A
21 66 C
41 48 88 A
41 50 88 B
36 68 B
52 21 80 B
12 74 B
15 87 C
33 86 A
30 84 A
42 74 A
31 86 C
32 98 C
45 72 B
16 90 D
20 74 A
15 80 C
30 80 A
28 82 C
25 68 D
15 80 C
29 94 A
28 82 C
35 76 A
31 72 D
25 79 B
45 75 D
43 86 C
28 85 D
17 78 D
43 86 B
26 75 B
30 80 A
26 95 B
17 78 D
31 66 A
38 86 C
35 88 B
37 92 C
40 84 A
20 74 D
13 75 B
43 86 A

First published 1984 by

Ordnance Survey   and   Newnes Books
Romsey Road   84-88 The Centre
Maybush   Feltham
Southampton SO9 4DH   Middlesex TW13 4BH

Copyright © Crown Copyright 1984

Second impression 1984

Newnes Books is a division of The Hamlyn Publishing Group
Limited.

ISBN: 0 600 35768 6
Printed in Great Britain

Discover Beautiful Britain
with
Ordnance Survey MAPS

**MAPS
YOU CAN
RELY ON**